4 NOW READ THE CHAPTER AGAIN, SLOWLY AND CAREFULLY

Pay particular attention to the key terms, which are printed in bold type and defined again in the margins. Highlight the three or four most important points in each major section, and copy them into your notes. Be sure to include the page number where they appear for reference later. Look for answers to any questions you jotted in the margins. Study the artwork in the chapter too, because the figures present important data and summarize key points; write your own brief note detailing each figure's main point in the margin. Read the photo captions carefully and test your judgment by tackling the questions posed in each.

5 USE THE EXTRA STUDY FEATURES IN EACH CHAPTER TO MAKE YOUR STUDY AN ACTIVE LEARNING EXPERIENCE

- Try to answer the boxed "Thinking Critically" questions at the end of each section; if you can't, review the section you just read and try again before you move on.

- The "Myth/Fact" boxes correct common misconceptions about criminal justice; test the accuracy of your thinking against these myths.

- The "CJ Online" activities direct you to Internet sites to research real-world data and criminal cases. Make notes to help you recall what you learn there.

- Use the "Careers in Criminal Justice" boxes as a study break. These boxes introduce you to real people working in the field of criminal justice and the day-to-day challenges they encounter on the job.

Continued on inside back cover

INTRODUCTION TO

Criminal**Justice**

SIXTH EDITION

INTRODUCTION TO
CriminalJustice
SIXTH EDITION

Robert M. Bohm
University of Central Florida

Keith N. Haley
Tiffin University

McGraw Hill

Connect
Learn
Succeed™

Connect
Learn
Succeed™

Published by McGraw-Hill, an imprint of The McGraw-Hill Companies, Inc., 1221 Avenue of the Americas, New York, NY 10020. Copyright © 2010. All rights reserved. No part of this publication may be reproduced or distributed in any form or by any means, or stored in a database or retrieval system, without the prior written consent of The McGraw-Hill Companies, Inc., including, but not limited to, in any network or other electronic storage or transmission, or broadcast for distance learning.

This book is printed on acid-free paper.

1 2 3 4 5 6 7 8 9 0 DOW/DOW 0 9

ISBN: 978-0-07-352795-6
MHID: 0-07-352795-5

Editor in Chief: *Michael J. Ryan*
Executive Sponsoring Editor: *Katie Stevens*
Executive Marketing Manager: *Leslie Oberhuber*
Director of Development: *Rhona Robbin*
Development Editor: *Teresa Treacy*
Senior Production Editor/Art Editor: *Mel Valentín*
Manuscript Editor: *Stacey C. Sawyer*
Design Manager: *Andrei Pasternak*
Text Designer: *Andrei Pasternak*
Cover Designer: *Kirk DouPonce, www.DogEaredDesign.com/Andrei Pasternak*
Cover Photo Illustration: *Kirk DouPonce, www.DogEaredDesign.com*
Lead Photo Research Coordinator: *Alexandra Ambrose*
Photo Research: *Judy Mason*
Senior Production Supervisor: *Tandra Jorgensen*
Composition: *9.5/12 Melior, Aptara®, Inc.*
Printing: *45 # New Era Thin Plus, R.R. Donnelley and Sons*

Cover: © *Nic Cleave/Alamy*

Credit: The credit section for this book begins on page C1 and is considered an extension of the copyright page.

Library of Congress Cataloging-in-Publication Data

Bohm, Robert M.
  Introduction to criminal justice / Robert M. Bohm, Keith N. Haley. —6th ed.
      p. cm.
  Includes bibliographical references and index.
  ISBN-13: 978-0-07-352795-6 (alk. paper)
  ISBN-10: 0-07-352795-5 (alk. paper)
  1. Criminal justice, Administration of—United States. 2. Crime—United States. 3. Criminal law—United States. I. Haley, Keith N. II. Title.
  HV9950.B63 2009
  364.973—dc22
                                                                    2009030632

The Internet addresses listed in the text were accurate at the time of publication. The inclusion of a website does not indicate an endorsement by the authors or McGraw-Hill, and McGraw-Hill does not guarantee the accuracy of the information presented at these sites.

www.mhhe.com

To my wife, Linda Taconis, with love.

Robert M. Bohm

To my wife, Shelby, and daughter, Jill, with love.

Keith N. Haley

About the Authors

Robert M. Bohm is professor of Criminal Justice and Legal Studies at the University of Central Florida in Orlando. He has also been a faculty member in the Departments of Criminal Justice at the University of North Carolina at Charlotte (1989–1995) and at Jacksonville State University in Alabama (1979–1989). In 1973 and 1974, he worked for the Jackson County Department of Corrections in Kansas City, Missouri, first as a corrections officer and later as an instructor/counselor in the Model Inmate Employment Program, a Law Enforcement Assistance Administration sponsored–work-release project. He received his Ph.D. in Criminology from Florida State University in 1980. He has published numerous journal articles, book chapters, and books in the areas of criminal justice and criminology. Besides being the coauthor of *Introduction to Criminal Justice,* 6th ed. (McGraw-Hill, 2010), he is the author of *A Concise Introduction to Criminal Justice* (McGraw-Hill, 2008), *Deathquest III: An Introduction to the Theory and Practice of Capital Punishment in the United States,* 3rd ed., and *A Primer on Crime and Delinquency Theory,* 2nd ed. He is also editor of *The Death Penalty in America: Current Research, The Death Penalty Today,* and, co-editor (with James R. Acker and Charles S. Lanier) of *America's Experiment with Capital Punishment: Reflections on the Past, Present, and Future of the Ultimate Sanction,* 2nd ed., and *Demystifying Crime and Criminal Justice* (with Jeffery T. Walker). He has been active in the American Society of Criminology, the Southern Criminal Justice Association, and especially the Academy of Criminal Justice Sciences, having served as Trustee-at-Large (1987–1990), Second Vice-President (1990–1991), First Vice-President (1991–1992), and President (1992–1993). In 1989, the Southern Criminal Justice Association selected him as the Outstanding Educator of the Year. In 1999, he was elected a Fellow of the Academy of Criminal Justice Sciences; in 2001, he was presented with the Founder's Award of the Academy of Criminal Justice Sciences; and, in 2008, he received the Bruce Smith, Sr., Award of the Academy of Criminal Justice Sciences.

Keith N. Haley is professor of Criminal Justice and chair of graduate studies programs in the School of Criminal Justice and Social Sciences at Tiffin University in Ohio. Mr. Haley has also been the dean of the School of Criminal Justice, chair of the criminal justice department, and the dean and associate vice president of the School of Off-Campus Learning at Tiffin University. He has acted as the primary contact for the TU MBA program in Bucharest, Romania, and the head of the Tiffin University Romania Study team that worked to establish a Master of Community Justice Administration degree program at the University of Bucharest. He has also served as coordinator of the criminal justice programs at Collin County Community College in Texas; executive director of the Ohio Peace Officer Training Commission; chair of the criminal justice department at the University of Cincinnati; police officer in Dayton, Ohio; community school director in Springfield, Ohio; director of the criminal justice program at Redlands Community College in Oklahoma; and electronics repairman and NCO in the U.S. Marine Corps. Haley holds a B.S. in Education from Wright State University and an M.S. in Criminal Justice from Michigan State University. He is the author, coauthor, and/or editor of twenty-two books, including revised editions, several book chapters, and many articles in criminal justice publications. He has served as a consultant to many public service, university, business, and industrial organizations on management, online learning, criminal justice research, and memory skills. Haley has also served as the secretary of the police section of the Academy of Criminal Justice Sciences. Haley received the 2001 Nikolai N. Khaladjan International Award for Innovation in Higher Education for helping to establish a graduate school of criminal justice administration in Bucharest, Romania. The Khaladjan Award is given to the higher education program that is the most innovative and has the widest potential for impact on postsecondary education. Bohm and Haley's *Introduction to Criminal Justice* has been translated into the Romanian language under the title *Justitia Penala.*

Brief Contents

Contents

4 The Rule of Law 98

Part **Two** Law Enforcement 141

5 History and Structure of American Law Enforcement 142

6 Policing: Roles, Styles, and Functions 204

Part **Four** Corrections 375

10 Institutional Corrections 376

11 Prison Life, Inmate Rights, Release, and Recidivism 428

12 Community Corrections 458

Part Five Additional Issues in Criminal Justice 503

Careers in Criminal Justice Boxes

Preface

We are convinced that a good education in criminal justice—and in liberal arts generally—can significantly improve the performance of most criminal justice personnel by equipping them, as this text does, to think critically, act ethically, and solve problems effectively. *Introduction to Criminal Justice,* Sixth Edition, is not just for students interested in pursuing a career in criminal justice, however. It is also for students who simply want to learn more about this important social institution, which is vital to a free and democratic society.

All citizens need to know their legal rights and responsibilities. The better informed citizens are, the better able they are to protect themselves. A major theme of this book is that much of what the public "knows" about criminal justice in the United States is myth—that is, either wrong or significantly misunderstood. Consequently, in addition to presenting current, accurate information about criminal justice in the United States and generally accepted interpretations of historical and modern developments, this book "sets the record straight" in areas where, we believe, many people are being misled.

With the help of a quality education in criminal justice, people will feel more comfortable and better equipped to participate in criminal justice policy formulation. They will also be more effective in solving problems in their communities. They will have the critical thinking skills they need if they are to be constructive participants in a democratic nation and to have greater control over their own destinies.

The Sixth Edition

Since 9/11, many people who once had no fear of public transportation, especially air travel, now fear it, afraid that a bomb might explode on board or that an airplane, for example, will be commandeered by terrorists who turn it into a weapon of mass destruction. People are even more suspicious of strangers, particularly of members of certain ethnic groups who before 9/11 caused little concern. We now live with a color-coded warning system that alerts us to the risk of terrorist attacks. In short, we now live in the Age of Terrorism.

The Sixth Edition of *Introduction to Criminal Justice* continues the examination of criminal justice's new expanded role in the "war against terrorism," which we introduced in the Fourth Edition. As noted in the Fourth

Edition, this war has caused the most dramatic transformation of the U.S. government in more than 50 years and has altered in many ways criminal justice at all levels of government. For example, the massive Department of Homeland Security was created, and, as in the last edition, its current organization is described. Also, following 9/11, the FBI's top priority shifted from being a federal police agency to being an intelligence and counterterrorism agency. In this Sixth Edition, the FBI's new National Security Branch is examined. New laws have been passed to provide governments with broad new powers to combat terrorism. These laws have changed many of the traditional rules of criminal justice. In addition to the "first" USA PATRIOT Act and the USA PATRIOT Act Improvement and Reauthorization Act of 2005, this new edition analyzes the Protect America Act of 2007 and the FISA Amendments Act of 2008. In short, in this Sixth Edition, the criminal justice response to terrorism continues to receive serious treatment in several chapters. A list of those additions and many others is provided below.

In addition to integrating detailed coverage of terrorism and updating the text throughout with the latest available statistics, research, and court cases, this Sixth Edition, like the previous one, also features coverage of some of today's highest-profile criminal investigations and cases—from Casey Anthony (who allegedly murdered her 2-year-old daughter, Caylee) to Rod Blagojevich (the former Illinois governor who allegedly tried to sell President Barack Obama's vacated senate seat) to the 8-year-old Arizona boy who shot and killed his father and his father's friend, as well as expanded discussion of some of today's most pressing issues in criminal justice:

- Chapter 4, "The Rule of Law," has new material on the Protect America Act of 2007 and the FISA Amendments Act of 2008.
- Chapter 5, "The History and Structure of American Law Enforcement," features a major new section on the history of federal law enforcement, focusing on the histories of the U.S. Marshals Service, the Secret Service, the FBI, and the DEA. The chapter also addresses new developments in the FBI's fight against terrorism, including the FBI's new National Security Branch.
- Chapter 7, "Policing America: Issues and Ethics," includes the selection standards for Seattle police officers and the results of a recent study of police and public contacts.

- Chapter 11, "Prison Life, Inmate Rights, Release, and Recidivism," has added coverage of the first annual self-report prison sexual victimization survey.
- Chapter 13, "Juvenile Justice," includes the results of a new nationwide survey of abuse in juvenile correctional institutions.
- Chapter 14, "The Future of Criminal Justice in the United States," features added material on law enforcement technology, including digital video surveillance cameras and automatic license number plate recognition systems, and new developments in neuroscience and their application to the administration of justice.

Organization

This book is divided into fourteen chapters that are organized into five parts. Part One, "The Foundations of Criminal Justice," introduces students to the concepts of crime and justice as well as how crime impacts society, how it can be explained, and the rule of law. Part Two, "Law Enforcement," is dedicated to the law enforcement component of criminal justice—its history, structure, roles, ethical issues, and challenges. Part Three, "The Courts," focuses on the administration of justice, sentencing, appeals, and the court process as a whole. Part Four, "Corrections," introduces students to the corrections system, jails, prisons, alternative sanctions, community corrections, and release of prisoners back into the community. And finally, Part Five, "Additional Issues in Criminal Justice," touches on some of the most pressing challenges in the system today: juvenile crime/justice, terrorism, transnational organized crime, and more.

Pedagogical Aids

Working together, the authors and editors have developed a learning system designed to help students get the most out of their first criminal justice course. This commitment to student success is evident from the very first pages of the text, which feature a unique roadmap to student success. This roadmap, entitled "10 Steps to Success" and printed on the text's inside front and back covers, gives students all the tips and tools they need to excel in their first criminal justice course.

The Bohm/Haley commitment to student success goes well beyond these unique guidelines, however; the learning system as a whole is without peer in Introduction to Criminal Justice textbooks. In addition to the many changes already mentioned, we have included many new photographs to make the book even more inviting and relevant for students. We have added new

and current chapter-opening *Crime Story* vignettes, giving the material a fresh flavor intended to motivate students to read on. Carefully updated tables and figures highlight and amplify the text coverage; and chapter outlines, objectives, marginal definitions, and an end-of-book glossary all help students master the material. Other innovative learning tools include:

- *Myth vs. Fact.* These inserts debunk common misconceptions about the system and alert students to the need to question what they see in the media.
- *Thinking Critically.* These sections challenge students to think about and apply chapter concepts.
- *Careers in Criminal Justice.* These mini-biographies highlight some of the most exciting career options available to criminal justice majors and keep the book relevant for students. For a complete list of these boxes, see page xi.
- *CJ Online.* These inserts enable students to explore chapter topics on the Net in a directed fashion.
- *FYI.* These sidebars present eye-opening additional information to retain students' interest and keep them thinking about what they are reading.

We are especially proud of our comprehensive end-of-chapter review sections. In these sections, we provide every kind of review and study tool students could need:

- *Summary*—a terrific study tool, because it is organized into sections that mirror the chapter-opening objectives exactly.
- *Key Terms*—a comprehensive list of the terms defined in the chapter, complete with page references to make it easy for students to go back and review .
- *Review Questions*—study questions that allow students to test their knowledge and prepare for exams.
- *In the Field Activities*—unique experiential exercises that enable students to broaden their understanding of chapter material by taking it to the next level.
- *On the Net Exercises*—still more Internet-based exercises for today's Net-oriented learner.
- *Critical Thinking Questions*—unique scenario-based activities that challenge students to apply what they've learned in the chapter.

Supplements Package

As a full-service publisher of quality educational products, McGraw-Hill does much more than just sell textbooks. The company creates and publishes an extensive array of print, video, and digital supplements for students and instructors. This edition of *Introduction to Criminal Justice* is accompanied by a comprehensive supplements package.

FOR THE STUDENT

An *Online Learning Center (OLC) Website* features innovative, text-specific, and interactive cases, as well as flashcards that can be used to master vocabulary, quizzes with feedback that students can use to study for exams, downloadable state supplements, and more.

FOR THE INSTRUCTOR

The following *Instructor Resources* can be downloaded through the book's website:

- *Instructor's Manual/Testbank*—detailed chapter outlines, key terms, overviews, lecture notes, and a complete testbank.
- *Computerized Testbank*—easy-to-use computerized testing program for both Windows and Macintosh computers.
- *PowerPoint Slides*—complete, chapter-by-chapter slide shows featuring text, art, figures, and tables.

In addition, the *Online Learning Center Website* provides password-protected access to downloadable state supplements and other important instructor support materials and additional resources.

- State-specific supplements for Texas, California, and Florida are available on the OLC.
- *Full-Length Videotapes*—a wide variety of videotapes from the *Films for the Humanities and Social Sciences* series is available to adopters of the text. For additional information, please contact your local sales representative.
- *Course Management Systems*—whether you use WebCT, Blackboard, e-College, or another course-management system, McGraw-Hill will provide you with a cartridge that enables you either to conduct your course entirely online or to supplement your lectures with online material. And if your school does not yet have one of these course-management systems, we can provide you with PageOut, an easy-to-use tool that allows you to create your own course Web page and access all material on the Online Learning Center.

- *Primis Online*—a unique database publishing system that allows instructors to create a customized text from material in this text or elsewhere and deliver that text to students electronically as an e-book or in print format via the bookstore.
- *McGraw-Hill Online Introduction to Criminal Justice Course*—our online courses provide interactive digital content and activities aligned to learning objectives that work with most major learning management systems. McGraw-Hill Online Learning's innovative online courses combine cutting-edge technology and comprehensive instructional design to provide a unique resource for educational institutions to reach a broader audience and offer a wide range of subjects and curriculum in a flexible teaching environment. Visit www.OnlineLearning.com to learn more about our library of courses.

In closing we would like to acknowledge the help and support we received from the McGraw-Hill staff: sponsoring editor Katie Stevens, development editor Teresa Treacy, production editor Mel Valentín, Andrei Pasternak for the design, Alexandra Ambrose for photo research, and the rest of the team.

Robert Bohm
Keith Haley

Acknowledgments

This textbook, like any book, is the product of a collaborative effort. We would like to acknowledge and thank the many people who helped to make this and previous editions possible. First, our thanks go to **Kevin I. Minor** and **H. Preston Elrod,** both at Eastern Kentucky University, for their significant contributions to the chapters on corrections and the juvenile justice system, respectively. We would also like to thank the following colleagues for their substantial help with revisions: **James R. Acker,** State University of New York at Albany (Chapter 4: "The Rule of Law"); **John O. Smykla,** University of West Florida (Chapter 12: "Community Corrections"); and **Donna M. Bishop,** Northeastern University (Chapter 13: "Juvenile Justice"). In addition, for their insightful reviews, criticism, helpful suggestions, and information, we would like to thank:

Brandon Applegate
University of Central Florida

Thomas Arnold
College of Lake County

Richard L. Ashbaugh
Clackamas Community College

Gregg Barak
Eastern Michigan University

David Barlow
Fayetteville State University

Michael Barrett
Ashland University

Denny Bebout
Central Ohio Technical College

Brenda Berretta
Middle Tennessee State University

Anita Blowers
University of North Carolina at Charlotte

Robert J. Boyer
Luzerne Country Community College

William D. Burrell
Probation Services Division, State of New Jersey

Michael Cain
Coastal Bend Community College

Vincent J. Capozzella
Jefferson Community College

Jonathan Cella
Central Texas Community College

Brenda Chappell
University of Central Oklahoma

Charles Chastain
University of Arkansas at Little Rock

David E. Choate
Arizona State University

Daryl Cullison
Columbus State Community College

Beth DeValve
Fayetteville State University

Hank DiMatteo
New Mexico State University

Vicky Dorworth
Montgomery College

Joyce K. Dozier
Wilmington College

Mary Ann Eastep
University of Central Florida

Randy Eastep
Brevard Community College

Robert R. Eiggins
Cedarville College

Linda L. Fleischer
Community College of Beaver County—Essex

John W. Flickinger
Tiffin University

Mike Flint
University of Central Florida

Kenneth A. Frayer
Schoolcraft College at Radcliff

Aric Steven Frazier
Vincennes University

David O. Friedrichs
University of Scranton

Rodney Friery
Jacksonville State University

Harold Frossard
Moraine Valley Community College

James N. Gilbert
University of Nebraska at Kearney

Brian J. Gorman
Towson University

Alex Greenberg
Niagara County Community College

Bob Hale
Southeastern Louisiana University

David O. Harding
Ohio University at Chillicothe

Stuart Henry
San Diego State University

Joseph Hogan
Central Texas College

Thomas E. Holdren
Muskingum Technical College

James Houston
Grand Valley State University

James L. Hudson
Clark State Community College

Pearl Jacobs
Sacred Heart University

W. Richard Janikowski
University of Memphis

Patricia Joffer
South Dakota State University

Mark A. Jones
Community College of Philadelphia

Michelle Jones
The Community College of Baltimore County—Catonsville

Lamar Jordan
Southern Utah University

Don Knueve
Defence College

Peter C. Kratcoski
Kent State University

Hamid R. Kusha
East Carolina University

Gregory C. Leavitt
Green River Community College

Vivian Lord
University of North Carolina at Charlotte

Karol Lucken
University of Central Florida

Richard Lumb
State University of New York at Brockport

Kathleen Maguire
Hindelang Criminal Justice Research Center

Bradley Martin
University of Findlay

Richard M. Martin
Elgin Community College

Alida Merlo
Indiana University of Pennsylvania

Dale Mooso
San Antonio College

James Newman
Rio Hondo College

Sarah Nordin
Solano Community College

Lisa S. Nored
University of Southern Mississippi—Hattiesburg

Les Obert
Casper College

Nancy Oesch
Everest University

Angela Ondrus
Owens Community College

Mary Carolyn Purtill
San Joaquin Delta College

Jerome Randall
University of Central Florida

Matthew Robinson
Appalachian State University

Joseph B. Sanborn, Jr.
University of Central Florida

Martin D. Schwartz
Ohio University

Lance Selva
Middle Tennessee State University

Jo Ann M. Short
Northern Virginia Community College, Annandale Campus

David Slaughter
University of Central Florida

James E. Smith
West Valley College

Jeffrey B. Spelman
North Central Technical College

Domenick Stampone
Raritan Valley Community College

Clayton Steenberg
Arkansas State University at Mountain Home

Gene Stephens
University of South Carolina

James Stinchcomb
Miami-Dade Community College

David Streater
Catawba Valley Community College

David Striegel
Wor-Wic Community College

William L. Tafoya
University of New Haven

Mike Tatum
Brigham Young University—Idaho

Henry A. Townsend
Washtenaw Community College

Roger D. Turner
Shelby State Community College

Ronald E. Vogel
California State University Dominguez Hills

Arnold R. Waggoner
Rose State College

Katina Whorton
Delgado Community College

Harold Williamson
Northeastern Louisiana University

Jeremy R. Wilson
Catawba Valley Community College

Ross Wolf
University of Central Florida

Peter Wood
Eastern Michigan University

Jeffrey Zack
Fayetteville Technical Community College

We would also like to thank **Jack Bohm,** Bob's late father; **Richard Bohm,** New York, New York; and **Lorie Klumb,** Denver, Colorado, for their help with this book. Finally, we would like to express our appreciation to our families and friends for their understanding and patience over the several years we have worked on this project.

Constitutional Issues

You will find coverage of key constitutional issues throughout this book. Use this handy guide to coverage as you study *Introduction to Criminal Justice.*

Article I

Article III

The Bill of Rights
Amendment 1

Congress shall make no law respecting an establishment of religion, or prohibiting the free exercise thereof; or abridging the freedom of speech, or of the press; or the right of the people peaceable to assemble; and to petition the Government for a redress of grievances. Chapter 8, pp. 287–288.

Amendment 2

A well-regulated militia, being necessary to the security of a free State, the right of the people to keep and bear arms shall not be infringed.

Amendment 3

No soldier shall, in time of peace be quartered in any house without the consent of the owner; nor in time of war but in a manner to be prescribed by law.

Amendment 4

The right of the people to be secure in their persons, houses, papers, and effects, against unreasonable searches and seizures, shall not be violated, and no warrants shall issue but upon probable cause, supported by oath or affirmation, and particularly describing the place to be searched, and the persons or things to be seized. Chapter 4, pp. 110–123.

Amendment 5

No person shall be held to answer for a capital or otherwise infamous crime, unless on a presentment or indictment of a Grand Jury, except in cases arising in the land or naval forces, or in the militia, when in actual service in time of war or public danger; nor shall any person be subject for the same offense to be twice put in jeopardy of life or limb; nor shall be compelled in any criminal case to be a witness against himself, not deprived of life, liberty, or property, without due process of law; nor shall private property be taken for public use without just compensation. Chapter 4, pp. 123–126.

Amendment 6

In all criminal prosecutions, the accused shall enjoy the right to a speedy and public trial, by an impartial jury of the State and district wherein the crime shall have been committed, which districts shall have been previously ascertained by law, and to be informed of the nature and cause of the accusation; to be confronted with the witnesses against him; to have compulsory process for obtaining witnesses in his favor, and to have the assistance of counsel for his defense. Chapter 4, pp. 126–130.

Amendment 7

In suits at common law, where the value in controversy shall exceed twenty dollars, the right of trial by jury shall be preserved, and no fact tried by a jury shall be otherwise re-examined in any court of the United States than according to the rules of the common laws.

Amendment 8

Excessive bail shall not be required, nor excessive fines imposed, nor cruel and unusual punishments inflicted. Chapter 4, pp. 130–132; Chapter 9, pp. 358–372; Chapter 11, pp. 445–447; Chapter 14, pp. 556–557.

Amendment 9

The enumeration in the Constitution of certain rights shall not be construed to deny or disparage others retained by the people.

Amendment 10

The powers not delegated to the United States by the Constitution, nor prohibited by it to the States, are reserved to the States respectively, or to the people.

Post-Civil War Amendments
Amendment 14

No State shall make or enforce any law which shall abridge the privileges or immunities of citizens of the United States, nor shall any State deprive any person of life, liberty, or property, without due process of law; nor deny to any person within its jurisdiction the equal protection of the laws. Chapter 4, pp. 109–110; Chapter 9, pp. 358–372; Chapter 11, pp. 447–448.

INTRODUCTION TO
Criminal**Justice**

SIXTH EDITION

PART **ONE**

The Foundations of Criminal Justice

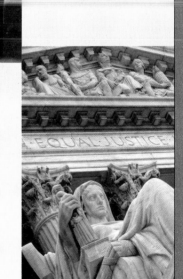

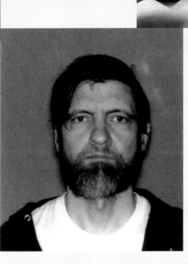

Have You Seen Me?
REWARD
Caylee Marie Anthony
3 Year Old, White Female, Brown hair, Hazel eyes,
Birthmark on left shoulder, Approximately 3 feet tall.
The Orange County Sheriff's Office is currently trying to determine the whereabouts and well being of this child. If you have seen Caylee Marie Anthony in the company of another since June 9, 2008 call 407-254-7000.
www.HelpFindCaylee.com
Please Contact The

Crime and Justice in the United States

1

Chapter Outline

Chapter Objectives

After completing this chapter, you should be able to:

1. Describe how the type of crime routinely presented by the media compares with crime routinely committed.

2. Identify institutions of social control, and explain what makes criminal justice an institution of social control.

3. Summarize how the criminal justice system responds to crime.

4. Explain why criminal justice in the United States is sometimes considered a nonsystem.

5. Point out major differences between Packer's crime control and due process models.

6. Describe the costs of criminal justice in the United States, and compare those costs among federal, state, and local governments.

7. Explain how myths about crime and criminal justice affect the criminal justice system.

CRIME STORY

Beginning in the summer of 2008, the American public has been captivated by the unfolding drama involving Orlando, Florida, toddler Caylee Marie Anthony and her mother, Casey. The story began on July 15, when Cindy Anthony, Caylee's grandmother, called the Orange County Sheriff's Office and asked to have a deputy sent to her home, where she, her husband George, her 22-year-old daughter Casey, and her then 2-year-old granddaughter Caylee lived. Cindy wanted the deputy to arrest her daughter for stealing the family car and money. Cindy also reported a "possible missing child" and stated that the car her daughter had been driving "smelled like there's been a dead body" in it. Cindy had last seen her granddaughter on June 15.

On July 16, Casey was arrested and charged with child neglect, filing false official statements, and obstructing a criminal investigation. She told investigators that she had left Caylee with a baby-sitter weeks before, but the sitter had disappeared. Investigators discovered that Casey had lied about being employed and that the apartment where she claimed to have left Caylee had been vacant for 142 days. Investigators also learned that between June 18 and June 20, a

continued

3

neighbor saw Casey back her car into her parents' driveway. The same neighbor reported that Casey borrowed her shovel. Casey abandoned her car on June 27 in the parking lot of a check-cashing business. The car was towed on June 30. On July 17, a cadaver dog alerted investigators to the odor of human decomposition in the trunk of Casey's car; they also found hair similar to Caylee's, dirt, and a stain. Cindy Anthony, who, with her husband George, consistently maintained that Caylee was alive and Casey was innocent, later stated that the foul odor in her daughter's car "could have been a [dead] squirrel."

On August 5, the state attorney's office charged Casey with child neglect, a third-degree felony, and filing a false statement, a misdemeanor. During the next several weeks, check-fraud charges were also filed. On August 27, a sheriff's official revealed that air samples indicated the car trunk once held a decomposing body. On September 1, sheriff's investigators announced that laboratory evidence suggested there was a strong possibility that Caylee was dead. On September 3, preliminary results from the FBI showed that chloroform, a chemical that can put people to sleep but also kill in large-enough doses, was found in the trunk of Casey's car.

On October 14, despite Caylee's body not having been found, a grand jury indicted Casey on charges of first-degree murder, aggravated child abuse, aggravated manslaughter of a child, and four counts of providing false information to law enforcement. Since July 16, Casey had been in and out of the Orange County jail on child-neglect and check-fraud charges but before the indictment was free on $500,000 bail and living with her parents on court-ordered home confinement. Following the indictment, Casey's release on bail was revoked, and she was returned to jail. On November 26, prosecutors released documents showing that someone used the Anthony family computer in March to search the Internet for words such as "neck-breaking," "shovel," "chloroform," and "household weapons." On December 11, a meter reader found a child's remains in a wet, wooded area a quarter-mile from the Anthony home. Law enforcement officers and hundreds of volunteers had spent months and thousands of hours searching for the missing child, and people from across the country had sent tips and pictures to the sheriff's office and the Anthony family claiming to have spotted Caylee. On December 19, law enforcement authorities announced that DNA tests confirmed the remains matched Caylee's genetic profile. On January 23, 2009, George Anthony, Caylee's grandfather, attempted suicide. In text messages to family and friends, he wrote that "he did not want to live anymore and that he wanted to be with Caylee . . . he wanted to make sure Caylee was in God's arms."

A trial originally was scheduled for March 2009 but was postponed until October 2009. As of this writing, the October date has been canceled, and no new trial date has been set. On April 13, 2009, prosecutors announced that they would seek the death penalty for Casey. In doing so, they reversed their decision, announced on December 5, 2008, less than a week before investigators found remains of Caylee, that they would not seek the death penalty.

Among the topics examined in Chapter 1 is how the media shapes peoples' understanding of crime. The Anthony case is a good example. Each new development in the case has been reported widely in newspapers and on television newscasts. On the Internet, "googling" "the Anthony case" reveals more than 25 million search results (as of July 13, 2009), and hundreds of videos about Casey Anthony have been viewed by thousands of people on YouTube. Comments about the case are regularly posted on blogs and message boards. Popular television shows have also featured the Anthony case. For example, just before Caylee's remains were discovered, Cindy and George Anthony appeared in "an exclusive interview" on *Larry King Live*. The Anthony case is a frequent topic on CNN's *Nancy Grace*, and *Dateline NBC* devoted an entire episode to the case. Casey's attorney, Jose Baez, appeared on NBC's *Today* show with Matt Lauer. One of the questions Lauer asked Baez was whether Casey could get a fair trial in Orlando or anywhere, for that matter, given all the media attention to the case. What do you think? Can Casey Anthony get a fair trial? If convicted, should she receive the death penalty?

Crime in the United States

Every day we are confronted with reports of crime in newspapers, magazines, and radio and television news programs. We also see crime in TV docudramas; on such popular shows as the fictional *Criminal Minds*, *The Closer*, and *Bones*; on the long-running franchises *Law & Order* and *CSI*; and on the reality-based shows *America's Most Wanted*, *Cops*, and *Unsolved Mysteries*. So popular are crime shows on television, they accounted for 9 of the top 20 and 4 of the top 10 network primetime series during the 2008–2009 season

Table 1.1 Top 20 Network Primetime Series, by Viewers, 2008–2009 Season (through 1/11/09)

Rank	Program Name	Total Viewers (millions)
1	*Dancing with the Stars*	19.15
2	*CSI**	18.12
3	*NCIS**	17.44
4	*Dancing w/Stars Results*	17.42
5	*NBC Sunday Night Football*	16.84
6	*The Mentalist**	16.44
7	*Desperate Housewives*	15.85
8	*60 Minutes*	15.37
9	*Criminal Minds**	15.15
10	*Grey's Anatomy*	14.21
11	*Two and a Half Men*	13.99
12	*CSI: NY**	13.63
13	*CSI: Miami**	13.06
14	*Survivor: Gabon*	12.91
15	*24**	12.61
16	*Biggest Loser 7*	11.92
17	*Without a Trace**	11.84
18	*Cold Case**	11.70
19	*Sunday Night NFL Pre-Kick*	11.35
20	*The OT*	11.14

Note: * = crime-related program

Source: Nielsen Media Research, Inc. at http://tv.zap2it.com/tveditorial/tve_main/1,1002,272|||season2,00.html (accessed January 14, 2009).

(see Table 1.1). Furthermore, in some of the other 2008–2009 top 20 series, crime was a significant storyline element. There is also truTV (formerly Court TV), which prominently features crime and justice issues. Crime is also a favorite subject of movies and novels. Unfortunately, some of us encounter crime more directly, as victims. No wonder crime is a top concern of the American public.

We should keep in mind, however, that the crimes presented by the media are usually more sensational than the crimes routinely committed. Consider some of the top crime news stories in the United States in 2008.[1]

- In February, tragedy struck another university campus. In a large lecture hall at Northern Illinois University in DeKalb, Illinois, a gunman dressed in black shot 21 people, five of them fatally, and then shot and killed himself. The gunman, a former graduate student at the university but not enrolled that semester, stepped from behind a curtain on stage shortly after 4 P.M. EST and began shooting. Witnesses said the gunman fired about 30 shots from three guns: first a shotgun and then a Glock handgun followed by a small-caliber pistol. The university with 25,000 students is 65 miles west of downtown Chicago.
- In March, Eve Marie Carson, the 22-year-old student body president and senior at the University of North Carolina at Chapel Hill, was murdered. Her body was found early in the morning lying in a city street, her car

 Crime & the Media

According to a 2006 ABCNEWS.com survey, among Americans who perceive a crime problem nationally, 82% say their belief is based on crime reports they have seen in the news. Only 17% say it is based on their personal experiences.

Source: Daniel Merkle, "Crime Fears Linger—Public Still Concerned Despite Improvements" (June 2006) at http://abcnews.go.com/sections/politics/DailyNews/poll000607.html.

about a mile away. She had been shot several times, including once in the right temple. She was last seen alive at 1:30 A.M., when she stayed home to do schoolwork while her roommates went out. Carson, from Athens, Georgia, was a prestigious Morehead-Cain scholar and a North Carolina Fellow. She was also a premed student, majoring in political science and biology. Two young men, Demario James Atwater, 21, and Lawrence Alvin Lovette Jr., 17, were arrested by Durham police and charged with first-degree murder.

- In April, Texas authorities investigating allegations of abuse and the forced marriage of young teenage women to much older men took more than 400 children into custody from the remote Yearning for Zion Ranch owned by a polygamist religious sect. The ranch built and run by the Fundamentalist Church of Jesus Christ of Latter Day Saints is affiliated with sect leader and prophet Warren Jeffs, who was convicted in 2007 of being an accomplice to the rape of a 14-year-old girl. In May, the Texas Supreme Court, in one of the largest custody cases in U.S. history, ruled that Child Protective Services (CPS) had overreached by putting all the children into foster care when it could show that no more than a handful of girls may have been abused. Although nearly all the children were returned to their parents, the court ordered the parents to take parenting classes, cooperate with CPS, and not leave the state. One by one, the state dropped the children from court oversight.

- In June, Wesley Neal Higdon, 25, of Henderson, Kentucky killed five co-workers and then himself at the Atlantis Plastics factory. Higdon was sent home from work by his supervisor following a dispute with a co-worker at a convenience store during a break. Two hours before the shootings, Higdon called his girlfriend and told her he was going to kill his boss. He then returned to the factory shortly after midnight with a handgun and opened fire, killing his supervisor, the co-worker he argued with at the convenience store, and three other co-workers.

- In October, O.J. Simpson was convicted of several felonies as part of a 2007 armed robbery in a Las Vegas hotel. The case involved sports memorabilia and personal mementoes he claimed were still his—but were the property of two dealers. In December, Simpson was sentenced to a maximum of 33 years in prison but is eligible for parole in nine. The judge stressed the sentence was not "payback" for his 1995 acquittal in the brutal killings of his former wife, Nicole Brown Simpson, and her friend, Ronald Goldman.

- Also in October, William Balfour, the estranged husband of Jennifer Hudson's sister, allegedly murdered Hudson's mother, brother, and nephew. Hudson was a finalist in the 2004 season of *American Idol* and won an Oscar in 2007 for her supporting role in the movie *Dreamgirls*.

- In December, the remains of missing 3-year-old Caylee Anthony were found in swampy woods less than a half mile from her home. The discovery came after months of searching. Caylee's mother, 22-year-old Casey Anthony, was indicted in October on first-degree murder and other charges, even though no body had been found. The mother had insisted that she left her daughter with a baby-sitter in June, but she did not report her missing until July. If convicted of first-degree murder, Casey Anthony faces the death penalty.

- Also in December, 70-year-old investment manager Bernard Madoff, former chairman of the Nasdaq Stock Market, was arrested for bilking mostly wealthy investors, corporations, nonprofit organizations, foundations, and charities of $50 billion in what is likely the largest such fraud in history. Madoff employed a classic "Ponzi" or "pyramid" scheme, whereby he used new investments in his hedge fund, Ascot Partners, to consistently

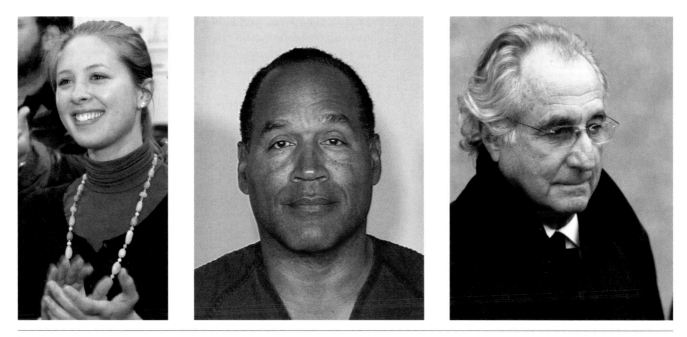

Criminal cases involving Eve Marie Carson, O.J. Simpson, and Bernard Madoff were among the top crime news stories of 2008. *What factors made these crimes so sensational?*

pay high single and double-digit returns to some of his fund's earlier investors. Madoff's investors recommended him to their friends, and Madoff accepted their money only reluctantly and as a favor. Some people had to literally beg Madoff to allow them to invest with him. Had Madoff not faced requests for $7 billion in redemptions as a result of the worldwide economic crisis, his Ponzi scheme might not have been discovered.

• On Christmas Eve, Bruce Jeffrey Pardo, dressed in a Santa Claus suit and carrying a large, wrapped package, entered the house of his former in-laws in Covina, California, and began firing a semiautomatic handgun into the crowd of 25 holiday revelers. He then doused the house with a flammable liquid from a pressurized fuel tank concealed in the package and set the house on fire. Nine people were killed, including his former wife and her parents. Pardo fled to his brother's house about 40 miles away and shot himself. Pardo had been unemployed since July and was described as "a reliable church usher and a good, but quiet, neighbor."

Some of these crime stories are likely to remain top news stories for 2009 and beyond. Furthermore, the fight against domestic terrorism occasioned by the tragedies of September 11, 2001, is likely to remain newsworthy for the foreseeable future. However, taken together, these sensational crime news stories do not provide a very accurate image of the types of crime by which the average citizen is victimized. Nor do such stories accurately depict the kinds of crime to which the police respond on a daily basis.

To provide a more accurate idea of the kinds of crimes more typically committed, we reviewed a list of calls for police service in Houston, Texas, for the month of January 2006.[2] There were 109,370 calls for police service in Houston during the period selected. A close examination of the list of police calls (see Table 1.2) reveals that the most frequent type of call for service in Houston involves disturbances (for example, domestic quarrels, neighbor or landlord-tenant squabbles, gang altercations, bar or street fights, or even loud music or a dog barking). This type of call accounted for 17.5% of the

FYI Ponzi and His Scheme

In 1920, Carlo "Charles" Ponzi, an Italian immigrant, began promising investors he could provide them a 50% return on their money in only 45 days. People from all over New England and New Jersey began mortgaging their homes and sending Ponzi their life savings. Tens of millions of dollars were invested with him, and, by July 1920, Ponzi was making millions of dollars. Ponzi's scam involved paying early investors with money raised from later ones. Ponzi's fraud was discovered, and he was indicted on multiple counts of fraud. He served time in prison and subsequently was deported to Italy.

Source: Charles Ponzi at www.u-s-history.com/pages/h1800.html (accessed January 3, 2009).

 **CJ Online**

Crime in the News

You can read more about past and present crime news stories by visiting the CRIMEBLOG website at www.crimeblog.com/news. *Does this website provide a balanced picture of crime in the United States, or does it primarily provide sensational news coverage?*

Table 1.2 Distribution of Calls for Police Service

Police Calls	Percentage
Disturbance	17.5
Alarm	15.5
On view*	12.1
Suspicious person, package, or vehicle	6.3
Auto accident	6.1
Burglary	4.9
Theft	3.9
Assault	3.2
Traffic	2.2
Criminal mischief	2.0
Trespasser/prowler	1.8
Illegal parking complaint	1.8
Auto theft	1.6
Discharge firearm	1.1
Recover stolen vehicle	1.1
Narcotics complaint	1.0

Note: These figures represent calls for police service to the Houston, Texas, Police Department during January 2006. There were a total of 109,370 police calls.

*Officer on patrol actually sees accident.

total. As shown in previous editions of this book, disturbance calls also accounted for the largest number of calls for police service in the Rampart Precinct of Los Angeles from mid-March through mid-April 1997, and in Chicago, Illinois, in June 2000. Other calls for service in Houston ranged from burglar alarms (15.5%) to suspicious persons, packages, or vehicles (6.3%); from auto accidents (6.1%) to burglaries (4.9%); and from thefts (3.9%) to assaults (3.2%). The calls for police service listed in Table 1.2 represent only those that accounted for at least 1% of the total calls. In all, there were 127 categories of calls for police service. Some crimes had multiple categories. For example, burglary was divided into 11 categories. There were also serious crimes or potential crimes not included in the list (because they accounted for less than 1% of the total calls): 977 robbery calls, 148 death investigation calls, 34 kidnapping calls, and 17 arson calls. Police are also called to assist motorists and to provide escorts for funeral processions—to name just two additional services. Police services and responsibilities are discussed further in Chapter 6.

Here it is important to observe that the calls to which the police routinely respond rarely involve the sensational crimes reported by the media. In many cases, they do not involve crimes at all. Critics argue that the news media have a dual obligation to (1) present news that reflects a more balanced picture of the overall crime problem and (2) reduce their presentation of sensational crimes, especially when such crimes are shown not so much to inform as to pander to the public's curiosity and its simultaneous attraction *and* repulsion to heinous crimes. The more fundamental problem, however, is that the public's conception of crime is to a large extent shaped by the media, and what the media present, for the most part, misleads the public about the nature of crime.

As shown in Table 1.2, Houston police respond to disturbance calls more often than any other type of call for service. *To what types of disturbances should the police respond and not respond?*

THINKING CRITICALLY

1. Do you think the news media are obligated to present a balanced picture of the overall crime problem and reduce their presentation of sensational crimes? Why or why not?

2. How much do you think the public conception of crime is influenced by the media? How do you think the media select crime stories on which to focus?

3. In what ways is crime entertainment?

Criminal Justice: An Institution of Social Control

In the United States, there are a variety of responses to crime. When a child commits a criminal act, even if that act does not come to the attention of the police, parents or school authorities nevertheless may punish the child for the offense (if they find out about it). Attempts to prevent crime by installing burglar alarms in automobiles and homes are other ways of responding to crime. Throughout this book, we focus on the criminal justice response to crime.

Like the family, schools, organized religion, the media, and the law, criminal justice is an **institution of social control** in the United States. A primary role of such institutions is to persuade people, through subtle and not-so-subtle means, to abide by the dominant values of society. Subtle means of persuasion include gossip and peer pressure, whereas expulsion and incarceration are examples of not-so-subtle means.

As an institution of social control, criminal justice differs from the others in two important ways. First, the role of criminal justice is restricted officially to persuading people to abide by a limited range of social values: those values whose violation constitutes crime. Thus, although courteous behavior is desired of all citizens, rude behavior is of no official concern to criminal justice unless it violates the criminal law. Dealing with noncriminal rude behavior is primarily the responsibility of the family. Second, criminal justice is generally society's "last line of defense" against people who refuse to abide by dominant social values and commit crimes. Usually, society turns to criminal justice only after other institutions of social control have failed.

institution of social control An organization that persuades people, through subtle and not-so-subtle means, to abide by the dominant values of society.

THINKING CRITICALLY

1. Given what you know about crime in the United States, do you think that the criminal justice system is a strong institution of social control? Why?

2. Do you think that other institutions such as the family, schools, and organized religion are better institutions of social control than the criminal justice system? If so, which ones? Why?

Criminal Justice: The System

Criminal justice in the United States is administered by a loose confederation of more than 50,000 agencies of federal, state, and local governments. Those agencies consist of the police, the courts, and corrections. Together they are commonly referred to as the *criminal justice system.* Although there are differences in the ways the criminal justice system operates in different jurisdictions, there are also similarities. The term **jurisdiction,** as used here, means a politically defined geographical area (for example, a city, a county, a state, or a nation).

The following paragraphs provide a brief overview of a typical criminal justice response to criminal behavior. Figure 1.1 is a graphic representation of the process. It includes the variations for petty offenses, **misdemeanors** (less serious crimes), **felonies** (serious crimes), and juvenile offenses. A more detailed

 Confidence in the Criminal Justice System

In a recent public opinion poll, 8% of Americans responded they had a "great deal" of confidence in the criminal justice system, 12% had "quite a lot" of confidence, 44% had "some" confidence, 32% had "very little" confidence, 2% had no ("none") confidence, and 2% had no opinion.

Source: The Gallup Poll (June 9–12, 2008) at www.gallup.com/poll/1597/Confidence-Institutions.aspx.

jurisdiction A politically defined geographical area.

misdemeanor A less serious crime generally punishable by a fine or by incarceration in jail for not more than 1 year.

felony A serious offense punishable by confinement in prison for more than 1 year or by death.

Figure 1.1

Overview of the Criminal Justice System

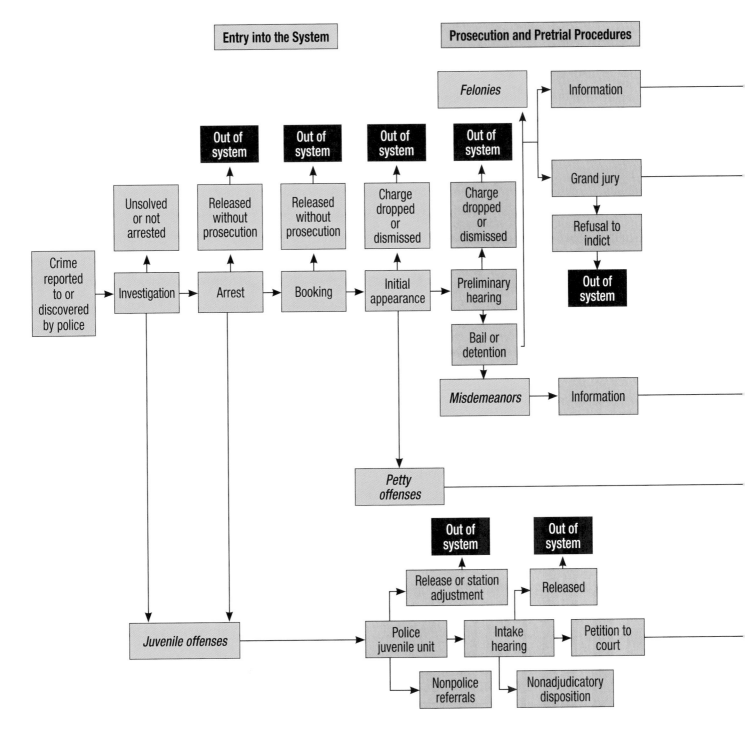

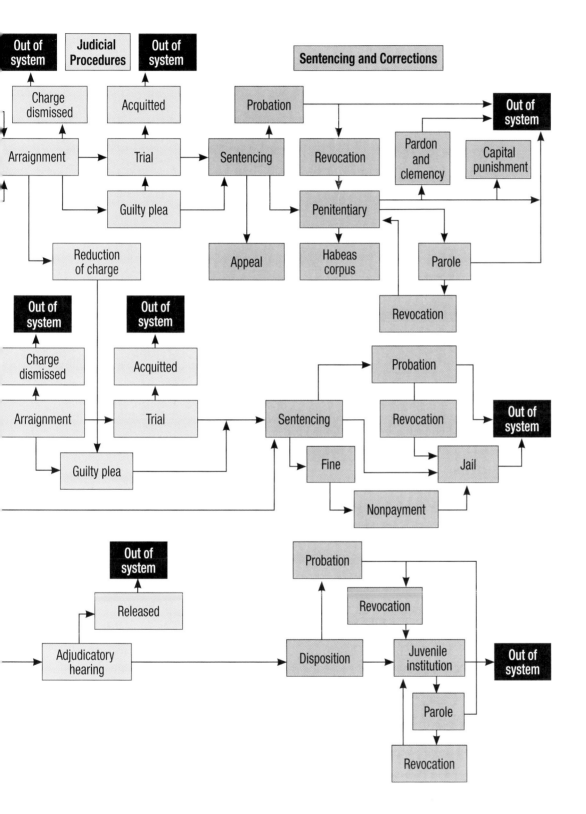

Judicial Procedures

Out of system

Charge dismissed

Arraignment

Acquitted

Trial

Guilty plea

Reduction of charge

Sentencing and Corrections

Probation

Sentencing

Revocation

Pardon and clemency

Capital punishment

Out of system

Penitentiary

Appeal

Habeas corpus

Parole

Revocation

Out of system

Charge dismissed

Out of system

Acquitted

Arraignment

Trial

Guilty plea

Sentencing

Probation

Revocation

Fine

Nonpayment

Jail

Out of system

Out of system

Released

Adjudicatory hearing

Disposition

Probation

Revocation

Juvenile institution

Parole

Revocation

Out of system

Getting fingerprints is generally a part of the booking into jail process. Pictured here is an inmate being fingerprinted with a technologically advanced "Printrat Livescan Finger Machine." *Why are inmates fingerprinted?*

examination of the criminal justice response to crime and delinquency is provided in later chapters of this book.

POLICE

The criminal justice response to crime begins when a crime is reported to the police or, far less often, when the police themselves discover that a crime has been committed. Sometimes solving the crime is easy—the victim or a witness knows the perpetrator or where to find him or her. Often, an arrest supported by witness statements and crime scene evidence is sufficient to close a case, especially with a less serious crime. More often, though, the police must conduct an in-depth investigation to determine what happened in a particular crime. Even when the police start with a known crime or a cooperative victim or witness, the investigation can be lengthy and difficult.

If police investigation of the crime is successful, a suspect is arrested. An **arrest** is the seizing and detaining of a person by lawful authority. After an arrest has been made, the suspect is brought to the police station to be booked. **Booking** is the administrative recording of the arrest. It typically involves entering the suspect's name, the charge, and perhaps the suspect's fingerprints and/ or photograph in the police blotter.

COURTS

Soon after a suspect has been arrested and booked, a prosecutor reviews the facts of the case and the available evidence. Sometimes a prosecutor reviews the case before arrest. The prosecutor decides whether to charge the suspect with a crime or crimes. If no charges are filed, the suspect must be released.

Pretrial Stages After the charge or charges have been filed, the suspect, who is now the **defendant,** is brought before a lower-court judge for an initial

arrest The seizing and detaining of a person by lawful authority.

booking The administrative recording of an arrest. Typically, the suspect's name, the charge, and perhaps the suspect's fingerprints or photograph are entered in the police blotter.

defendant A person against whom a legal action is brought, a warrant is issued, or an indictment is found.

Arrestees can spend up to 48 hours or more in a jail holding cell before a judge decides whether an arrest was justified. *What problems could occur as a result of this practice?*

appearance. At the **initial appearance,** the defendant is given formal notice of the charge or charges against him or her and advised of his or her constitutional rights (for example, the right to counsel). In the case of a misdemeanor or an ordinance violation, a **summary trial** (an immediate trial without a jury) may be held. In the case of a felony, a hearing is held to determine whether the defendant should be released or whether there is probable cause to hold the defendant for a preliminary hearing. **Probable cause** is a standard of proof that requires trustworthy evidence sufficient to make a reasonable person believe that, more likely than not, the proposed action is justified. If the suspect is to be held for a preliminary hearing, bail is set if the judge believes release on bail is appropriate. **Bail,** usually a monetary guarantee deposited with the court, is meant to ensure that the defendant will appear at a later stage in the criminal justice process. In states that do not utilize preliminary hearings, an arraignment date is scheduled at the initial appearance.

In about half of all states, a preliminary hearing follows the initial appearance. Preliminary hearings are used only in felony cases. The purpose of the **preliminary hearing** is for a judge to determine whether there is probable cause to believe that the defendant committed the crime or crimes with which he or she is charged. If the judge finds probable cause, the defendant is bound over for possible indictment in a state with grand juries or for arraignment on a document called *an information* (see below) in a state without grand juries.

Grand juries are involved in felony prosecutions in about half the states. A **grand jury** is a group of citizens who meet in closed sessions for a specified period to investigate charges coming from preliminary hearings and to fulfill other responsibilities. Thus, a primary purpose of the grand jury is to determine whether there is probable cause to believe that the accused committed the crime or crimes with which the prosecutor has charged her or him. The grand jury can either indict or issue a "true bill" or fail to indict a suspect or "issue no bill." If the grand jury fails to indict or issues no bill, the prosecution must be dropped. In states that do not use grand juries, prosecutors charge defendants with a document called an information. An **information** outlines

initial appearance A pretrial stage in which a defendant is brought before a lower court to be given notice of the charge(s) and advised of her or his constitutional rights.

summary trial An immediate trial without a jury.

probable cause A standard of proof that requires evidence sufficient to make a reasonable person believe that, more likely than not, the proposed action is justified.

bail Usually a monetary guarantee deposited with the court to ensure that suspects or defendants will appear at a later stage in the criminal justice process.

preliminary hearing In a felony case, a pretrial stage at which a judge determines whether there is probable cause.

grand jury A group of citizens who meet to investigate charges coming from preliminary hearings.

information A document that outlines the formal charge(s) against a suspect, the law(s) that have been violated and the evidence to support the charge(s).

the formal charge or charges, the law or laws that have been violated, and the evidence to support the charge or charges.

Once an indictment or information is filed with the trial court, the defendant is scheduled for arraignment. The primary purpose of **arraignment** is to hear the formal information or indictment and to allow the defendant to enter a plea. About 95% of criminal defendants plead guilty to the charges against them, in an arrangement called *plea bargaining*. **Plea bargaining** is the practice whereby the prosecutor, the defense attorney, the defendant, and, in many jurisdictions, the judge agree on a specific sentence to be imposed if the accused pleads guilty to an agreed-on charge or charges instead of going to trial.

arraignment A pretrial stage to hear the information or indictment and to allow a plea.

plea bargaining The practice whereby a specific sentence is imposed if the accused pleads guilty to an agreed-on charge or charges instead of going to trial.

Trial If a defendant pleads not guilty or not guilty by reason of insanity, a trial date is set. Although all criminal defendants have a constitutional right to a trial (when imprisonment for 6 months or more is a possible outcome), only about 5% of all criminal cases are disposed of by trial. Approximately 2% of criminal cases involve jury trials. The remaining cases that are not resolved through plea bargaining are decided by a judge in a **bench trial** (without a jury). Thus, approximately 95% of all criminal cases are resolved through plea bargaining, about 2% through jury trials, and about 3% through bench trials. (See Figure 1.2.) In most jurisdictions, the choice between a jury trial and a bench trial is the defendant's to make.

bench trial A trial before a judge without a jury.

If the judge or the jury finds the defendant guilty as charged, the judge begins to consider a sentence. In some jurisdictions the jury participates to varying degrees in the sentencing process. The degree of jury participation depends on the jurisdiction and the crime. If the judge or jury finds the defendant not guilty, the defendant is released from the jurisdiction of the court and becomes a free person.

Figure 1.2

Criminal Case Dispositions

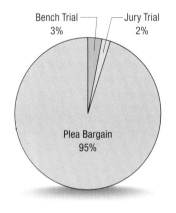

Bench Trial
3%

Jury Trial
2%

Plea Bargain
95%

CORRECTIONS

Judges cannot impose just any sentence. There are many factors that restrict sentencing decisions. The U.S. Constitution's Eighth Amendment prohibiting cruel and unusual punishments and various statutory provisions limit judges. Judges are guided by prevailing philosophical rationales, by organizational considerations, and by presentence investigation reports. They are also influenced by their own personal characteristics. Presentence investigation reports are used in the federal system and in the majority of states to help judges determine appropriate sentences.

Currently, five general types of punishment are in use in the United States: fines, probation, intermediate punishments, imprisonment, and death. Intermediate punishments are various punishments that are more restrictive than probation but less restrictive and less costly than imprisonment. **Probation** is a sentence in which the offender, rather than being incarcerated, is retained in the community under the supervision of a probation agency. Probation is the most frequently imposed criminal sentence in the United States. As long as a judge imposes one or a combination of the five punishments and the sentence length and type are within statutory limits, the judge is free to set any sentence.

probation A sentence in which the offender, rather than being incarcerated, is retained in the community under the supervision of a probation agency.

Defendants who are found guilty can appeal their convictions either on legal grounds or on constitutional grounds. Examples of legal grounds include defects in jury selection, improper admission of evidence at trial, and mistaken interpretations of law. Constitutional grounds include illegal search and seizure, improper questioning of the defendant by the police, identification of the defendant through a defective police lineup, and incompetent assistance of counsel.

The appellate court can *affirm* the verdict of the lower court and let it stand; modify the verdict of the lower court, without totally reversing it; reverse the verdict of the lower court, which requires no further court action; or reverse

Careers in Criminal Justice

Law Enforcement/Security
BATF Agent
Border Patrol Agent
Campus Police Officer
Crime Prevention Specialist
Criminal Investigator
Criminal Profiler
Customs Officer
Deputy Sheriff
Deputy U.S. Marshal
Drug Enforcement Officer
Environmental Protection Agent
FBI Special Agent
Federal Agency Investigator
Fingerprint Technician
Forensic Scientist
Highway Patrol Officer
INS Officer
Insurance Fraud Investigator
Laboratory Technician
Loss Prevention Officer
Military Police Officer
Park Ranger
Police Administrator

Police Dispatcher
Police Officer
Polygraph Examiner
Postal Inspector
Private Investigator
Secret Service Agent
State Trooper

Courts/Legal
Arbitrator
Attorney General
Bailiff
Clerk of Court
Court Reporter
District Attorney
Judge
Jury Assignment Commissioner
Jury Coordinator
Juvenile Magistrate
Law Clerk
Law Librarian
Legal Researcher
Mediator
Paralegal

Public Defender
Public Information Officer
Trial Court Administrator
Victim Advocate

Teaching/Research
Agency Researcher
Community College, College, or
   University Lecturer or
   Professor

Corrections/Rehabilitation
Activity Therapy Administrator
Business Manager
Case Manager
Chaplain
Chemical Dependency Manager
Child Care Worker
Children's Services Counselor
Classification Officer
Client Service Coordinator
Clinical Social Worker
Community Liaison Officer
Correctional Officer
Dietary Officer
Drug Court Coordinator
Field Administrator

Fugitive Apprehension Officer
Home Detention Supervisor
Human Services Counselor
Job Placement Officer
Juvenile Detention Officer
Juvenile Probation Officer
Mental Health Clinician
Parole/Probation Officer
Presentence Investigator
Prison Industries Superintendent
Program Officer/Specialist
Programmer/Analyst
Psychologist
Recreation Coordinator
Rehabilitation Counselor
Researcher
Residence Supervisor
Sex Offender Therapist
Social Worker
Statistician
Substance Abuse Counselor
Teacher
Vocational Instructor
Warden or Superintendent
Youth Service Worker/
   Coordinator
Youth Supervisor

---

the decision and *remand,* or return, the case to the court of original jurisdiction for either a retrial or resentencing.

A defendant sentenced to prison may be eligible for parole (in those jurisdictions that grant parole) after serving a portion of his or her sentence. **Parole** is the conditional release of prisoners before they have served their full sentences. Generally, the decision to grant parole is made by a parole board. Once offenders have served their sentences, they are released from criminal justice authority.

parole The conditional release of prisoners before they have served their full sentences.

THINKING CRITICALLY

1. Do you think the criminal justice system "works" in the United States? Why or why not?

2. What improvements do you think should be made to the criminal justice system?

3. Do you think judges should be limited in the sentences they are allowed to impose? Why or why not?

Criminal Justice: The Nonsystem

As noted earlier, the many police, court, and corrections agencies of the federal, state, and local governments, taken together, are commonly referred to as the criminal justice system. However, the depiction of criminal justice—or, more specifically, of the interrelationships and inner workings of its various components—as a "system" may be inappropriate and misleading for at least two reasons.

First, there is no single "criminal justice system" in the United States. Rather, as noted earlier, there is a loose confederation of many independent criminal justice agencies at all levels of government. This loose confederation is spread throughout the country with different, sometimes overlapping, jurisdictions. Although there are some similarities among many of those agencies, there are also significant differences. The only requirement they all share, a requirement that is the basis for their similarities, is that they follow procedures permitted by the U.S. Constitution.

system A smoothly operating set of arrangements and institutions directed toward the achievement of common goals.

MYTH

The agencies that administer criminal justice in the United States form a unified system: the criminal justice system.

FACT

There is no single "criminal justice system" in the United States. Instead, there is a loose confederation of many independent criminal justice agencies at all levels of government. Moreover, instead of operating together as a system, agencies of criminal justice in the United States interact but generally operate independently of one another, each agency often causing problems for the others.

Second, if a **system** is thought of as a smoothly operating set of arrangements and institutions directed toward the achievement of common goals, one is hard-pressed to call the operation of criminal justice in the United States a system. Instead, because there is considerable conflict and confusion among different agencies of criminal justice, a more accurate representation may be that of a criminal justice "nonsystem."

For example, police commonly complain that criminal offenders who have been arrested after weeks or months of time-consuming and costly investigation are not prosecuted or are not prosecuted vigorously enough. Police often maintain that prosecutors are not working with them or are making their jobs more difficult than necessary. Prosecutors, however, often gripe about shoddy police work. Sometimes, they say, they are unable to prosecute a crime because of procedural errors committed by the police during the investigation or the arrest.

Even when a criminal offender is prosecuted, convicted, and sentenced to prison, police often argue that the sentence is not severe enough to fit the seriousness of the crime, or they complain when the offender is released from prison after serving only a portion of his or her sentence. In such situations, police frequently argue that the courts or the correctional agencies are undermining their efforts by putting criminals back on the streets too soon.

Conflicts between the courts and corrections sometimes occur when judges continue to impose prison sentences on criminal offenders, especially so-called petty offenders, even though the judges know that the prisons are under court orders to reduce overcrowding.

Additionally, there is a mostly separate process for juvenile offenders. Criminal justice officials frequently complained that their jobs were made more difficult because of the practice, which used to be common in many states, of sealing juvenile court records. That practice withheld juvenile court records from the police, prosecutors, and judges even though the records may have been relevant and helpful in making arrests, prosecuting criminal cases, and determining appropriate sentences. Today, formerly confidential juvenile court records are made available to a wide variety of individuals, including prosecutors, law enforcement officers, social service personnel, school authorities, victims, and the public. However, access is not necessarily unlimited or automatic. Access still may be restricted to certain parts of the record and may require a court order.[3] A rationale for concealing juvenile court records is to prevent, as much as possible, the labeling of juvenile offenders as delinquents, which could make them delinquents. (Labeling theory is discussed in Chapter 3.)

In short, rather than operating together as a system, agencies of criminal justice in the United States generally operate independently of one another, each agency often causing problems for the others. Such conflicts may not be entirely undesirable, however, since they occur in a context of checks and balances by which the courts ensure that the law is enforced according to constitutional principles.

THINKING CRITICALLY

1. What do you think are some of the positive aspects of having a criminal justice nonsystem?

2. What do you think are some of the disadvantages of having a criminal justice nonsystem?

Two Models of Criminal Justice

In his influential 1968 book entitled *The Limits of the Criminal Sanction*, legal scholar Herbert Packer describes the criminal justice process in the United States as the outcome of competition between two value systems.[4] Those two value systems, which represent two ends of a value continuum, are the basis

Figure 1.3

Two Models of the Criminal Justice Process

Due Process Model	**Crime Control Model**
Traditional liberal values	Traditional conservative values

for two models of the operation of criminal justice—the crime control model and the due process model; Figure 1.3 depicts this continuum. From a political standpoint, the **crime control model** reflects traditional conservative values, while the **due process model** embodies traditional liberal values.[5] Consequently, when politically conservative values are dominant in society, as they have been for many of the past thirty years, the principles and policies of the crime control model seem to dominate the operation of criminal justice. During more politically liberal periods, such as the 1960s and 1970s, and perhaps under the Obama administration, the principles and policies of the due process model seem to dominate criminal justice activity.

The models are ideal types, neither of which corresponds exactly to the actual day-to-day practice of criminal justice. Rather, they both provide a convenient way to understand and discuss the operation of criminal justice in the United States. In practice, the criminal justice process represents a series of conflicts and compromises between the value systems of the two models. In the following sections, we describe Packer's two models in detail.

THE CRIME CONTROL MODEL

In the crime control model, the control of criminal behavior is by far the most important function of criminal justice. Although the means by which crime is controlled are important in this view (illegal means are not advocated), they are less important than the ultimate goal of control. Consequently, the primary focus of this model is on the efficiency of the criminal justice process. Advocates of the crime control model want to make the process more efficient—to move cases through the process as quickly as possible and to bring them to a close. Packer characterizes the crime control model as "assembly-line justice." Bohm has called it "McJustice."[6] To achieve "quick closure" in the processing of cases, a premium is placed on speed and finality. Speed requires that cases be handled informally and uniformly; finality depends on minimizing occasions for challenge, that is, appeals.

To appreciate the assembly-line or McJustice metaphors used by Packer and Bohm and to understand how treating cases uniformly speeds up the process and makes it more efficient, consider the way that McDonald's sells billions of hamburgers. When you order a Big Mac from McDonald's, you know exactly what you are going to get. All Big Macs are the same, because they are made uniformly. Moreover, you can get a Big Mac in a matter of seconds most of the time. However, what happens when you order something different, or something not already prepared, such as a hamburger with ketchup only? Your order is taken, and you are asked to stand to the side, because your special order will take a few minutes. Your special order has slowed down the assembly line and reduced efficiency. This happens in criminal justice, too! If defendants ask for something special, such as a trial, the assembly line is slowed and efficiency is reduced.

As described in Chapter 8 ("The Administration of Justice"), even when criminal justice is operating at its best, it is a slow process. The time from

crime control model One of Packer's two models of the criminal justice process. Politically, it reflects traditional conservative values. In this model, the control of criminal behavior is the most important function of criminal justice.

due process model One of Packer's two models of the criminal justice process. Politically, it embodies traditional liberal values. In this model, the principal goal of criminal justice is at least as much to protect the innocent as it is to convict the guilty.

Gary Ridgway, the so-called Green River Killer, was allowed to plead guilty to 48 counts of murder in exchange for helping authorities find some of his victims' remains. The plea bargain allowed him to escape the death penalty. He was sentenced to 48 consecutive life sentences without parole instead. *Was the plea bargain in this case justified? Why or why not?*

arrest to final case disposition can typically be measured in weeks or months. If defendants opt for a jury trial, as is their right in most felony cases, the cases are handled formally and are treated as unique; no two cases are the same in their circumstances or in the way they are handled. If defendants are not satisfied with the outcome of their trials, then they have the right to appeal. Appeals may delay by years the final resolution of cases.

To increase efficiency—meaning speed and finality—crime control advocates prefer plea bargaining. As described previously and as you will see in Chapter 8, plea bargaining is an informal process that is used instead of trial. Plea bargains can be offered and accepted in a relatively short time. Also, cases are handled uniformly because the mechanics of a plea bargain are basically the same; only the substance of the deal differs. Additionally, with successful plea bargains, there is no opportunity for challenge; there are no appeals. Thus, plea bargaining is the perfect mechanism for achieving the primary focus of the crime control model—efficiency.

The key to the operation of the crime control model is "a presumption of guilt." In other words, advocates of this model assume that if the police have expended the time and effort to arrest a suspect and the prosecutor has formally charged the suspect with a crime, then the suspect must be guilty. Why else would police arrest and prosecutors charge? Although the answers to that question are many (see the discussions in Chapters 7 and 8 of the extralegal factors that influence police and prosecutorial behavior), the fact remains that a presumption of guilt is accurate most of the time. That is, most people who are arrested and charged with a crime or crimes are, in fact, guilty. A problem—but not a significant one for crime control advocates—is that a presumption of guilt is not accurate all the time; miscarriages of justice do occur (see the discussion in Chapter 4, "The Rule of Law"). An equally important problem is that a presumption of guilt goes against one of the oldest and most cherished principles of American criminal justice—that a person is considered innocent until proven guilty.

Reduced to its barest essentials and operating at its highest level of efficiency, the crime control model consists of an administrative fact-finding process with two possible outcomes: a suspect's exoneration or the suspect's guilty plea.

THE DUE PROCESS MODEL

Advocates of the due process model, by contrast, reject the informal fact-finding process as definitive of factual guilt. They insist, instead, on formal, adjudicative fact-finding processes in which cases against suspects are heard publicly by impartial trial courts. In the due process model, moreover, the factual guilt of suspects is not determined until the suspects have had a full opportunity to discredit the charges against them. For those reasons, Packer characterizes the due process model as "obstacle-course justice."

What motivates this careful and deliberate approach to the administration of justice is the realization that human beings sometimes make mistakes. The police sometimes arrest the wrong person, and prosecutors sometimes charge the wrong person. Thus, contrary to the crime control model, the demand for finality is low in the due process model, and the goal is at least as much to protect the innocent as it is to convict the guilty. Indeed, for due process model advocates, it is better to let a guilty person go free than it is to wrongly convict and punish an innocent person.

The due process model is based on the doctrine of legal guilt and the presumption of innocence. According to the **doctrine of legal guilt,** people are not to be held guilty of crimes merely on a showing, based on reliable evidence, that in all probability they did in fact do what they are accused of doing. In other words, it is not enough that people are factually guilty in the due process model; they must also be legally guilty. Legal guilt results only when factual guilt is determined in a procedurally regular fashion, as in a criminal trial, and when the procedural rules, or due process rights, designed to protect suspects and defendants and to safeguard the integrity of the process are employed. The conditions of legal guilt—that is, procedural, or due process, rights—are described in Chapter 4. They include:

- Freedom from unreasonable searches and seizures.
- Protection against double jeopardy.
- Protection against compelled self-incrimination.
- A speedy and public trial.
- An impartial jury of the state and district where the crime occurred.
- Notice of the nature and cause of the accusation.
- The right to confront opposing witnesses.
- Compulsory process for obtaining favorable witnesses.
- The right to counsel.
- The prohibition of cruel and unusual punishment.

In short, in the due process model, factual guilt is not enough. For people to be found guilty of crimes, they must be found *both* factually and legally guilty.

This obstacle-course model of justice is championed by due process advocates, because they are skeptical about the ideal of equality on which U.S. criminal justice is supposedly based. They recognize that there can be no equal justice where the kind of trial a person gets, or whether he or she gets a trial at all, depends substantially on how much money that person has. It is assumed that in an adversarial system of justice (as described in Chapter 8 and employed in the United States), an effective defense is largely a function of the resources that can be mustered on behalf of the accused. It is also assumed that there are gross inequalities in the financial means of criminal defendants. Most criminal defendants are indigent or poor, and because of their indigence, they are frequently denied an effective defense. Although procedural safeguards, or conditions of legal guilt, cannot by themselves correct the inequity in resources, they do provide indigent defendants, at least theoretically, with a better chance for justice than they would receive without them.

Fundamentally, the due process model defends the ideal of personal freedom and its protection. The model rests on the assumption that preventing tyranny by the government and its agents is the most important function of the criminal justice process.

doctrine of legal guilt The principle that people are not to be held guilty of crimes merely on a showing, based on reliable evidence, that in all probability they did in fact do what they are accused of doing. Legal guilt results only when factual guilt is determined in a procedurally regular fashion, as in a criminal trial, and when the procedural rules designed to protect suspects and defendants and to safeguard the integrity of the process are employed.

CRIME CONTROL VERSUS DUE PROCESS

As noted earlier, which of the models dominates criminal justice policy in the United States at any particular time depends on the political climate. Until the election of Barak Obama, the United States was in the midst of a prolonged period—beginning in the mid-1970s—in which politically conservative values have dominated the practice of criminal and juvenile justice. Thus, it should come as no surprise that the crime control model of criminal justice more closely resembled the actual practice of criminal and juvenile justice in the United States immediately prior to Obama's election. At the time Packer wrote and published his book, however, politically liberal values and, thus, the principles and policies of the due process model, dominated the operation of criminal and juvenile justice. At least in the near future, the due process model of criminal and juvenile justice is likely to guide the Obama administration.

In any event, neither model is likely to completely represent the practices of criminal justice. Even though the current operation of criminal and juvenile justice reflects the dominance of the crime control model, elements of the due process model remain evident. The election of Barak Obama suggests that the American people have gotten tired of seeing their tax dollars spent on programs and a process that are not providing them with the safety from criminal behavior that they so desperately desire. If Packer's model of criminal justice is correct, we should expect a shift in criminal justice practice that will coincide with the shift in the values held by American political leaders and, of course, American citizens.

THINKING CRITICALLY

1. What do you think are some of the fundamental problems with the crime control model? What are the benefits of this model?

2. What do you think are some of the fundamental problems with the due process model? What are the benefits of this model?

Costs of Criminal Justice

Each year in the United States, an enormous amount of money is spent on criminal justice at the federal, state, and local levels. In 2006 (the latest year for which figures are available), a total of $214.5 billion was spent on civil and criminal justice. That represents approximately $718 for every resident of the United States. Table 1.3 shows the breakdown of spending among the three main segments of the criminal justice system and among the federal, state, and local levels. The $214.5 billion was an increase of about 10.5% from 2004 and nearly 500% from 1982.[7]

Criminal justice is primarily a state and local function; state and local governments spent about 83% of the 2006 total. Note that state and local governments share the costs of criminal justice by making police protection primarily a local function and corrections primarily a state function. In 2006, local governments spent 69% of the total spent on police protection, while state governments spent nearly 59% of the total spent on corrections. The expense of judicial and legal services was more evenly divided between state and local governments; still, local governments (primarily counties) spent more than state governments on those services (41% versus 38%).

Note that although the bulk of government spending on criminal justice is at the state and local levels, the federal government uses its expenditures strategically to influence criminal justice policy at the other levels of government. For example, the federal government develops and tests new approaches to criminal justice and crime control. It then encourages state and local criminal justice agencies to duplicate effective programs and practices by awarding monetary grants to interested and willing agencies. Grants are also

Table 1.3 Costs of Criminal Justice

In 2006, federal, state, and local governments spent $214.5 billion in direct expenditures for the criminal and civil justice systems.

Police Protection	In Millions ($)
69% Local	67,996
11% States	10.838
20% Federal	20,039
100%	98,873
Judicial/Legal Services	
41% Local	19,033
38% States	17,790
21% Federal	10,051
100%	46,874
Corrections	
32% Local	22,176
59% States	40,413
9% Federal	6,158
100%	68,747

Note: Detail may not add to 100% because of rounding.

Source: Steven W. Perry, "Justice Expenditure and Employment Extracts, 2006," *Bureau of Justice Statistics*, U.S. Department of Justice at www.ojp.usdoj.gov/bjs/eande.htm#selected,filename:cjee0601.cvs (date of version: 8/29/08).

awarded to state and local criminal justice agencies to implement programs that address the federal government's crime control priorities, such as its recent emphasis on violent and drug-related crimes. In 2006, the federal government spent nearly 17% of the total expenditures on criminal and civil justice.

It is also noteworthy that despite the billions of dollars spent on criminal and civil justice at the state and local levels, as a percentage of all government expenditures, the amount spent on criminal justice represents only a tiny fraction—about 7% (3% for police protection, about 2.5% for corrections, and 1.5% for judicial and legal services). In other words, only about 7 cents of every state and local tax dollar is spent on criminal justice. Include federal tax dollars, and only about 4 cents of every tax dollar is spent on criminal justice—an amount that has stayed about the same for approximately 20 years. Thus, compared with expenditures on other government services, such as social insurance, national defense, international relations, interest on debt at the federal level, public welfare, education, health and hospitals, and interest on debt at the state and local levels, spending on criminal justice remains a relatively low priority—a point apparently not missed by the American public.[8]

For almost three decades, public opinion polls have shown that more than half of all Americans believe that too little money is spent on crime control. Very few people think that too much is being spent.[9] What is not clear, however, because no data are available, is whether those people who believe more money should be spent to fight crime are willing to pay higher taxes to provide that money.

The data presented so far in this section provide a general overview of the aggregate costs of criminal justice in the United States. They do not, however, reveal the expenses of individual-level justice, which vary greatly. On the one hand, administering justice to people who commit capital or death-eligible crimes costs, on average, between $2.5 and $5 million per case (the cost of the entire process); extraordinary cases can cost much more. For example, the state of Florida reportedly spent $10 million to administer justice to serial murderer Ted Bundy in 1989, and the federal government spent more than $100 million to execute mass murderer Timothy McVeigh in 2001.[10]

FYI Money and Crime

Americans have definite opinions about crime and the money spent to fight it. For example, in 2003, 69% of Americans thought that to lower the crime rate in the United States, more money and effort should be spent attacking social and economic problems through better education and job training. Twenty-nine percent thought more money and effort should be spent on improving law enforcement by providing more prisons, police, and judges, and 2% didn't know or refused to answer.

Source: *Sourcebook of Criminal Justice Statistics Online*, Table 2.0007, at www.albany.edu/sourcebook/pdf/t20007.pdf.

The state of Florida reportedly spent $10 million to administer justice to serial murderer Ted Bundy in 1989, and the federal government spent more than $100 million to execute mass murderer Timothy McVeigh in 2001. *Were the executions worth the expense? Why or why not?*

Figure 1.4

Total Costs of the Orange County, Florida, Burglary Case by Specific Criminal Justice Functions

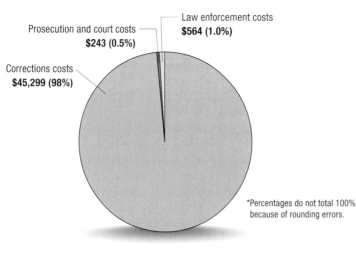

Law enforcement costs
$564 (1.0%)

Prosecution and court costs
$243 (0.5%)

Corrections costs
$45,299 (98%)

*Percentages do not total 100% because of rounding errors.

Total = $46,106

- Law enforcement costs include the time spent capturing and arresting the offender, writing reports, and conducting the investigation.

- Prosecution costs include the time spent reviewing the case and filing charges, negotiating a plea with the public defender, attending the sentencing hearing, and the support staff who performed various tasks such as filing and forwarding documents.

- Defense costs include the time spent reviewing the case, talking to the defendant, negotiating a plea, and attending the sentencing hearing.

- Judicial costs include time spent at the initial appearance and arraignment and completing required paperwork.

- Court support staff costs include time spent filing the charges, entering the file into the computer, assigning the case number, scheduling the arraignment, preparing subpoenas, and recording minutes of the formal proceedings.

- Corrections costs include the costs of booking the offender, detaining him in jail while awaiting the adjudication of the case, and incarcerating him in prison as a result of the sentence imposed.

On the other hand, the routine crimes processed daily cost much less. A better idea of the costs of justice in more typical cases comes from an examination of the costs of each stage of the local criminal justice process. The results of such a study are presented in the following text.[11] A 39-year-old male burglar was arrested in Orange County, Florida, in 1995. The state of Florida and Orange County spent $46,106 to administer justice to that offender, who had stolen approximately $5,100 of merchandise and caused about $1,000 in damages to the store. Of course, the costs of the crime include more than just the stolen merchandise and damaged property. They also include the psychological costs of victimization (for example, the loss of a sense of security, a greater fear of crime), which are difficult to place a dollar figure on. Figure 1.4 displays the total cost of the case and the costs for each of the specific criminal justice functions. As shown, corrections costs accounted for the bulk of expenditures (98%). Law enforcement, prosecution, and court costs were minimal in comparison. An interesting postscript is that in 2002, the offender was adjudicated guilty on several charges stemming from separate incidents in 1999 and 2000. The charges included: battery on a law enforcement officer, resisting arrest with violence, burglary of a conveyance, possession of burglary tools, and grand theft. His combined sentence for all charges was 20 years with credit for 3 years' time served. Florida law mandates that offenders serve at least 85% of their initial sentence. Therefore, this offender is not scheduled for release until 2017. Given the severity of the offenses and the duration of his prison sentence, it now appears that this offender is anything but typical.

THINKING CRITICALLY

1. Do you think more money needs to be spent on criminal justice? Why or why not?

Myths About Crime and Criminal Justice

A major theme of this book is to expose and correct misconceptions the American public has about crime and criminal justice. Much of the public's understanding of crime and criminal justice is wrong; it is based on myths. **Myths** are "simplistic and distorted beliefs based upon emotion rather than rigorous analysis" or "at worst . . . dangerous falsifications."[12] More specifically, myths are "credible, dramatic, socially constructed representation[s] of perceived realities that people accept as permanent, fixed knowledge of reality while forgetting (if they were ever aware of it) [their] tentative, imaginative, creative, and perhaps fictional qualities."[13] For example, during the Middle Ages in Europe, people commonly believed that guilt or innocence could be determined through *trial by ordeal*. The accused might be required to walk barefoot over hot coals, hold a piece of red-hot iron, or walk through fire. The absence of any injury was believed to be a sign from God that the person was innocent. Although we may now wonder how such a distorted and simplistic belief could have been taken as fact and used to determine a person's guilt or innocence, people did not consider the belief a myth during the time that it was official practice. The lesson to be learned from this example is that a belief that is taken as fact at one time may in retrospect be viewed as a myth. In this book, we attempt to place such myths about crime and criminal justice in perspective.[14]

Throughout this text, we present generally accepted beliefs about crime and the justice system that can be considered myths, because they can be contradicted with facts. In some instances it can be demonstrated that the perpetuation and acceptance of certain myths by the public, politicians, and criminal justice practitioners have contributed to the failure to significantly reduce predatory criminal behavior and to increase peace. It is also possible that acceptance of these myths as accurate representations of reality or as facts results in the waste of billions of dollars in the battle against crime.

During the Middle Ages, Holy Roman Emperor Otto III married the King of Aragon's daughter, who fell in love with a count of the court. When the count refused her advances, the emperor's wife accused him of making an attempt on her honor. The scene shows the count's wife attempting to prove his innocence by trial by fire (a red-hot rod in her hand). When she was not burned, the count's innocence was proved and the emperor's wife was burned alive for making the false accusation. *How could people believe that guilt or innocence could be proven in this way?*

myths Beliefs based on emotion rather than analysis.

✳ Summary

1. Describe how the type of crime routinely presented by the media compares with crime routinely committed.

   Crime presented by the media is usually more sensational than crime routinely committed.

2. Identify institutions of social control, and explain what makes criminal justice an institution of social control.

   Institutions of social control include the family, schools, organized religion, the media, the law, and criminal justice. Such institutions attempt to persuade people to abide by the dominant values of society. Criminal justice is restricted to persuading people to abide by a limited range of social values, the violation of which constitutes crime.

3. Summarize how the criminal justice system responds to crime.

   The typical criminal justice response to the commission of a crime involves the following: investigation; arrest (if the investigation is successful); booking; the formal charging of the suspect; an initial appearance; a preliminary hearing (for a felony); either indictment by a grand jury followed by arraignment or arraignment on an information; either a plea bargain or a trial; sentencing; possible appeal; and punishment (if the defendant is found guilty).

4. Explain why criminal justice in the United States is sometimes considered a nonsystem.

   Criminal justice in the United States is sometimes considered a nonsystem for two major reasons. First, there is no single system but instead a loose confederation of more than 50,000 agencies on federal, state, and local levels. Second, rather than being a smoothly operating set of arrangements and institutions, the agencies of the criminal justice system interact with one another but generally operate independently, often causing problems for one another.

5. Point out major differences between Packer's crime control and due process models.

   From a political standpoint, the crime control model of criminal justice reflects traditional conservative values, while the due process model embodies traditional liberal values. In the crime control model, the control of criminal behavior is by far the most important function of criminal justice. Consequently, the primary focus of this model is on efficiency in the operation of the criminal justice process. The goal of the due process model, in contrast, is at least as much to protect the innocent as it is to convict the guilty. Fundamentally, the due process model defends the ideal of personal freedom and its protection and rests on the assumption that the prevention of tyranny on the part of government and its agents is the most important function of the criminal justice process.

6. Describe the costs of criminal justice in the United States, and compare those costs among federal, state, and local governments.

   An enormous amount of money is spent each year on criminal justice in the United States. In 2006, federal, state, and local governments spent a total of $214.5 billion on police protection ($99 billion), judicial/legal services ($47 billion), and corrections ($69 billion). The bulk of government spending on criminal justice is at the state and local levels, but the federal government spends money strategically to influence criminal justice policy at the other levels of government.

7. Explain how myths about crime and criminal justice affect the criminal justice system.

   The acceptance and perpetuation of myths, or simplistic beliefs based on emotion rather than rigorous analysis, can harm the criminal justice system by contributing to the failure to reduce crime and to the waste of money in the battle against crime.

✳ Key Terms

institution of social
  control 9
jurisdiction 9
misdemeanor 9
felony 9
arrest 12
booking 12

defendant 12
initial appearance 13
summary trial 13
probable cause 13
bail 13
preliminary hearing 13
grand jury 13

information 13
arraignment 14
plea bargaining 14
bench trial 14
probation 14
parole 15
system 16

crime control model 17
due process model 17
doctrine of legal guilt 19
myths 23

✳ Review Questions

1. What is the fundamental problem with the types of crime routinely presented by the media?

2. What was the most frequent type of call for police service in Houston during the period examined in the text (see Table 1.2)?

3. What is an *institution of social control*?

4. Why is criminal justice sometimes considered society's "last line of defense"?

5. What three agencies make up the criminal justice system?

6. What is a *jurisdiction*?

7. What is the difference between a *misdemeanor* and a *felony*?

8. What is the difference between an *arrest* and a *booking*?

9. Who decides whether to charge a suspect with a crime?

10. What is a *defendant*, and when does a suspect become a defendant?

11. What is the difference between an *initial appearance* and a *preliminary hearing?*

12. Define *bench trial, summary trial, bail, grand jury, arraignment, plea bargaining,* and *parole.*

13. What is meant by *probable cause?*

14. Why are the conflicts between the different agencies of criminal justice not entirely undesirable?

15. Why does Packer use the metaphors of *assembly-line justice* and *obstacle-course justice* to characterize his crime control and due process models of criminal justice?

16. What are the bases (that is, the presumptions or doctrines) of Packer's crime control and due process models of criminal justice?

17. Which levels of government—federal, state, and local—bear most of the costs of criminal justice in the United States?

18. What is a lesson to be learned from myths about crime and criminal justice?

✳ In the Field

1. **Crime and the Media** Watch a local television station's broadcast of the evening news for one or more days and record the crimes reported. Then obtain from your local police department a copy of the log of calls for police service for one of those days. Compare the crimes reported on the nightly news with the calls for police service. Describe similarities and differences between the two different sources of crime information. What have you learned?

2. **Costs of Crime** Follow a criminal case in your community and determine the costs of processing the case. You will have to contact the police, the prosecutor, the defense attorney, the judge, and other relevant participants. Remember to consider both monetary and psychological costs. After you have determined the costs, decide whether you think they were justified. Defend your answer.

3. **Costs of Justice** Only about 7% of state and local spending is for criminal justice. By contrast, states and localities spend more for education and public welfare, and about the same for health care and hospitals. Divide into groups. Using the preceding information, debate within your group whether states and localities spend enough of their budgets on criminal justice. Share group results with the class.

✳ On the Net

1. **Criminal Justice in Other Countries** Learn about the criminal justice systems of other countries by visiting the U.S. Justice Department's website, *The World Factbook of Criminal Justice Systems,* at www.ojp.usdoj.gov/bjs/abstract/wfcj.htm.

2. **FBI's Most Wanted** Access the FBI's "Top Ten Most Wanted Fugitives" at www.fbi.gov/mostwant.htm. Read the descriptions of the fugitives. Write a report describing the characteristics they share. Also, try to determine what unique features qualify these fugitives, and not others, for the list.

✳ Critical Thinking Exercises

PLEA BARGAINING

1. Shirley Smith pleaded guilty to third-degree murder after admitting she had put rat poison in drinks her husband ingested at least 12 times during the course of their 13-month marriage. Sentenced to a maximum of 20 years in prison, she would have to serve at least 10 years before she could be considered for parole. The prosecutor defended the plea bargain against much public criticism. The prosecutor claimed that the costs of a murder trial and subsequent appeals were not paramount. However, the prosecutor did acknowledge that the case could have been the most expensive in county history, that it exhausted his entire $2 million budget for the fiscal year, and that it required a tax increase to cover the costs. As an elected official, the prosecutor attempted to seek justice while exercising a sense of fiscal responsibility.
   a. Do you think the prosecutor made the correct decision to plea bargain? Defend your answer.
   b. In potentially expensive cases, should the prosecutor seek a referendum on the matter (to determine whether residents are willing to pay additional taxes to try a defendant rather than accept a plea bargain)?

PRISON VERSUS REHABILITATION

2. The city council of a midsize East Coast city is locked in a debate concerning how to address the rising incidence of violent crime. John Fogarty, one of the most influential people in the city, is pushing for more police and stiffer penalties as the solution. He is the leader of a group that is proposing the construction of a new prison. Another group thinks putting more people in prison is not the answer. They believe that early intervention, education, and prevention programs will be most effective. There is not enough money to fund both sides' proposals.
   a. Which side would you support? Why?
   b. What do you think is the number-one crime problem in your community? List ways of dealing with that problem. What would be the most cost-effective way to lower the rate of that crime?

To access more information and resources, including study questions, chapter summaries, and links, go to www.mhhe.com/bohm6e.

Crime and Its Consequences

Chapter Outline

Chapter Objectives

After completing this chapter, you should be able to:

1. Distinguish between a social definition and a legal definition of crime, and summarize the problems with each.

2. List the technical and ideal elements of a crime.

3. Identify some of the legal defenses or legal excuses for criminal responsibility.

4. Explain why crime and delinquency statistics are unreliable.

5. Identify the two major sources of crime statistics in the United States.

6. Describe the principal finding of the national crime victimization surveys.

7. Summarize the general finding of self-report crime surveys.

8. Identify the costs of crime.

9. Describe the extent of fear of crime in the United States and the characteristics of people most likely to fear crime.

10. List the characteristics of people who are the most likely and the least likely to be victims of crime.

CRIME STORY

On June 5, 2008, Robert S. Benjo, 82, shot and killed his 76-year-old wife, Peggy, while she slept. The couple had been married for 52 years. Peggy had surgery for colon cancer in December, had lost about 50 pounds and had become incontinent. She had also been suffering from Alzheimer's disease. Doctors gave her about a year to live. Robert was her caregiver, who cleaned up after her and tried to feed her. No one doubted that he loved his wife.

Before her health started to fail, Peggy was a vibrant woman, but she had become a shell of her former self, according to Robert, who was becoming increasingly depressed. She pleaded

continued

with him that she did not want to live that way. She wanted her pain to end. Peggy told her daughter that she had lost everything, that she was unhealthy, and did not have the will or energy to live.

Robert was arrested on a second-degree murder charge after admitting he shot his wife. He told investigators that he did what he had to do and that he would have to live with it. He was released without bond after an emotional hearing during which his children pleaded for his release. They told the judge their father acted out of mercy and should not be in jail. He had been in custody since his arrest. Rather than face trial, Robert was allowed to plead guilty to manslaughter, and prosecutors waived any mandatory sentences, giving the judge discretion on the punishment. The judge sentenced Robert to a 15-year prison term but suspended the sentence and ordered Robert to serve two years of community control, which is similar to house arrest, plus 13 years of probation. The judge commented on the dilemma he faced. On the one hand, any prison sentence probably would be a death sentence. On the other hand, he did not "want to open the door to a bunch of people who think it's OK to kill their wives if they're old and sick." Robert walked out of the courtroom relieved that he could live with his family, especially his 3-year-old grandson. He said he was appreciative of what the court did.

Robert Benjo's case is a clear example of caregiver homicide or mercy killing, which occurs about 2,500 times annually and appears to be increasing with the increase in the elderly population. What is unusual about Benjo's case is that it did not end with the more common murder-suicide. In this case, Benjo knew his daughter-in-law and grandson were coming to visit, so he called and told her he had killed his wife and was going to kill himself. The daughter-in-law talked him out of suicide.

Among the topics examined in Chapter 2 are definitions of crime. Should caregiver homicide or mercy killing be a crime? One of the elements of crime is harm. What is the harm in caregiver homicide or mercy killing? Fear of crime and victims of crime are other topics addressed in the chapter. Should the public fear Robert Benjo? Is Benjo a real danger to society? Was his wife a crime victim? Did Benjo deserve to be sent to prison? The answers to these questions reveal much about crime and its consequences.

norm Any standard or rule regarding what human beings should or should not think, say, or do under given circumstances.

Definitions of Crime

The object of criminal justice in the United States is to prevent and control crime. Thus, to understand criminal justice, one must understand crime. An appropriate definition of crime, however, remains one of the most critical unresolved issues in criminal justice today. One problem is that many dangerous and harmful behaviors are not defined as crimes, while many less dangerous and less harmful behaviors are. We begin, then, by examining how crime is defined and the problems with defining what a crime is.

SOCIAL DEFINITIONS

The broadest definitions of crime are social definitions. A typical social definition of crime is behavior that violates the norms of society—or, more simply, antisocial behavior. A **norm** is any standard or rule regarding what human beings should or should not think, say, or do under given circumstances. Because social definitions of crime are broad, they are less likely than narrower definitions to exclude behaviors that ought to be included. Nevertheless, there are several problems with social definitions of crime.

First, norms vary from group to group within a single society. There is no uniform definition of antisocial behavior. Take, for example, the acts involved in gambling, prostitution, abortion, and homosexual behavior. As current public debates indicate, there is much controversy in the United States over whether those acts should be crimes. Even with acts about which there seems to be a consensus, like murder and rape, there is no agreement on what constitutes such acts. For example, if a patient dies from a disease contracted from a doctor who did not wash his or her hands before examining the patient, has the doctor committed murder? Or, if a man has forcible sexual intercourse with a woman against her will but, before the act, at the woman's request, puts on a condom so that the woman will not get a sexually transmitted disease, has the man committed rape? Those examples illustrate the difficulty of determining what, in fact, constitutes antisocial behavior, let alone crime.

Second, norms are always subject to interpretation. Each norm's meaning has a history. Consider abortion, for example. For some people, abortion is the killing of a fetus or a human being. For other people, abortion is not killing, because, for them, human life begins at birth and not at conception. For the latter group, the abortion issue concerns women's freedom to control their own bodies. For the former group, abortion constitutes an injustice to the helpless.

Third, norms change from time to time and from place to place. For example, the consumption of alcohol was prohibited in the United States during the 1920s and early 1930s but is only regulated today. Until the passage of the Harrison Act in 1914, it was legal in the United States to use opiates such as opium, heroin, and morphine without a doctor's prescription. Such use is prohibited today.

Casino gambling is allowed in some states but forbidden in other states. Prostitution is legal in a few counties in Nevada but illegal in the rest of the United States. Prior to the mid-1970s, a husband could rape his wife with impunity in all but a handful of states. Today, laws in every state prohibit a husband from raping or assaulting his wife.

A LEGAL DEFINITION

In an attempt to avoid the problems with social definitions of crime, a legal definition of crime is used in criminal justice in the United States. A typical **legal definition of crime** is this: an intentional violation of the criminal law or penal code, committed without defense or excuse and penalized by the state. The major advantage of a legal definition of crime, at least on the surface, is that it is narrower and less ambiguous than a social definition of crime. If a behavior violates the criminal law, then by definition it is a crime. However, although a legal definition eliminates some of the problems with social definitions of crime, a legal definition of crime has problems of its own.

First, some behaviors prohibited by the criminal law arguably should not be. This problem of **overcriminalization** arises primarily in the area of so-called victimless crimes. Lists of victimless crimes typically include gambling, prostitution involving consenting adults, homosexual acts between consenting adults, and the use of some illegal drugs, such as marijuana. Ultimately, whether those acts should or should not be prohibited by criminal law depends on whether they are truly victimless—an issue we will not debate here. Perhaps less controversial are some of the following illegal behaviors:

legal definition of crime An intentional violation of the criminal law or penal code, committed without defense or excuse and penalized by the state.

overcriminalization The prohibition by the criminal law of some behaviors that arguably should not be prohibited.

- It is illegal to buy a bag of peanuts after sunset and before sunrise the next day in Alabama.
- In California, it is illegal to trip horses for entertainment, to possess bear gall bladders, or to peel an orange in your hotel room.
- It is illegal to throw shoes at weddings in Colorado.
- In Connecticut, it is illegal to walk across the street on your hands.
- Women in Florida may be fined for falling asleep under a hair dryer, as can the salon owner.
- Idaho state law makes it illegal for a man to give his sweetheart a box of candy weighing less than 50 pounds.
- It is illegal to take a bath in the wintertime in Indiana.
- Kisses may last for as much as, but no more than, 5 minutes in Iowa.
- In Michigan a woman isn't allowed to cut her own hair without her husband's permission.
- It is illegal to slurp soup in New Jersey.
- Beer and pretzels can't be served at the same time in any bar or restaurant in North Dakota.
- Violators in Oklahoma can be fined, arrested, or jailed for making ugly faces at a dog.

More and more states are legalizing casino gambling as a means of generating income. *Is this a desirable trend? Why or why not?*

nonenforcement The failure to routinely enforce prohibitions against certain behaviors.

undercriminalization The failure to prohibit some behaviors that arguably should be prohibited.

- The state law of Pennsylvania prohibits singing in the bathtub.
- In South Dakota, a woman over 50 is not allowed to go outside and strike up a conversation with a married man older than 20.
- In Tennessee it is illegal to shoot any game other than whales from a moving automobile.
- In Texas, it is illegal to take more than three sips of beer at a time while standing.
- It is an offense in Washington State to pretend your parents are rich.[1]

A second problem with a legal definition of crime is that for some behaviors prohibited by criminal law, the law is not routinely enforced. **Nonenforcement** is common for many white-collar and government crimes. It is also common for blue laws, for example, those that require stores and other commercial establishments to be closed on Sundays. Many jurisdictions in the United States have blue laws, or they did until recently. The principal problem with the nonenforcement of prohibitions is that it causes disrespect for the law. People come to believe that because criminal laws are not routinely enforced, there is no need to routinely obey them.

A third problem with a legal definition of crime is the problem of **undercriminalization.** That is, some behaviors that arguably should be prohibited by criminal law are not. Have you ever said to yourself that there ought to be a law against whatever it is you are upset about? Of course, most of the daily frustrations that people claim ought to be crimes probably should not be. Some people argue, however, that some very harmful and destructive actions or inactions that are not criminal should be. Examples include the government allowing employers (generally through the nonenforcement of laws) to maintain unsafe working conditions that cause employee deaths and injuries, and corporations' intentional production of potentially hazardous products to maximize profits.[2]

ELEMENTS OF CRIME

A legal definition of crime is the basis of criminal justice in the United States. The legal definition of crime provided earlier in this chapter, however, is only a general definition. It does not specify all the elements necessary to make a behavior a crime. Technically and ideally, a crime has not been committed unless all seven of the following elements are present.[3]

1. Harm
2. Legality
3. *Actus reus*
4. *Mens rea*
5. Causation
6. Concurrence
7. Punishment

Only in a technical and ideal sense must all seven elements be present. In practice, a behavior is often considered a crime when one or more of the elements of crime are absent. We will examine each of the seven elements in turn, indicating exceptions to the technical and the ideal where relevant.

Harm For crime to occur, there must be an external consequence, or **harm.** A mental or emotional state is not enough. Thus, thinking about committing a crime or being angry enough to commit a crime, without acting on the thought or the anger, is not a crime.

The harm may be physical or verbal. Physically striking another person without legal justification is an example of an act that does physical harm. An example of an act that does verbal harm is a threat to strike another person, whether or not the threat is carried out. Writing something false about another person that dishonors or injures that person is a physical harm called *libel.* The spoken equivalent of libel is called *slander.*

Whether the legal element of harm is present in all crimes is sometimes questioned. Some crimes, such as gambling, prostitution, marijuana consumption, and certain consensually committed sexual acts such as sodomy, have come to be called "victimless crimes" by those who argue that only those people involved in these behaviors are harmed, if at all. Other people maintain that the participants, their families, and the moral fabric of society are jeopardized by such behavior. In short, there is considerable debate as to whether so-called victimless crimes really are harmless.

Ever since criminal sanctions were established for illegal drug use, some have argued for decriminalization by elimination or reduction of criminal penalties for possession or distribution of certain drugs. *Do you agree with this argument? Why or why not?*

harm The external consequence required to make an action a crime.

Legality The element of **legality** has two aspects. First, the harm must be legally forbidden for a behavior to be a crime. Thus, violations of union rules, school rules, religious rules, or any rules other than those of a political jurisdiction may be "wrong," but they are not crimes unless they are also prohibited by criminal law. Furthermore, rude behavior may be frowned upon, but it is not criminal.

Second, a criminal law must not be retroactive, or *ex post facto.* An **ex post facto law** (1) declares criminal an act that was not illegal when it was committed, (2) increases the punishment for a crime after it is committed, or (3) alters the rules of evidence in a particular case after the crime is committed. The first meaning is the most common. The U.S. Constitution (Article I, Section 10.1) forbids *ex post facto* laws.

legality The requirement (1) that a harm must be legally forbidden for the behavior to be a crime and (2) that the law must not be retroactive.

ex post facto law A law that (1) declares criminal an act that was not illegal when it was committed, (2) increases the punishment for a crime after it is committed, or (3) alters the rules of evidence in a particular case after the crime is committed.

Actus reus The Latin term ***actus reus*** refers to criminal conduct—specifically, intentional or criminally negligent (reckless) action or inaction that causes harm. Crime involves not only things people do but also things they do not do. If people do not act in situations in which the law requires them to act, they are committing crimes. For example, parents are legally required to provide their children with adequate food, clothing, and shelter. If parents fail to provide those necessities—that is, if they fail to act when the law requires them to—they are committing a crime.

actus reus Criminal conduct—specifically, intentional or criminally negligent (reckless) action or inaction that causes harm.

Mens rea The Latin term ***mens rea*** refers to criminal intent or a guilty state of mind. It is the mental aspect of a crime. Ideally, criminal conduct is limited to intentional or purposeful action or inaction and not to accidents. In practice, however, reckless actions or *negligence* may be criminal. **Negligence** is the failure to take reasonable precautions to prevent harm.

In some cases, offenders lack the capacity (sometimes called competence) to form *mens rea.* If they do not have that capacity, they are not to be held responsible for their criminal conduct. If they have a diminished capacity to form *mens rea,* they are to be held less than fully responsible. In other cases, offenders who have the capacity to form *mens rea* are not held responsible for

mens rea Criminal intent; a guilty state of mind.

negligence The failure to take reasonable precautions to prevent harm.

their crimes or are held less responsible for them, either because they did not have *mens rea* when they acted or because there were extenuating circumstances when they did act with *mens rea*.

Legal Defenses for Criminal Responsibility In the United States, an offender is not considered responsible or is considered less responsible for an offense if he or she, for example, (1) acted under duress, (2) was underage, (3) was insane, (4) acted in self-defense or in defense of a third party, (5) was entrapped, or (6) acted out of necessity. Those conditions are legal defenses or legal excuses for criminal responsibility.

If a person did not want to commit a crime but was forced or coerced to do so against his or her will, he or she committed the crime under **duress** and is generally excluded from criminal liability. Suppose that an intruder held a gun to the head of a loved one and threatened to kill that person if you did not rob a local convenience store and return immediately to give the intruder the money. If you committed the robbery to save the life of your loved one, you would probably not be held legally responsible for the crime, because you committed it under duress. There were extenuating circumstances when you acted with *mens rea*. To prevent all offenders from claiming duress, the burden of proof is placed on the defendant.

Another legal excuse or legal defense against criminal responsibility is being underage. Although the age at which a person is considered legally responsible for his or her actions varies by jurisdiction, in most American jurisdictions a child under the age of 7 is not held responsible for a crime. It is assumed that a child under 7 years of age does not have the capacity to form *mens rea*. A child under 7 years of age is considered a *legal infant* or of *legal nonage*. Such a child is protected by criminal law but not subject to it. Thus, if a 6-year-old child picks up a shotgun and shoots his or her parent, the child is unlikely to be charged with a crime. However, if a parent abuses a child, the criminal law protects the child by holding the abusive parent responsible for his or her actions.

In most developed countries children under 18 years of age are not considered entirely responsible for their criminal acts. It is assumed that their capacity to form *mens rea* is not fully developed. A special category of offense called **juvenile delinquency** has been created for those children. In most American jurisdictions, the upper age limit for juvenile delinquency is 18. The lower limit is usually 7. Criminal law generally treats anyone who is 18 or older as an adult. However, the upper age limit of juvenile delinquency is lower in some jurisdictions and sometimes varies with the sex of the offender. In some jurisdictions there is a legal borderland between the ages of 16 and 18. An offender in that age range may be treated as a juvenile or as an adult, depending on the severity of the offense. In some cases, an offense is considered heinous enough for a court to certify a juvenile, regardless of age, as an adult and to treat him or her accordingly. The subject of juvenile delinquency is discussed more fully in Chapter 13.

A third legal defense or legal excuse from criminal responsibility is insanity. **Insanity** is a legal term, not a medical one. It refers to mental or psychological impairment or retardation. Like many of the other legal defenses or excuses, an insanity defense rests on the assumption that someone who is insane at the time of a crime lacks the capacity, or has diminished capacity, to form *mens rea*. Thus, that person either should not be held responsible or should be held less responsible for a given crime.

In most western European nations, legal insanity is determined solely by the judgment and testimony of medical experts. British and American law, by contrast, provide guidelines for judges, juries, and medical experts to follow in determining whether a defendant is legally insane. The oldest of those guidelines is the M'Naghten rule or some variation of it, which was first used in an English trial in 1843 and is now used in 21 states (see Figure 2.1).

duress Force or coercion as an excuse for committing a crime.

Legal Infancy

On February 29, 2000, a Mount Morris Township, Michigan, 6-year-old first-grader pulled a gun from his pants and shot and killed a 6-year-old classmate in front of his teacher and classmates. He had quarreled with her on the playground the day before. Because of his age, he was neither charged nor held criminally responsible because, legally, he could not form *mens rea* or the intent to kill.

Source: "A 1st-grader turns killer," *The Orlando Sentinel* (March 1, 2000), p. A-1; "6-year-old boy who killed girl lived in 'flophouse,'" *The Orlando Sentinel* (March 2, 2000), p. A-1.

juvenile delinquency A special category of offense created for young offenders, usually those between 7 and 18 years of age.

insanity Mental or psychological impairment or retardation as a defense against a criminal charge.

Figure 2.1

Insanity Tests by State

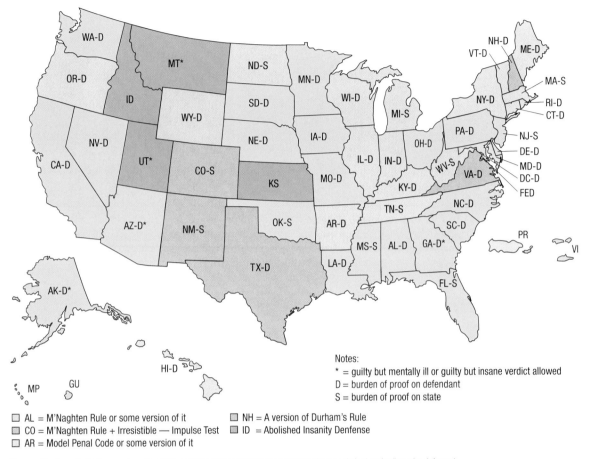

Notes:
* = guilty but mentally ill or guilty but insane verdict allowed
D = burden of proof on defendant
S = burden of proof on state

☐ AL = M'Naghten Rule or some version of it   ☐ NH = A version of Durham's Rule
☐ CO = M'Naghten Rule + Irresistible — Impulse Test   ☐ ID = Abolished Insanity Denfense
☐ AR = Model Penal Code or some version of it

Source: The Insanity Defense among the States at http://criminal.findlaw.com/crimes/more-criminal-topics/insanity-defense/
the-insanity-defense-among-the-states.html (accessed November 16, 2008).

Under the M'Naghten rule:

> Every man is to be presumed to be sane, and . . . to establish a defense on the ground of insanity, it must be clearly proved that, at the time of the committing of the act, the party accused was laboring under such a defect of reason, from disease of the mind, as not to know the nature and quality of the act he was doing; or if he did know it, that he did not know he was doing what was wrong.[4]

In short, according to the M'Naghten rule, which is also referred to as the "right-and-wrong test," a person is legally insane if, at the time of the commission of the act, he or she (1) did not know the nature and quality of the act or (2) did not know that the act was wrong. The burden of proof is on the defendant.

One problem with the M'Naghten rule is the difficulty of determining what a person's state of mind was at the time of the commission of the criminal act. The rule has also been criticized for its ambiguity. What is a "defect of reason," and by whose standards is the act a product of defective reason? Does "disease of the mind" refer to organic diseases, nonorganic diseases, or both? What does it mean to "know" the nature and quality of the act? Does it mean an intellectual awareness, an emotional appreciation, or both? Does "wrong" mean legally wrong, morally wrong, or both?

Perhaps the most serious problem with the M'Naghten rule is that it does not address the situation of a defendant who knew the difference between right and wrong but was unable to control his or her actions. To remedy that problem,

CJ Online

Daniel M'Naghten

Daniel M'Naghten was acquitted of the murder of a person he had mistaken for his real target, Sir Robert Peel, then the Prime Minister of Great Britain. M'Naghten claimed that he was delusional at the time of the killing. Go to http://wings.buffalo.edu/law/bclc/web/mnaghten.htm and research the M'Naghten case. *Explain the insanity defense in that case and give your opinion about the court's ruling.*

In a 1994 trial in Virginia, attorneys for Lorena Bobbitt, who had sliced off her husband's penis with a kitchen knife while he was sleeping, successfully used the *irresistible-impulse* defense against charges of malicious wounding. She claimed that she had been subjected to physical and sexual abuse for years during her marriage. She was acquitted of the crime. *Was Bobbitt's act uncontrollable or uncontrolled? Defend your answer.*

four states have adopted the *irresistible-impulse* or *control test* and use it in conjunction with the M'Naghten rule (see Figure 2.1). In those states a defense against conviction on grounds of insanity is first made by using the M'Naghten rule. If the conditions of M'Naghten are met, the irresistible-impulse or control test is applied. If it is determined that the defendant knew that he or she was doing wrong at the time of the commission of the criminal act but nevertheless could not control his or her behavior, the defendant is entitled to an acquittal on the grounds of insanity. The major problem with the irresistible-impulse or control test is distinguishing between behavior that is uncontrollable and behavior that is simply uncontrolled.

The test for insanity used by another 21 states is the *substantial-capacity test* of the American Law Institute's Model Penal Code or some version of it. Under that test, a defendant is not to be found guilty of a crime "if at the time of such conduct as a result of mental disease or defect he lacks substantial capacity either to appreciate the criminality of his conduct or to conform his conduct to the requirements of law." By using the term *substantial capacity*, the test does not require that a defendant be completely unable to distinguish right from wrong. The test has been criticized for its use of the ambiguous terms *substantial capacity* and *appreciate*. It also does not resolve the problem of determining whether behavior is uncontrollable or uncontrolled.

A final insanity test used only in New Hampshire is a version of Durham's Rule and is referred to as "the product test." The *product test* is a two-prong test in which the defense must show that (1) the defendant suffered from a mental disease or defect and (2) the murder was a product of that disease or defect. A problem with the *product test* is that neither the New Hampshire legislature nor New Hampshire courts have defined the terms "mental disease" and "defect," leaving interpretation entirely to juries.

Following the public uproar over the 1982 acquittal of John Hinckley, the would-be assassin of President Ronald Reagan, on the grounds that he was legally insane, five states, including two states that have otherwise abolished the insanity defense, enacted "guilty but insane" or "guilty but mentally ill" laws (See Figure 2.1). Defendants who are found guilty but insane generally receive sentences that include psychiatric treatment until they are cured. Then they are placed in the general prison population to serve the remainder of their sentences.

States are free to abolish insanity as a defense. The first state to do so was Montana in 1979. Idaho, Utah, and Kansas are the only other states that have eliminated any possibility of a criminal defendant's being found not guilty by reason of insanity.[5] Figure 2.1 shows the insanity test used by each state (and D.C.), as well as which party, either the defendant or the state, has the burden of proof, and the states that allow guilty but mentally ill or guilty but insane verdicts.

A fourth legal defense or legal excuse from criminal responsibility is self-defense or the defense of a third party. Generally, people are relieved of criminal responsibility if they use only the amount of force reasonably necessary to defend themselves or others against an apparent threat of unlawful and immediate violence. When it comes to the protection of property, however, the use of force is much more limited. Deadly force is not allowed, but nondeadly force may be used to protect one's property. In 2005, Florida became the first state to pass the NRA-backed "castle doctrine" law or, as it is sometimes called, the "stand your ground" law. Since then, at least 15 other states have followed suit, though the wording varies among states. The law generally provides that someone attacked in his or her home can use reasonable force, including deadly force, to protect his or another's life without any duty to retreat from the attacker. In Florida, the "no duty to retreat" language also applies to street crimes. In some states, the law applies to other locations besides a home, such as a place where a person is a guest or a workplace. Some versions provide criminal or civil immunity for someone who legally uses force in self-defense. Most of the laws presume that a person breaking into someone's house has the intent of a violent or forceful act. The law's name comes from the notion that "one's home is one's castle."[6] The reason people are not held legally responsible for acting in self-defense or in defense of a third party is that, because of extenuating circumstances, they do not act with *mens rea*.

Entrapment is a fifth legal defense or legal excuse from criminal responsibility. People are generally considered either not responsible or less responsible for their crimes if they were entrapped, or induced into committing them, by a law enforcement officer or by someone acting as an agent for a law enforcement officer, such as an informer or an undercover agent. A successful entrapment defense, however, requires proof that the law enforcement officer or his or her agent instigated the crime or created the intent to commit the crime in the mind of a person who was not already predisposed to committing it. Thus, it is not entrapment if a law enforcement officer merely affords someone an opportunity to commit a crime, as, for example, when an undercover agent poses as a drug addict and purchases drugs from a drug dealer.

The final legal defense or legal excuse from criminal responsibility to be discussed here is necessity. A **necessity defense** can be used when a crime has been committed to prevent a greater or more serious crime. In such a situation, there are extenuating circumstances, even though the act was committed with *mens rea*. Although it is rarely used, the necessity defense has been invoked occasionally, especially in cases of "political" crimes. The necessity defense was used successfully by Amy Carter (daughter of former President Jimmy Carter), Jerry Rubin, and other activists who were charged with trespassing for protesting apartheid on the property of the South African embassy in Washington, D.C. The court agreed with the protesters that apartheid was a greater crime than trespassing. Interestingly, the law does not recognize economic necessity as a defense against or an excuse from criminal responsibility. Therefore, the unemployed and hungry thief who steals groceries cannot successfully employ the necessity defense.

Causation A fifth ideal legal element of crime is causation, or a causal relationship between the legally forbidden harm and the *actus reus*. In other words,

entrapment A legal defense against criminal responsibility when a person, who was not already predisposed to it, is induced into committing a crime by a law enforcement officer or by his or her agent.

necessity defense A legal defense against criminal responsibility used when a crime has been committed to prevent a more serious crime.

the criminal act must lead directly to the harm without a long delay. In a recent case in Georgia, for example, a father was accused of murdering his baby daughter. The murder charges were dropped, however, because too much time had passed between the night the 3½-month-old girl was shaken into a coma and her death 18 months later. Because of Georgia's year-and-a-day rule, the father was not charged with murder, but he still faced a charge of cruelty to children, which in Georgia carries a maximum sentence of 20 years. The purpose of the requirement of causation is to prevent people from facing the threat of criminal charges the rest of their lives.

Concurrence Ideally, for any behavior to be considered a crime, there must be concurrence between the *actus reus* and the *mens rea.* In other words, the criminal conduct and the criminal intent must occur together. For example, suppose you call someone to repair your broken washing machine, and that person comes to your home, fixes your washing machine, and on the way out takes your television set. The repair person cannot be found guilty of entering your home illegally (trespass) because that was not his or her initial intent. However, the repair person can be found guilty of stealing your television set.

Punishment The last of the ideal legal elements of a crime is punishment. For a behavior to be considered a crime, there must be a statutory provision for punishment or at least the threat of punishment. Without the threat of punishment, a law is unenforceable and is therefore not a criminal law.

DEGREES OR CATEGORIES OF CRIME

Crimes can be classified according to the degree or severity of the offense, according to the nature of the acts prohibited, or on some other basis, such as a statistical reporting scheme. One way crimes are distinguished by degree or severity of the offense is by dividing them into *felonies* and *misdemeanors.* The only way to determine whether a crime is a felony or misdemeanor is by knowing the legislated punishment. Consequently, a felony in one jurisdiction might be a misdemeanor in another, and vice versa. Generally, a felony, as noted in Chapter 1, is a relatively serious offense punishable by death, a fine, or confinement in a state or federal prison for more than 1 year. A misdemeanor, in contrast, is any lesser crime that is not a felony. Misdemeanors are usually punishable by no more than a $1,000 fine and 1 year of incarceration, generally in a county or city jail.

mala in se Wrong in themselves; a description applied to crimes that are characterized by universality and timelessness.

mala prohibita Offenses that are illegal because laws define them as such; they lack universality and timelessness.

Another way of categorizing crimes is to distinguish between offenses that are *mala in se* and offenses that are *mala prohibita.* Crimes **mala in se** are "wrong in themselves." They are characterized by universality and timelessness. That is, they are crimes everywhere and have been crimes at all times. Examples are murder and rape. Crimes **mala prohibita** are offenses that are illegal because laws define them as such. They lack universality and timelessness. Examples are trespassing, gambling, and prostitution.

For statistical reporting purposes, crimes are frequently classified as *crimes against the person* or *violent crimes* (for example, murder, rape, assault), *crimes against property* or *property crime* (for instance, burglary, larceny, auto theft), and *crimes against public decency, public order,* and *public justice* or *public order crimes* (for example, drunkenness, disorderly conduct, vagrancy).

Table 2.1 is a list of selected crimes and their definitions, grouped by type. The selection, placement, and definition of the crimes are somewhat arbitrary. There are many different types of crime, and some crimes can be placed in more than one category. Legal definitions of crime vary among jurisdictions and frequently list numerous degrees, conditions, and qualifications. A good source of legal crime definitions is *Black's Law Dictionary.*

Table 2.1 Types and Definitions of Selected Crimes

Violent Crimes	Crimes that involve force or threat of force.
Murder	The unlawful killing of another human being with malice aforethought.
Manslaughter	The unlawful killing of another human being without malice aforethought.
Aggravated assault	An assault committed (1) with the intention of committing some additional crime, (2) with peculiar outrage or atrocity, or (3) with a dangerous or deadly weapon.
Forcible rape	The act of having sexual intercourse with a woman, by force and against her will.
Robbery	Theft from a person, accompanied by violence, threat of violence, or putting the person in fear.
Kidnapping	The unlawful taking and carrying away of a human being by force and against his or her will.
Property Crimes	Crimes that involve taking money or property, but usually without force or threat of force.
Larceny	The unlawful taking and carrying away of another person's property with the intent of depriving the owner of that property.
Burglary	Entering a building or occupied structure to commit a crime therein.
Embezzlement	The willful taking or converting to one's own use another person's money or property, which was lawfully acquired by the wrongdoer by reason of some office, employment, or position of trust.
Arson	Purposely setting fire to a house or other building.
Extortion/blackmail	The obtaining of property from another by wrongful use of actual or threatened force, violence, or fear, or under color of official right.
Receiving stolen property	Knowingly accepting, buying, or concealing goods that were illegally obtained by another person.
Fraud	The false representation of a matter of fact, whether by words or by conduct, by false or misleading allegations, or by concealment of that which should have been disclosed, which deceives and is intended to deceive, and causes legal harm.
Forgery	The fraudulent making of a false writing having apparent legal significance.
Counterfeiting	Under federal law, falsely making, forging, or altering any obligation or other security of the United States, with intent to defraud.
"Morals" Offenses	Violations of virtue in sexual conduct (for example, fornication, seduction, prostitution, adultery, illicit cohabitation, sodomy, bigamy, and incest).
Public Order Offenses	Violations that constitute a threat to public safety or peace (for example, disorderly conduct, loitering, unlawful assembly, drug offenses, driving while intoxicated).
Offenses against the Government	Crimes motivated by the desire to effect social change or to rebel against perceived unfair laws and governments (for example, treason, sedition, hindering apprehension or prosecution of a felon, perjury, and bribery).
Offenses by the Government	Harms inflicted on people by their own governments or the governments of others (for example, genocide and torture, police brutality, civil rights violations, and political bribe taking).
Hate Crimes	Criminal offenses committed against a person, property, or society and motivated, in whole or in part, by the offender's bias against a race, a religion, an ethnic/national origin group, or a sexual-orientation group.
Organized Crimes	Unlawful acts of members of highly organized and disciplined associations engaged in supplying illegal goods and services, such as gambling, prostitution, loan-sharking, narcotics, and labor racketeering.
White-Collar and Corporate Crimes	Generally nonviolent offenses committed for financial gain by means of deception by entrepreneurs and other professionals who utilize their special occupational skills and opportunities (for example, environmental pollution, manufacture and sale of unsafe products, price fixing, price gouging, and deceptive advertising).
Occupational Crimes	Offenses committed through opportunities created in the course of a legal business or profession and crimes committed by professionals, such as lawyers and doctors, acting in their professional capacities.
"Victimless" Crimes	Offenses involving a willing and private exchange of goods or services that are in strong demand but are illegal (for example, gambling, prostitution, drug law violations, and homosexual acts between consenting adults).

THINKING CRITICALLY

1. Are there any acts that are currently legal that you think should be illegal? If so, what?

2. Do you think there should be other elements of crime besides the seven listed in this section? If so, name them.

Many people learn about crime from the media. *How do the media determine which crimes to report?*

dark figure of crime The number of crimes not officially recorded by the police.

crime index An estimate of crimes committed.

Figure 2.2

Dark Figure of Crime

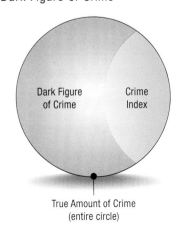

True Amount of Crime
(entire circle)

Measurement of Crime

At the end of 2008, 44% of Americans believed there was more crime in their area than there was a year ago (31% believed there was less, 19% thought it was about the same, and 5% had no opinion). Eleven percent of Americans believed the crime problem in their area was "extremely" or "very" serious; another 32% thought it was "moderately" serious. At the same time, 67% of Americans believed there was more crime in the United States than there was a year ago (15% believed there was less, 9% thought it was about the same, and 9% had no opinion). Fifty-one percent of Americans believed the crime problem in the United States was "extremely" or "very" serious; another 43% thought it was "moderately" serious.[7]

Many people who read the daily newspaper or watch the nightly news on television believe that crime is a pressing problem in the United States. But is it? How do you know how much crime is committed? How do you know whether crime is, in fact, increasing or decreasing? How do you know how serious the crime problem is? Besides what you learn from the media, perhaps you have been the victim of crime or know someone who has been. Although that information is important, it does not indicate whether your experience with crime or the experience of someone you know is typical. The fact is that what we and the media know about crime, by and large, is based on statistics supplied by government agencies.

CRIME STATISTICS

The difficulty in relying on crime statistics to measure the prevalence of crime is that "statistics about crime and delinquency are probably the most unreliable and most difficult of all social statistics."[8] In other words, "it is impossible to determine with accuracy the amount of crime [or delinquency] in any given jurisdiction at any particular time."[9] Why? There are several reasons. First, "some behavior is labeled . . . 'crime' by one observer but not by another."[10] If a behavior is not labeled a crime, it is not counted. However, if a behavior is wrongly labeled a crime, then it may be wrongly counted as a crime. Both situations contribute to the inaccuracy of crime statistics. Second, a large proportion of crimes are undetected. Crimes that are not detected obviously cannot be counted. Third, some crimes may not be reported to the police. If they are not reported to the police, they are unlikely to be counted. Fourth, crimes that are reported to the police may not be officially recorded by them, for various reasons (discussed later), or may be inaccurately recorded. Crimes that are not officially recorded by the police are called the **dark figure of crime** (see Figure 2.2).

For all of the foregoing reasons, any record of crimes—such as "offenses known to the police," arrests, convictions, or commitments to prison—can be considered at most a **crime index,** or an estimate of crimes committed. Unfortunately, no index or estimate of crimes is a reliable indicator of the actual amount of crime. The indexes or estimates vary independently of the true amount of crime, whatever that may be. Figure 2.2 portrays one possible relationship of a crime index to the dark figure of crime and the true amount of crime. It shows how great a discrepancy there can be between the index and the actual amount of crime.

Adding to the confusion is the reality that any index of crime varies with changes in police practices, court policies, and public opinion—to name just three factors. Suppose, for example, that a large city is hosting a major convention and city leaders want to make a good impression on visitors. The mayor asks the police chief to order officers to "sweep" the streets of prostitutes. As a result of that police policy, there is a dramatic increase in arrests for prostitution and in the index measuring prostitution. Does the increase in the index mean that the true amount of prostitution increased in the city? The answer is that we do not know and, for that matter, can never know. All we do know is that the index measuring prostitution increased as a result of police practices.

Thus, despite what some government agencies or the media may suggest, we do not know, nor can we ever know, the true amount of crime. For the same reasons, we can never know for sure whether crime is increasing, decreasing, or remaining at the same level. The sophisticated student of crime knows only that indexes of crime are imperfect estimates that vary widely. Those variations, which are independent of variations in the true amount of crime, depend on such things as police practices, court policies, and public opinion. Therefore, comparisons of crime measures are an especially dubious exercise. Criminal justice officials and professors routinely compare crime measures in different jurisdictions and at different times. What they are doing, though they rarely acknowledge it, even when they are aware of it, is comparing indexes or estimates of crime. Although such comparisons tell us nothing about differences in true amounts of crime, they do provide insights into police practices, court policies, and public opinion.

Probably the best index of crime—that is, the least inaccurate!—is **offenses known to the police.** That index, which is reported in the FBI's uniform crime reports (discussed later), is composed of crimes that are both reported to and recorded by the police. The reason it is an inaccurate measure of the true amount of crime is that the number of offenses known to the police is always much smaller than the number of crimes actually committed. One reason is that victims do not report all crimes to the police. According to the national crime victimization survey in 2007, for example, victims did not report to the police 54% of all violent crime victimizations and 63% of all property crime victimizations.[11] There are many reasons for the nonreporting of crimes:[12]

> **offenses known to the police** A crime index, reported in the FBI's uniform crime reports, composed of crimes that are both reported to and recorded by the police.

1. Victims may consider the crime insignificant and not worth reporting.
2. They may hope to avoid embarrassing the offender, who may be a relative, school friend, or fellow employee.
3. They may wish to avoid the publicity that might result if the crime were reported.
4. They might have agreed to the crime, as in gambling offenses and some sexual offenses.
5. They may wish to avoid the inconvenience of calling the police [filling out a report, appearing in court, and so on].
6. They may be intimidated by [or afraid of] the offender.
7. They may [dislike] the police or [be] opposed to the punitive policies of the legal system.
8. They may feel that the police are so inefficient that they will be unable to catch the offender even if the offense is reported.

Another reason the number of offenses known to the police is necessarily much smaller than the number of crimes actually committed is that the police do not always officially record the crimes that are reported to them. In practice, police officers often use their discretion to handle informally an incident reported to them; that is, they do not make an official report of the incident. Or they may exercise discretion in enforcing the law (for instance, by not arresting the customer in a case of prostitution). The law is often vague, and officers may not know the law or how to enforce it. Still another reason is that some police officers feel they are too busy to fill out and file police reports. Also, some officers, feeling an obligation to protect the reputations of their cities or being pressured by politicians to "get the crime rate down," may manipulate statistics to show a decrease in crime.[13] Consider the following examples. Since before the 1996 Olympics, Atlanta police have systematically underreported crime. An audit of the city's crime statistics revealed more than

CJ Online
Crime on Campus

Go to the U.S. Department of Education's Office of Post Secondary Education Campus Security Statistics website at http://ope.ed.gov/security/ for information and statistics on reported criminal offenses at colleges and universities across the United States. *What do the statistics say about crime at schools in your area?*

22,000 police reports missing in 2002 and 4,281 crimes that should have been counted as violent but were not.[14] In 1998, Philadelphia police failed to report 13,000 to 37,000 major crimes including robberies, aggravated assaults, and thefts. The review of the city crime statistics by the city controller's office also showed that other crimes were wrongly classified as less serious crimes.[15] According to the Florida Department of Law Enforcement (FDLE), Florida's crime rate dropped 1.7% from 1995 to 1996. Using that statistic, state officials claimed success for the state's emphases on imprisonment and juvenile crime. However, the FDLE report failed to mention that 20 Florida police agencies had not submitted crime reports for 1996. Rather than exclude those 20 agencies from the analysis, the FDLE instead recorded no crimes for the 348,231 residents of those 20 jurisdictions. If the FDLE had used numbers only from those agencies that reported, its calculation of the Florida crime rate would have been 0.2% higher in 1996 than it was in 1995, not 1.7% lower.[16]

Additionally, the number of offenses included in the index is much smaller than the actual number of crimes because of the way crimes are counted. For the FBI's uniform crime reports, when more than one crime is committed during a crime event, only the most serious is counted for statistical purposes. The seriousness of the crime is determined by the maximum legal penalty associated with it. Thus, for example, if a robber holds up 10 people in a tavern, takes their money, shoots and kills the bartender, and makes a getaway in a stolen car, only one crime, the murder, is counted for statistical purposes. However, the offender could legally be charged with several different crimes. (The practice of counting only the most serious offense in a multiple-crime event is being changed with the implementation of the National-Incident-Based Reporting System, which is discussed later in this chapter.)

Despite the problems in recording crime events, *offenses known to the police* is a more accurate index of crime than arrest statistics, charging statistics, trial statistics, conviction statistics, sentencing statistics, and imprisonment statistics.

Los Angeles police officers respond to a bungled bank robbery. The heavily armed, masked robbers fired hundreds of shots in a gun battle getaway that left 2 dead and at least 11 hurt. *In this crime event, what crimes would be officially recorded for purposes of the FBI's uniform crime reports?*

Figure 2.3

Indexes of Crime

Most Accurate   **Least Accurate**

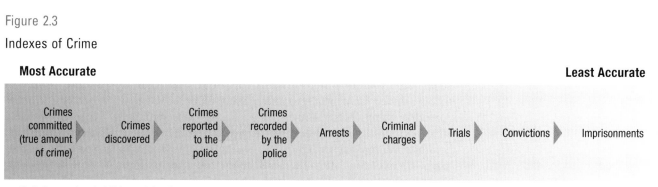

The farther away from the initial commission of a crime, the more inaccurate crime indexes are as measures of the true amount of crime.

As shown in Figure 2.3, the farther a crime index is from the initial commission of crime, the more inaccurate it is as a measure of the true amount of crime.

CRIME RATES

When crime indexes are compared, rarely are total numbers of crimes used. Instead, crime is typically reported as rates. A **crime rate** is expressed as the number of crimes per unit of population or some other base. Crime rates are used instead of total numbers, because they are more comparable. For example, suppose you wanted to compare the crime of murder in the United States for the years 1960 and 2000. There were 9,110 murders and nonnegligent manslaughters reported to and recorded by the police in 1960; there were 15,517 murders and nonnegligent manslaughters reported to and recorded by the police in 2000. According to those data, the total number of murders and nonnegligent manslaughters reported to and recorded by the police in 2000 increased about 70% from the number reported and recorded by the police in 1960. Although this information may be helpful, it ignores the substantial increase in the population of the United States—and thus in the number of potential murderers and potential murder victims—between 1960 and 2000.

crime rate A measure of the incidence of crime expressed as the number of crimes per unit of population or some other base.

A better comparison—though, of course, not an accurate one—would be a comparison that takes into account the different population sizes. To enable such a comparison, a population base, such as "per 100,000 people" is arbitrarily chosen. Then the total number of murders and nonnegligent manslaughters for a particular year is divided by the total population of the United States for the same year. The result is multiplied by 100,000. When those calculations are made for the years 1960 and 2000, the rate of murders and nonnegligent manslaughters is 5.1 per 100,000 people for 1960 and 5.5 per 100,000 people for 2000 (see Figure 2.4). According to those figures, the rate of murder and nonnegligent manslaughter in 2000 was about 8% higher than it was in 1960. Thus, although both sets of data show that murders and nonnegligent manslaughters reported to and recorded by the police increased between 1960 and 2000, the increase is not nearly as great when the increase in the size of the population (which was 57%) is taken into account. Crime rates provide a more accurate indication of increases or decreases in crime indexes than do total numbers of crimes. Remember, however, that what are being compared are indexes and not true amounts.

A variety of factors indirectly related to crime can affect crime rates. For example, burglary rates might

Figure 2.4

Calculating Crime Rates

1960

$$\frac{9,110 \text{ murders \& nonnegligent manslaughters}}{179,323,175 \text{ (1960 U.S. population)}} \times 100,000 = 5.1 \text{ per } 100,000 \text{ people}$$

2000

$$\frac{15,517 \text{ murders \& nonnegligent manslaughters}}{281,421,906 \text{ (2000 U.S. population)}} \times 100,000 = 5.5 \text{ per } 100,000 \text{ people}$$

increase, not because there are more burglaries but because more things are insured, and insurance companies require police reports before they will reimburse their policyholders. Changing demographic characteristics of the population can also have an effect. For example, because of the post–World War II baby boom (1945–1964), between 1963 and 1988 there were more people in the age group most prone to committing recorded crime (18- to 24-year-olds). All other things being equal, higher crime rates would be expected between 1963 and 1988 simply because there were more people in the age group that commits the most recorded crime. By the same token, a decrease in crime rates might be expected after 1988, all other things being equal, because the baby boom generation is no longer at those crime-prone ages. (That, in fact, occurred, at least with regard to violent crimes. See the discussion below.) However, an increase in crime might be expected when their children reach the age range 18 to 24. It has been estimated that changes in the age structure of the population account for approximately 40% of the changes in the crime rate.[17]

Urbanization is another factor, especially with regard to violent crime. Violent crime is primarily a big-city phenomenon. Thus, violent crime rates might increase as more of the population moves from rural to urban areas or as what were once rural areas become more urban.

In 2007, data reported by the Federal Bureau of Investigation showed that the violent crime rate in the United States decreased 1.4% from 2006.[18] The decrease continued a downward trend in the violent crime rate that began in 1991. In other words, except for the years 2004–2005 and 2005–2006, which had modest rate increases of 1.3% and 1%, respectively, the violent crime rate in the United States declined every other year since 1991.[19] Note that the rate for 2001 does include the murder and nonnegligent manslaughters that occurred as a result of the September 11 tragedy. Among the factors that police chiefs and academics have cited for the decline are these:

1. Aging-out of the crime-prone years by the postwar baby boom generation.
2. Fewer turf battles over crack cocaine distribution because of market maturation and consolidation.
3. Police efforts to disarm criminals and juveniles.
4. More police officers on the beat.
5. Smarter policing.
6. Tougher criminal justice legislation, such as the federal law that ties financial aid for prison building to a requirement that states keep violent offenders incarcerated for at least 85% of their sentences.
7. Increased interest in "grass-roots" crime prevention.
8. A better economy that provided jobs and gave cities more to invest in crime control.[20]

UNIFORM CRIME REPORTS (UCR)

uniform crime reports A collection of crime statistics and other law enforcement information gathered under a voluntary national program administered by the FBI.

A primary source of crime statistics in the United States is the **uniform crime reports** (UCR), which are a collection of crime statistics and other law enforcement information published annually under the title *Crime in the United States*. They are the result of a voluntary national program begun in the 1920s by the International Association of Chiefs of Police.[21] The program was turned over to the FBI in 1930 by the attorney general, whose office Congress had authorized to serve as the national clearinghouse for crime-related statistics. In 2007 (the latest year for which data were available), more than 17,000 city, university and college, county, state, tribal, and federal law enforcement agencies were active in the program; they represented about 95% of the U.S. population.[22]

Until June 2004, the uniform crime reports included two major indexes: (1) offenses known to the police, discussed earlier, and (2) statistics about persons arrested. The section on offenses known to the police, or offenses reported to the police, provided information about the **eight index crimes,** or Part I offenses:

1. Murder and nonnegligent manslaughter
2. Forcible rape
3. Robbery
4. Aggravated assault
5. Burglary
6. Larceny/theft
7. Motor vehicle theft
8. Arson (added in 1979)

eight index crimes The Part I offenses in the FBI's uniform crime reports. They are (1) murder and nonnegligent manslaughter, (2) forcible rape, (3) robbery, (4) aggravated assault, (5) burglary, (6) larceny/theft, (7) motor vehicle theft, and (8) arson, which was added in 1979.

The first four offenses were considered violent offenses; the last four were considered property offenses. The crime index was discontinued and replaced in 2004 with a violent crime total and a property crime total until a better index could be developed. The problem was that the crime index was skewed upward by the offense with the highest number; larceny/theft currently accounts for nearly 67% of reported crime. This creates a bias against jurisdictions with high numbers of larceny/thefts but low numbers of other more serious but less frequently committed crimes such as murder and forcible rape.[23]

The 1996 edition of the uniform crime reports included for the first time data reported on crimes motivated by bias against individuals on account of race, religion, disability, sexual orientation, or ethnicity/national origin. The UCR designated these as hate crimes or bias crimes. Beginning in 2005, the FBI began producing *Hate Crime Statistics* exclusively as a separate (from the UCR) Web publication. Agencies that participated in the 2007 data collection program procedure represented more than 86% of the nation's population. In 2007, 7,624 hate crime incidents were reported to the FBI, about 6% more than reported in 2005.[24] Of all the hate crimes reported (2005 percentages in parentheses), 50.8% (54.7%) were motivated by racial bias, 18.4% (17.1%) by religious bias, 16.6% (14.2%) by sexual-orientation bias, 13.2% (13.2%) by ethnic or national origin bias, and 1.0% (0.7%) by disability bias.[25]

MYTH

When the media report that crime has increased or decreased from one year to the next, they are generally referring to increases or decreases in the true amount of crime.

FACT

What the media are usually referring to when they report that crime has increased or decreased from one year to the next is an increase or decrease in the aggregate rate of the eight index crimes (that is, the "crime index total") or now the violent and property crime totals, not the rates of other crimes or the true amount of crime.

The other major crime index in the uniform crime reports is based on arrest statistics. Arrest data are provided for the previous eight index crimes, as well as 21 other crimes and status offenses. The 21 other crimes and status offenses were previously referred to as Part II offenses. A **status offense** is an act that is illegal for a juvenile but would not be a crime if committed by an adult (such as truancy or running away from home). Table 2.2 lists the now combined former Part I and Part II offenses in the FBI's uniform crime reports.

status offense An act that is illegal for a juvenile but would not be a crime if committed by an adult.

According to the UCR, law enforcement agencies made about 14 million arrests for the 29 offenses nationwide in 2007, nearly the same as the previous year. The number of arrests for violent crimes decreased 1.1%, while the number of arrests for property crimes increased 5.4% in 2007 compared to 2006.[26] The offenses for which the most arrests were made in 2007 (approximately 1.8 million and 1.4 million arrests, respectively) were drug-abuse violations and driving under the influence.[27] The third largest number of arrests (about 1.3 million) was for simple assault.[28] Arrestees generally were young (44.4% were under 25 years of age), male (75.8%), and white (69.7%).[29] The index crime for which women were most frequently arrested was larceny/theft. In 2007, the number of arrests of females was 6.6% higher than in 1998; the number of arrests of males was 6.1% lower.[30]

In addition to statistics on offenses known to the police and persons arrested, the UCR include statistics on crime index offenses cleared or "closed" by the police. **Crime index offenses cleared** (also called *clearance rates* or *percent cleared by arrest*) is a rough index of police performance in solving crimes. According to the UCR, offenses can be cleared in one of two ways: by arrest or

crime index offenses cleared The number of offenses for which at least one person has been arrested, charged with the commission of the offense, and turned over to the court for prosecution.

Table 2.2 Former Part I and Part II Offenses of the FBI's Uniform Crime Reports

PART I OFFENSES—INDEX CRIMES	PART II OFFENSES
Violent Crime 1. Murder and nonnegligent manslaughter 2. Forcible rape 3. Robbery 4. Aggravated assault **Property Crime** 5. Burglary—breaking or entering 6. Larceny/theft 7. Motor vehicle theft 8. Arson	1. Other assaults (simple) 2. Forgery and counterfeiting 3. Fraud 4. Embezzlement 5. Stolen property: buying, receiving, possessing 6. Vandalism 7. Weapons: carrying, possessing, etc. 8. Prostitution and commercialized vice 9. Sex offenses 10. Drug abuse violations 11. Gambling 12. Offenses against the family and children 13. Driving under the influence 14. Liquor laws 15. Drunkenness 16. Disorderly conduct 17. Vagrancy 18. All other offenses 19. Suspicion 20. Curfew and loitering laws 21. Runaway

by exceptional means. An offense that is cleared by arrest is one for which "at least one person is arrested, charged with the commission of the offense, and turned over to the court for prosecution."[31] The arrest of one person may clear several crimes, or one offense may be cleared by the arrest of several people. An offense cleared by exceptional means is one for which a law enforcement agency, for reasons beyond its control, cannot arrest and formally charge an offender. Examples of exceptional clearances include the offender's death or the refusal of a victim to cooperate with the prosecution after the offender has been identified. To clear an offense by exceptional means an offender must be identified; enough evidence must be available to support an arrest, a charge, and prosecution; the offender's exact location must be identified so that he or she can be taken into custody immediately; and a circumstance beyond the control of law enforcement must have occurred that prevented the offender's arrest, charging, and prosecution.[32] Clearances recorded in one year may be for offenses committed in previous years. Clearance rates remain remarkably stable from year to year. In 2007, the police were able to clear about 61% of murders and nonnegligent manslaughters, 40% of forcible rapes, 26% of robberies, 54% of aggravated assaults, 12% of burglaries, 19% of larceny/thefts, 13% of motor vehicle thefts, and 18% of acts of arson.[33] In 2007, the police were able to clear 44.5% of violent crimes and about 16.5% of property crimes.[34]

The UCR also provide statistics about law enforcement personnel, such as the number of full-time sworn officers in a particular jurisdiction and the number of law enforcement officers killed in the line of duty.

Finally, in recent editions of the UCR, special sections have been devoted to topical studies. For example, the 1996 special section is entitled "Drugs in America: 1980–1995," and the 1999 special section is entitled "The Chances of Lifetime Murder Victimization, 1997." The 2001 UCR has two special sections: "The Terrorist Attacks of September 11, 2001: A Compilation of Data" and "Injuries from Violent Crime, 2000: A Study Using NIBRS Data" (the NIBRS is discussed in the next section). The 2003 and 2004 UCRs also have two special sections: "Violence among Family Members and Intimate Partners" and "Homicide as a Community Problem in the United States" (2003), and "Arrest of Juveniles for Drug Abuse Violations 1994–2003" and "Infant Victims: An Exploratory Study" (2004).[35] Beginning in 2005, such studies have been released separately from the UCR as monographs.

NATIONAL INCIDENT-BASED REPORTING SYSTEM (NIBRS)

In 1982, a joint task force of the Bureau of Justice Statistics (BJS) and the Federal Bureau of Investigation (FBI) was created to study and recommend ways to improve the quality of information contained in the uniform crime reports.[36] The result is the National Incident-Based Reporting System (NIBRS), which collected its first data in 1991. Under NIBRS, participating law enforcement authorities provide offense and arrest data on 22 broad categories of crime, covering 46 offenses (as compared to the former 8 UCR index offenses), and provide only arrest information on 11 other offenses (as compared to the former 21 Part II UCR offenses) (see Table 2.3).

Perhaps the greatest and most important difference between the NIBRS and the UCR is that the NIBRS contains more data on each crime, making it possible to examine crimes in much more detail. The NIBRS contains more than

Table 2.3 The National Incident-Based Reporting System

GROUP A OFFENSES	GROUP B OFFENSES
Arson	Bad checks
Assault offenses	Curfew/loitering/vagrancy
Bribery	Disorderly conduct
Burglary/breaking and entering	Driving under the influence
Counterfeiting/forgery	Drunkenness
Destruction/damage/vandalism	Liquor law violations
Drug/narcotic offenses	Nonviolent family offenses
Embezzlement	Peeping Tom
Extortion/blackmail	Runaways
Fraud offenses	Trespassing
Gambling offenses	All other offenses
Homicide offenses	
Kidnapping/abduction	
Larceny/theft offenses	
Motor vehicle theft	
Pornography/obscene material	
Prostitution offenses	
Robbery	
Sex offenses, forcible	
Sex offenses, nonforcible	
Stolen property offenses	
Weapons law violations	

The National Incident-Based Reporting System provides the FBI more data on crime. *How will the new data help the FBI more effectively combat crime?*

50 different pieces of information about a crime, divided into six segments, or categories. It is hoped that the increased amount of information in the NIBRS will provide the basis for a much greater understanding of crime and its causes (or at least of crime reporting and recording behavior) than is possible with the data from the UCR. Table 2.4 lists the NIBRS data elements.

The BJS and the FBI hope that eventually the NIBRS will replace the UCR as the source of official FBI crime counts. As of December 2007, 31 states have been

Table 2.4 NIBRS Data Reporting Elements

Administrative Segment

1. ORI (originating agency identifier) number
2. Incident number
3. Incident date/hour
4. Exceptional clearance indicator
5. Exceptional clearance date

Offense Segment

6. UCR offense code
7. Attempted/completed code
8. Alcohol/drug use by offender
9. Type of location
10. Number of premises entered
11. Method of entry
12. Type of criminal activity
13. Type of weapon/force used
14. Bias crime code

Property Segment

15. Type of property loss
16. Property description
17. Property value
18. Recovery date
19. Number of stolen motor vehicles
20. Number of recovered motor vehicles
21. Suspected drug type
22. Estimated drug quantity
23. Drug measurement unit

Victim Segment

24. Victim number (ID)
25. Victim UCR offense code
26. Type of victim
27. Type of activity (officer)/circumstance
28. Assignment type (officer)
29. ORIB other jurisdiction (officer)
30. Age of victim
31. Sex of victim
32. Race of victim
33. Ethnicity of victim
34. Resident status of victim
35. Homicide/assault circumstances
36. Justifiable homicide circumstances
37. Type of injury
38. Related offender murder
39. Relationship of victim to offender

Offender Segment

40. Offender number (ID)
41. Age of offender
42. Sex of offender
43. Race of offender

Arrestee Segment

44. Arrestee number (ID)
45. Transaction number
46. Arrest date
47. Type of arrest
48. Multiple clearance indicator
49. UCR arrest offense code
50. Arrestee armed indicator
51. Age of arrestee
52. Sex of arrestee
53. Race of arrestee
54. Ethnicity of arrestee
55. Resident status of arrestee
56. Disposition of arrestee under 18

Careers in Criminal Justice

Social Science Statistician

My name is Tracy Snell. I am a statistician for the Bureau of Justice Statistics (BJS), U.S. Department of Justice. BJS collects, analyzes, publishes, and disseminates information on crime, criminal offenders, victims of crime, and the operation of justice systems at all levels of government.

BJS is divided into four units: Victimization Statistics; Law Enforcement, Adjudication, and Federal Statistics; Corrections Statistics; and Special Analysis and Methodology. I work in the corrections unit, and, over the years, I have worked on data collections pertaining to probationers, prison inmates, jail inmates, parolees, and correctional facilities. Currently, I am responsible for an annual collection of information on persons under sentence of death. I also recently finished work on a survey of inmates in state and federal correctional facilities. For this nationally representative survey, which BJS conducts every 5 to 7 years, we create the questionnaire, develop a sampling design, oversee the administration of the survey, edit and analyze the data, and prepare a file to be used by the general public.

I have a BS in psychology with a minor in political science from Denison University and a Masters of Public Policy (MPP) from the University of Michigan. While I was in graduate school, I did an internship with the Inspections Division of the New York City Police Department. I helped design and collect preliminary data for an evaluation of the Community Patrol Officer Program. Prior to coming to BJS, I worked as an information specialist at a clearinghouse for drugs and crime statistics, research, and information.

In addition to designing surveys and analyzing statistics, a social science statistician writes reports summarizing the information collected in our surveys, and we respond to information requests from policymakers, criminal justice practitioners, reporters, researchers, students, and inmates. We must be aware of current issues in the corrections and legal fields that will allow us to better understand the information that we collect and discuss the finer points in our findings.

Getting respondents to submit information to us in a timely fashion can be challenging. We are working with staff of criminal justice agencies whose primary purpose is running a prison or jail, so our surveys are not their top priority. However, I find it very satisfying to provide accurate, reliable information that is often unavailable from any other source.

NIBRS certified, that is, have shown that they are capable of meeting NIBRS's data submission requirements, 13 of those states submit all their data via NIBRS, 9 states are in the process of testing NIBRS, and an additional 6 states are developing NIBRS with plans to test in the future.[37] As of December 2003, only 6 states (Alaska, Florida, Georgia, Mississippi, Nevada, and Wyoming) had no formal plans or no current interest in participating in NIBRS. More than 5,000 law enforcement agencies, representing 20% of the U.S. population, contribute NIBRS data to the national program.[38] So far, the biggest impediment to implementation of the NIBRS is that it is a "paperless" reporting system and thus requires the use of a computerized records management system. Many larger law enforcement agencies have older computer systems that require extensive and costly modifications. Many smaller agencies do not have computer systems. Although some agencies have received federal and state grants to upgrade or buy computer systems for the NIBRS, the amounts allocated have covered only a small part of the need.

Adding to the implementation problem are benefit and policy concerns.[39] Some law enforcement agencies question who, other than researchers, will benefit from their reporting NIBRS data. Others fear that, because NIBRS reports multiple offenses within an incident, crime will appear to increase, causing a public relations nightmare for law enforcement officials. Some law enforcement administrators are concerned that the detailed incident reporting required for NIBRS will tie up patrol officers, keeping them from responding to the needs of the community. In 1997, the state of Florida decided to abandon incident-based reporting after using it for nearly 8 years. The Florida Department of Law Enforcement expects to save $1 million a year by switching to summary-based reporting, which requires less information.[40]

NATIONAL CRIME VICTIMIZATION SURVEYS (NCVS)

The **national crime victimization surveys (NCVS)** are the other major source of crime statistics in the United States. The surveys provide a detailed picture of crime incidents, victims, and trends from the victim's perspective. Formerly

national crime victimization surveys
A source of crime statistics based on interviews in which respondents are asked whether they have been victims of any of the FBI's index offenses (except murder, nonnegligent manslaughter, and arson) or other crimes during the past 6 months. If they have, they are asked to provide information about the experience.

called the national crime surveys (NCS), they have been conducted annually since 1972 by the Bureau of the Census for the U.S. Department of Justice's Bureau of Justice Statistics.[41] The NCVS, published under the title *Criminal Victimization in the United States,* were created not only as a basis for learning more about crime and its victims but also as a means of complementing and assessing what is known about crime from the FBI's uniform crime reports. (From 1996 on, the NCVS are available only in electronic formats; see www.ojp.usdoj.gov.)

From a nationally representative sample of 41,500 households (in 2007—the latest year for which data were available), 73,600 respondents age 12 or older were asked in interviews whether they had been victims of any of the FBI's former index offenses (except murder, nonnegligent manslaughter, and arson) or any other crimes during the past 6 months. If they had, they were asked to provide information about the experience. Because major changes were made in the format and methodology of the NCVS in 1992, adjustments have been made to the data before 1993 to make them comparable with data collected since the changes. Like the UCR, the NCVS are merely an index of crime and not an accurate measure of the true amount of crime that is committed.

Generally, the national crime victimization surveys produce different results from the FBI's uniform crime reports. For nearly all offenses, the NCVS show more crimes being committed than the UCR do. This underestimation by the UCR may result from victims' failure to report crimes to the police or from failure by the police to report to the FBI all the crimes they know about. The UCR count more of some kinds of offenses (such as assault) and count them differently. For example, the UCR count each report of a domestic assault at the same address separately; the NCVS count the repeated assaults as one victimization. The UCR count crimes reported by people and businesses that the NCVS don't reach. Unlike the UCR, the NCVS rely on random samplings of victims and their memories of things that may have happened months ago, both of which are subject to some degree of error. Other problems with the NCVS are interviewers who may be biased or who may cheat, and respondents who may lie or exaggerate, or may respond without understanding the questions.

Differences in the data sources help explain the differences in the trends indicated by the NCVS and the UCR. For example, in one year (1990), NCVS respondents indicated that they had experienced about 50% more crimes, on average, than were recorded by the FBI. However, the differences varied by offense. The smallest difference between the two indexes for that year was for motor vehicle theft (20%). The largest difference was for burglary (67%). The smaller difference for motor vehicle theft was probably due to insurance companies requiring a police report before reimbursing policyholders for their losses.

Sometimes overall changes in the two indexes differ. For example, between 1984 and 1985, the total number of crimes in the UCR increased 4.6%, while the total number of crimes in the NCVS decreased 1.9%. The difference probably stems from the difference in what the two indexes measure. Thus, between 1984 and 1985, there was an apparent increase in the number of crimes reported to and recorded by the police but an apparent decrease in the number of crimes to which people said they had been subjected. Figure 2.5 displays the trends in four measures or indexes of serious violent crime. Remember that serious violent crimes include murder, rape, robbery, and aggravated assault.

SELF-REPORT CRIME SURVEYS

self-report crime surveys Surveys in which subjects are asked whether they have committed crimes.

Whereas other tallies of crime rely on summary police reports, incident-based reports, or victim interviews, **self-report crime surveys** ask selected subjects whether they have committed crimes. Self-report crime surveys, like all crime measures, are indexes of crime; they are not accurate measures of the true amount of crime. To date, most self-report crime surveys conducted in the United States

Figure 2.5

Four Measures of Serious Violent Crime

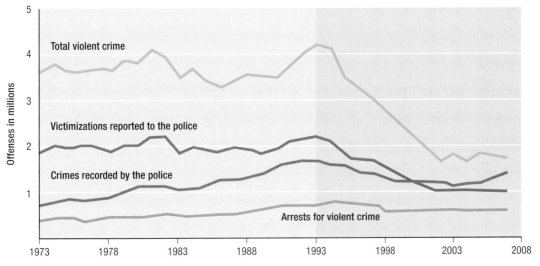

Notes:

1. The serious violent crimes included are rape, robbery, aggravated assault, and homicide. (For related data about homicide trends, see *Homicide Trends in the U.S.*) The National Crime Victimization Survey redesign was implemented in 1993: the area with the lighter shading is before the redesign and the darker area, after the redesign. The data before 1993 are adjusted to make them comparable with data collected since the redesign. The adjustment methods are described in *Criminal Victimization 1973–1995*. Estimates for 1993 and beyond are based on collection year, whereas earlier estimates are based on data year. For additional information about the methods used, see *Criminal Victimization 2004*.

2. The measures of serious violent crime come from two sources of data:

   • **The National Crime Victimization Surveys** (NCVS), household surveys ongoing since 1972, that interview about 75,000 persons age 12 and older in 42,000 households twice each year about their victimizations from crime.

   • **The Uniform Crime Reports** (UCR), which collects information on crimes and arrests reported by law enforcement authorities to the FBI.

   Although each measure is different, both the NCVS and the UCR show that serious violent crime levels declined in recent years. For a discussion of UCR and NCVS trends that use these data, see "True Crime Stories? Accounting for Differences in our National Crime Indicators" from *Chance* by BJS staff members Michael R. Rand and Callie Marie Rennison.

3. Definitions:

   Total serious violent crime: The number of homicides recorded by police plus the number of rapes, robberies, and aggravated assaults from the victimization survey whether or not they were reported to the police.

   Victimizations reported to the police: The number of homicides recorded by police plus the number of rapes, robberies, and aggravated assaults from the victimization survey that victims said were reported to the police.

   Crimes recorded by the police: The number of homicides, forcible rapes, robberies, and aggravated assaults included in the Uniform Crime Reports of the FBI excluding commercial robberies and crimes that involved victims under age 12.

   Arrests for violent crimes: The number of persons arrested for homicide, forcible rape, robbery, or aggravated assault as reported by law enforcement agencies to the FBI.

Source: www.ojp.us.doj.gov/bjs/glance/cv2.htm and www.ojp.usdoj.gov/bjs/glance/tables/4meastab.htm. 2007 data calculated from Michael R. Rand, "Criminal Victimization, 2007," U.S. Department of Justice, Bureau of Justice Statistics, National Crime Victimization Survey (Washington, D.C.: GPO, December 2008) at www.ojp.usdoj.gov/bjs/pub/pdf/cv07.pdf and Federal Bureau of Investigation, *Crime in the United States 2007* at www.fbi.gov/ucr/cius2007/data/table_01.html.

have been administered to schoolchildren, especially high school students. Some examples of such nationwide self-report crime survey efforts are the National Youth Survey, begun in 1975, and the effort to ascertain and gauge fluctuations in the levels of smoking, drinking, and illicit drug use among secondary school students, begun by the National Institute on Drug Abuse in 1975.

Earlier self-report crime surveys of adults interestingly enough found an enormous amount of hidden crime in the United States. Those self-report crime surveys indicated that more than 90% of all Americans had committed crimes for which they could have been found guilty and imprisoned.[42] This is not to say that all Americans are murderers, thieves, or rapists, for they are not, but only that crime serious enough to warrant an individual's imprisonment is more widespread among the U.S. population than many people might think or

MYTH

Criminal activity is concentrated among certain groups of people.

FACT

Early self-report crime surveys of adults found an enormous amount of hidden crime in the United States. They found that more than 90% of all Americans had committed crimes for which they could have been imprisoned.

Self-report crime surveys ask selected subjects whether they have committed crimes. *What are some problems with getting accurate information about crime from these surveys?*

imagine. The most commonly reported offenses in self-report crime surveys are larceny, indecency, and tax evasion.[43] It is unlikely that the pervasiveness of crime in the population has lessened significantly since the earlier self-report crime surveys were conducted.

One lesson that can be learned from the aforementioned survey findings is that people's criminality is better described as a continuum, that is, as having committed more crime or less crime, rather than simply being described as criminal or noncriminal. In society, there are probably few angels, that is, people who have never committed a crime. Likewise, there are probably few criminals whose whole lives are totally oriented toward the commission of crimes. Most people have committed a crime at some point in their lives and some have committed crimes repeatedly. It probably makes more sense for us, then, to talk about relative degrees of criminality, rather than to talk about all-encompassing criminality or its absence.

One of the criticisms of the National Youth Survey, and a problem with many self-report crime surveys, is that it asks about less serious offenses, such as cutting classes, disobeying parents, and stealing items worth less than $5, while omitting questions about serious crimes, such as robbery, burglary, and sexual assault. Self-report crime surveys also suffer from all the problems of other surveys, problems that were described in the last subsection—they produce results different from other surveys, and they are not an accurate measure of crime.

THINKING CRITICALLY

1. Of the various methods of measuring crime presented in this section, which one do you think is the most accurate? Why? Which one do you think is the least accurate? Why?

2. Do you think there are ways to get more victims of crime to report criminal incidents? If so, what would you suggest?

Costs of Crime

According to data from the national crime victimization survey, in 2006 the total economic loss to victims of crime in the United States was $18.4 billion.[44]

Table 2.5 shows the breakdown of this amount among categories of personal and property crimes. The total includes losses from property theft or damage, cash losses, medical expenses, and income lost from work because of injuries, police and court-related activities, or time spent repairing or replacing property.[45] It does not include the cost of the criminal justice process (described in Chapter 1), increased insurance premiums, security devices bought for protection, losses to businesses (which are substantial), or corporate crime. Regarding corporate crimes, the estimated $260 billion in annual losses to corporate crime victims are more than 14 times greater than the $18.4 billion cost to victims of crimes reported in the 2006 national crime victimization survey. The crime of price-fixing, alone, in which competing companies explicitly agree to keep prices artificially high to maximize profits, is estimated to cost consumers about $60 billion a year.[46]

The NCVS probably provides the best estimates of the annual costs of crime. Those cost estimates, however, are deficient in two ways. First, they include only a limited number of personal and property crimes. And, as noted previously, they do not include the cost of the criminal

Table 2.5 Total Economic Loss to Victims of Personal and Property Crimes, 2006

Type of Crime	Gross Loss in Millions ($)
All crimes	18,410
Personal Crimes	**1,896**
Crimes of violence	1,860
Rape/sexual assault	45
Robbery	904
Assault	911
Purse snatching	4
Pocket picking	32
Property Crimes	**16,513**
Household burglary	4,427
Motor vehicle theft	5,646
Theft	6,441

Note: Detail may not add to total shown because of rounding.

Source: *Criminal Victimization in the United States, 2006 Statistical Tables,* Table 82, www.ojp.usdoj.gov/bjs/pub/pdf/cvus/current/cv0682.pdf.

justice process, increased insurance premiums, security devices bought for protection, losses to businesses, or corporate crime. Second, they report estimates only of relatively short-term and tangible costs. They do not include long-term and intangible costs associated with pain, suffering, and reduced quality of life.

To compensate for the deficiencies of the NCVS, a 1996 study was sponsored by the National Institute of Justice.[47] In addition to the more standard cost estimates in the NCVS, the admittedly dated study estimated long-term costs as well as the intangible costs of pain, suffering, and reduced quality of life. Intangible costs were calculated in a number of ways. For example, the costs of pain, suffering, and reduced quality of life for non-fatal injuries were estimated by analyzing jury awards to crime and burn victims. Only the portion of the jury award intended to compensate the victim for pain, suffering, and reduced quality of life was used; punitive damages were excluded from the estimates.

Furthermore, although the study included only "street crimes" and "domestic crime," it expanded on the crime categories and information included in the NCVS by (1) including crimes committed against people under the age of 12, (2) using better information on domestic violence and sexual assault, (3) more fully accounting for repeat victimizations, and (4) including child abuse and drunk driving. Excluded from the study were crimes committed against business and government, personal fraud, white-collar crime, child neglect, and most "victimless" crimes, including drug offenses. The study, although dated and with its own problems, provides a rough idea of the degree to which the NCVS underestimates the costs of crime.

The study estimated that the annual tangible cost of personal and property crime—including medical costs, lost earnings, and public program costs related to victim assistance—were $105 billion, or more than $400 per U.S. resident. When the intangible costs of pain, suffering, and reduced quality of life were added, the annual cost increased to an estimated $450 billion, or about $1,800 per U.S. resident. Figure 2.6 shows how the $450 billion was divided into specific costs of crime.

Violent crime (including drunk driving and arson) accounted for $426 billion of the total, while property crime accounted for the remaining $24 billion. The study found that violence against children accounted for more than 20% of all tangible costs and more than 35% of all costs (including pain, suffering, and reduced quality of life).

Of the crimes included in the study, rape had the highest annual victim costs, at $127 billion a year (excluding child sexual abuse). Second was assault, with victim costs of $93 billion a year, followed by murder (excluding arson and drunk driving deaths), at $71 billion annually. Drunk driving (including fatalities) was next at $61 billion a year, and child abuse was estimated to cost $56 billion annually.

Among the tangible costs of crime excluded from the study were the costs of the criminal justice process and private security expenditures. Omitted also were the intangible costs of fear of crime, a fear that makes people prisoners in their own homes, divides people, and destroys communities.

Figure 2.6

Annual Cost of Crime in the United States

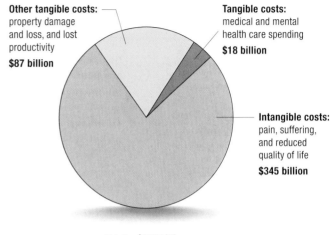

Other tangible costs: property damage and loss, and lost productivity
$87 billion

Tangible costs: medical and mental health care spending
$18 billion

Intangible costs: pain, suffering, and reduced quality of life
$345 billion

Total = $450 billion

Source: Ted R. Miller, Mark A. Cohen, and Brian Wiersema, *Victim Costs and Consequences: A New Look,* U.S. Department of Justice, National Institute of Justice Research Report (Washington, D.C.: GPO, February 1996), p. 17.

THINKING CRITICALLY

1. What would you estimate is the cost of crimes that go unreported?

2. Why are the highest costs of crimes the intangible costs?

Fear of Crime

A by-product of crime, beyond actual physical or material loss, is fear. For many crime victims, it is the most burdensome and lasting consequence of their victimizations. However, fear of crime is also contagious. One does not have to be a victim of violent crime to be fearful of violent crime. In fact, research shows that people who have heard about other people's victimizations are nearly as fearful as the people who have been victimized themselves.[48]

WHAT PEOPLE FEAR

When Americans are asked specifically what they fear, surveys show the following:

- 46% worry about their homes being burglarized when they are not there.
- 43% worry about having their car stolen or broken into.
- 37% worry about walking alone at night within a mile of where they live.
- 31% worry about being a victim of terrorism.
- 31% worry about having a school-aged child physically harmed while attending school.
- 29% worry about getting mugged.
- 28% worry about their homes being burglarized when they are there.
- 21% worry about being attacked while driving their car.
- 19% worry about being sexually assaulted.
- 17% worry about getting murdered.
- 16% worry about being the victim of a hate crime.
- 6% worry about being assaulted or killed by a co-worker or other employee where they work.[49]

WHO FEARS CRIME

Fear of criminal victimization is neither evenly distributed across the population nor commensurate with the statistical probability of being the victim of crime. Following are the percentages of respondents in each demographic group who replied "yes" to the survey question: "Is there any area right around here (referring to the respondent's own neighborhood)—that is, within a mile— where you would be afraid to walk alone at night?"[50]

- **Gender**—Females (47%) were more fearful than males (19%).
- **Race/Ethnicity**—Nonwhites (41%) were more fearful than whites (30%).
- **Age**—People 18 to 20 years old (41%) were more fearful than people in other age categories (21 to 29 = 30%; 30 to 49 = 27%; and 50 years and older = 37%).
- **Religion**—Jews (60%) were more fearful than Catholics (35%), Protestants (31%), or those who did not claim a religion (30%).
- **Region**—People living in the West (38%) were more fearful than people living in the Northeast (35%), South (33%), or Midwest (23%).
- **Education**—High school graduates (34%) were slightly more fearful than people with some college (31%) or people who did not graduate from high school (32%).
- **Politics**—Democrats (39%) were more fearful than either Republicans (30%) or Independents (28%).
- **Income**—Fear declined with increasing family income. People whose family income was $50,000 or more (22%) were less fearful than people whose family income was $30,000–$49,999 (32%), $20,000–$29,999 (37%), and under $20,000 (41%).

CJ Online

Gallup Crime Polls

The Gallup Organization conducts public opinion polls on a variety of topics that affect Americans. You can learn more about the public's view of crime issues by visiting the Gallup website at www.gallup.com. *What connection, if any, is there between public opinion toward crime and crime statistics?*

FYI   Seattle Safest City

According to a 2006 Gallup poll that asked Americans which of 16 major U.S. cities were safe or unsafe places to live or visit, Seattle was rated the safest, with Minneapolis, San Francisco, Dallas, and Boston also receiving high safety ratings. Detroit and New Orleans were rated as the least safe cities, along with Los Angeles and Washington, D.C.

Source: "Seattle Tops List of Safe Cities," The Gallup Poll at http://poll.gallup.com/content/default.aspx?ci525240.

HOW PEOPLE RESPOND TO A FEAR OF CRIME

Fear of crime has many detrimental consequences. It makes people feel vulnerable and isolated, it reduces a person's general sense of well-being, it motivates people to buy safety devices with money that otherwise could be used to improve their quality of life, and it also contributes to neighborhood decline and the crime problem. As criminologist Wesley Skogan explains:

> Fear . . . can work in conjunction with other factors to stimulate more rapid neighborhood decline. Together, the spread of fear and other local problems provide a form of positive feedback that can further increase levels of crime. These feedback processes include (1) physical and psychological withdrawal from community life; (2) a weakening of the informal social control processes that inhibit crime and disorder; (3) a decline in the organizational life and mobilization capacity of the neighborhood; (4) deteriorating business conditions; (5) the importation and domestic production of delinquency and deviance; and (6) further dramatic changes in the composition of the population. At the end lies a stage characterized by demographic collapse.[51]

In response to their fear of crime, Americans are employing a number of different strategies. Below is the percentage of Americans who had taken various defensive measures against crime as of 2007:

- 48% avoided going to certain places or neighborhoods that they might otherwise have wanted to go to.
- 31% kept a dog for protection.
- 31% had a burglar alarm installed in their home.
- 23% bought a gun for self-protection or home protection.
- 14% carried mace or pepper spray.
- 12% carried a knife for defense.
- 12% carried a gun for defense.[52]

THINKING CRITICALLY

1. What steps could be taken, if any, to reduce people's overall fear of crime?

2. Why do you think there is no correlation between those who fear crime the most and the most likely victims of crime?

3. What factors contribute to people's fear of crime?

4. What are the costs, if any, of a fear of crime?

Victims of Crime

Findings from the 2007 NCVS reveal that in 2007 an estimated total of 23 million crimes were attempted or completed against U.S. residents age 12 or older—about the same number of crimes attempted or completed in 2005. Approximately 5.2 million of the crimes were violent crimes (rape, sexual assault, robbery, aggravated assault, and simple assault), again about the same number as in 2005; about 17.5 million were property crimes (burglary, motor vehicle theft, and other thefts), about a half million fewer than in 2005; and 194,100 personal thefts (pocket picking, completed purse snatching, and attempted purse snatching), about 33,000 fewer than in 2005.[53]

VICTIMIZATION TRENDS

According to 2007 NCVS data, the violent and property crime victimization rates were 20.7 and 146.5 per 1,000 persons age 12 or older, respectively. The 2007 violent crime rate was 1.9% lower than the 2005 rate, a decline that continued

Many people take extraordinary measures to protect themselves from crime. *Why are people so fearful of crime? Should they be? Why or why not?*

Figure 2.7

Trends in Violent and Property Crime Rates

Violent crime victimization rate per 1,000 persons age 12 or older, 1973–2007

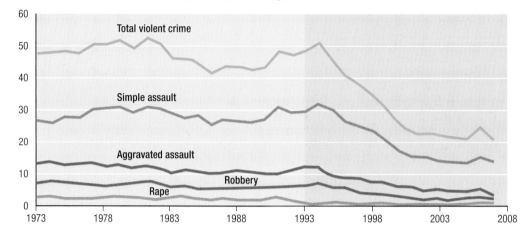

Property crime victimization rate per 1,000 households, 1973–2007

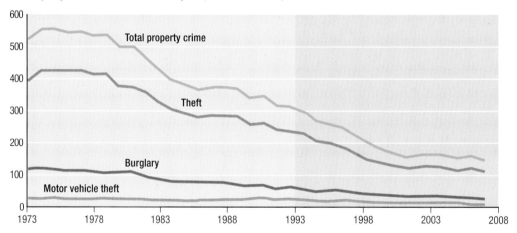

Note: From 1973 through June 1992, data were collected under the National Crime Survey (NCS) and made comparable to data collected under the redesigned methods of the NCVS that began in July 1992.

Source: Michael R. Rand, *Criminal Victimization, 2007,* U.S. Department of Justice, Bureau of Justice Statistics, National Crime Victimization Survey (Washington, D.C.: GPO, December 2008), pp. 2–3 at www.ojp.usdoj.gov/bjs/pub/pdf/cv07.pdf.

a trend that began in 1994 (see Figure 2.7, top graph).[54] The 2007 property crime rate decreased 5% from the 2005 rate, a decline that continued a trend that began in 1974 (see Figure 2.7, bottom graph).[55] The only crime rates that increased between 2005 and 2007 were rape/sexual assault and simple assault, which increased 25% and 3%, respectively.[56] Combined, the 2007 violent and property crime rates were the lowest recorded since the survey was first administered in 1973.[57] Figure 2.7 shows that the decline in the violent crime rate is primarily a result of a decline in simple assaults, while the decrease in the property crime rate is almost entirely attributable to a decrease in thefts.

WHO THE VICTIMS ARE

Although each year millions of people are victimized by crime, victimization—like the fear of crime—is not spread evenly throughout the population. Certain types of people are much more likely to be crime victims. The types of people that were most vulnerable to victimization in the past continue to be the most vulnerable.

Based on 2005 and 2007 NCVS data the demographic groups with the highest rates of violent crime victimization per 1,000 persons age 12 or older (from highest to lowest overall rate) were (year of data in parentheses):[58]

- **Multirace Persons** (2007)—The rate of violent crime victimization for blacks was 24.3; for whites, 19.9; and for others, 11.4. The rate for Hispanics was 18.6. The violent victimization rate for those who are of two or more races was 73.8.
- **Younger Persons** (2007)—Persons age 16 to 19 had the highest violent crime victimization rate (50.1), followed by persons age 12 to 15 (43.4) and persons age 20 to 24 (35.2). Rates dropped as victims got older. The rate for persons age 25 to 34 was 24.7, 35 to 49, 17.7, 50 to 64, 11.6, and 65 or older, 2.5. Persons age 16 to 19 were more than 20 times more likely than persons 65 and older to be victims of violent crime.
- **Never Married, Divorced, or Separated Persons** (2005)—Never married, divorced, or separated persons were more than 3.5 times more likely than married persons and about 7 times more likely than widowed persons to be violent crime victims. The rates for never married and divorced or separated persons were 38.4 and 32.3, respectively, compared to the rate of 10.0 for married persons and 5.0 for widowers.
- **Poorer Persons** (2005)—Persons with annual household incomes of less than $7,500 had violent victimization rates more than twice as high as victims with annual household incomes of $75,000 or more. The rate for the lower income category was 38.1; the rate for the highest income category was 16.7.
- **Urban Residents** (2005)—The violent crime victimization rates for urban, suburban, and rural residents were 29.4, 18.3, and 18.1, respectively.

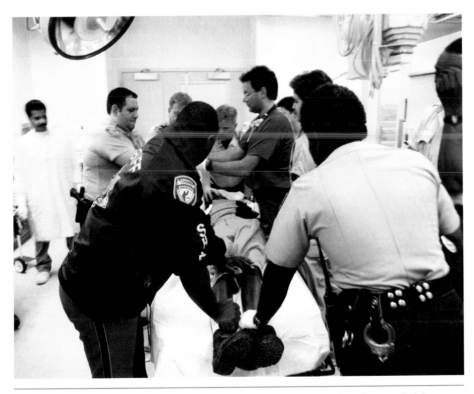

Young, economically disadvantaged black males are the most likely victims of personal violent crime. *Why, and what can be done about it?*

- **Persons Living in the West** (2005)—Persons living in the West had a violent crime victimization rate of 25.7, while persons living in the Midwest, South, and Northeast had rates of 23.4, 19.1, and 17.7, respectively.
- **Men** (2007)—The violent crime victimization rate for men was 22.5; the rate for women was 18.9.

Whereas violent crime victimization rates are measures of the characteristics of victims age 12 and older, property crime victimization rates are measures of the characteristics of victimized households or heads of households. Consequently, there are no property crime victimization rates recorded by gender, age, or marital status, but there is the category of home ownership. The characteristics of households or heads of households with the highest 2004 and 2007 rates of property crime victimization per 1,000 households (from highest to lowest overall rate) were (year of data in parentheses):[59]

- **Larger Households** (2007)—The rate of property victimization for households of six or more persons was 277.5. The rate for households of four or five persons was 207.5; for households with two or three persons, 137.7; and households with one person, 105.7.
- **Western Households** (2004)—The rate of property crime victimization for households in the West was 206.5; in the Midwest, 155.8; in the South, 146.8; and in the Northeast, 103.9.
- **Urban Residences** (2004)—The property crime victimization rates for urban, suburban, and rural residences were 200.0, 141.4, and 125.1, respectively.
- **Renters** (2004)—The rate of property crime victimization of renters was 192.3; the rate for homeowners was 136.5.

Property crime victimization rates in 2007 decreased as household incomes increased, with one exception. The rate for households with incomes of less than $7,500 was 213.1, while the rate for households with incomes of $75,000 or more was 146.3. Households with incomes from $50,000 to $74,999 had the lowest rate at 144.3 and were the lone exception.

There were two other interesting findings in the 2007 NCVS. The first deals with the victim-offender relationship. While strangers victimized half of all men (50%), a majority of women (69%) were victimized by someone they knew.[60] The second finding was that in 72% of violent victimizations no weapon was used. A weapon was known to be used in 47% of robberies, 18% of assaults, and only 6% of rapes or sexual assaults.[61]

THINKING CRITICALLY

1. Why do you think that certain types of people are more likely than others to become crime victims?

2. Why do you think that certain types of households or heads of households are more likely than others to become victimized by crime?

❋ Summary

1. Distinguish between a social definition and a legal definition of crime, and summarize the problems with each.

   A typical social definition of crime is behavior that violates the norms of society or, more simply, antisocial behavior. A typical legal definition of crime is an intentional violation of the criminal law or penal code, committed without defense or excuse and penalized by the state. There are problems with both definitions. Problems with the social definition are that (1) there are no uniform norms of behavior accepted by all of society, (2) norms of behavior are subject to interpretation, and (3) norms change from time to time and from place to place. Problems with the legal definition of crime are (1) overcriminalization, (2) nonenforcement, and (3) undercriminalization.

2. List the technical and ideal elements of a crime.

   The technical and ideal elements of a crime are (1) harm, (2) legality, (3) *actus reus,* (4) *mens rea,* (5) causation, (6) concurrence, and (7) punishment.

3. Identify some of the legal defenses or legal excuses for criminal responsibility.

   Among the legal defenses or legal excuses for criminal responsibility in the United States are these: the defendant (1) acted under duress, (2) was underage, (3) was insane, (4) acted in self-defense or in defense of a third party, (5) was entrapped, or (6) acted out of necessity.

4. Explain why crime and delinquency statistics are unreliable.

   Among the reasons why crime and delinquency statistics are unreliable are the following: First, some behaviors are labeled crime by one observer but not by another. Second, a large proportion of crimes are undetected. Third, not all crimes are reported to the police. Fourth, not all crimes that are reported are officially recorded by the police.

5. Identify the two major sources of crime statistics in the United States.

   The two major sources of crime statistics in the United States are the uniform crime reports (UCR) compiled by the FBI and the national crime victimization surveys (NCVS) compiled by the Bureau of Justice Statistics.

6. Describe the principal finding of the national crime victimization surveys.

   The national crime victimization surveys (NCVS) produce different results from the FBI's uniform crime reports (UCR). The NCVS generally show more crimes being committed than the UCR do. The NCVS count more of some kinds of crimes and count them differently.

7. Summarize the general finding of self-report crime surveys.

   Self-report crime surveys show that the amount of hidden crime in the United States is enormous; more than 90% of all Americans have committed crimes for which they could have been imprisoned.

8. Identify the costs of crime.

   According to data from the NCVS, in 2007 the total economic loss to victims of crime in the United States was $18.4 billion. This figure does not include the tangible costs of the criminal justice process, security devices bought for protection, losses to businesses, losses from corporate crimes, or the intangible costs of pain, suffering, and reduced quality of life. When all costs are totaled, it is estimated that crime costs about $450 billion annually (in the mid-1990s).

9. Describe the characteristics of people most likely to fear crime.

   In general, those more likely to fear crime are females, nonwhites, people 18 to 20 years old, Jews, Westerners, high school graduates, Democrats, and people whose family income is less than $20,000.

10. List the characteristics of people who are the most likely and the least likely to be victims of crime.

    According to data from the 2005 and 2007 NCVS, the most likely victims of personal violent crimes are multiracial, young (12–24 years old), never married, divorced, or separated, poor, black, and urban men living in the West. The group least likely to experience violent crime victimization is people age 65 or older. The most likely victims of household property crimes are large and poor Western households in urban areas headed by renters.

❋ Key Terms

norm 28	*actus reus* 31	*mala in se* 36	eight index crimes 43
legal definition of crime 29	*mens rea* 31	*mala prohibita* 36	status offense 43
overcriminalization 29	negligence 31	dark figure of crime 38	crime index offenses
nonenforcement 30	duress 32	crime index 38	cleared 43
undercriminalization 30	juvenile delinquency 32	offenses known to the	national crime victimization
harm 31	insanity 32	police 39	surveys 47
legality 31	entrapment 35	crime rate 41	self-report crime
ex post facto law 31	necessity defense 35	uniform crime reports 42	surveys 48

❋ Review Questions

1. What is a *norm?*

2. What is the *harm* of crime?

3. What is the *mens rea* of crime?

4. What is *legal infancy* or *legal nonage?*

5. What is *juvenile delinquency?*

6. What is *insanity?*

7. Does the availability of the insanity defense allow a large number of dangerous criminals to go free?

8. What is the difference between a *felony* and a *misdemeanor?*

9. What percentages of all crime are violent crime, property crime, and public order crime?

10. Why aren't any records or indexes of crime very reliable measures of the true amount of crime?

11. What are "offenses known to the police," and what are advantages and disadvantages of using it?

12. What is a *crime rate,* and why are crime rates used?

13. What is a *status offense?*

14. When the media report that crime has increased or decreased from one year to the next, to what are they referring?

15. What is the NIBRS?

16. What are some of the detrimental consequences of a fear of crime?

17. What are the most common ways people respond to a fear of crime?

18. What long-term trends in violent and property crime victimization rates are revealed by the national crime victimization surveys?

✳ In the Field

1. **Crime Victimization Survey** As an individual project or a group project, construct and conduct a crime victimization survey. (Use the national crime victimization survey as a model.) Either orally or in writing, present and discuss the results. Be sure to discuss problems encountered in constructing the survey and problems with the accuracy and trustworthiness of responses.

2. **Self-Report Crime Survey** As an individual project or a group project, construct and conduct a self-report crime survey. (Make sure you tell respondents not to put their names or any other identifying information on the survey. Also, be sure to include both serious and less serious crimes.) Either orally or in writing, present and discuss the results. Be sure to discuss problems encountered in constructing the survey and problems with the accuracy and trustworthiness of responses.

✳ On the Net

1. **Crime Statistics** Examine the latest edition of the FBI's uniform crime reports at www.fbi.gov/ucr/ucr .htm#cius. Then choose one of the former eight index crimes, and search the site for statistics about that crime. Write a brief report summarizing the results of your research.

2. **Victimization Data** Examine the latest edition of the NCVS at the Bureau of Justice Statistics site at www .ojp.usdoj.gov/bjs. Click on "criminal victimization," and scroll to the newest edition (hard copies of the NCVS are no longer available). Compare the latest victimization data with the data presented in your textbook. Write a brief report summarizing any changes.

✳ Critical Thinking Exercises

THE TWINKIE DEFENSE

1. Dan White had been elected as a city supervisor of San Francisco. White resigned on November 10, 1978. Four days later, he changed his mind and asked Mayor George Moscone to reappoint him to his former position. The mayor refused. On the morning of November 27, White confronted the mayor and demanded to be reappointed. When the mayor refused, White shot the mayor five times. White reloaded the gun, walked across the hall to City Supervisor Harvey Milk's office, and shot him four times. Milk was a leader in San Francisco's gay community with whom White frequently clashed. After shooting Moscone and Milk, White fled but shortly thereafter went to the police and confessed. He was charged with first-degree murder. During his trial, several psychologists called by the defense testified that White's behavior was the result of long-term depression exacerbated by a craving for junk food. They testified that White's judgment and ability to control his behavior were altered by the huge amount of sugar he had consumed the night before the killings. The so-called Twinkie defense worked. White was convicted of voluntary manslaughter instead of first-degree murder, and on May 21, 1979, he was sentenced to a prison term of 5 years to 7 years, 8 months. White was released from prison after serving 5 years, 1 month, and 9 days of his sentence. He committed suicide on October 21, 1985.

   a. What is the legal rationale for accepted legal defenses against or excuses from criminal responsibility? Do you agree with the rationale?

   b. Should all legal defenses or excuses be abolished? Why or why not?

THE SLEEPWALKING DEFENSE

2. Twenty-eight-year-old Justin Cox told a Florida jury that he was sleepwalking when he touched a 12-year-old girl's upper thigh at a friend's house one night in 2006. He stated that he would never do anything like that if he were awake, and he apologized to the girl when he awoke with her under him. Following a night of drinking, Cox ended up at a friend's house and went to sleep alone in a bedroom. The victim, who was spending the night with her girlfriend, had fallen asleep on the living-room couch. At some point, Cox wandered into the living room, sat down on the couch, put the victim's legs over his lap, and fondled her. When she moved and woke him up, Cox said he was "freaked" about what was happening and apologized to the girl. She started to cry and asked him to leave the house, which he did. Until investigators informed him, Cox stated that he did not know he had done more than put his hand on her leg. Cox was arrested for lewd and lascivious acts, placed on house arrest, and made to wear an ankle monitor.

   Cox's sleepwalking defense was unusual, but it had been used successfully in previous cases. However, juries are usually skeptical of it. Cox's attorney said, "It's almost like an insanity defense where you are not in your reality and therefore you are not conscious." Cox had a family history of sleepwalking and had sleepwalked since he was a child. After evaluating Cox, a doctor testified for the defense that at the time of the incident, Cox was sleepwalking. The state's sleepwalking expert said it was possible Cox was sleepwalking at the time of the crime, but not a "high medical probability." The jury believed the defense's doctor and, on May 8, 2008, acquitted Cox of the charges.

   a. In this case, do you think the sleepwalking defense was reasonable? Why or why not?
   b. Do you think the jury made the right decision? Why or why not?
   c. Do you think it was fair to place Cox on house arrest and make him wear an ankle monitor for nearly two years? Why or why not?

FIGHTING ILLEGAL DRUGS

3. Activists are advocating a different strategy in the fight against illegal drugs. In agreement with the American Medical Association, they maintain that drug addiction is a disease. They believe it should be treated as a public health problem, not as a law enforcement problem. They propose a change in strategy from prohibition to decriminalization or legalization. According to these activists, decriminalization or legalization would do the following:
   • Reduce profits from drug trafficking, crime caused by the need to support drug habits, and the prison population.
   • Allow money used for incarceration to fund new models of drug control.
   • Allow drugs such as marijuana to be regulated and taxed.
   • Reduce the negative health consequences from using drugs of unknown potency and purity.
   • Improve pain control options for certain medical conditions.
   • Free physicians from fear of entrapment for prescribing certain drugs.
   • Shift the focus of criminal justice to more serious crime problems.
   a. One of the seven elements of a crime is harm. Do you think that illegal drug use is harmful? Explain.
   b. If the use of addictive drugs is illegal, should addictive substances such as nicotine (in cigarettes) or caffeine (in coffee) also be made illegal? Explain.

To access more information and resources, including study questions, chapter summaries, and links, go to www.mhhe.com/bohm6e.

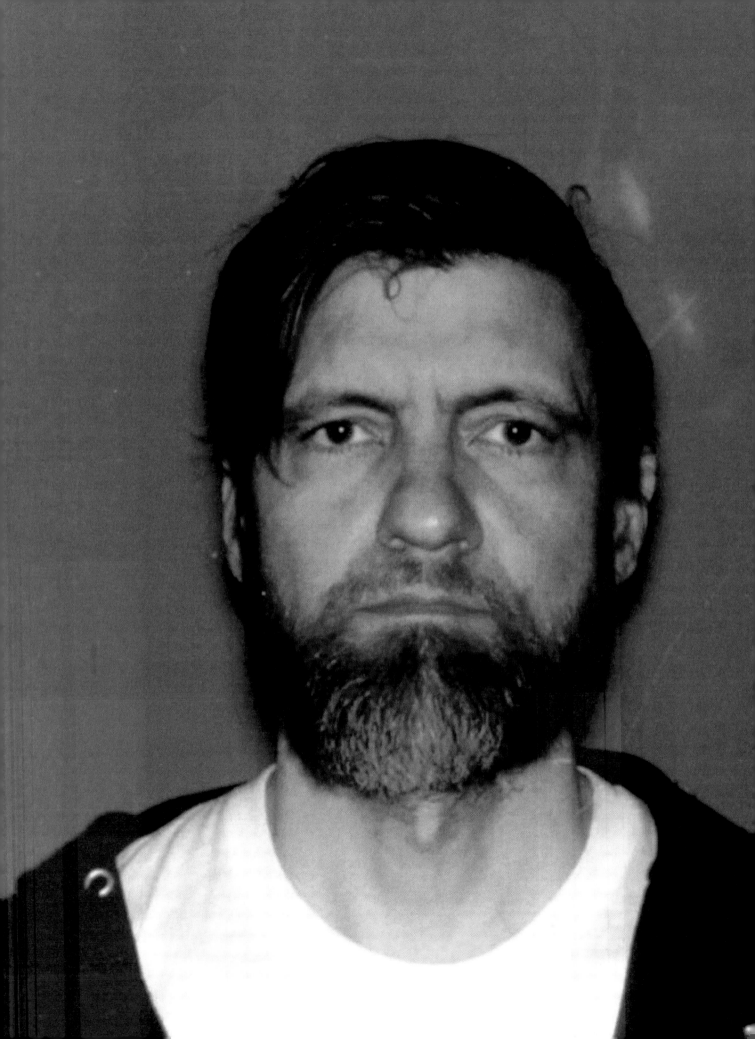

Explaining Crime

Chapter Outline

Chapter Objectives

After completing this chapter, you should be able to:

1. Define criminological theory.

2. State the causes of crime according to classical and neoclassical criminologists.

3. Describe the biological theories of crime causation and their policy implications.

4. Describe the different psychological theories of crime causation and their policy implications.

5. Explain sociological theories of crime causation and their policy implications.

6. Distinguish major differences among classical, positivist, and critical theories of crime causation.

7. Describe how critical theorists would explain the causes of crime.

CRIME STORY

In January 2009, Christine McCallum, a 29-year-old married fifth-grade teacher in Abington, Massachusetts, was charged with seven counts of statutory rape. She was being held on $10,000 bond and was placed on administrative leave from her job. The *Boston Herald* reported that she had sex with a student about 300 times beginning when he was 13 years old. The affair began in February 2006, when McCallum had sex with the boy on her couch, while her husband was asleep upstairs. She reportedly gave the young boy alcoholic drinks. The affair presumably ended in November 2007, when she became jealous that he was using the cell phone she gave him to text other girls. The alleged victim is now 16. An assistant district attorney observed: "The defendant is obsessed with this young child." In a MySpace message, McCallum admitted she was unable to control herself around him.

McCallum is only one among dozens, perhaps hundreds, of female

continued

teachers who, during the past couple of decades, have had sexual relations with underage male students. Perhaps the most infamous case involved Mary Kay Letourneau, a 34-year-old Seattle teacher whose relationship with a sixth-grade student ultimately produced two children. Letourneau was arrested in 1997 and spent seven years in prison for statutory rape. Following her release from prison Mary Kay and her former student, then 21, were married.

Another female teacher who had sex with an underage male student was Pamela Rogers Turner, a 28-year-old married Tennessee elementary school physical education teacher. In 2005, Turner was charged with 13 counts of statutory rape and 15 counts of sexual battery for having a 3-month long sexual relationship with a 13-year-old student. She pleaded guilty to four counts of sexual battery by an authority figure, was sentenced to 9 months in jail, and was required to surrender her state teaching certificate for life. After serving a little more than 6 months of her jail sentence, she was released for good behavior and placed on probation for 8 years. Just 2 months after her release from jail, Turner, now Rogers (her maiden name), was arrested for probation violation. Against the judge's orders, she repeatedly contacted the boy with whom she had sex and his family, by calls, emails, and text messages. She also sent the boy nude photos and sex videos of her. On July 14, 2006, the judge revoked Turner's probation and sent her to prison to serve the remainder of her suspended 7-year sentence. On January 10, 2007, the judge tacked on 2 more years to Turner's sentence after she pleaded guilty to two counts of solicitation of sexual exploitation of a minor for sending the boy the nude pictures of her.

With little research on the subject, it is not clear whether more teachers today are committing such crimes or whether students are simply reporting the behavior more often. One trend is certain, however: the number of disciplinary cases involving sexual misconduct among female teachers is increasing. The use of modern technology appears to be a part of the problem. About half of the teachers who have been reprimanded, suspended, put on probation, or had their teaching certificates revoked used cell phones, email, MySpace pages, and text messaging to flirt and talk about sex with students. The most comprehensive study to date, commissioned by the U.S. Department of Education in 2004, revealed that nearly 10% of the country's public-school students—approximately 4.5 million children—had received unwanted sexual attention from school employees, including teachers (both male and female). The study also found that only 11% of students who were sexually abused by teachers reported it.

Chapter 3 examines the causes of criminal behavior. A variety of theories are described under the general categories of classical, positivist, and critical explanations. Although most of these theories offer some insights into the origins of criminality, none is able to provide a complete picture of the factors that contribute to individual decisions to commit criminal acts. What caused Christine McCallum, Mary Kay Letourneau, and Pamela Rogers Turner to prey on their young male students? Did they know the difference between right and wrong at the time they committed those acts? How should society respond to their actions? When respected and trusted members of the community commit crimes and display behaviors suggestive of a mental breakdown, citizens are sometimes torn between the desire to offer help and support and the feeling that people must be held accountable for their actions. The criminal justice system includes processes that may recognize reduced responsibility when severe mental illness at the time was a factor in the commission of crime. Would the use of those processes in these cases be appropriate?

Introduction to Criminological Theory

theory An assumption (or set of assumptions) that attempts to explain why or how things are related to each other.

A **theory** is an assumption (or set of assumptions) that attempts to explain why or how things are related to each other. A theory of crime attempts to explain why or how a certain thing or certain things are related to criminal behavior. For example, some theories assume that crime is part of human nature, that some human beings are born evil. In those theories, human nature is examined in relation to crime. Other theories assume that crime is caused by biological things (for example, chromosome abnormalities, hormone imbalances), psychological things (for example, below-normal intelligence, satisfaction of basic needs), sociological things (for example, social disorganization, inadequate socialization), economic things (for example, unemployment, economic inequality), or some combination of all of these. In this chapter, we examine a variety of crime theories and discuss the policy implications of each. (Unless indicated otherwise, the term *crime* includes delinquency.)

criminological theory The explanation of criminal behavior, as well as the behavior of police, attorneys, prosecutors, judges, correctional personnel, victims, and other actors in the criminal justice process.

Criminological theory is important, because most of what is done in criminal justice is based on criminological theory, whether we or the people who propose and implement policies based on the theory know it or not. The failure to understand the theoretical basis of criminal justice policies leads to at least two undesirable consequences. First, if criminal justice policy makers do not know the theory or theories on which their proposed policies are based, then they will be unaware of the problems that are likely to undermine the success of the policies. Much time and money could be saved if criminal justice policies were based on a thorough theoretical understanding. Second, criminal justice policies invariably intrude on people's lives (for example, people are arrested and imprisoned). If people's lives are going to be disrupted by criminal justice policies, it seems only fair that there be very good reasons for the disruption.

Technically, criminological theory refers not only to explanations of criminal behavior but also to explanations of police behavior and the behavior of attorneys, prosecutors, judges, correctional personnel, victims, and other actors in the criminal justice system. However, in this chapter, our focus is on theories of crime causation. Table 3.1 outlines the crime causation theories presented in this chapter.

THINKING CRITICALLY

1. What is a theory?

2. Why is it important to understand the various theories of criminal behavior?

Classical and Neoclassical Approaches to Explaining Crime

The causes of crime have long been the subject of much speculation, theorizing, research, and debate among scholars and the public. Each theory of crime has been influenced by the religious, philosophical, political, economic, social, and scientific trends of the time. One of the earliest secular approaches to explaining the causes of crime was the classical theory, developed in Europe at the time of profound social and intellectual change. Before classical theory, crime was generally equated with sin and was considered the work of demons or the devil.

CLASSICAL THEORY

Classical theory is a product of the Enlightenment period, or the Age of Reason, a period of history that began in the late 1500s and lasted until the late 1700s. The Enlightenment thinkers, including members of the classical school of criminology, promoted a new, scientific view of the world. In so doing, they rejected the then-dominant religious view of the world, which was based on revelation and the authority of the Church. The Enlightenment thinkers assumed that human beings could understand the world through science—the human capacity to observe and to reason. Moreover, they believed that if people could understand the world and its functioning, they could change it. The Enlightenment thinkers rejected the belief that either the nature of the world or the behavior of the people in it was divinely ordained or predetermined.

Instead, the Enlightenment thinkers believed that people exercise *free will,* or the ability to choose any course of action, for which they are completely responsible. Human behavior was considered motivated by a *hedonistic rationality,* in which a person weighs the potential pleasure of an action against the possible pain associated with it. In that view, human beings commit crime because they rationally calculate that the crime will give them more pleasure than pain.

Classical criminologists, as Enlightenment thinkers, were concerned with protecting the rights of humankind from the corruption and excesses of the existing legal institutions. Horrible and severe punishments were common both before and during the Enlightenment. For example, in England during the eighteenth century, almost 150 offenses (some authorities claim more than 200 offenses) carried the death penalty, including stealing turnips, associating with gypsies, cutting down

classical theory A product of the Enlightenment, based on the assumption that people exercise free will and are thus completely responsible for their actions. In classical theory, human behavior, including criminal behavior, is motivated by a hedonistic rationality, in which actors weigh the potential pleasure of an action against the possible pain associated with it.

Table 3.1 Theories of Crime Causation

CLASSICAL AND NEOCLASSICAL THEORIES

Theories	Theorists	Causes	Policy Implications
Classical	Beccaria	Free-willed individuals commit crime because they rationally calculate that crime will give them more pleasure than pain.	Deterrence: Establish social contract. Enact laws that are clear, simple, unbiased, and reflect the population's consensus. Impose punishments that are proportionate to the crime, prompt, certain, public, necessary, the least possible in the given circumstances, and dictated by law, not judges' discretion. Educate the public. Eliminate corruption from the administration of justice. Reward virtue.

POSITIVIST THEORIES

Theories	Theorists	Causes	Policy Implications
Biological	Lombroso, Sheldon	Biological inferiority or biochemical processes cause people to commit crimes.	Isolate, sterilize, or execute offenders. For specific problems, brain surgery, chemical treatment, improved diets, and better mother and child health care.
Psychological			
Intelligence	Goddard	Mental inferiority (low IQ) causes people to commit crimes.	Isolate, sterilize, or execute offenders.
Psychoanalytic	Freud	Crime is a symptom of more deep-seated problems.	Provide psychotherapy or psychoanalysis.
Humanistic	Maslow	Crime is a means by which individuals can satisfy their basic human needs.	Help people satisfy their basic needs legally.
	Halleck	Crime is an adaptation to helplessness caused by oppression.	Eliminate sources of oppression. Provide legal ways of coping with feelings of helplessness caused by oppression; psychotherapy.
Sociological			
Durkheim	Durkheim	Crime is a social fact. It is a "normal" aspect of society, although different types of societies should have greater or lesser degrees of it. Crime is also functional for society.	Contain crime within reasonable boundaries.
Chicago School	Park, Burgess, Shaw, McKay	Delinquency is caused by detachment from conventional groups, which is caused by social disorganization.	Organize and empower neighborhood residents.
Anomie or strain	Merton, Cohen	For Merton, crime is caused by *anomie* or strain, which is the contradiction between cultural goals and the social structure's capacity to provide the institutionalized means to achieve those goals. For Cohen, gang delinquency is caused by *anomie* or strain, which is the inability to conform to middle-class values or to achieve status among peers legally.	Reduce aspirations. Increase legitimate opportunities. Do both.
Learning	Tarde, Sutherland, Burgess, Akers, Jeffery	Crime is committed because it is positively reinforced, negatively reinforced, or imitated.	Provide law-abiding models. Regulate associations. Eliminate crime's rewards. Reward law-abiding behavior. Punish criminal behavior effectively.

(continued)

<u>Table 3.1</u> **Theories of Crime Causation** *(continued)*

Theories	Theorists	Causes	Policy Implications
Control	Reiss, Toby, Nye, Reckless, Hirschi	Crime is a result of improper socialization.	Properly socialize children so that they develop self-control and a strong moral bond to society.

CRITICAL THEORIES

Theories	Theorists	Causes	Policy Implications
Labeling	Becker, Lemert	Does not explain the initial cause of crime and delinquency (primary deviance); explains only secondary deviance, which is the commission of crime after the first criminal act with the acceptance of a criminal label.	Do not label. Employ radical nonintervention. Employ reintegrative shaming.
Conflict	Vold, Turk	Crime is caused by relative powerlessness.	Dominant groups give up power to subordinate groups. Dominant groups become more effective rulers and subordinate groups better subjects.
Radical	Quinney, Chambliss, Platt	Competition among wealthy people and among poor people as well as between rich and poor (the class struggle) and the practice of taking advantage of "socialist" justice.	Define crime as a violation of basic human rights. Replace the criminal justice system with "popular" or "socialist" justice. Create a socialist society appreciative of human diversity.
British or Left Realism	Young	Relative deprivation is a potent, although not exclusive, cause of crime.	Employ police power to protect people in working-class communities.
Peacemaking	Quinney, Pepinsky	Same as radical (different prescription for change).	Transform human beings so that they are able to experience empathy with those less fortunate and respond to other people's needs. Reduce hierarchical structures. Create communities of caring people. Champion universal social justice.
Feminist theory	Daly, Chesney-Lind, Simpson	Patriarchy (men's control over women's labor and sexuality) is the cause of greater crime.	Abolish patriarchal structures and relationships. Champion equality for women in all areas.
Postmodernism	Henry, Milovanovic	Crime is caused by processes that result in the denial of responsibility for other people and to other people.	Similar to peacemaking criminological theory.

a tree, and picking pockets. Barbarous punishments were not the only problem. At the time, crime was rampant, yet types of crime were poorly defined. What we today call *due process of law* was either absent or ignored. Torture was employed routinely to extract confessions. Judgeships were typically sold to wealthy persons by the sovereign, and judges had almost total discretion. Consequently, there was little consistency in the application of the law or in the punishments imposed.

It was within that historical context that Cesare Beccaria, perhaps the best known of the classical criminologists, wrote and published anonymously in 1764 his truly revolutionary work, *An Essay on Crimes and Punishments* (*Dei Delitti e delle Pene*). His book is generally acknowledged to have had an enormous practical influence on the establishment of a more humane system of criminal law and procedure.[1] In the book, Beccaria sets forth most of what we now call classical criminological theory.

According to Beccaria, the only justified rationale for laws and punishments is the principle of **utility,** that is, "the greatest happiness shared by the greatest number."[2] The basis of society, as well as the origin of punishments

utility The principle that a policy should provide "the greatest happiness shared by the greatest number."

social contract An imaginary agreement to sacrifice the minimum amount of liberty necessary to prevent anarchy and chaos.

special or **specific deterrence** The prevention of individuals from committing crime again by punishing them.

general deterrence The prevention of people in general or society at large from engaging in crime by punishing specific individuals and making examples of them.

Cesare Beccaria believed that the only justified rationale for laws and punishments is the principle of utility, that is, "the greatest happiness shared by the greatest number." *Do you agree with him? Why or why not?*

FYI Cesare Beccaria and the Death Penalty

Cesare Beccaria, the best known of the classical criminologists, opposed the death penalty. In *An Essay on Crimes and Punishments,* he wrote: "The death penalty cannot be useful, because of the example of barbarity it gives. . . . It seems to me absurd that the laws, which are an expression of the public will, which detest and punish homicide, should themselves commit it, and that to deter citizens from murder, they order a public one."

neoclassical theory A modification of classical theory in which it was conceded that certain factors, such as insanity, might inhibit the exercise of free will.

and the right to punish, is the **social contract.** The social contract is an imaginary agreement entered into by persons who sacrifice the minimum amount of their liberty necessary to prevent anarchy and chaos.

Beccaria believed that the only legitimate purpose of punishment is deterrence, both special and general.[3] **Special** or **specific deterrence** is the prevention of the punished persons from committing crime again. **General deterrence** is the use of the punishment of specific individuals to prevent people in general or society at large from engaging in crime. To be both effective and just, Beccaria argued, punishments must be "public, prompt, necessary, the least possible in the given circumstances, proportionate to the crime, dictated by the laws."[4] It is important to emphasize, however, that Beccaria promoted crime prevention over punishment.

In addition to the establishment of a social contract and the punishment of people who violate it, Beccaria recommended four other ways to prevent or to deter crime.[5] The first was to enact laws that are clear, simple, and unbiased and that reflect the consensus of the population. The second was to educate the public. Beccaria assumed that the more educated people are, the less likely they are to commit crimes. The third was to eliminate corruption from the administration of justice. Beccaria believed that if the people who dispense justice are themselves corrupt, people lose respect for the justice system and become more likely to commit crimes. The fourth was to reward virtue. Beccaria asserted that punishing crime is not enough; it is also important to reward law-abiding behavior. Such rewards might include public recognition of especially meritorious behavior or, perhaps, an annual tax deduction for people who have not been convicted of a crime.

The application of classical theory was supposed to make criminal law fairer and easier to administer. To those ends, judges would not select sentences. They could impose only the sentences dictated by legislatures for specific crimes. All offenders would be treated alike, and similar crimes would be treated similarly. Individual differences among offenders and unique or mitigating circumstances about the crime would be ignored. A problem is that all offenders are not alike, and similar crimes are not always as similar as they might appear on the surface. Should first offenders be treated the same as those who commit crime repeatedly? Should juveniles be treated the same as adults? Should the insane be treated the same as the sane? Should a crime of passion be treated the same as the intentional commission of a crime? The classical school's answer to all of those difficult questions would be a simple yes.

Despite those problems, Beccaria's ideas were very influential. France, for example, adopted many of Beccaria's principles in its Code of 1791—in particular, the principle of equal punishments for the same crimes. However, because classical theory ignored both individual differences among offenders and mitigating circumstances, it was difficult to apply the law in practice. Because of that difficulty, as well as new developments in the emerging behavioral sciences, modifications of classical theory and its application were introduced in the early 1800s.

NEOCLASSICAL THEORY

Several modifications of classical theory are collectively referred to as **neoclassical theory.** The principal difference between the two theories has to do with classical theory's assumption about free will. In the neoclassical revision, it was conceded that certain factors, such as insanity, might inhibit the exercise of free will. Thus, the idea of premeditation was introduced as a measure of the degree of free will exercised. Also, mitigating circumstances were considered legitimate grounds for an argument of diminished responsibility.

Those modifications of classical theory had two practical effects on criminal justice policy. First, they provided a reason for nonlegal experts such as medical doctors to testify in court as to the degree of diminished responsibility of an offender. Second, offenders began to be sentenced to punishments that were considered rehabilitative. The idea was that certain environments, for example, environments free of vice and crime, were more conducive than others to the exercise of rational choice.

The reason we have placed so much emphasis on the classical school of criminology and its neoclassical revisions is that, together, they are essentially the model on which criminal justice in the United States is based today. During the past 30 years or so, at least in part because the public frequently perceived as too lenient the sentences imposed by judges for certain crimes, such measures as legislatively imposed sentencing guidelines have limited the sentencing authority of judges in many jurisdictions. Public outrage over the decisions of other criminal justice officials has led to similar measures. For example, parole has been abolished in the federal jurisdiction and in some states because many people believe that parole boards release dangerous criminals from prison too soon.

Historians of criminal law credit Beccaria's arguments in his book, *An Essay on Crimes and Punishments,* with ending legal torture throughout Christendom. However, in 1999, Haitian immigrant Abner Louima was brutally tortured by New York City police officers. *How could this have happened?*

The revival of classical and neoclassical theories during the past three decades, and the introduction of a more modern version called *rational choice theory,* are also probably a reaction to the allegation of some criminologists and public officials that criminologists have failed to discover the causes of crime. As a result of that belief, there has been a renewed effort to deter crimes by sentencing more offenders to prison for longer periods of time and, in many jurisdictions, by imposing capital punishment for heinous crimes. Ironically, one reason the theory of the classical school lost favor in the nineteenth century was the belief that punishment was not a particularly effective method of preventing or controlling crime.

THINKING CRITICALLY

1. Name four of the ways that classical criminologist Cesare Beccaria thought were best to prevent or deter crime. Do you agree with Beccaria? Why or why not?

2. What are the main differences between classical and neoclassical theories?

Positivist Approaches to Explaining Crime

The theory of the positivist school of criminology grew out of positive philosophy and the logic and basic methodology of empirical or experimental science. Positive philosophy was an explicit rejection of the critical and "negative" philosophy of the Enlightenment thinkers. Among the founders of positivism was Auguste Comte, who also has been credited with founding sociology. Comte acknowledged that the Enlightenment thinkers had contributed to progress by helping to break up the old system and by paving the way for a new one.[6] However, Comte argued that the ideas of the Enlightenment period had outlived their usefulness and had become obstructive.

At about the same time that positivist philosophy was developing, experimentation with animals was becoming an increasingly accepted way of learning about human beings in physiology, medicine, psychology, and psychiatry.

In his *Politique Positive* (1854), Comte proclaimed himself Pope of the new positive religion. *What did he mean by that?*

Human beings were beginning to appear to science as one of many creatures, with no special connection to God. Human beings were beginning to be understood, not as free-willed, self-determining creatures who could do anything that they wanted, but rather as beings whose action was determined by biological and cultural factors.

Positivism was a major break with the classical and neoclassical theories that had preceded it. The following are key assumptions of the positivist school of thought:

1. Human behavior is determined and not a matter of free will. Consequently, positivists focus on cause-and-effect relationships.
2. Criminals are fundamentally different from noncriminals. Positivists search for such differences by scientific methods.
3. Social scientists (including criminologists) can be objective, or value-neutral, in their work.
4. Crime is frequently caused by multiple factors.
5. Society is based on consensus but not on a social contract.

As the social sciences developed and social scientists directed their attention to the problem of crime, they adopted, for the most part, positivist assumptions. For example, theories of crime were (and continue to be) based on biological positivism, psychological positivism, sociological positivism, and so on. However, as theories based on positivist assumptions were developed, it became apparent to close observers that there were problems, not only with the theories but with the positivist assumptions as well. We will briefly discuss five of those problems.[7] In subsequent subsections, we will also describe problems peculiar to specific positivist theories of crime causation.

The first problem with positivism is overprediction: positivist theories generally account for too much crime. They also do not explain exceptions very well. For example, a positivist theory that suggests crime is caused by poverty overpredicts because not all poor people commit crime.

Second, positivist theories generally ignore the criminalization process, the process by which certain behaviors are made illegal. They separate the study of crime from a theory of the law and the state and take the legal definition of crime for granted. Ignored is the question of why certain behaviors are defined as criminal while other, similar behaviors are not.

A third problem with positivism is its consensual worldview, the belief that most people agree most of the time about what is good and bad and right and wrong. Such a view ignores a multitude of fundamental conflicts of value and interest in society. It also tends to lead to a blind acceptance of the status quo.

A fourth problem is positivism's belief in determinism, the idea that choice of action is not free but is determined by causes independent of a person's will. Positivists generally assume that humans only adapt or react—but humans also create. How else could we explain new social arrangements or ways of thinking? A belief in determinism allows positivists to present an absolute situation uncomplicated by the ability to choose.

Finally, a fifth problem with positivist theories is the belief in the ability of social scientists (criminologists) to be objective, or value-neutral, in their work. Positivists fail to recognize that to describe and evaluate such human actions as criminal behavior is fundamentally a moral endeavor and, therefore, subject to bias.

BIOLOGICAL THEORIES

Biological theories of crime causation (biological positivism) are based on the belief that criminals are physiologically different from noncriminals.

FYI

Charles Darwin

In *The Descent of Man* (1871), British naturalist Charles Darwin suggested that some people were "less highly evolved or developed than others," that some people "were nearer their apelike ancestors than others in traits, abilities, and dispositions."

Source: George B. Vold, *Theoretical Criminology*, 2nd ed. (New York: Oxford, 1979).

Careers in Criminal Justice

Criminologist

My name is Alida Merlo, and I am a professor of criminology at Indiana University of Pennsylvania. I have taught criminal justice and criminology for more than 25 years. I have a Ph.D. in sociology from Fordham University, a master's degree in criminal justice from Northeastern University, and a bachelor's degree from Youngstown State University. As an undergraduate, I majored in sociology and corrections.

I became interested in criminology while taking an undergraduate course in juvenile delinquency. That course inspired me to pursue a career in criminal justice as a probation officer and then as an intake supervisor for the Mahoning County Juvenile Court in Youngstown, Ohio. These experiences led me to enroll in graduate school to learn more about crime causation and the criminal justice process.

During graduate school, I realized I would like to teach criminology and criminal justice. I was attracted to the profession for a variety of reasons: It would enable me to do research, teach, develop programs, and pursue professional activities and community service. Teaching and studying criminal justice and criminology seemed a wonderful opportunity.

Being a criminologist involves developing and teaching courses, reading and contributing to the literature in the field, serving on departmental and university committees, advising students about courses, research, career options, and graduate education, meeting prospective students and their families, applying for research funding, conducting research, sharing research findings with colleagues at state, regional, national, and international meetings, being involved in professional organizations, and serving on community boards or assisting in community programs.

One great joy of teaching criminology and criminal justice is assisting students as they develop and blossom in the discipline. Many of my students work in the field. Former students have been awarded doctoral degrees and teach criminal justice. It is exciting to have played a part in their professional development.

One disadvantage of being a criminologist is the inability to communicate to the public and to policy makers the realities of criminal justice and the implications of one's research. Confronting the fact that policies are often developed and enforced with little enlightenment is frustrating, but I am confident that criminologists will play a greater role in the future.

What qualities does a criminologist need to succeed? Why?

Early biological theories assumed that structure determined function. In other words, criminals behave differently because, structurally, they are different. Today's biocriminologists are more likely to assume that biochemistry determines function or, more precisely, that the difference between criminals and noncriminals is the result of a complex interaction between biochemical and environmental factors. To test biological theories, efforts are made to demonstrate, through measurement and statistical analysis, that there are or are not significant structural or biochemical differences between criminals and noncriminals.

Historically, the cause of crime, from this perspective, was **biological inferiority.** Biological inferiority in criminals was assumed to produce certain physical or genetic characteristics that distinguished criminals from noncriminals. It is important to emphasize that in these theories, the physical or genetic characteristics themselves did not cause crime; they were only the symptoms, or *stigmata,* of the more fundamental inferiority. The concept of biological inferiority has lost favor among today's biocriminologists who generally prefer to emphasize the biological differences between criminals and noncriminals without adding the value judgment. In any event, several different methodologies have been employed to detect physical differences between criminals and noncriminals. They are criminal anthropology; study of body types; heredity studies, including family trees, statistical comparisons, twin studies, and adoption studies; and, in the last 15 to 20 years or so, studies based on new scientific technologies that allow, for example, the examination of brain chemistry processes.

biological inferiority According to biological theories, a criminal's innate physiological makeup produces certain physical or genetic characteristics that distinguish criminals from noncriminals.

Criminal Anthropology **Criminal anthropology** is the study of "criminal" human beings. It is associated with the work of an Italian army doctor and later, university professor, Cesare Lombroso. Lombroso first published his theory of a physical criminal type in 1876.

criminal anthropology The study of "criminal" human beings.

Lombroso's theory consisted of the following propositions:[8]

1. Criminals are, by birth, a distinct type.
2. That type can be recognized by physical characteristics, or stigmata, such as enormous jaws, high cheekbones, and insensitivity to pain.
3. The criminal type is clearly distinguished in a person with more than five stigmata, perhaps exists in a person with three to five stigmata, and does not necessarily exist in a person with fewer than three stigmata.
4. Physical stigmata do not cause crime; they only indicate an individual who is predisposed to crime. Such a person is either an **atavist**—that is, a reversion to a savage type—or a result of degeneration.
5. Because of their personal natures, such persons cannot desist from crime unless they experience very favorable lives.

atavist A person who reverts to a savage type.

Lombroso's theory was popular in the United States until about 1915, although variations of his theory are still being taught today. The major problem with Lombroso's criminal anthropology is the assumption that certain physical characteristics are indicative of biological inferiority. Unless there is independent evidence to support that assumption, other than the association of the physical characteristics with criminality, then the result is circular reasoning. In other words, crime is caused by biological inferiority, which is itself indicated by the physical characteristics associated with criminality.

Body-Type Theory Body-type theory is an extension of Lombroso's criminal anthropology. William Sheldon, whose work in the 1940s was based on earlier work by Ernst Kretchmer in the 1920s, is perhaps the best known of the body-type theorists. According to Sheldon, human beings can be divided into three basic body types, or *somatotypes,* which correspond to three basic temperaments.[9] The three body types are the endomorphic (soft, fat), the mesomorphic (athletically built), and the ectomorphic (tall, skinny).

Sheldon argued that everyone has elements of all three types, but that one type usually predominates. In a study of 200 Boston delinquents between 1939 and 1949, Sheldon found that delinquents were more mesomorphic than nondelinquents and that serious delinquents were more mesomorphic than less serious delinquents. Subsequent studies by the Gluecks in the 1950s and by Cortes in the 1970s also found an association between mesomorphy and delinquency.

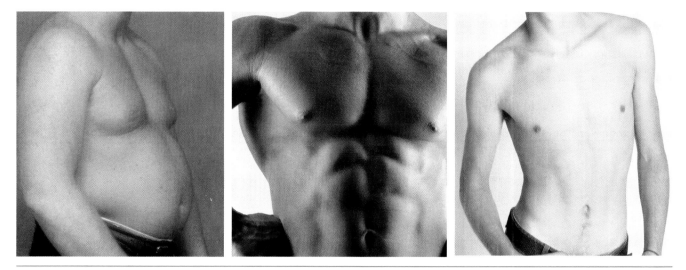

William Sheldon, a well-known body-type theorist, divided humans into three basic body types. Left: endomorphic (soft, fat); center: mesomorphic (athletically built); right: ectomorphic (tall, skinny). *Why would delinquents more likely have a mesomorphic body type rather than an endomorphic or ectomorphic body type?*

The major criticism of the body-type theory is that differences in behavior are indicative of the social selection process and not biological inferiority. In other words, delinquents are more likely to be mesomorphic than nondelinquents, because, for example, mesomorphs are more likely to be selected for gang membership. Also, the finding that delinquents are more likely than nondelinquents to be mesomorphic contradicts, at least with regard to physique, the theory's general assumption that criminals (or delinquents) are biologically inferior.

In any event, if one believes that crime is the product of biological inferiority, then the policy implications are limited. Either criminals are isolated from the rest of the population by imprisoning them, for example, or they are executed. If they are isolated, they may also need to be sterilized to ensure that they do not reproduce.

Heredity Studies A variety of methods has been employed to test the proposition that criminals are genetically different from noncriminals.

Family Tree Studies Perhaps the earliest method was the use of family trees, in which a family known to have many "criminals" was compared with a family tree of "noncriminals." (See FYI.) However, a finding that criminality appears in successive generations does not prove that criminality is inherited or is the product of a hereditary defect. For example, the use of a fork in eating has been a trait of many families for generations, but that does not prove that the use of a fork is inherited. In short, the family tree method cannot adequately separate hereditary influences from environmental influences.

Statistical Comparisons A second method used to test the proposition that crime is inherited or is the product of a hereditary defect is statistical comparison. The rationale is that if criminality exhibits the same degree of family resemblance as other physical traits, such as eye or hair color, then criminality, like those other traits, must be inherited. Although there is some evidence to support the notion, statistical comparisons also fail to separate adequately hereditary influences from environmental influences.

Twin Studies A third, more sophisticated method of testing the proposition that crime is inherited or is the result of a hereditary defect is the use of twin studies. Heredity is assumed to be the same in identical twins, because they are the product of a single egg. Heredity is assumed to be different in fraternal twins, because they are the product of two eggs fertilized by two sperm. The logic of the method is that if there is greater similarity in behavior between identical twins than between fraternal twins, the behavior must be due to heredity, since environments are much the same. More than a half century of this methodology has revealed that identical twins are more likely to demonstrate concordance (both twins having criminal records) than are fraternal twins, thus supporting the hereditary link. A problem with the twin studies, however, is the potential confounding of genetic and environmental influences. Identical twins tend to be treated more alike by others, spend much more time together, and have a greater sense of shared identity than do fraternal twins.

Adoption Studies A fourth method, the most recent and most sophisticated method of examining the inheritability of criminality, is the adoption study. The first such study was conducted in the 1970s. In this method, the criminal records of adopted children (almost always boys) who were adopted at a relatively early age are compared with the criminal records of both their biological parents and their adoptive parents (almost always fathers). The rationale is that if the criminal records of adopted boys are more like those of their biological fathers than like those of their adoptive fathers, the criminality of the adopted boys can be assumed to be the result of heredity.

 FYI The Family Tree Method

The family tree method was used by Dugdale (1877) and Estabrook (1916), who both compared the Jukes family with the Jonathan Edwards family. The Jukes family presumably had 7 murderers, 60 thieves, 50 prostitutes, and assorted other criminals. The Edwards family, in contrast, presumably had no criminals but, instead, had presidents of the United States, governors, Supreme Court justices, federal court justices, and assorted writers, preachers, and teachers. As it turns out, the Edwards family was not as crime-free as originally believed. Apparently, Jonathan Edwards's maternal grandmother had been divorced on grounds of adultery, a grandaunt had murdered her son, and a granduncle had murdered his sister.

Source: Richard L. Dugdale, *The Jukes: A Study in Crime, Pauperism, Disease and Heredity* (New York: Putnam, 1877); Arthur H. Estabrook, *The Jukes in 1915* (Washington, D.C.: Carnegie Institute of Washington, 1916).

The findings of the adoption studies reveal that the percentage of adoptees who are criminal is greater when the biological father has a criminal record than when the adoptive father has one. However, there also is an interactive effect. A greater percentage of adoptees have criminal records when both fathers have criminal records than when only one of them does. Like the twin studies, the adoption studies presumably demonstrate the influence of heredity but cannot adequately separate it from the influence of the environment. A problem with the adoption studies is the difficulty of interpreting the relative influences of heredity and environment, especially when the adoption does not take place shortly after birth or when, as is commonly the case, the adoption agency attempts to find an adoptive home that matches the biological home in family income and socioeconomic status.

If criminals are genetically different from noncriminals or the product of genetic defect, then the policy implications are the same as for other theories that propose that criminals are biologically inferior: isolate, sterilize, or execute. However, in the future, new technologies may make possible genetic engineering—that is, the removal or alteration of defective genes.

Modern Biocriminology Ongoing research has revealed numerous biological factors associated either directly or indirectly with criminal or delinquent behavior. Among such factors are certain chemical, mineral, and vitamin deficiencies in the diet, diets high in sugar and carbohydrates, hypoglycemia (low blood sugar level), certain allergies, ingestion of food dyes and lead, exposure to radiation from fluorescent tubes and television sets, and all sorts of brain dysfunctions such as attention deficit/hyperactivity disorder.[10] This section focuses on a few more of the biological factors linked to criminality and delinquency: disorders of the limbic system and other parts of the brain, brain chemical dysfunctions, minimal brain damage, and endocrine abnormalities.

limbic system A structure surrounding the brain stem that, in part, controls the life functions of heartbeat, breathing, and sleep. It also is believed to moderate expressions of violence; such emotions as anger, rage, and fear; and sexual response.

Limbic System Disorders At least some unprovoked violent criminal behavior is believed to be caused by tumors and other destructive or inflammatory processes of the limbic system.[11]

The **limbic system** (see Figure 3.1) is a structure surrounding the brain stem that, in part, controls the life functions of heartbeat, breathing, and sleep. It also is believed to moderate expressions of violence; such emotions as anger,

Figure 3.1

The Limbic System

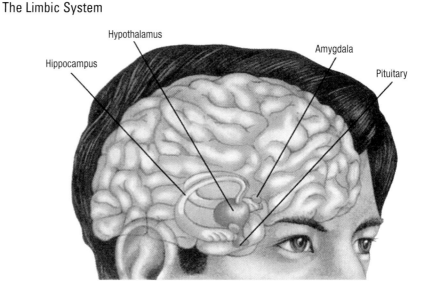

rage, and fear; and sexual response. Violent criminal behavior has also been linked to disorders in other parts of the brain. Recent evidence suggests that chronic violent offenders have much higher levels of brain disorder when compared to the general population. Surgical removal of the affected area sometimes eliminates expressions of violence. A problem with that type of intervention, however, is that it can cause unpredictable and undesirable behavior changes and, of course, is irreversible. Irreversibility is less a problem with newer chemical interventions, but the problem of unpredictable and undesirable behavior changes remains.

Chemical Dysfunctions Some criminal behaviors are believed to be influenced by low levels of brain neurotransmitters (substances brain cells use to communicate).[12] For example, low levels of the brain neurotransmitter *serotonin* have been found in impulsive murderers and arsonists. Research is currently being conducted to determine whether low levels of another neurotransmitter, *norepinephrine,* are associated with compulsive gambling. Another interesting discovery in this area may help explain cocaine use. Apparently cocaine increases the level of the neurotransmitter *dopamine,* which activates the limbic system to produce pleasure. If such chemical deficiencies are linked to those behaviors, chemical treatment or improved diets might help. Neurotransmitters are products of the foods people eat.

Minimal Brain Damage Research on minimal brain damage has found that it increases an individual's chances of being identified as delinquent.[13] Minimal brain damage is believed to be most commonly caused by nutritional or oxygen deficiencies during pregnancy, or during or shortly after birth, or by insufficient protein and sensory stimulation during a child's formative years. Because minimal brain damage is also strongly associated with lower socioeconomic status, social deprivation must be considered a crucial element in its occurrence.

To reduce minimal brain damage in the population, adequate prenatal medical care and nutrition must be provided to all expectant mothers. To minimize complications during birth, adequate medical assistance must be provided. Further reductions in minimal brain damage would require providing adequate protein and social and intellectual stimulation to developing infants and young children.

Endocrine Abnormalities Criminal behaviors have also been associated with endocrine, or hormone, abnormalities, especially those involving *testosterone* (a male sex hormone) and *progesterone* and *estrogen* (female sex hormones).[14] For example, administering estrogen to male sex offenders has been found to reduce their sexual drives. A similar effect has been achieved by administering the drug Depo-Provera, which reduces testosterone levels. However, a problem with Depo-Provera is that it is successful only for male sex offenders who cannot control their sexual urges. The drug does not seem to work on offenders whose sex crimes are premeditated. Studies have also found that a large number of crimes committed by females are committed during the menstrual or premenstrual periods of the female hormonal cycle. Those periods are characterized by a change in the estrogen-progesterone ratio.

In sum, there are probably no positivist criminologists today who would argue that biology or genetics makes people criminals. Nor, for that matter, are there many criminologists today who would deny that biology has some influence on criminal behavior. The position held by most criminologists today is that criminal behavior is the product of a complex interaction between biology and environmental or social conditions. What is inherited is not criminal behavior but rather the way in which the person responds to his or her environment. In short, biology or genetics gives an individual a predisposition, or

CJ Online

Biological Causes of Crime

Learn more about the biological causes of criminal, violent, and psychopathic behavior. Go to www.crime-times.org for the Crime Times website. Review the issue and/or subject index and read a few articles related to biology and criminal behavior. *Do you think that biological theories of crime causation adequately explain criminal behavior?*

FYI Chemical Castration

In 1996, California became the first state to require chemical castration of repeat child molesters. Under the law, molesters who commit a second crime against a child under 13 must receive weekly injections of Depo-Provera. In 1997, Florida and Georgia passed similar legislation requiring repeat offenders to be chemically castrated, and Texas approved voluntary castration for repeat molesters. Montana and Louisiana also have chemical castration laws.

Source: Cameron Cowan, "Is Chemical Castration a Viable Option for Child Sex Offenders?" at www.associatedcontent.com/article/308225/is _chemical_castration_a_viable_option.html?cat=17 (accessed November 19, 2008).

a tendency, to behave in a certain way. Whether a person actually behaves in that way and whether that behavior is defined as a crime depend primarily on environmental or social conditions.

PSYCHOLOGICAL THEORIES

This section examines psychological theories of crime causation, namely, the relationship between intelligence and criminality and delinquency and discusses psychoanalytic and humanistic psychological theories. Learning or behavioral theories will be discussed along with sociological theories.

FYI IQ & Crime

One of the earliest promoters in the United States of the relationship between low IQ and crime was H. H. Goddard. In 1914, he published *Feeblemindedness: Its Causes and Consequences.* In the book, Goddard argues that criminals are feebleminded, an old-fashioned term that means below-normal intelligence.

Source: Henry H. Goddard, *Feeblemindedness: Its Causes and Consequences* (New York: Macmillan, 1914).

Intelligence and Crime The idea that crime is the product primarily of people of low intelligence was popular in the United States from about 1914 until around 1930. It received some attention again during the mid-1970s and in the mid-1990s. The belief requires only a slight shift in thinking from the idea that criminals are biologically inferior to the idea that they are mentally inferior.

In 1931, Edwin Sutherland reviewed approximately 350 studies on the relationship between intelligence and delinquency and criminality.[15] The studies reported the results of intelligence tests of about 175,000 criminals and delinquents. Sutherland concluded from the review that although intelligence may play a role in individual cases, given the selection that takes place in arrest, conviction, and imprisonment, the distribution of the intelligence scores of criminals and delinquents is very similar to the distribution of the intelligence scores of the general population.

For the next 40 years or so, the issue of the relationship between intelligence and crime and delinquency appeared resolved. However, in the mid-1970s, two studies were published that resurrected the debate.[16] Those studies found that IQ was an important predictor of both official and self-reported juvenile delinquency, as important as social class or race. Both studies acknowledged the findings of Sutherland's earlier review. Both also noted that a decreasing number of delinquents had been reported as being of below-normal intelligence over the years. However, in both studies, it was maintained that the difference in intelligence between delinquents and nondelinquents had never disappeared and had stabilized at about eight IQ points. The studies failed to note, however, that the eight-point IQ difference found between delinquents and nondelinquents was generally within the normal range. The authors of the studies surmised that IQ influenced delinquency through its effect on school performance.

At this time, we cannot conclude with any degree of confidence that delinquents, as a group, are less intelligent than nondelinquents. We do know that most adult criminals are not of below-normal intelligence. Obviously, low-level intelligence cannot account for the dramatic increase in the crime rate over the last couple of decades—except recently—unless one is prepared to conclude that the population of offenders is getting less intelligent. Low-level intelligence certainly cannot account for complex white-collar and political crimes.

Nevertheless, to the degree, if any, that crime is caused by low-level intelligence, the policy implications are the same as for theories of biological inferiority: isolate, sterilize, or execute. Intelligence is believed to have a large genetic component.

Psychoanalytic Theories Psychoanalytic theories of crime causation are associated with the work of Sigmund Freud and his followers.[17] Freud did not theorize much about criminal behavior itself, but a theory of crime causation can be deduced from his more general

In "Criminality from a Sense of Guilt" (1915), Sigmund Freud, founder of psychoanalysis, suggested that some people commit crimes in order to be caught and punished—not for the crime for which they had been caught, but for something that they had done in the past about which they felt guilty and for which they were not caught or punished. *Do you think Freud was right? Why or why not?*

theory of human behavior and its disorders. Had he contemplated the issue, Freud probably would have argued that crime, like other disorders, was a symptom of more deep-seated problems and that if the deep-seated problems could be resolved, the symptom of crime would go away.

Freud believed that some people who had unresolved deep-seated problems were psychopaths (sociologists call them *sociopaths*). **Psychopaths, sociopaths, or antisocial personalities** are characterized by no sense of guilt, no subjective conscience, and no sense of right and wrong. They have difficulty in forming relationships with other people; they cannot empathize with other people. Table 3.2 provides an extended list of the characteristics of psychopaths.

The principal policy implication of considering crime symptomatic of deep-seated problems is to provide psychotherapy or psychoanalysis. *Psychoanalysis* is a procedure first developed by Freud that, among other things, attempts to make patients conscious or aware of unconscious and deep-seated problems in order to resolve the symptoms associated with them. Methods used include a variety of projective tests (such as the interpretation of Rorschach inkblots), dream interpretation, and free association. Another policy implication that derives logically from Freudian theory is to provide people with legal outlets to sublimate or redirect their sexual and aggressive drives. (Freud believed that all human beings are born with those two drives and that those drives are the primary sources of human motivation.)

Psychoanalysis, and the psychoanalytic theory on which it is based, are components of a medical model of crime causation that has, to varying degrees, informed criminal justice policy in the United States for a century. The general conception of this medical model is that criminals are biologically or, especially, psychologically "sick" and in need of treatment.

Despite the enduring popularity of this theory, a number of problems have been identified with it. First, the bulk of the research on the issue suggests that most criminals are not psychologically disturbed or, at least, are no more disturbed than the rest of the population.[18]

Second, if a person who commits a crime has a psychological disturbance, that does not mean that the psychological disturbance caused the crime. Many people with psychological disturbances do not commit crimes, and many people without psychological disturbances do commit crimes.

Third, psychoanalytic theory generally ignores the environmental circumstances in which the problematic behavior occurs. The problem is considered a personal problem and not a social one.

Fourth, there are problems with psychoanalysis and other forms of psychotherapy. Psychotherapy rests on faith. Much of its theoretical structure is scientifically untestable. The emphasis of psychotherapy as an approach to rehabilitation is on the individual offender and not on the offender in interaction with the environment in which the criminal behavior occurs. The behaviors that are treated in psychotherapy are not criminal; they are the deep-seated problems. It is assumed that criminal behavior is symptomatic of those problems. That assumption may not be true. Many people who do not engage in crime have deep-seated problems, and many people who do not have those problems do engage in crime.

Humanistic Psychological Theory Humanistic psychological theory, as described here, refers primarily to the

psychopaths, sociopaths, or **antisocial personalities** Persons characterized by no sense of guilt, no subjective conscience, and no sense of right and wrong. They have difficulty in forming relationships with other people; they cannot empathize with other people.

 CJ Online

Serial Killers

Serial killers are characterized as psychopaths or sociopaths. Go to www.crimelibrary.com/serialkillers.htm to read more about serial killers who are under investigation and some of the most well-known cases involving serial killers in the United States. *Were you able to note any of the characteristics of a psychopath listed in Table 3.2 in these articles?*

Table 3.2 Characteristics of the Psychopath

1. Superficial charm and good "intelligence."
2. Absence of delusions and other signs of irrational "thinking."
3. Absence of "nervousness" or psychoneurotic manifestations.
4. Unreliability.
5. Untruthfulness and insincerity.
6. Lack of remorse or shame.
7. Inadequately motivated antisocial behavior.
8. Poor judgment and failure to learn by experience.
9. Pathologic egocentricity and incapacity for love.
10. General poverty in major affective reactions.
11. Specific loss of insight.
12. Unresponsiveness in general interpersonal relations.
13. Fantastic and uninviting behavior, with drink and sometimes without.
14. Suicide rarely carried out.
15. Sex life impersonal, trivial, and poorly integrated.
16. Failure to follow any life plan.

Source: From Hervey Cleckley's "The Mask of Sanity," *Institutions, Etc.: A Journal of Progressive Human Services* 8, no. 9 (September 1985), p. 21. Reprinted by permission of Dolan, Pollak, and Schram.

Jeffery Dahmer was accused by the prosecutor in his case of being "an evil psychopath who lured his victims and murdered them in cold blood." He was convicted of 15 counts of murder and sentenced to serve 15 consecutive life sentences or a total of 957 years in prison. Dahmer was killed in prison in 1994. *Was Dahmer a psychopath? Why or why not?*

work of Abraham Maslow and Seymour Halleck. The theories of Maslow and Halleck are fundamentally psychoanalytic, but they are called humanistic because they assume that human beings are basically good even though they are sometimes influenced by society to act badly. By contrast, Freudian theory assumes that human beings are inherently bad, motivated by sexual and aggressive drives.

Maslow did not apply his theory to crime itself, so we must infer from Maslow's work what we think he would have said about the causes of crime had he addressed the subject. Abraham Maslow believed that human beings are motivated by a hierarchy of basic needs. (See Figure 3.2.)

1. Physiological (food, water, and procreational sex)
2. Safety (security; stability; freedom from fear, anxiety, chaos, etc.)
3. Belongingness and love (friendship, love, affection, acceptance)
4. Esteem (self-esteem and the esteem of others)
5. Self-actualization (being true to one's nature, becoming everything that one is capable of becoming)[19]

According to Maslow, during a given period, a person's life is dominated by a particular need. It remains dominated by that need until the need has been relatively satisfied, at which time a new need emerges to dominate that person's life. From this view, crime may be understood as a means by which individuals satisfy their basic human needs. They choose crime, because they cannot satisfy their needs legally or, for whatever reason, choose not to satisfy their needs legally. An obvious policy implication of the theory is to help people satisfy their basic human needs in legitimate ways. That may require governments to ensure adequate food, shelter, and medical care for those in need or to provide educational or vocational opportunities for those who are unable to obtain them. Those strategies are implied by several sociological theories as well. On a basic, interpersonal level, Maslow's theory might imply the need to make sympathetic listeners available to people who would benefit from sharing their problems.

Seymour L. Halleck views crime as one of several adaptations to the help-lessness caused by oppression.[20] For Halleck, there are two general types of

Figure 3.2

Maslow's Hierarchy of Needs

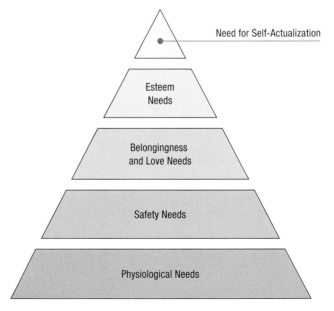

Need for Self-Actualization

Esteem Needs

Belongingness and Love Needs

Safety Needs

Physiological Needs

Source: From Abraham Maslow, *Toward a Psychology of Being,* Van Nostrand, 1968. This material is used by permission of John Wiley & Sons, Inc.

oppression, *objective* and *subjective.* Each has two subtypes. The subtypes of objective oppression are (a) social oppression (for example, oppression resulting from racial discrimination) and (b) the oppression that occurs in two-person interactions (for example, a parent's unfair restriction of the activities of a child). The subtypes of subjective oppression are (a) oppression from within (guilt) and (b) projected or misunderstood oppression (a person's feeling of being oppressed when, in fact, he or she is not).

For Halleck, the emotional experience of either type of oppression is helplessness, to which the person sometimes adapts by resorting to criminal behavior. Halleck suggests that criminal adaptation is more likely when alternative adaptations, such as conformity, activism, or mental illness, are not possible or are blocked by other people. He also maintains that criminal behavior is sometimes chosen as an adaptation over other possible alternatives because it offers gratifications or psychological advantages that could not be achieved otherwise. Halleck's psychological advantages of crime are listed in Table 3.3.

There are at least three crime policy implications of Halleck's theory. First, sources of social oppression should be eliminated wherever possible. Affirmative action programs, which attempt to rectify historic patterns of discrimination in such areas as employment, are an example of such efforts. Second, alternative, legal ways of coping with oppression must be provided. An example is the opportunity to file claims with the Equal Employment Opportunity Commission (EEOC) in individual cases of employment discrimination. Third, psychotherapy should be provided for subjective oppressions. Psychotherapy could make the individual aware of oppressive sources of guilt or sources of misunderstood oppression so that the individual could better cope with them.

Table 3.3 Halleck's 14 Psychological Advantages of Crime

1. The adaptational advantages of crime in changing one's environment are more desirable than illness or conformity.

2. Crime involves activity, and when man is engaged in motoric behavior, he feels less helpless.

3. However petty a criminal act may be, it carries with it a promise of change in a favorable direction.

4. During the planning and execution of a criminal act, the offender is a free man. (He is immune from the oppressive dictates of others.)

5. Crime offers the possibility of excitement.

6. Crime calls for the individual to maximize his faculties and talents which might otherwise lie dormant.

7. Crime can relieve feelings of inner oppression and stress.

8. Crime increases external stresses, which allows the individual to concentrate upon these threats to his equilibrium and temporarily allows him to abandon his chronic intrapsychic problems.

9. Once a person has convinced himself that the major pressures in his life come from without, there is less tendency to blame himself for this failure.

10. Adopting the criminal role provides an excellent rationalization for inadequacy.

11. Crime has a more esteemed social status than mental illness.

12. America has an ambivalent attitude toward crime. Although crime is regularly condemned, it is also glamorized.

13. Deviant behavior sometimes helps the criminal to form close and relatively nonoppressive relations with other criminals.

14. Crime can provide pleasure or gratify needs.

Source: Seymour L. Halleck, *Psychiatry and the Dilemmas of Crime* (New York: Harper and Row, 1967), pp. 76–80.

Émile Durkheim wrote in his volume, *Moral Education*, that, "The more detached from any collectivity man is, the more vulnerable to self-destruction he becomes." *Do you agree? Why? Why not?*

anomie For Durkheim, the dissociation of the individual from the collective conscience.

collective conscience The general sense of morality of the times.

A major problem with the theories of Maslow and Halleck is that they do not go far enough. Neither Maslow nor Halleck asks the basic questions: Why can't people satisfy their basic needs legally, or why do they choose not to? Why don't societies ensure that basic needs can be satisfied legally so that the choice to satisfy them illegally makes no sense? Similarly, why does society so oppress many people, and why aren't more effective measures taken to greatly reduce that oppression?

SOCIOLOGICAL THEORIES

Sociologists emphasize that human beings live in social groups and that those groups and the social structure they create (for example, political and economic systems) influence behavior. Most sociological theories of crime causation assume that a criminal's behavior is determined by his or her social environment, which includes families, friends, neighborhoods, and so on. Most sociological theories of crime explicitly reject the notion of the born criminal.

The Contributions of Durkheim Many of the sociological theories of crime (actually delinquency) causation have their roots in the work of the French sociologist Émile Durkheim. Durkheim rejected the idea that the world is simply the product of individual actions. His basic premise is that society is more than a simple aggregate of individuals; it is a reality *sui generis* (unique).[21] Rejecting the idea that social phenomena, such as crime, can be explained solely by the biology or psychology of individuals, Durkheim argued that society is not the direct reflection of the characteristics of its individual members, because individuals cannot always choose. For Durkheim, social laws and institutions are "social facts" that dominate individuals, and all that people can do is submit to them. The coercion may be formal (for example, by means of law) or informal (for instance, by means of peer pressure). Durkheim maintained that with the aid of positive science, all that people can expect is to discover the direction or course of social laws so that they can adapt to them with the least amount of pain.

For Durkheim, crime, too, is a social fact. It is a normal aspect of society, because it is found in all societies. Nevertheless, different types of societies should have greater or lesser degrees of it. The cause of crime for Durkheim is **anomie,** that is, the dissociation of the individual from the **collective conscience,** or the general sense of morality of the times. He also believed that crime is functional for society by marking the boundaries of morality. In other words, people would not know what acceptable behavior is if crime did not exist. Crime is also functional because it provides a means of achieving necessary social change through, for example, civil disobedience and, under certain circumstances, directly contributes to social change, as in the repeal of Prohibition. Durkheim advocated containing crime within reasonable boundaries. He warned, however, that too much crime could destroy society.

The Theory of the Chicago School In the 1920s, members of the Department of Sociology at the University of Chicago tried to identify environmental factors associated with crime. Specifically, they attempted to uncover the relationship between a neighborhood's crime rate and the characteristics of the neighborhood. It was the first large-scale study of crime in the United States and was to serve as the basis for many future investigations into the causes of crime and delinquency.

The research of the **Chicago School** was based on a model taken from ecology, and as a result, that school is sometimes called the Chicago School of Human Ecology.[22] Ecology is a branch of biology in which the interrelationship of plants and animals is studied in their natural environment. Robert Park was the first of the Chicago theorists to propose this organic or biological analogy—that is, the similarity between the organization of plant and animal life in nature and the organization of human beings in societies.

Park and his colleagues described the growth of American cities like Chicago in ecological terms, saying growth occurs through a process of invasion, dominance, and succession.[23] That is, a cultural or ethnic group *invades* a territory occupied by another group and *dominates* that new territory until it is displaced, or *succeeded,* by another group, and the cycle repeats itself.

This model of human ecology was used by other Chicago theorists, most notably Clifford R. Shaw and Henry D. McKay in their studies of juvenile delinquency in Chicago.[24] From the life histories of delinquents, Shaw and McKay confirmed that most of the delinquents were not much different from nondelinquents in their personality traits, physical condition, and intelligence.[25] However, Shaw and McKay did find that the areas of high delinquency were "socially disorganized." For the Chicago theorists, **social disorganization** is the condition in which the usual controls over delinquents are largely absent, delinquent behavior is often approved of by parents and neighbors, there are many opportunities for delinquent behavior, and there is little encouragement, training, or opportunity for legitimate employment.

In 1932, Shaw and his colleagues established the Chicago Area Project (CAP), which was designed to prevent delinquency through the organization and empowerment of neighborhood residents. Neighborhood centers, staffed and controlled by local residents, were established in six areas of Chicago. The centers had two primary functions. One was to coordinate community resources, such as schools, churches, labor unions, and industries, to solve community problems. The other function was to sponsor activity programs, such as scouting, summer camps, and sports leagues, to develop a positive interest by individuals in their own welfare and to unite citizens to solve their own problems. CAP operated continuously for 25 years, until Shaw's death in 1957. Evaluations of the project suggest that it had a negligible effect on delinquency.

Chicago School A group of sociologists at the University of Chicago who assumed in their research that delinquent behavior was a product of social disorganization.

social disorganization The condition in which the usual controls over delinquents are largely absent, delinquent behavior is often approved of by parents and neighbors, there are many opportunities for delinquent behavior, and there is little encouragement, training, or opportunity for legitimate employment.

From his analysis of the life histories of individual delinquents, Chicago sociologist Clifford Shaw discovered that many delinquent activities began as play activities at an early age. *What kind of play activities do you think are delinquent activities?*

One of the problems with the theory of the Chicago School is the presumption that social disorganization is a cause of delinquency. Both social disorganization and delinquency may be the product of other, more basic factors. For example, one factor that contributes to the decline of city neighborhoods is the decades-old practice of *redlining,* in which banks refuse to lend money in an area because of the race or ethnicity of the inhabitants. Though illegal today, the practice continues. What usually happens in redlined areas is that neighborhood property values decline dramatically. Then land speculators and developers, typically in conjunction with political leaders, buy the land for urban renewal or gentrification and make fortunes in the process. In other words, political and economic elites may cause both social disorganization and delinquency—perhaps not intentionally, but by the conscious decisions they make about how a city will grow—making social disorganization appear to be the basic cause of delinquency.

Anomie or Strain Theory In an article published in 1938, Robert K. Merton observed that a major contradiction existed in the United States between cultural goals and the social structure.[26] He called the contradiction **anomie,** a concept first introduced by Durkheim. Specifically, Merton argued that in the United States the cultural goal of achieving wealth is deemed possible for all citizens, even though the social structure limits the legitimate "institutionalized means" available for obtaining the goal. For Merton, legitimate institutionalized means are the Protestant work ethic (hard work, education, and deferred gratification); illegitimate means are force and fraud. Because the social structure effectively limits the availability of legitimate institutionalized means, a *strain* is placed on people (hence the other name of the theory). Merton believed that strain could affect people in all social classes, but he acknowledged that it would most likely affect members of the lower class.

Merton proposed that individuals adapt to the problem of anomie or strain in one of several different ways: (1) conformity, (2) innovation, (3) ritualism, (4) retreatism, and (5) rebellion. Table 3.4 displays these different adaptations. According to Merton, most people adapt by conforming; they "play the game." Conformers pursue the cultural goal of wealth only through legitimate institutional means. Innovation is the adaptation at the root of most crime. After rejecting legitimate institutional means, innovators pursue the cultural goal of wealth through illegitimate means. Ritualism is the adaptation of the individual who "takes no chances," usually a member of the lower middle class. Ritualists do not actively pursue the cultural goal of wealth (they are willing to settle for less) but follow the legitimate institutional means anyway. Retreatists include alcoholics, drug addicts, psychotics, and other outcasts of society. Retreatists "drop out"; they do not pursue the cultural goal of wealth, so they do not employ legitimate institutional means. Last is the adaptation of

anomie For Merton, the contradiction between the cultural goal of achieving wealth and the social structure's inability to provide legitimate institutional means for achieving the goal. For Cohen, it is caused by the inability of juveniles to achieve status among peers by socially acceptable means.

Table 3.4 Merton's Typology of Modes of Individual Adaptation

Modes of Adaptation	Culture Goals	Institutional Means
I. Conformity	+	+
II. Innovation	+	−
III. Ritualism	−	+
IV. Retreatism	−	−
V. Rebellion	±	±

Note: + signifies "acceptance," − signifies "rejection," and ± signifies "rejection of prevailing values and substitution of new values."

Source: Reprinted with permission of The Free Press, a Division of Simon & Schuster Adult Publishing Group from *Social Theory and Social Structure* by Robert K. Merton. Copyright © 1968, 1967 by Robert K. Merton. All rights reserved.

According to Albert K. Cohen's version of anomie theory, juveniles who are unable to achieve status among their peers by socially acceptable means sometimes turn to gangs for social recognition. *What are some other reasons why juveniles join gangs?*

rebellion. Rebels reject both the cultural goal of wealth and the legitimate institutional means of achieving it. They substitute both different goals and different means. Rebellion can also be a source of crime.

In summary, Merton believed that a source of some, but not all, crime and delinquency was anomie or strain, a disjunction or contradiction between the cultural goal of achieving wealth and the social structure's ability to provide legitimate institutional means of achieving the goal.

Beginning in the mid-1950s, concern developed over the problem of juvenile gangs. Albert K. Cohen adapted Merton's anomie or strain theory to his attempt to explain gang delinquency.[27] In attempting to explain such behavior, Cohen surmised that it was to gain status among peers. Thus, Cohen substituted the goal of status among peers for Merton's goal of achieving wealth.

For Cohen, anomie or strain is experienced by juveniles who are unable to achieve status among peers by socially acceptable means, such as family name and position in the community or academic or athletic achievement. In response to the strain, either they can conform to middle-class values (generated primarily through the public school) and resign themselves to their inferior status among their peers, or they can rebel and establish their own value structures by turning middle-class values on their head. Juveniles who rebel in this way tend to find one another and to form groups or gangs to validate and reinforce their new values. Like Merton, Cohen believed that anomie can affect juveniles of any social class but that it disproportionately affects juveniles from the lower class.

Richard Cloward and Lloyd Ohlin extended Merton's and Cohen's formulations of anomie theory by suggesting that not all gang delinquents adapt to anomie in the same way. Cloward and Ohlin argue that the type of adaptation made by juvenile gang members depends on the *illegitimate opportunity structure* available to them.[28] They identified three delinquent subcultures: the criminal, the violent, and the retreatist. According to Cloward and Ohlin, if illegitimate opportunity is available to them, most delinquents will form

FYI Youth Gangs

The 2007 National Youth Gang Survey sponsored by the Office of Juvenile Justice and Delinquency Prevention estimated that 27,000 youth gangs with a total of 788,000 members were active in the United States in 2007. That represented a 64% increase in gangs and a 36% increase in gang members since 2002. A youth gang is defined as "a group of youths or young adults in [the respondent's] jurisdiction that [the respondent] or other responsible persons in [the respondent's] agency or community are willing to identify or classify as a 'gang.' Motorcycle gangs, hate or ideology groups, prison gangs, and exclusively adult gangs were excluded from the survey."

Source: Arlen Egley, Jr. and Christina E. O'Donnell, "Highlights of the 2007 National Youth Gang Survey," U.S. Department of Justice, Office of Juvenile Justice and Delinquency Prevention Fact Sheet (Washington, D.C.: GPO, April 2009).

Juvenile Delinquency
Prevention and Control

When Robert Kennedy was Attorney General of the United States under his brother, President John F. Kennedy, he read Cloward and Ohlin's book *Delinquency and Opportunity: A Theory of Delinquent Gangs* (1960). Kennedy asked Lloyd Ohlin to help shape a new federal policy on juvenile delinquency. That effort, based on anomie theory, produced the Juvenile Delinquency Prevention and Control Act of 1961. The act included a comprehensive action program to provide employment opportunities and work training, in combination with community organization and improved social services, to disadvantaged youths and their families.

Source: George B. Vold and Thomas J. Bernard, *Theoretical Criminology,* 3rd ed. (New York: Oxford, 1986), p. 201.

imitation or **modeling** A means by which a person can learn new responses by observing others without performing any overt act or receiving direct reinforcement or reward.

differential association Sutherland's theory that persons who become criminal do so because of contacts with criminal patterns and isolation from anticriminal patterns.

criminal gangs to make money. However, if neither illegitimate nor legitimate opportunities to make money are available, delinquents often become frustrated and dissatisfied and form *violent* gangs to vent their anger. Finally, there are delinquents who, for whatever reason, are unable to adapt by joining either criminal or violent gangs. They *retreat* from society, as in Merton's retreatist adaptation, and become alcoholics and drug addicts.

The policy implications of anomie or strain theory are straightforward: reduce aspirations or increase legitimate opportunities, or do both. Increasing legitimate opportunities, already a cornerstone of the black civil rights movement, struck a responsive chord as the 1960s began. Examples of this strategy are affirmative action employment programs, expansion of vocational education programs, and government grants that enable low-income students to attend college. Reducing aspirations (that is, desires to be wealthy) received little attention, however, because to attempt it would be to reject the "American dream," a principal source of motivation in a capitalist society.

Among the problems with the anomie theories of Merton, Cohen, and Cloward and Ohlin is their reliance on official statistics (police and court records) as measures of crime. Because these theorists relied on official statistics, their theories focus on lower-class crime and delinquency and ignore white-collar and government crimes.

Learning Theories Gabriel Tarde was one of the first theorists to believe that crime was something learned by normal people as they adapted to other people and the conditions of their environment. His theory was a product of his experience as a French lawyer and magistrate and was described in his book *Penal Philosophy,* published in 1890. Reflecting the state of knowledge about the learning process in his day, Tarde viewed all social phenomena as the product of imitation. Through **imitation,** or **modeling,** a person can learn new responses, such as criminal behavior, by observing others, without performing any overt act or receiving direct reinforcement or reward.[29]

The first twentieth-century criminologist to forcefully argue that criminal behavior was learned was Edwin H. Sutherland. His theory of **differential association,** developed between 1934 and 1947, was that persons who become criminal do so because of contacts with criminal patterns and isolation from noncriminal patterns. Together with its more recent modifications, his theory remains one of the most influential theories of crime causation.[30] The nine propositions of Sutherland's theory are presented in Table 3.5.

Borrowing a premise from the theory of the Chicago School, Sutherland maintained that differential associations would not produce criminality if it were not for *differential social organization.* In other words, the degree to which communities promote or inhibit criminal associations varies with the way or the degree to which they are organized (that is, the extent of *culture conflict*).

Since its final formulation in 1947, modifications and additions have been made to Sutherland's theory as new developments in learning theory have emerged. For example, Daniel Glaser modified Sutherland's theory by introducing *role theory* and by arguing that criminal behavior could be learned by identifying with criminal roles and not just by associating with criminals.[31] Thus, a person could imitate the behavior of a drug dealer without actually having met one. Glaser obviously believed that the media had a greater influence on the learning of criminal behavior than Sutherland believed they had.

Robert L. Burgess and Ronald L. Akers, as well as C. Ray Jeffery, adapted the principles of *operant conditioning* and *behavior modification,* developed by the psychologist B. F. Skinner, and the principles of *modeling,* as developed by Albert Bandura, to the explanation of criminal behavior. Burgess, Akers, and Jeffery integrated psychological concepts with sociological ones. Although

Table 3.5 Sutherland's Propositions of Differential Association

1. Criminal behavior is learned.

2. Criminal behavior is learned in interaction with other persons in a process of communication.

3. The principal part of the learning of criminal behavior occurs within intimate personal groups.

4. When criminal behavior is learned, the learning includes (a) techniques of committing the crime, which are sometimes very complicated, sometimes very simple; and (b) the specific direction of motives, drives, rationalizations, and attitudes.

5. The specific direction of motives and drives is learned from definitions of the legal codes as favorable and unfavorable.

6. A person becomes delinquent because of an excess of definitions favorable to violation of law over definitions unfavorable to violation of law. This is the principle of differential association.

7. Differential associations may vary in frequency, duration, priority, and intensity.

8. The process of learning criminal behavior by association with criminal and anticriminal patterns involves all of the mechanisms that are involved in any other learning.

9. While criminal behavior is an expression of general needs and values, it is not explained by those general needs and values, since noncriminal behavior is an expression of the same needs and values.

Source: Edwin H. Sutherland and Donald R. Cressey, *Criminology,* 9th ed. (Philadelphia: J. B. Lippincott, 1974), pp. 75–77. Reprinted by permission.

they referred to their theories by different names, we will use the more general term *learning theory.*

Learning theory explains criminal behavior and its prevention with the concepts of *positive reinforcement, negative reinforcement, extinction, punishment,* and *modeling,* or *imitation.* In this view, crime is committed because it is positively reinforced, negatively reinforced, or imitated. We described the imitation, or modeling, of criminal behavior in our earlier discussion of Tarde. Here we will focus on the other concepts.[32]

Positive reinforcement is the presentation of a stimulus that increases or maintains a response. The stimulus, or *reward,* can be either material, like money, or psychological, like pleasure. People steal (a response) because of the rewards—for example, the objects or money—that they receive. They use drugs (at least at first) because of the rewards, the pleasure, that the drugs give them.

Negative reinforcement is the removal or reduction of a stimulus whose removal or reduction increases or maintains a response. The stimulus in negative reinforcement is referred to as an *aversive stimulus.* Aversive stimuli, for most people, include pain and fear. Stealing may be negatively reinforced by removing or reducing the aversive stimuli of the fear and pain of poverty. For drug addicts, the use of addictive drugs is negatively reinforced because the drugs remove or reduce the aversive stimulus of the pain of drug withdrawal. In short, both positive and negative reinforcement explain why a behavior, such as crime, is maintained or increases. Both types of reinforcement can simultaneously affect the same behavior. In other words, people may commit crime, in this view, both because the crime is rewarded and because it removes an aversive stimulus.

According to learning theory, criminal behavior is reduced, but not necessarily eliminated, through *extinction* or *punishment.* **Extinction** is a process in which behavior that previously was positively reinforced is no longer reinforced. In other words, the rewards have been removed. Thus, if burglars were to continually come up empty-handed in their quests—not to receive rewards for their efforts—they would no longer continue to commit burglary. **Punishment** is the

learning theory A theory that explains criminal behavior and its prevention with the concepts of positive reinforcement, negative reinforcement, extinction, punishment, and modeling, or imitation.

positive reinforcement The presentation of a stimulus that increases or maintains a response.

negative reinforcement The removal or reduction of a stimulus whose removal or reduction increases or maintains a response.

extinction A process in which behavior that previously was positively reinforced is no longer reinforced.

punishment The presentation of an aversive stimulus to reduce a response.

In 1994, then 18-year-old American student Michael Fay pled guilty to vandalism charges in Singapore and was sentenced to 3 months in jail, a $2,200 fine, and 6 strokes of the cane. *Should the flogging of convicted offenders be allowed in the United States? Why or why not?*

presentation of an aversive stimulus to reduce a response. It is the principal method used in the United States and in other countries, to prevent crime or, at least, reduce it. For example, one of the reasons offenders are imprisoned is to punish them for their crimes.

Among the policy implications of learning theory is to punish criminal behavior effectively, that is, according to learning theory principles. For a variety of reasons, punishment is not used effectively in criminal justice in the United States. For example, to employ punishment effectively, one must prevent escape. Escape is a natural reaction to the presentation of an aversive stimulus like imprisonment. In the United States, the chances of an offender's escaping punishment are great. Probation probably does not function as an aversive stimulus, and most offenders, especially first-time offenders, are not incarcerated.

To be effective, punishment must be applied consistently and immediately. As for immediacy, the process of criminal justice in the United States generally precludes punishment immediately after a criminal act is committed. The process is a slow and methodical one. Consistent application of punishment is rare because most criminal offenders are not caught.

In addition, extended periods of punishment should be avoided, or the effectiveness of the punishment will be reduced. The United States currently imprisons more of its offenders for longer periods than any other country in the world, except perhaps Russia, though in many cases inmates actually serve only a fraction of their original sentences.

A related issue is that punishment is far less effective when the intensity with which the aversive stimulus is presented is increased gradually than when the stimulus is introduced at full intensity. Prolonged imprisonment is a gradual process of punishment that lacks the full intensity and immediacy of corporal punishment, for example. Figure 3.3 shows how the corporal punishment of caning is done in Singapore.

To be effective, punishment must also be combined with extinction. That is, the rewards that maintain the behavior must be removed. In the United States, after imprisonment, offenders are generally returned to the environments in which their crimes originally were committed and rewarded.

Finally, for punishment to be effective, it must be combined with the positive reinforcement of alternative, pro-social behaviors.

We must emphasize that for learning theorists, positive reinforcement is a much more effective and preferred method of manipulating behavior than is punishment, because positive reinforcement does not suffer the disadvantages associated with punishment. That point is often overlooked by criminal justice decision makers. Among the disadvantages of punishment are the effort to escape punishment by means other than law-abiding behavior; the development of negative self-concepts by offenders, who come to view themselves (instead of their criminal behaviors) as bad, making rehabilitation difficult; and the causing of aggression.

Among the problems with a learning theory of crime causation is that it ignores the criminalization process. It fails to consider why the normal learned behaviors of some groups are criminalized while the normal learned behaviors

Figure 3.3

How Caning Is Done in Singapore

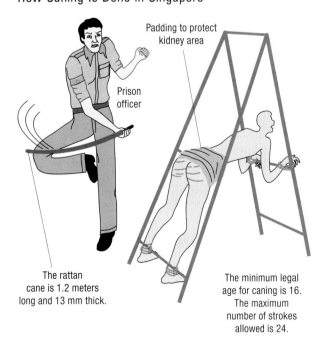

Padding to protect kidney area

Prison officer

The rattan cane is 1.2 meters long and 13 mm thick.

The minimum legal age for caning is 16. The maximum number of strokes allowed is 24.

of other groups are not. For example, why is marijuana consumption illegal, while cigarette or alcohol consumption is not? Learning theory ignores the effect that political and economic power have on the definition of criminal behavior.

Social Control Theories The key question for social control theorists is not why people commit crime and delinquency, but rather why do they not. Why do people conform? From the perspective of **social control theory,** people are expected to commit crime and delinquency unless they are prevented from doing so. They will commit crime, that is, unless they are properly socialized.

Like many of the other sociological theories of crime causation, social control theories have their origins in the work of Durkheim. It was not until the 1950s, however, that social control theories began to emerge to challenge other, more dominant theories, such as strain and differential association. Among the early social control theorists were Albert J. Reiss, Jackson Toby, F. Ivan Nye, and Walter C. Reckless. Despite the important contributions of those early theorists, modern social control theory in its most detailed elaboration is attributed to the work of Travis Hirschi. Hirschi's 1969 book, *Causes of Delinquency,* has had a great influence on current criminological thinking.

As did proponents of earlier social control theories, Hirschi argued that delinquency (his was not a theory of adult criminality) should be expected if a juvenile is not properly socialized. For Hirschi, proper socialization involves the establishment of a strong moral bond between the juvenile and society. This *bond to society* consists of (1) *attachment* to others, (2) *commitment* to conventional lines of action, (3) *involvement* in conventional activities, and (4) *belief* in the moral order and law. Thus, delinquent behavior is likely to occur if there is (1) inadequate attachment, particularly to parents and school, (2) inadequate commitment, particularly to educational and occupational success, (3) inadequate involvement in such conventional activities as scouting and sports, and (4) inadequate belief, particularly in the legitimacy and morality of the law. For Hirschi, the units of social control most important in the establishment of the bond are the family, the school, and the law.

In a more recent book, Michael Gottfredson and Travis Hirschi argue that the principal cause of many deviant behaviors, including crime and delinquency, is ineffective child-rearing, which produces people with low self-control.[33] Low self-control impairs a person's ability to accurately calculate the consequences of his or her actions and is characterized by impulsivity, insensitivity, physical risk taking, shortsightedness, and lack of verbal skills. This theory posits that everyone has a predisposition toward criminality; therefore, low self-control makes it difficult to resist.

One of the appealing aspects of Hirschi's social control theory—and Gottfredson and Hirschi's theory, too—is their seemingly commonsense policy implications. To prevent delinquency, juveniles must be properly socialized; they must develop a strong moral bond to society. As part of that strategy, children must be reared properly so that they develop a high level of self-control.

Although social control theory is currently very influential in the thinking of many criminologists, it has not escaped extensive criticism. Perhaps the major problem, at least for some criminologists, is the theory's assumption that delinquency will occur if not prevented. Some criminologists find it troublesome that the theory rejects altogether the idea of delinquent motivation. Another problem with social control theory is that it does not explain how juveniles are socialized. For example, how are attachments to others produced and changed? Finally, Hirschi's argument, as stated, does not allow for delinquency by juveniles who are properly socialized, nor does it allow for conformity by juveniles who are not properly socialized.

social control theory A view in which people are expected to commit crime and delinquency unless they are prevented from doing so.

1. What are the five key assumptions of the positivist school of thought?

2. How much crime do you think is related to biological factors? Which factors are most important?

3. Explain psychoanalytic and humanistic psychological theory. What are some of the problems associated with those theories?

4. Which one of the sociological theories do you think explains the most crime? Defend your choice.

Critical Approaches to Explaining Crime

Critical theories are, in part, a product of a different conception of American society that began to emerge toward the end of the 1950s. Concepts such as racism, sexism, capitalism, imperialism, monopoly, exploitation, and oppression were beginning to be employed with greater frequency to describe the social landscape. In the 1960s, the period of naive acceptance of the status quo and the belief in the purely benevolent actions of government and corporations ended for many social scientists, and critical theory emerged.

Not surprisingly, the basic assumptions of critical theories differ both from those of classical and neoclassical theories and from those of positivist theories. First, unlike classical and neoclassical theories, which assume that human beings have free will, and positivist theories, which assume that human beings are determined, critical theories assume that human beings are both determined *and* determining. In other words, critical theories assume that human beings are the creators of the institutions and structures that ultimately dominate and constrain them. Second, in contrast to both classical and neoclassical theories and positivist theories, critical theories assume that conflict is the norm, that society is characterized primarily by conflict over moral values. Finally, unlike positivist theorists, many critical theorists assume that everything they do is value-laden by virtue of their being human; that is, they believe it is impossible to be objective or value-neutral in anything a person does.

LABELING THEORY

labeling theory A theory that emphasizes the criminalization process as the cause of some crime.

criminalization process The way people and actions are defined as criminal.

The focus of **labeling theory** is the **criminalization process**—the way people and actions are defined as criminal—rather than the positivist concern with the peculiarities of the criminal actor. From this perspective, the distinguishing feature of all "criminals" is that they have been the object of a *negative social reaction.* In other words, they have been designated by the state and its agents as different and "bad."

Note that labeling theorists attempt to explain only what Edwin Lemert called *secondary deviance.*[34] For our purposes, *secondary deviance* is the commission of crime subsequent to the first criminal act and the acceptance of a criminal label. Secondary deviance begins with an initial criminal act, or what Lemert called *primary deviance.* The causes of initial criminal acts are unspecified. Nevertheless, if society reacts negatively to an initial criminal act, especially through official agents of the state, the offender is likely to be *stigmatized,* or negatively labeled. It is possible, even likely, that there will be no reaction at all to an initial criminal act or that the offender will not accept or internalize the negative label. However, if the negative label is successfully applied to the offender, the label may become a *self-fulfilling prophecy,* in which the offender's self-image is defined by the label. Secondary deviance is the prophecy fulfilled.

As is well known, once a person is labeled and stereotyped as a "criminal," he or she probably will be shunned by law-abiding society, have difficulty finding a good job, lose some civil rights (if convicted of a felony), and suffer a variety of other disabilities. The *criminal* (or *delinquent*) label is conferred by all of the agencies of criminal justice—the police, the courts, and the correctional apparatus—as well as by the media, the schools, churches, and other social institutions. The irony is that in its attempt to reduce crime and delinquency, society may inadvertently be increasing it by labeling people and producing secondary deviance.

A policy implication of labeling theory is simply not to label or to employ *radical nonintervention*.[35] This might be accomplished through decriminalization (the elimination of many behaviors from the scope of the criminal law), diversion (removing offenders from involvement in the criminal justice process), greater due-process protections (replacing discretion with the rule of law), and deinstitutionalization (a policy of reducing jail and prison populations and construction).[36]

An alternative to the nonintervention strategy is John Braithwaite's *reintegrative shaming*.[37] In this strategy, disappointment is expressed for the offender's actions, and the offender is shamed and punished. What is more important, however, is that following the expression of disappointment and shame is a concerted effort on the part of the community to forgive the offender and reintegrate him or her back into society. Braithwaite contends that the practice of reintegrative shaming is one of the principal reasons for Japan's relatively low crime rate.

A problem with labeling theory is that it tends to overemphasize the importance of the official labeling process.[38] On the one hand, the impression is given that innocent people are arbitrarily stigmatized by an oppressive society and that as a result, they begin a life of crime. That probably does not happen very much. On the other hand, the impression is given that offenders resist the criminal label and accept it only when they are no longer capable of fighting it. However, in some communities, the criminal label, or some variation of it, is actively sought. Perhaps the most telling problem with labeling theory is the question of whether stigmatizing someone as criminal or delinquent causes more crime and delinquency than it prevents. To date, the answer is unknown.

CONFLICT THEORY

Unlike classical and neoclassical and positivist theories, which assume that society is characterized primarily by consensus, **conflict theory** assumes that society is based primarily on conflict between competing interest groups—for instance, the rich against the poor, management against labor, whites against minorities, men against women, adults against children. In many cases, competing interest groups are not equal in power and resources. Consequently, one group is dominant and the other is subordinate.

One of the earliest theorists in the United States to apply conflict theory to the study of crime was George B. Vold. For Vold and other conflict theorists, such as Austin T. Turk, many behaviors are defined as crimes because it is in the interest of dominant groups to do so.[39]

According to conflict theorists, criminal law and the criminal justice system are used by dominant groups to control subordinate ones. However, the public image is quite different. The public image of the criminal law and the criminal justice system is that they are value-neutral institutions—that is, that neither institution has a vested interest in who "wins" a dispute. The public image is that the only concern of the criminal law and the criminal justice system is resolving disputes between competing interest groups justly and—more importantly—peacefully. According to conflict theorists, this public image legitimizes the authority and practices of dominant groups and allows them to

 Shaming as a Crime Prevention Strategy

Current crime prevention programs based on the theoretical proposition that shame will prevent crime include programs that publicize the names and faces of people arrested for trying to buy or sell sex or require convicted DUI offenders to put bumper stickers on their cars identifying them as such. For the most part, these strategies ignore reintegration.

conflict theory A theory that assumes that society is based primarily on conflict between competing interest groups and that criminal law and the criminal justice system are used to control subordinate groups. Crime is caused by relative powerlessness.

achieve their own interests at the expense of less powerful groups. In this view, crime also serves the interest of dominant groups. It deflects the attention of subordinate group members from the many problems that dominant groups create for them and turns that attention to subordinate group members who are defined as criminal.

All behavior, including criminal behavior, in this view, occurs because people act in ways consistent with their social positions. Whether white-collar crime or ordinary street crime, crime is a response to a person's social situation. The reason members of subordinate groups appear in official criminal statistics more frequently than members of dominant groups is that the dominant groups have more control over the definition of criminality. Thus they are better able to ensure that the responses of subordinate group members to their social situations will be defined and reacted to as criminal. For conflict theorists, the amount of crime in a society is a function of the extent of conflict generated by **power differentials,** or the ability of some groups to dominate other groups in that society. Crime, in short, is caused by **relative powerlessness,** the inability to dominate other groups.

There are two principal policy implications of conflict theory. One is for dominant groups to give up some of their power to subordinate groups, making the weaker more powerful and reducing conflict. Increasing equality in that way might be accomplished by redistributing wealth through a more progressive tax system, for example. Another way to increase equality, at least in the political arena, would be to strictly limit or eliminate altogether the contributions of wealthy people and corporations to political candidates. The other policy implication is for dominant group members to become more effective rulers and subordinate group members, better subjects. To do so, dominant group members would have to do a better job of convincing subordinate group members that the current unfair distribution of power in society is in their mutual interests.

A problem with conflict theory is that it generally fails to specify the sources of power in society. When those sources are identified, they are usually attributed to the personal characteristics of elites; that is, people with power are said to be smarter, better educated, luckier, and better able to defer

power differentials The ability of some groups to dominate other groups in a society.

relative powerlessness In conflict theory, the inability to dominate other groups in society.

For conflict theorists, conflict between competing interest groups can sometimes lead to crime. *What kinds of group conflicts are more likely to lead to crime?*

gratification. Conflict theorists seem to ignore that power in society comes primarily from the ownership of private property.

Another criticism of conflict theory is that it is basically reformist in its policy implications. Conflict theorists generally assume that crime, as well as other social problems, can be corrected by existing social institutions. For example, if only the agencies of criminal justice were more effective, a conflict theorist might argue, crime would be reduced greatly. Historical evidence suggests that this assumption may not be true.

RADICAL THEORY

The social and political turmoil in the United States during the 1960s and 1970s created a renewed interest in Marxist theory. Although Karl Marx wrote very little about crime and criminal justice, **radical theories** of crime causation are generally based on Marx's ideas. Among the first criminologists in the United States to employ Marxist theory to explain crime and justice were Richard Quinney, William J. Chambliss, and Anthony M. Platt.

Radical criminologists argue that *capitalism* is an economic system that requires people to compete against each other in the individualistic pursuit of material wealth. A defining characteristic of a capitalist society is that a very small percentage of people are the big winners in the competitive struggle for material wealth. Table 3.6 shows the distribution of income (a proxy for wealth) in the United States in 2007.

The winners do everything in their considerable power to keep from becoming losers, including taking advantage of other people, preying on them. Their power is considerable, by virtue of their ownership of material wealth. (The really big winners are members of the *ruling class.*) Losers—relatively speaking, members of the *working class* and the *nonworking class*—in an effort to become winners, usually do what the winners do: prey on weaker people. Radical criminologists believe that the more unevenly wealth is distributed in a society, the more likely people are to be able to find persons weaker than themselves.

It is important to understand that for radical criminologists, the destructive effects of capitalism, such as crime, are not caused by income or property inequality or by poverty. Rather, the competition among wealthy people and among poor people and between rich and poor people—the **class struggle**—and the practice of taking advantage of other people cause crime. They also cause

radical theories Theories of crime causation that are generally based on a Marxist theory of class struggle.

FYI Karl Marx

In an article entitled "Population, Crime and Pauperism," which appeared in the *New York Daily News* on September 16, 1859, Karl Marx observed that "there must be something rotten in the very core of a social system which increases its wealth without decreasing its misery; and increases in crimes even more than in numbers."

class struggle For radical criminologists, the competition among wealthy people and among poor people and between rich people and poor people, which causes crime.

Table 3.6 Distribution of 2007 Income in the United States Received by Each Fifth of Families (Households)

Families (Households) by Fifths	Percentage of Total Income	Average Household Income[a]
Lowest fifth	3.4%	$11, 551
Second fifth	8.7	29,442
Third fifth	14.8	49,968
Fourth fifth	23.4	79,111
Highest fifth	49.7	167,971
Top 5%[b]	21.2	287,191

Notes:

[a] Average income of all families (households) in 2007 = $50,233.

[b] The table fails to accurately convey the inequitable distribution of income/wealth in the highest category. In 2008, there were at least 449 billionaires in the United States. The richest individual (not household) was William Gates III (Microsoft), whose net worth was conservatively estimated to be $57 billion. The second and third richest individuals in the United States were Warren Buffett (Berkshire Hathaway) worth about $50 billion, and Lawrence Ellison (Oracle), worth approximately $27 billion.

Sources: U.S. Census Bureau, Historical Income Tables-Household, Table H-1 and H-3 at www.census.gov/hhes/www/income/histinc/inchhtoc.html; and Forbes.com at www.forbes.com/400richest/.

income or property inequality, poverty, and many of the other problems that are characteristic of a capitalist society. Crime in capitalist societies is a rational response to the circumstances in which people find themselves in the competitive class struggle to acquire material wealth. "Senseless" violent crime, which is most often committed by poor people against each other, is frequently a product of the demoralizing and brutalizing conditions under which many people are forced to live.

Radical criminologists argue that noncapitalist societies should have different types of crime and much lower rates of crime, as traditionally defined, "because the less intense class struggle should reduce the forces leading to and the functions of crime."[40]

Radical criminologists also define crime as a violation of human rights. As Tony Platt explains:

> A radical perspective defines crime as a violation of politically defined human rights: the truly egalitarian rights to decent food and shelter, to human dignity and self-determination, rather than the so-called right to compete for an unequal share of wealth and power.[41]

A radical definition of crime includes "imperialism, racism, capitalism, sexism and other systems of exploitation which contribute to human misery and deprive people of their human potentiality."[42] Although many behaviors currently proscribed by criminal law would be included in this radical definition, other behaviors now considered crimes would be excluded, such as prostitution, gambling, and drug use, and some behaviors not now considered crimes would be added, such as racism, sexism, and imperialism.

Consequently, the policy implications of radical theory include demonstrating that the current legal definition of crime supports the ruling class in a capitalist system and redefining crime as a violation of human rights. For nearly all radical criminologists—anarchists are exceptions—the solution to the crime problem is a benevolent socialist society governed by democratically elected representatives of the population. Arguably the biggest difference between the envisioned socialist society and the current capitalist society in

Radical criminologists define crime as a violation of politically defined human rights, such as the right to shelter. *Do you think that Americans should have a right to shelter? Why or why not?*

the United States is that governments in the socialist society would regulate the economy to promote public welfare. Governments in capitalist America regulate the economy to promote the accumulation of material wealth by individuals. Radical criminologists stress that the difference is primarily a matter of priorities. Some accumulation of private material wealth would probably exist in the socialist society, and even capitalist America provides for the public welfare through such socialistic programs as Social Security, Medicare, and Medicaid. Another important difference between the two societies is that in the socialist society, human diversity in all areas of life would be not only tolerated but also appreciated by government agents (and, one would hope, by the rest of society). In the socialist society, the criminal law would be based on a slightly modified version of the positive sanction of the classical school: that every member of society has a right to do anything that is not prohibited by law without fearing anything but natural consequences. Acts prohibited by law would be those that violate basic human rights or the public welfare, interpreted as liberally as possible. The recognition of "hate crimes" by federal legislation in the United States is an example of an attempt to protect human diversity.

Radical criminologists maintain that creating such a socialist society would first require the development of political awareness among all people disadvantaged by the capitalist system. Such people must be made aware that they are in a class struggle. Once enough people are aware, according to radical criminologists, then only through *praxis* (human action based on theoretical understanding) will the new socialist society be achieved.

One objection to radical theory is that the radical definition of crime as the violation of human rights is too broad and vague. Although radical criminologists concede that it may be difficult to determine what a human right is, they generally assume that most people know when a human right has been violated.

Other criticisms of radical theory are that its adherents are pursuing a political agenda and thus are not objective in their work; that its causal model is wrong, that is, that social arrangements do not cause people to commit crime, as radical theorists argue, but rather that crime is committed by people who are born evil and remain evil; that it has not been tested satisfactorily; that it cannot be tested satisfactorily; and that it is utopian in its policy implications.

OTHER CRITICAL THEORIES

The law-and-order climate of the 1980s and 1990s was not a period in which critical theories of crime causation received much attention from government bureaucrats and criminal justice practitioners. Nevertheless, critical scholars continued to produce and to refine critical analyses of government efforts to understand and to address the crime problem. In this subsection we will briefly describe some of the new directions taken by critical theorists. These descriptions will show the diversity of current critical thought.

British or Left Realism The focus of many critical criminologists has been on crimes committed by the powerful. While pursuing that area of study, however, they have tended either to ignore or to romanticize working-class crime and criminals. By the mid-1980s, a group of social scientists in Great Britain had begun to criticize that tendency and to argue that critical criminologists needed to redirect their attention to the fear and the very real victimization experienced by working-class people.[43] These **left realists** correctly observed that crimes against the working class were being perpetrated not only by the powerful but also by members of their own class. They admonished their critical colleagues to take crime seriously, especially street crime and domestic violence.

FYI Utopians

Early socialists criticized the rise of industry as the cause of great hardship among working people. During the early 1800s, socialists, who were sometimes called *utopians*, tried to foster communities with ideal social and economic conditions. Their name came from Sir Thomas More's *Utopia*, published in England in 1516. More's book describes an ideal society, with justice and equality for all citizens.

left realists A group of social scientists who argue that critical criminologists need to redirect their attention to the fear and the very real victimization experienced by working-class people.

relative deprivation Refers to inequalities (in resources, opportunities, material goods, etc.) that are defined by a person as unfair or unjust.

Recently, one of the leading exponents of left realism, Jock Young, has identified relative deprivation as a potent, though not exclusive cause of crime.[44] **Relative deprivation** refers to inequalities (in resources, opportunities, material goods, etc.) that are defined by a person as unfair or unjust. Left realists have argued that police power must be employed to protect people living in working-class communities. Certain versions of community policing are examples of such policy.

Left realism has been criticized for holding a contradictory position regarding the police (and other agencies of criminal justice).[45] On the one hand, left realists want to give the police more power to combat crime, especially crime committed against the working class. On the other hand, they want to reduce the power of the police to intervene in people's lives and want to make the police more accountable for their actions. Another criticism of left realism is that its emphasis on the reform of criminal justice practice, rather than on radical change, makes it little different in that regard from conflict theory, classical and neoclassical theories, and many positivist theories.[46]

peacemaking criminology An approach that suggests that the solutions to all social problems, including crime, are the transformation of human beings, mutual dependence, reduction of class structures, creation of communities of caring people, and universal social justice.

Peacemaking Criminology This perspective rejects the idea that predatory criminal violence can be reduced by repressive state violence. In this view, "wars" on crime make matters only worse. Consisting of a mixture of anarchism, humanism, socialism, and Native American and Eastern philosophies, **peacemaking criminology** suggests that the solutions to all social problems, including crime, are the transformation of human beings, mutual dependence, reduction of class structures, creation of communities of caring people, and universal social justice. For peacemaking criminologists, crime is suffering, and, therefore, to reduce crime, suffering must be reduced.[47] Policy emphasis is placed on the transformation of human beings through an inner rebirth or spiritual rejuvenation (inner peace) that enables individuals to experience empathy with those less fortunate and gives them a desire to respond to the needs of other people.

Peacemaking criminologists advocate restorative justice, compassion, and community action. *Should these principles replace the punitive justice that currently guides criminal justice in the United States? Why or why not?*

Peacemaking criminology has been criticized for its extreme idealism and its emphasis on the transformation of individuals as a way of transforming society rather than on the transformation of society as a way of transforming individuals.

Feminist Theory   Although feminism is not new, the application of feminist theory to the study of crime is.[48] Recognizing that the study of crime has always been male-centered, feminist criminologists seek a feminine perspective. Specifically, the focus of **feminist theory** is on women's experiences and ways of knowing, because, in the past, men's experiences have been taken as the norm and generalized to the population. As a result, women and girls have been omitted almost entirely from theories of crime and delinquency.

Three areas of crime and justice have commanded most of the attention of feminist theorists: (1) the victimization of women, (2) gender differences in crime, and (3) *gendered justice,* that is, differing treatment of female and male offenders and victims by the agencies and agents of criminal justice. Regarding gender differences in crime, two questions seem to dominate: (1) Do explanations of male criminality apply to women? (2) Why are women less likely than men to engage in crime?

Not all feminists share the same perspective on the issues noted. At least four different types of feminist thought have been identified: liberal, radical, Marxist, and socialist. (Conspicuously omitted from this typology are women of color, whose gender and race place them in a uniquely disadvantaged position.) Radical, Marxist, and socialist feminist thought share, to varying degrees, a belief that the problems of women, including female victimization, lie in the institution of **patriarchy,** men's control over women's labor and sexuality. The principal goal of most feminist theory is to abolish patriarchal relationships.

Liberal feminists are the exception. They do not generally view discrimination against women as the product of patriarchy. For them, the solution to women's subordinate position in society is the removal of obstacles to their full participation in social life. Liberal feminists seek equal opportunity, equal rights, and freedom of choice. As for crime, liberal feminists point to gender socialization (that is, the creation of masculine and feminine identities) as the primary culprit.

One of the principal criticisms of feminist criminology is the focus on gender as a central organizing theme. Such a focus fails to appreciate differences among women—for example, differences between the experiences of black women and white women.[49] Another problem similar to the one associated with left realism is many feminists' contradictory position regarding the police (and the criminal justice system in general). On the one hand, several feminists call for greater use of the police to better protect women from abuse; on the other hand, some feminists concede that giving more power to the police, under present circumstances, will lead only to further discrimination and harassment of minority males and females.[50] A similar contradictory position is held by many feminists toward using the law to improve gender relations. The law, after all, is almost entirely the product of white males.

Postmodernism   **Postmodernism** originated in the late 1960s as a rejection of the "modern" or Enlightenment belief in scientific rationality as the route to knowledge and progress. Among the goals of this area of critical thought are to understand the creation of knowledge and how knowledge and language create hierarchy and domination. Postmodernist ideas began to be introduced in law and criminology during the late 1980s.[51] As applied to the area of crime and criminal justice, the major foci have been critical analyses of the privileged position of "the Law" and the construction of crime theories.

feminist theory A perspective on criminality that focuses on women's experiences and seeks to abolish men's control over women's labor and sexuality.

patriarchy Men's control over women's labor and sexuality.

postmodernism An area of critical thought that, among other things, attempts to understand the creation of knowledge and how knowledge and language create hierarchy and domination.

With regard to the Law, postmodernist criminologists reject the idea "that there is only one true interpretation of a law or for that matter the U.S. Constitution."[52] They argue, instead, that there is a plurality of interpretations that are dependent, in part, on the particular social context in which they arise. As in other critical criminologies, the law, from a postmodernist view, always has a human author and a political agenda.[53] As for crime theories, postmodernist criminologists typically abandon the usual notion of causation. From the postmodernist perspective:

> Crime is seen to be the culmination of certain processes that allow persons to believe that they are somehow not connected to other humans and society. These processes place others into categories or stereotypes and make them different or alien, denying them their humanity. These processes result in the denial of responsibility for other people and to other people.[54]

Postmodernist criminologists would, among other things, replace the prevailing description of the world with new conceptions, words, and phrases that convey alternative meanings, as Sutherland did when he introduced the concept of white-collar crime. These new descriptions would tell different stories about the world as experienced by historically subjugated people.[55] Postmodernist criminologists would also replace the formal criminal justice apparatus with informal social controls so that the current functions of criminal justice are handled by local groups and local communities.[56] This strategy is consistent with the one advocated by peacemaking criminologists. Postmodernist criminology has been criticized for its relativism and subjectivism or for being an "anarchy of knowledge": "If truth is not possible, how can we decide anything?"[57]

THINKING CRITICALLY

1. How would you explain labeling theory?

2. What is peacemaking criminology? Is this theory realistic?

3. Explain feminist theory and its key criticisms.

4. How might postmodernists explain acts of domestic terrorism?

✳ Summary

1. Define criminological theory.

   Criminological theory is the explanation of the behavior of criminal offenders, as well as the behavior of police, attorneys, prosecutors, judges, correctional personnel, victims, and other actors in the criminal justice process. It helps us understand criminal behavior and the basis of policies proposed and implemented to prevent and control crime.

2. State the causes of crime according to classical and neo-classical criminologists and their policy implications.

   Classical and neoclassical criminologists theorize that human beings are free-willed individuals who commit crime when they rationally calculate that the crime will give them more pleasure than pain. In an effort to deter crime, classical criminologists advocate the following policies: (1) establish a social contract, (2) enact laws that are clear, simple, unbiased, and reflect the consensus of the population, (3) impose punishments that are proportionate to the crime, prompt, certain, public, necessary, the least possible in the given circumstances, and dictated by law rather than by judges' discretion, (4) educate the public, (5) eliminate corruption from the administration of justice, and (6) reward virtue. Neoclassical criminologists introduced the concepts that mitigating circumstances might inhibit the exercises of free will and that punishment should be rehabilitative.

3. Describe the biological theories of crime causation and their policy implications.

   The basic cause of crime for biological positivists has been biological inferiority, which is indicated by physical or genetic characteristics that distinguish criminals from noncriminals. The policy implications of biological theories of crime causation include a choice of isolation, sterilization, or execution. Biological theorists also advocate brain surgery, chemical treatment, improved diets, and better mother and child care.

4. Describe the different psychological theories of crime causation and their policy implications.

   According to psychological theories, crime results from individuals' mental or emotional disturbances, inability to empathize with others, inability to legally satisfy their basic needs, or oppressive circumstances of life. To combat crime, psychological positivists would isolate, sterilize, or execute offenders not amenable to treatment. For treatable offenders, psychotherapy or psychoanalysis may prove effective. Other policy implications are to help people satisfy their basic needs legally, to eliminate sources of oppression, and to provide legal ways of coping with oppression.

5. Explain sociological theories of crime causation and their policy implications.

   Sociological theories propose that crime is caused by *anomie,* or the dissociation of the individual from the *collective conscience;* by *social disorganization;* by *anomie* resulting from a lack of opportunity to achieve aspirations; by the learning of criminal values and behaviors; and by the failure to properly socialize individuals. Among the policy implications of sociological theories of crime causation are containing crime within reasonable boundaries; organizing and empowering neighborhood residents; reducing aspirations, increasing legitimate opportunities; providing law-abiding models, regulating associations, eliminating crime's rewards, rewarding law-abiding behavior, punishing criminal behavior effectively; and properly socializing children so that they develop self-control and a strong moral bond to society.

6. Distinguish major differences among classical, positivist, and critical theories of crime causation.

   Unlike classical theories, which assume that human beings have free will, and positivist theories, which assume that human beings are determined, critical theories assume that human beings are both determined and determining. In contrast to both classical and positivist theories, which assume that society is characterized primarily by consensus over moral values, critical theories assume that society is characterized primarily by conflict over moral values. Finally, unlike positivist theorists, who assume that social scientists can be objective or value-neutral in their work, many critical theorists assume that everything they do is value-laden by virtue of their being human, that it is impossible to be objective.

7. Describe how critical theorists would explain the causes of crime and their policy implications.

   Depending on their perspective, critical theorists explain crime as the result of labeling and stigmatization; of relative powerlessness, the class struggle, and the practice of taking advantage of other people; or of patriarchy. Those who support labeling theory would address crime by avoiding labeling people as criminals or by employing radical nonintervention or reintegrative shaming. Conflict theorists would address crime by having dominant groups give up some of their power to subordinate groups or having dominant group members become more effective rulers and subordinate group members, better subjects. Radical theorists would define crime as a violation of basic human rights, replace the criminal justice system with popular or socialist justice, and (except for anarchists) create a socialist society appreciative of human diversity. Left realists would use police power to protect people living in working-class communities. Peacemaking criminologists would transform human beings so that they were able to empathize with those less fortunate and respond to other people's needs, would reduce hierarchical structures, would create communities of caring people, and would champion universal social justice. Feminist theorists would address crime by eliminating patriarchal structures and relationships and promoting greater equality for women. Postmodernist criminologists would replace the prevailing description of the world with new conceptions, words, and phrases that convey alternative meanings, as experienced by historically subjugated people. They would also replace the formal criminal justice system with informal social controls handled by local groups and local communities.

❋ Key Terms

theory 62
criminological theory 62
classical theory 63
utility 65
social contract 66
special or specific
    deterrence 66
general deterrence 66
neoclassical theory 66
biological inferiority 69
criminal anthropology 69

atavist 70
limbic system 72
psychopaths 75
sociopaths 75
antisocial personalities 75
anomie (Durkheim) 78
collective conscience 78
Chicago School 79
social disorganization 79
anomie (Merton and
    Cohen) 80

imitation or modeling 82
differential association 82
learning theory 83
positive reinforcement 83
negative reinforcement 83
extinction 83
punishment 83
social control theory 85
labeling theory 86
criminalization process 86
conflict theory 87

power differentials 88
relative powerlessness 88
radical theories 89
class struggle 89
left realists 91
relative deprivation 92
peacemaking
    criminology 92
feminist theory 93
patriarchy 93
postmodernism 93

❋ Review Questions

1. What are two undesirable consequences of the failure to understand the theoretical basis of criminal justice policies?

2. Before the Enlightenment and classical theory, what was generally believed to be the cause of crime?

3. Who was arguably the best known and most influential of the classical criminologists, and how did his ideas become known?

4. What is the difference between *special* or *specific deterrence* and *general deterrence?*

5. What are five problems with positivist theories?

6. What is the position held by most criminologists today regarding the relationship between biology and crime?

7. What does research indicate about the relationship between intelligence and both juvenile delinquency and adult criminality?

8. What are problems with psychological or psychoanalytic theories of crime and their policy implications?

9. In what ways did Durkheim believe that crime was functional for society?

10. What is a potential problem with the theory of the Chicago School?

11. What is a criticism of most anomie theories?

12. Who was the first twentieth-century criminologist to argue forcefully that crime was learned, and what is his theory called?

13. What is arguably the major problem with social control theory?

14. What is *secondary deviance,* and how does it occur, according to labeling theorists?

15. What are major criticisms of conflict theory? Radical theory?

16. What contributions to criminological theory have been made by British or left realism, peacemaking criminology, feminist theory, and postmodernism?

❋ In the Field

1. **Professional Perspectives on Crime** Interview representatives of the criminal justice process—a police officer, a prosecutor, a defense attorney, a judge, a correctional officer, and a probation or parole officer. Ask each to explain why crimes are committed. Ask them how they would prevent or reduce crime. After completing the interviews, identify the theories and policy implications described in the textbook that best correspond to their responses. Explain any differences in responses that emerged. Present your findings in a brief written report.

2. **Literary Perspectives on Crime** Read a nonfiction book about crime. Explain the criminal behavior, orally or in writing, using the theories in this chapter. Some good books are Truman Capote's *In Cold Blood,* Vincent Bugliosi's *Helter Skelter,* and Norman Mailer's *The Executioner's Song.*

3. **Explaining Crimes** Select several crimes from Table 2.1, and explain them by using the theories in Chapter 3.

✳ On the Net

1. **Comparing Crime Rates** Use the Internet to research crime rates of several capitalist and noncapitalist countries. (Remember that crime rates, as discussed in Chapter 2, are not accurate measures of the true amount of crime.) Then write a paragraph in which you support or oppose the proposition that capitalist countries have higher crime rates than noncapitalist countries.

2. **Criminologists** Go to www.asc41.com to learn more about professional, mostly academic criminologists. Read about the history of the American Society of Criminology. Examine the annual meeting information to see the topics on which criminologists are currently working. Explore specialty areas in criminology. Scan employment information to discover the types of jobs available.

✳ Critical Thinking Exercises

THE DAHMER CASE

1. Jeffrey Dahmer, a white male, was sentenced to 957 years in prison (Wisconsin had no death penalty) for the murder and dismemberment of 15 young males—mostly black and homosexual—in Milwaukee, Wisconsin.

   Dahmer was arrested without a struggle at his apartment on Milwaukee's crime-infested west side in August 1991, after one of his victims had escaped and notified the police. Dahmer was 31 years old and had recently been fired from his job at a chocolate factory. He immediately confessed to 11 murders. He told the police that he lured men from bars and shopping malls by promising them money to pose for pictures. He would then take them to his apartment, drug them, strangle them, and dismember their bodies. He boiled the heads of some of his victims to remove the flesh and had sex with the cadaver of at least one of them. Police found rotting body parts lying around his apartment, along with bottles of acid and chemical preservatives. Photographs of mutilated men were on a freezer that contained two severed heads. Another severed head was in the refrigerator. Dahmer told the police that he had saved a heart to eat later.

   Dahmer's stepmother told the press that as a child, he liked to use acid to scrape the meat off dead animals. When he was 18, his parents divorced. He lived with his mother until, one day, she took his little brother and disappeared, leaving him alone. He went to live with his grandmother, where he started to abuse alcohol. During the 6 years he lived with his grandmother, mysterious things were occurring in the basement and garage. Dahmer's father, a chemist, discovered bones and other body parts in containers. Dahmer told

his father that he had been stripping the flesh from animals he found.

   In 1988, Dahmer spent 10 months in prison for fondling a 13-year-old Laotian boy. On his release from prison, he was placed on probation, but his probation officer never visited him.

   Dahmer's defense attorney claimed that his client was insane at the time of the murders. The jury rejected the insanity defense.
   a. Which theory or theories of crime causation described in this chapter best explain Jeffrey Dahmer's criminal behavior?
   b. What crime prevention and correctional policies described in this chapter should be employed with criminal offenders like Jeffrey Dahmer?

BREAKING THE LAW

2. Stacey Raines drives from Indianapolis to Fort Wayne, Indiana, twice a month as part of her job as a sales representative for a pharmaceutical company. Although the posted speed limit is 65 miles per hour, Stacey generally cruises at 80 to 85, intentionally exceeding the speed limit.
   a. Which theory or theories of crime causation described in this chapter best explain the behavior of intentional speeders?
   b. What crime prevention and correctional policies described in this chapter should be used with intentional speeders?

To access more information and resources, including study questions, chapter summaries, and links, go to: www.mhhe .com/bohm6e.

The Rule of Law

Chapter Objectives

After completing this chapter, you should be able to:

1. Distinguish between criminal law and civil law.

2. Distinguish between substantive law and procedural law.

3. List five features of "good" criminal laws.

4. Explain why criminal law is a political phenomenon.

5. Summarize the origins of American criminal law.

6. Describe the procedural rights in the Fourth Amendment.

7. Describe the procedural rights in the Fifth Amendment.

8. Describe the procedural rights in the Sixth Amendment.

9. Describe the procedural rights in the Eighth Amendment.

10. Explain why procedural rights are important to those accused of crimes.

CRIME STORY

In 2002, Bosnian police arrested Lakhdar Boumediene and five other Algerians, because U.S. intelligence officers believed they were planning an attack on the U.S. embassy in Sarajevo. The U.S. government classified the five suspects as enemy combatants in the war on terror and sent them to the U.S. prison at Guantanamo Bay Naval Base, which is located on leased land from Cuba. Alleging violations of the Constitution's Due Process Clause, various statutes and treaties, the common law, and international law, Boumediene filed a petition for a writ of *habeas corpus,* which is a court order to produce a prisoner in court, most frequently to ensure a prisoner is being legally detained or imprisoned. The government asked the U.S. District Court judge to dismiss Boumediene's claims on the ground that Boumediene had no right to a habeas petition, because he was an alien detained at an overseas military base. The judge granted the government's motion, and the U.S. Court of Appeals for the D.C. Circuit affirmed. However, in 2004, in *Rasul* v. *Bush,* the Supreme Court reversed the lower courts,

continued

holding that the habeas statute extended to noncitizen detainees at Guantanamo.

Congress responded to the Court's decision by passing the Detainee Treatment Act of 2005 (DTA), which specified the rights of enemy combatants, and the Military Commissions Act of 2006 (MCA), which eliminated the federal courts' jurisdiction to hear *habeas* applications from detainees who had been designated as enemy combatants. The Algerians again appealed their case to the D.C. Circuit, this time arguing that the MCA did not apply to their petitions, and, if it did, it was in violation of the U.S. Constitution's Suspension Clause. The Suspension Clause prescribes: "The Privilege of the Writ of Habeas Corpus shall not be suspended, unless when in Cases of Rebellion or Invasion the public Safety may require it." The D.C. court again ruled against the petitioners on both points. The court referred to language in the MCA applying the law to "all cases, without exception" that deal with detention. The court added that a purpose of the MCA was to overrule the Supreme Court's opinion in *Hamdan* v. *Rumsfeld*, which had allowed petitions like Boumediene's to proceed. The court concluded that the Suspension Clause protected the writ of *habeas corpus* only under conditions

that existed in 1789, which did not include an overseas military base leased from a foreign government. The court proclaimed that constitutional rights do not apply to aliens outside the United States, and the leased military base in Cuba was not in the United States.

The U.S. Supreme Court granted *certiorari* on June 29, 2007, to address four questions: (1) Should the MCA be interpreted to strip federal court jurisdiction over *habeas* petitions filed by foreign citizens detained at the U.S. Naval Base at Guantanamo Bay, Cuba? (2) If so, does the MCA violate the Suspension Clause of the Constitution? (3) Are the detainees at Guantanamo Bay entitled to the Fifth Amendment's right not to be deprived of liberty without due process of law and to the Geneva Conventions? (4) Can the detainees challenge the adequacy of judicial review provisions of the MCA before they have sought to invoke that review?

On June 12, 2008, in *Boumediene* v. *Bush,* five U.S. Supreme Court justices answered yes to each of the four questions and ruled that detainees were not barred either from seeking a writ of *habeas corpus* or invoking the Suspension Clause merely because they had been designated as enemy combatants or were held at the prison at Guantanamo Bay. Justice

Anthony Kennedy, writing for the majority, reasoned the rights granted in the DTA did not constitute an adequate substitute for *habeas corpus;* therefore, the MCA is an unconstitutional attempt to suspend the writ. The Court reversed the D.C. Circuit's ruling and found in favor of the detainees.

Chapter 4 examines the constitutional protections that limit the law enforcement power of government and ensure an appropriate balance between social control and individual liberty. When these two important priorities collide, the courts provide new case law to guide the government and its citizens to a revised perspective concerning these two American imperatives. Should detainees have the right to seek a writ of *habeas corpus* or invoke the Suspension Clause even though they have been designated as enemy combatants or are or were held at the prison at Guantanamo Bay, or did the Supreme Court err in its judgment? (On January 22, 2009, President Obama signed an order to close the Guantanamo Bay prison within a year.) Should Congress be able to create laws that overrule the Supreme Court's interpretation of the Constitution? These questions go to the very heart of the rule of law and the separation of powers.

---

criminal law One of two general types of law practiced in the United States (the other is civil law); "a formal means of social control [that uses] rules . . . interpreted [and enforced] by the courts . . . to set limits to the conduct of the citizens, to guide the officials, and to define . . . unacceptable behavior."

penal code The criminal law of a political jurisdiction.

tort A violation of the civil law.

civil law One of two general types of law practiced in the United States (the other is criminal law); a means of resolving conflicts between individuals. It includes personal injury claims (torts), the law of contracts and property, and subjects such as administrative law and the regulation of public utilities.

100

Two Types of Law: Criminal Law and Civil Law

As discussed in Chapter 2, the conventional, although not necessarily the best, definition of *crime* is "a violation of the criminal law." **Criminal law** is one of two general types of law practiced in the United States; the other is civil law. Criminal law is "a formal means of social control [that] involves the use of rules that are interpreted, and are enforceable, by the courts of a political community. . . . The function of the rules is to set limits to the conduct of the citizens, to guide the officials (police and other administrators), and to define conditions of deviance or unacceptable behavior."[1] The purpose of criminal justice is to enforce the criminal law.

A crime, as noted, is a violation of the criminal law, or of the **penal code** of a political jurisdiction. Although crime is committed against individuals, it is considered an offense against the state, that is, the political jurisdiction that enacted the law.[2] A **tort,** in contrast, is a violation of the **civil law** and is considered a private matter between individuals. Civil law includes the law of contracts and property as well as subjects such as administrative law (which deals with the rules and regulations created by government agencies) and the regulation of public utilities.

For legal purposes, a particular act may be considered an offense against an individual or the state or both. It is either a tort or a crime or both, depending on how it is handled. For example, a person who has committed an act of assault may be charged with a crime. If that person is convicted of the crime, the criminal court may order the offender to be imprisoned in the county jail for 6 months and to pay a fine of $2,000. Both the jail sentence and the fine are punishments, with the fine going to the state or local treasury (in federal court to the national treasury). The criminal court could also order the offender to pay restitution to the victim. In that case, the offender would pay the victim a sum of money either directly or indirectly, through an intermediary. In addition, the victim may sue the offender in civil court for damages, such as medical expenses or wages lost because of injury. If the offender is found liable (responsible) for the damages because he or she has committed a tort (civil courts do not "convict"), the civil court may also order the offender to compensate the victim in the amount of $2,000 for damage to the victim's interests. The payment of compensation in the civil case is not punishment; it is for the purpose of "making the victim whole again."

SUBSTANTIVE VERSUS PROCEDURAL LAW

There are two types of criminal law: substantive and procedural. **Substantive law** is the body of law that defines criminal offenses and their penalties. Substantive laws, which are found in the various penal codes, govern what people legally may and may not do. Examples of substantive laws are those that prohibit and penalize murder, rape, robbery, and other crimes. **Procedural law,** sometimes called *adjective* or *remedial* law, governs the ways in which the substantive laws are to be administered. It covers such subjects as the way suspects can legally be arrested, searched, interrogated, tried, and punished. In other words, procedural law is concerned with **due process of law**, or the rights of people suspected of or charged with crimes. The last part of this chapter is devoted to a detailed description of procedural law.

substantive law The body of law that defines criminal offenses and their penalties.

procedural law The body of law that governs the ways substantive laws are administered; sometimes called *adjective* or *remedial* law.

due process of law The rights of people suspected of or charged with crimes.

IDEAL CHARACTERISTICS OF THE CRIMINAL LAW

Legal scholars identify five features that all "good" criminal laws ideally ought to possess. To the extent that those features are absent in criminal laws, the laws can be considered "bad" laws, and bad laws do exist. The five ideal features of good criminal laws are (1) politicality, (2) specificity, (3) regularity, (4) uniformity, and (5) penal sanction (see Figure 4.1).

Figure 4.1

Ideal Characteristics of Criminal Law

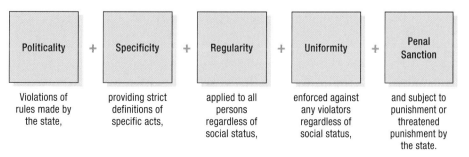

politicality An ideal characteristic of criminal law, referring to its legitimate source. Only violations of rules made by the state, the political jurisdiction that enacted the laws, are crimes.

specificity An ideal characteristic of criminal law, referring to its scope. Although civil law may be general in scope, criminal law should provide strict definitions of specific acts.

regularity An ideal characteristic of criminal law: the applicability of the law to all persons, regardless of social status.

uniformity An ideal characteristic of criminal law: the enforcement of the laws against anyone who violates them, regardless of social status.

penal sanction An ideal characteristic of criminal law: the principle that violators will be punished or at least threatened with punishment by the state.

Politicality **Politicality** refers to the legitimate source of criminal law. Only violations of rules made by the state (that is, the political jurisdiction that enacted the laws) are crimes. Violations of rules made by other institutions, such as families, churches, schools, and employers, may be "bad," "sinful," or "socially unacceptable," but they are not crimes, because they are not prohibited by the state.

Specificity **Specificity** refers to the scope of criminal law. Although civil law may be general in scope, criminal law should provide strict definitions of specific acts. The point is illustrated by an old case in which a person stole an airplane but was found not guilty of violating a criminal law that prohibited the taking of "self-propelled vehicles." The judge ruled that at the time the law was enacted, *vehicles* did not include airplanes. Ideally, as the Supreme Court ruled in *Papachristou* v. *City of Jacksonville* (1972), a statute or ordinance "is void for vagueness . . . [if] it fails to give a person of ordinary intelligence fair notice that his contemplated conduct is forbidden."

Regularity **Regularity** is the applicability of the criminal law to all persons. Ideally, anyone who commits a crime is answerable for it, regardless of the person's social status. Thus, ideally, when criminal laws are created, they should apply not only to the women who violate them, but also to the men; not only to the poor, but also to the rich. In practice, however, this ideal feature of law has been violated. Georgia's pre–Civil War criminal laws, for example, provided for a dual system of crime and punishment, with one set of laws for "slaves and free persons of color" and another for all other persons. Another example of the violation of this principle is illustrated by the case of *Michael M.* v. *Superior Court of Sonoma County* (1981). In this case, the U.S. Supreme Court upheld California's statutory rape law that made men alone criminally responsible for the act of illicit sexual intercourse with a minor female.

Uniformity **Uniformity** refers to the way in which the criminal law should be enforced. Ideally, the law should be administered without regard for the social status of the persons who have committed crimes or are accused of committing crimes. Thus, when violated, criminal laws should be enforced against both young and old, both rich and poor, and so on. However, as is the case with regularity, the principle of uniformity is often violated because some people consider the strict enforcement of the law unjust in some cases. For example, juveniles who are caught misbehaving in violation of the criminal law are sometimes ignored or treated leniently through the exercise of police or judicial discretion.

Penal Sanction The last ideal feature of criminal law is **penal sanction,** the principle that violators will be punished, or at least threatened with punishment, by the state. Conventional wisdom suggests that there would be no point in enacting criminal laws if their violation were not responded to with punishment or threat of punishment. Most people assume that sanctionless criminal laws would be ignored. Because all criminal laws carry sanctions, the power of sanctionless laws can be left to philosophers to debate. Table 4.1 shows the five general types of penal sanctions currently used in the United States, as well as the purpose and focus of each sanction. Combining different penal sanctions in the administration of justice is not uncommon.

Table 4.1 Five General Types of Penal Sanctions

Type	Purpose	Focus
Punishment	Prevent undesired conduct. Provide retribution ("an eye for an eye").	Offending conduct
Restitution	Make the victim "whole again" by having the offender directly or indirectly pay the victim.	Crime victim
Compensation	Make the victim "whole again" by having the state pay for damages to the victim.	Crime victim
Regulation	Control future conduct toward the best interests of the community (e.g., making it a crime or traffic violation to operate a motor vehicle with a blood alcohol content higher than a specified level).	The entire community
Treatment or rehabilitation	Change the offender's behavior and, perhaps, personality.	Criminal offender

CRIMINAL LAW AS A POLITICAL PHENOMENON

People sometimes forget that criminal law is a political phenomenon, that it is created by human beings to regulate the behavior of other human beings. Some people, for example, view the criminal law as divinely inspired, something that should not be questioned or challenged. That viewpoint probably comes from a belief in the biblical story of Moses receiving the Ten Commandments from God on Mount Sinai. However, as critical theorists are quick to point out, criminal law frequently promotes the interests of some groups over the interests of other groups. Thus, regardless of the law's source of inspiration, we must understand that what gets defined as criminal or delinquent behavior is the result of a political process in which rules are created to prohibit or to require certain behaviors. Nothing is criminal or delinquent in and of itself; only the response of the state makes it so.

Origins of Laws Formal, written laws are a relatively recent phenomenon in human existence. The first were created about 5,000 years ago. They emerged with the institutions of property, marriage, and government. "Stateless" societies apparently managed without them for two primary reasons.[3] First, most stateless societies were governed by rigid customs to which citizens strictly adhered. Second, crimes of violence were considered private matters and were usually resolved through bloody personal revenge. Formal, written laws partially replaced customs when nation-states appeared, although customs often remained the force behind the laws. Formal laws also replaced customs with the advent of writing, which allowed recorded legislation to replace the recollections of elders and priests.

The first known written laws (approximately 3000 C.E.) were found on clay tablets among the ruins of Ur, one of the city-states of Sumeria. Attributed to King Urukagina of Lagash, the laws were truly enlightened for their time and attempted to free poor people from abuse by the rich and everybody from abuse by the priests. For example, one law forbade the high priest from coming into the garden of a poor mother and taking wood or fruit from her to pay taxes. Laws also cut burial fees to one-fifth of what they had been and forbade the clergy and high

MYTH

Law makes people behave.

FACT

The existence of a law prohibiting a particular behavior does not necessarily prevent an individual from engaging in that behavior. Common sense suggests the implausibility of the notion. Ask yourself, if it were not for laws prohibiting murder, prostitution, or heroin use, for example, would you murder, engage in prostitution, or use heroin? How effective are speed limits in preventing you from exceeding them?

Bas relief depicting King Hammurabi with his code of laws. *Why do people believe that criminal laws come from God?*

officials from sharing among themselves the cattle that were sacrificed to the gods. By 2800 C.E., the growth of trade had forced the city-states of Sumeria to merge into an empire governed by a single, all-powerful king.

Around 2200 C.E., a war settlement between the Sumerians and the Akkadians produced the Babylonian civilization. Babylonia's best-known king was Hammurabi (1792–1750 C.E.), who ruled for 43 years. Hammurabi is famous for the first great code of laws. The Code of Hammurabi, like the laws of Moses later, presumably was a gift from God. Hammurabi was said to have received it from the sun god, Shamash, about 1780 C.E. There was a total of 285 laws in the code, arranged under the headings of personal property, real estate, trade and business, the family, injuries, and labor. The Code of Hammurabi combined very enlightened aims, such as "to prevent the strong from oppressing the weak, . . . to enlighten the land and to further the welfare of the people," with very barbaric punishments.

All the ancient nation-states or civilizations had formal legal codes. In addition to the laws of King Urukagina of Lagash (Sumeria) and the Code of Hammurabi (Babylonia), legal codes were established by the Egyptians, the Assyrians, the Hebrews, the Persians, the Indians, the Chinese, the Greeks (especially the codes of Lycurgus, Draco, Solon, and Plato), and the Romans (for example, the Twelve Tables, the Justinian Code, and the Law of the Nations). The development and the content of those legal codes are of mostly historical interest. The criminal law of the United States, for the most part, is derived from the laws of England.

England's Contribution to American Criminal Law Before the Norman Conquest in 1066, England was populated by Anglo-Saxon tribes that regulated themselves through custom.[4] Wars between those tribes resulted in the taking of the tribal lands of the losers by the leader of the victorious tribe, who, by force, made the newly acquired land his own private property and himself the feudal lord. By the time of the Norman Conquest, there were about eight large and relatively independent feudal landholdings. In an effort to increase their power, the feudal lords took it on themselves to dispense justice among their subjects and began to require that disputes between subjects be settled in local courts rather than by relatives, as had previously been the custom.

When William I of Normandy conquered England in 1066 and proclaimed himself king, he declared that all land, and all land-based rights, including the administration of justice, were now vested in the king. King William also rewarded the Norman noblemen who had fought with him with large grants of formerly Anglo-Saxon land.

FYI

Felony

The term *felony* originally meant an offense serious enough "to break the relationship between [the landowner and his lord] and to cause the [land] holding to be forfeited to the lord."

Source: S. Francis Milson, *The Historical Foundations of the Common Law* (London: Butterworths, 1969), p. 355.

To make the dispensing of justice a profitable enterprise for the king and to make sure the local courts remained under his control, the institution of the *eyre* was created early in the twelfth century. The eyre was composed of traveling judges who represented the king and examined the activities of the local courts.

Of particular interest to the eyre was the resolution of cases of sufficient seriousness as to warrant the forfeiture of the offender's property as punishment. The notion of forfeiture was based on the feudal doctrine that the right to own private property rested on a relationship of good faith between the landowner and his lord. The Norman kings expanded the notion of forfeiture to include any violation of the "king's peace," which enabled the king to claim forfeited property for a variety of offenses, including such minor ones as trespassing. It was the responsibility of the judges in eyre to make sure the king received his portion of forfeited property.

A secondary responsibility of the eyre was to hear common pleas, which consisted primarily of disputes between ordinary citizens. Although common pleas could be handled in the local courts, which in many instances were still influenced by Anglo-Saxon customs, the Norman settlers frequently felt more comfortable having their cases heard in the king's courts, of which the eyre was one. It was the common-plea decisions made by judges in eyre that formed the body of legal precedent that became known as the *common law*, that is, the rules used to settle disputes throughout England. Thus, as the judges of eyre resolved common-plea disputes, they created precedents to be followed in similar cases. Because the common law was built case by case, it is sometimes also called *case law*. Many of the precedents that were created in medieval England became the basis of statutory law in modern England, as well as in the United States. In both countries, some of the early precedents are still used as the basis for settling disputes not covered by statutes.

The efforts of the Norman kings to centralize their power over all of England were only partially successful. In 1215, powerful landholding nobles rebelled against the heavy taxation and autocratic rule of King John and forced him to sign the Magna Carta (the Great Charter). The primary purpose of the Magna Carta was to settle the dispute between the king and his nobles by placing checks on royal power. (It did little for the common person.) From that time forward, kings and queens of England were supposed to be governed by laws and customs rather than by their own wills, and the laws were supposed to be applied in a regular and fair way by the king or queen and his or her judges. Thus, the Magna Carta not only created the idea of the rule of law but also formed the basis of what would later be called *due process of law*.

The Magna Carta, signed by England's King John in 1215, placed limits on royal power and established the principle of the rule of law. *Which is preferable: unregulated royal power or the rule of law? Why?*

CREATING CRIMINAL LAWS IN THE UNITED STATES

In the United States, criminal laws (or criminal statutes) are almost entirely a product of constitutional authority and the legislative bodies that enact them. They are also influenced by common law or case law interpretation and by administrative or regulatory agency decisions.

Constitutions and Legislative Bodies Constitutions generally provide for the creation of legislative bodies empowered to enact criminal and other laws. The U.S. Constitution, for example, created Congress and gave it lawmaking power. The Bill of Rights of the Constitution (the first 10 amendments), as well as similar amendments to state constitutions, also describe procedural laws that dictate how substantive laws are to be administered. Constitutions are important to the substantive criminal law because they set limits on what can be defined as a crime.

As noted, criminal laws are products of the lawmaking bodies created by constitutional authority. Thus, federal statutes are enacted by Congress, and state statutes are enacted by state legislatures. Laws created by municipalities, such as by city councils, are generally called *ordinances*. Both the federal criminal

Federal statutes are enacted by Congress. *How does Congress create statutes?*

statutes and the criminal statutes of particular states, including the definitions of crimes and the penalties associated with them, can be found in penal codes, one for each jurisdiction.

Generally, statutes and ordinances apply only in the particular jurisdiction in which they were enacted. A crime must be prosecuted in the jurisdiction in which it was committed, and it is generally held to have been committed in the jurisdiction in which it was completed or achieved its goal. Federal crimes violate federal statutes, and state crimes violate state statutes. A crime in one state may not be a crime in another state, but a violation of a federal statute is a crime if committed anywhere in the United States. When a certain behavior violates both federal and state statutes, and possibly local ordinances, as is the case with many drug law violations, there is overlapping jurisdiction. In such cases, there is frequently confusion over which jurisdiction should assume responsibility for the enforcement of the law and the prosecution of the crime.

Common Law Common law, also called *case law*, is a by-product of decisions made by trial and appellate court judges, who produce case law whenever they render a decision in a particular case. The decision becomes a potential basis, or **precedent,** for deciding the outcomes of similar cases in the future. Although it is possible for the decision of any trial court judge to become a precedent, it is primarily the written decisions of appellate court judges that do. The reasons on which the decisions of appellate court judges are based are the only ones required to be in writing. This body of recorded decisions has become known as *common law.* Generally, whether a precedent is binding is determined by the court's location. (The different levels of courts in the United States will be described in detail in Chapter 8.)

The principle of using precedents to guide future decisions in court cases is called ***stare decisis*** (Latin for "to stand by decided cases"). Much of the time spent by criminal lawyers in preparing for a case is devoted to finding legal precedents that support their arguments. The successful outcome of a case depends largely on the success of lawyers in that endeavor.

Although common law was an important source of criminal law in colonial America, it is less so today. Currently, what were originally common law

precedent A decision that forms a potential basis for deciding the outcomes of similar cases in the future; a by-product of decisions made by trial and appellate court judges, who produce case law whenever they render a decision in a particular case.

stare decisis The principle of using precedents to guide future decisions in court cases; Latin for "to stand by decided cases."

Ordinances are the laws of municipalities and are created by city councils, for example, often with more citizen input than laws created at the state or federal levels of government. *How much input should citizens have in the creation of criminal laws? Defend your answer.*

crimes, as well as many new crimes, have been defined by statutes created by legislatures in nearly all states. There is no federal criminal common law. Nevertheless, as noted previously, common law or case law remains important for purposes of statutory interpretation.

Administrative or Regulatory Agency Decisions Administrative or regulatory agencies are the products of statutes enacted by the lawmaking bodies of different jurisdictions. Those agencies create rules, regulate and supervise activities in their areas of responsibility, and render decisions that have the force of law. Examples of federal administrative or regulatory agencies are the Federal Trade Commission (FTC), the Federal Communications Commission (FCC), the Nuclear Regulatory Commission (NRC), the Drug Enforcement Administration (DEA), and the Occupational Safety and Health Administration (OSHA). There are administrative or regulatory agencies at the state and local levels as well. Although violations of the rules and regulations of such agencies are generally handled through civil law proceedings, some violations—especially habitual violations—may be addressed through criminal proceedings if provided for by statute. Additionally, legislatures often enact criminal statutes based on the recommendations of regulatory agencies.

The Interdependency Among Sources of Legal Authority Although federal and state criminal statutes are essentially independent of one another, and although almost all of the action in the enforcement of criminal laws is at the state level, there is an important interdependency among sources of legal authority. For example, during the 1984 Republican National Convention in Dallas, Texas, Gregory Lee Johnson was part of a political protest of Reagan administration policies. As part of the protest, Johnson burned an American flag. Johnson was arrested and convicted of violating a Texas statute prohibiting the desecration of a venerated object. Several witnesses testified that the flag burning seriously offended them. A state court of appeals affirmed the conviction, but the Texas Court of Criminal Appeals reversed it, holding that to punish Johnson for burning the flag in this situation was inconsistent with the First Amendment. The U.S. Supreme Court agreed (*see Texas* v. *Johnson,* 1989). Provisions of the Constitution always take precedence over state statutes. However, if the state statute were not challenged, it would remain in effect in the particular state that enacted it.

THINKING CRITICALLY

1. Which of the five features of good criminal laws do you think are most important? Why?

2. Are there any other features that could or should be added to good criminal laws?

Procedural Law: Rights of the Accused

Most of the procedural, or due process rights, given to criminal suspects or defendants in the United States are found in the Bill of Rights. The Bill of Rights went into effect on December 15, 1791. Other procedural rights are found in state constitutions and federal and state statutes. Probably the best systematic collection of due process rights is the *Federal Rules of Criminal Procedure.* Those rules apply only to federal crimes prosecuted in federal courts. Most states also have collections of rules regarding criminal procedures in state courts. Ohio, for example, has 60 such rules in its *Ohio Rules of Criminal Procedure.*

THE BILL OF RIGHTS

The ink was barely dry on the new Constitution before critics attacked it for not protecting the rights of the people. The First Congress quickly proposed a set of 12 amendments and sent them to the states for ratification. By 1791, the states had ratified 10 of the amendments, which became known as the Bill of Rights (the first 10 amendments of the Constitution). Although the Bill of Rights originally applied only to the national government, almost all of its provisions have also been applied to the states through a series of U.S. Supreme Court decisions. Table 4.2 lists the 12 provisions in the Bill of Rights that are applicable to the criminal justice process. Note that only two of the provisions—the prohibition against excessive bail and fines and the right to a grand jury indictment—are not yet applicable to the states.

Table 4.2 **The 12 Provisions in the Bill of Rights Applicable to the Criminal Justice Process**

Procedural Right	Amendment
1. Freedom from unreasonable searches and seizures	Fourth
2. Grand jury indictment in felony cases*	Fifth
3. No double jeopardy	Fifth
4. No compelled self-incrimination	Fifth
5. Speedy and public trial	Sixth
6. Impartial jury of the state and district where crime occurred	Sixth
7. Notice of nature and cause of accusation	Sixth
8. Confront opposing witnesses	Sixth
9. Compulsory process for obtaining favorable witnesses	Sixth
10. Counsel	Sixth
11. No excessive bail and fines*	Eighth
12. No cruel and unusual punishment	Eighth

Note: *This right has not been incorporated by and made applicable to the states.

THE FOURTEENTH AMENDMENT AND THE SELECTIVE INCORPORATION OF THE BILL OF RIGHTS

The Fourteenth Amendment was finally ratified by the required three-fourths of all states in 1868, shortly after the conclusion of the Civil War. In part, the amendment reads as follows:

> No State shall make or enforce any law which shall abridge the privileges or immunities of citizens of the United States, nor shall any State deprive any person of life, liberty, or property, without due process of law; nor deny to any person within its jurisdiction the equal protection of the laws.

One of the interesting and long-debated questions about the Fourteenth Amendment was whether its original purpose was to extend the procedural safeguards described in the Bill of Rights to people charged with crimes at the state level. Before the passage of the Fourteenth Amendment, the Bill of Rights applied only to people charged with federal crimes; individual states were not bound by its requirements. Some justices of the Supreme Court—for example, William Douglas (justice from 1939 to 1975), Hugo Black (justice from 1937 to 1971), and Frank Murphy (justice from 1940 to 1949)—believed that the Fourteenth Amendment was supposed to *incorporate* the Bill of Rights and make it applicable to the states. However, other justices, perhaps even a majority of them, did not. Thus, until the 1960s, the Supreme Court did not interpret the Fourteenth Amendment as incorporating the Bill of Rights.

There are at least three different explanations for the actions or, in this case, inactions of the Supreme Court.[5] First, there is little evidence that supporters of the Fourteenth Amendment intended it to incorporate the Bill of Rights. Second, by 1937, a series of court decisions had established the precedent that the due process clause of the Fourteenth Amendment did not require states to follow trial procedures mandated at the federal level by provisions in the Bill of Rights. The Supreme Court had held that due process was not violated if procedures followed in state courts were otherwise fair. Third, there was the states' rights issue. Because the administration of justice is primarily a state and local responsibility, many people resented what appeared to be unwarranted interference by the federal government in state and local matters. Indeed, the Constitution, for the most part, leaves questions about policing and administering justice to the states, unless a state's procedure violates a fundamental principle of justice.

Regardless of the reason, it was not until the early 1960s that the Supreme Court, then headed by Chief Justice Earl Warren, began to selectively incorporate most of the procedural safeguards contained in the Bill of Rights, making them applicable to the states.

Thus, it took nearly 100 years after the ratification of the Fourteenth Amendment for suspects charged with crimes at the state level to be afforded most of the same due process protections as people charged with crimes at the federal level. During the past 40 years, however, the composition of the Supreme Court has changed dramatically, and with the change in personnel, the Court's views of due process rights have changed as well. Whereas the politically liberal Warren Court of the 1960s championed the rights of criminal suspects by extending procedural safeguards, the politically conservative Burger and Rehnquist Courts of the 1970s, 1980s, 1990s, and the first few years of the twenty-first century have actively reversed or altered in other ways the work of the Warren Court.[6] The Roberts Court is likely to resemble the conservative Rehnquist Court not only because Chief Justice Roberts was appointed by conservative President George W. Bush but also because Justice Roberts was a former law clerk for Justice Rehnquist.

 CJ Online

ACLU

The American Civil Liberties Union is a nonprofit, nonpartisan, advocacy group devoted to the protection of civil liberties for all Americans. You can learn more about the organization and its defense of the Constitution—especially the Bill of Rights—by going to www.aclu.org. Review "The Issues" section, and look at issues such as criminal justice, cyber-liberties, and drug policy. *Do you think that organizations like the ACLU are necessary? Why or why not?*

FYI "Evolving Standards of Decency"

In *Trop* v. *Dulles* (1958) Chief Justice Warren wrote that the protections of the Bill of Rights "must draw [their] meaning from evolving standards of decency that mark the progress of a maturing society."

From left to right: Chief Justices John Roberts, Jr., William Rehnquist, Warren Burger, and Earl Warren. Whereas the politically liberal Warren Court of the 1960s championed the rights of criminal suspects by extending procedural safeguards, the politically conservative Burger and Rehnquist courts of the 1970s, 1980s, 1990s, and the first few years of the twenty-first century have actively reversed or altered in other ways the work of the Warren Court. The Roberts Court is likely to follow the direction of the Burger and Rehnquist courts. *How can the different direction in criminal procedure taken by the Burger, Rehnquist, and Roberts courts be explained?*

In the rest of this section, we consider the procedural rights in the Bill of Rights, which are found in the Fourth, Fifth, Sixth, and Eighth Amendments to the Constitution.[7] Before we do, however, note that the specific interpretation of each of the procedural or due process rights has evolved over time through dozens of Supreme Court and lower-court decisions, or precedents. In this introductory examination, we limit our consideration of the legal development of those rights to what we believe are the most consequential cases, the landmark cases.

THE FOURTH AMENDMENT

The Fourth Amendment reads as follows:

> The right of the people to be secure in their persons, houses, papers, and effects, against unreasonable searches and seizures, shall not be violated, and no warrants shall issue, but upon probable cause, supported by Oath or affirmation, and particularly describing the place to be searched, and the person or things to be seized.

The Fourth Amendment (as well as other provisions of the Constitution) protects individual privacy against certain types of governmental interference. However, it does not provide a general constitutional "right to privacy," as many people wrongly believe. Nearly every governmental action interferes with personal privacy to some extent. Thus, the question in Fourth Amendment cases is limited to whether a governmental intrusion violates the Constitution.[8]

The procedural rights in the Fourth Amendment influence the operation of criminal justice in the United States nearly every day. They concern the legality of searches and seizures and the question of what to do with evidence that is illegally obtained. **Searches** are explorations or inspections, by law enforcement officers, of homes, premises, vehicles, or persons, for the purpose of discovering evidence of crimes or persons who are accused of crimes. A search occurs "when an expectation of privacy that society is prepared to consider

searches Explorations or inspections, by law enforcement officers, of homes, premises, vehicles, or persons, for the purpose of discovering evidence of crimes or persons who are accused of crimes.

reasonable is infringed [by the government]."[9] **Seizures** are the taking of persons or property into custody in response to violations of the criminal law. A seizure of property occurs "when there is some meaningful interference [by the government] with an individual's possessory interests in that property."[10]

In *United States* v. *Mendenhall* (1980), the Supreme Court created the following test for determining whether an encounter constitutes a Fourth Amendment seizure: "A person has been 'seized' within the meaning of the Fourth Amendment only if, in view of all the circumstances surrounding the incident, a reasonable person would have believed that he was not free to leave." The Court provided these examples of situations that might be construed as seizures, even if the person did not attempt to leave: (1) the threatening presence of several officers, (2) the display of a weapon by an officer, (3) some physical touching of the person, or (4) the use of language or a tone of voice that indicated that compliance with the officer's request might be compelled. In *California* v. *Hodari D.* (1991), the Court modified the plurality holding in *Mendenhall*. In *Hodari D.*, the suspect ran from the police, and an officer pursued, thereby creating a circumstance in which a "reasonable person would have believed that she or he was not free to leave" or to disobey the officer's command to halt. There was no physical touching of the suspect. The Court held that in cases involving a "show of authority," as distinguished from physical touching, no "seizure" occurs unless and until the suspect yields or submits to the assertion of authority.

According to the Supreme Court, the Fourth Amendment allows two kinds of searches and seizures: those made with a warrant and those made without a warrant. A **warrant** is a written order from a court directing law enforcement officers to conduct a search or to arrest a person. An **arrest** is the seizure of a person or the taking of a person into custody. An arrest can be either taking actual physical custody, as when a suspect is handcuffed by a police officer, or constructive custody, as when a person peacefully submits to a police officer's control. An arrest can occur without an officer's physically touching a suspect.

The Fourth Amendment requires only that searches and seizures not be "unreasonable." Searches and seizures conducted with a legal warrant are generally considered reasonable. However, what is "reasonable" in warrantless searches remained vague for more than 100 years after the ratification of the amendment. It was not until a series of cases beginning in the 1960s that the Supreme Court began to provide a more precise definition of the term. Because the law concerning warrantless searches and seizures is complex, only a relatively brief and simplified overview will be provided in that section.

Searches and Seizures with a Warrant

First, law enforcement officers must have *probable cause* before a judicial officer can legally issue a search or arrest warrant. Probable cause for a search warrant requires substantial and trustworthy evidence to support two conclusions: (1) that the specific objects to be searched for are connected with criminal activity and (2) that the objects will be found in the place to be searched. In nearly all jurisdictions, law enforcement officers seeking a search warrant must specify in a signed *affidavit*, a written and sworn declaration, the facts that establish probable cause. The facts in the affidavit are the basis for determining later whether there was probable cause to issue the warrant in the first place. Some jurisdictions allow sworn oral testimony to establish probable cause. Figure 4.2 shows the search warrant affidavit in the Duke lacrosse rape case.

The Fourth Amendment requires that a search warrant contain a particular description of the place to be searched and the person or things to be seized. Thus, the warrant must be specific enough that a law enforcement officer executing it would know where to search and what objects to seize, even if the

seizures The taking of persons or property into custody in response to violations of the criminal law.

warrant A written order from a court directing law enforcement officers to conduct a search or to arrest a person.

arrest The seizure of a person or the taking of a person into custody, either actual physical custody, as when a suspect is handcuffed by a police officer, or constructive custody, as when a person peacefully submits to a police officer's control.

Figure 4.2

Affidavit and Application for Search Warrant in the Duke University Lacrosse Rape Case

STATE OF NORTH CAROLINA § IN THE GENERAL COURT OF
JUSTICE
DURHAM COUNTY § DISTRICT COURT DIVISION

ATTACHMENT FOR APPLICATION FOR SEARCH WARRANT

IN THE MATTER OF: 610 N. Buchnan Blvd. Durham, NC 27701

I, Investigator Benjamin Himan being a duly sworn officer, request that the COURT issue a warrant to search the place, person, vehicles, and any other items or places described in this application; and to find and seize the property described in this application.

Description of items to be seized.

1. Any DNA evidence to include hair, semen, blood, salvia related to the suspects and victim

2. Blue bathroom carpet/rug

3. Any clothing related to the suspects and the victim

4. Any documentation identifying the suspects

5. Collection of latent prints identifying persons in the residence

6. Documentation of ownership of residence

7. Property belonging to include but not limited to a purse, wallet, make-up and make-up bag, cellular camera telephone, and a shoe

8. Still photographs, video footage and digital recordings of the party

9. Any cameras or video devices which could contain photographs or footage of the party on 03/13/2006 to 3/14/2006

10. Artificial Fingernails with a reddish color polish

11. United States Currency totaling $400.00 or portions of said currency (all twenty dollar bills)

MAGISTRATE/JUDGE

DATE __3.16.06__

APPLICANT

DATE __3.16.06__

STATE OF NORTH CAROLINA § IN THE GENERAL COURT OF
JUSTICE
DURHAM COUNTY § DISTRICT COURT DIVISION

ATTACHMENT FOR APPLICATION FOR SEARCH WARRANT

Description of items to be seized - Continued

12. Any electronic data processing and storage devices, computers and computer systems including central processing units; internal and peripheral storage devices such as fixed disks, external hard disks, floppy disk drives and diskettes, tape drives and tapes, cartridges, optical storage devices or other memory storage devices; peripheral input/output devices such as keyboards, printers, video display-monitors, optical reader/write devices, and related communications devices such as modems; together with system documentation, operating logs and documentation, software and instruction manuals Any e-mail correspondence, other electronic communications, memos, or documents of any type referring to First Degree Rape, Robbery, Kidnapping, First Degree Sexual Offense, Hate Crimes, Felony Strangulation, and Assault on a female.

Description of Crimes

First Degree Forcible Rape (N.C.G.S. 14-27.3), First Degree Kidnapping (N.C.G.S.14-39), First Degree Forcible Sexual Offense (N.C.G.S.14-27.4), Common Law Robbery (N.C.G.S., 14-87.1), Felonious Strangulation (N.C.G.S. 14-32 4(b))

Description of Premises to be Searched

The residence to be searched is located at 610 North Buchanan Blvd. in Durham, North Carolina. From the Durham Police District 2 Substation located at 1058 W. Club Blvd, officers will turn left traveling south on Guess Rd which turns into North Buchanan. The residence is on the east side of the street just after W. Markham. The premise to be searched is a one story single family dwelling white in color with black shutters. The shutters are only on the front and right side of the home if looking at the residence from the street. The front door faces west towards the street. There is a green motor vehicle parked in the garage on the East side of the dwelling. The numbers 610 are black and are on the front door of the residence. There are two brick chimney protruding from the roof of the dwelling. A chain link fence runs along the East side of the dwelling.

MAGISTRATE/JUDGE

DATE __3.16.06__

APPLICANT

DATE __3.16.06__

STATE OF NORTH CAROLINA § IN THE GENERAL COURT OF
JUSTICE
DURHAM COUNTY § DISTRICT COURT DIVISION

ATTACHMENT FOR APPLICATION FOR SEARCH WARRANT

Description of Vehicle to be Searched

1996 Green Honda Accord, Virginia License Plate Number JBM-5999
VIN: 1HGCD5654TA199992
And / or
Any vehicle on the curtilage

Description of Person to be Searched

Not applicable - -

IN THE MATTER OF: 610 N. Buchanan, Durham N.C.

Probable Cause Affidavit

The affiant swears to the following facts to establish probable cause for the issuance of a search warrant. I, Inv. B. W. Himan, am a sworn law enforcement officer and have been since 2003. I have been employed as a sworn police officer with the Durham City Police Department since 2003. I am currently an investigator with the Durham City Police Department's Criminal Investigation Division Violent Crimes Unit.

The Criminal Investigations Division has the responsibility of follow-up investigations of the crimes committed by adults and juveniles involving crimes against person and property. The primary objectives of this Division are to provide both investigative and general support to the other Divisions of the Durham Police Department in the accomplishment of establishing departmental goals and objectives. The Violent Crimes and Property Crimes Units are a part of the District 2 Criminal Investigations Division, dedicated to investigation matters of the people within the city of Durham, NC concerning persons.

I have been assigned to the Criminal Investigations Division as an Investigator in District 2. I have been involved in numerous investigations to include domestic violence assaults, robberies, sexual assaults, and homicide investigations. I have received specialized training in the area of criminal investigation over my years with the Durham City Police Department. I have attended the following classes related to Law enforcement:

Interview and Interrogation, Police Law Institute, Field Training Officers School, Street Drug Enforcement for Patrol Officers, and Child Death Investigation. These classes are in addition to hundreds of hours of In-Service Training with the Durham Police.

MAGISTRATE/JUDGE

DATE __3.16.06__

APPLICANT

DATE __3.16.06__

STATE OF NORTH CAROLINA § IN THE GENERAL COURT OF
JUSTICE
DURHAM COUNTY § DISTRICT COURT DIVISION

ATTACHMENT FOR APPLICATION FOR SEARCH WARRANT

On 3/14/06 at 1:22am Durham City Police Officers were called to the Kroger on Hillsborough Road. The victim reported to the officers that she had been sexually assaulted at 610 North Buchanan Blvd. The investigation revealed that the victim and another female had an appointment to dance at 610 North Buchanan Blvd. The victim arrived at the residence and joined the other female dancer. The victim reported that they began to perform their dance in master bedroom area. After a few minutes, the males watching them started to get excited and aggressive. The victim and her fellow dancer decided to leave because they were concerned for their safety. As the two women got into a vehicle, they were approached by one of the suspects. He appoligized and requested they go back inside and continue to dance. Shortly after going back into the dwelling the two women were separated. Two males, Adam and Matt pulled her into the bathroom. Someone closed the door to the bathroom where she was, and said "sweet heart you can't leave." The victim stated she tried to leave and the three males (Adam, Bret, and Matt) force fully held her legs and arms and sexually assaulted her anally, vaginally and orally. The victim stated she was hit, kicked and strangled during the assault and she attempted to defend herself, but was overpowered. The victim reported she was sexually assaulted for an approximate 30 minute time period by the three males. Police went to the residence in the early morning hours shortly after the victim reported the event. The Green Honda was parked at the residence at that time. Officers documented that vehicle was present, and no one would come to the door.

This Affiant is requesting the COURT to issue a warrant to search the residence, outbuildings, trash, and any vehicles on the curtilage of 610 North Buchanan Blvd Durham, North Carolina. In order to search and seize any evidence described under "Evidence to be Seized" from inside the residence of 610 North Buchanan Blvd. Durham, North Carolina.

MAGISTRATE/JUDGE

DATE __3.16.06__

APPLICANT

DATE __3.16.06__

officer was not originally involved in the case. However, absolute technical accuracy in the description of the place to be searched is not necessary. It is required only that an officer executing a warrant can find, perhaps by asking questions of neighborhood residents, the place to be searched.

A warrant may also be issued for the search of a person or an automobile, rather than a place. A warrant to search a person should provide the person's name or at least a detailed description. A warrant to search an automobile should include either the car's license number or its make and the name of its owner.

Search warrants are required to be executed in a reasonable amount of time. For example, federal law requires that a search be conducted within 10 days after the warrant is issued. The federal government and nearly half of the states also have laws limiting the time of day during which search warrants may be executed. In those jurisdictions, searches may be conducted only during daytime hours unless there are special circumstances.

Generally, before law enforcement officers may enter a place to conduct a search, they must first announce that they are law enforcement officers, that they possess a warrant, and that they are there to execute it. The major exceptions to this requirement are situations in which it is likely that the evidence would be destroyed immediately on notification or in which notification would pose a threat to officers. Judges in many jurisdictions also are authorized to issue "no-knock" warrants in some circumstances such as drug busts. However, if officers are refused entry after identifying themselves, they may then use force to gain entry, but only after they have given the occupant time to respond. In short, they cannot legally yell "police officers" and immediately kick down the door. The Supreme Court has held that under ordinary circumstances they must wait at least 15 to 20 seconds (see *United States* v. *Banks*, 2003). Finally, if in the course of conducting a legal search, law enforcement officers discover **contraband** (an illegal substance or object) or evidence of a crime not covered by the warrant, they may seize that contraband or evidence under the plain-view exception (discussed later) without getting a new warrant specifically covering it.

contraband An illegal substance or object.

Arrests with a Warrant Most arrests are made without a warrant. Generally, an arrest warrant is legally required when law enforcement officers want to enter private premises to make an arrest unless there is consent or exigent circumstances (discussed later). An arrest warrant is issued only if substantial and trustworthy evidence supports these two conclusions: (1) a violation of the law has been committed and (2) the person to be arrested committed the violation.

Searches and Seizures without a Warrant In guaranteeing freedom from illegal searches and seizures, the Fourth Amendment protects a person's privacy. Under most circumstances, the amendment requires a warrant signed by a judge to authorize a search for and seizure of evidence of criminal activity. However, Supreme Court interpretations of the Fourth Amendment have permitted warrantless searches and seizures in some circumstances. A person is generally protected from searches and seizures without a warrant in places, such as home or office, where he or she has a legitimate right to privacy. That same protection, however, does not extend to all places where a person has a legitimate right to be. For example, the Supreme Court has permitted the stopping

Samar Kaukab sued the Illinois National Guard and O'Hare International Airport security officers for strip-searching her at the Chicago airport before a flight simply because she was wearing a hijab—a Muslim head scarf. *Were the security officers justified in conducting the strip-search? Why or why not?*

E-mail does not have the same privacy protections as does "regular mail." Depending on where the e-mail is sent from and where it is sent to, privacy rights vary greatly. However, under no circumstances can e-mail messages ever be considered confidential. Both government employees (federal, state, and local) and employees in the private sector have few, if any, privacy rights in the e-mail messages they send or receive. Employers are free to examine all electronic communications stored on their systems. The e-mail messages of government employees may also be available to the public through a freedom of information request. In addition, commercial service providers (such as *America Online*) are permitted to disclose messages to law enforcement officials when they "inadvertently" come across messages containing references to illegal activity. Finally, regardless of the setting (work or home), e-mail can be subpoenaed, discovered, and intercepted under existing wiretap laws.

Source: Erik C. Garcia, "E-mail and Privacy Rights," www.wings.buffalo.edu.

and searching of automobiles under certain circumstances and with probable cause. Several doctrines concerning search and seizure without a warrant have developed over time.

Before 1969, when law enforcement officers arrested a suspect, they could legally search, without a warrant, the entire premises surrounding the arrest. That kind of search is called a *search incident to arrest*, and like a search with a warrant, it required probable cause. Evidence obtained through a search incident to arrest was admissible as long as the arrest was legal.

In 1969, in the case of *Chimel* v. *California*, the Supreme Court limited the scope of *searches incident to an arrest*. The Court restricted the physical area in which officers could conduct a search to the area within the suspect's immediate control. The Court interpreted the area within the suspect's immediate control as an area near enough to the suspect to enable him or her to obtain a weapon or destroy evidence. The Court also ruled that it is permissible for officers, incident to an arrest, to protect themselves, to prevent a suspect's escape by searching the suspect for weapons, and to preserve evidence within the suspect's grabbing area.

The Supreme Court has continued to refine the scope of warrantless searches and seizures incident to an arrest. For example, in 1981, in *New York* v. *Belton*, the Court ruled that after police have made a lawful arrest of the occupant of an automobile, they may, incident to an arrest, search the automobile's entire passenger compartment and the contents of any opened or closed containers found in the compartment. The police had long been able to legally search the automobile's trunk, providing there was probable cause (see *Carroll* v. *United States*, 1925). In *United States* v. *Ross* (1982) the Court held that when police "have probable cause to search an entire vehicle, they may conduct a warrantless search of every part of the vehicle [including the trunk] and its contents, including all containers and packages, that may conceal the object of the search." Then, in 1991, in the case of *California* v. *Acevedo*, the Court ruled that the police, "in a search extending only to a container within an automobile, may search the container without a warrant where they have probable cause to believe that it holds contraband or evidence." The Court will also allow the police, with probable cause, to search an automobile passenger's belongings, if he or she is capable of concealing the object of the search (see *Wyoming* v. *Houghton*, 1999).

In 2008, in *Brendlin* v. *California*, the Court ruled that when police make a traffic stop, a passenger in the car, like the driver, is seized for Fourth Amendment purposes and so may challenge the stop's constitutionality. In this case, Brendlin, a parole violator and passenger in a car that was stopped for a routine registration check, was recognized by one of the police officers, arrested, and searched. The driver and car were searched as well. The police found, among other things, methamphetamine paraphernalia. Brendlin was charged with possession and manufacture of the drug. He moved to suppress the evidence, arguing that the officers had neither probable cause nor reasonable suspicion to make the traffic stop, which was an unconstitutional seizure of his person. The Court agreed with Brendlin and remanded the case for further proceedings not inconsistent with its opinion.

Other Supreme Court decisions have established principles governing when private areas may be searched incident to an arrest. In 1968, for instance, in the case of *Harris* v. *United States*, the Court established the *plain-view doctrine*. Under this doctrine, the police may seize an item—evidence or contraband—without a warrant if they are lawfully in a position to view the item and if it is immediately apparent that the item is evidence or contraband. In 1990, the Court clarified its ruling in *Harris* by adding that the discovery of the item in plain view need not be "inadvertent." That is, the plain-view doctrine applies even when the police expect in advance to find the item in plain view

(*Horton* v. *California*). Also, in 1990, in the case of *Maryland* v. *Buie*, the Court addressed the issue of *protective sweeps*. The Court held that when a warrant-less arrest takes place in a suspect's home, officers, with reasonable suspicion, may make only a "cursory visual inspection" of areas that could harbor an accomplice or a person posing danger to them.

Even a warrantless search not incident to an arrest may be justified under the Supreme Court's *exigent circumstances* doctrine. It permits police to make warrantless searches in exigent, or emergency, situations. Such situations could include a need to prevent the imminent destruction of evidence, a need to prevent harm to individuals, or the hot pursuit of suspects.

Frequently, law enforcement officers are not hampered by the warrant requirement, because suspects often consent to a search. In other words, law enforcement officers who do not have enough evidence to obtain a search war-rant, or who either cannot or do not want to take the time and trouble to obtain one, may simply ask a suspect whether they may conduct a search. If the sus-pect consents voluntarily, the search can be made legally. Law enforcement officers call this strategy "knock and talk." In 1973, in the case of *Schenckloth* v. *Bustamonte*, the Supreme Court upheld the legality of *consent searches*. The Court also ruled that officers do not have to tell suspects that they have a right to withhold consent unless they ask.

It is not surprising that consent searches have become the most common type of searches performed by law enforcement officers. They are used fre-quently in traffic stops and drug interdiction efforts at airports and bus termi-nals. In the 1980s, as a new tool in the war on drugs, several police departments adopted programs in which officers boarded buses and asked passengers to consent to searches. The practice was challenged in a 1985 Florida case in which a bus passenger had consented to having his luggage searched. When the police found cocaine, the passenger was arrested and subsequently con-victed. The Florida Supreme Court ruled that the search was unconstitutional. In 1991, the U.S. Supreme Court reversed the Florida Supreme Court (in *Florida* v. *Bostick*) and held that the search was not unconstitutional and that law enforcement officers may make such a search without a warrant or suspicion of a crime—as long as the passenger feels free to refuse the search.

Critics argue that, in most cases, consent searches cannot be truly volun-tary, even when permission is granted, because most people are intimidated by the police and would have a hard time telling them no. Moreover, most people probably do not know that they may refuse a warrantless search except under the conditions described earlier.

Recently, in the case of *Georgia* v. *Randolph* (2006), the U.S. Supreme Court restricted consent searches of a home. In this case Randolph's estranged wife, concerned about his cocaine use, called the police and, when they arrived, told them they could find cocaine in their bedroom. The police asked her if they could conduct a search, and she consented. Randolph, a lawyer, who was pres-ent at the time, objected to the search, but the police ignored him, entered the house, and found cocaine in the bedroom. Randolph was arrested and subse-quently convicted of drug possession. On appeal, the U.S. Supreme Court, citing the Fourth Amendment's central value of "respect for the privacy of the home," ruled that warrantless searches of a home, even when a co-habitant consented to the search, are prohibited if the other co-habitant is physically present and objects to the search. As a result of the decision, the incriminating evidence was suppressed (that is, not admitted at the retrial). However, the consent of one co-occupant in the absence of another is generally considered sufficient to permit a home search by the police (see *United States* v. *Matlock*, 1974).

In a new twist on consent searches, Boston police recently instituted a new anti-crime program called "Safe Homes," in which they ask parents or legal guardians in high-crime areas for permission to conduct a warrantless search of their children's bedrooms for guns. The police believe that parents who fear their children will become involved in gun violence will let police into their homes to search for guns. If parents refuse, the police will leave. Such searches will not be conducted in the homes of teens suspected in shootings or homicides so as not to jeopardize prosecutions. If officers find drugs in the warrantless search, it will be up to them to decide to arrest; however, according to police brass, modest amounts of drugs such as marijuana will simply be confiscated. Civil libertarians are concerned.[11]

Arrests without a Warrant Officers may not enter a private home to make a warrantless arrest unless there is consent or the offense is a serious one and there are exigent circumstances, such as the likely destruction of evidence or the hot pursuit of a felony suspect. This is the same *exigent circumstances* doctrine that applies to warrantless searches and seizures.

A suspect who is arrested without a warrant and remains confined is entitled to have a judge determine whether there was probable cause for the arrest. Ordinarily, judges must make such a determination within 48 hours of arrest. The purpose of this proceeding is to ensure that the suspect's continuing custody is based on a judicial determination of probable cause and not merely on the police officer's judgment that probable cause supported an arrest.

Standards of Proof As mentioned previously and as specified in the Fourth Amendment, neither search nor arrest warrants can be issued legally unless law enforcement officers convince a judge or a magistrate that there is probable cause to believe either that the specific items to be searched for are related to criminal activity and the items will be found in the place to be searched or that a violation of the law has been committed and the person to be arrested committed the violation. Probable cause is one among a number of standards of proof for various criminal justice activities. The amount of proof necessary depends on the activity in question. Figure 4.3 shows various standards of proof, along a continuum of certainty, and the criminal justice activities that correspond to them.

Toward one end of the continuum is the standard of proof with the least certainty: *mere suspicion*. **Mere suspicion** is equivalent to a "gut feeling." In other words, a law enforcement officer may have a feeling that something is wrong—an uncanny knack that some experienced law enforcement officers possess—but be unable to state exactly what it is. With only mere suspicion, law enforcement officers cannot legally even stop a suspect.

mere suspicion The standard of proof with the least certainty; a "gut feeling." With mere suspicion, a law enforcement officer cannot legally even stop a suspect.

Figure 4.3

Standards of Proof and Criminal Justice Activities

Mere suspicion	Reasonable suspicion	Probable cause	Preponderance of evidence	Clear and convincing evidence	Beyond a reasonable doubt	Absolute certainty
None	Stop and frisk	Search or arrest	Determine "good faith" exception to exclusionary rule; show waiver of right to counsel "knowingly and intelligently"	Make successful claim of insanity in federal courts	Determine guilt in a criminal trial	None

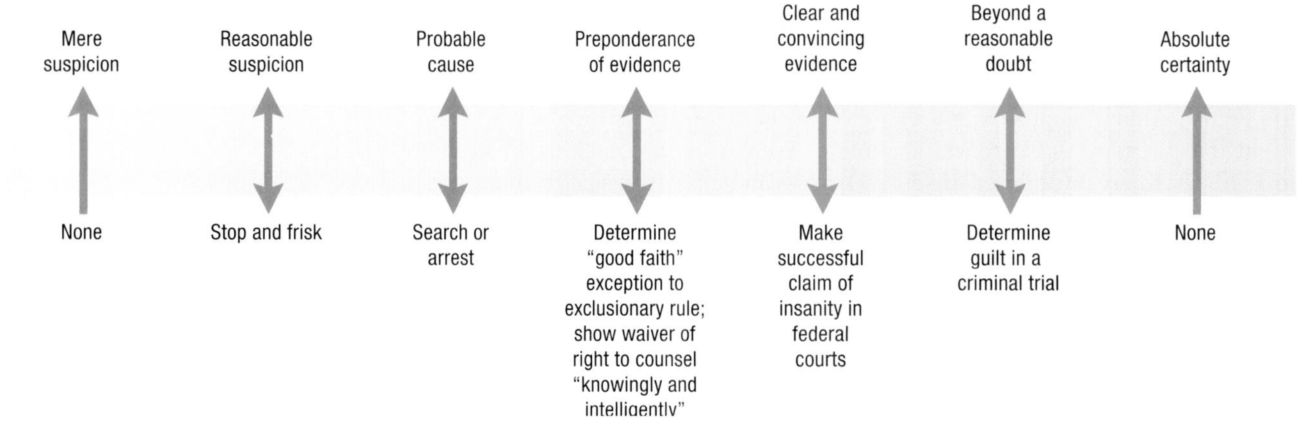

A standard of proof with greater certainty is *reasonable suspicion*. **Reasonable suspicion** is more than a gut feeling. It includes the ability to articulate reasons for the suspicion. For example, if a law enforcement officer observes a person in front of a bank wearing a heavy trench coat on a hot summer day, the officer might have a reasonable suspicion that something is wrong. The officer could state that idling in front of a bank while wearing a heavy trench coat on a hot summer day is suspect behavior. Until recently, an anonymous tip, as long as there were other reliable indicators, could be the basis for reasonable suspicion. However, in *Florida* v. *J.L.* (2000), the Supreme Court ruled that an uncorroborated anonymous tip was unconstitutional.[12] But the Court, in *Illinois* v. *Wardlow* (2000), confirmed that running from the police when they enter a high-crime area is reasonably suspicious behavior.[13] With reasonable suspicion, a law enforcement officer is legally permitted to stop and frisk a suspect (*Terry* v. *Ohio*, 1968). **Frisking** a suspect means conducting a search for weapons by patting the outside of a suspect's clothing, feeling for hard objects that might be weapons. Only if an officer feels something that may be a weapon may he or she search inside a pocket or an article of clothing. If evidence of a crime is discovered, the officer is permitted to make an arrest.

The standard of proof needed to conduct a search or to make an arrest is *probable cause*. The conventional definition of **probable cause** is the amount of proof necessary for a reasonably intelligent person to believe that a crime has been committed or that items connected with criminal activity can be found in a particular place. Although its meaning is not entirely clear—what is "reasonably intelligent"?—probable cause has a greater degree of certainty than reasonable suspicion. For probable cause, law enforcement officers must have some tangible evidence that a crime has been committed, but that evidence does not have to be admissible at trial. Such evidence might include a tip from a reliable informant or the pungent aroma of marijuana in the air. As noted in Chapter 1, probable cause is also the standard of proof used in initial appearances and preliminary hearings.

The line between probable cause and reasonable suspicion, or even mere suspicion, is a fine one and a matter of interpretation. In practice, there are many gray areas. Consequently, criminal courts and the judicial officers who are authorized to approve search warrants have been given the responsibility of determining whether a standard of proof has been met in a particular situation. As noted, search warrants, for example, must generally be approved by a judicial officer before they can be executed. The way courts and judicial officers determine whether a standard of proof has been met will be discussed in detail in Chapter 8. Here we simply observe that, for much of the public, one of the frustrating aspects of criminal justice is that offenders who are factually guilty of their crimes sometimes escape punishment because a judicial officer did not have probable cause to issue a warrant, or a police officer did not have probable cause to make an arrest or have reasonable suspicion to stop and frisk the suspect.

The next standard of proof along the continuum of legal certainty is *preponderance of evidence*. **Preponderance of evidence** is evidence that more likely than not outweighs the opposing evidence, or sufficient evidence to overcome doubt or speculation. It is the standard of proof necessary to find a defendant liable in a civil lawsuit. This standard is also used in determining whether the *inevitable-discovery rule* applies. That is, the prosecution must prove by a preponderance of the evidence that evidence actually uncovered as a result of a constitutional violation would inevitably have been discovered through lawful means, independent of the action constituting the violation. Finally, preponderance of evidence is the standard of proof in criminal proceedings by which the state must show that the right to counsel has been waived "knowingly and intelligently."

reasonable suspicion A standard of proof that is more than a gut feeling. It includes the ability to articulate reasons for the suspicion. With reasonable suspicion, a law enforcement officer is legally permitted to stop and frisk a suspect.

frisking Conducting a search for weapons by patting the outside of a suspect's clothing, feeling for hard objects that might be weapons.

probable cause The amount of proof necessary for a reasonably intelligent person to believe that a crime has been committed or that items connected with criminal activity can be found in a particular place. It is the standard of proof needed to conduct a search or to make an arrest.

preponderance of evidence Evidence that more likely than not outweighs the opposing evidence, or sufficient evidence to overcome doubt or speculation.

clear and convincing evidence The standard of proof required in some civil cases and, in federal courts, the standard of proof necessary for a defendant to make a successful claim of insanity.

beyond a reasonable doubt The standard of proof necessary to find a defendant guilty in a criminal trial.

Next along the continuum of certainty is **clear and convincing evidence,** which is evidence indicating that the thing to be proved is highly probable or reasonably certain. It is the standard of proof required in some civil cases and, in federal courts, the standard of proof necessary for a defendant to make a successful claim of insanity.

Of greater certainty still is proof **beyond a reasonable doubt,** the standard of proof necessary to find a defendant guilty in a criminal trial. "Reasonable doubt," as a standard of proof is a relatively recent concept. It appears to have been used for the first time in the Boston Massacre trials in 1770. Until then, no standards of proof existed in English colonies, and juries only had to return "true verdicts." Not until 1970 (in *In re Winship*) was reasonable doubt, as a standard of proof, made a constitutional requirement in all criminal cases, both federal and state.[14] Reasonable doubt is the amount of doubt about a defendant's guilt that a reasonable person might have after carefully examining all the evidence. In the case of *Sandoval* v. *California* (1994), the Court upheld the following definition of *reasonable doubt:*

> It is *not a mere possible doubt;* because everything relating to human affairs, and *depending on moral evidence,* is open to some possible or imaginary doubt. It is that state of the case which, after the entire comparison and consideration of all the evidence, leaves the minds of the jurors in that they cannot say they feel an abiding conviction, *to a moral certainty,* of the truth of the charge. [Emphasis in original.]

Thus, to convict a criminal defendant in a jury trial, a juror must be convinced of guilt by this standard. However, what is considered reasonable varies, and reasonableness is thus a matter of interpretation. Therefore, the procedural laws in most jurisdictions require that 12 citizens all agree that a defendant is guilty beyond a reasonable doubt before that defendant can be convicted. No criminal justice activity requires absolute certainty as a standard of proof, although standards of "beyond any doubt," "beyond all doubt," "no doubt," "no doubt about the guilt of the defendant," and "moral certainty" (a concept popular in the 17th century) have been proposed for use in capital cases.[15]

exclusionary rule The rule that illegally seized evidence must be excluded from trials in federal courts.

The Exclusionary Rule The **exclusionary rule** was created by the Supreme Court in 1914 in the case of *Weeks* v. *United States.* In *Weeks,* the Supreme Court held that illegally seized evidence must be excluded from trials in federal courts. In 1961, the Warren Court extended the exclusionary rule to state courts in the case of *Mapp* v. *Ohio.* The exclusionary rule originally had three primary purposes: (1) to protect individual rights from police misconduct, (2) to prevent police misconduct, and (3) to maintain judicial integrity (for citizens to have faith in the administration of justice, courts should not admit evidence that is tainted by the illegal activities of other criminal justice officials). Today, however, the principal purpose of the exclusionary rule is to deter the police from violating people's Fourth Amendment rights.

In practice, when suspects want to claim that incriminating evidence was obtained through an illegal search and seizure, that a confession was obtained without the required warnings or was involuntary, that an identification was made as a result of an invalid police lineup, or that evidence was in some other way illegally obtained, they attempt, through their attorneys, to show at a suppression hearing that the search and seizure, for example, violated the Fourth Amendment. If they are successful in their claims, the evidence that was obtained as a result of the illegal search and seizure will not be admitted at trial.

By the late 1970s, public opinion polls showed that Americans were becoming increasingly alarmed about the problem of crime and especially about what they perceived as the practice of allowing a substantial number of criminals to escape punishment because of legal technicalities. One so-called legal technicality that received much of the public's scorn was the exclusionary rule. In 1984, responding at least in part to public opinion, the Supreme Court, under Chief Justice Warren Burger, decided three cases that had the practical effect of weakening the exclusionary rule.

In two of the three cases, *United States* v. *Leon* and *Massachusetts* v. *Sheppard*, a *good faith exception* to the *exclusionary rule* was recognized. The Court ruled that as long as the police act in good faith when they request a warrant, the evidence they collect may be used in court, even if the warrant is illegal or defective. In the *Leon* case, the judge's determination of probable cause turned out to be wrong. Prior to *Leon*, such an error by a judge would have been recognized as a violation of the Fourth Amendment, and the evidence seized with the warrant would have been excluded at trial. The Court reasoned that it was unfair to penalize law enforcement officers who conduct searches in which incriminating evidence is found, when those officers conduct the search in good faith that they have a legal warrant. In the *Sheppard* case, the judge had used the wrong form for the warrant. As in *Leon*, the Court reasoned that it was unfair to penalize law enforcement officers, and the public, just because there was a flaw in the warrant, when the officers had conducted a search in good faith and found incriminating evidence.

The third case, *Nix* v. *Williams*, established an *inevitable-discovery exception* to the *exclusionary rule*. The *Nix* case involved a murderer whom police had tricked into leading them to the hidden body of his victim. In *Nix*, the Court held that evidence obtained in violation of a defendant's rights can be used at trial if the prosecution can show, by a preponderance of the evidence, that the information ultimately or inevitably would have been discovered by lawful means.

The exclusionary rule was again weakened in 1995. In the case of *Arizona* v. *Evans*, the Supreme Court ruled that unlawful arrests based on computer errors do not always require the exclusion of evidence seized by police. In the *Arizona* case, the Court held that a good faith exception to the exclusionary rule could be made as long as the illegal seizure of evidence was caused by the errors of court employees and not the police. In that case, a Phoenix man who had been stopped for a traffic violation was arrested, because a computer record showed an outstanding arrest warrant for some traffic violations. In fact, the warrant had been dropped 17 days earlier, but the action had not been entered into the computer. After the arrest, marijuana was seized from the man's car, and he was arrested for illegal possession.

The PATRIOT Act[16] Less than 2 months after the terrorist attacks of 9/11, and with little debate or scrutiny, Congress passed the "Uniting and Strengthening America by Providing Appropriate Tools Required to Intercept and Obstruct Terrorism Act of 2001" or the USA PATRIOT Act, for short. Among a host of provisions, the law gives broad new powers to the FBI, the CIA, and other U.S. foreign intelligence agencies to spy on American citizens. It also eliminates checks and balances on those powers such as judicial oversight, public accountability, and the ability to challenge government searches in court. For example, the law now allows the FBI to search private records (financial, medical, library, student—any recorded activity) *without a warrant and probable cause* and without having to reveal to anyone what it has done. It is able to do this through the use of "national-security letters," which are administrative subpoenas. According to a recent audit by the Justice Department's Inspector General, the FBI used the "letters" to collect more data than allowed in dozens of cases from 2003 through 2006, and underreported to Congress how many "letters" were requested by more than 4,600. The Inspector General blamed agent error and shoddy record keeping for the problems, while FBI Director Mueller attributed the problem in part to banks, telecommunication companies, and other private businesses providing the FBI more personal client data than was requested.

Under the PATRIOT Act, activist groups such as Operation Rescue, Greenpeace, or the World Trade Organization protesters could be charged with domestic terrorism if they committed specifically defined federal terrorism crimes. *Do you believe those groups engage in domestic terrorism? Why or why not?*

CJ Online

To see the long list of federal terrorism crimes, go to Title 18, Part I, 113B, Section 2332b(g)(5) of the U.S. Code at: http://www.law.cornell.edu/ uscode/html/uscode18/usc_sec_18_ 00002332---b000-.html. Do you agree that all the listed crimes should be considered terrorism crimes? Why or why not?

Also, under the act, the FBI no longer needs probable cause to conduct wiretaps of criminal suspects when "a significant purpose" is gathering intelligence.

The act also creates the new crime of "domestic terrorism." Under the act, members of controversial activist groups, such as Operation Rescue, Greenpeace, or the World Trade Organization protesters, could be charged with domestic terrorism if they committed specifically defined federal terrorism crimes. Even providing lodging or aid to such "terrorists" could initiate surveillance or prosecution. Another provision of the new law allows the U.S. Attorney General to detain noncitizens in the United States after certifying that there are "reasonable grounds to believe" that the noncitizen endangers national security. If a foreign country will not accept such noncitizens who are to be deported, they can be detained indefinitely without trial.

Ironically, as critics point out, most of the PATRIOT Act's changes to surveillance laws were part of a long-standing law enforcement wish list that Congress had repeatedly rejected. The events of 9/11 changed that. Critics also argue that the law was hurriedly passed without determining whether problems with existing surveillance laws contributed to the terrorist attacks and whether the new law would help prevent further attacks. Many of the law's provisions do not even deal with terrorism. Particularly troublesome to many critics is the law's elimination of the checks and balances placed on the government's surveillance powers. Most of those checks and balances were created after it was learned in the 1970s that the government had misused those powers. Among other things, the FBI and the CIA had illegally spied on more than half a million U.S. citizens during the McCarthy era and later. Perhaps the most notorious example of this clandestine activity was the illegal surveillance of Martin Luther King, Jr., during the 1960s. Critics took some comfort that several of the surveillance provisions of the PATRIOT Act were scheduled to expire on December 31, 2005.

However, on March 9, 2006, President Bush signed into law the USA PATRIOT Act Improvement and Reauthorization Act of 2005 (after Congress had temporarily extended the original Act). The legislation made permanent 14 of the 16 USA PATRIOT Act provisions set to expire and placed four-year sunsets on the other two—the authority to conduct "roving" surveillance under the Foreign Intelligence Surveillance Act (FISA) and the authority to request production of business records under FISA. The new act also purportedly added dozens of additional safeguards to protect Americans' privacy and civil liberties. Critics contend the safeguards are inadequate. Among the provisions of the new legislation are the following:

- Authorized the Attorney General to reorganize the Department of Justice by placing the Department's primary national security elements under the leadership of a new Assistant Attorney General for National Security. The new Assistant Attorney General will serve as the Department's primary liaison to the new Director of National Intelligence, and the new Division will gather expertise from across the Department to create a focal point for providing advice on the numerous legal and policy issues raised by the Department's national security missions.

- Provided tools to protect U.S. waterways and seaports from terrorists and thieves, including new or enhanced penalties for crimes such as smuggling goods into or out of the United States or bribing a public official to affect port security with the intent to commit international or domestic terrorism. Would-be terrorists will now face a U.S. Coast Guard empowered with new law enforcement tools for use at sea, including penalties for refusal to stop when ordered to do so and for transporting an explosive, biological agent, chemical weapon, or radioactive or nuclear materials knowing that the item is intended to be used to commit a terrorist act.

- Enhanced penalties for terrorism financing and closed a loophole in terrorist financing through hawalas, informal money transfer networks, rather than traditional financial institutions.

- The Combat Methamphetamine Act made certain drugs used in manufacturing "meth" "scheduled listed chemical products" harder to obtain in unlimited quantities and easier for law enforcement to track. It also enhanced penalties for the manufacture, smuggling, and selling of "meth."

- Eliminated confusion about the appropriate death penalty procedures for certain cases under the Controlled Substances Act and expanded on the authorities governing provision of counsel for death penalty–eligible defendants who are unable to afford counsel.

- Provided clear intent standards and tough penalties for terrorist attacks and other violence targeted at U.S. rail systems and other mass transportation systems regardless of whether they operate on land, on water, or through the air.

- Continued to allow investigators to use so-called section 215 orders—court orders requiring production of business records or any "tangible things"—in all phases of national security investigations. Documents considered more sensitive, such as library, bookstore, medical, tax return, and gun sale records, require that applications to the FISA court for section 215 orders be signed by either the Director or the Deputy Director of the FBI. Recipients of section 215 orders may seek judicial review and disclose receipt of the order to attorneys to obtain legal advice or assistance (something they were prohibited from doing under the original PATRIOT Act). Nevertheless, any employee who discloses a demand for such records, other than to the aforesaid attorney, can be imprisoned for 5 years under the new law.

- Amended the FISA court's authority to issue an electronic surveillance order that attaches to a particular target rather than a particular phone or computer by increasing the level of detail needed to obtain an order and, in most cases, requiring the government to provide notice to the court within 10 days that surveillance had been directed at a new facility or place.

- To avoid adverse consequences such as endangering an individual's life or physical safety, allowed investigators to obtain court permission to delay giving notice that a search warrant had been executed for a presumptive limit of 30 days and extensions of 90 days.

- Limited the PATRIOT Act's broad definition of domestic terrorism to specific federal terrorism crimes, instead of any acts "dangerous to human life" to "influence the policy of a government by intimidation or coercion."[17]

FYI FISA Court

Since its creation in 1978, a secretive federal court known as the Foreign Intelligence Surveillance Act Court, or FISA court, has approved thousands of Justice Department requests to conduct secret searches and surveillance of people in the United States who are suspected of having links to foreign agents or powers, often involving terrorism and espionage. The legislation that created the now 11-member FISA court also established a 3-member Foreign Intelligence Surveillance Court of Review, which has never been used because the FISA court almost always grants the government's requests, and suspects are never notified that they are the target of a search or surveillance. The U.S. Supreme Court has the final authority to review cases from the Court of Review. The Supreme Court's chief justice appoints all members of both courts. The 11 FISA court judges are selected from among U.S. district court judges, and the three judges of the Court of Review are selected from the U.S. district courts or courts of appeals. Judges serve for a maximum of 7 years.

Source: Federal Judicial Center, "Foreign Intelligence Surveillance Court," www.fjc.gov/public/home.nsf/hisc.

As of this writing, the newest developments in PATRIOT Act-related legislation are the "Amendment to the Foreign Intelligence Surveillance Act of 1978," which is referred to as the "Protect America Act of 2007" and the "Foreign Intelligence Surveillance Act of 1978 Amendments Act of 2008," which is also called the "FISA Amendments Act of 2008."[18] The 2008 legislation, which President Bush signed into law on July 10, 2008, reauthorizes many of the provisions in the 2007 legislation. The 2007 Act, which was signed into law by President Bush on August 5, 2007, clarifies the use of electronic surveillance of non-U.S. persons outside the U.S. Under the new laws, a court order is no longer required to collect foreign intelligence information against such a target located overseas. That authority now rests solely with the Attorney General and the Director of National Intelligence. The law thus removes an obstacle from U.S. intelligence agencies to obtain real-time information about the intent of enemies located outside the United States.

Specifically, the law allows U.S. intelligence agencies to collect foreign-to-foreign phone calls and emails as well as all international communications where one party is in the United States, so long as no one particular person in the United States is being targeted. It also requires, under penalty of law, third parties such as telecommunication companies and electronic communication service providers to provide information, facilities, and assistance necessary to conduct the surveillance. Finally, it protects those third parties from past or future lawsuits arising from the assistance they provide the government. Several companies, such as AT&T and Verizon, had been sued for allegedly violating their customers' privacy.

The law does empower the FISA Court to review the efforts of U.S. intelligence agencies to gather foreign intelligence, although, according to critics, it will have no information about how extensive the breach of American privacy is, or the authority to remedy it. Critics contend that the law allowed the Bush Administration, especially the National Security Agency (NSA), to resume a once-secret warrantless wiretapping program it created after 9/11, but was brought under court oversight in January 2007. The ACLU calls the "Protect America Act of 2007" the "Police America Act" and has filed a lawsuit challenging the "FISA Amendments Act of 2008," claiming the new law violates Americans' rights of free speech and privacy under the First and Fourth Amendments.

Clearly, the catastrophic events of 9/11 have had a dramatic effect on American law enforcement and administration of justice. However, whether the changes

Police helicopter conducting aerial surveillance. *Do you believe visual aerial observation without a warrant should be legally allowed? Why or why not?*

that have been implemented and proposed in the wake of those events, such as the PATRIOT Act, the USA PATRIOT Act Improvement and Reauthorization Act of 2005, the Protect America Act of 2007, and the FISA Amendments Act of 2008, are desirable is a fair subject of debate in a free and democratic country.

Of all the due process guarantees in the Bill of Rights, those in the Fourth Amendment are the ones likely to require the most interpretation by the Supreme Court in the future. With advances in the technology of surveillance, the Court will have to determine the legality of increasingly more intrusive ways of gathering evidence. The star of a 1983 science fiction movie was a police helicopter named *Blue Thunder*. The helicopter was able to hover silently outside apartment buildings, record what was being said inside the apartments, and take pictures of what was being done. Although the movie was fictional, it will probably not be long before law enforcement has such equipment—if it does not have at least some of that equipment already. Will evidence obtained by means of the futuristic surveillance technology of *Blue Thunder* violate the Fourth Amendment prohibition against unreasonable searches and seizures?

The Supreme Court likely provided an answer to that question in *Kyllo* v. *United States* (2001). Danny Kyllo was convicted on a federal drug charge after federal agents, suspicious that Kyllo was growing marijuana in his home, used a thermal-imaging device to determine whether the heat coming from his house was consistent with the high-intensity lamps typically used in growing marijuana indoors. Based partly on the thermal imaging, a warrant was issued to search Kyllo's home, where agents found more than 100 marijuana plants growing. The Supreme Court, in a 5–4 ruling, held that the use of the thermal-imaging device before the warrant was issued was an impermissible search of Kyllo's home, violating the Fourth Amendment's prohibition of unreasonable searches and seizures. According to the Court, law enforcement agents must first obtain a search warrant before using high-tech devices to gather information from inside a home. At least for now, then, the use of futurist technology in the surveillance of a home, without a warrant, is legally prohibited. The use of a helicopter for visual aerial observation, however, probably is not (see *Florida* v. *Riley*, 1989).

THE FIFTH AMENDMENT

The Fifth Amendment reads as follows:

> No person shall be held to answer for a capital, or otherwise infamous crime, unless on a presentment or indictment of a Grand Jury, except in cases arising in the land or naval forces, or in the Militia, when in actual service in time of War or public danger; nor shall any person be subject for the same offence to be twice put in jeopardy of life or limb, nor shall be compelled in any criminal case to be a witness against himself, nor be deprived of life, liberty, or property, without due process of law; nor shall private property be taken for public use without just compensation.

Right to Grand Jury Indictment and Protection Against Double Jeopardy The Fifth Amendment right to a grand jury indictment in felony cases, to be described in detail in Chapter 8, is one of the two Bill of Rights guarantees that has not yet been extended to the states (see *Hurtado* v. *California*, 1884). However, the Fifth Amendment protection against **double jeopardy** has been (see *Benton* v. *Maryland*, 1969). The protection provides that no person shall "be subject for the same offence to be twice put in jeopardy of life or limb."

When most people think of double jeopardy, they probably think of the classic case in which a defendant cannot be retried for the same crime or a related crime after he or she has been acquitted or convicted by a jury. However, the protection against double jeopardy can apply even without an acquittal or conviction. Technically, it does not apply until jeopardy has attached. If a trial ends before jeopardy has attached, the prosecution has the right to

double jeopardy The trying of a defendant a second time for the same offense when jeopardy attaches in the first trial and a mistrial was not declared.

retry the defendant for the same charge in a new trial. But, when does jeopardy attach? In jury trials, jeopardy attaches when the entire jury has been selected and sworn in. In a bench trial (a trial before a judge without a jury), jeopardy attaches when the first witness has been sworn in. In cases that are resolved through a guilty plea, jeopardy attaches when the court unconditionally accepts the defendant's plea. Even after jeopardy has attached, however, the prosecution is generally not barred from retrying a defendant when a mistrial has been declared or when a defendant appeals and is granted a new trial.

The theoretical rationale behind the protection against double jeopardy is that the state should have one and only one chance to convict a defendant charged with a crime. Otherwise, the state could endlessly harass its citizens, as sometimes happens in countries without this protection.

Protection Against Compelled Self-Incrimination Arguably, the most important procedural safeguard in the Fifth Amendment is the protection against compelled **self-incrimination.** The protection guarantees that in criminal cases, suspects or defendants cannot be forced to be witnesses against themselves. The protection is based on the belief that confessions may not be truthful if they are not made voluntarily. It also expresses an intolerance for certain methods used to extract confessions, even if the confessions ultimately prove to be reliable. A **confession** is an admission by a person accused of a crime that he or she committed the offense as charged. According to the Supreme Court's **doctrine of fundamental fairness,** confessions are inadmissible in criminal trials if they were obtained by means of either psychological manipulation or "third-degree" methods—for example, beatings, subjection to unreasonably long periods of questioning, or other physical tactics.

Although the Fifth Amendment protection against compelled self-incrimination has long been observed in federal trials, it was not until the 1960s, in the case of *Malloy* v. *Hogan* (1964), that the Fifth Amendment protection against compelled self-incrimination was extended to trials in state courts. In *Miranda* v. *Arizona* (1966), the Court broadened the protection against compelled self-incrimination to cover nearly all custodial police interrogations. (Custodial police interrogations essentially mean questionings that take place after an arrest or the functional equivalent of an arrest; they may or may not take place at the police station.) In *Miranda,* the Court added that confessions obtained without suspects being notified of their specific rights could not be admitted as evidence. Perhaps even more important, it established specific procedural safeguards that had to be followed to avoid violation of the protection against compelled self-incrimination. The Court said:

> Procedural safeguards must be employed to protect the privilege [against self-incrimination], and unless other fully effective means are adopted to notify the person of his right of silence and to assure that the exercise of the right will be scrupulously honored, the following measures are required. [The suspect] must be warned prior to any questioning (1) that he has the right to remain silent, (2) that anything he says can be used against him in a court of law, (3) that he has the right to the presence of an attorney, and (4) that if he cannot afford an attorney one will be appointed for him prior to any questioning if he so desires.

If suspects indicate, before or during questioning, that they wish to remain silent, the interrogation must cease; if they state that they want an attorney, the questioning must cease until an attorney is present. Where an interrogation is conducted without the presence of an attorney and a statement is taken, a heavy burden rests on the government to demonstrate that a suspect knowingly and intelligently waived his or her right to counsel. However, if an individual being questioned is not yet in custody, the *Miranda* warnings do not have to be given. Also, volunteered confessions do not violate *Miranda* or the Fifth Amendment. In 1980, in the case of *Rhode Island* v. *Innis,* the Supreme Court

self-incrimination Being a witness against oneself. If forced, it is a violation of the Fifth Amendment.

confession An admission by a person accused of a crime that he or she committed the offense charged.

doctrine of fundamental fairness The rule that makes confessions inadmissible in criminal trials if they were obtained by means of either psychological manipulation or "third-degree" methods.

FYI Coerced Confessions

The first time the Supreme Court held that a coerced confession, brutally beaten out of the suspect, was inadmissible in a state trial was in 1936, in the case of *Brown* v. *Mississippi.* However, in the *Brown* case, the Court did not find that the coerced confession violated the Fifth Amendment protection against self-incrimination. Rather, the Court found that it violated the Fourteenth Amendment right to due process.

expanded the meaning of interrogation under *Miranda* beyond express questioning "to any words or actions on the part of the police (other than those normally attendant to arrest and custody) that the police should know are reasonably likely to elicit an incriminating response from the suspect."

The Fifth Amendment protection against compelled self-incrimination also has been weakened by the Supreme Court. For example, in *New York* v. *Quarles* (1984), the Supreme Court created a public-safety exception to the Fifth Amendment protection. Also, in *Arizona* v. *Fulminante* (1991), the Court ruled that improper use of a coerced confession is a harmless trial error if other evidence is strong enough to convict the defendant. The burden of proof is on the state to show that a coerced confession is harmless error. The case involved a defendant who had been sentenced to death for killing his 11-year-old stepdaughter. While in prison, the defendant confessed to an FBI informant after the informant promised to protect the defendant from other inmates. Prior to *Fulminante,* such a conviction would most likely have been reversed on appeal because of the use of the coerced confession.

However, in *Dickerson* v. *United States* (2000), the Court reaffirmed the importance of *Miranda,* even when it inconveniences law enforcement officers. In *Dickerson,* a bank robbery suspect asked the Court to throw out incriminating statements he made to FBI agents because he was not given *Miranda* warnings prior to questioning. Prosecutors argued that the suspect made voluntary statements, which were admissible under a law approved by Congress in 1968. The law gives federal judges authority to admit statements from suspects if the judges believe that the statements are voluntary. The Court disagreed and held that Congress did not have the authority to supersede the Supreme Court's interpretation of the Constitution. Therefore, the incriminating statements made by the bank robbery suspect were inadmissible.[19]

The Fifth Amendment protection against compelled self-incrimination also applies to trial procedures. If defendants do not voluntarily take the stand to testify, not only do they have a right to refuse to answer any questions put

Lee Malvo asserted his Fifth Amendment right against self-incrimination at a pretrial hearing in the Washington, D.C. sniper case, when he was asked whether he would testify. He also "took the Fifth" when he was asked whether he knew John Allen Muhammad, Malvo's alleged co-conspirator. *Should Malvo have been compelled to answer the questions? Why or why not?*

to them by the prosecution during a trial (by "pleading the fifth"), but they also have the right not to take the witness stand in the first place. Moreover, the prosecution is forbidden to comment on the defendant's silence or refusal to take the witness stand. This protection rests on a basic legal principle: the government bears the burden of proof. Defendants are not obligated to help the government prove they committed a crime. In 1964 and 1965, those Fifth Amendment rights were extended to defendants being tried in state courts in the cases of *Malloy* v. *Hogan and Griffin* v. *California,* respectively.

THE SIXTH AMENDMENT

The Sixth Amendment reads as follows:

> In all criminal prosecutions, the accused shall enjoy the right to a speedy and public trial, by an impartial jury of the State and district wherein the crime shall have been committed; which district shall have been previously ascertained by law, and to be informed of the nature and cause of the accusation; to be confronted with the witnesses against him; to have compulsory process for obtaining witnesses in his favor, and to have the assistance of counsel for his defence.

Right to a Speedy and Public Trial The Sixth Amendment right to a speedy and public trial applies directly to trials in federal courts. It was extended to trials in state courts in 1967, in the case of *Klopfer* v. *North Carolina* (right to a speedy trial), and in 1948, in the case of *In re Oliver* (right to a public trial). Delays in a trial can severely hamper a defendant's case if favorable witnesses have died, have moved and cannot be found, or have forgotten what they saw. Delays can also adversely affect defendants by forcing them to remain in jail for long periods of time while awaiting trial. A long wait in jail can be a very stressful and sometimes dangerous experience.

In *United States* v. *Marion* (1971), the Supreme Court held that the right to a speedy trial "is activated only when a criminal prosecution has begun and extends only to those persons who have been 'accused' in the course of that prosecution." It added that "invocation of the right need not await indictment, information, or other formal charge but begins with the actual restraints imposed by arrest if those restraints precede the formal preferring of charges." In determining what constitutes a speedy trial, the Supreme Court has created a balancing test that weighs both the defendant's and the prosecution's behavior (see *Barker* v. *Wingo,* 1972). Thus, the reason for the delay in a trial is critical. For example, a search for a missing witness would probably be considered an acceptable reason for delay. Court congestion, on the other hand, typically would not.

The acceptable length of delay in a trial also depends partly on the nature of the charge. In *Barker,* the Court held that "the delay that can be tolerated for an ordinary street crime is considerably less than for a serious, complex conspiracy charge." There has been great variation in the length of delay tolerated by specific courts.

Federal courts are regulated by the Speedy Trial Act of 1974, which specifies two separate time limits: one for the period between arrest and charging, and the other for the period between charging and trial. The act stipulates that, generally, a delay between arrest and charging (that is, the filing of an indictment or information) may be no more than 30 days, and a delay between charging and trial may be no more than 70 days. The act also specifies periods of delay that do not count—for example, delay due to the unavailability of an essential witness or continuances (that is, postponements) that serve "the ends of justice." If the delay, excluding periods of delay that do not count, is longer than the number of days allowed, the court must dismiss the charges. A dismissal with prejudice, which is given when there are no good reasons for the delay, prevents the re-prosecution of the case. A dismissal without prejudice gives the prosecutor the option of prosecuting the case again.

The Sixth Amendment right to a public trial means that a trial must be open to the public, but it need not be open to all who want to attend. Obviously, the number of people who can attend a trial depends on the size of the courtroom. The right would be violated only if the trial were held, for example, in a prison or in a closed judge's chambers against a defendant's wishes. Defendants have no right to a private trial.

A trial may be closed to the public if the defendant's right to a public trial is outweighed by "a compelling state interest." However, before a trial is closed, "the party seeking to close the hearing must advance an overriding interest that is likely to be prejudiced, the closure must be no broader than necessary to protect that interest, the trial court must consider reasonable alternatives to closing the proceeding, and it must make findings adequate to support the closure" (*Waller* v. *Georgia,* 1984). In some cases, parts of a trial may be closed—for example, to protect the identity of an undercover informant during his or her testimony.

Right to Impartial Jury of the State and District Wherein the Crime Shall Have Been Committed

The right to an impartial jury promises not only that a jury will be unbiased but also that there will be a jury trial. As interpreted by the Supreme Court, this right means that defendants charged with felonies or with misdemeanors punishable by more than 6 months' imprisonment are entitled to be tried before a jury. The right was extended to the states in 1968, in the case of *Duncan* v. *Louisiana.* Most states also allow defendants to be tried by a jury for less serious misdemeanors, but states are not constitutionally required to do so.

For practical purposes, the right to an impartial jury is achieved by providing a representative jury, that is, a jury randomly selected from a fair cross section of the community. However, whether members of such a jury will be impartial in a particular case is a question that defies an easy answer. Juries will be discussed more extensively in Chapter 8.

Finally, the Sixth Amendment guarantees the specific **venue,** or the place of trial. (Venue is also mentioned in the Constitution in Article 3, Section 2: "Trial shall be held in the State where the said Crimes shall have been committed. . . .") The venue of a trial must be geographically appropriate. Generally, a crime must be tried in the jurisdiction—the politically defined geographical area—in which it was committed. However, if a defense attorney believes that a client cannot get a fair trial in the appropriate venue because of adverse publicity or for some other reason, the attorney can ask the court for a change of venue. If the change of venue is granted, the trial will be moved to another location (within the state in cases of state law violations), where, presumably, the adverse publicity or other factors are not as great. In 1994, the state of Florida passed a law allowing a jury selected in one county to hear a trial in another county. Before the law, trials—not juries—were moved, often causing hardship to victims' families.

Right to Be Informed of the Nature and Cause of the Accusation

The right to notice and a hearing is the very core of what is meant by due process. In *Twining* v. *New Jersey* (1908), for example, the Supreme Court held that "due process requires . . . that there shall be notice and opportunity for hearing given the parties. . . . [T]hese two fundamental conditions . . . seem to be universally prescribed in all systems of law established by civilized countries." Later, in *In re Oliver* (1948), the Court opined, "A person's right to reasonable notice of a charge against him, and an opportunity to be heard in his defense—a right to his day in court—are basic in our system of jurisprudence." The reason for the

 Jury Trials

The fundamental right to a jury trial, itself, is provided in Article 3, Section 2.3, of the U.S. Constitution: "The Trial of all Crimes, except in Cases of impeachment, shall be by Jury, and such Trial shall be held in the State where the said crimes shall have been committed; but when not committed within any State, the Trial shall be at such Place or Places as the Congress may by Law have directed."

venue The place of the trial. It must be geographically appropriate.

Disorderly defendant removed from courtroom. *Should courts be able to use stun belts to keep disorderly defendants in line? Why or why not?*

subpoena A written order issued by a court that requires a person to appear at a certain time and place to give testimony. It can also require that documents and objects be made available for examination by the court.

right is to prevent the practice, common in some countries, of holding suspects indefinitely without telling them why they are being held.

Right to Confront Opposing Witnesses The Sixth Amendment right to confront opposing witnesses was extended to trials in state courts in 1965, in the case of *Pointer* v. *Texas.* In essence, it means that defendants have a right to be present during their trials (otherwise, they could not confront opposing witnesses) and to cross-examine witnesses against them. However, the right to be present during the trial may be forfeited by a defendant's disruptive behavior. Thus, if a defendant continues to scream, use profanity, or refuse to sit quietly after being warned by the judge, the judge may have the defendant removed from the trial (see *Illinois* v. *Allen,* 1970).

In about 30 states, potentially disruptive defendants may have a stun belt strapped to their waist instead of being shackled. If they become violent or try to escape during court proceedings, a deputy can push a remote-control button that will deliver an 8-second charge of 50,000 volts and 4 milliamps of electricity to the defendants' kidneys. The jolt of electricity will likely knock them to the floor, incapacitate them, and cause them to writhe in pain. They may also lose control of their bladder and bowels. Apparently, the fear of being shocked is enough to keep defendants in line. Nationally, between about 1991 and 2002, the belt had been strapped on 62,000 defendants and had been activated only 34 times.[20]

Right to Compulsory Process for Obtaining Favorable Witnesses This right ensures a defendant the use of the subpoena power of the court to compel the testimony of any witnesses who may have information useful to the defense. A **subpoena** is a written order issued by a court that requires a person to appear at a certain time and place to give testimony. It can also require that documents and objects be made available for examination by the court. Even though the right to compulsory process for obtaining favorable witnesses was already applicable in many states because of its inclusion in state constitutions and laws, the Supreme Court officially extended it to state trials in 1967, in the case of *Washington* v. *Texas.*

Right to Counsel The Sixth Amendment right to privately retained and paid-for counsel has existed in federal courts since the ratification of the Bill of Rights. (The terms *counsel, attorney,* and *lawyer* are interchangeable.) Criminal defendants in state courts did not gain the right until 1954. In the case of *Chandler* v. *Fretag,* the Supreme Court held that the right to a privately retained lawyer is "unqualified," that is, as long as a criminal defendant (or suspect) can afford to hire an attorney, he or she has the right to be represented by that attorney, not only at trial, but at any stage of the criminal justice process. But what if a criminal defendant were indigent, lacking the funds to hire an attorney? The Supreme Court first extended the right to court-appointed counsel to indigents in *Powell* v. *Alabama* (1932). The right, however, was extended only to indigents in death penalty cases who were "incapable adequately of making [their] own defense because of ignorance, feeblemindedness, illiteracy or the like." Moreover, the Court's decision in *Powell* was based on the Fourteenth Amendment right to due process and not on the Sixth Amendment right to counsel. It was not until 1938, in the case of *Johnson* v. *Zerbst,* that the Supreme Court first extended the Sixth Amendment right to court-appointed counsel to indigent defendants facing felony charges in federal trials. Another 25 years passed before the right to court-appointed counsel was extended to indigent defendants facing felony charges in state courts. That right was granted in the famous case of *Gideon* v. *Wainwright* (1963). In 1972, in the case of *Argersinger* v. *Hamlin,* the Court extended the Sixth Amendment right to court-appointed counsel to defendants in misdemeanor trials in which a sentence to jail might result. Thus, as a result of those decisions, no person may be imprisoned for any offense, whether classified as petty, misdemeanor, or felony, unless he or she is represented by counsel. If the person cannot afford to hire an attorney, then the court is required to appoint one. However, if there is no possibility of incarceration, then a defendant has no right to state-furnished counsel (see *Scott* v. *Illinois,* 1979). Later, in *Alabama* v. *Shelton* (2002), the Court added that indigents have a right to court-appointed counsel even when a defendant is given "a suspended sentence that may 'end up in the actual deprivation of a person's liberty.'"

In other Supreme Court decisions, the Sixth Amendment right to counsel has been extended to indigents at additional *critical stages* (described in Chapter 8 and elsewhere in this book) and other circumstances in the administration of justice, "where substantial rights of the accused may be affected." Those include (by date of Supreme Court decision):

1. Arraignment, under most circumstances (*Hamilton* v. *Alabama,* 1961)
2. The plea bargaining process (*Carnley* v. *Cochran,* 1962)
3. Initial appearances where defendants may be compelled to make decisions that may later be formally used against them (*White* v. *Maryland,* 1963)
4. Interrogations after formal charges (*Massiah* v. *United States,* 1964)
5. Post-charge police lineups (*United States* v. *Wade,* 1967; *Gilbert* v. *California,* 1967)
6. Sentencing (*Mempa* v. *Rhay,* 1967)
7. Preliminary hearings (*Coleman* v. *Alabama,* 1970)
8. A psychiatric examination used by the prosecution to show that a murder defendant remains dangerous and should receive the death penalty (*Estelle* v. *Smith,* 1981)

To date, the Court has not extended the Sixth Amendment right to counsel to preindictment lineups, booking, grand jury investigations, or appeals after the first one.

The Sixth Amendment not only guarantees the right to counsel in the areas to which it has been extended, it also guarantees the right to the "effective assistance of counsel" (see *McMann* v. *Richardson,* 1970). However, it was not until 1984, in the case of *Strickland* v. *Washington,* that the Supreme Court first established standards to define "ineffective assistance of counsel." The Court ruled that two facts must be proved to show that counsel was ineffective: (1) that counsel's performance was "deficient," meaning that counsel was not a "reasonably competent attorney" or that his or her performance was below the standard commonly expected, and (2) that the deficiencies in the attorney's performance were prejudicial to the defense, meaning that there is a "reasonable probability that, but for the counsel's unprofessional errors, the result of the proceeding would have been different." In other words, not only must it be shown that an attorney was incompetent, it must also be shown that there is a reasonable probability that the incompetence led to the final result. Thus, if the defendant were clearly guilty of the crime with which he or she was charged, it would most likely be impossible to win a claim of "ineffective assistance of counsel."

Finally, the right to counsel may be waived, but only if the waiver is made knowingly, intelligently, and voluntarily. Thus, the Sixth Amendment has also been interpreted to mean that defendants have the right to represent themselves, that is, to conduct the defense *pro se* (see *Faretta* v. *California*, 1975). However, if defendants choose to represent themselves, they cannot claim later, on appeal, that their defense suffered from ineffective assistance of counsel.

THE EIGHTH AMENDMENT

The Eighth Amendment reads as follows:

> Excessive bail shall not be required, nor excessive fines imposed, nor cruel and unusual punishments inflicted.

Protection Against Excessive Bail and Fines The Eighth Amendment protection against excessive bail and fines is the second Bill of Rights guarantee dealing directly with criminal justice that has not been extended to the states. (The first is the right to a grand jury indictment in felony cases.) However, there is a good possibility that the protection against excessive bail will be incorporated and made applicable to state-level criminal cases when the issue is finally brought before the Supreme Court.

In any event, it is important to note that the Eighth Amendment to the Constitution does not require that bail be granted to all suspects or defendants, only that the amount of bail not be excessive. What constitutes excessive bail is determined by several factors, including the nature and circumstances of the offense, the weight of evidence against the suspect or defendant, the character of the suspect or defendant, the suspect or defendant's ties to the community, and the ability of the suspect or defendant to pay bail. The subject of bail will be discussed more fully in Chapter 8.

The Eighth Amendment also prohibits excessive fines. What is excessive depends on the seriousness of the crime. For example, in a conviction for illegal possession of a small amount of marijuana, a defendant's having to forfeit his or her home might be considered an excessive fine.

FYI Bills of Attainder

The Constitution—in Article 1, Sections 9.3 and 10.1—prohibits bills of attainder. Under English common law, these legal documents stripped convicted offenders of their citizenship and allowed the Crown to confiscate all of their property. Bills of attainder also extended to include offenders' families, who were judged "attainted" and could not inherit the offender's property. Recent civil forfeitures of property in drug violations seem to circumvent the constitutional prohibition. In some cases, property has been confiscated even though the suspect was never arrested or convicted of a crime.

Protection Against Cruel and Unusual Punishments The final prohibition of the Eighth Amendment is against "cruel and unusual punishments." That prohibition was extended to trials in state courts in 1962, in *Robinson* v. *California*. Generally, discussions of this issue involve the practice of capital punishment, or the death penalty, which will be discussed in detail in Chapter 9. Here we will provide only a brief history of the definition of cruel and unusual punishments.

For approximately 120 years after the adoption of the Bill of Rights, the Supreme Court employed a fixed, historical meaning for "cruel and unusual punishments." In other words, the Court interpreted the concept's meaning in light of the practices that were authorized and were in use at the time the Eighth Amendment was adopted (1791). Thus, only the most barbarous punishments and tortures were prohibited. Capital punishment itself was not prohibited, because there was explicit reference to it in the Fifth Amendment and it was in use when the Eighth Amendment was adopted.

The Court, in *Wilkerson* v. *Utah* (1878), provided examples of punishments that were prohibited by the Eighth Amendment because they involved "torture" or "unnecessary cruelty." They included punishments in which the criminal "was emboweled alive, beheaded, and quartered." In another case, *In re Kemmler* (1890), the Court expanded the meaning of cruel and unusual punishments to include punishments that "involve torture or lingering death . . . something more than the mere extinguishment of life." The Court also provided some examples of punishments that would be prohibited under that standard: "burning at the stake, crucifixion, breaking on the wheel, or the like."

Careers in Criminal Justice

Public Defender

My name is Junior A. Barrett, and I am an assistant public defender in the Major Crimes Unit of the Public Defender Office in the Ninth Judicial Circuit (Orange and Osceola Counties in Florida). I have a Bachelor of Science degree in Criminal Justice Administration and Planning from John Jay College of Criminal Justice, City University of New York. I also have a Juris Doctor from Union University, Albany Law School, Albany, New York.

My decision to represent indigent clients was made before I even started college. I wanted to do something that was not only challenging, but where I felt I could help the poor. Growing up on the island of Jamaica and in Brooklyn, New York, I saw what can happen to people who don't receive proper legal representation. I knew people who were railroaded by the criminal justice system and by lawyers who did not really care, but instead saw what they did as just a job.

I started working for the Public Defender's Office in July of 1991 doing misdemeanor and traffic-related offenses. About six years ago, I was promoted to the Major Crimes Unit where I represent clients charged with capital sexual battery and first-degree murder.

My days are never typical. Sometimes they start with a trip to the Orange County Jail to talk to a client about his case and what we will need to do to prepare for court. Another day might begin with me sitting down with an investigator to talk about locating witnesses.

A large portion of my day is spent trying to reconstruct my client's life and reviewing evidence. Reconstructing my client's life involves contacting family and friends of my client. It also involves my spending a lot of time contacting different agencies in order to get copies of my client's school records, medical records, mental health records, military records, job records, and even records of time the client spent in jail or prison. This information is then used to try and convince a jury that my client should not be executed.

Ultimately, everything I do is in preparation for trying the case. A first-degree murder trial usually takes about a week to try. If the death penalty is involved, it can take two weeks. Often, the case does not end at a trial. There are appeals, rehearings, and sometimes even retrials. It is hard to say what I like best and least about my job. Sometimes it is seeing the tears of joy running down the cheeks of my client as a jury says not guilty. Sometimes it is knowing that the State of Florida will not be able to execute my client. Other times it is the camaraderie that I find in the Public Defender's Office. On the flip side, one of the things I enjoy least about my job is a verdict of guilty in spite of the evidence. I also dislike the fact that even after a verdict of not guilty, my client's life is ruined forever. I have had clients who have lost many months of their lives because they were in jail awaiting a final disposition of their case. There is no way to give back to an innocent client the months he sat in jail waiting to be tried by a jury.

The job of an Assistant Public Defender is a morally rewarding one. You deal with real-life situations that are often interesting, challenging, and fast-paced. You put in long hours for little pay. You have to deal with assistant state attorneys who think your clients are scum, judges who care little for your clients' rights, and clients who sometimes verbally abuse you. If you can handle all that, at the end of the day you will feel that you have truly helped another human being. You have to be prepared to fight the good fight.

Would you choose to defend indigent clients? Why or why not?

In 1910, in the noncapital case of *Weems* v. *United States,* the Supreme Court abandoned its fixed, historical definition of cruel and unusual punishments and created a new one. Weems was a U.S. government official in the Philippines who was convicted of making two false accounting entries, amounting to 612 pesos (about $12.40 in 2008 dollars).[21] He was sentenced to 15 years of hard labor and was forced to wear chains on his ankles and wrists. After completing his sentence, he was to be under surveillance for life, and he was to lose his voting rights as well. Weems argued that his punishment was disproportionate to his crime, and, therefore, cruel and unusual.

The Court agreed with Weems and, breaking with tradition, held "(1) that the meaning of the Eighth Amendment is not restricted to the intent of the Framers, (2) that the Eighth Amendment bars punishments that are excessive, and (3) that what is excessive is not fixed in time but changes with evolving social conditions." Thus, the Court no longer interpreted the concept of cruel and unusual punishments in the context of punishments in use when the Eighth Amendment was adopted. Instead, it chose to interpret the concept in the context of "evolving social conditions."

The Court further clarified its position nearly 50 years later, in another noncapital case, *Trop* v. *Dulles* (1958). As punishment for desertion during World War II, Trop was stripped of his U.S. citizenship. In reviewing the case on appeal, the Court ruled that the punishment was cruel and unusual, because

During the Inquisition, heretics were subjected to fire torture on the wheel. *Do you consider this cruel and unusual punishment in violation of the Eighth Amendment? Why or why not?*

it was an affront to basic human dignity. Noting that the "dignity of man" was "the basic concept underlying the Eighth Amendment," the Court held that Trop's punishment exceeded "the limits of civilized standards." Referring to the earlier *Weems* case, the Court emphasized that "the limits of civilized standards . . . draws its meaning from the evolving standards of decency that mark the progress of a maturing society." Those "evolving standards of decency" are, in turn, determined by "objective indicators, such as the enactments of legislatures as expressions of 'the will of the people,' the decisions of juries, and the subjective moral judgments of members of the Supreme Court itself." In short, it appears that a punishment enacted by a legislature and imposed by a judge or jury will *not* be considered cruel and unusual, as long as the U.S. Supreme Court determines that (1) it is not grossly disproportionate to the magnitude of the crime, (2) it has been imposed for the same offense in other jurisdictions, and (3) it has been imposed for other offenses in the same jurisdiction (see *Solem* v. *Helm*, 1983; *Harmelin* v. *Michigan*, 1991; *Ewing* v. *California*, 2003; *Lockyer* v. *Andrade*, 2003).

THINKING CRITICALLY

1. Which of the amendments within the Bill of Rights do you think are the most protective of the rights of the accused? Why?

2. Why is the Bill of Rights subject to interpretation by the Supreme Court?

Protecting the Accused from Miscarriages of Justice

The legal system of the United States is unique in the world in the number of procedural rights that it provides people suspected or accused of crimes. The primary reason for procedural rights is to protect innocent people, as much as possible, from being arrested, charged, convicted, or punished for crimes they did not commit. One of the basic tenets of our legal system is that a person is considered innocent until proven guilty. However, even with arguably the most highly developed system of due process rights in the world, people continue to be victims of miscarriages of justice. For example, attorney Barry Scheck and his colleagues report, "Of the first eighteen thousand results [of DNA tests] at the FBI and other crime laboratories, at least five thousand prime suspects were excluded *before* their cases were tried." In other words, more than 25% of the prime suspects were wrongly accused. Scheck is a co-founder of the Innocence Project at the Cardoza School of Law in New York City.[22]

Unfortunately, there is no official record of miscarriages of justice, so it is impossible to determine precisely how many actually occur each year. Nevertheless, in an effort to provide some idea of the extent of the problem, a study was conducted of wrongful convictions—miscarriages of justice at just one of the stages in the administration of justice.[23] In the study, *wrongful convictions* were defined as cases in which a person [is] convicted of a felony but later . . . found innocent beyond a reasonable doubt, generally due to a confession by the actual offender, evidence that had been available but was not sufficiently used at the time of conviction, new evidence that was not previously available, and other factors.

The conclusions of the study were based on the findings of a survey. All attorneys general in the United States and its territories were surveyed, and in Ohio, all presiding judges of common pleas courts, all county prosecutors, all county public defenders, all county sheriffs, and the chiefs of police of seven major cities were also surveyed. The authors of the study conservatively estimated that approximately 0.5% of all felony convictions are in error. In other words, of every 1,000 persons convicted of felonies in the United States, about 5 are probably innocent. The authors believe that the frequency of error is probably higher in less serious felony and misdemeanor cases.

Although an error rate of 0.5% may not seem high, consider that in 2007, a typical year, approximately 14 million people were arrested in the United States.[24] Assuming conservatively that 50% of all people arrested are convicted[25]— about 7 million convictions in 2005—then approximately 35,000 people were probably wrongfully convicted!

Eyewitness misidentification is the most important factor contributing to wrongful convictions. For example, a study of DNA exonerations by the Innocence Project found that more than 80% of wrongful convictions could be attributed, at

Death Row Reversals

From 1973 through 2008, 130 inmates in 26 states have been freed from death row because of problems or errors in the legal process. Common reasons for reversals include (1) key witnesses lied or recanted their testimony, (2) police overlooked or withheld important evidence, (3) DNA testing showed someone else committed the crime, (4) the defense lawyer was incompetent or negligent, and (5) prosecutors withheld exculpatory evidence from the defense.

Source: The Death Penalty Information Center, www.deathpenaltyinfo.org; Jonathan Alter, "The Death Penalty on Trial," *Newsweek*, June 12, 2000.

Roberto Miranda is one of more than 100 inmates since 1973 who have been released from death row because of evidence of their innocence. Mr. Miranda spent 14 years on Nevada's death row. *What, if anything, does the state of Nevada owe Mr. Miranda?*

least in part, to eyewitness or victim misidentification.[26] The second and third most important contributing factors are police and prosecutorial errors, respectively. They accounted for nearly 65% of the DNA exonerations in the Innocence Project study.[27] Overzealous police officers and prosecutors, convinced that a suspect or defendant is guilty, may prompt witnesses, suggest to witnesses what may have occurred at the time of the crime, conceal or fabricate evidence, or even commit perjury. Another factor contributing to wrongful convictions is guilty pleas made "voluntarily" by innocent defendants. Innocent defendants are more likely to plead guilty to crimes they did not commit when they are faced with multiple charges and when the probability of severe punishment is great. They are also more likely to plead guilty to crimes they did not commit when they are mentally incompetent.

When the charge is a less serious one, innocent people who are unable to post bail sometimes admit guilt to be released from jail immediately. For many people, release from jail is more important than a minor criminal record. Besides, it is often difficult to prove one's innocence. (Remember that in the United States the prosecution is required to prove, beyond a reasonable doubt, that defendants are guilty. Defendants are not required to prove their innocence.) Problems faced by innocent people wrongly accused of crimes include inability to establish an alibi; misidentification by witnesses who swear they saw the defendant commit the crime; a lawyer who lacks the skill, time, or resources to mount a good defense; and a lawyer who is unconvinced of the defendant's innocence. Inadequate legal representation is one of the most important factors in wrongful convictions in death penalty cases.[28] It accounted for nearly a third of the wrongful convictions discovered in the Innocence Project study.[29] Other factors contributing to wrongful convictions are community pressures, especially in interracial and rape cases; false accusations; knowledge of a defendant's prior criminal record; judicial errors, bias, or neglect of duty; errors made by medical examiners and forensic experts; and errors in criminal record keeping and computerized information systems.[30] In short, numerous factors can cause wrongful convictions. And remember, the foregoing discussion addresses only wrongful convictions; it does not consider wrongful arrests or other miscarriages of justice.

What, if anything, can be done about miscarriages of justice? Scheck and his colleagues suggest the following reforms:

- **DNA Testing** Allow postconviction DNA testing nationwide. Test DNA on unsolved crimes where evidence exists.
- **Witness IDs** An independent, trained examiner who does not know the suspect should conduct live lineups and videotape lineups, and handle photo IDs and photo spreads to ensure investigators don't influence witnesses and thereby to ensure neutrality.
- **Confessions** Videotape all interrogations.
- **Informants** A committee of prosecutors should screen all informant testimony before permission to use at trial. All deals between prosecutors and informants must be in writing.
- **Forensics** Crime labs should function and be funded separately from police, prosecution, or defense. Strengthen accreditation programs for labs and establish postgraduate forensic programs at universities.
- **Police, Prosecutors** Establish disciplinary committees to deal with legal misconduct by police and prosecution.
- **Defense Attorneys** Increase fees to attract competent lawyers. Public defenders' pay should equal prosecutors' pay.
- **Wrongful Convictions** Establish innocence commissions to investigate wrongful convictions. Create and fund innocence projects at law schools to represent clients. Provide compensation to those who were clearly wrongly convicted. Have a moratorium on death penalty.[31]

Despite miscarriages of justice, many people still resent the provision of procedural safeguards to criminal suspects. The accusation is frequently made that procedural rights protect criminals and penalize victims—that many criminals escape conviction and punishment because of procedural technicalities. For example, a driving force behind the good faith and inevitable-discovery exceptions was the belief that a substantial number of criminal offenders escaped punishment because of the exclusionary rule. The available evidence, however, does not support the belief. One of the most thorough studies of the effect of the exclusionary rule was conducted by the National Institute of Justice (NIJ).[32] The NIJ study examined felony cases in California between 1976 and 1979—a period during which the American public was becoming increasingly alarmed about the problem of crime and especially about what was perceived as the practice of allowing a substantial number of criminals to escape punishment because of legal technicalities. The study found that only a tiny fraction (fewer than 0.5%) of the felony cases reaching the courts were dismissed because of the exclusionary rule. It is important to emphasize that the study examined only the cases that reached the courts. It excluded cases that prosecutors elected not to pursue to trial because they assumed that the exclusionary rule would make the cases impossible to win. However, studies show that although there is some variation between jurisdictions, fewer than 1% of cases overall are dropped by prosecutors before trial because of search and seizure problems.[33] Interestingly, 71.5% of the California cases affected by the exclusionary rule involved drug charges. The problem in most of the drug cases was that in the absence of complaining witnesses, overaggressive law enforcement officers had to engage in illegal behavior to obtain evidence.

A study of the effect of the exclusionary rule at the federal level was conducted by the General Accounting Office (GAO).[34] The GAO examined 2,804 cases handled by 38 different U.S. attorneys in July and August of 1978. The GAO found results similar to those found by the NIJ in California. In only 1.3% of the nearly 3,000 cases was evidence excluded in the federal courts. Again, note that the study included only cases that went to trial. However, as noted earlier, evidence shows that, overall, fewer than 1% of cases are dropped by prosecutors before trial because of search and seizure problems. Moreover, having evidence excluded from trial does not necessarily mean that a case is impossible to win and that the defendant will escape punishment. A defendant may still be convicted on the basis of evidence that was not illegally obtained.

The *Miranda* mandates, like the exclusionary rule, are also viewed by many people as legal technicalities that allow guilty criminals to escape punishment. That view is fortified by Supreme Court Justice Byron White's dissent in *Miranda:* "In some unknown number of cases the rule will return a killer, a rapist or other criminal to the streets." No doubt, Justice White's warning is true, but the evidence suggests that only a very small percentage of cases are lost as a result of illegal confessions. In one large survey, for example, fewer than 1% of all cases were thrown out because of confessions illegally obtained.[35]

In another study of decisions made by the Indiana Court of Appeals or the Indiana Supreme Court from November 6, 1980, through August 1, 1986, the researchers found that in only 12 of 2,354 cases (0.51%) was a conviction overturned because of the failure of the police to correctly implement the *Miranda* safeguards.[36] In only 213 of the 2,354 cases (9%) was a claim even made about improper interrogation procedures by the police, and in 201 of those 213 cases, the conviction was affirmed by the appellate court, resulting in a reversal rate of 5.6% for the cases raising a *Miranda* question.

The authors of that study speculated on possible reasons for the low rate of successful appeals. One was that the police routinely comply with the

CJ Online

NIJ

Learn more about the National Institute of Justice and its various research findings by accessing their website at www.ojp.usdoj.gov/nij. *Why is it important to have research organizations such as the NIJ?*

MYTH

Many criminals escape punishment because of the Supreme Court's decision in *Miranda* v. *Arizona.*

FACT

Very few criminals escape punishment because of that decision.

My name is Renée Daniel, and I have an Associate of Applied Science Degree in Paralegal Studies from State Technical Institute at Memphis now called Southwest Tennessee Community College. Currently I am a senior pursuing a Bachelor of Arts Degree in Criminology and Criminal Justice from the University of Memphis. After graduating from State Tech, I was chosen by the chairperson and associate professors of the Paralegal Studies Department to be the recipient of a scholarship to pursue my Bachelor's Degree and also work as a paralegal in the Shelby County Jail Law Library.

Prior to graduating from State Tech, I interned as a paralegal for the Shelby County Division of Corrections. As a paralegal intern I had the opportunity to learn the various duties and responsibilities a paralegal encounters. During my internship I was able to review and answer inmate disciplinary appeals, draft documents, review discovery for litigation, and research case law and brief cases.

As a paralegal in the County Jail I assist inmates/pretrial detainees with legal research. Inmates are scheduled to report to the law library through program services in groups. My job involves assisting them in locating case law, statutes, sentencing guidelines, information pertaining to criminal procedure, pretrial motions, and petitions. I act as a liaison between the inmates and the courts by verifying all outgoing legal calls. I have contacted

attorneys, probation officers, parole officers, court clerks, and on some occasions, Immigration and Naturalization Services. My duties as a paralegal not only involve assisting inmates with preparation for trial/appeal but also managing and organizing the law library. I log and inventory all legal material that comes to the library and supervise the placement and rotation of books and supplements. In order to adequately assist the inmates with significant research, the legal material must be monitored at all times. I consult frequently with practicing attorneys regarding relevant substantive and procedural legal material that would help those who are preparing for trial or filing motions. If we do not already have the material, I submit a request to the director of programs to order necessary items.

The aspect I like most about my job is the opportunity I have to utilize the skills I have learned in the Paralegal Studies and Criminology and Criminal Justice programs. I enjoy legal research and applying legal principles to substantive crimi-

nal law. My job allows me to see firsthand how the criminal justice system works from arrest to sentencing and appeal. What I like least about my job are the imperfections that exist in the criminal justice system. I often see several inmates who have been detained in the jail for a year or more before they are indicted. There have been cases where inmates have served their entire sentences in the jail by the time they go to trial. Another aspect about my job that I like least is the destructive behavior that some inmates display by destroying legal books. Once these books are destroyed it is difficult to have them replaced.

Paralegals work in several areas of the legal system with knowledge of substantive and procedural law. A paralegal has the opportunity to work in numerous areas of the law. I would advise paralegal students to intern first to gain insight and experience in the area of law in which they wish to work.

What type of growth opportunities would you expect as a paralegal?

Miranda decision. In fact, most police support *Miranda* and the other reforms because it makes them appear more professional. The second possible reason was that the police are able to solve most cases without having to question suspects. Studies show that the *Miranda* warnings rarely stop suspects from confessing anyway. Nearly 80% of suspects waive their Miranda rights. As many as 75% of suspects attempt to clear themselves in the eyes of the police and end up incriminating themselves instead; other suspects simply do not understand that they have a right to remain silent.[37] Third, the police are able to evade *Miranda* by using more-sophisticated strategies, such as skillfully suggesting that suspects volunteer confessions or casually talking with suspects in the back of squad cars.[38] And, fourth, prosecutors, knowing that they cannot win cases involving illegal interrogations, screen them out before trial or settle them through alternative means, such as plea bargaining. However, as with the exclusionary rule, fewer than 1% of cases overall are dismissed or handled in other ways by prosecutors because of *Miranda*.[39] In short, the available evidence suggests that the effects of both *Miranda* and the exclusionary rule in Fourth and Fifth Amendment contexts have been minor.[40]

THINKING CRITICALLY

1. Do you think miscarriages of justice are on the increase? Decrease? Why or why not?
2. Do you think that anything can be done to combat miscarriages of justice?

✳ Summary

1. Distinguish between criminal law and civil law.

   There are two general types of law practiced in the United States—criminal and civil. Criminal law is a formal means of social control that involves the use of rules that are interpreted, and are enforceable, by the courts of a political community. The violation of a criminal law is a crime and is considered an offense against the state. Civil law is a means of resolving conflicts between individuals. The violation of a civil law is a tort—an injury, damage, or wrongful act—and is considered a private matter between individuals.

2. Distinguish between substantive law and procedural law.

   There are two types of criminal law—substantive and procedural. Substantive law defines criminal offenses and their penalties. Procedural law specifies the ways in which substantive laws are administered. Procedural law is concerned with due process of law—the rights of people suspected of or charged with crimes.

3. List five features of "good" criminal laws.

   Ideally, good criminal laws should possess five features: (1) politicality, (2) specificity, (3) regularity, (4) uniformity, and (5) penal sanction.

4. Explain why criminal law is a political phenomenon.

   Criminal law is the result of a political process in which rules are created by human beings to prohibit or regulate the behavior of other human beings. Nothing is criminal in and of itself; only the response of the state makes it so.

5. Summarize the origins of American criminal law.

   The criminal law of the United States is, for the most part, derived from the laws of England and is the product of constitutions and legislative bodies, common law, and, if provided for by statute, some administrative or regulatory agency rules and decisions.

6. Describe the procedural rights in the Fourth Amendment.

   The Fourth Amendment protects persons from unreasonable searches and seizures (including arrests). Under most circumstances, it requires that a judge issue a search warrant authorizing law officers to search for and seize evidence of criminal activity, but the warrant can be issued only when there is probable cause. In 1914, the Supreme Court adopted the *exclusionary rule,* which barred evidence seized illegally from being used in a criminal trial; in 1961, the rule was made applicable to the states. Subsequent Supreme Court decisions have narrowed the application of the exclusionary rule. The Fourth Amendment also protects persons from warrantless searches and seizures in places where they have a legitimate right to expect privacy. The protection, however, does not extend to every place where a person has a legitimate right to be. The Court has permitted stopping and searching an automobile when there is probable cause to believe the car is carrying something illegal.

7. Describe the procedural rights in the Fifth Amendment.

   The Fifth Amendment provides many procedural protections, the most important of which is the protection against compelled self-incrimination. This protection was extended to most police custodial interrogations in the 1966 case of *Miranda* v. *Arizona.* According to *Miranda,* police custody is threatening and confessions obtained during custody can be admitted into evidence only if suspects have been (1) advised of their constitutional right to remain silent, (2) warned that what they say can be used against them in a trial, (3) informed of the right to have an attorney, and (4) told that if they cannot afford an attorney, one will be appointed for them prior to questioning, if they so desire. Suspects may waive their *Miranda* rights, but only if the waiver is made knowingly, intelligently, and voluntarily. Other due process rights in the Fifth Amendment are the right to a grand jury indictment in felony cases (in federal court) and protection against double jeopardy.

8. Describe the procedural rights in the Sixth Amendment.

   Many due process rights are provided by the Sixth Amendment: the right to a speedy and public trial, the right to an impartial jury of the state and district where the crime occurred, the right to be informed of the nature and cause of the accusation, the right to confront opposing witnesses, the right to compulsory process for obtaining favorable witnesses, and the right to counsel. In the 1963 case of *Gideon* v. *Wainwright,* the Supreme Court extended the right to court-appointed counsel to any poor state defendant charged with a felony.

9. Describe the procedural rights in the Eighth Amendment.

   The Eighth Amendment protects against "cruel and unusual punishments." The Supreme Court has rarely ruled on this provision, generally approving a punishment as long as it has been enacted by a legislature, it has been imposed by a judge or jury, and the Court determines that (1) it is not grossly disproportionate to the magnitude of the crime, (2) it has been imposed for the same offense in other jurisdictions, and (3) it has been imposed for other offenses in the same jurisdiction. The Eighth Amendment also protects against excessive bail and fines, but those protections have not been made binding on state courts.

10. Explain why procedural rights are important to those accused of crimes.

    The primary reason for procedural rights is to protect innocent people, as much as possible, from being arrested, charged, convicted, or punished for crimes they did not commit. However, even with the most highly developed system of procedural, or due process, rights in the world, criminal defendants in the United States still face miscarriages of justice.

✳ Key Terms

criminal law 100	substantive law 101	specificity 102	precedent 106
penal code 100	procedural law 101	regularity 102	*stare decisis* 106
tort 100	due process of law 101	uniformity 102	searches 110
civil law 100	politicality 102	penal sanction 102	seizures 111

warrant 111	probable cause 117	beyond a reasonable	confession 124
arrest 111	preponderance of	doubt 118	doctrine of fundamental
contraband 113	evidence 117	exclusionary rule 118	fairness 124
mere suspicion 116	clear and convincing	double jeopardy 123	venue 127
reasonable suspicion 117	evidence 118	self-incrimination 124	subpoena 128
frisking 117			

✳ Review Questions

1. How does one know whether a particular offense is a *crime* or a *tort?*

2. How did the institution of the *eyre* contribute to the development of American criminal law?

3. What is the importance of the Magna Carta for American criminal law?

4. To what jurisdiction do federal and state criminal statutes (and local ordinances) apply?

5. What is *stare decisis?*

6. Why did it take nearly 100 years after the ratification of the Fourteenth Amendment before suspects charged with crimes at the state level were afforded most of the same due process protections as people charged with crimes at the federal level?

7. What are *searches* and *seizures?*

8. What is an *arrest?*

9. What two conclusions must be supported by substantial and trustworthy evidence before either a search warrant or an arrest warrant is issued? (The two conclusions are different for each type of warrant.)

10. In *Chimel* v. *California* (1969), what limitations did the U.S. Supreme Court place on searches incident to an arrest?

11. What is *probable cause?*

12. Today, what is the principal purpose of the exclusionary rule?

13. What are the major provisions of the PATRIOT Act?

14. To what critical stages in the administration of justice has the Sixth Amendment right to counsel been extended, and to what critical stages has it not been extended?

15. What two conditions must be met to show that counsel was ineffective?

16. What are some of the factors that contribute to wrongful convictions?

17. Do many criminals escape conviction and punishment because of procedural technicalities, such as the exclusionary rule or the *Miranda* mandates?

✳ In the Field

1. **Make a Law** By yourself or as part of a group, create a law. Choose a behavior that is currently not against the law in your community, and write a statute to prohibit it. Make sure that all five features of "good" criminal laws are included. (If this is a group exercise, decide by majority vote any issue for which there is not a consensus.) Critique the outcome.

2. **Exclusionary Rule** Make an oral or a written evaluation of the good faith and inevitable-discovery exceptions to the exclusionary rule. Has the Supreme Court gone too far in modifying the exclusionary rule? Defend your answer.

✳ On the Net

1. **Historical Perspectives** "The Timetable of World Legal History" found at www.duhaime.org/LegalResources/ LawMuseum/LawArticle-44/Duhaimes-Timetable-of-World-Legal-History.aspx provides brief descriptions of important historical legal developments. (This website also provides links to other sources of legal information.) Choose among the available topics (for instance, the actual text of the Magna Carta), and write a summary of the information you find.

2. **Supreme Court Decisions** Access the Supreme Court website at www.supremecourtus.gov. Then select subjects of interest (especially Fourth, Fifth, Sixth, and Eighth Amendment cases), and read the Supreme Court's most recent decisions.

✳ Critical Thinking Exercises

MEGAN'S LAW

1. The sexual assault and murder of 7-year-old Megan Kanka in New Jersey on October 31, 1994, struck a national nerve. Megan was assaulted and killed by a neighbor, Jesse Timmendequas, who had twice been convicted of similar sex offenses and was on parole. In response to the crime and public uproar, the state of New Jersey enacted "Megan's Law." The law, as originally passed, required sex offenders, upon their release from prison, to register with New Jersey law enforcement authorities, who are to notify the public about their release. The public was to be provided with the offender's name; a recent photograph; a physical description; a list of the offenses for which he or she was convicted; the offender's current address and place of employment or school; and the offender's automobile license plate number. The Supreme Court has upheld Megan's Law.

   Currently, all 50 states and the federal government have Megan's laws that require sex offenders released from prison to register with local law enforcement authorities. Many of those laws, like New Jersey's, require that law enforcement officials use the information to notify schools and day-care centers and, in some cases, the sex offender's neighbors. In 1997, California enacted a law allowing citizens access to a CD-ROM with detailed information on 64,000 sex offenders living in California who had committed a broad range of sex crimes since 1944. Megan's laws are not uniform across states. For example, not all states require active community notification; many of them (including the U.S. government) make the information available only to the public.

   In 1996, President Clinton signed into law the Pam Lyncher Sexual Offender Tracking and Identification Act, which called for a national registry of sex offenders, to be completed by the end of 1998. The national registry allows state officials to submit queries, such as the name of a job applicant at a day-care center, and to determine whether the applicant is a registered sex offender in any of the participating states.

   a. Is Megan's Law a good law? (Consider the ideal characteristics of the criminal law.)
   b. Is Megan's Law fair to sex offenders who have served their prison sentences (that is, "paid their debt to society")?
   c. What rights does a sex offender have after being released from prison?
   d. What rights does a community have to protect itself from known sex offenders who have been released from prison?
   e. When the rights of an individual and the rights of a community conflict, whose rights should take precedence? Why?

SURVEILLANCE CAMERAS

2. In January 1998, police in Cincinnati, Ohio, began using a special video camera to monitor activity on a "crime-ridden street corner." The camera, which cost $11,000, rotates, enabling it to observe activity in a 1,000-foot radius. It records 24 hours a day, and it can read a license plate number from more than a block away. To protect privacy, policy requires that all tapes be erased after 96 hours if they show no criminal activity. Residents of the area claim that the camera's presence has cleaned up the area by, among other things, scaring away drug dealers. A 2006 report estimated that a quarter of major American cities were investing in the surveillance technology. Critics worry about government spying on residents. The Cincinnati city council is considering putting cameras in other parts of the city.

   a. Should the city council have surveillance cameras installed in other parts of the city? Why or why not?
   b. What legal or procedural issues should be considered before making a decision?

To access more information and resources, including study questions, chapter summaries, and links, go to: www.mhhe.com/bohm6e.

PART **TWO**

Law Enforcement

History and Structure of American Law Enforcement

Chapter Outline

Chapter Objectives

After completing this chapter, you should be able to:

1. Briefly describe the jurisdictional limitations of American law enforcement.

2. Trace the English origins of American law enforcement.

3. Discuss the early development of American law enforcement.

4. Describe the major developments that have occurred in American policing.

5. Describe the structure of American law enforcement.

6. Explain the relationship between the FBI and the Department of Homeland Security.

7. Discuss the development and growth of private security in the United States.

On December 8, 2008, the FBI arrested Illinois Governor Rod Blagojevich and his Chief of Staff, John Harris, on federal corruption charges. Both men were charged with conspiracy to commit mail and wire fraud and solicitation of bribery for (1) attempting to obtain personal financial benefits for Blagojevich by leveraging his sole authority to appoint a United States Senator to the seat vacated by President Barack Obama; (2) threatening to withhold substantial assistance to the Tribune Company in connection with the sale of the Chicago Cubs baseball team's Wrigley Field to induce the firing of *Chicago Tribune* editorial board members sharply critical of Blagojevich; and (3) obtaining campaign contributions in exchange for official actions before a new state ethics law took effect January 1, 2009.

A 76-page FBI affidavit alleges that Blagojevich was intercepted on court-authorized wiretaps conspiring to sell or trade Illinois' U.S. Senate seat vacated by President Barack Obama for financial and other personal benefits for himself and his wife, including (1) substantial salary for himself at either a nonprofit foundation or an organization affiliated with labor unions; (2) placing his wife on paid corporate boards where he speculated she might receive as much as $150,000 a year; (3) promises

of campaign funds, including cash up front; and (4) a cabinet post or ambassadorship for himself. The affidavit further revealed that, while talking on the phone about the Senate seat with Harris and an advisor, Blagojevich said he needed to consider his family and that he was "financially hurting." Harris allegedly said they were considering what would help the financial security of the Blagojevich family and what would keep Blagojevich "politically viable." Blagojevich replied, "I want to make money," adding later he was interested in making $250,000 to $300,000 a year. In another phone conversation Blagojevich and others discussed various ways Blagojevich could "monetize" the relationships he had made as governor to make money after leaving office.

In the earliest intercepted conversation, Blagojevich was overheard saying that if he were not going to get anything of value for the open Senate seat, then he would take it for himself. His reasons for doing so were: (1) frustration at being "stuck" as governor; (2) a belief that he would be able to obtain greater resources if he were indicted as a sitting senator as opposed to a sitting governor; (3) a desire to remake his image in consideration of a possible run for president in 2016; (4) avoiding impeachment by the Illinois legislature; (5) making corporate contacts that would be of value to him after leaving public office; (6) facilitating his wife's employment as a lobbyist; and (7) generating speaking fees should he decide to leave public office.

The investigation was part of Operation Board Games, a 5-year-old

public corruption investigation of pay-to-play schemes, including insider dealing, influence peddling and kickbacks involving private interests and public duties. Blagojevich has proclaimed his innocence. Nevertheless, on January 29, 2009, Blagojevich was unanimously convicted at his impeachment trial and removed from office. Blagojevich still faces a federal indictment and likely trial on the corruption charges.

Chapter 5 examines the history and structure of American law enforcement. Law enforcement agencies often cooperate with one another in criminal investigations. That way, they can draw on the special expertise and jurisdiction of officers in different agencies. For example, in the Blagojevich case, Patrick Fitzgerald, U.S. Attorney for the Northern District of Illinois, and Robert Grant, Special Agent-in-Charge of the FBI's Chicago Office, thanked the Chicago offices of the Internal Revenue Service Criminal Investigation Division, the U.S. Postal Inspection Service, and the U.S. Department of Labor Office of Inspector General for their assistance in the investigation. The FBI may not have been able to make a case, or as strong a case, against Blagojevich without the cooperation of those other agencies. Cooperation among law enforcement agencies is especially important in the war on terrorism; yet, many of these agencies have a history of "guarding their own turf." How can law enforcement agencies be made to cooperate more fully with one another? That is an important issue for political leaders at all levels of government.

The Limited Authority of American Law Enforcement

The United States has almost 18,000 public law enforcement agencies at the federal, state, and local levels of government. The vast majority of those agencies, however, are local, serving municipalities, townships, villages, and counties. The authority of each agency—whether it is the FBI, a state highway patrol, or a county sheriff's department—is carefully limited by law. The territory within which an agency may operate is also restricted. The city police, for example, may not patrol or answer calls for service outside the city's boundaries unless cooperative pacts have been developed. **Jurisdiction,** which is defined as a specific geographical area, also means the right or authority of a justice agency to act in regard to a particular subject matter, territory, or person. It includes the laws a particular police agency is permitted to enforce and the duties it is allowed to perform. The Oklahoma Highway Patrol, for example, has investigative and enforcement responsibilities only in traffic matters, while the Kentucky State Police have a broader jurisdiction that includes the authority to conduct criminal investigations throughout the state. Each of the 69 federal law enforcement agencies, large and small, has a specific jurisdiction, although one criminal event may involve crimes that give several federal agencies concurrent jurisdiction. For example, in a bank robbery, if mail of any sort is taken, both the Postal Inspection Service and the FBI are likely to investigate the case.

Beyond the statutes that create and direct law enforcement agencies, the procedural law derived from U.S. Supreme Court decisions also imposes limitations on the authority of those agencies. Giving arrested suspects the familiar *Miranda* warnings before questioning is a good example of the Court's role in limiting the authority of the police. In addition, police civilian review boards, departmental policies and procedures, and civil liability suits against officers who have abused their authority curtail the power of the police in the United States.

jurisdiction The right or authority of a justice agency to act in regard to a particular subject matter, territory, or person.

The only police contact most citizens have is in a traffic situation in a local or state jurisdiction. *Should citizens have more contact with the police in non-law-enforcement situations? Why or why not?*

Thus, there is a great difference between law enforcement with limited authority, operating under the rule of law in a democratic nation, and law enforcement in countries where the law is by decree and the police are simply a tool of those in power. Even in comparison with other democratic nations of the world, however, the United States has remarkably more police agencies that operate under far more restrictions on their authority. To understand the origin of those unique qualities of law enforcement in the United States, it is necessary to look first at the history of law enforcement in England, the nation that provided the model for most of American criminal justice.

THINKING CRITICALLY

1. Why do you think it is important that law enforcement agencies have limited authority?

English Roots

If you are the victim of a crime, you might expect that a uniformed patrol officer will respond quickly to your call and that a plainclothes detective will soon follow up on the investigation. Because there are thousands of police departments in local communities across the nation, you might also take for granted that the police handling your case are paid public servants employed by your city or county. Such was not always the case in the United States—or in England, where the basic concepts of American law enforcement and criminal justice originated. The criminal justice system in England took hundreds of years to develop, but eventually the idea arose of a locally controlled uniformed police force with follow-up plain clothes investigators.

THE TITHING SYSTEM

tithing system A private self-help protection system in early medieval England, in which a group of 10 families, or a *tithing,* agreed to follow the law, keep the peace in their areas, and bring law violators to justice.

shire reeve In medieval England, the chief law enforcement officer in a territorial area called a *shire;* later called the *sheriff.*

posses Groups of able-bodied citizens of a community, called into service by a sheriff or constable to chase and apprehend offenders.

constable-watch system A system of protection in early England in which citizens, under the direction of a constable, or chief peacekeeper, were required to guard the city and to pursue criminals.

constable The peacekeeper in charge of protection in early English towns.

Before the twelfth century in England, justice was primarily a private matter based on revenge and retribution.[1] Victims of a crime had to pursue perpetrators without assistance from the king or his agents. Disputes were often settled by blood feuds, in which families would wage war on each other. By the twelfth century, a system of group protection had begun to develop. Often referred to as the **tithing system** or the frankpledge system, it afforded some improvements over past practices. Ten families, or a *tithing,* were required to become a group and agree to follow the law, keep the peace in their areas, and bring law violators to justice. Over even larger areas, 10 tithings were grouped together to form a *hundred,* and one or several hundred constituted a *shire,* which was similar to a modern American county. The shire was under the direction of the **shire reeve** (later called the *sheriff*), the forerunner of the American sheriff. The shire reeve received some assistance from elected constables at the town and village levels, who organized able-bodied citizens into **posses** to chase and apprehend offenders.[2] County law enforcement agencies in the United States still sometimes use posses to apprehend law violators. The Maricopa County (Arizona) Sheriff's Department, for example, has a 3,000-member volunteer posse, whose members are trained and often-former deputies.[3]

THE CONSTABLE-WATCH SYSTEM

The Statute of Winchester, passed in 1285, formalized the **constable-watch system** of protection. The statute provided for one man from each parish to be selected as **constable,** or chief peacekeeper. The statute further granted constables the power to draft citizens as watchmen and require them to guard the city at night. Watchmen were not paid for their efforts and, as a result, were often found sleeping or sitting in a pub rather than performing their duties. In addition, the statute required all male citizens between the ages of 15 and 60 to maintain weapons and to join in the *hue and cry*, meaning to come to the aid of the constable or the watchman when either called for help. If they did not come when called, the male citizens were subject to criminal penalties for aiding the offender. This system of community law enforcement lasted well into the 1700s.

Two features of this system are worthy of note. First, the people were the police, and second, the organization of the protection system was local. These two ideas were transported to the American colonies centuries later.

THE BOW STREET RUNNERS

In 1748, Henry Fielding, a London magistrate, founded a group of professional law enforcement agents to apprehend criminals and recover stolen property in the entertainment district of London, known as Bow Street Covent Garden. This publicly funded detective force, named the Bow Street Runners, was by far the most effective official law enforcement organization of its day. Efforts to duplicate it in other parts of London proved unsuccessful, but Fielding's work in organizing the first British detective force, and his writing addressing the shortcomings of the criminal justice system, had a great deal of influence. They helped pave the way for a more professional and better-organized response to the crime problems that were dramatically increasing in London by the end of the eighteenth century.[4]

THE LONDON METROPOLITAN POLICE

Because of the Industrial Revolution, urban populations in cities like London swelled with an influx of people from the countryside looking for work in factories. A major result of this social transformation was that England began experiencing increasing poverty, public disorder, and crime. There was no clear consensus about what to do. Several efforts to establish a central police force for London had been opposed by people who believed that police of any

Henry Fielding

Henry Fielding, founder of the Bow Street Runners, is perhaps better known for his literary accomplishments. His most famous work is *Tom Jones,* which first appeared in 1749 and is considered by literary scholars as the first "satisfactory" novel written in English.

Source: William H. McNeill, *History Handbook of Western Civilization* (Chicago: University of Chicago Press, 1965), p. 526.

The London Metropolitan Police discover another victim of Jack the Ripper. *What do you suppose were some of the unique problems encountered by the first bobbies, or peelers?*

Table 5.1 Robert Peel's Principles of Policing

1. The police must be stable, efficient, and organized along military lines.

2. The police must be under governmental control.

3. The absence of crime will best prove the efficiency of police.

4. The distribution of crime news is essential.

5. The deployment of police strength both by time and area is essential.

6. No quality is more indispensable to a policeman than a perfect command of temper; a quiet, determined manner has more effect than violent action.

7. Good appearance commands respect.

8. The securing and training of proper persons is at the root of efficiency.

9. Public security demands that every police officer be given a number.

10. Police headquarters should be centrally located and easily accessible to the people.

11. Policemen should be hired on a probationary basis.

12. Police records are necessary to the correct distribution of police strength.

Peel's Principles of Policing A dozen standards proposed by Robert Peel, the author of the legislation resulting in the formation of the London Metropolitan Police Department. The standards are still applicable to today's law enforcement.

kind were a throwback to the absolute power formerly wielded by English kings. Parliament eventually responded, in 1829, with the London Metropolitan Police Act. It created a 1,000-officer police force with professional standards to replace the patchwork of community law enforcement systems then in use. Members of the London Police became known as *bobbies*, or *peelers*, after Robert Peel, the British Home Secretary who had prodded Parliament to create the police force.

To ensure discipline, the London Police were organized according to military rank and structure and were under the command of two magistrates, who were later called commissioners. According to Peel, the main function of the police was to prevent crime, not by force but by preventive patrol of the community. Londoners, who resented such close scrutiny, did not at first welcome this police presence in the community. Eventually, though, the bobbies (the term was originally derogatory) showed that the police could have a positive effect on the quality of life in the community. Peel's military approach to policing and some of his other principles remain in effect today throughout the world. **Peel's Principles of Policing** are outlined in Table 5.1.[5]

THINKING CRITICALLY

1. Do you think any of the early English systems of law enforcement (e.g., tithing) could work today? Why or why not?

The Development of American Law Enforcement

The United States has more police departments than any other nation in the world. The major reason for this is that local control is highly regarded in the United States. Thus, like many other services, even small communities that can barely afford police service provide it locally. This practice is primarily responsible for the disparity in the quality of American police personnel and service. The struggle to improve American law enforcement began even before formal police departments came into existence.

The "Leatherheads"

In Dutch-influenced New York in the seventeenth century, the first paid officers on the night watch were known as *leatherheads* because they wore leather helmets similar in appearance to the helmets worn by today's firefighters. The leatherheads were not known for their attention to duty and often spent entirely too much of their watch schedule inside.

Source: Carl Sifakis, "Leatherheads: First New York Police," *The Encyclopedia of American Crimes* (New York: Smithmark Publishers, Inc., 1992).

EARLY AMERICAN LAW ENFORCEMENT

The chance for a better life, free of government intervention, was key in the decision of many colonists to cross the Atlantic and settle in the New World. American colonists from England brought with them the constable-watch system, with which they were familiar if not completely satisfied. Boston established a night watch as early as 1634. Except for the military's intervention in major disturbances, the watch system, at least in the cities, was the means of preventing crime and apprehending criminals for the next two centuries. As in England, the people were the police. Citizens could pay for watch replacements, and often the worst of the lot ended up protecting the community. In fact, Boston and other cities frequently deployed the most elderly citizens and occasionally sentenced minor offenders to serve on the watch.[6] Later, in rural and southern areas of the country, the office of sheriff was established and the power of the posse was used to maintain order and apprehend offenders. In essence, two forms of protection began to evolve—the watch in the villages, towns, and cities and the sheriff in the rural areas, unincorporated areas, and counties. Communities in the North often had both systems.

LAW ENFORCEMENT IN THE CITIES

As had happened in England, the growth of the Industrial Revolution lured people away from the farms to cities. Large groups of newcomers, sometimes immigrants from other countries, settled near factories. Factory workers put in long days, often in unsafe and unhealthy working conditions. Some workers organized strikes, seeking better working conditions, but the strikes were quickly suppressed. As the populations of cities swelled, living conditions in some areas became overcrowded and unhealthy. Major episodes of urban violence occurred in the first half of the nineteenth century because of the social and economic changes transforming American cities. Racial and ethnic tensions often reached a boiling point, resulting in mob disturbances that lasted for days. A particular source of trouble was the drinking establishments located throughout working-class districts of cities. Regular heavy drinking led to fights, brawls, and even full-scale riots.

Unlike London, which organized its police force in 1829, American citizens resisted the formation of police departments, relying instead on the constable-watch system, whose members lit streetlights, patrolled the streets to maintain order, and arrested some suspicious people. Constables often had daytime duties, which included investigating health hazards, carrying out orders of the court, clearing the streets of debris, and apprehending criminals against whom complaints had been filed. Neither the night watch nor the constables tried to prevent or discover crime, nor did they wear any kind of uniform. This weak protection system was unable to contain the increasing level of lawlessness.

Municipal Police Forces   In 1844, New York City combined its day and night watches to form the first paid, unified police force in the United States. Close ties developed between the police and local political leaders. As with the first police in London, citizens were suspicious of the constant presence of police

New York had a watch system as early as 1658. *Why did the watch system of policing last so long?*

officers in their neighborhoods. Also, citizens had little respect for the New York police because they thought they were political hacks, appointed by local officials who wanted to control the police for their own gain. During the next several years, the struggle to control the police in New York built to a fever pitch.[7]

In 1853, the New York state legislature formed the Municipal Police Department, but within 4 years that force was so corrupt from taking bribes to overlook crime that the legislature decided to abolish it. It was replaced by the Metropolitan Police, which was administered by five commissioners appointed by the governor. The commissioners then selected one superintendent. Each commissioner was to oversee the others, as well as the superintendent, and keep them all honest. The new structure was an improvement, in the minds of the legislature, that would prevent corruption in the top level of the department. But when the Metropolitan Police Board called on Mayor Fernando Wood to abolish the Municipal Police, he refused. Even after New York's highest court upheld a decision to disband the Municipals, the mayor refused. The Metropolitans even tried to arrest Mayor Wood, but that failed attempt resulted in a pitched battle between the two police forces. When the National Guard was called in, Mayor Wood submitted to arrest but was immediately released on bail.

During the summer of 1857, the two police forces often fought over whether to arrest certain criminals. A particularly troubling practice was one police force's releasing from custody the criminals arrested by the other force. Lawbreakers operated freely during the dispute between the two police forces. Criminal gangs had a free hand to commit robberies and burglaries during most of that summer. The public became enraged over this neglect of duty and the increased danger on the streets of New York City. Only when another court order upheld the decision to disband the Municipal Police did Mayor Wood finally comply.

Following the course charted by New York City, other large cities in the United States soon established their own police departments. In 1855, Boston combined its day and night watches to form a city police department. By the end of the decade, police departments had been formed in many major cities east of the Mississippi. The duties of the officers did not vary substantially from the duties of those who had served on the watch. After the Civil War, however, peace officers began to take on the trappings of today's police. They began to wear uniforms, carry nightsticks, and even carry firearms, although many citizens resisted giving this much authority to the police.

A street arrest in 1878 Manhattan, New York. *What problems did the police of this era encounter?*

Tangle of Politics and Policing Until the 1920s in most American cities, party politics prevented the development of professional police departments. Local political leaders understood that controlling the police was a means of maintaining their own political power and of allowing criminal friends and political allies to violate the law with impunity. In fact, in some cities, the police were clearly extensions of the local party machine, which attempted to dominate all activity in a community. If local politicians gave police applicants a job, it became the hired officers' job to get out the vote so that the politicians could keep their positions. The system was so corrupt in some cities that police officers bought their jobs, their promotions, and their special assignments. In collaboration with local politicians, but often on their own, the police were more than willing to ignore violations of the law if the lawbreakers gave them money, valuables, or privileges.

By the early 1900s, most American cities had organized, uniformed police forces similar to the police force of Newport, Rhode Island, pictured circa 1910. *How do current police officers differ from those depicted in the photo?*

A Brief History of Blacks in Policing For most of American history blacks who have wanted to be police officers have faced blatant discrimination and have generally been denied the opportunity.[8] The first black police officers in the United States were "free men of color." They were hired around 1805 to serve as members of the New Orleans city watch system. They were hired primarily because other people did not want the job. In addition to serving on the watch, they were responsible for catching runaway slaves and generally policing black slaves in New Orleans.

By 1830, policing had become more important in New Orleans, and the "free men of color" lost their jobs on the city police force to others who wanted them. Not until after the Civil War were black Americans allowed to be police officers again. During Reconstruction, black Americans were elected to political office and hired as police officers throughout the South. This did not last long. By 1877, the backlash to Reconstruction drove black Americans and their white Republican allies from elective offices, and black police officers throughout the South lost their jobs. By 1890, most southern cities had all-white police departments. The few black police officers in the southern cities that retained them generally could not arrest white people and were limited to patrolling only areas and communities where other black Americans lived. By 1910, there were fewer than 600 black police officers in the entire United States, and most of them were employed in northern cities.

It was not until the 1940s and 1950s that black police officers began to be hired again in most southern cities. They were hired primarily to patrol black communities, to prevent crime, and to improve race relations. Still, few black Americans ever rose to command positions in their departments. Indeed, prior to the 1950s, only two black Americans had ever been promoted to the command position of captain: Octave Rey of New Orleans and John Scott of Chicago. Both served relatively short tenures in the position: Rey from 1868 to 1877 and Scott from 1940 to 1946.

LAW ENFORCEMENT IN THE STATES AND ON THE FRONTIER

The development of law enforcement on the state level and in the frontier territories was often peculiar to the individual location. Without large population centers that required the control of disorderly crowds, law enforcement was more likely to respond to specific situations—for example, by rounding up cattle rustlers or capturing escaped slaves. Still, out of this kind of limited law enforcement activity, the basic organizational structure of police units with broader responsibilities was born.

slave patrols The earliest form of policing in the South. They were a product of the slave codes. The plantation slave patrols have been called "the first distinctively American police system."

Southern Slave Patrols In the South, the earliest form of policing was the plantation **slave patrols.**[9] They have been called "the first distinctively American police system."[10] The slave patrols were created to enforce the infamous slave codes, the first of which was enacted by the South Carolina legislature in 1712. Eventually all the Southern colonies enacted slave codes. The slave codes protected the slaveholders' property rights in human beings, while holding slaves responsible for their crimes and other acts that were not crimes if committed by free persons. Under some slave codes, enslaved people could not hold meetings, leave the plantation without permission from the master, travel without a pass, learn to read and write, carry a firearm, trade, or gamble. Both the slave codes and the slave patrols were created in part because of a fear of bloody slave revolts, such as had already occurred in Virginia and other parts of the South.

The most publicized slave revolt was the Nat Turner Rebellion of 1831 in Virginia. Turner and five other slaves killed Joseph Travis, Turner's owner, and his family. Approximately 70 more rebels joined Turner, whose immediate plan was to capture the county seat, where munitions were stored. Turner was unsuccessful in his plan, but during the siege, he and his rebels killed 57 whites. Turner was tried, convicted, and hanged, along with 16 other rebels. In response to the revolt, white mobs lynched nearly 200 blacks, most of whom were innocent.[11]

Slave patrols generally consisted of three men on horseback who covered a beat of 15 square miles. They were responsible for catching runaway slaves, preventing slave uprisings, and maintaining discipline among the slaves. To maintain discipline, the patrols often whipped and terrorized black slaves who were caught after dark without passes. The slave patrols also helped enforce the laws prohibiting literacy, trade, and gambling among slaves. Although the law required that all white males perform patrol services, the large plantation owners usually hired poor, landless whites to substitute for them. The slave patrols lasted until the end of the Civil War, in 1865. After the Civil War, the Ku Klux Klan served the purpose of controlling blacks just as the slave patrols had before the Civil War.

The plantation slave patrols have been called "the first distinctively American police system." *Have any elements of the slave patrols influenced contemporary American policing? If yes, what are they?*

Frontier Law Enforcement In the remote and unpopulated areas of the nation, and particularly on the expanding frontier, justice was often in the hands of the people in a more direct way. Vigilantism was often the only way that people could maintain order and defend themselves against renegades and thugs.[12] Even when formal law enforcement procedures were provided by the sheriff or a marshal, courts in many communities were held only once or twice a year, leaving many cases unresolved. This idea of self-protection remains very popular in the

The Texas Rangers, organized in the early 1800s to fight Native Americans, patrol the Mexican border, and track down rustlers, were the first form of state police. *Why and how do you think the Rangers have endured for so long?*

South and the West, where firearms laws in many states permit people to carry loaded weapons in a vehicle, or even on their persons if they have completed a qualification and licensing procedure.

State Police Agencies Self-protection did not prove sufficient as populations and their accompanying problems increased. As early as 1823, mounted militia units in Texas protected American settlers throughout that territory. Called *rangers,* these mounted militia fought Native Americans and Mexican bandits. The Texas Rangers were officially formed in 1835, and the organization remains in existence today as an elite and effective unit of the Texas Department of Public Safety.[13]

The inefficiency and unwillingness of some sheriffs and constables to control crime, along with an emerging crime problem that exceeded the local community's ability to deal with it, prompted other states to form state law enforcement agencies. In 1905, Pennsylvania established the first modern state law enforcement organization with the authority to enforce the law statewide, an authority that made it unpopular in some communities where enforcement of state laws had been decidedly lax.[14] The Pennsylvania state police officially had been created to deal with crime in rural areas, but in its early years it frequently responded to industrial discord. The event that led directly to the formation of the state agency was the 1902 anthracite coal strike, which caused a national crisis and the intervention of President Theodore Roosevelt. Industrialists believed municipal police departments and the state militia were too unreliable during strikes because officers were overly sympathetic to workers with whom they often shared community ties and social origins. Industrialists assumed that a centralized mobile force, recruited statewide with ties to no particular community would eliminate any sympathy between officers and workers.[15] The authority of state police agencies was extended with the advent of the automobile and the addition of miles of state highways. Some form of state law enforcement agency existed in every state by the 1930s.

CJ Online

Texas Rangers

To learn more about the history of the Texas Rangers, visit the Texas Ranger Hall of Fame and Museum website at www.texasranger.org/index.htm. *Why do you think the Texas Rangers have elite status?*

PROFESSIONALISM AND REFORM

You will recall that the people themselves were once the police, as they served on the watch. Being an adult citizen was about the only qualification. No training was required, and it was common practice for citizens who did not want to serve to hire replacements, sometimes hiring sentenced offenders. Because of the few services and the little order the watch provided, not much else seems to have been required. Even when organized police forces were developed in the 1840s and 1850s in the United States, qualifications for the job mattered little beyond the right political connections or the ability to purchase one's position outright.

Not until the latter part of the nineteenth century did qualifications for the position of police officer begin to evolve. In the 1880s, Cincinnati posted two qualifications to be a police officer.[16] First, an applicant had to be a person of high moral character—an improvement over earlier times. Three citizens had to vouch for the applicant's character at a city council meeting. If deemed acceptable by the council, the applicant was immediately taken to a gymnasium and tested for the second qualification, foot speed.

Both Cincinnati and New York began police academies in the 1880s, but the curriculum was meager and recruits were not required to pass any examinations to prove their competence. The lack of adequate standards and training for police officers was recognized as a major stumbling block to improved policing. A group of reformers within policing allied themselves with the Progressives, a movement for political, social, and economic change. Among the reformers was August Vollmer, who became chief of police of Berkeley, California, in 1909. During his tenure as chief from 1909 to 1932, Vollmer attempted to create a professional model of policing. With Vollmer and a succession of internal reformers who followed, a new era of professional policing began.

August Vollmer. *Do you agree with Vollmer's idea that police should focus on law enforcement and leave social services and the maintenance of order to others? Why or why not?*

Vollmer and his followers advocated training and education as two of the key ingredients of professionalism in policing. He also believed strongly that the police should stay out of politics and that politics should stay out of policing. Vollmer believed that the major function of the police was fighting crime, and he saw great promise in professionalizing law enforcement by emphasizing that role.[17] He began to hire college graduates for the Berkeley Police Department, and he held college classes on police administration.

Within a few decades, this professional model, sometimes called the reform model, had taken root in police departments across the country. To eliminate political influences, gain control of officers, and establish crime-fighting priorities, departments made major changes in organization and operation. Those changes included the following:

- Narrowing of the police function from social service and the maintenance of order to law enforcement only.
- Centralization of authority, with the power of precinct captains and commanders checked.
- Creation of specialized, centrally based crime-fighting units, as for burglary.
- A shift from neighborhood foot patrol to motorized patrol.
- Implementation of patrol allocation systems based on such variables as crime rates, calls for service, and response times.
- Reliance on technology, such as police radios, to both control and aid the policing function.
- Recruitment of police officers through psychological screening and civil service testing.
- Specific training in law enforcement techniques.

Policewomen It took a long time for policewomen to gain the opportunity to perform the same roles and duties as their male counterparts. From the early 1900s until 1972, when the Equal Employment Opportunity Commission began to assist women police officers in obtaining equal employment status with male officers, policewomen were responsible for protection and crime prevention work with women and juveniles, particularly with girls. The Los Angeles Police Department created the City Mother's Bureau in 1914 and hired policewomen to work with delinquent and predelinquent children whose mothers did not want formal intervention by a law enforcement agency. Policewomen were also used to monitor, investigate, and punish young girls whose behavior flouted social and sexual conventions of the times.

The first woman to have full police power (1905) was Lola Baldwin of Portland, Oregon. The first uniformed policewoman was Alice Stebbins Wells, who was hired by the Los Angeles Police Department in 1910. By 1916, 16 other police departments had hired policewomen as a result of the success in Los Angeles.[18]

CONFLICTING ROLES

Throughout their history, Americans have never been sure precisely what role they want their police officers to play. Much of the ambivalence has to do with American heritage, which makes many Americans suspicious of government authority. At one time or another, local police have acted as peacekeepers, social workers, crime fighters, and public servants, completing any task that was requested. Often, the police have been asked to take on all those roles simultaneously.

For most of the nineteenth century, distrust of government was so strong and the need to maintain order in the cities so critical that the police operated almost exclusively as peacekeepers and social service agents, with little or no concern for enforcing the law beyond what was absolutely necessary to maintain tranquility.[19] In this role, the police in many American cities administered the laws that provided for public relief and support of the poor. They fed the hungry and housed the homeless at the request of the politicians who controlled them. Later, other social service agents, such as social workers, began to replace them, and a reform effort developed to remove policing from the direct control of corrupt politicians. As a result, the police began to focus on crime-fighting as early as the 1920s. Having the police enforce the law fairly and objectively was thought to be a major way of professionalizing law enforcement. This approach also fit the professional model of policing advocated by Vollmer and other reformers.

By the end of the 1960s, strong doubts about the role of the police emerged again. The role they had been playing encouraged them to ferret out crime and criminals through such practices as aggressive patrol, undercover operations, and electronic surveillance. In some neighborhoods, the police came to be viewed as armies of occupation. Some confrontations between police and citizens resulted in violence. The civil rights movement produced a series of demonstrations and civil disorders in more than 100 cities across America, beginning in 1964. As in the labor struggles of the late nineteenth and early twentieth centuries, the police were called in to restore order. Some police officers suppressed the demonstrations with brutal tactics. The anti–Vietnam War movement during the 1960s sparked protests all over the country, especially on college campuses. Again, police officers were called on to maintain and sometimes to restore order. Thousands of students were sprayed with tear gas, and some were beaten and even killed by police.

By the end of the 1960s, it was clear that police standards and training had to be improved. To many observers, fast response and proactive patrols did not seem effective in reducing crime, and officers increasingly were seeing their work world through the windshield of a cruiser. The likelihood of establishing rapport with the people they served was remote as officers dashed from one crime scene to another.

Brutal tactics by some police officers to suppress civil rights protests during the 1960s led to calls for improved standards of police conduct and training. *Have new standards of conduct and training ended brutal police tactics?*

Four blue-ribbon commissions studied the police in the United States. The names of the four commissions and the years in which they released their reports are as follows:

National Advisory Commission on Civil Disorders, 1967

President's Commission on Law Enforcement and the Administration of Justice, 1967

National Advisory Commission on Criminal Justice Standards and Goals, 1973

American Bar Association's Standards Relating to Urban Police Function, 1973

All four reports made the same major recommendations: They pointed out the critical role police officers play in American society, called for careful selection of law enforcement officers, and recommended extensive and continuous training. The reports also recommended better police management and supervision, as well as internal and external methods of maintaining integrity in police departments.

In an attempt to follow many of the specific recommendations of the reform commissions' reports, police selection became an expensive and elaborate process. It was designed to identify candidates who had the qualities to be effective law enforcement officers: integrity, intelligence, interpersonal skills, mental stability, adequate physical strength, and agility. Attempts were also made to eliminate discriminatory employment practices that had prevented minorities and women from entering and advancing in law enforcement. Finally, it became more common for police officers to attend college, and some police agencies began to set a minimum number of college credit hours as an employment qualification.

COMMUNITY POLICING

By the 1970s, research began to show that a rapid response to crime does not necessarily lead to more arrests and that having more police officers using methods made popular under the professional or reform model does not significantly reduce crime.[20] What was emerging was the view that unattended disorderly behavior in neighborhoods—such as unruly groups of youths, prostitution, vandalism, drunk and disorderly vagrants, and aggressive street people—is a signal to more serious criminals that residents do not care what goes on in their community and that the criminals can move in and operate with impunity.

The 1970s and 1980s saw some experimentation with community- and neighborhood-based policing projects.[21] Those projects got mixed results, and many were abandoned because of high costs, administrative neglect, and citizen apathy. However, higher crime rates, continued community deterioration, and recognition of the failure to control crime caused law enforcement to again question the role it was playing. The enforcer role still was not working well enough. It appeared senseless simply to respond to calls for service and arrive at scenes of crime and disorder time and time again without resolving the problems or having any lasting effect on the lives of the residents of the community. Out of this failure and frustration came the contemporary concept of **community policing.**

Under a community policing philosophy, the people of a community and the police form a lasting partnership, in which they jointly approach the problems of maintaining order, providing services, and fighting crime.[22] If the police show they care about the minor problems associated with community disorder, two positive changes are likely to occur: citizens will develop better relations with the police as they turn to them for solutions to the disorder, and criminals will see that residents and the police have a commitment to keeping all crime out of the neighborhood. Once again, the emphasis has shifted from fighting crime to keeping peace and delivering social services. The goal is eradicating the causes of crime in a community, not simply responding to symptoms.

In the early 1990s, many communities across the nation began implementing community policing strategies. Community policing called for a shift from incident-based crime fighting to a problem-oriented approach, in which police would be prepared to handle a broad range of troublesome situations in a city's neighborhoods. There was greater emphasis on foot patrol so that officers could come to know and be known by the residents of a neighborhood. Those citizens would then be more willing to help the police identify and solve problems in the neighborhood. Many other aspects of community policing are discussed more fully in Chapter 6.

COMPSTAT

At about the same time that community policing was becoming popular in many American cities, a new policing strategy was being implemented in New York City.[23] By the beginning of the new millennium, a third of the nation's largest police departments had adopted it, and another 25% were planning to do so. The new strategy was called CompStat, an abbreviation of "compare stats" or "computer statistics meetings." **CompStat** is a technological and management system that aims to make the police better organized and more effective crime fighters. It combines innovative crime analysis and geographic information systems, that is, crime mapping (described in Chapter 6), with the latest management principles.

CompStat is based on four interrelated crime-reduction principles: (1) provide accurate and timely crime data to all levels of the police organization, (2) choose the most effective strategies for specific problems, (3) implement those strategies by the rapid deployment of personnel and resources, and

MYTH

Random patrol, as opposed to directed patrol, reduces crime. It is important to have police out in patrol cars, scouting neighborhoods and business districts.

FACT

There is not much value to such random patrols other than perhaps helping people feel safe. They would probably feel even safer if the police were walking a beat. However, little research supports the idea that officers who ride around for 3 to 5 hours of their shifts are repressing crime. Even being available to respond to calls from the public is not a strong argument for such patrols. Only a small percentage of reported crimes and other incidents require a rapid response.

community policing A contemporary approach to policing that actively involves the community in a working partnership to control and reduce crime.

CompStat A technological and management system that aims to make the police better organized and more effective crime fighters. It combines innovative crime analysis and geographic information systems, that is, crime mapping (described in Chapter 6) with the latest management principles.

(4) diligently evaluate the results and make adjustments to the strategy as necessary. Problems are identified by crime analysts who collect data, analyze it, and then map it to show trends or trouble spots. Armed with this information, precinct commanders are responsible for formulating a response and solving the problem. Failure to get the job done results in harsh reprimands from top administrators, and repeated failures can lead to removal from command.

Supporters of CompStat claim that it has reduced crime, and FBI statistics show that crime rates have declined in those cities that have implemented it. However, the simultaneous decrease in crime rates reported by the FBI and the implementation of CompStat may be nothing more than a coincidence. In fact, a few studies reveal that crime rates were already declining in cities before CompStat was implemented. Critics contend that CompStat is incompatible with community policing. Whereas community policing is based on the decentralization of decision-making authority and the empowerment of patrol officers to make decisions in their communities, CompStat concentrates decision-making power among command staff who issue orders to the rank and file. Centralized command and control are key features of the traditional model of police organizations, and therein lies the appeal of CompStat to police administrators who are uncomfortable giving up too much control. CompStat allows the chief of police to judge the performance of precinct commanders and precinct commanders to hold their officers accountable. CompStat returns the control of everyday policing to police administrators and requires minimal disruption to the traditional police organization. At the same time it allows police administrators to tout their use of innovative technologies and problem-solving techniques. It will be interesting to see whether policing's future is community policing, CompStat, or some other system.

THINKING CRITICALLY

1. Which of the major changes in the organization and operation of police departments listed on page 154 do you think brought about the most significant change? Why?

2. What do you think are the key benefits of community policing? Why?

3. Which system of policing do you believe will best serve the interests of the American public: community policing or CompStat? Why?

Federal Law Enforcement

Since the United States was formed, the American public has held a healthy skepticism about a centralized police system. That is why law enforcement in the United States, unlike in many other countries, is primarily a state and local matter. However, the creation of a federal system of government and laws necessitated a national law enforcement presence. The result has been dozens of federal law enforcement agencies. Although space limitations preclude an examination of all these agencies' histories, the histories of four of the more prominent ones—the U.S. Marshals Service, the Secret Service, the Federal Bureau of Investigation, and the Drug Enforcement Administration—are described below.

U.S. MARSHALS SERVICE

The first federal law enforcement agents in the United States were the U.S. Marshals, which were a product of the Judiciary Act of 1789.[24] The Act fleshed out details of the new federal judicial system, as provided for in the U.S. Constitution. Duties of the federal Marshals and their deputies included protecting the federal courts, supporting their operation, and enforcing federal court decisions and federal laws. In supporting the operation of the federal courts, U.S. Marshals served summonses, subpoenas, writs, warrants and other process (that is, proceedings in any action or prosecution) issued by the courts; arrested people suspected of committing federal crimes; were responsible for all federal prisoners; disbursed funds as ordered by the federal courts; paid the fees and expenses of court clerks, U.S. Attorneys, jurors and witnesses; rented courtrooms and jail space and hired bailiffs, court criers, and janitors; and made sure that prisoners were present, jurors were available, and witnesses were punctual. U.S. Marshals also were charged with carrying out the lawful orders of Congress and the president. The position of U.S. Marshal was modeled after the position of county sheriff. In Virginia, between 1619 and about 1634, local sheriffs were called provost marshals or marshals. The same was true in Georgia between 1733 and 1773.

President George Washington personally selected the first thirteen Marshals—one for each state. The president still nominates U.S. Marshals who must be confirmed by the Senate. Washington wanted men who would support the federal government without jeopardizing states' rights. Most of his appointees had a previous association with him, including service under his command during the Revolutionary War. The first Marshals helped to establish the federal judicial system and place the new federal government on sound footing because of their local ties, which made the exercise of federal power a little more palatable to the American public. Throughout their history, U.S. Marshals have been required to live within the districts they served. As civilian law enforcers, the availability of the U.S. Marshals frequently prevented military intervention in state and local affairs.

The U.S. Marshals represented the federal government's interests at the local level and performed a variety of non-law enforcement duties needed to keep the central government functioning effectively. For example, they conducted the first national census in 1790, and continued to do so until 1870. They also distributed presidential proclamations and collected statistical information on commerce and manufacturing. Until 1861, they reported directly to the Secretary of State; in 1861, Congress assigned their supervision to the Attorney General. Nevertheless, until the 1960s, and the establishment of a centrally administered U.S. Marshals Service with control over district budgets and the hiring of deputies, the U.S. Marshals operated with little supervision. Working with federal judges and U.S. Attorneys, U.S. Marshals prior to the 1960s were relatively free to determine how they would enforce the law.

One of the first law enforcement duties of the Marshals—one they still perform today—was to conduct executions authorized by the federal courts. U.S. Marshal Henry Dearborn of Maine conducted the first federal execution in 1790. He executed Thomas Bird for a murder committed at sea. Another early duty of the U.S. Marshals was to enforce the Sedition Act of 1798. The Act punished unlawful combinations against the government and publishing "false, scandalous, and malicious writing" about the government. Prior to the creation of the U.S. Secret Service in 1865, U.S. Marshals and their deputies were used by the Treasury Department to investigate and pursue counterfeiters nationwide. U.S. Marshals also were charged with enforcing the Fugitive Slave Act of 1850. The Marshals arrested fugitive slaves and returned them to their southern masters. During the Civil War, U.S. Marshals confiscated property used to support the confederacy and aided in the capture of confederate spies.

Following the Civil War, U.S. Marshals and their deputies were instrumental in keeping law and order in the "Wild West." One of the most infamous incidents involving the Marshals occurred in Tombstone, Arizona, in 1881. The gunfight at the O.K. Corral pitted U.S. Marshall Virgil Earp and his deputies, brothers Wyatt and Morgan Earp and John "Doc" Holiday, against the Clanton gang. The U.S. Marshals became a part of the newly created Justice Department in 1870. During the Pullman railroad strike of 1894, President Grover Cleveland and the federal courts ordered the U.S. Marshals to help United States Army troops break the strike and keep the trains rolling.

U.S. Marshals helping to break the Pullman railroad strike of 1894. *Was this an appropriate use of the U.S. Marshals? Why or why not?*

In 1896, U.S. Marshals began to receive an annual salary for the first time. They had previously worked under a fee system in which they would collect set amounts for performing specific tasks. Getting paid under the fee system was frequently an ordeal. During World War I, U.S. Marshals helped protect the home front from enemy aliens, spies, and saboteurs. They also arrested draft dodgers and people who tried to disrupt Selective Service operations. With the ratification of the 18th Amendment in 1919, which prohibited the manufacture, sale, and transportation of intoxicating beverages in the United States, the U.S. Marshal Service assumed the primary responsibility for enforcing the Prohibition laws. They continued in that role until 1927, when the Treasury Department gave the responsibility to the newly created Bureau of Prohibition. After that, the Marshals, along with other federal agencies, assisted in prohibition efforts.

In the 1960s, U.S. Marshals helped enforce desegregation orders. For example, when James Meredith, a black man, enrolled in the University of Mississippi in 1962, deputies protected him 24 hours a day for an entire year. Following passage of the Organized Crime Control Act of 1970, the U.S. Marshal Service was given responsibility for the Witness Security Program. In 1979, the U.S. Attorney General transferred primary jurisdiction for the apprehension of escaped federal prisoners from the FBI to the U.S. Marshals Service. In 1985, U.S. Marshals were given the task of managing and disposing of properties seized and forfeited by federal law enforcement agencies and U.S. Attorneys nationwide. In 1996, following a series of bombings, the U.S. Marshal Service was charged with protecting abortion clinics and doctors.

Throughout their more than 220-year history, U.S. Marshals and their deputies have been "general practitioners within the law enforcement community," capable of responding quickly to new problems. Unlike other federal law enforcement agencies, the U.S. Marshals have not been restricted by legislation to specific, well-defined duties and jurisdictions. Today, their major responsibilities include:

- Judicial security
- Fugitive investigations

- Witness security
- Prisoner services (for example, detaining pre-sentenced federal prisoners)
- Transporting federal prisoners and criminal aliens
- Managing and disposing of seized and forfeited property
- Serving federal court criminal and some civil process
- Conducting special operations (for instance, providing security assistance when Minuteman and cruise missiles are moved between military facilities)

THE SECRET SERVICE

In 1865, the United States Secret Service was created as a branch of the Treasury Department to combat the counterfeiting of U.S. currency.[25] During the mid-nineteenth century, approximately 1,600 state banks designed and printed their own bills, making it difficult to distinguish between counterfeit bills and the more than 7,000 uniquely designed legitimate bills. Counterfeiting was a serious problem. It was estimated that one-third to one-half of all currency in circulation was counterfeit. By comparison, the counterfeit rate today is a fraction of a percent. To resolve the counterfeiting problem, a national currency was adopted in 1862, but the national currency was soon counterfeited extensively too. The enforcement of anti-counterfeiting laws was clearly necessary, and the Secret Service was and continues to be effective in suppressing the problem.

In 1867, Secret Service responsibilities were expanded to include "detecting persons perpetrating frauds against the government." This resulted in investigations into the Ku Klux Klan, nonconforming distillers, smugglers, mail robbers, land frauds, and a number of other federal law violations. In 1984, Congress enacted legislation further expanding the Secret Service's investigative responsibilities to violations relating to credit and debit card fraud, federal-interest computer fraud, and fraudulent identification documents.

In 1894, the Secret Service began informal part-time protection of President Grover Cleveland, and, in 1902, a year after the assassination of President William McKinley, it was given full-time responsibility for the protection of the U.S. president. In 1951, Congress enacted legislation permanently authorizing Secret Service protection of the president, his or her immediate family, the president-elect, and the vice president, if he or she wishes. Ten years later, Congress authorized Secret Service protection of former presidents for a reasonable period of time. In 1962, Congress expanded Secret Service protection to include the vice president or the next officer to succeed the president and the vice president-elect. Congress passed legislation in 1963 to provide Secret Service protection of Mrs. John F. Kennedy and her minor children for two years. In 1965, Congress authorized Secret Service protection of former presidents and their spouses during their lifetime and minor children until age 16. Following the assassination of Robert F. Kennedy in 1968, Congress expanded Secret Service protection to major presidential and vice presidential candidates and nominees; it also authorized protection of widows of presidents until death or remarriage, and their children until age 16.

In 1922, President Warren Harding requested the creation of the White House Police, which was placed under the supervision of the Secret Service in 1930. The White House Police was renamed the Executive Protection Service in 1970, and the Secret Service Uniformed Division in 1977. The Treasury Police Force was merged into the Secret Service Uniformed Division in 1986. The Secret Service was transferred from the Treasury Department to the Department of Homeland Security in 2003. Today, "the mission of the United States Secret Service is to safeguard the nation's financial infrastructure and payment systems to preserve the integrity of the economy, and to protect national leaders, visiting heads of state and government, designated sites and National Special Security Events."

CJ Online

Secret Service

To learn more about the U.S. Secret Service, visit their website at www .treas.gov/usss. *Based on what you have learned from the website, do you think that you would be interested in a career with the Secret Service? Why or why not?*

FYI Counterfeiting Today

The Secret Service reported that ink-jet counterfeiting accounted for 60% of the $103 million in counterfeit money it removed from circulation from October 2007 to August 2008. The figure in 1995 was less than 1%. Many of today's counterfeiters simply use pictures of bills from their computers, buy paper at an office supply store, and print out a few bills, usually for $1, $5, or $10. They cut the bills apart, go into a store or bar and pass one or two. Many offenders are involved with drugs, especially methamphetamine. In the past, the best counterfeiters were skilled printers who used heavy offset presses to make decent 20s, 50s, and 100s. Now that kind of work is rare and almost all comes from abroad.

Source: Joe Lambe, "Fake Money Isn't What It Used to Be," *The Kansas City Star* (December 26, 2008), p. A1.

U.S. Secret Service agent Tim McCarthy "took a bullet" protecting President Ronald Reagan from would-be assassin John Hinckley Jr. in 1981. *Could you be a U.S. Secret Service agent?*

THE FEDERAL BUREAU OF INVESTIGATION (FBI)

When he assumed the presidency following President McKinley's assassination in 1901, Theodore Roosevelt, who had served as New York City Police Commissioner from 1895–1897, began his crusades to break up big-business monopolies in the East and to stop land theft in the West.[26] He successfully employed Secret Service agents in that effort. Four years later, Roosevelt appointed Charles Bonaparte as U.S. Attorney General. As head of the Justice Department, Bonaparte had only a few special agents of his own and a group of Examiners, who were trained as accountants and charged with reviewing the federal courts' financial transactions. Since its establishment in 1870, the Justice Department had to hire private detectives and later investigators from other federal agencies to investigate federal crimes. By 1907, the Justice Department primarily relied on Secret Service agents to conduct its investigations. These Secret Service agents reported to the Chief of the Secret Service and not to the Attorney General. Bonaparte did not like the arrangement and wanted complete control of investigations under his jurisdiction. In 1908, big business and land interests were successful in getting Congress to pass a law prohibiting the Justice Department and all other executive agencies, except the Treasury Department, from hiring Secret Service agents to conduct investigations. The law was intended to thwart President Roosevelt's reform agenda. A month after the law was passed, Roosevelt ordered Bonaparte to appoint a force of what turned out to be 34 Special Agents within the Justice Department. Ten of his new appointees were former Secret Service agents. The primary purpose of the new force was to investigate violations of the Sherman Anti-Trust Act, which was passed in 1890, and was intended to prevent business monopolies from artificially raising prices by restriction of trade or supply. On July 26, 1908, Bonaparte ordered his new agents to report to Chief Examiner Stanley W. Finch. This act is considered the beginning of the FBI. The force of 34 agents became a permanent part of the Justice Department in 1909, following the recommendations of both Attorney General Bonaparte and President Roosevelt. Later in 1909, George Wickersham, who succeeded Bonaparte as Attorney General, named the force the Bureau of Investigation and the Chief Examiner as the Chief of the Bureau of Investigation.

When the Bureau was created, there were few federal crimes. Investigations were limited mostly to crimes involving national banking, bankruptcy, naturalization, antitrust, land fraud, and peonage. Peonage was the system by which debtors or legal prisoners were held in servitude to labor for their creditors or for persons who leased their services from the state. The Bureau began to expand in 1910, after Congress passed the Mann ("White Slave") Act. The Mann Act made it a crime to transport women across state lines for immoral purposes. When the U.S. entered World War I in 1917, President Woodrow Wilson enlarged the Bureau's responsibility to include crimes of espionage and sabotage and violations of the Selective Service Act. The Bureau also assisted the Labor Department in the investigation of enemy aliens. In 1919, William J. Flynn, a former chief of the Secret Service, became the head of the Bureau of Investigation and was the first to use the title of Director. Also in 1919,

Congress passed the National Motor Vehicle Theft Act, which further expanded the Bureau's investigative responsibilities.

In 1921, President Warren Harding's Attorney General Harry M. Daugherty appointed William J. Burns Director of the Bureau. Burns, like Flynn, had been chief of the Secret Service but gained notoriety by running the William J. Burns International Detective Agency. Because of his involvement in the infamous Teapot Dome Scandal, Burns was asked by Attorney General Harlan Fiske Stone to resign from the Bureau in 1924. Burns's short-lived career as Director of the Bureau is perhaps best remembered for his appointment to the position of Assistant Director of the Bureau a 26-year-old graduate of George Washington University Law School named John Edgar Hoover. Hoover had worked for the Justice Department since 1917, where he headed the enemy alien operations during World War I and assisted in the investigation of suspected anarchists and communists in the General Intelligence Division under Attorney General A. Mitchell Palmer. Following Burns's resignation in 1924, Attorney General Stone appointed then 29-year-old J. Edgar Hoover as Director of the Bureau of Investigation, a position he would hold for the next 48 years.

Under Hoover's leadership, the Bureau of Investigation became a major factor in policing. A few spectacular and well-publicized crimes in the early 1930s, coupled with the problem of Prohibition and gangland killings in Chicago in the 1920s, fueled a public panic about a national crime emergency. The pivotal event was probably the Lindberg baby kidnapping in 1932. Because of Charles Lindberg's fame, the kidnapping received international attention. In response, Congress quickly passed a federal kidnapping statute dubbed the "Lindberg Law." Prior to 1932, Hoover's only major accomplishment was getting the Bureau designated as the national clearinghouse and publisher of the new Uniform Crime Reports (UCR) in 1930. However, following passage of the Lindberg Law, the Bureau at Hoover's direction mounted a massive publicity campaign that emphasized the threat of crime and the Bureau's role as the guardian of law and order. Through Bureau

FBI Director J. Edgar Hoover was considered by many as the nation's "top cop." *Did FBI Director J. Edgar Hoover have too much power? Why or why not?*

press releases about the killing of John Dillinger in 1934, and, in the next few years, the killing or apprehension of Pretty Boy Floyd, Baby Face Nelson, Ma Barker, and Alvin "Creepy" Karpis, a mythology was created about the Bureau's success in fighting crime. This mythology, which was promoted and exploited by Hoover over his long FBI career, appealed to many Americans, who found the sensationalized crime stories about "G-Men" and "Public Enemies" a titillating diversion from life's demoralizing daily drudge during the Great Depression.

In the next few years, the FBI expanded in size and prominence and gained increasing influence over local policing. This influence began in 1930, when the Bureau became responsible for the Uniform Crime Reports system. It received added momentum in 1932, when the Bureau established its own crime lab and, in 1935, when it founded the National Police Academy. In the midst of what appeared to be a mounting crime wave, few people objected to the establishment of a "national police force." As a result, in 1935, under Hoover's leadership the Bureau of Investigation became the Federal Bureau of Investigation (FBI), and thanks to his aggressive public relations department, Hoover managed to win for himself the image of the nation's "top cop." The FBI's influence over local policing increased further in 1940, when it was given responsibility for coordinating domestic security during World War II.

When the war ended and the Cold War began, the FBI continued its domestic security responsibilities. For example, it was given the job of investigating allegations of disloyalty among federal employees and was relentless in combating the communist threat, which Hoover always equated with U.S. labor union activity. Hoover began to consider himself as internal security czar, who was not subordinate to the Attorney General but rather a coequal consultant and advisor. The Bureau also began devoting a larger portion of its resources to helping state and local law enforcement agencies. In the 1960s, Congress passed new laws giving the FBI the authority to fight civil rights violations, racketeering, and gambling. However, under Hoover, the FBI "dragged its feet" in the field of civil rights, primarily because Hoover, a virulent racist, maintained, despite evidence to the contrary, that civil rights organizations such as the Southern Christian Leadership Conference (SCLC) had been infiltrated and were being led by Communists. The leader of the SCLC was Martin Luther King, Jr. Hoover also was less than enthusiastic about enforcement of the civil rights laws, because he did not want to jeopardize mutually beneficial relationships with powerful southern Congressmen and local law enforcement agencies, whose officers were often sympathetic to Ku Klux Klan activities. As for organized crime, new laws passed by Congress enabled the FBI to engage in court-ordered electronic surveillance, and together with increased undercover work, to successfully develop cases against nearly all the heads of the U.S. organized crime families. This was accomplished despite Hoover's insistence that an organization called the "Mafia" did not exist. Hoover used the term "La Cosa Nostra" when reality could not be denied.

As just shown with regard to civil rights, the FBI and its long-time Director had a darker, more sinister side, which was epitomized by the FBI's infamous covert domestic counterintelligence programs ("COINTELPROS"), which from 1956 through 1971 were used against dissidents and their organizations. The purpose of COINTELPROS, according to Hoover, was to "expose, disrupt, misdirect, discredit and otherwise neutralize" specific groups and individuals. To impede constitutionally protected political activity against groups and individuals who opposed government domestic and foreign policy, the FBI used surveillance, infiltration, harassment, intimidation, sabotage, provocation, media manipulation, and other oftentimes illegal tactics, including complicity in the alleged assassination of Black Panther leader Fred Hampton. COINTELPROS' targets included the Communist Party; the Socialist Worker's Party; the National Association for the Advancement of Colored People (NAACP); the American Civil Liberties Union (ACLU); the National Lawyer's Guild; the American

Friends Service Committee (a Quaker service organization that received the Nobel Peace Prize in 1947); the American Indian Movement; Black Nationalist groups, such as the Black Panther Party; White Hate groups, such as the Ku Klux Klan; and many members of the New Left including the Students for a Democratic Society (SDS) and numerous antiwar, antiracist, feminist, lesbian and gay, environmentalist, and other groups. It also targeted individuals such as civil rights leader Martin Luther King, Jr., whom the Bureau set out to destroy in 1963, and civil rights leader and labor organizer Cesar Chavez. Some of the aforementioned groups, such as the ACLU, had been under FBI surveillance since the 1920s because of their criticism of the Bureau.

Hoover was able to freely pursue these clandestine and often illegal activities because he was able to successfully insulate himself and the Bureau from executive and legislative control. He was able to do this by amassing secret files on the conduct and associations of presidents and legislators that might prove embarrassing to them if revealed. He also kept extensive investigative files on thousands of other individuals who had been involved in controversial causes and dissident organizations, including deaf and blind educator Helen Keller; U.S. Supreme Court Justice Felix Frankfurter; football player Joe Namath; actors Marlon Brando, Paul Newman, and Rock Hudson; and boxers Joe Louis and Muhammad Ali. Yet, as an enduring monument to his government service,

Top (L/R): Helen Keller, Felix Frankfurter, Joe Namath, and Marlon Brando. Bottom (L/R): Paul Newman, Rock Hudson, Joe Louis, and Muhammad Ali. *Why did the FBI keep secret files on these individuals?*

adoration, and power, the mammoth FBI headquarters in Washington, D.C., the preoccupation of his last years, was named the J. Edgar Hoover Building. The building, formally dedicated in 1975, dwarfs the Justice Department headquarters building and dominates the inaugural route between the Capitol and the White House.

The day after Hoover's death in 1972, President Richard Nixon appointed L. Patrick Gray III as the FBI's Acting Director. Gray, who most recently had been the Justice Department's Assistant Attorney General for the Civil Division, allowed the Bureau to become a part of the Watergate cover-up, authorized and approved illegal break-ins and burglaries, and even coached Deputy Attorney General Richard Kleindienst on his testimony before the Senate Judiciary Committee. The Justice Department had been charged with compromising its case against the International Telephone and Telegraph Company (ITT) in exchange for promised campaign contributions and other favors. When Gray's personal involvement in these nefarious activities became public, he resigned and withdrew his name from Senate consideration to be Director. Hours after Gray resigned in 1973, William Ruckleshaus, a former Congressman and the first head of the Environmental Protection Agency, was appointed Acting Director and served in that capacity for three months until Clarence Kelley was appointed Director. Kelly, who had been an FBI agent from 1940 to 1961, was Kansas City, Missouri, Police Chief at the time of his appointment. Kelley labored to restore public trust in the FBI; he also established three national priorities for the FBI: foreign counterintelligence, organized crime, and white-collar crime. To accomplish his priorities, Kelley intensified the Bureau's recruitment of accountants, women, and minorities.

In 1978, Kelley resigned as FBI Director and was replaced by former federal Judge William H. Webster. Webster made terrorism a fourth FBI national priority in 1982, following a series of worldwide terrorist incidents. Also in 1982, the Attorney General gave the FBI concurrent jurisdiction with the Drug Enforcement Administration (DEA) over the War on Drugs. The FBI also served as lead security agency at the 1984 Los Angeles Olympics. In the mid-1980s, the FBI was successful in solving several espionage cases, the most serious of which involved John Walker and his spy ring. Under Webster's leadership, the FBI also attacked public corruption and white-collar crime nationwide. FBI operations led to convictions of members of Congress (ABSCAM), the judiciary (GREYLORD), defense procurement officials (ILLWIND), and state legislators in California and South Carolina. FBI investigations in the 1980s successfully uncovered massive fraud in the Savings and Loan debacle, too. Webster left the Bureau in 1987 to become Director of the Central Intelligence Agency (CIA). Webster was temporarily replaced by FBI Executive Assistant Director John E. Otto, who during his five-month tenure made drug investigations the FBI's fifth national priority. Later in 1987, federal Judge William S. Sessions was appointed as the eighth FBI Director. Following the fall of the Berlin Wall in 1989, and a steep rise in violent crime over the preceding ten years, Sessions designated the investigation of domestic violent crimes as the FBI's sixth national priority. To address the new priority, he reassigned 300 Special Agents from foreign counterintelligence responsibilities to domestic violent crime investigations. By 1991, the FBI has instituted "Operation Safe Streets" in Washington, D.C., which involved the coordination of federal, state, and local police task forces in the targeting of fugitives and gangs. With the FBI's assistance, the program would soon be expanded nationwide. At about the same time, the FBI Crime Laboratory revolutionized violent criminal identification by successfully employing DNA technology. Under Sessions's leadership, the FBI refocused resources to combat a new wave of large-scale insider bank fraud and other financial crimes, complex health care frauds, and newly created environmental crimes. National security priorities were also refocused from the threats of communism and nuclear war to protecting U.S. information and technologies; the proliferation of biological, chemical, and nuclear weapons; and the theft of economic trade secrets and proprietary information. Also under Sessions' watch, the FBI's image was tarnished by the mishandling of two crisis situations: one in 1992, at Ruby Ridge, Idaho, where the wife of fugitive Randall Weaver was accidentally shot and killed by an FBI sniper, and the other in 1993, at Waco, Texas, where 74 members of the Branch Davidian religious sect, including women and children, died as a result of the government's misguided attack of their compound. During the summer of 1993, President Bill Clinton removed Director Sessions from office when he refused to resign following allegations of ethics violations involving the misuse of government planes and limousines. President Clinton appointed Deputy Director Floyd I. Clarke as Acting FBI Director.

In the fall of 1993, Louis J. Freeh was sworn in as the ninth Director of the FBI. Freeh had been a federal judge at the time of his appointment and a former FBI agent. Freeh's primary goal was to forge strong international police partnerships to fight evolving crime problems at home and abroad. He was instrumental in the establishment of the first International Law Enforcement Academy in Budapest, Hungary, in 1995. Between 1993 and 1996, the FBI conducted successful investigations into the 1993 World Trade Center bombing in New York City, the 1995 bombing of the Murrah Federal Building in Oklahoma City, the UNABOMBER Theodore Kaczynski in 1996, and the arrests of Russian crime boss Vyacheslav Ivankov in 1995 and Mexican drug-trafficker Juan Garcia-Abrego in 1996. The Bureau under Freeh also created the Critical Incident Response Group (CIRG) in response to the tragedies at Ruby Ridge, Idaho, and Waco, Texas. To deal with crime in cyberspace, the Bureau under Freeh established the Computer Investigations and Infrastructure Threat Assessment Center (CITAC) and employed its Computer Analysis and Response Teams (CART) to successfully investigate and prevent computer crimes. In 1998, the FBI under Freeh instituted its National Infrastructure Protection Center (NIPC) to monitor the spread of computer viruses, worms, and other malicious programs and to warn government and businesses about these threats to their computers. Freeh resigned from the Bureau in the summer of 2001, amid criticism that the FBI needed stronger leadership, especially after allegations that 25-year FBI agent Robert Hanssen had been a spy for the Soviet Union and Russia since 1985, the FBI bungling of the investigation of Los Alamos National Laboratory scientist Wen Ho Lee, and allegations of incompetence at the FBI crime laboratory.

On September 4, 2001, President George W. Bush appointed U.S. Attorney Robert S. Mueller to succeed Director Freeh. At this writing, Mueller is the FBI's current Director. Mueller's mandate as FBI Director was to refine the Bureau's information technology infrastructure, to improve its records management system, and to upgrade FBI foreign counterintelligence analysis and security because of the damage done by former Special Agent and convicted spy Robert Hanssen. However, only days after Mueller took office, the terrorist attacks of September 11 occurred, and Mueller's mandate changed. Today, the mission of the FBI is "to protect and defend the United States against terrorist and foreign intelligence threats, to uphold and enforce the criminal laws of the United States, and to provide leadership and criminal justice services to federal, state, municipal, and international agencies and partners." Its priorities are these:

1. Protect the United States from terrorist attack.
2. Protect the United States against foreign intelligence operations and espionage.

CJ Online

FBI Fights Terrorism

To learn more about the FBI's efforts to combat terrorism, visit its website at www.fbi.gov. Click on "Terrorism" and then click on "Counterterrorism Website." *From what you have learned, do you think the FBI will be effective in combating terrorism?*

FBI Director Robert S. Mueller. *What attributes are needed to succeed in this position?*

3. Protect the United States against cyber-based attacks and high-technology crimes.
4. Combat public corruption at all levels.
5. Protect civil rights.
6. Combat transnational/national criminal organizations and enterprises.
7. Combat major white-collar crime.
8. Combat significant violent crime.
9. Support federal, state, local, and international partners.
10. Upgrade technology to successfully perform the FBI's mission.

THE DRUG ENFORCEMENT ADMINISTRATION (DEA)

President Richard Nixon created the Drug Enforcement Administration by executive order in 1973.[27] His goal was to establish a single unified command to wage "an all-out global war on the drug menace." The DEA traces its history through several Treasury Department bureaus: the Bureau of Internal Revenue (1915–1927), the Bureau of Prohibition (1927–1930), and the Bureau of Narcotics (1930–1968), and the Justice Department's Bureau of Narcotics and Dangerous Drugs (1968–1973).

The federal law that inaugurated America's War on Drugs was the Harrison Narcotics Tax Act of 1914. The Act provided that all persons who produced, imported, manufactured, compounded, dealt in, dispensed, sold, distributed, or gave away opium or coca leaves, their salts, derivatives (such as morphine, heroin, and cocaine), or preparations had to register with the Bureau of Internal Revenue, pay a special tax, and keep records of all transactions. The Act further authorized the Commissioner of Internal Revenue, with the approval of the Secretary of the Treasury, to appoint such agents as necessary to enforce the provisions of the Act. The Act stipulated that any person who violated the law could be fined not more than $2,000 or be imprisoned for not more than five years, or both. On its face the Harrison Act was a tax law and not a prohibition law, but the Treasury Department interpreted the law to mean that it was illegal for a doctor to prescribe any of the aforementioned drugs to an addict to maintain his or her use and comfort. The U.S. Supreme Court made that interpretation official in 1919 in *Webb* v. *U.S.*

In 1922, the Court in *U.S.* v. *Behrman* added that a narcotic prescription for an addict was illegal, even if the drugs were prescribed as part of a cure program. (Cocaine was included although it is not a narcotic.) These decisions made it nearly impossible for addicts to legally obtain their drugs. And despite the Court's reversing its *Behrman* decision in *Lindner* v. *U.S* in 1925 (holding that addicts were entitled to medical care), the damage was done because physicians refused to treat addicts under any circumstances. As a result, a well-developed illegal drug marketplace arose to cater to addicts' needs.

Controversial is how large the hardcore drug addict problem was before passage of the law. However, several indicators suggest that the use of the drugs among Americans, albeit unbeknownst to most of them, was relatively widespread. First, in the eighteenth, nineteenth, and early twentieth centuries, a booming so-called patent medicine (they were not patented) and elixir industry flourished. The active ingredient in many of these medicines and elixirs was the prohibited drugs. In 1804, about 90 brands of elixirs were advertised; by 1905, the list had increased to more than 28,000. As for advertising, following the Civil War, the patent-medicine industry was the leader in national advertising, with some individual proprietors spending more than $1 million a year. A second indicator of the widespread use of the drugs is an ad in the 1897 Sears Roebuck catalog that offered "hypodermic kits, which included a syringe, two needles, two vials, and a carrying case for as little as $1.50, with extra needles available at 25 cents each or $2.75 per dozen." A third indicator is the law, itself. It is unlikely Congress would have passed a tax act unless it believed that revenue from the tax would be substantial. Finally, a fourth indicator comes from an editorial in *American Medicine,* published six months after the Harrison Act was signed into law. The editorial also sounded a warning about the legislation: "Narcotic drug addiction is one of the gravest and most important questions confronting the medical profession today. Instead of improving conditions the laws recently passed have made the problem more complex." The complex problems to which the editorial referred were made explicit in an editorial published in the *New York Medical Journal* just six weeks after the Harrison Act went into effect:

> As was expected . . . the immediate effects of the Harrison antinarcotic law were seen in the flocking of drug habitues to hospitals and sanatoriums. Sporadic crimes of violence were reported too, due usually to desperate efforts by addicts to obtain drugs, but occasionally to a delirious state induced by sudden withdrawal. . . . The really serious results of this legislation, however, will only appear gradually and will not always be recognized as such. These will be the failures of promising careers, the disrupting of happy families, the commission of crimes which will never be traced to their real cause, and the influx into hospitals to the mentally disordered of many who would otherwise live socially competent lives.

The Bureau of Prohibition originated in 1920 as the Prohibition Unit of the Bureau of Internal Revenue. The purpose of the Prohibition Unit was to enforce the National Prohibition Act of 1919 (also known as the Volstead Act). The Act was passed to support the U.S. Constitution's newly ratified Eighteenth Amendment, which prohibited the manufacture, sale, and transportation of alcoholic beverages. In 1927, Congress passed the Bureau of Prohibition Act, which created the Bureau of Prohibition and the Bureau of Customs as independent agencies within the

ALLEN'S COCAINE TABLETS.

For Colds, Sore Throat, Nervousness, Neuralgia, Headache, Sleeplessness, Dyspepsia, Indigestion, Heartburn, and Flatulency.

USED BY ELOCUTIONISTS, VOCALISTS, AND ACTORS.

NASAL TABLOIDS.

For Catarrh, Asthma, Hay Fever, Cold in the Head.

COCAINE OINTMENT.

For Burns, Scalds, Sunburn, Prickly Heat, Eczema, Hives, Itching Skin Eruptions, Mosquito Bites.

PRICE LIST.

TABLETS, - - - - - - $4.00 PER DOZEN.
OINTMENT, - - - - - - 4.00 " "
NASAL TABLOIDS, - - - - 8.00 " "

For Sale by Wholesale Druggists and

ALLEN COCAINE MFG. CO.,

1254 BROADWAY, NEW YORK.

A patent-medicine advertisement. *Why were narcotics so popular with the American public?*

Treasury Department. The Bureau of Prohibition's most famous agent was Eliot Ness of *The Untouchables* fame. In 1930, the largely ineffective and corrupt Bureau was transferred from the Treasury Department to the Justice Department. With the ratification of the Twenty-First Amendment in 1933, the failed national experiment with alcohol prohibition was abandoned and with it, its primary enforcement agency. Commenting on the experiment's demise, early supporter of Prohibition John D. Rockefeller, Jr., had this to say:

> When Prohibition was introduced, I hoped that it would be widely supported by public opinion and the day would soon come when the evil effects of alcohol would be recognized. I have slowly and reluctantly come to believe that this has not been the result. Instead, drinking has generally increased; the speakeasy has replaced the saloon; a vast army of lawbreakers has appeared; many of our best citizens have openly ignored Prohibition; respect for the law has been greatly lessened; and crime has increased to a level never seen before.

In 1930, Congress created the Federal Bureau of Narcotics (FBN) in the Treasury Department following the collapse of the Department's Narcotics Division the year before amid evidence of corruption. The first and only commissioner of the FBN was Harry J. Anslinger, who held the post for 32 years. Before his appointment to the FBN, Anslinger was the Assistant Commissioner in the Bureau of Prohibition. Anslinger is considered the United States' first "drug czar" and is best known for his sensational campaign to demonize marijuana, which he used to elevate himself to national prominence. To fuel his national anti-marijuana campaign, Anslinger maintained a "gore file" of reefer madness-style exploitation stories that linked the drug to heinous offenses featuring ax murderers and crazed black men sexually assaulting white women. Anslinger's campaign resulted in the Marijuana Tax Act passed by Congress in 1937.

Advertisement for the 1936 movie *Reefer Madness*. Why did the FBN sensationalize the effects of marijuana consumption? Was it a good idea? Why or why not?

Like the Harrison Narcotics Tax Act of 1914, the Marijuana Tax Act of 1937, on its face, was not intended to prohibit the popular and therapeutic use of marijuana. The ostensible purpose of the legislation was to levy a token tax on anyone who imported, manufactured, produced, compounded, sold, dealt, dispensed, prescribed, administered, or gave away marijuana or any of its derivatives. The Act granted Commissioner Anslinger and his Bureau absolute administrative, regulatory, and enforcement authority. For most individuals, the tax was either one or three dollars a year or fraction thereof; for importers, manufacturers, and compounders the tax was $24 a year or fraction thereof. Those people who provided the drug, including physicians, also were required to maintain detailed records of their transactions (names, addresses, dates, amounts, and so on) that had to be made available on request to Bureau agents for inspection.

Also like the Harrison Act, the Marijuana Tax Act's ostensible purpose was belied by the punishment provisions of the law: five years' imprisonment, a $2,000 fine, or both. The penalties are curiously severe for failing to pay a tax that, even if collected, would produce only a tiny amount of revenue for the government. (A later version of the Act made it possible to impose a life sentence for selling just one marijuana cigarette to a minor.) Another telltale sign of the Act's "real" purpose was the onerous record-keeping requirement that had a chilling effect on

The United States' first "drug czar" Harry J. Anslinger. *In what ways were FBN Director Anslinger and FBI Director Hoover alike, and in what ways were they different?*

anyone who wanted to legally provide the drug. Finally, the Act erroneously classified marijuana as a narcotic; thus, placing it in the same category and under the same controls as opium and coca products. (Marijuana is still included in the same category as heroin today.)

Although Anslinger is best known for criminalizing marijuana, he also was instrumental in strengthening the Harrison Narcotics Tax Act of 1914 and lobbying for severe penalties for illegal drug usage generally. For example, in the 1950s, federal laws were passed that set mandatory sentences for drug-related offenses, including marijuana. A first-offense for possession of marijuana, for instance, carried a minimum sentence of 2 to 10 years with a fine of up to $20,000. Still, the main focus of the FBN during Anslinger's long tenure was combating opium and heroin smuggling. To that end, he opened offices in France, Italy, Turkey, Lebanon, Thailand, and other countries involved in the illegal drug trade. However, Anslinger's efforts in this area were handicapped by U.S. foreign policy considerations that shielded U.S. allies. For example, during the Vietnam War, investigations of large-scale smuggling operations in allied countries such as Thailand were never completed.

In 1968, the Justice Department's Bureau of Narcotics and Dangerous Drugs (BNDD) was formed by combining the Treasury Department's Bureau of Narcotics with the Food and Drug Administration's Bureau of Drug Abuse Control. The Food and Drug Administration was under the Department of Health, Education, and Welfare. The Bureau of Narcotics was responsible for the control of marijuana and narcotics such as heroin, while the Bureau of Drug Abuse Control was charged with the control of other dangerous drugs, including depressants, stimulants, and hallucinogens, such as LSD. The only Director of the BNDD was John E. Ingersoll, who had been Charlotte, North Carolina, Police Chief immediately before his appointment. Under Ingersoll's leadership, the BNDD became the primary U.S. drug law enforcement agency. The Bureau's goals were fourfold: (1) to consolidate the authority and preserve the experience and manpower of the Bureau of Narcotics and Bureau of Drug Abuse Control; (2) to work with state and local governments in their crackdown on illegal trade in drugs and narcotics, and help to train local agents and investigators; (3) to maintain worldwide operations, working closely with other nations, to suppress the trade in illicit narcotics and marijuana; and (4) to conduct an extensive campaign of research and a nationwide public education program on drug abuse and its tragic effects.

In 1970, under the BNDD, the first joint narcotics task force, comprising federal, state, and local law enforcement officers, was formed in New York to conduct complex drug investigations into the heroin trade. In 1971, the BNDD was given authority to enforce what became the Diversion Control Program, which investigated the large-scale diversion of such legitimate drugs as amphetamines and barbiturates to illicit markets. The BNDD also was responsible for the successful 1972 French Connection heroin investigation.

In 1973, the short-lived BNDD became a part of the newly created Drug Enforcement Administration (DEA) within the Justice Department. In addition to the BNDD, the DEA combined the Justice Department's Office of National Narcotics Intelligence and the Office of Drug Abuse Law Enforcement, the Treasury Department's Drug Investigation Unit of the U.S. Customs Service, and the Narcotics Advance Management Research Team in the Executive Office of the President. The official rationale for combining the various drug enforcement agencies was (1) the growing availability of illegal drugs in most areas of the United States, (2) the lack of coordination and the perceived lack of cooperation between U.S. Customs and the BNDD, and (3) the need for better intelligence gathering on drug trafficking organizations. The anticipated benefits of the new DEA included:

1. Putting an end to the interagency rivalries that have undermined federal drug law enforcement, especially the rivalry between the BNDD and the U.S. Customs Service;
2. Giving the FBI its first significant role in drug enforcement by requiring that the DEA draw on the FBI's expertise in combating organized crime's role in the trafficking of illicit drugs;
3. Providing a focal point for coordinating federal drug enforcement efforts with those of state and local authorities, as well as with foreign police forces;
4. Placing a single Administrator in charge of federal drug law enforcement in order to make the new DEA more accountable than its component parts had ever been, thereby safeguarding against corruption and enforcement abuses;
5. Consolidating drug enforcement operations in the DEA and establishing the Narcotics Division in Justice to maximize coordination between federal investigation and prosecution efforts and eliminate rivalries within each sphere;
6. Establishing the DEA as a superagency to provide the momentum needed to coordinate all federal efforts related to drug enforcement outside the Justice Department, especially the gathering of intelligence on international narcotics smuggling.

Multiple bombing suspect Eric Robert Rudolph is escorted by law enforcement officials from The Cherokee County Courthouse and Jail in Murphy, N. C., June 2, 2003, to a federal court hearing in Ashville, N. C. *What causes interagency rivalries, and how can they be reduced?*

The official version of the DEA's origins omits the DEA's link to the Watergate scandal that ultimately led to President Nixon's humiliating resignation from office.

Many of the key participants in the DEA's creation were key conspirators in the Watergate affair. The Nixon White House wanted to establish its own domestic-intelligence system and private police force, so it could control and eliminate Nixon Administration enemies. The war on heroin provided the needed cover, and the Offices of National Narcotics Intelligence (ONNI) and Drug Abuse Law Enforcement (ODALE) became the vehicles. (No information could be found on the Narcotics Advance Management Research Team.) The new offices, which were created in 1972 by executive order, were placed in the Justice Department instead of the White House to satisfy concerns of BNDD Director Ingersoll and Deputy Attorney General Richard Kleindienst. ONNI and ODALE agents installed illegal "national security" wiretaps and committed burglaries, warrantless raids, and other crimes on the orders of John Ehrlichman, who was counsel and Assistant to the President for Domestic Affairs, and other high-ranking Nixon Administration officials.

Besides the Watergate break-in, one of the more notorious operations of OMNI agents, called "plumbers," was the burglary of Daniel Ellsberg's psychiatrist's office. The "plumbers" were a special investigative unit charged with fixing "leaks" to the press, something with which the Nixon White House was obsessed. Ellsberg was a former military analyst, who "leaked" to the *New York Times* and other newspapers the *Pentagon Papers,* a top-secret Pentagon study that revealed faulty government decision making about the Vietnam War that was embarrassing to the Kennedy, Johnson, and Nixon administrations. The plumbers were seeking information to discredit Ellsberg, who had also been the subject of illegal wiretapping.

Today, the mission of the Drug Enforcement Administration (DEA) is this:

> to enforce the controlled substances laws and regulations of the United States and bring to the criminal and civil justice system of the United States, or any other competent jurisdiction, those organizations and principal members of organizations, involved in the growing, manufacture, or distribution of controlled substances appearing in or destined for illicit traffic in the United States; and to recommend and support non-enforcement programs aimed at reducing the availability of illicit controlled substances on the domestic and international markets.

In carrying out its mission, the agency's primary responsibilities include:

- Investigation and preparation for the prosecution of major violators of controlled substance laws operating at interstate and international levels.
- Investigation and preparation for prosecution of criminals and drug gangs who perpetrate violence in our communities and terrorize citizens through fear and intimidation.
- Management of a national drug intelligence program in cooperation with federal, state, local, and foreign officials to collect, analyze, and disseminate strategic and operational drug intelligence information.
- Seizure and forfeiture of assets derived from, traceable to, or intended to be used for illicit drug trafficking.
- Enforcement of the provisions of the Controlled Substances Act as they pertain to the manufacture, distribution, and dispensing of legally produced controlled substances.
- Coordination and cooperation with federal, state and local law enforcement officials on mutual drug enforcement efforts and enhancement of such efforts through exploitation of potential interstate and international investigations beyond local or limited federal jurisdictions and resources.
- Coordination and cooperation with federal, state, and local agencies, and with foreign governments, in programs designed to reduce the availability of illicit abuse-type drugs on the United States market through nonenforcement methods such as crop eradication, crop substitution, and training of foreign officials.

- Responsibility, under the policy guidance of the Secretary of State and U.S. Ambassadors, for all programs associated with drug law enforcement counterparts in foreign countries.
- Liaison with the United Nations, Interpol, and other organizations on matters relating to international drug control programs.

A detailed critique of America's War on Drugs is presented in Chapter 6.

THINKING CRITICALLY

1. Which of the four federal law enforcement agencies described in this section—the U.S. Marshals Service, the Secret Service, the Federal Bureau of Investigation, and the Drug Enforcement Administration—is the most important, and why?

2. Do you think it is a good idea for any individual to head a federal law enforcement agency as long as J. Edgar Hoover or Harry J. Anslinger did? Why or why not?

3. Why do you suppose the DEA continues to include marijuana in the same category as heroin?

The Structure of American Law Enforcement

Describing American law enforcement and its structure is especially difficult today because of its ongoing restructuring and transformation, from community policing at the local level to the new Department of Homeland Security at the federal level and increasing privatization at all levels. It is also difficult to describe because law enforcement agencies are so diverse. To begin with, you must decide which law enforcement agency you are talking about. For example, Oklahoma Highway Patrol officers cruise the highways and back roads, enforcing traffic laws, investigating accidents, and assisting motorists over seemingly endless miles of paved and unpaved routes. They do not ordinarily investigate criminal violations unless the violations are on state property. In contrast, a sheriff and two deputies in rural Jenkins County, Georgia, conduct criminal investigations, serve subpoenas, and investigate accidents. In the towns of Danvers, Homer, and Newman, Illinois, only one employee, the chief of police, works in each department, and that person is responsible for all law enforcement, public order, and service duties. About 60 sworn law enforcement officers at the University of Texas in Austin are also a part of American law enforcement.[28]

Altogether, tens of thousands of law enforcement officers at the federal, state, county, and municipal levels protect life and property and serve their respective publics. They are employed by government, private enterprise, and quasi-governmental entities. Their responsibilities are specific and sometimes unique to the kind of organization that employs them. Examples of these organizations are airports, transit authorities, hospitals, and parks.

At the state level, there are highway patrols, bureaus of investigation, park rangers, watercraft officers, and other law enforcement agencies and personnel with limited jurisdictions. Colleges and universities employ police officers, and some of those forces are comparable to many medium-sized police departments in the United States.

At the federal level, there are about 65 law enforcement agencies if all of the small agencies with very specific jurisdictions are included. The Federal Bureau of Investigation (FBI), the U.S. Secret Service, and the Drug Enforcement Administration (DEA) are three of the better-known agencies. The U.S. Marshals Service, the Bureau of Alcohol, Tobacco, Firearms and Explosives (ATF), and the U.S. Immigration and Customs Enforcement (ICE) are other federal law enforcement agencies, as are the Internal Revenue Service's

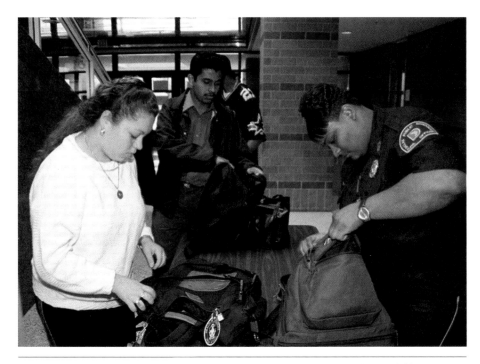

Before entering some schools, students have their bags checked every day by special law enforcement officers with limited jurisdiction. *Is this practice necessary? Why or why not?*

Criminal Investigation Division, the United States Postal Inspection Service, the U.S. Customs and Border Protection (CBP), and several dozen other agencies. As of September 2004, federal law enforcement agencies employed more than 105,000 full-time personnel authorized to make arrests and carry firearms.[29]

As the aforementioned list of law enforcement agencies suggests, explaining the law enforcement mandate and its execution in the United States is difficult. The structure of American police services is different from those of other countries. Japan and many other nations have only one police department. The United States has almost 18,000 public law enforcement agencies, and probably more when all the special police jurisdictions in the public sector are counted—including game protection agencies, water conservancies, and mental health institutions. Figure 5.1 summarizes the various law enforcement agencies in the United States.

You have already learned that law enforcement in America is fragmented, locally controlled, and limited in authority; to that, you can also add the terms *structurally* and *functionally different*. Virtually no two police agencies in America are structured alike or function in the same way. Police officers themselves are young and old; well-trained and ill-prepared; educated and uninformed; full-time and part-time; rural, urban, and suburban; generalists and specialists; paid and volunteer; and public and private. These differences lead to the following generalizations about law enforcement in the United States:

1. The quality of police services varies greatly among states and localities across the nation.
2. There is no consensus on professional standards for police personnel, equipment, and practices.
3. Expenditures for police services vary greatly among communities.
4. Obtaining police services from the appropriate agency is often confusing for crime victims and other clients.

Figure 5.1

Public Law Enforcement Agencies in the United States

The United States has almost 18,000 public law enforcement agencies.

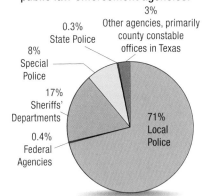

Source: Calculated from material in Brian A. Reaves, *Census of State and Local Law Enforcement Agencies, 2004*, U.S. Department of Justice, Bureau of Justice Statistics *Bulletin* (Washington, D.C.: GPO, June 2007); Brian A. Reaves, *Federal Law Enforcement Officers, 2004*, U.S. Department of Justice, Bureau of Justice Statistics (Washington, D.C.: GPO, July 2006).

LOCAL POLICING AND ITS DUTIES

If a person knows a law enforcement agent at all, it is probably a local police officer. The officer may have given the person a traffic ticket or investigated an automobile accident. The officer may have conducted a crime prevention survey. Children meet local police officers through Drug Abuse Resistance Education (D.A.R.E.) in public or private schools. Almost everyone has seen the beat cop drive by in a patrol car. Some people have reported thefts or burglaries, but it is doubtful that even they understand what local police officers in America really do, besides what they see on television and in movies.

Municipal Police Departments The more than 12,500 municipal police departments in the United States come in all sizes, but most of them are small in the number of officers employed. The overwhelming majority of police departments in America employ fewer than 50 sworn officers. Figure 5.2 shows the number of sworn officers in local police agencies in the United States. As shown, nearly one-half of all local police departments in the United States employ fewer than 10 officers, and fewer than 1% employ more than 1,000 sworn personnel.

What are some of the characteristics of the sworn personnel who occupy the ranks of municipal police agencies in the United States? Most police officers are white males. In 2003 (the latest year for which data were available), 69.4% of full-time sworn officers were white men, down from 78.4% in 1997. The

Figure 5.2

Number of Sworn Personnel in Local Departments, 2003

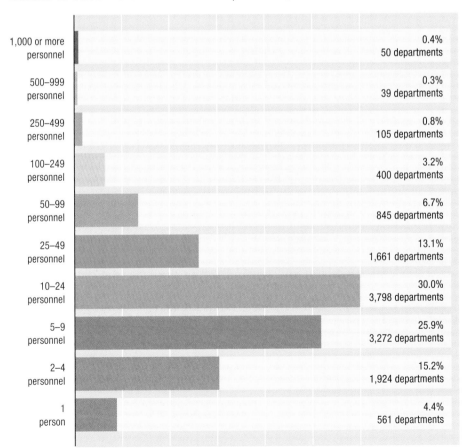

Source: Matthew J. Hickman and Brian A. Reaves, *Local Police Departments, 2003,* U.S. Department of Justice, Bureau of Justice Statistics (Washington, D.C.: GPO, May 2006).

Figure 5.3

Characteristics of Local Full-Time Police Officers

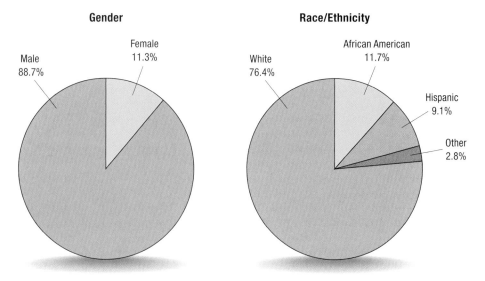

Source: Matthew J. Hickman and Brian A. Reaves, *Local Police Departments, 2003,* U.S. Department of Justice, Bureau of Justice Statistics (Washington, D.C.: GPO, May 2006).

larger the police agency, the more likely it is to employ minority officers. Women represented about 11.3% of all sworn officers in the nation's local police departments in 2003. Figure 5.3 provides a breakdown of police employment in local agencies by gender, race, and ethnicity.

A high school diploma or higher educational achievement was required by 99% of the local police departments of the nation in 2003. Eight percent of local police departments in 2003 required some college courses (up from 6% in 1990), but only 9% of the agencies required recruits to have a minimum of 2 years of college. Just 1% required new recruits to have a 4-year college degree.[30]

Local Police Duties The local police are the workhorses of the law enforcement system in America. They have many duties and tasks that will never be included in police detective novels or in movies about law enforcement. Their duties have been categorized in several different ways. One general grouping lists these four categories of local police duties:

1. **Law Enforcement**—examples are investigating a burglary, arresting a car thief, serving a warrant, or testing in court.
2. **Order Maintenance or Peacekeeping**—examples are breaking up a fight, holding back a crowd at a sporting event, or intervening in a domestic dispute before it gets violent.
3. **Service**—examples are taking people to the hospital, escorting funeral processions, delivering mail for city officials, or chasing bats out of a caller's house.
4. **Information Gathering**—examples are determining neighborhood reactions to a proposed liquor license in the community, investigating a missing child case, or investigating and reporting on a dangerous road condition.

Some police academies teach recruits the duties of a police officer through the use of the acronym *PEPPAS:*

P—Protect life and property (patrol a business district at night, keep citizens from a fire scene, recover and return lost property).

E—Enforce the law (ensure traffic laws are obeyed, warn jaywalkers of the inherent danger, make out criminal complaints, seize illegal weapons).

Local police departments, which make up the bulk of law enforcement agencies in America, are responsible for law enforcement, order maintenance, service, and information gathering. *How important is public relations for local police departments? Why?*

P—Prevent crime (give home security advice, patrol high crime areas, work as a D.A.R.E. officer in schools).

P—Preserve the peace (disband disorderly groups, have a visible presence at sporting events, intervene in neighbor conflicts).

A—Arrest violators (apprehend fleeing suspects, give citations to alcohol permit holders who sell to minors, conduct drug raids).

S—Serve the public (give directions to travelers, deliver emergency messages, administer first aid).

There are literally dozens of other duties that the police of a city, town, or village carry out, and much of the work falls into the category of helping out when no one else seems to be available. Because the police are on duty 24 hours a day in nearly every community, they are often called on to perform services that have nothing to do with law enforcement. That round-the-clock availability also significantly affects the structure, work life, and activity of a police agency.

Organizational Structure How a police agency is structured depends on the size of the agency, the degree of specialization, the philosophy the leadership has chosen (such as community policing), the political context of the department (the form of municipal government), and the history and preferences of a particular community. Most medium- to large-staffed police agencies are subdivided into patrol, criminal investigation, traffic, juvenile, and technical and support services. Subspecialties include robbery, gangs, training, bombs, property, victims' services, jail, and mounted patrol. Table 5.2 lists the specialty units of the Seattle (Washington) Police Department (SPD). The SPD has approximately 1,250 sworn officers and about 500 civilian employees. The SPD usually requires officers to work at least their first 3 years in uniformed patrol assignments. Many officers choose to remain in patrol much longer or return to patrol after assignments in other units. Others choose to vary their assignments within the Department. Some assignments outside of uniformed patrol

Table 5.2 Specialty Units of the Seattle Police Department

K-9	Traffic Enforcement	Special Activities (Seattle Center)
Auto Theft	Arson/Bomb Squad	Pawn Shop Detail
DUI Squad	Audit/Inspections	Traffic Collision Unit (T.C.I.)
Training	Anti-Crime Teams	Mounted (horses)
Bias Crimes	Community Police	Domestic Violence
Gang Unit	School Emphasis	Sexual Assault
Robbery	Vice	Burglary/Theft
Narcotics	Media Relations	Crime Analysis
Juvenile	Harbor (boats, divers)	Motorcycle
Homicide	Checks & Forgery	SWAT
C.S.I. Unit	Recruitment	Homeland Security
Background Unit	Violent Crimes	Fugitive Warrants
Internet Crimes	Child Exploitation	Cold Cases—Homicide
Missing Persons	Criminal Intelligence	Crisis Intervention Team

Source: www.seattlepolicejobs.com.

are officer positions and some are detective positions. After 3 years in patrol, officers are eligible to attend a weeklong detective school. Upon completion of the course, officers are placed on the Detective Eligibility List and are then available for assignment to a detective position. This is considered a lateral move, not a promotion.

To be promoted within the SPD, officers are required to take a civil service test, which is administered every other year. Tests are given for the rank of sergeant, lieutenant, and captain. The chief appoints assistant chiefs from the rank of captain. Officers may be promoted to sergeant after 5 years of experience with the SPD and passing the sergeant's test. Lieutenants must have at least 3 years experience as sergeants and captains must have at least 3 years experience as lieutenants. A bachelor's degree may substitute for one year of experience but can be used only for one promotional exam.

The Dallas (Texas) Police Department has about 3,000 sworn officers and 550 civilian employees and, like the Seattle Police Department, is large, sophisticated, and very specialized. For example, it has a separate detective unit for each major category of crime. Evidence technicians collect and preserve evidence during the preliminary investigation of a crime. An entire contingent of officers is assigned to traffic regulation and enforcement duties. Bicycle patrol officers work the popular West End entertainment and restaurant section downtown. The Dallas police even have sworn officers who serve as crime analysts and collect, analyze, map, and report crime data to enable better prevention and repression of crime by means of scientific deployment of officers and other strategies. Figure 5.4 presents the organizational structure of the Dallas Police Department.

Most police agencies in the United States do not have or need elaborate organizational structures. Police officers on the beat are generalists, and when special circumstances arise, such as a homicide or a complex financial investigation, they can usually rely on state bureaus of investigation to assist them. Moreover, local cooperation pacts among departments in a particular region often provide for sharing resources and specialized assistance when needed.

The infrequent need for homicide investigation skills in communities under 30,000 people, for example, makes it impractical to train one or more officers in the methods of conducting a thorough death investigation. An officer so trained might have to wait an entire career to put into practice the acquired skills, and it is most likely that by the time they were needed, the officer would have forgotten them. The lack of a trained specialist for the infrequent complex

Figure 5.4

Dallas Police Department Organization Chart

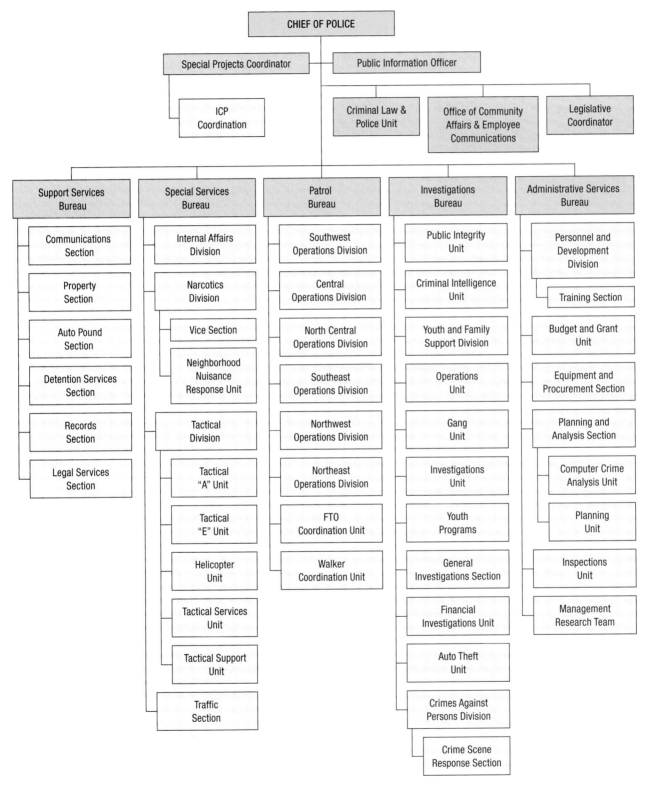

investigation, however, is one of the major reasons criminal investigation services in small communities are not equal to those in larger police departments.

The question has been raised whether larger, regional police departments would be more efficient providers of police services. However, as you have already discovered, policing in America is a local concern, and that is not likely to change.

The police are organized militarily with regard to accountability, discipline, rank, dress, and decorum. Many people believe that the military structure of a chain of command may be dysfunctional because police work is so varied. Some people believe that a military structure is best suited for situations where the objectives are simple and few, which is not the case in municipal policing. Some commentators think the military structure impedes the flow of communication and the development of good community relations because people are suspicious of the police or even fear them in some neighborhoods. Despite these criticisms, most police departments retain this organizational structure, which originated in the hiring of military leaders as the first police chiefs. Attempts to change the military structure of policing have generally failed. One reason is that police officers have often resisted any type of reorganization.

The Political Context of Policing A police department of any size is part of a larger government entity. Municipalities generally operate under one of four forms of municipal government:[31]

Strong Mayor-Council—Voters elect the mayor and the city council; the mayor appoints heads of departments.

Weak Mayor-Council—Voters elect the mayor and the city council; the city council appoints heads of departments.

City Manager—Voters elect the city council and, in some cities, a mayor; the city council selects the city manager, who appoints heads of departments.

Commission—Voters elect a board of commissioners, who become the heads of departments; the commission or the voters may choose one commissioner to be mayor.

As you can see, the forms of municipal government vary in the amount of control citizens have over the municipality's leaders, the source of the executive authority of the chief of police, and the degree of insulation a chief of police has from interference by the executive head of the city (mayor or city manager) or the city council. Each form has advantages and disadvantages. At one time it was thought that city manager government was the system under which the police were most likely to develop professionally, be free of political meddling from city lawmakers, and be insulated from local corruption. Although many progressive and effective police departments operate under a city manager form of government, other municipal forms of government have records of both success and failure in local police effectiveness and integrity.

You have probably noticed from reading newspapers and listening to radio and television that chief executives of local police agencies have different titles, depending on the locale. Popular titles are chief of police (Kansas City), director of police (Dayton, Ohio), and commissioner (New York City).

COUNTY LAW ENFORCEMENT

A substantial portion of law enforcement work in the United States is carried out by sheriffs' departments. In 2004 (the latest year for which data were available), the nation had 3,067 sheriffs' departments, employing 326,531 full-time

Figure 5.5

Characteristics of Sheriffs' Personnel, 2003

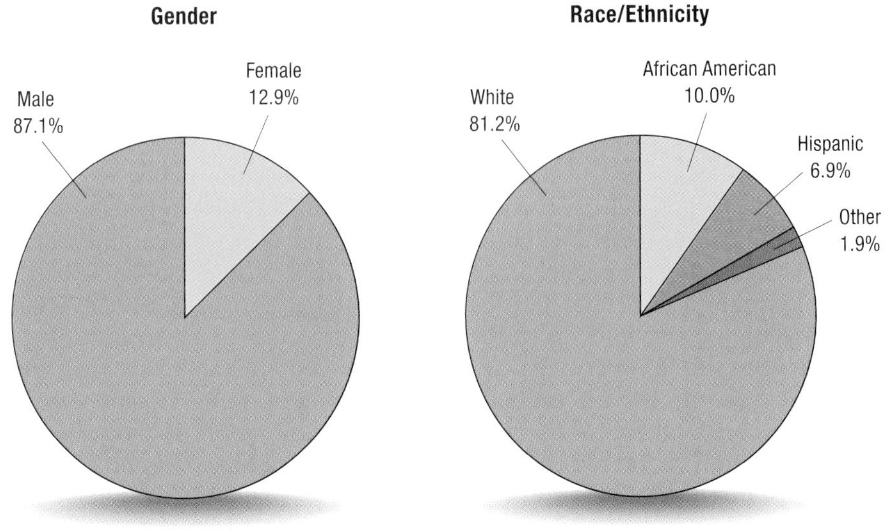

Gender

Male
87.1%

Female
12.9%

Race/Ethnicity

White
81.2%

African American
10.0%

Hispanic
6.9%

Other
1.9%

Source: Matthew J. Hickman and Brian A. Reaves, *Sheriffs' Offices, 2003,* Bureau of Justice Statistics (Washington, D.C.: GPO, 2006).

FYI Female Sheriffs

Before 1992, no woman had ever been elected to the position of sheriff in the United States. The first two were elected in 1992: The first was Jackie Barrett in Fulton County, Georgia, and the second was Judy Pridgen in Saline County, Arkansas.

personnel. About 53% of the personnel were sworn peace officers. Sheriffs frequently employ part-time personnel who work as special deputies, assisting with posses, disasters, county fairs, traffic control, and other duties. Sheriffs' departments represent about 17% of all the law enforcement departments in the United States. In 2003, the cost to provide county law enforcement was $22.3 billion, 18% more than in 2000 after adjusting for inflation.[32]

Sheriffs' personnel are 81.2% white, 10.0% black, 6.9% Hispanic, and 1.9% other. Women make up 12.9% of the sworn personnel working for sheriffs' departments.[33] (See Figure 5.5.) As are most municipal police departments, most sheriffs' departments in America are small. Figure 5.6 shows the number of departments and their respective sizes. More than one-half of all sheriffs' departments employ fewer than 25 sworn personnel.

Sheriffs' departments often have employment qualifications similar to those of municipal police agencies. A high school diploma or higher educational achievement was required by 99% of sheriffs' departments in 2003. Four percent of sheriffs' departments in 2003 required some college courses (the same as in 1990), and 5% of the departments required recruits to have a 2-year college degree. Fewer than one-half of 1% of departments required new recruits to have a 4-year college degree.[34]

County Law Enforcement Functions The sheriff and department personnel perform functions that range from investigation to supervision of sentenced offenders. Even in the smallest departments, sheriffs are responsible for investigating crimes and enforcing the criminal and traffic laws of the state. They also perform many civil process services for the court, such as serving summonses, warrants, and various writs. In addition, they provide courtroom security and confine and transport prisoners. The larger the sheriff's department, the more confinement and corrections responsibilities it has. Sheriffs' departments frequently operate the county jail, which houses hundreds and even thousands of prisoners, depending on the particular county. In some counties, the sheriff's department shares law enforcement duties with a separate police department.

Figure 5.6

Number of Sworn Personnel in Sheriffs' Departments, 2003

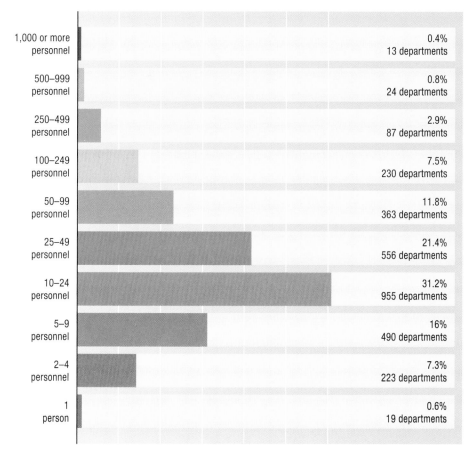

Source: Matthew J. Hickman and Brian A. Reaves, *Sheriffs' Offices, 2003,* Bureau of Justice Statistics (Washington, D.C.: GPO, 2006).

Politics and County Law Enforcement Most sheriffs are directly elected and depend on an elected board of county commissioners or supervisors for their funding and some oversight of their operations. Sheriffs generally have a freer hand in running their agencies than do police chiefs. In many counties, local politics govern the operation of the sheriff's department, and the sheriff must operate as a partisan politician to remain in office. The authority to appoint special deputies and to award patronage jobs contributes to the sheriff's power and influence in a county.

STATE LAW ENFORCEMENT

Filling the complement of law enforcement agencies in a particular state are one or more state law enforcement agencies, which provide criminal and traffic law enforcement, as well as other services peculiar to the needs of that state government. In 2004 (the latest year for which data were available), the 49 primary state law enforcement agencies (Hawaii has no state police agency) had 89,265 employees, of which 58,190, or 65%, were full-time sworn officers. Seventeen state agencies employ more than 1,000 personnel. The California Highway Patrol is the largest state law enforcement agency, with more than 10,000 personnel, of which about two-thirds are sworn officers.[35]

For the most part, each state has chosen one of two models for providing law enforcement services at the state level. The first model is the **state police model,**

state police model A model of state law enforcement services in which the agency and its officers have the same law enforcement powers as local police but can exercise them anywhere within the state.

State police agencies in every state except Hawaii have statewide jurisdiction and may be set up according to state police or highway patrol models. *Are state police agencies necessary? Why or why not?*

in which the agency and its officers have essentially the same enforcement powers as local police in the state and can work cases and enforce the law anywhere within the state's boundaries. One of the best-known state police agencies is the Texas Rangers, part of the Texas Department of Public Safety, which also employs state troopers to enforce criminal and traffic laws. The Rangers usually focus on special and complex investigations, such as the Branch Davidian case in Waco in 1993. A number of states have placed some restrictions on state police activities to avoid clashes with local politicians and local police agencies.

The second model for state law enforcement services is the **highway patrol model,** in which officers focus almost exclusively on highway traffic safety, enforcement of the state's traffic laws, and investigation of accidents on the state's roads and highways. Even highway patrols, however, may retain responsibility for investigating criminal violations on state property and in state institutions or for conducting drug interdictions.

States that employ the highway patrol model often have other state law enforcement agencies with narrow service mandates, such as these:

- Bureaus of criminal investigation (to investigate white-collar and organized crime, narcotics, and so on)
- State criminal identification services
- Forest, game, and watercraft protection services
- Alcoholic beverage control and enforcement
- Crime laboratory and criminalistics services
- Driver's license examinations
- Drug interdiction activities
- Peace officer training and certification

Both state police and highway patrol agencies help regulate commercial traffic, conduct bomb investigations, protect the governor and the capitol grounds and buildings, and administer computer-based information networks for the state, which link up with the National Crime Information Center (NCIC) run by the FBI.

highway patrol model A model of state law enforcement services in which officers focus on highway traffic safety, enforcement of the state's traffic laws, and the investigation of accidents on the state's roads, highways, and property.

Some tension always seems to exist between state police agencies and local law enforcement over legal jurisdiction and recognition for conducting investigations and making arrests. Recall that policing in America and the political system that governs it are local. Much of the resentment by locals over state interference is similar to the suspicions and doubts concerning federal involvement at the local level.

A significant function performed by a special category of state law enforcement officers is university or campus policing. Some of the large state and private universities and colleges have full-blown police agencies with many special subdivisions. They are very much like municipal police departments—and rightly so, because a community's problems with crime and public order do not end at the university gate.

FEDERAL LAW ENFORCEMENT

Everyone has heard of a few of the better-known federal law enforcement agencies. The FBI, the U.S. Secret Service, and even the T-men and T-women of the Treasury Department have had their own television shows, creating wider public recognition of those agencies. The unrelenting war on drugs has brought to the attention of the American public the activities of the Drug Enforcement Administration (DEA). There are also other, lesser-known federal police agencies. Their law enforcement jurisdictions are narrowly defined by specific statutes, and their work is unlikely to come to the attention of most American citizens.

Three major differences exist between federal law enforcement and the local and state police agencies with which we are likely to be more familiar. First, federal agencies such as the FBI operate across the entire nation and even have agents serving abroad. Second, federal police agencies do not, as a rule, have the peacekeeping or order maintenance duties typical in local policing. Finally, some federal law enforcement agencies have extremely narrow jurisdictions. (The U.S. Supreme Court Police, for example, provide protective and investigative services for the Supreme Court only.)

Federal law enforcement agencies investigate violations of federal law, enforce laws that involve interstate crimes, and conduct activities to prevent and control domestic and international terrorism. *How do the jobs of federal law enforcement agents differ from the jobs of other law enforcement officers?*

Federal Law Enforcement Personnel As of September 2004 (the latest year for which data were available), federal agencies employed nationwide about 105,000 full-time personnel authorized to make arrests and carry firearms—an increase of about 13% since June 2002 and 52% since the end of 1993.[36] Another 1,500 federal officers worked in U.S. territories, and some were employed in foreign countries. (Data for the Transportation Security Administration's Federal Air Marshals were not available because of security concerns, but see later in this chapter.) Approximately 60% of federal officers were employed by the four largest agencies: the U.S. Customs and Border Protection, the Federal Bureau of Prisons, the Federal Bureau of Investigation, and U.S. Immigration and Customs Enforcement.[37] (Note that on March 1, 2003, the former Immigration and Naturalization Service, the border and agency functions of the U.S. Customs Service, and the Federal Protective Service were reorganized into the Bureau of Immigration and Customs Enforcement in the new Department of Homeland Security, which is described in detail in the next section.) Table 5.3 shows the major employers of federal officers authorized to make arrests and carry firearms. Nearly 40% of federal law enforcement officers have criminal investigation and enforcement duties; about 20% engage in police response and patrol; 16% do inspections related to immigration or custom laws; another 16% perform corrections or detention-related roles; 5% have court-related duties; and 4% are directly involved with security and protection. Combined, the federal law enforcement agencies spent approximately $20 billion on police protection in 2006, which represented an increase of about 45% since 2004.[38]

Of the federal officers with arrest and firearm authority in 2004, about 84 were men and 16 were women—an increase in women from 14 in 1996. The Administrative Office of the U.S. Courts employed the largest percentage of women (44%), while the Veteran's Health Administration employed the fewest women (7%).[39] About one-third of federal officers were members of a racial or ethnic minority—an increase from 28% in 1996. Approximately 18% of them were Hispanic or Latino, about 11% were non-Hispanic blacks, 3% were Asians or Pacific Islanders, and 1% were American Indians. U.S. Customs and Border Protection had the largest minority percentage (approximately 47%, of which about 37% were Hispanic or Latino.) The agency with the fewest minorities was the National Park Service, Ranger Activities Division (with fewer than 10.3%). The largest percentage of black officers (about 29%) was employed by the U.S. Capitol Police, the Forest Service employed the largest percentage of American Indians (about 7%), and the Postal Inspection Service employed the largest percentage of Asians and Pacific Islanders (4.4%).[40] Table 5.3 also shows the gender and race or ethnicity of federal officers with arrest and firearm authority who were working for agencies that employed 500 or more full-time officers in 2004.

Training Federal Law Enforcement Officers The Federal Law Enforcement Training Center (FLETC) is the largest law enforcement-training establishment in the United States.[41] It provides some or all of the training for a majority of federal law enforcement agencies, as well as for many state, local, and international law enforcement agencies. Notable exceptions are the FBI and DEA, which train their special agents at their respective academies in Quantico, Virginia. Until 2003, when it became a part of the Department of Homeland Security, FLETC was a bureau of the Treasury Department with an annual budget of about $200 million.

The FLETC got its start in the late 1960s, when a federal government study disclosed that the training of most federal law enforcement personnel was inadequate at worst and substandard at best. With only a few exceptions, part-time

FYI Offices of Inspector General

Offices of Inspector General (IG) investigate criminal violations and prevent and detect fraud, waste, and abuse related to federal programs, operations, and employees. In September of 2004, there were 57 statutory federal IG offices, 27 of which employed criminal investigators with arrest and firearm authority. Overall, these agencies employed nearly 3,000 officers. The largest IG employer of federal officers authorized to arrest and carry firearms in 2004 was the Department of Health and Human Services (with 374 officers).

Source: Brian A. Reaves, *Federal Law Enforcement Officers, 2004,* U.S. Department of Justice, Bureau of Justice Statistics (Washington, D.C.: GPO, July 2006), p. 5.

Table 5.3 Gender and Race or Ethnicity of Federal Officers with Arrest and Firearm Authority, Agencies Employing 500 or More Full-Time Officers, September 2004

| | | | | PERCENTAGE OF FULL-TIME FEDERAL OFFICERS WITH ARREST AND FIREARM AUTHORITY | | | | |
| | | | | | RACE/ETHNICITY | | | |
Agency	Number of Officers*	Female	Total Minority	American Indian	Black or African American	Asian or Pacific Islander	Hispanic or Latino, Any Race	Other Race
U.S. Customs and Border Protection	28,200	15.3%	46.8%	0.6%	5.0%	4.2%	36.9%	0%
Federal Bureau of Prisons	15,361	13.3	39.7	1.3	24.2	1.5	12.7	0
Federal Bureau of Investigation	12,414	18.5	17.2	0.4	5.8	3.6	7.4	0
U.S. Immigration and Customs Enforcement	10,691	13.7	33.9	0.6	8.6	2.7	22.0	0
U.S. Secret Service	4,780	10.5	19.6	0.6	11.2	2.6	5.2	0
Drug Enforcement Administration	4,500	8.9	19.4	0.4	7.6	2.5	8.9	0
Administrative Office of the U.S. Courts	4,166	44.2	32.2	0.5	15.3	1.6	14.1	0.6
U.S. Marshals Service	3,233	10.2	20.0	0.7	7.3	2.3	9.6	0.1
U.S. Postal Inspection Service	2,999	19.6	36.4	0.5	21.6	4.7	9.6	0
Internal Revenue Service, Criminal Investigation	2,791	30.0	24.0	0.8	10.2	4.5	8.1	0.4
Veterans Health Administration	2,474	6.9	40.1	0.9	26.8	2.5	10.0	0
Bureau of Alcohol, Tobacco, Firearms & Explosives	2,398	13.3	19.9	1.1	9.3	2.1	7.5	0
National Park Service—Ranger Division	1,547	18.2	10.3	2.1	2.5	2.4	3.0	0.3
U.S. Capitol Police	1,535	18.8	34.7	0.3	28.9	1.2	4.2	0
Bureau of Diplomatic Security	825	11.8	20.0	0.7	9.7	3.4	5.5	0.7
U.S. Fish and Wildlife Service	713	8.7	13.6	3.5	1.7	1.4	7.0	0
National Park Service—U.S. Park Police	612	11.4	18.8	0	10.9	2.8	5.1	0
USDA Forest Service	604	17.5	17.4	6.5	3.3	1.3	6.3	0

Note: Data on gender and race or ethnicity of officers were not provided by the Administrative Office of the U.S. Courts. Detail may not add to total because of rounding or because of personnel classified as "other" race.

*Includes employees in U.S. Territories.

Source: Brian A. Reaves, *Federal Law Enforcement Officers, 2004,* U.S. Department of Justice, Bureau of Justice Statistics *Bulletin* (Washington, D.C.: GPO, July 2006), p. 6, Table 4.

instructors, on an irregular basis, conducted most training in inferior facilities. Much of the training duplicated the training of other federal agencies or was inconsistent with it. A government task force recommended that a federal law enforcement training center be established to provide the training for most federal law enforcement personnel. The center would have a professionally trained, full-time staff that offered consistent and high-quality programs in state-of-the-art facilities.

FLETC first opened in Washington, D.C., in 1970. That year it graduated 848 students. In 1975, its first full year of operation at its current headquarters location on a 1,500-acre campus in Glenn County ("Glynco"), Georgia (near Brunswick, Georgia), it graduated more than 5,000 students. At year-end 2005, more than 19,000 students graduated from the FLETC at Glynco, including 566 state and local officers. Another 4,910 students graduated from the FLETC Office of Artesia Operations (OAO) in New Mexico, which opened in 1989 to provide training for the Bureau of Indian Affairs and agencies with a large number of officers in the western United States. It also

CJ Online

Federal Law Enforcement Training Center

To learn more about the FLETC, visit its website at www.fletc.gov. Access its Catalog of Training Programs. *Which programs, if any, would be of interest to you? Why?*

hosts the new U.S. Border Patrol Academy. A temporary satellite training campus was opened in Charleston, South Carolina, in 1995, to train an increasing number of INS and border patrol agents. In 2003, the Charleston facility became the third FLETC-residential campus and, in 2004, all of the Border Patrol training operations were moved to FLETC-Artesia. Besides some of the same training programs offered at FLETC-Glynco and FLETC-Artesia, the FLETC-Charleston facility specializes in maritime law enforcement training. In 2005, the facility graduated nearly 1,850 officers. A fourth training facility that was developed in 2002 in Cheltenham, Maryland, is used primarily for in-service and requalification training for officers and agents in the Washington, D.C., area. It also serves as the new home for the U.S. Capitol Police Training Academy. In 2005, it graduated 15,591 students. FLETC also provides training at other temporary sites in the United States and in foreign countries.

Because basic training requirements for federal officers vary by agency and by position within agencies, FLETC provides more than 150 different agency-specific training programs. About half the instructors are permanent employees, and the other half are federal officers on short-term assignment from their respective agencies. Depending on the agency, classroom instruction ranges from about 8 to 22 weeks for criminal investigators and from 4 to 26 weeks for patrol officers. Field training requirements range from 2 weeks to 6 months for patrol officers and up to 2 years for investigators.

THINKING CRITICALLY

1. What do you think are the pros and cons of working at the local, state, and federal levels of law enforcement?

2. Do you think that any one of the three major areas of law enforcement (local, state, federal) is most prestigious? Why?

The Department of Homeland Security

The U.S. Congress responded to the terrorist attacks of September 11, 2001 (described in Chapter 6), by enacting the Homeland Security Act of 2002.[42] Among other provisions, such as allowing commercial pilots to carry guns in cockpits, the act established the Department of Homeland Security (DHS). According to the legislation, this new executive department was created to

1. Prevent terrorist attacks within the United States.
2. Reduce the vulnerability of the United States to terrorism.
3. Minimize the damage, and assist in the recovery, from terrorist attacks that do occur within the United States.
4. Carry out all functions of entities transferred to the department, including by acting as a focal point regarding natural and manmade crises and emergency planning.
5. Ensure that the functions of the agencies and subdivisions within the department that are not related directly to securing the homeland are not diminished or neglected except by an explicit act of Congress.
6. Ensure that the overall economic security of the United States is not diminished by efforts, activities, and programs aimed at securing the homeland.
7. Monitor connections between illegal drug trafficking and terrorism, coordinate efforts to sever such connections, and otherwise contribute to efforts to interdict illegal drug trafficking.

The act also stipulates that "primary responsibility for investigating and prosecuting acts of terrorism shall be vested not in the Department, but rather in

A UH-60 Black Hawk helicopter from the Department of Homeland Security's new Bureau of Immigration and Customs Enforcement patrolling restricted airspace over the New York metropolitan area to detect unauthorized intrusions. *Is this an effective defensive strategy against terrorism? Why or why not?*

Federal, State, and local law enforcement agencies with jurisdiction over the acts in question."

The creation of the Department of Homeland Security represents the most dramatic transformation of the U.S. government since 1947, when President Harry S. Truman combined the various branches of the U.S. military into the Department of Defense. On an even grander scale, President George W. Bush combined 22 previously separate domestic agencies into the new department to protect the country from future threats. To head the new department, President Bush selected former Pennsylvania Governor Tom Ridge. On February 15, 2005, Michael Chertoff, former U.S. Court of Appeals judge, was sworn in as the second Secretary of DHS, and on January 21, 2009, former Arizona Governor Janet Napolitano became the third Secretary of DHS.

DEPARTMENT COMPONENTS

The new department, which has been reorganized since its inception, comprises the following major components:

1. The **Directorate for Management** is responsible for Department budgets and appropriations, expenditure of funds, accounting and finance, procurement, human resources, information technology systems, facilities and equipment, and the identification and tracking of performance measurements.
2. The **Directorate for Science and Technology** is the primary research and development arm of the Department. It provides federal, state, and local officials with the technology and capabilities to protect the homeland.
3. The **Directorate for National Protection and Programs** works to advance the Department's risk-reduction mission. Reducing risk requires an integrated approach that encompasses both physical and virtual threats and their associated human elements.
4. The **Office of Policy** is the primary policy formulation and coordination component for the Department of Homeland Security. It provides a centralized,

CJ Online

Department of Homeland Security

To learn more about the Department of Homeland Security, visit its website at www.dhs.gov/index.shtm. *Based on what you have learned, do you think the DHS will be effective in preventing terrorism on American soil?*

coordinated focus to the development of Department-wide, long-range planning to protect the United States.

5. The **Office of Health Affairs** coordinates all medical activities of the Department of Homeland Security to ensure appropriate preparation for and response to incidents having medical significance.

6. The **Office of Intelligence and Analysis** is responsible for using information and intelligence from multiple sources to identify and assess current and future threats to the United States.

7. The **Office of Operations Coordination** is responsible for monitoring the security of the United States on a daily basis and coordinating activities within the Department and with governors, Homeland Security Advisors, law enforcement partners, and critical infrastructure operators in all 50 states and more than 50 major urban areas nationwide.

8. The **Federal Law Enforcement Training Center** provides career-long training to law enforcement professionals to help them fulfill their responsibilities safely and proficiently.

9. The **Domestic Nuclear Detection Office** works to enhance the nuclear detection efforts of federal, state, territorial, tribal, and local governments, and the private sector and to ensure a coordinated response to such threats.

10. The **Transportation Security Administration (TSA)** protects the nation's transportation systems to ensure freedom of movement for people and commerce.

11. **United States Customs and Border Protection (CBP)** is responsible for protecting our nation's borders in order to prevent terrorists and terrorist weapons from entering the United States, while facilitating the flow of legitimate trade and travel.

12. **United States Citizenship and Immigration Services** is responsible for the administration of immigration and naturalization adjudication functions and establishing immigration services policies and priorities.

13. **United States Immigration and Customs Enforcement (ICE),** the largest investigative arm of the Department of Homeland Security, is responsible for identifying and shutting down vulnerabilities in the nation's border, economic, transportation, and infrastructure security.

14. The **United States Coast Guard** protects the public, the environment, and U.S. economic interests—in the nation's ports and waterways, along the coast, on international waters, or in any maritime region as required to support national security.

15. The **Federal Emergency Management Agency (FEMA)** prepares the nation for hazards, manages federal response and recovery efforts following any national incident, and administers the National Flood Insurance Program.

16. The **United States Secret Service** protects the President and other high-level officials and investigates counterfeiting and other financial crimes, including financial institution fraud, identity theft, computer fraud; and computer-based attacks on our nation's financial, banking, and telecommunications infrastructure.

17. The **Office of the Secretary** oversees activities with other federal, state, local, and private entities as part of a collaborative effort to strengthen our borders, provide for intelligence analysis and infrastructure protection, improve the use of science and technology to counter weapons of mass destruction, and create a comprehensive response and recovery system. The Office of the Secretary includes the following multiple offices that contribute to the overall Homeland Security mission.

18. **Office of the General Counsel** integrates approximately 1,700 lawyers from throughout the Department into an effective, client-oriented, full-service

---

FYI TSA and Federal Air Marshals

The Transportation Security Administration (TSA) was created in response to 9/11. One of its first actions was to significantly expand the Federal Air Marshals program to provide security on commercial aircrafts. Although exact numbers are not available, there are an estimated 3,000 to 4,000 Federal Air Marshals.

Source: Brian A. Reaves, *Federal Law Enforcement Officers, 2004*, U.S. Department of Justice, Bureau of Justice Statistics (Washington, D.C.: GPO, July 2006), p. 11, Exhibit B.

Careers in Criminal Justice

U.S. Immigration and Customs Special Agent

My name is Jose Pagan and I became a U.S. Customs Special Agent/Criminal Investigator in 1987 (before the creation of the Department of Homeland Security). During my career, I have served as a federal law enforcement officer in the U.S. Virgin Islands, Puerto Rico, and Orlando, Florida, where I have been assigned since December 2000.

I have had the opportunity to conduct and participate in numerous narcotic interdiction investigations, as well as become a liaison officer between U.S. Customs and other federal and international law enforcement agencies.

As a U.S. Immigration and Customs special agent, I have learned the value of organization and sound criminal investigation procedures as the primordial law enforcement tools. The investigation of crimes, regardless of type (passion, violence, financial, fraud, narcotic smuggling, counterfeiting, etc.), depends on sound standardized investigatory procedures. I have also mastered many investigative techniques. Among these techniques are interviewing skills such as detecting and utilizing flaws in elicited responses from a suspect, as well as observing behavior that could assist me in assessing the subject's veracity.

By utilizing proven criminal investigation procedures, in conjunction with the officer's experience, crime investigation becomes a scientific, measurable, and reliable method of protecting the public. Even in the investigation of the most heinous crimes, a reliable investigation, based on facts properly discovered and presented in an orderly, organized, and logical fashion, will always portray a fair, just, and clear case for the jury.

I have participated in operations such as the marine interdiction of narcotics and illegal aliens, as well as serving dozens of search warrants, all of which have demanded a great deal of physical exertion (added to the emotional stress that an assertive law enforcement action creates on the officers). Cases such as joint international investigations of narcotic smuggling have given me the opportunity to learn other countries' law enforcement techniques, customs, and points of view. At the same time, counterfeiting cases offer the opportunity to learn about the U.S. and international trade systems, as well as to teach the true impact that unfair trade practices have on the U.S. economy.

There are no typical days at the office in this career. On any given day, I could be on a vessel, sailing to prevent narcotic smuggling into the U.S., or interviewing the operation manager of a large company whose product has been counterfeited.

What parts of the U.S. Immigration and Customs Special Agent's role do you find most and least appealing? Why?

---

legal team and comprises a headquarters office with subsidiary divisions and the legal programs for eight Department components.

19. The **Office of Legislative Affairs** serves as primary liaison to members of Congress and their staffs, the White House and Executive Branch, and to other federal agencies and governmental entities that have roles in assuring national security.

20. **Office of Public Affairs** coordinates the public affairs activities of all of the Department's components and offices, and serves as the federal government's lead public information office during a national emergency or disaster. Led by the Assistant Secretary for Public Affairs, it comprises the press office, incident and strategic communications, speechwriting, Web content management, employee communications, and the Department's Ready campaign.

21. The **Office of Inspector General** is responsible for conducting and supervising audits, investigations, and inspections relating to the programs and operations of the Department, recommending ways for the Department to carry out its responsibilities in the most effective, efficient, and economical manner possible.

22. The **Citizenship and Immigration Services Ombudsman** provides recommendations for resolving individual and employer problems with the United States Citizenship and Immigration Services in order to ensure national security and the integrity of the legal immigration system, increase efficiencies in administering citizenship and immigration services, and improve customer service.

23. The **Privacy Office** works to minimize the impact on the individual's privacy, particularly the individual's personal information and dignity, while achieving the mission of the Department of Homeland Security.

24. The office for **Civil Rights and Civil Liberties** provides legal and policy advice to Department leadership on civil rights and civil liberties issues, investigates and resolves complaints, and provides leadership to Equal Employment Opportunity Programs.
25. **Office of Counternarcotics Enforcement**
26. The Office of the **Executive Secretariat** (ESEC) provides all manner of direct support to the Secretary and Deputy Secretary, as well as related support to leadership and management across the Department. This support takes many forms, the most well known being accurate and timely dissemination of information and written communications from throughout the Department and our homeland security partners to the Secretary and Deputy Secretary.
27. **Military Advisor's Office**

ADVISORY PANELS AND COMMITTEES

- The **Homeland Security Advisory Council** provides advice and recommendations to the Secretary on matters related to homeland security. The Council comprises leaders from state and local government, first responder communities, the private sector, and academia.
- The **National Infrastructure Advisory Council** provides advice to the Secretary of Homeland Security and the President on the security of information systems for the public and private institutions that constitute the critical infrastructure of our nation's economy.
- The **Homeland Security Science and Technology Advisory Committee** serves as a source of independent, scientific and technical planning advice for the Under Secretary for Science and Technology.
- The **Critical Infrastructure Partnership Advisory Council** was established to facilitate effective coordination between federal infrastructure protection programs with the infrastructure protection activities of the private sector and of state, local, territorial, and tribal governments.
- The **Interagency Coordinating Council on Emergency Preparedness and Individuals with Disabilities** was established to ensure that the federal government appropriately supports safety and security for individuals with disabilities in disaster situations.
- The **Task Force on New Americans** is an inter-agency effort to help immigrants learn English, embrace the common core of American civic culture, and become fully American.

The organization chart of the Department of Homeland Security is shown in Figure 5.7.

HOMELAND SECURITY AND THE FBI

Before the creation of the Department of Homeland Security, the FBI had primary responsibility for locating terrorist groups and preventing terrorist acts in the United States. It had many successes. According to FBI data, for example, the agency prevented 130 terrorist acts between 1980 and 1999.[43] However, following the al-Qaeda attacks on New York and Washington, the FBI was heavily criticized for missing clues and intelligence failures.[44] For example, Senator John Edwards of North Carolina, who had oversight responsibility for the FBI as a member of both the Intelligence and Judiciary committees, remarked, "The FBI is clearly broken, and we can accept no further delay in the effort to fix it." He added, "The FBI should do what it does best: law enforcement [rather than] collecting information, fitting it into a bigger picture and sharing that information with people who can act on it." To root out terrorists within the United States, legislators on Capitol Hill called for

Figure 5.7

Department of Homeland Security Organization Chart

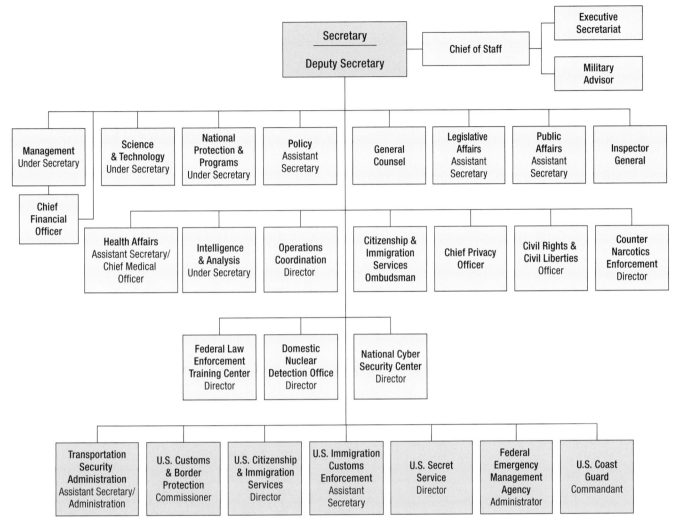

Source: Department of Homeland Security at www.dhs.gov/dhspublic (accessed April 20, 2009).

the creation of a new domestic intelligence-gathering agency similar to the MI-5 in Great Britain.

FBI Director Robert Mueller defended his agency. He responded, "Establishing a new domestic intelligence agency would constitute a step backward in the war on terror, not a step forward." He maintained that rather than "create a new agency from whole cloth, the public would be better served by improving what the FBI is already doing."

Director Mueller won a reprieve for the FBI and quickly began implementing fundamental changes. First, he shifted the top priority of the FBI from being a federal police agency to being an intelligence and counterterrorism agency. In doing so, he no longer allows local field offices to establish their own distinct agendas. As a result, by 2008, the FBI had referred 40% fewer criminal investigations to the Justice Department than it did two decades ago.

Second, he restructured the management hierarchy at FBI headquarters in Washington to support counterterrorism efforts. Figure 5.8 shows the FBI's post-9/11 organization chart with the new emphasis on counterterrorism.

Third, he reassigned about one-quarter of the FBI's then 11,000 agents to work on counterterrorism. That represents a doubling of the number of agents handling

Figure 5.8

Federal Bureau of Investigation Organization Chart

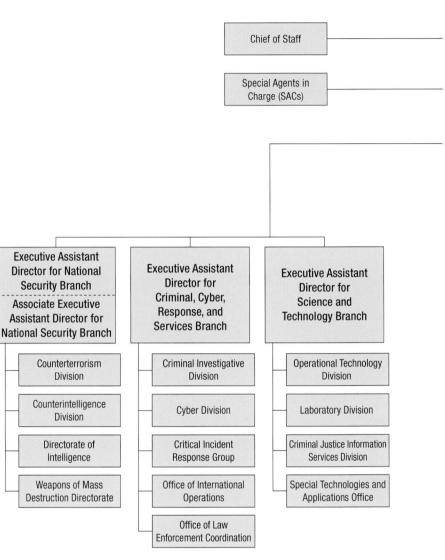

Source: www.fbi.gov/filelink.html?file=/aboutus/todaysfbi/orgchart.pdf (accessed April 20, 2009).

terrorism cases, a quadrupling of the number of strategic analysts at FBI headquarters, but a decrease of about one-third of all agents in criminal programs. Consequently, although the FBI official in charge of criminal investigations correctly predicted the recent mortgage crisis in 2004, and believed the FBI could prevent it from spiraling out of control, by 2007, the FBI had only about 100 agents pursuing mortgage fraud. By comparison, during the Savings and Loan debacle of the 1980s and 1990s, the FBI had about 1,000 agents investigating banking fraud.[45] (In response to the recent financial collapse, the FBI is planning to double the number of agents working financial crimes, but it is unclear from where those agents will come and whether there will be enough of them. Since 2004, the Bush Administration had refused to approve new agents to investigate financial crimes.)[46]

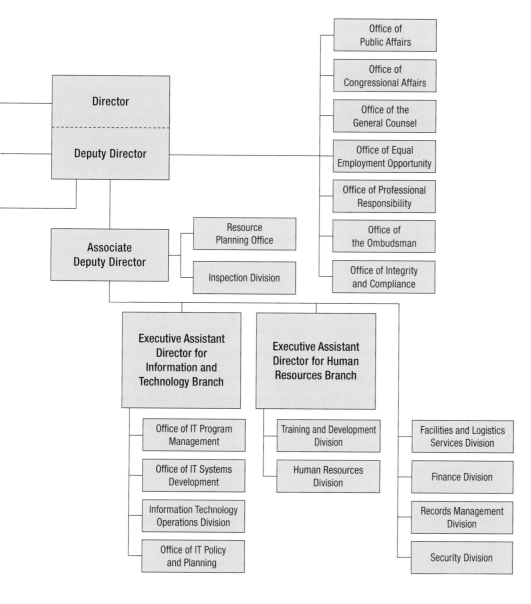

Fourth, he established a National Joint Terrorism Task Force at FBI headquarters that includes staffers from federal, state, and local agencies. They are responsible for coordinating the flow of information with task forces in each of the bureau's 56 field offices.

Fifth, to more directly address the global threat of al-Qaeda and other terrorist groups, he planned on opening FBI offices in Kabul, Afghanistan; Sarajevo, Bosnia; Jakarta, Indonesia; Tashkent, Uzbekistan; and Belgrade, Serbia. As of 2008, he had opened FBI offices in Kabul, Sarajevo, and Jakarta but not in Tashkent or Belgrade. He also planned on expanding FBI offices in Ottawa, Canada; Seoul, South Korea; London, Berlin, and Moscow. Since the tragic events of 9/11, about 500 FBI agents and 200 support personnel have been working outside the United States on terrorism investigation. Already working outside the United States in 75 key cities worldwide were FBI agents known as permanent legal attaches, or "legats." The job of legats is to feed information gathered from interviews back to the United States for further investigation. Unlike CIA agents, legats, who will

Careers in Criminal Justice

FBI Special Agent

My name is Michelle L. Rankin and I am an FBI special agent in the Washington, D.C. (PCU), field office, Public Corruption Unit. The Washington, D.C., field office is the second largest field office in the FBI. I thoroughly enjoy my career with the FBI.

The PCU investigates allegations of bribery involving public officials, including extortion or using the mail to defraud the public. Examples include the issuance of licenses, permits, contracts, or zoning variances; judicial case fixing; and law enforcement corruption.

The PCU's responsibilities are divided into two squads. My squad focuses on the District of Columbia government. The other squad concentrates on the executive branch of the federal government in the Washington, D.C., area. Twelve agents are assigned to my squad, along with nonagent support specialists.

Prior to transferring to the PCU, I worked on a special inquiry squad, conducting background investigations for White House staff and presidential appointees. It was in this capacity that I had the opportunity to interview Attorney General Janet Reno as well as other prominent politicians.

People often ask about training at the FBI Academy. The program is 16 weeks of rigorous and intellectually challenging work. You have to study 12–15 major subject areas, you often have 3 hours of homework for the next day's classes, and you may also have an exam in another course the next day. Some agents realize that the FBI is not what they thought it was. Others find it difficult to be away from family and friends.

I have a B.A. in Criminal Justice from California State University at San Bernardino. While working on a Certificate in Crime and Intelligence Analysis through the California State University system and the California Department of Justice, I began to volunteer with the Riverside County Sheriff's Department. I eventually obtained a full-time position as an analyst there. Later I went to the Santa Clara Police Department as a Certified Crime and Intelligence Analyst. I designed and directed their crime analysis unit for 4 years. I left Santa Clara in 1999 to become an FBI agent.

To become an FBI Special Agent, applicants must be between the ages of 23 and 37. The FBI prefers to hire people who are already successful in some other field. Prior work experience need not be in law enforcement. The FBI hires agents from four career categories: law; accounting; foreign languages; and "diversified"—which includes criminal justice. You need to have a minimum of 3 years of work experience in your chosen field before applying to be an agent. When hired, new FBI Special Agents start at a GS-10, step 1 pay grade, which is now approx-imately $40,000 per year before overtime. My advice to some-one who wants to become an FBI agent is to maintain the highest standards of conduct in your life. Your first job out of college does not have to be in criminal justice, but be sure to be successful in whatever you do.

After reading this account, what do you think is a key quality of a good FBI agent?

---

work more closely with the CIA, do not operate covertly and are involved more with investigations than with gathering intelligence.

In 2005, in response to a presidential directive to establish a "National Security Service" that combined the missions, capabilities, and resources of the FBI's counterterrorism, counterintelligence, and intelligence units, the FBI cre-ated a National Security Branch (NSB). In 2006, the Weapons of Mass Destruc-tion (WMD) Directorate was established within the NSB to integrate WMD units that previously had been spread throughout the FBI. The NSB also includes the Terrorist Screening Center, whose role is to provide actionable intelligence to state and local law enforcement. In creating the NSB, the FBI has moved beyond case-focused intelligence to building a Bureau-wide intelligence collection, anal-ysis, and dissemination program that combines intelligence from across the Bureau. The FBI now uses intelligence not just to pursue investigations but to have greater awareness of national security threats and the total threat environ-ment. The FBI now looks at information for its predictive value and shares that information—save that which it is legally proscribed from releasing—with its partners in law enforcement and the Intelligence Community.

An integral part of the FBI's information-sharing capabilities is the Guard-ian Terrorist Threat and Suspicious Incident Tracking System, which was intro-duced in 2002. However, according to a November 2008 Justice Department inspector general report, although Guardian is an improvement over the FBI's former program, the FBI could be more effectively using the new computer system and central database. For example, between July 2004 and November 2007, the FBI collected information on 108,000 potential threats, suspicious incidents, and encounters with people on a terrorist suspect watch list. The information triggered 600 investigations from October 2006 to December 2007. The FBI failed to enter into the Guardian system about half of those investigations, and supervisors had not reviewed 12% of the threat information among 218 incidents included in the audit. The report noted that the FBI did a good job following up on high-priority threats but generally failed to follow up low-priority threats within its 30-day goal.[47]

In sum, through the efforts of Director Mueller, the FBI remains an independent agency, albeit with a new top priority, and retains its traditional responsibility of intelligence gathering and analysis. However, it now closely coordinates its antiterrorism activities with personnel from the Office of the Director of National Intelligence (ODNI), Central Intelligence Agency (CIA), Department of Defense (DOD), and Department of Homeland Security (DHS) at the new National Counterterrorism Center (NCTC) and with state, local, and tribal partners in task forces around the country. Today, the FBI shares intelligence gathered in the United States and overseas to provide a coordinated strategic and tactical response to threats.

THE WAR ON TERRORISM: AN EVALUATION

Advocates of the Department of Homeland Security are confident that the DHS will have the financial, intelligence, and tactical resources necessary to prevent and control domestic terrorism. At this writing, the DHS is assessing the threats against the United States and coordinating the resources of law enforcement and other kinds of agencies that are necessary to defeat terrorism at home. One of its first efforts was the creation of a color-coded warning system to alert citizens to the likelihood of a terrorist attack. The hope is that as the warning level is raised, the vigilance of Americans will increase and information will be discovered that will prevent a terrorist act.

The war on terrorism is an ongoing battle with no end in sight. Nevertheless, there already have been some successes. For example, since September 11, 2001, as a result of cooperation among law enforcement agencies, thousands of al-Qaeda members or their associates have been captured and detained in more than 100 countries.[48] In addition, most of al-Qaeda's top leadership has been killed or captured.[49] The financial resources of terrorist groups have also been successfully attacked. Leaders of 173 countries have ordered the freezing of more than $136 million terrorist-related financial assets.[50] In the United States, under the authority of Executive Order 13224, which was issued by President Bush on September 23, 2001, about 460 terrorist groups and entities have been listed as possible targets for the freezing of their U.S.-based assets (as of the end of 2007).[51] Further, any American citizen who contributes money or other aid to any of the 460 organizations and entities automatically becomes suspect. Most important, the United States, as of February 1, 2009, has not experienced a repeat of the 9/11 tragedy. However, Osama bin Laden (probably) and other key al-Qaeda leaders were still at large (as of February 1, 2009) despite the best efforts of the United States and its coalition partners and a reward of up to $25 million authorized by then Secretary of State Colin Powell for information leading to their capture.[52] Also, as of November 2008, few countries were freezing the financial assets of terrorist groups and entities, and many countries had not even created the legal framework necessary to do so. Persian Gulf countries, especially Iran, Syria, and Saudi Arabia, remain significant sources of terrorist funds.[53]

THINKING CRITICALLY

1. Do you think the United States has too many law enforcement agencies? Why or why not?

2. With the creation of the Department of Homeland Security, is the FBI needed any longer? Defend your answer.

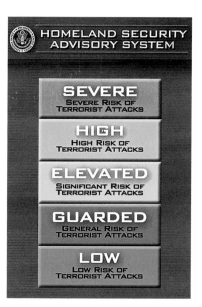

The Homeland Security Department's color-coded national threat alert system is intended to help citizens better prepare for potential terrorist attacks. *Do you believe the system is effective? Why or why not?*

 Rewards for Justice

Rewards of up to $25 million are available through the Rewards for Justice program for information that prevents or favorably resolves acts of international terrorism against U.S. citizens or property anywhere in the world. Since its inception in 1984, Rewards for Justice has paid more than $77 million to more than 50 people (as of November 24, 2008).

Source: Rewards for Justice at www.rewardsforjustice.net/index.cfm?page=success_stories&language=english; Federal Bureau of Investigation at www.fbi.gov/page2/feb07/rewards021207.htm.

American Private Security

Private security is a huge enterprise that complements public law enforcement in the United States. The Department of Labor's Bureau of Labor Statistics projects the continued growth of private security employment well into this century.[54] It has been estimated that twice as many people work in private security as in public law enforcement. A recent study found that in major American cities, the ratio is three or four private security officers to each police officer.[55] Until recently, substantially more money was being spent on private security than on public policing, but that gap has been narrowing somewhat because of the increases in spending on public law enforcement during the 1990s and the federalizing of airport security (through the Transportation Security Administration) in the wake of the 9/11 terrorist assault.

A common way to categorize private security employment is to classify the agencies and personnel as either contract or proprietary. **Contract security** companies offer protective services for a fee to people, agencies, and companies that do not employ their own security personnel or that need extra protection. A state university, for example, may employ private security officers to work at a football game. Contract security employees are not peace officers. **Proprietary security** agents and personnel provide protective services for the entity that employs them. They are also not classified as sworn peace officers. For example, the Ford Motor Company employs its own security forces at its large manufacturing plants. Primarily for cost reasons, the number of contract security jobs is likely to increase faster than the number of proprietary security jobs.

contract security Protective services that a private security firm provides to people, agencies, and companies that do not employ their own security personnel or that need extra protection.

proprietary security In-house protective services that a security staff provides for the entity that employs it.

Private security is assuming an increasing role in maintaining order, investigating crime, and apprehending criminals. *Is this a positive trend? Why or why not?*

PRIVATE SECURITY OFFICERS

Private security officers, or guards, are hired to provide protection.[56] They typically work 8-hour shifts, 5 days a week. In 2007, the average salary for a private security officer was $24,840. Managers and corporate officers made more. More than half of private security officers in 2007 worked for investigation and security services, such as armored car services.

Because of relatively low wages, private security officers frequently work part-time or have another "primary" job and use their security job wages to supplement their incomes. In 2007, there were more than one million private security officers. A private security officer's duties vary and depend on the employers' particular needs. Private security officers generally specialize in one of the following areas:

- Protecting people, records, merchandise, money, and equipment in department stores; also working with undercover store detectives to prevent theft by customers or store employees and helping in the apprehension of shoplifting suspects before the police arrive.
- Patrolling the parking lots of shopping centers and theaters, sometimes on horseback or bicycles, to deter car theft and robberies.
- Maintaining order and protecting property, staff, and customers in office buildings, banks, and hospitals.

- Protecting people, freight, property, and equipment at air, sea, and rail terminals as well as other transportation facilities; also screening passengers and visitors for weapons and explosives using metal detectors and high-tech equipment, ensuring that nothing is stolen while being loaded or unloaded, and watching for fires and criminals.
- Protecting paintings and exhibits by inspecting people and packages entering and leaving public buildings such as museums or art galleries.
- Protecting information, products, computer codes, and defense secrets and checking the credentials of people and vehicles entering or leaving the premises of factories, laboratories, government buildings, data-processing centers, and military bases.
- Performing crowd control, supervising parking and seating, and directing traffic at universities, parks, and sports stadiums.
- Preventing access by minors, collecting cover charges at the door, maintaining order among customers, and protecting property and patrons while stationed at the entrance to bars and places of adult entertainment such as nightclubs.
- Protecting money and valuables during transit in armored cars; also protecting individuals responsible for making commercial bank deposits from theft or bodily injuries.
- Observing casino operations for irregular activities, such as cheating or theft, by employees or patrons.

REASONS FOR GROWTH

A number of factors have stimulated the phenomenal growth of private security since the 1970s.

Declining Revenues for Public Policing In virtually all major cities and in state governments in the United States, the competition for limited funds to operate public services is fierce. Public police agencies have experienced their share of across-the-board government belt-tightening, and that has caused limitations and even freezes on the hiring of additional police officers. As a result, police departments have curtailed services no longer deemed critical. Often, businesses have filled the service gap by employing private security personnel.

The Private Nature of Crimes in the Workplace A business depends on a positive reputation to remain competitive. Widespread employee theft, embezzlement scandals, and substance abuse harm an organization's public image and may cause potential customers to question the quality of a company's products and services. By employing private security personnel to prevent and repress crime in their facilities, businesses can either hide the crimes that occur or minimize the negative publicity.

Better Control and Attention to the Problem By employing in-house security personnel or by contracting with an outside firm, the management of a business can direct security personnel to do precisely what is needed to prevent crime, minimize substance abuse, and discipline wayward employees. Public police would have to combine the concerns of a business with the priorities of the citizens of the community.

Fewer Constitutional Limitations Some of the constitutional restrictions that would limit the actions of public police officers working undercover to curtail drug trafficking in an industrial plant, for example, would not restrict private security personnel employed directly by that industry. U.S. Supreme Court prohibitions that restrict a public police officer's right to search and seize property, for instance, would not limit the actions of a private security agent.

ISSUES INVOLVING PRIVATE SECURITY

A number of unresolved problems and issues impinge on the potential for development of the private security industry. Some of them put the industry at odds with public law enforcement.

Legal Status and Authority Private security officers' legal status and authority derive from the rights of the owner who employs them to protect property on the premises. These rights are essentially the same ones you have to protect your life and property at home.

If this view prevails, private security personnel face few constitutional limitations in investigating crime, obtaining evidence, employing reasonable force, searching personal property stored in corporate spaces, and interrogating suspects. Although this is not a unanimous view among courts, it is the most prevalent one. However, private security officers and their employers face the possibility of being held civilly or criminally liable for violating an individual's civil rights or for false arrest.

Public Policing in a Private Capacity Although some police departments prohibit moonlighting, thousands of police officers still work in a private capacity during their off-duty hours. Some police agencies even cooperate with private agencies in scheduling their officers for off-duty assignments. With regard to their legal status and authority, are these officers considered public police or private security personnel? The private organization that employs them believes that off-duty police officers are better qualified, have more authority to arrest, and will have a greater deterrent effect on the crimes and disturbances of the peace the employer is trying to prevent.

An equally important question is, Who is liable should moonlighting officers abuse their authority or make a mistake? At present, it seems police agencies that take an active role in scheduling off-duty assignments accept greater liability than the police departments that do not. Many agencies limit the assignments officers are allowed to accept and the number of hours they are permitted to work.

Qualifications and Training Many superbly qualified people work in private security at all levels throughout the United States, but those people are not the norm. Although the minimum qualifications for private security personnel at all levels of employment are increasing, they lag far behind those of the public police. Few states enforce any educational, physical, or background integrity qualifications for private security personnel. In most states, the training required to become a private security officer is less than a week long. However, private security officers at nuclear power plants, for example, receive months of training before they are placed on the job under close supervision. In some states, armed security officers must attend a firearms course, including a section on the laws applicable to the use of deadly force, and must successfully complete a practical firearms qualification test. In nearly all states, public police officers who work off duty in a private policing capacity are exempt from any private security training, even if the nature of their private police work is substantially different from their police department functions.

The qualifications of proprietary security officers are generally higher than those of contract security officers, demonstrating corporate demand for high-quality security services even when they cost more.

Diminished Public Responsibility The current mixture of public and private protection is a matter of concern to many. What does it say about a government's ability to govern and provide for the general welfare—let alone what it says about American society—that ever more frequently it is shifting responsibility for protecting life and property to private security enterprises? To some, it seems to mean that public police officers and the governments that employ them have defaulted on a major portion of the social contract.

Private Security's Role in the Fight Against Terrorism Private security officers are often the first line of defense against terrorism in the United States and other nations. They guard government buildings, utilities, schools, courts, corporate headquarters, office complexes, laboratories, and transportation facilities, to name only a few. Security experts believe that 15% to 20% of the private security officers in the United States protect sites designated by the government as "critical infrastructure."[57] Unfortunately, with relatively few exceptions, most of the nation's more than one million security officers are unlicensed, untrained, and do not undergo background checks (see the FYI in the margin).

The private security industry and its officers have been given more protection responsibilities as the threat of domestic terrorism in the United States has increased. Public law enforcement alone cannot begin to meet the protection responsibilities necessary to prevent terrorism. This means that the private security industry, comprising 11,000 companies throughout America, will have to begin improving its selection standards and training if the nation's people, visitors, and assets are to be protected. As unbelievable as it is, hundreds of security guards employed to protect the Statue of Liberty were found in 2002 to have no licenses, and their ranks included ex-convicts. According to a recent report, tens of thousands of security guard applicants were found to have criminal backgrounds.[58]

Because it is so difficult to find enough capable private security officers, the proprietary security firms, motivated by large profits, have been employing hundreds if not thousands of unqualified and unmotivated applicants. For many of the guards, the position is a second or low-paying job that they can easily quit if they find a better-paying job or simply choose to do so. More troublesome is that foreign and domestic terrorists could easily obtain a private security position and inflict physical and emotional havoc on the nation by initiating some terrorist activity inside a vulnerable site.

Seldom is throwing money at a problem a solution in and of itself; yet, if the private security industry is to fulfill its obligation to protect the homeland, it is going to need more financial resources. It may be necessary, for example, to provide government subsidies for training and background checks and a significant increase in the amount of cooperation between the public police and the private security industry. That sort of investment and training can bring positive results. Following the 1993 World Trade Center bombing, the security officers at the World Trade Center were provided in-depth and regular follow-up training on such topics as emergency evacuation procedures and building layout. On September 11, 2001, security officers helped thousands of building workers safely out of the World Trade Center before the twin towers fell.

 Laws Governing Private Security

There are no federal laws governing the private security industry. No training is required for unarmed guards in 29 states and the District of Columbia. Private security officers do not have to be licensed in 22 states. In 16 states, background checks are not required.

Source: Mimi Hall, "Private Security Guards: Homeland Defense's Weak Link," *USA Today* (January 23, 2003), p. 1A.

THINKING CRITICALLY

1. What do you think are some of the benefits and drawbacks of being a private security officer?

2. Do you think that stricter qualification standards should be established for private security personnel? Why or why not?

✳ Summary

1. Briefly describe the jurisdictional limitations of American law enforcement.

   The authority of public law enforcement agencies in the United States, whether they are local, state, or federal agencies, is carefully limited by law. The territory within which each may operate is also restricted.

2. Trace the English origins of American law enforcement.

   Many institutions of American law enforcement evolved from the English tradition. The medieval tithing system and the constable-watch system were early methods of community protection that led to the development of the positions of sheriff and constable. The Bow Street Runners in the city of London in the 1750s were an early group of crime fighters who patrolled neighborhoods and pursued lawbreakers. The London Metropolitan Police, founded in 1829, became the model for municipal police departments in the United States.

3. Discuss the early development of American law enforcement.

   Americans at first adopted the British system of community protection. When the constable-watch system proved inadequate in meeting the peacekeeping needs of the nation's major cities, municipal police forces were established in the mid-1800s. They soon became entangled with local politics. In the states and on the frontier, law enforcement reflected regional differences. In the South, the earliest policing was the plantation slave patrols. On the frontier, vigilantism and later, local sheriffs or U.S. marshals dealt with lawbreakers. In some states, state police agencies, such as the Texas Rangers, were established to enforce laws statewide.

4. Describe the major developments that have occurred in American policing.

   During the period of professionalism and reform that lasted from about 1920 to 1970, the police became professional crime fighters, relying on the centralization of authority, motorized patrols, specialization, and technological aids. In the 1960s, the crime-fighting role of the police came into conflict with the social and political upheavals of the time, causing critics to call for improved standards and training. By the early 1990s, some police agencies began to turn to community policing, attempting to eliminate crime problems in neighborhoods and return to their role as peacekeepers. At the start of the twenty-first century, the prevention and repression of domestic terrorism has also become a major priority of police in America.

5. Describe the structure of American law enforcement.

   Law enforcement agencies are found at all levels of government in the United States. Most law enforcement officers work for local governments and are responsible for enforcing laws, maintaining order, providing service, and gathering information. In rural areas, the county sheriff's department is responsible for law enforcement. Every state, except Hawaii, has a state law enforcement agency. The law enforcement agencies of the federal government are concerned primarily with violations of federal laws, especially violations that cross state boundaries; maintaining homeland security; and preventing domestic terrorism.

6. Explain the relationship between the FBI and the Department of Homeland Security.

   Since 9/11, the FBI has undergone fundamental changes. The biggest change is that it has shifted its top priority from being a federal police agency to being an intelligence and counterterrorism agency. Although it remains an independent agency in the Justice Department, it will now closely coordinate its antiterrorism activities with the CIA and the Department of Homeland Security.

7. Discuss the development and growth of private security in the United States.

   The private security industry has grown rapidly over the past 35 years for a number of reasons: revenues for public policing have declined (until recently); crimes in the workplace are often private, costly, and embarrassing; employers have better control of private security officers; and fewer constitutional limits restrict private security officers.

✳ Key Terms

jurisdiction 145	constable-watch system 146	slave patrols 152	highway patrol model 184
tithing system 146	constable 146	community policing 157	contract security 197
shire reeve 146	Peel's Principles of	CompStat 157	proprietary security 197
posses 146	Policing 148	state police model 183	

✳ Review Questions

1. What is meant by *jurisdiction?*
2. What was the *tithing system?*
3. Who were the Bow Street Runners?
4. In what year was the London Metropolitan Police founded?
5. Who was Robert Peel?
6. What system of English policing did the colonists bring to America?
7. What were the *slave codes?*
8. What group is considered to be the first state police agency?
9. How did August Vollmer change policing?
10. How did police response to the demonstrations and civil disorders of the 1960s affect policing?
11. What is *community policing?*
12. What is *CompStat?*
13. Why were the U.S. Marshals Service, the Secret Service, the Federal Bureau of Investigation, and the Drug Enforcement Agency created?
14. What are the four main functions of local police?

15. Why do county sheriffs have more political clout than police chiefs?

16. What is the difference between a *state police model* and a *highway patrol model* of state law enforcement?

17. Name some federal law enforcement agencies.

18. Distinguish between *contract* and *proprietary private security services.*

19. What are some successes and problems with private security in the war on terrorism?

20. How do the employment qualifications for private security personnel in the United States compare and contrast with the qualifications to be a police officer, deputy sheriff, state police, or federal agent?

❋ In the Field

1. **Your Local Law Enforcement** Identify all the local law enforcement agencies in your area. Divide up the list among your classmates and arrange to visit your assigned agency. On the day that you visit, find out how many calls the department received and/or how many crimes the agency personnel investigated in the 24-hour period prior to your visit, what types of calls were received or crimes were investigated, and how the agency handled the situation. Categorize the actions of the agency personnel into law enforcement, order maintenance, service, or information gathering. Identify the category with the most action. Share your findings with others in the class. What conclusions can you draw about the operation of the local law enforcement agencies in your area?

2. **Local and Private Police** Describe the possibilities you see for local police departments and private security agencies to work together more closely. To prepare for this activity, interview a local police official and a private security manager, either by telephone or in person, asking them what obstacles prevent closer cooperation between local policing and private security.

❋ On the Net

1. **Local Police Jobs** Go to the following links for sites dedicated to law enforcement careers and select two municipal police departments, one large and one small, and one county sheriff's department that list the agency's employment qualifications on their Web page:

   http://govtjobs.com/safe/index.html

   http://www.jobs4police.com

   http://www.lawenforcementjobs.com

   http://www.policecareer.com

   http://www.policeemployment.com

   Then find the qualifications for a private security officer through other applicable career sites provided at www.securityjobs.net or www.bls.gov/oco/ocos159.htm. Make a list of the similarities and differences between police and deputy sheriff qualifications and private security officer qualifications. Given your background and abilities, for which type of work would you be best suited? Why? Compile your findings in a two-page report and present it to the class.

2. **Federal Law Enforcement** To learn about the responsibilities of some of the lesser-known federal law enforcement agencies, access their websites: (a) *Food and Drug Administration, Office of Criminal Investigations,* www.fda.gov/ora/inspect_ref/iom/ChapterText/980.html; (b) *National Park Service, U.S. Park Police,* www.nps.gov/personnel/parkpolice.htm; (c) *U.S. Fish and Wildlife Service, Division of Law Enforcement,* www.le.fws.gov; and (d) *U.S. Capitol Police,* www.fedquest.com/opmrefs/tei51.htm. Which agency seems the most interesting? Why?

❋ Critical Thinking Exercises

NEIGHBORHOOD WATCH

1. You live in a middle-class community of single-family homes close to the center of a midsize city. Over the past 5 years, everyone in your neighborhood has noted the rise in burglaries and many people feel that it is not safe to walk around the neighborhood after dark. You think that setting up a neighborhood watch would help lower the burglary rate and make people feel safer. Prepare an oral presentation of your ideas for a community meeting. Use the following questions as a guide.
   a. How would you go about organizing a night watch?
   b. How would you select volunteers?
   c. What training, if any, would volunteers have to have?
   d. How would you maintain interest and participation in the watch?

PUBLIC OFFICER OR PRIVATE CITIZEN?

2. An off-duty police officer was seated in a restaurant when two men entered, drew guns, and robbed the cashier. The officer made no attempt to prevent the robbery or apprehend the robbers. Later the officer justified the conduct by stating that an officer, when off duty, is a private citizen with the same duties and rights as all private citizens. Do you agree? Explain.

To access more information and resources, including study questions, chapter summaries, and links, go to: www.mhhe.com/bohm6e.

Policing: Roles, Styles, and Functions

Chapter Outline

Chapter Objectives

After completing this chapter, you should be able to:

1. Identify characteristics of police work.

2. Distinguish among James Q. Wilson's three operational styles in policing.

3. List the four major functions of police departments.

4. List the drug enforcement strategies of local police agencies.

5. Explain the main components of community policing.

6. Identify the four steps in a community policing approach to problem solving.

7. Define terrorism, and identify different types of terrorism.

CRIME STORY

On January 6, 2009, Dallas, Texas police officer Norman Smith, an 18-year veteran of the agency, was shot and killed while serving an arrest warrant. Officer Smith's death is believed to be the nation's first fatal shooting of a police officer in the line of duty in 2009. Officer Smith and about six other gang-unit officers were in search of a violent felon at an apartment complex, long known as a haven for drug and gang activity. Officer Smith, flanked by two other officers, approached the apartment door and knocked. Someone inside asked who was there, and Smith responded with a fake name. When the suspected gunman opened the door, Smith yelled they were the police. The suspect then tried to close the door, and Smith pushed back. That is when the suspect shot Officer Smith in the face. Officers returned fire, frantically trying to pull their fallen comrade out of the line of fire as the gunman opened the door and continued shooting.

continued

No one else was injured in the gun battle. The three men inside the apartment then surrendered, one at a time, within minutes of the shooting. Officer Smith was taken to the Baylor University Medical Center at Dallas, where he was pronounced dead about an hour later.

Officer Smith was a member of the gang unit for 14 years and was considered an expert on Dallas-area gangs. He was well liked by his fellow officers who knew him by a number of nicknames, including "Normando" and "the big Russian." He was remembered as having a strong passion for his job and was a former officer of the year. He is survived by his wife, Regina, who is also a Dallas police officer, and a teenage son and daughter.

Officer Smith's death represents a sad story that is heard repeatedly in cities and towns across the land. The peacemakers become the targets of a criminal element that has no regard for their dedication and commitment. And yet, we can look at the statistics and put this enduring image of what must be a dangerous profession in perspective. In a nation with more than 800,000 sworn police officers, attackers kill approximately 50 officers a year, a rate of 6.25 per 100,000 officers. This rate is substantially lower than the general homicide rate for all citizens in many major American cities. The death of one valiant public servant is too many, but training and technology have significantly reduced the professional casualties in the war on crime. The worthless thug who shot Officer Smith will be the subject of a vigorous and serious prosecution effort, while Smith's friends and family are left to wonder why Smith was killed.

Among the topics addressed in Chapter 6 are the characteristics of police work. Officer Smith died in the line of duty, and his dedication underscores the risks inherent in professional efforts to maintain order in a modern society. Could Officer Smith's death been prevented? Police officers can quickly become the targets of angry and disturbed individuals, and no amount of equipment or training offers total protection.

Policing in America

The police are at the forefront of the criminal justice process and, for most people, the only personal experience they have with that process is contact with a local police officer. Most people have never been in a courthouse for a criminal matter or in a jail or prison for any reason. This chapter examines what the police do and the qualities they need to do it.

THE ROLES OF THE POLICE

Our expectations of police behavior depend on where we live and when we consider the question. For example, we saw in the last chapter that Cincinnati wanted its police officers in the 1880s to be fleet-footed and honest. In Dallas, Miami, and New York City, citizens may expect police officers to have a working knowledge of Spanish. In Alaska, we would expect police officers to be self-reliant, enjoy the outdoors, and not mind working by themselves in lonely surroundings. In essence, what we expect from the police depends on how we view their role in society.

A **role** consists of the rights and responsibilities associated with a particular position in society. A related concept is **role expectation,** the behavior and actions that people expect from a person in a particular role. Suppose, for example, that teenagers living in a wealthy neighborhood have been caught drinking alcohol. Their parents probably expect police officers to warn the young people and bring them home. In a less affluent neighborhood, however, the expectation of community residents might be that the police will arrest the teenagers and bring them into juvenile court. This example illustrates a problem that often arises in our attempt to understand the police role in America. When the public's expectations differ from the official police role, the public may become disenchanted and sometimes hostile toward law enforcement officers. Such negative feelings cause officers personal frustration and role conflict. **Role conflict** is the psychological strain and stress that result from trying to perform two or more incompatible responsibilities. A common source of role

role The rights and responsibilities associated with a particular position in society.

role expectation The behavior and actions that people expect from a person in a particular role.

role conflict The psychological stress and frustration that results from trying to perform two or more incompatible responsibilities.

conflict for the police is the expectation that they should be social or helping agents at the same time they are expected to be control agents by arresting law violators.

What we expect from police officers, then, depends on how we view the police role—a role that has been described as complex, ambiguous, changing, and repressive. Obviously, not everyone views the role of the police in the same way, but a definition that includes the majority of perspectives is possible. The police:

1. Are community leaders in public safety. (By nature, this makes the work potentially dangerous.)
2. Possess broad discretion.
3. Solve sociological and technological problems for people on a short-term basis.
4. Occasionally serve in a hostile or dangerous environment.[1]

Think about some of the common situations in which police officers find themselves when people call and want something "fixed." One example would be an officer's response to freeway accidents where vehicles are overturned and burning and people are trapped inside. Such situations require leadership, informed and quick decisions, the solving of numerous immediate problems, and the use of extreme caution to prevent further injury to citizens or the police officer. Another example would be intervention in a long-running family dispute that has suddenly turned violent. Such a situation requires caution, quick thinking, and the solving of a number of problems in an effort to ensure the safety of all parties. Still another typical role of a police officer is to provide protection at protests and strikes. Those potentially volatile circumstances clearly illustrate the key elements of the police role. Of course, sometimes an officer's role may be simply to solve problems in the course of providing service, as when retrieving a citizen's dropped keys from below a sewer grate.

Police officers are expected to respond to traffic accidents. *How might such experiences affect them?*

CHARACTERISTICS OF POLICE WORK

Police work requires a combination of special characteristics. Personnel with the following qualities are best able to carry out the difficult service role mandated for law enforcement officers.

Quick Decision Making Sometimes police officers must make on-the-spot decisions about whether to use force, how to maneuver a patrol car, or whether to stop a suspect. Making the wrong decision can be fatal for the officer or the other person. All of the work in a lengthy investigation can be ruined by a single procedural law violation if an officer unintentionally makes a wrong decision.

The Independent Nature of Police Work The position of peace officer in all states in the United States is a position of honor and trust. After patrol officers attend roll call, stand inspection, check out their equipment, and depart into the streets in their patrol cars, they work virtually unsupervised until the end of their tour of duty.

Figure 6.1 shows the Law Enforcement Officer's Code of Ethics, which was written as a guide for working police officers. It offers some professional direction in a line of work with many opportunities to go astray. The independent nature of police work increases the chances of malfeasance and corruption—topics discussed in the next chapter.

"Dirty Work" Most people agree that police work needs to be done, but police work is sometimes distasteful—for example, dealing with people who have committed horrible acts and viewing mangled, broken, and decomposed bodies. Oftentimes, the police must deal with people at their worst—angry, drunk, in trouble, victimized, violent, and so forth. The distasteful part of policing has been referred to as "dirty work."[2]

Danger Police officers in the United States spend a substantial amount of their time trying to resolve conflicts, frequently in hostile environments.[3] Table 6.1 identifies dangerous circumstances in which officers find themselves. Contrary to the media image, police officers are often afraid on the job, and far too many are injured or killed. The data reveal that disturbance calls (for example, a family quarrel or a man with a gun) and arrests of suspects are the most dangerous circumstances for police officers. Because of the danger they face, many departments require their field officers to wear body armor while on duty. Table 6.2 shows the percentage of local police departments, by size of population served, that required field officers to wear body armor while on duty in 2003.

Despite the use of body armor and other precautions, each year police officers are killed while on duty. In 2007, for example, 57 officers were feloniously killed in the line of duty, many fewer than the 142 officers killed feloniously in 2001, and two more than the 55 officers killed feloniously in 2005. However, 2001 was an unusual year. Among the 142 officers feloniously killed were the 72 federal, state, and local officers killed during the tragedy of September 11—the most officers killed in the United States on a single day. In 1999, only 42 officers were feloniously killed in the line of duty, which was the lowest recorded figure in more than 35 years.[4]

Of the 57 officers feloniously killed in the line of duty in 2007, 16 died in arrest situations, 16 were ambushed by their assailants, 11 were killed during traffic pursuits and stops, 5 were murdered answering disturbance calls, 4 while investigating suspicious persons or circumstances, 3 during tactical situations (for example, barricaded offender, hostage taking, and so on), 2 while handling mentally deranged individuals, 1 while conducting investigative

FYI Killed in the Line of Duty

Today, more than 800,000 sworn officers put their lives on the line for our protection each day. The first known line-of-duty death was that of U.S. Marshal Robert Forsyth, who was shot and killed on January 11, 1794, while serving court papers in a civil suit. Wilmington, Delaware, police matron Mary T. Davis was the first female officer killed on duty. She was beaten to death in 1924 while guarding a prisoner in the city jail.

Figure 6.1

Law Enforcement Officer Code of Ethics

The purpose of the Code of Ethics is to ensure that all peace officers are fully aware of their individual responsibility to maintain their own integrity and that of their agency. Every peace officer, during basic training, or at the time of appointment, shall be administered the [following] Code of Ethics.

As a law enforcement officer, my fundamental duty is to serve mankind; to safeguard lives and property; to protect the innocent against deception, the weak against oppression or intimidation, and the peaceful against violence or disorder; and to respect the constitutional rights of all men to liberty, equality, and justice.

I will keep my private life unsullied as an example to all; maintain courageous calm in the face of danger, scorn, or ridicule; develop self-restraint; and be constantly mindful of the welfare of others. Honest in thought and deed in both my personal and official life, I will be exemplary in obeying the laws of the land and the regulations of my department. Whatever I see or hear of a confidential nature or that is confided to me in my official capacity will be kept ever secret unless revelation is necessary in the performance of my duty. I will never act officiously or permit personal feelings, prejudices, animosities, or friendships to influence my decisions. With no compromise for crime and with relentless prosecution of criminals, I will enforce the law courteously and appropriately without fear or favor, malice or ill will, never employing unnecessary force or violence, and never accepting gratuities.

I recognize the badge of my office as a symbol of public faith, and I accept it as a public trust to be held so long as I am true to the ethics of the police service. I will constantly strive to achieve these objectives and ideals, dedicating myself to my chosen profession—law enforcement.

Canons

1. The primary responsibility of police officers and organizations is the protection of citizens by upholding the law and respecting the legally expressed will of the whole community and not a particular party or clique.

2. Police officers should be aware of the legal limits on their authority and the "genius of the American system," which limits the power of individuals, groups, and institutions.

3. Police officers are responsible for being familiar with the law and not only their responsibilities but also those of other public officials.

4. Police officers should be mindful of the importance of using the proper means to gain proper ends. Officers should not employ illegal means, nor should they disregard public safety or property to accomplish a goal.

5. Police officers will cooperate with other public officials in carrying out their duties. However, the officer shall be careful not to use his or her position in an improper or illegal manner when cooperating with other officials.

6. In their private lives, police officers will behave in such a manner that the public will "regard (the officer) as an example of stability, fidelity, and morality." It is necessary that police officers conduct themselves in a "decent and honorable" manner.

7. In their behavior toward members of the public, officers will provide service when possible, require compliance with the law, respond in a manner that inspires confidence and trust, and will be neither overbearing nor subservient.

8. When dealing with violators or making arrests, officers will follow the law; officers have no right to persecute individuals or punish them. And officers should behave in such a manner so the likelihood of the use of force is minimized.

9. Police officers should refuse to accept any gifts, favors, or gratuities that, from a public perspective, could influence the manner in which the officer discharges his or her duties.

10. Officers will present evidence in criminal cases impartially because the officer should be equally concerned with both the prosecution of criminals and the defense of innocent persons.

Source: Commission on Peace Officer Standards and Training, *Administrative Manual* (State of California: POST, 1990), p. c-5.

Table 6.1 Law Enforcement Officers Assaulted in the United States, 2007

Circumstances at Scene of Incident	Total	Percentage of Total
Total	59,201	100%
Disturbance calls (family quarrel, man with gun, etc.)	18,789	31.7
Burglaries in progress or pursuit of burglary suspects	905	1.5
Robberies in progress or pursuit of robbery suspects	515	0.9
Other arrest attempts	8,935	15.1
Civil disorders (mass disobedience, riot, etc.)	759	1.3
Handling, transporting, custody of prisoners	7,347	12.4
Investigation of suspicious persons and circumstances	5,333	9.0
Ambush (no warning) situations	198	0.3
Handling mentally deranged persons	1,114	1.9
Traffic pursuits and stops	6,424	10.9
All other	8,882	15.0

Source: United States Department of Justice, Federal Bureau of Investigation, Law Enforcement Officers Killed and Assaulted, *www.fbi.gov/ucr/killed/2007/data/table_69.html, October 2008, Table 69.*

activities (for instance, surveillance, search, interview, and so forth), and 1 while handling and transporting prisoners.[5] Accidents, such as automobile accidents, during the performance of official duties claimed the lives of an additional 83 officers in 2007, up from the 67 in 2005.[6]

From 1972 through 2007, 5,089 law enforcement officers were killed in the line of duty: 2,820 were feloniously killed and 2,269 were accidentally killed. The most officers killed in any one year were 218 in 2001, while the least in any year was 107 in 1999. In general, and with few exceptions, the number of law enforcement officers killed while on duty has declined since the early 1970s.[7]

OPERATIONAL STYLES

After police officers are trained and begin to gain experience and wisdom from their encounters with veteran police officers and citizens on the street, it is believed that they develop **operational styles** that characterize their overall approach to the police job. If these styles actually exist, it means that the effort of the police department to systematically train and deploy officers

operational styles The different overall approaches to the police job.

Table 6.2 Body Armor Requirements for Field Officers in Local Police Departments, by Size of Population Served, 2003

Population Served	PERCENTAGE OF AGENCIES REQUIRING FIELD OFFICERS TO WEAR ARMOR WHILE ON DUTY		
	Total	At All Times	In Some Circumstances
All Sizes	71%	59%	12%
1,000,000 or more	63	44	19
500,000–999,999	79	60	19
250,000–499,999	68	56	12
100,000–249,999	68	50	18
50,000–99,999	69	52	17
25,000–49,999	74	61	13
10,000–24,999	74	63	11
2,500–9,999	80	69	11
Under 2,500	63	52	11

Source: Matthew J. Hickman and Brian A. Reaves, *Local Police Departments, 2003,* U.S. Department of Justice, Bureau of Justice Statistics (Washington, D.C.: GPO, May 2006), p. 25, Table 56.

with the same philosophy and practical approach to policing in the community has not been entirely successful. The research on operational styles shows that they vary both between departments and among officers of the same department.

One of the earliest scholars to report on the existence of policing styles was political scientist James Q. Wilson, who found the following three styles in a study of eight police departments:

1. **Legalistic Style**—The emphasis is on violations of law and the use of threats or actual arrests to solve disputes in the community. In theory, the more arrests that are made, the safer a community will be. This style is often found in large metropolitan areas.
2. **Watchman Style**—The emphasis is on informal means of resolving disputes and problems in a community. Keeping the peace is the paramount concern, and arrest is used only as a last resort to resolve any kind of disturbance of the peace. This style of policing is most commonly found in economically poorer communities.
3. **Service Style**—The emphasis is on helping in the community, as opposed to enforcing the law. Referrals and diversion to community treatment agencies are more common than arrest and formal court action. The service style is most likely to be found in wealthy communities.[8]

Sociologist John Broderick, who also studied operational styles among the police, classified police officers by their degree of commitment to maintaining order and their respect for due process:

1. **Enforcers**—The emphasis is on order, with little respect for due process.
2. **Idealists**—The emphasis is on both social order and due process.
3. **Optimists**—The emphasis is on due process, with little priority given to social order.
4. **Realists**—Little emphasis is given to due process or social order.[9]

Another classification is based on the way officers use their authority and power in street police work. The two key ingredients of this scheme are passion and perspective. Passion is the ability to use force or the recognition that force is a legitimate means of resolving conflict; perspective is the ability to understand human suffering and to use force ethically and morally. According to political scientist William Muir's styles of policing, police officers include:

1. **Professionals**—Officers have the necessary passion and perspective to be valuable police officers.
2. **Enforcers**—Officers have passion for the job, for enforcing the law, for taking decisive action; their inner drive or value system allows them to be comfortable using force to solve problems.
3. **Reciprocators**—Officers lack the passion to do the job; they have a difficult time taking action, making arrests, enforcing the law; their values make it difficult for them to use force to solve problems.
4. **Avoiders**—Officers have neither passion nor perspective, resulting in no recognition of people's problems and no action to resolve them.[10]

Are there identifiable styles of policing? What value do these styles hold for us? In any area of human endeavor, classifications have been constructed. We have developed classifications for leaders, prisoners, quarterbacks, and teachers. These classifications give us a framework of analysis, a basis for discussion. But can they be substantiated when we go into a police agency to see if they actually exist?

Social scientist Ellen Hochstedler examined the issue of policing styles with 1,134 Dallas, Texas, police officers and was not able to confirm the officer styles identified in the literature by Broderick, Muir, and others. Her conclusion was that it is not possible to "pigeonhole" officers into one style or another because the way officers think and react to street situations varies, depending on the particular situation, the time, and the officers themselves.[11]

THINKING CRITICALLY

1. Which characteristics do you think are the most important for police officers to have? Why?

2. Is there an operational style of policing that you think is the most effective? If so, which one?

3. Do you think it is possible to identify styles of policing? If so, how can it be done? If not, what obstacles prevent identification?

Police Functions

The list of functions that police are expected to carry out is long and varies from place to place. In the following sections, we look at the major operations of police departments and the services they provide.

PATROL

Police administrators have long referred to patrol as the backbone of the department. It is unquestionably the most time-consuming and resource-intensive task of any police agency. More than half of the sworn personnel in any police department are assigned to patrol. In Houston, Chicago, and New York, for example, patrol officers make up more than 65% of the sworn personnel in each department.

Patrol officers respond to burglar alarms, investigate traffic accidents, care for injured people, try to resolve domestic disputes, and engage in a host of other duties that keep them chasing radio calls across their own beats and the entire city and county when no other cars are available to respond. Precisely

Street patrol is the most resource-intensive task of any police agency. *Are there acceptable alternatives to street patrol? If yes, what are they?*

how to conduct patrol activities, however, is a matter of much debate in the nation today. Indeed, it seems that there are many ways to police a city.

Preventive Patrol For decades, police officers patrolled the streets with little direction. Between their responses to radio calls, they were told to be "systematically unsystematic" and observant in an attempt to both prevent and ferret out crime on their beats. In many police departments, as much as 50% of an officer's time is uncommitted and available for patrolling the beats that make up a political jurisdiction. The simultaneous increases in the official crime rate and the size of police forces beginning in the 1960s caused police managers and academics to question the usefulness of what has come to be known as **preventive patrol** or random patrol. To test the usefulness of preventive patrol, the now famous Kansas City (Missouri) Preventive Patrol Experiment was conducted in 1972.

The Kansas City, Missouri, Police Department and the Police Foundation set up an experiment in which 15 patrol districts were divided into three matched groups according to size, record of calls for service, and demographic characteristics. In the first group, the "control beats," the police department operated the same level of patrol used previously in those beats. In the second group of districts, the "proactive beats," the police department doubled or even tripled the number of patrol officers normally deployed in the area. In the third group of districts, the "reactive beats," the police department deployed no officers at all on preventive patrol. Officers only responded to calls for service and did no patrolling on their own. At the end of the 1-year study, the results showed no significant differences in crime rates among the three groups of patrol districts. In other words, a group of districts that had no officers on preventive patrol had the same crime rates as groups that had several times the normal level of staffing engaged in patrol activity. The number of officers made no difference in the number of burglaries, robberies, vehicle thefts, and other serious crimes experienced in the three groups of police districts. Perhaps even more important is that the citizens of Kansas City did not even notice that the levels of patrol in two of the three districts had been changed.[12]

The law enforcement community was astounded by the results of the study, which showed that it made no difference whether patrol officers conducted preventive, or random, patrol. The research was immediately attacked on both philosophical and methodological grounds. How could anyone say that having patrol officers on the street made no difference?

One of the criticisms of the study was that no one in the community was told that there were no officers on patrol in reactive districts. What might have happened to the crime rates had the community known no officers were on patrol? Moreover, during the course of the study, marked police cars from other departments and districts crossed the reactive districts to answer calls but then left when the work was completed. Thus, there appeared to be a police presence even in the so-called reactive districts.

This study has forced police executives and academics to reconsider the whole issue of how patrol is conducted, once considered a closed issue. Police administrators have begun to entertain the possibility of reducing the number of officers on patrol. Innovations in patrol methods have also been proposed.

Directed Patrol In **directed patrol,** officers are given guidance or orders on how to use their patrol time. The guidance is often based on the results of crime analyses that identify problem areas. Evidence shows that directed patrol can reduce the incidence of targeted crimes such as thefts from autos and robberies.[13]

preventive patrol Patrolling the streets with little direction; between responses to radio calls, officers are "systematically unsystematic" and observant in an attempt to both prevent and ferret out crime. Also known as random patrol.

MYTH

Adding more police officers will reduce crime.

FACT

Short of having a police officer on every corner, evidence indicates no relationship between the number of police officers and the crime rate.

directed patrol Patrolling under guidance or orders on how to use patrol time.

CJ Online

GIS Crime Mapping

To learn more about GIS crime mapping and how it works, visit the GIS Lounge at http://gislounge.com/features/aa101100.shtml. *Why is crime mapping important?*

Crime Mapping One technological innovation in crime analysis that has aided directed patrol is Geographic Information Systems (GIS) crime mapping. **GIS crime mapping** is a technique that involves the charting of crime patterns within a geographic area. Crime mapping makes it possible to keep a closer watch on crime and criminals through the generation of crime maps capable of displaying numerous fields of information. If, for example, a series of armed robberies of dry cleaning stores had been committed over a period of several weeks in three adjacent police beats, police crime analysts would be able to record, analyze, determine a definite pattern to these robberies, and make a reasonable prediction as to when and where the next robbery in the series is likely to occur. The patrol and investigation forces could be deployed at a prescribed time to conduct surveillance of the prospective target dry cleaning store or stores with a good chance the robber can be arrested. This use of crime mapping is referred to as "resource reallocation" and is probably the most widely used crime-mapping application. Figure 6.2 is an example of a crime map.

Crime mapping is also used as a tool to help evaluate the ability of police departments to resolve the problems in their communities. This is the primary purpose of the New York City Police Department's CompStat process, for example.[14] Begun in 1994, CompStat is a divisional unit responsible for statistical analysis of daily precinct crime reports frequently using crime mapping. The information produced by CompStat is used by the chief of police to judge the performance of precinct commanders and by precinct commanders to hold their officers accountable (see the discussion of Comp-Stat in Chapter 5).

Figure 6.2

Crime Map of Total Crime Index in the City of Atlanta, Georgia, 2008

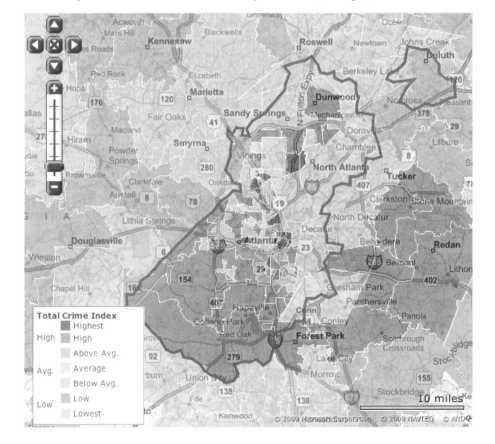

Crime mapping is likely to be used increasingly in crime scene investigations and the forensic sciences. For example, a GIS-based system has been created that can determine the origin of gunshots through sound triangulation. Crime mapping will also be combined with other technologies such as aerial photography so that geocoded data can be superimposed on aerial photographs rather than computer-generated maps. This should aid community policing efforts by making census data, liquor license locations, drug-market data, and probationer addresses, for example, readily available in a more useful form. Another technology that will be combined with crime mapping is Global Positioning Systems (GPS) technology. Such technology would allow beat officers to track and monitor probationers and parolees in the area, for example. It is currently used in some departments to help manage the department's fleet of vehicles.[15]

Aggressive Patrol In nearly all police departments, some patrol officers have used aggressive patrol tactics and have been rewarded as high performers because they made many arrests for both minor and serious offenses. When the entire patrol section is instructed to make numerous traffic stops and field interrogations, the practice is referred to as **aggressive patrol.** A **field interrogation** is a temporary detention in which officers stop and question pedestrians and motorists they find in suspicious circumstances. Such procedures have been found to reduce crime in targeted areas.[16]

aggressive patrol The practice of having an entire patrol section make numerous traffic stops and field interrogations.

field interrogation A temporary detention in which officers stop and question pedestrians and motorists they find in suspicious circumstances.

At least two problems can occur as a result of aggressive patrol. First, random traffic stops and field interrogations inconvenience innocent citizens. To avoid conflict, the police must be certain that those tactics are necessary, and they must explain the necessity to the public. Second, it is often difficult to get all officers on each work shift and in each patrol division motivated to use aggressive patrol tactics. Many officers are reluctant to carry out their duties in an aggressive way. Nevertheless, with crime rates high and research confirming that aggressive patrol can reduce crime, aggressive patrol tactics are likely to continue.

Foot Patrol For some time, there has been renewed interest in having police officers patrol their beats on foot. Is there value in this practice, or is it just nostalgia for a more romantic period in law enforcement? The use of motorized patrols has allowed the police to respond rapidly to citizen calls and to cover large geographical areas. Yet, officers working a busy shift, perhaps responding to more than two dozen calls, come to feel as if they are seeing the world through a windshield. Moreover, it is now generally accepted that rapid response time is useful in only a small portion of the incidents and crimes to which the police are asked to respond.

Challenging conventional wisdom about rapid response, two cities—Flint, Michigan, and Newark, New Jersey—launched substantial programs in foot patrol. In Newark, the results of the foot patrol experiment showed that foot patrol had little or no effect on the level of crime. However, positive effects were identified:

1. Newark residents noticed whether foot patrol officers were present.
2. They were more satisfied with police service when foot patrol officers delivered it.
3. They were less afraid than citizens being served by motorized patrol.[17]

Field interrogation has been found to reduce crime in targeted areas. *What are some of the problems with field interrogations?*

Table 6.3 Types of Patrol Used on a Routine Basis by Local Police Department, by Size of Population Served, 2003

| Population Served | PERCENTAGE OF AGENCIES USING EACH TYPE OF PATROL ON A ROUTINE BASIS | | | | | |
	Auto-mobile*	Foot	Bicycle	Motor-cycle	Marine	Horse
All sizes	100%	59%	38%	14%	4%	2%
1,000,000 or more	100	75	100	81	63	63
500,000–999,999	100	79	95	100	41	63
250,000–499,999	100	76	83	93	32	59
100,000–249,999	100	57	83	89	14	18
50,000–99,999	100	54	64	63	14	7
25,000–49,999	100	47	60	49	8	2
10,000–24,999	100	53	58	21	5	2
2,500–9,999	100	61	43	8	3	—
Under 2,500	100	61	18	3	2	—

Note: Less than 0.5%; As of 2000, all local police departments surveyed reported routine use of automobile patrols.

Source: Matthew J. Hickman and Brian A. Reaves, *Local Police Departments, 2003,* U.S. Department of Justice, Bureau of Justice Statistics (Washington, D.C.: GPO, May 2006), p. 13, Table 24.

In Flint, Michigan, the extensive neighborhood foot patrol experiment also had positive results:

1. Flint residents had a decreased fear of crime.
2. Their satisfaction with police service increased.
3. There were moderate decreases in crime.
4. There were decreased numbers of calls for police service.

Citizens would wait to talk to their neighborhood foot patrol officer about a problem instead of calling the police department through 911 and speaking with an officer they were not likely to know. One astounding result of the Flint program was that the foot patrol officers became so popular that citizens saw them as real community leaders. They often became more influential than some elected officials. Evidence of the degree of satisfaction with the foot patrol program in Flint was that the community voted three times to continue and expand foot patrol at a time when the city was experiencing one of the nation's highest unemployment rates.[18] Perhaps even more important, the findings of foot patrol research provided the seeds of a much broader concept for law enforcement: community policing, which we will discuss later in this chapter. Table 6.3 shows the percentage of agencies, by size of population served, that used various types of patrol on a routine basis in 2003 (the latest year for which data were available).

INVESTIGATION

The role of the detective has generally been glorified by media sources in both fiction and nonfiction accounts. Homicide investigation, in particular, has captured the imagination of fiction readers worldwide. Most police officers aspire to be investigative specialists by attaining the position of detective. But it should be noted that detectives represent only one unit in a police department that conducts investigations. Investigators work in a variety of capacities in a police agency:

1. Traffic homicide and hit-and-run accident investigators in the traffic section.
2. Undercover investigators in narcotics, vice, and violent gang cases.
3. Internal affairs investigators conducting investigations of alleged crimes by police personnel.

4. Investigators conducting background checks of applicants to the police department.
5. Uniformed patrol officers investigating the crimes they have been dispatched to or have encountered on their own while on patrol.
6. Detectives of criminal investigation divisions who conduct investigations into reports of criminal activity made by patrol officers.

What Is Criminal Investigation? Criminal investigation has been defined as a lawful search for people and things to reconstruct the circumstances of an illegal act, apprehend or determine the guilty party, and aid in the state's prosecution of the offender.[19] The criminal investigation process is generally divided into two parts: the preliminary, or initial, investigation and the continuing, or follow-up, investigation. Most of the time the preliminary investigation in both felony and misdemeanor cases is conducted by patrol officers, although for homicides and other complex, time-consuming investigations, trained investigators are dispatched to the crime scene immediately. The continuing investigation in serious crimes is ordinarily conducted by plainclothes detectives, although small and medium-sized agencies may require patrol officers or a patrol supervisor to follow up on serious criminal offenses.

For less serious crimes, many police departments use solvability-factor score sheets or software programs to assess information collected at crime scenes. The assessment, which is done by the responding officer, a case-screening officer, or a felony-review unit, determines which cases are likely to be solved, given the initial information obtained. Promising cases are turned over to detectives for follow-up investigation. The rest are often closed on the basis of the preliminary investigation and are reopened only if additional information is uncovered.[20]

Investigative Functions In any type of investigation in a police agency, all investigators share responsibility for a number of critical functions. They must:

1. Locate witnesses and suspects.
2. Arrest criminals.

Criminal investigation is a time-consuming task that requires much attention to detail. *What aspects of criminal investigations are the most time-consuming and why?*

3. Collect, preserve, and analyze evidence.
4. Interview witnesses.
5. Interrogate suspects.
6. Write reports.
7. Recover stolen property.
8. Seize contraband.
9. Prepare cases and testify in court.

The specific application and context of those functions vary considerably, depending on whether the investigation is of the theft of expensive paintings, for example, or the rape of an elderly widow living alone.

The Role of the Detective At first glance, the role of the detective seems highly desirable. To a patrol officer who has been rotating work shifts for several years, seldom getting a weekend off, detectives in the police department seem to have a number of advantages:

1. They do not have to wear uniforms.
2. They have anonymity during work hours if they choose it.
3. They have steady work hours, often daytime hours with weekends off.
4. They have offices and desks.
5. They enjoy the prestige associated with the position.
6. In many agencies, detectives receive higher compensation and hold a higher rank.
7. Perhaps most important, they enjoy more freedom than patrol officers from the police radio, geographical boundaries, and close supervision.

All these advantages add up to a high-status position, both within the police department and in the eyes of the public.

Productivity Despite all the advantages of being a detective, investigators are often faced with insurmountable obstacles and stressful work conditions. Noting the next of kin in a homicide is one of the worst tasks:

> Of all the dirty tasks that go with the dirty work of chasing a killer, noting the next of kin is the job that homicide detectives hate most. It's worse than getting up at 3 A.M. on a February night to slog through a field of freezing mud toward a body that needed burying two days ago. Worse than staring into the flat cold eyes of a teenager who bragged about dragging a man through the streets to his death. Worse than visiting every sleazy dive in town until you finally find the one person who can put the murderer away and having that person say as cool as a debutante with a full dance card, "I don't want to get involved."[21]

MYTH

Improvements in detective work and criminal investigation will significantly raise clearance rates or lower the crime rate.

FACT

"Cleared" crimes generally solve themselves. The offender either is discovered at the scene or can be identified by the victim or a witness. Investigation rarely solves "cold" or "stranger" crimes.

Detectives have the cards stacked against them most of the time. Unless they discover, during the preliminary investigation, a named suspect or a description or other information that leads to a named suspect, the chances of solving the crime are low. Property crimes with no witnesses are particularly hard to solve. In 2007, for example, the clearance rates for crimes against persons were 61.2% for murder, 54.1% for aggravated assault, 40% for forcible rape, and 25.9% for robbery. In crimes against property, the clearance rates were 12.4% for burglary, 18.6% for larceny-theft, and 12.6% for motor vehicle theft. Clearances for crimes against persons are generally higher than for property crimes, because crimes against persons receive more intensive investigative effort and because victims and witnesses frequently identify the perpetrators. In 2007, for example, the nationwide clearance rate for violent crimes was 44.5% and for property crimes, 16.5%.[22] Studies have found that much of what a detective does is not needed and that an investigator's technical knowledge often does little to help solve cases.[23] In one study, for example, fewer than 10% of all arrests for robbery were the result of investigative work by detectives.[24] Nevertheless, police agencies retain detectives and plainclothes investigators for a number of reasons:

1. Detectives have interrogation and case presentation skills that assist in prosecution.
2. Technical knowledge, such as knowing about burglary tools, does help in some investigations and prosecutions.
3. Law enforcement executives can assign detectives to a major, high-profile case to demonstrate to the public that they are committing resources to the matter.

The major studies of investigative effectiveness emphasize the value of improving the suspect-identification process. Once a suspect is identified by name or some other clearly distinguishing characteristic, the chances of making an arrest are increased substantially.

Recent Identification Developments in Criminal Investigation Two of the most significant advances in criminal investigation have been the development of fingerprinting and DNA profiling. Fingerprinting has resulted in the arrest and conviction of millions of criminal suspects who otherwise might never have been brought to justice. DNA profiling holds even greater promise.

DNA Profiling DNA (deoxyribonucleic acid) is a molecule present in all forms of life. A unique genetic profile can be derived from blood, hair, semen, or other bodily substances found at the scene of a crime or on a victim. Not only can bodily substances found at a crime scene be matched with DNA samples from a suspect to give an extremely high probability of identing the perpetrator, but it is believed that soon DNA from a sample as small as a flake of dandruff will yield a positive, unique identification, with no need to consider mathematical probabilities.

DNA profiling has three distinct functions: linking or eliminating identified suspects to a crime; identing "cold hits," whereby a sample from a crime scene is matched against numerous cases in a DNA database and a positive match is made; and clearing convicted rapists and murderers years after they began serving their sentences. DNA profiling would be very useful, for example, in cases where a murderer's blood was found at the scene of a crime after a deadly struggle or in a rape case where seminal fluid could be obtained from the victim. In approximately one-third of DNA examinations, the suspect's DNA cannot be matched with biological evidence from the crime scene. Thus, potential suspects can be eliminated from consideration early in the investigative process, allowing investigators to focus their efforts more effectively on other suspects or cases. Potential suspects also can be eliminated from an investigation years after the crime occurred, as happened recently in the JonBenet Ramsey murder case. The then 6-year-old beauty queen was killed in 1996, and her brother and parents remained suspects for more than a decade. In 2008, based on results obtained from a new technology called "touch DNA," the cloud of suspicion was finally removed from the Ramsey family. Touch DNA involves scraping genetic material from an object that otherwise could not be seen. In this case, newly discovered DNA from a few minute skin cells matched DNA found earlier and was not from the Ramsey family. Investigators will try to locate a match in the national DNA database, which has more than 5 million offenders' profiles. For now, the murder remains unsolved.[25]

A serious issue at present is whether DNA databases ought to be assembled and from whom the samples should be taken. Many states permit the taking of DNA samples from arrested and convicted subjects. Some enthusiasts believe that DNA samples should be taken from all suspects in crimes, while a smaller number believe the samples should be collected from all people at birth.

CJ Online

DNA Evidence

The National Commission on the Future of DNA Evidence is a program sponsored by the National Institute of Justice. Visit the program's website at www.ojp.usdoj.gov/nij/topics/forensics/dna/commission/welcome.html. *How big a role should DNA play in criminal investigations?*

Figure 6.3

How DNA Profiling Is Performed

DNA, deoxyribonucleic acid, is the material that carries the genetic pattern that makes each person unique. Scientists in the laboratory can map DNA patterns in samples of skin, blood, semen, or other body tissues or fluids. The DNA patterns can then be analyzed and compared.

There are two main DNA testing procedures used in criminal forensics.

1. Samples are taken of tissue or body fluids at crime scenes. Comparison samples are taken from victims and suspects.

RFLP (Restriction Fragment Length Polymorphism)

2. In the laboratory, DNA genetic material is extracted from the samples and mixed with enzymes to cut the DNA into fragments.

3. The DNA fragments are put in a special gel and exposed to an electrical charge to sort the fragments by size.

4. Genetic tracers are used to search out and lock onto specific fragments of the DNA.

5. The tracers reveal a pattern. Each evidence sample will have a pattern that can be compared with the sample from the victim and the sample from the suspect.

PCR (Polymerase Chain Reaction)

2. In the laboratory, DNA is extracted from the samples.

3. Part of the DNA molecule is amplified in a test tube to produce billions of copies of that part.

4. The amplified DNA is analyzed.

5. The analysis of the evidence sample can be compared with the analysis of the sample from the victim and the sample from the suspect.

Comparing the patterns in the samples results in a DNA profile representing distinctive features of the samples that may or may not match.

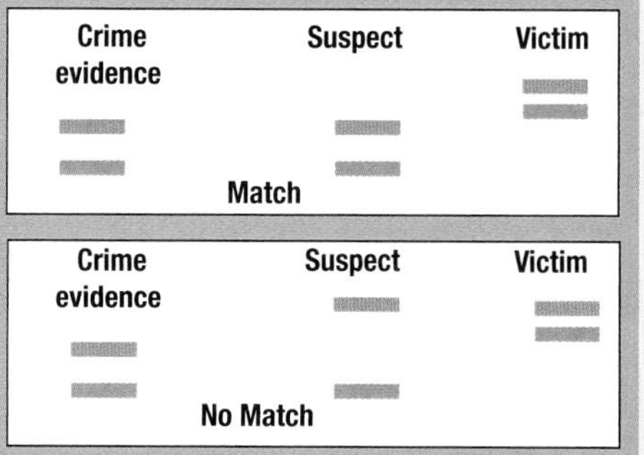

Crime evidence	Suspect	Victim
Match

Crime evidence	Suspect	Victim
No Match

Another controversial issue is how long DNA samples should be kept. In December 2008, 17 judges on the European Court of Human Rights, Europe's highest human-rights court, struck down a British law that allowed the government to store DNA and fingerprints of people with no criminal record. The law had allowed the government to keep samples until an individual died or reached the age of 100. Britain's DNA databases, with more than 4.5 million samples, have been taken from arrestees, regardless of whether they have been charged, convicted, or acquitted and, occasionally, from crime victims. The court unanimously ruled that Britain's "blanket and indiscriminate" storage of DNA samples and fingerprints of people with no criminal record violated people's right to privacy—a protection under the Human Rights Convention to which the United Kingdom is a signatory. The ruling likely will require Britain to destroy about 1 million samples in its DNA database.[26]

Currently, the most complete DNA database in the United States, with nearly 6.4 million samples (as of October 2008), is the Combined DNA Index System

(CODIS), which is managed by the Federal Bureau of Investigation.[27] CODIS comprises DNA profiles that have been entered into local, state, and other national databases. The profiles are from either biological evidence left at crime scenes or individuals convicted of violent crimes and other felonies. Undoubtedly the more collected samples in a database, the more likely a match is going to be found. But privacy concerns and the potential for misuse of DNA samples are likely to hinder any more intrusive measures on the part of agents of the justice system.

Automated Fingerprint Identification System An expensive but invaluable tool in criminal investigation is the Automated Fingerprint Identification System (AFIS). This relatively new technology allows investigators to sort through thousands of sets of stored fingerprints for a match with those of a suspect in a crime. In fact, many of the current attempts to match prints would not have been made without AFIS, because the old process would have taken thousands of hours. Large metropolitan police agencies use it to identify 200–500 suspects a year who would have escaped apprehension before the implementation of AFIS. The initial and maintenance costs for an AFIS, however, are expensive. The FBI's IAFIS (Integrated Automated Fingerprint Identification System) is the world's largest, with more than 55 million prints on file. The Florida Department of Law Enforcement's system, by contrast, has only about 5 million prints on file.[28]

Cybercrime The use of computer technology to commit crime is of increasing concern to law enforcement officials. The FBI reports that the losses from **cybercrime** each year total $10 billion even though two-thirds of computer crime victims fail to notify the authorities. Some of the reasons for not reporting computer crime are the fear of loss of the public's confidence in the organization, the attention to vulnerability that a crime report would attract, and the shame of not providing adequate security to protect trusted assets.

> **cybercrime** The use of computer technology to commit crime.

Since so little hardware and expense is involved, any person with a computer and modem connection to the Internet has the potential to attack computer systems and people online. The knowledge to carry out these attacks is often available online at hacker websites, message boards, and chat rooms. The cybercriminal can be as unsophisticated as a teenage amateur hacker just out for some fun or a talented computer specialist possessing skills on par with technical experts employed by the nation's top security organizations. Each of these types of computer criminal can wreak destructive havoc on a computer system, invade the privacy of thousands of citizens, and engage in the theft of millions of dollars' worth of trade secrets or steal large sums of money. At present, unfortunately, most law enforcement agencies in America are ill prepared to detect, investigate, and prosecute cybercriminals.[29]

A variety of offenses can be committed using computer and Internet technology.

- **Sex Crimes**—Predators search the Internet looking for sexually explicit content as well as child pornography. Much of the sexually explicit and pornographic content is in JPEG and MPEG formats, which allow it to be downloaded to a person's hard drive easily.[30] Downloading much of this material is illegal in a number of states. The origin of some of this content is often from other nations of the world, thus complicating investigation and prosecution.

- **Illegal Access, Destruction, and Manipulation of Data**—Cybercriminals break into computer systems and obtain data that is illegal for them to have, such as credit card numbers, bank records, and software codes. In October of 2000, someone illegally entered Microsoft's computer system and stole software codes for some of its future products. Hackers often illegally enter computer systems and introduce viruses or worms that infect that computer system and any other storage device that interacts with it. Computer data can also be illegally manipulated

CJ Online

Combating Cybercrime

To learn more about what the U.S. government is doing to combat cybercrime, visit the U.S. Department of Justice cybercrime website at www.usdoj.gov/criminal/cybercrime. *Do you think that there is anything more the government can do to prevent cybercrime?*

Scientific traffic accident investigation requires technical expertise. *Should all patrol officers be trained to conduct traffic investigations? Why or why not?*

in a variety of ways. Computer records can be altered at financial, business, and educational institutions. Millions of dollars have been illegally transferred to the accounts of cybercriminals since the inception of electronic data storage. (The crime of identity theft, which can involve cybercrime, is discussed at length in Chapter 14.)

In a survey involving 114 state and local law enforcement agencies, it was revealed that these agencies lacked the adequate training, equipment, and staff to confront present and future incidents of cybercrime.[31] Cooperative efforts are now underway among law enforcement, business, high-tech, and national security organizations to better prepare the nation's police agencies to combat cybercrime.

TRAFFIC

When loss of life, serious injury, suffering, and property damage are all considered, the regulation and control of vehicle and pedestrian traffic are important, if not the most important, police responsibilities. Each year, nearly twice as many people are killed in automobile accidents on the streets and highways of the nation than are murdered.

A large percentage of this highway death and suffering is attributable to alcohol. Enforcement of DUI (driving under the influence) laws is critical to the safety of a community. In addition, automobile insurance rates are based to some degree on a community's level of traffic enforcement. Thus, if the police neglect traffic regulation and enforcement, they are likely to hear about it from both insurance companies and premium payers.

Some of the debate about traffic enforcement concerns whether the major enforcers of traffic regulations should be specialized personnel or uniformed patrol officers. Some traffic responsibilities are already delegated to specialized personnel, such as enforcement of parking regulations and investigations of hit-and-run accidents and traffic fatalities. In some agencies, special **traffic accident investigation crews** are assigned to all traffic accident investigations. Otherwise, patrol officers investigate accidents and attend to other traffic-related duties as a normal part of their everyday workload.

traffic accident investigation crews In some agencies, the special units assigned to all traffic accident investigations.

Traffic units exist in nearly all medium-to-large police agencies. Some of their more important functions are these:

• To educate motorists in a community about traffic safety and proper driving procedures.
• To enforce traffic laws, particularly when violations of those laws cause traffic accidents.
• To recommend traffic engineering changes that will enhance the flow of traffic and promote safety.

Enforcing traffic laws may also reduce criminal activity because stopping vehicles for traffic violations both day and night is likely to put police officers in contact with criminals.

Many veteran officers consider working in the traffic division "clean" police work, because it does not normally involve responding to radio calls that take them to the scene of fights, domestic disturbances, or other distasteful incidents, such as those involving drunks. Traffic officers in large police agencies are usually well schooled in scientific accident investigation, a skill that makes them employable in the private sector, usually doing traffic reconstruction for insurance companies. The Traffic Institute at Northwestern University is one of the

Ohio State Highway Patrol Officer

My name is Lieutenant Brenda Sue Collins. I have had an exciting career with the Ohio State Highway Patrol and have worked in a variety of assignments since 1985. Currently I am the post commander for the Fremont post of the State Highway Patrol, responsible for the leadership of all operational and staff personnel serving at the Fremont post. I have also served as a cadet dispatcher (my first job with the patrol), a highway trooper, an academy instructor, an officer in the Traffic and Drug Interdiction Unit, a supervisor in the recruiting section, and a public information officer. I am married to Captain Richard Collins, a district commander of the patrol stationed in Findlay.

An Ohio State Highway Patrol Officer's major responsibility is to patrol the roadways and keep them safe. That responsibility includes investigating vehicle crashes, gaining obedience to the traffic laws by enforcement and other means, giving assistance to motorists 24 hours a day, keeping the roadway free of obstructions, enforcing the extensive commercial vehicle laws, and checking for signs of criminal activity during vehicle stops. One of the toughest parts of the patrol officer's job is to make death notifications to family members of loved ones who have been killed in a fatal crash.

I graduated in the 116th Academy class and was assigned to the Portsmouth post as a trooper, where I was somewhat of a novelty with the citizens since there were not that many female highway patrol officers. But when people see that you do your job effectively and professionally just like your male counterparts, the novelty soon wears off. Now we have about 130 female troopers out of a total of approximately 1,400 troopers.

I attended Ohio University, where I studied forensic chemistry and law enforcement, and I also attended Ohio State University in Marion. The OSHP provides tuition assistance that varies depending on the grades you receive in courses.

Being married to another highway patrol officer really has its advantages. First, you can learn from each other, because you have worked in different assignments and have experienced common things at different times in your career. Richard and I also know the language and values of the highway patrol, therefore allowing us to communicate a lot more clearly than a married couple working at entirely different jobs. The only disadvantage that I can see is that when both of you are senior officers in the patrol, you have to deal with the issue of promotions. As a married couple we are not allowed to serve in the same posts of the patrol but can be in adjacent districts if there are openings for our rank. Consequently when promotional opportunities come up for one or the other of us, we have to think of what kind of disruption that will cause in our home life.

The advice I would offer to somebody that wants to be a highway patrol officer is to work in a job you really want until the highway patrol officer's job becomes available. The selection process is long and difficult. I would suggest that you investigate and really find out what a highway patrol officer's job is like. The job entails round-the-clock duty in all sorts of weather, including the worst weather. In fact, you may be the only one out on the highways during bad weather. You are more likely to stick with it when you know these things up front.

What characteristics of your personality do you think would make you best suited to be a highway patrol officer?

major schools that prepare officers for sophisticated accident investigation, although many state peace officer and highway patrol academies now have comparable training programs.

DRUG ENFORCEMENT

Illegal drug use in the United States is widespread and stable. According to the Substance Abuse and Mental Health Services Administration's *2007 National Survey on Drug Use and Health,* 19.9 million Americans age 12 and older (8% of the population age 12 or older) reported using an illegal drug in the month before the survey was conducted. The use rate has remained stable since at least 2002.[32] Illegal drugs included marijuana/hashish, cocaine (including crack), heroin, hallucinogens (for example, LSD, PCP, peyote, mescaline, mushrooms, and "Ecstasy" or MDMA), inhalants (for instance, amyl nitrite, cleaning fluids, gasoline, paint, and glue), or prescription-type psychotherapeutics (pain relievers, tranquilizers, stimulants, and sedatives) used nonmedically. Among past-month illegal drug users, 53.3% used only marijuana, 19.4% used marijuana and another illegal drug, and 27.2% used only an illegal drug other than marijuana. During 2007, 3.6 million Americans age 12 or older were

Table 6.4 The Extent of Illegal Drug Use in the United States Among Population Age 12 or Older

Drug	DURING LIFETIME		DURING 2007		DURING MONTH BEFORE SURVEY CONDUCTED	
	Number	**%**	**Number**	**%**	**Number**	**%**
Marijuana	100.5 m	40.6%	25.1 m	10.1%	14.4 m	5.8%
Cocaine	35.9 m	14.5	5.7 m	2.3	2.1 m	0.8
Crack	8.6 m	3.5	1.45 m	0.6	610,000	0.2
Hallucinogens	34.2 m	13.8	3.8 m	1.5	1.0 m	0.4
Inhalants	22.5 m	9.1	2.1 m	0.8	616,000	0.2
Heroin	3.8 m	1.5	366,000	0.1	153,000	0.1
Methamphetamine	13.1 m	5.3	1.3 m	0.5	529,000	0.2
MDMA	12.4 m	5.0	2.1 m	0.9	503,000	0.2
Psychotherapeutics used nonmedically*	50.4 m	20.3	16.3 m	6.6	6.9 m	2.8

Notes: m = million; % = percentage of overall population; * = pain relievers, tranquilizers, and sedatives.

Source: Constructed from data in *2007 National Survey on Drug Use and Health* at www.oas.samhsa.gov/nsduh/2k7nsduh/2k7Results.cfm#1.1 and www.oas.samhsa.gov/nsduh/2k7nsduh/AppG.htm.

daily marijuana users. Table 6.4 provides the number of Americans age 12 or older who used a specific drug or category of drug at least once during their lifetime, during 2007, and during the month before the survey was conducted, and their percentage of the overall population.

Given the extent of illegal drug use in the United States, it is not surprising that drug enforcement has become an increasingly important responsibility of police departments across the nation. Although the war on drugs is a priority of state and federal law enforcement agencies as well, it has been at the local level that many of the battles have been fought. Approximately 90% of local police departments regularly engaged in drug enforcement in 2003 (the latest year for which data were available), and nearly all police departments that served 100,000 or more residents did so.[33]

Eighteen percent of local police departments in 2003 had a special drug enforcement unit with one or more officers assigned to it full-time. Larger departments were much more likely than smaller departments to have special drug enforcement units and more full-time officers assigned to them. For example, all departments serving one million or more residents had such units, and a majority of departments serving at least 50,000 residents had them. The average number of full-time officers assigned to drug enforcement units was 6, but departments serving one million or more residents averaged 233 full-time officers. In departments serving less than 10,000 residents, only an average of 1.5 full-time officers were assigned to the special drug enforcement unit in those departments that had one.

In 2003, approximately one in four local police departments had one or more officers assigned full-time to a multiagency drug enforcement task force. Again, larger departments were more likely than smaller departments to participate in these task forces and assign full-time officers to them. More than 75% of local police departments serving 50,000 or more residents participated in a multiagency drug enforcement task force in 2003, and nearly two-thirds of the departments serving 25,000 or more residents participated in them. About 6,000 local police officers were assigned full-time to a task force in 2003. The average number of officers assigned ranged from 39 in departments serving one million or more residents to about 1 or 2 in departments serving fewer than 50,000 residents.

Although all levels of government are waging the war on drugs, the focus of the remainder of this section is the drug enforcement strategies of local police (and sheriffs') agencies. The particular strategies employed by individual agencies vary widely, but the most common strategies are street-level enforcement, midlevel investigations, major investigations, crop eradication, smuggling interdiction, problem-oriented and community policing strategies, drug demand reduction, and asset forfeiture. It is important to note at the outset that none of these strategies has had much of a long-term effect on the U.S. drug problem.

Street-Level Enforcement Patrol officers, officers assigned to special drug enforcement units, and plainclothes officers do most of the street-level enforcement. Their tactics include surveillance, interruption of suspected transactions, raids of "shooting galleries" and "crack houses," buy-and-bust operations, and "reverse stings," in which plainclothes officers offer to sell drugs to willing customers. Street-level enforcement is responsible for most drug arrests and seizures. However, typically, the people arrested are either drug users or small-time dealers, and the seizures are for small amounts of drugs. In 2007, a typical year, more arrests were made for drug abuse violations than for any other offense. About 1.8 million drug arrests were made, which represented 13% of all arrests reported to the FBI.[34]

Mid-Level Investigations Informants or undercover police officers are frequently employed in mid-level investigations. The primary purpose of these investigations is to identify and make cases against mid-level dealers. Although mid-level dealers generally occupy relatively low-level positions in a drug distribution network and are easily replaced, they often are the highest-ranking drug traffickers that local police agencies can catch. The basic tactic used in these investigations is for undercover officers to gain the confidence of street-level dealers and work their way up to mid-level dealers by requesting to buy larger quantities of drugs than the street-level dealer can provide. Another tactic is for an informant to simply introduce an undercover officer to a mid-level dealer. Street-level dealers often become informants when they are

Drug busts can be dangerous. *As a law enforcement officer, would you be willing to participate in drug busts? Why or why not?*

arrested and agree to inform on their suppliers in return for some consideration in prosecution.

Major Investigations The goal of major investigations is to arrest drug king-pins and shut down the organizations responsible for producing, importing, and distributing large quantities of illegal drugs. Major investigations are conducted primarily by federal and state law enforcement agencies, but sometimes the largest local police agencies are involved as well. Most local police agencies do not have the resources to engage in major investigations, which often require long-term commitments, extensive travel, and specialized expertise. In some cases, however, local police agencies participate in major investigations as part of a multiagency task force.

Crop Eradication Crop eradication is a tactic employed by federal, state, and local law enforcement agencies. However, the only crop targeted by local police agencies is cannabis (marijuana), because it is the only major illegal drug grown in the United States. Because cannabis eradication intervenes at the beginning of the trafficking process, in theory it should have the greatest potential for eliminating or at least significantly reducing marijuana availability and use. In practice, however, a number of problems reduce the effectiveness of the eradication strategy. First, large quantities of marijuana are generally grown in remote, largely inaccessible areas. This makes locating and destroying crops by hand difficult, time-consuming, labor-intensive, and dangerous. Second, spraying crops with chemicals can be hazardous to people, water supplies, animals, and other vegetation. Third, even when crop eradication is successful in one area, a new crop can easily be grown in another area. The huge profits that can be made from a marijuana crop create a powerful incentive not to be deterred by eradication efforts. In 2007, the DEA reported that nearly 6.6 million marijuana plants cultivated outdoors were eradicated (as well as about 435,000 plants cultivated indoors).[35]

Smuggling Interdiction Federal law enforcement agencies have the primary responsibility for smuggling interdiction, but local police agencies can play a role. Local police officers in jurisdictions near the U.S. borders or those in jurisdictions with international airports or even small airports and airfields can be on the lookout for drug smugglers.

Problem-Oriented and Community Policing Strategies Problem-oriented policing is a strategy that focuses on the underlying problems that cause crime rather than focusing on each specific criminal event. The strategy involves identing the underlying problems, analyzing them in detail, applying solutions to them, and then evaluating the effectiveness of the solutions. The problem-oriented approach to drug enforcement has been adopted by many local police agencies to address drug problems in public housing projects, drug abuse among teenagers, and drug abuse in abandoned buildings. The strategy makes sense because it promotes careful analysis of a community's unique drug problem before action is taken, advocates customizing responses and targeting resources, and recommends working with other public and private agencies in the problem-solving process.

Community policing, which is addressed in more detail later in the chapter, is both a philosophy and a set of methods. The philosophy is that citizens and the police must form a partnership and work collectively to identify problems, propose solutions, implement action, and evaluate results in the community. Methods include foot patrol, storefronts and other mini-stations in the community, door-to-door contact with citizens, community organizing, ombudsperson-like activities, provision of social services, and problem-oriented policing.

MYTH

Drug interdiction and eradication are effective strategies.

FACT

Despite the regular seizure of huge quantities of illegal drugs, federal, state, and local law enforcement efforts net only about 10% to 15% of the total supply. As for drug interdiction, if correctional officials cannot keep illegal drugs out of maximum security prisons, how effective is the government going to be in keeping illegal drugs from entering the country?

Community policing can contribute to drug enforcement in several ways. For example, foot patrol and problem-oriented policing can reduce street-level dealing. Successful community policing may increase public support for drug enforcement efforts by encouraging citizens to report drug crimes and identify drug dealers. Community organizing may empower citizens to resist drug dealers and drug abusers who invade their communities. The provision of enhanced social services, whether provided by police officers or through police ombudspersons, may help individuals resist the temptation of illegal drugs.

Drug Demand Reduction Local police agencies can play a role in drug demand reduction strategies in at least four ways. First, through visible drug enforcement efforts, the police may discourage some people from using drugs in the first place because of a fear of arrest. Second, the police may stop some people from continuing to use drugs by arresting them so that they can get court-ordered treatment or by diverting them to drug treatment programs. Third, through public education programs, especially in the schools, the police may get young people to resist the temptations of drugs or the peer pressure to use them. Fourth, the police can lend their stature and credibility to efforts to increase funding for drug treatment, prevention, and education programs.

D.A.R.E. (Drug Abuse Resistance Education) is the nation's largest and best-known substance abuse prevention program. It was developed in 1983 by Los Angeles Police Chief Daryl Gates and is now taught in more than 50% of the school districts nationwide, down from more than 80% of school districts just a few years ago. It is a school-based collaborative effort among police departments, schools, parents, and community leaders to teach children how to recognize and resist the direct and subtle pressures that influence them to experiment with alcohol, tobacco, marijuana, and other drugs. Usually addressing children in the fifth or sixth grade, a specially trained uniformed police officer comes to the school 1 day a week for 17 weeks and teaches the children for about an hour. The D.A.R.E. curriculum is integrated with other regular subjects. Although D.A.R.E. programs are hugely popular, no scientific study, among the many evaluations that have been conducted, has discovered any

D.A.R.E. programs are taught in more than 80% of the nation's school districts. *Why haven't these programs been more effective in reducing illegal drug use among the nation's youth?*

statistically significant difference in drug-usage rates between students who had taken D.A.R.E. and those who had not.[36]

Asset Forfeiture A huge incentive for local police departments to participate in drug enforcement activities is *asset forfeiture*. Asset forfeiture for crimes is an ancient practice that is referred to in the Bible. It was part of English common law and helped instigate the American Revolution. Partly because of asset forfeiture abuses, the due process clause of the Fifth Amendment was included in the U.S. Constitution to guarantee that property could not be taken from citizens without a judicial hearing.

Congress enacted the first drug-related civil asset forfeiture law in 1970, as part of the Comprehensive Drug Abuse and Prevention Act. The law authorized the government to seize and forfeit illegal drugs, manufacturing and storage equipment, and vehicles used to transport drugs. A major rationale for the law was the belief that drug traffickers should not benefit financially from their illegal activities or be able to use property or money obtained illegally in future drug crimes. In 1978 and throughout the 1980s, Congress passed several more antidrug laws that enhanced the government's power to seize and forfeit property.

Note that the government can seize a person's property under both criminal and civil law. A reason why civil asset forfeiture has been the preferred tool in drug enforcement is that property can be forfeited under criminal law only if the property owner has been convicted of a crime (beyond a reasonable doubt). Under civil forfeiture law, however, the government is required only to have probable cause to seize a person's property. Furthermore, until the passage of the Civil Asset Forfeiture Reform Act of 2000 (CAFRA), an owner under civil forfeiture law had to be proactive to get his or her property back: An owner had to prove in a civil proceeding by a preponderance of the evidence that the property was not used in a crime. CAFRA shifted the burden of proof so that, today, the government has to prove by a preponderance of evidence that the property should be forfeited.

Assets can be forfeited under either federal or state law. When federal agencies are involved in a successful drug enforcement operation, they can return up to 80% of forfeited assets to other participating state or local law enforcement agencies. The amount of money or property returned depends on the particular agency's level of involvement in the case. Federal law requires that all funds returned to state and local law enforcement agencies be used for law enforcement activities. Each state has its own formula for how forfeited assets are to be distributed and used. For example, some states require all forfeitures to be used for drug enforcement activities; some states require forfeited assets to be given to the state educational system; and other states require the proceeds from forfeitures be deposited in the state treasury to be used at the legislature's discretion.

Prior to CAFRA, critics pointed to many problems with civil asset forfeiture laws. First, as noted previously, civil asset forfeiture laws placed the burden of proof on the owner of the property seized to show that the property was not used in a drug-related crime. Not only was it difficult to prove a negative—that the property was *not* used in a drug-related crime—the government also had to prove almost nothing. CAFRA shifted the burden of proof to the government.

Second, the costs involved in a civil asset forfeiture proceeding could be prohibitively high. For example, to contest a federal forfeiture, a property owner had to post a bond equal to 10% of the seized property's value. This requirement placed a burden on the poor. CAFRA abolished the bond requirement. The poor were further handicapped in civil asset forfeiture proceedings, because the government was not obligated to provide counsel, as the Sixth

FYI

Civil Forfeiture

Civil forfeiture is based on the legal fiction that the property that facilitates or is connected to a crime has itself committed a wrong and can be seized and tried in civil court. Such judicial hearings are referred to as *in rem* proceedings, meaning "against the thing."

Source: Scott Ehlers, *Policy Briefing: Asset Forfeiture*, The Drug Policy Foundation (Washington, D.C.: GPO, 1999), p. 4.

Amendment required in criminal trials. In many cases, property owners simply forfeited the seized property because of the high costs of getting it back. In some cases, the costs of getting property back were higher than the value of the seized property itself. CAFRA provides for court-appointed counsel for indigent owners if (1) the indigent owner makes a "good faith" claim and is already represented by court-appointed counsel in the related criminal case, and (2) the subject of the forfeiture is the indigent's primary residence. Additionally, nonindigent claimants may be entitled to court and litigation costs provided they "substantially prevail" in the civil forfeiture action. Finally, before CAFRA, the government was generally exempt from claims stemming from seizure and possession of an owner's property in civil forfeiture actions. CAFRA now provides for compensation to victims of forfeiture where their property was seized and they were not convicted of a crime giving rise to that forfeiture.

Third, innocent owners could lose their property when someone else used it without their permission or knowledge to commit a drug crime. In the case of *Calero-Toledo* v. *Pearson Yacht Leasing Company* (1974), for example, law enforcement officers found a marijuana cigarette onboard a yacht rented by the Pearson Yacht Leasing Company. The yacht was forfeited to the government, because it was used to transport a controlled substance. The U.S. Supreme Court upheld the forfeiture, establishing the principle that the government can seize an innocent owner's property in a civil proceeding. This seeming injustice was corrected somewhat in 1988, when Congress passed the Asset Forfeiture Amendments Act. The act created forfeiture exceptions for some, but not all, innocent owners and for violations involving the possession of personal-use quantities of drugs. However, innocent owners were not fully protected by the exception. For example, in 1999, a Wichita, Kansas, couple had their motel forfeited and sold because drugs had been sold on the property. The couple had tried to keep drug dealers off the property by installing floodlights and fences and calling the police, but their property was forfeited anyway. CAFRA created an innocent owner defense applicable to all civil asset forfeiture statutes.

Still, critics argue that the standard of proof in civil forfeiture cases is too low. Because probable cause is the standard of proof necessary to seize property that was used to facilitate a drug crime, little more than hearsay evidence is required. Another problem with probable cause as the standard of proof in civil asset forfeiture proceedings is exemplified by the sheriff of Volusia County, Florida (near Daytona Beach), who defined probable cause for purposes of asset forfeiture as having more than $100 in cash.

Finally, critics maintain that civil asset forfeiture policy undermines the integrity of the police and the criminal justice system. The proceeds that can be had from civil asset forfeitures are a corrupting influence for many law enforcement officers. Sometimes officers are more concerned with seizing assets than they are with getting drugs off the streets. In some cases, law enforcement officers simply extort money and property from innocent people. Civil asset forfeiture laws sometimes promote other illegal practices such as racial profiling (described in Chapter 7). Sometimes resources are diverted from more serious crimes to drug cases that promise asset forfeitures. In short, although civil asset forfeiture helps fuel the war on drugs and can reduce the profits from the illegal drug trade, there are many reasons to question its fairness and utility, despite the significant reforms of CAFRA. Its harshest critics contend that civil asset forfeiture should be eliminated altogether because criminal asset forfeiture is available and has procedures that better protect the innocent.

Criticisms of the War on Drugs

In addition to the already mentioned problems with specific aspects of drug enforcement, the war on drugs, itself, has been

Illegal drug use causes crime.

Illegal drug use is not a significant cause of crime. Although the effects of some illegal drugs may cause a very small number of violent crimes, the vast majority of drug-related crimes are caused by the drug laws, which make the possession, distribution, cultivation, or manufacture of certain drugs a crime. The drug laws also cause crime by creating an illegal market in which drug prices are artificially and dramatically increased. This makes it necessary for some drug users, especially addicts, to steal or deal to get money to buy drugs. It also contributes to the violence of rival drug dealers seeking to monopolize a market. The illegality of desired drugs also puts otherwise law-abiding people in contact with members of the criminal underworld from whom they can learn criminal skills. Ironically, alcohol is the only drug that has been found to cause a significant amount of crime, and alcohol is legal for adults.

severely criticized. First, critics contend that the government has exaggerated the dangers of illegal drug use to gain public support for the war on drugs and has generally ignored the harms caused by the drug laws themselves. For example, it has been estimated that about 3,600 people die each year from the consumption of all illegal drugs combined. While any death from illegal drug consumption is regrettable, the 3,600 deaths attributed to illegal drugs pale in comparison to the approximately 200,000 alcohol-related and 400,000 tobacco-related deaths each year. Moreover, rarely are drug-related deaths the result of abuse or misuse of the drugs. Instead, most of the drug-related deaths are directly attributable to the drug laws that prohibit their use. For example, most heroin overdoses occur because the heroin is adulterated (that is, the drug is "cut" or mixed with dangerous substances to increase the quantity of the drug available to sell or to produce a more readily ingestible form of the drug). The reason why the heroin is adulterated is because it is illegal and unregulated; there is no quality control in its production and distribution. Also, because it is illegal, heroin addicts share needles, which spreads disease and illness. It has been estimated that 25% of AIDS cases in the United States are a direct result of the unsafe and unsanitary conditions in which illegal drugs are consumed. The same is true of cocaine. Because of the drug laws, the price of using powder cocaine is too high for many people so they substitute the more affordable and more dangerous crack cocaine. A person is more likely to die or suffer injury from smoking the drug than he or she is from snorting it. As for marijuana, no one has ever died from using marijuana. The greatest danger to marijuana smokers is in smoking the drug after it has been adulterated by government control programs, such as the spraying of herbicides on marijuana crops.

Another way the government has tried to rally support for the drug war has been to try to persuade the public of a direct connection between illegal drug use and crime. However, as described in the myth/fact box on this page, it is not drugs that cause crime, but rather the drug laws that cause crime.

Second, critics have argued that the drug war is racist. Of the approximately 1.8 million people arrested in 2007 for drug abuse violations, 64% were white and 35% were black. Yet, blacks are only about 14% of all drug users, and a National Institute on Drug Abuse (NIDA) survey showed that the prevalence of drug use is nearly the same among whites and blacks. Furthermore, in many jurisdictions the penalties are much more severe for possession of crack cocaine than they are for the possession of powder cocaine, although pharmacologically they are identical drugs. For example, federal sentencing guidelines provide for a 100-to-1 sentencing disparity, which means that conviction for possessing 5 grams of crack results in the same mandatory minimum 5-year sentence as conviction for possessing 500 grams of powder cocaine. On average, federal crack-cocaine defendants receive sentences that are 50% longer than those received by federal powder-cocaine defendants. When Congress passed the Anti-Drug Abuse Act in 1986, crack was a relatively new drug and was believed to be more dangerous than powder cocaine. About 60% of people arrested for possession of powder cocaine are white, while about 90% of the people arrested for possession of crack cocaine are black. Ironically, relatively low-level crack cocaine dealers have received longer prison sentences than wholesale-level powder cocaine dealers from whom the crack dealer originally bought the powder to make the crack.

About 60% of people arrested for possession of powder cocaine are white, while about 90% of people arrested for possession of crack cocaine are black. *Should law enforcement authorities distinguish between powder cocaine and crack cocaine when making arrests for possession? Why or why not?*

In two recent cases, the U.S. Supreme Court has ameliorated somewhat the harsh federal sentencing guidelines for cocaine. In *United States* v. *Booker* (2005), the Court held that the formerly mandatory sentencing guidelines are now only advisory. Under the new rule, the guidelines are to serve as only one factor among others that must be considered in determining an appropriate sentence. If judges believe that deviating from the guidelines is reasonable under the circumstances, they may do so. In *Kimbrough* v. *United States* (2007), the Court reversed the Fourth Circuit of Appeals, which ruled that "a sentence outside the guidelines range is *per se* unreasonable when it is based on a disagreement with the sentencing disparity for crack and powder offenses." As a result, in December 2007, the federal sentencing commission voted unanimously to allow about 20,000 federal inmates to seek reductions in their crack sentences. The sentencing commission estimated the average reduction would likely be a little more than two years. Of course, these developments only apply to federal cocaine cases; they do not apply to those that originate at the state level.

Third, as noted previously, critics point out that the war on drugs and the huge amount of money involved in the drug trade have corrupted many law enforcement personnel, who have been found guilty of drug dealing, providing protection for drug dealers, conspiracy, extortion, bribery, robbery, theft, and murder. Unfortunately, examples abound. A *New York Times* report disclosed that each year more than 100 law enforcement officers are prosecuted in state and federal courts on drug corruption charges.

Fourth, critics maintain that the war on drugs is hugely expensive, diverts resources from arguably more important projects, and has had little lasting effect on illegal drug use. Since 1980, the United States has spent hundreds of billions of dollars on federal, state, and local antidrug efforts, more than is spent on medical research into cancer, heart disease, or AIDS—to name just three worthwhile projects. Furthermore, despite the huge amount of money and effort spent on the drug war, the prices of many illegal drugs have not increased and in many cases have fallen, and the purity of illegal drugs and their availability have not decreased but in many cases have increased. If the drug war were successfully reducing supply or demand, one would expect prices to increase, and the purity and availability of illegal drugs to decline.

Although the measurement of illegal drug use is fraught with all sorts of reliability problems, according to the Substance Abuse and Mental Health Services Administration's annual *National Survey on Drug Use and Health*, there was a significant decline in illegal drug use among both youths and adults between 1979 and 1992 (from 25 million past-month illegal drug users to 12 million past-month illegal drug users). However, the number of past-month illegal drug users has increased unevenly between 1992 and 2008. The estimated number of past-month illegal drug users aged 12 or older in the United States in 2007 was 19.9 million. The higher number is attributed to a much higher rate of use among youths, a small increase in the rate of use among adults, and a 10% increase in the size of the U.S. population. Critics are calling for an end to the drug war. Some critics want illegal drugs to be decriminalized or legalized. Other critics want the drug problem treated as a public health problem and not as a criminal justice problem. Perhaps it is time to seriously rethink America's strategy for dealing with illegal drug use.

FYI Drug Offenders in Prison

In 2007, 53% of federal prisoners and, in 2005, 19.5% of state prisoners were incarcerated for drug offenses. That compares with 58% of federal prisoners and 21% of state prisoners who were incarcerated for drug offenses in 1998.

Source: Heather C. West and William J. Sabol, "Prisoners in 2007," U.S. Department of Justice, Bureau of Justice Statistics *Bulletin* (Washington, D.C.: GPO, December 2008), p. 22, Appendix tables 11 and 12; Allen J. Beck, "Prisoners in 1999," U.S. Department of Justice, Bureau of Justice Statistics *Bulletin* (Washington, D.C.: GPO, August 2000), p. 10, Table 15, and p. 12, Table 21.

THINKING CRITICALLY

1. What do you think are the pros and cons of being an investigator/detective? Does this type of work sound attractive to you?

2. Do you think state and federal law enforcement agencies should be able to collect and store DNA and fingerprints of people who have not been convicted of crimes? Why or why not? If they should be allowed, for how long should the DNA and fingerprints be kept?

3. Do you think there are any ways to protect individuals and businesses from becoming victims of cyber-crime? If so, what do you propose?

4. Do you think the United States should change its drug enforcement strategy? If so, in what ways? If not, why not?

Community Policing

For decades, police followed the professional model, which rested on three foundations: preventive patrol, quick response time, and follow-up investigation. Sensing that the professional model did not always operate as efficiently and effectively as it could, criminal justice researchers set out to review current procedures and evaluate alternative programs. One of the first and best-known of these studies was the Kansas City, Missouri, Preventive Patrol Experiment, discussed earlier in this chapter. That study's conclusion was that preventive patrol did not necessarily prevent crime or reassure citizens. Following the study, some police departments assigned police units to proactive patrol, giving them specific assignments rather than having them randomly cruise the streets.

Another study, again with the Kansas City Police Department, examined the effects of police response time. The study found that police response time was unrelated to the probability of making an arrest. Researchers discovered that the time it takes a citizen to report a crime—not the speed with which police respond—was the major determinant of whether an on-scene arrest took place or witnesses could be located. In 90% of crimes, citizens wait 5 to 10 minutes to call the police, precluding catching the criminal at the scene.

As preventive patrol and fast response time were being questioned, so too was follow-up investigation. A study by the Rand Corporation reviewed the criminal investigation process for effectiveness. The researchers concluded that the work of a criminal investigator alone rarely leads to an arrest and that the probability of arrest is determined largely by information that patrol officers obtain at the crime scene in their preliminary investigation.[37]

Criminal justice researchers continued their review of accepted police functions with the aim of making policing more effective by initiating new techniques and procedures. One of the interesting findings of the foot patrol research was that foot patrol officers were better able to deal with minor annoyances—such as rowdy youths, panhandlers, and abandoned cars—that irritate citizens.

In a theory called "broken windows," noted police scholars James Q. Wilson and George Kelling proposed that those minor annoyances are signs of crime and cause a fear of crime and that if they are not dealt with early, more serious and more costly problems are likely to occur.[38] Wilson and Kelling concluded that to help solve both minor and major problems in a neighborhood and to reduce crime and fear of crime, police officers must be in close, regular contact with citizens. That is, police and citizens should work cooperatively to build a strong sense of community and should share responsibility in the neighborhood to improve the overall quality of life within the community.

THE PHILOSOPHY AND COMPONENTS OF COMMUNITY POLICING

With community policing, citizens share responsibility for their community's safety. Citizens and the police work collectively to identify problems, propose solutions, implement action, and evaluate the results in the community. A community policing perspective differs in a number of ways from a traditional policing perspective. For example, in community policing, the police must

MYTH

Shorter police response time contributes to more arrests.

FACT

For most crimes, police response time is irrelevant. Approximately two-thirds of crimes are "cold"; the offender is gone long before the crime is discovered. In cases in which time counts, the critical delay often occurs in the time it takes the victim to call the police.

Community police officers visit with a citizen. *How does such activity contribute to crime fighting?*

share power with residents of a community, and critical decisions need to be made at the neighborhood level, not at a downtown police headquarters. Such decentralization of authority means that credit for bringing about a safer and more secure community must be shared with the people of the community, a tall order for any group of professionals to accept. Achieving the goals of community policing requires successful implementation of three essential and complementary components or operational strategies: community partnership, problem solving, and change management.[39]

Community Partnership Establishing and maintaining mutual trust between citizens of a community and the police is the main goal of the first component of community policing. Police have always recognized the need for cooperation with the community and have encouraged members of the community to come forward with crime-fighting information. In addition, police have spoken to neighborhood groups, worked with local organizations, and provided special-unit services. How are those cooperative efforts different from the community partnership of community policing?

In community policing, the police become an integral part of the community culture, and the community, in turn, helps the police define future crime prevention strategies and allocate community protection services. Establishing a community partnership means adopting a policing perspective that exceeds the standard law enforcement emphasis. The police no longer view the community as a passive presence connected to the police by an isolated incident or series of incidents. The community's concerns with crime and disorder become the target of efforts by the police and the community working together.

For patrol officers, building police-community partnerships entails such activities as talking to local business owners to identify their concerns, visiting residents in their homes to offer advice on security, and helping to organize and support neighborhood watch groups and regular community meetings. It also involves ongoing communication with residents. For example, a patrol officer might canvass a neighborhood for information about a string of burglaries and then revisit those residents to inform them when the burglar is caught.

FYI The Crime Act and COPS

The Violent Crime Control and Law Enforcement Act of 1994—popularly known as the Crime Act—authorized $8.8 billion over 6 years for grants to local policing agencies to add 100,000 officers and promote community policing in innovative ways. To implement the law, the Office of Community Oriented Policing Services (COPS) was created in the U.S. Department of Justice. As of this writing, COPS has invested $12.4 billion to add community policing officers to the nation's streets and schools, enhance crime-fighting technology, support crime prevention initiatives, and provide training and technical assistance to advance community policing. As of April 30, 2008, COPS had funded more than 118,000 community policing officers and deputies, and more than 100,000 of these officer and deputies are currently on the beat.

Source: U.S. Department of Justice, Office of Community Oriented Policing Services, www.cops.usdoj.gov/Default.asp?Item=35 and www.cops.usdoj.gov/Default.asp?Item=37.

A community police officer talks to a boy at the Puerto Rico Day Parade. *What, if anything, is the police officer trying to accomplish?*

Problem Solving Problem solving requires a lot more thought, energy, and action than traditional incident-based police responses to crime and disorder. In full partnership, the police and a community's residents and business owners identify core problems, propose solutions, and implement a solution. Thus, community members identify the concerns that they feel are most threatening to their safety and well-being. Those areas of concern then become priorities for joint police-community interventions.

For this problem-solving process to operate effectively, the police need to devote time and attention to discovering a community's concerns, and they need to recognize the validity of those concerns. Police and neighborhood groups may not always agree on the specific problems that deserve attention first. For example, the police may regard robberies as the biggest problem in a particular neighborhood, while residents find derelicts who sleep in doorways, break bottles on sidewalks, and pick through garbage cans the number one problem. In community policing, both problems should receive early attention from the police, other government agencies, and the community.

Some community policing advocates recommend a four-step problem-solving process referred to as SARA: *S*canning—identifying problems; *A*nalysis—understanding underlying conditions; *R*esponse—developing and implementing solutions; *A*ssessment—determining the solutions' effect. One useful tool in working toward a solution is known as the *crime triangle.* The crime triangle is a view of crime and disorder as an interaction among three variables: a victim, an offender, and a location. Solutions can be developed that affect one or more of the three elements of the crime triangle. For example, suppose elderly residents are being jeopardized by speeding teenagers in automobiles as they walk across the streets of a suburban residential neighborhood. Using a crime triangle analysis might result in the following police-community solutions: using the juvenile court to alter the probation period of offending drivers (focus on the offender), installing speed bumps in the pavement or changing the cycles of traffic signals on opposite ends of the street so that motorists cannot build up speed (focus on the location), holding safety education classes at the senior center to educate elderly residents to use marked crosswalks (focus on the victim). More than likely, in community policing, a combination of those solutions would be used. Such a response to a community problem is much more thorough than merely having a squad car drive by the location when a citizen calls in a complaint.

Community police officers discussing neighborhood problems with residents. *In what ways can elderly citizens contribute to crime fighting?*

Change Management Forging community policing partnerships and implementing problem-solving strategies necessitate assigning new responsibilities and adopting a flexible style of management. Traditionally, patrol officers have been accorded lower status in police organizations and have been dominated by the agency's command structure. Community policing, in contrast, emphasizes the value of the patrol function and the patrol officer as an individual. It requires the shifting of initiative, decision making, and responsibility downward within the police organization. The neighborhood police officer or deputy sheriff becomes responsible for managing the delivery of police services to the community or area to which he or she is permanently assigned. Patrol officers are the most familiar with the needs and concerns of their communities and are in the best position to forge the close ties with the community that lead to effective solutions to local problems.

Under community policing, police management must guide, rather than dominate, the actions of the patrol officer and must ensure that patrol officers have the necessary resources to solve the problems in their communities. Management must determine the guiding principles to convert the philosophy of the agency to community policing and then to evaluate the effectiveness of the strategies implemented.

IMPLEMENTING COMMUNITY POLICING

Implementation plans for community policing vary from agency to agency and from community to community. The appropriate implementation strategy depends on conditions within the law enforcement agency and the community embarking on community policing. Successful implementation requires that the police and the members of the community understand the underlying philosophy of community policing and have a true commitment to the community policing strategy. Communication, cooperation, coordination, collaboration, and change are the keys to putting community policing into action. Until recently, the community policing philosophy had become so popular and broadly implemented that it existed as the operating method of police departments in colleges and universities, transit systems, and even airports. At Dallas Love Field, City of Dallas police officers maintain a community police substation in the airport

FYI School Resource Officers

School resource officers use a community policing approach to provide a safe environment for students and staff. They respond to calls for service within the school and work with school administrators and staff to prevent crime and disorder by monitoring crime trends, problem areas, cultural conflicts, and other concerns. As of June 2003, local police departments had about 14,300 full-time sworn personnel serving as school resource officers.

Source: Matthew J. Hickman and Brian A. Reaves, *Local Police Departments, 2003*, U.S. Department of Justice, Bureau of Justice Statistics (Washington, D.C.: GPO, May 2006), p. iii.

as part of the regular security force and receive specially marked federal funds and airport community police training.

All this may be changing, however, because grant funding is being shifted from the federal Office of Community Oriented Policing Services (COPS) to the Department of Homeland Security. If, as some have argued, the philosophies of community policing and homeland security are incompatible, the era of community policing may be ending, as the era of homeland security policing begins.[40] According to a recent survey, 14% of local police departments, employing 44% of all officers, maintained or created a written community policing plan during the 12-month period ending June 30, 2003. Nearly half (47%) of departments, employing 73% of all officers, had a mission statement that included some aspect of community policing. Fifty-eight percent of all departments, employing 82% of all officers, used full-time community policing officers in 2003; 54,800 local police officers were designated community policing officers in 2003. These numbers are down substantially from those reported in 2000.[41]

THINKING CRITICALLY

1. Can you think of ways to make community policing even more effective?

2. Do you think there is a certain operational style that is most appropriate for community policing? If so, which one?

Terrorism and Homeland Security

Terrorism is one of the oldest forms of human conflict. Before societies began waging war against each other, individuals and small groups used acts of terror to achieve their goals, such as deposing existing leaders and frightening and repelling adversaries from territory they claimed for themselves.[42] Terrorism has been used by both right-wing and left-wing political organizations, by ethnic and nationalistic groups, by revolutionaries, and by the armies and secret police of established governments. However, according to the FBI, the modern era of terrorism did not begin until the late 1960s, and U.S. soil remained largely free from serious acts of international terrorism until the bombing of the World Trade Center in 1993.[43] Before then, the vast majority of deadly terrorist acts carried out in the United States were committed by domestic terrorists, such as Timothy McVeigh and Terry Nichols, who were responsible for the 1995 bombing of the Alfred P. Murrah Federal Building in Oklahoma City.[44] All that changed on September 11, 2001, when, according to Ambassador Francis X. Taylor, the U.S. Department of State's Coordinator for Counterterrorism, "the United States suffered its bloodiest day on American soil since the Civil War, and the world experienced the most devastating international terrorist attack in recorded history."[45] On that infamous day in September, 19 hijackers belonging to the al-Qaeda terrorist network commandeered four aircraft to commit the most audacious terrorist act in American history.

- Five terrorists hijacked American Airlines flight 11, which departed Boston for Los Angeles at 7:45 A.M. An hour later it was deliberately piloted into the North Tower of the World Trade Center in New York City.
- Five terrorists hijacked United Airlines flight 175, which departed Boston for Los Angeles at 7:58 A.M. At 9:05 A.M. the plane crashed into the South Tower of the World Trade Center. Both towers collapsed shortly thereafter, killing approximately 3,000 persons, including hundreds of firefighters and rescue personnel who were helping to evacuate the buildings.
- Four terrorists hijacked United Airlines flight 93, which departed Newark for San Francisco at 8:01 A.M. At 10:10 A.M. the plane crashed in Stony Creek

terrorism The systematic use of terror or unpredictable violence against governments, publics, or individuals to attain a political objective; the unlawful use of force and violence against persons or property to intimidate or coerce a government, the civilian population, or any segment thereof, in furtherance of political or social objectives; or premeditated, politically motivated violence perpetrated against noncombatant targets by subnational groups or clandestine agents, usually intended to influence an audience.

domestic terrorism The unlawful use, or threatened use, of force or violence by a group or individual based and operating entirely within the United States or its territories without foreign direction committed against persons or property to intimidate or coerce a government, the civilian population, or any segment thereof, in furtherance of political or social objectives.

Township, Pennsylvania, killing all 45 persons onboard. The intended target of this hijacked plane is not known, but it is believed that passengers overpowered the terrorists, thus preventing the aircraft from being used as a missile.

- Five terrorists hijacked American Airlines flight 77, which departed Washington Dulles Airport for Los Angeles at 8:10 A.M. At 9:39 A.M. the plane was flown directly into the Pentagon in Arlington, Virginia, near Washington, D.C. A total of 189 persons were killed, including all who were onboard the plane.[46]

DEFINITIONS AND TYPES OF TERRORISM

There is no single, universally accepted definition of terrorism, and types of terrorism can be distinguished by perpetrators, motives, methods, and targets. Whatever the definition, the key elements of terrorism are fear, panic, violence, and disruption.[47] The FBI defines **terrorism** as "the systematic use of terror or unpredictable violence against governments, publics, or individuals to attain a political objective."[48] In the U.S. Code of Federal Regulations (28 C.F.R. Section 0.85), terrorism is defined as "the unlawful use of force and violence against persons or property to intimidate or coerce a government, the civilian population, or any segment thereof, in furtherance of political or social objectives."[49] Title 22 of the U.S. Code, Section 2656f(d), defines terrorism as "premeditated, politically motivated violence perpetrated against noncombatant targets by subnational groups or clandestine agents, usually intended to influence an audience."[50]

The FBI divides terrorism into two broad categories: *domestic terrorism* and *international terrorism.*

- **Domestic terrorism** is the unlawful use, or threatened use, of force or violence by a group or individual based and operating entirely within the United States or its territories without foreign direction committed against persons or property to intimidate or coerce a government, the civilian population, or any segment thereof, in furtherance of political or social objectives.[51]
- **International terrorism** involves violent acts dangerous to human life that are a violation of the criminal laws of the United States or any state, or that would be a criminal violation if committed within the jurisdiction of the United States or any state. These acts appear to be intended to intimidate or coerce a civilian population, influence the policy of a government by intimidation or coercion, or affect the conduct of a government by assassination or kidnapping. International terrorist acts occur outside the United States or transcend national boundaries in terms of the means by which they are accomplished, the persons they appear intended to coerce or intimidate, or the locale in which the perpetrators operate or seek asylum.[52]

The FBI further divides domestic terrorism into "right-wing terrorism," "left-wing terrorism," "special interest terrorism," and "individual terrorism." *Right-wing terrorist groups,* such as the Aryan Nations and the World Church of the Creator, generally oppose government in general and government regulation in particular. Members typically are virulent racists who believe in racial supremacy and conspiracy theories.[53] *Left-wing terrorist groups* generally

Before 9/11, the bombing of the Alfred P. Murrah Federal Building in Oklahoma City on April 19, 1995, by Timothy McVeigh was the worst incident of domestic terrorism in American history. *What are the similarities and differences between the bombing of the Murrah Federal Building by McVeigh and the 9/11 terrorist assaults on the World Trade Center and the Pentagon?*

international terrorism Violent acts dangerous to human life that are a violation of the criminal laws of the United States or any state, or that would be a criminal violation if committed within the jurisdiction of the United States or any state. These acts appear to be intended to intimidate or coerce a civilian population, influence the policy of a government by intimidation or coercion, or affect the conduct of a government by assassination or kidnapping. International terrorist acts occur outside the United States or transcend national boundaries in terms of the means by which they are accomplished, the persons they appear intended to coerce or intimidate, or the locale in which the perpetrators operate or seek asylum.

believe in revolutionary socialist doctrine and seek radical change outside the established political process. They want to liberate people from the dehumanizing effects of capitalism and imperialism. With the collapse of the Soviet Union and the fall of communism in Eastern Europe in the 1980s, left-wing terrorist groups no longer pose much of a threat to the United States.[54] The goal of *special interest terrorist groups* is to change the attitudes of the public about specific issues that are important to the group rather than to bring about fundamental political change. These groups generally are fringe elements of antinuclear, environmental, pro-life, animal rights, and other movements.[55] As of this writing, the FBI considers the Animal Liberation Front (ALF) and the Earth Liberation Front (ELF) as two of the most active special interest terrorist groups. *Individual terrorist acts* are committed by "lone wolf" extremists who operate alone or in small groups and defy detection both as to their identities and their plans for destruction. Timothy McVeigh and Eric Robert Rudolph are examples of this category of terrorist.[56]

The FBI estimates that about 20% to 30% of international terrorist incidents that occur annually in the United States and abroad are directed at U.S. interests.[57] These threats to U.S. interests are divided into three categories: state sponsors of international terrorism, formalized terrorist organizations, and loosely affiliated extremists and rogue international terrorists.[58] As of this writing, the principal *state sponsors of terrorism* are Cuba, Iran, Sudan, and Syria. For these countries, terrorism is a tool of foreign policy.[59] Three countries recently have been removed from the state sponsors of terrorism list: Iraq in 2004, Libya in 2006, and North Korea in 2008. *Formal terrorist organizations* are autonomous, generally transnational, and have their own personnel, infrastructures, financial arrangements, and training facilities.[60] Table 6.5 lists the 45 foreign terrorist organizations recognized by the U.S. State Department. *Loosely affiliated extremists* and *rogue international terrorists* include the World Trade Center bombers and rogue terrorists such as Osama bin Laden and members of al-Qaeda.[61]

Table 6.5 45 Foreign Terrorist Organizations Recognized by the U.S. State Department

Abu Nidal Organization (ANO)	Jaish-e-Mohammed (JEM) (Army of Mohammed)	Popular Front for the Liberation of Palestine (PFLP)
Abu Sayyaf Group	Jemaah Islamiya organization (JI)	PFLP-General Command (PFLP-GC)
Al-Aqsa Martyrs Brigade	al-Jihad (Egyptian Islamic Jihad)	Tanzim Qa'idat al-Jihad fi Bilad
Al-Shabaab	Kahane Chai (Kach)	al-Rafidayn (QJBR) (al-Qaida in Iraq)
Ansar al-Islam	Kata'ib Hizballah	(formerly Jama'at al-Tawhid wa'al-
Armed Islamic Group (GIA)	Kongra-Gel (KGK, formerly Kurdistan	Jihad, JTJ, al-Zarqawi Network)
Asbat an-Ansar	Workers' Party, PKK, KADEK)	al-Qa'ida
Aum Shinrikyo	Lashkar-e Tayyiba (LT) (Army of the	al-Qaida in the Islamic Maghreb
Basque Fatherland and Liberty (ETA)	Righteous)	(formerly GSPC)
Communist Party of the Philippines/New	Lashkar i Jhangvi	Real IRA
People's Army (CPP/NPA)	Liberation Tigers of Tamil Eelam (LTTE)	Revolutionary Armed Forces of Colombia
Continuity Irish Republican Army	Libyan Islamic Fighting Group (LIFG)	(FARC)
Gama'a al-Islamiyya (Islamic Group)	Moroccan Islamic Combatant Group	Revolutionary Nuclei (formerly ELA)
HAMAS (Islamic Resistance Movement)	(GICM)	Revolutionary Organization 17 November
Harakat ul-Jihad-i-Islami/Bangladesh	Mujahedin-e Khalq Organization	Revolutionary People's Liberation Party/
(HUJI-B)	(MEK)	Front (DHKP/C)
Harakat ul-Mujahidin (HUM)	National Liberation Army (ELN)	Shining Path (Sendero Luminoso, SL)
Hizballah (Party of God)	Palestine Liberation Front (PLF)	United Self-Defense Forces of Colombia
Islamic Jihad Group	Palestinian Islamic Jihad (PIJ)	(AUC)
Islamic Movement of Uzbekistan (IMU)		

Source: U.S. State Department, "Foreign Terrorist Organizations" at www.state.gov/s/et/rls/other/des/123085.htm (accessed July 7, 2009).

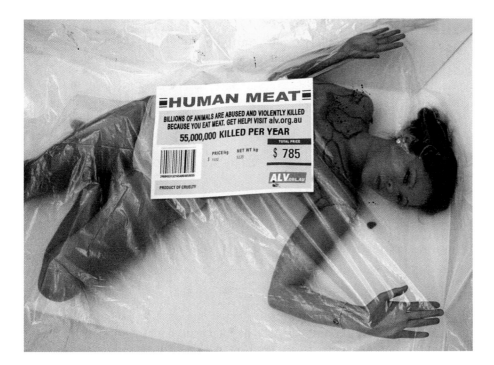

The FBI considers the Animal Liberation Front (ALF) and the Earth Liberation Front (ELF) as two of the most active special interest terrorist groups. *What do these two groups have in common with terrorist groups such as the Irish Republican Army, Palestinian Hamas, and the Revolutionary Armed Forces of Colombia (FARC)? How do they differ?*

Table 6.6 Terrorism Incidents between September 10, 2001 and January 16, 2007, by Type of Terrorist Group

Group Classification	DOMESTIC			INTERNATIONAL		
	Incidents	Injuries	Fatalities	Incidents	Injuries	Fatalities
Anarchist	48	2	0	7	0	0
Anti-Globalization	12	4	0	13	4	0
Communist/Socialist	1,618	3,084	1,421	57	200	31
Environmental	40	0	0	0	0	0
Leftist	28	27	7	22	26	4
Nationalist/Separatist	2,305	10,521	4,583	270	3,728	1,109
Other	21	30	33	15	26	4
Racist	20	3	1	1	0	0
Religious	1,671	11,543	5,694	303	7,654	4,790
Right-Wing Conservative	43	10	110	7	1	9
Right-Wing Reactionary	9	8	14	0	0	0

Source: MIPT Terrorism Knowledge Base at www.tkb.org/IncidentClassModule.jsp.

Table 6.6 shows the number of both domestic and international terrorist incidents committed between September 10, 2001 and January 16, 2007, by type of terrorist group. It also displays the number of injuries and fatalities attributed to those terrorist incidents. Note that the classification of terrorist group types provided in Table 6.6 is more detailed than the FBI's classification described previously. Domestic terrorist incidents refer to incidents perpetrated by local nationals against a purely domestic target. International terrorist incidents are those in which terrorists go abroad to strike the targets, select domestic targets associated with a foreign state, or create an international incident by attacking airline passengers, personnel, or equipment. Nearly 90% of terrorist incidents committed between September 10, 2001 and January 16, 2007 were acts of domestic terrorism. Three types of groups—Nationalist/Separatist, Religious, and Communist/Socialist—accounted for 96% of those domestic terrorist incidents. They also can claim the greatest number of injuries and fatalities, especially the Nationalist/Separatist and Religious groups.

The number of recent terrorist incidents in each region of the world, along with the injuries and the fatalities each caused, is shown in Table 6.7. Separate data for the United States were not available. However, as of February 1, 2009, the

Table 6.7 Terrorism Incidents between September 10, 2001 and January 16, 2007, by Region

Region	DOMESTIC			INTERNATIONAL		
	Incidents	Injuries	Fatalities	Incidents	Injuries	Fatalities
Africa	145	615	649	57	675	287
East and Central Asia	47	65	26	13	2	28
Eastern Europe	795	2,831	1,168	39	698	179
Latin America and the Caribbean	1,059	1,176	1,038	80	131	38
Middle East/Persian Gulf	9,331	32,275	18,736	989	4,838	1,750
North America	63	51	6	5	2,340	2,985
South Asia	3,828	12,766	5,316	224	700	379
Southeast Asia and Oceania	1,073	2,706	936	42	846	272
Western Europe	1,422	680	93	131	623	194
Total	**17,766**	**53,765**	**27,968**	**1,580**	**10,853**	**6,112**

Source: MIPT Terrorism Knowledge Base at www.tkb.org/IncidentRegionModule.jsp.

Table 6.8 Terrorism Incidents between September 10, 2001 and January 16, 2007, by Target

Target	DOMESTIC			INTERNATIONAL		
	Incidents	Injuries	Fatalities	Incidents	Injuries	Fatalities
Airports and airlines	69	126	66	19	115	28
Business	948	3,866	869	268	2,947	3,037
Diplomatic	32	11	11	232	1,349	225
Educational institutions	510	1,263	619	8	60	11
Food or water supply	5	0	0	0	0	0
Government	3,771	7,373	4,012	96	628	439
Journalists and media	269	169	170	57	104	57
Maritime	7	32	14	3	12	1
Military	74	933	424	18	45	9
NGO	87	80	66	81	46	89
Other	1,126	1,412	1,579	280	384	505
Police	3,805	13,097	7,507	64	385	133
Private citizens and property	3,971	15,633	8,835	290	2,380	669
Religious figures/Institutions	831	4,432	1,819	28	204	101
Telecommunication	110	81	59	4	0	9
Terrorists/Former terrorists	97	49	103	1	1	5
Tourists	51	201	19	27	955	364
Transportation	720	3,883	1,195	44	1,180	389
Unknown	474	719	285	40	44	24
Utilities	809	405	316	20	14	17
Total	**17,766**	**53,765**	**27,968**	**1,580**	**10,853**	**6,112**

Source: MIPT Terrorism Knowledge Base at www.tkb.org/IncidentTargetModule.jsp.

United States had not suffered an international terrorist act since September 11, 2001. More than half of the terrorist incidents between September 10, 2001, and January 16, 2007, were committed in the Middle East/Persian Gulf region. That region was also the source of most injuries and fatalities. The five international terrorist incidents committed in North America were the infamous acts of 9/11.

Terrorist incidents also can be distinguished by the type of target selected. Table 6.8 shows that the largest number of terrorist incidents between September 10, 2001, and January 16, 2007, were targeted at private citizens and property, the police, and government. Those targets also accounted for the largest number of injuries and fatalities.

Still another way of characterizing terrorism is by the methods used by terrorists. The traditional method has involved a conventional bomb, and it continued to be the preferred method between September 10, 2001 and January 16, 2007 (see Table 6.9). However, today, the most feared method involves weapons of mass destruction (WMDs), such as nuclear, radiological, and biological devices. Agroterrorism is another method and is an attack on a food source or the distribution of food supplies. Cyberterrorism, dubbed "information warfare," may take various forms, including the hacking into or destroying of the nation's electronic infrastructure, thus rendering mass communications via the Internet inoperable. High-energy radio frequency (HERF) and electromagnetic pulse weapons (EMPs) can shut down mass communication systems almost instantly.[62]

For purposes of this textbook, note that terrorists are criminals, according to the FBI's counterterrorism policy.[63] However, also remember that one person's terrorist is another person's freedom fighter. The British, for example, accused the American revolutionaries of being terrorists.[64]

Table 6.9 Terrorism Incidents between September 10, 2001
and January 16, 2007, by Method

Method	DOMESTIC			INTERNATIONAL		
	Incidents	**Injuries**	**Fatalities**	**Incidents**	**Injuries**	**Fatalities**
Armed attack	5,208	5,864	9,250	398	849	684
Arson	471	160	286	33	0	5
Assassination	1,174	817	1,615	60	30	83
Barricade/Hostage	21	743	411	4	667	175
Bombing	9,522	45,581	14,840	784	6,933	1,980
Hijacking	9	0	0	4	0	20
Kidnapping	892	84	1,001	260	19	156
Other	111	260	100	11	2	5
Unconventional attack	30	22	12	8	2,344	2,982
Unknown	328	234	453	18	9	22
Total	**17,766**	**53,765**	**27,968**	**1,580**	**10,853**	**6,112**

Source: MIPT Terrorism Knowledge Base at www.tkb.org/IncidentTacticModule.jsp.

THE LAW ENFORCEMENT RESPONSE TO TERRORISM

Terrorists' acts are often perpetrated by disaffected and angry individuals and groups who are far removed from the everyday American scene. Yet, through the media, American citizens are learning more about terrorism than ever before. Still, terrorism is a complex phenomenon. American law enforcement officers have no choice anymore. They must learn all they can to protect the nation and its people.

Since the tragedy of September 11, 2001, terrorism has been at the top of the national agenda. People are frightened without knowing exactly what to do about it. Local, state, and federal law enforcement agencies have new responsibilities for the prevention of both domestic and international terrorism and for reducing America's fear. To guide them, especially at the national level, President Bush laid out four general policy principles:

1. Make no concessions to terrorists and strike no deals (even if U.S. citizens are held hostage).
2. Bring terrorists to justice for their crimes (no matter how long it takes).
3. Isolate and apply pressure on states that sponsor terrorism to force them to change their behavior.
4. Bolster the counterterrorist capabilities of those countries that work with the United States and require assistance.[65]

To prevent terrorism, billions of dollars are being committed and spent, and some civil liberties have been curtailed or severely restricted. The typical business or pleasure trip by airplane, for example, has become an even more taxing and intrusive experience. Even a simple trip to the library can make a person suspect should he or she select literary works that trigger the suspicion of a federal law enforcement agency. In a nation that was founded on the principles of freedom, openness, and anonymity for the most part, the new security, surveillance, and intelligence initiatives implemented since 9/11 have created concerns for many Americans.

Attempting to prevent terrorism is a daunting task. How can law enforcement officers protect every soft and hard target in America: all schools, all local water supplies, all food supply lines, all religious institutions, every public building in large and small communities, and all sources of energy?

Although Herculean does not adequately describe the charge, the protection of the American people and the nation's physical assets, as well as the reduction of fear from the threat of terrorism, is precisely what American law enforcement aims to do.

American law enforcement is now engaged in both defensive and offensive strategies to combat terrorism. However, in a free, open, and largely anonymous society, terrorists and potential terrorists know that the United States is fertile ground for terrorism. The police are faced with a dilemma. If the police are too aggressive trying to find and capture terrorists, American citizens are likely to become more fearful, anxious, and either resistant to or overly enthusiastic about repressive measures. If that occurs, terrorists win because fear, intimidation, disruption, and media attention to their cause are principal goals. However, if American law enforcement is not firm enough in its resolve and tactics to repress terrorism, terrorists will be able to again perpetrate a disaster on the public such as the events of 9/11, with loss of life, serious injury, fear, and anger. Such an event would likely encourage even tighter domestic security procedures, which would be resented by many members of the public, and the entire terror cycle would start over again. Law enforcement officers walk a fine line between preserving liberty and tranquility and providing security that may be perceived as excessive and repressive.

To illustrate, on June 17, 2003, President Bush issued guidelines barring federal agents from using race or ethnicity in routine investigations, but the policy permits exceptions in investigations involving terrorism and national security issues. Consequently, if law enforcement and intelligence officials receive information that terrorists of a certain ethnic group plan to hijack a plane in a particular state in the near future, officials are allowed to heighten security on people of that ethnicity that board planes in that area (also see the description of the PATRIOT Act in Chapter 4).[66]

HOW PREPARED IS THE UNITED STATES TO DEFEND AGAINST TERRORISM?

The answer depends on whom you ask, and there are many people and groups willing to give an answer. As noted in the last chapter, there already have been some successes. Terrorist acts have been prevented; terrorists have been captured and brought to justice; and the nation, as of February 1, 2009, has avoided another tragedy of 9/11 proportions. Nevertheless, U.S. borders remain porous, and U.S. assets are still vulnerable.

In 2003, two reports critical of the nation's preparedness to respond to terrorist attacks were released. The independent and bipartisan Council on Foreign Relations concluded that the United States was "drastically underfunding local emergency responders and remains dangerously unprepared to handle another September 11 event."[67] The nonprofit Partnership for Public Service determined that the United States is likely to be overwhelmed in the event of a bioterrorism attack because of serious shortages in skilled medical and scientific personnel.[68]

At the end of 2005, the "Final Report on 9/11 Commission Recommendations" was issued, and the news was not good. Congress created the bipartisan Commission in 2002 to investigate aspects of the 9/11 terrorists attacks. Thomas Kean, the Republican chairperson of the Commission, told NBC's *Meet the Press* that enacting the changes is "not a priority for the government right now." He added, "A lot of the things we need to do really to prevent another 9/11 just simply aren't being done by the president or by the Congress." Lee Hamilton, the Commission's Democratic vice-chairperson, predicted another

FYI Americans Not Very Satisfied with War on Terrorism

In a recent public opinion poll, 52% of Americans were "very satisfied" (11%) or "somewhat satisfied" (41%) with the way things are going for the United States in the war on terrorism, while 47% of Americans were "not too satisfied" (23%) or "were not at all satisfied" (24%).

Source: The Gallup Poll, September 5–7, 2008 at www.gallup.com/poll/5257/War-Terrorism.aspx.

attack would occur. He maintained, "It's not a question of if."[69] The conclusion, it seems, is that the United States has much more to do in its preparation to fight terrorism.

None of this has been lost on the American public. In a 2007 Harris Poll, substantial majorities of Americans responded that the United States is "likely" to experience the following types of terrorist attacks (percentages in parentheses): (1) "a suicide bomber in a shopping mall" (82%), "a chemical attack using a poison gas" (70%), "a biochemical attack using diseases such as anthrax or small pox" (69%), and "an attack on a nuclear power station" (62%). More than 40% of respondents thought the United States was "likely" to experience "another attack using airplanes like 9/11" (48%) and "a nuclear bomb exploding in a city" (42%). A much smaller percentage believed any of the terrorist incidents was "very likely."[70]

THINKING CRITICALLY

1. What type of terrorism do you think poses the greatest threat to the United States and why?

2. Which of America's assets do you think are most vulnerable to terrorist attacks, and what do you think can be done to better defend them?

✳ Summary

1. Identify characteristics of police work.

   The role of the police officer is complex and requires a combination of special characteristics, which involve quick decision making, invisible work, "dirty work," and danger.

2. Distinguish among James Q. Wilson's three operational styles in policing.

   Wilson's three operational styles in policing are legalistic, which emphasizes violations of the law and the use of arrests to resolve community disputes; watchman, emphasizing informal means of resolving disputes and using arrest only as a last resort; and service, which emphasizes helping in the community over enforcing the law.

3. List the four major functions of police departments.

   The four major functions of police departments in the United States are patrol, investigation, traffic, and drug enforcement.

4. List the drug enforcement strategies of local police agencies.

   Although the particular drug enforcement strategies employed by individual agencies vary widely, the most common strategies are street-level enforcement, mid-level investigations, major investigations, crop eradication, smuggling interdiction, problem-oriented and community policing strategies, drug demand reduction, and asset forfeiture.

5. Explain the main components of community policing.

   The three main components of community policing are community partnership, problem solving, and change management.

6. Identify four steps in a community policing approach to problem solving.

   Community policing relies heavily on problem solving. The four steps in a community policing approach to problem solving are often referred to as SARA: Scanning—identing problems, Analysis—understanding underlying conditions, Response—developing and implementing solutions, and Assessment—determining the solutions' effect.

7. Define terrorism, and identify different types of terrorism.

   Terrorism has been defined as the systematic use of terror or unpredictable violence against governments, publics, or individuals to attain a political objective; the unlawful use of force and violence against persons or property to intimidate or coerce a government, the civilian population, or any segment thereof, in furtherance of political or social objectives; or premeditated, politically motivated violence perpetrated against noncombatant targets by subnational groups or clandestine agents, usually intended to influence an audience. Two broad categories of terrorism are domestic terrorism and international terrorism. Specific types of domestic terrorism are right-wing terrorism, left-wing terrorism, special interest terrorism, and individual terrorism. International terrorism is divided into state-sponsored terrorism, formalized terrorist organizations, and loosely affiliated extremists and rogue international terrorists.

✳ Key Terms

role 206
role expectation 206
role conflict 206
operational styles 210
preventive patrol 213
directed patrol 213
GIS crime mapping 214
aggressive patrol 215
field interrogation 215
cybercrime 221
traffic accident investigation crews 222
terrorism 237
domestic terrorism 237
international terrorism 237

✳ Review Questions

1. What is a common source of role conflict for the police?
2. Distinguish among the three sets of operational styles identified by criminal justice scholars.
3. How are preventive patrol, directed patrol, and aggressive patrol different?
4. What are the major uses of GIS crime mapping in law enforcement?
5. What are some of the functions of a criminal investigator?
6. What are three distinct functions of DNA profiling?
7. What are two broad categories of cybercrime?

8. What are some of the more important functions of traffic units?

9. What are some of the problems with the use of civil asset forfeiture in drug enforcement?

10. What is the philosophy of community policing?

11. What are the three complementary operational strategies of community policing?

12. How frequently has the United States been victimized by domestic and international terrorism?

13. What were President Bush's four general terrorism policy principles?

✳ In the Field

1. **SARA Approach** In groups of three or four, select a local crime or disorder problem. Using the first three components of the SARA approach to problem solving (scanning, analysis, and response) and considering the elements of the crime triangle, formulate some options to deal with the problem. Present your options to the class, and let the whole class vote to determine which option is the best to solve the problem. Do you agree with the class vote? Why or why not? What do the results of this vote say about attitudes toward crime-related problem solving?

2. **Law Enforcement Resources** Look through several police periodicals, such as *Law and Order, Police Chief,* or other professional police magazines. What do the advertised products tell you about law enforcement? What law enforcement issues are addressed in the articles? Write a brief summary of your findings.

✳ On the Net

1. **Cybercrime** Ask a local police officer what the needs of the police in combating cybercrime in your area are. Make a list of the types of cybercrimes that have actually occurred in your area. Compare and contrast that list with what experts on CNET (go to their Web page at www.CNET.com) and the material in your text describe as the important concerns in addressing cybercrime. Is there cause for concern? Why or why not?

2. **Drug Enforcement** To learn more about illegal drugs and drug control policy, visit the website of the Office of National Drug Control Policy at www .whitehousedrugpolicy.gov. Based on what you have learned, write an essay or prepare an oral presentation on whether national drug control policy has been or will be effective in reducing drug use and abuse among the American public.

✳ Critical Thinking Exercises

POLICE PATROL

1. Assume that you are the patrol commander in a southern city that has large numbers of African American and Hispanic residents. All shifts of your patrol division have embraced and supported a "broken windows" and "zero-tolerance" approach to patrol work. Your patrol division's style could clearly be called aggressive, but for the past 5 years the city's violent, property, and minor offense rates have been dropping steadily. Some citizens have complained each month about the aggressive and sometimes intrusive vehicle stops. Most of the complainants have been African Americans who live in neighborhoods where the recorded crime rate has dropped the most dramatically since the implementation of the aggressive patrol style. They accuse officers of racial profiling. Racial profiling is illegal and occurs when minority citizens are stopped in their cars and on the street for little or nothing more than their race as the cause. (Racial profiling is discussed in greater detail in the next chapter.) When applied to motorists, racial profiling has even acquired a popular name, "Driving While Black," or DWB, or DWBB, "Driving While Black or Brown."

   a. What steps would you take as patrol commander to assure the chief of police, the city's leaders, and the public at large that racial profiling is not occurring in your patrol division, nor are infringements on citizens' liberties beyond what are legal and necessary?

   b. What impact would validated cases of "Driving While Black or Brown" (or racial profiling) in other cities have on your plan?

COMMUNITY POLICING

2. You are a new community police officer assigned with seven other officers to a low-income, heterogeneous, high-turnover, high-crime neighborhood. How should you and your fellow officers address the following problems?

   a. Neighborhood residents, neighborhood business owners, and community leaders disagree about the most important problems of the neighborhood and what to do about them. What should you and your fellow officers do?

   b. You organize and heavily publicize a meeting to discuss neighborhood problems and their solutions. However, only about 10% to 20% of neighborhood residents attend, and most of them are white and more affluent homeowners who live in the better parts of the neighborhood. Few minorities or renters attend. What should you and your fellow officers do?

   c. Your precinct captain disagrees with neighborhood residents about the most important problems in the neighborhood. Your precinct captain's top priority is abandoned cars used for drug dealing. The top priority of neighborhood residents is the overall appearance of the neighborhood. What should you and your fellow officers do?

To access more information and resources, including study questions, chapter summaries, and links, go to www.mhhe .com/bohm6e.

Policing America: Issues and Ethics

Chapter Outline

Chapter Objectives

After completing this chapter, you should be able to:

1. Describe the general attitude of the public toward the police.

2. Summarize the steps in an effective police officer selection process.

3. Identify factors that affect the exercise of police discretion and methods of limiting discretion.

4. Describe two general ways that law enforcement agencies can reduce stress on the job.

5. Explain the circumstances under which police officers may be justified in using deadly force.

6. List some of the ways to control and reduce police corruption.

CRIME STORY

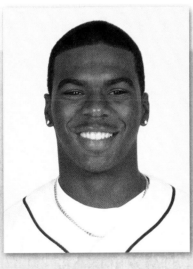

On November 25, 2006, Sean Bell, an unarmed bridegroom, was shot by New York City police officers hours before his wedding ceremony. A fusillade of fifty police bullets smashed through the car in which Bell and two friends were riding in the Jamaica neighborhood of the Borough of Queens. The friends were wounded, and Sean Bell was killed. One of the police officers fired 31 shots at the car, an attack that required reloading the weapon. On March 16, 2007, a grand jury handed down indictments charging two of the police officers with manslaughter, reckless endangerment, and assault in connection with the shootings. Another officer was charged with the lesser crime of reckless endangerment. All three officers pleaded not guilty at arraignment. At least one police organization criticized the indictments as unfair reactions to community pressure for some government response.

The Queens nightclub where the shootings occurred was under police surveillance at the time because of its history of narcotics, prostitution, and weapons incidents, and the involved officers were part of a seven-officer

continued

249

team working in an undercover capacity. Sean Bell and his two companions had been celebrating his imminent wedding. The groom was driving the car, and Bell's vehicle had reportedly struck one of the officers and one of the police vehicles prior to the shootings.

Following their bench trial on April 25, 2008, a judge cleared the three officers of all charges. In announcing his verdict, the judge stated that the inconsistent testimony, courtroom demeanor, and rap sheets of the prosecution witnesses— mainly Bell's friends—"had the effect of eviscerating" their credibility. The judge added, "At times, the testimony just didn't make sense." The verdict does not entirely resolve the matter. The U.S. Attorney's Office said it would review the case and "take appropriate action if the evidence indicates a prosecutable violation of federal criminal civil-rights statutes." Additionally, relatives of the victims have filed lawsuits against the city, and those cases could either go to trial or be settled out of court with the potential for multimillion-dollar payouts. Also, the officers, who had been on paid leave, still faced possible departmental charges that could result in their firing.

Chapter 7 examines the implementation of the police power in America. The authorization to use force to make an arrest is the essence of American police power. This authority is a fundamental feature of governments throughout the world. With this significant power comes great responsibility, however, and the use of deadly force represents a monumental issue at the extreme end of the social control spectrum. Police actions must, of course, be legal. They must also be justified and reasonable to the extent that the community and the greater society will approve of the actions. The use of force may occur in a context where time is very compressed and critical decisions must literally be made in seconds. Evaluations of the actions that are performed later proceed at a much more leisurely pace. Was the police shooting that killed Sean Bell justified? Was it reasonable? Were the indictments of the involved officers an appropriate response to the incident and to community consternation concerning the shooting? Were the officers' acquittals on all charges the correct outcome? Great public safety challenges provide profound satisfaction for police practitioners when things go well, but this sense of purpose and fulfillment quickly evaporates when serious mistakes are made.

The Police and the Public

To carry out the duties of law enforcement, order maintenance, service, and information gathering successfully, the police must have the trust and cooperation of the public. The manner in which they carry out those functions, especially law enforcement and order maintenance, determines the community's respect for and trust in the police. Citizens who trust and respect the police are much more likely to help them carry out their duties; citizens who lack that trust and respect may rebel against the police in particular and government in general.

PUBLIC ATTITUDES TOWARD THE POLICE

What do people think of the police? The answer depends on what and whom you ask. It also depends on people's previous experience with the police. Research shows that citizens who have experienced positive contacts with the police generally have positive attitudes toward the police.[1] Figure 7.1 reveals that, overall, 58% of the public have "a great deal" or "quite a lot" of confidence in the police, 30% have "some" confidence, 10% have "very little," and 1% has "no confidence at all." However, among blacks, only 22% have "a great deal" or "quite a lot" of confidence in the police, while 43% have "some" confidence, 34% have "very little confidence," and 1% has "no confidence at all." What is it about the police that the public has or does not have confidence?

To begin with, a majority or nearly a majority of the public rate the police "excellent" or "good" at being part of the community, responding quickly to calls for help and assistance, preventing crimes, solving crimes, being helpful and friendly, treating people fairly, not using excessive force, and

Figure 7.1

Views of the Public toward the Police in the United States, by Race, 2007 and 2008

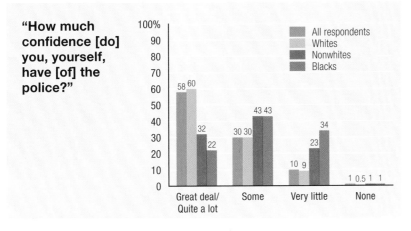

Note: Owing to rounding, percentages may not add up to 100%.

Source: Harris Interactive® online survey conducted between June 9 and 12, 2008 at www.gallup.com/poll/1597/ Confidence-Institutions.aspx and Sourcebook of Criminal Justice Statistics Online, Table 2.12.2007 at www.albany.edu/ sourcebook/pdf/t2122007.pdf (both accessed January 11, 2009).

preventing terrorist attacks. As shown in Figure 7.2, between 45% and 60% of the public rate the police "excellent" or "good" on the eight aforementioned issues. Between 30% and 40% rate the police "fair," and between 9% and 16% rate them "poor" or "terrible." A different poll shows that 60% of the public have "a great deal" or "quite a lot" of confidence in the police's ability to protect it from violent crime; 31% do "not [have] very much confidence"; 8% have "none at all"; and 1% have "no opinion." The public's confidence in the police's ability to protect it from violent crime has not changed much in more than two decades. In short, a majority of the public has at least some confidence in the ability of the police to do its job in a professional manner.

Among minorities, however, confidence in the police is much lower. On every measure of performance in Figure 7.2, blacks and Hispanics rate the police lower than whites. Other polls that measure other aspects of police performance reveal the same pattern:

- Only 43% of blacks and 41% of Hispanics, compared to 61% of whites, believe that "the police treat all races fairly."
- Eighty percent of blacks and 66% of Hispanics are much more likely to believe that "police brutality against minorities happens 'occasionally' (or more often) in their communities." Fifty-one percent of whites also agree with the statement.
- Thirty-two percent of blacks and 24% of Hispanics, compared to 6% of whites, believe that "police brutality against minorities in their communities happens 'often.'"
- Forty-two percent of blacks and 39% of Hispanics, compared to 16% of whites, are sometimes "afraid that they will be arrested when they are completely innocent."[2]

When asked to rate the honesty and ethical standards of the police, 13% of the general public rate the police as "very high" on this measure, 43% rate them as "high," 35% rate them as "average," 7% rate them as "low," and 2% rate them as "very low." Blacks rate the honesty and ethical standards of police

About 50% of Americans rate the police as either good or excellent at solving crimes. *Why isn't the percentage higher?*

Figure 7.2

Respondents' Ratings of Police Performance in Own Community, United States, by Race, 2005

How would you rate the police in your community on the following—excellent or good, fair, or poor or terrible?

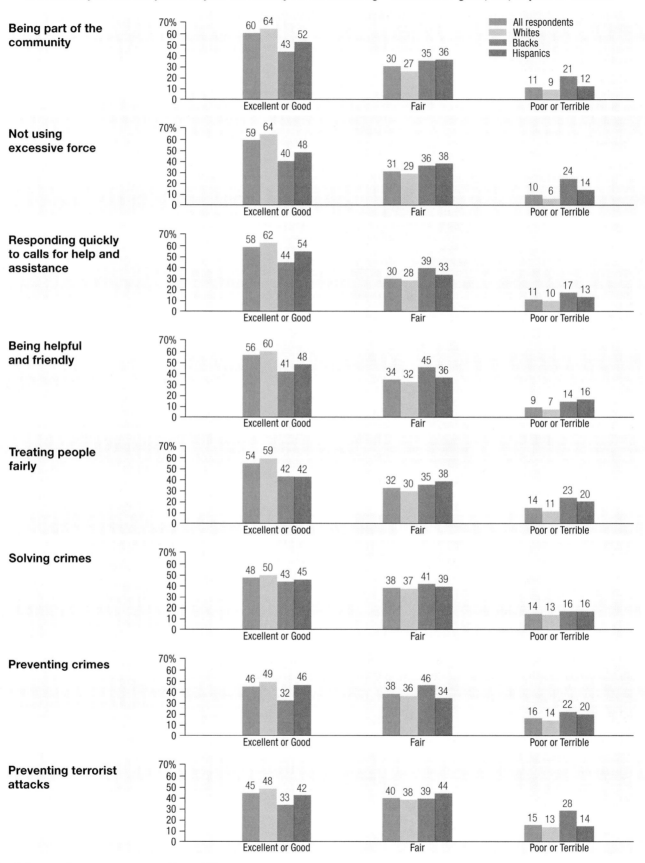

Note: Owing to rounding, percentages may not add up to 100%.

Source: Harris Interactive® online survey conducted between September 6 and 12, 2005, among 2,242 U.S. adults aged 18 and older. Sampling error for the overall results is +/−2 percentage points. Data generously provided to author.

Figure 7.3

Views of the Public Toward the Police in the United States, 2007 and 2008

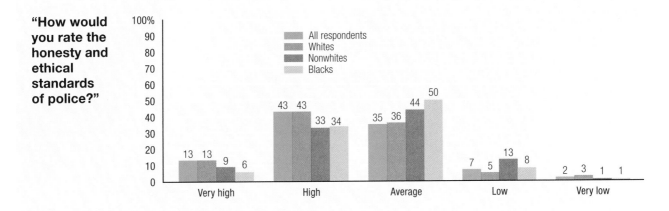

"How would you rate the honesty and ethical standards of police?"

Legend:
- All respondents
- Whites
- Nonwhites
- Blacks

Very high: 13, 13, 9, 6
High: 43, 43, 33, 34
Average: 35, 36, 44, 50
Low: 7, 5, 13, 8
Very low: 2, 3, 1, 1

Source: Bureau of Justice Statistics, *Sourcebook of Criminal Justice Statistics Online,* Table 2.21. 2007 at www.albany.edu/sourcebook/pdf/t2212007.pdf and The Gallup Poll at www.gallup.com/poll/1654/Confidence-Institutions.aspx (conducted between November 7 and 9, 2008) (both accessed January 11, 2009).

lower: Only 6% rate the police as "very high," 34% rate them as "high," 50% rate them as "average," 8% rate them as "low," and 1% rate them as "very low." (See Figure 7.3.)

In sum, these data clearly show that the public as a whole has more respect for the police and their honesty and ethical standards than it does for a variety of other occupations.[3] Yet, the level of respect and confidence is not particularly high, nor is it uniform across races. Although most of the public believes that the police do a pretty good job, it also believes there is much room for improvement. One way to improve the police is to employ better police officers.

The level of respect and confidence the public has for the police is not particularly high, especially among minorities. *Why is this the case?*

THINKING CRITICALLY

1. Why do you think that racial groups differ so greatly in their attitudes toward the police?

2. What do you think could be done to improve public attitudes toward the police?

3. How accurate do you think the public's perceptions of the police are?

4. How do the perceptions presented in this section compare with your own?

Police Recruitment and Selection

Deciding whom to employ should be simple: hire the type of police officer that the citizens of the community want. Of course, that approach assumes that the citizens of a community have some idea of what it takes to be a police officer. Then, there is the matter of which people to consult. Who should decide? The wealthy? The middle class? The poor? The politically conservative? The politically liberal? The young? The old? The business community? Community leaders? Crime victims? Those people most likely to be policed? Some consensus is needed on the type of police officer desired. Seeking that consensus in metropolitan communities is filled with conflict. Police administrators need to be very careful in choosing police officers, who may well be with the agency for 20 years or more. A police department will never reach its full potential without selecting the best available personnel. Selection decisions have momentous long-term implications for a police department.[4]

QUALITIES OF A SUCCESSFUL POLICE OFFICER

Given the complexity of the role of the police officer, it comes as no surprise that deciding what qualities the successful police officer needs is not easy. Indeed, police officers require a combination of qualities and abilities that is rare in any pool of applicants. Robert B. Mills, a pioneer in the psychological testing of police officers, believes that police applicants should possess the following psychological qualities:

- Motivation for a police career
- Normal self-assertiveness
- Emotional stability under stress
- Sensitivity toward minority groups and social deviates
- Collaborative leadership skills
- A mature relationship with social authority
- Flexibility
- Integrity and honesty
- An active and outgoing nature[5]

The Berkeley, California, Police Department lists these qualities:

- Initiative
- Ability to carry heavy responsibilities and handle emergencies alone
- Social skills and ability to communicate effectively with persons of various cultural, economic, and ethnic backgrounds
- Mental capacity to learn a wide variety of subjects quickly and correctly
- Ability to adapt thinking to technological and social changes
- Understanding of other human beings and the desire to help those in need
- Emotional maturity to remain calm and objective and provide leadership in emotionally charged situations
- Physical strength and endurance to perform these exacting duties[6]

Police officers must have a variety of qualities to be successful on the job. *What qualities would you bring to the position?*

Three qualities seem to be of paramount importance. One commentator refers to them as the **three I's of police selection:** intelligence, integrity, and interaction skills. In short, police officers need to be bright enough to complete rigorous training. They should be honest enough to resist—and have a lifestyle that allows them to resist—the temptation of corrupting influences in law enforcement. They should also be able to communicate clearly and get along with people of diverse backgrounds.

Nearly as important as the three I's, however, are common sense and compassion. In resolving conflicts and solving problems they encounter, police officers must often choose a course of action without much time to think about it. Common sense is a key quality, for example, in locating a suspect who has just fled a crime scene on foot or in deciding when to call off a high-speed vehicle pursuit that suddenly endangers innocent citizens and other police officers.

Police agencies also seek to employ officers with the core value of compassion. Without a genuine concern for serving one's fellow human beings, a police officer is not likely to sustain a high level of motivation over a long period of time. Many people the police meet on a daily basis simply need help, sometimes required by law; but more often these officers are spurred by a compassion for helping people no matter what their need.

Other qualities, such as physical strength, endurance, and appearance, seem less important. If you were the one who needed to be dragged from a burning automobile, however, the physical strength of the police officer might be important to you.

THE POLICE RECRUITMENT PROCESS

Few occupations have selection processes as elaborate as the ones used in choosing police officers in most departments of the nation. Before choices are made, a wide net must be cast in the recruiting effort to come up with enough

three I's of police selection Three qualities of the American police officer that seem to be of paramount importance: intelligence, integrity, and interaction skills.

potential applicants to fill the vacancies for an academy class. Police departments, often working with city personnel agencies, are generally guided in their selection decisions by civil service regulations. Those regulations are developed either locally or at the state level. They guarantee a merit employment system with equal opportunity for all.

Because employment qualifications are supposed to be based on perceived needs in policing, law enforcement agencies must be careful not to set unnecessary restrictions that have no bearing on an officer's ability to complete training and perform successfully on the job. The addition of just one seemingly minor qualification, such as requiring four pull-ups instead of three during physical ability testing, or making the eyesight requirement slightly more stringent, may eliminate thousands of men and women from the selection process in a large metropolitan area. It is difficult enough to find capable police candidates without needlessly eliminating them from the selection process.

Recruitment Most police agencies have finally realized that the kind of officers they desire will not gravitate naturally to the doors of the department. The search for top-notch applicants is very competitive, and many chiefs and sheriffs believe that they have to look at larger pools of applicants than in the past to find the same number of qualified officers. The reasons for the increased difficulty in finding good police candidates involve social maturity and lifestyle issues. Problems with drugs and alcohol, sexually transmitted diseases, personal debt, and dependability have reduced the number of qualified police applicants. Table 7.1 provides the selection standards for Seattle police officers.

The major goal of the recruiting effort is to cast police work as an attractive and sustaining career, even to those who might initially be turned off by it. Research supports the allure of policing for many people who view a career in law enforcement as financially rewarding and status enhancing. In addition, the work itself is intrinsically satisfying because it is nonroutine, exciting, generally outdoors, and people oriented.[7]

In recruiting new police officers, efforts are made to cast police work as an attractive and sustaining career. *What should people interested in becoming police officers be told about the job?*

Table 7.1 Selection Standards for Seattle Police Officers, 2009

The following standards apply to all candidates for Police Officer:

Minimum Standards:

- Applicant must be at least 20.5 years of age at the time of taking the exam to be hired.
- United States Citizenship is required.
- Proof of high school diploma or a certified GED.
- A valid Washington State Driver's License is required prior to being hired.
- Military discharge under honorable conditions, if applicable (fair employment laws apply).

Drug Use:

- Have **not** used Marijuana within the three (3) years prior to the date of this Acknowledgment of Minimum Standards Regarding Illegal Drug Use, **and**
- Have **not** used Marijuana more than twenty-five (25) times within the past ten (10) years prior to the date of this Acknowledgment of Minimum Standards Regarding Illegal Drug Use, **and**
- Have **not** used cocaine or crack within the ten (10) years prior to the date of this Acknowledgment of Minimum Standards Regarding Illegal Drug Use, **and**
- Have **not** used club drugs such as, but not limited to, ketamine, GHB, rohypnol, and MDMA (ecstasy) within the five (5) years prior to the date of this Acknowledgment of Minimum Standards Regarding Illegal Drug Use, **and**
- Have **not** used any Hallucinogens, LSD, Mushrooms, or Psylocybin within the ten (10) years prior to the date of this Acknowledgment of Minimum Standards Regarding Illegal Drug Use, **and**
- Have **not** used PCP, Angel Dust, Wet or Phencyclidine within the ten (10) years prior to the date of this Acknowledgment or Minimum Standards Regarding Illegal Drug Use, **and**
- Have **not** used Opium, Morphine, or Heroin within the ten (10) years prior to the date of this Acknowledgment of Minimum Standards Regarding Illegal Drug Use, **and**
- Have **not** used Methamphetamine, Crank, Crystal, Ice, Speed, Glass, or Amphetamine within the ten (10) years prior to the date of this Acknowledgment of Minimum Standards Regarding Illegal Drug Use, **and**
- Have **not** inhaled aerosols, sometimes referred to as Huffing (paint) or Whippits (Nitrous Oxide) or used Khat within the five (5) years prior to the date of this Acknowledgment of Minimum Standards Regarding Illegal Drug Use, **and**
- Have **not** used four (4) or more controlled substances within the ten (10) years prior to the date of this Acknowledgment of Minimum Standards Regarding Illegal Drug Use, **and**
- Have **not** used any illegal drug(s) or illegally used pharmaceuticals more than twenty-five (25) times within the ten (10) years prior to the date of this Acknowledgement of Minimum Standards Regarding Illegal Drug Use, **and**
- Have **not** used any illegal drug(s) while employed in a criminal justice and/or law enforcement capacity, **and**
- Have **not** manufactured or cultivated illegal drug(s) for the purpose of the sales/marketing of the drug(s).

Please note that use of illegal drugs and the illegal use of prescription drugs, referred to in this acknowledgment, means the use of one or more drugs, the possession or distribution of which is unlawful under the Uniform Controlled Substances Act.

Traffic Record:

An applicant's driving record will be thoroughly assessed and may be a factor for disqualification. Examples of infractions/traffic crimes that may be disqualifying:

- Driving While Intoxicated (DWI), Reckless Driving, or Hit & Run Driving.
- Suspension of your driver's license within five (5) years of the date of application.
- Three (3) or more moving violations (speeding, negligent driving, etc.) in the past five (5) years of the date of application will be carefully reviewed.
- Two (2) or more accidents within five (5) years of the date of application, wherein applicant was judged to be at fault and/or charged with a moving violation.

Criminal Record:

An applicant's criminal record, including all arrests, prosecutions, deferred prosecutions, "Alford" pleas, and non-conviction information will be thoroughly assessed and may be grounds for disqualification. The following will be disqualifying:

- Any adult felony conviction.
- Any misdemeanor or felony conviction while employed in a criminal justice and/or law enforcement capacity.
- Any domestic violence conviction.

Employment Record:

An applicant's employment history, including any terminations, or leaving an employer in lieu of termination, will be thoroughly assessed and may be grounds for disqualification.

Financial Record:

An applicant's credit history, including excessive credit card debt or unresolved accounts in collection, will be thoroughly assessed and may be ground for disqualification. The following will be disqualifying:

- Failure to pay income tax or child support.

Table 7.2 Average Base Annual Salary for Selected Positions in Local Police Departments, by Size of Population Served, 2003

Population Served	ENTRY-LEVEL OFFICER		SERGEANT OR EQUIVALENT		CHIEF	
	Minimum	Maximum	Minimum	Maximum	Minimum	Maximum
All sizes	$28,200	$35,300	$36,600	$42,400	$ 48,800	$ 56,900
1,000,000 or more	37,700	57,800	60,200	73,500	113,000	157,100
500,000–999,999	36,600	54,900	58,000	69,600	109,700	143,200
250,000–499,999	38,300	53,500	54,600	66,900	94,400	129,200
100,000–249,999	39,600	54,000	56,000	68,000	95,000	123,100
50,000–99,999	37,400	51,200	54,500	65,300	85,500	106,900
25,000–49,999	35,900	48,600	53,400	62,400	77,700	94,500
10,000–24,999	33,000	45,000	47,400	55,200	65,900	77,800
2,500–9,999	29,000	36,200	37,400	43,600	48,900	56,200
Under 2,500	23,400	26,800	27,100	30,800	32,700	36,500

Note: Salary figures have been rounded to the nearest $100. Computation of average salary excludes departments with no full-time employee in that position.

Source: Matthew J. Hickman and Brian A. Reaves, *Local Police Departments, 2003,* U.S. Department of Justice, Bureau of Justice Statistics (Washington, D.C.: GPO, May 2006), p. 11, Table 20.

Table 7.2 shows the average base annual salary for selected positions in local police departments, by size of population served in 2003. Many departments also offer the opportunity to earn special pay. Table 7.3 shows the percentage of local police departments, by size of population served, that authorize various types of special pay.

Affirmative Action Since the passage of the Civil Rights Act of 1964 and the threat of court challenges to the fairness of the police selection process, police agencies have struggled to find the best-qualified applicants and yet achieve satisfactory race and gender representation within the ranks of the department. Failure to seriously pursue equitable representation has led to expensive lawsuits, consent decrees, and court-ordered quotas to achieve the desired diversity.

Table 7.3 Local Police Departments Authorizing Special Pay for Full-Time Sworn Personnel by Size of Population Served, 2003

Population Served	PERCENTAGE OF AGENCIES AUTHORIZING PAY FOR:							
	Tuition Reimbursement	Education Incentive	Merit	Shift Differential	Special Skills	Military Duty	Hazardous Duty	Bilingual Ability
All sizes	35%	32%	21%	21%	13%	10%	5%	4%
1,000,000 or more	81	75	44	81	56	19	69	50
500,000–999,999	72	54	30	65	30	30	54	32
250,000–499,999	83	61	54	76	44	27	49	44
100,000–249,999	76	72	44	57	33	25	29	38
50,000–99,999	76	68	39	44	39	23	24	27
25,000–49,999	72	67	30	44	26	19	10	14
10,000–24,999	61	57	30	37	24	14	5	6
2,500–9,999	38	35	21	23	13	11	3	2
Under 2,500	13	11	14	6	3	4	3	—

Note: — = less than 0.5%.

Source: Matthew J. Hickman and Brian A. Reaves, *Local Police Departments, 2003,* U.S. Department of Justice, Bureau of Justice Statistics (Washington, D.C.: GPO, May 2006), p. 12, Table 21.

Increasing the number of female officers is a major concern in police selection and employment. *What are some of the advantages of having a greater number of female police officers?*

Consequently, affirmative action has become a major concern in police selection and employment. Now affirmative action programs are being questioned on several legal grounds. That questioning may lead to more difficulty in trying to achieve race and gender balance in police departments.

How successful has affirmative action been in accomplishing the desired goal of race and gender balance in police departments? Affirmative action *has* been relatively successful in increasing the percentage of minority members in policing. It has been less successful in increasing the percentage of women. As noted previously, more than 70% of the sworn officers in the nation's police departments are white males. However, as shown in Table 7.4, the percentage of black and Hispanic officers in local departments in 2003 (the most recent year for which data were available) was 11.7% and 9.1%, respectively—up from 9.3% and 4.5% in 1987. The 2003 figures closely approximate the percentage of blacks and Hispanics in the general population of the United States (12.2% for blacks and 13.7% for Hispanics). However, women, who compose more than 50% of the United States population, represented only 11.3% of the police officers in local police departments in 2003; still, that was an increase from 7.6% in 1987.[8]

Education Given the amount of discretion that law enforcement officers have and the kinds of sociological problems with which they deal, selecting reasonably intelligent, college-educated officers seems a wise practice. Many police agencies in the country currently require some college background. As a result, the average level of education in policing today is nearly 2 years of college. Table 7.5 shows the minimum educational requirement for new officers in local departments, by size of population served. Among the advantages of hiring college-educated officers are the following:

1. Better written reports
2. Enhanced communication with the public
3. More effective job performance

Table 7.4 Minority Representation in Local Police Departments in the United States, 2003

Race/Ethnicity	Police	Population
Black	11.7%	12.2%
Hispanic	9.1	13.7
White	76.4	67.9
Other	2.8	6.2

Source: Matthew J. Hickman and Brian A. Reaves, *Local Police Departments, 2003,* U.S. Department of Justice, Bureau of Justice Statistics (Washington, D.C.: GPO, 2006), and U.S. Census Bureau.

Table 7.5 Minimum Educational Requirement for New Officers in Local Police Departments, by Size of Population Served, 2003

Population Served	Total with Requirement	PERCENTAGE OF AGENCIES REQUIRING A MINIMUM OF:			
		High School Diploma	Some College*	2-Year College Degree	4-Year College Degree
All sizes	98%	81%	8%	9%	1%
1,000,000 or more	98	72	18	7	1
500,000–999,999	99	72	13	9	5
250,000–499,999	99	84	8	4	3
100,000–249,999	98	81	13	3	2
50,000–99,999	100	76	17	6	1
25,000–49,999	99	77	10	11	1
10,000–24,999	99	82	7	9	1
2,500–9,999	99	83	7	9	—
Under 2,500	97	82	6	9	0

Notes: Detail may not add to total because of rounding.

*Nondegree requirements.

— = less than 0.5%.

Source: Matthew J. Hickman and Brian A. Reaves, *Local Police Departments, 2003,* U.S. Department of Justice, Bureau of Justice Statistics (Washington, D.C.: GPO, May 2006), p. 9, Table 16.

4. Fewer citizen complaints
5. Wiser use of discretion
6. Heightened sensitivity to racial and ethnic issues
7. Fewer disciplinary actions[9]

This list of advantages should impress police administrators and the public. Satisfied citizens, the savings of substantial amounts of money by avoiding lawsuits, and fewer disciplinary actions against officers are good reasons for law enforcement executives to search for police applicants with college backgrounds.

Recognition that college-educated police officers are generally better performers than officers without that level of education is long overdue. And the idea is catching on. Minnesota's Peace Officer Licensing Commission now requires a 4-year college degree for licensing. The Peace Officer Council in Ohio now has more than one dozen **college academies,** where students pursue a program that integrates an associate's degree curriculum in law enforcement or criminal justice with the state's required peace officer training. On receipt of the associate's degree, students sit for the peace officer certification exam. If they receive a passing score on the exam, they are eligible to be hired by any police agency and to go to work without any additional academy training.

college academies Schools where students pursue a program that integrates an associate's degree curriculum in law enforcement or criminal justice with the state's required peace officer training.

SUCCESSFUL RECRUITING PRACTICES

Where do you find the best-qualified police applicants? Some of the more successful recruiting practices have included going to colleges, neighborhood centers, and schools in minority communities; using television, radio, and newspaper advertisements; and working with local employment offices. Demystifying the nature of police work and the selection process and shortening the time from application to final selection have also helped to attract and retain qualified candidates.

Pictured here are police cadets searching a parking lot, where a woman was shot and killed by a sniper. *What are some of the advantages of police cadet programs?*

Public Safety Officers Another promising recruitment strategy has been the employment of 18-year-olds as **public safety officers** (sometimes called community service officers or public service aides), who perform many police service functions but do not have arrest powers. By the time they are 21, the department has had an excellent opportunity to assess their qualifications and potential to be sworn officers.

Police Cadets **Police cadet programs** have been around since the 1960s (Cincinnati Police), and as recently as the 1990s, the New York City Police launched a cadet program combining a college education with academy training and work experience in the police department. Upon graduation from the university, a cadet is promoted to police officer.

High School Tech Prep Programs Another program that is proving useful in attracting potentially capable police officers at an even earlier age is known as **tech prep** or **technical preparation** for a criminal justice career. Area community colleges and high schools team up to offer 6 to 9 hours of college law enforcement courses in the eleventh and twelfth grades, as well as one or two training certifications, such as police dispatcher or local corrections officer. Students who graduate are eligible for employment at age 18. They become interested in law enforcement work early and are ideal police applicants when they become old enough to apply. Accurate law enforcement career information can be passed on to high school students through a tech prep program because the teachers are required to either currently work in law enforcement or have police experience in their backgrounds.

Police Corps The federal Police Corps program was created as part of the Violent Crime Control and Law Enforcement Act of 1994.[10] Its purposes are to (1) address violent crime by increasing the number of police with advanced education and training on community patrol and (2) provide educational assistance to law enforcement personnel and students who possess a sincere interest in public service in the form of law enforcement. Through its state-level

public safety officers Police department employees who perform many police services but do not have arrest powers.

police cadet program A program that combines a college education with agency work experience and academy training. Upon graduation, a cadet is promoted to police officer.

tech prep (technical preparation) A program in which area community colleges and high schools team up to offer 6 to 9 hours of college law enforcement courses in the eleventh and twelfth grades, as well as one or two training certifications, such as police dispatcher or local corrections officer. Students who graduate are eligible for police employment at age 18.

affiliates, the program provides federal scholarships on a competitive basis to college students who agree to serve where needed on community patrol as police officers or sheriffs' deputies for at least 4 years. Students who are accepted into the Police Corps programs receive up to $3,750 a year to pay the expenses toward a bachelor's or graduate degree. A student may receive up to $15,000 under the program, including reasonable room and board. Undergraduate participants must be full-time students at an accredited public or nonprofit 4-year college or university. They may pursue a degree in any relevant field of study, including criminal justice or law enforcement. Shortly after graduation, participants begin their work as officers. Those who pursue a graduate degree complete their service in advance.

In addition to their college education, all Police Corps participants must satisfactorily complete a rigorous 16- to 24-week residential Police Corps basic law enforcement training program paid for by the federal government. The law enforcement agency with which the participant serves provides additional training as appropriate. If a Police Corps participant fails to complete his or her bachelor's degree, Police Corps training, and 4 years of required service with the assigned agency, he or she must repay all scholarships and reimbursements received through the program, plus 10% interest.

Police Corps participants are expected to work as community patrol officers in geographic areas that have a great need for additional officers and to be assigned to challenging beats where they can be most effective. The program encourages states, where feasible, to place participants in areas where they have community or family ties. Participants receive the same pay and benefits and have the same responsibilities as any other officer of similar rank and tenure.

THE POLICE SELECTION PROCESS

In many communities, selection of police officers takes place through a merit system. A **merit system** of employment is established when an independent civil service commission, in cooperation with the city personnel section and the police department, sets employment qualifications, performance standards, and discipline procedures. Officers employed under such a system are hired and tenured, in theory, only if they meet and maintain the employment qualifications and performance standards set by the civil service commission. Officers in such a system cannot be fired without cause.

To find the best possible recruits to fill department vacancies, police agencies use a selection process that includes some or all of the following steps.

merit system A system of employment whereby an independent civil service commission, in cooperation with the city personnel section and the police department, sets employment qualifications, performance standards, and discipline procedures.

Short Application This brief form registers the interest of the applicant and allows the agency to screen for such things as minimum age, level of education, residency, and other easily discernible qualifications.

Detailed Application This document is a major source of information for the department and background investigators. The applicant is asked for complete education and work histories, military status, medical profile, references, a record of residence over many years, and other detailed information. Applicants are also asked to submit copies of credentials, military papers, and other certificates.

Medical Examination This exam determines if applicants are free of disease, abnormalities, and any other medical problems that would disqualify them for police work. This information is critical because retiring a young officer on a

Table 7.6 Interviews, Tests, and Examinations Used in Selection of New Officer Recruits in Local Police Departments, by Size of Population Served, 2003

Population Served	Personal Interview	Medical Exam	Drug Test	Psychological Evaluation	Physical Agility Test	Written Aptitude Test	Personality Inventory	Polygraph Exam	Voice Stress Analysis	Second Language Ability Test
All sizes	98%	85%	73%	67%	50%	43%	26%	25%	4%	1%
1,000,000 or more	94	100	100	100	94	81	56	81	0	0
500,000–999,999	100	100	95	100	86	84	48	64	11	11
250,000–499,999	95	93	98	98	93	83	51	78	10	2
100,000–249,999	95	97	86	95	88	82	50	77	11	1
50,000–99,999	99	97	90	97	83	80	47	57	7	3
25,000–49,999	99	99	88	96	76	76	45	47	12	2
10,000–24,999	99	98	88	89	71	72	40	42	6	1
2,500–9,999	91	74	71	52	48	26	25	3	—	
Under 2,500	73	63	47	31	20	16	11	2	—	

Notes: List of selection methods is not intended to be exhaustive.

— = less than 0.5%

Source: Matthew J. Hickman and Brian A. Reaves, *Local Police Departments, 2003,* U.S. Department of Justice, Bureau of Justice Statistics (Washington, D.C.: GPO, May 2006), p. 8, Table 14.

medical disability shortly after employment could cost the public hundreds of thousands of dollars. Table 7.6 shows the percentage of local police departments by population served that use medical exams, as well as various interviews, tests, and other exams, in the selection of new officer recruits.

Physical Ability Test Physical ability tests are common in police selection despite having been challenged in the courts as having an adverse effect on the hiring of female applicants. Physical ability tests were initially a direct response to the elimination of height and weight standards, which were also discriminatory against female applicants. The first tests required exceptional speed and strength, such as going over walls that were taller than any of the walls in the cities that had such tests. Those tests were struck down by the courts as not being job-related. Today, any physical ability tests must be based on a thorough analysis of the actual work of police officers. See Table 7.6 for the percentage

Physical ability tests are common in police selection. *Why are they important?*

of local police departments that use physical agility tests in the selection of new officer recruits.

Written Examination Police agencies once used intelligence tests in their selection process. Most agencies now use some type of aptitude, personality, general knowledge, reading comprehension, writing, or police skill exam. The courts have held that those tests must be true measures of the knowledge and abilities needed to perform police work successfully. Pre-employment tests have been the subject of much controversy in the courts.

Background Investigation Investigators in this process look for any factors in the backgrounds of applicants that would prevent them from performing successfully as police officers. Past drug use or excessive alcohol use, a poor driving record, employer problems, a bad credit history, criminal activity, and social immaturity are areas of concern in the background investigation. The investigator relies heavily on the detailed application, verifies its contents, explores any discrepancies, and develops additional leads to follow. Table 7.7 shows the percentage of local police departments by population served that use various types of background checks in the selection of new officer recruits.

Psychological Testing Emotional stability and good mental health are critical to the ability to perform police work, which can be very stressful. Departments have been held liable for not screening their applicants for those psychological traits.[11]

Systematic psychological testing of police officers began in the 1950s. At first, the typical approach was to have the psychological evaluators look for disqualifying factors. The process included a pencil-and-paper test and a one-on-one interview with a psychologist. Today, the testing focus has generally shifted to a search for the positive psychological qualities required in police work. Current tests include multiple versions of both written and clinical evaluations.

The validity of psychological tests has been an issue for decades. Psychologists are often reluctant to rate with any specificity the police candidates

Table 7.7 Background Checks Used in Selection of New Officer Recruits in Local Police Departments, by Size of Population Served, 2003

Population Served	Criminal Record Check	Background Investigation	Driving Record Check	Credit History Check	Volunteer Service Check
All sizes	99%	98%	98%	55%	8%
1,000,000 or more	100	100	100	81	0
500,000–999,999	100	100	100	89	19
250,000–499,999	100	100	98	88	7
100,000–249,999	100	99	98	88	12
50,000–99,999	99	100	99	87	8
25,000–49,999	100	100	99	83	11
10,000–24,999	99	99	99	76	8
2,500–9,999	99	98	99	55	9
Under 2,500	98	97	92	39	6

Note: List of selection methods is not intended to be exhaustive.

Source: Matthew J. Hickman and Brian A. Reaves, *Local Police Departments, 2003,* U.S. Department of Justice, Bureau of Justice Statistics (Washington, D.C.: GPO, May 2006), p. 8, Table 15.

they evaluate. Candidates considered "unacceptable" are sometimes classified as "uncertain" to avoid lawsuits. It is important to remember that understanding and predicting human behavior is an inexact art. So it is easy to appreciate the reluctance of psychologists to be more specific. See Table 7.6 for the percentage of local police departments by population served that use psychological tests and evaluation in the selection of new officer recruits.

Oral Interview/Oral Board This step is frequently the final one in the selection process. Members of the interview team have the results of the previous selection procedures, and they now have an opportunity to clear up inconsistencies and uncertainties that have been identified. The board normally restricts itself to evaluating the following qualities:

1. Appearance, poise, and bearing
2. Ability to communicate orally and organize thoughts
3. Attitude toward law enforcement and the job required of police officers
4. Speech and the ability to articulate
5. Attitude toward drug, narcotic, and alcohol use
6. Sensitivity to racial and ethnic issues[12]

See Table 7.6 for the percentage of local police departments by population served that use personal interviews in the selection of new officer recruits.

Academy Training The police academy is part of the selection process. Virtually every academy class in any sophisticated police department loses up to 10% of its students. Thus, to survive academy training, students must be committed to the process. Students undergo from 400 to more than 1,000 hours of academic, skill, and physical training and are tested virtually every week of the process. In 2003, for example, state-mandated field and academy training requirements for new officers averaged about 750 hours combined. Additional training beyond state requirements averaged about 200 hours (see Table 7.8). At the end of many academy training programs, students must take a state licensing or certification examination.

Table 7.8 Training Requirements for New Officer Recruits in Local Police Departments, by Size of Population Served, 2003

| Population Served | AVERAGE NUMBER OF HOURS REQUIRED | | | | | |
| | ACADEMY | | | FIELD | | |
	Total	State-Mandated	Other Required	Total	State-Mandated	Other Required
All sizes	628	588	40	326	147	179
1,000,000 or more	1,016	689	327	513	153	360
500,000–999,999	920	588	332	561	104	456
250,000–499,999	950	620	330	652	200	452
100,000–249,999	815	642	173	624	253	371
50,000–99,999	721	657	64	598	268	330
25,000–49,999	702	657	46	527	210	317
10,000–24,999	672	642	30	442	164	279
2,500–9,999	630	597	32	314	151	162
Under 2,500	577	542	35	199	106	93

Note: Average number of training hours excludes departments not requiring training.

Source: Matthew J. Hickman and Brian A. Reaves, *Local Police Departments, 2003,* U.S. Department of Justice, Bureau of Justice Statistics (Washington, D.C.: GPO, May 2006), p. 9, Table 17.

At the end of many police academy training programs, there is a state licensing or certification examination. *Do you believe those examinations are necessary? Why or why not?*

Probation Under local or state civil service requirements, employers may keep a new police officer on probation for 6 months to a year. The probation period gives the new police officer a chance to learn policing under the guidance of a well-qualified field training officer. Formal field training is a wise investment, and it ensures that new officers get as much knowledge and experience as possible before an agency commits to them for their careers.

A problem is that with police academy training now often extending 5 or 6 months, a 6-month probation period no longer seems logical. The agency is, in effect, offering the police officer tenure in a matter of weeks after graduation from the academy. This practice defeats the purpose of probation, which was designed to allow the employer to see whether the newly trained officer can successfully perform the job.

THE SELECTION OF A LAW ENFORCEMENT EXECUTIVE

No less important than the selection of operations-level officers is the choice of the chief executive of a police agency. This executive might be a chief of police, a sheriff, or the head of a state law enforcement organization. A crucial decision in the selection process is whether to allow people from outside the agency to apply. In some police agencies in the United States, civil service regulations prohibit the selection of outside candidates. The rationale for this rule is that there must be qualified internal candidates. In addition, it is discouraging to hard-working and talented police administrators to be denied a chance to lead the agency they have spent many years serving.

Actual hiring decisions are usually shared by members of a selection committee. Frequently, an executive search firm is also employed. The selection committee usually consists of representatives of the local government, the police department, the search firm, and the community. Applicants are put through a rigorous process that includes several visits to the city, written exams, interviews, and assessment center testing, in which candidates try to resolve real-world management problems. Once the interviews and testing have been completed, applicants are normally ranked, and the list is presented to the city manager, the mayor, or others so that a final selection can be made.

The pursuit of a police chief's job is very competitive. Often several hundred candidates contend for a position even in a small suburban community. A typical police chief rarely serves longer than 10 years, and life in the chief's seat may not be very comfortable, particularly if a new chief intends to change things. Much of the political controversy and many of the social problems in major cities and counties end up at the door of the police department, so police chiefs must be politically savvy to survive. Many chiefs discover that they cannot please everybody, particularly if they are trying to change the department. Should police chiefs have protection under civil service? Most commentators say no, arguing that mayors and city managers ought to have the authority to pick the management teams that work immediately under their direction. A small number of cities give their police chiefs civil service protection to insulate them from unnecessary political interference. Police chief salaries based on the size of the population served are shown in Table 7.2.

The selection of a sheriff of one of the nation's counties is just as important as choosing a police chief. The difference in the two processes has to do

Police Officer

My name is Robert Bour. I really enjoy being a police officer in Tiffin, Ohio, a small city of about 20,000 people. My assignment is in the patrol section, but I also work as a bike patrol officer, a field training officer, and a member of the SWAT team. As a SWAT officer, I go out mainly on search warrant and drug raids and in cases where someone has barricaded him- or herself in, and a life is in danger. In a small police department, you have the opportunity to be involved in a number of specialized assignments.

As a patrol officer, I have the opportunity to interact with the public a great deal. We have always done community policing here in one form or another. Small communities have to. You stop people on the street and say hello, chat with business owners, and meet as many residents as you can. People always have questions for you; often they are about traffic laws and enforcement.

I also have to respond to calls for services and these calls take precedence over everything else. I get one to three calls per hour on the evening and early morning shift, but there are rare times when I don't get any calls during the entire 10 hours of work.

My third area of activity involves self-initiated patrol activity. That includes traffic enforcement, of course, but also patrolling the alleys and streets around bars when they are closing in order to protect inebriates who may have passed out outside the establishment. The patrol also includes guarding against people who may be driving under the influence of alcohol. Tiffin has two universities, so sometimes college students may get a little more disorderly than they should and we have to respond.

I graduated in 1992 from a police academy that was hosted by a local community college. Before becoming a police officer in Tiffin, I worked as a sheriff's deputy and a village police officer, both full- and part-time. The Tiffin Police Department now requires a 2-year college degree as the minimum to become employed. At the time I came on, it was not necessary, but I intend to go back to college and finish my degree anyway.

I can offer a few suggestions for anyone who wants to be a police officer. First, you should have a desire to work with people from diverse backgrounds, because that is what police work is. Second, you must genuinely want to help people, keeping in mind that you are not always able to help everybody; sometimes that is frustrating. Finally, you must think about your family. They must support you in being a cop because there is some danger involved in the job. Still, police work is one of the best jobs a person can have.

What are the pros and cons of being a police officer?

with who does the selecting. In all but a few of the nation's counties, sheriffs are elected by the county's eligible voters. Not all sheriffs have a law enforcement background. In most states, they are not required to be licensed or certified peace officers as their deputies or municipal officers are. As a result, people from various occupations often succeed in being elected sheriff. To be elected, sheriffs must be good politicians. They often have a much better idea of the priorities of a community and wield more influence with prosecutors and in the legislature than chiefs of police. Sheriffs who do not exhibit this political acumen are not likely to be reelected. In 2003 (the latest year for which data were available), the average salary of county sheriffs ranged from a low of $54,500 to a high of $59,800. In counties with a population of one million or more, the salary range was $119,300 to $135,000. In counties with populations of fewer than 2,500 the salary range was $37,000 to $40,000.[13]

THINKING CRITICALLY

1. What do you think are the most important qualities for police officers to have? Why?

2. How much formal education do you think police officers should have? Why?

Issues in Policing

The discussion of law enforcement thus far has made it clear that not all matters of policing in America are settled. In this final section of the chapter, some of the issues that continue to be major topics of debate in law enforcement and have significant impact on the quality of life in neighborhoods and communities across the nation are highlighted.

DISCRETION

discretion The exercise of individual judgment, instead of formal rules, in making decisions.

Discretion is the exercise of individual judgment, instead of formal rules, in making decisions. No list of policies and procedures could possibly guide police officers in all of the situations in which they find themselves. Even the police officer writing a ticket for a parking meter violation exercises a considerable amount of discretion in deciding precisely what to do.[14] Police even have the discretion to ignore violations of the law when they deem it appropriate in the context of other priorities.

The issue of police discretion is very controversial. Some believe that the discretion of police officers should be reduced. The movement to limit the discretion of police officers is the result of abuses of that discretion, such as physical abuse of citizens or unequal application of the law in making arrests. Other people argue that we should acknowledge that officers operate with great discretion and not attempt to limit it. Advocates of this view believe that better education and training would help officers exercise their judgment more wisely.

Patrol Officer Discretion Patrol officers frequently find it necessary to exercise their discretion. Within the geographical limits of their beats, they have the discretion to decide precisely where they will patrol when they are not answering radio calls. They decide whom to stop and question. For example, they may tell some children playing ball in the street to move, while they ignore others. Patrol officers decide for themselves which traffic violators are worth chasing through busy traffic and which ones are not. They even have the right not to arrest for a minor violation when, for example, they are on the way to investigate a more serious matter.

Some of the more critical situations involve decisions about stopping, searching, and arresting criminal suspects. Many citizens have been inconvenienced and some have been abused because of a police officer's poor use of discretion in those areas.

full enforcement A practice in which the police make an arrest for every violation of law that comes to their attention.

Police officers cannot make an arrest for every violation of law that comes to their attention—that is, they cannot provide **full enforcement.** The police do not have the resources to enforce the law fully, nor can they be everywhere at

Police officers can exercise discretion in arrest situations. *Should police officers be allowed to use discretion in arrest situations? Why or why not?*

once. And even if full enforcement were possible, it may not be desirable. For example, persons intoxicated in front of their own homes may not need to be arrested, but only to be told to go inside. Motorists slightly exceeding the speed limit need not be arrested if they are moving with the flow of traffic. Prostitution may be widely practiced in large metropolitan areas, but police officers have little to gain by searching hotels and motels to stamp it out, particularly when judges will turn the prostitutes right back out on the street. Generally, only when such an activity becomes a clear nuisance, is the subject of a public outcry, or threatens health and safety do the police department and its officers choose to take formal action.

The practice of relying on the judgment of the police leadership and rank-and-file officers to decide which laws to enforce is referred to as **selective enforcement.** The practice allows street police officers to decide important matters about peacekeeping and enforcement of the law. For most violations of the law, but not all felonies, a police officer can usually exercise a number of options:

selective enforcement The practice of relying on the judgment of the police leadership and rank-and-file officers to decide which laws to enforce.

1. Taking no action at all if the officer deems that appropriate for the situation
2. Giving a verbal warning to stop the illegal action
3. Issuing a written warning for the violation
4. Issuing a citation to the perpetrator to appear in court
5. Making a physical arrest in serious matters or in situations with repeat offenders

Factors Affecting Discretion
Dozens of studies have been conducted on the exercise of discretion by police patrol officers. A number of significant factors affect discretion:

-   **The Nature of the Crime**—The more serious the crime, the more likely it is that police officers will formally report it. In cases involving lesser felonies, misdemeanors, and petty offenses, police officers are more likely to handle the offenses informally. A minor squabble between over-the-fence neighbors is an example of a matter that would probably be handled informally.
-   **Departmental Policies**—If the leadership of a police department gives an order or issues a policy demanding that particular incidents be handled in a prescribed way, then an officer is not supposed to exercise discretion but is to do as the order or policy directs. Thus, if a city has had many complaints about dangerous jaywalking in a certain downtown area, the chief of police may insist that citations be issued to those found jaywalking, even though, in the past, citations had not been issued.
-   **The Relationship between the Victim and the Offender**—Particularly for minor offenses, the closer the relationship between the victim of an alleged offense and the suspected perpetrator, the more discretion the officer is able to exercise. For example, police officers are not likely to deal formally with a petty theft between two lovers if they believe that the victim will not prosecute his or her partner.
-   **The Amount of Evidence**—If officers do not have enough evidence to substantiate an arrest or to gain a conviction in court, they are likely to handle the case in some way other than making an arrest.
-   **The Preference of the Victim**—Sometimes the victim of a crime may simply want to talk the matter over with someone, and the police are available on a 24-hour basis. Also, if the officer senses that the victim of a minor assault does not wish to prosecute the perpetrator of the offense, the patrol officer will not make a formal complaint, and the complainant will most likely never know that a report was not made.
-   **The Demeanor of the Suspect**—Suspects who are disrespectful and uncooperative may very well feel the full brunt of the law. Patrol officers often choose the most severe option possible in dealing with such suspects.

- **The Legitimacy of the Victim**—Patrol officers are bound to pass some kind of judgment on the legitimacy of the victim. An assault victim who is belligerent and intoxicated, for instance, will not be viewed favorably by the investigating officer. Criminals victimized by other criminals are also seen as less than fully authentic victims, no matter what the offense.
- **Socioeconomic Status**—The more affluent the complainant, the more likely a patrol officer is to use formal procedures to report and investigate a crime. Contrary to popular belief, the personal characteristics of an officer (such as race, gender, and education) do not seem to influence the exercise of discretion.

Discretion and Domestic Violence Police officers have intervened in domestic violence cases and other kinds of family disputes, sometimes off-duty, since the inception of public policing. For the longest period of time, these interventions were viewed as peacekeeping activities when, in fact, they should have been treated as criminal matters. Many women and some men were hurt, and some killed, as a result of the restrictions on the police in making arrests for assault misdemeanors not made in their presence and a view among the police that these calls were the private business of the family instead of real police matters. Traditionally, law enforcement has been less interested in arresting perpetrators of crimes when the victim and the perpetrator have a close relationship.

Approximately one million women are victims of domestic violence each year. Even today, with every state requiring the police to have domestic violence intervention training, some commentators believe that the police are not the best qualified of available community helpers to intervene. However, if crimes are committed in the form of physical abuse, the police are not only the best qualified to intervene but are also required by law to do so. Certainly, the availability of 24-hour service has always made the police the major responder to domestic violence calls.

Many states have mandatory arrest laws that require police officers to arrest any suspect that has battered a spouse or domestic partner. *Do you support mandatory arrest laws in domestic violence cases? Why or why not?*

The police in general do not relish the task of responding to domestic violence calls for several reasons. First, the calls can be dangerous, although generally no more dangerous than other disturbance calls. Nevertheless, officers are hurt each year by responding to domestic violence complaints. Second, police officers know from experience that many of the tense and hostile dynamics that exist between quarreling spouses, couples, and other family members have a way of dissipating over time or at least subsiding for a while. Third, the police know that they have often conducted investigations, even arrested the suspected batterer, and the victim has later chosen to drop charges. Finally, the police know that responding to the minor assault cases in domestic violence calls is not always the best thing for the family because the arrest creates its own complications that may, in fact, exacerbate the family crisis to a state of irreparable harm.

Police have responded to domestic violence in three distinct ways: mediate the dispute, separate domestic partners in minor disputes, and arrest the perpetrator of the assault. Which of these ways is the most effective? This question was put to the test in a 3-year study in the city of Minneapolis. In minor domestic dispute cases, Minneapolis police officers gave up their discretion in handling domestic violence calls. Instead of deciding for themselves the appropriate disposition for each call, they randomly chose arrest, separation, or mediation. The results of the study showed that the arrested perpetrators were about half as likely to repeat their violence against the original victim.[15] This study may have been the impetus for many states to implement a mandatory arrest domestic violence law. Subsequent studies, however, have not been able to clearly support the mandatory arrest disposition as the most effective way to handle the problem of domestic violence. Yet today nearly half of the states have a mandatory arrest law requiring the arrest of any suspect that has battered a spouse or domestic partner. While victim safety and welfare are indeed the major reasons for police intervention, more research is clearly needed to determine the best approaches to handling domestic violence calls.

Discretion and Racial Profiling **Racial profiling** is of growing concern to law enforcement officials and the public. Just how frequently this illegal practice occurs is difficult to discern, particularly since the term *racial profiling* is seldom defined in the discussions found in the national media. Racial profiling is a law enforcement infringement on a citizen's liberty based solely on race. It is widely believed that on freeways, highways, and streets throughout the nation blacks and other minorities are stopped for traffic violations and field interrogations in numbers disproportionate to their representation in the population. It is further assumed that many of these stops are pretext stops where the stop is justified by a minor equipment or moving traffic violation that might otherwise be ignored. Where the practice is considered widely experienced, it has been called "driving while black or brown" (DWBB). It is presumed that at the root of such a practice is racial stereotyping and prejudice. According to a recent national survey, 53% of Americans think that the practice of stopping motorists because of their race or ethnicity is widespread among law enforcement officers. Sixty-seven percent of blacks and 63% of Hispanics believe the practice is widespread, while 50% of non-Hispanic whites believe it to be true. Only 31% of Americans believe the practice is justified: 23% of blacks, 30% of Hispanics, and 31% of non-Hispanic whites.[16]

Results of a recent federal study of police and public contacts show that the police in 2005 stopped white, black, and Hispanic drivers at similar rates (8.9%, 8.1%, and 8.9%, respectively) and that 86% of the drivers felt they were pulled over for a legitimate reason (87.6% of whites, 76.8% of blacks, and 85.1% of Hispanics).[17] However, a smaller percentage of blacks felt they were pulled over by the police for a legitimate reason when the stop involved a vehicle defect (66.5% believed the stop was legitimate), a record check (72.2%), and a stop sign/light violation (56.8%). Comparable rates for whites were 90.5%, 91.8%, and 77.1%, respectively, and for Hispanics, 85.5%, 85.4%, and 72.3% respectively. The study also found that of the approximately 18 million drivers stopped by the police in 2005, black and Hispanic drivers were more likely than white drivers to be searched and arrested. About 5% of all drivers stopped by the police were searched, and police found evidence of a crime in nearly 12% of the searches. Of the stopped drivers searched, 3.6% were white, 9.5% were black, and 8.8% were Hispanic. Racial breakdowns were not provided for the searches in which evidence of a crime was found. Arrests were made in 2.4% of the traffic stops: 2.1% of the arrestees were white, 4.5% were black, and 3.1% were Hispanic. Thus, although these data do not support the contention that minorities, especially blacks, experience traffic stops at rates substantially higher than rates for whites, they do show that when the police stop minorities, they are more likely than whites to be searched and arrested. These data also show that a larger percentage of blacks than whites or Hispanics are more likely to believe the reasons for certain stops are illegitimate. Less

racial profiling The stopping and/or detaining of individuals by law enforcement officers based solely on race.

CJ Online
ACLU
To learn more about what is being done to combat racial profiling, visit the American Civil Liberties Union (ACLU) website on racial profiling at www.aclu.org/profiling. *What can police departments do to prevent racial profiling?*

clear is whether disparate rates of searching and arresting are a function of racial stereotyping and prejudice or legitimate legal factors.

Racial profiling is a hot topic in the U.S. Congress, state legislatures, county commissions, and city councils, as well as in the meeting rooms of civil rights and professional police organizations. The American Civil Liberties Union, for example, has started a national project to eliminate racial profiling and even provides citizens with a "Bust Card" that tells them how to respectfully interact with the police (acknowledging the difficulty of their job) even when falling victim to racial profiling. At the end of 2006, 31 states had laws prohibiting racial profiling by law enforcement officers, but only 19 of those states required police departments to collect information on the race of motorists they stop.[18]

Racial profiling to any degree is a blight on the record of professional law enforcement and democracy. Some of the methods that have been prescribed to stop racial profiling include racial and cultural diversity training for police personnel, strong discipline for errant officers, videotaping all traffic stops, collecting data on the race of stopped motorists and pedestrians and the disposition of the encounter, and having police officers distribute business cards to all motorists and pedestrians they stop.

The business card may reduce race-based stops, because it would allow an officer to be easily identified at a later time. But city leaders throughout the United States are in a quandary as to precisely what to do to stop racial profiling. Thirty-six members of the National League of Cities' public safety committees met in Oklahoma City and determined that they oppose police profiling of suspects when it violates a person's civil rights, but they could not agree whether all profiling should be banned.[19]

Factors Limiting Discretion Several methods are employed to control the amount of discretion exercised by police officers. One method is close supervision by a police agency's management. For example, a department may require that officers consult a sergeant before engaging in a particular kind of action. Department directives or policies also limit the options police officers have in particular situations. Decisions of the U.S. Supreme Court, such as one restricting the use of deadly force to stop a fleeing felon, limit the options available to officers on the street. Finally, the threat of civil liability suits has reduced the discretion an officer has, for example, in the use of deadly force or in the pursuit of fleeing suspects in an automobile.

The debate over how much control should be placed on the exercise of police discretion is ongoing. Few other professionals have experienced a comparable attack on their authority to make decisions for the good of the clients they serve. The continuing attempt to limit discretion also seems out of place at a time when community policing is being widely advocated. Remember that community policing decentralizes authority and places it in the hands of the local beat officers and their supervisors. Community policing is bound to fail if citizens see that the police they work with every day do not have the authority and discretion to make the decisions that will ultimately improve the quality of life in a community.

JOB STRESS

Stress in the workplace is common today. A recent survey revealed that 80% of responding workers reported at least some degree of stress.[20] Given the nature of police work, no one is surprised to discover that a law enforcement officer's job is stressful. Police officers intervene in life's personal emergencies and great tragedies. Working extended shifts, for example, at the scene of the bombing of the federal building in Oklahoma City or the World Trade Center disaster would tax the resources of even the most resourceful police officer.

Working extended shifts at the World Trade Center disaster was very stressful for police officers and other first responders. *In what ways is a police officer's job more stressful than other jobs?*

Who would deny the stress involved in working deep undercover on a narcotics investigation over a period of several months? Some officers are able to manage stress on the job better than others.

Job stress is defined as the harmful physical and emotional outcomes that occur when the requirements of a job do not match the capabilities, resources, or needs of the worker. Poor health and injury are possible results of prolonged job stress. Police work has long been identified as one of the most stressful of all occupations, and many police officers suffer each year from the deleterious effects of a job that tests their physical and emotional limits.

job stress The harmful physical and emotional outcomes that occur when the requirements of a job do not match the capabilities, resources, or needs of the worker.

Sources and Effects of Stress A number of conditions can lead to stress: (1) design of tasks—heavy lifting, long hours without breaks, and monotonous repetition of dangerous maneuvers; (2) management style—lack of participation by workers in decision making, poor communication, lack of family-friendly policies; (3) interpersonal relationships—poor social environment and lack of support from co-workers and supervisors; and (4) work roles—conflicting or uncertain job expectations, wearing too many hats, too much responsibility.[21] The signs that stress is becoming a problem with an officer are frequent headaches, difficulty in concentrating, short temper, upset stomach, job dissatisfaction, abuse of alcohol and drugs, and low morale. Individually and collectively these symptoms can have other origins, but job stress is often the source.

Copicide As if the work of confronting dangerous suspects and preserving the peace were not stressful enough, "copicide," or "death by cop," has entered the work life of some police officers. **Copicide** is a form of suicide in which a person

copicide A form of suicide in which a person gets fatally shot after intentionally provoking police officers.

Police officers sometimes manage stress by seeking counseling. *Are there ways that you handle stress that you think would work particularly well in policing?*

gets fatally shot after intentionally provoking police officers.[22] A study of police shootings resulting in the death of a citizen in Los Angeles found that 10% could be attributed to copicide.[23] One commentator believes that "dozens of times each year during jittery hostage dramas and routine traffic stops, desperate people lure police officers into shooting them in a phenomenon known in law enforcement circles as 'suicide by cop.'"[24] The truth is that no one knows exactly how many times copicide incidents occur each year. Most police officers require a lot of time to emotionally recover from a fatal shooting in circumstances where they were fully authorized to use deadly force. To later discover that they were provoked into killing people who simply used police as a tool in a suicide scheme creates an extra emotional burden to bear.

Stress Management and Reduction Fortunately, there are ways to manage and reduce stress without leaving police work. The "fixes" for stress come in two general categories. Stress management now encompasses a variety of programs and procedures that include discussing stressful events with colleagues and mental health professionals, regular exercise, relaxation techniques such as structured visualization, a healthy diet that also eliminates caffeine and nicotine, enriched family support, religious support, prayer, meditation, and stress management classes that often involve spouses.

Organizational change can also reduce the potential for stress in the police work environment. Officers, for example, may be given more discretion in determining their work hours and shifts as long as the police agency is able to respond effectively to the workload requirements of the community. Flattening the organizational structure can help reduce stress by giving officers more discretion in carrying out the responsibilities of their job. Community policing is an effective paradigm for increasing officers' ability to control their work and perhaps minimize stress. Job redesign can assist assigning the right number and type of tasks to a police position when one job requires too much of an officer to maintain emotional stability and good health. Finally, excellent public safety equipment can minimize stress. Proper police weaponry, dependable vehicles, and the best of protective equipment such as high-grade body armor not only can protect officers but can also put their minds a little more at ease on those important concerns.[25]

USE OF FORCE

No issue in policing has caused as much controversy in recent decades as the use of force. In New York, Los Angeles, Detroit, Miami, and many other cities, excessive-force charges against police officers have been made and documented and have resulted in the loss of public confidence in the police. Although the vast majority of police officers of this country go to work every day with no intention of using excessive force, far too many instances of brutality still occur.

A precise definition of brutality is not possible. However, the use of excessive physical force is undoubtedly a factor in everyone's definition. For many people, particularly members of racial and ethnic minorities, brutality also includes verbal abuse, profanity, harassment, threats of force, and unnecessary stopping, questioning, and searching of pedestrians or those in vehicles.

Excessive Force Why do the police have to use force as frequently as they do? A major responsibility of police officers is to arrest suspects so that they can answer criminal charges. No criminal suspect wants his or her liberty taken away, so some of them resist arrest. Invariably, a few suspects are armed with some kind of weapon, and some are prepared to use that weapon against the police to foil the arrest. The police need to establish their authority to control such conflicts. They have a variety of nonlethal weapons at their disposal to accomplish that task (see Table 7.9). The disrespect and physical resistance that are frequently the result of encounters with suspects have caused the police on occasion to use **excessive force,** which is a measure of coercion beyond that necessary to control participants in a conflict.

Not only is the persistent use of excessive force by the police against citizens unethical, civilly wrong, and criminally illegal, but it also creates a situation in which nobody wins. Police may face criminal and civil prosecution in such cases, citizens build up layers of resentment against the police, and law enforcement agencies pay out millions of dollars in damages while losing respect in the eyes of the community. Disturbing events such as the brutal beating and sexual assault of Abner Louima in 1997, and the shooting deaths of Amadou Diallo in 1999 and Sean Bell in 2006, by New York City police officers received nationwide media attention while causing great concern by citizens and law enforcement over the use of excessive force. There were also charges of racism by the police because all three incidents involved the use of excessive force by white police officers against black men.

Abner Louima, a 30-year-old Haitian immigrant, was accused of assaulting a police officer outside a nightclub in the city. Louima claimed that following his arrest and arrival at the station house, a white officer, Justin Volpe, savagely beat and sodomized him with a toilet plunger. In 1999, Volpe pled guilty to charges stemming from the beating. Charles Schwarz, another police officer accused of holding Louima down while Volpe attacked him, was convicted separately in a federal trial of violating Louima's rights. Three other NYPD officers said to be involved in the event were acquitted of all charges.

Amadou Diallo, a 22-year-old West African immigrant, was hit by 19 of the 41 bullets shot by police officers from the NYPD street crimes unit. Diallo died at the scene. The officers claimed that Diallo fit the description of a rape suspect for whom they had been searching. When the officers tried to stop Diallo, he reached for what police officers thought was a weapon; they then began to shoot. Apparently Diallo, who spoke little English, was reaching for his wallet. The officers involved in the shooting were charged with second-degree murder; however, a state jury found the officers innocent.

Although past and recent incidents of excessive force have been disturbing, research reveals that police brutality does not occur as often as some people might think. For example, according to a recent survey of large state and local law enforcement agencies with 100 or more sworn officers, more than 26,000 citizen complaints about officer use of force were received during 2002. The rate of complaints was 33 per agency and 6.6 per 100 full-time sworn officers. However, of the 94% of complaints with a final disposition, only about 8% were sustained (that is, there was sufficient evidence of the allegation to justify disciplinary action against the officer or officers); 34% of the complaints were not sustained (that is, there was insufficient evidence to prove the allegation), 25% were unfounded (that is, the complaint was not based on facts, or the reported incident

excessive force A measure of coercion beyond that necessary to control participants in a conflict.

 Taser Use

According to a recent study, Houston, Texas police officers used Tasers 1,417 times between December 2004 and June 2007, and in about two-thirds of the cases the suspect was black. About 25% of Houston's population is black. The study also found that black officers were less likely than white or Hispanic officers to use Tasers on a black suspect. A Houston police spokesperson said the "use of Tasers was not tied to race but to a person's behavior."

Source: "If You're Black in Houston, Look Out: Cops Are More Likely to Taser You," *The Orlando Sentinel* (September 11, 2008), p. A2.

There is much debate on how much control should be placed on the decisions of police officers in arrest situations. *How much control should be placed on them and why?*

Table 7.9 Types of Nonlethal Weapons Authorized for Personal Use by Sworn Personnel in Local Police Departments, by Size of Population Served, 2003

| | PERCENTAGE OF AGENCIES AUTHORIZING | | | | | | | |
| | CHEMICAL AGENTS—PERSONAL USE | | | | BATONS | | | |
Population Served	Any Type in Survey	Pepper Spray	Tear Gas	CS	Any Type in Survey	Collapsible	Traditional	PR-24
All sizes	99%	98%	16%	14%	95%	88%	49%	42%
1,000,000 or more	94	94	19	19	100	88	56	44
500,000–999,999	97	97	19	22	100	89	60	38
250,000–499,999	98	95	24	22	100	83	54	44
100,000–249,999	99	99	22	24	99	93	56	44
50,000–99,999	99	97	25	27	99	92	45	39
25,000–49,999	100	100	24	21	99	93	44	39
10,000–24,999	99	98	22	17	97	91	47	45
2,500–9,999	98	98	13	14	94	88	47	41
Under 2,500	99	98	14	12	93	86	52	42

(continued on pg 277)

did not occur), 23% resulted in officer exoneration (that is, the incident occurred, but the officer's action was deemed lawful and proper), and 9% had some other disposition, such as the complaint was withdrawn).[26] Note that just because a complaint was not sustained does not necessarily mean unlawful use of force did not occur. Also, the use of force data described above includes less than "excessive" forms of force. However, the study's authors report that nearly all the 2,124 sustained complaints (8% of all complaints) may have involved excessive force. If that were the case, the excessive-force use rate is about 1 incident per every 200 full-time sworn officers and almost 1% of every 100 officers that respond to calls for service. A newer federal study found that 1.6% of the 43.5 million persons who had at least one contact with the police in 2005 (approximately 696,000 people) had force used or threatened against them—a rate relatively unchanged from 2002; 83% of them considered the force excessive.[27] Widespread media coverage of high-profile cases, such as the Los Angeles police officers' assault on Rodney King, can lead the public to believe that brutality is much more common than it really is. The Los Angeles police, however, had a higher rate of wounding and killing suspects than did any other police department in the nation, according to the Christopher Commission, which investigated the assault on Rodney King.

Deadly Force The greatest concern over the use of force by the police has to do with the infliction of death or serious injury on citizens and criminal suspects. Since the U.S. Supreme Court's 1985 decision in *Tennessee* v. *Garner,* the use of deadly force has been severely restricted, and police shootings of suspects and citizens have been reduced. In the *Garner* case, an unarmed teenage boy was shot as he fled a house burglary, failing to heed the warning to stop given by a Memphis police officer. The boy later died of a gunshot wound to the head. He was found with $10 in his pocket that he had stolen from the home. The Memphis officer was acting in compliance with his department's policy on the use of deadly force and with the law in Tennessee and in most other states in the nation.

Giving law enforcement officers the authority to use deadly force to stop a fleeing felon, even when they know the suspect is unarmed and not likely to be a danger to another person, derives from the common law in England and the United States, which permitted such a practice. At the time the rule

Table 7.9 Types of Nonlethal Weapons Authorized for Personal Use by Sworn Personnel in Local Police Departments, by Size of Population Served, 2003 (continued)

Population Served	Soft Projectile	Electrical Devices[a]	Holds/Neck Restraints	Rubber Bullet	Blackjack	High Intensity Light
All sizes	28%	23%	13%	8%	5%	1%
1,000,000 or more	69	75	31	25	6	0
500,000–999,999	48	43	16	16	3	0
250,000–499,999	59	56	39	22	7	2
100,000–249,999	66	50	36	22	2	2
50,000–99,999	72	46	30	22	3	2
25,000–49,999	57	39	12	19	3	1
10,000–24,999	42	31	12	10	3	—
2,500–9,999	28	21	9	6	4	0
Under 2,500	13	15	13	6	6	1

PERCENTAGE OF AGENCIES AUTHORIZING — OTHER WEAPONS/ACTIONS

Notes: — = less than 0.5%.

[a]Includes handheld direct contact devices (such as stun gun) and handheld stand-off devices (such as Taser).

Source: Matthew J. Hickman and Brian A. Reaves, *Local Police Departments, 2003*, U.S. Department of Justice, Bureau of Justice Statistics (Washington, D.C.: GPO, May 2006), p. 26, Table 57.

developed, however, unlike today, dozens of crimes were capital offenses, and the fleeing suspect, if apprehended and convicted, would have been executed. The *Garner* decision, no doubt, was long overdue, and it included a rule that many police agencies in the nation had adopted years earlier. The perspective that professional law enforcement agencies had already begun to adopt on deadly force was from the Model Penal Code, Section 307(2)(B). It reads:

The use of deadly force is not justifiable under this section unless:

1. The arrest is for a felony.
2. The person effecting the arrest is authorized to act as a peace officer or is assisting a person whom he believes to be authorized to act as a peace officer.
3. The actor believes that the force employed creates no substantial risk of injury to innocent persons.
4. The actor believes that: (a) The crime for which the arrest is made involved conduct including the use or threatened use of deadly force. (b) There is substantial risk that the person to be arrested will cause death or serious bodily harm if his on her apprehension is delayed.

In 2003 (the latest year for which data were available), 95% of local police departments, employing 99% of all officers, had a written policy on the use of deadly force. Ninety percent of departments, employing 97% of all officers, had a written policy on the use of nonlethal force.[28] Even with explicit guidelines, however, the decision to use deadly force is seldom clear-cut for police officers, because of the violent and occasionally ambiguous situations in which they find themselves. For example, consider the confrontation a Dallas, Texas, police officer had in the summer of 1993. As a plainclothes officer, he responded to a call at an apartment complex where it was reported that a man had fired shots. It was nighttime, and when he arrived at the parking lot of the complex, he saw a man perhaps 50 feet from him with the butt end of a pistol sticking out of the waistband of his trousers. The police officer told him to stop and put his hands in the air. Instead of doing what he was ordered to do, the man pulled the gun from his waistband and moved it toward the officer. The officer responded by firing his weapon several times at the man and killing him. Later, it was discovered that the man was a Mexican citizen who spoke no English.

Some members of the Hispanic community were enraged that the officer did not offer commands in Spanish, because Dallas officers were required to study 20 hours of the language in the police academy. After several months of investigation and the grand jury's ignoring the case, the officer was exonerated. However, the chief of police assured the community that new police recruits would study three times the previously required amount of Spanish and that annual in-service training would also require the study of Spanish. In addition, the chief stated that in situations such as the one in question, undercover and plainclothes officers would be required, if possible, to put on jackets that would readily identify them as police officers. Some people argue that the man with the gun in this situation not only did not understand English but also had no idea that the officer with drawn gun was a police officer.

Not all "deadly force" cases involve shootings. In 2007, for example, in the case of *Scott* v. *Harris*, the issue was a high-speed police chase. In 2001, a Georgia deputy attempted to pull over Victor Harris, who was clocked driving at 73 miles per hour on a road with a 55-mile-an-hour speed limit. Instead of stopping, Harris sped away on the two-lane road at speeds exceeding 85 miles an hour. The deputy radioed his dispatcher to report he was pursuing a fleeing vehicle. Deputy Timothy Scott heard the radio communication and joined pursuit, as did other officers. At one point the officers had Harris cornered in a shopping-center parking lot, but Harris was able to evade the officers by making a sharp turn and colliding with Scott's police car. At that point, Officer Scott took the lead in the pursuit. After 6 minutes and about 10 miles, Officer Scott sought permission from his supervisor to perform a "Precision Intervention Technique" ("PIT") maneuver, which causes a fleeing vehicle to spin to a stop. The supervisor told Scott to "go ahead and take him out." However, instead of using the PIT maneuver, Officer Scott hit the rear of Harris's car with his push bumper and, as a result, Harris lost control of his car and crashed, leaving him a quadriplegic.

Harris sued Officer Scott and others, claiming that the use of excessive force constituted an unreasonable seizure in violation of his Fourth Amendment right. Officer Scott filed a motion for a summary judgment based on an assertion of qualified immunity. The District Court denied Officer Scott's motion. On appeal, the U.S. Court of Appeals for the 11th Circuit concluded that Scott's actions could constitute "deadly force" under *Tennessee* v. *Garner*, and that Officer Scott was not entitled to qualified immunity. The U.S. Supreme Court granted certiorari and reversed. The Court ruled: "Because the car chase respondent initiated posed a substantial and immediate risk of serious physical injury to others, Scott's attempt to terminate the chase by forcing respondent off the road was reasonable, and Scott is entitled to summary judgment." The Court further noted that the *Garner* decision did not apply to the facts of this case. The major issue, according to the Court, was whether Officer Scott's actions were reasonable and not whether they constituted "deadly force." According to Highway Traffic Safety Administration records, 357 people were killed in police chases in 2005.[29]

We should not forget that citizens and criminal suspects also attack the police. Mentally ill persons, parties to a family dispute, and suspects trying to avoid arrest feloniously kill between 50 and 100 officers each year. More than 90% of officers are killed by assailants using firearms. In response, police officers exercise caution by wearing protective vests, they proactively use what they learn in courses on self-defense (unarmed and armed), and they attempt to defuse hostile situations through peaceful techniques they learn in training. When all else fails, they can use their sidearms to protect themselves. In 2003 (the latest year for which data were available), nearly all local police departments authorized patrol officers to carry one or more types of semiautomatic sidearms.

Table 7.10 Semiautomatic Sidearms Authorized for Use
by Sworn Personnel in Local Police Departments,
by Size of Population Served, 2003

Population Served	PERCENTAGE OF AGENCIES AUTHORIZING SEMIAUTOMATIC SIDEARMS						
	Total	.40	9 mm	.45	.357	10 mm	.380
All sizes	100%*	62%	34%	34%	16%	10%	3%
1,000,000 or more	100	50	63	31	6	0	0
500,000–999,999	100	65	48	24	17	3	3
250,000–499,999	100	61	59	39	15	7	7
100,000–249,999	99	59	52	47	19	9	6
50,000–99,999	99	68	43	37	12	11	3
25,000–49,999	99	65	31	31	8	7	1
10,000–24,999	100	69	29	30	12	6	2
2,500–9,999	100	63	27	31	12	9	3
Under 2,500	100	58	41	37	22	13	4

Notes: Some departments authorized more than one type of sidearm.

*Rounded from less than 100%.

Source: Matthew J. Hickman and Brian A. Reaves, *Local Police Departments, 2003,* U.S. Department of Justice, Bureau of Justice Statistics (Washington, D.C.: GPO, 2006), p. 25, Table 55.

This was up from 73% of departments in 1990. Table 7.10 shows the percentage of local police agencies by size of population served that authorized officers to carry specific types of semiautomatic sidearms in 2003. The table reveals that the largest percentage of agencies (62%) authorized their officers to carry the .40-caliber semiautomatic sidearm. Sixty-five percent of local departments, employing 81% of all officers, supplied regular field officers with their primary sidearm.[30]

POLICE CORRUPTION

Almost from the beginning of formal policing in the United States, corruption of law enforcement officers has been a fact of life. Almost nothing is more distasteful to the public than a police officer or a whole department gone bad. Throughout history, police officers have bought their positions and promotions, sold protection, and ignored violations of the law for money.

Why is policing so susceptible to bribery and other forms of corruption? Perhaps it has to do with the combination of two critical features of the police role in society. On the one hand, the police have authority to enforce laws and to use power to make sure that those laws are obeyed. On the other hand, they also have the discretion *not* to enforce the law. The combination of those two features makes the police vulnerable to bribes and other forms of corruption. Other features of police work add to the potential for corruption: low pay in relation to important responsibilities, cynicism about the courts' soft handling of criminals that the police spend so much time trying to apprehend, society's ambivalence about vice (most citizens want the laws on the books, but many of them are willing participants), and the practice of recruiting officers from

Policing is susceptible to bribery and other forms of corruption. *Who is policing the police? Are controls adequate?*

working-class and lower-class backgrounds, where skepticism about obeying the law might be more prevalent.

Some of those factors undoubtedly help explain the following four examples of corruption. In November 2006, the sheriff of small, rural, economically depressed Henry County, Virginia (which is about 50 miles south of Roanoke), 12 of his 96 deputies, and 7 others were indicted by federal prosecutors on racketeering conspiracy, narcotics distribution, obstruction of justice, perjury, and weapons charges. The sheriff, a former state trooper who was first elected in 1991, also was charged with impeding the investigation by the FBI and federal drug-enforcement agents and with money laundering. Prosecutors presented evidence showing that for 8 years, the sheriff's department confiscated cocaine, steroids, marijuana, and other drugs and then sold them to the public. The sheriff was quoted as saying the only way to acquire wealth is to be "a little crooked and not get caught." Prosecutors reported the sheriff owns large tracts of land and a trucking company and earns more than $20,000 a year in dividends. The salary range for sheriffs in counties the size of Henry County, according to state law, is $85,000 to $93,500 a year.[31]

In April 2006, two former New York City police detectives were convicted in U.S. District Court of participating in a racketeering conspiracy that included eight Mafia-related murders, witness tampering, witness retaliation, and obstruction of justice. Prosecutors said the two detectives had accepted $375,000 in payments over 6 years while using their police status to aid an underboss of the Luchese organized crime family.[32]

An 8-month investigation by the *Miami Herald* in 1997, documented a police scam involving hundreds of officers in thousands of cases in Dade County. Dubbed "collars for dollars," the scam worked like this. Police officers listed one another as witnesses in drunken-driving and misdemeanor cases even if they did little or no police work on the cases. They then went to court on overtime and received pay they did not deserve. According to the newspaper report, "collars for dollars" happened often and cost Dade County taxpayers millions of dollars.[33]

In 1993, before a commission investigating charges of police corruption in the New York City police department, one former patrol officer testified that fellow officers called him "the mechanic" because he "tuned people up"—slang for beating people up. When asked whether his victims were suspects, the officer replied that they were just ordinary citizens, approximately 400 of them over a 4-year period. Other officers testified that they randomly broke into apartments; stole drugs, guns, and money; lied to grand juries; "tuned up" people with leather gloves packed with lead; and generally broke more laws than they enforced. One officer described how he received $8,000 a week to protect a drug dealer.[34]

Types of Corruption In 1972, the Knapp Commission issued a report on corruption in the New York City Police Department. Two types of corrupt officers were identified: "grass eaters" and "meat eaters." **Grass eaters** were officers who occasionally engaged in illegal or unethical activities, such as accepting small favors, gifts, or money for ignoring violations of the law during the course of their duties. **Meat eaters**, in contrast, actively sought ways to make money illegally while on duty. For example, they would solicit bribes, commit burglaries, or manufacture false evidence for a prosecution.[35]

More than 30 years ago, sociologist Ellwyn Stoddard identified a more complete list of types of police misconduct, with examples, in what he described as the "blue-coat code":

1. **Bribery**—Accepting cash or gifts in exchange for nonenforcement of the law
2. **Chiseling**—Demanding discounts, free admission, and free food
3. **Extortion**—The threat of enforcement and arrest if a bribe is not given

grass eaters Officers who occasionally engage in illegal and unethical activities, such as accepting small favors, gifts, or money for ignoring violations of the law during the course of their duties.

meat eaters Officers who actively seek ways to make money illegally while on duty.

4. **Favoritism**—Giving breaks on law enforcement, such as for traffic violations committed by families and friends of the police
5. **Mooching**—Accepting free food, drinks, and admission to entertainment
6. **Perjury**—Lying for other officers apprehended in illegal activity
7. **Prejudice**—Unequal enforcement of the law with respect to racial and ethnic minorities
8. **Premeditated Theft**—Planned burglaries and thefts
9. **Shakedown**—Taking items from the scene of a theft or a burglary the officer is investigating
10. **Shopping**—Taking small, inexpensive items from a crime scene or an unsecured business or home[36]

Controlling Corruption Corruption in law enforcement strikes at the core of the profession and takes a heavy toll. All peace officer positions are positions of honor and trust, and agencies invest money and time in selecting officers with integrity. To see this investment lost is disheartening. But more than anything else, public confidence and trust plummet after a widely publicized corruption case, such as the police drug-trafficking episode in Miami. In the following list, some ways to control and reduce corruption in policing are described.

- **High Moral Standards** Selecting and maintaining officers with high moral standards is a step in the right direction. Some police agencies in the United States still hire convicted felons to do police work. In-depth academy and in-service training on ethical issues that officers are likely to face would prepare officers for the compromises they may be asked to make later in their careers.
- **Police Policies and Discipline** A police department should develop rigid policies that cover the wide range of activities that corruption comprises. Drug testing of officers, particularly those in narcotics-sensitive positions, may be necessary, although unpopular. Policies mean nothing unless they are enforced. Discipline should be imposed and prosecutions should go forward when officers are found guilty of violating established policies and laws.
- **Proactive Internal Affairs Unit** The **internal affairs investigations unit** of a police department should ferret out illegal and unethical activity. Any internal affairs unit that waits for complaints probably is not going to receive many of them. First-line supervisors should know whether their subordinates are engaging in unethical and illegal violations of department rules and state laws. They should also be held responsible for the actions of their subordinates.
- **Uniform Enforcement of the Law** If a police agency makes it clear that no group of citizens, no matter what their affiliation with the police department, is going to receive special treatment from the police department, the incentive for offering bribes and other forms of corruption will be minimized. This process starts with clear policies and procedures and must be backed up with discipline, when necessary.
- **Outside Review and Special Prosecutor** Heavily resisted by police leadership and police labor associations is any kind of outside review of their actions. However, both the Christopher Commission and the Knapp Commission are examples of outside reviews that brought about improvements in the agencies they investigated. Special prosecutors are recommended in serious cases to relieve the police and the government of any accusations of a whitewash.
- **Court Review and Oversight** Criminal prosecutions or civil liability suits deriving from police corruption cases can be very costly to a police agency. Such visible forms of oversight often result in adverse media coverage, civil liability awards, and higher insurance rates—all of which should encourage police agencies to control corruption.[37]

internal affairs investigations unit The police unit that ferrets out illegal and unethical activity engaged in by the police.

THINKING CRITICALLY

1. What do you think are the best ways for police officers to handle stress on the job?

2. What do you think are the best ways to reduce police corruption?

Professionalizing Law Enforcement

Many people would argue that policing in America has already reached professional status. Law enforcement is a valued service. Its agents make important decisions daily that substantially affect the lives of people and the quality of life in a community. The police officer's position is one of honor and trust. There are academy programs consisting of hundreds of hours of instruction, as well as law enforcement degree programs. Now there are even signs that law enforcement is attempting to police its own profession. Professional accreditation for police agencies is a rite of passage that is needed if law enforcement is to join the list of the most respected professions. Nevertheless, resistance to it and the other developments is still widespread.

Not everyone has the qualities to be a police officer. To allow into law enforcement those people with no desire to serve, low intelligence, a shady past, poor work habits, and no ability to communicate effectively is to court disaster for every department that does so—and for the entire profession.

Some police officers and their leaders resist 600 hours of initial training and do all they can to avoid continuing education and training. Real professionals seek advanced training.

Professionals in any field make mistakes, and a caring public should forgive most of them. In police work, there are incomplete interviews, evidence left at crime scenes, and bad reports written. In the long run, the consequences of such mistakes are generally insignificant as long as corrections are made. Mistakes can also be technological, such as the failure of a radar gun. No one should blame the police for technological mishaps that are not the result of negligence.

One kind of mistake, however, stands out more than any other: the condoning of racist and brutal tactics like the Los Angeles police officers' beating of Rodney King. The findings of the Christopher Commission confirmed that such tactics were generally condoned and even encouraged. The videotaped replay of that performance will be an embarrassment to professional policing for years to come. Police departments need to remove from the profession officers who would participate in or overlook such violence.

Many police officers go to work each day with a negative attitude, and some may take out their frustrations on the citizens they meet. Police officers need to treat their on-duty time as a professional performance and render the best service possible on any given day. If they treat the citizens they serve with respect and concern, officers will make great progress in improving the public's perception of law enforcement as a profession worthy of trust and admiration.

FYI Accreditation

By December 2008, 739 police agencies in the United States, Canada, Mexico, and Barbados were accredited or recognized (for smaller law enforcement agencies) by the Commission on Accreditation for Law Enforcement Agencies (CALEA).

Source: "CALEA, Commission on Accreditation for Law Enforcement Agencies," www.calea.org (personal communication).

✳ Summary

1. Describe the general attitude of the public toward the police.

   According to surveys, the American public is generally satisfied with the quality of the service the police provide. The level of confidence varies across racial and ethnic groups. As with most services, the public believes there is room for improvement.

2. Summarize the steps in an effective police officer selection process.

   Police applicants go through several different kinds of testing to become law enforcement officers. Steps in an effective police officer selection process include: recruitment, short application, detailed application, medical examination, physical ability test, written examination, background investigation, psychological testing, oral interview/oral board, academy training, and a probationary employment period.

3. Identify factors that affect the exercise of police discretion and methods of limiting discretion.

   Factors that affect the exercise of police discretion include the nature of the crime, departmental policies, the relationship between the victim and the offender, the amount of evidence, the preference of the victim, the demeanor of the suspect, the legitimacy of the victim, and the suspect's socioeconomic status. Methods of limiting police discretion are close supervision by a police agency's management, department directives and policies, U.S. Supreme Court decisions, and the threat of civil liability suits.

4. Describe two general ways that law enforcement agencies can reduce stress on the job.

   Two general ways that law enforcement agencies can reduce job stress for police officers are (1) to employ *stress management* strategies, such as discussing stressful events with colleagues and mental health professionals, regular exercise, relaxation techniques, healthy diet, religious support, enriched family support, prayer, meditation, and stress management classes that often involve spouses, and (2) to implement *organizational change,* such as allowing officers more discretion in determining work hours and shifts, flattening the organizational structure and giving officers more discretion in carrying out their responsibilities, job redesign that assigns unwanted or unnecessary tasks for a police officer to another position, and having excellent public safety equipment such as weaponry, vehicles, and body armor.

5. Explain the circumstances under which police officers may be justified in using deadly force.

   The use of deadly force by a police officer may be justifiable if (1) the arrest is for a felony; (2) the person effecting the arrest is authorized to act as a peace officer or is assisting a person whom he believes to be authorized to act as a peace officer; (3) the officer believes that the force employed creates no substantial risk of injury to innocent persons; (4) the officer believes that the crime for which the arrest is made involved conduct including the use or threatened use of deadly force; and (5) the officer believes there is substantial risk that the person to be arrested will cause death or serious bodily harm if his or her apprehension is delayed.

6. List some of the ways to control and reduce police corruption.

   Ways to control and reduce police corruption include selecting and maintaining officers with high moral standards, developing rigid departmental policies that cover the wide range of activities that corruption comprises, disciplining and prosecuting officers who are guilty of violating established policies and laws, utilizing a proactive internal affairs investigations unit, holding first-line supervisors responsible for the actions of their subordinates, employing outside review and special prosecutors, and emphasizing to officers the costs to police agencies of criminal prosecutions and civil liability suits.

✳ Review Questions

1. Explain how the three I's of police selection (intelligence, integrity, and interaction skills) relate to the success of a police officer.

2. What are some advantages of hiring college-educated police officers?

3. What are some arguments in favor of and opposing the reduction of police discretion?

4. Why do police generally not like to respond to domestic violence calls?

5. What is *racial profiling* in law enforcement, and what are some of the methods that have been prescribed to stop it?

6. What are some of the conditions that can lead to police job stress?

7. What is meant by *copicide?*

8. What is meant by *excessive force?*

9. What are some types of police misconduct?

✳ Key Terms

three I's of police
  selection 255
college academies 260
public safety officers 261
police cadet program 261

tech prep (technical
  preparation) 261
merit system 262
discretion 268
full enforcement 268

selective enforcement 269
racial profiling 271
job stress 273
copicide 273
excessive force 275

"grass eaters" 280
"meat eaters" 280
internal affairs
  investigations unit 281

✳ In the Field

1. **Neighborhood Survey** Conduct a survey about the police in your neighborhood. Use the same survey questions and categories as in Figures 7.1, 7.2, and 7.3. Try to get respondents from as many races, genders, and age groups as possible. Compare the results of your survey with the results in Figures 7.1, 7.2, and 7.3. Note any gender, race, or age differences in responses.

2. **Police Recruiting** Contact your local police department, and find out what it does to recruit police candidates. Does it run a police academy? Does it generally recruit officers from other jurisdictions? Compare your findings with those of others in the class and what you have learned from your textbook.

✳ On the Net

1. **Racial Profiling** Go to the website of the American Civil Liberties Union at www.aclu.org/RacialEquality/RacialEquality.cfm?ID=18163&c=133 and look at its report on "Driving While Black: Racial Profiling on Our Nation's Highways," by Professor David A. Harris from the University of Toledo College of Law. Read Professor Harris's report and his five recommendations for ending racial profiling. Which of the five recommendations do you agree with and why? Which do you disagree with and why? Discuss these findings in class and see if other students share your views.

2. **Job Qualifications** Go to the websites of four large police departments (New York City at www.ci.nyc.ny.us/html/ nypd/home.html; Los Angeles at www.lapdonline.org; Philadelphia at www.ppdonline.org; and Houston at www.houstontx.gov/police, and identify the major qualifications to be a police officer that are listed there. What qualifications are the same or similar among the agencies you examined? What qualifications are unique among those listed by the four agencies? Which employment qualifications are the most difficult to meet? Do you agree that all of the qualifications most difficult to meet are necessary? Would you add any qualifications? If so, what would they be? What would be the impact of your new qualifications on the recruitment and selection of police officers?

✳ Critical Thinking Exercises

POLICE ACADEMY

1. Recently, "Police Corps," a new military-style police academy, has opened in cities such as Jacksonville and Tampa, Florida. The cadets of the mentally exhausting 6-month program eat, sleep, and live together in rooms near the academy with no televisions and with the constant threat of surprise inspections. Their days involve marching in military formation with a platoon leader barking out cadences, weight lifting, and classes on self-defense as well as law and criminal procedure. Afternoons are spent at the firing range, where they train with pistols, MP-5 submachine guns, and AR-15 assault rifles. After ending their days at 10 P.M. with little or no time for themselves to relax or study, they are occasionally awakened at 2 A.M. as instructors push them for practice in high-speed driving and patrolling tactics. At some point in the course, the cadets are put through 24 to 72 hours of sleep deprivation to teach them the effects of stress and lack of sleep on their bodies. The punishment for not following orders correctly is pushups.

   Supporters of the new academy maintain that the Navy SEAL–type training will help officers become more disciplined and community-oriented. Critics contend that the program is too extreme and isn't necessary for a community police force, that it "isn't needed in our society unless we're in a warfare environment."

   a. What are the pros and cons of this new military-style police academy training?
   b. What effects, if any, are such training methods likely to have on police recruitment?
   c. Is such training needed in our society?

STRESS

2. You are the commander of the operations division of a medium-sized police department, in charge of the patrol, criminal investigation, and traffic sections.
   a. What would you do if several officers from each of the sections came to you and said that they believed that job stress was hindering officer performance and endangering the health of several officers in each of the units?
   b. How would you go about validating their claims of job stress in the work environment?
   c. If it were determined that stressors such as too frequent shift changes, poor communication among the various ranks, and a lack of sufficient safety equipment were present, what would be your plan to improve working conditions and reduce job stress?
   d. Provide a step-by-step summary of what you would do.

To access more information and resources, including study questions, chapter summaries, and links, go to www.mhhe.com/bohm6e.

PART THREE

The Courts

Chapter 8
The Administration of Justice

Chapter 9
Sentencing, Appeals, and the Death Penalty

The Administration of Justice

Chapter Outline

Chapter Objectives

After completing this chapter, you should be able to:

1. Identify the type of court structure in the United States, and describe its various components.

2. Summarize the purposes of courts.

3. Identify the most powerful actors in the administration of justice, and explain what makes them so powerful.

4. Summarize the types of attorneys available to a person charged with a crime.

5. Describe the responsibilities of a judge.

6. Describe the purposes of an initial appearance.

7. Explain what bail is, and describe the different methods of pretrial release.

8. Define grand jury, and explain its purposes.

9. Describe the purposes of the arraignment and the plea options of defendants.

10. Describe the interests served and not served by plea bargaining.

11. List and define the stages in a criminal trial.

CRIME STORY

On April 23, 2008, a federal prosecutor announced that he would try for the third time to convict six suspected terrorists accused of plotting to blow up Chicago's Sears Tower and federal buildings in Miami. On December 13, 2007, after deliberating nine days, a Miami jury in the first trial acquitted one of the defendants of all charges and deadlocked on the charges brought against the other six. In the second trail, the jury deadlocked on April 16, 2008, after 13 days of deliberations. Arguing for a third trial, the prosecutor reminded the U.S. District judge of taped conversations obtained by the

continued

FBI in which the leader of the "Liberty City Seven," Narseal Batiste, made threatening comments about U.S. citizens. Batiste, referring to Americans, said he wanted "to kill all the devils we can" and compared the U.S. government to "the Kingdom of Satan."

The "Liberty City Seven" were arrested on June 23, 2006, at a warehouse in Miami's impoverished Liberty City neighborhood. FBI informants, posing as al-Qaeda operatives, obtained the warehouse for the group and had it wired for video and sound. The informants persuaded the men to pledge allegiance to the terrorist organization and Osama bin Laden and offered them $50,000 to participate in a terror plot. During both of the previous trials, Batiste testified that he and his followers agreed to the informants' proposal only because they believed they could con them out of the money. The government maintained that the defendants planned to use the money to finance the plot. Batiste and one of his codefendants have remained in jail since their arrests; the other four defendants were released on bail after the second mistrial. The accused men face up to 70 years in prison if convicted on all four charges, including conspiracy to support al-Qaeda and to levy war against the United States.

Although it is not unusual for prosecutors to retry a case once if a jury deadlocks, a second retrial is very rare and is usually reserved for murder cases. A third retrial on terrorism-related charges is unprecedented and raises serious questions about whether prosecutors are more concerned with saving face than seeking justice. In the first two trials, prosecutors presented hundreds of video and audio recordings, including the oath-taking ceremony, but they could not show that the men had any weapons, explosives, or ammunition on them at the time of their arrest. At the time of the indictment, a Justice Department official said the terrorist plot was more "aspirational than operational."

Undeterred, on May 12, 2009, federal prosecutors on their third attempt successfully convicted five of the remaining six "Liberty City Seven," including Batiste. The sixth defendant, who had spent two years incarcerated, was acquitted of all charges. Sentencing for the other five was scheduled for July 27, 2009. Defense attorneys said they would appeal, arguing that their clients were harmless dupes who were entrapped by government informants. The case has cost millions of dollars.

Chapter 8 examines the officials and processes involved with the adjudication of criminal cases in American courts. The "Liberty City Seven" case raises several important questions about how the United States wages its war on terrorism. Law enforcement officers and prosecutors have a difficult and thankless task when they try to preempt terrorist attacks. If they learn of possible plots and fail to stop them, they will be held accountable for failing to protect the public. However, when they attempt to disrupt what they believe to be a plot in the making, they risk charging people who may have expressed anti-American feelings but who have committed no crimes. Should the remaining members of the "Liberty City Seven" have been retried for a third time? Was a third retrial a good use of scarce prosecutorial and court resources? Were the prosecutors in this case more concerned with saving face than seeking justice? The more prosecutors insist on retrials when they do not like the previous trials' outcomes, the more the legitimacy of the justice system is called into question. Should the convictions in this case cause concern?

dual court system The court system in the United States, consisting of one system of state and local courts and another system of federal courts.

jurisdiction The authority of a court to hear and decide cases.

original jurisdiction The authority of a court to hear a case when it is first brought to court.

appellate jurisdiction The power of a court to review a case for errors of law.

general jurisdiction The power of a court to hear any type of case.

special jurisdiction The power of a court to hear only certain kinds of cases.

subject matter jurisdiction The power of a court to hear a particular type of case.

personal jurisdiction A court's authority over the parties to a lawsuit.

The American Court Structure

The United States has a **dual court system**—a separate judicial system for each of the states and a separate federal system. Figure 8.1 displays this dual court system and routes of appeal from the various courts. The only place where the two systems connect is in the U.S. Supreme Court.

The authority of a court to hear and decide cases is called the court's **jurisdiction.** It is set by law and is limited by territory and type of case. A court of **original jurisdiction** has the authority to hear a case when it is first brought to court. Courts having the power to review a case for errors of law are courts of **appellate jurisdiction.** Courts having the power to hear any type of case are said to exercise **general jurisdiction.** Those with the power to hear only certain types of cases have **special jurisdiction. Subject matter jurisdiction** is the court's power to hear a particular type of case. **Personal jurisdiction** is the court's authority over the parties to a lawsuit.

THE FEDERAL COURTS

The authority for the federal court system is the U.S. Constitution, Article III, Section 1, which states, "The judicial Power of the United States, shall be vested in one Supreme Court, and in such inferior courts as the Congress may

Figure 8.1

Dual Court System of the United States

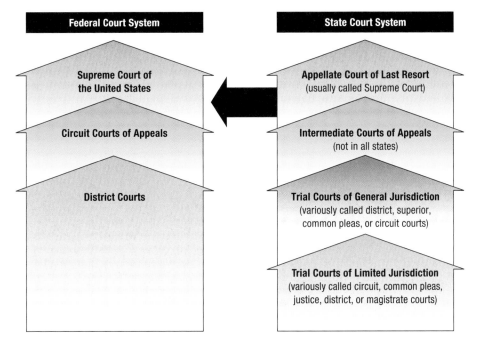

from time to time ordain and establish." The federal court system includes the Supreme Court, the federal courts of appeals, and the federal district courts. The federal court system is shown in Figure 8.2.

U.S. District Courts Forming the base of the federal court structure are the U.S. district courts. These are courts of original jurisdiction, or courts where most violations of federal criminal and civil law are first adjudicated. Today, there are 94 district courts divided into 13 circuits, with at least one federal district court in each state, one each in the District of Columbia and the commonwealths of Puerto Rico and the Northern Mariana Islands, and one each in the U.S. territories of the Virgin Islands and Guam. In some states, the courts are divided into districts geographically. New York, for example, has northern, eastern, southern, and western district courts.

Two factors determine the jurisdiction of federal district courts: the subject matter of a case and the parties to a case. Federal district courts have subject matter jurisdiction over cases that involve federal laws, treaties with foreign nations, or interpretations of the Constitution. Cases involving admiralty or maritime law—the law of the sea, including ships, their crews, and disputes over actions and rights at sea—also come under federal district court jurisdiction.

Federal district courts have personal jurisdiction in cases if certain parties or persons are involved. These include (1) ambassadors and other representatives of foreign governments, (2) two or more state governments, (3) the U.S. government or one of its offices or agencies, (4) citizens of different states, (5) a state and a citizen of a different state, (6) citizens of the same state claiming lands under grants of different states, and (7) a state or its citizens and a foreign country or its citizens.

U.S. district courts are presided over by district court judges who are appointed by the President, are confirmed by the Senate, and, except for the territorial judges who serve 10-year terms, serve for life (if they choose, do not resign, or are not impeached and convicted by Congress). In 2008, there were 667 authorized federal district judgeships (including 11 temporary judgeships). Several district courts,

FYI The Judicial Conference of the United States

The Judicial Conference of the United States governs the federal court system. The conference is composed of 27 federal judges and is presided over by the Chief Justice of the U.S. Supreme Court. The conference meets twice a year to consider policies affecting the federal courts, to make recommendations to Congress on legislation affecting the judicial system, to propose amendments to the federal rules of practice and procedure, and to address administrative problems of the courts.

Sources: Administrative Office of the U.S. Courts, Federal Judiciary website at www.uscourts.gov/judconf.html.

Figure 8.2

The Federal Court Structure

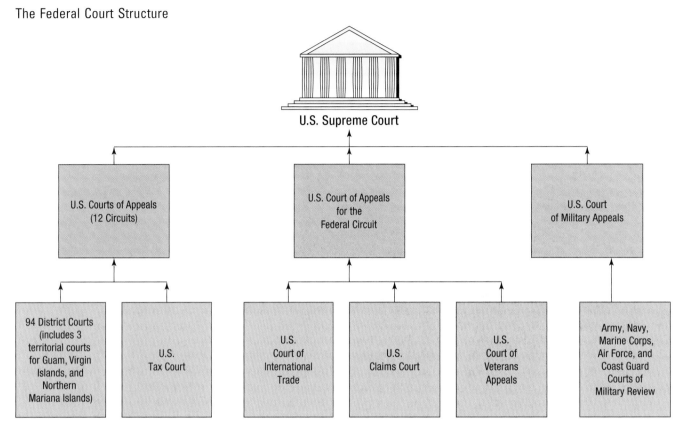

such as the district court of North Dakota had only two judges; the southern-district court of New York in New York City had the most with 28.[1] The annual salary of a U.S. district court judge is $169,300 (as of November 30, 2008).[2]

Usually a single federal judge presides over a trial, and trial by jury is allowed if requested by a defendant. Some complex civil cases are heard by a special panel of three judges. The bulk of the workload of the U.S. district courts is devoted to civil cases, the number of which has risen dramatically in recent years, to 267,257 in 2008.[3] Federal criminal cases involve such crimes as bank robbery, counterfeiting, mail fraud, kidnapping, and civil rights abuses. Until 1980, the number of criminal cases in federal district courts remained relatively stable at about 30,000 a year. However, as a result of the federal government's war on drugs and an increase in illegal immigration cases, the number of criminal cases had more than doubled to 70,896 by the end of 2008. The 70,896 criminal cases represented a 4% increase from 2007. About 22% of the criminal cases filed in U.S district courts in 2008 were drug cases and about 30% were immigration cases.[4]

To ease the caseload of U.S. district court judges, Congress created the judicial office of federal magistrate in 1968. The title changed to magistrate judge in 1990. As their caseloads require and as funding from Congress permits, district judges may appoint magistrate judges to part-time or full-time positions. Magistrate judges handle civil consent cases, misdemeanor trials, preliminary hearings, pretrial motions and motion hearings, and conferences in felony cases.[5] The behavior of most United States judges is governed by a code of conduct, presented in Figure 8.3.

Circuit Courts of Appeals A person or group that loses a case in district court may appeal to a federal circuit court of appeals or, in some instances, directly to the Supreme Court. Congress created the U.S. circuit courts of appeals in 1891 to reduce the case burden of the Supreme Court. The U.S. circuit courts of

Figure 8.3

Code of Conduct for United States Judges

Canon 1	A Judge Should Uphold the Integrity and Independence of the Judiciary
Canon 2	A Judge Should Avoid Impropriety and the Appearance of Impropriety in All Activities
Canon 3	A Judge Should Perform the Duties of the Office Impartially and Diligently
Canon 4	A Judge May Engage in Extra-Judicial Activities to Improve the Law, the Legal System, and the Administration of Justice
Canon 5	A Judge Should Regulate Extra-Judicial Activities to Minimize the Risk of Conflict with Judicial Duties
Canon 6	A Judge Should Regularly File Reports of Compensation Received for Law-Related and Extra-Judicial Activities
Canon 7	A Judge Should Refrain from Political Activity

The Code of Conduct for United States Judges was initially adopted by the Judicial Conference on April 5, 1973, and was known as the "Code of Judicial Conduct for United States Judges." At its March 1987 session, the Judicial Conference deleted the word "Judicial" from the name of the Code. Substantial revisions to the Code were adopted by the Judicial Conference at its September 1992 session. This Code applies to United States Circuit Judges, District Judges, Court of International Trade Judges, Court of Federal Claims Judges, Bankruptcy Judges, and Magistrate Judges. Certain provisions of this Code apply to special masters and commissioners. In addition, the Tax Court, Court of Appeals for Veterans Claims, and Court of Appeals for the Armed Forces have adopted this Code. Persons to whom the Code applies must arrange their affairs as soon as reasonably possible to comply with the Code and should do so in any event within one year of appointment.

Source: Administrative Office of the U.S. Courts, Federal Judiciary website, "Judges and Judgeships" at www.uscourts .gov/guide/vol2/ch1.html.

appeals have only appellate jurisdiction and review a case for errors of law, not of fact. Most appeals arise from the decisions of district courts, the U.S. Tax Court, and various territorial courts (see Figure 8.2). Federal courts of appeals also hear appeals of the rulings of regulatory agencies, such as the Federal Trade Commission. An appeal to the U.S. circuit court of appeals is a matter of right— the court cannot refuse to hear the case. However, unless appealed to the Supreme

The 9th U.S. Circuit Court of Appeals in San Francisco, California (pictured here), has the most judges (28) of all the circuit courts of appeals. *What determines how many judges are selected to serve on a U.S. circuit court of appeals?*

Figure 8.4

The 13 U.S. Circuits

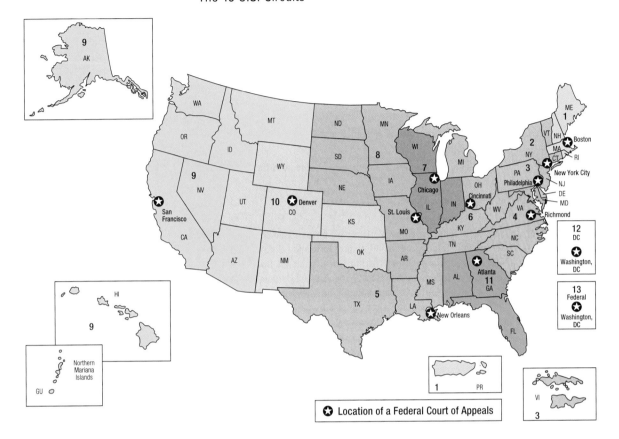

Location of a Federal Court of Appeals

Court, decisions of the courts of appeals are final. U.S. courts of appeals heard 61,104 cases in 2008, an increase of about 5% from 2007. About 22% of those cases were criminal, and another 28% were prisoner cases.[6]

There are currently 13 U.S. circuit courts of appeals (see Figure 8.4). Twelve of them have jurisdiction over cases from particular geographic areas. The Court of Appeals for the Federal Circuit, created in 1982, has national jurisdiction over specific types of cases, such as appeals from the U.S. Court of International Trade.[7] Like U.S. district judges, federal appellate judges are nominated by the President, are confirmed by the Senate, and may serve for life. Currently, 179 judges serve on the 13 U.S. circuit courts (167 on the 12 regional courts and 12 on the federal circuit).[8] The yearly salary of a U.S. circuit court of appeals judge is $179,500 (as of November 30, 2008).[9] The number of judges assigned to each court of appeals ranges from 6 (the First Circuit) to 28 (the Ninth Circuit) and, normally, 3 judges sit as a panel.[10] Jury trials are not allowed in these courts. In highly controversial cases, all the judges in a circuit may sit together and hear a case. Those *en banc* hearings are rare; there probably are no more than 100 of them in all circuits in 1 year.

The U.S. Supreme Court The U.S. Supreme Court is the court of last resort in all questions of federal law (see Figure 8.2). It has the final word in any case involving the Constitution, acts of Congress, and treaties with other nations. Under the Supreme Court's appellate jurisdiction, the Court hears cases appealed from federal courts of appeals, or it may hear appeals from federal district courts in certain circumstances in which an act of Congress has been held unconstitutional.

FYI Circuit Courts

The circuit courts are so named because early in the nation's history, federal judges traveled by horseback to each of the courts in a specified region, or "circuit," in a particular sequence. In short, they rode the circuit.

Source: Howard Ball, "The Federal Court System," in R. J. Janosik (ed.), *Encyclopedia of the American Judicial System: Studies of the Principal Institutions and Processes of Law* (New York: Charles Scribner's Sons, 1987), p. 556.

The Supreme Court may also hear cases that are appealed from the high court of a state, if claims under federal law or the Constitution are involved. In such cases, however, the Court has the authority to rule only on the federal issue involved, not on any issues of state law. For example, suppose a state tries a person charged with violating a state law. During the trial, the accused claims that the police violated Fourth Amendment rights with an illegal search at the time of the arrest. The defendant may appeal to the Supreme Court on the constitutional issue only. The Supreme Court generally has no jurisdiction to rule on the state issue (whether the accused actually violated state law). The Court would decide only whether Fourth Amendment rights were violated. Decisions of the Supreme Court are binding on all lower courts.

The Supreme Court is composed of a chief justice, officially known as the Chief Justice of the United States, and eight associate justices. They are appointed for life by the President with the consent of the Senate and, like other federal judges, can be removed from office against their will only by "impeachment for, and Conviction of, Treason, Bribery, or other high Crimes and Misdemeanors." The Chief Justice, who is specifically nominated by the President for the position, presides over the Court's public sessions and private conferences, assigns justices to write opinions (when the Chief Justice has voted with the majority), and supervises the entire federal judiciary. (When the Chief Justice has voted with the minority, the Associate Justice who has the greatest seniority, that is, has been on the Court the longest, assigns who writes the opinion.) The salary of the Chief Justice is $217,400; the salaries of the Associate Justices are $208,100 (as of November 30, 2008).[11]

For a case to be heard by the Supreme Court, at least four of the nine justices must vote to hear the case (the "rule of four"). When the required number of votes has been achieved, the Court issues a **writ of *certiorari*** to the lower court whose decision is being appealed, ordering it to send the records of the case forward for review. The Court is limited by law and custom in the types of cases for which it issues writs of *certiorari*. The Court will issue a "writ" only if the defendant in the case has exhausted all other avenues of appeal and the case involves a substantial federal question as defined by the appellate court. A substantial federal question, as noted, is one in which there is an alleged violation of either the U.S. Constitution or federal law.

When the Supreme Court decides a case it has accepted on appeal, it can take one of these actions:

1. Affirm the verdict or decision of the lower court and "let it stand."
2. Modify the verdict or decision of the lower court, without totally reversing it.
3. Reverse the verdict or decision of the lower court, requiring no further court action.
4. Reverse the verdict or decision of the lower court and remand the case to the court of original jurisdiction, for either retrial or resentencing.

In some cases, the Supreme Court has ordered trial courts to resentence defendants whose original sentences violated the Eighth Amendment prohibition against cruel and unusual punishment. In other cases, prison authorities have been ordered to remedy unconstitutional conditions of imprisonment.

Appeals to the Supreme Court are heard at the discretion of the Court, in contrast to appeals to the U.S. circuit courts, which review cases as a matter of right. In 2007, for example, the Supreme Court heard only 75 of the 8,241 cases filed for review and disposed of 72 of the cases, 67 with signed opinions.[12] In other words, in 2007, the Court opted not to review more than 99% of the appealed cases—a figure typical of Court practice. Generally, the Supreme

CJ Online

Supreme Court Justices

The Supreme Court Justices of the United States have varied biographical, legal, and educational backgrounds. Learn more about the current justices by going to the following website: www.oyez.org/oyez/portlet/justices. *What do the justices have in common? How do their backgrounds differ?*

writ of *certiorari* A written order, from the U.S. Supreme Court to a lower court whose decision is being appealed, to send the records of the case forward for review.

FYI

Court Fees

The fee for filing an appeal with the U.S. Supreme Court is $300. Fees are waived for indigent defendants. Approximately 90% of the criminal proceedings appealed to the Supreme Court involve indigent defendants. The fees do not include the costs of printing various documents required under other court rules.

Source: Clerk of the Supreme Court; 28 U.S.C. § 1911.

U.S. Supreme Court Justices. (L-R): Associate Justices Anthony Kennedy, Stephen Breyer, John Paul Stevens, Clarence Thomas, Chief Justice John Roberts, Jr., Associate Justices Ruth Bader Ginsburg, Antonin Scalia, Samuel Alito, Jr., David Souter. (On August 8, 2009, Judge Sonia Sotomayor was officially sworn in as the newest Supreme Court Justice, replacing retired Justice David Souter.)

writ of *habeas corpus* An order from a court to an officer of the law to produce a prisoner in court to determine if the prisoner is being legally detained or imprisoned.

Court's refusal to hear a case ends the process of direct appeal. In certain circumstances, an imprisoned defendant whose appeal has been denied may still try to have the Supreme Court review his or her case on constitutional grounds by filing a writ of *habeas corpus*. A **writ of *habeas corpus*,** which is guaranteed by Article I, Section 9, of the Constitution, the Federal Habeas Corpus Act, and state *habeas corpus* laws, is a court order directing a law officer to produce a prisoner in court to determine if the prisoner is being legally detained or imprisoned. The *habeas corpus* proceeding does not test whether the prisoner is guilty or innocent.

The Supreme Court also has original jurisdiction. However, Article III, Section 2.2, of the Constitution limits the Court's original jurisdiction to two types of cases: (1) cases involving representatives of foreign governments; and (2) certain cases in which a state is a party. Many cases have involved two states and the federal government. When Maryland and Virginia argued over oyster fishing rights, and when a dispute broke out between California and Arizona over the control of water from the Colorado River, the Supreme Court had original jurisdiction in the matters. Original jurisdiction cases are a very small part of the Court's yearly workload. Most of the cases the Court decides fall under its appellate jurisdiction.

THE STATE COURTS

The state courts have general power to decide nearly every type of case, subject only to the limitations of the U.S. Constitution, their own state constitutions, and state law. State and local courts are the courts with which citizens most often have contact. These courts handle most criminal matters and the majority of day-to-day legal matters. The laws of each state determine the organization, function, and even the names of its courts. Thus, no two state court systems are exactly alike. For discussion purposes, it is useful to distinguish four levels of state courts: trial courts of limited jurisdiction, trial courts of general jurisdiction, intermediate appellate courts, and state courts of last resort.[13]

Trial Courts of Limited Jurisdiction At the base of the state court structure (see Figure 8.1) are the approximately 13,500 trial courts of limited jurisdiction, sometimes referred to generally as "inferior trial courts" or simply as "lower courts." Depending on the jurisdiction, those courts are called city courts, municipal courts, county courts, circuit courts, courts of common pleas, justice-of-the-peace courts, district courts, or magistrate courts. (Technically, most of the lower courts are not really part of the state judicial structure because they are the creation of, and funded by, either city or county governments.) In several states, judges of the lower courts are not required to have any formal legal training.

The lower courts typically deal with minor cases, such as ordinance and traffic violations, some misdemeanors, and—in many jurisdictions—civil cases involving less than $1,000. For those types of offenses, the lower courts in many states are allowed to conduct **summary** or **bench trials,** or trials without a jury. Typically, the greatest penalty that can be imposed is a fine of $1,000 and a maximum of 12 months in jail. Unlike trial courts of general jurisdiction, the lower courts are not courts of record, where detailed transcripts of the proceedings are made. Because they are not courts of record, an appeal from such a lower court requires a **trial *de novo,*** in which the entire case must be reheard by a trial court of general jurisdiction.

In addition to handling minor cases, the lower courts in most states hear the formal charges against persons accused of felonies, set bail, appoint counsel for indigent defendants, and conduct preliminary hearings for crimes that must be adjudicated at a higher level. The legal proceedings in these courts are typically less formal, and many cases are resolved without defense attorneys. Lower courts process and quickly dispose of large numbers of cases, approximately 90 million a year.

Trial Courts of General Jurisdiction Variously called district courts, superior courts, and circuit courts, depending on the jurisdiction, the more than 3,000 trial courts of general jurisdiction have the authority to try all civil and criminal cases and to hear appeals from lower courts. They are courts of record (formal transcripts of the proceedings are made), and judges and lawyers in those courts have formal legal training. Trial courts of general jurisdiction are funded by the state.

Augmenting trial courts of general jurisdiction are specialty courts that have been created during the past two decades to deal with increases in certain types of crimes or chronic social problems.[14] "Drug courts" were the first of these new "problem-solving" courts, the first of which was established in Dade County (Miami), Florida, in 1989. Within a decade, all but 10 states had at least one such court. Drug courts were created to (1) help handle the dramatic increase in drug cases resulting from the War on Drugs that have been overwhelming the trial courts of general jurisdiction, and (2) use the court's authority to reduce crime by changing defendants' drug-using behavior. In exchange for the possibility of dismissed charges or reduced sentences, defendants accept diversion to drug treatment programs during the judicial process. Drug court judges preside over drug court proceedings, monitor the progress of defendants by means of frequent status hearings, and prescribe sanctions and rewards as appropriate, in collaboration with prosecutors, defense attorneys, treatment providers, and others.

Drug courts are popular. Research shows that active drug court participants, especially those who graduate from the program, are less likely to be rearrested than those in comparison groups; that recidivism reductions are maintained for substantial amounts of time after participants complete the drug court program; and that there is a positive cost-benefit ratio for drug court participants. In 1999, drug courts were officially endorsed by the National

summary or **bench trials** Trials without a jury.

trial *de novo* A trial in which an entire case is reheard by a trial court of general jurisdiction because there is an appeal and there is no written transcript of the earlier proceeding.

 **CJ Online**

Court TV

Over the past several years, there has been a growing interest in the inner workings of the American court system. This is evident in the popularity of the television network Court TV (now truTV). Go to the truTV website at www.trutv.com. Review the list of featured cases and the programming schedule for the network. *Why do you think that shows on truTV are so popular?*

Noelle Bush, daughter of former Florida Governor Jeb Bush, is shown with her brother George P. Bush in Orange County, Florida drug court during her status hearing. Noelle was charged with contempt of court and spent 43 hours in jail for violating her court-ordered drug treatment plan. She was ordered to continue in the drug program. *Are drug courts a good idea? Why or why not?*

District Attorney's Association and the National Sheriff's Association. At the beginning of 2008, there were 2,147 drug courts—an increase of 32% since 2004 and 223% since 2000. They were located in all 50 states, the District of Columbia, Guam, Northern Mariana Islands, Puerto Rico, the Virgin Islands, and a number of Native American Tribal Courts. California had the most drug courts (217), followed by New York (172) and Missouri (124). More than 70,000 drug court clients are served at any given time throughout the United States and its territories.

Drug courts are so popular and the need for them is perceived as so great that more specialized drug courts have been established. The first of these "sub-specialty" drug courts was a women's drug court, which opened in Kalamazoo, Michigan, in 1992. That was followed in 1995 by the first juvenile drug court in Visalia, California, and the first family drug court in Reno, Nevada. Juvenile drug courts operate within juvenile courts and handle delinquency cases or status offenders who have alcohol and/or drug problems. Family drug courts deal with selected abuse, neglect, and dependency cases where parental substance abuse is a primary factor. Other specialized drug courts include adult drug courts (for nonviolent substance abusing adult offenders), campus drug courts (for students with substance-abuse-related disciplinary cases that would otherwise result in expulsion from college), DWI (driving while intoxicated) drug courts (for alcohol/drug dependent offenders arrested for DWI), integrated-treatment courts (for juveniles and their families/guardians who need services to help juveniles make better choices about their lives and drug and alcohol abuse), reentry drug courts (for drug-involved offenders being released from local or state correctional facilities), and "tribal healing to wellness" drug courts (for Native American alcohol and/or drug-related offenders living in Native communities).

Drug courts have also provided the general model for the 1,057 (as of the start of 2008) other, nondrug specialty courts. Rhode Island led the way with 143 of these other problem-solving courts; California was next with 139; and Florida was third with 112. These other problem-solving courts include child-support courts (for defendants with child-support issues), collections courts (for offenders, particularly probationers, who are having problems paying or are unwilling to pay court costs and restitution),[15] community courts (for low-level, nonviolent offenders who are required, as punishment for their crimes, to help in the restoring of distressed neighborhoods by cleaning streets and removing graffiti),[16] domestic-violence courts (for defendants facing domestic-violence charges and victims of domestic violence who need help), environmental courts (for defendants charged with housing, community health, solid waste, fire, building and zoning violations), gambling courts (for defendants suffering from a pathological or compulsive gambling disorder), gun courts (for defendants charged with illegal firearm possession), homeless courts (for homeless individuals with records of misdemeanor offenses, who, because of the records, are ineligible for government aid and, in some jurisdictions, such things as driver's licenses), mental-health courts (for mentally ill or developmentally disabled individuals who have been charged with nonviolent misdemeanors and are in need of treatment),[17] and truancy courts (for children trying to overcome the underlying causes of truancy). Teen courts (also called peer courts or youth courts; youths who commit minor offenses receive consequences for their behavior from a jury of their peers) are not included in the 1,057 total of other, nondrug specialty courts because a majority of teen courts do not operate under the judicial branch, All of these specialty courts share three common characteristics: (1) they focus on one type of case; (2) court personnel receive specialized training for the particular type of case; and (3) judges closely monitor compliance with court dispositions. Figure 8.5 presents a timeline of drug courts and other problem-solving courts in the United States.

Intermediate Appellate Courts In some of the geographically smaller and less-populous states, there is only one appellate court, the state court of last resort, usually called the state supreme court. Many states, however, have created intermediate appellate courts to reduce the overwhelming case burden of the state supreme court. As of November 19, 2008, 40 states had intermediate courts of appeal.[18]

The intermediate appellate courts have no trial jurisdiction. They hear only appeals in both civil and criminal cases from the trial courts of general jurisdiction. An appeals court is charged with reviewing a case for errors of law and ensuring that legal procedures were followed. The decision rendered by the appeals court is based on a review of the trial court's official transcript and any other legally relevant information that may be submitted. Brief oral arguments by the attorneys for both sides are also allowed.

Like their federal counterparts, the intermediate appellate courts cannot refuse to hear any legally appealed case. Intermediate appellate courts range in size from 3 to 105 judges, although the states with the largest number of intermediate appellate judges (California, Florida, Texas, and New York) are divided into regional district courts. The largest intermediate appellate court with statewide jurisdiction is New Jersey, which has 32 judges.[19] Normally, three judges sit as a panel to decide cases.

State Courts of Last Resort In most states, the state court of last resort is referred to as the state supreme court, although, as noted above, some states use different names. In Massachusetts and Maine, for example, the state court of last resort is called the supreme judicial court; in Maryland and New York, it is called the court of appeals. Oklahoma and Texas have two courts of last resort: the court of criminal appeals (for criminal appeals) and the supreme court (for civil cases). The court of last resort in 13 states or the chief justice of the court of last resort in 36 states is the designated head of a state's judicial branch. In one state, Utah, the Judicial Council is the designated head of the judicial branch.

As previously noted, the primary responsibility of state courts of last resort is to hear appeals from either trial courts of general jurisdiction (in those states without intermediate appellate courts) or intermediate appellate courts. In states with intermediate courts of appeal, the state court of last resort, like the U.S. Supreme Court, has discretion in which cases it will hear. And, like the U.S. Supreme Court, most state courts of last resort have original jurisdiction over a few types of cases.

Depending on the state, the number of judges that serve on the state court of last resort ranges from five to nine, though more than half the states have seven.[20] However, unlike judges of intermediate courts of appeal, judges of the state court of last resort are not divided into panels to hear cases. Instead, all of the judges hear all of the cases; that is, they *sit en banc*. State courts of last resort have the final word on matters involving interpretation of state law. Although defendants dissatisfied with a verdict rendered in a state court of last resort may appeal the decision to the Supreme Court, the Supreme Court will hear the appeal only if it involves an alleged violation of the Constitution or federal law. In deciding cases, most state courts of last resort follow procedures similar to those employed by the Supreme Court.

Figure 8.5

Timeline of Drug Courts and Other Problem-Solving Courts in the United States

Timeline of Drug Courts and Other Problem-Solving Courts in the United States

1989
- Height of crack cocaine epidemic in the U.S.
- First drug court opens in Miami, Florida

1990
- Spending on corrections exceeds $26 billion nationally

1991
- 5 drug courts in existence
- Drug offenses account for 31% of all convictions in state courts
- State prison costs for low-level drug offenders exceed $1.2 billion annually

1992
- 10 drug courts in existence
- One-third of women inmates in state prisons are drug offenders
- First women's drug court opens in Kalamazoo, Michigan

1993
- 19 drug courts in existence
- Drug offenders account for 60% of federal prisoners
- First community court opens in Brooklyn, New York

1994
- 44 drug courts in existence
- U.S. total incarceration figure tops 1 million
- Congress passes Violent Crime Control and Law Enforcement Act (the Crime Bill)
- National Association of Drug Court Professionals (NADCP) founded

1995
- 75 drug courts in existence
- Drug Courts Program Office (DCPO) established in U.S. Department of Justice
- 2 out of 3 police chiefs favor court-supervised treatment over prison for drug abusers
- NADCP holds first national drug court training conference in Las Vegas, Nevada
- First State Drug Court Association incorporated in California
- First juvenile drug court opens in Visalia, California
- First family drug court opens in Reno, Nevada

1996
- 139 drug courts in existence
- 5.7 million people in the U.S. are under criminal justice supervision
- Congress of State Drug Courts of NADCP holds its first meeting
- NADCP Mentor Drug Court established
- First DWI court opens in Dona Ana, New Mexico
- First felony domestic violence court opens in Brooklyn, New York

1997
- 230 drug courts in existence
- NADCP, DCPO, and the Bureau of Justice Assistance (BJA) release *Defining Drug Courts: The Key Components*
- First tribal healing to wellness court opens in Fort Hall, Idaho
- First mental health court opens in Broward County, Florida

1998
- 347 drug courts in existence
- National Drug Court Institute (NDCI) founded
- Federal funding for drug courts reaches $40 million for FY 1999

1999
- 472 drug courts in existence
- U.S. total incarceration figure tops 2 million
- 10th anniversary of the first drug court
- National District Attorneys Association passes resolution in support of drug courts
- National Sheriffs' Association passes resolution in support of drug courts

2000
- 665 drug courts in existence
- First Juvenile and Family Drug Court Training Conference held in Phoenix, Arizona
- American Bar Association releases Proposed Standard 2.77 - Procedures in Drug Treatment Courts
- Conference of Chief Justices/Conference of State Court Administrators passes resolution in support of problem-solving courts (CCJ/COSCA)

2001
- 847 drug courts in existence
- NADCP and National Council of Juvenile and Family Court Judges release *Best Strategies for Juvenile Drug Courts*
- First campus drug court opens at Colorado State University
- DCPO merges into BJA

2002
- 1,048 drug courts in existence
- 1,667 problem-solving courts in existence
- The National Institute of Justice reports drug court recidivism rates are as low as 16.4% nationwide one year after graduation

2003
- 1,183 drug courts in existence
- 2,558 problem-solving courts in existence
- NADCP holds 10th Annual Drug Court Training Conference
- CCJ/COSCA reaffirms support for problem-solving courts by passing a second joint resolution

2004
- 1,621 drug courts in existence
- 23% of adult drug courts accept impaired driving population, a 165% increase from 2004
- 33 U.S. states report an increase in drug court clients whose primary drug of choice is methamphetamine

2005
- 1,756 drug courts in existence
- U.S. incarcerated population reaches 2.2 million
- National study finds that parents in Family Dependency Treatment Courts were significantly more likely to be reunified with their children than with their comparison group parents

2006
- 1,926 drug courts in existence
- 7.2 million people in the U.S. are under criminal justice supervision

2007
- 2,147 drug courts in existence
- 3,204 problem-solving courts in existence
- National Center for DWI Courts (NCDC) founded

Source: C. West Huddleston, III, Douglas B. Marlowe, and Rachel Casebolt, *Painting the Current Picture: A National Report Card on Drug Courts and Other Problem-Solving Court Programs in the United States*, Vol. III, Number 1, Alexandria, VA: National Drug Court Institute (May 2008), p. 1 at www.ndci.org/sites/default/files/ndci/PCPII1_web%5D.pdf

THINKING CRITICALLY

1. What are some of the benefits of a dual court system?

2. Why is it difficult for a case to make it all the way to the Supreme Court? Should it be that difficult? Why or why not?

Purposes of Courts

Ted Rubin, former juvenile court judge and noted expert on juvenile justice, court, and rehabilitation issues, outlines ten purposes of courts.[21] The first is to "do justice." However, whether justice is done usually depends on the interests and viewpoints of the parties involved in a dispute. Typically, the "winning" party believes that justice has been done, while the "loser" thinks otherwise.

A second purpose of courts is "to appear to do justice." Even when a decision rendered by a court seems unjust to some people, it is still important that the court appear to "do justice." The appearance of justice is accomplished primarily by providing due process of law. **Due process of law,** as noted in Chapter 4, refers to the procedures followed by courts to ensure that a defendant's constitutional rights are not violated.

A third purpose of courts is "to provide a forum where disputes between people can be resolved justly and peacefully." Until the creation of courts of law, disputes were often settled violently, through blood feuds and other acts of revenge. Aggrieved parties would gather their extended families and friends and make war against the families and friends of the person or persons who had presumably violated their rights. Sometimes those feuds would span generations, as did the legendary battles between the Hatfields and the McCoys. Courts were instituted, at least in part, to prevent those calamities. Thus, regardless of which side in a dispute "wins," what is important, from the standpoint of the court, is that the dispute be resolved justly and, perhaps more important, peacefully.

A fourth purpose of courts is "to censure wrongdoing." To "censure" means to condemn or to blame. In this context, it refers to condemning or blaming people who have violated the law.

Purposes five through eight involve specific outcomes that courts hope to achieve by their actions. They are **incapacitation,** or the removal or restriction of the freedom of those found to have violated criminal laws; **punishment,** or the imposition of a penalty for criminal wrongdoing; **rehabilitation,** or the attempt to "correct" the personality and behavior of convicted offenders through educational, vocational, or therapeutic treatment and to return them to society as law-abiding citizens; and **general deterrence,** or the attempt to prevent people in general from engaging in crime by punishing specific individuals and making examples of them. (Omitted from Rubin's list is special or specific deterrence.) These purposes are discussed at greater length in the next chapter under the goals of sentencing.

A ninth purpose of courts is to determine legal status. For example, courts determine marital status by dissolving marriages and granting divorces. Similarly, parental status is determined by approving adoptions.

A tenth and critically important purpose of courts is to protect individual citizens against arbitrary government action. Recourse through the courts is available to citizens who have been abused by government agencies and agents. Examples of such abuses include illegal invasion of a person's privacy; interference with a person's First Amendment rights of religious choice, speech, press, and assembly; and denial of public employment because of race, gender, or age. In summary, by custom and law, courts have become an integral and seemingly indispensable part of modern life.

due process of law The procedures followed by courts to ensure that a defendant's constitutional rights are not violated.

incapacitation The removal or restriction of the freedom of those found to have violated criminal laws.

punishment The imposition of a penalty for criminal wrongdoing.

rehabilitation The attempt to "correct" the personality and behavior of convicted offenders through educational, vocational, or therapeutic treatment and to return them to society as law-abiding citizens.

general deterrence The attempt to prevent people in general from engaging in crime by punishing specific individuals and making examples of them.

A purpose of courts is to provide a forum where disputes between people, such as the legendary feud between the Hatfields and McCoys (pictured here), can be resolved justly and peacefully. *How successful have the courts been in achieving this purpose? Defend your answer.*

THINKING CRITICALLY

1. The first purpose of the court is to "do justice." Given what you know about the American court system, do you think that justice is done? Why or why not?

2. Of the remaining nine purposes of the courts, which ones do you think can be most easily achieved? Why?

Key Actors in the Court Process

The three key actors in the court process are the prosecutor, the defense attorney, and the judge. In this section, we will examine the roles those three officers of the court play in the administration of justice.[22]

THE PROSECUTOR

Because most crimes violate state laws, they fall under the authority, or jurisdiction, of the state court system and its prosecutors. The prosecutor is a community's chief law enforcement official and is responsible primarily for the protection of society.[23] Depending on the state, the prosecutor may be referred to as the district attorney, the prosecuting attorney, the county attorney, the state's attorney, the commonwealth's attorney, or the solicitor. In large cities, the day-to-day work of the prosecutor's office is performed by assistant district attorneys.

Whatever the name, the prosecutor is the most powerful actor in the administration of justice. Not only do prosecutors conduct the final screening of each person arrested for a criminal offense, deciding whether there is enough evidence to support a conviction, but in most jurisdictions they also have unreviewable discretion in deciding whether to charge a person with a crime and whether to prosecute the case. In other words, regardless of the amount (or lack) of incriminating evidence, and without having to provide any reasons to anyone, prosecutors have the authority to charge or not charge a person with a crime and to prosecute or not prosecute the case. If they decide to prosecute, they also

 U.S. Attorneys

Violations of federal laws are prosecuted by the U.S. Justice Department. The Justice Department is headed by the U.S. Attorney General and staffed by 94 U.S. attorneys (Guam and the Northern Mariana Islands share 1), each of whom is nominated to office by the President and confirmed by the Senate. One U.S. attorney is assigned to each of the federal district court jurisdictions. There were approximately 5,700 assistant U.S. attorneys in 2007.

Source: Sourcebook of Criminal Justice Statistics Online at www.albany.edu/sourcebook/pdf/t1792007.pdf.

determine what the charge or charges will be. (The charge or charges may or may not be the same as the one or ones for which the person was arrested.) In most cities, prosecutors refuse to formally charge a person in about one-half of all felony arrests. Prosecutors are not required to prosecute a person for all the charges that the evidence will support. However, the more charges they bring against a suspect, the more leverage prosecutors have in plea bargaining, which will be discussed later in this section. Regardless of the reason, when prosecutors elect not to prosecute, they enter a notation of **_nolle prosequi (nol. pros.)_** on the official record of the case and formally announce in court the decision to dismiss the charge or charges. Insufficient evidence is the most frequent reason given by prosecutors for not prosecuting cases.

The Decision to Charge and Prosecute The exercise of prosecutorial discretion in charging contrasts sharply with the way prosecutors are supposed to behave in their professional capacities. Ideally, prosecutors are supposed to charge an offender with a crime and to prosecute the case if after full investigation three, and only three, conditions are met:

District Attorney Mike Nifong responds to reporters' questions about the Duke University lacrosse rape case. _Was it appropriate for D. A. Nifong to respond to reporters' questions? Why or why not?_

1. They find that a crime has been committed.
2. A perpetrator can be identified.
3. There is sufficient evidence to support a guilty verdict.

However, prosecutors are not supposed to charge suspects with more criminal charges or for more serious crimes than can be reasonably supported by the evidence. They are not supposed to be deterred from prosecution because juries in their jurisdiction have frequently refused to convict persons of particular kinds of crimes. Conversely, they are not supposed to prosecute simply because an aroused public demands it. Prosecutors are not supposed to be influenced by the personal or political advantages or disadvantages that might be involved in prosecuting or not prosecuting a case. Nor, for that matter, are they supposed to be swayed by their desire to enhance their records of successful convictions. It would be naive, however, to believe that those factors do not have at least some influence on prosecutors' decisions to pursue or to drop criminal cases.

Prosecutors sometimes choose not to charge or prosecute criminal cases for any of the following nine additional reasons. The first is their belief that an offense did not cause sufficient harm. This decision is usually a practical one. Given limited time and resources, overworked and understaffed prosecutors often have to choose which cases go forward and which do not.

A second reason involves the relationship between the statutory punishment and the offender or the offense. In today's legal climate of increasingly harsh sentencing laws, a prosecutor may feel that the statutory punishment for a crime is too severe for a particular offender (for example, a first-time offender) or for a particular offense. In an effort to be fair, at least in their own minds, prosecutors in such cases impose their own sense of justice.

A third reason for not prosecuting, even when the three ideal conditions are met, is an improper motive on the part of a complainant. The prosecutor may feel that a criminal charge has been made for the wrong reasons. For example, if a prosecutor were convinced that a woman who had caught her husband cheating lied when charging her husband with beating her, the prosecutor might elect not to charge the husband with assault or some other crime.

A fourth reason prosecutors sometimes choose not to prosecute a case is that the particular law has been violated with impunity for a long time with few complaints by the public. In the case of "blue laws," for example, which may require stores to be closed on Sundays, prosecutors would occasionally get complaints from outraged churchgoers. In some cases, prosecutors simply ignored the complaints because the law, although on the books for decades,

nolle prosequi (nol. pros.) The notation placed on the official record of a case when prosecutors elect not to prosecute.

had not been enforced for years and few complaints had been received. In most states, incidentally, blue laws have been declared unconstitutional.

A fifth reason prosecutors often choose not to prosecute a case, even though, ideally, prosecution is required, is that a victim may refuse to testify. In rape cases, for example, prosecutors realize that it is nearly impossible to secure a conviction without the testimony of the victim. Thus, if the victim refuses to testify, the prosecutor may decide to drop the case, knowing that the chances of obtaining a conviction are reduced dramatically without the cooperation of the victim.

A sixth reason for not prosecuting has to do with humanitarian concerns for the welfare of the victim or the offender. In child sexual molestation cases, for example, conviction depends on the victim's testimony. Prosecutors may decline to prosecute because of the possible psychological injury to a child who is forced to testify. When offenders are suffering from mental illness, prosecutors may decide that diverting the offender to a mental health facility rather than prosecuting for a crime is in the best interests of all concerned.

Seventh, prosecutors sometimes do not prosecute a case otherwise worthy of prosecution because the accused person cooperates in the apprehension or conviction of other criminal offenders. In drug cases, for example, prosecutors often "cut deals" (make promises not to prosecute) with users or low-level dealers in order to identify "higher-ups" in the drug distribution network. Prosecutors make similar deals with low-level operatives in organized crime.

An eighth reason prosecutors sometimes choose not to prosecute is that the accused is wanted for prosecution of a more serious crime in another jurisdiction. Thus, there is little reason to expend resources prosecuting a case if an offender is likely to receive greater punishment for a crime committed elsewhere. It is easier and cheaper simply to extradite, or to deliver, the offender to the other jurisdiction.

Finally, if an offender is on parole when he or she commits a new crime, prosecutors may not prosecute the new crime because they consider it more cost-effective to simply have the parole revoked and send the offender back to prison.

The Decision to Plea-Bargain

Unreviewable discretion in deciding whether to charge and prosecute citizens for their crimes is the principal reason the prosecutor is considered the most powerful figure in the administration of justice, but it is by no means the prosecutor's only source of power. Probably the most strategic source of power available to prosecutors is their authority to decide which cases to "plea bargain." **Plea bargaining** or **plea negotiating** refers to the practice whereby the prosecutor, the defense attorney, the defendant, and—in many jurisdictions—the judge agree to a negotiated plea. For example, they may agree on a specific sentence to be imposed if the accused pleads guilty to an agreed-upon charge or charges instead of going to trial. It is the prosecutor alone, however, who chooses what lesser plea, if any, will be accepted instead of going to trial. Contrary to popular belief, justice in the United States is dispensed mostly through plea bargaining. Criminal trials are relatively rare events; plea bargaining is routine. About 95% of all convictions in felony cases are the result of guilty pleas. Guilty pleas account for an even higher percentage of convictions in misdemeanor cases.[24] Plea bargaining and the different types of plea bargains will be discussed in more detail later in this chapter.

Recommending the Amount of Bail

In addition to control over charging, prosecuting, and plea bargaining, another source of power for the prosecutor in many jurisdictions is the responsibility of recommending the amount of bail. Although the final decision on the amount or even the opportunity for bail rests with the judge, the prosecutor makes the initial recommendation. By recommending a very high bail amount, an amount that a suspect is unlikely to be

plea bargaining or **plea negotiating** The practice whereby the prosecutor, the defense attorney, the defendant, and—in many jurisdictions—the judge agree on a specific sentence to be imposed if the accused pleads guilty to an agreed-upon charge or charges instead of going to trial.

Actor Robert Downey Jr. departs Riverside County Superior Court after pleading no contest to a felony count for cocaine possession and a misdemeanor count for being under the influence of the drug in a plea bargain that allowed him to continue live-in drug treatment, rather than face jail time. *What factors might influence a prosecutor's plea-bargaining decision? Are all those factors legitimate?*

able to raise, a prosecutor can pressure a suspect to accept a plea bargain. Bail will be discussed later in this chapter.

Rules of Discovery Perhaps the only weakness in a prosecutor's arsenal of weapons is the legal rules of discovery. The **rules of discovery** mandate that a prosecutor provide defense counsel with any exculpatory evidence in the prosecutor's possession. Exculpatory evidence is evidence favorable to the accused that has an effect on guilt or punishment. Examples of possible exculpatory evidence are physical evidence, evidentiary documents (such as a defendant's recorded statements to police and reports of medical examinations or scientific tests), and lists of witnesses. A prosecutor's concealment or misrepresentation of evidence is grounds for an appellate court's reversal of a conviction. Defense attorneys, however, are under no constitutional obligation to provide prosecutors with incriminating evidence. However, most states and the federal system have by statute or by court rules given the prosecution some discovery rights (for example, the right to notice of the defense's intent to use an alibi or an insanity defense). The rationale for the rules of discovery is that, ideally, the prosecutor's job is to see that justice is done and not necessarily to win cases.

rules of discovery Rules that mandate that a prosecutor provide defense counsel with any exculpatory evidence (evidence favorable to the accused that has an effect on guilt or punishment) in the prosecutor's possession.

Selection and Career Prospects of Prosecutors Given the power of prosecutors in the administration of justice, the public can only hope that prosecutors wield their power wisely and justly. We believe that many of them do. Unfortunately, political considerations and aspirations may be too enticing to some prosecutors, causing them to violate the canons of their position. The partisan political process through which the typical prosecutor is elected increases the chances that political influence will affect the prosecutor's decisions. In most jurisdictions, prosecutors run for office on either the Democratic or Republican ticket, although in some jurisdictions, they are elected in nonpartisan races—that is, without party affiliation. In 2005, all chief prosecutors were elected, except for those in Alaska, Connecticut, the District of Columbia, and New Jersey, where they were appointed. Eighty-five percent of chief prosecutors were

Careers in Criminal Justice

Assistant State Attorney

My name is Wilson Green and I am an assistant state attorney (prosecutor) in Orlando. I received a B.A. from Vanderbilt, an M.Div. from Reformed Theological Seminary, and my J.D. from the University of Mississippi, with some navy time along the way. I interviewed for and began my current job about 20 years ago here at the State Attorney's Office.

I am in the homicide unit. Most of us deal either with misdemeanor or felony cases that are set for trial. Most

cases are resolved by defendants pleading guilty (or no contest) and being sentenced by a judge, while others proceed to a jury trial. The prosecutor is assigned cases as they come to our office from law enforcement agencies and after the defendants have been formally charged by other attorneys in our office.

The first step is to "work-up" each case—to review the entire file (police reports, witness statements, photos, tape recordings, lab reports, etc.) and to send out appropriate "discovery" to the defendant's attorney. Witnesses must be listed and subpoenaed for trial. Requests for further investigation may be needed as

the prosecutor anticipates what the defense will probably be. Often the defense attorney will take depositions of state witnesses before trial, which we attend. There may also be pretrial hearings on legal issues, as well as plea negotiations.

Jury trials generally may last a day or so or up to a week or more. A prosecutor may have as many as a hundred cases pending at one time (spread over a few months period), with new ones coming in as fast as others are resolved. The stress level can be high at times, due to the caseload, problem cases, witness problems, cases being postponed at the last minute, not knowing which case will actually go to trial until the last minute, and having to make appropriate plea offers. On the plus side, prosecutors (who are to be "ministers of justice," not just win cases) have a beneficial role in society, have much discretion

in handling their cases, are in the courtroom on a regular basis, and are in touch with the "real world" through their contact with police agencies, witnesses, victims, families of victims, judges, and juries. They can use both common sense and legal training. Each case seems to have something new.

Those considering becoming prosecutors might think about sampling criminal justice and prelaw undergraduate courses, taking advantage of internships with law enforcement agencies or prosecutors' offices, or simply observing court proceedings as a citizen. Use any employment opportunities as a way to gain common-sense experience that will help in a later career. Take advantage of any group or public speaking opportunities as well.

What do you think is the most challenging part of a prosecutor's job? Explain.

---

elected or appointed to 4-year terms.[25] Although prosecutors can be removed from office for criminal acts or for incompetence, removal is rare.

The potential for political influence is increased even further by prosecutors' frequent use of the position as a stepping-stone to higher political office (several mayors, governors, and presidents have been former prosecutors). There are very few career prosecutors. Those who are not elected to higher political office and those who choose not to seek it typically go into private law practice.

Assistant District Attorneys The workhorses of the big-city prosecutor's office, as already noted, are the assistant district attorneys (or deputy district attorneys), who are hired by the prosecutor. Generally, assistant district attorneys are hired right out of law school or after a brief and usually unsuccessful stint in private practice. Most of them remain in the prosecutor's office for only 2 to 4 years and then go into, or back into, private law practice. Reasons for leaving the prosecutor's office include low pay, little chance for advancement, physical and psychological pressures, boredom, and disillusionment with the criminal adjudication process. Assistant district attorneys provide an important social service, and the job is a good way of gaining legal experience. Lawyers who occupy the position, however, usually do not consider it anything more than temporary employment before they go into private practice.

National Survey of Prosecutors The most recent government survey of prosecutors reported that, in 2005, 2,344 prosecutors' offices prosecuted felony cases in state courts of general jurisdiction.[26] About 78,000 attorneys, investigators, victim advocates, and support staff worked in those offices. The average number of employees across all prosecutor offices was nine, including the chief prosecutor. Full-time offices in large districts averaged staffs of 419, with an average of 141 assistant prosecutors (including attorneys who also had managerial responsibilities),

20 legal services personnel (law clerks and paralegals), 13 victim advocates, 39 staff investigators, and 136 support staff (secretaries, clerks, and computer specialists). A prosecutorial district consists of one or more counties.

State law determines the number of chief prosecutors. States with the largest number of chief prosecutors in 2005 were Texas (155), Virginia (120), and Missouri (115). Chief prosecutors served for an average of 8 years. Nearly a third of the chief prosecutors had served 4 years or less, while two in five had served 12 or more years. The longest term of service reported in the survey was 35 years. A chief prosecutor's annual salary depended primarily on whether the job was part-time or full-time and the size of the prosecutorial district. In 2005, half of all offices reported that the chief prosecutor earned $85,000 a year or more. Nearly 40% had a salary of $100,000 or more. In 2005, the median salary for full-time large offices was $149,000 compared to a median of $42,000 for part-time offices.

The total amount spent for prosecutorial services nationwide in 2005 was approximately $4.9 billion. The average (mean) annual budget was about $2 million. (The median annual budget was $355,000.) Annual budgets ranged between $5,000 and $285 million. Most of the funding for prosecutors' offices came from county governments, although funding in some offices was also received from state governments and state and federal grants.

In 2005, prosecutors' offices closed more than 2.4 million felony cases and nearly 7.5 million misdemeanor cases. The median number of felony and misdemeanor cases closed per office was 250 and 630, respectively. With regard to felonies, that amounted to about 90 cases per assistant prosecutor. As an indication of the importance of plea bargaining, the median number of felony jury trial verdicts per office was six, or 2.4% of all felony cases closed. Large, full-time offices prosecuted a median of 230 felony jury trials, while the median number for part-time offices was two.

The survey found an element of danger in the work of prosecutors. About 40% of prosecutors' offices reported a work-related threat or assault against a staff member in 2005. Consequently, various security measures were used for protection, such as electronic security systems, building guards, metal detectors, electronic surveillance, and police protection. About one in five chief prosecutors carried a firearm for personal security.

THE DEFENSE ATTORNEY

The Sixth Amendment to the U.S. Constitution and several modern Supreme Court decisions, discussed in Chapter 4, guarantee the right to the "effective assistance" of counsel to people charged with crimes.[27] (The terms *counsel, attorney,* and *lawyer* are interchangeable.)

The right to counsel extends not only to representation at trial but also to other critical stages in the criminal justice process, "where substantial rights of the accused may be affected." Thus, defendants have a right to counsel during custodial interrogations, preliminary hearings, and police lineups. They also have a right to counsel at certain posttrial proceedings, such as their first (and only the first) appeal that is a matter of right, and probation and parole revocation hearings. The Supreme Court has also extended the right to counsel to juveniles in juvenile court proceedings.

A defendant may waive the right to counsel and appear on his or her own behalf. However, given the technical nature of criminal cases and the stakes involved (an individual's freedom!), anyone arrested for a crime is well advised to secure the assistance of counsel at the earliest opportunity. The phone call routinely given to arrested suspects at the police station is for the specific purpose of obtaining counsel. If a suspect cannot afford an attorney and is accused of either a felony or a misdemeanor for which imprisonment could be the result of conviction, the state is required to provide an attorney at the state's expense.

FYI Female Lawyers

In 1971, just 3% of all lawyers in the United States were women. By 1980, the percentage of female lawyers had increased to 8%, and by 2008, about 32% of all lawyers were women. In 1961, only 4% of the 16,489 first-year law students were women. In 2008, about 47% of the 49,082 first-year law students were women. Still, women make up only about 18% of the partners in the nation's approximately 50,000 major law firms. The percentage of associates is much higher (about 45%). In 1981, Sandra Day O'Connor became the first female justice of the U.S. Supreme Court. Ruth Bader Ginsburg became the second in 1993. Also, in 1993, Janet Reno became the first female Attorney General of the United States.

Source: American Bar Association, Commission on Women in the Profession, "A Current Glance at Women in the Law 2008" at www.abanet .org/women/CurrentGlanceStatistics2008.pdf; "Despite Gains, Women Lawyers Still Face Bias," *The Orlando Sentinel* (August 18, 1996), p. A20; "Where My Girls At? Women Are Finally Catching Up to Men in Law School Enrollment," *The Princeton Review* at www .princetonreview.com/law/research/articles/ decide/gender.asp.

Lawyers are sometimes vilified by the media and the public for defending people unquestionably guilty of crimes. That lawyers sometimes succeed in getting guilty persons "off" by the skillful use of legal technicalities only makes matters worse. However, what some people fail to understand is that in the American system of justice, it is not the role of defense lawyers to decide their clients' guilt or innocence. Rather, the role of defense lawyers is to provide the best possible legal counsel and advocacy within the legal and ethical limits of the profession. Legal and ethical codes forbid lawyers, for example, to mislead the court by providing false information or by using perjured testimony (false testimony under oath). The American system of justice is based on the premise that a person is innocent until proven guilty. In the attempt to ensure, as far as possible, that innocent people are not found guilty of crimes, all persons charged with crimes are entitled to a rigorous defense. The constitutional right to counsel and our adversarial system of justice would be meaningless if lawyers refused to defend clients that they "knew" were guilty.

Not all lawyers are adequately trained to practice in the specialized field of criminal law. Law schools generally require only a one-semester course in criminal law and a one-semester course in criminal procedure, though additional courses may be taken as electives in a typical 6-semester or 3-year program. Many lawyers prefer to practice other, often more lucrative, areas of law, such as corporate, tax, or tort law. Compared with those other areas of legal practice, the practice of criminal law generally provides its practitioner less income, prestige, and status in the community.

For those reasons, criminal defendants in search of counsel are limited by practical considerations. They can choose a privately retained lawyer who specializes in criminal law, if they can afford one. Or, if they are indigent and cannot afford one, they will receive a court-appointed attorney (who may or may not be skilled in the practice of criminal law), a public defender, or a "contract" lawyer. In large cities, there is little problem in locating a criminal lawyer. They are listed in the Yellow Pages of the local telephone book. In rural areas, however, finding a lawyer who specializes in criminal law may be more difficult. Because of the lower volume of criminal cases in rural areas, attorneys who practice in those areas generally must practice all kinds of law to make a living; they cannot afford to specialize. Outside large cities, then, a criminal defendant may have no better option than to rely on the services of a court-appointed attorney, a public defender, or a contract lawyer, whichever is provided in that particular jurisdiction. Court-appointed attorneys, public defenders, and contract lawyers are discussed further later in this section.

Criminal Lawyers In discussing privately retained criminal lawyers, it is useful to think of a continuum. At one end are a very few nationally known, highly paid, and successful criminal lawyers, such as Gerry Spence, Thomas A. Mesereau, Jr., and Alan Dershowitz. Those criminal lawyers generally take only three kinds of cases: (1) those that are sensational or highly publicized, (2) those that promise to make new law, or (3) those that involve large fees. A little further along the continuum is another small group of criminal lawyers, those who make a very comfortable living in the large cities of this country by defending professional criminals, such as organized crime members, gamblers, pornographers, and drug dealers. Toward the other end of the continuum are the vast majority of criminal lawyers who practice in the large cities of this country.

Most criminal lawyers must struggle to earn a decent living. They have to handle a large volume of cases to make even a reasonable salary. To attract clients, some criminal lawyers engage in the unethical practice of paying kickbacks to ambulance drivers, police officers, jailers, and bail bonds people for client referrals. Some criminal lawyers also engage in the unethical practice of soliciting new clients in courthouse hallways.

 Public Opinion and Lawyers

In 2008, only 18% of Americans rated the honesty and ethical standards of lawyers "high" (15%) or "very high" (3%), 45% rated lawyers' honesty and ethical standards "average," and 37% rated them "low" (25%) or "very low" (12%).

Source: The Gallup Poll, www.gallup.com/poll/1654/Honesty-Ethics-Professions.aspx (conducted November 7–9, 2008; accessed November 30, 2008).

Thomas A. Mesereau, Jr., Gerry Spence, and Alan Dershowitz (from left to right) are among the very few nationally known, highly paid, and successful criminal lawyers. *What do you think distinguishes these lawyers from all other lawyers?*

Although a few criminal lawyers are known for their criminal trial exper- tise, most relatively successful criminal lawyers gain their reputations from their ability to "fix" cases, that is, their ability to produce the best possible outcome for a client, given the circumstances of the case. Fixing cases usually involves plea bargaining but may also include the strategic use of motions for continuances and for changes in the judge assigned to the case. *Who* a lawyer knows is often more important than *what* the lawyer knows. In other words, a close personal relationship with the prosecutor or a hearing before the "right" judge is often far more important to the case's outcome (for example, a favor- able plea bargain) than is an attorney's legal ability.

Besides legal expertise and good relationships with other actors in the adjudication process, the only other commodity criminal lawyers have to sell is their time. Thus, for the typical criminal lawyer, time is valuable. As a result, criminal lawyers try to avoid time-consuming court battles and are motivated to get their clients to plead guilty to reduced charges.

Another reason most criminal lawyers prefer plea bargaining to trials is that they are more likely to receive a fee, however small, from their typically poor clients for arranging the plea. When cases go to trial and the legal fee has not been paid in advance, there is the possibility that the lawyer will receive no compensation or inadequate compensation from his or her client, especially if the case is lost.

To prevent nonpayment for services, criminal lawyers sometimes engage in unethical, if not illegal, behavior. Sometimes criminal lawyers plea-bargain cases that they know they can win at trial. They do this because they know that their clients do not have the money to compensate them for the time they would put into a trial. If clients have only a few hundred dollars, some unscrupulous crim- inal lawyers reason that those clients can afford only "bargain" justice. Another unethical tactic employed by some criminal lawyers to secure a fee from their clients is to seek delays in a case and allow their clients to remain in jail until they have been paid for services yet to be performed. Getting a client to pay a legal fee is not a legitimate basis for seeking a court delay.

Criminal lawyers often spend more time at the county jail and the court- house, where their clients are, than in their offices, which generally are spartan

 **CJ Online**

Rules of Conduct

As noted previously, the American public generally does not rate the honesty and ethical standards of lawyers very high. Go to the American Bar Association's website at www .abanet.org and review the Model Rules of Professional Conduct. Although individual states have their own rules, most states modeled their rules after these. *From what you have read and heard, which of the rules do you think are most commonly violated?*

compared with the plush offices of their corporate counterparts. They are sometimes told by their clients about grisly crimes that have been committed or will
be committed in the future. Because of attorney-client privilege, the lawyer in
possession of this information cannot reveal it, under penalty of disbarment
(the revocation of his or her license to practice law). In short, many criminal
lawyers are considered somewhat less than respectable by their professional
colleagues and much of the general public, because their clients are "criminals," they deal with some of the more unsavory aspects of human existence,
and a few may engage in unethical behavior to earn a living.

The Court-Appointed Lawyer In some jurisdictions, criminal suspects or
defendants who cannot afford to hire an attorney are provided with court-
appointed lawyers. The court-appointed lawyer is usually selected in one of
two ways. In some jurisdictions, lawyers volunteer to represent indigent offenders and are appointed by judges on a rotating basis from a list or from lawyers
present in the courtroom. In other jurisdictions, lawyers are appointed by a
judge from a list of attorneys who are members of the county bar association.

In the past, appointed lawyers frequently represented indigent clients *pro
bono* (without pay). Today, however, the vast majority of appointed lawyers
are paid by the jurisdiction. Hourly fees are usually much less than would be
charged by privately retained counsel. Seldom is money available to hire investigators or to secure the services of expert witnesses, the lack of which weak-
ens the defense that can be provided a client.

In addition, although appointed attorneys may be experts in some areas of
law, they may not be familiar with the intricacies of a criminal defense. They
may have never before represented a client charged with a crime. Nevertheless,
many lawyers view their appointments as a public service and do their best
to represent their clients in a professional manner. Some, however, take cases
grudgingly (they can refuse an appointment only for very good reasons) and
regard an appointment as a financially unrewarding and unpleasant experience. They perform well enough only to escape charges of malpractice. In many
cases, an appointed attorney first meets his or her client in the courtroom,

Determining Indigency

In some jurisdictions, indigency is
determined by the examination of
tax returns or the filing of affidavits
documenting resources. Generally,
defendants are deemed indigent if
their resources place them below the
government's official poverty level.
In other jurisdictions, indigency is
determined simply by defendants'
response to the judge's question
whether they can afford an attorney.

Source: See, for example, Steven K. Smith and
Carol J. DeFrances, "Indigent Defense," U.S.
Department of Justice, *Bureau of Justice
Statistics Selected Findings* (Washington, D.C.:
GPO, February 1996).

Defense lawyers spend much of their time at the local jail. *Do you think that the jail setting
influences a lawyer's opinion of his or her client?*

where they have a brief conference before a guilty plea is arranged. When they go to trial, they often fail their clients. An estimated 35,000 people are convicted wrongfully in American courts every year.[28]

The Public Defender In many jurisdictions today, people who are charged with crimes and cannot afford an attorney are provided with public defenders. Public defenders are paid a fixed salary by a jurisdiction (city, county, state, or federal) to defend indigents charged with crimes. Frequently, public defenders are assigned to courtrooms instead of to specific clients. They defend all of the indigent clients who appear in their courtrooms. As a result, a defendant may have a different public defender at different stages in the process (for example, preliminary hearing, arraignment, and trial). Public defenders commonly spend only 5 to 10 minutes with their clients. In addition, this bureaucratic arrangement makes the public defender a part of a courtroom work group that includes the judge, the prosecutor, and the other courtroom actors with whom the public defender interacts daily. This work group, in turn, may be more interested in processing cases efficiently and maintaining cooperative relationships with each other than in pursuing adversarial justice. Nevertheless, despite the method of assignment, the impersonal nature of the defense, and the potential conflict of interest, most indigent clients in criminal cases prefer public defenders to court-appointed attorneys because public defenders practice criminal law full-time.

Like prosecutors, many public defenders regard their position not as a career but as a valuable learning experience that will eventually lead to private law practice.

The Contract Lawyer A relatively new and increasingly popular way of providing for indigent defense is the contract system. In this system, private attorneys, law firms, and bar associations bid for the right to represent a jurisdiction's indigent defendants. Terms of contracts differ, but in the typical contract, counsel agrees to represent either all or a specified number of indigent defendants in a jurisdiction during a certain period of time, in exchange for a fixed dollar amount. Contracts are awarded on the basis of costs to the jurisdiction, qualifications of bidders, and other factors.

In certain situations, some jurisdictions employ a combination of indigent defense systems. For example, jurisdictions that regularly use public defenders sometimes contract out the defense of cases where there is a conflict of interest (for example, multiple-defendant cases) or cases that require special expertise (such as some death penalty cases).

Indigent Defense Systems In 2005, all 50 states except Maine had public defender systems for indigent defendants, although some states, such as Alabama, North Carolina, and Texas, relied more on court-appointed and/or contract lawyers.[29] Counties, states, and the federal government spent an estimated $4.1 billion on indigent defense in 2005, up from $3.3 billion in 2002 and just under $1 billion in 1986. The federal government's share of the 2005 bill was $669 million. (These figures do not include indigent defense expenditures of municipalities or in-kind costs such as supplying office space.) Many death penalty states have special indigent defense systems for capital cases, especially at the appellate level. Death penalty states with large death rows such as California, Florida, and Texas, have much higher indigent defense costs. Costs also are higher in states that prohibit representation of codefendants or limit joint representation to preliminary matters. Some states, such as California, pay their public defenders much higher salaries than do other states, such as Virginia. Also, some states, such as New York, are required by statute to appoint counsel to indigent defendants charged with misdemeanors, including traffic offenses, which are treated as jailable

Table 8.1 State and County Expenditures for Indigent Defense Services FY 2005

State	Fiscal Year	State Expenditure	County Expenditure	Total Expenditure	Percentage of State Funds
Alabama	2005	$ 41,791,344		$ 41,791,344	100.0%
Alaska	2005	27,183,800		27,183,800	100.0
Arizona	2005	820,900	$103,169,343	103,990,243	0.8
Arkansas	2005	15,032,000	1,440,395	16,472,395	91.3
California	2005	27,460,000	545,417,808	572,877,808	4.8
Colorado	2005	47,473,830		47,473,830	100.0
Connecticut	2005	35,547,327		35,547,327	100.0
Delaware	2005	10,621,400		10,621,400	100.0
District of Columbia	2005			59,535,000	0.0
Florida	2005	232,700,000		232,700,000	100.0
Georgia	CY 2005	37,227,081	57,000,000	94,227,081	39.0
Hawaii	2005	10,530,386		10,530,386	100.0
Idaho	2005	1,265,800	9,921,192*	11,186,992	11.3
Illinois	2005	24,342,584	100,435,199*	124,777,783	19.5
Indiana	2005	17,467,000	25,000,000	42,467,000	41.1
Iowa	2005	43,194,649		43,194,649	100.0
Kansas	2005	18,114,857	5,308,134*	23,422,991	77.3
Kentucky	2005	29,970,270	1,528,140	31,498,410	95.1
Louisiana	CY 2005	4,381,640	21,561,889	25,943,529	16.9
Maine	2005	10,841,372		10,841,372	100.0
Maryland	2005	70,330,970		70,330,970	100.0
Massachusetts	2005	120,033,457		120,033,457	100.0
Michigan	2005	5,634,400	73,221,713	78,856,113	7.1
Minnesota	2005	61,110,000	4,500,000	65,610,000	93.1
Mississippi	2005	1,456,121	11,364,919	12,821,040	11.4
Missouri	2005	30,156,416		30,156,416	100.0
Montana	2005	13,786,495		13,786,495	100.0
Nebraska	2004/2005[i]	845,781	22,693,906	23,539,687	3.6
Nevada	2005	726,178*	26,806,108*	27,532,286	2.6
New Hampshire	2005	15,718,938		15,718,938	100.0
New Jersey	2005	104,552,000		104,552,000	100.0
New Mexico	2005	30,798,000		30,798,000	100.0
New York	2005	157,636,127	244,843,703	402,479,830	39.2
North Carolina	2005	85,526,000		85,526,000	100.0
North Dakota	2005	2,549,663		2,549,663	100.0

(continued on pg 311)

offenses. Other states punish such offenses with fines only, which eliminate the counsel requirement. Twelve states with public defender systems use assigned counsel when conflicts of interest arise, and 3 states use contract attorneys. In Georgia, regional conflict defender offices handle conflicts of interest.

Indigent defense systems (IDS) can be distinguished by sources of political and economic control. Five types of IDS are: (1) fully state funded IDS, (2) more than 50% state funded IDS, (3) full county funded IDS, (4) more than 50% county funded IDS, and (5) municipally funded IDS. (Data were not provided for municipal IDS.) The state government fully funds the public defender offices in 28 states and funds more than half of their expenditures in 3 states (Alabama, Kansas, and Oklahoma). In about half of the states, state government provides indigent defendants with public defenders who work out of field offices. In 2005, Florida had the highest state expenditure for indigent defense: $233 million. All Florida funding came from the state. Nevada had the lowest state expenditure: $726,000. However, most of Nevada's funding came from counties: $27 million in 2005. The other half of states allows counties to select their own method of indigent representation. Assigned counsel is an option for indigent defendants in 22 states; contract attorneys are an option in 19 states.

Table 8.1 State and County Expenditures for Indigent Defense Services FY 2005 (continued)

State	Fiscal Year	State Expenditure	County Expenditure	Total Expenditure	Percentage of State Funds
Ohio	2005	41,100,978	70,357,402	111,458,380	36.9
Oklahoma	2005	17,513,364	10,926,734*	28,440,098	61.6
Oregon	2005	88,123,000		88,123,000	100.0
Pennsylvania	2005		100,652,582*	100,652,582	0.0
Rhode Island	2005	9,326,000		9,326,000	100.0
South Carolina	2005	9,356,488	13,283,625	22,640,113	41.3
South Dakota	2005	927,726	8,073,281	9,001,007	10.3
Tennessee	2005	51,038,008	4,422,300	55,460,308	92.0
Texas	2005	16,370,412	128,313,242	144,683,654	11.3
Utah	2005		12,896,632*	12,896,632	0.0
Vermont	2005	9,019,910		9,019,910	100.0
Virginia	2005	90,129,365		90,129,365	100.0
Washington	2005	4,397,900	80,392,300	84,727,200	5.2
West Virginia	2005	29,565,099		29,565,099	100.0
Wisconsin	2005	68,088,536		68,088,536	100.0
Wyoming	2005	5,233,755	921,493	6,155,248	85.0
State Total	2005	1,777,017,327	1,684,389,040	3,520,941,367	50.5
Federal Expenditure: Criminal Justice Act Funding	2005	668,800,000			
National Total	2005	$4,189,741,367			

Notes: *Figure represents estimate—see notes for explanation.
ⁱState money for Nebraska is from FY 2005; county money is from FY 2004; CY 5 calendar year.
In a number of states we were required to estimate the indigent defense expenditure. This is due to a lack of reliable data, either at the state or county level. Below are the states in which the indigent defense expenditures were estimated and the methodology used to makes these estimates.
Arizona: We were able to obtain FY 2005 expenditures only for Maricopa and Pima Counties, and state-level expenditures. In FY 2002 (the last year for which statewide data was collected), Maricopa and Pima Counties made up 77% of the total countywide indigent defense expenditures in the state. Using this 77% expenditure figure, we were able to estimate the remaining 23% of county expenditures.
Idaho and Illinois: We were able to obtain accurate state expenditure data in Idaho and Illinois; however, there is no state entity that tracks county expenditures in each state. Therefore, using Idaho's and Illinois' FY 2002 expenditure data from our last state and county expenditure report, we calculated each state's county expenditure by estimating a 5% increase in expenditures annually since 2002.

Source: The Spangenberg Group. "State Indigent Defense Commissions," Final Draft. Prepared for the Bar Information Program Upon Request of the Indigent Defense Advisory Group of the American Bar Association Standing Committee on Legal Aid and Indigent Defendants (October 2006). Generously provided by Robert Spangenberg.

Some states have both options. In 17 of the states, the state provides at least 50% of the county's costs. For example, New York's indigent defense system, which spent $402.5 million in 2005 and was second only to California's in total funding, received $245 million from the state and $157.5 million from counties. California counties spent the most on indigent defense in 2005: $545 million. The state contributed another $27.5 million. Pennsylvania ($101 million) and Utah ($13 million) are the only states that fund their indigent defense systems entirely through county funds. In three states, Florida, Georgia, and Tennessee, judicial circuits or districts exercise control over the public defender system. In Florida, the state contributes 100% of funding; in Georgia, counties contribute 60%; the state, 40%; and in Tennessee, the state contributes 92%; counties provide 8%. Table 8.1 shows the indigent defense funding of the 50 states, the District of Columbia, and the federal government in 2005. Funding critics claim that indigent defense systems are chronically underfunded regardless of how they are funded.

The trend in indigent defense systems is toward greater centralized control through increased state funding and the establishment of state oversight bodies or commissions, usually with a director and/or a chief public defender. The primary purpose of the state oversight bodies or commissions is to ensure that indigent defense remains independent of political and judicial influence. Other functions include monitoring costs and caseloads, creating standards, and enforcing compliance with the standards. Forty-two states have some sort of state indigent defense oversight body. The actual authority of state oversight bodies or commissions is tied closely to the amount and source of funding.

A study of the IDS in the 100 most populous counties found that indigent defense was provided in more than four million cases in 1999. More than 80% of the cases were handled by public defenders, 15% were handled by court-appointed private attorneys, and 3% by contract attorneys. Conviction rates for indigent defendants in federal and state courts were about the same as they were for defendants with privately retained counsel.[30] However, incarceration rates were higher for defendants with publicly financed attorneys than for those with privately retained counsel: in the federal courts, 88% to 77%, and in the state courts, 71% to 54%. Ironically, the length of jail or prison sentence was shorter for defendants with publicly financed attorneys. Those defendants with publicly financed attorneys received sentences in federal courts that averaged just less than 5 years; those with privately retained counsel averaged sentences of a little more than 5 years. In the state courts, defendants with publicly financed attorneys received sentences that averaged about 2.5 years, while those with privately retained counsel received sentences that averaged about 3 years.

The study discovered that, in 1999, nearly 70% of state prison inmates had attorneys appointed by the court. However, among minorities the percentage was higher: 77% of black inmates and 73% of Hispanic inmates. Among federal prison inmates, 65% of blacks, 57% of whites, and 56% of Hispanics had publicly financed attorneys.

THE JUDGE

According to the Bible, the idea of judges was first suggested to Moses by his father-in-law, Jethro. Following their exodus from Egypt, the Hebrews, having been slaves, had no formal government. Because Moses was the only one among them with evident authority, he served as arbiter of domestic controversies—a time-consuming and exhausting job. Jethro recognized the problem with this arrangement and suggested to Moses that he create a kind of theocracy. Moses would be the supreme judge and would represent the people before God. He would also teach the people laws governing everyday behavior. The actual administration of the laws, which came from God through Moses, was to be handled "by able men, . . . such as fear God, men who are trustworthy and who hate a bribe." These "judges" were to be established in a hierarchical order, so that the highest would be rulers over thousands of people; beneath them would be, successively, rulers of hundreds, fifties, and tens.[31]

For most people, black-robed judges are the embodiment of justice, and although they are generally associated with trials, judges actually have a variety of responsibilities in the criminal justice process.[32] Among their nontrial duties are determining probable cause, signing warrants, informing suspects of their rights, setting and revoking bail, arraigning defendants, and accepting guilty pleas. Judges spend much of the workday in their chambers (offices), negotiating procedures and dispositions with prosecutors and defense attorneys. The principal responsibility of judges in all their duties is to ensure that suspects and defendants are treated fairly and in accordance with due process of law.

Furthermore, in jurisdictions without professional court administrators, judges are responsible for the management of their own courtrooms and staff. Judges in some jurisdictions are also responsible for the entire courthouse and its personnel, with the added duties of supervising building maintenance, budgeting, and labor relations.

In jury trials, judges are responsible for allowing the jury a fair chance to reach a verdict on the evidence presented. Judges must ensure that their behavior does not improperly affect the outcome of the case. Before juries retire to deliberate and reach a verdict, judges instruct them on the relevant law. This involves

Judges spend much of their workday in their chambers (offices). *How does this differ from what the public generally believes about judges?*

interpreting legal precedents and applying them to the unique circumstances of the case. Those jury instructions are reviewable by an appellate court.

Characteristics of Judges In the United States, judges are overwhelmingly white and male. They generally come from upper-middle-class backgrounds, are Protestant, are better educated than most citizens, and average over 50 years of age. A majority of them were in private legal practice before becoming judges. Most were born in the communities in which they preside and attended college and law school in that state.

Selection of Judges States vary in the ways they select judges. The two most common selection methods are election and merit selection. Other, less common, ways of selecting judges are gubernatorial appointment and legislative election.

Like prosecutors, many state judges are elected to their positions in either partisan (with political party designation) or nonpartisan elections. This selection process exposes judges, like prosecutors, to potential charges of political influence. For many years, individuals campaigning for elected judgeships were required by judicial codes of conduct to refrain from revealing their positions on controversial political and legal issues. This prohibition set judicial campaigns apart from those of all other elected officials. The prohibition was intended to preserve fair and impartial justice and public trust in the judiciary. In 2002, in *Republican Party of Minnesota* v. *White*, the U.S. Supreme Court ruled that the prohibition was unconstitutional in violation of the First Amendment's protection of speech, especially speech about the qualifications of candidates for public office. The Court's decision has raised many concerns. For example, U.S. Supreme Court Justice John Paul Stevens contends that "electing judges is like allowing football fans to select their referees—an unwise practice." Stevens noted that "a campaign promise to 'be tough on crime' or to 'enforce the death penalty' is evidence of bias that should disqualify a candidate from sitting in criminal cases." He concluded that "making the retention of judicial office dependent on the popularity of the judge inevitably affects the decisional process in high-visibility cases, no matter how conscientious the judge may be."[33] Electing judges may also discourage some of the best lawyers from becoming judges. Successful lawyers with lucrative practices may not want to interrupt their careers to take the chance of becoming a judge, only to lose the position in the next election. Besides, successful lawyers generally earn much more

Table 8.2 Salaries of State Court Judges, 2008

	Mean	Median	Range	Average Annual Change (%) 2003–2008
Chief, Highest Court	$154,825	$151,328	$107,404 to 228,856	3.14%
Associate Justice, Court of Last Resort	150,042	145,984	106,185 to 218,237	3.24%
Judge, Intermediate Appellate Courts	145,445	141,250	105,050 to 204,599	3.13%
Judge, General Jurisdiction Trial Courts	134,207	130,312	99,234 to 178,789	3.18%

Source: National Center for State Courts, "Survey of Judicial Salaries" (as of January 1, 2009) at www.ncsconline.org/D_KIS/salary_survey/.

money than judges. Table 8.2 summarizes the 2008 salaries of state court judges. The table provides mean and median salaries of the chief and associate-justices of a state's highest court, intermediate appellate court judges, and general jurisdiction trial court judges, as well as the range of salaries and the average annual change in salaries between 2003 and 2007 for judges of each level of court. Table 8.3 shows 2008 judicial salaries for each state and the District of Columbia.

In an attempt to reduce the appearance of possible political influence, several states have adopted merit selection, sometimes referred to as the "Missouri Plan," as their method of selecting judges. First used in Missouri in 1940, merit selection is a process in which the governor appoints judges from a list of qualified lawyers compiled by a nonpartisan nominating commission composed of both lawyers and other citizens. After serving a short term on the bench, usually 1 year, the appointed judges face the voters in an uncontested election. Voters are instructed to vote yes or no on whether the judge should be retained in office. If a majority vote yes, the judge remains in office for a full term (usually 6 years; the range is 4 years to life). In Illinois, a judge must receive at least 60% of the votes. Toward the end of the term, the judge must face the voters again in the same kind of election. The merit plan does not entirely eliminate political influence from the selection process, but it seems to have less potential for influence than the direct popular election of judges.

In 2008, states used the following methods for initially selecting their highest *appellate court judges*:

• Merit selection—23 states (and the District of Columbia)
• Nonpartisan election—15 states
• Partisan election—7 states
• Appointment by the governor—2 states
• Election by the legislature—2 states
• Appointment by the legislature—1 state

In 2008, states used the following methods for initially selecting their *general-jurisdiction court judges*:

• Nonpartisan election—21 states
• Merit selection—15 states (and the District of Columbia)
• Partisan election—11 states
• Appointment by the governor—2 states
• Election by the legislature—2 states
• Appointment by the legislature—1 state

Four states—Arizona, Kansas, Maryland, and Missouri—provide for two methods of selecting general-jurisdiction judges. In those states, counties choose the method or, as in Arizona, the method depends on the size of the county.[34]

FYI Choosing State Court Judges

According to a recent public opinion poll, 43% of adult Americans aged 18 and over believe state court judges should be chosen by nonpartisan elections, 12% by partisan elections, 19% by gubernatorial appointment from candidates suggested by a citizen nominating committee, 4% by another method, and 24% were not at all sure.

Source: "Most Americans Want State Judges to Be Elected," The Harris Poll (survey conducted between September 15 and 22, 2008) at www.harrisinteractive.com/harris_poll/index.asp?PID=960 (accessed January 11, 2009).

Table 8.3 2008 Salaries for Appellate and General Jurisdiction Judges, and Rank

	HIGHEST COURT		INTERMEDIATE APPELLATE COURT		GENERAL-JURISDICTION TRIAL COURT	
	Salary	Rank	Salary	Rank	Salary	Rank
Alabama	$ 180,005	8	$ 178,878	3	$ 134,943	22
Alaska	179,520	9	169,608	6	165,996	5
Arizona	155,000	20	150,000	14	145,000	14
Arkansas	139,821	31	135,515	23	131,206	25
California	218,237	1	204,599	1	178,789	1
Colorado	139,660	32	134,128	25	128,598	29
Connecticut	162,520	15	152,637	12	146,780	12
Delaware	185,050	5			168,850	4
District of Columbia	184,500	6			174,000	2
Florida	161,200	17	153,140	11	145,080	13
Georgia	167,210	11	166,186	8	120,252	41
Hawaii	159,072	19	147,288	17	143,292	15
Idaho	119,506	47	118,506	37	112,043	46
Illinois	196,322	2	184,775	2	169,555	3
Indiana	151,328	22	147,103	18	125,647	32
Iowa	163,200	14	147,900	16	137,700	18
Kansas	135,905	38	131,518	30	120,037	42
Kentucky	134,160	40	128,760	34	123,384	36
Louisiana	136,967	37	130,194	32	124,085	35
Maine	119,594	46			112,145	45
Maryland	162,352	16	149,552	15	140,352	16
Massachusetts	145,984	26	135,087	24	129,694	27
Michigan	164,610	12	151,441	13	139,919	17
Minnesota	145,981	27	137,552	22	129,124	28
Mississippi	112,530	50	105,050	39	104,170	50
Missouri	137,034	36	128,207	35	120,484	39
Montana	106,185	51			99,234	51
Nebraska	135,881	39	129,087	33	125,690	31
Nevada	170,000	10			160,000	8
New Hampshire	146,917	25			137,084	20
New Jersey	185,482	4	175,534	5	165,000	6
New Mexico	123,691	44	117,506	38	111,631	47
New York	151,200	23	144,000	19	136,700	21
North Carolina	137,249	34	131,531	29	124,382	33
North Dakota	118,121	49			108,236	49
Ohio	141,600	29	132,000	28	121,350	38
Oklahoma	137,655	33	130,410	31	124,373	34
Oregon	125,688	43	122,820	36	114,468	44
Pennsylvania	186,450	3	175,923	4	161,850	7
Rhode Island	152,403	21			137,212	19
South Carolina	137,171	35	133,741	26	130,312	26
South Dakota	118,173	48			110,377	48
Tennessee	159,288	18	153,984	10	148,668	11
Texas	150,000	24	141,250	20	132,500	23
Utah	145,350	28	138,750	21	132,150	24
Vermont	129,245	41			122,867	37
Virginia	183,839	7	168,322	7	158,134	9
Washington	164,221	13	156,328	9	148,832	10
West Virginia	121,000	45			116,000	43
Wisconsin	141,566	30	133,552	27	125,992	30
Wyoming	126,500	42			120,400	40

Source: National Center for State Courts, "Survey of Judicial Salaries" (as of January 1, 2009) at www.ncsconline.org/D_KIS/salary_survey/.

Qualifications and Training   Although in most jurisdictions lower-court judges
are not required to be lawyers or to possess any special educational or professional training, nearly all states require judges who sit on the benches of appellate courts and trial courts of general jurisdiction to be licensed attorneys and
members of the state bar association. However, being a lawyer is not the same
as being a judge. Many judges come to the bench without any practical experience with criminal law or procedure. Consequently, many states now require
new appellate court and trial court judges to attend state-sponsored judicial
training seminars. In addition, more than 1,500 judges a year take 1- to 4-week
summer courses offered by the National Judicial College, founded in 1963 and
located at the University of Nevada, Reno. Despite those efforts, most judges
still learn the intricacies of their profession on the job.

THINKING CRITICALLY

1. Do you think prosecutors have too much power? Why or why not?

2. Of the different types of attorneys a defendant might have, which one do you think will do the best
job of defending the accused? Why?

3. Which method of selecting judges do you think is best? Why?

Pretrial Stages

As described in Chapter 2, probably fewer than one-half of the crimes committed each year are reported to the police and, of those, only a fraction are officially recorded. Of the crimes that are recorded by the police, only about 20%
are "cleared by arrest." Still, an arrest by no means guarantees prosecution and
conviction. As a result of initial prosecutorial screening, for example, about
25% of all arrests are rejected, diverted, or referred to other jurisdictions.
Another 20% or so of all people arrested are released later for various reasons
during one of the pretrial stages. Thus a powerful "funneling" or screening
process in the administration of justice eliminates about one-half of all persons
arrested. Figures 8.6 and 8.7 illustrate this funneling or screening process.

Figure 8.6

Funneling Effect

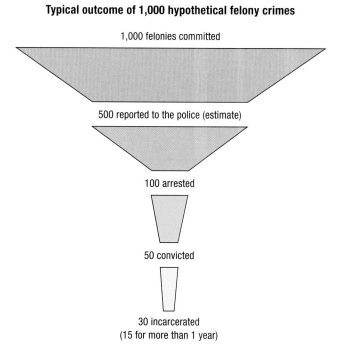

Typical outcome of 1,000 hypothetical felony crimes

1,000 felonies committed

500 reported to the police (estimate)

100 arrested

50 convicted

30 incarcerated
(15 for more than 1 year)

Figure 8.7

Outcome of 100 Criminal Cases in State Courts of Large Urban Counties

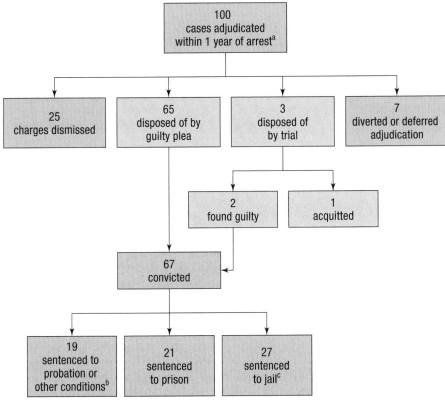

Notes: [a]From May 2002–May 2003.

[b]Other conditions include fines, community service, and treatment.

[c]Includes split sentences (jail and probation).

Source: Adapted from Thomas H. Cohen and Brian A. Reaves, *Felony Defendants in Large Urban Counties, 2002,* U.S. Department of Justice, Bureau of Justice Statistics (Washington, D.C.: GPO, February 2006).

The pretrial stages do not have the same names or order in every jurisdiction. So what follows should be considered only a general overview. States are required to provide only a prompt, neutral review of the evidence to determine whether there is probable cause that the suspect/defendant committed the crime or crimes with which he or she is charged. *Probable cause*, which was described in more detail in Chapter 4, is an abstract term that basically means that a law enforcement officer or a judge has trustworthy evidence that would make a reasonable person believe that, more likely than not, the proposed action, such as an arrest, is justified. Figure 1.2 in Chapter 1 provides a simplified view of the caseflow through the criminal justice process, highlighting pretrial stages.[35] Following a brief consideration of caseflow management, we describe the pretrial stages typical of many jurisdictions.

CASEFLOW MANAGEMENT

Increasingly large caseloads in the state and federal courts are requiring new management skills that enable the courts to process a huge volume of civil and criminal cases as efficiently as possible. In a recent book on the subject, caseflow management was called "the conceptual heart of judicial administration in the new millennium."[36] Today's court administrators (see the Careers in Criminal Justice box on the next page) are being influenced by basic business principles. Among the subjects being learned about managing jury trials, for example, are "How to Relieve Juror Boredom," "Routine Use of Anonymous

 Trial Court
Administrator Salaries

As of January 1, 2009 state trial court administrators earned a median annual salary of $126,738. The mean annual salary was $132,984. Annual salaries ranged from a low of $76,500 to a high of $211,272.

Source: National Center for State Courts, "Survey of Judicial Salaries" (as of January 1, 2009) at www.ncsconline.org/D_KIS/Salary_Survey/.

Juries," "Juror Questions to Witnesses," and "Post-Verdict Debriefings with the Trial Judge."[37] There is even a manual for *Managing Notorious Cases.*[38]

FROM ARREST THROUGH INITIAL APPEARANCE

Soon after most suspects are arrested, they are taken to the police station to be "booked." **Booking** is the process in which suspects' names, the charges for which they were arrested, and perhaps their fingerprints or photographs are entered on the police blotter. Following booking, a prosecutor is asked to review the facts of the case and, considering the available evidence, to decide whether a suspect should be charged with a crime or crimes (sometimes prosecutors review a case prior to the arrest). As a result of the review, the prosecutor may tell the police that they do not have a case or that the case is weak, requiring further investigation and additional evidence.

However, if the prosecutor decides that a suspect is "chargeable," the prosecutor prepares a charging document. The crime or crimes with which the suspect is charged may or may not be the same crime or crimes for which the suspect was originally arrested.

There are three primary kinds of charging documents: (1) a complaint, (2) an information, and (3) a grand jury indictment. If the offense is either a misdemeanor or an ordinance violation, then the prosecutor in many jurisdictions prepares a complaint. A **complaint** is a charge that an offense has been committed by a person or persons named or described. Complaints must be supported by the oath or affirmation of either the arresting officer or the victim. If the offense is a felony, an information is used in those states that do not rely on a grand jury indictment. An **information** outlines the formal charge or charges, the law or laws that have been violated, and the evidence to support the charge or charges. A **grand jury indictment,** on the other hand, is a written accusation by a grand jury charging that one or more persons have committed a crime. Informations and grand juries are described later in this section.

booking The process in which suspects' names, the charges for which they were arrested, and perhaps their fingerprints or photographs are entered on the police blotter.

complaint A charging document specifying that an offense has been committed by a person or persons named or described; usually used for misdemeanors and ordinance violations.

information A document that outlines the formal charge or charges, the law or laws that have been violated, and the evidence to support the charge or charges.

grand jury indictment A written accusation by a grand jury charging that one or more persons have committed a crime.

318

On rare occasions, the police obtain an arrest warrant from a lower-court judge before making an arrest. An **arrest warrant** is a written order directing law enforcement officers to arrest a person. The charge or charges against a suspect are specified on the warrant. Police officers more frequently make an arrest and then apply for an arrest warrant. Some jurisdictions have created joint police-prosecution teams so that decisions about arrest and chargeability can be coordinated and can be made early on. If no charges are filed, the suspect must be released.

After the charge or charges have been filed, suspects, who are now *defendants,* are brought before a lower-court judge for an initial appearance, where they are given formal notice of the charges against them and advised of their constitutional rights (for example, the right to counsel). For misdemeanors or ordinance violations, a summary trial may be held at the initial appearance. About 75% of misdemeanants and ordinance violators plead guilty at the initial appearance and are sentenced on the spot. For felonies, a hearing is held to determine whether the suspect should be released or whether there is probable cause to hold the suspect for a preliminary hearing. If the suspect is to be held for a preliminary hearing, bail may be set if the judge believes release on bail is appropriate. In states that do not utilize preliminary hearings, an arraignment date is scheduled at the initial appearance.

One of the critical questions about the initial appearance is how long suspects may be held in jail before being brought before a judge. In some countries the answer to the question is "indefinitely," but in the United States there is a limit so that innocent persons are not left in jail too long. If suspects are freed after having posted station-house bail (based on a bail fee schedule for minor offenses posted at the police station), then the initial appearance may be several days after the arrest. However, if suspects remain in custody (the usual scenario), they must be brought for an initial appearance "without unnecessary delay." In 1975, in *Gerstein* v. *Pugh,* the Supreme Court held that a "prompt" judicial hearing is required in a warrantless arrest to determine whether the officer had probable cause to make the arrest. The vast majority of arrests are warrantless. If suspects are not brought before a judge promptly, then they are to be released. The one exception to this requirement is suspects arrested on a Friday night and not brought before a judge until Monday morning.

A problem with the Supreme Court's promptness requirement is that the Court did not define *prompt.* The norm in most jurisdictions was between 24 and 72 hours. Even after the ruling, however, some jurisdictions held suspects much longer than that. For example, in 1975, a district court judge in Birmingham, Alabama, ruled that because of abusive holding practices in that city, suspects arrested on a felony charge could not be held longer than 24 hours. In 1984, the same judge set a new limit of 8 hours for holding suspects, because his previous order had been ignored. The judge added, however, that in certain cases a limited time extension could be obtained. In 1991, in *County of Riverside* v. *McLaughlin,* the Supreme Court finally clarified the situation by ruling that anyone arrested without a warrant may be held no longer than 48 hours before a judge decides whether the arrest was justified.

BAIL AND OTHER METHODS OF PRETRIAL RELEASE

A **bail bond** or **bail** is usually a monetary guarantee deposited with the court that is supposed to ensure that the suspect or defendant will appear at a later stage in the criminal justice process. In other words, it allows suspects or defendants to remain free while awaiting the next stage in the adjudication process. It is *not* a fine or a penalty; it is only an incentive to appear. Opportunities for bail follow arrest, initial appearance, preliminary hearing, arraignment, and conviction.

arrest warrant A written order directing law enforcement officers to arrest a person. The charge or charges against a suspect are specified on the warrant.

FYI Bail

The granting of bail and pretrial release to criminal suspects was common practice in England by the twelfth century. It was officially recognized and legally regulated by the Statute of Westminster in 1275.

Source: No author, "Bail: An Ancient Practice Reexamined," *Yale Law Journal* 70 (1961), pp. 966–977.

bail bond or **bail** Usually a monetary guarantee deposited with the court that is supposed to ensure that the suspect or defendant will appear at a later stage in the criminal justice process.

Without the cooperation of the bail bond industry, jail populations would be unmanageable. *Is that reason enough to allow the bail bond industry to exist?*

preventive detention Holding suspects or defendants in jail without giving them an opportunity to post bail, because of the threat they pose to society.

MYTH

Preventive detention will reduce violent crime.

FACT

Preventive detention is not new and has always been used by judges in the United States, even though it was not referred to by that name. Judges simply set bail at a level beyond the financial means of a person suspected of violent crime.

Although bail-setting practices vary widely by jurisdiction, the amount of bail, assuming that bail is granted, generally depends on the likelihood that the suspect or defendant will appear in court as required. If the suspect or defendant has strong ties to the community—for example, a house, a family, or a job—then the amount of bail will be relatively low (depending on the seriousness of the offense and other factors). However, if the suspect or defendant has few or no ties to the community, the amount of bail will be relatively high, or the judge may refuse to grant bail.

Next to likelihood of appearance, the most important factor in a judge's determination of the amount of bail—and, perhaps, whether bail is granted at all—is the seriousness of the crime. Generally, the more serious the crime, the higher the bail amount. Table 8.4 shows the percentage of felony defendants released before or detained until case disposition by most serious arrest charge in 2004 (the latest year for which data were available). A third influence on the amount of bail is prior criminal record. A prior criminal record usually increases the amount of bail. Jail conditions are a fourth influencing factor—at least on whether bail is set. If the jail is overcrowded, as are many of the jails in the United States, judges are more likely to grant bail, particularly in borderline cases.

In rare cases, when a judge believes that a suspect or defendant would pose a threat to the community if released, the judge can refuse to set bail. Holding suspects or defendants in jail without giving them an opportunity to post bail, because of the threat they pose to society, is called **preventive detention.** Preventive detention is used most often in cases involving violent crimes, drug crimes, and immigration offenses. However, in *U.S.* v. *Salerno* (1987), the Supreme Court made clear that before a judge can legally deny bail for reasons of preventive detention, a suspect or defendant must have the opportunity for a hearing on the decision. At the hearing, the individual circumstances of the suspect or defendant (such as community ties, convictions, and past dangerous tendencies) must be considered. About 60% of all states and the federal jurisdiction have enacted laws that provide for some form of preventive detention, although the laws, at least at the state level, are rarely implemented. The reason is that they are unnecessary. Judges have traditionally imposed high bail amounts on dangerous suspects or defendants. Preventive detention has been employed more frequently at the federal level.

For suspects or defendants who cannot afford to post bail, professional bonds people, who are private entrepreneurs, are available to post it for them for a nonrefundable fee. The fee is typically 10% of the required amount. Thus, a bonds person would collect $500 for posting a $5,000 bond. If a suspect or a defendant is considered a greater than average risk, then the bonds person can require collateral—something of value like money or property—in addition to the fee.

Bail bonds people are under no obligation to post a surety bond if they believe that a suspect or a defendant is a bad risk. If bonds people believe that a client might flee and not appear as required, they have the right to revoke the bond without refunding the fee. Bail bonds people or their agents (modern-day bounty hunters known as "skip tracers") are also allowed, without a warrant, to track down clients who fail to appear and to return them forcibly, if

Table 8.4 Felony Defendants Released Before or Detained Until Case Disposition by Most Serious Arrest Charge, 2004

Most Serious Arrest Charge	Number of Defendants	PERCENT OF DEFENDANTS IN THE 75 LARGEST COUNTIES		
		Total	Released Before Case Disposition	Detained Until Case Disposition
All offenses	54,979	100%	57%	43%
Violent offenses	12,532	100%	51%	49%
Murder	348	100	12	88
Rape	499	100	52	48
Robbery	3,001	100	42	58
Assault	6,609	100	55	45
Other violent	2,076	100	57	43
Property offenses	16,840	100%	57%	43%
Burglary	4,359	100	46	54
Larceny/theft	4,291	100	58	42
Motor vehicle theft	2,011	100	39	61
Forgery	1,999	100	72	28
Fraud	1,771	100	73	27
Other property	2,409	100	64	36
Drug offenses	20,074	100%	60%	40%
Trafficking	8,275	100	60	40
Other drug	11,799	100	60	40
Public-order offenses	5,533	100%	65%	35%
Weapons	1,710	100	58	42
Driving-related	1,730	100	69	31
Other public-order	2,093	100	66	34

Note: Data on detention/release outcome were available for 98% of all cases. Detail may not add to total because of rounding.

Source: Tracy Kyckelhahn and Thomas H. Cohen, "Felony Defendants in Large Urban Counties, 2004—Statistical Tables," Table 9, U.S. Department of Justice, Bureau of Justice Statistics (Washington, D.C.: GPO, revised April 25, 2008) at www.ojp.usdoj.gov/bjs/pub/html/fdluc/2004/tables/fdluc04st9.htm

necessary, to the jurisdiction from which they fled. If the client crosses state lines, the bonds person does not have to seek extradition, as would a law enforcement official, to bring the client back. Clients sign extradition waivers as a condition of receiving bail.

In practice, most bail bonds people assume little risk. Many of them use part of their fee (generally 30%) to secure a surety bond from a major insurance company, which then assumes financial liability if the bail is forfeited. However, even this practice is unnecessary in many jurisdictions, because the courts do not collect forfeited bonds. Judges are able to use their discretion to simply vacate outstanding bonds and, by doing so, relieve the bail bonds person or the insurance company of any financial obligation. Judges vacate bonds because they realize that without the cooperation of bail bonds people, the courts would be faced with an unmanageably large jail population and prohibitively high pretrial detention costs. If the bond is not vacated, the bonds person will generally stop looking for the fugitive after 2 years because, by then, there is little chance that the bonds person will get his or her money back.[39]

Suspects or defendants who post their own bail ("full cash bond," 100% of the amount required), or have family members or friends do it for them, get it all back after they appear. Sometimes the court will accept property instead of cash. If the suspect or defendant does not appear, the bail is forfeited and

CJ Online

Bail Agents

You can learn more about how bail agents work by going to the website of The Professional Bail Agents of the United States at www.pbus.com, where you can review the code of ethics for bail agents. *What does the code of ethics tell you about the different responsibilities of a bail agent?*

Table 8.5 Released Felony Defendants Who Failed to Make a Scheduled Court Appearance, by Most Serious Arrest Charge, 2004

Most Serious Arrest Charge	Number of Defendants	Made All Court Appearances	PERCENT OF RELEASED FELONY DEFENDANTS IN THE 75 LARGEST COUNTIES WHO: FAILED TO APPEAR IN COURT		
			Total	Returned to Court	Remained a Fugitive
All offenses	31,280	79%	21%	16%	5%
Violent offenses	6,309	86%	14%	11%	3%
Murder	42	100	0	0	0
Rape	249	90	10	9	2
Robbery	1,238	82	18	13	5
Assault	3,619	87	13	10	3
Other violent	1,162	87	13	9	4
Property offenses	9,470	77%	23%	18%	6%
Burglary	1,973	80	20	17	3
Larceny/theft	2,473	80	20	17	4
Motor vehicle theft	782	68	32	26	6
Forgery	1,420	72	28	22	7
Fraud	1,282	82	18	13	5
Other property	1,541	73	27	17	11
Drug offenses	11,973	76%	24%	18%	6%
Trafficking	4,974	76	24	18	6
Other drug	6,999	77	23	18	6
Public-order offenses	3,523	83%	17%	14%	3%
Weapons	990	80	20	16	5
Driving-related	1,189	83	17	14	3
Other public-order	1,345	85	15	13	3

Note: Data on the court appearance record for the current case were available for 99% of cases involving a defendant released prior to case disposition. All defendants who failed to appear in court and were not returned to the court during the 1-year study period are counted as fugitives. Some of these defendants may have been returned to the court at a later date. Detail may not add to total because of rounding.

Source: Tracy Kyckelhahn and Thomas H. Cohen, "Felony Defendants in Large Urban Counties, 2004—Statistical Tables," Table 16, U.S. Department of Justice, Bureau of Justice Statistics (Washington, D.C.: GPO, revised April 25, 2008) at www.ojp.usdoj.gov/bjs/pub/html/fdluc/2004/tables/fdluc04st16.htm

bench warrant or *capias* A document that authorizes a suspect's or defendant's arrest for not appearing in court as required.

the judge issues a **bench warrant,** or *capias,* authorizing the suspect's or defendant's arrest. It is estimated that about 10,000 criminal defendants skip bail each year, costing local governments tens of millions of dollars. Part of the problem is that overburdened courts are not pursuing many criminal defendants on bond that fail to appear. Another problem is that new companies are writing bonds for more high-risk defendants. However, not all bail skippers flee. Some are just irresponsible and do not come to court until someone drags them in. Others change their address so often they do not receive the notices to appear. Still others do not appear because they are in jail or prison in other counties or states.[40] Once arrested, the absconder must be brought before the judge who issued the warrant and cannot be released on bail again. Failure to appear also constitutes a new offense, "bond jumping," that carries criminal penalties. Table 8.5 shows the percentage of released felony defendants who failed to make a scheduled court appearance by most serious arrest charge in 2004 (the latest year for which data were available).

Courts in Illinois, Kentucky, and Pennsylvania, as well as the federal courts, allow defendants to post 10% of the required bond (*deposit bond*) directly with the court, thereby circumventing the need for bail bonds people. When a defendant makes all required court appearances, 90% of the amount

Table 8.6 Median and Mean Bail Amounts Set for Felony Defendants, by Pretrial Release/Detention Outcome and Most Serious Arrest Charge, 2004

| | FELONY DEFENDANTS IN THE 75 LARGEST COUNTIES | | | | | |
| | MEDIAN BAIL AMOUNT | | | MEAN BAIL AMOUNT | | |
Most Serious Arrest Charge	Total	Released	Detained	Total	Released	Detained
All offenses	$10,000	$6,000	$25,000	$52,500	$16,600	$85,800
Violent offenses	$25,000	$10,000	$50,000	$99,900	$20,700	$166,700
Murder	500,000	25,000	500,000	819,500	50,800	926,600
Rape	50,000	25,000	150,000	142,400	37,000	253,600
Robbery	25,000	10,000	50,000	68,700	22,900	92,200
Assault	15,000	7,500	50,000	72,400	15,300	130,900
Other violent	25,000	15,000	75,000	125,800	30,600	224,300
Property offenses	$10,000	$5,000	$20,000	$33,500	$12,900	$49,600
Burglary	20,000	10,000	25,000	43,100	15,300	58,800
Larceny/theft	7,500	5,000	15,000	27,700	9,400	43,900
Motor vehicle theft	20,000	5,000	20,000	32,600	17,000	37,700
Forgery	5,000	5,000	15,000	27,100	6,800	64,300
Fraud	7,500	5,000	10,000	35,500	23,600	52,500
Other property	10,000	5,000	20,000	28,600	10,200	44,700
Drug offenses	$10,000	$5,700	$25,000	$39,200	$18,200	$61,200
Trafficking	15,000	10,000	25,000	54,400	26,900	85,600
Other drug	10,000	5,000	20,000	26,000	9,900	41,600
Public-order offenses	$10,000	$5,000	$25,000	$31,300	$11,300	$57,700
Weapons	15,000	8,000	35,000	39,300	14,100	66,600
Driving-related	5,000	3,500	20,000	18,900	7,700	39,900
Other public-order	10,000	5,000	15,000	35,600	12,900	61,400

Note: Data on bail amount were available for 96% of all defendants for whom a bail amount was set. Table excludes defendants given nonfinancial release.

Source: Tracy Kyckelhahn and Thomas H. Cohen, "Felony Defendants in Large Urban Counties, 2004—Statistical Tables," Table 12, U.S. Department of Justice, Bureau of Justice Statistics (Washington, D.C.: GPO, revised April 25, 2008) at www.ojp.usdoj.gov/bjs/pub/html/fdluc/2004/tables/fdluc04st12.htm

posted is refunded (the remaining 10% covers administrative costs). Defendants who fail to appear are still liable for the entire bail amount.

As noted in Chapter 4, the Eighth Amendment to the Constitution does not require that bail be granted to all suspects or defendants. It requires only that the amount of bail, when granted, not be excessive. What constitutes excessive bail is determined by several factors, including the nature and circumstances of the offense, the weight of evidence against the suspect/defendant, the character of the suspect/defendant, and the ability of the suspect/defendant to provide bail. Table 8.6 shows the median and mean bail amounts set for felony defendants by pretrial release/detention outcome and most serious arrest charge in 2004 (the latest year for which data were available).

The bail system has been criticized for unfairly discriminating against the poor, who are the least likely to have the assets for their own bail and are least able to pay the fee to a bail bonds person. About 85% of all suspects or defendants are released before the final disposition of their cases, but, in some jurisdictions, as many as 90% of them are held in jail because they are unable to afford bail. In most jurisdictions, defendants held in jail because they are unable to post bail (about one-half of the jail population nationwide) are mixed with the rest of the jail population, that is, convicted offenders. They are also treated in the same way as the rest of the jail population. One of the tragedies of this practice is the occasional brutalization (for example, rape) of the jailed indigent

MYTH

The most dangerous defendants released on bail are the ones least likely to appear as required.

FACT

Defendants accused of minor offenses and released on bail have the highest rates of failure to appear.

defendant whose case is later dismissed for lack of evidence or who is found not guilty at trial. Although brutalization of any prisoner is horrible and reprehensible, it is particularly so when the prisoner is an innocent person.

Jailed indigent defendants are also likely to lose their jobs and have their personal lives disrupted in other ways as a result of their detention. Studies consistently show that jailed defendants, who are frequently brought into court in jail clothes and handcuffs, are more likely to be indicted and convicted and are sentenced more severely than defendants who have been released pending the next stage in the process. However, it is not clear whether those disparities are the result of pretrial detention or of the selection process in which suspects or defendants charged with more serious crimes and with prior criminal records are more likely to be denied bail.

When the crime is minor and suspects or defendants have ties to the community, they are generally released on their own recognizance. **Release on own recognizance (ROR)** is simply a release secured by a suspect's written promise to appear in court. Another nonfinancial means of release, more restrictive than ROR, is **conditional release.** This form of release (sometimes called *supervised release*) usually requires that a suspect/defendant maintain contact with a pretrial release program or undergo regular drug monitoring or treatment. Some conditional release programs also require a third-party custody agreement (that is, a promise by a reputable person to monitor the person released). Another way that suspects or defendants are released without a financial requirement is by **unsecured bond.** Under this arrangement, bail is set, but no money is paid to the court. Suspects or defendants are liable for the full amount of bail if they do not appear as required. Table 8.7 shows the type of pretrial release or detention of felony defendants by most serious arrest charge in 2004 (the latest year for which data were available).

INFORMATION

If the decision is made to prosecute a defendant, in states that do not use grand juries, the prosecutor drafts a document called an *information.* The information outlines the formal charge or charges, the law or laws that have been violated, and the evidence to support the charge or charges. The information is generally filed with the court at the preliminary hearing or, if the preliminary hearing is waived, at the arraignment.

PRELIMINARY HEARING

The purpose of the **preliminary hearing,** used in about one-half of all states, is for a judge to determine whether there is probable cause to support the charge or charges imposed by the prosecutor. Preliminary hearings are used only in felony cases, and defendants may waive the right to the hearing. A preliminary hearing is similar to a criminal trial in two ways but also differs from a criminal trial in two ways. It is similar in that defendants can be represented by legal counsel and can call witnesses on their behalf. It differs in that the judge must determine only that there is probable cause that the defendant committed the crime or crimes with which he or she is charged. At criminal trials, guilt must be determined "beyond a reasonable doubt." Also, at preliminary hearings, unlike criminal trials, defendants have no right to be heard by a jury.

If the judge determines that there is probable cause that a defendant committed the crime or crimes with which he or she is charged, then the defendant is bound over for possible indictment in states with grand juries or for arraignment on an information in states without grand juries. In grand jury states, even if the judge at the preliminary hearing rules that there is insufficient evidence to proceed, the case is not necessarily dropped. The

release on own recognizance (ROR) A release secured by a suspect's written promise to appear in court.

conditional release A form of release that requires that a suspect/defendant maintain contact with a pretrial release program or undergo regular drug monitoring or treatment.

unsecured bond An arrangement in which bail is set but no money is paid to the court.

preliminary hearing A pretrial stage used in about one-half of all states and only in felony cases. Its purpose is for a judge to determine whether there is probable cause to support the charge or charges imposed by the prosecutor.

Table 8.7 Type of Pretrial Release or Detention of Felony Defendants, by Most Serious Arrest Charge, 2004

PERCENT OF FELONY DEFENDANTS IN THE 75 LARGEST COUNTIES

Most Serious Arrest Charge	RELEASED BEFORE CASE DISPOSITION									DETAINED UNTIL CASE DISPOSITION	
	FINANCIAL RELEASE					NONFINANCIAL RELEASE					
	Total Financial	Surety Bond	Deposit Bond	Full Cash Bond	Property Bond	Total Non-financial	Recognizance	Conditional	Unsecured	Held on Bail	Denied Bail
All offenses	32%	25%	5%	1%	1%	26%	14%	9%	2%	37%	6%
Violent offenses	34%	26%	6%	1%	1%	17%	7%	9%	1%	41%	8%
Murder	9	6	0	0	3	3	3	1	0	52	36
Rape	37	26	6	3	1	15	8	7	1	41	8
Robbery	26	20	6	0	0	16	7	9	—	52	7
Assault	38	28	7	1	1	17	7	9	1	38	7
Other violent	38	34	3	2	—	19	10	8	1	37	7
Property offenses	27%	23%	3%	1%	1%	29%	17%	9%	3%	37%	6%
Burglary	25	22	3	1	1	20	11	7	3	47	8
Larceny/theft	29	25	3	1	1	29	15	11	4	36	5
Motor vehicle theft	18	16	2	1	0	21	11	9	1	55	6
Forgery	34	26	4	1	3	38	24	13	2	21	7
Fraud	32	29	2	1	0	40	26	11	4	23	4
Other property	26	19	5	2	2	38	25	8	4	31	5
Drug offenses	32%	24%	7%	1%	1%	28%	15%	10%	3%	35%	5%
Trafficking	37	25	11	1	1	23	12	10	2	36	4
Other drug	28	23	4	1	1	32	17	11	4	35	5
Public-order offenses	38%	31%	5%	1%	—%	27%	18%	7%	3%	30%	5%
Weapons	39	26	12	1	1	19	13	5	2	37	5
Driving-related	46	41	2	2	—	24	15	8	1	27	4
Other public-order	30	27	3	1	1	36	24	7	5	28	6

Note: Data on specific type of pretrial release or detention were available for 90% of all cases.

Detail may not add to total because of rounding.

—Less than 0.5%.

Source: Tracy Kyckelhahn and Thomas H. Cohen, "Felony Defendants in Large Urban Counties, 2004—Statistical Tables," Table 10, U.S. Department of Justice, Bureau of Justice Statistics (Washington, D.C.: GPO, revised April 25, 2008) at www.ojp.usdoj.gov/bjs/pub/html/fdluc/2004/tables/fdluc04st10.htm

prosecutor could take the case directly to the grand jury. If the case is not dropped for lack of evidence, then the judge may set bail again or may continue the previous bail to ensure that the defendant appears at the next stage in the process.

Although judges at preliminary hearings are supposed to examine the facts of the case before making a probable cause determination, in practice they seldom do. In big cities, judges do not generally have the time to inquire into the facts of a case. Consequently, at most preliminary hearings, judges simply assume that if a police officer made an arrest and a prosecutor charged the defendant with a crime or crimes, then there must be probable cause that the defendant, in fact, committed the crime or crimes. Few cases are dismissed for lack of probable cause at preliminary hearings.

GRAND JURY

grand jury Generally a group of 12 to 23 citizens who meet in closed sessions to investigate charges coming from preliminary hearings or to engage in other responsibilities. A primary purpose of the grand jury is to determine whether there is probable cause to believe that the accused committed the crime or crimes.

A **grand jury** is generally a group of 12 to 23 citizens who, for a specific period of time (generally 3 months), meet in closed sessions to investigate charges coming from preliminary hearings or to engage in other responsibilities. Thus a primary purpose of the grand jury is to determine whether there is probable cause to believe that the accused is guilty of the charge or charges brought by the prosecutor. Grand juries do not convene every day. Many federal grand juries meet only once a week, and some may meet only twice a month. State practice varies, but a state grand jury may meet only twice a month, or even only once a month. Sometimes a grand jury does not convene unless it is asked to do so by a prosecutor with cases to hear.

indictment A document that outlines the charge or charges against a defendant.

Before appearing before a grand jury, the prosecutor drafts an **indictment,** a document that outlines the charge or charges against a defendant. Because the grand jury has to determine only whether there is probable cause that a defendant committed the crime or crimes with which he or she is charged, only the prosecution's evidence and witnesses are heard. In most jurisdictions, neither the defendant nor the defendant's counsel has a right to be present during the proceedings. Furthermore, in grand jury proceedings, unlike criminal trials, prosecutors are allowed to present *hearsay* evidence (information learned from someone other than the witness who is testifying). They may also use illegally obtained evidence because the exclusionary rule does not apply to grand jury proceedings. Prosecutors can subpoena witnesses to testify. A **subpoena** is a written order to testify issued by a court officer. A witness who refuses to testify can be held in contempt and can be jailed until he or she provides the requested information. In practice, however, a witness jailed for contempt is generally held only as long as the grand jury is in session and no longer than 18 months in the federal jurisdiction.

subpoena A written order to testify issued by a court officer.

After hearing the prosecutor's evidence and witnesses, the grand jury makes its probable cause determination and, usually on a majority vote, either indicts (issues a *true bill*) or fails to indict (issues *no bill*). If the grand jury fails to indict, then in most jurisdictions, the prosecution must be dropped. However, in some jurisdictions, the case can be brought before another grand jury.

All but two states and the District of Columbia use grand juries to indict. Twenty-three states plus the District of Columbia require that indictments be used to charge certain crimes, generally serious crimes. Twenty-five states make the use of indictments optional. Connecticut and Pennsylvania have abolished the use of grand juries to return indictments, but they have retained them to investigate crimes and the conduct of public affairs. The most common civil matter they investigate is the operation and condition of local jails and other confinement facilities. In the federal system, a grand jury indictment is required in all felony prosecutions, unless the defendant waives that right. The alternative to the grand jury is the filing of an information.[41]

In practice, the grand jury system is criticized for merely providing a rubber stamp for whatever the prosecutor wants to do. In other words, in cases where the prosecutor wants an indictment, the grand jury is likely to indict. Likewise, in cases where the prosecutor does not want to indict, the grand jury tends to fail to indict. The reason that prosecutors are so successful with grand juries is that they manage the entire proceedings (remember, only the prosecution's evidence and witnesses are heard). So it should not be surprising that suspects waive the right to a grand jury hearing in about 80% of cases. Defendants may also waive the right to a grand jury hearing to speed up their trial date.

You might be wondering why prosecutors would want a grand jury to fail to indict after they have gone to the trouble of bringing a case to the grand jury in the first place. The reason is political. To avoid losing marginal cases or looking cowardly by dropping charges, prosecutors can bring a case to the grand jury, have the grand jury fail to indict, and then blame the grand jury for its failure. The strategy deflects criticism from the prosecutor to the anonymous members of the grand jury. Sometimes prosecutors delay preliminary hearings to await a grand jury action to avoid disclosing evidence in open court that might help defense attorneys at trial. Because of the way the grand jury is used today, some critics of the system suggest that it ought to be abolished.

ARRAIGNMENT

The primary purpose of an **arraignment** is to hear the formal information or indictment and to allow the defendant to enter a plea. The two most common pleas are "guilty" and "not guilty." "Not guilty" is the most common plea at arraignments. However, some states and the federal courts allow defendants to plead *nolo contendere* to the charges against them. **Nolo contendere** is Latin for "no contest." When defendants plead "*nolo*," they do not admit guilt but are willing to accept punishment anyway. The *nolo* plea is used for strategic purposes. If a defendant does not admit guilt in a criminal trial, admission of guilt cannot be the basis for a subsequent civil lawsuit. If there is a subsequent civil lawsuit, the lack of an admission of guilt in a criminal trial may allow the defendant to avoid a penalty of treble, or triple, damages. Furthermore, in some states, defendants can stand mute or can plead "not guilty by reason of insanity." Standing mute at arraignment is interpreted as pleading "not guilty." In states that do not accept a plea of "not guilty by reason of insanity," defendants plead "not guilty" and assume the burden of proving insanity at trial.

If a defendant pleads guilty, the judge must determine whether the plea was made voluntarily and whether the defendant is fully aware of the consequences of his or her action. If the judge doubts either of those conditions, then the judge can refuse to accept the guilty plea and can enter in the record a plea of "not guilty" for the defendant.

At arraignment, the judge also determines whether a defendant is competent to stand trial. Defendants can seek a delay before trial to consult further with their attorneys. A defendant who does not already have an attorney can ask for one to be appointed. Finally, defendants sometimes attempt to have their cases dismissed at arraignment. For example, they may assert that the state lacks sufficient evidence or that improper arrest procedures were used.

arraignment A pretrial stage; its primary purpose is to hear the formal information or indictment and to allow the defendant to enter a plea.

nolo contendere Latin for "no contest." When defendants plead *nolo,* they do not admit guilt but are willing to accept punishment.

THINKING CRITICALLY

1. Do you agree with the criticism that the poor are unfairly discriminated against because they are the least able to pay their own bail and the least able to pay the fee to a bail bonds person? Why or why not?

2. Do you think a preliminary hearing is necessary? Should it be abolished? Why or why not?

3. Are grand jury proceedings fair to the suspect? Why or why not?

FYI   Plea Bargaining

Plea bargaining became a common practice in state courts shortly after the Civil War. The practice was instituted at the federal level during Prohibition, in the 1930s, as a result of the tremendous number of liquor law violations.

Sources: Albert W. Alschuler, "Plea Bargaining and Its History," *Law and Society Review* 13 (1979), pp. 211–245; John F. Padgett, "Plea Bargaining and Prohibition in the Federal Courts, 1908–1934," *Law and Society Review* 24 (1990), pp. 413–450.

Plea Bargaining

As noted earlier in this chapter, justice in the United States is dispensed mostly through plea bargaining.[42] About 95% of all convictions in felony cases are the result of guilty pleas; criminal trials are relatively rare. We already saw in Figure 8.7 the typical outcome of 100 felony arrests and the prevalence of plea bargaining.

There are three basic types of plea bargains. First, the defendant may be allowed to plead guilty to a lesser offense. For example, a defendant may be allowed to plead guilty to manslaughter rather than to first-degree murder. Second, at the request of the prosecutor, a defendant who pleads guilty may receive a lighter sentence than would typically be given for the crime. Note, however, that the prosecutor can only recommend the sentence; the judge does not have to grant it. Third, a defendant may plead guilty to one charge in return for the prosecutor's promise to drop other charges that could be brought.

The bargain a prosecutor will strike generally depends on three factors. The most important factor is the seriousness of the offense. Generally, the more serious the crime, the more difficult it is to win concessions from the prosecutor. A second factor is the defendant's criminal record. Defendants with criminal records usually receive fewer concessions from prosecutors. The final factor is the strength of the prosecutor's case. The stronger the case, the stronger is the position of the prosecutor in plea negotiations.

Surprisingly, there is neither a constitutional basis nor a statutory basis for plea bargaining. It is a custom that developed because of the mutual interests it serves. The custom received formal recognition from the Supreme Court in 1970 in the case of *Brady* v. *United States*. In that case, the Court upheld the use of plea bargaining because of the "mutuality of advantage" it provided the defendant and the state. In two later cases, the Court provided safeguards for the bargaining process. In the 1971 case of *Santobello* v. *New York*, the Court held that the "deal" offered by a prosecutor in a plea negotiation must be kept. In 1976, in the case of *Henderson* v. *Morgan*, the Court held that to be valid, a guilty plea must be based on full knowledge of its implications and must be made voluntarily. However, prosecutors are under no obligation to plea-bargain. Once defendants plead guilty and are sentenced, they are almost always stuck with the bargain, even if they have a change of heart. Nevertheless, in most jurisdictions, defendants are allowed to withdraw their guilty pleas before sentencing.

As just noted, the reason justice in the United States is administered primarily through plea bargaining is that the process seemingly serves the interests of all the court participants by, among other things, reducing uncertainty. Uncertainty is a characteristic of all criminal trials, because neither the duration of the trial, which may be a matter of minutes or of months, nor the outcome of the trial can ever be predicted with any degree of accuracy. Plea bargaining eliminates those two areas of uncertainty by eliminating the need for a trial.

Plea bargaining also serves the interests of the individual participants in the administration of justice. Prosecutors, for example, are guaranteed high conviction rates. For prosecutors and, apparently, the general public, a conviction is a conviction, whether it is obtained through plea bargaining or as the result of a trial. A prosecutor's conviction rate is one of the principal indicators of job performance, and job performance certainly helps determine whether the prosecutor will fulfill his or her aspirations for higher political office.

Plea bargaining also serves the interests of judges by reducing their court caseloads, allowing more time to be spent on more difficult cases. In addition, if a large proportion of the approximately 90% of felony cases that are handled each year by plea bargaining were to go to trial instead, the administration of justice in the United States would be even slower than it already is.

Federal judges and the judges in seven states are legally prohibited from participating in plea negotiations. In other states, their role in the process is limited by law.

Plea bargaining serves the interests of criminal defense attorneys by allowing them to spend less time on each case. It also allows them to avoid trials. Trials are relatively expensive events. Because most criminal defendants are poor, they are usually unable to pay a large legal fee. Thus, when criminal defense attorneys go to trial, they are frequently unable to recoup all of their expenses. Plea bargaining provides many criminal defense attorneys with the more profitable option of charging smaller fees for lesser services and handling a larger volume of cases.

Even most criminal defendants are served by plea bargaining. A guilty plea generally results in either no prison sentence or a lesser prison sentence than the defendant might receive if found guilty at trial. Plea bargaining also often allows defendants to escape conviction of socially stigmatizing crimes, such as child abuse. By "copping" a plea to assault rather than to statutory rape, for example, a defendant can avoid the embarrassing publicity of a trial and the wrath of fellow inmates or of society in general.

Two types of criminal defendants are not served by the practice of plea bargaining. The first are innocent, indigent, highly visible defendants who fear being found guilty of crimes they did not commit and receiving harsh sentences. Such defendants are sometimes pressured by unscrupulous defense attorneys into waiving their constitutional right to trial. The second type is the habitual offender. In this context, a habitual offender is a person who has been convicted under a state's habitual-offender statute (sometimes called a "three strikes and you're out" law). Most such statutes provide that upon conviction of a third felony, a defendant must receive life imprisonment. Although habitual-offender statutes would seem to imprison offenders for life, they actually are used mostly as bargaining chips by prosecutors in plea negotiations and not as they were intended.

A problem with those statutes is illustrated by the Supreme Court case of *Bordenkircher* v. *Hayes* (1978). The defendant, who had previously been convicted of two minor felonies, was arrested and charged with forging an $88 check. The prosecutor in the case told the defendant that if he did not plead guilty to the charge and accept a 5-year prison sentence, which on its face seemed very harsh, then the prosecutor would invoke the state's habitual-offender statute. The statute required the judge to impose a sentence of life imprisonment if the defendant were found guilty at trial. The defendant elected to play "you bet your life" and turned down the prosecutor's plea offer. At trial, the defendant was found guilty of forging the check and was sentenced to life imprisonment. Clearly, the defendant in this case was not served by plea bargaining or, perhaps, was not served by refusing the prosecutor's offer. In either case, with the possible exception of habitual offenders and innocent people, plea bargaining serves the interests of all the actors in the administration of justice. It does so by allowing cases to be disposed of predictably, quickly, and with little of the adversarial conflict associated with criminal trials.

THINKING CRITICALLY

1. Do you think that the plea-bargaining process is beneficial? Why or why not?

2. Why is murder the crime least likely by far to be resolved through a guilty plea (see Table 8.1)?

3. How could the plea-bargaining process be improved?

MYTH

Abolishing plea bargaining would reduce the level of serious crime.

FACT

Despite the administrative nightmare it would cause, the abolition of plea bargaining would probably only shift discretion to another area. It would be unlikely to have any effect on crime.

 Three Strikes Laws

Although habitual-offender statutes have existed in many jurisdictions for decades, the first state to enact a "three strikes and you're out" law was Washington, in 1993. The Washington law, called the Persistent Offender Accountability Act, allows three-time felons to be imprisoned for life without parole. In August 1996, the Washington Supreme Court upheld the law as constitutional. More than half the states and the federal government have three-strike laws on their books.

Source: "Washington Court Deems '3 Strikes' Constitutional," *The Orlando Sentinel* (August 9, 1996), p. A-12.

The Criminal Trial

One of the distinctive features of criminal justice in the United States is trial by a jury of one's peers.[43] The principal purpose of jury trials—and of criminal trials without juries—is to discover the truth of whether defendants are guilty or innocent of the crimes with which they are charged. The process by which truth is sought is an adversarial one regulated by very specific procedures and rules. The adversaries in a criminal trial are the state (represented by the prosecutor) and the defendant (usually represented by defense counsel). The burden of proof is on the prosecution to show, beyond a reasonable doubt, that the defendant is guilty. The goal of defense counsel is to discredit the prosecution's case and to create reasonable doubt about the defendant's guilt. It is the responsibility of the jury (in jury trials) or the judge (in trials without juries) to determine and assign guilt.

Although all criminal defendants have a constitutional right to a jury trial (when imprisonment for 6 months or more is a possible outcome), only about 2% of all criminal cases are disposed of in this way. Approximately 95% of cases are resolved through a guilty plea, and the remaining cases are decided by a judge in a **bench trial** (without a jury). In most jurisdictions, defendants may choose whether they want to exercise their right to a jury trial or whether they prefer a bench trial. The principal reason that so few criminal cases are decided by criminal trials is undoubtedly the advantages associated with plea bargaining.

THE JURY

Trial by an impartial jury of one's peers is an exalted American tradition and a Sixth Amendment right.[44] Its principal purposes are these:

1. To protect citizens against arbitrary law enforcement.
2. To prevent government oppression.
3. To protect citizens from overzealous or corrupt prosecutors and from eccentric or biased judges.

But jury trials in the United States are relatively rare. So on those rare occasions when defendants are tried by a jury, seldom is the jury composed of their peers. Until the mid-twentieth century, many states excluded women and people of color from jury service. Even today, class, gender, and racial biases enter into the jury selection process.

In many jurisdictions, jury pools are selected from voter registration lists. About 30% of eligible voters do not register; in some jurisdictions, the rate is as high as 60%. People not registered to vote are excluded from jury service. Studies show that the poor, the poorly educated, the young, and people of color are least likely to register to vote and, as a result, are least likely to be called for jury service. To remedy this problem, some jurisdictions now use multiple-source lists for obtaining jurors. In addition to voter registration lists, their sources include lists of licensed drivers, lists of utility users, and names listed in the telephone directory. Appellate courts have ruled that master jury lists must reflect an impartial and representative cross-section of the population. People of color and women cannot be excluded systematically from juries solely because of race, ethnicity, or gender. But this does not mean that people of color and women must be included on all juries, only that they cannot be denied the opportunity of being chosen for jury service.

From the master list of all eligible jurors (sometimes called the *master wheel* or the *jury wheel*), a sufficient number of people are randomly chosen to make up the jury pool, or **venire.** Those chosen are summoned for service by the sheriff. However, not all those summoned will actually serve on the venire. Potential jurors must generally be U.S. citizens, residents of the locality of the trial, of a certain minimum age, and able to understand English. Convicted

---

MYTH

Criminal justice in the United States is dispensed primarily through jury trials.

FACT

Jury trials are relatively rare. Approximately 95% of all criminal cases are resolved through guilty pleas. Only about 5% are decided by bench or jury trials.

bench trial A trial before a judge without a jury.

FYI Trial by Jury

Trial by a jury of one's peers originated in England as a way of limiting the power of the king. When the Magna Carta was signed in 1215, it contained the following provision: No freeman shall be taken, or imprisoned, or disseized, or outlawed, or exiled, or in any way harmed—nor will we go upon or send upon him—save by the lawful judgment of his peers or by the law of the land.

Source: "Magna Carta" at www.britannia.com/history/magna2.html.

venire The pool from which jurors are selected.

felons and insane persons are almost always excluded. Most jurisdictions also require that jurors be of "good character" and be "well-informed," which eliminates other potential jurors. In addition, members of other groups often escape jury service. Professionals such as doctors, lawyers, and teachers; some elected officials; military personnel on active duty; and law enforcement personnel frequently are not called for jury duty because their professional services are considered indispensable or because they are connected to the criminal justice process. Many jurisdictions allow citizens to be excused from jury service if it would cause them physical or economic difficulties.

Compensation for jury service varies widely among states.[45] In 2005, 18 states and the federal courts paid jurors a flat daily rate, ranging from $10 in Alabama, Idaho, Iowa, and Tennessee to $40 in New York, West Virginia, and the federal courts. Technically, New Mexico paid the highest flat daily rate of $41.20, which was based on federal minimum wage of $5.15 for an 8-hour day. Several of these flat-rate jurisdictions pay for half a day service. Twenty-one states and the District of Columbia use a graduated rate system in which jurors receive either no fee or a significantly reduced fee usually for one to three days of service; after that, they receive an increased fee. In 1986, Massachusetts became one of the first states to employ a graduated rate system. Under the Massachusetts' system, jurors receive no fee for the first three days of service, and $50 per day thereafter. Massachusetts' law also requires employers to pay their employees on jury service their regular pay for the first three days of service. Unemployed jurors or jurors with child care needs in Massachusetts are paid the $50 fee from day one. Texas recently switched from a flat $6 per day rate to a $40 per day rate beginning on the second day of service. The five states that pay jurors the highest rate for service—Colorado, Connecticut, Massachusetts, North Dakota, and South Dakota—pay jurors $50 a day under a graduated rate system. Some states are moving from local funding of jurors to state funding to equalize what some people consider unfair pay differentials among counties. Twelve states still have state-mandated minimum funding for jury service and encourage counties to supplement the mandated minimum. Illinois, for example, has the lowest state mandated minimum of $4 per day with county supplements ranging from $5 to $25 per day. Not all employers pay for time lost from work. Consequently, only about 25% of adult Americans have ever served on juries; still, that is up from only 6% in 1977.[46]

From the venire, as many as 30 people (in felony prosecutions that mandate 12 jurors) are randomly selected by the court clerk for the jury panel from which the actual trial jury is selected. To ensure a fair trial, potential trial jurors go through ***voir dire,*** a process in which persons who might be biased or unable to render a fair verdict are screened out. During *voir dire,* which means "to speak the truth," the defense, the prosecution, and the judge question jurors about their backgrounds and knowledge of the case and the defendant. If it appears that a juror might be biased or unable to render a fair verdict, the juror can be challenged "for cause" by either the defense or the prosecution. If the judge agrees, the juror is dismissed from jury service. In death penalty trials, for example, death penalty opponents can be excluded from juries for cause if they are opposed to the death penalty under any circumstances (*Lockhart* v. *McCree,* 1986). Generally, there is no limit to the number of jurors that can be eliminated for cause. In practice, however, few potential jurors are eliminated for cause, except in high-profile trials, such as the O. J. Simpson murder trial in 1995.

Another way that either the defense or the prosecution can eliminate potential jurors from jury service is by the use of *peremptory challenges,* which allow either prosecutors or defense attorneys to excuse jurors without having to provide a reason. Peremptory challenges are frequently used to eliminate jurors whose characteristics place them in a group likely to be unfavorable to the case of either the prosecution or the defense. For example, in death penalty cases,

voir dire The process in which potential jurors who might be biased or unable to render a fair verdict are screened out.

FYI

SmartJURY

Software, called SmartJURY, has been developed that can evaluate the demographic profile and verbal and nonverbal clues given by potential jurors to calculate with precision whether they will acquit or convict a criminal defendant. The cost of the software is $995 a year.

Source: Amie K. Streater, "High-Tech, Cheap Way Found to Pick a Jury," *The Orlando Sentinel* (January 5, 2003), p. B5.

prosecutors often use their peremptory challenges to eliminate people of color and women from the juries, because, statistically, people of color and women are less likely to favor capital punishment. However, prosecutors must be careful in their use of peremptory challenges for such purposes, because the Supreme Court has forbidden the use of peremptory challenges to exclude potential jurors solely on account of their race (*Batson* v. *Kentucky*, 1989) or gender (*J. E. B.* v. *Alabama*, 1994). The number of peremptory challenges is limited by statute. In most jurisdictions, the prosecution is allowed from 6 to 8 peremptory challenges and the defense from 8 to 10. *Voir dire* continues until the required number of jurors has been selected. The *voir dire* process may take an hour or two or, in rare cases, months.

Traditionally, a jury in a criminal trial, sometimes called a *petit jury* to distinguish it from a grand jury, consists of 12 citizens plus one or two alternates, who will replace any jurors unable to continue because of illness, accident, or personal emergency. Recently, however, primarily to reduce expenses, some states have gone to six-, seven-, and eight-member juries in noncapital criminal cases. The Supreme Court will not allow criminal trial juries with five or fewer members, and 12-member juries are still required in all states in capital (death penalty) cases.

Recently, attempts have been made to reduce the burden of jury service. In many jurisdictions, jurors can now call a number to find out whether they will be needed on a particular day during their term of service. Some jurisdictions have instituted "1 day/1 trial" jury systems, which require jurors to serve either for 1 day or for the duration of one trial. Once they have served, they are exempt from jury service for 1 or 2 years. Each year in the United States, approximately 2 million jurors serve in about 200,000 criminal and civil trials.

THE TRIAL PROCESS

Before a criminal trial formally begins, attorneys in about 10% of felony cases file pretrial motions. A motion is an application to a court, requesting a judge to order a particular action. Motions can also be made during and after a trial. Common pretrial motions are to obtain discovery of the prosecution's evidence and to have some of the prosecution's evidence suppressed (for example, to have a confession ruled inadmissible because of *Miranda* violations).

The following is a general description of the stages in a criminal trial.[47] Figure 8.8 shows that process and includes some pretrial stages as well (not all

Figure 8.8

Stages in a Criminal Trial

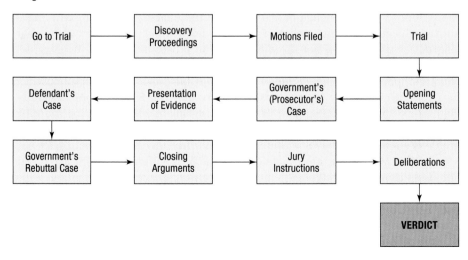

stages occur in every trial). After the jury has been sworn in (if the case is tried before a jury) and the court clerk has read the criminal complaint, the prosecution begins the trial with an opening statement, outlining its case. Next is the opening statement by the defense. However, the defense is not required to make an opening statement. In some jurisdictions, the defense is allowed to defer its opening statement until after the prosecution has presented its case. Opening statements are rarely made in bench trials.

The prosecution then submits its evidence and questions its witnesses. The prosecution must establish beyond a reasonable doubt each element of the crime. The elements of a crime vary by offense and jurisdiction. In other words, two jurisdictions (for example, two states) may have different elements for the same crime. The specific elements of each crime are provided in state and federal statutes. Some of the elements common to most crimes were described in Chapter 2 and include *actus reus, mens rea,* and concurrence.

If the defense believes that the prosecution has failed to make its case, then the defense may choose to *rest,* that is, not to defend against the charge or charges. At this point, the defense in most states is allowed to request a *directed verdict* or to make a motion for dismissal. If the judge agrees with the defense that the prosecution's evidence is insufficient for conviction, then the judge can either direct the jury to acquit the defendant or "take the case from the jury" and grant the motion for dismissal.

If the defense does not seek a dismissal or a dismissal is not granted, the defense follows the prosecution with its witnesses and any contrary evidence. Then the prosecution and the defense take turns offering rebuttals to the other side's evidence, cross-examining witnesses, and reexamining their own witnesses. Following the rebuttal period, the prosecution summarizes its case. The defense then summarizes its case and makes its closing statement. The closing statement by the prosecution ends the adversarial portion of the trial.

Normally, after the closing statement by the prosecution, the judge instructs, or *charges,* the jury concerning the principles of law the jurors are to utilize in determining guilt or innocence. The judge also explains to the jury the charges, the rules of evidence, and the possible verdicts. In some jurisdictions, the judge summarizes the evidence presented from notes taken during the trial. The jury then retires to deliberate until it reaches a verdict. In a room where it has complete privacy, the jury elects from its members a foreperson to preside over the

Attorneys from opposing sides in a trial sometimes confer with the judge. *Why does this happen and what do you think is discussed?*

FYI Are Juries Fair
and Impartial?

A recent public opinion poll found that 58% of the American public believed that defendants had fair and impartial juries "all of the time" (3%) or "most of the time" (55%). Another 21% of Americans believed that defendants had fair and impartial juries "occasionally," while 8% of Americans believed that defendants "rarely" (7%) or "never" (1%) had fair and impartial juries. Thirteen percent of Americans were not sure.

Source: The Harris Poll #9, January 21, 2008 at www.harrisinteractive.com/harris_poll/index. asp?PID=861.

hung jury The result when jurors cannot agree on a verdict. The judge declares a mistrial. The prosecutor must decide whether to retry the case.

subsequent deliberations. Jurors are not allowed to discuss the case with anyone other than another juror. In some cases, a jury is sequestered at night in a hotel or motel to prevent any chance of outside influence.

To find a defendant guilty as charged, the jury must be convinced "beyond a reasonable doubt" that the defendant has committed the crime. Some juries reach a verdict in a matter of minutes; some juries have taken weeks or more. If the jury finds the defendant guilty as charged, as it does in two-thirds of criminal cases, the judge begins to consider a sentence. In some jurisdictions, the jury participates to varying degrees in the sentencing process. If the jury finds the defendant not guilty, the defendant is released from the jurisdiction of the court and is a free person. After the verdict has been read in the courtroom, either the defense or the prosecution may ask that the jury be polled individually, with each juror stating publicly how he or she voted.

In the federal courts and in nearly every state, a unanimous verdict is required. If, after serious deliberation, even one juror cannot agree with the others on a verdict, the result is a **hung jury.** Even in jurisdictions that do not require a unanimous verdict, a hung or deadlocked jury results when a jury cannot reach a verdict by the required voting margin. Judges hate hung juries. Not only do they fail to produce a decisive trial outcome, either a conviction or an acquittal, but they also result in a huge waste of time and money for all parties involved. In the fourteenth century, judges would routinely confine deadlocked juries "without meat, drink, fire, or candle, or conversation with others, until they were agreed."[48] Judges continued to force deadlocked juries to reach a verdict well into the twentieth century, for example, by requiring them to deliberate all night, threatening to deprive them of food from Saturday to Monday, or warning them on a frigid winter day that water and heat would be turned off in the jury room until they reached a unanimous verdict.[49] Judges have special instructions for deadlocked juries. These instructions have been referred to as "shotgun charges," "hammer charges," "the third-degree charges," "dynamite charges," and "nitroglycerine charges." As the names imply, the purpose of the instructions is to blast a verdict out of a deadlocked jury.[50] Following is a typical dynamite charge:

> You have informed the Court of your inability to reach a verdict in this case. At the outset, the Court wishes you to know that although you have a duty to reach a verdict, if that is not possible, the Court has neither the power nor the desire to compel agreement upon a verdict. The purpose of these remarks is to point out to you the importance and the desirability of reaching a verdict in this case, provided, however, that you as individual jurors can do so without surrendering or sacrificing your conscientious scruples or personal convictions. You will recall that upon assuming your duties in this case each of you took an oath. The oath places upon each of you as individuals the responsibility of arriving at a true verdict upon the basis of your opinion and not merely upon acquiescence in the conclusions of your fellow jurors. However, it by no means follows that opinions may not be changed by conference in the jury room. The very object of the jury system is to reach a verdict by a comparison of views and by consideration of the proofs with your fellow jurors. During your deliberations you should be open-minded and consider the issues with proper deference to and respect for the opinions of each other and you should not hesitate to re-examine your own views in the light of such discussions. You should consider also that this case must at some time be terminated; that you are selected in the same manner and from the same source from which any future jury must be selected; that there is no reason to suppose that the case will ever be submitted to twelve persons more intelligent, more impartial or more competent to decide it, or that more or clearer evidence will ever be produced on one side or the other. You may retire now, taking as much time as is necessary for further deliberations upon the issues submitted to you for determination.[51]

If the jury remains deadlocked, the judge declares a mistrial, and the prosecutor must decide whether to retry the case. Recent data show that in the

Court Reporter

My name is Debora Randolph, and I am an official court reporter with the Johnson County, Kansas District Court. I have an Associate of Applied Science degree in court reporting and also an Associate's degree in specialized business.

I began thinking about a career in court reporting when I was in high school. At the time, Kansas City Business College was the only school that had a court reporting program, but it was being phased out. I then enrolled in another program and received my specialized business degree. I worked as a secretary at first. Still having a desire to be a court reporter, I opened the phonebook hoping to find a school that offered such a program and came across Brown Mackie College. I enrolled in the evening program and attended school for 2 years while working a full-time job as an administrative assistant. I successfully completed the program and received an AA degree. I then took and passed the required state certification test and was hired by the state of Kansas. I subsequently received my national certification. I have also taught court reporting courses.

As an official court reporter for the state of Kansas, my job entails recording verbatim reports of judicial trials, conferences, and hearings. Notes are taken at a high rate of speed through the use of a stenotype machine. As an officer of the court, it is my responsibility to prepare a complete and accurate report of proceedings, which may involve highly technical terminology used in a number of different fields. Although the proceedings may not be transcribed until sometime later, I also provide "realtime" or instant-text translation feed to the attorneys and judges. Text is displayed on computer monitors for attorneys and judges to view during the proceedings. Additionally, I provide input to the judge and administrative assistant regarding docket management.

One of the things I like best about my job is I am constantly learning because of the varied cases I take. I also get to listen to some very interesting life experiences. Court reporting is an interesting, challenging, and rewarding career; however, because of the long hours involved, it can be overwhelming. I often work evenings and weekends producing transcripts. I would advise anyone who is thinking of court reporting as a career to be prepared to dedicate a considerable amount of time to the profession. Many aspiring court reporters do not make it past the first year of school. Training requires much practice time to learn to "write" up to 25 words per minute in addition to the other core requirements.

Which aspect of this job would you find the most rewarding?

small number of jury trials (less than 3% of all criminal case dispositions), hung juries occur infrequently: only in about 6% of state court criminal jury trials and in fewer than 3% of federal court criminal jury trials. The percentage of hung juries in the state courts ranged from 0% to nearly 19%. In state court criminal trials that end in hung juries, possible outcomes include case dismissal, guilty plea, another jury trial, or a bench trial. The average percentage of hung juries in criminal trials has not varied much in the past 40 years.[52]

THINKING CRITICALLY

1. What are some of the benefits of having a trial by jury?

2. How could the jury system be improved so that there is a more diverse mix of people?

✳ Summary

1. Identify the type of court structure in the United States, and describe its various components.

   The United States has a dual court system—a separate judicial system for each of the states and a separate federal system. The only place where the two systems "connect" is in the U.S. Supreme Court. The federal court system is composed of U.S. district courts, U.S. circuit courts of appeals, and the U.S. Supreme Court. The state court system consists of trial courts of limited jurisdiction, trial courts of general jurisdiction, intermediate appellate courts (in most states), and state courts of last resort.

2. Summarize the purposes of courts.

   The purposes of courts are (1) to do justice, (2) to appear to do justice, (3) to provide a forum where disputes between people can be resolved justly and peacefully, (4) to censure wrongdoing, (5) to incapacitate criminal offenders, (6) to punish offenders, (7) to rehabilitate offenders, (8) to deter people from committing crimes, (9) to determine legal status, and (10) to protect individual citizens against arbitrary government action.

3. Identify the most powerful actors in the administration of justice, and explain what makes them so powerful.

   Prosecutors are the most powerful actors in the administration of justice because they conduct the final screening of all persons arrested for criminal offenses, deciding whether there is enough evidence to support a conviction, and because, in most jurisdictions, they have unreviewable discretion in deciding whether to charge a person with a crime and prosecute the case.

4. Summarize the types of attorneys available to a person charged with a crime.

   People charged with crimes may have privately retained counsel, or if indigent, they may have court-appointed attorneys, public defenders, or "contract" lawyers, depending on which is provided by the jurisdiction.

5. Describe the responsibilities of a judge.

   Judges have a variety of responsibilities in the criminal justice process. Among their nontrial duties are determining probable cause, signing warrants, informing suspects of their rights, setting and revoking bail, arraigning defendants, and accepting guilty pleas. Judges spend much of the workday in their chambers, negotiating procedures and dispositions with prosecutors and defense attorneys. The principal responsibility of judges in all of those duties is to ensure that suspects and defendants are treated fairly and in accordance with due process of law. In jury trials, judges are responsible for allowing the jury a fair chance to reach a verdict on the evidence presented. A judge must ensure that his or her behavior does not improperly affect the outcome of the case. Before juries retire to deliberate and reach a verdict, judges instruct them on the relevant law. Additionally, in jurisdictions without professional court administrators, each judge is responsible for the management of his or her own courthouse and its personnel, with the added duties of supervising building maintenance, budgets, and labor relations.

6. Describe the purposes of an initial appearance.

   At the initial appearance—the first pretrial stage—defendants are given formal notice of the charges against them and are advised of their constitutional rights. For a misdemeanor or an ordinance violation, a summary trial may be held. For a felony, a hearing is held to determine whether the suspect should be released or whether the suspect should be held for a preliminary hearing.

7. Explain what bail is, and describe the different methods of pretrial release.

   Bail is usually a monetary guarantee deposited with the court that is supposed to ensure that the suspect or defendant will appear at a subsequent stage in the criminal justice process. Different pretrial release options include station-house bail, surety bonds, full cash bonds, deposit bonds, release on own recognizance (ROR), conditional release, and unsecured bonds.

8. Define what a grand jury is, and explain its purposes.

   A grand jury is a group of generally 12 to 23 citizens who, for a specific period of time, meet in closed sessions to investigate charges coming from preliminary hearings or to engage in other responsibilities. A primary purpose of the grand jury is to determine whether there is probable cause to believe that the accused committed the crime or crimes with which he or she is charged by the prosecutor. Other purposes of a grand jury are to protect citizens from unfounded charges and to consider the misconduct of government officials.

9. Describe the purposes of the arraignment and the plea options of defendants.

   The primary purpose of arraignment is to hear the formal information or grand jury indictment and to allow defendants to enter a plea. Plea options include "guilty," "not guilty," and in some states and the federal courts, "nolo contendere." In some states, defendants can also stand mute or can plead "not guilty by reason of insanity."

10. Describe the interests served and not served by plea bargaining.

    Plea bargaining seemingly serves the interests of all the court participants by, among other things, reducing uncertainty about the length or outcome of trials. Plea bargains serve prosecutors by guaranteeing them high conviction rates; judges by reducing court caseloads; defense attorneys by allowing them to avoid trials and spend less time on each case; and even some criminal offenders by enabling them to escape a prison sentence altogether, to receive a lesser sentence than they might have received if convicted at trial, or to escape conviction of socially stigmatizing crimes. Two types of criminal offenders are not served by plea bargaining: (1) innocent, indigent defendants who fear being found guilty of crimes they did not commit and receiving harsh sentences, and (2) habitual offenders.

11. List and define the stages in a criminal trial.

    The stages in a criminal trial are as follows: (1) selection and swearing in of the jury, in jury trials; (2) opening statements by the prosecution and the defense; (3) presentation of the prosecution's case; (4) presentation of the defense's case; (5) rebuttals, cross-examination, and reexamination of witnesses; (6) closing arguments by the defense and the prosecution; (7) the judge's instructing, or charging, the jury; and (8) deliberation and verdict.

✳ Key Terms

dual court system 288	trial *de novo* 295	booking 318	unsecured bond 324
jurisdiction 288	due process of law 299	complaint 318	preliminary hearing 324
original jurisdiction 288	incapacitation 299	information 318	grand jury 326
appellate jurisdiction 288	punishment 299	grand jury indictment 318	indictment 326
general jurisdiction 288	rehabilitation 299	arrest warrant 319	subpoena 326
special jurisdiction 288	general deterrence 299	bail bond or bail 319	arraignment 327
subject matter jurisdiction 288	*nolle prosequi (nol.*	preventive detention 320	*nolo contendere* 327
personal jurisdiction 288	*pros.)* 301	bench warrant or *capias* 322	bench trial 330
writ of *certiorari* 293	plea bargaining or plea	release on own recognizance	venire 330
writ of *habeas corpus* 294	negotiating 302	(ROR) 324	*voir dire* 331
summary or bench trials 295	rules of discovery 303	conditional release 324	hung jury 334

✳ Review Questions

1. What is the difference between *original* and *appellate jurisdiction?* Between *general* and *special jurisdiction?* Between *subject matter* and *personal jurisdiction?*

2. Under what circumstances will the U.S. Supreme Court issue a writ of *certiorari?*

3. Ideally, what are the three conditions that must be met before a prosecutor charges a person with a crime and prosecutes the case?

4. Why do prosecutors sometimes choose not to prosecute criminal cases?

5. In general, when does an individual accused of a crime have the right to counsel?

6. By what methods are judges selected?

7. Describe the "funneling" or screening process in the administration of justice.

8. When do suspects officially become defendants?

9. How long may suspects arrested without a warrant be held in jail before being brought before a judge for an initial appearance?

10. In what two ways are preliminary hearings similar to criminal trials, and in what two ways do preliminary hearings differ from criminal trials?

11. What is the primary purpose of a grand jury?

12. What are three basic types of plea bargains?

13. What are three principal purposes of jury trials?

14. What is *voir dire,* and what is its purpose?

15. What are the stages of a criminal trial?

✳ In the Field

1. **Bail Bonds** Visit the office of a local bail bonds person. It is generally near the courthouse and well marked. Ask the bonds person to describe the job. Ask about major problems with the business and satisfactions of the job. Specific questions could be: (1) For what type of offender is it most risky to provide bail? (2) How does a bail transaction work? (3) Do bonds people actually have to give money to the court when they put up bail?

2. **Court Proceedings** Visit several different types of courts, such as a lower court, a trial court, an appellate court, state courts, and federal courts. Observe the proceedings and describe how they differ from or are similar to those described in this chapter and to each other.

3. **Report on a Criminal Trial** Scan a local newspaper for a story of a criminal trial. Write a report that includes information about (1) the type of court in which the trial is being held and why it has jurisdiction, (2) the type of case being tried (misdemeanor or felony), (3) the outcome of the case.

✳ On the Net

1. **District Courts** Go to the Federal Judiciary website at www.uscourts.gov and find the directory of district courts. Look up the number of districts your state is divided into, where the courts for the districts are located, and how many judgeships are authorized for each district. Report the results to your class or instructor.

2. **State Courts** Go to the U.S. Department of Justice, Bureau of Justice Statistics's *State Court Organization 2004* document at www.ojp.usdoj.gov/bjs/pub/pdf/sco04 .pdf. Examine the material in each table for your state. Write a report about your state court system.

✳ Critical Thinking Exercises

WHAT WOULD YOU DO?

1. As a defense attorney, what would you do under the following circumstances?
   a. Your client tells you that he committed the crime or crimes for which he is being prosecuted.
   b. Your client tells you about a serious crime that will be committed sometime next week.
   c. Your client tells you that if you lose the case, his friends will harm your family.
   d. You learn that your client, who has paid you nothing so far for your services, will not be able to pay your fee.
   e. Your client insists on testifying, even though you believe that it is not in his best interests to do so.

JURY NULLIFICATION

2. In John Grisham's 1992 novel, *A Time to Kill,* the defendant, a black man whose young daughter was viciously raped by two white men, is on trial for gunning down the two men on the courthouse steps in full view of many bystanders. Even though it was obvious to all that the defendant had killed the two men, the jury in the case returned a not-guilty verdict, and the defendant was allowed to walk free. This is an example of *jury nullification,* the power of a jury in a criminal case to acquit a defendant despite overwhelming evidence. The jury can acquit for any reason or for no reason at all, and the decision of the jury cannot be appealed. Jury nullification is one of the problems cited by critics who call for the abolition of the present American jury system. Another complaint about the jury system is the inability of some jurors in some trials to understand legal arguments, the evidence presented, or the instructions of the judge. Critics of the jury system suggest replacing jury trials with bench trials or with trials before a panel of judges or substituting professionally trained jurors for the current "amateur" jurors.
   a. Should the American jury system be abolished? Why or why not?
   b. Do you believe that any of the alternatives suggested by jury critics would produce a better or more just system? Defend your answer.

To access more information and resources, including study questions, chapter summaries, and links, go to: www.mhhe .com/bohm6e.

Sentencing, Appeals, and the Death Penalty

9

Chapter Outline

Chapter Objectives

After completing this chapter, you should be able to:

1. Identify the general factors that influence a judge's sentencing decisions.

2. Describe how judges tailor sentences to fit the crime and the offender.

3. Distinguish between indeterminate and determinate sentences.

4. Explain the three basic types of determinate sentences.

5. List five rationales or justifications for criminal punishment.

6. Explain the purposes of presentence investigation reports.

7. List the legal bases for appeal.

8. Identify the type of crime for which death may be a punishment.

9. Summarize the three major procedural reforms the U.S. Supreme Court approved for death penalty cases in the *Gregg* decision.

CRIME STORY

On January 26, 2009, five members of the "Beatrice Six," Joann Taylor, James Dean, Debra Shelden, Kathy Gonzales, and Thomas Winslow, were exonerated and received rare full pardons from the Nebraska Pardons Board. They had been convicted for the 1985 brutal rape and murder of 68-year-old Helen Wilson in Beatrice, Nebraska. Another co-defendant, Joseph White, already had his conviction overturned in October 2008. DNA evidence, using technology not available in the 1980s, proved that none of the six was involved in the crime. According to Deputy Attorney General Cory O'Brien, "They were absolutely, positively not present. Not beyond a reasonable doubt but beyond any and all doubt." The evidence proved Bruce Allen Smith of Oklahoma City, who was living in Beatrice at the time, alone raped and killed Wilson. Smith died in an Oklahoma prison of AIDS in 1992. A witness had placed Smith near the crime scene early in the investigation, but based on a blood test, using forensic evidence available at the time, police excluded him as the killer. Governor Dave Heineman, a member of the three-person pardons board with

continued

Attorney General Jon Bruning and Secretary of State John Gale, stated, "I believe the evidence is overwhelming and conclusive that we should grant a pardon today." Winslow, White, and Taylor had each spent nearly 20 years in prison. The other three were already out of prison, having served more than 4 years of their 10-year sentences for lesser charges. Together, the Beatrice Six had served 70 years in prison.

Five of the six defendants had pleaded guilty because they were threatened with the death penalty and told that others had implicated them in the crime. They were offered plea deals to confess and implicate the others. Dean said, "When you're life's on the line, you do things that normal people wouldn't do." Winslow received a life sentence, but has maintained all along that he has no memory of the incident. Taylor implicated Winslow and White but later recanted. She maintains she was coerced into taking a plea bargain and her testimony was coached. She said, "I had a 14-month old baby [and] was told they'd make me the first female on death row." Police also told Gonzalez that she would be the first woman executed in state history. A psychiatrist told Gonzalez, Shelden, and Dean they probably had repressed their memories of the murder and helped them "recover" them, sometimes through their dreams. Deputy Attorney General O'Brien said Shelden and others might have been brainwashed. White was the only defendant who continued to deny being involved in the murder. All six of the defendants had a history of alcohol and drug abuse and some of them had a history of mental illness.

The Six had former state senator Ernie Chambers to thank for sponsoring the law, adopted in 2001, that granted DNA testing in certain criminal cases. The Beatrice Six case was the first time in Nebraska that DNA testing overturned murder convictions. All of the exonerated said there should be another law that compensates those who are wrongly convicted. State senator Kent Rogert recently introduced such a bill that would give at least $50,000 for each year served plus additional expenses for anyone wrongly convicted of a crime.

Chapter 9 examines sentencing, appeals, and the death penalty. How could the miscarriages of justice in the Beatrice Six case have occurred? Clearly, a confession is persuasive evidence. It is hard for jurors to believe that people would admit to crimes they did not commit. Yet, about one quarter of documented wrongful convictions cleared by DNA evidence result from false confessions or guilty pleas. In many of these cases, defendants are worn down and influenced by the police and confess to escape from the interrogation process. Their confessions seem credible because the police provide them with details of the crime. Police are able to convince other innocent people, especially those who are emotionally vulnerable or mentally unstable, they committed the crime. In cases such as the one involving the Beatrice Six, fear of the death penalty is a powerful tool for extracting guilty pleas from innocent suspects who do not want to take their chances at trial.

The case of the Beatrice Six raises several important questions. Should DNA be tested in all criminal cases where it is available? Should all police interrogations be video and audio recorded? Should people wrongfully convicted and imprisoned for crimes they did not commit be compensated by the state? If so, how much should they receive? Should a criminal justice system that can wrongfully convict six people for a murder they did not commit be allowed to condemn people to death?

Sentencing

If a criminal defendant pleads guilty or is found guilty by a judge or jury, then the judge must impose a sentence.[1] In a few jurisdictions, sentencing is the responsibility of the jury for certain types of offenses (for example, capital crimes). Table 9.1 displays, by offense, the amount of time between conviction and sentencing for felony defendants in state courts in 2004 (the latest year for which data were available). As Table 9.1 shows, for most offenses a majority of defendants are sentenced either on the day of conviction or the next day.

Sentencing is arguably a judge's most difficult responsibility. Judges cannot impose just any sentence. They are limited by the U.S. Constitution's Eighth Amendment prohibition of cruel and unusual punishments (discussed in Chapter 4) and statutory provisions; guided by prevailing philosophical rationales, organizational considerations, and presentence investigation reports; and influenced by their own personal characteristics.

STATUTORY PROVISIONS

As described in Chapter 4, state and federal legislative bodies enact penal codes that specify appropriate punishments for each statutory offense or class of offense, such as a class B felony or class C felony. Currently, five general

FYI Sentencing by Judge or Jury?

According to a recent public opinion poll, 48% of Americans would trust a judge more than a jury to give a fair sentence, while 31% of Americans would trust a jury more than a judge to give a fair sentence. Twenty-one percent of Americans were not sure.

Source: The Harris Poll #9, January 21, 2008 at www.harrisinteractive.com/harris_poll/index .asp?PID=861.

Table 9.1 Time between Felony Conviction and Sentencing
in State Courts, by Offense, 2004

Most Serious Conviction Offense	Number of Defendants	Total	PERCENT OF DEFENDANTS IN THE 75 LARGEST COUNTIES WHO WERE SENTENCED WITHIN:			
			0–1 Day	2–30 Days	31–60 Days	61 Days or More
All offenses	32,680	100%	65%	15%	12%	8%
All felonies	28,512	100%	63%	17%	12%	8%
Violent offenses	4,733	100%	56%	17%	16%	11%
Murder	98	100	41	26	27	7
Rape	145	100	34	15	28	23
Robbery	1,169	100	57	18	15	11
Assault	2,346	100	61	15	14	9
Other violent	976	100	47	17	21	15
Property offenses	9,469	100%	64%	16%	12%	8%
Burglary	2,303	100	63	17	14	6
Larceny/theft	2,754	100	69	12	10	9
Motor vehicle theft	1,307	100	55	25	13	7
Forgery	834	100	64	11	13	11
Fraud	929	100	60	14	15	11
Other property	1,345	100	64	19	11	6
Drug offenses	10,847	100%	66%	17%	10%	7%
Trafficking	4,129	100	59	18	14	9
Other drug	6,720	100	69	17	8	5
Public-order offenses	3,360	100%	62%	17%	14%	7%
Weapons	1,066	100	56	21	16	7
Driving-related	1,153	100	64	15	14	7
Other public-order	1,143	100	66	15	13	6
Misdemeanors	4,168	100%	82%	4%	8%	6%

Note: Data on time from conviction to sentencing were available for 94% of convicted defendants. Total for all felonies includes cases that could not be classified into 1 of the 4 major offense categories. Detail may not add to total because of rounding.

Source: Felony Defendants in Large Urban Counties, 2004—Statistical Tables (Table 24) at www.ojp.usdoj.gov/bjs/pub/html/fdluc/2004/tables/fdluc04st24.htm (accessed December 3, 2008).

types of punishment are in use in the United States: fines, probation, intermediate punishments (various punishments that are more restrictive than probation but less restrictive and costly than imprisonment), imprisonment, and death. As long as judges impose one or a combination of those five punishments, and the sentence type and length are within statutory limits, judges are free to set any sentence they want.

Thus, within limits, judges are free to tailor the punishment to fit the crime and the offender. As noted, judges can impose a combination sentence of, for example, imprisonment, probation, and a fine. They can suspend the imprisonment portion of a combination sentence, or they can suspend the entire sentence if the offender stays out of trouble, makes **restitution** (pays money or provides services to victims, their survivors, or the community to make up for the injury inflicted), or seeks medical treatment. If the offender has already spent weeks, months, or sometimes even years in jail awaiting trial, judges can give the offender credit for jail time and deduct that time from any prison sentence. When jail time is not deducted from the sentence, it is called "dead time." In some cases, the sentence that a judge intends to impose closely matches the time an offender has already spent in jail awaiting trial. In such cases, the judge may impose a sentence of "time served" and release the offender. When an offender is convicted of two or more crimes, judges can

restitution Money paid or services provided by a convicted offender to victims, their survivors, or the community to make up for the injury inflicted.

Table 9.2 Distribution of Types of Felony Sentences Imposed in State Courts, by Offense, 2004

Most Serious Conviction Offense	Number of Defendants	PERCENT OF CONVICTED FELONY DEFENDANTS IN THE 75 LARGEST COUNTIES SENTENCED TO:						
		Total	INCARCERATION			NONINCARCERATION		
			Total	Prison	Jail	Total	Probation	Other
All offenses	33,181	100%	72%	31%	41%	28%	24%	4%
All felonies	28,796	100%	75%	36%	40%	25%	24%	1%
Violent offenses	4,799	100%	83%	47%	36%	17%	16%	1%
Murder	112	100	96	96	0	4	4	0
Rape	155	100	95	65	30	5	5	0
Robbery	1,198	100	84	63	21	16	15	1
Assault	2,356	100	81	37	44	19	18	1
Other violent	978	100	84	43	41	16	15	1
Property offenses	9,545	100%	79%	37%	43%	21%	20%	1%
Burglary	2,327	100	85	45	41	15	14	1
Larceny/theft	2,770	100	77	36	41	23	21	2
Motor vehicle theft	1,309	100	91	38	52	9	9	—
Forgery	840	100	69	28	42	31	30	—
Fraud	933	100	66	30	36	34	32	2
Other property	1,365	100	78	33	46	22	20	2
Drug offenses	10,940	100%	67%	29%	38%	33%	31%	1%
Trafficking	4,166	100	80	35	45	20	19	1
Other drug	6,773	100	60	25	35	40	39	2
Public-order offenses	3,417	100%	78%	37%	41%	22%	21%	1%
Weapons	1,077	100	84	48	36	16	16	—
Driving-related	1,175	100	79	36	43	21	18	3
Other public-order	1,163	100	72	28	43	28	28	1
Misdemeanors	4,385	100%	50%	3%	47%	50%	29%	21%

Note: Data on type of sentence were available for 97% of convicted defendants. Sentences to incarceration that were wholly suspended are included under probation. Seven percent of prison sentences and 64% of jail sentences included a probation term. Sentences to incarceration or probation may have included a fine, restitution, community service, treatment, or other court-ordered conditions. Other sentences may include fines, community service, restitution, and treatment. Total for all felonies includes cases that could not be classified into 1 of the 4 major offense categories. Detail may not add to total because of rounding.

—Less than 0.5%.

Source: Felony Defendants in Large Urban Counties, 2004—Statistical Tables (Table 25) at www.ojp.usdoj.gov/bjs/pub/html/fdluc/2004/tables/fdluc04st25.htm (accessed December 3, 2008).

FYI

The Longest Sentences

The longest prison sentence in the United States is believed to be a 10,000-year sentence imposed on Dudley Wayne Kyzer, 40, on December 4, 1981, in Tuscaloosa, Alabama, for a triple murder committed in 1976. The longest federal prison sentence is presumably the 960-year sentence imposed on Pierre Ernest Falgout III, 35, on April 25, 2008, in Birmingham, Alabama, for photographing and videotaping young children while he tortured them sexually.

Source: George E. Rush, *The Dictionary of Criminal Justice,* 5th ed. (Sluice Dock, Guilford, CT: Dushkin/ McGraw-Hill, 2000), p. 295; "Alabama Man Gets 960 Years for Sexual Torture of Children," *The Orlando Sentinel* (April 26, 2008), p. A16.

order the prison sentences to run concurrently (together) or consecutively (one after the other). Judges can also delay sentencing and retain the right to impose a sentence at a later date if conditions warrant. Table 9.2 shows, by offense, the types of felony sentences imposed by state courts in 2004. Note that 72% of all offenders were incarcerated; only 24% received probation. The remaining 4% were sentenced to fines, community service, restitution, and/or treatment. The largest percentage of offenders incarcerated was violent offenders (83%).

The sentence of death is generally limited to offenders convicted of "aggravated" murder, and because most criminal offenders are poor, fines are seldom imposed for serious crimes. (When they are, it is generally for symbolic reasons.) Thus, in practice, judges have three sentencing options—probation, intermediate punishments, and imprisonment. Later chapters in this text will cover those options. The death penalty will be discussed at the end of this chapter.

The type of sentence imposed on an offender can be a highly volatile issue. Also controversial is the length of the sentence imposed. Judges in states that have indeterminate sentencing statutes generally have more discretion in sentencing than do judges in states with determinate sentencing laws. An **indeterminate sentence** has a fixed minimum and maximum term of incarceration, rather than a set period. Sentences of 10 to 20 years in prison or of not less than 5 years and not more than 25 years in prison are examples of indeterminate sentences. The amount of the term that is actually served is determined by a parole board. In 2006, a third of prison releases were determined by a parole board decision.[2]

Indeterminate sentences were a principal tool in the effort to rehabilitate offenders in the United States from about 1875 to about 1975. They are based on the idea that correctional personnel must be given the flexibility necessary to successfully treat offenders and return them to society as law-abiding members. The rationale underlying indeterminate sentencing is that the time needed for "correcting" different offenders varies so greatly that a range in sentence length provides a better opportunity to achieve successful rehabilitation.

Beginning in the early 1970s, social scientists and politicians began to question whether the rehabilitation of most criminal offenders was even possible. Skepticism about rehabilitation of offenders, a public outcry to do something about crime, and a general distrust of decisions made by parole boards continued to grow. By the mid-1970s, several state legislatures had abandoned or at least deemphasized the goal of rehabilitation and had begun to replace indeterminate sentencing with determinate sentencing. Maine was the first state to replace indeterminate sentencing with determinate sentencing in 1975. It abolished parole at the same time.[3]

A **determinate sentence** has a fixed period of incarceration, which eliminates the decision-making responsibility of parole boards. The hope of determinate sentencing is that it will at least get criminals off the street for longer periods of time. Some people also consider a determinate sentence more humane because prisoners know exactly when they will be released, something that they do not know with an indeterminate sentence. Several states and the federal government have developed guidelines for determinate sentencing; other states have established sentencing commissions to do so.

There are three basic types of determinate sentences: flat-time, mandatory, and presumptive. With **flat-time sentencing,** judges may choose between probation and imprisonment but have little discretion in setting the length of a prison sentence. Once an offender is imprisoned, there is no possibility of a reduction in the length of the sentence. Thus, parole and **good time** (the number of days deducted from a sentence by prison authorities for good behavior or for other reasons) are not options under flat-time sentencing. Before New York imposed the first indeterminate sentence in the United States in 1924, nearly all sentences to prison in the United States were flat-time sentences. Flat-time sentences are rarely imposed today.

With **mandatory sentencing,** the second type of determinate sentencing, a specified number of years of imprisonment, usually within a range, is provided for particular crimes. Mandatory sentencing usually allows credit for good time but does not allow release on parole. Beginning in the 1980s, two principal variations of mandatory sentencing emerged. The first was *mandatory minimum* sentences, which require that offenders serve a specified amount of prison time. Mandatory minimum sentences are most frequently imposed on offenders who commit certain types of offenses such as drug offenses, offenses committed with weapons, and offenses committed by repeat or habitual ("three strikes and you're out") offenders. All states and the federal government have one or more mandatory minimum sentencing laws.

Similar to mandatory minimum sentences are sentences based on *truth-in-sentencing* laws. First enacted in the state of Washington in 1984,

indeterminate sentence A sentence with a fixed minimum and maximum term of incarceration, rather than a set period.

determinate sentence A sentence with a fixed period of incarceration, which eliminates the decision-making responsibility of parole boards.

flat-time sentencing Sentencing in which judges may choose between probation and imprisonment but have little discretion in setting the length of a prison sentence. Once an offender is imprisoned, there is no possibility of reduction in the length of the sentence.

good time The number of days deducted from a sentence by prison authorities for good behavior or for other reasons.

mandatory sentencing Sentencing in which a specified number of years of imprisonment (usually within a range) is provided for particular crimes.

MYTH

Determinate sentencing, especially mandatory sentencing, has a significant effect on serious crime.

FACT

In practice, this myth has at least two problems. First, "mandatory" aspects of the laws are easy to evade. Second, the basic assumption on which the myth rests is wrong: that "soft" judges release too many dangerous offenders on probation. A recent study shows that 70% of all felons convicted in state courts were sentenced to either prison or jail; only 30% received probation or another sentence that did not involve incarceration. Seventy-six percent of violent offenders and 67% of drug offenders were incarcerated. In the federal courts, 79% of felons were sentenced to incarceration.

Source: Matthew R. Durose and Patrick A. Langan, "Felony Sentences in State Courts, 2004," U.S. Department of Justice, Bureau of Justice Statistics *Bulletin* (Washington, D.C.: GPO, July 2007), p. 2; Sourcebook of Criminal Justice Statistics Online at www.albany.edu/sourcebook/pdf/t5192004.pdf.

presumptive sentencing Sentencing that allows a judge to retain some sentencing discretion, subject to appellate review. The legislature determines a sentence range for each crime.

CJ Online

U.S. Sentencing Commission

To learn more about the U.S. Sentencing Commission, visit its website at www .ussc.gov. *Why do you think sentencing commissions are necessary?*

"Three strikes and you're out" laws have been used against offenders whose third felony was a relatively minor offense. *Are "three strikes" laws good laws? Why or why not?*

truth-in-sentencing laws require offenders to serve a substantial portion of their prison sentence, usually 85% of it. Most truth-in-sentencing laws target violent offenders and restrict or eliminate parole eligibility and good-time credits. Probably because of incentive grants authorized by Congress in 1994 to build or expand correctional facilities, nearly all states and the District of Columbia have enacted truth-in-sentencing laws modeled after the federal government's, which requires that for certain offenses 85% of a prison sentence must be served.

In practice, however, offenders sentenced under truth-in-sentencing laws rarely serve 85% of their sentences. For example, in 2002, violent offenders sentenced to prison were sentenced to serve an average of 84 months. It is estimated that they will serve 62% of their prison sentences or 52 months prior to release. Under a truth-in-sentencing law requiring 85% of the sentence to be served, violent offenders would be expected to serve an estimated 19 months longer.[4]

The third type of determinate sentencing is presumptive sentencing. **Presumptive sentencing** allows a judge to retain some sentencing discretion, subject to appellate review. In presumptive sentencing, the legislature determines a sentence range for each crime usually based on the seriousness of the crime and the criminal history of the offender. The judge is expected to impose the typical sentence, specified by statute, unless mitigating or aggravating circumstances justify a sentence below or above the range set by the legislature. Any sentence that deviates from the norm, however, must be explained in writing and is subject to appellate review. Generally, with presumptive sentencing, credit is given for good time, but there is no opportunity for parole. Presumptive sentencing is a compromise between legislatively mandated determinate sentences and their indeterminate counterparts. Figure 9.1 displays Minnesota's presumptive sentencing guidelines grid.

Presumptive sentences may also be based on *sentencing guidelines* developed, not by legislatures, but by *sentencing commissions* comprised of both criminal justice professionals and private citizens. Sentencing guidelines are a different way of restricting the sentencing discretion of judges. In 1984, Congress created the nine-member U.S. Sentencing Commission, which is charged with creating and amending federal sentencing guidelines.

Figure 9.1

Sample Sentencing Guidelines

MINNESOTA SENTENCING GUIDELINES GRID
Presumptive Sentence Lengths in Months

Italicized numbers within the grid denote the range within which a judge may sentence without the sentence being deemed a departure. Offenders with non-imprisonment felony sentences are subject to jail time according to law.

SEVERITY LEVEL OF CONVICTION OFFENSE (Common offenses listed in italics)		CRIMINAL HISTORY SCORE						
		0	1	2	3	4	5	6 or more
Murder, 2nd Degree (intentional murder; drive-by-shootings)	XI	306 *261–367*	326 *278–391*	346 *295–415*	366 *312–439*	386 *329–463*	406 *346–480²*	426 *363–480²*
Murder, 3rd Degree Murder, 2nd Degree (unintentional murder)	X	150 *128–180*	165 *141–198*	180 *153–216*	195 *166–234*	210 *179–252*	225 *192–270*	240 *204–288*
Assault, 1st Degree Controlled Substance Crime, 1st Degree	IX	86 *74–103*	98 *84–117*	110 *94–132*	122 *104–146*	134 *114–160*	146 *125–175*	158 *135–189*
Aggravated Robbery, 1st Degree Controlled Substance Crime, 2nd Degree	VIII	48 *41–57*	58 *50–69*	68 *58–81*	78 *67–93*	88 *75–105*	98 *84–117*	108 *92–129*
Felony DWI	VII	36	42	48	54 *46–64*	60 *51–72*	66 *57–79*	72 *62–84²*
Controlled Substance Crime, 3rd Degree	VI	21	27	33	39 *34–46*	45 *39–54*	51 *44–61*	57 *49–68*
Residential Burglary Simple Robbery	V	18	23	28	33 *29–39*	38 *33–45*	43 *37–51*	48 *41–57*
Nonresidential Burglary	IV	12¹	15	18	21	24 *21–28*	27 *23–32*	30 *26–36*
Theft Crimes (Over $5,000)	III	12¹	13	15	17	19 *17–22*	21 *18–25*	23 *20–27*
Theft Crimes ($5,000 or less) Check Forgery ($251–$2,500)	II	12¹	12¹	13	15	17	19	21 *18–25*
Sale of Simulated Controlled Substance	I	12¹	12¹	12¹	13	15	17	19 *17–22*

☐ Presumptive commitment to state imprisonment. First-degree murder has a mandatory life sentence and is excluded from the guidelines by law. See Guidelines Section II.E., Mandatory Sentences, for policy regarding those sentences controlled by law.

▨ Presumptive stayed sentence; at the discretion of the judge, up to a year in jail and/or other non-jail sanctions can be imposed as conditions of probation. However, certain offenses in this section of the grid always carry a presumptive commitment to state prison. See Guidelines Sections II.C. Presumptive Sentence and II.E. Mandatory Sentences.

¹ One year and one day

² M.S. § 244.09 requires the Sentencing Guidelines to provide a range for sentences which are presumptive commitment to state imprisonment of 15% lower and 20% higher than the fixed duration displayed, provided that the minimum sentence is not less than one year and one day and the maximum sentence is not more than the statutory maximum. See Guidelines Sections II.H. Presumptive Sentence Durations that Exceed the Statutory Maximum Sentence and II.I. Sentence Ranges for Presumptive Commitment Offenses in Shaded Areas of Grids.

Source: Minnesota Sentencing Guidelines Commission at www.msgc.state.mn.us/guidelines/grids/grid_2008.pdf

Effective August 1, 2008

In today's "law and order" climate, state legislatures, as noted, are increasingly replacing indeterminate sentences with determinate ones. This trend, however, has not escaped criticism. For example, it has been argued that the consequences of determinate sentencing include longer prison sentences and overcrowded prisons. Whether it is the result of a shift in sentencing philosophy or some other factor or factors, there is no question that the United States has been experiencing a dramatic increase in the number of people sentenced to prison and in the length of terms of incarceration. A result has been a crisis of prison overcrowding. In recent years, the United States has had one of the highest imprisonment rates in the world. Furthermore, as of 2007, the entire adult correctional departments of 8 states (Alabama, California, Colorado, Florida, Michigan, Mississippi, New Hampshire, and New York) were under court orders to reduce overcrowding or improve other conditions of confinement. In another 3 states (Montana, Ohio, and Wisconsin), one or more institutions were under court orders to reduce overcrowding or improve other conditions of confinement. (No information was available for Connecticut, Georgia, Idaho, Illinois, Nevada, New Jersey, Oregon, Utah, and Washington. However, in 2005, the entire adult correctional departments of Connecticut, Idaho, and New Jersey were under courts orders, as was at least one institution in Illinois.)[5]

A related criticism of determinate sentencing is that it produces an unusually harsh prison system. For example, because of prison overcrowding, many states have all but abandoned even the pretense of rehabilitating offenders. Prisons are increasingly becoming places where offenders are simply "warehoused." In addition, because of the abolition of good time and parole under some determinate sentencing schemes, prison authorities are having a more difficult time maintaining discipline and control of their institutions. Eliminating good time and parole removed two of the most important incentives that prison authorities use to get inmates to behave and to follow prison rules. Also, because of the perceived harshness of some of the determinate sentencing schemes, some judges simply ignore the guidelines. Other judges have ignored sentencing guidelines, because they believe they are too lenient. In short, many judges resent sentencing guidelines and refer to their use as "justice by computer."

In response to overcrowding, some states erected tents on prison grounds, as in this Huntsville, Texas, facility. *Do you think that the use of tents to deal with prison overcrowding is acceptable? Why or why not?*

A third criticism of determinate sentencing is that it merely shifts sentencing discretion from judges to legislatures and prosecutors (through plea bargaining). Whether this shift in sentencing responsibility is desirable is a matter of debate. On the one hand, prosecutors generally exercise their discretion in secret, whereas judges exercise discretion in the open. Also, prosecutors and legislators are generally subject to more political influence than are judges.

Yet, on the other hand, one of the major criticisms of indeterminate sentencing and a principal reason for the adoption of determinate sentencing schemes by some states is judicial disparity in sentencing. Judges vary widely in the sentences they impose for similar crimes and offenders. For example, in one study, 41 New York state judges were asked to review files of actual cases and to indicate the sentences they would impose. Sentences for the same crime were quite different. In one case, a heroin addict robbed an elderly man at gunpoint. The assailant was unemployed, lived with his pregnant wife, and had a minor criminal record. He was convicted of first-degree robbery, and under New York's indeterminate sentencing statute, the actual sentence was between 0 and 5 years. When the 41 judges were asked what sentence they would impose in the case, 22% of them chose the actual sentence (between 0 and 5 years), 29% chose a sentence of 5 to 10 years, another 29% selected a sentence of 10 to 15 years, 12% opted for a sentence of 15 to 20 years, and 7% of them chose a sentence of 20 to 25 years.[6] Figure 9.2 displays the judges' choices. Table 9.3 provides a comparison of the outcomes of felony convictions in state and federal courts in 2004. Obviously, different judges view the same circumstances very differently. Critics have charged that disparity in sentencing has resulted in discrimination against people of color and the poor.

A fourth, related criticism of determinate sentencing in those jurisdictions that retain good time is that sentencing discretion, at least to some degree,

Figure 9.2

Sentencing Choices of 41 New York State Judges

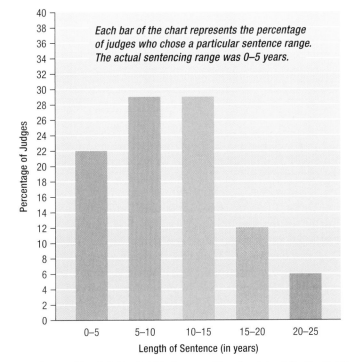

Each bar of the chart represents the percentage of judges who chose a particular sentence range. The actual sentencing range was 0–5 years.

Percentage of Judges

Length of Sentence (in years)

Source: Adapted from "Sentence Disparity in New York: The Response of Forty-One Judges," *The New York Times* (March 30, 1979), p. B3.

Table 9.3 Comparison of the Outcomes of Felony Convictions in State and Federal Courts, 2004

| Most Serious Conviction Offense | FELONY CONVICTIONS | | | Federal Felony Convictions as Percent of Total | PERCENT OF FELONS SENTENCED TO INCARCERATION (PRISON OR JAIL) | | MEAN MAXIMUM SENTENCE LENGTH (IN MONTHS) FOR FELONS SENTENCED TO INCARCERATION (PRISON OR JAIL) | |
	Total	State	Federal		State	Federal	State	Federal
All offenses	1,145,438	1,078,920	66,518	5.8%	70%	85%	37 mo	61 mo
Violent offenses	197,138	194,570	2,568	1.3	78	94	68	96
Murder[a]	8,590	8,400	190	2.2	92	92	232	111
Sexual assault[b]	33,605	33,190	415	1.2	81	94	93	112
Rape	12,409	12,310	99	0.8	89	88	123	141
Other sexual assault	21,196	20,880	316	1.5	76	96	72	105
Robbery	40,230	38,850	1,380	3.4	87	98	86	105
Aggravated assault	94,845	94,380	465	0.5	73	83	41	45
Other violent[c]	19,868	19,750	118	0.6	73	82	38	88
Property offenses	322,501	310,680	11,821	3.7	68	60	29	26
Burglary	93,923	93,870	53	0.1	75	83	40	28
Larceny[d]	120,705	119,340	1,365	1.1	69	54	21	31
Motor vehicle theft	16,968	16,910	58	0.3	86	67	17	27
Other theft	103,737	102,430	1,307	1.3	67	53	22	31
Fraud	107,873	97,470	10,403	9.6	60	60	26	26
Fraud[e]	57,883	48,560	9,323	16.1	56	60	24	26
Forgery	49,990	48,910	1,080	2.2	63	64	28	24
Drug offenses	387,322	362,850	24,472	6.3	67	93	31	84
Possession	163,112	161,090	2,022	1.2	64	90	23	82
Trafficking	224,210	201,760	22,450	10	69	93	37	84
Weapon offenses	41,092	33,010	8,082	19.7	72	93	32	84
Other offenses[f]	197,385	177,810	19,575	9.9	69	86	24	30

Note: Federal statistics shown in the above table are from the same database that was used to create tables 5.1 and 5.2 of the BJS publication "Compendium of Federal Statistics, 2004." Tables 5.1 and 5.2 figures differ from the above figures because of offense definitions.

[a]Includes nonnegligent manslaughter.
[b]Includes rape.
[c]Includes offenses such as negligent manslaughter and kidnapping.
[d]Includes motor vehicle theft.
[e]Includes embezzlement.
[f]Composed of nonviolent offenses such as receiving stolen property and vandalism.

Source: State Court Sentencing of Convicted Felons, 2004—Statistical Tables at www.ojp.usdoj.gov/bjs/pub/html/scscf04/tables/scs04110tab.htm.

actually shifts from legislators and prosecutors to correctional personnel. By charging inmates with violations of prison rules, correctional personnel can reduce (if the charges are upheld) the amount of good time earned by inmates and, by doing so, increase an inmate's time served.

A fifth criticism of determinate sentencing is that it is virtually impossible for legislatures or sentencing commissions to define in advance all of the factors that ought to be considered in determining a criminal sentence. You may recall from the discussion in Chapter 3 that this was a problem with one of the crime prevention implications of the classical school (equal punishment for equal crime) and the major reason for neoclassical reforms.

PHILOSOPHICAL RATIONALES

At the beginning of Chapter 2, the goals of criminal justice in the United States were identified as the prevention and the control of crime. Those are also the goals of **criminal sanctions** or **criminal punishment**—the penalties that are imposed for violating the criminal law. What has always been at issue, however,

criminal sanctions or **criminal punishment** Penalties that are imposed for violating the criminal law.

is how best to achieve those goals. This decision is the main problem faced by legislators who determine what the criminal sanctions will be in general and by judges who make sentencing decisions in individual cases. Historically, four major rationales or justifications have been given for the punishment imposed by the criminal courts: retribution, incapacitation, deterrence, and rehabilitation. A fifth rationale, restoration, has also been receiving greater attention.

Frequently, judges impose sentences for all five reasons, but at certain times in history, one or more of the reasons have been seen as less important than the others. Today, for example, punishment is imposed less for rehabilitative purposes than it once was because of the prevalent view that we do not know how to change the behavior of criminal offenders. We will now examine each of the rationales for criminal punishment.

Retribution From biblical times through the eighteenth century, **retribution** was the dominant justification for punishment. It implies repayment for an offense committed. Although it has probably always played some role in sentencing decisions, it is now increasingly popular with the public as a rationale for punishment. However, *retribution* is an imprecise term that has been defined in many ways.[7] Nevertheless, when people say that criminal punishment should be imposed for retribution, what most of them want is probably either *revenge* or *just deserts*. **Revenge** is the justification for punishment expressed by the biblical phrase, "An eye for an eye, and a tooth for a tooth." People who seek revenge want to pay back offenders by making them suffer for what they have done. The concept of **just deserts** is another justification in which punishment is seen as a payback, one that is based on something more than vindictive revenge. It supposedly does not contain the emotional element of vengeance. *Just deserts* draws part of its meaning from the idea, attributed to the German philosopher Immanuel Kant (1724–1804), that offenders should be punished automatically, simply because they have committed a crime—they "deserve" it. Another aspect of *just deserts* is proportionality of punishment. That is, a punishment should fit the crime and should not be more nor less than the offender deserves.

Based on the assumption that the desire for revenge is a basic human emotion, retributivists generally believe that state-authorized punishment greatly reduces the likelihood that individual citizens will take it upon themselves to pay back offenders for what they have done. Vigilante justice is thereby avoided. Retributivists also believe that if offenders are not punished for their crimes, then other people will lose respect for the criminal law and will not obey it.

Finally, retribution is the only rationale for criminal punishment that specifically addresses what has happened in the past; that is, to pay back offenders for their crimes. All the other rationales focus on the future and seek to influence it; for example, to restrain or prevent an offender from committing future crimes.

Incapacitation **Incapacitation** is the removal or restriction of the freedom of those found to have violated criminal laws. Incapacitation makes it virtually impossible for offenders to commit crimes during the period of restraint. Banishment or exile was once used to achieve incapacitation. Even today, foreign nationals are deported after conviction of certain crimes. Currently, incapacitation is achieved primarily through imprisonment, which keeps inmates from committing further crimes (at least outside the prison). Some states, as noted previously, have habitual-offender statutes, "three strikes and you're out" laws, or "life without opportunity of parole" (LWOP) laws that are intended to incapacitate for life repeat felons or, in the case of LWOP laws, offenders who commit capital crimes. All but two states (Alaska and New Mexico) have LWOP laws. Currently, approximately 40,000 prisoners in the United States have been sentenced to LWOP, which contrasts sharply with many European countries where the longest sentence imposed for a single offense, including murder, is

retribution A justification for punishment that implies repayment for an offense committed.

revenge The punishment rationale expressed by the biblical phrase, "An eye for an eye, and a tooth for a tooth." People who seek revenge want to pay back offenders by making them suffer for what they have done.

just deserts The punishment rationale based on the idea that offenders should be punished automatically, simply because they have committed a crime—they "deserve" it—and the idea that the punishment should fit the crime.

incapacitation The removal or restriction of the freedom of those found to have violated criminal laws.

Historically, many people have believed that public executions have a general deterrent effect. *Do you agree? Why or why not?*

14 years.[8] Because of policies that allow child offenders to be transferred to adult courts (discussed in Chapter 13), children as young as 12 years old have been sentenced to LWOP and will spend the rest of their lives in prison.[9] Capital punishment is the ultimate means of incapacitation. An executed offender can never commit a crime again.

Deterrence As described in Chapter 3, in keeping with their goal of achieving the "greatest happiness for the greatest number," Beccaria and other classical theorists believed that the only legitimate purpose for punishment is the prevention or deterrence of crime. They generally viewed punishment for purely retributive reasons as a pointless exercise.

special or **specific deterrence** The prevention of individuals from committing crimes again by punishing them.

general deterrence The prevention of people in general from engaging in crime by punishing specific individuals and making examples of them.

There are two forms of deterrence. **Special deterrence,** or **specific deterrence,** is the prevention of individuals from committing crime again by punishing them. **General deterrence** is the prevention of people in general from engaging in crime by punishing specific individuals and making examples of them.

One of the problems with general deterrence as a rationale for punishment is that even though it makes intuitive sense, social science is unable to measure its effects. Only those people who have not been deterred come to the attention of social scientists and criminal justice personnel.

rehabilitation The attempt to correct the personality and behavior of convicted offenders through educational, vocational, or therapeutic treatment and to return them to society as law-abiding citizens.

Rehabilitation For nearly 100 years, between the 1870s and 1970s, the primary rationale for punishing criminal offenders was **rehabilitation,** which is the attempt to correct the personality and behavior of convicted offenders through educational, vocational, or therapeutic treatment. The goal was to return them to society as law-abiding citizens. However, the goal of rehabilitating offenders was challenged on the grounds that we simply do not know how to correct or cure criminal offenders because the causes of crime are not fully understood. Beginning in the mid-1970s, the goal of rehabilitation was abandoned altogether in some states, or at least deemphasized in favor of the goals of retribution and incapacitation. In other states, attempts at rehabilitation continue in an institutional context that seems to favor retribution and incapacitation (as it probably always has). Some critics have suggested that punishment and rehabilitation are incompatible ways of preventing and controlling crime and that rehabilitation generally cannot be achieved in a prison setting. This criticism, however, has apparently not influenced judges, who continue to send criminal offenders to prison to rehabilitate them.

Restoration and Victims' Rights Until recently, victims of crime and their survivors have generally been forgotten or neglected in criminal justice. They have not been important or respected participants in the adjudication process except, perhaps, as witnesses to their own or their loved ones' victimization. Beginning in the 1980s, however, because of increased scholarly attention to their plight and a fledgling victims' rights movement, attempts have been made to change the situation. Today, in many jurisdictions, a greater effort is being made to do something for victims and their survivors—to restore them, as much as possible, to their previous state and to make them "whole" again.

In the early 1980s, only four states had laws that protected the basic rights of crime victims in the criminal justice system. Now, every state has such laws. In fact, there has been an explosion of activity in this area over the last 25 years. States have enacted more than 30,000 crime-victim-related statutes, at least 32 state victims' rights constitutional amendments have been passed, and the federal government has passed legislation providing basic rights and services to federal crime victims, such as victim assistance and victim compensation programs.[10]

The federal government, through its Crime Victims Fund, has also made millions of dollars available for state crime victim compensation, local victim assistance programs, and national training and technical assistance. The Crime Victims Fund is derived from fines, forfeited bonds, and penalties paid by federal criminal offenders, as well as gifts, bequests, and donations. Since the fund was established in 1984 and, through 2004, about $6.7 billion have been awarded, and 2 to 4 million victims have been helped each year.[11]

Among the rights now granted crime victims in at least some jurisdictions are these:

- The right to notice of victims' rights.
- The right to be treated with fairness, dignity, and respect.
- The right to be informed, present, and heard at important criminal justice proceedings.
- The right to confer with the prosecutor.
- The right of sexual assault victims to be paid for forensic exams.
- The right to HIV testing of sex offenders and notification of the results.
- The right to reasonable protection from the accused.
- The right to privacy (including a prohibition against compelling testimony about personal information in open court, exclusion or limited disclosure of victim-identifying information in criminal justice records, and protection from release of addresses and phone numbers provided for notice purposes).
- The right to a speedy resolution of the case.
- The right to a prompt return of the victim's property.
- The right to notice of the offender's release.
- The right to restitution from the offender or compensation from the state.[12]

In the sentencing process, the U.S. Supreme Court ruled in 1991 in *Payne v. Tennessee* that judges and juries may consider *victim-impact statements* in their sentencing decisions. **Victim-impact statements** are descriptions of the harm and suffering that a crime has caused victims and their survivors. Before the Court's 1991 decision, victim-impact statements were considered irrelevant and potentially inflammatory and were not allowed.

FYI Rehabilitation

In 2003, 72% of Americans either completely agreed (29%) or mostly agreed (43%) that the criminal justice system should try to rehabilitate criminals and not just punish them; only 25% either mostly disagreed (14%) or completely disagreed (11%).

Source: *Sourcebook of Criminal Justice Statistics online*, www.albany.edu/sourcebook/pdf/t20012.pdf (Table 2.0012).

CJ Online

Victim Assistance

The U.S. Department of Justice established the Office for Victims of Crime (OVC) in 1983. OVC provides federal funding for victim assistance and compensation programs throughout the country. It also develops policies and works with criminal justice professionals in order to support crime victims. Visit the OVC website at www.ojp.usdoj.gov/ovc. *Do you think that enough is being done to support crime victims?*

victim-impact statements Descriptions of the harm and suffering that a crime has caused victims and their survivors.

Careers in Criminal Justice

Victim Advocate

My name is Dori DeJong, and I am a victim advocate with the Denver District Attorney's Office in Denver, Colorado. I have a Bachelor's degree in education from the University of Northern Colorado, a Master's degree in social work and a Juris Doctor from the University of Denver. Prior to working in the district attorney's office, I worked as a counselor at a children's psychiatric hospital, as a children's counselor at a battered women's shelter, and as a legal advocate for a community agency that provided assistance to victims of domestic violence. I decided to become a victim advocate because it was a great way to combine my educational background in both social work and law.

A typical day as a victim advocate includes contacting the victims of crimes (domestic violence, stranger assault, sex assault, child abuse, etc.) and explaining the criminal justice system to them; providing details about their specific case; giving notification of their rights as a victim; referring victims to various outside assistance agencies; and obtaining their input as to the best possible outcome of the case in which they are involved. Additionally, I coordinate and participate in the meetings between the victims and the assistant district attorneys to assist in the preparation of the victims for trial and to answer any questions they have about the process. I accompany the victims in the courthouse on the day of the trial to provide encouragement, support, and understanding of the process in order for them to get through a very difficult experience. I also send update letters and victim impact statements to victims, notify other agencies and jurisdictions of active cases, run criminal background checks on defendants to identify habitual offenders, and maintain statistics on domestic violence cases. I have regular contact and communication with police officers, detectives, district attorneys, investigators, and other victim advocates. I also communicate with staff from outside assistance agencies to help sustain continuing support for the victim.

The most positive aspect of the job is the ability to help people and feel that you are really making a difference in someone's life. It is so encouraging when you have a client call you, months or even years after you've assisted them, to thank you and tell you what a difference you've made in their lives and their children's lives. It is also rewarding to be a part of the prosecution team that holds criminals responsible and accountable for their behavior.

Being a victim advocate can sometimes be difficult and frustrating because you work with people who are in crisis and often are not appreciative of your involvement in their lives. Sometimes their anger about the incident is misdirected at the victim advocate and the system, which is trying to provide justice.

The job of a victim advocate is interesting, challenging, often fast paced, and can be very rewarding. However, the job can also be overwhelming, since it frequently involves dealing with offensive criminal defendants and their actions, and the sometimes inequitable system of justice. If you are considering a job as a victim advocate, I would encourage you to volunteer or do an internship in an agency that works with victims. This invaluable experience will provide you with the knowledge to determine if this career suits you.

Do you have any characteristics and/or abilities that you think would make you particularly suited to being a victim's advocate? If so, what?

Despite the many rights that have been granted crime victims in the United States, there are many problems with the victims' rights laws and their implementation. Victims' rights vary greatly among states and at the federal level. Even in states that have constitutional rights for victims, those rights often are ignored, suffer from arbitrary implementation, or depend on the whims of criminal justice officials. Victims from other cultures and those with disabilities frequently are not informed of their rights or given the opportunity to participate in criminal and juvenile justice proceedings. There are also gaps in the laws. For example, many states do not provide comprehensive rights for the victims of crimes committed by juveniles. Victims' rights in tribal, military, and administrative proceedings are generally nonexistent.[13]

Another effort at restoration places equal emphasis on victims' rights and needs and the successful reintegration (and, in some cases, initial integration) of offenders into the community. Unlike retribution, which focuses almost entirely on offenders and their punishments, restorative justice seeks to restore the health of the community, repair the harm done, meet victims' needs, and require the offender to contribute to those repairs. Following Braithwaite's theory of reintegrative shaming, described in Chapter 3, in restorative justice the criminal act is condemned, offenders are held accountable, participants are involved, and repentant offenders are encouraged to earn their way back into society.[14]

Brendan Costin, the 14-year-old son of hockey dad victim Michael Costin, becomes emotional as he delivers a victim-impact statement about his deceased father while sitting next to a framed memorial the family set up on the witness stand at the sentencing hearing of hockey dad Thomas Junta. *Should victim-impact statements be allowed at sentencing hearings? Why or why not?*

Restitution and community service are two examples of restorative practices (they are used for other purposes as well). Restitution is a court requirement that a victim's convicted offender pay money or provide services to victims, survivors, or the community that has been victimized. Typically, laws specify that restitution may be ordered to cover medical expenses, lost wages, counseling expenses, lost or damaged property, funeral expenses, and other direct out-of-pocket expenses. The 1984 Federal Comprehensive Crime Control Act requires that when offenders convicted of federal violations are sentenced to probation, they must pay a fine, make restitution, perform community service, or do all three. In more than one-third of all states, courts are required by law to order restitution unless there are compelling or extraordinary circumstances.[15] Unfortunately, a problem with restitution is that most offenders have neither the financial means nor the abilities to provide adequate restitution.

ORGANIZATIONAL CONSIDERATIONS

A judge's sentence is also guided by organizational considerations. We have already discussed at some length the practice of plea bargaining and have shown that without it, the judicial process could not function. For practical reasons, judges almost always impose the sentence agreed on during plea negotiations. If they did not, plea bargaining would not work. That is, if defendants could not be sure that judges would impose the agreed-on sentence, there would be no reason for them to plead guilty. They might as well take their chances at trial.

Another organizational consideration is the capacity of the system. As we already have noted, many of the prisons in this country and some entire state prison systems are overcrowded and are under federal court order to reduce the problem. Judges in jurisdictions with overcrowded prisons are generally less inclined to sentence offenders to prison.

A third organizational consideration is the cost-benefit question. Every sentence involves some monetary and social cost. Judges must be sensitive to this issue and must balance the costs of the sentence they impose with the benefits that might be derived from it.

PRESENTENCE INVESTIGATION REPORTS

presentence investigation reports Reports, often called PSIs or PSIRs, that are used in the federal system and the majority of states to help judges determine the appropriate sentence. They are also used in classing probationers, parolees, and prisoners according to their treatment needs and security risk.

A purpose of **presentence investigation reports** (PSIs or PSIRs), used in the federal system and by the majority of states, is to help judges determine the appropriate sentence for particular defendants. They are also used in classing probationers, parolees, and prisoners according to their treatment needs and security risk. Generally, a PSI is prepared by a probation officer, who conducts as thorough a background check as possible on a defendant. In some jurisdictions, probation officers recommend a sentence based on the information in the PSI. In other jurisdictions, they simply write the report and do not make a sentencing recommendation. Studies show that judges follow the sentencing recommendations in PSIs most of the time, although they are not required to do so.

allocution The procedure at a sentencing hearing in which the convicted defendant has the right to address the court before the sentence is imposed. During allocution, a defendant is identified as the person found guilty and has a right to deny or explain information contained in the PSI if his or her sentence is based on it.

In most jurisdictions, after the PSI has been submitted to the judge, a sentencing hearing is held at which the convicted defendant has the right to address the court before the sentence is imposed. This procedure is called **allocution.** During allocution, a defendant is identified as the person found guilty and has a right to deny or explain information contained in the PSI if his or her sentence is based on it. The defendant also has the opportunity to plead for a **pardon** (a "forgiveness" for the crime committed that stops further criminal processing). He or she may also attempt to have the sentencing process stopped or may explain why a sentence should not be pronounced. However, defendants are not entitled to argue during allocution about whether they are guilty. Among the claims that a convicted offender can make at allocution are the following:

pardon A "forgiveness" for the crime committed that stops further criminal processing.

1. That he or she is not the person who was found guilty at trial.
2. That a pardon has been granted for the crime in question.
3. That he or she has gone insane since the verdict was rendered. Rules of due process prohibit the sentencing of convicted offenders if they do not understand why they are being punished. Punishment must be deferred until they are no longer insane.
4. That she is pregnant. The sentence of a pregnant offender must be deferred or adjusted, especially in a capital case.

PERSONAL CHARACTERISTICS OF JUDGES

Although extralegal factors are not supposed to influence a judge's sentencing decision, studies show that they invariably do. Judges, after all, are human beings with all of the human frailties and prejudices of other human beings. Among the personal characteristics of judges that have been found to affect their sentencing decisions are these:

1. Their socioeconomic backgrounds.
2. The law schools they attended.
3. Their prior experiences both in and out of the courtroom.
4. The number of offenders they defended earlier in their careers.
5. Their biases concerning various crimes.
6. Their emotional reactions and prejudices toward the defendants.
7. Their own personalities.
8. Their marital and sexual relations.

A judge's sentencing is the result of a complex set of factors. *Which factors do you consider to be the most important and the least important? Why?*

In summary, a judge's sentencing decision is the result of the complex interplay of several different factors.

Those factors include statutory provisions, philosophical rationales, organizational considerations, presentence investigation reports, results of the allocution, and personal characteristics of the judge.

THINKING CRITICALLY

1. What do you think are some of the most important issues to consider when sentencing a convicted criminal?

2. Do you think that victims should play more or less of a role in sentencing?

Appeals

As described previously, defendants can appeal their convictions either on legal grounds (for example, defects in jury selection, improper admission of evidence at trial, mistaken interpretations of law) or on constitutional grounds (for instance, illegal search and seizure, improper questioning of the defendant by the police, identification of the defendant through a defective police lineup, incompetent assistance of counsel). However, they are not entitled to present new evidence or testimony on appeal if that evidence or testimony could have been presented at trial. If new evidence is discovered that was unknown or unknowable to the defense at trial, then an appeal can sometimes be made on the basis of that new evidence. Still, in *Herrera* v. *Collins,* 1993, a death penalty case, the Supreme Court ruled that, absent constitutional grounds, new evidence of innocence is no reason for a federal court to order a new state trial. In any event, because the defendant has already been found guilty, the presumption of innocence no longer applies during the appellate process, and the burden of showing why the conviction should be overturned shifts to the defendant.

Generally, notice of intent to appeal must be filed within 30 to 90 days after conviction. Also, within a specified period of time, an *affidavit of errors* specifying the alleged defects in the trial or pretrial proceedings must be submitted. If those two steps are followed, the appellate court must review the case. Nevertheless, very few appeals are successful. Nearly 80% of state trial court decisions are affirmed on appeal. (See Chapter 8 for more on the appellate courts.)

THINKING CRITICALLY

Why do you think so few appeals are successful? Do you think the appeals process works effectively? Why or why not?

The Death Penalty

Before concluding this chapter, we will examine in some detail the death penalty in the United States, because, as the Supreme Court has acknowledged, "death is different."[16] Other sentencing options are discussed in later chapters of this book. As a punishment for the most heinous of crimes, the death penalty, or capital punishment, differs from all other criminal sanctions, not only in the nature of the penalty itself (the termination of life) but also in the legal procedures that lead to it. However, before describing the unique way in which capital punishment is administered in the United States, we provide some background about the penalty.

For a century after the ratification of the Eighth Amendment, hanging was the only legally authorized method of execution in the United States. The one exception was that spies, traitors, and deserters convicted under federal statutes could be shot. Hanging is no longer authorized as the sole or principal method of execution in any executing jurisdiction. *Why was hanging as a method of execution abandoned?*

A BRIEF HISTORY OF THE DEATH PENALTY IN THE UNITED STATES

When the first European settlers arrived in America, they brought with them the legal systems from their native countries, which included the penalty of death for a variety of offenses. For example, the English Penal Code at the time, which was adopted by the British colonies, listed more than 50 capital offenses, but actual practice varied from colony to colony. In the Massachusetts Bay Colony, 12 crimes carried the death penalty:

- Idolatry
- Witchcraft
- Blasphemy
- Rape
- Statutory rape
- Perjury in a trial involving a possible death sentence

- Rebellion
- Murder
- Assault in sudden anger
- Adultery
- Buggery (sodomy)
- Kidnapping

In the statute, each crime was accompanied by an appropriate biblical quotation justifying the capital punishment. Later the colony added arson, treason, and grand larceny to the list of capital offenses. In contrast, the Quakers adopted much milder laws. The Royal Charter for South Jersey (1646), for example, did not permit capital punishment for any crime, and in Pennsylvania, William Penn's Great Act of 1682 limited the death penalty to treason and murder. Most colonies, however, followed the much harsher British Code.

The earliest recorded lawful execution in America was in 1608 in the colony of Virginia. Captain George Kendall, a councilor for the colony, was executed for being a spy for Spain. Since Kendall, about 20,000 legal executions have been performed in the United States under civil authority. However, only about 3% of those people executed since 1608 have been women. Ninety percent of the women executed were executed under local, as opposed to state, authority, and the majority (87%) were executed before 1866. The first woman executed was Jane Champion in the Virginia colony in 1632. She was hanged for murdering and concealing the death of her child, who had not been fathered by her husband. Since 1962, only 11 women have been executed in the United States (as of January 1, 2009).[17]

In addition, about 2% of those executed in the United States since 1608 have been juveniles—those whose offenses were committed before their eighteenth birthdays. The first juvenile executed in America was Thomas Graunger in the Plymouth Colony in 1642, for the crime of bestiality. Between 1990 and 2005, the United States was one of only seven countries that had executed anyone under 18 years of age at the time of the crime; the others were the Democratic Republic of Congo, Iran, Nigeria, Pakistan, Saudi Arabia, and Yemen. Pakistan, Yemen, and the United States (as of March 1, 2005) no longer execute juveniles. The United States had executed 22 juveniles since 1976.[18]

ENTER THE SUPREME COURT

For more than one hundred fifty years, the United States Supreme Court ("the Court") has exercised its responsibility to regulate capital punishment in the United States

During the twentieth century, more people were executed by electrocution than by any other method. *Why have states abandoned electrocution as an execution method?*

and its territories. Among the principal issues the Supreme Court considered in relation to capital punishment before 1968 concerned the means of administering the death penalty. The Court upheld the constitutionality of shooting (*Wilkerson* v. *Utah,* 1878), electrocution (*In re Kemmler,* 1890), and a second electrocution after the first attempt had failed to kill the offender (*Louisiana ex rel. Francis* v. *Resweber,* 1947). Currently, there are five methods of execution authorized: lethal injection, electrocution, lethal gas, hanging, and firing squad. However, lethal injection is now the primary method of execution used in all executing states, as well as the U.S. government and the U.S. military. In 2008, in *Baze v. Rees,* the Court upheld the constitutionality of lethal injection.

Between 1968 and 1972, a series of lawsuits challenged various aspects of capital punishment as well as the constitutionality of the punishment itself. During this period, an informal moratorium on executions was observed, pending the outcome of the litigation, and no death row inmates were executed. Some of the suits were successful, and some of them were not. Finally, on June 29, 1972, the Supreme Court set aside death sentences for the first time in its history. In its decisions in *Furman* v. *Georgia, Jackson* v. *Georgia,* and *Branch* v. *Texas* (hereafter referred to as the *Furman* decision), the Court held that the capital punishment statutes in those three cases were unconstitutional because they gave the jury complete discretion to decide whether to impose the death penalty or a lesser punishment in capital cases. Although nine separate opinions were written—a very rare occurrence—the majority of five justices (Douglas, Brennan, Stewart, White, and Marshall) pointed out that the death penalty had been imposed arbitrarily, infrequently, and often selectively against people of color. According to the majority, those statutes constituted "cruel and unusual punishment" under the Eighth and Fourteenth Amendments. (The four dissenters were Chief Justice Burger and justices Blackmun, Powell, and Rehnquist.) Note that the Supreme Court did not rule that the death penalty itself was unconstitutional, only the way in which it was being administered.

The practical effect of the *Furman* decision was that the Supreme Court voided the death penalty laws of some 35 states, and more than 600 men and women had their death sentences vacated and commuted to a term of imprisonment. Although opponents of capital punishment were elated that the United States had finally joined all the other Western industrialized nations in abolishing capital punishment either in fact or in practice, the joy was short-lived. By the fall of 1974, 30 states had enacted new death penalty statutes that were designed to meet the Court's objections.

The new death penalty laws took two forms. Some states removed all discretion from the process by mandating capital punishment upon conviction for certain crimes (mandatory statutes). Other states provided specific guidelines that judges and juries were to use in deciding if death was the appropriate sentence in a particular case (guided-discretion statutes).

The constitutionality of the new death penalty statutes was quickly challenged, and on July 2, 1976, the Supreme Court announced its rulings in five test cases. In *Woodson* v. *North Carolina* and *Roberts* v. *Louisiana,* the Court rejected mandatory statutes that automatically imposed death sentences for defined capital offenses. However, in *Gregg* v. *Georgia, Jurek* v. *Texas,* and *Proffitt* v. *Florida* (hereafter referred to together as the *Gregg* decision), the Court approved several different forms of guided-discretion statutes. Those statutes, the Court wrote, struck a reasonable balance between giving the jury some guidance and allowing it to consider the background and character of the defendant and the circumstances of the crime.

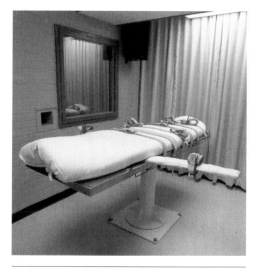

Lethal injection has become the sole or principal method of execution in all executing jurisdictions in the United States. *Why?*

The most celebrated recent execution by firing squad was the January 17, 1977, execution of Gary Gilmore in Utah. It no longer is authorized as the sole or principal method of execution in any executing jurisdiction. *Does execution by firing squad have any advantages over other methods of execution? If so, what are they?*

The most dramatic effect of the *Gregg* decision was the resumption of executions on January 17, 1977, when the state of Utah executed Gary Gilmore (at his own request) by firing squad. Since then, 1,143 people have been executed in 34 states and by the federal government, which has executed three (as of January 30, 2009).[19] More than half of the 1,143 executions have taken place in just three states—Texas (428), Virginia (102), and Oklahoma (89). Figure 9.3 shows the states in which executions have taken place. Note that Texas alone accounts for more than one-third of all post-*Furman* executions. Texas has executed more than four times as many offenders as any other state.

Table 9.4 shows the race or ethnicity and gender of the defendants executed and their victims, as well as defendant-victim racial or ethnic combinations. As shown, nearly all the people executed since Gilmore's execution in 1977 have been male, whereas the gender of the victims is divided nearly evenly between males and females. As for race, nearly 57% of all people executed under post-*Furman* statutes have been white; about 35% have been black. Thus, the percentage of blacks who have been executed far exceeds their proportion of the general population (about 13%). Particularly interesting is that nearly 80% of the victims of those executed have been white. What makes this finding interesting is that murders, including capital murders (all post-*Furman* executions have been for capital murders; see the following discussion), tend to be intraracial crimes. However, the death penalty is imposed primarily

Figure 9.3

State-by-State Count of Inmates Executed in 34 States Since Executions Resumed in 1977

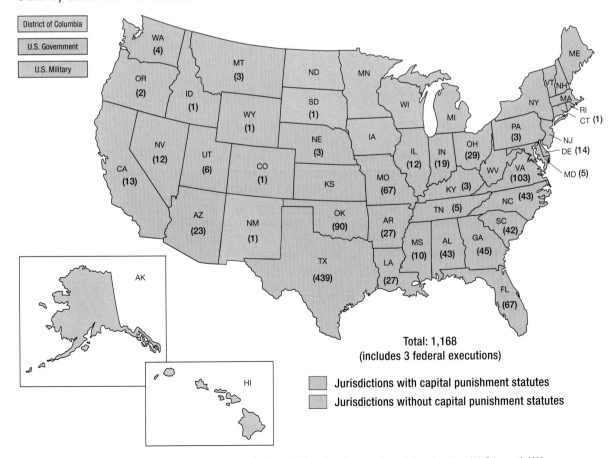

Total: 1,168
(includes 3 federal executions)

Jurisdictions with capital punishment statutes

Jurisdictions without capital punishment statutes

Source: Adapted from Death Penalty Information Center at www.deathpenaltyinfo.org/number-executions-state-and-region-1976, February 2, 2009.

Table 9.4 Race or Ethnicity and Sex of Defendants Executed and Their Victims and Defendant-Victim Racial or Ethnic Combinations

GENDER OF DEFENDANTS EXECUTED			GENDER OF VICTIMS		
Total Number 1,136	(Number)	(%)	Total Number 1,683	(Number)	(%)
Female	11	(.97%)	Female	832	(49.44%)
Male	1,125	(99.03)	Male	851	(50.56)

RACE OF DEFENDANTS EXECUTED			RACE OF VICTIMS		
White	643	(56.60)	White	1,324	(78.67)
Black	393	(34.60)	Black	239	(14.20)
Latino/a	78	(6.87)	Latino/a	82	(4.87)
Native American	15	(1.32)	Native American	5	(0.30)
Asian	7	(0.62)	Asian	33	(1.96)

DEFENDANT-VICTIM RACIAL COMBINATIONS

White Defendant and			Asian Defendant and		
White Victim	602	(52.99)	White Victim	2	(0.18)
Black Victim	15	(1.32)	Black Victim	0	(0.00)
Latino/a Victim	13	(1.14)	Latino/a Victim	0	(0.00)
Asian Victim	4	(0.35)	Asian Victim	5	(0.44)
Native American Victim	0	(0.00)	Native American Victim	0	(0.00)
Black Defendant and			Native American Defendant and		
White Victim	236	(20.77)	White Victim	13	(1.14)
Black Victim	125	(11.00)	Black Victim	0	(0.00)
Latino/a Victim	15	(1.32)	Latino/a Victim	0	(0.00)
Asian Victim	10	(0.88)	Asian Victim	0	(0.00)
Native American Victim	0	(0.00)	Native American Victim	2	(0.18)
Latino/a Defendant and			TOTAL		
White Victim	38	(3.25)	White Victim	891	(78.43)
Black Victim	2	(0.18)	Black Victim	142	(12.50)
Latino/a Victim	33	(2.89)	Latino/a Victim	61	(5.37)
Asian Victim	2	(0.18)	Asian Victim	21	(1.85)
Native American Victim	0	(0.00)	Native American Victim	2	(0.18)

Note: In addition, there were 19 defendants executed for the murders of multiple victims of different races. Of those, 11 defendants were white, 5 black, and 3 Latino (1.67%).

Source: Death Row, U.S.A., *NAACP Legal Defense and Educational Fund* (January 1, 2009).

on the killers of white people, regardless of the race or ethnicity of the offender. The figures on defendant-victim racial or ethnic combinations (see Table 9.4) further support this conclusion. Note that about 53% of executions have involved white killers of white victims, and about 21% of executions have involved black killers of white victims. However, only 11% of executions have been of black killers of black victims, and there have been only 15 executions of white killers of black persons (less than 2%).

Currently (as of May 16, 2009), 37 jurisdictions have capital punishment statutes; 16 jurisdictions do not have capital punishment statutes. (In 2004, New York's death penalty statute was declared unconstitutional; in 2007, New Jersey abolished its death penalty; and, in 2009, New Mexico abolished its death penalty.) Figure 9.4 shows the jurisdictions with and without capital punishment statutes.

In decisions since *Gregg*, the Supreme Court has limited the crimes for which death is considered appropriate and has further refined death penalty

Figure 9.4

Jurisdictions with and without Capital Punishment Statutes

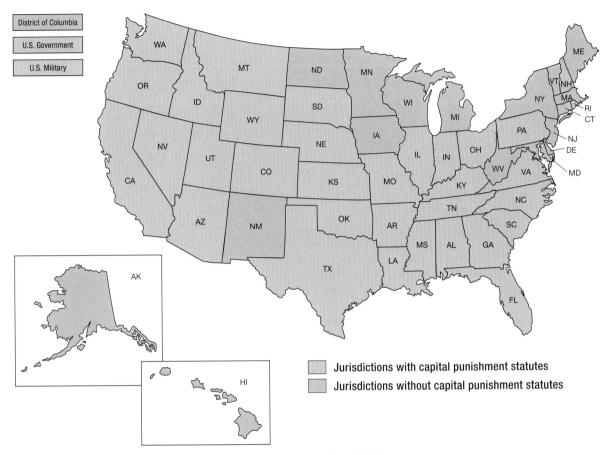

Source: Adapted from the Death Penalty Information Center, www.deathpenaltyinfo.org (May 16, 2009).

MYTH

Capital punishment is no longer administered in a way that is racially discriminatory and legally impermissible.

FACT

Dozens of scientific studies clearly show that the death penalty continues to be administered in a legally impermissible and discriminatory fashion against blacks and the killers of whites.

Source: For a summary of those studies, see Robert M. Bohm, *Deathquest III: An Introduction to the Theory and Practice of Capital Punishment in the United States*, 3rd ed. (Cincinnati, OH: Anderson, 2007), Chapter 8. For the view that the evidence does not show racial discrimination, see William Wilbanks, *The Myth of a Racist Criminal Justice System* (Monterey, CA: Brooks/ Cole, 1987).

jurisprudence. In 1977, in the cases of *Coker* v. *Georgia* and *Eberheart* v. *Georgia,* the Court held that rape of an adult female (in *Coker*) and kidnapping (in *Eberheart*) when the victim was not killed do not warrant death. In 2008, in *Kennedy* v. *Louisiana,* the Court ruled that the rape of a child, when the victim was not killed, also did not warrant death. Those three decisions effectively limit the death penalty to those offenders convicted of capital, or aggravated, murder.

In 1986, in *Ford* v. *Wainwright,* the Court barred states from executing inmates who have developed mental illness while on death row, and, in 2002, in *Atkins* v. *Virginia,* the Court held that it is cruel and unusual punishment to execute the mentally retarded. In the 2005 case of *Roper* v. *Simmons,* the Court, again referring to "evolving standards of decency," effectively limited capital punishment to offenders who are 18 years of age or older at the time of their offenses. Another death penalty decision of the Supreme Court is the 1987 case of *McCleskey* v. *Kemp,* in which the Court held that state death penalty statutes are constitutional even when statistics indicate that they have been applied in racially biased ways. The Court ruled that racial discrimination must be shown in individual cases. The *McCleskey* decision was particularly disheartening to opponents of capital punishment because, for them, the case was the last best chance of having the Supreme Court declare the death penalty unconstitutional once and for all.

The 1994 federal crime bill (the Violent Crime Control and Law Enforcement Act) expanded the number of federal crimes punishable by death to about 50. (Estimates vary depending on whether statutes or offenses are counted, and how offenses are counted.) All but four of the federal crimes involve murder. The four exceptions are treason; espionage; drug trafficking in large quantities; and attempting, authorizing, or advising the killing of any public officer, juror, or witness in a case involving a continuing criminal enterprise—regardless of whether such a killing actually occurs. In addition, the bill reinstated the death penalty for federal crimes for which previous death penalty provisions could not pass constitutional muster. The new law brought the earlier statutes into compliance with guidelines established by the Supreme Court. The U.S. government executed Timothy McVeigh and Juan Raul Garza in 2001, and Louis Jones, Jr., in 2003. They were the first federal executions in nearly 40 years. Prior to those three, the last execution by the U.S. government was on March 15, 1963, when Victor H. Feguer was hanged at Iowa State Penitentiary.

THE PROCEDURAL REFORMS APPROVED IN *GREGG*

It is important to emphasize that the Supreme Court approved the new death penalty statutes in *Gregg* "on their face." That is, the Court assumed, without any evidence, that the new guided-discretion statutes would eliminate the arbitrariness and discrimination that the Court found objectionable in its *Furman* decision. The Court was particularly optimistic about the following procedural reforms: bifurcated trials, guidelines for judges and juries, and automatic appellate review.

Bifurcated Trials A **bifurcated trial** is a two-stage trial—unlike the one-stage trial in other felony cases—consisting of a guilt phase and a separate penalty phase. If, in the guilt phase, the defendant is found guilty as charged, then at the penalty phase, the jury must determine whether the sentence will be death or life in prison (there are no other choices except, in most death penalty states, life imprisonment without opportunity for parole).

Some states require the selection of two separate juries in capital trials, one for the guilt phase and one for the penalty phase. During *voir dire* in capital cases, each side is generally allowed more peremptory challenges, necessitating a larger panel from which to select the jury. California, for example, allows 20 peremptory challenges in capital cases and only 10 in noncapital cases. During both phases of a bifurcated capital trial, evidence may be introduced and witnesses may be called to testify. In short, all of the procedures of due process apply to both phases of the bifurcated trial.

Guidelines for Judges and Juries What the Court found especially appealing about the guided-discretion statutes approved in *Gregg* is that judges and juries are provided with standards that presumably restrict, but do not eliminate, their sentencing discretion. Specifically, judges and juries, in most states, are provided with lists of aggravating and, at least in some states, mitigating factors. **Aggravating factors,** or **aggravating circumstances,** are facts or situations that increase the blameworthiness for a criminal act. **Mitigating factors, or mitigating circumstances,** are facts or situations that do not justify or excuse a criminal act but reduce the degree of blameworthiness and thus may reduce the punishment. The Court has since ruled (in *Lockett* v. *Ohio,* 1978; *Bell* v. *Ohio,* 1978; and *Hitchcock* v. *Dugger,* 1987) that judges and juries must consider any mitigating circumstance offered by the defense, whether it is listed in the statute or not. Table 9.5 lists the aggravating and mitigating factors in Florida's current death penalty statute. The factors are typical of most states that provide them.

Under Florida's death penalty statute, which is an "aggravating-versus-mitigating" type, at least one aggravating factor must be found before death may be considered as a penalty. If one or more aggravating factors are found, it is

bifurcated trial A two-stage trial (unlike the one-stage trial in other felony cases) consisting of a guilt phase and a separate penalty phase.

aggravating factors or **circumstances** In death sentencing, facts or situations that increase the blameworthiness for a criminal act.

mitigating factors or **circumstances** In death sentencing, facts or situations that do not justify or excuse a criminal act but reduce the degree of blameworthiness and thus may reduce the punishment.

Table 9.5 Aggravating and Mitigating Factors in Florida's Death Penalty Statute

Aggravating Factors

1. The capital felony was committed by a person previously convicted of a felony and under sentence of imprisonment or placed on community control or on felony probation.

2. The defendant was previously convicted of another capital felony or of a felony involving the use or threat of violence to the person.

3. The defendant knowingly created a great risk of death to many persons.

4. The capital felony was committed while the defendant was engaged, or was an accomplice, in the commission of, or an attempt to commit, or flight after committing or attempting to commit, any: robbery; sexual battery; aggravated child abuse; abuse of an elderly person or disabled adult resulting in great bodily harm, permanent disability, or permanent disfigurement; arson; burglary; kidnapping; aircraft piracy; or unlawful throwing, placing, or discharging of a destructive device or bomb.

5. The capital felony was committed for the purpose of avoiding or preventing a lawful arrest or effecting an escape from custody.

6. The capital felony was committed for pecuniary gain.

7. The capital felony was committed to disrupt or hinder the lawful exercise of any governmental function or the enforcement of laws.

8. The capital felony was especially heinous, atrocious, or cruel.

9. The capital felony was a homicide and was committed in a cold, calculated, and premeditated manner without any pretense of moral or legal justification.

10. The victim of the capital felony was a law enforcement officer engaged in the performance of his or her official duties.

11. The victim of the capital felony was an elected or appointed public official engaged in the performance of his or her official duties if the motive for the capital felony was related, in whole or in part, to the victim's official capacity.

12. The victim of the capital felony was a person less than 12 years of age.

13. The victim of the capital felony was particularly vulnerable due to advanced age or disability, or because the defendant stood in a position of familial or custodial authority over the victim.

14. The capital felony was committed by a criminal street gang member, as defined in § 874.03.

15. The capital felony was committed by a person designated as a sexual predator pursuant to § 775.21 or a person previously designated as a sexual predator who had the sexual predator designation removed.

Mitigating Factors

1. The defendant has no significant history of prior criminal activity.

2. The capital felony was committed while the defendant was under the influence of extreme mental or emotional disturbance.

3. The victim was a participant in the defendant's conduct or consented to the act.

4. The defendant was an accomplice in the capital felony committed by another person, and his or her participation was relatively minor.

5. The defendant acted under extreme duress or under the substantial domination of another person.

6. The capacity of the defendant to appreciate the criminality of his or her conduct or to conform his or her conduct to the requirements of law was substantially impaired.

7. The age of the defendant at the time of the crime.

8. The existence of any other factors in the defendant's background that would mitigate against imposition of the death penalty.

Source: Online Sunshine View Statutes (2008) "The 2008 Florida Statutes," www.leg.state.fl.us/statutes/index.cfm?mode=View%20Statutes&SubMenu=1&App_mode=Display _Statute&Search_String=aggravating+circumstances&URL=Ch0921/Sec141.HTM.

weighed against any mitigating factors. If the aggravating factors outweigh the mitigating factors, the sentence is death. However, if the mitigating factors outweigh the aggravating factors, the sentence is life imprisonment without opportunity for parole. Currently, in Florida (and Alabama) the jury's recommendation is only advisory to the judge. That is, in those states, the judge may impose death even if the jury recommends life, or may impose life even if the jury recommends death. This override provision may not survive constitutional challenge because in *Ring* v. *Arizona* (2002) the U.S. Supreme Court ruled that juries and not judges alone must determine whether death is the appropriate penalty in a capital case.

Another type of guided-discretion statute is Georgia's "aggravating-only" statute. In Georgia, if a jury finds at least one statutory aggravating factor, then it may, but need not, recommend death. The jury may also consider any mitigating factors, although mitigating factors are not listed in the statute, as they are in some states. The judge must follow the jury's recommendation.

A third type of guided-discretion statute is Texas's "structured-discretion" statute. In Texas, aggravating or mitigating factors are not listed in the statute. Instead, during the sentencing phase of the trial, the state and the defendant or the defendant's counsel may present evidence about any matter that the court deems relevant to sentence, that is, any aggravating or mitigating factors. On conclusion of the presentation of the evidence, the court submits the following issues to the jury:

1. Whether the defendant would possibly commit criminal acts of violence that would constitute a continuing threat to society.
2. Whether the defendant actually caused the death of the deceased or did not actually cause the death of the deceased but intended to kill the deceased or another or anticipated that a human life would be taken (if raised by the evidence).

During penalty deliberations, juries in Texas must consider all evidence admitted at the guilt and penalty phases. Then, they must consider the two aforementioned issues. To answer "yes" to the issues, all jurors must answer "yes"; to answer "no" to the issues, 10 or more jurors must answer "no." If the two issues are answered in the affirmative, jurors are then asked if there is a sufficient mitigating factor or factors to warrant that a sentence of life imprisonment rather than a death sentence be imposed. To answer "no" to this issue, all jurors must answer "no"; to answer "yes," 10 or more jurors must agree. If the jury returns an affirmative finding on the first two issues and a negative finding on the third issue, then the court must sentence the defendant to death. However, if the jury returns a negative finding on either of the first two issues or an affirmative finding on the third issue, then the court must sentence the defendant to life imprisonment.

Automatic Appellate Review The third procedural feature of most of the new death penalty statutes is automatic appellate review. Currently, 34 of the 35 states with death penalty statutes provide for automatic appellate review of all death sentences, regardless of the defendant's wishes. South Carolina allows the defendant to waive sentence review if the defendant is deemed competent by the court; also, the federal jurisdiction does not provide for automatic appellate review. Most of the 34 states automatically review both the conviction and the sentence (Idaho, Montana, Oklahoma, South Dakota, and Tennessee review only the sentence).[20] Generally, the automatic review is conducted by the state's highest appellate court. If either the conviction or the sentence is overturned, then the case is sent back to the trial court for additional proceedings or for retrial. It is possible that the death sentence may be reimposed as a result of this process.

Some states are very specific in defining the review function of the appellate courts, while other states are not. Although the Supreme Court does not require it (*Pulley* v. *Harris,* 1984), some states have provided a proportionality review. In a **proportionality review,** the appellate court compares the sentence in the case it is reviewing with penalties imposed in similar cases in the state. The object of proportionality review is to reduce, as much as possible, disparity in death penalty sentencing.

In addition to the automatic appellate review, there is a dual system of collateral review for capital defendants. In other words, capital defendants may appeal their convictions and sentences through both the state and the federal appellate systems. Table 9.6 shows the general appeals process in death penalty cases.

proportionality review A review in which the appellate court compares the sentence in the case it is reviewing with penalties imposed in similar cases in the state. The object is to reduce, as much as possible, disparity in death penalty sentencing.

Table 9.6 The Appellate Process in Capital Cases

Stage 1

Step 1: Trial and Sentence in State Court
Step 2: Direct Appeal to the State Appeals Court
Step 3: U.S. Supreme Court for Writ of *Certiorari*

Stage 2

Step 1: State Post Conviction
Step 2: State Court of Appeals
Step 3: U.S. Supreme Court for Writ of *Certiorari*

Stage 3

Step 1: Petition for Writ of *Habeas Corpus* in Federal District Court
Step 2: Certificate of Probable Cause and Request for Stay of Execution
Step 3: U.S. Court of Appeals
Step 4: U.S. Supreme Court for Writ of *Certiorari*
Step 5: Request for a Stay of Execution

Source: Raymond Paternoster, *Capital Punishment in America* (New York: Lexington, 1991), p. 203. Reprinted by permission of Raymond Paternoster.

The death row population in the United States has grown steadily in recent years. *What factors have kept it from growing even faster?*

Some death row inmates whose appeals have been denied by the U.S. Supreme Court may still try to have the Supreme Court review their cases on constitutional grounds by filing a writ of *habeas corpus.* Recall that a writ of *habeas corpus* is a court order directing a law officer to produce a prisoner in court to determine whether the prisoner is being legally detained or imprisoned. Critics maintain that abuse of the writ has contributed to the long delays in executions (currently averaging nearly 13 years after conviction) and to the high costs associated with capital punishment.

Congress passed the Antiterrorism and Effective Death Penalty Act of 1996, in part to speed up the process and reduce costs. President Clinton signed it into law on April 24, 1996. The law requires that second or subsequent *habeas* petitions be dismissed when the claim had already been made in a previous petition. It also requires that new claims be dismissed, unless the Supreme Court hands down a new rule of constitutional law and makes it retroactive to cases on collateral review. Under the act, the only other way the Supreme Court will hear a claim made for the first time is when the claim is based on new evidence not previously available. Even then, the new evidence must be of sufficient weight, by a clear and convincing standard of proof, to convince a judge or jury that the capital defendant was not guilty of the crime or crimes for which he or she was convicted.

The act also made the federal appellate courts "gatekeepers" for second or subsequent *habeas corpus* petitions. Thus, to file a second or subsequent claim under the new law, a capital defendant must first file a motion in the appropriate appellate court announcing his or her intention. A panel of three judges must then hear the motion within 30 days. The judges must decide whether the petitioner has a legitimate claim under the new act. If the claim is denied, the new law prohibits any review of the panel's decision, either by a rehearing or writ of *certiorari* to the Supreme Court. So far, the Supreme Court has upheld the constitutionality of the law.

Some people argue that the appellate reviews are unnecessary delaying tactics (at least those beyond the automatic review). However, the outcomes of the reviews suggest otherwise. Nationally, between

Figure 9.5

The Total Number of Death Row Inmates, by Race and Gender

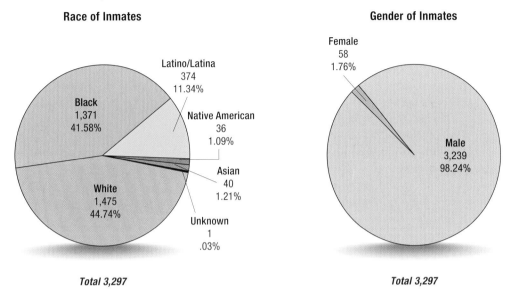

Race of Inmates

Latino/Latina
374
11.34%

Black
1,371
41.58%

Native American
36
1.09%

Asian
40
1.21%

White
1,475
44.74%

Unknown
1
.03%

Total 3,297

Gender of Inmates

Female
58
1.76%

Male
3,239
98.24%

Total 3,297

Source: Adapted from *Death Row, U.S.A.,* NAACP Legal Defense and Educational Fund (Winter 2009). Data depicted are as of January 1, 2009.

1973 and 2006, 35% of the initial convictions or sentences in capital cases were overturned on appeal,[21] and, contrary to popular belief, those reversals were generally not the result of so-called legal technicalities. They were the product of "such fundamental constitutional errors" as denial of the right to an impartial jury, problems of tainted evidence and coerced confessions, ineffective assistance of counsel, and prosecutors' references to defendants who refuse to testify.[22]

The number of persons currently on death rows in the United States is 3,297 (as of January 1, 2009). Figure 9.5 shows the race, ethnic, and gender distributions of the death row population. The size of the death row population in the United States does not fluctuate very much from year to year, despite the relatively few executions each year (the largest number since 1977 was 98, in 1999).[23] One reason is that the number of new death sentences has been declining in recent years (see Figure 9.6).[24] Another reason, as noted above, is that since January 1, 1973, approximately 2,800 of the nearly 8,000 defendants sentenced to death (35%) have been removed from death row by having their convictions or sentences reversed. In addition, since January 1, 1973, 245 death row inmates have received **commutations** (reductions in sentences, granted by a state's governor or the president of the United States), and approximately 365 have died of natural causes or have been killed.[25]

commutations Reductions in sentences, granted by a state's governor.

PROSPECTS FOR THE FUTURE

These are interesting times when it comes to the death penalty in the United States. It appears that capital punishment is receiving more attention than usual. Although less than half of the world's nations still have a death penalty, those that do have one seldom use it. Among Western, industrialized nations, the United States stands alone as the only nation to employ capital punishment. However, even within the United States, 16 jurisdictions do not have a death penalty, and among the 37 jurisdictions that do have one, only a handful of them use it more than occasionally, and almost all of them are located geographically in the South.

Figure 9.6

Death Sentences and Executions in the United States, 1976–2008

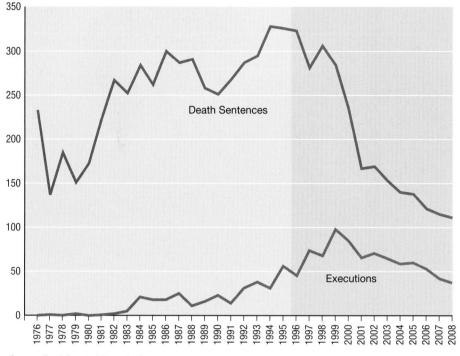

Death sentences and executions in the United States, 1976–2008

Sources: Death Penalty Information Center at www.deathpenaltyinfo.org/death-sentences-year-1977–2008 and www
.deathpenaltyinfo.org/executions-year.

Consider the distribution of the 1,143 executions conducted in the United States between January 17, 1977 and January 30, 2009:[26]

- The 1,143 executions have occurred in 35 of 38 death penalty jurisdictions (New Mexico had 1 execution, but abolished the death penalty on March 18, 2009.).
- Three jurisdictions with death penalty statutes (Kansas, New Hampshire, and the U.S. military) have not had a single execution.
- Sixteen of the 35 "executing" jurisdictions (46%) have held fewer than 10 executions.
- Only 19 executing jurisdictions (54%) have conducted 10 or more executions.
- Two-thirds of all executions have taken place in just five states—Texas, Virginia, Oklahoma, Missouri, and Florida.
- Fifty-four percent of all executions have taken place in just three states—Texas, Virginia, and Oklahoma.
- Texas, alone, accounts for 37% of all the executions.
- More than 80% of all executions have occurred in the South.[27]

Thus, for all intents and purposes, the death penalty today is a criminal sanction that is used more than occasionally in only a few non-Western countries and a few states in the American South. This is an important point because it raises the question of why those death penalty—or more precisely, executing—jurisdictions in the world need the death penalty, while all other jurisdictions in the world—the vast majority—do not.

There are several other reasons to believe that the death penalty in the United States may be a waning institution. First, although abstract support for the death penalty remains relatively high—it was 64% in 2008—it was equal

According to public opinion polls, a majority of Americans support the death penalty. *Why?*

to the lowest level recorded by Gallup since 1978. When respondents are provided an alternative, such as life imprisonment with absolutely no possibility of parole (LWOP), support for the death penalty falls to about 50% (47% in 2006). In a 2005 *CBS News* poll, support for the death penalty was only 39% when respondents were provided with alternatives: 39% chose life with no parole, 6% picked a long sentence with parole, and 13% volunteered the answer "depends." The level of interest in both the death penalty and LWOP was lower in the *CBS News* poll primarily because of the percentage of the public that responded "depends."[28]

Second, the American public continues to express some concern about the way the death penalty is being administered. For example, the 2008 Gallup poll found that 38% of the American public did not believe that the death penalty is applied fairly, up from 35% in 2005. However, the 73% of Americans in 2003 that believed an innocent person had been executed in the last 5 years dropped to 63% in 2006. Most people believe that the execution of innocent people is a rare occurrence. For example, in the 2005 Gallup poll, 57% of respondents believed that an executed person was innocent no more than 5% of the time. Only about 11% of respondents believed that more than 20% of executions involved innocent people.[29] Although concern about the death penalty's administration has waned somewhat from the level of concern expressed in 2000, it remains higher than it was prior to revelations about the quality of justice in capital murder trials, the overturning of several convictions as a result of DNA tests, and the resulting moratorium on executions in Illinois and elsewhere.

A third factor is the positions taken by respected organizations within the United States, such as the American Bar Association (ABA) and organized religions. In 1997, the ABA adopted a resolution that requested death penalty jurisdictions to refrain from using the sanction until greater fairness and due process could be assured. In July 2000, the ABA's president, Martha Barnett, a "reluctant supporter" of the death penalty, reiterated the call for a moratorium on executions. Besides inadequate counsel and a lack of due process, she cited racial bias, racial

MYTH

Innocent people are never executed.

FACT

As many as 25 people (and likely more) may have been executed in error in the United States since 1976.

Source: Talia Roitberg Harmon and William S. Lofquist, "Too Late for Luck: A Comparison of Post-*Furman* Exonerations and Executions of the Innocent." *Crime and Delinquency* 51 (2005), pp. 498–520; Patrick Lehner, "Abolition Now!!!" at www.abolition-now.com; The Death Penalty Information Center, www.deathpenaltyinfo.org/innocothers.html#executed.

profiling, and the execution of the mentally retarded and juveniles as problems with the death penalty's administration.[30] The leaders of most organized religions in the United States—whether Catholic, Protestant, or Jewish—openly oppose capital punishment. A recent survey of religious organizations in the United States found that of the 126 religious organizations that responded to the survey, 61% (77) officially oppose capital punishment, 17% (22) officially support capital punishment, and 2% (27) leave it up to individual congregations or individual religious leaders to determine their own position on capital punishment.[31]

A fourth factor is world opinion. All of our major allies except Japan have abolished the death penalty. In Europe the death penalty is viewed as a violation of human rights.[32] Demonstrations protesting against the U.S. death penalty have been held in France, Spain, and Norway.[33] A condition for admittance into the European Union (EU) is the abolition of the death penalty. That is why Turkey recently abolished its death penalty. Admittance into the 40-nation Council of Europe also requires the renouncing of the death penalty. Georgia, a former republic of the Soviet Union, effectively abolished its death penalty in 1997 so that it could join the Council. Russia has promised to end its death penalty so that it, too, can secure membership in the Council. Figure 9.7 lists the principal executing countries of the world in 2008. The United Nations Commission on Human Rights has repeatedly condemned the death penalty in the United States, urging the U.S. government to stop all executions until it brings states into compliance with international standards and laws. Of particular importance, some foreign businesses may make economic decisions based on a state's use of the death penalty. In a 1998 letter to then Texas governor George W. Bush, a European Parliament official wrote, "Many companies, under pressure from shareholders and public opinion to apply ethical business practices, are beginning to consider the possibility of restricting the investment in the U.S. to states that do not apply the death penalty."

However, capital punishment in some states has proven stubbornly resilient. There are reasons to believe that in those U.S. states the death penalty

Figure 9.7

Countries with the Most Confirmed Executions in 2008

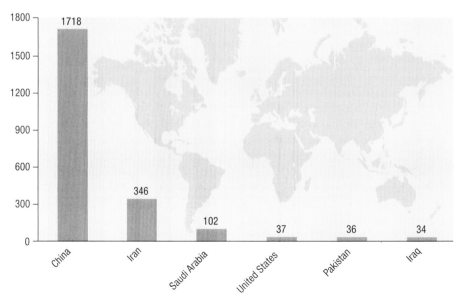

Note: These figures include only cases known to Amnesty International; the true figures were certainly higher. In 2008, at least 2,390 people were executed in 25 countries. The six countries shown in the figure carried out 95% of the total.

Source: The Death Penalty Information Center, "The Death Penalty: An International Perspective," www.deathpenaltyinfo .org/death-penalty-international-perspective (accessed May 16, 2009).

will remain a legal sanction for the foreseeable future. One reason is that death penalty support among the American public, at least according to the major opinion polls, remains relatively strong. It is unlikely that the practice of capital punishment could be sustained if a majority of American citizens were to oppose it. In no year for which polls are available has a majority of Americans opposed the death penalty (the first national death penalty opinion poll was conducted in December 1936).[34]

Although life imprisonment without opportunity for parole (LWOP) seems to be a popular alternative to the death penalty in polls, a problem with the LWOP alternative is that many people are very skeptical about the ability of correctional authorities to keep capital murderers imprisoned for life. Thus, although more than half of the public may say that it prefers LWOP to capital punishment, in practice, it may be reluctant to make the substitution because it fears that the alternative might not adequately protect it from the future actions of convicted capital offenders.

The abiding faith of death penalty proponents in the ability of legislatures and courts to fix any problems with the administration of capital punishment is another reason for its continued use in some places. However, the more than three-decade record of "fine-tuning" the death penalty process remains ongoing. Legislatures and courts are having a difficult time "getting it right," despite spending inordinate amounts of their resources trying. Former Supreme Court Justice Harry A. Blackmun, who for more than 20 years supported the administration of capital punishment in the United States, finally gave up. On February 22, 1994, in a dissent from the Court's refusal to hear the appeal of a Texas inmate scheduled to be executed the next day, Blackmun asserted that he had come to the conclusion that "the death penalty experiment has failed" and that it was time for the Court to abandon the "delusion" that capital punishment could be administered in a way that was consistent with the Constitution. He noted that "from this day forward, I no longer shall tinker with the machinery of death."[35]

As for the positions against capital punishment taken by respected organizations in the United States, "true believers" in the death penalty could care less what others think, especially in the case of organizations such as the American Bar Association. This holds true for world opinion as well. In the case of organized religions, the situation is probably more complex. Although most people who consider themselves religious and are affiliated with religions whose leadership opposes capital punishment probably respect the views of their leaders, they obviously live their daily lives and hold beliefs about capital punishment (and other issues such as abortion) based on other values.

Some death penalty opponents believe that a principal reason for the continuing support of capital punishment is that most people know very little about the subject and what they think they know is based almost entirely on myth. It is assumed that if people were educated about capital punishment, most of them would oppose it. Unfortunately, research suggests that educating the public about the death penalty may not have the effect that abolitionists desire. Although information about the death penalty can reduce support for the sanction—sometimes significantly—rarely is the support reduced to less than a majority, and any reduction in support may be only temporary.[36]

What else, then, sustains the public's death penalty support? We believe that there are at least three more major factors:

1. The desire for vindictive revenge.
2. The incapacitative power of the penalty.
3. The symbolic value it has for politicians and law enforcement officials.

In a recent Gallup poll on the subject, 50% of all respondents who favored the death penalty selected "An eye for an eye/Convicted deserve to be executed" as a reason.[37] The reasons selected second most often (by only 11%) were "Save taxpayers money/Cost associated with prison and deterrence." No other reasons were selected by more than 10% of the death penalty proponents.

The choice of "An eye for an eye/Convicted deserve to be executed" indicates support of the penal purpose of retribution. Those who chose this reason want to repay the offender for what he or she has done. This response, moreover, at least the "eye for an eye" part, has a strong emotional component and thus has been called "vindictive revenge."[38] That the public may support the death penalty primarily for vindictive revenge raises two important questions. First, is the satisfaction of the desire for vindictive revenge a legitimate penal purpose? And second, does pandering to or legitimizing this desire for vindictive revenge contribute to the violence in our nation?

Another factor that sustains death penalty support is the unquestionable incapacitative power of the penalty: Once a capital offender has been executed, he or she can never kill again. Although this seems persuasive, it is not a reason often given by the public. Only 7% of Gallup-polled death penalty proponents chose it.

Nevertheless, research confirms that a small percentage of capital offenders released from prison have killed again. The execution of all convicted capital offenders would have prevented those killings. However, a problem with simply executing all convicted capital offenders is that, inevitably, innocent people would be executed. The possibility of executing an innocent person does not seem to be a crucial problem for a majority of Supreme Court justices, given the Court's 1993 ruling in *Herrera* v. *Collins* (see the FYI). It might, however, be a problem for many Americans. In any event, to prevent capital offenders from killing again, doesn't it make sense simply to keep them imprisoned? At least then, if errors are made, they can be rectified to some degree.

A final factor that sustains death penalty support is the symbolic value it has for politicians and criminal justice officials. Politicians use support for the death penalty as a symbol of their toughness on crime. Opposition to capital punishment is invariably interpreted as symbolic of softness on crime. Criminal justice officials and much of the public often equate support for capital punishment with support for law enforcement in general. It is ironic that although capital punishment has virtually no effect on crime, the death penalty continues to be a favored political silver bullet—a simplistic solution to the crime problem used by aspiring politicians and law enforcement officials.

In short, the reasons provided for supporting capital punishment do not stand up well to critical scrutiny, but the American public has not been deterred from supporting it anyway. Together with the movement to replace indeterminate sentencing with determinate sentencing and to abolish parole, the death penalty is part of the "law and order" agenda popular in the United States since the mid-1970s. Whether this direction in criminal justice has run its course is anyone's guess. However, it appears that the effort to "get tough" with criminals has not produced the results desired by its advocates.

FYI *Herrera v. Collins*

In *Herrera* v. *Collins* (1993) the Supreme Court held that in the absence of constitutional grounds, new evidence of innocence is no reason for the Court to order a new trial. According to the majority opinion: "Where a defendant has been afforded a fair trial and convicted of the offense for which he was charged, the constitutional presumption of innocence disappears. . . . Thus, claims of actual innocence based on newly discovered evidence [are not] grounds for . . . relief absent an independent constitutional violation occurring in the course of the underlying state criminal proceedings." For some, the decision is a reasonable response to the Court's need to limit its jurisdiction in *habeas corpus* cases.

THINKING CRITICALLY

1. Do you think the death penalty helps to prevent crime in the United States? Why or why not?

2. Do you think the death penalty should continue to be legal in this country? Why or why not?

✳ Summary

1. Identify the general factors that influence a judge's sentencing decisions.

   In sentencing, judges are limited by statutory provisions; guided by prevailing philosophical rationales, organizational considerations, and presentence investigation reports; and influenced by their own personal characteristics.

2. Describe how judges tailor sentences to fit the crime and the offender.

   Judges have several ways to tailor sentences to fit the crime and the offender. They can impose a combination sentence of imprisonment, probation, and a fine. They can suspend the imprisonment portion of a combination sentence, or they can suspend the entire sentence if the offender stays out of trouble, makes restitution to the victim, or seeks medical treatment. Judges can give offenders credit for time spent in jail while awaiting trial, deducting that time from any prison sentence. A judge may even impose a sentence of "time served" and release the offender. When an offender is convicted of two or more crimes, a judge can order the prison sentences to run concurrently or consecutively. Judges can also delay sentencing and retain the right to impose a sentence at a later date if conditions warrant it.

3. Distinguish between indeterminate and determinate sentences.

   An indeterminate sentence has a fixed minimum and maximum term of incarceration, rather than a set period. A determinate sentence, in contrast, has a fixed period of incarceration and eliminates the decision-making responsibility of parole boards.

4. Explain the three basic types of determinate sentences.

   There are three basic types of determinate sentences: flat-time, mandatory, and presumptive. With flat-time sentencing, judges may choose between probation and imprisonment but have little discretion in setting the length of a prison sentence. With mandatory sentencing, a specified number of years of imprisonment (usually within a range) is provided for particular crimes. Mandatory sentencing generally allows credit for good time but does not allow release on parole. Presumptive sentencing allows a judge to retain some sentencing discretion (subject to appellate review). It requires a judge to impose the normal sentence, specified by statute, on a "normal" offender who has committed a "normal" crime. However, if the crime or the offender is not normal—if there are mitigating or aggravating circumstances—then the judge is allowed to deviate from the presumptive sentence.

5. List five rationales or justifications for criminal punishment.

   Five rationales or justifications for criminal punishment are retribution, incapacitation, deterrence, rehabilitation, and restoration.

6. Explain the purposes of presentence investigation reports.

   Presentence investigation reports (PSIs) help judges determine the appropriate sentences for particular defendants. PSIs are also used in the classification of probationers, parolees, and prisoners according to their treatment needs and their security risks.

7. List the legal bases for appeal.

   Defendants can appeal their convictions either on legal grounds (such as defects in jury selection, improper admission of evidence at trial, mistaken interpretations of law) or on constitutional grounds (such as illegal search and seizure, improper questioning of the defendant by the police, identification of the defendant through a defective police lineup, and incompetent assistance of counsel).

8. Identify the type of crime for which death may be a punishment.

   In the United States, death is the ultimate punishment. At the state level, death can be imposed only for the crime of aggravated murder and a few other seldom-committed offenses.

9. Summarize the three major procedural reforms the U.S. Supreme Court approved for death penalty cases in the *Gregg* decision.

   The three major procedural reforms the Court approved in *Gregg* were bifurcated trials, guidelines for judges and juries to follow, and automatic appellate review.

✳ Key Terms

restitution 343	retribution 351	presentence investigation	mitigating factors or
indeterminate sentence 345	revenge 351	reports 356	circumstances 363
determinate sentence 345	just deserts 351	allocution 356	proportionality review 365
flat-time sentencing 345	incapacitation 351	pardon 356	commutations 367
good time 345	special or specific	bifurcated trial 363	
mandatory sentencing 345	deterrence 352	aggravating factors or	
presumptive sentencing 346	general deterrence 352	circumstances 363	
criminal sanctions or criminal	rehabilitation 352		
punishment 350	victim-impact statements 353		

✳ Review Questions

1. What are five general types of punishment currently being used in the United States?

2. What are some criticisms of determinate sentencing?

3. Which rationale for criminal punishment is the only one that specifically addresses what has happened in the past, and what are its two major forms?

4. What are three organizational considerations that may influence a judge's sentencing decision?

5. What is *allocution?*

6. What two steps must be taken before an appellate court will hear an appeal?

7. What was the landmark 1972 decision in which the Supreme Court set aside death sentences for the first (and only) time in its history?

8. What are the five methods of execution currently available in the United States?

✳ In the Field

1. **Sentencing** Select a criminal case that is currently receiving publicity in your community. Conduct an informal survey, asking respondents what sentence they believe would be appropriate in the case. Ask them why they chose the sentence. Determine whether respondents tended to agree with each other. If they did not tend to agree, speculate on the reasons for the disagreement.

2. **Death Penalty Opinion** With family members or friends, discuss the death penalty. Ask them why they hold their particular positions (in favor, opposed, undecided). Also, ask them under what circumstances they would change their positions. Would any of the mitigating circumstances listed in the second Critical Thinking exercise that follows cause any of them to change their positions?

✳ On the Net

1. **Death Penalty** Access the Death Penalty Information Center website at www.deathpenaltyinfo.org and the "Pro Death Penalty pages" at www.prodeathpenalty.com. Choose the same topic included in both sources, and review the information provided. Write a brief summary of the information you discovered and how it affected your view of capital punishment.

2. **Mandatory Minimums** Access the website of Families Against Mandatory Minimums at www.famm.org. After studying information provided at the site, write an essay or prepare an oral presentation critiquing mandatory minimum sentences.

✳ Critical Thinking Exercises

THE THREE STRIKES LAW

1. In March 1995, a 27-year-old man who had stolen a slice of pizza from a group of children sitting outside a pizza parlor became the first person to be sentenced to 25 years to life in prison under California's "three strikes and you're out" law. Enacted March 7, 1995, the law was reinforced November 8, 1995, by a constitutional amendment supported by 72% of California voters. The "three strikes" law is triggered by two past felony convictions. In this case, the defendant was convicted of "petty theft with a prior felony conviction." He had already been convicted of robbery, attempted robbery, drug possession, and riding a stolen motorcycle.
   a. It will cost the taxpayers of California about $26,000 a year to incarcerate the man. Is it worth it? Is it a wise expenditure of tax dollars?
   b. Is the punishment proportional to the crime or crimes? Should it be?
   c. Do you think "petty theft with a prior conviction" is a legitimate trigger of a "three strikes" law?
   d. There is no question that the offender was a criminal. He had a reputation for being a bully. Nevertheless, are "three strikes and you're out" laws an ethically defensible way of dealing with such criminals? Why or why not?

SENTENCING

2. You are a juror in a death penalty case. The defendant in the case has already been found guilty of capital murder during the guilt phase of the trial. During the penalty phase, you have to determine whether the defendant is to be sentenced to death or to life imprisonment without opportunity for parole (LWOP). The judge has instructed you (and the rest of the jury) to consider the aggravating and mitigating circumstances of the case. If the aggravating circumstances outweigh the mitigating circumstances, you are expected to vote for death. However, if the mitigating circumstances outweigh the aggravating circumstances, you are expected to vote for LWOP. The lone aggravating circumstance in the case is that the defendant committed the capital murder during the commission of a robbery. Though they are not aggravating circumstances, the defendant also has two prior convictions for robbery and one prior conviction for the sale of illegal drugs. Under which of the following mitigating circumstances would you vote for LWOP or death in this case? Explain the reasons for your decision.
   a. The defendant is a female with children.
   b. The defendant acted under extreme duress or under the substantial domination of another person.
   c. The defendant was seriously abused, both mentally and physically, as a child.
   d. The capacity of the defendant to appreciate the criminality of his or her conduct to the requirements of law was substantially impaired.

To access more information and resources, including study questions, chapter summaries, and links, go to: www.mhhe.com/bohm6e.

PART **FOUR**

Corrections

Institutional Corrections

10

Chapter Outline

Chapter Objectives

After completing this chapter, you should be able to:

1. Summarize the purposes of confinement in Europe before it became a major way of punishing criminals.

2. Describe how offenders were punished before the large-scale use of confinement.

3. Explain why confinement began to be used as a major way of punishing offenders in Europe.

4. Describe the recent trends in the use of incarceration in the United States.

5. List some of the characteristics of the incarcerated population in the United States.

6. Describe how incarceration facilities are structured, organized, and administered by the government in the United States.

7. Name some of the common types of correctional facilities in the United States.

8. Identify some of the procedures that institutions employ to maintain security and order.

9. List the services and programs that are commonly available to inmates.

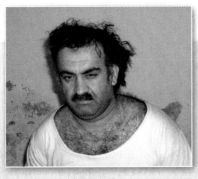

CRIME STORY

On January 22, 2009, President Obama signed executive orders for the purpose of closing the Guantanamo Bay, Cuba, detention facility within a year. He explained that he wanted to return the United States to the "moral high ground" in the war on terrorism. During the signing ceremony at the White House, Obama reaffirmed his inauguration pledge that the United States does not have "to continue with a false choice between our safety and our ideals." The president said he issued the prison-closing order to "restore the standards of due process and the core constitutional values that have made this country great even in the midst of war, even in dealing with terrorism."

A second order established an interagency task force charged with

continued

conducting a systematic review of detention policies, procedures, and all individual cases. The task force, remarked Obama, will "provide me with information in terms of how we are able to deal [with] the disposition of some of the detainees that may be currently in Guantanamo that we cannot transfer to other countries, who could pose a serious danger to the United States." Senator John McCain, appearing on CNN's *Larry King Live,* supported the president's position on closing the Guantanamo prison but also voiced the major concern of Obama's critics: where to send the remaining 245 prisoners, especially such prisoners as Khalid Sheikh Mohammed, the professed architect of the September 11 attack? Intelligence reports indicate that the remaining detainees are either committed, highly skilled al-Qaeda operatives too dangerous to ever be released, or Islamists whose native countries would do little to prevent them from rejoining the jihad. Commented McCain, "So, the easy part, in all due respect, is to say we're going to close Guantanamo. Then I think I would have said where they were going to be taken. Because you're going to run into a NIMBY [not in my backyard] problem here in the United States of America."

Defense Secretary Robert Gates revealed possible prisons in the United States to which the detainees could be sent. He added, however, that he had heard from members of Congress representing the states in which the selected prisons are located, and they were not happy about having the detainees in their states. Possible sites included military prisons at Fort Leavenworth, Kansas; the Naval Consolidated Brig near Charleston, South Carolina; Camp Pendleton, California; and Marine Corps Air Station Miramar, California. The nonmilitary federal supermax prison in Florence, Colorado also was mentioned.

Obama is gambling that his orders will not haunt him in the 2012 election. The worst-case scenario is that a freed Guantanamo prisoner returns to American soil and takes part in a terrorist attack that kills Americans. Already, a detainee released in 2007 (by the Bush administration), Said Ali al-Shihri, has been implicated in a deadly bombing at the U.S. embassy in Yemen in 2008. At least that bombing was not on U.S. soil. Al-Shihri had been sent to Saudi Arabia, where he supposedly was rehabilitated, and then released. Another nightmare is that terrorists try to free their comrades by attacking a prison on American soil.

Chapter 10 examines institutional corrections. The primary purpose of correctional institutions is to protect the public from an offender's continuing criminal behavior. As the aforementioned discussion shows, sending the Guantanamo detainees to prisons on American soil raises a number of concerns. Are the personnel at the prison or prisons to which the detainees are sent capable of adequately protecting and managing the suspected terrorists, who, most certainly, will be a target for some American prisoners? Will the detainees present a heightened risk of harm to correctional officers, other prison personnel, and other inmates? Will special accommodations to prison policies and procedures for the detainees, such as special dietary or religious requirements, disrupt the daily prison routine? No matter how those and other concerns are addressed, Senator McCain is probably right. President Obama's decision to close the Guantanamo prison is the easy part.

Historical Overview of Institutional Corrections

Students often wonder why they must learn about the history of institutional corrections. One reason is that it is impossible to fully understand (and improve) the present state of affairs without knowledge of the past; the present developed out of the past. To paraphrase the philosopher George Santayana, people who fail to remember the past are destined to repeat its mistakes. Another reason is that nothing helps us see how institutional corrections is linked to our larger society and culture better than the study of history.

EUROPEAN BACKGROUND

In Europe, institutional confinement did not become a major punishment for criminals until the 1600s and 1700s. (In the United States, institutional confinement was not used extensively as a punishment until the 1800s.) As a practice, though, institutional confinement has existed since ancient times. Before the 1600s, however, it usually served functions other than punishment for criminal behavior. For example, confinement was used to:

1. Detain people before trial.
2. Hold prisoners awaiting other sanctions, such as death and corporal punishment.

MYTH

Throughout history, imprisonment has been the primary sentence for lawbreakers, and it still is today.

FACT

Viewed historically, imprisonment is a relatively recent sentence for lawbreaking. Even today in the United States, the number of people in prison is small compared with the number on probation or under other types of supervision in the community.

3. Coerce payment of debts and fines.
4. Hold and punish slaves.
5. Achieve religious indoctrination and spiritual reformation (as during the Inquisition).
6. Quarantine disease (as during the bubonic plague).[1]

Forerunners of Modern Incarceration Unlike modern incarceration, which strives to change the offender's character and is carried out away from public view, popular early punishments for crime, which predated the large-scale use of imprisonment, were directed more at the offender's body and property; one basic goal was to inflict pain.[2] Furthermore, those punishments were commonly carried out in public to humiliate the offender and to deter onlookers from crime. Examples of such early punishments are fines, confiscation of property, and diverse methods of corporal and capital punishment. Some popular methods of corporal and capital punishment were beheading, stoning, hanging, crucifixion, boiling and burning, flogging, branding, and placement in the stocks or pillory.[3] As this brief list illustrates, the eventual shift to incarceration reduced the severity and violence of punishment.

Two additional forerunners of modern incarceration were banishment and transportation. In essence, they were alternatives to the more severe corporal punishments or capital punishment. Originating in ancient times, **banishment** required offenders to leave the community and live elsewhere, commonly in the wilderness. The modern version of banishment is long-term incarceration (for example, life imprisonment without opportunity for parole). As population and urban growth displaced frontiers across Europe and as demands for cheap labor increased with the rise of Western capitalism, **transportation** of offenders from their home nation to one of that nation's colonies gradually replaced banishment. England, for instance, was transporting hundreds of convicts a year to North America by the early 1600s.[4] Transportation fell into disuse as European colonies gained independence.

FYI Mamertine Prison

Although it surely did not resemble today's prisons, one of the earliest known prisons was the Mamertine Prison, built around 64 B.C.E. under the sewers of Rome.

Source: Robert Johnson, *Hard Time: Understanding and Reforming the Prison*, 3rd ed. (Belmont, CA: Wadsworth, 2002), p. 19.

banishment A punishment, originating in ancient times, that required offenders to leave the community and live elsewhere, commonly in the wilderness.

transportation A punishment in which offenders were transported from their home nation to one of that nation's colonies to work.

Besides being painful, placement in the stocks or pillory was intended to humiliate and shame offenders. *Is a greater emphasis on the shame of punishment needed today? If so, how should it be accomplished?*

workhouses European forerunners of the modern U.S. prison, where offenders were sent to learn discipline and regular work habits.

The closest European forerunners of the modern U.S. prison were known as **workhouses** or *houses of correction.* Offenders were sent to them to learn discipline and regular work habits. The fruits of inmate labor were also expected to pay for facility upkeep and even to yield a profit. One of the first and most famous workhouses, the London Bridewell, opened in the 1550s, and workhouses spread through other parts of Europe thereafter. Such facilities were used extensively throughout the next three centuries, coexisting with such responses to crime as transportation, corporal punishment, and capital punishment. In fact, crowding in workhouses was a major impetus for the development of transportation as a punishment.

Reform Initiatives As described in Chapter 3, the Enlightenment was a time of faith in science and reason as well as a period of humanistic reform. The Enlightenment thinkers and reformers of the 1700s and 1800s described the penal system of their day with such terms as *excessive, disorderly, inefficient, arbitrary, capricious, discriminatory* (against the poor), and *unjust.* Three reformers who were important to initiatives in corrections were Cesare Beccaria (1738–1794), John Howard (1726–1790), and Jeremy Bentham (1748–1832).

Criminologists Graeme Newman and Pietro Marongiu contend that Milanese philosopher Cesare Beccaria's famous book, *On Crimes and Punishments* (1764), although often acclaimed for its originality, actually brought together the reformist principles espoused by other thinkers of the era, such as Montesquieu and Voltaire.[5] One of those principles concerned replacing the discretionary and arbitrary administration of justice with a system of detailed written laws describing the behaviors that constitute crime and the associated punishments. People need to know, Beccaria believed, exactly what punishments are prescribed for various offenses if the law is to deter criminal behavior. As part of his quest to deter crime, Beccaria declared that the punishment should fit the crime in two senses. First, the severity of punishment should parallel the severity of harm resulting from the crime. Second, the punishment should be severe enough to outweigh the pleasure obtainable from the crime. Furthermore, to deter crime, he believed, punishment needed to be certain and swift. Certainty implies that the likelihood of getting caught and punished is perceived as high. Swiftness implies that punishment will not be delayed after commission of the crime.

MYTH

The reason punishment fails to adequately deter crime in the United States is that it is not severe enough.

FACT

The United States has a higher rate of imprisonment and longer sentences than virtually any other nation. It is also one of the few advanced, industrialized nations to have retained the death penalty. It is hard indeed to support the argument that our punishment is not severe enough. Certainty and swiftness, however, are lacking, and that is the failure to which Beccaria would probably point.

Beccaria did not ground his thinking firmly in empirical observations and did little to actively campaign for the reforms he advocated.[6] The work of John Howard, an English sheriff and social activist, presents an interesting contrast in that regard. Howard's 1777 book, *The State of the Prisons in England and Wales,* was based on his visits to penal institutions in various parts of Europe. The crowding, overall poor living conditions, and disorderly and abusive practices he observed in those facilities appalled Howard. He advocated that penal environments be made safe, humane, and orderly. Howard's opinion was that incarceration should do more than punish—that it should also instill discipline and reform inmates. Toward that end, he proposed an orderly institutional routine of religious teaching, hard work, and solitary confinement to promote introspection and penance.[7] Howard's work inspired the growing popularity of the term *penitentiary* to refer to penal confinement facilities.

penology The study of prison management and the treatment of offenders.

panopticon A prison design consisting of a round building with tiers of cells lining the inner circumference and facing a central inspection tower.

In **penology,** the study of prison management and the treatment of offenders, English philosopher Jeremy Bentham is perhaps best remembered for his idea that order and reform could be achieved in a prison through architectural design. His **panopticon** ("all-seeing" or "inspection-house") prison design consisted of a round building with tiers of cells lining the circumference and facing a central inspection tower so that staff from the tower could watch prisoners. Although no facilities completely true to Bentham's panopticon plan were ever constructed, structures similar in design were erected at Illinois's Stateville Penitentiary (now Stateville Correctional Center), which opened in 1925.

In sum, the historical roots of the modern prison lie in Europe. It was in America, however, that the penitentiary concept was first put into wide practice.

DEVELOPMENTS IN THE UNITED STATES

In colonial America, penal practice was loose, decentralized, and unsystematic, combining private retaliation against wrongdoing with fines, banishment, harsh corporal punishments, and capital punishment. Local jails were scattered about the colonies, but they were used primarily for temporary holding rather than for punishment.[8] Some people, such as William Penn, the famous Quaker and founder of Pennsylvania, promoted incarceration as a humane alternative to the physically brutal punishments that were common. However, that idea was largely ignored because there was no stable central governmental authority to coordinate and finance (through tax revenue) the large-scale confinement of offenders.

Stateville Correctional Center in Illinois is similar in design to Bentham's panopticon plan. *Why wasn't this prison design used more widely in the United States?*

The Penitentiary Movement In the aftermath of the American Revolution, it rapidly became apparent that the colonial system of justice would not suffice. Economic chaos and civil disorder followed the war. Combined with population growth and the transition from an agricultural society to an industrial one, they created the need for a strong, centralized government to achieve political and economic stability. The rise of the penitentiary occurred in that context.[9] Philosophically, it was guided by Enlightenment principles. In 1790, the Walnut Street Jail in Philadelphia was converted from a simple holding facility to a prison to which offenders could be sentenced for their crimes. It is commonly regarded as the nation's first state prison. In a system consistent with Howard's plan, its inmates labored in solitary cells and received large doses of religious teaching. Later in the 1790s, New York opened Newgate Prison. Other states quickly followed suit, and the penitentiary movement was born. By 1830, Pennsylvania and New York had constructed additional prisons to supplement their original ones.

Pennsylvania and New York pioneered the penitentiary movement by developing two competing systems of confinement.[10] The **Pennsylvania system,** sometimes called the *separate system,* required that inmates be kept in solitary cells so that they could study religious writings, reflect on their misdeeds, and perform handicraft work. In the New York system, or the **Auburn system** (named after Auburn Penitentiary and also referred to as the *congregate* or *silent system*), inmates worked and ate together in silence during the day and were returned to solitary cells for the evening. Ultimately, the Auburn system prevailed over the Pennsylvania system as the model followed by other states. It avoided the harmful psychological effects of total solitary confinement and allowed more inmates to be housed in less space, because cells could be smaller. In addition, the Auburn system's congregate work principle was more congruent with the system of factory production emerging in wider society than was the outdated craft principle of the separate system. If prison labor

Pennsylvania system An early system of U.S. penology in which inmates were kept in solitary cells so that they could study religious writings, reflect on their misdeeds, and perform handicraft work.

Auburn system An early system of penology, originating at Auburn Penitentiary in New York, in which inmates worked and ate together in silence during the day and were placed in solitary cells for the evening.

The Elmira Reformatory, which opened in 1876 in Elmira, New York, was the first institution for men that was based on reformatory principles. *What caused the change in penal philosophy?*

was to be profitable, it seemed that the Auburn plan was the one to use.

It is interesting that although penitentiary construction flourished and the United States became the model nation in penology during the first half of the nineteenth century, there was serious discontent with the penitentiary by the end of the Civil War. There were few signs penitentiaries were deterring crime, reforming offenders, or turning great profits from inmate labor. In fact, prisons were becoming increasingly expensive to run, and opposition was growing to selling prisoner-made goods on the open market. With faith in the penitentiary declining, the stage was set for a new movement—a movement that, rather than challenging the fundamental value of incarceration as a punishment, sought to improve the method of incarceration.

The Reformatory Movement The reformatory movement got its start at the 1870 meeting of the National Prison Association, in Cincinnati. The principles adopted there were championed by such leaders in the field as Enoch Wines (1806–1879) and Zebulon Brockway (1827–1920).[11] A new type of institution, the reformatory, was designed for younger, less hardened offenders, between 16 and 30 years of age. Based on a military model of regimentation, it emphasized academic and vocational training in addition to work. A classification system was introduced, in which inmates' progress toward reformation was rated. The sentences for determinate periods of time (for example, 5 years) were replaced with indeterminate terms, in which inmates served sentences within given ranges (for example, between 2 and 8 years). Parole or early release could be granted for favorable progress in reformation.

It has been observed that indeterminate sentences and the possibility of parole facilitate greater control over inmates than do determinate sentences. Many inmates are interested, above all else, in gaining their freedom. The message conveyed by indeterminate sentences and the possibility of parole is this: "Conform to institutional expectations or do more time."

Institutions for Women Until the reformatory era, there was little effort to establish separate facilities for women. Women prisoners were usually confined in segregated areas of male prisons and generally received inferior treatment. The reformatory movement, reflecting its assumptions about differences between categories of inmates and its emphasis on classification, helped feminize punishment.[12] The first women's prison organized according to the reformatory model opened in Indiana in 1873. By the 1930s, several other women's reformatories were in operation, mainly in the Northeast and the Midwest. Most employed cottages or a campus and a family-style living plan, not the cell-block plan of men's prisons. Most concentrated on molding inmates to fulfill stereotypical domestic roles, such as cleaning and cooking, upon release.

Twentieth-Century Prisons Criminologist John Irwin has provided a useful typology for summarizing imprisonment in the last century.[13] According to Irwin, three types of institutions have been dominant. Each has dominated a different part of the century. The dominant type for about the first three decades was the "big house." In Irwin's words:

> The Big House was a walled prison with large cell blocks that contained stacks of three or more tiers of one- or two-man cells. On the average, it held 2,500 men. Sometimes a single cell block housed over 1,000 prisoners in six tiers of cells. Most of these prisons were built over many decades and had a mixture of old and new cell blocks. Some of the older cell blocks were quite primitive.[14]

Note that big houses were not new prisons, distinct from earlier penitentiaries and reformatories. They were the old penitentiaries and reformatories, expanded in size to accommodate larger inmate populations. Originally, big-house prisons exploited inmate labor through various links to the free market. Industrial prisons predominated in the North, while plantation prisons characterized much of the South. With the rise of organized labor and the coming of the Great Depression, free-market inmate labor systems fell into demise during the 1920s and 1930s. Big houses became warehouses oriented toward custody and repression of inmates.

What Irwin calls the "correctional institution" arose during the 1940s and became the dominant type of prison in the 1950s. Correctional institutions generally were smaller and more modern in appearance than big houses. However, correctional institutions did not replace big houses; they simply supplemented them, though correctional-institution principles spread to many big houses. Correctional institutions emerged as penologists turned to the field of medicine as a model for their work. During that phase of corrections, a so-called **medical model** came to be used, as crime was seen as symptomatic of personal illness in need of treatment. Under the medical model, shortly after being sentenced to prison, inmates were subjected to psychological assessment and diagnosis during classification processes. Assessment and diagnosis were followed by treatment designed to address the offender's supposed illness. The main kinds of treatment, according to Irwin, were academic and vocational education and therapeutic counseling. After institutional treatment came parole, which amounted to follow-up treatment in the community. Importantly,

medical model A theory of institutional corrections, popular during the 1940s and 1950s, in which crime was seen as symptomatic of personal illness in need of treatment.

Big-house prisons, which consisted of large cell blocks containing stacks of cells, were the dominant prison design of the early twentieth century. *What are some problems with the big-house prison design?*

the ways of achieving control over inmate behavior shifted from the custodial repression typical of the big house to more subtle methods of indirect coercion: inmates knew that failure to participate in treatment and exhibit "progress" in prison meant that parole would be delayed.

During the 1960s and 1970s, both the effectiveness and the fairness of coerced prison rehabilitation programming began to be challenged,[15] and the correctional institution's dominance began to wane. In Irwin's view, the third type of prison, the "contemporary violent prison," arose by default as the correctional institution faded. Gone were many of the treatment-program control mechanisms of the correctional institution. Further, many of the repressive measures used to control inmates in the big house became illegal after the rise of the inmates' rights movement during the 1960s (to be discussed later). In essence, what emerged in many prisons was a power vacuum that was filled with inmate gang violence and interracial hatred.

Privatization and Shock Incarceration

As will be readily apparent in the next section of this chapter, the last three decades are likely to be remembered for the largest incarceration boom to date and for desperate attempts to deal with prison crowding by developing alternatives to traditional incarceration.

One alternative to traditional confinement is the move toward **privatization,** the involvement of the private sector in the construction and operation of confinement facilities. The private sector has a long tradition in institutional corrections. For instance, such diverse services as food, legal aid, medical and psychiatric care, and education have long been provided through private vendors. There is a rich history of private labor contracting in the operation of prisons, and it is now witnessing something of a revival in certain jurisdictions. Also, the private sector has operated juvenile institutions for many years. But mounting prison populations, combined with space and budget limitations, have helped give privatization new twists. One of those twists entails having the private sector finance construction of institutions under what amounts to a lease-purchase agreement. The Potosi Correctional Center in Missouri was constructed under such a strategy. In another twist, the state contracts with private companies like Corrections Corporation of America to have them operate prisons. One of the earliest privately operated state prisons for adult felons, Kentucky's minimum-security Marion Adjustment Center, was opened in January 1986.

At the beginning of 2008, 32 states and the federal prison system reported that 125,975 prison inmates (7.9% of all state and federal prison inmates) were held in privately operated facilities. Private facilities confined 6.8% of all state prisoners and 15.7% of all federal prisoners. Since 2000, the percentage of state prison inmates held in private facilities has increased nearly 32%, while the percentage of federal prison inmates in private facilities has increased about 100%. The federal prison system with 31,310 inmates, Texas with 18,871 inmates, and Florida with 8,769 inmates had the largest number of prison inmates held in private facilities at the beginning of 2008. States with the largest percentage of their prison populations in private facilities at the beginning of 2008 were New Mexico (42%), Montana (38%), Hawaii (36%), Wyoming (30%), and Alaska (29.5%). Regionally, the West had the most state prison inmates in private facilities (9.2%) followed by the South (8.8%), the Northeast (2.4%), and the Midwest (1.9%).[16]

In 2007, private contractors operated only about 7.5% of all state and federal prisons (61): 48 state prisons and 13 federal prisons. The vast majority of privately operated prisons were either minimum- or medium-security facilities. Few of them were maximum-security institutions, which gives rise to the criticism that private prisons are relatively successful because they do not house the most difficult and dangerous inmates.[17]

privatization The involvement of the private sector in the construction and the operation of confinement facilities.

The Convict Lease System

One of the darkest chapters in the history of American corrections involves the convict lease system that was adopted by many southern states following the Civil War. It perpetuated slavery in the states that embraced it. Counties and states leased thousands of prisoners (mostly black) to private individuals and companies to work (and die) in cotton fields, mines, and forests of the Deep South. Governments made millions of dollars in lease payments, and those who leased prisoners and brutally exploited them made millions more. The practice did not end until the 1930s.

Source: Fletcher M. Green, "Some Aspects of the Convict Lease System in the Southern States," *Essays in Southern History,* vol. 31 (Durham: University of North Carolina Press, 1949).

State and federal prisons represent only a small part of private contactors' correctional-institution inventory. Private contractors operate many more community-based and juvenile institutions. They also operate county and local jails, detention facilities for the U.S. Marshals Service and the Bureau of Immigration and Customs Enforcement, as well as correctional institutions in other countries, such as Canada, Australia, South Africa, and the United Kingdom.

Two corporations dominate the industry: Corrections Corporation of America (CCA) and the GEO Group, Inc. (formerly the Wackenhut Corrections Corporation). The Cornell Companies is the third largest business in the industry. CCA is the founder of the private corrections industry and is the fifth largest correctional system in the United States, behind only the federal system and the systems of California, Texas, and Florida. CCA manages more than 50% of all beds in the U.S. under contract with private contractors. It has more than 80,000 beds in more than 60 facilities in 19 states and the District of Columbia. The corporation owns 42 of those facilities. CCA manages about 80,000 inmates, including males, females, and juveniles, at all security levels for the Federal Bureau of Prisons, the U.S. Marshals Service, Immigration and Customs Enforcement, nearly half of the states, and more than a dozen municipalities. The GEO Group, Inc., has a 25% share of the U.S. market. In 1997, it became the first private company hired by the Federal Bureau of Prisons to manage one of its major facilities: the 2,048-bed Taft Correctional Institution in Taft, California. In 2000, the BOP awarded the GEO Group a contract to design, construct, finance, and manage the 1,200-bed Rivers Correctional Institution in Winton, North Carolina. The GEO Group, Inc., currently has 62,134 beds in 18 states. At this writing, the Cornell Companies manage 18,550 beds in 71 facilities in 15 states.[18]

Private contractors are poised to take advantage of what promises to be a huge increase in the number of illegal immigrants detained in the United States. By the fall of 2007, for example, the Bush Administration was expecting to detain about 27,500 illegal immigrants—an increase of 6,700 over the number in custody in 2006. The annual cost of detaining that many illegal immigrants is estimated to be nearly $1 billion. CCA and the GEO Group housed fewer than 20% of the detained immigrants in 2006, but they are competing with several smaller companies for a greater share of the growing business. In 2006, CCA and the GEO Group were operating 8 of the 16 federal detention centers, but the federal detention centers are full and the federal government is not planning on building more of them. Consequently, most of the new money for illegal immigrant detention will go to private companies and to county governments, which currently hold 57% of detained illegal immigrants in county jails. Private companies already manage some of those jails.[19]

Proponents of states' contracting to have the private sector finance construction and operate prisons often point to efficiency, flexibility, and cost-effectiveness. Opponents frequently worry about liability issues, about creating a profit motive for incarcerating people, and about the incentive to trim inmate services and programs to maximize profits.

Research shows the following about private correctional facilities:

- Private facilities can be constructed and opened more quickly. Following contract awards, private facilities can be constructed within 12 to 18 months; similar facilities constructed by governments usually take 36 to 48 months to be brought "on line."
- Construction cost savings of 25% or more and operating cost savings of 10% to 15% are common for private facilities. However, other research shows that these cost savings can be illusory, that there are wide variations among facilities. For example, a survey of private correctional management

Figure 10.1

Cost Comparison Data: *Texas Private* v. *Government Prison Provision*

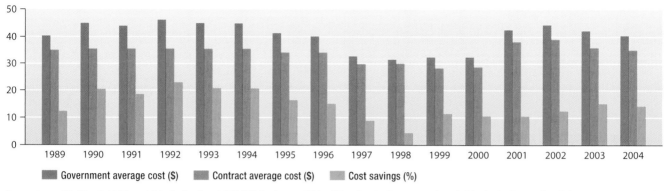

Legend: ■ Government average cost ($)   ■ Contract average cost ($)   ■ Cost savings (%)

Source: Leonard C. Gilroy (ed.), "Annual Privatization Report 2006: 20th Anniversary Edition." *Transforming Government through Privatization.* Reason Foundation at www.reason.org/apr2006/.

companies found that the average savings from privatization was only about 1%, achieved mostly through reduced labor costs. It is also unclear whether any cost savings can be sustained over time. Figure 10.1 provides a cost comparison between government and privately operated prisons in Texas from 1989 through 2004. The figure shows that in every year privately operated prisons were more cost effective than government operated prisons.

- The quality of services and programs in private facilities is frequently superior to that in publicly operated facilities.
- Private contractors can frequently deliver correctional services more cost effectively than public employees can.
- Privatization can substantially reduce legal liability costs of operating prisons and jails.
- Necessary changes in the nature and scope of prisoner programs can be made quicker and easier in private facilities.
- The existence of private facilities in a jurisdiction sometimes encourages improvements in the public facilities in that jurisdiction.
- Prisoners in private facilities have a broader array of legal remedies when challenging conditions of confinement than prisoners in public facilities.[20]

Despite this list of advantages, the future of correctional privatization may depend on the answer to a philosophical question: To what degree should governments cede their correctional responsibilities to the private sector?

shock incarceration The placement of offenders in facilities patterned after military boot camps.

A second confinement alternative to traditional incarceration is **shock incarceration,** the placement of offenders in facilities patterned after military boot camps. Such facilities are ordinarily designed for young, nonviolent offenders without extensive criminal records. Instead of being given traditional prison sentences, those offenders are sentenced to shock incarceration facilities for relatively short periods (for instance, 90 days). There, they are subjected to a strict, military-style program of work, physical conditioning, and discipline. Boot camps vary considerably in their emphasis on treatment. After completing the program, inmates are released into the community on probation or parole. Shock incarceration is appealing to those who wish to convey a "tough on crime" message to the general public. However, as criminologists Doris Layton MacKenzie and James Shaw observe, the "studies examining the recidivism of boot camp releasees have been disappointing for those who expect the programs to affect offenders' activities after release."[21]

Boot-camp prisons are considered an intermediate sanction, which is discussed in Chapter 12 ("Community Corrections").

Cycles in History The history of institutional corrections has evolved in cycles of accumulation. Developments viewed as innovative replacements for old practices almost always contain vestiges of the old practices, and the old practices seldom disappear when "new" ones are introduced. The new is implemented alongside the old and contains elements of the old. Penitentiaries were not torn down when reformatories were introduced, nor were big houses abolished when correctional institutions arose. Similarly, many jurisdictions have recently moved away from indeterminate sentences toward determinate ones. Those determinate sentences, although often seen as innovative, are hard to distinguish from the fixed sentences that preceded the move to indeterminate sentencing. Likewise, the modern trend toward boot camps revives the quasi-military organization that was present at Elmira Reformatory. An interesting question is whether penological history represents progress or the coming back around of what went around before.

Chain gangs are another recent example of the "what goes around comes around" phenomenon. In 1995, Alabama became the first state to reintroduce the chain gang. Arizona, Oklahoma, and Wisconsin (which used stun belts instead of chains) soon followed. Arizona is also the first state to allow female prisoners to work on chain gangs.[22] These states (except Wisconsin, see above) put shackled prisoners to work along the roadside, cutting high weeds, picking up trash, and clearing muddy ditches. Arizona's female chain gang members also dig graves and bury indigents who have died, paint curbs, and remove graffiti. Gun-toting guards supervise prisoners. Alabama's experiment with chain gangs lasted less than 4 years. Among problems blamed for its demise were escape attempts, inmate fights, lack of productivity (people chained together move slowly), and the need for more guards inside prisons. Oklahoma and Wisconsin also no longer employ chain gangs. As of this writing, Arizona was still using chain gangs, but participation was voluntary. In addition, unlike in Alabama where inmates were chained together, in Arizona, inmates are chained individually. Widespread

Chain-gang prisoners on burial detail. *Do you think chain gangs are a good idea? Why or why not?*

use of chain gangs ended between the Depression and World War II, though it was not until the late 1970s that Alabama abolished the practice.

THINKING CRITICALLY

1. Do you think any of the early forerunners to modern corrections (such as banishment, etc.) could be used today? Why or why not?

2. Do you think that shock incarceration has any merit? Why or why not?

The Incarceration Boom

For most of the past 65 years, the incarceration rate was fairly steady. Only since 1973 has there been a continuing increase, with each year showing a new high. Figure 10.2 shows the incarceration rate from the 1920s to the present. Because of the growing incarceration rate, several states in the United States now have as many or more prisons in operation as some entire Western nations. At the beginning of 2008, the states and the federal government, combined, operated about 1,000 adult prisons. The states operated nearly 900 of them, and the Federal Bureau of Prisons managed 114.[23]

RECENT TRENDS

There were 329,821 inmates in state and federal prisons at the end of 1980 (305,458 state prison inmates and 24,363 federal prison inmates). By mid-decade, the total number of prison inmates had increased 52%, to 502,752 inmates, and by the end of the 1980s, there were a total of 712,967 inmates, an increase of 116% over 1980.[24] That represents an average increase of about 9% per year.

Figure 10.2

Sentenced Prisoners in State and Federal Institutions

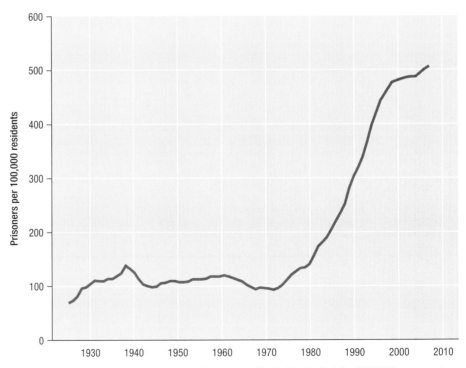

Sources: Kathleen Maguire and Ann L. Pastore (eds.), *Sourcebook of Criminal Justice Statistics 1996,* U.S. Department of Justice, Bureau of Justice Statistics (Washington, D.C.: GPO, 1997), p. 517, Table 6.4 and p. 518, Table 6.21; Heather C. West and William J. Sabol "Prisoners in 2007," U.S. Department of Justice, *Bureau of Justice Statistics Bulletin* (Washington, D.C.: GPO, December 2008).

More than a decade and a half later, at year-end 2007, the adult prison population stood at 1,598,316 (1,398,698 state prison inmates and 199,618 federal prison inmates), an increase of 124% over the beginning of 1990 and an increase of 385% over 1980. About 12.5% of all inmates at year-end 2007 were in federal prisons. The remaining 87.5% were in state prisons.[25] The total number of prison inmates at year-end 2007 was about 14% more than the record high of 1,404,032 inmates at year-end 2001. (Between 1980 and year-end 2007, the state prison population increased 358% and the federal prison population increased 719%.) In other words, between 1980 and year-end 2007, the adult prison population (both state and federal) had more than quadrupled.[26]

However, the growth of the prison population slowed somewhat in the 1990s to an average of about 6.5% per year (from approximately 9% per year during the 1980s). Between year-end 2000 and year-end 2007, the state and federal prison population increased at an average annual rate of 2% (the state prison population increased only 1.7% per year, while the federal prison population increased 4.8% per year). The overall growth of the state (but not federal) prison population has been slowing since 1995. For example, between year-end 2006 and year-end 2007, the prison population grew 1.8% (the state prison population increased only 1.5%, while the federal prison population increased 3.4%). The level of growth (1.1%) in the state and federal prison population in 2001 was the lowest annual rate recorded since 1972 and is entirely attributable to the slower growth in the state prison population.[27] Table 10.1 shows the jurisdictions with the largest and smallest numbers of prison inmates and the highest and lowest incarceration rates per 100,000 residents at year-end 2007. (We will discuss incarceration rates later in this section.)

The approximately 1.5 million state and federal prison inmates incarcerated in the United States and its territories at year-end 2007 include 125,975 prisoners held in privately operated facilities and 80,371 state and federal prisoners held in local jails or other facilities operated by county or local

Table 10.1 Jurisdictions with the Largest and Smallest Numbers of Prison Inmates and Incarceration Rates per 100,000 Residents in 2007

Prison Population	Number of Inmates	Prison Population	Incarceration Rate per 100,000 State Residents[a]
5 Largest:			
Federal	199,618	Louisiana	865
California	174,282	Mississippi	734
Texas	171,790	Texas	669
Florida	98,219	Oklahoma	665
New York	62,623	Alabama	615
5 Smallest:			
North Dakota	1,416	Maine	159
Wyoming	2,084	Minnesota	181
Vermont	2,145	North Dakota	221
Maine	2,222	New Hampshire	222
New Hampshire	2,943	Rhode Island	235

Note: [a] The number of prisoners with a sentence of more than 1 year per 100,000 residents in the state population. Based on census estimates for January 1, 2008.

Source: Calculated from Heather C. West and William J. Sabol, "Prisoners in 2007," U.S. Department of Justice, *Bureau of Justice Statistics Bulletin* (Washington, D.C.: GPO, December 2008), p. 2, Table 2 and p. 18, Appendix Table 6.

Table 10.2 **The 10 Largest Local Jail Jurisdictions with Their Average Daily Populations at Mid-Year 2008**

Jurisdiction	Average Daily Population
Los Angeles County, CA	19,836
New York City, NY	13,849
Harris County, TX	10,000
Cook County, IL	9,900
Maricopa County, AZ	9,265
Philadelphia City, PA	8,811
Dade County, FL	7,050
Dallas County, TX	6,385
Orange County, CA	6,000
Shelby County, TN	5,765

Source: Adapted from Todd D. Minton and William J. Sabol, "Jail Inmates at Midyear 2008-Statistical Tables," U.S. Department of Justice, *Bureau of Justice Statistics Bulletin,* March 2009, p. 7, Table 10 at www.ojp.usdoj.gov/bjs/pub/pdf/jim08st.pdf.

incarceration rate A figure derived by dividing the number of people incarcerated by the population of the area and multiplying the result by 100,000; used to compare incarceration levels of units with different population sizes.

CJ Online

Incarceration Rates

For the incarceration rates of 216 nations, access the International Centre for Prison Studies website at www.kcl.ac.uk/depsta/law/research/icps/worldbrief/wpb_stats.php?area=all&category=wb_poprate. *Why do you think incarceration rates vary so greatly among different nations?*

authorities. This figure does not include the 780,581 local jail inmates (more about the jail population later); the 14,678 inmates held in territorial and commonwealth prisons; the 9,720 inmates held in facilities operated by or exclusively for the Bureau of Immigration and Customs Enforcement (formerly the U.S. Immigration and Naturalization Service); the 1,794 inmates in military facilities; the 2,163 inmates in jails in Indian country; or the 92,845 inmates (as of 2006) in juvenile facilities (discussed in Chapter 13). Overall, the United States had more than 2.5 million people incarcerated at year-end 2007.[28]

Similar, although somewhat less drastic, trends are evident when local jails are examined. Between 1982 and 1990, the number of jail inmates increased nearly 89%, from 209,582 to 395,553. On June 30, 2008, the local jail population stood at a record high of 785,556 inmates, an increase of about 99% over the beginning of 1990 and 275% over 1982.[29] If the additional 72,852 persons being supervised outside a jail facility (in community service programs, weekender programs, by electronic monitoring, and so on) at mid-year 2008 are added to the 785,556 confined inmates, the total number of people under the supervision of local jails increases to 858,408, an increase of about 1% over the previous year.[30] Table 10.2 lists the 10 largest local jail jurisdictions in the United States, along with their average daily populations at mid-year 2008.

We must be cautious about looking exclusively at changes in the sheer number of people incarcerated, because such changes do not take into consideration changes in the size of the general population. We might wonder whether big increases in the number of people incarcerated simply reflect growth in the U.S. population. Researchers typically convert a raw figure to an **incarceration rate** to deal with that problem. The incarceration rate is calculated by dividing the number of people incarcerated by the population of the area and multiplying the result by 100,000:

Incarceration rate = number incarcerated/population × 100,000

As shown in Figure 10.2, the U.S. adult prison incarceration rate was comparatively stable from the period before 1930 until the mid-1970s, at which time the dramatic upward climb began. Between 1980 and year-end 2007, the prison incarceration rate rose 264%, from 139 to 506 prisoners per 100,000 residents.[31] Likewise, between 1982 and mid-year 2008, the jail incarceration rate rose from 90 to 258 per 100,000 residents, or approximately 187%.[32]

Incarceration rates also differ significantly among nations. The data in Figure 10.3 show the prison population rates for 20 selected nations as of the most recent year available. Note that the United States has the highest rate of incarceration in the world. An article on the front page of the April 23, 2008 *The New York Times* entitled "Inmate Count in U.S. Dwarfs Other Nations'" noted that the United States has less than 5% of the world's population but almost a quarter of the world's prisoners.[33]

Annual incarceration rates such as those depicted in Figure 10.3 and discussed earlier reflect the numbers of people admitted to institutions, the lengths of time those people serve, and (for purposes of international comparisons) the nations' levels of crime. Nations with higher levels of crime, with more people admitted to prison, and with prisoners serving longer terms can be expected to have higher annual rates of incarceration. Thus, James Lynch argues that the

Figure 10.3

Incarceration Rates for Selected Nations

Nation	
United States	762
Russian Federation	628
St. Kitts and Nevis	588
Virgin Islands	549
Belarus	426
Bermuda	394
Puerto Rico	356
South Africa	343
Israel	319
Chile	305
Mexico	200
England and Wales	153
China	119
Greece	99
Germany	89
Switzerland	76
Haiti	72
Cambodia	71
Norway	69
Denmark	63
Japan	63
Pakistan	55
Iceland	44
India	33
Nigeria	29
Nepal	24

Source: Kings College London: International Centre for Prison Studies, www.kcl.ac.uk/depsta/law/research/icps/worldbrief/
wpb_stats.php?area=all&category=wb_poprate (accessed December 10, 2008).

type of international comparisons depicted in Figure 10.3 may be misleading, because the United States has a more serious crime problem than most other nations.[34] Lynch contends that if the analysis is controlled for nations' levels of crime, the differences between the United States and other nations in the use of imprisonment are smaller. Still, Americans are incarcerated for such crimes as writing bad checks or using marijuana, which would rarely result in prison sentences in other countries.[35]

Cost Estimates Total spending on state and federal prisons in 2007 was approximately $45 billion (about 10% more than in 2005). Table 10.3 shows the 10 states with the highest correctional budgets in 2007. If the Federal Bureau of Prisons were included, it would rank second behind California with a 2007 budget of about $5.7 billion. Of the approximately $45 billion spent in 2007, by far the largest amount was for salaries and benefits. About $5.9 billion were for inmate healthcare, $2.1 billion were for capital improvements (new construction, physical plant improvements, and equipment), about $1.2 billion for food, and about $1.1 billion for treatment programs.

Table 10.3 **Ten States with Highest Correctional Budgets (as of 2007)**

State	Budget
California	$7,824,565,000
New York	$3,672,506,798
Texas	$2,886,970,083
Florida	$2,460,339,030
Michigan	$2,078,269,100
Ohio	$1,686,124,536
Pennsylvania	$1,420,259,000
North Carolina	$1,302,165,885
Illinois	$1,125,856,200
Georgia	$1,124,626,358

Source: *American Correctional Association 2006 Directory: Adult and Juvenile Correctional Departments, Institutions, Agencies and Probation and Parole Authorities* (Lanham, MD: American Correctional Association, 2006), p. 12; Calculated from California Department of Corrections at www.cdcr.ca.gov/ Budget/Budget_Overview.html (accessed December 11, 2008); Pennsylvania Department of Corrections at www.cor.state.pa.us/stats/lib/stats/Budget2007. pdf (accessed December 11, 2008); Illinois Department of Corrections (personal communication, December 11, 2008).

California spent the most of any state (about $7.8 billion); South Dakota, the least (about $64 million).[36]

The average daily cost of incarceration per inmate in 2007 was $75.74 ($27,645 per inmate per year). Of the states reporting data (see endnote 36), Rhode Island had the highest daily cost ($164.28, or $59,962 per year), and South Carolina had the lowest ($38.61, or $14,092.65 per year). California spent the most on inmate health care ($1.8 billion), and North Dakota spent the least ($5.8 million). The state of Washington spent the most per inmate for health care ($5,860), and Alabama spent the largest percentage of its Department of Corrections budget for inmate health care (21%).[37] California also spent the most on food services ($245 million), while New Hampshire spent the least ($2.2 million). New York spent the most on treatment programs ($46 million), and Rhode Island spent the least ($1.7 million).[38]

The Crowding Issue Crowding has always been a problem in American prisons, but it has become especially troublesome over the past three decades. The increase in prison construction across the nation of late, while staggering, has failed to keep pace with the increase in prison populations, produced partly by the War on Drugs. At year-end 2007, for example, 19 states and the federal prison system reported operating at 100% or more of their highest capacity. The federal prison system was operating at 36% over its highest capacity. Moreover, these capacity figures do not include prison inmates held in local jails, in other states, or in private facilities because of insufficient prison space.[39] In 2007, at least 11 states had at least one institution under court order to rectify crowded conditions. Crowded prisons are often volatile prisons, and efforts to address problems related to crowding frequently end up diverting resources from inmate services and programs. How did we arrive at this state of affairs? The most obvious explanation is that a massive outbreak of crime in the United States has fueled the growth of the prison population. But as criminologist Nils Christie and a number of other observers have pointed out, that explanation is simply not supported by the data, which show relatively stable, and in some cases even declining, rates of crime for much of the period of the incarceration boom.[40] Likewise, there has not been an increase in the proportion of young adults, who constitute the most prison-prone age group, in the general population. Criminologist Michael Tonry, in a cross-national analysis, attributes high incarceration rates to high levels of income inequality, low levels of trust and legitimacy, weak welfare states, politicized as opposed to professionalized criminal justice systems (for example, the popular election of judges and prosecutors), and conflictual rather than consensual political cultures.[41]

Law professor Franklin Zimring offers an interesting public opinion explanation.[42] Zimring claims that members of the public will think punishment for crime is too soft and will demand more imprisonment as long as they think crime is too high. The problem is that prisons generally do an unsatisfactory job of controlling crime, so the public continues to perceive crime as high, despite increases in the prison population. The inability of prisons to control crime fuels the public demand for still more punishment (such as more imprisonment). Zimring uses the analogy of a person who finds that the medicine he or she has been taking for a headache is not helping and decides to increase the dose of the same medication.

We can expand a bit on Zimring's perspective. Over the last 200 years, Americans have developed a tradition of strong reliance on the prison to control crime. It has never done very well. As Zimring observes, the typical response to high crime and high recidivism is to conclude that criminals are not being punished enough and to gradually increase the use of imprisonment. In pursuing that strategy, we get caught in a loop. We are continually forced to direct the greatest portions of our overall correctional budgets toward

MYTH

Six percent of America's criminals commit 70% of all violent crimes. Thus, crime control could be improved dramatically if only those 6% were imprisoned.

FACT

This well-publicized statistic comes from a misinterpretation of two studies focusing on criminal activity by boys born in Philadelphia. Dr. Marvin Wolfgang of the University of Pennsylvania discovered that 6% of the boys born in Philadelphia in 1945 were responsible for more than half of the serious crimes committed by the entire group. Of those born in 1958, 7.5% committed 69% of the serious crimes. Those who cite these outdated studies focus erroneously on 6% of "criminals"—as if future high-rate offenders could be predicted—instead of 6% of all male children born in a given year, whose future criminal behavior is also not predictable.

Source: *Seeking Justice: Crime and Punishment in America*, Edna McConnell Clark Foundation (New York: 1997), p. 12.

imprisonment. Relatively few resources are left to develop effective programs in community corrections and crime prevention programs that might reduce reliance on imprisonment. Data show, for example, that about two-thirds of all money spent on corrections is used to finance institutions. Roughly a quarter of all persons under correctional supervision are incarcerated. Therefore, about three-quarters of the correctional population must be accommodated with one-third of the resources. The lack of resources devoted to community corrections and crime prevention helps ensure that programs in those areas will fail to control crime. So there will always be an abundant supply of offenders to feed the prison population and escalate the cost of maintaining that population. The irony is clear and substantial. While crowding in correctional institutions suggests the need for effective alternatives in community corrections and crime prevention, that same crowding and the resources it consumes preclude such alternatives. Ineffectiveness in community corrections and crime prevention simply makes the crowding worse, thereby consuming even more resources.

The incarceration boom of the past three decades has required the construction of dozens of new prisons. *Was this construction boom necessary? Why or why not?*

PRISON INMATE CHARACTERISTICS

Who are the people in prison, and why are they there? First, we must distinguish between federal and state prisoners. At year-end 2007, 87.5% of all prisoners in the United States were state prisoners, while only 12.5% were federal prisoners.[43] Because most prisoners are state prisoners, we will focus on them. At the end of this section, however, we will indicate some important differences between state and federal prisoners. One last point before we begin: the characteristics of both state and federal prisoners are remarkably stable over time, that is, they do not change much from one year to the next.

The largest proportion of state prisoners are male and black. *Why, and what can be done about it?*

Table 10.4 Selected Characteristics of State and Federal Prison Inmates

Characteristics	State Prison Inmates	Federal Inmates
Gender		
Male	92.8%	93.3%
Female	7.2	6.7
Race/Ethnicity		
White	39.2%	56.4%
Black	43.1	40.2
Hispanic	16.0	31.8
Other*	0.4	3.4
Age		
17 or younger	0.1%	0%
18–24	17.2	9.0
25–34	33.1	38.4
35–44	30.5	28.8
45–55	14.1	17.2
55–64	4.1	5.5
65 or older	1.0	1.1
Median age	34 yrs.	35 yrs.
Marital Status		
Married	16.4%	26.0%
Widowed	2.0	1.1
Separated	5.1	5.1
Divorced	19.7	20.3
Never married	56.8	47.5
Educational Attainment		
8th grade or less	12.3%	10.8%
Some high school	24.3	16.0
GED	29.9	28.8
High school graduate	21.6	24.1
Some college	8.8	13.7
College graduate or more	3.1	6.6
Median education	12 yrs.	12 yrs.
Employed in Month before Arrest		
Working	72.4%	72.4%
Not working	27.6	27.6

Notes: All data are based on 2004 data, except state and federal inmate gender and state inmate race/ethnicity data, which are based on 2007 data. Federal inmate race/ethnicity data are based on 2008 data. State and federal inmate race/ethnicity data are not directly comparable because the federal government records ethnicity separately from race, so Hispanics also could be either white or black. Some states record race and ethnicity differently. Some states combine race and ethnicity, so there is not separate category for Hispanics. They are recorded as either white or black.

In 2004, federal inmate data were missing on marital status for 0.2% of the inmates; on education, 2.2%; and on employment, 4.4%.

*Includes American Indians, Alaska Natives, Hawaiian Natives, Asians, Pacific Islanders, inmates who specified more than one race, and inmates whose race was unknown.

Source: Bureau of Justice Statistics, unpublished data from 2004 Survey of Inmates in State and Federal Correctional Facilities; Heather C. West and William J. Sabol, "Prisoners in 2007," U.S. Department of Justice, *Bureau of Justice Statistics Bulletin* (Washington, D.C.: GPO, December 2008) at www.ojp.usdoj.gov/bjs/pub/pdf/p07.pdf (accessed December 13, 2008); Bureau of Justice Statistics, unpublished preliminary 2007 data for race/ethnicity (disaggregated).

From Table 10.4 it is evident that the largest proportion of state prisoners are male and black. In addition, a large proportion had not completed high school or did not have a GED, were under 35 years of age and never married, and were employed prior to arrest. Three things about these data bear mention. First, even though there is actually a greater percentage of females than males

Table 10.5 Most Serious Offenses for Which State Inmates Were Serving Sentences in 2005

Offense	Percentage of Inmates	Offense	Percentage of Inmates	Offense	Percentage of Inmates
Violent Offenses	53.0	Property Offenses	19.2	Drug Offenses	19.5
Murder[a]	12.9	Burglary	9.6	Public Order Offenses[b]	7.6
Manslaughter	1.3	Larceny	3.5	Other/Unspecified	6.9
Rape	4.7	Motor vehicle theft	1.7	Offenses[c]	0.6
Other sexual assault	8.0	Fraud	2.5		
Robbery	13.7	Other property offenses	1.9		
Assault	10.0				
Other violent offenses	2.5				

Notes: Data are for inmates with a sentence of more than 1 year under the jurisdiction of state correctional authorities.

[a]Includes nonnegligent manslaughter.

[b]Includes weapons, drunk driving, court offenses, commercialized vice, morals and decency charges, liquor law violations, and other public-order offenses.

[c]Includes juvenile offenses and unspecified felonies.

Source: Heather C. West and William J. Sabol, "Prisoners in 2007," U.S. Department of Justice, *Bureau of Justice Statistics Bulletin* (Washington, D.C.: GPO, December 2008), p. 22, Appendix Table 11.

in the U.S. population, males make up about 93% of the state and federal prison population; that is what is meant by saying that men are disproportionately represented in prison. Put differently, at year-end 2007, the imprisonment rate for men was 955 per 100,000 men, compared with 69 per 100,000 for women.[44] Second, more than 72% of the prisoners were employed in the month preceding their arrests; however, many of them held low-paying jobs. Third, blacks are disproportionately represented in state prisons. While blacks make up approximately 13% of the general U.S. population, they account for approximately 43% of the state prison population. Further, the vast majority of blacks in prison are male, and black males constitute somewhere around half of all black persons in the United States. The overrepresentation of blacks in prison is a very heated issue in criminal justice today, and research has not established a consensus on the reasons for that overrepresentation. Currently, however, the weight of the evidence suggests that offense seriousness and prior criminal record generally exert a stronger impact on decisions to imprison than do extralegal factors such as race.[45]

At year-end 2005, about half of state prison inmates were serving sentences for violent offenses, about 19% were serving sentences for property offenses, 19.5% were serving terms for drug offenses, and most of the remainder were doing time for public order offenses. A more detailed breakdown for the violent and property offense categories is shown in Table 10.5.

The overall profile of federal prison inmates is very similar to the overall profile of state prison inmates (see Table 10.4). However, there are some differences. For example, a greater percentage of federal prison inmates are white; while median ages are about the same, federal prisons hold about half as many 18- to 24-year-old inmates as state prisons; and federal inmates are more likely to be married and have a higher level of education than state inmates, even though both state and federal inmates had the same median level of education. Also, about 53% of federal inmates were serving time for drug offenses in 2007 (not shown in table), compared to 19.5% of state inmates (in 2005).[46]

One last characteristic of both state and federal prison inmates is that many of them are parents. In 2004, for example, nearly 1.9 million children had at least one parent in state or federal prison (up from less than 1.5 million in 1999).[47]

THINKING CRITICALLY

1. What do the characteristics of prison inmates say about American society as a whole?

Incarceration Facilities

In the United States, the organizational and administrative structure of institutional corrections is diffuse and decentralized. Primary administrative responsibility for facilities lies with the executive branch of government, but the legislative and judicial branches are also involved. For example, the legislative branch appropriates resources and passes statutes that affect sentence length. The judicial branch sentences offenders to facilities and oversees the legality of institutional practices.

ORGANIZATION AND ADMINISTRATION BY GOVERNMENT

Incarceration facilities exist at all three levels of government (federal, state, and local), and power and decision-making responsibility are widely distributed both among and within levels. Within broad guidelines, the federal level and the various state and local (county and city) jurisdictions have much autonomy to organize and carry out incarceration practices. As a general rule, the federal government operates its own prison system, each state operates its own prison system, and local jurisdictions operate their own jail systems. Decentralization and autonomy notwithstanding, there are interrelationships between levels. For example, federal requirements affect the operation of state prisons, and local jails are affected by both federal and state regulations.

Federal institutions are administered by the Federal Bureau of Prisons (BOP), which was established within the U.S. Justice Department in 1930 under the Hoover Administration. Before the BOP was created, there were seven federal prisons, each separately funded and each operated under policies and procedures established by its warden. The BOP's mission is "to protect society by confining offenders in the controlled environments of prison and community-based facilities that are safe, humane, and appropriately secure and that provide work and other self-improvement opportunities to assist offenders in becoming law-abiding citizens."[48] The bureau's central office is in Washington, D.C., and there are six regional offices, in Philadelphia; Annapolis Junction, Maryland (near Baltimore); Atlanta; Dallas; Kansas City, Kansas; and Dublin, California (near San Francisco). The bureau also has two staff training centers and 28 community corrections offices. At the end of 2008, the BOP operated 114 institutions (see Figure 10.4), with more in various stages of construction. The bureau's facilities hold inmates convicted of violating the U.S. Penal Code. In 2001, the BOP assumed the added responsibility of incarcerating the District of Columbia's sentenced felons because of federal legislation passed in 1997.[49] By mid-year 2002, the federal prison system, with 161,681 inmates, for the first time in U.S. history had more inmates than did any state system. By year-end 2007, the federal prison population stood at 199,618 inmates and was still the largest. (California was second with 174,282 inmates. See Table 10.1.)[50] The administrative organization of the bureau is shown in Figure 10.5. The bureau has come to serve as a source of innovation and professionalization in the field of institutional corrections.

Although states vary in the way they organize institutional corrections, each state has a department of corrections or a similar administrative body to coordinate the various adult prisons in the state. Whether federal or state, correctional institutions are formal, bureaucratic organizations characterized by agency goals, rules and regulations, a staff chain of command, a staff division of labor, and similar features. Most adult prisons employ a quasi-military model of administration and management. Figure 10.6 displays the organizational chart for the California Department of Corrections and Rehabilitation, Division of Adult Institutions.

Harley G. Lappin, Director, Federal Bureau of Prisons. *What do you suppose are the major challenges for the director of the BOP?*

Figure 10.4

Locations of Institutions in Federal Bureau of Prisons

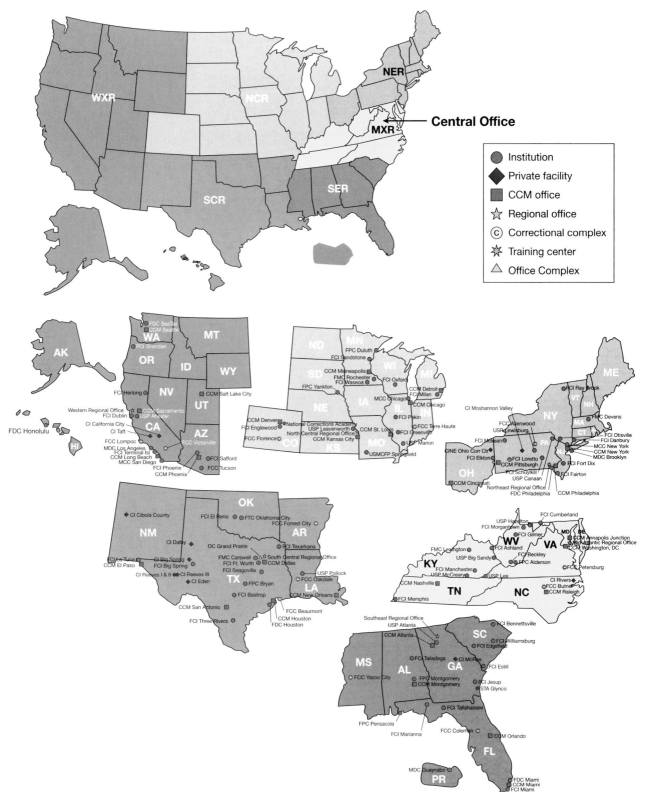

Source: Adopted from the Federal Bureau of Prisons at www.bop.gov/locations/locationmap.jsp, December 2008. Some locations have more than one institution.

Figure 10.5

Organization of Federal Bureau of Prisons

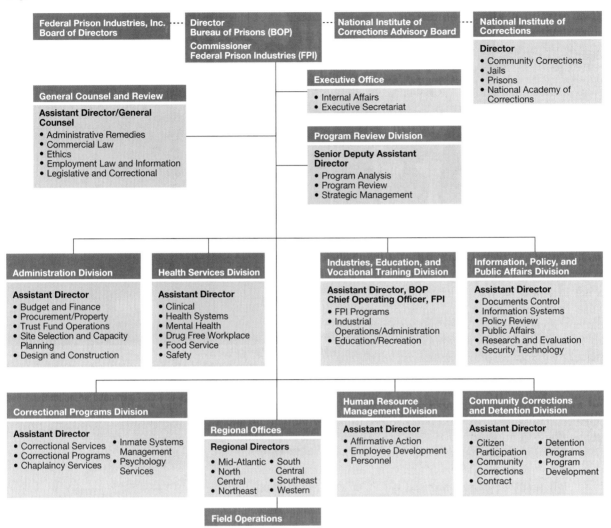

CLASSIFICATION AND OTHER SPECIAL FACILITIES

classification facility A facility to which newly sentenced offenders are taken so that their security risks and needs can be assessed and they can be assigned to a permanent institution.

When offenders are sentenced to the custody of the department of corrections in most states, they are transported initially to a **classification facility** (sometimes referred to as an assessment, reception, or diagnostic center). Stays at classification facilities are ordinarily short (for example, 60 days). The process of classification entails assessing an offender's security risk and determining which program services (for instance, counseling and education) the offender needs. Assessment information is used in deciding to which institution in the jurisdiction an offender will go to begin his or her term and which problems (such as alcohol dependency) the offender must address while imprisoned. A variety of other factors influence those decisions, including the nature of the offense, the offender's prior record (if any), propensity toward violence and escape, and vulnerability to victimization by other inmates; and the programs offered at the state's various institutions, as well as the levels of crowding at those institutions. The idea is to place inmates in facilities that can accommodate their risk-and-needs profiles.

Figure 10.6

Organization of the California Department of Corrections and Rehabilitation, Division of Adult Institutions

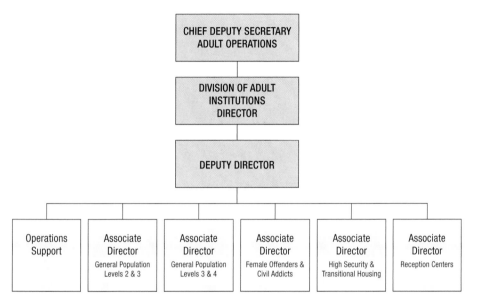

Classification is not a one-time process; it occurs periodically throughout an inmate's sentence. Inmates are routinely monitored and reclassified to preserve institutional security and for purposes of transfer, programming, and release decisions.

Classification centers are not the only short-term-stay facilities. For example, the Federal Bureau of Prisons administers a number of medical institutions that receive inmates with health problems and provide them with health care services. If an inmate's condition improves, he or she is returned to the institution of origin or sent to another institution to complete the sentence. Other short-term facilities in various jurisdictions provide services for offenders with mental disorders.

MEN'S PRISONS

Men's prisons, the most common general type of prison in the nation, are often distinguished from one another by **security level.** An institution's security level is determined by two related factors: (1) the degree of external or perimeter security surrounding the prison and (2) the measures taken to preserve internal security within the institution. The simplest security level categorization is maximum, medium, and minimum. Of the 830,721 male state prison inmates incarcerated on September 30, 2007 (see endnote 51), 12.4% were in maximum-security facilities, 36.4% were in medium-security facilities, 26.4% were in minimum-security facilities, and 8.0% were unclassified or in other facilities, such as multilevel-security facilities, reception and diagnostic facilities, admissions and orientation facilities, and community (low-security) facilities such as prerelease facilities. In addition, 15.5% of the inmates were in correctional facilities designated as "high/close," a security level between maximum and medium, and 1.2% were in supermaximum-security facilities.[51] Jurisdictions vary in the security categorizations they use.

Maximum-Security Facilities Maximum-security facilities (the BOP refers to them as high-security institutions or United States penitentiaries) are characterized by very tight external and internal security. A high wall or razor-wire fencing, with armed-guard towers, electronic detectors, or both, usually surrounds the prison. External armed patrol is also common. Some maximum-security

security level A designation applied to a facility to describe the measures taken, both inside and outside, to preserve security and custody.

Pottsville Prison in Pennsylvania (left) is an example of the radial prison design, and the Oregon State Correctional Institution (right) is an example of the telephone pole prison design. *What are advantages and disadvantages of each of these prison designs?*

institutions have a wide, open buffer zone between the outer wall or fence and the free community. In a recent national trend, however, prison watchtowers staffed with prison guards are being replaced with electronic security systems. Under the new system, the interior fence is outfitted with one device that detects movements such as the fence being shaken or cut and then sounds an alarm. Razor wire is then unrolled between the interior and exterior fences. Motion detectors that sound alarms when triggered also monitor that space. Once an alarm sounds, officers in the main control room can radio officers inside the prison and those circling the prison in vehicles. The electronic system is cheaper, too. It costs $175,000 to install the system, which should last 8 to 10 years. It costs about $800,000 to staff the watchtowers.[52]

Most maximum-security prison designs follow the radial plan or the telephone pole plan. Pottsville Prison is based on the radial plan, and the Oregon State Correctional Institution displays the telephone pole design. Internal security consists of such features as cell-block living, restrictions on inmate movement, and the capability of closing off areas of the institution to contain riots and disruptions.

"Supermax" Facilities A recent development is the construction of "ultra-maximum-" or "supermaximum-security" prisons intended to house notorious offenders and problem inmates from other institutions. These prisons utilize total isolation of inmates and constant lockdowns, during which inmates are not permitted to leave their cells. The Federal Bureau of Prisons opened one of the first of these types of prisons in November 1994 in Florence, Colorado. The $60 million state-of-the-art prison (a modern-day Alcatraz) was custom-built to hold the 400 most predatory convicts in the federal system. The new prison is divided into nine units. Security is controlled by means of 1,400 electronically controlled gates and doors and 168 television monitors. Each unit is self-contained and includes separate sick-call rooms, law libraries, and barber chairs. Inmates do not leave their cells for more than an hour a day. When they must leave their cells, they do so only with leg irons, handcuffs, and an escort of two or three guards per inmate. Each cell has a double-entry door, with the classic barred cage door backed up by a windowed steel door that minimizes voice contact among prisoners. After 3 years of this type of confinement, a successful inmate can gradually regain social contact by being allowed to go to the recreation yard or the cafeteria.[53] Currently, more than 40 states and the federal government are operating either one or more "supermax" units within existing maximum-security facilities or entire "supermax" facilities.[54] Pelican Bay State Prison in northern California and Red Onion State Prison in Virginia are examples of the ultramaximum- or supermaximum-security prison.

Camp Delta: A Special Supermaximum Facility

The war on terrorism gave rise to a new, special kind of supermaximum-security prison, Camp Delta, at the Guantánamo Bay Naval Base in Cuba.[55] The prison is composed of several camps and was built to hold more than 600 of what Pentagon officials call the "worst of the worst enemies in the war on terror." The U.S. government was holding the prisoners indefinitely without filing criminal charges or assigning them prisoner-of-war status, without giving them access to lawyers or allowing visits from family. The first prisoners arrived from Afghanistan in January 2002. They were to be held until they no longer had useful intelligence to provide, were cleared of criminal wrongdoing, and no longer posed a threat to the United States. They may be held until the war on terrorism is over, whenever that might be.

Camp Delta, on a bluff overlooking the Caribbean Sea, is surrounded by chain-link fence, lined with green nylon windscreen, and topped with spirals of razor wire. Troops patrol the perimeter on foot, in machine-gun-mounted Humvees, and aboard Piranha boats. Military Police guards watch rows of cell blocks from covered wooden watchtowers. A cell block consists of a long hallway with 7-by-8-foot green steel-grate cells on either side. Each cell holds one prisoner, and most prisoners remain in their cells 23.5 hours a day. Prisoners can see and talk to one another from their cells. Each cell has a sink with running water and a floor toilet. At the end of the cell block is a 30-by-30-foot enclosed and covered gravel exercise area that the best-behaved prisoners may use for up to 30 minutes a day. There are also individual outdoor showers.

Each Muslim prisoner receives a Quran, oils, beads, and a prayer mat. An arrow stenciled on each steel bed points east to Mecca. Prisoners may receive and write letters to family. Censors read all letters. Personnel from the military, CIA, FBI, and other agencies interrogate prisoners regularly. There have been no escape attempts. Most prisoners are well behaved, although a few of them

President Obama has promised to close down the Guántanamo Bay prison. *Is this a good idea? Why or why not?*

throw water and sometimes urine on the guards, yell insults and obscenities, refuse to return eating utensils after meals, and, at one point, went on a hunger strike. During the first six months of 2007, the U.S. military reported 385 "mass disturbances," defined as "assaults or other acts involving at least three detainees that were intended to disrupt operations." That was a 91.5% increase from the same period in 2006. However, the report also noted that for the 355 detainees remaining at the prison (260 as of February 7, 2008), there was a decrease in 10 of 11 disciplinary infraction categories. For example, assaults on guards declined from 180 to 70, dangerous-contraband incidents decreased from 51 to 14, and acts of "self harm" fell from eight to six. Camp officials claim that many of the prisoners arrived with mental-health problems. Mental-health professionals are on staff to serve them. Some prisoners were receiving psychotherapy, antidepressants, and antipsychotic drugs. Since Camp Delta opened, at least 37 prisoners have attempted suicide. Most have tried to hang themselves during an exercise period. Three have succeeded. Troublemakers are moved to solid-steel-walled cells that impede communication with other prisoners and are allowed to shower only twice a week. Cooperative prisoners may be moved to Camp Four, a medium-security section of Camp Delta. In Camp Four, prisoners live in open bays of 10 bunks and may gather and eat in open common areas. In February 2008, the existence of top-secret Camp 7 was revealed for the first time. Camp 7 holds 15 alleged "high value" al-Qaeda members, who had been transferred from CIA secret detention facilities.

Critics contend that not all of the prisoners are terrorists or have meaningful connections to the Taliban or al-Qaeda. Prisoners have been from 42 countries. Most of them have been from the Middle East and Central Asia, but some of them have been citizens of Great Britain, Canada, Australia, China, and Russia. Unfortunately, for them, until 2008, there was no way to challenge their detention. The Pentagon refused to hold the Geneva Convention hearings that would officially classify them as either prisoners of war or terror suspects, and the federal courts had determined that they did not have jurisdiction over the prisoners. As of June 2005, 3 prisoners had been charged with crimes, and 137 prisoners had been sent home. However, in *Boumediene* v. *Bush* (2008), the U.S. Supreme Court ruled that the Guantánamo detainees now have the constitutional privilege of habeas corpus. This may not matter much, because President Obama has promised to close down the Guantánamo Bay prison.

Medium-Security Facilities Compared with maximum-security prisons, medium-security institutions place fewer restrictions on inmate movement inside the facility. Cell blocks often coexist with dormitory- or barracks-type living quarters, and in some medium-security prisons, cells are relatively few. Typically, there is no wall for external security. Fences and towers exist but are less forbidding in appearance; razor wire may be replaced with less-expensive barbed wire.

Low-Security Facilities The BOP operates low-security facilities, a classification between medium- and minimum-security. Low-security facilities have double-fenced perimeters, mostly dormitory or cubicle housing, and strong work and program components.

Minimum-Security Facilities Compared with prisons at the other security levels, minimum-security prisons are smaller and more open. Inmates are frequently transferred to such prisons from more secure facilities after they have established records of good behavior or when they are nearing release. Dorm or barracks living quarters predominate, and often there are no fences. Some inmates may be permitted to leave the institution during the day to work (under *work release*) or study (under *study release*) in the community. Likewise, some inmates may be granted furloughs so that they can reestablish ties with family members, make living arrangements for their upcoming release, or establish employment contacts.

Custody Level versus Security Level *Custody level* should be distinguished from *security level*. Whereas institutions are classified by security level, individual inmates are classified by custody level. An inmate's **custody level** indicates the degree of precaution that needs to be taken when working with that inmate. Confusion arises because custody levels are sometimes designated by the same terms used to designate institutional security levels (maximum, medium, and minimum). However, the two levels are independent of each other. For example, some inmates with medium or minimum custody levels may be housed in maximum-security prisons.

custody level The classification assigned to an inmate to indicate the degree of precaution that needs to be taken when working with that inmate.

WOMEN'S PRISONS AND COCORRECTIONAL FACILITIES

As pointed out earlier, women make up about 7% of the population of both state and federal prisons. In recent years, however, incarceration rates for females in the United States have grown faster than incarceration rates for males. For example, between 1995 and 2008 the annual rate of growth of the female inmate population has averaged about 6%, compared to about a 4% average increase in the male inmate population. While the total number of male inmates has grown 53% between 1995 and 2008, the number of female inmates has increased 77%. Nevertheless, as noted previously, at year-end 2007 there were 69 sentenced female inmates per 100,000 women in the United States, compared to 955 sentenced male inmates per 100,000 men.[56] One difference between male and female state prisoners is that a somewhat greater proportion of women than men are serving sentences for property offenses (28.6% female vs. 18.5% male) and drug offenses (28.% female vs. 18.9% male), while a greater proportion of men are serving time for violent crimes (54.3% male vs. 35.4% female).[57] Other differences are that female inmates are more likely than male inmates to have dependent children and to be serving their first prison term. Figure 10.7 shows the percentage of the adult state prison population by security level and gender.

In 2007, 88% of all state adult prisons in the nation were for men only, 9% were for women only, and 3% were for both men and women.[58] Many states operate only one major prison for women. In general, prisons exclusively for women are smaller and house fewer inmates than institutions exclusively for men. Dorm and cottage plans are much more common than cell block plans in institutions for women.

Figure 10.7

Percentage of Adult State Prison Inmate Population by Security Level and Gender, 2007

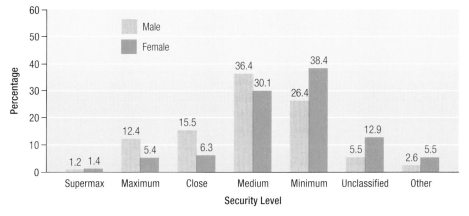

Source: American Correctional Association *2008 Directory: Adult and Juvenile Correctional Departments, Institutions, Agencies and Probation and Parole Authorities.* (Lanham, MD: American Correctional Association, 2008), calculated from data on pp. 52–53; figures do not include data from Alabama (females), Arizona, Connecticut, Delaware, Georgia, Hawaii, Illinois, Kentucky, Michigan, Mississippi, Nevada, South Dakota, Utah, and West Virginia.

cocorrectional facilities Usually small, minimum-security institutions that house both men and women with the goal of normalizing the prison environment by integrating the daytime activities of the sexes.

Cocorrectional facilities, which house both male and female inmates, have been in operation (in contemporary form) since the 1970s. The goal of cocorrections is to normalize the prison environment by integrating the daytime activities of the sexes. In 2007, 22 cocorrectional prisons were in operation in the United States (down from 27 in 2005) in addition to several other cocorrectional facilities and centers.[59] Cocorrectional prisons are usually small, and security is typically minimum. A comprehensive review of the effect of cocorrections on women prisoners paints a bleak picture: "cocorrections offers women prisoners few, if any, economic, educational, vocational, and social advantages. Cocorrections benefits male prisoners and system maintenance."[60]

JAILS AND LOCKUPS

lockup A very short-term holding facility that is frequently located in or very near an urban police agency so that suspects can be held pending further inquiry.

jail A facility, usually operated at the local level, that holds convicted offenders and unconvicted persons for relatively short periods.

A **lockup** is a very short-term (for instance, 24- to 48-hours) holding facility that is frequently located in or very near an urban police agency so that suspects can be held pending further inquiry into their cases by the police or the court. If there is cause, a suspect may be transferred from the lockup to the jail.

A **jail** is a facility that holds convicted offenders and unconvicted persons for relatively short periods. The modern term "jail" comes from the English term "gaol" (the pronunciation is identical), and English gaols have a history that dates to the 1100s. In contrast to prisons, most jails are administered at the county or city level of government. Excluding lockups, there are more jails (between 3,000 and 4,000) than any other kind of confinement facility in the United States. Although most jails in the United States are small (about half of them hold fewer than 50 people), some, such as those in Los Angeles and New York City, are very large (refer to Table 10.2).

Jail Functions Most people think of jails primarily as short-term holding facilities where suspects or defendants are detained pending further court processing, such as arraignment, trial, conviction, or sentencing. In practice, though, jails serve a catchall function in criminal justice and corrections. For example, jails also:

- Receive individuals pending arraignment and hold them awaiting trial, conviction, and sentencing.
- Readmit probation, parole, and bail-bond violators and absconders.
- Temporarily detain juveniles pending transfer to juvenile authorities.
- Hold mentally ill persons pending their movement to appropriate health facilities.
- Hold individuals for the military.
- Hold individuals for protective custody.
- Hold individuals for contempt (contempt refers to conduct that defies the authority or dignity of a court or legislature).
- Hold witnesses for the courts (witnesses are sometimes held in jails for their safety or if they are unlikely to appear in court when requested).
- Release convicted inmates to the community upon completion of sentence.
- Transfer inmates to federal, state, or other authorities.
- House inmates for federal, state, or other authorities because of crowding of their facilities.
- Sometimes operate community-based programs as alternatives to incarceration (those programs are described in Chapter 12).
- Hold inmates sentenced to short terms (generally 1 year or less).[61]

Because jails must be able to hold all types of people, including those who pose grave threats to the security and safety of others, the limited funds available through local taxes are directed primarily toward custody and security. Accommodations, services, and programs for inmates often suffer as a consequence.

Jail Populations   The number of people being held in local jails has risen dramatically in the past 25 years. The U.S. local jail population increased from 209,582 in 1982 to 785,556 at mid-year 2008, an increase of about 275% (see Figure 10.8). The jail incarceration rate was 96 inmates per 100,000 U.S. residents in 1983; by June 30, 2008, that number had climbed to 258 per 100,000, an increase of 169%. However, in recent years the growth rate of the jail population has been slowing substantially. Between 2000 and 2008, for example, the jail population increased only an average of 3.3% a year and, except for 2005, the growth rate of the jail population has decreased each year since 2002. The 0.7% growth rate in the 12 months ending June 30, 2008 was the smallest annual jail population growth rate since 2001 and the second smallest since 1981.[62]

Although less than 1% of the jail population in 2008 consisted of juveniles, that still amounted to 7,703 juveniles. The practice of holding juveniles in adult jails, where they are vulnerable to influence and victimization by adult criminals, is most common in rural areas, where there are no separate juvenile detention centers. That practice has been the target of much criticism and many policy initiatives for more than two decades. As a consequence, the number of juveniles held in adult jails has declined in recent years until lately: the number decreased by about 12% between mid-year 1995 and mid-year 2007 (from 7,800 to 6,837) but increased 26% between mid-year 2006 and mid-year 2008

CJ Online

Jail Statistics

To obtain the most recent jail statistics, go to the Bureau of Justice Statistics website at www.ojp.usdoj .gov/bjs/jails.htm. *How has the jail population changed between 1990 and 2008?*

Figure 10.8

Growth in Local Jail Population, 1982–Mid-Year 2008

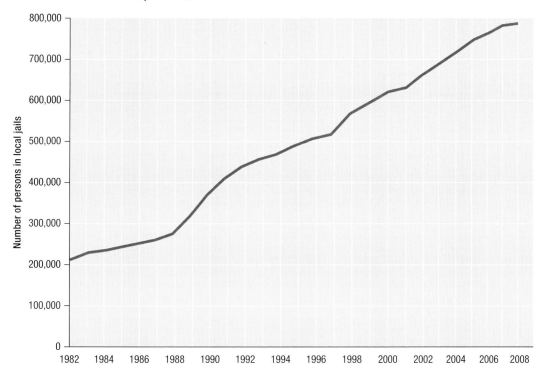

Sources: Adapted from Darrell K. Gilliard and Allen J. Beck, "Prison and Jail Inmates at Midyear 1997," U.S. Department of Justice, *Bureau of Justice Statistics Bulletin,* January 1998; Craig A. Perkins, James J. Stephan, and Allen J. Beck, "Jails and Jail Inmates 1993–1994," U.S. Department of Justice, *Bureau of Justice Statistics Bulletin,* April 1995; Allen J. Beck, "Prison and Jail Inmates at Midyear 1999," U.S. Department of Justice, *Bureau of Justice Statistics Bulletin,* April 2000; Paige M. Harrison and Jennifer C. Karberg, "Prison and Jail Inmates at Midyear 2002," U.S. Department of Justice, *Bureau of Justice Statistics Bulletin,* April 2003; Paige M. Harrison and Allen J. Beck, "Prison and Jail Inmates at Midyear 2004," U.S. Department of Justice, *Bureau of Justice Statistics Bulletin,* April 2005; Paige M. Harrison and Allen J. Beck, "Prison and Jail Inmates at Midyear 2005," U.S. Department of Justice, *Bureau of Justice Statistics Bulletin,* May 2006. William J. Sabol, Todd D. Minton, and Paige M. Harrison, "Prison and Jail Inmates at Midyear 2006," U.S. Department of Justice, *Bureau of Justice Statistics Bulletin,* June 2007; William J. Sabol and Todd D. Minton, "Jail Inmates at Midyear 2007," U.S. Department of Justice, *Bureau of Justice Statistics Bulletin,* June 2008; Todd D. Minton and William J. Sabol, "Jail Inmates at Midyear 2008-Statistical Tables," U.S. Department of Justice, Bureau of Justice Statistics, March 2009.

Table 10.6 Selected Characteristics of Jail Inmates Mid-Year, 2008

Inmate Characteristic	Percentage of Inmates (Total = 785,556)	Inmate Characteristic	Percentage of Inmates (Total = 785,556)
Age		**Race/Hispanic Origin**	
Juvenile	1.0%	White, non-Hispanic	42.5%
Adult	99.0%	Black, non-Hispanic	39.2%
Gender			
Male	87.3%	Hispanic	16.4%
Female	12.7%	Other	1.8%
		Two or more races	0.2%
		Legal Status (adults only)	
		Convicted	37.1%
		Unconvicted	62.9%

Source: Todd D. Minton and William J. Sabol, "Jail Inmates at Midyear 2008-Statistical Tables," *Bureau of Justice Statistics Bulletin* (Washington, D.C.: U.S. Department of Justice, March 2009), p. 5, Table 7.

(from 6,102 to 7,703).[63] Table 10.6, which displays selected characteristics of the jail population, also shows that the greatest proportions of jail inmates were male and racial or ethnic minorities in 2008. Less than half the jail population had been convicted of criminal activity. The remainder was unconvicted persons (usually awaiting trial or other case disposition).

In a classic study of jails[64] criminologist John Irwin found that, although members of the public tend to believe that jails are heavily populated with dangerous criminals, jails actually hold few such people. Jails are populated disproportionately with members of what Irwin calls the "rabble" class. The rabble class consists of people who are poor, undereducated, alienated from mainstream society, disreputable, and more likely than the general population to belong to an ethnic minority. Most of them have not committed serious offenses. In short, Irwin argues that the main function of the jail is to manage or control marginal members of our society and that as an unintended result of that process, the degradation those people experience in jail makes them even more marginal.

However, another study of jail bookings challenges Irwin's conclusion that jails tend to house mostly rabble. By analyzing the characteristics of persons booked into two jails (one urban, one rural), researchers found that nearly 47% had been charged with felonies, and more than 90% had been booked for a felony or a class A misdemeanor. Moreover, in 1-day counts of those jails, the researchers discovered that 82.5% of those held had been either charged with or convicted of a felony offense. As the authors of the study observe, "These data do not appear to support Irwin's claims about detached and disreputable persons whose real problem is offensiveness, not serious criminality."[65]

Jail Architecture and Management Philosophies Jails have traditionally represented, and continue to represent, one of the most problematic aspects of criminal justice. Many jails in the nation are old buildings plagued by overcrowding, a lack of services and programs for inmates, inadequate staffing, and unsanitary and hazardous living conditions. Some of the interrelated reasons for those problems are (1) the limited and unstable nature of local taxes to fund and staff jails, (2) a general lack of public support for jail reform, (3) rapid rates of inmate turnover, which make it difficult to coordinate programs, and (4) the sheer diversity of the risks and needs of the inmates. Also, in many areas, the chief jail administrator is the local sheriff, an elected or appointed political official. Because jails are usually under local administration, they are sometimes affected by the erratic and corrupt elements that often characterize local politics.

With increasing pressure from the courts to reform jail conditions and management practices,[66] efforts at jail reform continue. Historically, jails have progressed through three general overlapping stages of architectural design. Each design reflects a different philosophy about how to operate a jail.[67] The earliest jails, which date back to the eighteenth century, were built in a linear design. These *first-generation jails* have inmates live together in cells, dormitories, or "tanks." The cells line corridors, which make the supervision of inmates difficult (see Figure 10.9). Guards (they did not become "correctional officers" until the late 1960s or early 1970s—see the nearby FYI) at regular intervals walk up and down the corridors and observe inmates in their cells. To observe the inmates in the dormitories or tanks, guards periodically walk through the dormitories or along a perimeter catwalk, which separates them from the inmates by bars. (This type of supervision is referred to as "intermittent surveillance.") A "48-man tank," for example, is a large cage that might have six inner cells, each with eight bunks, that open into a "dayroom" or "bullpen" equipped with two long metal picnic-like tables attached to the floor and, perhaps, one television for the entire

FYI First-Generation Jails

The first-generation jail in which Robert Bohm (an author of this textbook) worked in the early 1970s was located on the eleventh to fifteenth floors of the Jackson County Courthouse in Kansas City, Missouri. When Bohm was hired as a guard, the official title of the jail was the Jackson County Jail. During the time he worked there, the official title of the jail was changed to the Jackson County Department of Corrections, and Bohm became a "correctional officer." Physically, the jail remained the same, and Bohm's work duties did not change.

Source: Personal experience.

Figure 10.9

A Typical First-Generation Jail Design

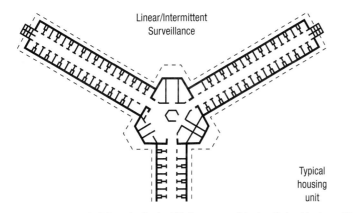

Linear/Intermittent Surveillance

Typical housing unit

Source: *Podular, Direct Supervision Jails: Information Packet,* U.S. Department of Justice, National Institute of Corrections, Jails Division, January 1993, at www.nicic.org/resources/topics/DirectSupervisionJails.aspx.

In first-generation jails, correctional officers cannot observe all inmate housing areas from one location, so they can only provide intermittent surveillance. *What are the advantages and disadvantages of working in this type of jail?*

tank. In the cells, beds, sinks, and toilets are made of reinforced metal and are bolted to the floor or wall. There is little direct contact between the guards and inmates, unless the guards have to respond to an incident, such as a fight or medical emergency. The first-generation jail is often a separate building or set of buildings surrounded by walls of reinforced concrete topped with razor wire (but see the FYI on p. 407). Many first-generation jails resemble early prisons.

Second-generation jails began to emerge in the 1960s. In these jails, correctional officers constantly supervise inmates from secure control booths that overlook inmate living areas, called "pods" or "modules." (This type of supervision is referred to as *indirect supervision* or *remote surveillance*.) Cells become rooms and are clustered around dayrooms or common living areas, where inmates can congregate for activities (see Figure 10.10). Inmate rooms have reinforced metal doors with unbreakable windows instead of bars and generally house only one

Figure 10.10

A Typical Second-Generation Jail Design

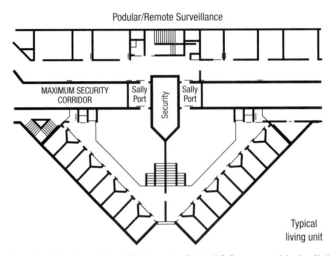

Podular/Remote Surveillance

MAXIMUM SECURITY CORRIDOR

Sally Port

Security

Sally Port

Typical living unit

Source (of diagram): *Podular, Direct Supervision Jails: Information Packet,* U.S. Department of Justice, National Institute of Corrections, Jails Division, January 1993, at www.nicic.org/resources/topics/DirectSupervisionJails.aspx.

In second-generation jails, correctional officers continuously observe inmates from a secure control booth that overlooks inmate living areas, called "pods" or "modules." They provide indirect or remote supervision. *What are the advantages and disadvantages of working in this type of jail?*

or two inmates. Beds, sinks, toilets, desks, and tables (in the dayrooms) are made of concrete or reinforced metal bolted to the floor or wall. There is very little direct interaction between inmates and correctional officers. Officers generally communicate with inmates by using a public address or intercom system. When trouble occurs inside the living area, a response team is called to intervene. The facility's perimeter walls continue to be made of reinforced concrete topped with razor wire or, in some cases, fences secured by razor wire.

Third-generation, new-generation, or *direct-supervision jails* emerged in the late 1970s. They use a "podular" or "modular" design similar to the one employed in second-generation jails in which inmates' rooms are arranged around a common area or dayroom. A third-generation jail may have one or more pods, with a pod typically containing 48 to 60 beds. However, in third-generation jails, there is no secure control booth for correctional officers, and there are no physical barriers between correctional officers and inmates (see Figure 10.11). Officers

Figure 10.11

A Typical Third-Generation Jail Design

Podular/Direct Supervision

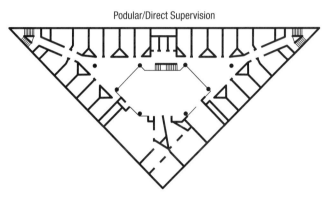

Source (of diagram): *Podular, Direct Supervision Jails: Information Packet,* U.S. Department of Justice, National Institute of Corrections, Jails Division, January 1993, at www.nicic.org/resources/topics/DirectSupervisionJails.aspx.

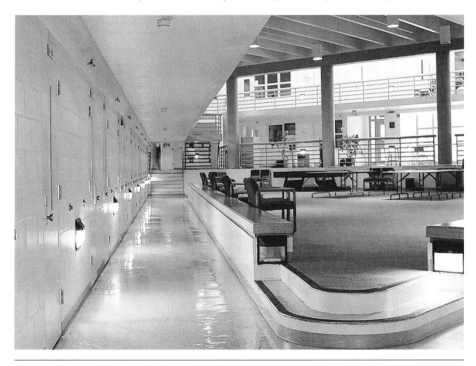

Third-generation jails employ a "podular" or "modular" design, but unlike in second-generation jails, correctional officers are stationed inside the housing unit where they directly supervise and interact with inmates. *What are the advantages and disadvantages of working in this type of jail?*

may have a desk or table for paperwork, but it is in the open dayroom area. Many new-generation jails have added amenities in inmate living areas, such as carpeting, upholstered furnishings, individual shower stalls, several television sets and viewing areas, collect-call telephones, game tables, and exercise equipment. Third-generation jails generally have strong perimeter security.

The pods in third-generation jails are self-contained to reduce costly and potentially dangerous inmate transport. Consider visitation, for example. In older jails, including many second-generation jails, inmates are moved from secure housing units to a visitation area. In many new-generation jails, visitors are taken to the housing unit by way of a nonsecure corridor and visit through a high-security glass barrier. The inmate stays securely in the housing unit and the visitor stays in the nonsecure corridor. Some new-generation jails are employing new technology for visitation. They are installing state-of-the-art video screens and phones in cubicles or carrels in inmate living areas and in remote video visitation centers for family members and friends. This arrangement also stops contraband from entering the institution by way of visitors. Attorneys, chaplains, or others visiting inmates for professional reasons, however, still are allowed to visit in person.[68] To reduce inmate transport, many new-generation jails also have their own courtroom, which is used primarily for arraignments and other pretrial proceedings.

The major difference between second- and third-generation jails is that third-generation jails are based on a different philosophy or management strategy called *direct supervision.* In this strategy, correctional officers continue to constantly supervise inmates, but rather than isolate themselves from the inmates, they are stationed inside the pod to give the inmates the opportunity to directly and regularly interact with them. (Direct supervision is also employed in some prisons.) In the new-generation jail, each congregate living area is a staff post, usually with one correctional officer in direct control of 40 to 50 inmates.

Correctional officers in direct-supervision jails are more than just turnkeys; they are professionals who need skills in interpersonal communication, crisis intervention, and counseling. Perhaps that is why research has found that female officers do at least as well as male officers while working in male units. Officers are taught to view the pods as space that they control, to be leaders and mentors in their pods, and to encourage inmates to change their destructive behaviors and ways of thinking. Correctional officers are more independent in direct-supervision jails and have the primary responsibility for daily decision making in the pods. Supervisors evaluate officer performance based on some of the following objectives:

- Being in daily contact with inmates in pods.
- Refraining from doing or saying anything that would belittle or degrade an inmate.
- Reporting promptly critical information to superior officers (for example, inmate escape plans).
- Engaging in continual visual observation of inmates.
- Investigating activity appearing out of the ordinary.[69]

Research suggests that direct-supervision jails provide a less-stressful, more positive, and safer environment for inmates and staff, may enhance supervision by reducing the number of unsupervised areas, and reduce inmate violations for contraband possession, destruction of property, escapes, disrespecting officers and staff, suicides, and violence, including sexual assaults.[70] In 2006, there were approximately 349 direct-supervision jails in all 50 states, the District of Columbia, and Puerto Rico—an increase of 19% over the approximately 293 direct-supervision jails in 2001.[71] Figure 10.12 shows the American Jail Association's Code of Ethics for Jail Officers. It

Figure 10.12

American Jail Association's Code of Ethics for Jail Officers

As an officer employed in a detention/correctional capacity, I swear (or affirm) to be a good citizen and a credit to my community, state, and nation at all times. I will abstain from questionable behavior which might bring disrepute to the agency for which I work, my family, my community, and my associates. My lifestyle will be above and beyond reproach and I will constantly strive to set an example of a professional who performs his/her duties according to the laws of our country, state, and community and the policies, procedures, written and verbal orders, and regulations of the agency for which I work.

On the Job I promise to:

KEEP	The institution secure so as to safeguard my community and the lives of the staff, inmates, and visitors on the premises.
WORK	With each individual firmly and fairly without regard to rank, status, or condition.
MAINTAIN	A positive demeanor when confronted with stressful situations of scorn, ridicule, danger, and/or chaos.
REPORT	Either in writing or by word of mouth to the proper authorities those things which should be reported, and keep silent about matters which are to remain confidential according to the laws and rules of the agency and government.
MANAGE	And supervise the inmates in an evenhanded and courteous manner.
REFRAIN	At all times from becoming personally involved in the lives of the inmates and their families.
TREAT	All visitors to the jail with politeness and respect and do my utmost to ensure that they observe the jail regulations.
TAKE	Advantage of all education and training opportunities designed to assist me to become a more competent officer.
COMMUNICATE	With people in or outside of the jail, whether by phone, written word, or word of mouth, in such a way so as not to reflect in a negative manner upon my agency.
CONTRIBUTE	To a jail environment which will keep the inmate involved in activities designed to improve his/her attitude and character.
SUPPORT	All activities of a professional nature through membership and participation that will continue to elevate the status of those who operate our nation's jails. Do my best through word and deed to present an image to the public at large of a jail professional, committed to progress for an improved and enlightened criminal justice system.

The American Jail Association's Board of Directors has approved the AJA Code of Ethics as part of an integral program to achieve a high standard of professional conduct among those officers employed in our nation's jails. Adopted by the American Jail Association Board of Directors on November 10, 1991. Revised May 19, 1993.

reflects the professionalism expected of correctional officers who work in today's jails.

THINKING CRITICALLY

1. What, if any, effect does a jail's architectural design have on inmates?

2. Do you agree that one of a jail's functions is to manage marginal members of society? Why or why not?

Institutional Security, Services, and Programs

In many ways, an incarceration facility is like a miniature society within the larger society. Institutions have many of the same features as the wider society, such as security procedures for maintaining order and preserving the safety of inhabitants, as well as a variety of services and programs meant to provide for inmate needs and encourage inmates to better themselves.

SECURITY AND INMATE DISCIPLINE

An orderly and safe environment is the foundation for all else that happens in an institution. When the environment is not stable, everything else tends to become secondary. For that reason, security procedures strongly affect the daily activities of both staff and inmates.

In any prison or jail, special security precautions are directed toward certain locations because of the importance of those locations to the institution's capacity for maintaining order. Examples of such locations include:

1. The front entry to the facility, through which all persons coming and going must pass.
2. The control room, which is usually located close to the front entry and is the heart of the institution's communication system.
3. The cell blocks or other quarters where the inmates live.
4. The dining area.
5. The area where the institution's confidential records and documents are maintained.
6. The indoor recreation areas and the outdoor recreation area or yard.
7. The sites where inmates work.

All institutions routinely employ a range of security procedures to maintain control over inmates. The classification of inmates by custody levels, mentioned earlier, is one such method. An inmate's custody level indicates the degree of precaution to be used when working with that inmate. In some facilities, certain inmates are given special custody designations that distinguish them from members of the general inmate population. Those inmates are not permitted to live among the general population of the facility. For example, inmates who are vulnerable to assault by other inmates may be designated for **protective custody,** meaning that they are to be kept segregated for their own safety. In contrast, inmates who represent a danger to other inmates or staff may be designated for **administrative segregation,** indicating that they must be kept in secure isolation so that they cannot harm others. Inmates who display signs of serious mental disorders may be segregated in a similar fashion.

As a basis for security procedures, institutions publish written rules that regulate the daily activities of inmates and staff alike. During the course of daily activities, staff routinely count inmates to detect escapes, and inmate whereabouts are constantly monitored within the facility. There are standard procedures for staff to follow when transporting certain inmates within the facility or from the facility to an outside location, such as to another prison, to court, or to a hospital in the community. Much

protective custody The segregation of inmates for their own safety.

administrative segregation The keeping of inmates in secure isolation so that they cannot harm others.

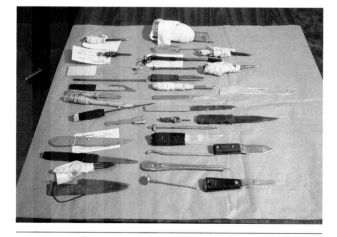

Handmade weapons such as those shown here are contraband and make prisons and jails dangerous places. *Where do inmates get the materials for these weapons?*

effort goes into controlling the property of the institution—for example, fire-arms, medicine, keys, tools, and basic commodities like clothes and food. In many prisons and jails, searches of inmates' clothing and bodies and shake-downs (usually random and warrantless searches) of their cells are common-place in an effort to control the flow of contraband, especially handmade knives and other weapons. There are special procedures and even special staff units for responding to riots, escapes, and other disturbances.

The mail and phone conversations of inmates may be monitored if there is sufficient security justification. Inmates may visit with relatives and friends only at designated times and may visit only those people the insti-tution has approved. Although a small number of prisons permit **conjugal visits**—in which an inmate and his or her spouse or significant other visit in private to maintain their personal relationship—routine visits usually occur in large, open rooms with other inmates, their visitors, and staff pres-ent. Visits are supervised closely because of the potential for contraband to enter the prison (but see the discussion of visitation in new-generation jails in the previous section).

Note that written rules and regulations are not the exclusive basis for institutional security. Written rules and regulations are part of an institu-tion's formal bureaucratic structure, which was discussed earlier in this chapter. Within that formal structure, there develops an unwritten, informal structure of norms and relations that is vital to the operation of the facility. For example, most institutions have an elaborate **snitch system** in which staff learn from inmate informants about the presence of contraband, the potential for disruptions, and other threats to security. Informants often receive special concessions and protection in exchange for snitching on other inmates. Such arrangements can be very elaborate, as illustrated by the research of criminologists James Marquart and Ben Crouch. In their study of a Texas prison, Marquart and Crouch found that certain elite inmates, known as building tenders, actually functioned as extensions of the uniformed guard force to achieve control of the institution.[72] The use of inmates (building tenders or trustees) to discipline other inmates was formally out-lawed in 1984.

Inmates who violate formal institutional regulations may be subjected to disciplinary measures. Staff members typically have broad discretion when they detect rule vio-lations. They may simply overlook the infraction or may issue an informal warning. Alternatively, they may file a disciplinary report so that formal sanctions can be consid-ered. The report usually leads to a disciplinary hearing, during which the charges and supporting evidence are pre-sented to the institution's disciplinary committee or hear-ing officer. If the report is found to be valid, a number of sanctions are possible. For example, the inmate may have some of his or her privileges temporarily restricted (for instance, no commissary or store privileges for 30 days), may be placed in solitary confinement or "the hole" for a specified number of days, may forfeit some of the time that has been deducted from his or her sentence for good behavior, or may even be transferred to another facility. Because institutions have many rules governing the behav-ior of inmates, it should come as no surprise that rule infractions and disciplinary measures occur frequently.[73]

conjugal visits An arrangement whereby inmates are permitted to visit in private with their spouses or significant others to maintain their personal relationship.

snitch system A system in which staff learn from inmate informants about the presence of contraband, the potential for disruptions, and other threats to security.

Family visitation is extremely important to inmate morale. *What are other advantages and disadvantages of family visitation?*

Careers in Criminal Justice

Visitation Coordinator

My name is Pat Bryant, and I am an administrative coordinator with the Central Visitation Center (CVC) for the South Carolina Department of Corrections (SCDC), Charleston, South Carolina. I have a Bachelor of Science degree in criminal justice from Benedict College, Columbia, South Carolina. I have held several positions with the South Carolina

Department of Corrections during the course of my career including administrative assistant, project developer, and business manager, to name a few. I have found these positions to be very rewarding.

The inmate visitation program is recognized by SCDC as an integral component of the rehabilitation process as it encourages inmates to have the opportunity to visit with family members and friends. The Central Visitation Center became operational in the fall of 1996 at which time I became the administrative coordinator.

A typical day as administrative coordinator for CVC involves communicating directly with family and friends of inmates in person, by telephone, or written correspondence and explaining to the prospective visitor the reason he/she may have been disapproved as a visitor, and providing guidance and technical assistance as it relates to inmate visitation to the 31 correctional institutions within the SCDC and other law enforcement agencies as requested. One of the most significant aspects of this job is ensuring that all Requests for Visiting Privileges forms are reviewed and approved (if deemed appropriate) and an automated record is created for the prospective visitor. The CVC

processes approximately 500 to 600 visitation applications per day. Some other aspects of this job include coordinating and conducting training for employees involved in the inmate visitation process and conducting semiannual visits to each institution to ensure visitation procedures are being implemented according to policy.

While the job of administrative coordinator is certainly an interesting one, it can also be a challenge. The reward is knowing that you have assisted someone who may not have had a clear understanding of the visitation process and being a part of the solution.

What do you think are the greatest challenges for a visitation coordinator?

SERVICES AND PROGRAMS

Many of the human services and programs found in the free society are duplicated within institutions. At a minimum, inmates must be fed, clothed, and provided with such basic shelter requirements as warmth, electricity, and plumbing, and their health care needs must be addressed.

Food services are an important part of an institution's operation. Waste and inefficiency must be avoided to control expense, but inmate demand and dietary standards must be met. Some institutions, particularly those under budgetary constraints, attempt to save money by serving cheaper food. For example, the Polk County, Florida Sheriff recently announced that he will be serving cheaper food to his jail's 2,400 inmates to shave approximately $161,000 from his annual budget. Instead of corn bread, he will be serving crackers and will save $33,304; tea and juice will be replaced by water, saving $56,630; one slice of bread will be served instead of two slices, saving $25,116; two fresh eggs will be replaced with one frozen egg patty, saving $24,545; bologna sandwiches will replace peanut butter and jelly sandwiches, saving $11,076; and fresh milk will be replaced with powdered milk, saving $10,545. All these changes meet the approval of a nutritionist, follow state jail nutrition guidelines, and still provide inmates with a 2,300–2,800-calorie daily diet.[74] Some institutions are notorious for serving cheap food even under normal budgetary circumstances. For example, Alabama counties still operate under an 80-year-old law that requires sheriffs to spend only $1.75 a day on food for jail inmates. The law also allows the sheriffs to keep any money they do not spend. No one knows how much money sheriffs' make on "food profits," because they are not required to report their private accounts to state auditors. Sheriffs are able to feed inmates on $1.75 a day by serving minimal portions, day-old bread, cut-rate vegetables, powdered food, and using inmate labor. Sheriffs argue that they do not make much money on food service, and the state holds them personally liable for budget shortfalls and possibly, lawsuits over jail food.[75]

Prisons and jails are buildings that, like all buildings, require maintenance and repair. Inmates as part of their job assignments perform a large portion of the maintenance and repair work.

Courts have held that inmates are entitled to medical and dental services. Prisons normally have an infirmary where less serious ailments can be treated. More serious problems necessitate transfer to either a prison with more extensive medical services or a hospital in the local community.

Institutions make an array of services available to inmates for their leisure time. We have already mentioned mail, phone, and visitation services. In addition, institutions operate commissaries where inmates can purchase such items as food, tobacco, radios, reading materials, and arts and crafts supplies. A number of recreational facilities are also provided, such as weight-lifting equipment, softball fields, basketball courts, game tables, and television viewing areas. In addition, legal resources and religious services are available (discussed in more detail in the next chapter). Although most prisons still offer a substantial number of services to prisoners, there has been a movement to reduce services over the past two decades.

Inmates with Special Needs All institutions have special-needs populations. Although those populations generally consist of far fewer inmates than the general prison population, it is still necessary to provide services for them. For example, elderly inmates frequently need more medical attention than younger inmates. Correctional officials generally consider 50-year-old inmates elderly inmates or geriatrics, because their lives have often been filled with violence, drug, alcohol and tobacco abuse, poor diets, and inadequate medical care.[76] The number of elderly prison inmates is increasing. At year-end 1991, 3.6% (or about 25,650) of state and federal prisoners were age 55 or older. At year-end 2007, 5.0% (or about 76,600) were age 55 or older—an increase of 39% in the percentage of inmates age 55 or older and an increase of nearly 200% in the number of inmates age 55 or older. In the federal prison system, each inmate age 55 or older costs the government about $69,000 a year in maintenance costs, two or three times as much as is spent on inmates younger than age 55. Most of the added expense is related to health costs. One health-related problem that has not been adequately addressed is the decreased mobility of older inmates—a problem that current prisons are rarely designed to accommodate.[77]

Another special-needs population is the mentally ill.[78] Since the deinstitutionalization of the mentally ill in the 1960s, in favor of treating them in the community, prisons and especially jails have become surrogate public mental hospitals. According to recent Justice Department research, more than half of all prison and jail inmates (more than 1.2 million inmates) had a mental health problem—that is, symptoms of mania, major depression, or a psychotic disorder: 56% of state inmates, 45% of federal inmates, and 64% of jail inmates. Symptoms of major depression or mania included persistent sadness, loss of interest in activities, insomnia or hypersomnia, psychomotor agitation, and persistent anger or irritability. A psychotic disorder was indicated by signs of delusions (a belief that other people were controlling their brain or thoughts, could read their mind, or were spying on them) or hallucinations (reports of seeing things others said they did not see or hearing voices others did not hear). To meet the criteria for mania, inmates had to report three symptoms or a persistent angry mood during the past 12 months; to meet the criteria for major depression, inmates had to report a depressed mood or decreased interest or pleasure in activities, along with four additional symptoms of depression during the past 12 months; and to meet the criteria for a psychotic disorder, inmates had to report one symptom of delusions or hallucinations during the past 12 months. The study did not address the severity and duration of the

Table 10.7 Prevalence of Mental Health Problems of Prison and Jail Inmates

Mental Health Problem	Percentage of State Prison Inmates	Federal Prison Inmates	Local Jail Inmates
Any mental health problem	56%	45%	64%
Mania disorder	43	35	55
Major depression	24	16	30
Psychotic disorder	15	10	24
No mental health problem	44	55	36

Source: Adapted from Doris J. James and Lauren E. Glaze, "Mental Health Problems of Prison and Jail Inmates," U.S. Department of Justice, Bureau of Justice Statistics *Special Report* (Washington, D.C.: GPO, September 2006).

symptoms nor did it exclude symptoms due to medical illness, bereavement, substance use, or the incarceration experience. Forty-three percent of state inmates, 35% of federal inmates, and 55% of jail inmates met the criteria for mania; 24% of state inmates, 16% of federal inmates, and 30% of jail inmates met the criteria for major depression; and 15% of state inmates, 10% of federal inmates, and 24% of jail inmates met the criteria for a psychotic disorder. These findings are shown in Table 10.7.

Inmate mental health problems varied by sex, race or ethnicity, and age, among other factors. Female inmates had much higher rates of mental health problems than male inmates: in state prisons, 73% of females compared to 55% of males; in federal prisons, 61% of females compared to 44% of males; and in local jails, 75% of females compared to 63% of males. As for race or ethnicity, white inmates had higher rates of mental health problems than either blacks or Hispanics: in state prisons, 62% of whites, 55% of blacks, and 46% of Hispanics; in federal prisons, 50% of whites, 46% of blacks, and 37% of Hispanics; and in local jails, 71% of whites, 63% of blacks, and 51% of Hispanics. Finally, regarding age, younger inmates had higher rates of mental health problems than older inmates. Inmates 24 or younger had the highest rates, whereas inmates age 55 or older had the lowest rates. These data are shown in Table 10.8.

The costs of incarcerating the mentally ill are huge. The Justice Department estimates that it costs at least $15 billion a year to house inmates with psychiatric disorders (about $50,000 per inmate per year). Such inmates may require segregated housing for their own protection and the protection of other inmates, frequent consultation with psychologists and psychiatrists, efforts to ensure that they take prescribed medication, and special safety precautions (for example, for a suicidal inmate, the use of paper sheets rather than cloth to prevent hanging).

The problem is particularly acute in jails. Mentally ill people are frequently held in jails even though they have not been charged with a crime. Many of them are held under state laws that permit emergency detentions of people suspected of being mentally ill. They are typically incarcerated pending a psychiatric evaluation or until they can be transported to a psychiatric hospital.

Most mentally ill inmates who are arrested are charged with misdemeanors such as trespassing or disorderly conduct. They are also frequently charged with drug- or alcohol-related offenses. Inmates with more serious psychiatric problems, such as paranoid schizophrenia, are sometimes arrested for assault because they mistakenly believe that someone was following them or trying to hurt them. Police also arrest people with severe psychiatric problems (so-called mercy bookings) to protect them from harm. This is especially true of women on the streets who are easily victimized, including being raped. Family members sometimes have mentally ill relatives arrested, because it is the easiest and most effective way to get the mentally ill relative needed treatment. Sometimes being incarcerated is the only way for mentally ill people to get needed treatment.

Table 10.8 Prison and Jail Inmates Who Had a Mental Health Problem, by Selected Characteristics

Characteristic	PERCENTAGE OF INMATES IN:		
	State Prison	**Federal Prison**	**Local Jail**
All inmates	56.2%	44.8%	64.2%
Gender			
Male	55.0%	43.6%	62.8%
Female	73.1	61.2	75.4
Race			
White[a]	62.2%	49.6%	71.2%
Black[b]	54.7	45.9	63.4
Hispanic	46.3	36.8	50.7
Other[a,b]	61.9	50.3	69.5
Age			
24 or younger	62.6%	57.8%	70.3%
25–34	57.9	48.2	64.8
35–44	55.9	40.1	62.0
45–54	51.3	41.6	52.5
55 or older	39.6	36.1	52.4

Notes: [a]Excludes persons of Hispanic origin.
[b]Includes American Indians, Alaska Natives, Asians, Native Hawaiians, other Pacific Islanders, and inmates who specified more than one race.

Source: Adapted from Doris J. James and Lauren E. Glaze, "Mental Health Problems of Prison and Jail Inmates," U.S. Department of Justice, Bureau of Justice Statistics *Special Report* (Washington, D.C.: GPO, September 2006).

Unfortunately, for the mentally ill, most jails do not provide adequate mental health services. More than 20% of jails provide no mental health services at all. Correctional officers in the vast majority of jails receive either no training or less than 3 hours of training in dealing with the special needs of inmates with severe mental illness. Prisons generally do a better job of accommodating the needs of mentally ill inmates. Most state public and private adult prisons provide mental health services to their inmates. In 2005, for example, nearly 34% of state prisoners with a mental problem received mental health treatment, compared to 24% of federal prison inmates and 17.5% of jail inmates. About 27% of state prisoners received prescribed medications for their mental illness, compared to 19.5 of federal prison inmates and about 15% of jail inmates.[79] Still, jails and prisons are often brutal places for mentally ill inmates, where they are vulnerable to assault, rape, and exposure to infectious diseases. Because many of them are unable to describe their symptoms to correctional officers, their needs, even in facilities equipped to deal with them, are often ignored.

Much controversy surrounds the presence of the human immunodeficiency virus (HIV) and acquired immune deficiency syndrome (AIDS) among institutional populations. As of year-end 2006, 1.8% of state and federal prison inmates (21,980) were reported by prison officials to be HIV-positive: 1.5% of state prison inmates (20,450) and 0.8% of federal prison inmates (1,530).[80] The total declined 3.1% from the previous year. Three states—New York (4,000), Florida (3,412), and Texas (2,693)—accounted for nearly half of all HIV-infected inmates at year-end 2006. New York, with 18% of the total, had the largest HIV-positive inmate population, but that population has been declining (down 440 at the end of 2006). The group most likely to test HIV-positive in either state or federal prisons was black, non-Hispanic, females, who were 35 years of age or older, had less than a high school education, and were separated from their husbands.

Table 10.9 Circumstances under Which Inmates Are Tested for the Antibody to HIV, by Jurisdiction, 2006

Jurisdiction	Entering	In Custody	Upon Release	High-Risk Groups	Inmate Request	Clinical Indication	Involvement in Incident	Random Sample	Court Order	Other
				ALL INMATES						
Federal System*				X	X	X	X	X	X	
Northeast										
Connecticut				X	X	X	X		X	
Maine					X	X			X	
Massachusetts					X					
New Hampshire	X									
New Jersey					X	X			X	
New York				X	X	X	X	X	X	
Pennsylvania				X	X	X	X		X	
Rhode Island	X				X	X	X		X	
Vermont					X	X	X			
Midwest										
Illinois	/	/	/	/	/	/	/	/	/	/
Indiana	X				X	X	X		X	
Iowa	X				X	X				
Kansas				X	X	X	X		X	X
Michigan	X				X		X		X	
Minnesota					X	X	X		X	
Missouri	X		X	X	X	X	X		X	
Nebraska	X				X	X	X		X	
North Dakota	X	X			X	X	X		X	
Ohio	X				X	X	X		X	
South Dakota					X	X	X			
Wisconsin					X	X	X		X	X

(continued on pg 419)

Of all the state and federal HIV-positive inmates, 26% (5,674) had confirmed cases of AIDS. This was an increase from the 5,422 confirmed cases of AIDS in 2005. In 2006, 155 state prison inmates died from AIDS-related causes, down from the 176 inmates who died from AIDS-related causes in 2005, and the 1,010 AIDS-related deaths recorded in 1995—the peak year. The 12 federal prison inmates who died from AIDS-related causes in 2006 were 15 fewer than the 27 who died from AIDS-related causes in 2005. In 2006, 4.6% of state prison inmate deaths were attributed to AIDS, down from 8% in 2003 and 34% in 1995. In 2006, less than 4% of federal prison inmate deaths were attributed to AIDS. At the end of 2006, the rate of confirmed AIDS cases in state and federal prisons was more than 2.5 times the rate in the total U.S. population. Intravenous drug use is the key risk factor for AIDS among inmates.

As shown in Table 10.9, at year-end 2006, 21 states tested all inmates for HIV at some point during their sentences, a controversial practice known as *mass screening*. Arkansas, Nevada, New York, Oregon, and the Federal Bureau of Prisons (BOP) test inmates chosen randomly. Forty-seven states test inmates if they have HIV-related symptoms or if inmates request a test. The BOP and 40 states test inmates if they have been involved in an incident, and 16 states and the BOP test "high-risk" inmates. Alabama, Florida, Missouri, Nevada, and Texas test inmates before their release, and Idaho, Nevada, and North Dakota test all inmates while

Table 10.9 Circumstances under Which Inmates Are Tested for the Antibody to HIV, by Jurisdiction, 2006 (continued)

Jurisdiction	Entering	In Custody	Upon Release	High-Risk Groups	Inmate Request	Clinical Indication	Involvement in Incident	Random Sample	Court Order	Other
South										
Alabama	X		X		X	X	X		X	
Arkansas	X			X	X	X	X	X	X	X
Delaware				X	X	X			X	
Florida			X		X	X	X			
Georgia	/	/	/	/	/	/	/	/	/	/
Kentucky				X		X	X			
Louisiana					X	X	X			
Maryland				X	X	X	X		X	X
Mississippi	X			X	X	X	X		X	
North Carolina				X		X	X		X	
Oklahoma	X				X	X	X		X	X
South Carolina	X				X	X	X		X	X
Tennessee					X	X	X		X	
Texas			X	X	X	X	X		X	
Virginia					X	X	X			
West Virginia					X	X	X		X	
West										
Alaska					X	X	X		X	
Arizona					X	X	X			
California					X	X	X		X	
Colorado	X				X	X	X		X	
Hawaii					X	X	X			
Idaho	X	X		X	X	X	X		X	
Montana					X	X	X		X	
Nevada	X	X	X			X	X	X	X	X
New Mexico					X	X				X
Oregon				X	X	X	X	X	X	
Utah	X			X		X	X			
Washington				X	X	X	X		X	
Wyoming	X				X	X				

Notes: *The Bureau of Prisons tests a random sample of inmates on alternate years.

/Not reported.

Source: Laura Maruschak, "HIV in Prisons, 2006," U.S. Department of Justice, Bureau of Justice Statistics at www.ojp.usdoj.gov/bjs/pub/html/hivp/2006/tables/hivp06t10.htm (accessed December 13, 2008).

in custody. The testing policies of each jurisdiction have not changed much since 1991. In addition to mass mandatory screening, other debated issues are whether HIV-positive inmates should be segregated and the degree to which HIV-positive test results should be kept confidential by attending medical staff. At present, the trend seems to be away from blanket segregation and toward confidentiality.

Inmate Rehabilitation Programs Inmates hoping to better themselves during their incarceration normally have the opportunity to participate in a number of rehabilitation programs. The particular programs offered vary across jurisdictions and institutions. Some examples:

1. Self-improvement programs offered by religious and civic groups (Alcoholics Anonymous, the Jaycees, a Bible club).
2. Work programs.
3. Education and vocational training.
4. Counseling and therapy.

CJ Online

U.S. Corrections

To learn more about a variety of issues that affect corrections in the United States, go to www.corrections.com. *What does this website tell you about the state of corrections in the United States?*

Work Programs Since the creation of the first houses of correction in Europe, there has been one constant: the belief that the imprisonment experience should improve inmates' work habits. Today, however, there is tremendous variation among institutions regarding work programs. In some institutions, all inmates who are physically able are required to work. In other institutions, the inmates who work are those who choose to do so. Likewise, there is great variation in the types of work inmates perform. Some inmates are employed to help the daily running of the institution and work in such areas as food services, maintenance and repair, laundry, health care, and clerical services. Other inmates work in factories at industrial tasks, such as wood or metal manufacturing. Still other inmates perform agricultural work. At the Cedar Creek Corrections Center in Washington state, most of the 400 inmates at the minimum-security facility work six to eight hours a day raising bees, growing organic tomatoes and lettuce (8,000 pounds worth in 2008), composting 100% of food waste, and even recycling shoe scraps that are made into playground turf. The work program not only reduces the prison's damaging impact on the environment, but it also reduces costs. The prison reduced water usage by 250,000 fewer gallons a year; reduced garbage bills $6,000 to $8,400 a year, and avoided a $1.4 million sewage-treatment plant upgrade.[81]

Institutions also vary in the degree to which the private sector is involved in work programming. Although extensive ties between inmate labor and the free market characterized the early history of the prison in the United States, those ties diminished during the first half of the 1900s. That change was due to concern by organized labor about unemployment among free citizens, concern by businesses that did not employ convict labor about their ability to compete on the open market, and concern by prison reformers about exploitation of inmates. Because of a series of laws restricting the private use of inmate labor, the *state-use system* became—and still is—the predominant way of arranging inmate work programs. Under that system, inmates are allowed to produce goods and services for the government. For example, in the main work program operated by the Federal Bureau of Prisons, known as UNICOR, inmates make a variety of products used by agencies of the federal government. Recently, however, legal restrictions on the private use of prison labor have been loosened, and the practice is witnessing somewhat of a resurgence in certain jurisdictions.

Education and Vocational Training It has long been assumed that rehabilitation can be facilitated by improving inmates' academic skills and providing them with job skills. Many offenders enter prison with deficits in their education. It is not at all uncommon to encounter adult inmates who are reading, writing, and performing math operations at an elementary school level. Therefore, much prison education amounts to remedial schooling designed to prepare inmates to obtain their GEDs. College courses are made available in some prisons through correspondence or study release arrangements or by bringing college instructors to the prison to offer courses. However, low educational levels render college courses inappropriate for many inmates.

A recent study found that two-thirds of prison inmates had such poor reading and arithmetic skills that they were unable to write a brief letter explaining a billing error or to interpret a bar graph. Only about half of all prisoners had completed high school or its equivalent, but even inmates who had a high school diploma demonstrated lower basic skills than did members of the general public with a high school diploma. Yet, over the past few years, while the prison population has expanded dramatically, more than half the states have cut back their educational and training budgets. The percentage of inmates enrolled in educational programs ranged from a high of 86% in Kentucky to a low of 7% in Nebraska. In most states, only 25% to 50% of

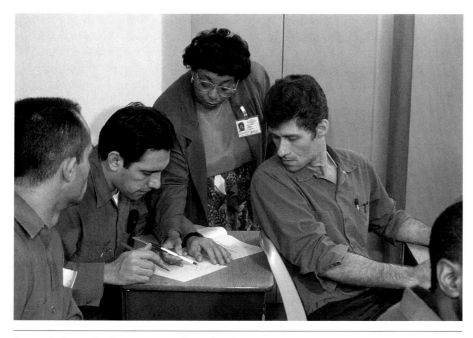

Research shows that inmates exposed to education programs have lower recidivism rates than nonparticipants. *Why do only 25% to 50% of inmates take part in some form of education?*

inmates take part in some form of education, even though several studies show that inmates exposed to education programs have lower recidivism rates than do nonparticipants.[82]

Some prison vocational programs operate as part of job assignments (on-the-job training), and others are separate from job assignments. Either way, the goal is to provide inmates with job skills that will improve their marketability upon release. Most prison vocational training is geared toward traditional blue-collar employment, such as welding and auto mechanics. Vocational programs offered in women's prisons have often been criticized for concentrating excessively on stereotypical women's jobs, such as cosmetology.

Counseling and Therapy A wide range of counseling techniques and therapy modalities are used in prisons across the nation. The description of specific techniques and modalities, however, is beyond the scope of this chapter.[83] Suffice it to say that the techniques and modalities used at a given institution ordinarily reflect the training and professional orientation of the treatment staff—caseworkers, religious counselors, social workers, psychologists, and psychiatrists.

A distinction is usually drawn between individual counseling, which involves one-on-one interaction between the counselor and the inmate, and group counseling, which involves the interaction of the counselor with a small group of inmates. Those categories of treatment may overlap, because an inmate receiving individual counseling may also be in group counseling, and many of the techniques and principles used in individual counseling are also applied to group settings. Still, the distinction has merit, because individual counseling is more appropriate for some inmates (for example, those with deep-seated problems who will require long-term help), and group counseling is more appropriate for other inmates (for example, those who are defensive, manipulative, and prone to denying their problems).

Group counseling is more popular than individual counseling in institutional settings, primarily because it is more economical and because there are large numbers of inmates who share similar backgrounds and problems. In fact,

milieu therapy A variant of group therapy that encompasses the total living environment so that the environment continually encourages positive behavioral change.

crisis intervention A counselor's efforts to address some crisis in an inmate's life and to calm the inmate.

FYI Rehabilitating Criminals

A national survey shows that 72% of the American public agrees (29% completely agree and 43% mostly agree) that "the criminal justice system should try to rehabilitate criminals, not just punish them"; 25% disagree (14% mostly disagree and 11% completely disagree); and 3% did not know.

Source: *Sourcebook of Criminal Justice Statistics 2003* (online), p. 139, Table 2.46.

less-eligibility principle The position that prisoners should receive no service or program superior to the services and programs available to free citizens without charge.

the members of a group are frequently selected on the basis of their common backgrounds and problem behavior patterns. For example, a group may consist of persons who have substance abuse problems or those who are sex offenders. Some institutions employ a variant of group therapy known as **milieu therapy** (also called a *therapeutic community*). Rather than having inmates attend periodic group sessions (one or two hourly sessions per week), milieu therapy encompasses the total living environment of inmates so that the environment continually encourages positive behavioral change. In effect, the entire inmate population becomes the group, and inmates have active roles in helping other inmates change.

Most counselors and therapists who work in prison spend a considerable portion of their time performing **crisis intervention.** Crisis intervention consists of a counselor's efforts to address some crisis that has erupted in an inmate's life (for example, suicidal thoughts, rejection by the spouse, a mental breakdown, or a conflict between inmates). Institutions are stressful living environments, so inmate crises are common. The counselor's task is to assist inmates in restoring a state of emotional calm and greater stability so that problems can be addressed rationally before inmates harm themselves or others.

Programs in Perspective We usually think of rehabilitation programs as serving one main objective: to help inmates better themselves. In practice, however, programs serve other, more subtle functions as well. Programs give inmates a way to occupy themselves; they help inmates manage time. They also help the institution achieve control over inmates. For example, inmates who are in counseling for displaying too much aggression toward other inmates may realize that unless they demonstrate "progress" in reducing their aggression, the counselor will not recommend them to the parole board for early release (in states where parole is available). Although such progress may be achieved quickly in prison, it may be short-lived upon release. Similarly, from the standpoint of inmates, the most desirable work assignments are those that give inmates access to valued resources (for instance, a kitchen job provides greater access to food). More desirable work assignments are routinely held out by the staff as privileges to be earned through good behavior.

Institutional programs are also plagued by a variety of problems that hinder their ability to effect rehabilitation. For example, prison work assignments frequently do not parallel work in the free world. In prison, workdays are often short and interrupted. In many cases, there is little concern for the quantity and quality of work. Furthermore, some of the jobs lack any real counterpart in the free world. The classic example is license plate manufacturing. In many prisons, educational programs suffer from a lack of funding. Vocational training focuses primarily on traditional blue-collar jobs and thus prepares inmates to enter jobs for which there is already abundant competition. A dilemma is created by the argument that inmates should not receive highly technical or professional training (such as training in computer programming) because many members of the free, law-abiding community cannot afford such training. That argument is based on the **less-eligibility principle,** the position that prisoners should receive no service or program superior to the services and programs available to free citizens without charge. Moreover, prison education and vocational programs can do little to create jobs. If an inmate returns to a community with a poor economy and high unemployment, the education and training received in prison may do little more than raise the inmate's expectations to unrealistic levels.

For their part, counseling and therapy programs must operate against the harsh realities of the prison environment, where custody and security ordinarily take priority over rehabilitation. Despite those obstacles, some programs are able to bring about positive changes in offenders' attitudes and behavior.

Psychologist Ted Palmer has observed that although no single type of treatment can be identified as the most effective, one feature that seems to characterize programs that consistently reduce offender recidivism is the quality of the program's implementation. Thus, when the integrity of treatment efforts is allowed to take priority over institutional concerns for security and custody, offending can be reduced.[84] Also, as criminologist Robert Johnson points out, many counseling programs place nearly exclusive emphasis on inmates' pasts and futures, with insufficient attention given to present coping patterns. Johnson recommends that programs begin teaching inmates to cope maturely and constructively with their present environment so that they will be better able to cope with life after release.[85]

THINKING CRITICALLY

1. Do you think inmate rehabilitation programs can truly make a difference? Why or why not?

2. Do you think inmates should earn money for the work they do while in prison? Why or why not?

✳ Summary

1. Summarize the purposes of confinement in Europe before it became a major way of punishing criminals.

   Confinement became a major way of punishing criminals in Europe in the 1600s and 1700s. Before that, it was used to (1) detain people before trial, (2) hold prisoners awaiting other sanctions, such as death and corporal punishment, (3) coerce payment of debts and fines, (4) hold and punish slaves, (5) achieve religious indoctrination and spiritual reformation (as during the Inquisition), and (6) quarantine disease (as during the bubonic plague).

2. Describe how offenders were punished before the large-scale use of confinement.

   Before the large-scale use of confinement, punishments were directed more at the offender's body and property. One basic goal was to inflict pain. Those punishments were commonly carried out in public to humiliate the offender and to deter onlookers from crime. Examples of such punishments are fines, confiscation of property, and diverse methods of corporal and capital punishment.

3. Explain why confinement began to be used as a major way of punishing offenders in Europe.

   Enlightenment-era reforms led to an emphasis on deterring and reforming criminals through confinement. Confinement was also advocated as a humane alternative to older punishments. In addition, during the 1500s and 1600s, workhouses were established as places where offenders could be sent to learn discipline and productive work habits.

4. Describe the recent trends in the use of incarceration in the United States.

   There has been a dramatic increase since the mid-1970s in the number of people incarcerated in the United States, partly because of the War on Drugs. That increase has been accompanied by much concern over rising costs and institutional crowding. In response to those problems, confinement alternatives to traditional incarceration have been developed. Two of those alternatives are contracts with the private sector for the construction or operation of some confinement facilities and the use of shock incarceration, or "boot camp" prisons, for young, nonviolent offenders without extensive prior criminal records.

5. List some of the characteristics of the incarcerated population in the United States.

   The incarcerated population in the United States is disproportionately male, black, young, single, undereducated, and poor. More than half of state prison inmates are serving time for violent offenses, whereas more than half of federal prison inmates are serving sentences for drug offenses. More than half of jail inmates are unconvicted, usually awaiting trial or other case disposition.

6. Describe how incarceration facilities are structured, organized, and administered by the government in the United States.

   Incarceration facilities in the United States are administered primarily by the executive branch of government. They exist at all three levels of government. Prisons are administered at the federal level and state levels, while jails tend to be locally administered. Despite this diversification, all the institutions have somewhat similar administrative structures, ranging from the warden or superintendent at the top to the correctional (line) officers at the bottom.

7. Name some of the common types of correctional facilities in the United States.

   Common types of adult correctional facilities in the United States include (1) classification and special facilities, (2) "supermaximum-," maximum-, medium-, and minimum-security men's prisons, (3) women's and cocorrectional facilities, and (4) jails and lockups.

8. Identify some of the procedures that institutions employ to maintain security and order.

   To maintain security and order, correctional institutions employ a number of procedures. Among them are the use of custody designations for inmates, inmate counts, property control, searches of inmates and their living quarters, and restrictions on inmate communication (mail, phone calls, and visits) with outsiders. Also, institutions commonly rely on inmate-informant, or snitch, systems to maintain security. Inmates found guilty of violating institutional rules may be subjected to a variety of disciplinary sanctions (such as loss of good time, restriction of privileges, and solitary confinement) to deter future rule infractions.

9. List the services and programs that are commonly available to inmates.

   Some of the services and programs available to inmates are subsistence services (food, clothing, and shelter), health care services, legal services, recreation, and religious services. There are also a number of programs designed to improve inmates' lives. They include low-paying work, education and vocational training, and group and individual counseling.

✳ Key Terms

banishment 379
transportation 379
workhouses 380
penology 380
panopticon 380
Pennsylvania system 381

Auburn system 381
medical model 383
privatization 384
shock incarceration 386
incarceration rate 390
classification facility 398

security level 399
custody level 403
cocorrectional facilities 404
lockup 404
jail 404
protective custody 412

administrative segregation 412
conjugal visits 413
snitch system 413
milieu therapy 422
crisis intervention 422
less-eligibility principle 422

✳ Review Questions

1. What did Cesare Beccaria, the Enlightenment thinker, mean when he said that a punishment should fit the crime?

2. What reforms in penal institutions did John Howard advocate in his book *The State of the Prisons in England and Wales* (1777)?

3. What is generally considered the first state prison in the United States, and of what did the daily routine of inmates in this prison consist?

4. How did the Pennsylvania system of confinement differ from the Auburn system of confinement, and which system became the model followed by other states?

5. What were the main features of the reformatory?

6. According to John Irwin, what three types of penal institutions dominated different parts of the last century?

7. What is an incarceration rate, and why is it used?

8. How does the incarceration rate of the United States compare with the incarceration rates of other countries?

9. How do the authors of this textbook explain the prison overcrowding crisis in the United States?

10. What are some differences between the federal prison and state prison populations?

11. What is the official mission of the Federal Bureau of Prisons?

12. What are the purposes of inmate classification?

13. What are prison security and custody levels, and how do they differ?

14. What are the purposes of a jail?

15. Why do jails represent one of the most problematic aspects of criminal justice?

16. What are some objectives of inmate rehabilitation programs?

17. What is the less-eligibility principle, as applied to corrections?

✳ In the Field

1. **Prison Tour** Many prisons and jails conduct tours for students in criminal justice courses. Arrange to visit one or more prisons and jails in your area. Compare and contrast what you see during your visit(s) with the material in this chapter. Also, if you tour both a prison and a jail, describe similarities and differences between the two institutions. Either present your findings orally in class or put them in writing for your instructor.

2. **Create a Prison** Design a prison conceptually and, perhaps, three-dimensionally. Decide what type of inmates the prison is to hold (men, women, or both; prisoners requiring maximum security, minimum security, and so on) and what the security level will be. Consider location, architectural design, bureaucratic structure, security and discipline procedures, and inmate services and programs.

✳ On the Net

1. **Federal Bureau of Prisons** Go to the Federal Bureau of Prisons website at www.bop.gov. Access "Public Info" and then "Quick Facts and Statistics" from the topic list. Use the data provided to construct a current profile of inmates. Then access the "Weekly Population Report," and search for data about any federal prisons in your state. Write a brief report on what you find.

2. **Incarceration Worldwide** Review the document, "Comparative International Rates of Incarceration: An Examination of Causes and Trends," at the Sentencing Project website at www.sentencingproject.org/PublicationDetails .aspx?PublicationID=423. Write a brief essay explaining why rates of incarceration vary so greatly among countries of the world.

✳ Critical Thinking Exercises

PRISON RESEARCH

1. A Florida prison has recently been transformed into a combination hospital and prison where most inmates have HIV. They participate in tests of some of the newest HIV drugs being developed and have access to some of the nation's leading AIDS researchers. Only about 120 of the 3,000 or so state inmates who are known to be HIV-positive are able to participate. Some inmates are due to be released in a few weeks or months; others are serving life sentences. On the street, the treatment would cost about $1,400 a month; participating inmates get it for free.

The program is controversial. Although it has been praised as a model for the rest of the country's prisons to copy, it has also been criticized for conducting drug trials or medical studies on inmates. Because inmates are a captive audience, a major question is whether they can truly give informed consent to participate in the voluntary program. Before they are allowed to participate, inmates must sign a five-page consent form that lists the possible benefits and side effects of the drugs. The state also has no relationship with the drug companies and accepts no money from them.

a. Should the program continue and be spread to other prisons? Why or why not?

b. Address these questions: Can inmates give informed consent? Does it matter? If inmates are allowed to participate, how should they be chosen from among all those who volunteer?

THE EX-CONVICT

2. To the average citizen, the ex-convict is an individual of questionable character. This image is reinforced by the fact that the only thing that is usually newsworthy about ex-convicts is bad news, such as when they are rearrested. Few citizens know a rehabilitated offender for obvious reasons. Yet, the rehabilitated ex-convict faces a variety of civil disabilities. Not the least among those is the difficulty of getting a "good" job. On virtually every job application, there is the question: "Have you ever been convicted of a felony or misdemeanor or denied bond in any state?" In addition, prospective employers generally ask applicants to reveal their former substance abuse, which is a problem that most former offenders had. An affirmative answer to either question almost always eliminates a person's chance for employment.

a. How can ex-offenders shed the ex-convict status? Should they be allowed to shed it? Why or why not?

b. Do your answers to the above questions change depending upon the ex-convict's conviction offense?

To access more information and resources, including study questions, chapter summaries, and links, go to: www.mhhe.com/bohm6e.

Prison Life, Inmate Rights, Release, and Recidivism

11

Chapter Outline

Chapter Objectives

After completing this chapter, you should be able to:

1. Distinguish between the deprivation and importation models of inmate society.

2. Explain how today's inmate society differs from those of the past.

3. Identify some of the special features of life in women's prisons.

4. Describe the profile of correctional officers, and explain some of the issues that they face.

5. Identify prisoners' rights, and relate how they were achieved.

6. List the two most common ways that inmates are released from prison, and compare those two ways in frequency of use.

7. Summarize what recidivism research reveals about the success of the prison in achieving deterrence and rehabilitation.

CRIME STORY

Khalid Duhham Al-Jawary was scheduled to be released from a federal prison on February 19, 2009. He had been convicted of terrorism charges in 1973 for his role in a failed attempt to bomb Israeli targets in New York City. Al-Jawary, 63 years old, would have served about half his 30-year sentence, which included time served prior to his sentence and credit for good behavior.

Al-Jawary entered the United States to carry out his plot on January 12, 1973. He flew to Boston by way of Montreal and then made his way to New York City. He built three powerful bombs composed of large containers filled with gasoline, propane tanks, plastic explosives, blasting caps, and batteries. Two of the bombs used alarm clocks, but the third used a sophisticated electronic-timing device commonly referred to as an "e-cell." Al-Jawary and presumably his accomplices put the bombs in rental cars and parked the cars by two Israeli banks on Fifth Avenue and the El-Al cargo terminal at JFK International airport. The bombing was to coincide

continued

with Israeli Prime Minister Golda Meir's visit to the city. However, the bombs failed to detonate, and Al-Jawary fled the country, escaping prosecution for nearly two decades. He was arrested in Italy in 1991 and returned to the United States to face trial. He was sentenced to the 30-year prison term on April 16, 1993. Al-Jawary claimed he was framed and that the government had the wrong person. However, FBI agents had lifted 60 incriminating fingerprints, all matching Al-Jawary's, including some on one of the bombs. They also found other evidence linking him to the plan such as a fake Jordanian passport in a hotel room he rented.

Among the topics examined in Chapter 11 is the release and recidivism of prison inmates. As the Al-Jawary example illustrates, nearly all inmates eventually are released from prison. Many will be rehabilitated and not engage in crime again, but as statistics clearly show, too many will return to crime. What should be done about prisoners such as Khalid Duhham Al-Jawary? Why is he being released after serving only about half his sentence? He supposedly has "paid his debt to society," but few people feel comfortable about his release from prison. Once he is released he will be turned over to U.S. Immigration and Customs Enforcement and held until his deportation. At this point no one is sure where he will go, because his true identity is unknown. FBI agents involved in his capture believe that following his release he will pick up where he left off. As one agent noted, "He'll be deported and received as a hero and go right back into his terrorist activities." Al-Jawary has been linked to the deadly letter-bombing campaign by the Palestinian terrorist group Black September that targeted world leaders in the 1970s and is suspected of having a role in the bombing of a TWA flight in 1974 off Greece that killed 88 people, including 17 Americans. If it is believed that he is a threat to himself or others, the government has the power to have him involuntarily committed to the care of a secure mental institution until physicians are convinced he is well. Is involuntary commitment to a mental institution a preferable alternative for Al-Jawary than release and deportation? Is involuntary commitment justifiable? Although correctional and other criminal justice authorities rarely have to deal with the release of terrorists from prison, they must address the release of potentially dangerous felons from prison on a regular basis.

Living in Prison

When people think of prisons, they usually imagine the big-house, maximum-security prison for men. Indeed, the majority of scholarly research on prison life has focused on this type of institution. In this chapter, we survey some of that research. However, we caution the reader to be careful about generalizing findings from studies of the big house to all institutions. As we have already seen, institutions are quite diverse.

INMATE SOCIETY

total institution An institutional setting in which persons sharing some characteristics are cut off from the wider society and expected to live according to institutional rules and procedures.

In his classic book *Asylums*, sociologist Erving Goffman described prisons as total institutions. Goffman defined a **total institution** as "a place of residence and work where a large number of like-situated individuals, cut off from the wider society for an appreciable period of time, together lead an enclosed, formally administered round of life."[1] As already pointed out and as further implied by Goffman's definition, a prison represents a miniature, self-contained society.

Although prisons are certainly influenced by the outside world,[2] they are also separated and closed off from that world. A society of prisoners, like any society, possesses distinctive cultural features (values, norms, and roles), and because prisoners do not serve their time completely isolated from other inmates, the features of the inmate society influence the way prisoners adjust to prison life.

convict code A constellation of values, norms, and roles that regulate the way inmates interact with one another and with prison staff.

Central to the inmate society of traditional men's prisons in the United States is the convict code. The **convict code** is a constellation of values, norms, and roles that regulate the way inmates interact with one another and with prison staff. For example, a principle of the convict code is that individual inmates should mind their own affairs and do their own time. Other principles are that inmates should not inform the staff about the illicit activities of other prisoners and that inmates' overall attitude and behavior should be indifferent to the staff and loyal to other convicts. Conning and manipulation skills are highly valued under the code, as is the ability to show strength, courage, and toughness.

Two major theories of the origins of the inmate society have been advanced: the deprivation model and the importation model. Advocates of the **deprivation model** (sometimes called the "indigenous origins model") contend that the inmate society arises in response to the prison environment and the painful conditions of confinement.[3] Specifically, imprisonment deprives inmates of such things as material possessions, social acceptance, heterosexual relations, personal security, and liberty. This environment of shared deprivation gives inmates a basis for solidarity. The inmate society and its convict code represent a functional, collective adaptation of inmates to this environment. When an inmate enters prison for the first time, the inmate is socialized into the customs and principles of the inmate society, a process former correctional officer Donald Clemmer termed **prisonization.**[4] Clemmer believed that the longer inmates stayed in prison, the more "prisonized" they became and the more likely they were to return to crime after their release from prison.

An alternative to the deprivation model is the **importation model,** which holds that the inmate society is shaped by factors external to the prison environment—specifically, the preprison experiences and socialization patterns that inmates bring with them when they enter prison.[5] For example, inmates who were thieves and persistently associated with other thieves before going to prison bring the norms and values of thieves into the prison. They will remain more loyal to those norms and values than to the staff while incarcerated. However, if an inmate primarily conformed to the law before entering prison, the inmate will probably exhibit greater loyalty to staff norms once in prison. In short, the deprivation model assumes that new inmates are socialized into the existing inmate society, which arises in response to the prison environment; the importation model suggests that the inmate society is the product of the socialization inmates experience before entering prison.

The deprivation and importation models were developed from studies of prisons of the pre-1960s era. Some scholars believe that the image of a fairly

deprivation model A theory that the inmate society arises as a response to the prison environment and the painful conditions of confinement.

prisonization The process by which an inmate becomes socialized into the customs and principles of the inmate society.

importation model A theory that the inmate society is shaped by the attributes inmates bring with them when they enter prison.

Conflict builds when inmates form competing gangs along ethnic, racial, and geographic lines. *Why do inmates form gangs in prison?*

unified inmate society with an overarching convict code fails to characterize many of today's crowded and violent prisons. According to those scholars, several factors have rendered the inmate society fragmented, disorganized, and unstable:

1. Increasing racial heterogeneity
2. The racial polarization of modern prisoners
3. Court litigation
4. The rise and fall of rehabilitation
5. The increased politicalization of inmates

The order and stability provided by the old inmate subculture have been replaced by an atmosphere of conflict and tension, in which inmates align themselves into competing gangs (such as the Aryan Brotherhood, the Mexican Mafia, and the Black Guerrilla Family) and other inmate organizations (such as the Lifer's Club and the Muslims).[6]

Violence and Victimization It is generally agreed that there is more physical violence by inmates in today's men's prisons than there was in earlier periods. In recent years, thousands of inmates and staff have been assaulted. In 2006, for example, 55 inmates and at least one staff member were killed by inmates in state prisons.[7] There is also consensus that staff violence against inmates is less common today. However, the number of inmates killed by staff in the last few years is unknown.

Commonly cited reasons for high rates of prison violence include improper management and classification practices by staff, high levels of crowding and competition over resources, the young age of most inmates in many prisons, and increases in racial tensions and prison gang activity. Although gang and racial conflicts surely play a role, it seems unlikely that the bulk of prison violence is extensively planned or gang-orchestrated. One reason is that many prisons across the United States lack well-developed gang structures and serious gang problems, but they are still plagued by violence. Furthermore, what

FYI Attica Prison Riot

The deadliest prison riot in the nation's history occurred at the Attica Correctional Facility in upstate New York in September 1971. The uprising began when inmates took over one of the prison yards, and held 49 guards hostage, demanding better living conditions within the facility. It ended 4 days later after state troopers, under orders from then-Governor Nelson Rockefeller, raided the prison, sparking violence that left 11 guards and 32 prisoners dead and more than 80 others wounded. On February 15, 2000, a U.S. District Court judge approved a settlement under which New York State, without admitting wrongdoing or liability, would pay $8 million to 1,280 inmates who were abused by law enforcement officials during the riot. The agreement concluded a long-stalled $2.8 billion class action lawsuit originally filed against prison and state officials in 1974.

Source: "$8 Million Award Ends Attica Prison Suit," *Facts on File: World News Digest with Index*, No. 3097 (April 13, 2000), p. 248.

Prison violence and disorder generally result spontaneously from particular circumstances. *What are some of those circumstances?*

we know about violent crime in general suggests that much prison violence is probably spontaneous, motivated by particular circumstances. Some common perpetrator motives for physical violence in prison are to (1) demonstrate power and dominance over others; (2) retaliate against a perceived wrong, such as the failure of another inmate to pay a gambling debt; and (3) prevent the perpetrator from being victimized (for example, raped) in the future.

A good deal of prison violence—but not all—has sexual overtones. Note that not all instances of sex in prison are violent, that not all instances are homosexual in nature, and that sexual encounters can involve both inmates and staff. Instances of prison sex can be further divided into three basic categories: (1) consensual sex for gratification, (2) prostitution, and (3) sexual assault. The third category obviously involves violence, and the first two sometimes have indirect links to violence. For example, a consensual sexual relationship between two inmates may have started out as a forced one. Likewise, an inmate who is vulnerable to sexual assault may perform sexual favors for an aggressive, well-respected prisoner in exchange for protection from other inmates. In the language of the prison, such vulnerable inmates are known as "punks." Prison sexual encounters can be intraracial or interracial; however, sexual assaults are more often interracial than intraracial.

In 2007, the first annual self-report sexual victimization survey was completed, as required by The Prison Rape Elimination Act of 2003. The survey of a sample of inmates in both state and federal prisons revealed that about 60,500 inmates, or 4.5% of the nation's prisoners, experienced sexual victimization. Sexual victimization was defined as "all types of sexual activity—for example, oral, anal, or vaginal penetration, handjobs, touching of the inmate's butt, thighs, penis, breasts, or vagina in a sexual way and other sexual acts." It included "nonconsensual sexual acts, abusive sexual contacts, and both willing and unwilling sexual activity with staff." The data showed that about 2.1% of inmates reported sexual victimization involving another inmate, 2.9% reported sexual victimization involving staff, and about 0.5% of inmates had been victimized by both other inmates and staff. Inmates were also asked the number of times they had experienced each type of sexual victimization from which rates were calculated. Nationwide, 123 incidents of sexual victimization per 1,000 inmates were reported, which included 49 incidents of inmate-on-inmate sexual acts per 1,000 inmates and 75 incidents of unwilling sex with staff per 1,000 inmates. The rates excluded unwanted touching by other inmates and willing sexual contacts with staff.[8]

Physical victimization is not the only or even the most frequent kind of victimization that takes place in prison. Sociologist Lee Bowker identifies three other kinds: economic, psychological, and social.[9] As with physical victimization, these three kinds may be perpetrated by inmates against other inmates, by inmates against staff, or by staff against inmates. In addition, the four kinds of victimization are interrelated: combinations can occur, and one can lead to another.

All societies have an economy, and most have a black-market component. The inmate society is no exception. The **sub-rosa** (secret or underground) **economy** of an institution consists of the exchange of goods and services that, although

Prostitution is part of prison culture in many institutions. *Why do some prisoners prostitute themselves?*

sub-rosa economy The secret exchange of goods and services among inmates; the black market of the prison.

often illicit, are in high demand among inmates. Examples of such goods and services include food, clothes, alcohol and other drugs, pornography, weapons, loan services, protection, sex, and gambling. Engaging in illicit economic exchanges is commonly referred to as "playing the rackets" or "hustling." Cigarettes often serve as the medium of exchange, because currency is typically contraband. The money inmates earn from prison work is usually maintained in accounts from which they may deduct only specified amounts for specified purposes. Hence, packs and cartons of cigarettes assume the symbolic value of money in the sub-rosa economy. However, currency may also be used. Like any kind of contraband (drugs, for example), currency can enter the institution via mail, visits, or staff.

One of the newest forms of prison contraband are cell phones, which have been used in escapes, arranging drug deals, kidnappings, and murders. Hundreds of illegal cell phones have been confiscated every year. In 2008, South Carolina prison officials confiscated 1,800 cell phones or components, which are smuggled into prisons despite metal detectors and X-ray machines. Some phones have been thrown over prison fences, including one incident where someone threw a football loaded with phones into the prison yard. Prison officials are lobbying the Federal Communications Commission to change current regulations that ban cell phone signal jamming technology in state prisons. New technology can "surgically" control jamming so that it affects only the reception of phones within specific areas of the prison. The cost of the jamming solution is about $100,000 for a 1,000-inmate institution.[10] A prison's sub-rosa economy is a major concern to prison officials because it sets the stage for various types of economic victimization, including theft, robbery, fraud, extortion, loan-sharking, and price-fixing by gangs and cliques.

Psychological victimization consists of subtle manipulation tactics and mind games that occur frequently in prison. For example, a staff member may obtain sensitive confidential information from an inmate's file and proceed to "mess" with the inmate's mind by threatening to convey the information to other inmates. Likewise, an inmate may threaten to convey to superiors some instance of a staff member's corruption or failure to follow procedure. Examples of psychological victimization are numerous. Combined with the crowded and noisy living conditions, separation from the outside world, and the threats to physical safety, psychological victimization contributes significantly to the stress of the prison environment. It is small wonder that many prisoners suffer from a host of psychological maladaptations, such as fear, paranoia, excess anxiety, depression, anger, and lack of trust in others.

Social victimization involves prejudice or discrimination against a person because of some social characteristic that person has. The social characteristic may be race, age, class background, religious preference, political position, or another factor. For example, racial segregation and discrimination against minorities was official policy in many prisons until the 1960s. Following the desegregation movement in the wider society, prisons, too, have become more racially integrated. Today, the segregation that remains is typically voluntary on the part of inmates.

Inmate Coping and Adjustment Living in prison is fundamentally different from living in the free community. In prison, for example, deprivation of personal freedom and material goods is much more pronounced. There is less privacy, there is more competition for scarce resources, and life is typified by greater insecurity, stress, and unpredictability. Moreover, prison life may encourage qualities counter to those required for functioning effectively in the free community. Criminologist Ann Cordilia, expanding on the work of Erving Goffman, argues that prisons "desocialize" and alienate inmates by discouraging personal responsibility and independence, creating excessive dependency on authority, and diminishing personal control over life events.[11] One result is what Goffman called *self-mortification,* a subduing or deadening of self-identity and self-determination.[12]

Therefore, a person coming from the free community into prison must learn to cope with and adjust to the institutional environment. Building on the ideas of criminologist Hans Toch,[13] criminologist Robert Johnson identifies two broad ways that inmates cope with imprisonment.[14] Some inmates enter what Johnson describes as the public domain of prison culture. Predatory, violent convicts, many of whom have lengthy prior records of incarceration (that is, are "state-raised youths") dominate this domain. Those convicts seek power and status in the prison world by dominating and victimizing others. Johnson claims that most inmates do not enter the public domain and live by its norms. Instead, most enter the prison's private culture. To understand this method of coping and adjustment, we must realize that each inmate brings a unique combination of personal needs into prison. That is, inmates vary in their needs for such things as privacy, environmental stimulation, safety, and emotional feedback. Entering the private culture of the prison means finding in the diverse environment of the institution a niche that will accommodate the inmate's unique combination of needs. For example, an inmate who has strong needs for privacy, safety, and intellectual stimulation may arrange to have a job in the prison library. The library becomes the inmate's niche. The private domain of prison culture consists of many diverse niches.

From another perspective, criminologist John Irwin suggests that in coping and adjusting to prison, an inmate will develop a prison career or lifestyle.[15] Three such lifestyles are "doing time," "jailing," and "gleaning." Inmates who adopt the "doing time" lifestyle are primarily concerned with getting out of prison as soon as possible and avoiding hard time in the process. Avoiding hard time means maximizing comfort and minimizing discomfort in a way that does not threaten to extend the sentence or place the inmate in danger. Inmates with lengthy prior records of incarceration, who are more accustomed to life in an institution than life outside one, often embrace the "jailing" lifestyle.

Inmates develop a variety of coping mechanisms in prison. *If you were in prison, how would you cope?*

Those inmates are concerned with achieving positions of influence in the inmate society; prison is their world. "Gleaning" entails trying to take advantage of the resources available for personal betterment, such as obtaining marketable vocational skills. The idea is to prepare for life after release. Relatively few inmates adopt the gleaning lifestyle.

LIFE IN WOMEN'S PRISONS

Life in women's prisons is similar to life in men's prisons in some respects, but there are also important differences. For example, both female and male inmates must cope with the deprivations, stress, depersonalization, and authoritarian atmosphere of prison life. However, women's prisons are usually not characterized by the levels of violence, interpersonal conflict, and interracial tension found in men's institutions. Nor is the antistaff mentality of male prisoners as common among female inmates. Consequently, the environments of women's institutions are often less oppressive.

Those observations should not be taken to mean that female inmates generally do easier time than male inmates. Indeed, it has been suggested that women experience imprisonment more negatively than men.[16] A major reason for this is separation from friends and family.[17] Female inmates are more likely than male inmates to have children and to have been living with those children immediately before incarceration. In recent years, for example, about 65% of female state prisoners had children under 18 years old, and about the same percentage of those women lived with their children before incarceration.[18]

Procedures for determining the custodial relationship between a female inmate and her child vary widely. In some cases, very young children of incarcerated women may live with their mothers in prison for a temporary period. In other cases, maternal custody might be terminated. The procedure depends on the jurisdiction and the particular circumstances. A common arrangement is for children to reside with their fathers, grandparents, or other relatives or friends during the period of incarceration. Visitation is often irregular or nonexistent, and the amount of visitation is dictated by institutional rules and the geographic distance between children and their mothers.[19]

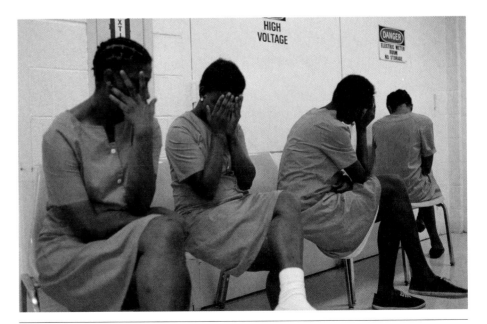

Female inmates are an increasing part of the nation's prison population. *Why?*

Many women in prison are mothers or mothers-to-be, and the restrictions imprisonment imposes on them as they try to maintain relationships with their children affect their physical and emotional well-being. *How could the stress of a prison mother's parent/child relationship be reduced?*

Pseudofamilies and Homosexuality A distinguishing feature of the inmate society in many women's prisons is the presence of make-believe families, known as pseudofamilies. Studies have discovered that some female inmates adopt family roles, such as mother, daughter, sister, husband, and father to form kinship networks.[20] The number of inmates who adopt masculine roles, known as "butches," appears to be small in comparison with the number who take on feminine roles.[21] Furthermore, kinship ties may cut across racial lines, reflecting that race is not the divisive factor in women's prisons that it is in men's institutions. Pseudofamily structures are central to inmate society in women's prisons, providing social interaction and emotional support. Sociologist Rose Giallombardo suggests that pseudofamilies provide imprisoned women with the family affiliation and bonding that they have been socialized to desire but have been deprived of by incarceration.[22]

Family activity and homosexual activity appear to be relatively independent of one another. A female prisoner who is involved in homosexuality may or may not be part of a family. Likewise, a female prisoner who is part of a make-believe family may or may not be involved in homosexuality. If she is, she may be having homosexual relations with someone who is part of the family or with someone who is not. The number of female prisoners who take part in family activities probably exceeds the number who participate in homosexuality. In addition, the majority of female inmates who participate in homosexuality are what sociologists David Ward and Gene Kassebaum call "turnouts," those who were heterosexual before incarceration and will return to heterosexuality upon release.[23] As in men's prisons, interracial homosexuality is quite common, but in contrast to men's prisons, the overwhelming majority of homosexual activity in women's institutions is consensual and is rooted in affection and attachment instead of dominance motives.

Inmate Roles Social scientist Esther Heffernan identified three roles that women commonly adopt when adjusting to prison. Heffernan's roles are very

MYTH

Virtually all female prisoners are lesbians.

FACT

Although there are no totally reliable data on the proportion of female inmates who engage in homosexuality while incarcerated, a reasonable estimate (based on the literature) is approximately half. This proportion is comparable to the proportion of male prisoners who do so.

similar to roles identified by sociologist Clarence Schrag in his work on male inmates.[24] The "square" role is adopted by women who were primarily noncriminals before coming to prison, and those women tend toward conventional behavior in prison. The square role discussed by Heffernan corresponds to the "square john" role identified by Schrag. Heffernan's "life" role is analogous to Schrag's "right guy" role. Inmates who assume the life role were habitual offenders before coming to prison, and they continue to adhere to antisocial and antiauthority norms in prison. Sophisticated professional criminals occupy the "cool" role, or what Schrag referred to as the "con politician." They try to do easy time by manipulating other inmates and the staff to their own advantage.

THINKING CRITICALLY

1. In comparison to male prisons, why do you think that there is less violence, interpersonal conflict, and interracial tension in women's prisons?

2. Should very young children of incarcerated women be allowed to temporarily live with their mothers in prison? Why or why not?

Correctional Officers

In 1976, criminologist Gordon Hawkins wrote, "It is in fact remarkable how little serious attention has been paid to prison officers in the quite extensive literature on prisons and imprisonment."[25] Although it has increased steadily since, research on prison staff remains sparse compared with research on inmates. Most studies of prison staff have concentrated on guards or correctional officers, and there is good reason for this. Correctional officers represent the majority of staff members in a prison, are responsible for the security of the institution, and have the most frequent and closest contact with inmates. Yet correctional officers should not be thought of as existing in isolation from the larger structure of the prison bureaucracy discussed in the last chapter.

As of September 30, 2007, there were about 460,000 employees of adult correctional agencies in the United States, an increase of about 8% from the same date in 2005.[26] Of those more than 400,000 employees, approximately 250,000 (about 54%) were uniformed staff, a decrease of about 6% from 2005. (The percentage of uniformed or custody staff in the Federal Bureau of Prisons was about 50%.) Uniformed staff consists of all correctional security staff, including majors, captains, lieutenants, sergeants, and officers. (The BOP does not use all of those designations.) Most of the uniformed staff were correctional officers.

About 92% of both uniformed staff and correctional officers were employed by state agencies. About 73% of uniformed staff, including correctional officers, were male, about 65% were white, 26% were black, 6% were Hispanic, and 3% were other. The average ratio of correctional officers to inmates across the states in 2007 was one officer for every 6.21 inmates (down from 6.6 in 2005), and the average ratio in federal prisons was one correctional officer for every 8.5 inmates (down from 10 in 2004). California had the highest ratio: 1 officer for every 26.25 inmates, and Vermont had the lowest ratio: 1 officer for every 2.61 inmates.[27]

In 2007, starting salaries for entry-level state correctional officers ranged from $18,356 in Louisiana to $45,549 in New Jersey. Salaries were subject to increases after completion of preservice training and a probationary period. The starting salary for entry-level federal correctional officers in 2008 was $25,093 plus a locality supplement for some areas.[28] In 2007, the turnover rate for correctional security staff in state facilities was 16.9%; the rate for correctional security staff in federal facilities was 6.3%. Maine had the highest turnover rate at 60%, and Rhode Island had the lowest turnover rate at 3.7%.[29]

Correctional officers face a number of conflicts in their work. Criminologists Richard Hawkins and Geoffrey Alpert observe that the job is characterized by both boredom and stimulus overload; officers assigned to the towers may experience the former, whereas officers assigned to work the cell blocks may experience the latter.[30] Much also has been written about the role ambiguity and role strain resulting from conflict between custody and treatment objectives. How does an officer supervise and discipline inmates and at the same time attempt to counsel and help them? Traditionally, the role of guards was clearer and less ambiguous; they were responsible for custody. With the advent of rehabilitation, guards became correctional officers, and the custodial role grew clouded with treatment considerations. In addition, a series of court decisions has given many officers the perception that they have lost power while inmates have gained it.[31] Officers generally have considerable discretion in discharging their duties within the constraints of rules, regulations, and policies. Yet, because they lack clear and specific guidelines on how to exercise their discretion, they feel vulnerable to second-guessing by their superiors and the courts.

A correctional officer's custodial role is of primary importance. *Why?*

A popular misconception has been that officers manage inmates with an iron fist and are therefore corrupted by the power they have over inmates. However, as sociologist Greshan Sykes realized, the limits on an officer's power may be the real source of corruption.[32] Although their formal role places them in a superior position over inmates, officers must still obtain a measure of voluntary compliance from inmates. In the modern prison, it is impossible to rely exclusively on force to gain compliance if bureaucratic inefficiency, mass inmate rebellion, and court litigation are to be avoided. Moreover, because of the nature of the prison environment, officers do not have many incentives they can use to solicit compliance, and they do not directly control many of the main rewards, such as release date. Still, officers' performances are often judged by how smoothly the officers interact with inmates and get inmates to go along with their wishes. Consequently, many officers seek inmate compliance through informal negotiation and exchange, and this practice can promote corruption. For example, an officer may gain compliance by becoming friendly with particular inmates, by granting inmates concessions in exchange for their cooperation, and by overlooking certain rule infractions in exchange for compliance with other rules. A study of a federal prison by criminologist John Hewitt and his colleagues found that inmates reported committing, and officers reported observing, far more prison rule infractions than were documented in the institution's official disciplinary files.[33]

How do correctional officers respond to their roles and their work conditions? According to Hawkins and Alpert, some officers become alienated and cynical and withdraw from their work. Withdrawal can be figurative: an officer may minimize his or her commitment to the job and may establish a safe and comfortable niche in the prison, such as prolonged tower duty. Withdrawal can also be literal: turnover and absenteeism are high in many prison systems. Other officers become overly authoritarian and confrontational in a quest to control inmates by intimidation. Those officers put up a tough facade similar to that displayed by some inmates. Still other officers respond by becoming

Careers in Criminal Justice

Correctional Sergeant

My name is Pietro DeSantis II, and I am a correctional sergeant employed by the California Department of Corrections, assigned to the California Correctional Center (CCC) in Susanville, California. I have an Associate of Science degree from Lassen Community College in Susanville. I began my career as a correctional officer with the department in November 1986 and was promoted to sergeant in February 1996. During my tenure with corrections I have also been chapter president and board member of the California Correctional Peace Officer Association and commissioner and curriculum review committee chair of the Correctional Peace Officer Standards and Training (CPOST) Commission.

A normal workday starts as soon as you arrive on grounds and start talking to staff that are either beginning or ending their shift. Normal shifts at CCC are first watch (2200–0600 hours), second watch (0600–1400 hours), and third watch (1400–2200 hours). A normal day on all three watches starts with a security check of our safety equipment and security locks. First watch staff normally read the incoming and outgoing mail, count the inmate population three times, and ensure workers for the culinary service are awake and report to work. Second watch staff normally feed breakfast and lunch to the inmates and supervise the inmate workers who clean the living quarters, inner perimeter yard areas, and the outside grounds. Third watch staff normally deliver the mail, count the inmates twice, feed them dinner, and house new arrivals from the transportation buses. As a sergeant, I could be assigned to supervise an office or unit with between zero and 40 correctional officers.

Before entering into a career within corrections, I strongly suggest you do everything possible to become an effective communicator.

Why do you think it is important for a correctional officer to be an effective communicator?

---

corrupt (for example, selling drugs to inmates in response to a low salary).[34] Finally, a number of officers respond by adopting a human-services orientation toward their work.[35] Those officers seek to make prison a constructive place for themselves and for inmates. They try to deliver goods and services to inmates in a regular and responsive manner, to advocate and make referrals on behalf of inmates when appropriate, and to assist inmates in coping with prison by providing protection and counseling.

Efforts are under way to transform prison work from a mere job into a profession, but a number of problems and issues surround those efforts. First, factors such as low pay, the nature and prestige of the work, and the remote location of many prisons make recruitment of new officers difficult in some jurisdictions. Some people take prison work simply because they believe that nothing better is currently available, with the intent of leaving as soon as a better job opens. Guards at the Federal Bureau of Prisons' supermax facility in Florence, Colorado—the nation's most secure prison reserved for "the worst of the worst"—have been complaining recently about staffing levels that are perilously low because of budget cutting. Officers contend that inmates are getting angrier and threats and assaults are becoming more frequent. As of August 2006, only 186 of the 221 correctional officer positions allocated to the supermax prison were filled, while the prison with 490 beds held 460 inmates. An arbitrator hearing the guards' complaints reported that staffing is so low that some cell blocks have been left unstaffed, cells are not being searched regularly, and job hazards have increased. In 2005, two inmates were beaten to death by other prisoners—the first killings in supermax history. Between March 2004 and March 2005, incident reports revealed 55 threats against staff members. The number of such threats doubled between March 2005 and March 2006. Assaults against staff went from 30 to 38 during the same time periods.[36] Although rates of inmate assaults on prison staff have been increasing generally, the likelihood of an individual staff member's being the victim of an inmate assault, especially a lethal assault, remains fairly low. The assault of staff by inmates is a serious problem and is always a threat in prison, but the risks should not be exaggerated. Second, the general lack of competition for prison jobs in many jurisdictions makes it difficult to impose restrictive criteria

Table 11.1 Percentage of Correctional Training Programs with
            Particular Program Components

Administration	92%	Inmate programs	86
Chemical agents	86	Organizational/prison culture	
Communicable diseases	98	assessment	70
Communications	98	Race relations	78
Conflict resolution	90	Report writing	98
CPR	94	Security devices	94
Crisis management	90	Self-defense	96
Diversity training	96	Sexual misconduct prevention: staff	96
Ethics	98	Sexual misconduct prevention:	
Firearms	86	inmates	98
Fire/safety	92	Spanish	14
First aid	96	Special inmate populations	78
Hostages	92	Stress reduction	76
Inmate classification	92	Substance abuse awareness	80
Inmate gangs	96	Suicide awareness	98
Inmate health care	78	Transportation	92
Inmate management	96	Use of force	100
Inmate manipulations	96	Working with female inmates	74
Inmate mental health	98	Workplace violence	74

Source: American Correctional Association, *Corrections Compendium* (Lanham, MD: American Correctional Association,
July/August 2008), calculated from pp. 15–19, Table 2, Parts A & B.

for choosing among applicants. Most states require that applicants be of a
certain age (18 or 21) and have completed high school or the GED. Some states
have additional requirements, such as no prior felony convictions, related work
experience, and the passing of certain tests. Third, in some jurisdictions, a
backlash against affirmative action—which has increased female and minority
representation among correctional officers—has resulted in tensions between
the genders and races[37] and resentment by some white male officers. In jurisdictions where this backlash has occurred, efforts toward professionalization
have been hampered. Fourth, once officers have been recruited and hired, they
need to be trained, and the move toward professionalization has been accompanied by increased attention to training. Officers are usually trained at the
outset of their jobs and then receive annual training thereafter. At present,
however, training standards are not uniform across or even within jurisdictions. For example, at least 70% of agencies require a minimum of 200 hours
of coursework during initial training sessions; Florida, New Jersey, and Utah
require more than 500 hours; and California and Michigan require 640 hours.[38]
(See Table 11.1 for the components of correctional training programs.) Still,
when turnover rates are high, training costs are high and training may start to
be viewed as a waste of money and time. Fifth, professionalization has been
accompanied by increased unionism among officers. As of 2007, only Arkansas,
the District of Columbia, Georgia, Idaho, Indiana, North Carolina, Oklahoma,
South Carolina, South Dakota, and Tennessee reported that unions were not
part of their correctional systems.[39] Although guard unions can help improve
pay levels, job benefits, and work conditions, unions can also divide the superior
and subordinate ranks. In addition, most guard unions have a very limited ability to engage in collective bargaining because strikes are commonly illegal.

THINKING CRITICALLY

1. What do you think could be done to further professionalize corrections work?

2. What are some ways you can think of to add selectivity to correctional worker recruitment?

Inmate Rights and Prison Reform

Over the past four decades, the major means of reforming prisons has been court intervention. Until the middle of the twentieth century, the courts followed a **hands-off philosophy** toward prison matters. Under this hands-off philosophy, court officials were reluctant to hear prisoners' claims regarding their rights while they were incarcerated. Among other considerations, court officials questioned whether they had the necessary expertise to evaluate prison administration, and judges did not want to undermine the power of prison authorities. As a consequence of this inaction, prisoners, for all practical purposes, had no civil rights. (Remember that civil rights are those rights an individual possesses as a member of the state, especially those guaranteed against encroachment by the government.) This situation began to change as progress was made in civil rights in the wider society. Inmates were first granted rights of access to the courts, and the courts subsequently turned their attention to other rights.

hands-off philosophy A philosophy under which courts are reluctant to hear prisoners' claims regarding their rights while incarcerated.

ACCESS TO THE COURTS AND LEGAL SERVICES

Ordinarily, prisoners want to get their cases into the federal courts because they perceive those courts as more receptive to their claims than state courts. In its 1941 landmark ruling in *Ex parte Hull,* the U.S. Supreme Court granted inmates the right of unrestricted access to the federal courts. Just 3 years later (in *Coffin* v. *Reichard*, 6th Cir., 1944), a federal circuit court held that prisoners may challenge in federal court not only the fact of their confinement but also the conditions under which they are confined. But the most important U.S. Supreme Court ruling in this area (*Cooper* v. *Pate*) did not occur until 1964, when Thomas Cooper, a Stateville inmate, first successfully used Section 1983 of the Federal Civil Rights Act of 1871 to challenge the conditions of confinement. Prior to the ruling in *Cooper,* inmates had relied primarily on *habeas corpus* petitions to obtain access to the federal courts. **Habeas corpus** is a court order requiring that a confined person be brought to court so that his or her claims can be heard. For various technical reasons, it has normally been easier for prisoners to win federal cases under Section 1983 than under *habeas corpus.* In effect, then, the *Cooper* decision launched the prisoners' rights movement by opening the door to a flood of Section 1983 claims from prisoners. Calling *Cooper* v. *Pate* "the Supreme Court's first modern prisoners' rights case," law professor James Jacobs writes:

habeas corpus A court order requiring that a confined person be brought to court so that his or her claims can be heard.

> But for the prisoners' movement it was not the breadth of the decision that mattered but the Supreme Court's determination that prisoners have constitutional rights; prison officials were not free to do with prisoners as they pleased. And the federal courts were permitted, indeed obligated, to provide a forum where prisoners could challenge and confront prison officials. Whatever the outcome of such confrontations, they spelled the end of the authoritarian regime in American penology.[40]

However, by the 1990s, Congress had become exasperated with the flood of claims by prisoners challenging their conditions of confinement in the federal courts. In response, it passed the Prison Litigation Reform Act (PLRA) of 1995.[41] The intent of the legislation was to restrict and discourage litigation by prison inmates. The PLRA mandates that prisoners must exhaust all available prison administrative remedies, that is, prison grievance procedures, before they can bring lawsuits in federal court challenging prison conditions. If all administrative remedies are not exhausted, that is, pursued to their conclusion, then the federal courts are obligated to dismiss the lawsuits. The PLRA applies to civil actions arising under federal law that challenge conditions of confinement or the effects of actions by government officials on the lives of prison inmates. It does not apply to *habeas corpus* proceedings that

Inmates are entitled to adequate law library facilities. *Why do inmates have this right and should they?*

challenge the fact or duration of prison confinement. The act also restricts the relief that courts may grant in successful lawsuits. Relief to correct the violation cannot extend any further than the particular plaintiff or plaintiffs that filed the lawsuit. Any relief that is granted must be narrowly drawn, extending no further than necessary to correct the violation of the federal right. It must also be the least intrusive means necessary to correct the violation. In granting relief, the court must give substantial weight to any adverse impact on public safety or the operation of a criminal justice system the relief may cause. The court is not authorized, in exercising its remedial powers, to order the construction of prisons or the raising of taxes. In 2007, state and federal prison inmates filed 53,945 petitions in federal district courts seeking release from prison (*habeas corpus;* 42%) alleging civil rights violations (31%), or complaining of prison conditions (14%). This was nearly 14% fewer petitions than were filed in 1997, even though the prison population had increased by about 32% during that period.[42]

To get their cases to court, prisoners need access to legal materials, and many of them need legal assistance from persons skilled in law. The U.S. Supreme Court has recognized those facts. In *Johnson* v. *Avery* (1969), the Court held that inmates skilled in legal matters (so-called **jailhouse lawyers**) must be permitted to assist other inmates in preparing cases unless the government provides a reasonable alternative. Furthermore, in *Bounds* v. *Smith* (1977), the U.S. Supreme Court ruled that inmates are entitled to either an adequate law library or adequate legal assistance. So if a correctional institution does not wish to allow a jailhouse-lawyer system and does not wish to provide adequate library facilities for inmates, the implication is that the correctional institution should allow inmates to consult with licensed attorneys to obtain legal assistance.

jailhouse lawyers Inmates skilled in legal matters.

PROCEDURAL DUE PROCESS IN PRISON

In the last chapter, we noted that inmates can face disciplinary action for breaking prison rules. The U.S. Supreme Court has moved to ensure that inmates receive minimal elements of due process during the disciplinary process.

CJ Online

The Fortune Society

The Fortune Society is a not-for-profit community-based organization staffed mostly by ex-offenders. The organization is dedicated to educating the public about prisons and prison life, criminal justice issues, and the root causes of crime. You can visit the website for the Fortune Society at www.fortunesociety.org. *Do you think organizations such as this one are necessary? Why or why not?*

Probably the most important case in this area is *Wolff* v. *McDonnell* (1974). In *Wolff,* the Court held that although inmates facing a loss of good time for a rule infraction are not entitled to the same due process protections as in a criminal trial, such inmates are entitled to (1) a disciplinary hearing by an impartial body, (2) 24 hours' written notice of the charges, (3) a written statement of the evidence relied on and the reasons for the disciplinary action, and (4) an opportunity to call witnesses and present documentary evidence, provided that this does not jeopardize institutional security. The Court ruled that inmates are not entitled to confront and cross-examine people who testify against them or to have legal counsel.

FIRST AMENDMENT RIGHTS

The First Amendment to the Constitution guarantees freedom of speech, press, assembly, petition, and religion. The U.S. Supreme Court has rendered numerous decisions affecting prisoners' rights to freedom of speech and expression and freedom of religion.

Free Speech The significant case of *Procunier* v. *Martinez* (1974) dealt with censorship of prisoners' outgoing mail but is generally regarded as applicable to other aspects of correspondence and expression. In *Procunier,* the Supreme Court ruled that censorship is legal only if it furthers one or more of the following substantial government interests: security, order, and rehabilitation. Moreover, the degree of censorship can be no greater than that required to preserve the government interest in question.

Religious Freedom With the demise of the hands-off policy, the first substantive right won by inmates was freedom of religion, which was awarded to Black Muslims in *Cooper* v. *Pate.* As a rule, inmates are free to practice either conventional or unconventional religions in prison, and prison officials are obligated to provide accommodations. However, restrictions may be imposed, for

As a rule, inmates are free to practice their religion in prison. Religious symbols and practices that interfere with institutional security can be restricted. *Should religious practices be allowed in prisons? Why or why not?*

example, where prison officials can demonstrate convincingly that religious practices compromise security or are unreasonably expensive. Granting special religious privileges can also be denied on the grounds that they will cause other groups to make similar demands. In general, the reasons given for restricting religious freedom must be compelling, and the restrictions imposed must be no more limiting than necessary.

EIGHTH AMENDMENT RIGHTS

As described in Chapter 4, the Eighth Amendment outlaws the imposition of cruel and unusual punishment. The courts have considered a number of issues under the umbrella of cruel and unusual punishment.

Medical Care In 1976, the Supreme Court decided *Estelle* v. *Gamble*. The Court ruled that inmates, under the Eighth Amendment, have a right to adequate medical care, but that inmates claiming Eighth Amendment violations on medical grounds must demonstrate that prison officials have shown deliberate indifference to serious medical problems. Under these conservative and subjective criteria, medical services and circumstances usually have to be really bad—even extreme—for inmates to win cases. Furthermore, the deliberate-indifference standard formulated in *Estelle* now applies to Eighth Amendment challenges to any condition of confinement, medical or otherwise.[43]

Staff Brutality Ironically, the Eighth Amendment has done little to protect inmates from staff brutality because brutality is normally construed as a tort rather than a constitutional issue.[44] (Recall that a tort is the breach of a duty to an individual that results in damage to him or her. It involves only duties owed to an individual as a matter of law.) However, whipping and related forms of corporal punishment have been prohibited under this amendment. Also, in *Hudson* v. *McMillian* (1992), the Supreme Court found that staff use of force against an inmate need not cause a significant physical injury to violate the Eighth Amendment.

Despite these protections, staff brutality remains a problem. For example, a recent Human Rights Watch report revealed that policies in five U.S. state prison systems—in Connecticut, Delaware, Iowa, South Dakota, and Utah—allow guards to use aggressive, unmuzzled dogs to extract inmates from their cells when they refuse to comply with orders. Dogs are ordered to bite inmates if they resist.[45]

Total Prison Conditions Totality-of-conditions cases involve claims that some combination of prison practices and conditions (crowding, lack of services and programs, widespread brutality, and labor exploitation, for example) makes the prison, as a whole, unconstitutional under the Eighth Amendment. It is primarily in this area that the Eighth Amendment has been used. For example, in the famous case of *Holt* v. *Sarver* (1971), the entire Arkansas prison system was declared unconstitutional on grounds of totality of conditions and was ordered to implement a variety of changes. Totality-of-conditions rulings were later handed down against prisons in Alabama (*Pugh* v. *Locke,* 1976) and Texas (*Ruiz* v. *Estelle,* 1982).

FYI *Brubaker*

In *Holt* v. *Sarver* (1971), the Supreme Court ordered the reform of the Arkansas prison system. The movie *Brubaker,* starring Robert Redford, is a fictionalized account of the real story of Tom Murton, warden of Arkansas's Tucker & Cummins prison in 1967–1968. Murton's evidence was instrumental in the Supreme Court's decision. The U.S. District Court characterized the Arkansas prison as "a dark and evil world completely alien to the free world."

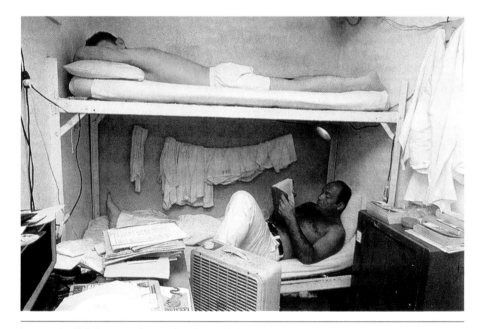

In 1981, the U.S. Supreme Court refused to hold that double-bunking in prison cells was cruel and unusual punishment. *Should double-bunking be allowed in prisons? Why or why not?*

Prisons have long had the right to provide only the minimal conditions necessary for human survival. Such conditions include the necessary food, shelter, clothing, and medical care to sustain life. Whether institutional crowding violates the Eighth Amendment is typically determined in relation to total prison conditions. Instead of being treated as a separate issue, crowding is viewed as part of the totality of conditions. The Supreme Court has been reluctant to side with inmates in their challenges to crowding. In both *Bell* v. *Wolfish* (1979) and *Rhodes* v. *Chapman* (1981), the Court refused to prohibit the placing of two inmates in cells designed for one person ("double-bunking") as a response to crowding.

Other Prison Conditions Found to Violate the Eighth Amendment Federal courts have found all of the following prison conditions to be in violation of the Eighth Amendment's prohibition of cruel and unusual punishments:

- Inadequate ventilation
- Excessive heat
- Excessive cold
- Lack of drinkable water (also lack of cold water where prison yard temperatures reached 100 degrees)
- Toxic or noxious fumes (pesticides sprayed into housing units; inadequate ventilation of toxic fumes in inmate workplaces)
- Exposure to sewage (exposure to flooding and human waste)
- Exposure to second-hand tobacco smoke (cell mates smoking five packs of cigarettes a day)
- Excessive noise
- Sleep deprivation
- Sleeping on the floor (failure to provide inmates with a mattress and bed or bunk)
- Lack of fire safety
- Risk of injury or death in the event of an earthquake
- Inadequate food or unsanitary food service
- Inadequate lighting or constant lighting
- Exposure to insects, rodents, and other vermin
- Defective plumbing
- Deprivation of basic sanitation
- Denial of adequate toilet facilities
- Exposure to asbestos (exposure to "moderate levels of asbestos" did not violate the Eighth Amendment)
- Exposure to the extreme behavior of severely mentally ill prisoners (exposure to constant screaming and feces-smearing of mentally ill prisoners "contributes to the problems of uncleanliness and sleep deprivation, and by extension mental health problems, for other inmates")
- Miscellaneous unhealthy or dangerous conditions (unsafe conditions for prisoners performing electrical work; prisoner injured in vehicle accident after transport officers refused to fasten his seat belt)[46]

FOURTEENTH AMENDMENT RIGHTS

As described in Chapter 4, the Fourteenth Amendment guarantees U.S. citizens due process of law and equal protection under law. The due process clause inspired the Supreme Court's decision in the previously discussed case of *Wolff* v. *McDonnell,* for example. Likewise, the equal-protection clause has led the Supreme Court to forbid racial discrimination (*Lee* v. *Washington,* 1968) and has led state courts to target gender discrimination (*Glover* v. *Johnson,* ED Mich., 1979). Compared with the rights of male inmates, however, the rights

 FYI Sexually Violent Predator Laws

By a 5–4 decision, in *Kansas* v. *Hendricks* (1997), the Supreme Court ruled that sexual predators judged to be dangerous may be confined indefinitely even after they finish serving their sentences. The decision allowed the state of Kansas to continue to hold an admitted pedophile, Leroy Hendricks, under the provisions of the state's Sexually Violent Predator Act. The Court's majority noted that such confinement, intended to protect society, does not violate the constitutional right to due process and is not double punishment for the same crime. At least 17 states, including Arizona, California, Minnesota, Washington, and Wisconsin, have laws similar to the Kansas Sexually Violent Predator Act.

Source: *Kansas* v. *Hendricks,* 117 S.Ct. 2072 (1997); "Court: Sex Predators Can Be Kept in Prison," *The Orlando Sentinel* (June 24, 1997), p. A-1; Roxanne Lieb and Kathy Gookin, "Involuntary Commitment of Sexually Violent Predators: Comparing State Laws." Olympia, WA: Washington State Institute for Public Policy (March 2005) at www.nicic.org/Library/020501.

of female prisoners remain underdeveloped. The inmates' rights movement has been primarily a male phenomenon, and the rights of female prisoners deserve more attention from the courts in the future.

THE LIMITS OF LITIGATION

The progress toward prison reform resulting from the inmates' rights movement should not be underestimated. Nevertheless, one can question on a number of grounds the almost exclusive reliance, during the past four decades, on court intervention to reform the nation's prisons. Perhaps the most basic and compelling argument is that the monies being spent by prison systems to defend against inmate lawsuits and to comply with court orders (when inmate suits are successful) could have been spent better to reform the unacceptable practices that sparked the suits in the first place. Meanwhile, those prison systems are unable to address problems that help generate further inmate lawsuits precisely because they are defending against new suits and trying to comply with past court orders. The result is that even more money must be spent for legal defense and compliance with court orders. This cycle is difficult to break.

Court litigation is not just an expensive way to reform prisons; it is also a very slow and piecemeal way. A high percentage of lawsuits filed by inmates are judged frivolous and are therefore dismissed. If an inmate's suit is not judged frivolous, the inmate must still win the case in court and many lose in the process. Even when inmates win a case, their success usually does not lead to wide-scale reforms. Successful, large-scale, class-action suits that have far-reaching impact on the prison system are relatively uncommon and will become more so under the Prison Litigation Reform Act of 1995. Moreover, winning a case and then getting the desired changes implemented can take many years. Prison systems do not comply automatically with court decrees. Achieving compliance with court orders often requires sustained monitoring by court-appointed officials as well as considerable negotiation and compromise by all parties involved to agree on a timetable and the specific nature of reforms. Finally, the transformation of traditional, ingrained practices in a prison system can render the prison environment chaotic and unstable, at least in the short run.

THINKING CRITICALLY

1. What do you think are legitimate complaints from prisoners?

2. What constitutional rights do you think should be extended to prisoners? Or do you think prisoners already have too many rights? Why?

Release and Recidivism

Most inmates (approximately 93%) will eventually be released from prison. The 7% of inmates who will not be released are serving death or life sentences and likely will die in prison. Figure 11.1 shows the causes of death of the 3,295 state prison inmates who died in prison in 2006. More than 80% died of illnesses other than AIDS.

Depending on the jurisdiction and the specific case, inmates may be released from prison in a number of ways. Examples include expiration of the maximum sentence allowed by law (known as "maxing out"); **commutation,** or reduction of the original sentence by executive authority; release at the discretion of a parole authority; and mandatory release. Of those ways, the two most common are release at the discretion of a parole authority and mandatory release.

The term **parole** has two basic meanings. It can refer to a way of being released from prison before the entire sentence has been served, or it can

commutation Reduction of the original sentence given by executive authority, usually a state's governor.

parole The conditional release of prisoners before they have served their full sentences.

refer to a period of community supervision following early release. We are concerned here with the former meaning. In jurisdictions that permit parole release, inmates must establish eligibility for parole. Eligibility normally requires that inmates have served a given portion of their terms minus time served in jail prior to imprisonment and minus good time. **Good time** is time subtracted from the sentence for good behavior and other meritorious activity in prison. Once eligible, an inmate submits a parole plan stipulating such things as where he or she plans to live and work upon release. The parole authority, which may consist of a board, members of the board, or a representative of the board, then considers the inmate's plan. The parole authority also considers reports from institutional staff who have worked with the inmate. The decision to grant or deny parole is announced at a parole-grant hearing. Parole will be discussed more fully in the next chapter.

Figure 11.1

Causes of State Prison Inmate Deaths, 2006 (Total = 3,295)

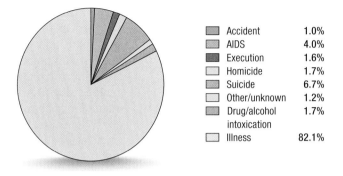

Accident	1.0%
AIDS	4.0%
Execution	1.6%
Homicide	1.7%
Suicide	6.7%
Other/unknown	1.2%
Drug/alcohol intoxication	1.7%
Illness	82.1%

Source: Calculated from data in Christopher J. Mumola and Margaret E. Noonan, "State Prison Deaths, 2001–2006," U.S. Department of Justice, Bureau of Justice Statistics at www.ojp.usdoj.gov/bjs/dcrp/tables/dcst06spt1.htm#top (last revised June 30, 2008). Execution data were taken from a different source.

Most offenders who receive lengthy prison terms (for example, 25 years) do not serve the entire term, and many do not even come close to doing so. The reason is the availability of parole, good time, and other mechanisms for reducing time served. Some opponents of those reductions in terms fail to understand that the mechanisms are essential to the operation of many current prison systems. Without them, many systems would be rendered dysfunctional by crowding. Additionally, without early release incentives for inmates, it would be extremely difficult to maintain order in prisons.

Mandatory release is release under the provisions of law, not at the discretion of a parole board. The inmate is released after serving his or her sentence or a legally required portion of the sentence, minus good-time credits. Mandatory release is similar to parole in that persons let out under either arrangement ordinarily receive a period of community supervision by a parole officer or the

good time Time subtracted from an inmate's sentence for good behavior and other meritorious activities in prison.

mandatory release A method of prison release under which an inmate is released after serving a legally required portion of his or her sentence, minus good-time credits.

Most parole decisions are made by administrative boards whose members are appointed by state governors. An inmate's eligibility for release on parole depends on requirements set by law and on the sentence imposed by the court. *Should parole be abolished? Why or why not? If not, how could the decision-making process be improved?*

equivalent. Their freedom from prison is conditioned on following the rules of their community supervision (for example, obeying curfew, abstaining from drug use, and maintaining gainful employment) and on avoiding criminal activity.

In 1977, approximately 72% of inmates released from state prisons were released at the discretion of parole boards; only about 6% left prison under mandatory release that year. By contrast, in 2006, 33% were released by parole boards, compared with approximately 48% who received mandatory release.[47] This shifting pattern indicates the strong emphasis placed on determinate sentencing during the 1980s and 1990s and the use of statistical guidelines to structure early-release decisions.

When inmates are released from correctional institutions, the hope is that as a result of deterrence or rehabilitation (discussed in Chapter 9), they will not return to criminal activity. Hence, we will conclude this chapter by considering **recidivism**—the return to illegal activity after release. Measuring recidivism and attributing the lack of recidivism to the influence of correctional programs are complicated by scientific methodological problems. Nevertheless, until recently, numerous studies conducted during the past couple of decades in several different jurisdictions revealed that recidivism rates, when recidivism was defined in a similar way, had remained remarkably stable.

For example, a comprehensive national study of recidivism among state prisoners conducted by U.S. Justice Department's Bureau of Justice Statistics found that 67.5% of nearly 300,000 former inmates released from prisons in 1994 had been rearrested for a new offense within 3 years of their release.[48] A similar study of inmates released in 1983 showed that 62.5% of them were rearrested within 3 years of their release.[49] Inmates in the more recent study were from Arizona, California, Delaware, Florida, Illinois, Maryland, Michigan, Minnesota, New Jersey, New York, North Carolina, Ohio, Oregon, Texas, and Virginia. The average prison sentence was about 5 years. On average, the inmates were released after serving 35% of their sentences, or about 20 months.

The study used four measures of recidivism: rearrest, reconviction, resentence to prison, and return to prison with or without a new sentence. In addition to the 67.5% of prisoners rearrested for a new offense (almost exclusively a felony or a serious misdemeanor), 46.9% were reconvicted for a new crime, 25.4% were resentenced to prison for a new crime, and 51.8% were returned to prison for a new crime (25.4%) or for a technical violation of release conditions (26.4%), such as failing a drug test or missing an appointment with their parole officer (see Figure 11.2). Not all reconvicted prisoners were sentenced to another prison term for their new offenses. Some were sentenced to confinement in a local jail or probation.

Released prisoners with the highest rearrest rates were motor vehicle thieves (78.8%), those in prison for possessing or selling stolen property (77.4%), larcenists (74.6%), burglars (74%), robbers (70.2%), and those in prison for possessing, using, or selling illegal weapons (70.2%). Released prisoners with the lowest rearrest rates were those in prison for homicide (40.7%), nonrape sexual assault (41.4%), rape (46%), and driving under the influence (51.5%). Rearrests of the released prisoners accounted for about 5% of all arrests for serious crime from 1994 to 1997. Among other notable findings:

- Men were more likely than women to be rearrested (68.4% vs. 57.6%), reconvicted (47.6% vs. 39.9%), resentenced to prison for a new crime (26.2% vs. 17.3%), and returned to prison with or without a new prison sentence (53% vs. 39.4%).
- Blacks were more likely than whites to be rearrested (72.9% vs. 62.7%), reconvicted (51.1% vs. 43.3%), resentenced to prison for a new crime (28.5% vs. 22.6%), and returned to prison with or without a new prison sentence (54.2% vs. 49.9%).

recidivism The return to illegal activity after release from incarceration.

Figure 11.2

Recidivism Rates of Prisoners Released in 1994 from Prisons in 15 States, by Time after Release

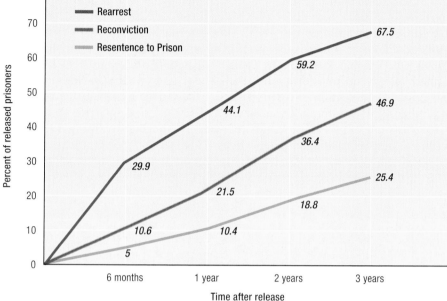

Source: Patrick A. Langan and David J. Levin, "Recidivism of Prisoners Released in 1994," U.S. Department of Justice, Bureau of Justice Statistics *Special Report* (Washington, D.C.: GPO, June 2002), p. 3.

- Non-Hispanics were more likely than Hispanics to be rearrested (71.4% vs. 64.6%), reconvicted (50.% vs. 43.9%), and returned to prison with or without a new prison sentence (57.3% vs. 51.9%). The difference between non-Hispanics and Hispanics in being resentenced to prison for a new crime was not significant.
- Younger persons were more likely to be rearrested than older persons. For example, more than 80% of those under age 18 were rearrested, while only 45.3% of those age 45 or older were rearrested.

Nearly 70% of the inmates released in 1994 had a record of violence. Seventy percent of the released inmates had five or more prior arrests (not counting the arrest that brought them to prison). Half of the inmates had two or more prior convictions (not including the conviction that resulted in their prison sentence). For 56% of the released inmates, the prison sentence they were serving when released was their first-ever sentence to prison; the other 44% had previously served time in prison.

The nearly 300,000 inmates released in 1994 had amassed 4.1 million arrest charges before their most recent imprisonment and an additional 744,000 charges within 3 years of release. A small percentage of offenders was responsible for a large number of the arrests. An estimated 6.4% of the inmates were each charged with 45 or more crimes before and after their release in 1994. About 7.6% of all released prisoners were rearrested for a new crime in a state other than the one that released them. They were charged with committing 55,760 such crimes. There was no evidence that spending more time in prison raised the recidivism rate. The evidence was mixed with regard to whether serving more time reduced recidivism. A good predictor of whether an inmate will continue to commit crimes following release is the number of times the inmate has been arrested in the past. Prisoners with longer prior records were more likely to be rearrested than prisoners with shorter prior records. As other recidivism research has shown, the first year of release is the most critical one. Nearly two-thirds of all the recidivism of the first 3 years occurred in the first year (see Figure 11.2).

The American Correctional Association recently reported 2007 data from 31 states, which suggest that recidivism rates may be declining.[50] The average recidivism rate for the 31 states was 38.3% for males and 31.4% for females, considerably lower than the 60%-plus rates of the earlier studies. Different definitions of recidivism were used (for example, rearrest, reconviction, reincarceration) but, for the most part, it appears to refer to a return to prison within 2 to 4 years. As shown in Table 11.2, in 2007, males in Alaska had the highest recidivism rate (60%) and both males and females in Wyoming had the lowest recidivism rate (8.9%). Whether these data represent the beginning of a new trend or simply an aberration will not be known for some time. Regardless, the fact that more than 3 of every 10 inmates are returned to prison within 4 years is nothing to celebrate.

Obviously, those research findings are not good news for people who believe that imprisonment can achieve large-scale deterrence of crime and

Table 11.2 Recidivism Rates of State Prisoners in 31 States, 2007

State	RECIDIVISM RATE		Number of Years Tracked
	Male	**Female**	
Alabama	28.7%	21.9%	3
Alaska	60.0	57.0	3
Arkansas	52.6	41.6	3
Colorado	50.1	47.5	3
Florida	33.5	19.7	3
Georgia	28.0 (male & female)		3
Indiana	33.0	40.1	3
Iowa	34.9	33.6	3
Louisiana	30.2	19.4	5
Maryland	48.5 (male & female)		3
Massachusetts	39.0	42.0	3
Michigan	47.0	38.9	2
Minnesota	37.0	29.0	3
Missouri	44.8	38.1	2
Montana	45.7	42.2	3
Nebraska	30.8	22.2	3
New Hampshire	42.3	34.9	3
New Jersey	32.0	22.0	3
New Mexico	44.0	34.0	3
New York	39.6	26.6	3
North Carolina	51.1	37.7	3
Ohio	40.3	26.8	3
Oklahoma	25.8	18.5	3
Pennsylvania	26.2	21.7	1
Rhode Island	48.0	40.0	2
South Carolina	34.0	22.7	3
Tennessee	45.0 (male & female)		3
Texas	28.6	21.7	3
Vermont	53.7	50.7	3
Virginia	29.7	19.3	3
Wyoming	8.9	8.9	3
Average	38.3	31.4	

Source: *American Correctional Association 2008 Directory: Adult and Juvenile Corrections Departments, Institutions, Agencies and Probation and Parole Authorities* (Lanham, MD: American Correctional Association, 2008), p. 64.

rehabilitation of criminals. More bad news for deterrence advocates comes from the research of sociologist Ben Crouch, who found that newly incarcerated offenders frequently express a preference for prison over probation sentences. Crouch explains:

> A fundamental irony emerges in our justice system. That is, the lawbreakers whom middle-class citizens are most likely to fear and want most to be locked away . . . tend to be the very offenders who view prison terms of even two or three years as easier than probation and as preferable. To the extent that these views among offenders are widespread, the contemporary demand for extensive incarceration (but often for limited terms) may foster two unwanted outcomes: less deterrence and more prisoners.[51]

Similar research by criminologist Kenneth Tunnell shows that most repeat property offenders are not threatened by the prospects of imprisonment.[52]

Unfavorable news for advocates of rehabilitation began trickling in even before the release, in 1974, of the famous Martinson report, which cast grave doubts on the ability of prisons to reform offenders.[53] In a later study, criminologist Lynne Goodstein demonstrated that the inmates who adjusted most successfully to prison had the most difficulty adjusting to life in the free community upon release. About her research, Goodstein writes:

> These findings provide a picture of the correctional institution as a place which reinforces the wrong kinds of behaviors if its goal is the successful future adjustment of its inmates. In the process of rewarding acquiescent and compliant behavior, the prison may, in fact, be reinforcing institutional dependence.[54]

Of course, some people are deterred from crime by the threat of imprisonment, and the prison experience does benefit some inmates in the way rehabilitation advocates envision. Criminologists Frank Cullen and Paul Gendreau conducted a comprehensive review of research that evaluated the effects of correctional interventions on recidivism rates.[55] They found that across studies, the correctional interventions reduced recidivism rates, on average, 10%. The most successful interventions reduced recidivism 25%. They used cognitive-behavioral treatments, targeted known predictors of crime for change, and intervened mainly with high-risk offenders. Cognitive-behavioral treatments emphasize the important role of thinking in how people feel and behave. Therapists help offenders identify the thinking that is causing their problematic feelings and behavior and then teach them how to replace those thoughts with thoughts that will lead to more desirable feelings and actions. Cullen and Gendreau also reported that punishment-oriented, correctional interventions generally had no effect on offender criminality.

We must be careful not to hold unrealistic expectations about what imprisonment can accomplish in our society. Traditionally, we have placed undue confidence in the ability of imprisonment to control crime. But imprisonment is a reactive (versus proactive) response to the social problem of crime, and crime is interwoven with other social problems, such as poverty, inequality, and racism, in our wider society. We should not expect imprisonment to resolve or control those problems.

Another impediment to the successful reintegration of released inmates is their loss of civil rights. Depending on the jurisdiction, convicted felons lose a variety of civil rights. Among the most common rights forfeited are the rights to vote, hold public office, serve on a grand or petit jury, practice a profession that requires an occupational or professional license, be a parent (termination of parental rights), and carry or possess firearms. In many states, women convicted of drug offenses may be denied welfare benefits. If convicted of a federal felony, a person is ineligible for enlistment in any of the armed services, may have public housing benefits restricted under certain circumstances, and, depending on the crime, may lose veteran benefits, including pensions and disability. A majority of jurisdictions provide a means for restoring lost rights. Some rights are restored automatically. Other rights are restored by executive or judicial proceedings that are often based on the ex-offender's demonstration that he or she has been rehabilitated. Some rights are lost permanently.[56] It is difficult enough for released prison inmates to reenter society and succeed. The loss of civil rights and the hurdles that make them difficult to restore (when they can be restored) do not make it any easier.

THINKING CRITICALLY

1. Do you think anything could be done to lower recidivism rates among offenders? If so, what?

2. In your opinion, should prisoners be allowed to reduce their time in prison through parole or good time? Why or why not?

3. Should convicted felons lose civil rights? If yes, which ones and why? If not, why not?

❈ Summary

1. Distinguish between the deprivation and importation models of inmate society.

   The deprivation model of inmate society emphasizes the role of the prison environment in shaping the inmate society. The importation model of inmate society emphasizes attributes inmates bring with them when they enter prison.

2. Explain how today's inmate society differs from those of the past.

   Compared with prisons of the past, the inmate society in today's prisons is much more fragmented and conflict-ridden. Physical, psychological, economic, and social victimization are facts of life in many contemporary institutions. Inmates must learn to cope with this state of affairs. Some do so by becoming part of the prison's violent public culture. Others carve out niches and meet their needs in the prison's private culture.

3. Identify some of the special features of life in women's prisons.

   Life in women's prisons is somewhat different from life in men's prisons. In particular, women's prisons often have less stringent security measures, are less violent, and are characterized by pseudofamily structures that help the inmates cope.

4. Describe the profile of correctional officers, and explain some of the issues that they face.

   The growing number of correctional officers who staff prisons are predominantly white and male. Correctional officers face a number of problems in their work, including low pay, work-related conflicts, and a potential for corruption. They are also subject to role conflict because of their dual objectives of custody and treatment. Some officers respond to those problems more constructively than others. Efforts are ongoing to transform prison work into a profession, and issues surrounding those efforts include recruitment and selection, the backlash against affirmative action and other hiring practices, training, and unionism.

5. Identify prisoners' rights, and relate how they were achieved.

   The main way that prisoners have gained rights during the past four decades is through intervention by the courts. Until the 1960s, inmates had minimal rights. As the hands-off policy was lifted, prisoners gained a number of important rights: greater access to the courts, easier access to legal services in prison, and improved prison disciplinary procedures. They also gained certain rights under the First, Eighth, and Fourteenth Amendments.

6. List the two most common ways that inmates are released from prison, and compare those two ways in frequency of use.

   Most inmates are released from prison at the discretion of a parole authority or under mandatory release laws. Mandatory release, a method of prison release under which an inmate is released after serving a legally required portion of his or her sentence minus good-time credits, has begun to rival parole release in frequency of use.

7. Summarize what recidivism research reveals about the success of the prison in achieving deterrence and rehabilitation.

   When inmates are released from prison, it is hoped that they will not return to crime. Studies show, however, that the rate of return to crime, or recidivism, is high. Studies also show that recidivism rates have remained fairly constant for a long time, at least until recently. Those studies call the deterrence and rehabilitation rationales into question. As a society, our expectations of what incarceration can accomplish are probably unrealistic.

❈ Key Terms

total institution 430
convict code 430
deprivation model 431
prisonization 431

importation model 431
sub-rosa economy 433
hands-off philosophy 442
habeas corpus 442

jailhouse lawyer 443
commutation 448
parole 448
good time 449

mandatory release 449
recidivism 450

❈ Review Questions

1. What did Erving Goffman mean when he wrote that prisons are *total institutions?*

2. What is the *convict code,* and why is it central to inmate society in traditional men's prisons?

3. What is *prisonization?*

4. What factors have rendered contemporary inmate society fragmented, disorganized, and unstable?

5. What are some of the reasons for high rates of prison violence?

6. What are four types of victimization that take place in prisons?

7. What are some of the general ways that inmates cope and adjust to the institutional environment, according to Johnson, Irwin, and Heffernan?

8. According to Hawkins and Alpert, what are four ways that correctional officers respond to their roles and their work conditions?

9. In *Wolff* v. *McDonnell* (1974), what rights were given to inmates facing disciplinary actions, and what rights were not extended?

10. What prison conditions are Eighth Amendment violations?

11. How has court intervention limited prison reform?

12. What civil rights can convicted felons lose in some jurisdictions?

✳ In the Field

1. **Rehabilitation Programs** Contact a local prison or jail, and arrange to investigate one or more rehabilitation programs. Obtain pertinent written material, and observe the program in operation as much as possible. Assess how successful the program is in achieving its goals. Consider these specific issues:

    a. What are the goals of the program?

    b. Are the goals of the program clearly defined in some document?

    c. Is the program administered in an effective way?

    d. Is instruction adequate?

    e. Is there adequate equipment (if applicable)?

    f. Will the skills learned in the program be important to inmates upon release?

    g. How likely are inmates to successfully complete the program?

    h. Does the program have an evaluation component that would allow officials to determine the program's success or failure?

    i. On what basis is the program's success or failure judged? After assessing the program, explain what changes, if any, you would recommend.

2. **Prison Films** Watch a video or movie about prison life. Good choices are *Murder in the First* with Kevin Bacon and Christian Slater, *The Shawshank Redemption* with Tim Robbins and Morgan Freeman, *Birdman of Alcatraz* with Burt Lancaster, *Brubaker* with Robert Redford, and *Cool Hand Luke* with Paul Newman. From what you have learned in this chapter, determine how realistic the portrayals are. Note common themes.

✳ On the Net

1. **Life in Prison** Visit the website of the North Carolina Department of Corrections at www.doc.state.nc.us/dop/CPtour/index.htm. Access "A Tour of Central Prison." Pretend you are an inmate and write an essay describing your experiences in the prison.

2. **Virtual Prison Tour** Access the Florida Department of Corrections website at www.dc.state.fl.us and take the virtual prison tour through Florida prisons. In either an oral or written presentation describe your impressions of the prison. What surprised you? What, if anything, disturbed you? What changes, if any, should be made? As an option include North Carolina's Central Prison in your description—see On the Net exercise 1.

✳ Critical Thinking Exercises

RIGHT TO VOTE

1. As of August 2005, more than 4 million Americans were denied the right to vote because they were felons or ex-felons. In 48 states and the District of Columbia, incarcerated felons were denied the right to vote (only Maine and Vermont permitted prison inmates to vote); 35 states disenfranchised felony probationers or parolees (or both); and 13 states additionally disenfranchised some or all ex-felons who completed their sentences. Regarding the latter category, Alabama, Florida, Iowa, Kentucky, Mississippi, Nevada, Virginia, and Wyoming denied the right to vote to all ex-offenders who completed their sentences; Arizona and Maryland disenfranchised recidivists; Tennessee disenfranchised ex-felons convicted prior to 1986; Washington disenfranchised ex-felons convicted prior to 1984; and Delaware disenfranchised some ex-offenders for 5 years following their release from prison.

    Each state has developed its own process of restoring voting rights to ex-offenders, but most of those processes are so cumbersome that few ex-offenders are able to take advantage of them. As a result, in the 2000 presidential election, for example, an estimated 4.7 million people (2.3% of the voting-age population) were disenfranchised by virtue of having a felony conviction on their record. Of those people disenfranchised, 13% were black men. In seven states, 25% of the black men were disenfranchised.

    A recent national opinion poll found that 80% of the public favors restoring voting rights to ex-felons, generally, while a low of 52% even favors restoring voting rights to sex offenders. Sixty percent support enfranchising felony parolees, and 66% favor enfranchising ex-felons convicted of a violent crime who have served their entire sentence.

    a. Should incarcerated felons have the right to vote? What about felony probationers or parolees? What about ex-felons who have completed their sentences? What about sex offenders who have completed their sentences? What about felons who were convicted of a violent crime and have completed their sentences? Justify your answers.

    b. If you believe that voting rights should be restored, should there be conditions? If so, what should they be?

    c. Currently, some states restore voting rights automatically; other states do so by executive or judicial action. If you believe that voting rights should be restored, what should the process entail?

INMATE ORGAN TRANSPLANTS

2. On January 3, 2003, a California prison inmate received a donor heart. He had suffered congestive heart failure the month before. The inmate was serving a 14-year sentence for robbery, and the transplant and treatment for his illness cost California taxpayers about $1 million. Medical professionals defended the transplant, saying the recipient met medical criteria. Prison officials cited a 1976 Supreme Court decision and a 1997 California ruling by the 9th U.S. Circuit Court of Appeals requiring them to meet inmate medical needs. Critics point out that, among other things, at the time of the surgery, more than 4,000 Americans were on a waiting list for heart transplants, and 700 would die that year waiting for one. The prison inmate died about a year after receiving the transplant. Prison authorities noted that he had failed to maintain rigorous medical routines following the transplant.

   a. Should prison inmates be eligible for organ transplants?
   b. Does it matter whether they can pay for them?
   c. What does the law require prison officials to do about organ transplants?
   d. Should the "less eligibility" principle apply to organ transplants? Why or why not?
   e. Should there be limits to the medical services provided to prison inmates and, if so, what should the limits be?

To access more information and resources, including study questions, chapter summaries, and links, go to: www.mhhe .com/bohm6e.

Community Corrections

Chapter Outline

Chapter Objectives

After completing this chapter, you should be able to:

1. Define community corrections, and identify the goals and responsibilities of community corrections agencies and their staffs.

2. Define probation, and summarize the research findings on recidivism rates.

3. Distinguish parole from probation.

4. Explain the functions of a parole board.

5. Describe how intermediate sanctions differ from traditional community corrections programs.

6. Explain two major concerns about intensive-supervision probation and parole (ISP).

7. Explain what day reporting centers and structured fines are.

8. Explain what home confinement and electronic monitoring are.

9. Identify the goal of halfway houses, and compare them with other community corrections programs.

10. Summarize the purposes and outcomes of temporary-release programs.

CRIME STORY

On December 3, 2008, 25-year-old Laura Garza was seen leaving a nightclub in the Chelsea neighborhood of New York City at 4 A.M. with a registered sex offender, 23-year-old Michael Mele. She was reported missing by her Brooklyn roommate because she did not return home. Garza, a native of Mexico, who had lived in Texas, was new to the city and probably was easily charmed by the good looking, smooth-talking, and wealthy Mele, who owned a Quizno's sandwich shop in Newburgh, New York, and is the son of a former high-ranking New York Police Department official who is now retired. High-tech surveillance cameras at the club showed the pair dancing, flirting, and talking for about 45 minutes. Police surmise that Mele drove Garza to his condo in Wallkill, New York, where he killed her.

continued

State police searched Mele's condo three days after Garza was reported missing. Detectives discovered blood even though Mele had scrubbed his condo with bleach, cut out a patch of hallway carpeting large enough to wrap a body in, vacuumed thoroughly, and tossed pieces of evidence in dumpsters, including a machete, a woman's shoe, and the vacuum. He said he cut out the carpet because he had spilled bleach on it. A blue piece of cloth that could have been from a woman's underpants also was found in some shrubbery near the condo. Neighbors reported Mele was acting weird and erratic.

Accompanied by his father and lawyer, Mele turned himself in to police, who held him on a probation violation for drinking alcohol at the club where he met Garza and violating his curfew. Mele was on probation for a 2007 forcible touching incident. He had a history of following young women to their cars in shopping mall parking lots, grabbing them just as they were about to get in, and then masturbating while they watched, sometimes in front of their young children. At the stationhouse, police observed that Mele had bite marks on his hands and scratches on his neck. Mele's DNA reportedly was on file with the FBI because of his sexual offenses. After he had surrendered to the police, Mele's bloodstained Lexis SUV, which was parked at his family's upstate home, was impounded. At this writing, Mele appears guilty, but Garza's body has not been found. Her family is hoping she is still alive.

If Mele is found guilty of Garza's killing, one question will beg for an answer. Why did Mele receive probation for his sex offenses? Had he been incarcerated, Laura Garza might still be alive (assuming she is not). Among the topics examined in Chapter 11 is probation, the most frequently imposed sentence in American criminal courts. In 2007, approximately 4 million adults in the United States were on probation; that represents about 2% of all adult residents and nearly 58% of all adults under correctional supervision.

Regarding his sex offenses, Mele had confessed to two parking lot attacks in April of 2008. His confession was subsequently corroborated by DNA evidence and identification by one of the victims. He was allowed to plead guilty to a misdemeanor—forcible touching and endangering the welfare of a child—the most serious charge. He also was charged with several public-lewdness counts and third-degree sexual abuse, also misdemeanors. He escaped prosecution for at least two other similar attacks. He was sentenced to 6 years' probation and required to undergo treatment for his sexual compulsion. Although he probably could have been charged with a felony, he was not, according to prosecutors, because he was young, a first-time offender, and could be supervised by authorities. If he were sentenced to 1 year in jail, he likely would be out in 8 months and free of any supervision.

Even if Mele's original probation sentence can be justified, another intriguing question is this: why was Mele allowed to remain on probation after missing an appointment with his probation officer in October, skipping three mandated sex offender treatment sessions within nine days in November, and failing to inform authorities he had moved from his parents' house in Newburgh to a condo in Wallkill? A spokesperson for the state probation office explained that "state law and regulations give all parties involved in probation—the probation officers and their supervisors, judges, prosecutors, treatment centers—a great deal of discretion in handling violations." He added, "What the probation officer is looking for is a 'course of conduct,' or a pattern or an indication that the probationer has essentially forsaken the probation alternative." Laura Garza's family and friends are unlikely to find much solace in that explanation.

Community Corrections: Definition and Scope

community corrections The subfield of corrections in which offenders are supervised and provided services outside jail or prison.

Community corrections can be broadly defined as the subfield of corrections consisting of programs in which offenders are supervised and provided services outside jail or prison. For this reason, community corrections is sometimes referred to as noninstitutional corrections. Community corrections includes such programs as diversion, restitution, probation, parole, halfway houses, and various provisions for temporary release from prison or jail. Those programs are the subject of this chapter.

Note that community corrections is a generic term. Federal, state, and local jurisdictions differ widely in the way they organize and administer community corrections and in the specific procedures they use. Criminologist David Duffee's delineation of three varieties of community corrections illustrates this diversity.[1] Community-run correctional programs are controlled by local governments, with minimal connection to state and federal authorities. In effect, local officials determine how such programs will be run within the broad guidelines of state and federal laws. In community-placed programs, as in community-run ones, offenders are handled by agencies within the local district, but agencies in community-placed programs are connected to central state or federal authorities, or both. Consequently, central authority affects program operation, and community-placed programs tend to be more isolated from local affairs than are community-run programs. Community-based correctional programs are a combination of the other two types. Connection to central authority for resources and other support services (a feature of community-placed programs) is combined with strong links between the program and the surrounding locality (a feature of community-run programs).

GOALS AND STAFF ROLES

As described in Chapter 9, the goals of sentencing, which also are the goals of corrections, include punishment, deterrence, incapacitation, and rehabilitation. Yet, as a subfield of corrections, community corrections has traditionally emphasized rehabilitation. Although community programs are concerned with supervising and controlling offenders and ensuring that they follow the rules of their sentences, there is frequently great emphasis on assisting offenders with personal problems and needs. Another emphasis is establishing stronger ties between the offender and the community, by helping the offender get and keep a job, for example. However, the traditional preoccupation of community corrections with rehabilitation has given way in recent years to concern with the other goals.

The staff of community correctional programs have two potentially competing roles that reflect different goals. The first amounts to a law enforcement role: seeing that offenders comply with the orders of community sentences. This means that staff must supervise offenders, investigate possible rule infractions, and take action to address any serious or repeated rule violations.

The other role of staff is to help offenders identify and address their problems and needs. This role has three aspects. The first is the direct provision of services, such as counseling, to offenders. The second is commonly described as the "resource broker" role. In this role, staff identify particular problems and needs and refer offenders to various community agencies for help. An important advantage of community corrections is that correctional agencies can draw on the services of other agencies in the locality. For example, a probation officer may refer a client to a local mental health center for counseling. The third aspect of the helping role is advocacy. A community may not offer services that a significant number of offenders require—for example, opportunities for vocational training. It is the responsibility of staff to advocate greater availability for services that are lacking and to work with community leaders to develop those services.

Many people believe that community correctional staff *should* occupy the dual roles of enforcing the law and helping clients. Those people maintain that supervision and control are necessary to facilitate rehabilitation and that rehabilitation enhances supervision and control. Opponents of that position point to the potential for conflict between roles. They argue that such conflict creates undue stress for staff and makes it difficult to accomplish anything of value.

A study of the attitudes of community correctional staff toward their work found that staff attitudes have been shifting away from the helping role and

MYTH

Modern community correctional programs are invariably "soft on crime." They focus too much on rehabilitation, to the exclusion of punishment, deterrence, and incapacitation.

FACT

Major prison crowding in the past 15 years or so has made it necessary to channel into the community, under supervision, many felons who formerly would have gone to (or stayed in) prison. The priorities and operations of community agencies have shifted to meet this challenge. Many community programs—especially the newer "intermediate sanctions," such as electronic monitoring—emphasize punishment, deterrence, and incapacitation as much as, if not more than, rehabilitation.

One aspect of probation and parole is client counseling. *What kinds of counseling problems are probation or parole officers likely to encounter?*

toward the law enforcement role. The findings of this study indicate the declining emphasis on rehabilitation in community corrections and suggest that the potential for role conflict may lessen as well.[2]

THE IMPORTANCE OF COMMUNITY CORRECTIONS

A discussion of the definition and scope of community corrections would not be complete without stressing how other components of criminal justice depend on community programs. It is not feasible to send all convicted persons—or even all felons—to jail or prison; resources are simply too limited. The sheer number of cases would overwhelm the courts and institutional corrections were it not for the availability of community programs.

To illustrate, examine Figure 12.1, which presents data on the number of adults under the supervision of state and federal corrections agencies at the end of 1980, compared with the end of 2007. Note that at the end of 2007, the number of offenders in jail and prison combined is considerably smaller than the number serving community sentences on probation and parole. Approximately five million adults were on probation or parole at the end of 2007, compared with more than two million in jail or prison.

Figure 12.1 also shows that large increases in the prison and jail populations have been accompanied by large increases in the probation and parole populations. Between 1980 and 2008, the probation population increased by 283%, and the parole population by 274%. The comparable increases in the prison and jail populations were 391% and 328%, respectively.

THINKING CRITICALLY

1. Which do you think is more beneficial to society: community corrections or prison? Why?

2. Which role of community corrections staff do you think is more important: the law enforcement role or the helping role? Why?

FYI Funding Corrections

Of all adults under some type of correctional supervision in the United States, approximately 30% are confined in prisons or jails. Approximately 70% are serving community sentences. Approximately 80% of all funds allocated to corrections in the United States are spent to build and run institutions, and about 20% are spent on community corrections. Thus, 80% of the funds are spent on 30% of the correctional population, and 20% of the funds are left to accommodate 70% of that population.

Source: Lauren E. Glaze and Thomas P. Bonczar, "Probation and Parole in the United States, 2007 Statistical Tables," U.S. Department of Justice, *Bureau of Justice Statistics* (Washington, D.C.: GPO, December 2008), Table 1, www.ojp.usdoj .gov/bjs/pub/pdf/ppus07st.pdf; *Sourcebook of Criminal Justice Statistics* Online, www.albany .edu/sourcebook/pdf/t192005.pdf.

Figure 12.1

Corrections Populations in the United States

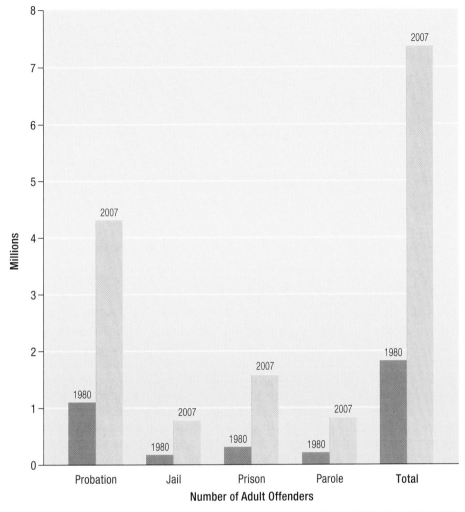

Source: Lauren E. Glaze and Thomas P. Bonczar, "Probation and Parole in the United States, 2007 Statistical Tables," U.S. Department of Justice, *Bureau of Justice Statistics* (Washington, D.C.: GPO, December 2008), Tables 1, 2, & 3 at www.ojp .usdoj.gov/bjs/pub/pdf/ppus07st.pdf; Heather C. West and William J. Sabol, "Prisoners in 2007," U.S. Department of Justice, *Bureau of Justice Statistics Bulletin* (Washington, D.C.: GPO, December 2008), p. 1 at www.ojp.usdoj.gov/bjs/pub/pdf/p07 .pdf; William J. Sabol and Todd D. Minton, "Jail Inmates at Midyear 2007," U.S. Department of Justice, *Bureau of Justice Statistics Bulletin* (Washington, D.C.: GPO, June 2008), p. 1 at www.ojp.usdoj.gov/bjs/pub/pdf/jim07.pdf. Figures for 1980 are from Ann L. Pastore and Kathleen Maguire (eds.), *Sourcebook of Criminal Justice Statistics 1999,* U.S. Department of Justice, Bureau of Justice Statistics (Washington, D.C.: GPO, 2000), p. 484, Table 6.1.

Probation

Probation can be defined as a sentence imposed by the courts on offenders who have either pleaded guilty or been found guilty. Instead of being incarcerated, an offender placed on probation is retained in the community under the supervision of a probation agency. The offender is provided with supervision and services. Continuation of probation (that is, avoidance of incarceration) depends on the offender's compliance with the rules and conditions of the probation sentence. Probation is the most frequently imposed criminal sentence in the United States. Table 12.1 shows the states with the largest probation populations and the highest and lowest rates of persons under probation supervision per 100,000 adult U.S. residents at year-end 2007.

Probation should be distinguished from diversion, although, in broad terms, probation can be thought of as a type of posttrial diversion from incarceration.

probation A sentence in which the offender, rather than being incarcerated, is retained in the community under the supervision of a probation agency and required to abide by certain rules and conditions to avoid incarceration.

Table 12.1 States with the Largest Probation Populations and the Highest and Lowest Rates of Persons under Probation Supervision per 100,000 Adult U.S. Residents at Year-End 2007

States with the Largest Probation Populations		States with the Highest Rates of Supervision		States with the Lowest Rates of Supervision	
Georgia	435,361	Georgia	6,144	New Hampshire	454
Texas	434,309	Idaho	4,405	West Virginia	553
California	353,969	Massachusetts	3,484	Utah	584
Florida	274,079	Minnesota	3,226	Nevada	697
Ohio	254,898	Rhode Island	3,167	Minnesota	754
Michigan	182,706	Ohio	2,917	Kansas	771
Pennsylvania	176,987	Indiana	2,646	New York	804
Massachusetts	175,419	Delaware	2,513	Virginia	877
Illinois	142,790	Texas	2,485	North Dakota	896
Minnesota	127,797	Michigan	2,392	South Dakota	972

Source: Lauren E. Glaze and Thomas P. Bonczar, "Probation and Parole in the United States, 2007 Statistical Tables," U.S. Department of Justice, *Bureau of Justice Statistics* (Washington, D.C.: GPO, December 2008), pp. 2–3, Table 2 at www.ojp.usdoj.gov/bjs/pub/pdf/ppus07st.pdf.

diversion Organized, systematic efforts to remove individuals from further processing in criminal justice by placing them in alternative programs; diversion may be pretrial or posttrial.

Diversion refers to organized and systematic efforts to remove people from the criminal justice process by placing them in programs that offer alternatives to the next, more restrictive stage of processing. Although diversion is commonly associated with juvenile justice, it is also used in adult criminal justice. Diversion can occur at any point from the initial police contact up to, and even in conjunction with, formal sentencing. For example, the police may divert a domestic-violence case by making a referral to a family-in-crisis center instead of making an arrest. Instead of filing charges against an arrestee who is an alcoholic, a prosecutor may divert the case to a detoxification and counseling agency. Those are examples of *pretrial* diversion. *Posttrial* diversion—for example, probation—occurs when an offender who has pleaded guilty or has been found guilty is placed in a program that is an alternative to a more restrictive sentence, such as incarceration.

There are five types of probation:

1. *Straight probation* occurs when an offender is sentenced only to probation, with no incarceration or other form of residential placement.
2. In *suspended-sentence probation*, the judge pronounces a jail or prison sentence but suspends the sentence on the condition that the offender performs well on probation.
3. With a *split sentence*, the judge divides a single sentence into a relatively short jail term followed by probation supervision (for example, a 5-year probation sentence with the first 6 months to be served in jail).
4. *Shock probation* usually involves two sentences. The offender is initially sentenced to prison but is soon (perhaps after 120 days) recalled to court and placed on probation.
5. *Residential probation* involves placement of the probationer in a structured, but generally open, living environment, such as a halfway house. When residential probation is used, it is common for the probationer to spend the early part of the sentence in the residential facility and then, upon successful discharge, to complete the probation sentence living in the free community.

At year-end 2007, 54% of adults on probation in the United States were sentenced to straight probation, 27% were sentenced to suspended-sentence

Alcoholics Anonymous and Al-Anon are frequently used as diversion programs for offenders who otherwise would be incarcerated. *Should some offenders be diverted from jail or prison? Why or why not?*

probation, 9% were sentenced to split-sentence probation, and the remainder were sentenced to other types of probation.[3]

A probation agency has three fundamental objectives. The first is to assist the court in matters pertaining to sentencing. Conducting inquiries and furnishing the court with information about offenders' backgrounds and current situations accomplish this objective. The second objective is to promote community protection by supervising and monitoring the activities of persons sentenced to probation. The third objective is to promote the betterment of offenders by ensuring that they receive appropriate rehabilitation services. Thus, probation agencies work closely with the courts to assist offenders and, when possible, help them avoid incarceration without compromising the safety and security of the community.

HISTORICAL CONTEXT

Probation developed out of various practices used under English common law. One such practice, known as benefit of clergy, allowed certain accused individuals to appeal to the court for leniency in sentencing by reading from the Bible. Another practice was judicial reprieve, whereby a convicted offender could ask the judge to suspend the sentence on the condition that the offender display good future behavior. Those and other practices were important forerunners of modern probation.

The more immediate origins of modern probation lie in the efforts of John Augustus (1785–1859), a prosperous Boston shoemaker, who is considered the "father" of probation. Starting in the early 1840s, Augustus volunteered to stand bail and assume custody for select, less serious offenders in exchange for the judge's deferring the sentence. Augustus was responsible for monitoring offenders' activities and later reporting to the judge on their performance in the community. If the judge was satisfied with community performance, charges were dropped; if not, sentencing proceeded. Augustus received no pay for his 18 years of court work. He used his own money and voluntary contributions from others to finance his efforts.[4]

FYI Characteristics of Adults on Probation, 2007

In 2007, 77% of all probationers in the United States were male and 23% were female. Fifty-five percent were white (non-Hispanic), 29% were black (non-Hispanic), 13% were Hispanic, and the remainder were of other races. Forty-seven percent of probationers had committed felonies, 51% had committed misdemeanors, and 3% had committed other infractions.

Source: Lauren E. Glaze and Thomas P. Bonczar, "Probation and Parole in the United States, 2007 Statistical Tables," U.S. Department of Justice, *Bureau of Justice Statistics* (Washington, D.C.: GPO, December 2008), Table 4, www.ojp.usdoj .gov/bjs/pub/pdf/ppus07st.pdf.

Influenced by the efforts of Augustus, Massachusetts passed the first formal probation law in 1878. By 1920, a majority of the states allowed probation. However, it was not until 1957 that all states had probation statutes. The federal probation system was established in 1925.[5] In more than 160 years, probation has grown from the efforts of a volunteer in Boston into the most frequently used sentence in criminal justice.

ADMINISTRATION

As mentioned earlier in the chapter, probation is administered in many different ways across the nation. The federal government administers its own probation system under the Administrative Office of the Courts, and each state has responsibility for determining how to administer probation. In some states, such as Kentucky, probation is administered at the state level as part of a department of corrections or other state agency. In other states, such as California and Indiana, probation administration is a local function. Still other states combine state and local administration. Under *probation subsidy*, which became popular in the 1960s, states agree to financially support locally administered probation services in exchange for the localities' not sentencing all their offenders to the state prison system. The goal is to give localities a financial incentive to retain offenders in their communities when possible.

There are other variations in the way probation is administered. Depending on the jurisdiction, administrative responsibility may lie with the executive branch, the judicial branch, or both. Adult and juvenile probation services can be administered separately or jointly, as can misdemeanor and felony services. Finally, probation administration can be combined with parole administration, or the two may be separate.

PROCESS AND PROCEDURES

A probation sentence can be viewed as a process with an identifiable beginning and ending. The process consists of three basic stages:

1. Placement of an offender on probation by a judge.
2. Supervision and service delivery for the probationer by probation officers.
3. Termination of the probation.

Before and during the process, probation agency staff employ a number of important procedures, which will be examined in the following subsections.

Placement on Probation In deciding whether an offender should be sentenced to probation, a judge usually considers a host of factors, such as statutes outlining eligibility for probation, structured sentencing guidelines (in jurisdictions where they are used), recommendations from the prosecuting and defense attorneys, the offender's freedom or detention in jail before and during trial, the presentence investigation report prepared by the probation agency, and characteristics of the offender and offense. Judges ordinarily give great consideration to the seriousness of the current offense and the prior legal record of the offender. Cases involving more serious offenses or offenders with more extensive prior records are less likely to receive probation.

The Presentence Investigation The **presentence investigation (PSI)** is conducted by the probation agency at the request of the judge, usually during the period between the finding or plea of guilt and sentencing. In performing a PSI, a probation officer conducts an inquiry into the offender's past and current social and psychological functioning as well as the offender's prior criminal

FYI Federal Probation Officers

As of December 2008, the Administrative Office of the U.S. Courts employed 4,995 probation officers. They supervise offenders placed on probation and supervised release and conduct presentence investigations to assess the risk to the community of future criminal behavior, the harm caused by the offense, the need for restitution, and the defendant's ability to pay restitution.

Source: Brian A. Reaves, "Federal Law Enforcement Officers, 2004," U.S. Department of Justice, *Bureau of Justice Statistics Bulletin* (Washington, D.C.: GPO, July 2006), p. 3; personal communication (December 18, 2008).

presentence investigation (PSI) An investigation conducted by a probation agency or other designated authority at the request of a court into the past behavior, family circumstances, and personality of an adult who has been convicted of a crime, to assist the court in determining the most appropriate sentence.

As part of a presentence investigation, a probation officer interviews an offender to obtain background information for the court. *What kinds of background information, if any, should influence the length and type of sentence? Why?*

record. The main tasks of the inquiry are to estimate the risk the offender presents to the community and to determine the offender's treatment needs. The probation officer obtains the necessary information by interviewing the offender and others who know the offender, such as an employer, family members, and victims. The officer also reviews relevant documents and reports. The information is assembled into a PSI report, which is submitted to the court.

A sample PSI checklist appears in Table 12.2. There are no universally accepted standards for PSI report format and content. However, reports typically contain these basic elements:

1. A face sheet of identifying demographic data.
2. A discussion of the instant or current offense as perceived by the police, the victim, and the offender.
3. A summary of the offender's prior legal record.
4. An overview of the offender's past and present social and psychological functioning.
5. The probation officer's evaluation of the offender and the officer's recommendation for an appropriate sentence.

The probation officer must convey the essential information in a concise and objective manner that supports the sentencing recommendation being offered.

Once prepared, the PSI report serves a variety of functions. It is useful in formulating supervision and treatment plans for persons who are given probation sentences. It also serves as the baseline for progress reports on probationers. When an offender is sent to prison, the report helps prison officials learn about and make decisions about the offender. However, the most well-known and immediate function of the PSI report is to assist judges in arriving at a proper sentence.

In most cases, there is a high degree of consistency between the sentencing recommendation in the PSI report and the actual sentence handed down by the judge. As shown in the Myth/Fact box, however, this does not mean that

MYTH

An essential function of the PSI report is to individualize justice by helping judges structure their sentencing decisions around the offender's unique circumstances.

FACT

In an important study, criminologist John Rosecrance found that experienced probation officers try to recommend sentences that are consistent with judicial expectations, given the seriousness of the offense and the offender's prior criminal record. Rosecrance found that officers selectively structure information in the report to support the recommendations they have already decided on. Information that is inconsistent with those recommendations is minimized in the report. Rosecrance's research implies that the PSI report merely gives the sentencing process a guise of individualized justice.

Source: John Rosecrance, "Maintaining the Myth of Individualized Justice: Probation Presentence Reports," *Justice Quarterly 5* (1988), pp. 235–256.

Table 12.2 Checklist for Completing a Presentence Investigation Report

Face Sheet of Identifying Demographic Information:
   Name, aliases, and address
   Physical description
   Social security number
   Date and place of birth
   School history, occupation, marital status, family members

Instant Offense:
   Offense and docket number
   Name(s) of codefendants, if any
   Prosecutor and defense attorney (names and addresses)
   Means of conviction (trial, plea agreement, etc.)
   Sentencing date

Presentence Investigation:
   Defendant's version of events relating to offense
   Victim impact, restitution needs
   Jail time served in connection with offense
   Previous record
   Social history (family, friends, self-image)
   Educational history
   Marital history
   Employment history
   Economic situation
   Religious association
   Outside interests
   Health (including drug and alcohol use)
   Present attitudes of defendant
   Plea agreement (if any)
   Fiscal impact of sentencing option(s) to victim and state
   Psychiatric insights
   Statement of probation officer
   Sentencing recommendation

Probation Plan:
   Length of probationary period
   Probationer reporting requirements
   Job placement
   Postemployment education training needs
   Community service requirements
   Other probation requirements

probation conditions Rules that specify what an offender is and is not to do during the course of a probation sentence.

judges are always strongly influenced by probation officers' sentencing recommendations. In some cases, probation officers recommend sentences that they believe are consistent with judicial expectations.

In addition to questions about the actual effect of PSI reports on sentencing decisions, another issue is whether courts should use PSIs conducted by private individuals and agencies rather than by probation agencies. Private PSIs became popular in the 1960s. Private individuals and agencies may conduct PSIs under contract with the defense or the court. Advocates of privately prepared PSIs argue that privatization reduces probation agency workloads and saves tax dollars (when such PSIs are commissioned by the defendant). Opponents argue that improper sentences may be recommended, that private PSIs can discriminate against the poor, and that the PSIs can reduce the credibility and funding of probation agencies.

The PSI report is usually the property of the court for which it is prepared. Once the report is submitted to the court, a copy is often provided to the defendant, defense counsel, and the prosecuting attorney. Both parties have the opportunity to review the report for accuracy and to bring any concerns to the court's attention. This process is known as *disclosure,* and there has been controversy about it. Those who oppose the practice of disclosure maintain that people with important information may not make it available if the offender will see it and know who provided it. Those who support disclosure, on the other hand, argue that it is a matter of fairness that the offender be able to see the information on which the sentence is based, to ensure that it is accurate.

The Probation Order When an offender is sentenced to probation, the court files the appropriate documents indicating the length and conditions of the probation sentence. Although the length of probation sentences varies between jurisdictions and between cases, it is common for adults placed on probation for misdemeanor offenses to receive 1- to 2-year terms. Those convicted of felonies and sentenced to probation generally receive longer terms (for example, 5 years). Some states allow sentences of lifetime probation. In some cases, the court has the authority to grant early discharge from probation for commendable performance or to extend the term of probation.

Probation conditions are rules that specify what an offender is and is not to do during the course of a probation sentence. They are of crucial significance because the success or failure of the probationer is evaluated with respect to those rules. There are two types of conditions. *Standard* or *general conditions* apply to all persons placed on probation and pertain primarily to control and supervision of the offender. Figure 12.2 shows the standard or general conditions of probation for the state of New Hampshire. *Special conditions* are imposed at the discretion of the judge and probation officials and are designed to address the offender's particular situation. Special conditions frequently deal with treatment matters. For example, an offender may be ordered to participate in drug abuse counseling. Figure 12.3 shows Indiana's special probation conditions for adult sex offenders. Special conditions can be creative. For example, in Massachusetts, Connecticut,

Figure 12.2

Rules of the Superior Court of the State of New Hampshire, Terms and Conditions of Probation

The terms and conditions of probation, unless otherwise prescribed, shall be as follows:

The probationer shall:

a. Report to the probation or parole officer at such times and places as directed, comply with the probation or parole officer's instructions, and respond truthfully to all inquiries from the probation or parole officer;

b. Comply with all orders of the Court, board of parole or probation or parole officer, including any order for the payment of money;

c. Obtain the probation or parole officer's permission before changing residence or employment or traveling out of State;

d. Notify the probation or parole officer immediately of any arrest, summons or questioning by a law enforcement officer;

e. Diligently seek and maintain lawful employment, notify probationer's employer of his or her legal status, and support dependents to the best of his or her ability;

f. Not receive, possess, control or transport any weapon, explosive, or firearm, or simulated weapon, explosive, or firearm;

g. Be of good conduct, obey all laws, and be arrest-free;

h. Submit to reasonable searches of his or her person, property and possessions as requested by the probation or parole officer and permit the probation or parole officer to visit his or her residence at reasonable times for the purpose of examination and inspection in the enforcement of the conditions of probation or parole;

i. Not associate with any person having a criminal record or with other individuals as directed by the probation or parole officer unless specifically authorized to do so by the probation or parole officer;

j. Not indulge in the illegal use, sale, possession, distribution, or transportation, or be in the presence, of controlled drugs, or use alcoholic beverages to excess;

k. Agree to waive extradition to the State of New Hampshire from any State in the United States or any other place and agree to return to New Hampshire if directed by the probation or parole officer; and

l. Comply with such of the following, or any other, special conditions as may be imposed by the Court, the parole board, or the probation or parole officer:

  1. Participate regularly in Alcoholics Anonymous to the satisfaction of the probation or parole officer;

  2. Secure written permission from the probation or parole officer prior to purchasing and/or operating a motor vehicle;

  3. Participate in and satisfactorily complete a specific designated program;

  4. Enroll and participate in mental health counseling on a regular basis to the satisfaction of the probation or parole officer;

  5. Not be in the unsupervised company of minors of one or the other sex at any time;

  6. Not leave the county without permission of the probation or parole officer;

  7. Refrain totally from the use of alcoholic beverages;

  8. Submit to breath, blood, or urine testing for abuse substances at the direction of the probation or parole officer; and

  9. Comply with designated house arrest provisions.

Source: http://www.courts.state.nh.us/rules/sror/sror-h3-107.htm.

Figure 12.3

Indiana Recommended Special Probation Conditions for Adult Sex Offenders

The _____ Circuit/Superior Court hereby imposes the following special probation conditions upon defendant _____ in Cause No. _____. The special conditions checked below apply to you as a result of your sex offense conviction and should be initialed by you after you have read these conditions or after these conditions have been read to you. Violation of any of the special conditions checked below can result in revocation of your probation and incarceration.

CHECK ALL CONDITIONS THAT APPLY:
Offender Ordered
Initials By Court

_____ _____ 1. *Applies only to sexually violent predators:* A sex offender who is a sexually violent predator (as defined in IC 35-38-1-7.5) shall register with local law enforcement authorities within seventy-two (72) hours of being released to probation in accordance with IC 11-8-8-7(h). ***Required as a condition of probation by IC 35-38-2-2.2 for sex offenses listed in IC 11-8-8-5.**

_____ _____ 2. *Applies only to sex offenders who are NOT sexually violent predators:* You shall register with local law enforcement authorities as a sex offender within seven (7) days of being released to/placed on probation in accordance with IC 11-8-8-7. ***Required as a condition of probation by IC 35-38-2-2.2 for sex offenses listed in IC 11-8-8-5.**

_____ _____ 3. *Applies only to "offenders against children" as defined in IC 35-42-4-11(a) (1) & (2).* You shall not reside within one thousand (1,000) feet of school property, a youth program center or a public park and you shall not establish a residence within one (1) mile of the victim of your sex offense in accordance with IC 35-42-4-11(c).

_____ _____ 4. You shall not reside within one thousand (1,000) feet of school property as defined in IC 35-41-1-24.7, unless written approval is obtained from the court. ***Required as a condition of probation by IC 35-38-2-2.2.**

_____ _____ 5. You shall not reside within one (1) mile of the residence of the victim of your sex offense (as defined by IC 35-38-2-2.5(b)) unless granted a waiver from the court. The court may not grant a waiver for a sexually violent predator. ***Required as a condition of probation by IC 35-38-2-2.5(c).**

_____ _____ 6. You shall not establish a new residence within one (1) mile of the residence of the victim of your sex offense (as defined in IC 35-38-2-2.5(b)) unless granted a waiver from the court. The court may not grant a waiver for a sexually violent predator. ***Required as a condition of probation by IC 35-38-2-2.5(e) and (f).**

_____ _____ 7. You shall attend, actively participate in and successfully complete a court-approved sex offender treatment program as directed by the court. Prompt payment of any fees is your responsibility and you must maintain steady progress towards all treatment goals as determined by your treatment provider. Unsuccessful termination from treatment or non-compliance with other required behavioral management requirements will be considered a violation of your probation. You will not be permitted to change treatment providers unless the court gives you prior written approval.

_____ _____ 8. You shall not miss any appointments for treatment, psychotherapy, counseling, or self-help groups (any 12 Step Group, Community Support Group, etc.) without the prior approval of your probation officer and the treatment provider involved, or a doctor's excuse. You shall comply with the attendance policy for attending appointments as outlined by the court. You shall continue to take any medication prescribed by your physician.

_____ _____ 9. You shall not possess obscene matter as defined by IC 35-49-2-1 or child pornography as defined in 18 U.S.C. § 2256(8), including but not limited to: videos, magazines, books, DVDs, and material downloaded from the Internet. You shall not visit strip clubs, adult bookstores, motels specifically operated for sexual encounters, peep shows, bars where partially nude or exotic dancers perform, or businesses that sell sexual devices or aids.

_____ _____ 10. You shall not consume alcohol or use any controlled substance.

_____ _____ 11. You shall submit to a substance abuse evaluation and follow all recommendations of your treatment provider at your own expense.

_____ _____ 12. You shall be required to inform all persons living at your place of residence about all of your sex-related convictions. You shall notify your probation officer of any changes in home situations or marital status. You shall have only one residence and one mailing address at a time.

_____ _____ 13. You shall not travel alone after 10 p.m. (including but not limited to: driving, walking, bicycling, etc.) unless given permission by your probation officer.

_____ _____ 14. You shall notify your probation officer of your establishment of a dating, intimate and/or sexual relationship. You shall notify any person with whom you are engaged in a dating, intimate or sexual relationship of your sex-related conviction(s). You shall not engage in a dating, intimate or sexual relationship with any person who has children under the age of 18 years.

_____ _____ 15. Your probation officer must first approve any employment and may contact your employer at any time. You will not work in certain occupations that involve being in the private residences of others, such as, but not limited to, door-to-door sales, soliciting, home service visits, or delivery.

_____ _____ 16. You shall have no contact with your victim's family unless approved in advance by your probation officer and treatment provider for the benefit of the victim. Contact includes face-to-face, telephonic, written, electronic, or any indirect contact via third parties.

_____ _____ 17. You must never be alone with or have contact with any person under the age of 18. Contact includes face-to-face, telephonic, written, electronic, or any indirect contact via third parties. You must report any incidental contact with persons under age 18 to your probation officer within 24 hours of the contact.

_____ _____ 18. You shall not be present at schools, playgrounds, or day care centers unless given permission by the court.

_____ _____ 19. You shall not participate in any activity which involves children under 18 years of age, such as, but not limited to, youth groups, Boy Scouts, Girl Scouts, Cub Scouts, Brownies, 4-H, YMCA, YWCA, or youth sports teams, unless given permission by the Court.

_____ _____ 20. You shall sign a waiver of confidentiality, releases of information, or any other document required that permits your probation officer and other behavioral management or treatment providers to examine any and all records relating to you to collaboratively share and discuss your behavioral management conditions, treatment progress, and probation needs as a team. This permission may extend to: (1) sharing your relapse prevention plan and treatment progress with your significant others and/or your victim and victim's therapist as directed by your probation officer or treatment provider(s); and (2) sharing of your modus operandi behaviors with law enforcement personnel.

_____ _____ 21. You shall participate in and complete periodic polygraph testing at your own expense at the direction of your probation officer or any other behavioral management professionals who are providing treatment or otherwise assisting your probation officer in monitoring your compliance with your probation conditions.

_____ _____ 22. You shall be under intensive supervision and report to your probation officer as directed. You shall complete a travel log and/or journal of daily activities as directed by your probation officer.

_____ _____ 23. You shall not access the Internet or any other on-line service through use of a computer, cell phone, iPod, Xbox, Blackberry, personal digital assistant (PDA), pagers, Palm Pilots, televisions, or any other electronic device at any location (including your place of employment) without prior approval of your probation officer. This includes any Internet service provider, bulletin board system, e-mail system, or any other public or private computer network. You shall not possess or use any data encryption technique or program.

_____ _____ 24. You shall allow your probation officer and/or probation computer service representative, based on reasonable suspicion, to conduct periodic unannounced examinations of your home computer(s) equipment or other electronic equipment with access to the Internet. Such examinations may include retrieval and copying of all memory from your computer(s) and other electronic equipment, and any internal or external peripherals to ensure compliance with your special probation conditions, and/or removal of such equipment for the purpose of conducting a more thorough inspection. Your probation officer may have installed on your computer(s) or other electronic equipment, at your expense, any hardware or software systems to monitor your computer use.

_____ _____ 25. _____ .
_____
_____ _____ 26. _____
_____ .

ORDERED BY THE COURT THIS _____ DAY OF _____, 20__.
_____   _____
Judge Defendant/Probationer

_____
Probation Officer
Adopted 09/2000, Revised 12/2006

Source: www.in.gov/judiciary/probation/docs/sex-offender-conditions-adult.pdf.

Texas, and a few other states, a special condition of probation for some offenders is participation in a reading program called "Changing Lives Through Literature." Eligible offenders agree to attend a class on a college campus each week for 10 or 12 weeks. They read and discuss such books as *The Old Man and the Sea*, *Deliverance*, *The Sea Wolf*, *Of Mice and Men*, and *One Flew over the Cuckoo's Nest*. If they complete the program, their probation is reduced, usually by 3 months. An evaluation of the first four classes in Massachusetts found that only 18% of the men who completed the class committed crimes again, compared with 43% in a comparable group of offenders.[6]

In recent years it has become increasingly common for jurisdictions to include restitution orders as part of probation, as either a standard condition or a special condition. **Restitution,** you may recall, usually means that the offender provides either the victim or the community with money or work service.

In some areas, the court may later amend or modify conditions outlined in the initial probation order. The conditions can be made more or less restrictive, depending on the probationer's behavior. However, to be legal, it is necessary for all conditions, regardless of when they are imposed, to be clear, reasonable, permitted by the Constitution, and related to the rehabilitation of the offender or the protection of society, or both.[7]

restitution Money paid or services provided to victims, their survivors, or the community by a convicted offender to make up for the injury inflicted.

Supervision and Service Delivery Once offenders have been placed on probation, the probation agency must shift attention to supervision and service delivery. At this point, probationers must be assigned to probation officers. In making assignments, it is important to match officer and probationer characteristics. For example, a manipulative probationer who poses a risk to community security might be assigned to an officer with a law enforcement orientation. An offender who poses little risk but has pressing treatment needs might be assigned to an officer with more of a helping background.

Because not all persons placed on probation require the same amounts and types of supervision and services, an important task is to determine what is appropriate for each client. In recent years, this task has been facilitated by the development of risk-and-needs assessment instruments such as the one shown in Figure 12.4. The probation agency can more objectively determine the amount and type of supervision a probationer requires by examining the risk score. For instance, a probationer with a risk score in the maximum range might receive weekly contacts from the probation officer, whereas a probationer with a minimum-range risk score might receive monthly contacts. Likewise, the amount and kind of services are directed by the needs score. The point is to ensure that the highest levels of supervision are reserved for probationers who present the greatest risk to the community and that the highest levels of treatment services are reserved for those who present the greatest needs.

Once risk-and-needs assessment has been completed, the probation agency can formulate supervision and treatment plans for its clients. In effect, those plans further specify the conditions of probation and describe what is expected of probationers. Some of the requirements might include weekly contacts with the probation officer, random drug tests, weekly Alcoholics Anonymous meetings, or obtainment of a GED. Once supervision and treatment plans are set, the monitoring of probationers and the periodic filing of progress reports for the court can begin.

Termination of Probation Ultimately, the probation agency must make recommendations to the court about how probation is to be terminated. Clients who have generally fulfilled the conditions of their sentences and have served their terms are recommended for successful discharges. If a client has violated the conditions of probation, the probation agency may recommend **revocation,** which entails repealing the probation sentence and substituting a more restrictive

revocation The repeal of a probation sentence or parole, and substitution of a more restrictive sentence, because of violation of probation or parole conditions.

Figure 12.4

Sample Risk and Needs Assessment Instrument

DEPARTMENT OF CORRECTIONS
DIVISION OF PROBATION & PAROLE

Client No. _____ Client Name: _____ Officer No. _____

CLIENT RISK ASSESSMENT
Instructions: Enter numerical rating in box at right.
1. TOTAL NUMBER OF PRIOR FELONY CONVICTIONS:
   (include juvenile adjudications, if known)
   a. None .... Enter 0
   b. One .... Enter 2
   c. Two or more .... Enter 4
2. PRIOR NUMBER OF PROBATION/PAROLE SUPERVISION PERIODS:
   (include juvenile, if known)
   a. None .... Enter 0
   b. One or more .... Enter 4
3. PRIOR PROBATION/PAROLE REVOCATIONS:
   (adult only)
   a. None .... Enter 0
   b. One or more .... Enter 4
4. AGE AT FIRST KNOWN CONVICTION OR ADJUDICATION:
   (include juvenile, if known)
   a. 24 years or older .... Enter 0
   b. 20 through 23 years .... Enter 2
   c. 19 years or younger .... Enter 4
5. HISTORY OF ALCOHOL ABUSE:
   a. No history of abuse .... Enter 0
   b. Occasional or prior abuse .... Enter 2
   c. Frequent current abuse .... Enter 4
6. HISTORY OF OTHER SUBSTANCE ABUSE:
   (prior to incarceration for parolees)
   a. No history of abuse .... Enter 0
   b. Occasional or prior abuse .... Enter 1
   c. Frequent current abuse .... Enter 2
7. AMOUNT OF TIME EMPLOYED IN LAST 12 MONTHS:
   (prior to incarceration for parolees, based on 35 hr. week)
   a. 7 months or more .... Enter 0
   b. 4 months through 6 months .... Enter 1
   c. Less than 4 months .... Enter 2
   d. Not applicable .... Enter 0
8. AGENT IMPRESSION OF OFFENDER'S ATTITUDE:
   a. Motivated to change, receptive to assistance .... Enter 0
   b. Dependent or unwilling to accept responsibility .... Enter 3
   c. Rationalizes behavior, negative, not motivated to change ..... Enter 5
9. RECORD OF CONVICTION FOR SELECTED OFFENSES:
   (include current offense, add categories and enter total)
   a. None of the following .... Enter 0
   b. Burglary, Theft, Auto Theft, Robbery .... Add 2
   c. Forgery, Deceptive Practices (Fraud, Bad Check, Drugs) ...... Add 3
10. ASSAULTIVE OFFENSES:
    a. Crimes against persons which include use of weapon, physical force, threat of
       force, all sex crimes, and vehicular homicide
       ☐ Yes   ☐ No

Total Score
(Range 0–34)

CLIENT NEED ASSESSMENT
Instructions: Enter numerical rating in box at right.
1. ACADEMIC/VOCATIONAL SKILLS:
   a. High school or above skill level .... Enter 0
   b. Has vocational training, additional not needed/desired ...... Enter 1
   c. Has some skills; additional needed/desired .... Enter 3
   d. No skills, training needed .... Enter 5
2. EMPLOYMENT:
   a. Satisfactory employment for 1 year or longer .... Enter 0
   b. Employed, no difficulties reported, or homemaker, student, retired,
      or disabled and unable to work .... Enter 1
   c. Part-time, seasonal, unstable employment or needs additional
      employment; unemployed, but has a skill .... Enter 4
   d. Unemployed & virtually unemployable; needs training .... Enter 7
3. FINANCIAL STATUS:
   a. Longstanding pattern of self-sufficiency .... Enter 0
   b. No current difficulties .... Enter 1
   c. Situational or minor difficulties .... Enter 4
   d. Severe difficulties .... Enter 6
4. LIVING ARRANGEMENTS (Within last six months):
   a. Stable and supportive relationships with family or others in
      living group .... Enter 0
   b. Client lives alone or independently within another household .. Enter 1
   c. Client experiencing occasional, moderate interpersonal problems
      within living group .... Enter 4
   d. Client experiencing frequent and serious interpersonal problems
      within living group .... Enter 6
5. EMOTIONAL STABILITY:
   a. No symptoms of instability .... Enter 1
   b. Symptoms limit, but do not prohibit adequate functioning ... Enter 5
   c. Symptoms prohibit adequate functioning .... Enter 8
6. ALCOHOL USAGE (Current):
   a. No interference with functioning .... Enter 1
   b. Occasional abuse, some disruption of functioning, may need
      treatment .... Enter 4
   c. Frequent abuse, serious disruption, needs treatment .... Enter 7
7. OTHER SUBSTANCE USAGE (Current):
   a. No interference with functioning .... Enter 1
   b. Occasional substance abuse, some disruption of functioning,
      may need treatment .... Enter 4
   c. Frequent substance abuse, serious disruption, needs treatment . Enter 6
8. REASONING/INTELLECTUAL ABILITY:
   a. Able to function independently .... Enter 1
   b. Some need for assistance, potential for adequate adjustment ... Enter 4
   c. Deficiencies suggest limited ability to function independently . Enter 7
9. HEALTH:
   a. Sound physical health, seldom ill .... Enter 1
   b. Handicap or illness interferes with functioning on a
      recurring basis .... Enter 2
   c. Serious handicap or chronic illness, needs frequent
      medical care .... Enter 3
10. AGENT'S IMPRESSION OF CLIENT'S NEEDS:
    a. None .... Enter 0
    b. Low .... Enter 1
    c. Moderate .... Enter 4
    d. High .... Enter 6

Total Score
(Range 5–61)

SCORING AND OVERRIDE
Instruction: Check appropriate block
SCORE BASED SUPERVISION LEVEL ☐ Maximum ☐ Medium ☐ Minimum
Check if there is an override ☐ Override Explanation _____

FINAL CATEGORY OF SUPERVISION ☐ Maximum ☐ Medium ☐ Minimum

APPROVED (Supervisor Signature and Date)   Agent

Date Supervision Level Assigned
MONTH   DAY   YEAR

Source: Anthony Walsh, *Understanding, Assessing, and Counseling the Criminal Justice Client* (Pacific Grove, CA: Brooks/Cole, 1988), p. 110. Reprinted with permission of Anthony Walsh.

sentence, such as a jail or prison term. If probation is revoked, the judge can impose any sentence, including incarceration that was authorized for the offense for which the offender was originally placed on probation. Furthermore, the time already spent on probation, even though it may be several years, does not count as credit against the new sentence.[8]

Revocation can be recommended for two general categories of violations. One category involves commission of new offenses. The second category, known as **technical violations,** involves failure to abide by the technical rules of the sentence. For example, a probationer might fail to report regularly to the probation officer or might leave the jurisdiction without the officer's consent. A recommendation of revocation is not automatic in the event of a violation, even if the violation is a new crime. Probation agents have considerable discretion on this matter. If the violation is a serious crime, a recommendation of revocation is very likely. However, a less serious offense or a technical violation may result in a warning, a tightening of probation conditions (perhaps the addition of a nightly curfew), or a brief jail term. Many probation agencies tend to let technical violations and petty offenses accumulate, with warnings and condition modifications along the way. However, repeated and excessive violations of this nature usually result in revocation recommendations.

> **technical violations** Failure to abide by the technical rules or conditions of probation or parole (for example, not reporting regularly to the probation officer), as distinct from commission of a new criminal act.

If the probation agency asks the court to consider revocation of probation, the court must work within the guidelines of case law established by the U.S. Supreme Court. Two landmark cases are *Morrissey* v. *Brewer* and *Gagnon* v. *Scarpelli*. The Court's 1972 ruling in *Morrissey* v. *Brewer* dealt with parole revocation, but by virtue of the 1973 ruling in *Gagnon* v. *Scarpelli*, it also applies to probation revocation. *Morrissey* established that revocation is to be a two-stage process. In the first stage, there must be an informal, preliminary inquiry to establish probable cause that a violation has occurred. If probable cause is established, then in the second stage, there must be a formal court hearing to determine whether the violation warrants revocation. Offenders have certain rights at both stages. They include the right to notice of the hearing and charges, the right to be present at the hearing and to present evidence and witnesses, and the right to a detached and neutral hearing body.

The *Gagnon* decision extended the requirements of *Morrissey* to include probationers and also addressed the issue of right to counsel, which the *Morrissey* decision did not address. In *Gagnon*, the Court ruled that there is no absolute right to counsel at revocation proceedings. Whether the offender is provided with counsel is determined on a case-by-case basis, and if there is no compelling reason for providing counsel, counsel is unnecessary. However, the Court added that in probation revocation hearings, counsel should be provided when probationers present a timely claim that (1) they did not commit the violation or (2) there are mitigating circumstances making revocation inappropriate. In other situations, attorneys are allowed at revocation hearings as long as defendants provide their own, at no cost to the state.

ISSUES IN PROBATION

Probation is an evolving, changing field with many controversial issues. Several such issues have already been considered in this chapter. We now turn our attention to some additional issues.

Committing a new crime or violating the conditions of probation may lead to revocation of probation. *How serious should a new crime or violation of probation conditions be before probation is revoked?*

FYI Probation Fees

In 1929, Michigan became the first jurisdiction in the United States to impose probation supervision fees.

Source: www.appa-net.org.

Probation Fees Increases in the probation population have been accompanied by increases in the financial costs of probation. Consequently, a trend has emerged toward having probationers pay fees (for example, $30 per month) to help offset the cost of their supervision and treatment. Probation fees—or supervision fees, as they are sometimes called—are distinct from fines, court costs, and restitution.

Advocates of probation fees argue that fees can help contain the increasingly high costs of probation. Advocates further contend that because the majority of probationers can afford reasonable monthly fees, it is only fair that those probationers be held responsible for supporting at least part of the services they receive. However, critics charge that fees are unfair for indigent offenders and that offenders should not have to pay for services they are mandated to receive. Critics also claim that the administrative costs associated with collecting fees can exceed the amount of money collected. Given the skyrocketing number of persons on probation and the high cost of supervision and treatment, it seems unlikely that the trend toward probation fees will decrease in the near future.

Legal Issues: Confidentiality and Privacy Counseling is often an aspect of probation. It can be argued that to protect the counseling relationship, the information a probationer shares with a counselor should not be divulged to outside parties. However, it can also be argued that the counselor, who could be the offender's probation officer or a counselor to whom the probation officer has referred the offender, has a duty to divulge information about certain activities, particularly new crimes and technical violations, to appropriate authorities, such as police officers and judges. To what degree, then, should confidentiality govern the relationship between probation officer and probationer? In *Minnesota* v. *Murphy* (1984), the U.S. Supreme Court held that this relationship is not governed by the same degree of confidentiality as that between attorney and client or between physician and patient. Counselors taking probationer referrals can reveal information about a probationer's illegal activities to the probation officer, and the probation officer can notify the police.

Another issue is the conditions under which a probation officer may search a probationer's home for evidence. In its decision in *Griffin* v. *Wisconsin* (1987), the Supreme Court held that a search warrant based on probable cause is unnecessary for a probation officer to search a probationer's home; reasonable grounds is a sufficient basis for the search. This decision and the *Murphy* decision show that probationers are generally entitled to fewer due process protections than are free citizens who are not on probation. Whether this is just and fair is open to debate.

recidivism The return of probationers to crime during or after probation.

Caseload and Recidivism With the probation population growing each year, it is not unusual for probation officers in larger urban jurisdictions to have as many as 200 offenders in their caseloads. Large caseloads, in turn, have been criticized for contributing to **recidivism** (the return of probationers to crime during or after probation). Clearly, it is difficult for probation officers with large caseloads to give each case individual attention and to provide proper supervision and services for all their clients.

Interestingly, however, research has generally failed to confirm that smaller caseloads, such as 25 cases per officer, are associated with decreased recidivism. In the words of criminologist Jay S. Albanese and his colleagues, "It appears from many studies that the simple expedient of reducing caseloads will not of itself assure a reduction of recidivism."[9] In fact, it is reasonable to suppose that caseload reduction may sometimes be associated with an *increase* in recidivism detected by probation officers, because officers with smaller caseloads are able to scrutinize each probationer's activities more closely. There is some support for this supposition.[10] However, to the extent that (1) large caseloads promote recidivism because of the inability of probation officers to provide sufficient supervision and services and (2) smaller caseloads inflate recidivism numbers because of greater scrutiny of probationers' activities, probation agencies are in a no-win situation with respect to the issue of optimal caseload.

How effective is probation in controlling recidivism? First, note that researchers attempting to address this question confront a variety of difficulties. One difficulty is deciding whether to define probationer recidivism in terms of technical violations, arrests for new crimes, new convictions, or revocations. The definition employed affects the amount of recidivism uncovered. Another important difficulty lies in accurately determining whether it is the probation experience or some additional factor that is responsible for the recidivism observed among a group of probationers. A simple finding that recidivism is low among a group of probationers does not necessarily mean that probation is containing recidivism. Other factors, such as improvements in the local economy or the selection of low-risk offenders for probation, may be responsible. To date, many studies of probation effectiveness have not been designed well enough to rule out the role of factors other than the probation experience. Difficulties like these must be kept in mind when reviewing studies on probation recidivism.

Research suggests that probation is less effective than many people would like in curtailing rearrests of felony offenders. In a well-known California study by criminologist Joan Petersilia and her colleagues, approximately 1,700 felony offenders placed on probation were tracked for a period of 40 months. During this period, about two-thirds of the probationers were rearrested, more than half were reconvicted, and about one-third were sent to jail or prison.[11] In a similar but larger-scale study by the U.S. Justice Department, 79,000 felons sentenced to probation in 1986 by state courts in 17 states were followed for 3 years. By 1989, 43% of those felons had been arrested for new felonies: 8.5% were rearrested for violent offenses, 14.8% for property crimes, 14.1% for drug offenses, and the remainder for other crimes.[12] According to data provided by the U.S. Justice Department's Bureau of Justice Statistics, in 2007, about 62% of the nearly 1.6 million adults discharged from probation whose outcome was known had successfully met the conditions of their supervision. These data show that the percentage of probationers successfully discharged has remained relatively constant since 1995, varying between 62% in 1995 and 2007 and 59% in 2005. In 2007, as in 2005, 16% of probationers were incarcerated because they had committed a new offense, a rule violation, or for some other reason. Probationers who have been incarcerated since 1995 have varied between 21% in 1995 and 15% in 2000. Another 3% of probationers in 2007, as in 2005, had absconded and 11% (down from 13% in 2005) had their probation revoked without incarceration. The remainder were discharged to a warrant or a detainer, transferred to another probation agency, had died, and so on.[13]

In general, the recidivism figures associated with probation do not seem substantially higher or lower than those associated with incarceration. (See Chapter 11 for data on recidivism following incarceration.) Accordingly, it can be argued that when feasible, probation should be the preferred sentence because probation costs less than imprisonment. Of course, this logic holds true only if probation does not culminate in revocation followed by incarceration. If revocation and subsequent incarceration do occur, the combined costs of probation followed by incarceration may well exceed the cost of incarceration alone.

THINKING CRITICALLY

1. What do you think makes an offender an ideal candidate for probation?

2. What are the benefits and drawbacks of probation vs. traditional jail time?

Careers in Criminal Justice

U.S. Probation Officer

My name is Steve E. Whisenant and I am an officer with the Federal Corrections and Supervision Division of the U.S. Courts, better known as the U.S. Pretrial and Probation Office. I supervise the Hickory and Statesville, North Carolina, offices, two of the five U.S. Pretrial and Probation Offices that serve the Western District of North Carolina.

My interest in criminal justice was initiated because law enforcement offered a challenging and exciting work environment. At age 20, I began employment with the Burke County, North Carolina, Sheriff's Office. While working as a deputy sheriff, I enrolled in a criminal justice program at Western Piedmont Community College in Morgantown, North Carolina. After receiving a police science Associate degree, I transferred to an evening program to earn a Bachelor of Science degree in social science/criminal justice from Gardner-Webb University in Boiling Springs, North Carolina.

During my service with the sheriff's office as a patrol officer, detective, and captain of law enforcement operations, I met the U.S. probation officer who worked in Burke County. After 9 rewarding years as a sheriff's deputy, the lure of a more stable work schedule and the absence of an election every 4 years made a position with the U.S. Probation Office appealing.

My career as a U.S. probation officer began in 1986. I worked in all three of our major units including (1) pretrial; (2) presentence writing; and (3) supervision. Each of these units offers unique and rewarding challenges. The pretrial unit completes background investigations, prepares written reports, and recommends release conditions for the magistrate's court. This unit also supervises defendants released under various bond conditions including electronic monitoring. Following a defendant's plea or verdict of guilty, the presentence unit conducts investigations and prepares detailed reports with sentencing recommendations for the district court. Its duties include contact with offenders, various law enforcement officers, U.S. attorneys, defense attorneys, and judges. The supervision unit supervises offenders who receive probation or who are released from imprisonment on parole or supervised release. They have contact with a number of persons including local law enforcement agencies, treatment providers, and offenders' employers, families, and acquaintances.

Some challenges faced by probation and pretrial staff include having little control over their workload numbers. Cases are generated by other federal agencies' arrests, releases from prison, and violations generated by the supervised offenders. Additionally, changes in the types of offenders and crimes committed, coupled with society's changing needs and expectations for supervising offenders, require a successful organization to be flexible and innovative.

Our district's leadership solicits input from every employee on how to best accomplish the organization's mission. Opportunities to work on various committees and projects abound. Employees are encouraged to promote our organization's national vision statement to exemplify the highest standards in community corrections.

As a supervisor, I support a very competent and highly professional organization. My recommendation for anyone seeking a career within this organization is to excel in fields like criminal justice, psychology, sociology, or human relations.

What do you think are the most important abilities that one must have to be a successful probation officer?

Parole

parole A method of prison release whereby inmates are released at the discretion of a board or other authority before having completed their entire sentences; can also refer to the community supervision received on release.

Recall that probation refers to the court-imposed sentence in which the offender, rather than being imprisoned, stays in the local community under the supervision of a probation officer. Two basic differences between probation and **parole** are that (1) parole is not a court-imposed sentence, and (2) parole is used with persons leaving prison. For purposes of definition, parole can be divided into two components. *Parole release* is one mechanism for releasing persons from prison. It involves releasing the inmate from prison, at the discretion of a parole board or similar paroling authority, before his or her sentence expires. *Parole supervision*, the aspect of parole that is often confused with probation, occurs after parole release. Essentially, parole supervision is a community-based continuation of the prison sentence. It involves supervision of the released offender in the community, often for a period roughly equal to the time remaining in the prison sentence.

Probation and parole supervision have similar features, which is why the two are sometimes confused. For example, both involve specific rules and conditions that offenders must follow to avoid revocation, and both entail providing offenders with supervision and services. In some instances, one officer may supervise both probationers and parolees. However, *probationer* and *parolee* are two distinct legal statuses. It is not uncommon for parole rules and conditions to be somewhat stricter and for officers to be less tolerant of violations committed by parolees; revocation of parole may be sought quickly, even for a technical parole violation. In addition, parolees often face greater adjustment problems because of the stigma attached to their prison records and because of the time they have spent away from the free community.

Just as there are different types of probation (suspended-sentence probation, split-sentence probation, and so on), there are two general types of parole. In *straight parole,* offenders are released from prison directly into the community under the supervision of the parole agency. In *residential parole,* offenders serve part of the parole term in a community residential facility or halfway house. There are two variants of residential parole. In the first variant, offenders are released from prison into the residential facility, where they spend a temporary, transitional period before returning home. The idea is to make the release process a gradual one. In the second variant, a person who violates the conditions of parole is kept on parole and is placed in the residential facility for a period of structured living, rather than having parole revoked and being returned to prison.

There are four fundamental objectives of parole. Two of these are also objectives of probation and were discussed earlier in this chapter. As with probation, parole is meant to provide community safety and to promote offender betterment and reintegration into society. The other two objectives of parole are more subtle, often unstated, but no less important. They are to (1) relieve and contain prison crowding and (2) control the behavior of prison inmates.

Since its inception, parole has functioned as a "safety valve" for institutional corrections; crowding levels can

Some offenders are released on parole before the end of their sentences, on the condition that they remain law-abiding and follow the rules designed to control their movement and to help them adjust to society. *Should parole be abolished? Why or why not?*

be better contained if more inmates are granted early release. One of the clearest manifestations of this objective is the growing popularity of emergency release laws that permit executive authorities (usually governors) to accelerate parole eligibility for selected inmates when prison crowding reaches a particular level. Parole also gives prison officials some control over the behavior of inmates. The prospect of early release gives inmates an incentive to cooperate with prison officials and to avoid infractions of prison rules.

HISTORICAL CONTEXT

As with probation, parole emerged from earlier practices. One of those is the *tickets-of-leave* concept pioneered around the mid-1800s by Captain Alexander Machonochie off the coast of Australia and by Sir Walter Crofton in Ireland. Under this concept, inmates, after serving a portion of their sentences and exhibiting good performance in prison, could be granted tickets of leave, whereby they were released into the community under supervision. Release was made conditional on continuation of good behavior, so the practice was also known as conditional pardon.

The idea of releasing some prisoners early to community supervision and making release contingent on good conduct found its way to the United States. The idea was initially implemented, along with indeterminate sentencing, in the 1870s by Zebulon Brockway at Elmira Reformatory in New York. Brockway's system allowed prison officials to grant parole release to inmates they perceived as ready for release. Parole spread rapidly after its inception at Elmira. By the turn of that century, 20 states had provisions for parole, and by 1920, the majority of states had adopted such provisions.[14]

ADMINISTRATION

It is helpful to divide parole administration into two areas. The first area is the parole board, or a similar paroling authority, which makes parole release decisions. The second is the parole field service agency, which provides parole supervision in the community after release.

Parole administration, like probation administration, exhibits much variation across the nation. At the federal level, the paroling authority is the United States Parole Commission, and the Administrative Office of the Courts administers field services. Only those offenders sentenced or under supervision before November 1, 1987, are still eligible for federal parole supervision. Federal parole has been abolished for anyone who has committed a federal crime after November 1, 1987. Offenders imprisoned for federal crimes after November 1, 1987, must serve their entire sentences, less a maximum of 54 days a year good time, if granted.[15]

Each state is responsible for administering its own parole system. Parole at the state level is generally an executive branch function, and each state has its own paroling authority. In most states, parole boards and field service agencies are administratively separate, although in some states, the board administers field services.[16] Whether probation and parole field services are jointly administered by the same government agency varies among the states. It has become quite common, however, for states to combine probation and parole administration. In Kentucky, for example, the same unit of the Department of Corrections administers both.

Another area of difference between states is whether the paroling authority or board is (1) administratively autonomous and independent of prison officials or (2) administratively consolidated with the department of corrections. Most parole boards are autonomous.[17]

In many ways the parole board is the centerpiece of parole administration; the board is very influential in establishing a jurisdiction's parole policies. A national survey of parole boards found that in most states, the governor, subject to legislative confirmation, appoints parole board members. Appointment terms in most states are 4 to 6 years, and the vast majority of states use renewable appointments. The professional qualifications required for appointment differ across states. Interestingly, law in many jurisdictions requires no minimum professional qualifications. The number of parole board members also varies by state, with five and seven members being common. A minority of states employs part-time parole board members. Most of the nations' board members are white, approximately one-quarter is female, and the average age of board members is about 50.[18]

PROCESS AND PROCEDURES

Besides helping establish the jurisdiction's parole policies, the parole board is generally responsible for managing parole release processes and making decisions to terminate parole supervision.

The Parole Board—Release and Termination   Prior to appearing before the parole authority for a parole-grant hearing, a prisoner must first become eligible for parole and complete a parole plan describing such things as where he or she plans to live and work after release. In addition, prison staff usually prepares a preparole report for the parole board. The report summarizes the characteristics of the inmate and his or her offense, reviews the inmate's adjustment to prison and his or her progress toward rehabilitation, and presents the inmate's parole plan. Reports sometimes contain a recommendation about whether the inmate should be paroled.

Depending on the jurisdiction and the particular case, the actual parole-grant hearing can be conducted by the full parole board, a partial board, or representatives of the board known as examiners or hearing officers. Roughly half of the states rely on hearing officers.[19] Other concerned parties, such as prison staff, prosecuting attorneys, and victims, may also be present. Parole hearings are typically quite short and routine. Parole authorities review relevant documents, such as the inmate's parole plan, the preparole report, and victim statements, and often interview the inmate. Authorities then vote on whether to grant or to deny parole release. In more than half of the states, the inmate is notified of the outcome of voting at the hearing or immediately thereafter. In the remaining states, notification time frames range from 1 week to more than 30 days.[20] If parole is denied, the inmate is automatically eligible for a future hearing. For example, in May 2007, Charles Manson, then 72, was denied parole for the eleventh time. He was sentenced to death in 1970 for his role in the 1969 Tate-LaBianca murders. When the Supreme Court declared capital punishment unconstitutional in 1972, his death sentence was automatically commuted to life imprisonment with opportunity for parole. His next parole hearing is scheduled for 2012.[21]

Increasingly, parole authorities are using structured instruments called **parole guidelines** to estimate the probability of recidivism and to direct their release decisions. Those guidelines are similar to the sentencing guidelines used by judges and the risk-and-needs assessment instruments used in probation work. Only about half the jurisdictions employ parole guidelines, and even in those jurisdictions, parole authorities often have the discretion to override guideline recommendations.[22] A sample parole guideline instrument, recently revised and updated by the Georgia Parole Board, is presented in Figure 12.5. The risk instrument accurately predicted that 39% of 33,000 offenders released, either discharged or paroled, from Georgia's prisons over a recent three-year period were at high risk of being reconvicted of a new crime.[23]

Parole authorities consider a variety of factors in determining whether to grant or to deny an inmate parole. Furthermore, those factors tend to be assigned

parole guidelines Structured instruments used to estimate the probability of parole recidivism and to direct the release decisions of parole boards.

Figure 12.5

Georgia Parole Guideline Instrument

Parole Decision Guidelines, Time to Serve GRID

Risk	Low (−5 to +2)			Medium (3−6)			High (7+)			Risk
CSL	Low	Mid	High	Low	Mid	High	Low	Mid	High	CSL
1	15	**17**	19	17	**20**	22	20	**22**	26	1
2	18	**20**	22	20	**22**	24	24	**26**	28	2
3	20	**22**	24	22	**24**	28	26	**28**	32	3
4	22	**24**	26	24	**28**	34	28	**32**	38	4
5	30	**34**	40	34	**42**	52	40	**50**	60	5
6	36	**40**	52	40	**50**	60	52	**65**	78	6
7	40	**44**	60	48	**60**	78	60	**76**	102	7
8	65% of sentence			75% of sentence			90% of sentence			8

GRID effective for cases considered on or after January 1, 2008

Notes: Risk = Risk to re-offend; CSL = Crime Severity Level (1 = least severe; 8 = most severe); numbers in figure represent months.

Source: "Georgia Parole Decision Guidelines" (October 19, 2007) at www.pap.state.ga.us/opencms/export/sites/default/resources/Proposed_Parole_Decision_Guidelines.pdf (accessed December 18, 2008).

different levels of importance. A recent analysis of national data found that the four most important factors, in order, are these:

1. Seriousness of the current offense.
2. History of prior violent behavior.
3. Prior felony convictions.
4. Use of a firearm in committing the current offense.

Other relevant factors include the number of prior incarcerations, prior adjustment on parole, prison disciplinary record, psychological reports, and victim input.[24]

The U.S. Supreme Court addressed due process in parole release decisions in *Greenholtz* v. *Inmates of the Nebraska Penal and Correctional Complex* (1979). Noting that parole release is an act of grace, the Court held that release on parole is distinct from parole revocation. Thus, the Court declined to apply the provisions outlined in *Morrissey* v. *Brewer,* discussed earlier in this chapter, to parole release. Consequently, what constitutes acceptable due process in release decision-making is largely case-specific. Jurisdictions vary considerably in their due process provisions for parole hearings. Most of the jurisdictions allow inmates to be represented by attorneys.[25]

Once inmates receive parole release, they begin the period of parole supervision, discussed later, which continues until it is terminated. In addition to its responsibility for release decisions, the parole board is responsible for parole termination decisions. In most jurisdictions, the board can discharge individuals from parole supervision; this is commonly done upon the recommendation of the parole supervision agency. Alternatively, if no board action is taken, the individual is discharged from parole upon expiration of the legal sentence.

Parole revocation is also the responsibility of the parole board and can occur in response to new crimes or technical violations. Parole revocation is quite similar to probation revocation and is governed by the same case law (*Morrissey* v. *Brewer* and *Gagnon* v. *Scarpelli*). As is true in the field of probation, parole officers enjoy considerable discretion when deciding whether to recommend revocation for violations. If revocation is sought, the two-stage hearing process required under *Morrissey* becomes applicable. Although parole authorities consider various factors in determining whether to revoke parole, research indicates that the two most important factors are the seriousness of the violation and the recommendation of the supervising parole officer.[26]

Field Services—Supervision and Service Delivery Traditionally, parole boards administered most parole supervision or field service agencies. This situation has changed dramatically since the 1960s. Currently, most field service agencies are administratively separate from the parole board.[27] In most of those jurisdictions, parole supervision is administered by the department of corrections. Nevertheless, the basic task of field service agencies has remained constant through the years—to provide control and assistance for persons re-entering the community from prison.

Virtually everything that was stated earlier in this chapter about probation supervision and service delivery applies to parole supervision and service delivery. The subtle differences between the two are overshadowed by the many similarities. However, one difference warrants mention. Specialization is more common in parole than in probation supervision. Under specialization, offenders who pose a similar threat to public safety or those who share similar treatment needs are grouped together and assigned to the same officers. Specialization by parole officers is used in slightly more than half the jurisdictions. The two most common areas for specialization are with sex offenders and substance-abusing offenders.[28]

Social scientist Richard McCleary conducted what is considered a classic sociological study of a parole supervision agency.[29] In his book *Dangerous Men,*

MYTH

If parole is revoked, return to prison is automatic.

FACT

Though reincarceration is common, other options are usually possible, such as placement in a halfway house or reinstatement of parole. Much discretion is involved.

McCleary observes that parole officers are very concerned with avoiding "trouble" from parolees. Trouble is defined broadly as anything that runs counter to the status quo of the parole agency. Trouble can threaten the agency's public image, thus bringing the agency pressure—and possibly increased structure—from political officials. The likelihood of trouble is reduced to the extent that officers can anticipate what clients might do in response to threats of various punishments and rewards from officers. "Dangerous men" are parolees who do not respond predictably to officers' threats and promises. Dangerous men are not necessarily prone to violent behavior; they are merely unpredictable. Because unpredictability implies possible trouble, officers try to identify dangerous men as soon as possible in the supervision process. The dangerous-man label is used sparingly because it means greater supervision and more documentation and paperwork for officers. However, the label can protect the supervising officer and the agency from subsequent criticism because, early on, it conveys that problems may be expected from a particular parolee. Concerned parties in the parole bureaucracy are alerted to what might happen, and the potential for "surprises" is reduced. Once parolees have acquired the dangerous-man label, the agency is quick to seek reasons to revoke their paroles. McCleary's research underscores the crucial significance of agency bureaucratic dynamics in shaping supervision practices.

PAROLE ISSUES

Since the 1970s, discretionary parole release has been among the most controversial issues in criminal justice. Proponents of parole release argue, for example, that early release provisions are essential for controlling prisoners' behavior and for containing institutional crowding. However, several criticisms have been directed at parole release. Some critics claim that parole undermines both retribution and deterrence because offenders are permitted to leave prison early, sometimes many years before finishing their maximum sentences. Similarly, critics argue that because prisons generally fail to reform offenders and it is impossible for parole boards to accurately predict which offenders will commit new crimes, parole does not sufficiently guarantee public safety. Other critics believe that parole is unfair to offenders. Those opponents charge that parole leads to significant disparities in time served in prison for offenders who should be serving equal amounts of time. For example, two offenders in the same jurisdiction with very similar prior legal backgrounds may be convicted of committing armed robbery under very similar circumstances. One offender may serve 5 years in prison and receive parole, whereas the other may serve twice as long before release. Another contention of critics is that linking the degree of participation in prison treatment programs to the possibility of early parole amounts to subtly coercing inmates into programs that are often of questionable effectiveness.

Those and other criticisms helped persuade a number of jurisdictions to curtail discretionary parole release. Instead, they moved from indeterminate sentencing to determinate sentencing, decreased reliance on parole release and increased reliance on mandatory release, and devised both sentencing and parole guidelines. There were even forceful calls and some initiatives

Parole officers frequently meet their clients at the clients' workplaces. *What problems, if any, might be created by this practice?*

undertaken to completely abolish parole release, although the movement to abolish parole seems to have peaked.[30] By 2005 (the latest year for which data were available), 19 states (Arizona, 1994; Arkansas, 1994; California, 1976 (but see below); Delaware, 1990; Florida, 1983; Illinois, 1978; Indiana, 1977; Kansas, 1993; Maine, 1976; Minnesota, 1980; Mississippi, 1995; New Mexico, 1979; North Carolina, 1994; Ohio, 1996; Oregon, 1989; South Dakota, 1996; Virginia, 1995; Washington, 1984; and Wisconsin, 2000) and the federal government had abolished early release by discretion of a parole board for all offenders. However, parole boards still have discretion over inmates who were sentenced for crimes committed prior to the effective date of the law that eliminated parole board release. A few other states have abolished parole release for certain violent or felony offenders (Alaska, Georgia, Louisiana, Massachusetts, Maryland, Missouri, New Jersey, New York, Oklahoma, South Carolina, and Tennessee). California allows discretionary release by a parole board only for offenders with indeterminate life sentences.[31] Note that although discretionary release from prison by a parole board has been eliminated by some states, postrelease supervision still exists and is generally referred to as community or supervised release. Parole boards, in various forms, have the responsibility to set conditions of release for offenders under community or supervised release, the authority to return an offender to prison for violating the conditions of supervised release, and the power to grant parole for medical reasons.[32]

Besides the issue of whether parole release should exist, there are a number of other pressing concerns surrounding parole. They include legal issues, strained parole resources, and parolee adjustment and recidivism.

Legal Issues There are two general categories of legal issues that relate to parole: (1) parolees' civil rights and (2) the liabilities of parole officials.

As noted previously, individuals forfeit a variety of civil rights when they are convicted of a felony. Some of those include the right to hold public office and certain other jobs, the right to jury service, and the right to obtain some types of licenses and insurance. Although the specific rights forfeited vary by jurisdiction, in many instances parolees must seek court action to restore their rights following release from incarceration. Only a few jurisdictions grant their parole boards authority to restore ex-offenders' rights.[33]

People who support denying released inmates certain rights argue that the practice is necessary to preserve public safety and maintain high moral standards in society. Opponents argue that it is unfair to continue penalizing individuals who have paid their debts. They point out that denial of civil liberties contributes to poor adjustment on parole. Given the current posture of the nation toward felons and exfelons, it seems unlikely, at least in the foreseeable future, that the majority of persons coming out of prison will have their rights fully restored.

Can parole board officials and field service agents be held legally liable if a parolee's actions cause harm to a victim or victims? The answer is a qualified yes. Even though the vast majority of paroling authorities enjoy some type of immunity from liability (through constitution, statute, or case law), such immunity has been eroding in recent years.

According to attorney and criminal justice professor John Watkins, Jr., three central elements must be proven to establish liability on the part of parole and probation officials.

1. The existence of a legal duty owed the public.
2. Evidence of a breach of the required standard of duty.
3. An injury or damage to a person or group proximately caused by the breach of duty.

Watkins further observes that as a general rule, tort liability applies to injuries, or damages, caused by the negligent or improper performance of ministerial functions but not to injuries caused by unsatisfactory performance of discretionary functions. A *discretionary* function is one "that may involve a series of possible choices from a wide array of alternatives, none of which may be absolutely called for in a particular situation." A *ministerial* function is "one regarding which nothing is left to discretion—a simple and definite duty imposed by law, and arising under conditions admitted or proved to exist."[34] An example of a breach of a ministerial function would be if a parole board were to completely disregard parole guidelines that the board is legally bound to consider before releasing inmates. Thus, if parole and probation officials wish to minimize the likelihood of being held liable, those officials should determine what is legally required of them in their jurisdiction and make good faith efforts to abide by those requirements.

Strained Parole Resources Parole supervision agencies across the nation are currently attempting to manage record numbers of parolees. On December 31, 2007, for example, 824,365 adults were under active parole supervision. That represents an increase of about 55% over the total number of parolees on December 31, 1990.[35] Table 12.3 shows the states with the largest parole populations and the highest and lowest rates of persons under parole supervision per 100,000 adult U.S. residents at year-end 2007. Moreover, an increasingly large proportion of parolees has been released from prison early because of pressures to relieve institutional crowding, rather than because those persons have been judged good candidates for parole. Such parolees often require above-average levels of supervision and services. Because most jurisdictions are facing pressure to expand prison space, it is not surprising that parole resources, such as budgets and staffing, have failed to keep pace with those developments.

The long-term implications of this predicament are often unappreciated. Parolee recidivism is normally quite high, partly because of the strained resources of parole agencies. The typical public and political response to high parolee recidivism is to demand a "get-tough" stance that culminates in the return of

FYI Characteristics of Adults on Parole, 2007

In 2007, 88% of all probationers in the United States were male and 12% were female. Forty-two percent were white (non-Hispanic), 37% were black (non-Hispanic), 19% were Hispanic, and the remainder were of other races. Twenty-six percent of parolees had committed violent offenses, 24% had committed property offenses, 37% had committed drug offenses, and 13% had committed public order or other offenses.

Source: Lauren E. Glaze and Thomas P. Bonczar, "Probation and Parole in the United States, 2007 Statistical Tables," U.S. Department of Justice, *Bureau of Justice Statistics* (Washington, D.C.: GPO, December 2008), Table 5, www.ojp.usdoj.gov/bjs/pub/pdf/ppus07st.pdf.

Table 12.3 **States with the Largest Parole Populations and the Highest and Lowest Rates of Persons under Parole Supervision per 100,000 Adult U.S. Residents at Year-End 2007**

States with the Largest Parole Populations		States with the Highest Rates of Supervision		States with the Lowest Rates of Supervision	
California	= 123,764	Arkansas	= 904	Maine	= 3
Texas	= 101,748	Pennsylvania	= 807	Florida	= 33
Pennsylvania	= 78,107	Oregon	= 779	North Carolina	= 48
New York	= 53,669	Louisiana	= 746	Rhode Island	= 56
Illinois	= 33,354	Texas	= 582	Nebraska	= 60
Louisiana	= 24,085	South Dakota	= 466	Massachusetts	= 64
Georgia	= 23,111	California	= 453	North Dakota	= 69
Oregon	= 22,658	Missouri	= 443	South Carolina	= 72
Michigan	= 21,131	Wisconsin	= 395	Delaware	= 81
Missouri	= 19,849	Kentucky	= 392	Connecticut	= 81

Note: This table excludes the District of Columbia.

Source: Lauren E. Glaze and Thomas P. Bonczar, "Probation and Parole in the United States, 2007 Statistical Tables," U.S. Department of Justice, *Bureau of Justice Statistics* (Washington, D.C.: GPO, December 2008), pp. 4–5, Table 3, www.ojp.usdoj.gov/bjs/pub/pdf/ppus07st.pdf.

reintegration The process of rebuilding former ties to the community and establishing new ties after release from prison.

large numbers of parolees to prison. This exacerbates both prison crowding and the tendency to rely on parole release to relieve crowding. The result is further strain on parole resources and, consequently, further recidivism.

Parolee Adjustment and Recidivism A key to successful community adjustment for inmates leaving prison is **reintegration,** which means rebuilding former prosocial ties to the community and establishing new ties. An important part of reintegration is finding a satisfactory job and obtaining adequate subsistence funds through legal means.

The stigma of a prison record can result in grim employment prospects, especially without the assistance of the parole agency. Yet, research suggests that obtaining employment improves adjustment to community life. In a study of the effects of postrelease employment on the emotional well-being of a sample of ex-felons in Texas and Georgia, it was found that employment enhanced emotional well-being by providing wages and improving perceptions of self-worth. The research discovered that sustained unemployment caused emotional distress. This distress reduced the motivation of releasees to search for jobs. In the words of the study's author, "Unemployment fed on itself by creating psychological stress which in turn reduced effectiveness in finding work."[36] Related evidence suggests that providing newly released ex-inmates with temporary unemployment benefits can decrease the recidivism rate, although it is important that such benefits not create a work disincentive.[37]

Research spanning three decades shows that fewer than half of all state prison inmates released on parole successfully complete their term of supervision. For example, during the 1990s, the percentage of successful parole discharges ranged from about 42% to about 49%.[38] In 2007, 44.5% of state parolees successfully completed their term of supervision, 38% were returned to prison or jail, and 17% absconded or in other ways failed to successfully meet the conditions of supervision.[39]

States vary widely in their rates of success, which can be attributed to a number of factors such as variations in the parole populations (for example, age at release, criminal history, and most serious offense), the level of supervision, and parole agency policies on the revocation of technical violators. Research shows that inmates released from prison on parole for the first time are more likely to succeed than re-releases. Re-releases are inmates who are being discharged from prison on parole who have served time for a previous violation of parole or conditional release or a new offense committed while under previous parole supervision. However, the success rate for first-time releases declines the longer the inmate has been in prison. Success rates also vary by method of release. State inmates released by a parole board (*discretionary parole*) almost always have a higher rate of success than inmates released through *mandatory parole* (that is, inmates who generally are sentenced under determinate sentencing statutes and are released from prison after serving a portion of their original sentence minus any good time earned). There is also a temporal element to parole success or failure. The chances of failure are generally highest during the early stages of parole. The first year appears to be the most critical if a successful discharge from parole is going to occur. Finally, parole success and failure have varied by parolee gender, race or ethnicity, age, and most serious offense for which he or she was incarcerated.

THINKING CRITICALLY

1. How much weight do victim impact statements get in the decision to grant parole?

2. Given what you have read, do you think there are ways to improve the parole process? If so, what can be done?

Parole Agent

My name is Arthur J. Ramirez and I am a parole agent III (PA III) for the California State Department of Corrections (CDC) Parole and Community Services Division (P&CSD). Since 1983, I have also taught undergraduate and graduate criminal justice courses at California State University, Long Beach. I hold a Bachelor of Science degree in criminal justice, two master's degrees (community clinical psychology and criminal justice), as well as a Doctorate degree in criminology. I chose to work with ex-felons in order to be in a unique position to improve the quality of life in our society.

As a PA III, I provide supervisory direction with respect to the philosophies, policies, and procedures of the CDC for the Long Beach I Parole Unit. I also complete a number of adjunct assignments for the department. A typical day includes reviewing my management formation system to ensure that the operations of the parole unit run smoothly. I hold case conferences with parole agents and/or review reports, written by them, related to the progress of parolees or parole violations committed by them. I review each case in order to determine the appropriate action. The actions may include: reviewing cases for discharge from parole; referring parolees to community programs that are in line with their needs; approving funds to assist parolees; and reviewing activity reports to continue parolees on parole as a disposition after a parole violation. This allows the parolee to remain in the community and is often accompanied with a referral to a social program. I also make decisions to return parolees back into custody for parole violations. This includes reviewing the violation reports prior to submitting them to the Board of Prison Terms. Additionally, I review reports to initiate warrants for the arrest of parolees when they abscond from parole. Another typical day may also include traveling to Sacramento to attend a Commission on Correctional Peace Officer Standards and Training (CPOST) Curriculum Review Committee meeting. In this capacity, I review lesson plans submitted by youth and adult corrections agencies statewide and health care services to ensure that they are in line with the professional training standards established and approved by CPOST.

It is very rewarding to see parolees making a positive adjustment in their reintegration into society from imprisonment. It is also frustrating to see them being returned to prison for parole violations despite effective casework by a parole agent. Our society is currently faced with the challenge to provide the highest quality criminal justice services in order to respond to our criminal justice problems. I enjoy being a part of this process at the local and state levels. The field of criminal justice provides many career position opportunities for students. I fully believe that students today need to plan for their future careers systematically. Students interested in working in the field of criminal justice need to contact practicing professionals in the community in order to find out more about the position opportunities available in the field. I also recommend that students interested in working in parole should volunteer or enroll in an internship program with an agency that works with parolees or offenders. This will assist them in deciding whether a career in parole is for them.

Compare the information above with the career box on probation officers. Which position would you be more attracted to? Why?

Intermediate Sanctions

Recent dramatic increases in prison, parole, and probation populations have fundamentally altered the field of community corrections. Community corrections has been forced to accommodate (1) growing numbers of the types of offenders the field has traditionally accommodated, plus (2) offenders who would have been sent to—or remained in—prison had sufficient space been available. At the same time, the field has witnessed a general decline in philosophical support for rehabilitation, coupled with a growing emphasis on punishing and controlling offenders. Since the 1980s, the intermediate-sanction trend has grown within this context.

In restrictiveness and punitiveness, **intermediate sanctions** lie somewhere between traditional probation and traditional imprisonment or, alternatively, between imprisonment and traditional parole supervision (see Figure 12.6). Intermediate sanctions are designed to widen the range of incarceration alternatives and to calibrate that range according to the differential risks and needs of offenders.

As a rule, the newer intermediate sanctions are oriented less toward rehabilitation and more toward retribution, deterrence, and incapacitation than older community correctional programs. However, the distinction between intermediate sanctions and older, more traditional programs has become

intermediate sanctions Sanctions that, in restrictiveness and punitiveness, lie between traditional probation and traditional imprisonment or, alternatively, between imprisonment and traditional parole.

Figure 12.6

Relationship of Intermediate Sanctions to Traditional Sanctions

No Sanction	Traditional Probation	Intermediate Sanctions	Traditional Imprisonment	Intermediate Sanctions	Traditional Parole Supervision

somewhat blurred because some traditional programs, such as restitution and halfway houses, have been incorporated into the intermediate-sanction category. The specific intermediate sanctions to be discussed in this section include intensive-supervision probation and parole, day reporting centers, structured fines (or day fines), home confinement and electronic monitoring, and halfway houses.

INTENSIVE-SUPERVISION PROBATION AND PAROLE (ISP)

intensive-supervision probation and parole (ISP) An alternative to incarceration that provides stricter conditions, closer supervision, and more treatment services than do traditional probation and parole.

Intensive-supervision probation and parole (ISP) provides stricter conditions, closer supervision, and more treatment services than do traditional probation and parole. Offenders are often selected for ISP on the basis of their scores on risk-and-needs-assessment instruments. Alternatively, they may be placed on ISP after violating regular probation or parole. Most ISP programs are for non-violent felons.

The ISP programs in existence across the nation are diverse, and some programs come much closer than others to providing supervision and services that are genuinely intensive. In theory, ISP programs have the following features:

1. Specially trained intensive-supervision officers with small caseloads (for example, 25 cases per officer)
2. Inescapable supervision, such as multiple weekly contacts between officers and clients and frequent testing for drug use
3. Mandatory curfews
4. Mandatory employment or restitution requirements, or both
5. Mandatory or voluntary participation in treatment
6. Supervision fees to be paid by clients

CJ Online

American Probation and Parole Association

The American Probation and Parole Association explores issues relevant to the field of community corrections. You can visit its website at www .appa-net.org/. *Would a career in probation or parole be of interest to you? Why or why not?*

ISP usually lasts 6 months to 2 years. Typically, offenders must pass through a series of phases that become progressively less restrictive during the period of intensive supervision.

The majority of states have implemented ISP programs for adult probationers and parolees.[40] However, of all persons placed on probation or parole, relatively few are placed under intensive supervision, because of resource limitations and the small caseloads required by ISP. Although it is commonly argued that ISP costs less money than incarceration, provided it is not followed by incarceration due to revocation, ISP generally costs more than traditional probation or parole. For this reason, it is used rather sparingly.

Although a number of concerns have been raised about ISP, two of the most important are (1) the potential for net widening and (2) the lack of demonstrated reduction of recidivism.

net widening A phenomenon that occurs when the offenders placed in a novel program are not the offenders for whom the program was designed. The consequence is that those in the program receive more severe sanctions than they would have received had the new program remained unavailable.

Net widening takes various forms and can plague virtually any type of community correctional program. Net widening occurs when the offenders placed in a novel program like ISP are not the offenders for whom the program was intended. The consequence is that those in the program receive more

Intensive-supervision probation and parole (ISP) provides stricter conditions, closer supervision, and more treatment services than do traditional probation and parole. *Is ISP worth the extra expense? Why or why not?*

severe sanctions than they would have received had the new program remained unavailable. Suppose, for example, that a jurisdiction facing a prison-crowding crisis establishes a new intensive probation program so that a substantial number of nonviolent offenders can be sentenced to ISP rather than prison. That is, the ISP target group consists of nonviolent felons who would have gone to prison had ISP not become available. If only persons who would formerly have gone to prison are placed on ISP, net widening has not taken place. However, if persons who would formerly have been placed on regular probation are now placed on ISP, net widening has occurred. To the degree that such net widening is the result, ISP becomes a costly addition to ordinary probation, instead of serving its intended function of providing a cost-efficient alternative to imprisonment.

Again, it is important to realize that almost all community correctional programs, especially those specifically designed to divert offenders from more severe sanctions, are vulnerable to net widening. Net widening can be avoided or minimized by establishing and following standard criteria for assigning offenders to programs. If the goal of an intensive probation program is to divert offenders from prison, then only prison-bound offenders should be placed in the program. Offenders who would have been placed on regular probation had the intensive program been unavailable should continue to be placed on regular probation. When modern ISP programs were introduced in the early 1980s, there was much optimism that a cost-efficient means of diverting offenders from prison and controlling their recidivism had been found. Writing about the Georgia ISP program, social scientists Billie Erwin and Lawrence Bennett stated that "the recidivism rates are considerably better than for groups under regular probation and for those released from prison. [ISP] offenders commit fewer and less serious crimes."[41] Erwin and Bennett also estimated that Georgia saved $6,775 for each case diverted from prison into ISP.

Unfortunately, the initial optimism surrounding ISP has not been sustained according to subsequent, well-designed research by Joan Petersilia and her

Table 12.4 **Offender Recidivism Averages in Petersilia and Turner's Study of ISP in 14 Jurisdictions**

Sanction	Percentage Arrested	Percentage with Technical Violations	Percentage Returned to Prison
ISP	37	65	24
Alternative	33	38	15

MYTH

Incarceration for technical violations prevents crime.

FACT

In the largest controlled experiment ever conducted nationwide on intensive-supervision probation and parole, researchers found that offenders who committed technical violations were no more likely to be arrested for new crimes than those who did not commit technical violations.

Source: Joan Petersilia and Susan Turner, *Evaluating Intensive Supervision Probation/ Parole: Results of a Nationwide Experiment,* U.S. Department of Justice, National Institute of Justice, Research in Brief (Washington, D.C.: GPO, 1993).

colleagues. In one study, criminologists Petersilia and Turner compared offenders who had been randomly assigned to either intensive or regular probation in three California counties. Efforts were made to ensure that only high-risk, serious offenders were included in the study, and offenders were followed for 6 months after program placement. Across counties, an average of 30% of the ISP cases had technical violations, and about 20% had new arrests. In two counties, ISP clients were significantly more likely than regular probationers to incur technical violations but neither more nor less likely to incur new arrests. In the other county, ISP cases and regular probationers did not differ significantly in technical violations or new arrests. Petersilia and Turner observe that in the first two counties, the increased supervision of ISP may simply have increased awareness of clients' technical violations. That is, regular probationers may have committed just as many technical violations, but more of the violations may have escaped detection because of less supervision. More important, Petersilia and Turner point out that if ISP simply increases awareness of technical violations and if the official response to such violations is swift revocation of ISP followed by incarceration, two things may occur. First, because offenders are no longer at risk of recidivism in the community once they are incarcerated, the artificial impression may be created that ISP is associated with low arrest rates. Second, ISP will fuel the prison crowding problem it is intended to relieve.[42]

In another study, Petersilia and Turner evaluated a national ISP demonstration project in 14 jurisdictions across nine states.[43] The 14 programs were implemented between 1986 and 1991 and involved approximately 2,000 offenders. In each program, offenders were assigned randomly to either ISP or an alternative sanction, such as regular probation, prison, or regular parole. They were then followed for 1 year. The average results across jurisdictions are summarized in Table 12.4. ISP was associated with a substantially higher percentage of technical violations than the alternative sanctions. Again it appears that ISP may have increased detection of technical violations and thereby inflated incarceration rates. The data suggest that if ISP is to relieve prison crowding in any meaningful way, officials will have to become more reluctant to revoke ISP and impose incarceration for technical violations.

DAY REPORTING CENTERS

day reporting centers Facilities that are designed for offenders who would otherwise be in prison or jail and that require offenders to report regularly to confer with staff about supervision and treatment matters.

Day reporting centers, a relatively new facet of the intermediate-sanction movement, emerged in Great Britain in the 1970s and were pioneered in the United States in Massachusetts in 1986. The centers can be administered publicly or privately and are designed primarily for offenders who would otherwise be in jail or prison. This includes offenders such as those on ISP and those awaiting trial who did not receive release on recognizance or bail. Offenders are permitted to live at home but must report to the center regularly to confer with center staff about supervision and treatment matters. Program components commonly focus on work, education, counseling, and community service.[44] The program objectives devised for offenders by the Metropolitan Day Reporting Center in

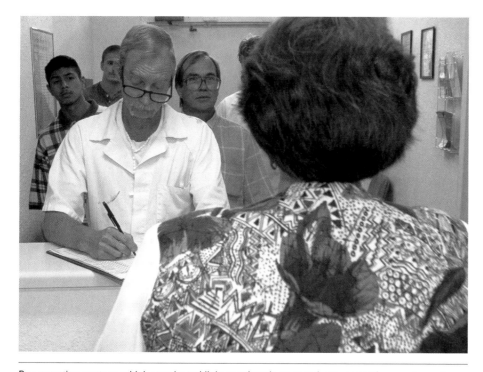

Day reporting centers, which may be publicly or privately operated, are corrections centers where offenders must report regularly to comply with a sentence. Most day center programs include employment, counseling, education, and community service components. *Should the use of day reporting centers be expanded? Why or why not?*

Boston are illustrated in Figure 12.7. In June 2007, 6,163 offenders nationwide were being supervised by personnel of day reporting centers instead of being confined in jails (down from 6,627 in June 2004 but up from 4,747 in June 2005). The 2007 figure represents about 9% of offenders being supervised outside a jail facility (excluding persons on probation or parole).[45]

STRUCTURED FINES, OR DAY FINES

Another relatively new intermediate sanction, at least in the United States, is structured fines, or day fines.[46] **Structured fines,** or **day fines,** differ fundamentally from the fines (called *tariff fines*) more typically imposed by American criminal courts. Whereas tariff fines require a single fixed amount of money, or an amount of money within a narrow range, to be paid by all defendants convicted of a particular crime, *without regard to their financial circumstances*, structured fines are based on defendants' ability to pay. The basic premise of structured fines is that "punishment by a fine should be proportionate to the seriousness of the offense and should have roughly similar impact (in terms of economic sting) on persons with differing financial resources who are convicted of the same offense."

The creation of a structured fine is a two-part process. In the first part, the number of fine units for a crime is determined from a scale that ranks crimes according to their seriousness. In the second part, the dollar amount of the fine is determined by multiplying the number of fine units by a proportion of the defendant's net daily income (hence the term *day fine*), adjusted to account for dependents and special circumstances.

Structured fines were first introduced in the 1920s in Sweden and soon thereafter were adopted by other Scandinavian countries. West Germany began employing them in the early 1970s. The western European nations have made day fines the sanction of choice in a large proportion of criminal cases, including

structured fines, or **day fines** Fines that are based on defendants' ability to pay.

 FYI No Time for Fine

The U.S. Supreme Court has ruled that an offender cannot be imprisoned for failure to pay a fine unless the default is willful, if imprisonment is not an authorized penalty for the offense of which the defendant was convicted.

Source: *Tate* v. *Short* (1971).

Figure 12.7

Metropolitan Day Reporting Center Participant Program Objectives

I ,_____, agree to participate in
the activities and to adhere to the schedule of this contract. I understand that
this contract may be modified during my participation in the Day Reporting
Center and I agree to those modifications as determined by my participation.

Objectives   *Time frame*

Reporting: I will report in to the Center at the times designated by my case
                 manager and as noted on my daily itinerary.

                 I will call in to the Center at the times designated by my ca
                 manager and as noted on my daily itinerary.

Supervision: I will be available for phone calls or house checks by Day
                 Reporting Center staff at the locations listed on my daily itine

Employment: Employer: _____
                 Address: _____

                 Contact Person: _____
                 Telephone: _____
                 Hours: _____
                 Salary: _____

Financial: I agree to submit my pay stub to the Center for verification (
                 my employment. I further agree to work with my case
                 manager on budgeting my money; including the payment of
                 any court-ordered fines or other restitution.
                 Details:_____

Substance Abuse Treatment: I agree to participate in the following program
                 address my substance abuse problems: _____

Urinalysis: I agree to submit to urinalysis testing upon the request of Day
                 Reporting Center staff. _____

Curfew: I understand that I am to be at my residence from the hours of
                 _____ P.M. to _____ A.M., and that I may be contacted by
                 Day Reporting Center staff during that time. _____

Other Objectives: _____
                 _____
                 _____
                 _____
                 _____
                 _____
                 _____
                 _____
                 _____
                 _____

Client _____   *Date* _____

I agree to assist _____ to achieve the
listed objectives of this contract in my capacity as case manager.

Case Manager _____   *Date* _____

FYI

Structured Fines

Regarding the use of structured fines,
or day fines, in the United States,
criminologists Norval Morris and
Michael Tonry make this interesting
observation: "It is paradoxical that a
society that relies so heavily on the
financial incentive in its social
philosophy and economic practice
should be so reluctant to use the
financial disincentive as a punishment
of crime."

Source: Norval Morris and Michael Tonry (eds.),
*Between Prisons and Probation: Intermediate
Punishments in a Rational Sentencing System*
(New York: Oxford University Press, 1990), p. 111.

many involving serious offenses. For example, in Germany, day fines are used as the only sanction for three-fourths of all offenders convicted of property crimes and for two-thirds of all offenders convicted of assaults.

The first structured-fine program in the United States began in 1988 in Richmond County (Staten Island), New York, as a demonstration project. Other structured-fine demonstration projects have been established in Maricopa County (Phoenix), Arizona; Bridgeport, Connecticut; Polk County (Des Moines), Iowa; and four counties in Oregon (Marion, Malheur, Josephine, and Coos). An evaluation of the Richmond County project, sponsored by the National Institute of Justice, showed very promising results.

Among the presumed advantages of structured-fine or day-fine programs are these:

1. **Offender Accountability**—"The offender is, quite literally, made to pay his or her debt to society."
2. **Deterrence**—"Structured fines provide an economic disincentive for criminal behavior."

3. **Fairness**—Structured fines are fairer than tariff fines because tariff fines frequently are too low to be meaningful to wealthier offenders and too high for poorer offenders to pay.
4. **Effective and Efficient Use of Limited System Resources**—"Structured fines are relatively inexpensive to administer compared with most other types of intermediate sanctions."
5. **Revenue**—"Structured fines can be more effective than tariff fines in generating revenue."
6. **Credibility for the Court**—Because offenders pay in full in a very large proportion of cases, the sanction has credibility with the offender and the community.

Among the problems with structured fines are these:

1. **Collection Problems**—"If judges are not convinced that such fines will be paid in a high proportion of cases, or if offenders assume that the fines need not be paid, the usefulness of the structured fine as a criminal sanction is seriously eroded."
2. **The Effect of Other Monetary Penalties**—In most U.S. jurisdictions, defendants convicted of crimes have a variety of monetary penalties to pay, for example, penalty assessment fees, crime victim compensation fees, indigent defense fees, and probation fees. Those monetary sanctions create a high cost to a defendant, even before a fine is imposed. A fine added to those costs may exceed the ability of poorer defendants to pay.

HOME CONFINEMENT AND ELECTRONIC MONITORING

In **home confinement** programs (also known as home incarceration, home detention, and house arrest), offenders are required by the court to remain in their homes except for preapproved periods of absence. For example, offenders may be permitted to leave home to go to work, school, or church or to run errands. Home confinement is usually considered more punitive than ISP but is often used in conjunction with ISP. For example, home confinement may be required during the initial phase of intensive probation or may be ordered if an offender violates probation or parole. Home confinement can also serve as an alternative to pretrial detention in jail.

House arrest has traditionally been employed in the military and has a long history of limited use in criminal justice. However, home confinement programs did not gain wide popularity until **electronic monitoring** equipment became readily available during the 1980s. The first statewide home confinement program without electronic monitoring was implemented in Florida in the early 1980s. St. Louis was one of the cities to pioneer such programming in the early 1970s. Among the first jurisdictions to implement an electronic monitoring program was Palm Beach County, Florida, in 1984.[47]

Electronic monitoring allows an offender's whereabouts to be gauged through the use of computer technology. Before the use of electronic monitoring, it was time consuming and expensive for officials to ensure that offenders were complying with home confinement orders. Electronic monitoring rendered home confinement more practical and cost effective because officials did not have to rely on personal phone calls and home visits to assess compliance with home detention orders. Today, it is very

home confinement A program that requires offenders to remain in their homes except for approved periods of absence; commonly used in combination with electronic monitoring.

electronic monitoring An arrangement that allows an offender's whereabouts to be gauged through the use of computer technology.

Home confinement requires offenders to remain in their homes except for preapproved periods of absence. Most programs use electronic monitoring equipment to verify that offenders are at their designated locations at particular times. *For what type of offenders are home confinement and electronic monitoring appropriate, and for what type of offenders are they not?*

common for home confinement programs to have electronic monitoring components. In June 2007, for example, 13,643 offenders nationwide who otherwise would have been confined in a jail facility were being supervised in a home detention program (up from 12,900 in June 2005). That represents about 20% of offenders being supervised outside a jail facility (excluding persons on probation or parole). Of those offenders participating in a home detention program, more than 96% were being electronically monitored.[48]

Electronic monitoring devices are used to verify, either through phone lines or radio signals, that offenders are at their designated locations at particular times. The two most popular electronic monitoring devices are the continuously signaling and programmed contact systems. In the continuously signaling system, an offender wears a small transmitter, usually on the ankle, that sends encoded signals to a nearby receiver at regular intervals. In essence, the receiver communicates with the monitoring agency's computer, which contains the offender's schedule, so staff can determine whether the offender is in the designated location at the required time. Under the programmed contact arrangement, the agency's computer generates either random or scheduled phone calls to the designated location, and the offender must respond to the calls. The type of response required from the offender depends on the specific device. For example, some devices require the offender to insert a wristlet into a verifier box hooked on the phone. Others require the offender to speak for purposes of voice verification.

Home confinement and electronic monitoring have not yet been evaluated extensively. However, a national survey found that electronic monitoring has expanded rapidly since its inception. Furthermore, there appears to be a trend toward using electronic monitoring with offenders who have committed more serious crimes.

As might be expected, home confinement and electronic monitoring are controversial practices. This is particularly true of monitoring. Supporters argue that home confinement and monitoring are cost-effective alternatives to incarceration in jail or prison that allow offenders to receive more supervision and punishment than they would receive on traditional probation or parole. Another argument is that offenders are spared the potentially harmful effects of institutionalization, one of the most important of which is the breaking of family ties.

Critics counter with a variety of claims. One important criticism is that home confinement and monitoring encroach on the constitutional rights to privacy, protection against self-incrimination, and protection against unreasonable search and seizure. Critics maintain that not only are the offender's rights threatened but also the rights of persons who share the offender's residence. However, it seems unlikely that the use of those sanctions will be severely restricted on constitutional grounds in the foreseeable future. As criminologists Rolando del Carmen and Joseph Vaughn observe, "A review of decided cases in probation and parole indicates that while the use of electronic devices raises constitutional issues, its constitutionality will most likely be upheld by the courts, primarily based on the concept of diminished rights [for offenders]."[49]

Some people worry that home confinement and electronic monitoring may discriminate against economically disadvantaged persons, who are less likely to have homes and telephone systems for the installation of monitoring devices. Others are concerned that offenders and manufacturers of monitoring equipment have become locked in a perpetual and costly battle to outwit one another. Manufacturers continually work to devise monitors that will resist offender tampering. Meanwhile, offenders seek ways to manipulate the latest monitoring innovations on the market. This situation, of course, is potentially lucrative for equipment vendors, but it is potentially costly for taxpayers and for offenders who must pay monitoring fees. A broader criticism is that a profit incentive is being created to subject more and more persons to government surveillance.

Some people object to monitoring on the grounds that it is impersonal, thus removing the human and helping elements from community corrections.

Those critics suggest that by reducing the need for skill and professionalism on the part of probation and parole officers, monitoring may undermine rehabilitation. As criminologist John Conrad writes:

> Probation and parole were once intended to help men and women in the worst kind of trouble to find ways to lead law abiding lives. No more. Official services to offenders in the community have been transformed into a cat-and-mouse game in which surveillance, not service, has become the primary, if not the exclusive requisite. . . . Electronic surveillance is a recent and welcomed contribution of high technology to the community control of convicted offenders. We settle for temporary control in place of a serious program for changes in attitude, behavior and style of life.[50]

An investigation of Florida's house-arrest program provides empirical support for these criticisms. It also reveals some problems heretofore overlooked by house-arrest critics.[51] Florida's house-arrest program, which the Florida Department of Corrections manages and calls "community control," is one of the largest such programs in the United States. In 2008, the state supervised 6,550 active program participants a day—9% of whom were electronically monitored. By contrast, in 2002, the state supervised about 10,000 active program participants a day—6% of whom were electronically monitored. Since its inception in 1983 and through 2008, more than 278,000 offenders have served time in the program.

A principal reason for the program's creation was the prospect of saving money by reducing the prison population. Whether the program has achieved that goal is a difficult question to answer. On the one hand, participation in house arrest is significantly cheaper than the costs of incarceration. In 2008, house-arrest program participants cost the state as little as $5.72 a day, while state prison inmates cost the state $55.09 a day. By that measure, the program has saved the state of Florida millions of dollars. However, if in the absence of the program, offenders would have been placed on regular probation, for which the average cost per probationer per day in 2008 was $5.72, then the program produced no cost savings.

The house-arrest program may have reduced the prison population, but that is not entirely clear, either. From June 1983 through June 2008, Florida's prison population increased each year except from June 1983 to June 1984. From June 1983 through June 2008, the prison population increased about 200%. Still, the program may have reduced the prison population by approximately 11,000 inmates per year—the number participating in the house-arrest program. However, if the program participants would have been sentenced to regular probation instead of prison in the absence of the program, then the program did not reduce the prison population.

In any event, in 2008, Florida's house-arrest program had about a 66% success rate. That is, about two of every three program participants completed a year in the program without being removed for committing new crimes or violating other program rules. The other "unsuccessful" 34% of Florida's house-arrest participants were removed from the program and usually incarcerated during the first year for committing crimes or violating program rules such as testing positive for drugs, leaving home without authorization, failing to pay restitution, or possessing a firearm.

In addition, during the past two and a half decades, program participants killed at least 462 people and committed at least 722 sex crimes (about 32% of the murderers and 17% of the sex offenders were in absconder status at the time the murder or sex offense was committed). Approximately 2,000 to 3,000 violent offenders are sentenced to house arrest each year. Of that number, about 400 are placed in the program even though state law prohibits it. In Florida, offenders are not to be placed on house arrest if (1) they have been convicted of a crime that appears on a specific list of violent felonies, including robbery, kidnapping, and assault; and (2) they have a prior conviction from that same list. Judges who sentence such offenders to house arrest either don't know the

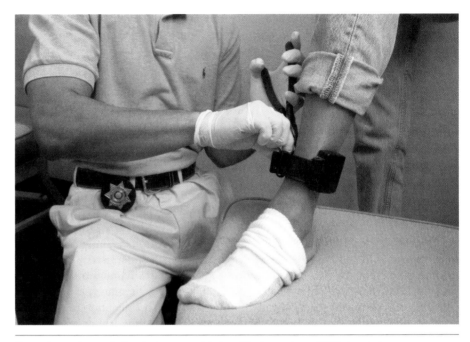

Some electronic monitoring devices use global positioning systems (GPS). *In what ways are GPS-equipped monitoring devices superior to conventional phone or radio signal devices?*

law or ignore it. Some judges claim that the law makes no sense. They argue that the law allows some violent offenders barred from house arrest to be placed on probation, where they get even less supervision.

Another problem is that, in 2008, 1,315 house-arrest participants fled the program. Although most of them eventually will be caught, some of them will not. The program is also understaffed. In 2008, for example, community control officers had an average caseload of 31.6 (down from 39 in 2002), with 17.2 community control cases, even though the state legislature set a limit at 25 cases per officer. By law, officers are supposed to check on program participants three times a week. In practice, however, most participants are checked on only twice a week. For one of those checks, the participant reports to a department of corrections office.

House-arrest participants who wear electronic monitors are 5 times more likely to successfully complete their sentences and half as likely to flee the program. However, as noted previously, only about 9% of house-arrest participants, in 2008, were electronically monitored. The problem is money, at least with monitoring by satellite. In 2008, it cost $8.94 a day to monitor an offender by satellite (down from $20.33 in 2002) and $1.97 a day to monitor an offender by radio frequency (down from $13.91 in 2002). By comparison, in 2008, it cost $5.72 to supervise a house-arrest participant without electronic monitoring. As noted, Florida uses two types of electronic monitoring tracking systems. The newer and more expensive technology uses Global Positioning System satellites that track an offender's whereabouts 24 hours a day. The other, older and less expensive technology sends signals over telephone lines. It is called "RF" (radio frequency) monitoring. It cannot tell the agency where an offender is, but it can tell when the offender is home or not and alert the department. Both types of monitoring have their problems. For example, the GPS system generates numerous false alarms. The GPS system's signal also will not penetrate most buildings. Even so, it would seem that electronic monitoring of house-arrest participants would be a good investment, but the Department of Corrections prefers to use the bulk of its resources on prisons.

HALFWAY HOUSES

Halfway houses (sometimes referred to as community correctional centers or residential community centers) are community-based residential facilities that are an alternative to confinement in jail or prison.[52] Although those facilities are an alternative to more secure and restrictive placements, they provide a much more controlled environment than is possible with traditional probation and parole, or even with ISP and home confinement. As the term *halfway* implies, the offender is midway between jail or prison and the free community.

The goal of halfway houses is to provide offenders with a temporary (for instance, 6-month) period of highly structured and supportive living so that they will be better prepared to function independently in the community upon discharge. To this end, most programs place a heavy emphasis on addressing offenders' educational and employment deficits. For example, persons who have not completed high school are encouraged to obtain the GED, individuals who have few marketable job skills are encouraged to complete vocational training, and those who lack employment are assisted in finding and keeping jobs.

Halfway houses have existed in the United States since the mid-1800s and, prior to the 1960s, were used primarily for persons coming out of prison and making the transition back into the community. During the 1960s, the number and functions of halfway house programs in the nation expanded. In addition to providing services for parolees and prereleasees (prisoners nearing their release dates), houses began to service probationers, pretrial detainees, and persons on furlough from prison. More recently, in the 1980s, halfway houses became an integral part of the intermediate-sanction movement. They are now sometimes used in conjunction with other intermediate sanctions. For example, as part of a probation sentence, an offender may complete a stay in a halfway house before being discharged to ISP, or a person who has violated a home confinement order may be placed in a halfway house program to give authorities added control.

Halfway houses are quite diverse. Not all houses are for offenders; some facilities serve other populations, such as those with mental disorders or drug addictions. Programs for offenders may serve a specific category of offenders, such as all probationers or all parolees, or some combination of offender groups. In addition, a halfway house's population may be all male, all female, or both male and female. Some houses rely heavily on referrals to other local agencies to ensure that offenders' treatment needs are met, whereas others provide extensive in-house treatment. Programs can be administered publicly or privately, but private administration is more common. Public programs may be administered at the federal, state, or local level of government.

Procedures Halfway house programming involves five basic procedures:

1. Referral
2. Administrative screening
3. Intake and orientation
4. Program participation
5. Termination of the stay

Referral of clients to a halfway house may be done by a correctional institution (as in the case of prereleasees), a court, or a probation or parole agency. The fundamental issue referral sources must confront is whether the offender will benefit from halfway house placement without compromising community safety. Thus, such factors as the offender's propensity for violence and degree of

halfway houses Community-based residential facilities that are less secure and restrictive than prison or jail but provide a more controlled environment than other community correctional programs.

 Halfway Houses for White-Collar Offenders

The Justice Department is no longer allowing the U.S. Bureau of Prisons to assign first-time nonviolent white-collar offenders to federal halfway houses instead of prisons. Advocates of the nearly two-decade-old practice argue that it reduced prison crowding and encouraged rehabilitation of low-risk offenders. Critics claim that the practice allowed wealthy white-collar offenders to circumvent sentencing guidelines and escape prison.

Source: Dan Eggen, "Wealthy Criminals Will Head for Prison," *The Orlando Sentinel* (January 7, 2003), p. A5.

Halfway houses may be operated by private-for-profit or not-for-profit contractors or by public agencies. Some provide room, board, and help with employment. Others provide remedial education, individual or group counseling, and other types of life skills training. *Should halfway houses be restricted in the type of offender that is accepted? If yes, what types of offenders should be barred?*

employment and educational deficits are generally given great weight in determining whether to make a referral.

When a referral is made, the next step is *administrative screening*, in which halfway house administrators examine the case and decide whether to accept the offender into the program. Some house administrators have more authority to reject referrals than others. Administrators of private houses often have more discretion to decline referrals than do administrators of public programs. An important point to note is that referral sources and house administrators are sometimes motivated by differing objectives. For instance, correctional institution staff may be motivated by the desire to reduce crowding in their facilities, whereas house administrators may wish to maximize the rate of successful discharge from their programs.

If administrative screening results in a decision to accept the referral, the focus shifts to *intake and orientation*. This entails assessing the new resident's risks and needs as well as orienting him or her to the rules, expectations, and routines of the program. An important aspect of intake and orientation is determining exactly what the resident should accomplish during the stay to improve his or her life and reduce the likelihood of recidivism. That determination is usually written as a treatment plan with specific goals and objectives.

With respect to *program participation*, many halfway houses have a series of levels, or phases, through which residents must pass to receive a successful discharge. Typically, each level is associated with progressively more demanding goals and responsibilities for the resident to meet and also with more privileges and freedoms. For example, a requirement for an offender to move from the entry level to the second level may be the successful completion of a job skills class. On promotion to level two, the offender may receive one weekend furlough per month to spend with family and friends. Promotion to level three may carry additional furlough time and require that the offender obtain a job and complete a class on job retention skills.

As noted previously, halfway houses usually provide a variety of treatment services, such as employment counseling and training, life skills training, substance abuse intervention, and remedial education. Those services are provided either directly by house staff or indirectly through referrals to community agencies. To allow control and supervision, houses have a number of rules that govern both the in-house behavior of residents and residents' activities away from the facility. Those rules cover such matters as interaction between residents, care of facility property, curfews, and the use of alcohol. Progress through program levels requires completion of the goals and responsibilities associated with a particular level, participation in relevant treatment components, and compliance with house rules. Failure to achieve goals, to complete treatment components, or to abide by rules can result in the resident's staying at a given level or being demoted to a lower level.

A resident's behavior must be monitored and periodically reviewed throughout the term of program participation because, ultimately, the house administration must decide the resident's *termination*, or discharge, status. Residents who have satisfactorily completed all of the required levels are discharged into the community, frequently under probation or parole supervision. If a resident fails to make satisfactory progress through levels in a reasonable time, compiles an excessive number of less serious rule violations, or commits a serious rule infraction (such as another felony), the resident can also be discharged from the facility. An unsuccessful discharge can be granted at any point in a resident's stay and is frequently followed by incarceration.

Issues Several issues surround the use of halfway houses. Two of the most critical issues are (1) the relations between a halfway house and the local community of which it is a part and (2) recidivism among persons who have been discharged from the house.

For a halfway house to be established in a community and to operate effectively, cooperative relations between the staff of the house and members of the community are essential. Halfway house staff often depend on the surrounding community for such things as resident health care, counseling services, educational programming, and job placements. Furthermore, unfavorable reactions from community members toward residents will simply reinforce the sense of marginalization and alienation that many offenders already experience. To the extent that community members feel threatened by residents or have poor relations with staff, the halfway house program is in jeopardy.

Virtually all halfway houses must confront the issue of community resistance, and some must confront outright hostility from community members. There are at least two keys to doing this effectively. First, halfway house officials must actively cultivate support and assistance from community members by engaging in open, honest communication with them from the earliest possible stage of the halfway house's existence. Many fears that community members have of residents are founded on inaccurate, media-fueled stereotypes and can be reduced with realistic, factual information. Second, it is very helpful if community members can see that the halfway house is contributing something of value to the community, rather than simply consuming resources. For example, house residents can be involved in well-publicized and highly visible community service projects that save tax dollars. Also, in houses where a high proportion of residents are employed, community residents should be frequently reminded that residents are contributing to the tax base instead of consuming public revenue as jail or prison inmates. If community members can be convinced that the halfway house has a positive, contributing side, they are likely to be more accepting of the house.

Just as there are ways to facilitate cooperative community relations, there also are ways to create unfavorable relations. One way to almost ensure poor relations is for the halfway house to be sprung on the community without any notice of the desire of officials to establish the house and without community input in the early planning process. Another common mistake is for halfway house officials to be content with a low-profile image once the house is established. Believing that adequate community relations will exist as long as offenders are controlled and unfavorable media exposure is avoided, officials may try to minimize exposure of house operations to the public. The typical result is an atmosphere of secrecy, suspicion, and distrust. When the inevitable negative incident occurs, such as a crime by a resident against a community member, public outcry against the house is likely.

How many persons placed in halfway houses successfully complete their stays, and how high is recidivism among former residents after discharge? Those questions were addressed in a study of 156 probationers admitted to a halfway house in Michigan.[53] The study found that nearly 60% of all probationers received unsuccessful discharges. However, other studies have discovered successful discharge figures as high as 60%.[54] The Michigan study tracked former halfway house residents for 7 years after their discharges. The researchers found that approximately 67% of the former residents were arrested at least once during the 7-year period for some type of criminal activity; about 60% were arrested at least once for felonies. However, persons who had successfully completed the halfway house program were significantly less likely to incur new arrests than the persons who had not done so. For instance, 44% of the persons who had received successful discharges were arrested for new felonies, compared with 68.8% of those who had received unsuccessful discharges.

In another study, the recidivism of offenders who had been placed in halfway house programs was compared with the recidivism of those placed on regular probation supervision. Using a 3-year follow-up period, the researchers found that 29.5% of the former halfway house residents and 30.7% of the regular probationers experienced new criminal convictions. Slightly more than 40% of the halfway house residents had failed to complete their programs successfully.[55]

MYTH

When an offender halfway house is established in a neighborhood, crime rates increase and property values fall.

FACT

Research on this subject has confirmed neither of those assumptions. Crime rates and property values tend to remain the same.

CJ Online

ICCA

To learn more about halfway houses, visit the website of the International Community Corrections Association (ICCA), formerly the International Halfway House Association, at www .iccaweb.org/. *Does working in a halfway house appeal to you? Why or why not?*

Research clearly suggests that a large number of offenders placed in halfway houses do not successfully complete their programs. However, those who do receive successful discharges seem less likely to commit new crimes than those who do not. Yet, there is little reason to believe that halfway houses are associated with less recidivism than other types of community corrections programs.

THINKING CRITICALLY

1. Do you think people should have the right to reject the placement of a halfway house in their neighborhood? Why or why not?

2. What could be done to bring about good relations between a community and the halfway house located within the community?

Temporary-Release Programs

temporary-release programs Programs that allow jail or prison inmates to leave the facility for short periods to participate in approved community activities.

Temporary-release programs allow inmates in jail or prison to leave the facility for short periods to participate in approved community activities. Those programs are designed to permit inmates to establish or maintain community ties, thereby gradually preparing them for reentry into society. The programs also give institutional authorities a means of testing the readiness of inmates for release as well as a means of controlling institutional behavior. Not surprisingly, opportunities for temporary release create a major incentive for inmates to engage in the conduct desired by officials.

Three common temporary-release programs are work release, study release, and furloughs. The persons involved in such programs may be prison or jail inmates, or halfway house residents. As should be apparent from the previous section of this chapter, temporary release is an integral aspect of halfway houses. In prisons and jails, temporary release is reserved for inmates who have demonstrated that they are appropriate candidates to participate in community-based activities.

Organized temporary-release programs are not new in American corrections. Although the programs date to the early 1900s, they did not gain widespread popularity until the 1960s, when the emphasis on community corrections began to grow. Today, almost all states offer temporary release.[56]

Temporary-release programs allow inmates in jail or prison to leave the facility for short periods to participate in approved community activities. *Should temporary release from jail or prison be allowed? Why or why not?*

In work-release programs, inmates leave the facility for certain hours each day to work for employers in the free community. Work-release inmates are paid prevailing wages, but they are usually required to submit their paychecks to corrections officials to deduct for such things as dependent support and restitution orders before placing the balance in inmates' accounts. Inmates may withdraw some money while in the facility but are usually required to save a certain amount for their ultimate release from incarceration. A limitation of such programs is that most inmates must settle for low-skilled and low-paying jobs. This limitation exists because:

1. A large proportion of inmates lack the educational and vocational backgrounds needed to secure higher-paying employment.
2. There is more competition for higher-paying jobs.
3. Many employers are reluctant to hire work-release inmates, especially for jobs that pay well and require skill and responsibility.

Study-release inmates can leave prison for high school equivalency classes, vocational training, or college coursework. A limitation of study release is that, unlike work release, it does not generate financial resources. If inmates cannot pay for their own educational programs or obtain financial aid, study release must be funded by the jurisdiction. Even in the unlikely event that a jurisdiction has resources to fund study release, there may still be reluctance to do so because of the argument that inmates are getting free education at taxpayers' expense.

In furlough programs, inmates are granted leaves of absence for brief periods (for example, 48 hours) to accomplish specific things. Inmates may be granted furloughs to spend time with family members, to attend funerals, or to search for employment and housing before release.

One commonly voiced fear about temporary-release programs is that inmates will flee or commit serious crimes while away from the facility. In fact, research shows that most inmates neither flee nor commit serious offenses. The most frequent problems are late returns and the use of alcohol and illegal drugs.

Temporary-release programs became a significant issue in the U.S. presidential election campaign of 1988. Massachusetts Governor Michael Dukakis, the Democratic presidential nominee, was heavily criticized by Vice President George H. W. Bush, the Republican nominee, for allowing temporary release of inmates with records of violence. Willie Horton, a black man who had been serving a first-degree murder sentence at a Massachusetts institution, committed violent crimes against a white couple during his tenth furlough from the institution. Bush made much of the "liberal" prison release policies of Massachusetts in an attempt to discredit Dukakis.

Around the same time, an evaluation of temporary release in Massachusetts was being conducted. The evaluation was published in 1991.[57] The researchers studied persons released from Massachusetts facilities between 1973 and 1983. Offenders were tracked for 1 year after release, and recidivism was defined as return to prison. The recidivism of persons who participated in furloughs, prerelease-center (halfway house) programs, and both furloughs and prerelease centers was compared with the recidivism of persons who participated in neither. Using statistical controls for differences in offenders' backgrounds, researchers concluded that "prerelease programs following prison furloughs, and prison furloughs alone, appear to reduce dramatically the risks to public safety after release." This study implies that eliminating or significantly curtailing temporary-release programs is likely to result in a long-term decline in community safety and an increase in recidivism.

THINKING CRITICALLY

1. Do you think offenders should be allowed to take college courses, at taxpayers' expense, through study-release programs? Why or why not?

2. Do you think temporary-release programs help rehabilitate offenders? Why or why not?

✳ Summary

1. Define community corrections, and identify the goals and responsibilities of community corrections agencies and their staffs.

    Although community corrections programs are very diverse across the nation, the common feature of those programs is that they provide supervision and treatment services for offenders outside jails and prisons. The dual emphasis on supervision and treatment creates a potential role conflict for community corrections staff. There is some indication, however, that the traditional focus on treatment has been declining relative to the growing emphasis on supervision.

2. Define probation, and summarize the research findings on recidivism rates.

    The most commonly used type of community sentence is probation. Offenders placed on probation are supervised and provided with various services in the community instead of being incarcerated. In return, they are required to abide by the rules of the probation sentence. Overall, studies indicate that probation is about as effective as incarceration in controlling recidivism. Available data indicate that recidivism is quite high among felons sentenced to probation. Furthermore, research has not found a strong association between probation officers' caseloads and the likelihood of probationer recidivism. If anything, reduced caseloads seem to increase the probability that instances of recidivism will be detected.

3. Distinguish parole from probation.

    Unlike probation, parole is not a court-imposed sentence. Parole is a mechanism of releasing persons from prison and a means of supervising them after release, instead of an alternative to an incarceration sentence. Parole supervision is often confused with probation because the two share many similarities. Four major objectives of parole agencies are to: (1) preserve community safety by supervising the behavior of parolees; (2) promote the betterment of parolees by responding to their treatment needs; (3) control prison crowding; and (4) control the behavior of prison inmates by providing early release opportunities in exchange for good prison conduct.

4. Explain the functions of a parole board.

    In general, a parole board directs a jurisdiction's parole policies and manages the parole release and termination processes. Parole board members (or their representatives) conduct parole-grant hearings to determine which inmates should receive early release from prison. Boards also determine whether to revoke the parole of persons who have violated parole conditions. In most states, field service agencies are administratively independent of parole boards. A field service agency provides community supervision and treatment services for persons who have been granted parole release by the board and makes recommendations to the board concerning termination of parole.

5. Describe how intermediate sanctions differ from traditional community corrections programs.

    Compared with traditional programs in community corrections, intermediate sanctions are oriented less toward rehabilitation and more toward retribution, deterrence, and incapacitation. They are more punitive and more restrictive. The recent popularity of intermediate sanctions is attributable largely to the record high levels of prison crowding that plague many jurisdictions and a corresponding need to devise acceptable alternatives to imprisonment.

6. Explain two major concerns about intensive-supervision probation and parole (ISP).

    Two major concerns about ISP are (1) the potential for net-widening, and (2) the lack of demonstrated reduction of recidivism. Net-widening occurs when offenders placed in a novel program such as ISP are not the offenders for whom the program was intended. The consequence is that those in the program receive more severe sanctions than they would have received had the new program been unavailable. Studies show that ISP is associated with a substantially higher percentage of technical violations than alternative sanctions such as regular probation, prison, or regular parole.

7. Explain what day reporting centers and structured fines are.

    Day reporting centers allow offenders to live at home but require them to report to the center regularly to confer with center staff about supervision and treatment matters. Program components commonly focus on work, education, counseling, and community service. Structured fines, or day fines, differ fundamentally from the fines (called *tariff fines*) more typically imposed by American criminal courts. Whereas tariff fines require a single fixed amount of money, or an amount within a narrow range, to be paid by all defendants convicted of a particular crime, without regard to their financial circumstances, structured fines, or day fines, are based on defendants' ability to pay. The basic premise of structured fines is that punishment by a fine should be proportionate to the seriousness of the offense and should have a roughly similar economic impact on persons with differing financial resources who are convicted of the same offense.

8. Explain what home confinement and electronic monitoring are.

    In home confinement programs (also known as home incarceration, home detention, and house arrest), offenders are required by the court to remain in their homes except for preapproved periods of absence. Electronic monitoring, which is generally coupled with home confinement, allows an offender's whereabouts to be gauged through the use of computer technology.

9. Identify the goal of halfway houses, and compare them with other community corrections programs.

    The goal of halfway houses is to provide offenders with a temporary (for instance, 6-month) period of highly structured and supportive living so that they will be better prepared to function independently in the community upon discharge. To this end, most programs place a heavy emphasis on addressing offenders' educational and employment deficits. Research clearly suggests that a large number of offenders placed in halfway houses do not successfully complete their programs. However, those who do receive successful discharges seem less likely to commit new crimes than those who do not. Yet, there is little reason to believe that halfway houses are associated with less recidivism than other community corrections programs.

10. Summarize the purposes and outcomes of temporary-release programs.

   By allowing incarcerated persons to temporarily leave their facilities to participate in approved activities in the community, temporary-release programs are intended to foster ties between inmates and their communities, thus gradually preparing inmates for return to society. These programs also give officials a way to judge the readiness of inmates for release, and since most inmates want to participate in temporary release, the programs give inmates an incentive to maintain good institutional behavior. Although fear and other forms of resistance from community members often plague the programs, there is evidence that participation in temporary release is associated with a decreased likelihood of recidivism upon release from incarceration. Some common types of temporary release include work release, study release, and furlough.

❋ Key Terms

community corrections 460
probation 463
diversion 464
presentence investigation
   (PSI) 466
probation conditions 468
restitution 471

revocation 471
technical violations 473
recidivism 474
parole 476
parole guidelines 479
reintegration 484
intermediate sanctions 485

intensive-supervision
   probation and
   parole (ISP) 486
net widening 486
day reporting centers 488
structured fines, or day
   fines 489

home confinement 491
electronic monitoring 491
halfway houses 495
temporary-release
   programs 498

❋ Review Questions

1. What are David Duffee's three varieties of community corrections, and how do they differ?

2. What are three aspects of the helping role of community corrections staff?

3. Why is community corrections important?

4. What are five types of probation?

5. What are three fundamental objectives of probation agencies?

6. What is a probation subsidy, and what is its goal?

7. What is the main task of the PSI?

8. What are two types of probation conditions, and how do they differ?

9. For what general types of violations can probation be revoked?

10. What two landmark Supreme Court cases define the procedural guidelines for revoking probation or parole?

11. What are two general types of parole, and what is their function?

12. According to a recent study, what are the four most important factors parole authorities consider before granting release on parole?

13. What are some criticisms of parole release?

14. What are two ways that halfway house officials might effectively confront community resistance?

❋ In the Field

1. **Tour a Probation Agency** Take a guided tour of the probation or parole agency in your community. (1) Ask the guide to explain the various activities of the agency. Also ask to speak with various officers about their work. (2) Request sample copies of agency documents, such as risk-and-needs-assessment instruments. (3) Write a short essay describing what the agency documents reveal about the work of the agency.

2. **Evaluate Halfway House Rules** Obtain a copy of the rules of behavior for a halfway house. (1) Evaluate the rules, and decide whether you think they are too strict, not strict enough, or on target. (2) Rewrite any rules that you think need changing.

❋ On the Net

1. **Local Community Corrections** Visit the Sedgwick County, Kansas, Department of Corrections, Community Corrections website at (www.sedgwickcounty.org/corrections/afs.html) or the North Carolina Department of Corrections, Division of Community Corrections website at (www.doc.state.nc.us/dcc/index8-22-08.htm). Choose from the topics provided, and write a brief summary of the information you find and how it is related to community corrections.

2. **U.S. Parole Commission** Visit the website of the United States Parole Commission at www.usdoj.gov/uspc and click on "Our History" to read a contextual history of the federal parole system. Then click on "Answering Your Questions" for the answers to many commonly asked questions about federal parole. Write a short essay explaining why you support or oppose the 1987 abolition of federal parole.

✳ Critical Thinking Exercises

PROBATION/PAROLE OFFICER

1. You are a probation or parole officer. Your caseload averages 100 clients.
   a. A client tells you that her boss is treating her unfairly at work because of her criminal record and probation or parole status. Your client is afraid of being fired and having her probation or parole revoked. What do you do?
   b. You discover that a client is using marijuana. You like the client, and other than the marijuana use, he has been doing well on probation or parole. What do you do?
   c. You have a problem client who is using drugs (marijuana and cocaine), hanging out with a "bad" group of people, and probably (although you have no hard evidence) committing petty thefts to support her drug habit. You have warned the client to stop this behavior, but she has ignored your warnings. Furthermore, the client has threatened to harm you and your family should you revoke her probation or parole. What do you do?
   d. You have a client who, as a condition of his probation or parole, is required to earn his GED. Although the client has been attending classes regularly and seems to be trying very hard, his teacher informs you that the client just does not have the intellectual capacity to earn the GED. What do you do?

HALFWAY HOUSE

2. As an employee of your state department of corrections, you have been asked to establish a halfway house for parolees, all of whom are former substance abuse offenders, in the nice, middle-class community where you live. Assuming that you take the job, how would you address the following questions?
   a. Would you communicate to the community your intention of establishing the halfway house? Why or why not?
   b. How would you address community resistance to the halfway house should it arise?
   c. Would you ask community residents to aid you in your efforts? Why or why not?
   d. Besides community resistance, what other problems might arise in your effort to establish the halfway house? How would you handle them?
   e. Would you be willing to remain a resident of the community after the halfway house is established (especially if you have a family with small children)? Why or why not?

To access more information and resources, including study questions, chapter summaries, and links, go to: www.mhhe.com/bohm6e.

PART **FIVE**

Additional Issues in Criminal Justice

Chapter 13
Juvenile Justice

Chapter 14
The Future of Criminal Justice
in the United States

Juvenile Justice

Chapter Objectives

After completing this chapter, you should be able to:

1. Describe some of the early institutions used to respond to wayward and criminal youths.

2. Explain the effects of some landmark U.S. Supreme Court cases on the juvenile justice system.

3. Identify and describe factors that influence the ways that police process juvenile cases.

4. Summarize the rationale for the use of diversion in juvenile justice.

5. Describe the adjudication hearing in juvenile justice.

6. Describe the disposition hearing and the types of dispositions available to the juvenile court.

7. Identify the types and describe the effectiveness of community-based correctional programs for juveniles.

8. Summarize recent trends in juvenile incarceration.

9. Identify the types and describe the effectiveness of institutional programs for juveniles.

CRIME STORY

On November 5, 2008, an 8-year-old boy allegedly shot and killed his father, 29-year-old Vincent Romero, and his friend, 39-year-old Timothy Romans, in St. Johns, Arizona, a town with 4,000 residents near the New Mexico border. (The boy's name was not released because of his age.) About 5 P.M. on the night of the shootings, neighbors heard three to four "pops," with a delay between each one. The boy's father died in an upstairs room of his house, and Romans died outside. Romans, who lived in Phoenix, stayed with the Romeros during the week in a rented room. Authorities reported that Romero and Romans were shot about five times each with a .22-caliber rifle that had to be reloaded after every shot. The boy initially told police he saw a white vehicle with rimless back tires speeding away. He said he "saw the door [was] open, and I saw Tim right there . . . and I ran and I said, 'Dad! Dad!' And I went upstairs and I saw him. And there was

continued

505

blood all over his face. And I think I touched him. I just kind of checked to see if he was a little bit alive." Police investigators believed the shootings were the result of a workplace dispute.

The day after the shootings, Romans' widow told a sheriff's sergeant she had spoken to her husband on his cell phone just before he was killed. She recounted hearing a child she believed to be Romero's son yell that "something's wrong" inside the house. She heard no gunshots. She suggested the police reinterview the boy, who, she said, "knows something," because "he was there when something bad happened to my husband." Two officers questioned the boy at a local clinic and after some prodding the boy stated, "I think, um, I think I shot my dad, because he was suffering, I think." The boy then confirmed that he shot his father twice. He said, "After I shot him once he was still moving. I think I shot him again." He later revealed, "He was mad at his dad" because his dad instructed the boy's stepmother, Tiffany, to give him "five swats." His father was angry with him, because he did not bring home some papers from school, as he should have. According to prosecutors, the boy kept a record of spankings and vowed that the 1,000th one would be his last.

The boy's father had been awarded custody of the boy after his mother filed for divorce in 2001. His father married Tiffany in September. The boy called her "Mom." Tiffany was not at home at the time of the shootings. Neighbors reported the boy "seemed OK with the world." He was described as "a happy little guy, the kind you'd want to hug." He routinely waved to neighbors while walking his boxer puppy. He had no history of violence. The boy's father, Vincent, was a well-liked, lifelong resident of St. Johns. One resident remarked about him: "If he didn't shake your hand, he gave you a hug." Ironically, Vincent Romero, an avid hunter, taught his son how to shoot and gave his son what is likely the murder weapon, after consulting with their local Catholic priest.

The boy was charged with two counts of premeditated murder, and Arizona law allows 8-year-olds to be tried as adults. Prosecutors in the case are conflicted. On the one hand, experts maintain that children that age are far from fully formed mentally, and most do not understand the finality of death and the consequences of murder. On the other hand, prosecutors believe the juvenile justice system is ill equipped to handle the third-grade boy. Prosecutors also have another problem. The boy confessed to police without having a lawyer or parent present, probably making the confession inadmissible at trial. The judge in the case stayed all proceedings pending a competency evaluation of the boy. Prosecutors have offered a plea deal, which would resolve the case without it being transferred to adult court.

What do you do with an 8-year-old boy charged with two counts of premeditated murder? Chapter 13 is about the juvenile justice system, and among the topics examined is the increasingly common practice of trying juveniles as adults. Should this 8-year-old (at the time of the shooting) boy be tried as an adult? Should the boy's defense attorney accept the prosecutors' deal? If the boy goes to trial and is convicted, should he be sentenced to an adult correctional facility? If he is not tried as an adult or if his attorney accepts the prosecutor's deal, what should be done with the boy? These are questions that arise when children commit heinous crimes.

Historical Development of Juvenile Justice

From a historical perspective, juvenile delinquency and a separate justice process for juveniles are recent concepts. So, too, are the ideas of childhood and adolescence. **Juvenile delinquency,** as you may recall from Chapter 2, is a special category of offense created for youths—that is, in most U.S. jurisdictions, persons between the ages of 7 and 18. Through most of recorded history, the young have not enjoyed the statuses of childhood and adolescence as special times during which they need nurturing and guidance for their healthy development.

Before the sixteenth century, the young were viewed either as property or as miniature adults who, by the age of 5 or 6, were expected to assume the responsibilities of adults. They were also subject to the same criminal sanctions as adults. However, in the sixteenth and seventeenth centuries, a different view of the young emerged that recognized childhood as a distinct period of life, and children as corruptible but worth correcting.[1] Youths began to be viewed not as miniature adults or as property but rather as persons who required molding and guidance to become moral and productive members of the community. American colonists brought with them those new ideas about childhood as well as European mechanisms for responding to violators of social and legal rules.

During the colonial period, the family was the basic unit of economic production and the primary mechanism through which social control was exerted. Survival depended on the family's ability to produce what it needed, rather than

juvenile delinquency A special category of offense created for youths who, in most U.S. jurisdictions, are persons between the ages of 7 and 18.

| Age (on discharge) .... | *11* | Photograph of Prisoner. |

Height............................... *4 ft 1 ¾*

Hair.................................. *Brown*

Eyes.................................. *Brown*

Complexion........................... *Fresh*

Where born........................... *Middlesex*

Married or single .... *Single*

Trade or occupation .... *None*

Any other distinguishing mark .... *Scar on*

forehead and on right shoulder

Description when liberated.

Until the early 1900s, children were subject to the same punishments as adults. *Should children be punished in the same way as adults? Why or why not?*

relying on the production of others. Consequently, a primary responsibility of the family was overseeing the moral training and discipline of the young. During this period, two age-old mechanisms were employed to teach a trade to children who were difficult to handle or needed supervision in order to allow them an opportunity to earn a livelihood. One of those mechanisms was the **apprenticeship system,** which served as a primary means for teaching skilled trades to the children of the middle and upper classes. The other tradition was the binding-out system, which was reserved for poor children. Under the **binding-out system,** children were bound over to masters for care. However, under this system, masters were not required to teach the youths a trade. As a result, boys were often given farming tasks, and girls were assigned to domestic duties.[2]

Religion, particularly in New England, was another powerful force that shaped social life in the colonies. Regular church attendance was expected, and religious beliefs dominated ideas about appropriate behavior. Present-day concerns about the separation of church and state were nonexistent. What was believed to be immoral was also unlawful and subject to punishment by the authorities. Punishments such as fines, whipping, branding, and the use of stocks and the pillory served as reminders to both young and old that violations of community norms would not go unpunished.[3]

By the early 1800s, the social organization of colonial life began to change as a result of economic and social developments. The family-based production unit that had characterized colonial social life was giving way to a factory-based system in the growing towns. As parents—particularly fathers—and children began to leave the home for work in a factory, fundamental changes occurred in the relationships between family members and in the role of the family in controlling the behavior of children. Further, as industry developed and as towns grew, communities became more diverse and experienced problems on a scale unheard of during earlier periods.

apprenticeship system The method by which middle- and upper-class children were taught skilled trades by a master.

binding-out system Practice in which children were "bound over" to masters for care. However, under the binding-out system, masters were not required to teach youths a trade.

 Juvenile Crime Wave

Each generation of Americans seems to believe that the country is experiencing a "juvenile crime wave."

Source: Thomas J. Bernard, *The Cycle of Juvenile Justice* (New York: Oxford University Press, 1992).

THE DEVELOPMENT OF INSTITUTIONS FOR YOUTHS

At the time of the American Revolution, Philadelphia had fewer than 20,000 residents, and other large towns, such as New York, Boston, Newport, and Charleston, had fewer than 15,000 inhabitants each. However, by 1820, the

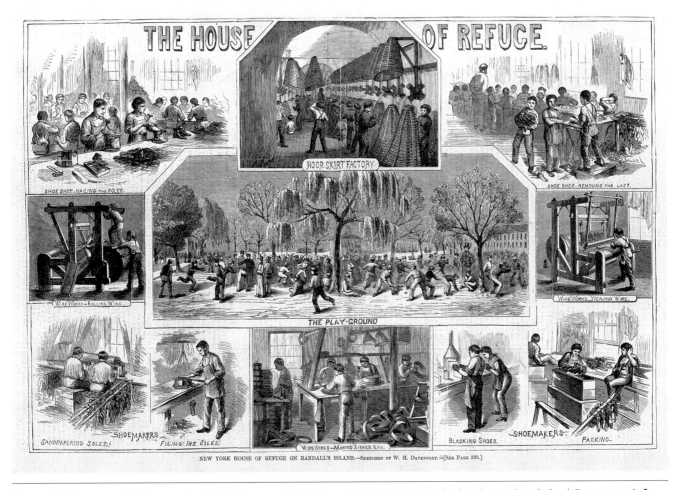

Houses of refuge were the first correctional institutions specifically for youths. *Should houses of refuge be used again for delinquent youths? Why or why not?*

population of New York City was about 120,000 and was growing rapidly as a result of immigration. Immigration, in turn, was changing the composition of communities, which had been more homogeneous during colonial times.

houses of refuge The first specialized correctional institutions for youths in the United States.

The Houses of Refuge Accompanying those changes in the social and economic life of the growing cities were a host of social problems, such as poverty, vagrancy, drunkenness, and crime, including crimes committed by children. In response to those conditions, the first correctional institutions specifically for youths developed. Those institutions were called **houses of refuge.** The first was established in New York City in 1825, and houses of refuge soon spread to other cities such as Boston and Philadelphia.[4]

A primary goal of the houses of refuge was to prevent pauperism and to respond to youths who were ignored by the courts. Houses of refuge were meant to be institutions where children could be reformed and turned into hard-working members of the community. To accomplish this mission, youths were placed in houses of refuge for indeterminate periods or until their 18th or 21st birthdays. Placement, moreover, did not require a court hearing. A child could be committed to a house of refuge by a constable, by a parent, or on the order of a city alderman.[5]

While there, children engaged in a daily regimen of hard work, military drills, and enforced silence, as well as religious and academic training. It was also common practice for outside contractors to operate shops within the houses of refuge. In those shops, children produced goods such as shoes or furniture, and in return, the houses of refuge were paid 10 to 15 cents per youth each day. This arrangement allowed houses of refuge to pay a substantial percentage of their daily operating expenses.[6] When the youthful inmates failed to meet production quotas, they were often punished. After "reformation," boys were frequently indentured to masters on farms or to tradesmen, and girls were placed in domestic service.[7]

Placing Out Soon after the establishment of houses of refuge, reformers began to recognize the inability of those institutions to accommodate the large numbers of children needing placement and to either reform or control youths. One early response to those problems was the development of placing out. **Placing out,** which involved the placing of children on farms in the West and Midwest, was believed to have several advantages over the houses of refuge. First, placing out was seen as a way of removing children from the supposedly corrupting influences of their parents, who frequently were immigrants, and especially of the cities, which reformers viewed as breeding grounds for idleness and crime. Second, many reformers recognized that the conditions in the houses of refuge were counterproductive to the goal of reform. Third, rural areas were assumed to be an ideal environment for instilling in children the values the reformers cherished—values that stressed discipline, hard work, and piety.

Agents hired by charitable organizations would take children west by train and place them with farm families. Although some children were placed in caring homes and were treated as members of the family, others were not so lucky. Many of the children who were placed out were required to work hard for their keep, were abused, were not accepted as members of the family, and never saw their own families again.

placing out The practice of placing children on farms in the Midwest and West to remove them from the supposedly corrupting influences of their parents and the cities.

Probation Another effort to deal with troubled children was initiated by a Boston shoemaker, John Augustus. As described in Chapter 12, Augustus spent considerable time observing the court and became convinced that many minor offenders could be salvaged. As a result of his concern and his willingness to work with offenders, Augustus was permitted to provide bail for his first probation client in 1841.

Augustus's first client was a drunkard who showed remarkable improvement during the period in which he was supervised. The court was impressed with Augustus's work and permitted him to stand bail for other minor offenders, including children.

After Augustus died, the Boston Children's Aid Society and other volunteers carried on his work. Then, in 1869, the state of Massachusetts formalized the existing volunteer probation system by authorizing visiting probation agents, who were to work with both adult and child offenders who showed promise. Under this arrangement, youths were allowed to return home to their parents, provided they obeyed the law.[8] In 1878, an additional law was passed in Boston that provided for paid probation officers.[9] Subsequently, several other states authorized the appointment of probation officers. However, it was not until after the turn of the twentieth century and the development of the first juvenile court that probation gained widespread acceptance.[10]

Reform Schools, Industrial Schools, and Training Schools By the late 1800s, the failure of houses of refuge was well known. Dislocations produced by the Civil War placed tremendous strain on houses of refuge and the placing out system. Perhaps most disappointing, the number of problem youths was growing. In response, state and city governments took over the administration of institutions for juvenile delinquents. Another response was the establishment

Juveniles incarcerated at the turn of the twentieth century were put into job training programs that would help them when they were released. Typically, male offenders learned industrial trades; female offenders learned ironing, laundry work, and cooking. *Should these practices be revived? Why or why not?*

reform, industrial, or **training schools** Correctional facilities for youths, first developed in the late 1800s, that focused on custody. Today, those institutions are often called training schools, and although they may place more emphasis on treatment, they still rely on custody and control.

cottage reformatories Correctional facilities for youths, first developed in the late 1800s, that were intended to closely parallel family life and remove children from the negative influences of the urban environment. Children in those facilities lived with surrogate parents, who were responsible for the youths' training and education.

of **reform, industrial,** or **training schools,** correctional facilities that focused on custody.[11] Those institutions were of two types: cottage reformatories and institutional reformatories.

Cottage reformatories were usually located in rural areas to avoid the negative influences of the urban environment. They were intended to closely parallel family life. Each cottage contained 20 to 40 youths, who were supervised by cottage parents charged with the task of overseeing residents' training and education.[12]

In addition to cottage reformatories, larger, more institutional reformatories were developed in many states. Like the cottage reformatories, the institutional reformatories were usually located in rural areas in an effort to remove youths from the negative influences of city life. However, the institutions were frequently large and overcrowded.

Another development, in the late 1800s, was the establishment of separate institutions for females. Previously, girls had been committed to the same institutions as boys, although there was strict gender segregation in those institutions. Moreover, parents or relatives often committed girls for moral, as opposed to criminal, offenses. Those moral offenses consisted of such actions as "vagrancy, beggary, stubbornness, deceitfulness, idle and vicious behavior, wanton and lewd conduct, and running away."[13] The expressed goal of those institutions was to prepare girls to be good housewives and mothers. Yet, the institutions, like those for boys, were little different from the prisons of that era.

The reform, industrial, and training schools placed more emphasis on formal education than did the houses of refuge, but in many other respects there was little difference. Indeed, those institutions confronted many of the same problems as the houses of refuge had. Moreover, the conditions in the reformatories were certainly no better than those in the houses of refuge, and in many cases they were worse.

THE DEVELOPMENT OF THE JUVENILE COURT

By the end of the 1800s, a variety of institutions and mechanisms had been developed in response to problem children. Still, the problems presented by children who were believed to be in need of correctional treatment—problems such as homelessness, neglect, abuse, waywardness, and criminal behavior—proved difficult to solve. Consequently, during the late 1800s a new group of reformers, the *child savers,* began to advocate a new institution to deal with youth problems. This new institution was the juvenile court.

The Social Context of the Juvenile Court The period from 1880 to 1920, a period historians refer to as the Progressive Era, was a time of major change in the United States. Although industrialization and urbanization were well underway, and previous waves of immigrants had added to the population of the country, the pace of industrialization, urbanization, and immigration quickened. The city of Chicago provides a good example of the changes experienced during the Progressive Era. Between 1890 and 1910, Chicago's population grew from one million to two million. Between 1880 and 1890, the number of factories nearly tripled. By 1889, nearly 70% of the inhabitants of the city were immigrants.[14]

In an effort to respond to the problem of youth crime and waywardness, reformers again sought to save children from the crime-inducing conditions of the cities. Supported by important philanthropic and civic organizations, the child savers worked to improve jail and reformatory conditions. However, the primary outcome of the child-saving movement was the extension of governmental control over children's lives. The child savers argued for stricter supervision of children, and they improved legal mechanisms designed to regulate children's activities.[15] In short, the child savers believed that children needed to be protected and that the best institutions for protecting them were government agencies such as the police and the courts, as well as local charitable organizations.

The Legal Context of the Juvenile Court By the late 1800s, legal mechanisms for treating children differently and separately from adults had existed for some time. For example, jurisdictions had set the minimum age at which a child could be considered legally responsible for criminal behavior. Minimum ages for placement in adult penitentiaries were also enacted during the first half of the 1800s.[16] Moreover, special institutions for dealing with youths had been in existence since 1825, when the first house of refuge was established in New York City. Yet, cases involving juveniles were still heard in criminal courts. Many of the child savers believed that criminal courts failed to respond adequately to many of the transgressions of the young.

The legal philosophy justifying state intervention in the lives of children, the doctrine of **parens patriae** ("the state as parent"), was given judicial endorsement in the case *Ex parte Crouse* (1838). Mary Ann Crouse had been committed to the Philadelphia House of Refuge by her mother against her father's wishes. Mary Ann's father contested his daughter's placement, arguing that she was being punished even though she had committed no criminal offense. However, the Pennsylvania Supreme Court ruled that Mary Ann's placement was legal, because (1) the purpose of the Philadelphia House of Refuge was to reform youths not to punish them, (2) formal due process protections provided to adults in criminal trials were unnecessary, because Mary Ann was not being punished, and (3) when parents were unwilling or unable to protect their children, the state had a legal obligation to do so.[17]

However, the right of the state to intervene in the lives of children did not go unchallenged. In *People* v. *Turner* (1870), for example, the Illinois Supreme Court ruled that Daniel O'Connell, who was committed to the Chicago House of Refuge against both his parents' wishes, was being punished and not helped by his placement. Like Mary Ann Crouse, who was committed by her mother against her father's wishes, Daniel O'Connell was institutionalized even though he had committed no criminal offense. He was placed

parens patriae The legal philosophy justifying state intervention in the lives of children when their parents are unable or unwilling to protect them.

The use of informal procedures is characteristic of the juvenile court system. *Are the juvenile court's informal procedures desirable? Why or why not?*

in the house of refuge because he was perceived to be in danger of becoming a pauper or a criminal. However, Daniel's case differed from Mary Ann's, because both his parents objected to his placement and, even more important, because the court ruled that Daniel's placement was harmful, not helpful. The court also decided that because placement in the house of refuge actually was punishment, due process protections were necessary.[18] The ruling, together with increasing concern over the willingness or ability of the criminal courts to protect or control youths, led reformers in Chicago to consider other mechanisms by which their aims might be achieved. The mechanism they created was the first juvenile court, which was established in Chicago in 1899 by passage of the Juvenile Court Act in Illinois.[19] Some scholars argue that the Juvenile Court Act was a means for the child savers, intent on salvaging poor children—especially poor immigrant children—to get around the *Turner* decision's requirement of due process protections for youths.

The Operation of Early Juvenile Courts

The Juvenile Court Act of 1899 gave the Chicago juvenile court broad jurisdiction over persons under the age of 16 who were delinquent, dependent, or neglected. In addition, the act required:

1. The court to be overseen by a special judge.
2. Hearings to be held in a separate courtroom.
3. Separate records to be kept of juvenile hearings.[20]

It also made probation a major component of the juvenile court's response to offenders and emphasized the use of informal procedures at each stage of the juvenile court process. Indeed, this informality has been a hallmark of the juvenile court since its beginning, a key feature distinguishing it from criminal court proceedings. The major reason for this informality is that the juvenile court has traditionally focused not on the act but on the *whole child*.

In practice, the informality of the juvenile court allowed complaints against children to be made by almost anyone in the community. It also allowed juvenile court hearings to be held in offices, instead of in traditional courtrooms, and to be closed to the public, unlike criminal trials, which were open to the public. In the typical juvenile court hearing, the only persons present were the judge, the parents, the child, and the probation officer, who met and discussed the case. Also, few (if any) records were kept of hearings, proof of guilt was not necessary for the court to intervene in children's lives, and little or no concern for due process existed. Finally, judges exercised wide discretion in how they dealt with children, ranging from a warning to placement in an institution.[21]

The idea of a juvenile court spread rapidly after the passage of the Juvenile Court Act. Within a decade, 10 states had established special courts for children, and by 1925 all but 2 states had juvenile courts.[22] Moreover, those juvenile courts followed closely the model developed in Chicago of an informal court intended to "serve the best interests of children."

Despite the growing popularity of the new courts, they did not go completely unchallenged. In the case *Commonwealth of Pennsylvania* v. *Fisher* (1905), for example, the Pennsylvania Supreme Court again examined the juvenile court's mission, the right to intervene, and the due process protections owed to children. In this case, Frank Fisher, a 14-year-old male, was indicted for larceny and committed to the house of refuge until his 21st

FYI Juvenile Courts

Each state has at least one court with juvenile jurisdiction, but only in a few states is it called juvenile court. Other names include district, superior, circuit, county, family, or probate court. Regardless of the name, courts with juvenile jurisdiction are generally referred to as juvenile courts.

Source: Melissa Sickmund, "Juveniles in Court," U.S. Department of Justice, Office of Juvenile Justice and Delinquency Prevention, *Juvenile Offenders and Victims National Report Series Bulletin* (Washington, D.C.: GPO, June 2003), p. 4.

birthday. Frank's father objected to his placement, claiming that Frank's 7-year sentence for a minor offense was more severe than he would have received in criminal court.[23]

In its ruling, the Pennsylvania Supreme Court upheld the idea of the juvenile court and in many respects repeated the arguments it had made in the *Crouse* decision. The court found that the state may intervene in families when parents are unable or unwilling to prevent their children from engaging in crime and that Frank was being helped by his placement in the house of refuge. It further ruled that due process protections were unnecessary when the state acted under its *parens patriae* powers.[24]

The *Fisher* case set the legal tone for the juvenile court from its beginnings until the mid-1960s, when new legal challenges began to be mounted. Those legal challenges attempted primarily to expand juveniles' due process protections. Critics of the juvenile courts recognized that despite their expressed goal of "serving the best interests of children," the established institutions of juvenile justice often did the opposite.

The Legal Reform Years: The Juvenile Court after *Gault* The 1960s and 1970s provided the social context for a more critical assessment of American institutions, including juvenile justice. Beginning in the mid-1960s and continuing through the mid-1970s, a number of cases decided by the U.S. Supreme Court altered the operation of the juvenile court. The most important of those cases was *In re Gault,* which expanded the number of due process protections afforded juveniles within the juvenile court. However, a number of other cases also helped define juveniles' rights within juvenile justice and contributed to the legal structure found in juvenile courts today. The first of those cases was *Kent* v. *United States* (1966).

Morris Kent was a 16-year-old juvenile on probation who was transferred to criminal court to stand trial on charges of robbery and rape. Although the juvenile court judge received several motions from Kent's attorney opposing the transfer, he made no ruling on them. Further, after indicating that a "full investigation" had been completed, the juvenile court judge transferred Kent to criminal court for trial.[25] Thus, an important decision had been made, the decision to try Kent as an adult, even though no hearing had been held. Kent's attorney had no opportunity to see or to question material that had been used to make the decision to transfer jurisdiction, and no reasons for the court's decision were given.

The *Kent* case is important for several reasons. It was the first major ruling by the U.S. Supreme Court that closely examined the operation of the juvenile courts. It also made clear the need for due process protections for juveniles who were being transferred to criminal court for trial. The Court noted that even though a hearing to consider transfer to criminal court is far less formal than a trial, juveniles are still entitled to some due process protections. Specifically, the Court ruled that before a juvenile court could transfer a case to criminal court, there must be a hearing to consider the transfer, the defendant must have the assistance of defense counsel if requested, defense counsel must have access to social records kept by the juvenile court, and the reasons for the juvenile court's decision to transfer must be stated.[26]

Having given notice that it would review the operations of the juvenile court, the Supreme Court, within a year of the *Kent* decision, heard another landmark case. This case, *In re Gault* (1967), went far beyond the ruling in *Kent* in its examination of juvenile court practices. The *Gault* case is important because it extended a variety of due process protections to juveniles. In addition, the facts of the case clearly demonstrate the potential for abuse in the informal practices of the traditional juvenile court.

FYI *In re*

The Latin phrase *in re* in the description of court cases (for example, *In re Gault*) means, literally, "in the matter of" or "concerning." It is used when a case does not involve adversarial parties.

In the 1967 landmark case of *In re Gault,* Supreme Court Justice Abe Fortas wrote, "Due process of law is the primary and indispensable foundation of individual freedom." *Do you agree with Justice Fortas? Why or why not?*

Gerald Gault was 15 years old when he, along with a friend, was taken into custody by the Gila County, Arizona, Sheriff's Department for allegedly making an obscene phone call to a neighbor, Ms. Cook. At the time of his arrest, Gerald was on 6-months' probation as a result of his presence when another friend had stolen a wallet from a woman's purse. Without notifying his mother, a deputy took Gerald into custody on the oral complaint of Ms. Cook and transported him to the local detention unit.

When Ms. Gault heard Gerald was in custody, she went to the detention facility. The superintendent of the facility told her that a juvenile court hearing would be held the next day. On the following day, Gerald, his mother, and the deputy who had taken Gerald into custody appeared before the juvenile court judge in chambers. The deputy had filed a petition alleging that Gerald was delinquent. Ms. Cook, the complainant, was not present. Without being informed that he did not have to testify, Gerald was questioned by the judge about the telephone call and was sent back to detention. No record was made of this hearing, no one was sworn, and no specific charge was made, other than an allegation that Gerald was delinquent. At the end of the hearing, the judge said he would "think about it." Gerald was released a few days later, although no reasons were given for his detention or release.

On the day of Gerald's release, Ms. Gault received a letter indicating that another hearing would be held a few days later about Gerald's delinquency. The hearing was held and, again, the complainant was not present. Again, there was no transcript or recording of the proceedings, and the parties later disputed what was said. Neither Gerald nor his parent was advised of a right to remain silent, a right to be represented by counsel, or any other constitutional rights. At the conclusion of the hearing, Gerald was found delinquent and was committed to the state industrial school until he was 21 years old, unless released earlier by the court. This meant that Gerald received a sentence of up to 6 years for an offense that if committed by an adult, would have been punished by a maximum sentence of 2 months in jail and a $50 fine.

When the case finally reached the Supreme Court, the Court held that a youth has procedural rights in delinquency hearings where there is the possibility of confinement in a state institution. Specifically, the Court ruled that juveniles have a right against self-incrimination, a right to adequate notice of charges against them, a right to confront and to cross-examine their accusers, and a right to assistance of counsel. In addition, the Court's ruling implied that juveniles also have the rights to sworn testimony and appeal.

The landmark *Gault* decision was not the last Supreme Court decision to influence juvenile court procedures. The Supreme Court further expanded protections for juveniles 3 years after *Gault.* In a 1970 case, *In re Winship,* the Court ruled that delinquency charges must be proven beyond a reasonable doubt where there was a possibility that a youth could be confined in a locked facility. Until the *Winship* ruling, the standard of proof typically employed at the adjudication stage of the juvenile justice process was a preponderance of the evidence, the level of proof employed in civil proceedings. **Adjudication** is the juvenile court equivalent of a trial in criminal court, or the process of rendering a judicial decision regarding the truth of the facts alleged in a petition. Under the preponderance-of-the-evidence standard of proof, juveniles could be adjudicated delinquent (found guilty) if the weight of the evidence was slightly against them, a much lower standard of proof than the standard required in criminal courts.

adjudication The juvenile court equivalent of a trial in criminal court, or the process of rendering a judicial decision regarding the truth of the facts alleged in a petition.

Note that both the *Gault* and *Winship* decisions not only increased procedural formality in juvenile court cases but also shifted the traditional focus from the "whole child" to the child's act. Once this shift occurred, it was only a short step to offense-based sentencing and the more punitive orientation that is characteristic of the juvenile justice system today.

The Supreme Court's extension of due process protections to juveniles slowed in the year following the *Winship* decision. In a 1971 ruling, *McKeiver* v. *Pennsylvania,* the Court held that juveniles were not entitled to a trial by jury. The Court cited several reasons for the decision:

1. The Court did not want to turn the juvenile court into a fully adversarial process.
2. The Court determined that bench trials could produce accurate determinations.
3. The Court felt that it was too early to completely abandon the philosophy of the juvenile court and its treatment mission.

To grant juveniles all of the protections accorded adults, the Court surmised, would make the juvenile court indistinguishable from the criminal court. Nevertheless, many states have required more due process protections for juveniles than have been mandated by the Supreme Court. For example, many state laws specify that juveniles have a right to trial (adjudication) by a jury. In fact, Texas requires that a jury hear all adjudications. Nevertheless, jury trials are rare in states that have this right, including Texas. This is because the right must be exercised or, as in Texas, the automatic right to a trial by jury can be waived. In practice, jury trials are often discouraged because they are time consuming and costly.

The continued informality of the juvenile court may explain why very few youths contest charges against them and why a surprising number of youths who are not adjudicated delinquent (found guilty) are placed on probation. Indeed, most youths who appear before the juvenile court admit to the charges against them.[27] Moreover, data collected by the National Center for Juvenile Justice indicate that in 2005 (the latest year for which data were available), about 6% of youths who were not adjudicated delinquent in juvenile courts were still placed on some form of probation (see also Figure 13.2 on page 525).[28]

Today, juveniles have been granted many, but not all, of the due process protections given adults in criminal trials. However, the daily operation of juvenile courts calls into question the extent to which court-mandated changes in juvenile justice procedures have influenced the traditional informality of the juvenile court. Juvenile court procedures are still characterized by an informality that most people would find unacceptable if it were applied to adults in criminal court.

THINKING CRITICALLY

1. Should youths in juvenile court proceedings be granted the same due process protections as adults in criminal trials? Why or why not?

2. Historically, what do you think was the most significant change in the treatment of juvenile offenders? How did the change occur?

The Processing of Juvenile Offenders

Juvenile delinquency in the United States is widespread, and people respond to it both formally and informally. Informal responses consist of actions taken by members of the public that do not rely on official agencies of juvenile justice. Formal responses, in contrast, rely on official agencies of juvenile justice such as the police and juvenile court. Figure 13.1 depicts the stages in the formal juvenile justice process. Before providing a detailed examination of the formal

Teachers are an important part of the informal juvenile justice process. *What can teachers do to keep students from becoming delinquent?*

informal juvenile justice The actions taken by citizens to respond to juvenile offenders without involving the official agencies of juvenile justice.

status offenses Acts that are not crimes when committed by adults but are illegal for minors (for example, truancy or running away from home).

CJ Online

Juvenile Justice by State

Go to www.acf.hhs.gov/programs/cb/law/pi/pi9902a7.htm to access the website for the National Center for Juvenile Justice to find descriptive information and analyses of the various juvenile justice systems in the United States. Compare your state's juvenile justice system to that of another state. *How are the two states similar? Different?*

juvenile justice process, however, we take a brief look at the informal juvenile justice process.

THE INFORMAL JUVENILE JUSTICE PROCESS

An examination of the juvenile justice process usually begins with the police, and the police do play a critical role in juvenile justice. However, any discussion of the juvenile justice process should really begin with the public, because police involvement with juveniles is typically the result of citizen complaints.

The informal actions taken by citizens to respond to delinquency constitute an **informal juvenile justice** process that operates outside the official agencies of juvenile justice. Neighbors, business owners, teachers, and others who are not part of the formal juvenile justice apparatus handle many illegal behaviors by juveniles informally. The informal processing of juveniles is important, because it is one of the mechanisms that operates to control youths' behavior. The more citizens rely on informal control and the more effective it is, the less necessary the formal processing of juveniles becomes.

Although many delinquent actions are handled informally, in other instances members of the public decide to call the police or the juvenile court and to request action from the formal agencies of juvenile justice. Thus, most youths become involved in the formal juvenile justice process when the people who make up the informal process decide, in their discretion, to involve the police or the juvenile court. This means that some combination of the public and the police plays a major role in determining who the clientele of juvenile justice will be.

THE FORMAL JUVENILE JUSTICE PROCESS

The police represent the primary gatekeepers to the formal juvenile justice process (see Figure 13.1). For example, in 2005 (the latest year for which data are available), 81% of delinquency cases referred to the juvenile courts came from police agencies.[29] This percentage has remained about the same for about two decades. In the case of status offenses, however, the percentage of cases referred from police agencies varies greatly by offense. In 2005, for example, 92% of status liquor law violation cases were referred by police agencies to the juvenile courts, while only 51% of cases of running away, 34% of ungovernability (being beyond the control of parents or guardians) cases, and 15% of truancy cases were referred from police agencies.[30] **Status offenses,** as you may recall, are acts that are not crimes when committed by adults but are illegal for minors.

The Police Response to Juveniles   Like citizens, the police exercise discretion in handling juvenile cases. Typical responses that police officers may employ are to:

1. Warn and release.
2. Refer to parents.
3. Refer to a diversionary program operated by the police or another community agency.
4. Refer to court.

In some communities, an officer may have a variety of options, whereas in other communities available options are more limited.

Figure 13.1

The Formal Juvenile Justice Process

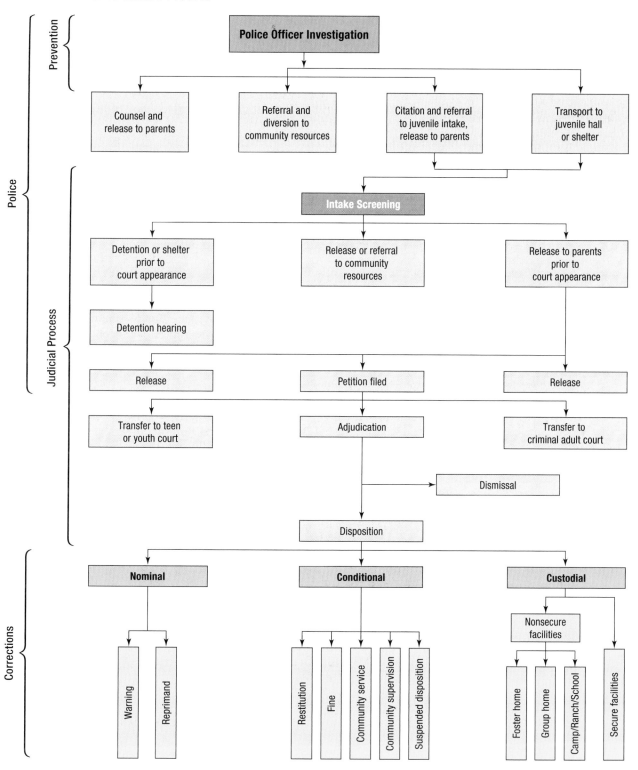

Describing the typical police response to juveniles in trouble is difficult, because there is considerable variation in the ways individual officers approach juvenile offenders. A number of factors influence the ways police officers handle juvenile suspects. Among them:

1. The seriousness of the offense.
2. The police organization.
3. The community.
4. The wishes of the complainant.
5. The demeanor of the youth.
6. The gender of the offender.
7. The race and social class of the offender.

Offense Seriousness The most important factor in the decision to arrest is the seriousness of the offense. Regardless of the subject's demeanor or other factors, as the seriousness of the offense increases, so does the likelihood of arrest. Most police-juvenile encounters involving felony offenses result in an arrest. However, most police-juvenile encounters involve minor offenses. When offenses are minor, a number of other factors have been found to influence police decision making.

The Police Organization As described in Chapter 6, police departments develop their own particular styles of operation. Those styles, in turn, help structure the way officers respond to juvenile offenders. For example, in one study that categorized police departments by the extent to which they employed a legalistic style of policing, characterized by a high degree of professionalism and bureaucratic structure, it was discovered that officers in most legalistic departments were more likely to arrest juvenile suspects than were officers in less legalistic departments.[31] Thus, the ways that police department personnel respond to juvenile offenders is to some extent a product of the organizational characteristics and policies developed by their individual departments. However, police departments do not operate in a political and social vacuum. The communities in which they operate also influence them.

The Community Communities influence policing in a variety of ways. Through their interactions with residents of a community, police develop assumptions

A juvenile's demeanor can influence arrest decisions. *How would you advise a juvenile to act if he or she is stopped by a police officer?*

about the communities they police, the people who live in those communities, and the ability and willingness of community residents to respond to crime and delinquency. Research suggests that police operate differently in lower-class communities than in wealthier communities. Police expect lower-class communities to have higher levels of crime and delinquency, because more arrests are made in those communities and because they know that lower-class communities have fewer resources with which to respond informally to the array of problems experienced there. Consequently, when police have contact with juveniles in lower-class communities, formal responses become more likely, because informal responses are believed to be ineffective in most cases. Indeed, research that has examined the effect of neighborhood socioeconomic status has found that as the socioeconomic status of the neighborhood increases, the likelihood that a police-juvenile encounter will end in arrest declines.[32]

The Wishes of the Complainant As noted earlier, many police-juvenile interactions occur because of a citizen complaint to the police. What police do in those situations often depends on whether the complainant is present, what the complainant would like the police to do, and, sometimes, who the complainant is.

The Demeanor of the Youth As one might expect, how youths behave toward the police can influence whether an arrest is made. Interestingly, youths who are either unusually antagonistic or unusually polite are more likely to be arrested. In contrast, youths who are moderately respectful to the police are less likely to be arrested—as long as the offense is not serious.[33]

The Gender of the Offender Gender also appears to influence the decision to arrest, particularly when status offenses are involved. A number of studies have found that female status offenders are more likely to be formally processed than male status offenders.[34]

When it comes to criminal offenses, however, research results are mixed. Some of the research shows that girls are less likely than boys to be arrested for criminal offenses, even when prior record and seriousness of offense are taken into account.[35] Other research suggests that any gender bias that existed in the past has diminished or disappeared.[36] In 2006, 29% of juvenile arrests involved females.[37] Table 13.1 shows the percentage change in arrests of

Table 13.1 Percentage Change in Arrests, 1997–2006, By Gender

Most Serious Offense	PERCENTAGE CHANGE IN ARRESTS 1997–2006	
	Female	**Male**
Violent Crime Index	−12%	−22%
Aggravated assault	−10%	−24%
Simple assault	19	−4
Property Crime Index	−35	−48
Burglary	−31	−38
Larceny-theft	−34	−51
Motor vehicle theft	−49	−54
Vandalism	−4	−15
Weapons	5	−11
Drug abuse violations	2	−14
Liquor law violations	1	−22
DUI	39	−6
Disorderly conduct	33	−2

Source: Howard N. Snyder, "Juvenile Arrests 2006," U.S. Department of Justice, Office of Juvenile Justice and Delinquency Prevention, *Juvenile Justice Bulletin* (Washington, D.C.: GPO, November 2008), p. 8 at www.ncjrs.gov/pdffiles1/ojjdp/221338.pdf.

females and males under age 18 between 1997 and 2006. The table reveals that between 1997 and 2006, arrests of juvenile females decreased less than male arrests in most offense categories and, in some categories, female arrests increased while male arrests decreased.

The Race and Social Class of the Offender There is strong evidence that a juvenile's race and social class influence police decision making. The evidence is clear that minority and poor youths are represented disproportionately in arrest statistics. For example, according to 2007 UCR data, white youths accounted for 67% of all arrests of persons less than 18 years of age. They accounted for 66% of arrests for index property offenses and about 47.5% of arrests for index violent offenses. In contrast, African American youths accounted for about 31% of all arrests of persons less than 18 years of age, 32% of index property-crime arrests, and approximately 51% of index violent-crime arrests. Other racial groups accounted for the remainder of arrests of persons less than 18 years of age.[38] Thus, although white youths account for the majority of juvenile arrests, African American youths are arrested in disproportionate numbers, since they make up only 15.4% of the U.S. population less than 18 years of age.[39]

The UCR does not report arrests by social class. However, self-report data reveal that the prevalence of delinquency (that is, the proportion of the youth population involved in delinquency) does not differ significantly between social classes when all types of offenses are considered. In other words, the proportions of middle-class and lower-class youths who engage in delinquency are similar. However, when different types of offenses are examined, significant social class differences appear. Middle-class youths have higher rates of involvement in such offenses as stealing from their families, cheating on tests, cutting classes, disorderly conduct, and drunkenness. Lower-class youths, in contrast, have higher rates of involvement in more serious offenses, such as felony assault and robbery.[40]

Police Processing of Juvenile Offenders When a police officer encounters a juvenile who has committed an illegal act, the officer must decide what to do. One option is to make an arrest. (In some jurisdictions, this is referred to as "taking into custody.") For practical purposes, an arrest takes place whenever a youth is not free to walk away.

As a general rule, the basis for arresting a juvenile is the same as for arresting an adult. An officer needs to have probable cause. There are, however, several differences between arrests of adults and juveniles. First, the police can arrest juveniles for a wider range of behaviors. For example, juveniles, but not adults, can be arrested for status offenses. (Technically, juveniles are not "arrested" for status offenses, because such offenses are not crimes. Also, because status offenses are not crimes, the apprehension of juveniles for status offenses does not require probable cause.) Second, at least in some jurisdictions, juveniles are given the *Miranda* warnings in the presence of a parent, guardian, or attorney. This is not necessary, however, because the Supreme Court, in *Fare* v. *Michael C.* (1979), ruled that parents or attorneys do not have to be present for juveniles to waive their rights. Third, in many jurisdictions, juveniles are more likely than adults who have committed similar offenses to be detained pending adjudication. In *Schall* v. *Martin* (1984), the Supreme Court ruled that preventive detention of juveniles is acceptable.

Concern about the detention of juveniles generally focuses on the use of preventive detention. Some critics argue that it amounts to punishment before a youth has been found guilty of an offense. The conditions juveniles are sometimes exposed to in detention units and adult jails raise additional concerns.

The exact procedures that the police must follow when taking a juvenile into custody vary from state to state and are specified in state juvenile codes.

FYI *"Child Delinquents"*

In 2007, the police arrested about one-half million (461,937) youths age 14 and younger. Such very young offenders represented about 28% of the total number of juvenile arrestees. These numbers may underestimate the number of child delinquents, because in many jurisdictions it is unusual for delinquents under age 12 to be arrested or referred to juvenile court.

Source: Federal Bureau of Investigation, *Crime in the United States 2007*, Table 38, www.fbi.gov/ucr/cius2007/data/table_38.html. *OJJDP Research 2000*, U.S. Department of Justice, Office of Juvenile Justice and Delinquency Prevention (Washington, D.C.: GPO, May 2001), p. 3.

However, those codes typically require officers to notify a juvenile's parents that the juvenile is in custody. Police often ask parents to come to the police station. Sometimes, an officer transports a youth home prior to any questioning. When an officer feels that detention of a juvenile is appropriate, the juvenile is transported to a juvenile detention facility. If such facilities are not available, the youth may be taken to an adult jail in some jurisdictions. In cases where a juvenile is released to his or her parents, the juvenile and the parents are informed that the court will contact them at a later date about the case. After a juvenile is released, an officer completes the complaint, collecting any additional information needed, and then forwards it to the next stage of the juvenile justice process for further action. When a juvenile is detained in a juvenile detention facility or an adult jail, the processing of the complaint is expedited because juvenile codes require a detention hearing (and therefore, a specific complaint) to determine the appropriateness of detention.

Trends in Police Processing of Juveniles In 2007, approximately 70% of all juveniles taken into police custody were referred to juvenile court, 19.5% were handled within the police department and released, and 9.4% were referred to adult or criminal courts.[41] However, an examination of such data over time reveals a trend toward increased formal processing of cases (referral to court) by police agencies. For example, in 1972, approximately 51% of youths taken into custody by the police were referred to the juvenile court, 45% were handled within the police department and released, and only about 1% was referred to criminal courts. Table 13.2 shows that there has been a trend toward:

1. Referring more youths to juvenile court.
2. Handling fewer cases within police departments.
3. Referring more cases to criminal courts.

Diversion The goal of juvenile diversion programs is to respond to youths in ways that avoid formal juvenile justice processing. Diversion can occur at any stage of the juvenile justice process, but it is most often employed before adjudication.

Diversion programs are based on the understanding that formal responses to youths who violate the law, such as arrest and adjudication, do not always protect the best interests of the youths or the community. Consequently, efforts to divert youths *from* the juvenile justice process by warning and releasing them, as well as efforts to divert youths *to* specific diversionary programs, such as counseling, have long been a part of juvenile justice practice. This is especially true for status offenders. Since the enactment of the Juvenile Justice and Delinquency Act of 1974, which stipulated that status offenders not be placed in secure detention facilities or secure correctional facilities, the number of status offenders diverted from formal juvenile justice processing has increased dramatically.

Today, diversion strategies are of two basic types. Some diversion strategies are based on the idea of radical nonintervention. Other strategies are designed to involve youths, and possibly parents, in a diversionary program. **Radical nonintervention** is based on the idea that youths should be left alone if at all possible, instead of being formally processed. The police practice of warning and releasing some juvenile offenders is an example of radical nonintervention. The practice of referring juveniles to community agencies for services such as individual or family counseling is an example of a strategy that involves youths in a diversionary program.

Both juvenile justice and community agencies operate contemporary diversion programs. Interventions employed in those programs include providing basic casework services to youths; providing individual, family, and group counseling; requiring restitution; and imposing community service. Even

radical nonintervention A practice based on the idea that youths should be left alone if at all possible, instead of being formally processed.

Table 13.2 Percentage Distribution of Juveniles Taken into Police Custody, by Method of Disposition

	Referred to Juvenile Court Jurisdiction	Handled Within Department and Released	Referred to Criminal or Adult Court	Referred to Other Police Agency	Referred to Welfare Agency
1974	47.0	44.4	3.7	2.4	2.5
1975	52.7	41.6	2.3	1.9	1.4
1976	53.4	39.0	4.4	1.7	1.6
1977	53.2	38.1	3.9	1.8	3.0
1978	55.9	36.6	3.8	1.8	1.9
1979	57.3	34.6	4.8	1.7	1.6
1980	58.1	33.8	4.8	1.7	1.6
1981	58.0	33.8	5.1	1.6	1.5
1982	58.9	32.5	5.4	1.5	1.6
1983	57.5	32.8	4.8	1.7	3.1
1984	60.0	31.5	5.2	1.3	2.0
1985	61.8	30.7	4.4	1.2	1.9
1986	61.7	29.9	5.5	1.1	1.8
1987	62.0	30.3	5.2	1.0	1.4
1988	63.1	29.1	4.7	1.1	1.9
1989	63.9	28.7	4.5	1.2	1.7
1990	64.5	28.3	4.5	1.1	1.6
1991	64.2	28.1	5.0	1.0	1.7
1992	62.5	30.1	4.7	1.1	1.7
1993	67.3	25.6	4.8	0.9	1.5
1994	63.2	29.5	4.7	1.0	1.7
1995	65.7	28.4	3.3	0.9	1.7
1996	68.6	23.3	6.2	0.9	0.9
1997	66.9	24.6	6.6	0.8	1.1
1998	69.2	22.2	6.8	0.9	1.0
1999	69.2	22.5	6.4	1.0	0.8
2000	70.8	20.3	7.0	1.1	0.8
2001	72.4	19.0	6.5	1.4	0.7
2002	72.8	18.1	7.0	1.4	0.7
2003	71.0	20.1	7.1	1.2	0.6
2004	69.5	20.8	7.9	1.3	0.5
2005	70.7	20.2	7.4	1.3	0.4
2006	69.3	20.8	8.2	1.2	0.5
2007	69.6	19.5	9.4	1.2	0.4

Note: Because of rounding, percentages may not add to 100.

Source: *Sourcebook of Criminal Justice Statistics Online,* Table 4.26 at www.albany.edu/sourcebook/1995/pdf/t426.pdf.; Federal Bureau of Investigation, *Crime in the United States,* 2002, 2003, 2005, 2006 and 2007 editions, www.fbi.gov.

though diversion programs are frequently touted as a way to reduce the number of youths involved in juvenile justice, some diversionary strategies contribute to net widening. Net widening occurs when a program handles youths who would have been left alone in the absence of the new program.

Recently, a relatively small number of juvenile offenders (estimates suggest more than 120,000 cases a year) have been adjudicated in teen courts or youth courts instead of juvenile courts or adult courts.[42] Teen courts or youth courts are a new way of dealing with relatively young and usually first-time offenders charged with offenses such as theft, misdemeanor assault, disorderly conduct, and possession of alcohol. At the end of 2008, there were 1,255 teen court programs in the United States, up from about 50 in 1991. Connecticut was the only state without at least one teen court at the end of 2008.

Teen courts are based on one of four models:

1. **Adult Judge**—An adult serves as judge and rules on legal matters and courtroom procedure. Youths serve as attorneys, jurors, clerks, bailiffs, and so on.

Teen Courts

To learn more about teen courts, visit the website of the National Youth Court Center at www.youthcourt.net. *Do you think teen courts are a good idea? Why or why not?*

All States except Connecticut have at least one teen court. *Are teen courts a good idea? Why or why not?*

2. **Youth Judge**—Similar to the adult judge model, but a youth serves as judge.
3. **Tribunal**—Youth attorneys present the case to a panel of three youth judges, who decide the appropriate disposition for the defendant. A jury is not used.
4. **Peer Jury**—This model does not use youth attorneys; the case is presented to a youth jury by a youth or adult. The youth jury then questions the defendant directly.

Nearly half of all teen courts use the adult judge model.

Most teen courts do not determine guilt or innocence. Rather they serve as diversion alternatives, and youths must admit to the charges against them to qualify for teen court. The most common disposition used in teen court cases is community service. Other frequently used dispositions included victim apology letters, apology essays, teen court jury duty, drug/alcohol classes, and monetary restitution.

Another new juvenile diversion program is restorative justice conferences or family group conferences.[43] Commonly used in Australia and New Zealand and increasingly being used throughout the world, restorative justice conferences bring together juvenile offenders, their victims, and other relevant parties (such as parents or guardians) with trained facilitators to discuss the offense and the harm done to victims and the other relevant parties. As is the case with teen courts, juvenile offenders who have been screened to participate in restorative justice conferences are generally nonviolent offenders who commit less-serious offenses and have not had a previous referral.

At the conferences, victims and the other relevant parties have an opportunity to explain how they have been affected by the offense and to question the offending juveniles. At the end of the conference, the participants determine how the offending juveniles can make amends to the victims for the wrong done and then sign a reparation agreement. These agreements typically include an apology and some type of restitution to the victims. They may also require the offenders to perform community service or complete other requirements such as improving school attendance, finishing homework, or doing chores at home or school. If an agreement cannot be reached or a juvenile challenges the allegations, then the matter proceeds to juvenile court.

Advocates of restorative justice conferences and teen courts maintain that the programs provide greater benefits to all parties involved than does the traditional juvenile court system. Advocates argue that restorative justice conferences and teen courts hold juveniles more accountable for their offenses, better enable offending juveniles to appreciate how their actions negatively affected others, better involve and meet the needs of victims, and create a more supportive community for offending juveniles. Additional benefits include the timelier handling of cases, cost savings because of the heavy reliance on volunteers, and higher levels of victim satisfaction. Because of the lack of rigorous studies, it is not possible at this time to determine whether restorative justice conferences and teen courts are more effective at reducing recidivism than is the traditional juvenile court system or other juvenile diversion programs. However, based on the research available, as well as anecdotal evidence, it appears that both restorative justice conferences and teen courts may be positive alternatives to the traditional juvenile court process, especially in jurisdictions that do not have a wide variety of intervention options for young, first-time juvenile offenders.

Detention Sometimes a youth is held in a secure detention facility during processing. There are three primary reasons for this practice: (1) to protect the community from the juvenile, (2) to ensure that the juvenile appears at a subsequent stage of processing, and (3) to secure the juvenile's own safety. In 2005, juveniles were held in detention facilities at some point between referral to court and case disposition in 21% of all delinquency cases disposed. The percentage of juveniles detained during processing has not changed very much since 1985.[44]

On a typical day in 2007, 6,837 juveniles were confined in adult jails in the United States—about a 10% decrease from 2000. Of the 6,837 juveniles confined in adult jails on a typical day in 2007, approximately 83% were tried or awaiting trial as adults.[45] In states that allow the jailing of juveniles, statutes usually prevent youths from being placed in cells with adults. This means that jail administrators must provide separate rooms and supervision for juveniles within their facilities. Federal rules require that a juvenile who is detained in an adult jail or lockup be held for no more than 6 hours and in a separate area out of sight or sound of adult inmates.[46] For juveniles, separation often means isolation, which is in turn related to an increased risk of self-destructive behavior. A recent study found that the suicide rate for juveniles in adult jails was 19 times the suicide rate for juveniles in the general population, and nearly 36 times the suicide rate of juveniles in juvenile detention facilities.[47]

Intake Screening When the decision to arrest a youth is made, or a social agency such as a school alleges that an offense has occurred, the next step in the juvenile justice process is **intake screening.** The purpose of intake screening is to make decisions about the continued processing of cases. Those decisions and others made during juvenile court processing of delinquency cases in 2005 are shown in Figure 13.2. The location of the intake screening and the educational background and training of the person who conducts it vary from jurisdiction to jurisdiction. Traditionally, probation officers have performed intake screening. However, in recent years there has been a move toward involving the prosecuting attorney in the intake process. In fact, in some jurisdictions, such as Colorado and Washington, intake screening is now the responsibility of the prosecuting attorney's office.[48] In other states, such as Michigan, intake screening is done by an intake officer (probation officer) who works for the juvenile court, although the prosecuting attorney's office reviews most complaints for legal sufficiency.

intake screening The process by which decisions are made about the continued processing of juvenile cases. Decisions might include dismissing the case, referring the youth to a diversion program, or filing a petition.

Figure 13.2

Juvenile Court Processing of Delinquency Cases, 2005, National Estimates

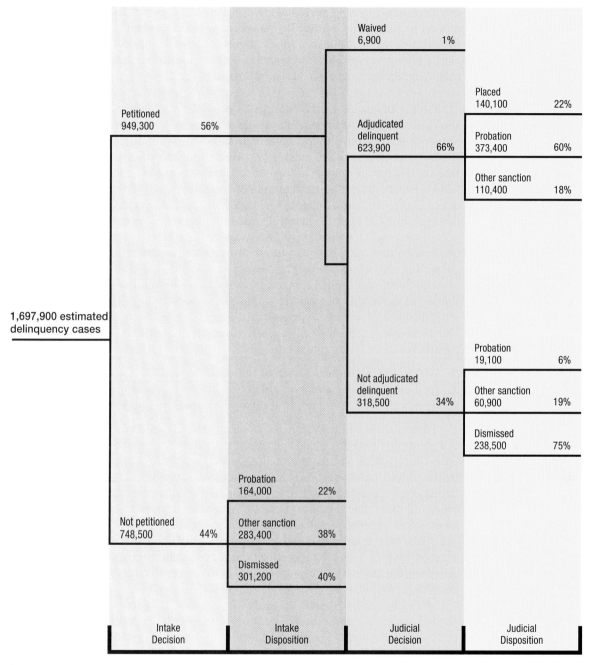

Note: Detail may not add to totals because of rounding.

Source: Charles Puzzanchera and Melissa Sickmund, *Juvenile Court Statistics 2005* (Pittsburgh, PA: National Center for Juvenile Justice, 2008), p. 58 at http://ncjj.servehttp.com/NCJJWebsite/pdf/jcsreports/jcs2005.pdf.

Possible intake decisions might include dismissing the case or having youths and parents in for a conference or an informal hearing to collect additional information for making the intake decision. Other decisions include referral of the youth to a diversion program (for example, informal probation or counseling at a community agency), filing a **petition** (a legal form of the police complaint that specifies the charges to be heard at the adjudication), and waiver or transfer of the case to criminal court.

petition A legal form of the police complaint that specifies the charges to be heard at the adjudication.

As in police decision making, a number of factors have been found to influence intake-screening decisions. For example, youths who have committed serious offenses, those with prior records, and those who are uncooperative are more likely to have petitions filed. In addition, lower-class minority males, at least in some jurisdictions, are more likely than other groups to receive more formal responses at intake. Finally, there is considerable evidence that female status offenders are likely to be treated more harshly at intake than are their male counterparts, at least in some jurisdictions.[49]

transfer, waiver, or **certification** The act or process by which juveniles who meet specific age, offense, and (in some jurisdictions) prior-record criteria are transferred to criminal court for trial.

Transfer, Waiver, or Certification to Criminal Court Since the early days of the juvenile court, state legislatures have given juvenile court judges statutory authority to transfer certain juvenile offenders to criminal court. In some jurisdictions, transfer is called waiver or certification. **Transfer, waiver,** or **certification** may occur in cases where youths meet certain age, offense, and (in some jurisdictions) prior-record criteria. For example, in Mississippi, waiver may occur if a youth has reached 13 years of age and has committed any criminal offense. In Michigan, a juvenile must be 14 years of age and must have committed one of a number of felonies specified by law. By contrast, in most other countries, juveniles as old as 13 or 14 cannot be criminally prosecuted no matter what their offense.[50] In many states, before a youth is transferred to an adult criminal court, a separate transfer or waiver hearing must be conducted to determine the waiver's appropriateness.

The judicial waiver process varies from state to state, but at the typical waiver hearing, probable cause must be shown. In addition, in many states the prosecutor must show that:

1. The youth presents a threat to the community.
2. Existing juvenile treatment programs would not be appropriate.
3. Programs within the adult system would be more appropriate.

Historically, judicial transfer authority has been exercised infrequently. For example, between 1985 and 2006, the percentage of petition cases transferred to criminal court remained around 1%. However, because of changes in the total number of petition cases between 1985 and 2006, the number of delinquency cases waived by juvenile court judges rose about 70% between 1985 and 1994, the peak year (from 7,100 cases to 12,100 cases), then dropped about 43% between 1994 and 2006 (from 12,100 cases to 6,900 cases). The net result was that the number of cases judicially waived was about 3% less in 2005 than in 1985. Between 1985 and 2006, the number of person offense cases waived increased from 33% of the waived caseload to 51% of the waived caseload, and waived property offense cases decreased from 53% of the waived caseload to 27% of the waived caseload. Throughout this period person offense cases were most likely to be judicially waived—except for 1989 through 1992, when drug offense cases were most likely to be waived. In 1985, 5% of the judicially waived delinquency cases were drug offense cases; in 2005, they constituted 12% of the waived caseload. In the 6,900 cases waived in 2005, 91% of the juveniles were male and 58% were white (39% were black). Regardless of offense, more than 99% of all petitioned delinquency cases waived to criminal court between 1985 and 2006 involved juveniles who were 16 or 17 years of age.[51]

The number of juvenile cases transferred to criminal court in recent years is actually much larger than the aforementioned data suggest. This is because there are no national statistics available on the number of prosecutorial transfers. However, it recently has been estimated that 200,000 juveniles a year are charged as adults nationwide.[52] Prosecutorial transfers occur in states that have passed legislation giving prosecutors concurrent jurisdiction. In the 15 concurrent jurisdiction states (as of 2007), both the juvenile court and the criminal court have original jurisdiction in cases that meet certain age, offense, and (in some jurisdictions) prior-record criteria. In those states, prosecutors have discretion to file eligible cases in either court.[53] In Florida alone, more than 2,000 juvenile cases were transferred to criminal court in fiscal year 2001 through prosecutorial transfer. Today, because of the availability of prosecutorial transfer, judicial waiver is almost never used in Florida.[54]

One of the concerns with trying juveniles as adults is whether they are competent to stand trial. A recent study suggests that thousands of juveniles tried as adults in the United States are incompetent to stand trial, because they are emotionally or intellectually unable to contribute to their own defense. When compared with young adults, children ages 11 to 13 were more than 3 times as likely to be found "seriously impaired" in understanding the judicial process and aiding their own defense. Children 14 or 15 years old were twice as likely to be "seriously impaired" in such awareness and reasoning. Youths age 16 and 17 did not differ in these categories from those at least 18 years of age.[55]

Besides an increase in the use of prosecutorial transfer, additional developments in this area include (1) an expansion of the number of transfer mechanisms, (2) simplification of the transfer process in some states, including the *exclusion* of offenders charged with certain offenses from juvenile court jurisdiction, or their *mandatory* or *automatic waiver* to criminal court, and (3) the lowering by some states of the maximum age for juvenile court jurisdiction. Statutory exclusion ("legislature transfers") accounts for the largest number of transfers.[56] As for lowering the maximum age, since 1995, all 17-year-olds in at least 10 states (Georgia, Illinois, Louisiana, Massachusetts, Michigan, Missouri, New Hampshire, South Carolina, Texas, and Wisconsin) and all 16- and 17-year-olds in at least 3 states (Connecticut, New York, and North Carolina) have been subject only to criminal court jurisdiction. Additionally, in 34 states, juveniles who have been convicted as adults must be prosecuted in criminal court for any subsequent offenses (the "Once an adult, always an adult" provision). Those developments reflect a shift in many jurisdictions toward a more punitive orientation toward juvenile offenders. However, some jurisdictions are moving in the opposite direction with "reverse waivers" and "criminal court blended sentencing." In 22 states, reverse waivers allow juveniles whose cases are handled in criminal courts to petition to have the case heard in juvenile court. Regarding criminal court blended sentencing, 17 states give juveniles convicted in criminal court the opportunity to be sanctioned in the juvenile system.[57]

The Adjudication Hearing When a petition is filed at intake and the case is not transferred to criminal court, the next step is adjudication. As noted previously, adjudication is the juvenile court equivalent of a trial in criminal court. In some states, such as Michigan, adjudication is now called a trial. It is at adjudication, moreover, that a juvenile begins to develop an official court record.

Before adjudication can take place, several preliminary actions are necessary. A petition must be filed, a hearing date must be set, and the necessary parties (such as the youth, the parents, and witnesses) must be given notice of the hearing. Notice is typically given through a summons or subpoena. A summons, which is an order to appear in court, is issued to the youth; copies are also given to the parents or guardians. The summons specifies the charges and the date, time, and location of the hearing, and it may list the youth's rights, such as a right to an attorney. Subpoenas are issued to witnesses, instructing them to appear on a certain day, time, and place to provide testimony or records.

When charges specified in the petition are contested by a juvenile and the juvenile is represented by an attorney, another critical event often takes place before adjudication—a plea bargain. Plea bargaining, including its problems, was discussed in detail in Chapter 8. Although the extent of plea bargaining

Nathaniel Abraham was 11 when he was charged with first-degree murder for shooting an 18-year-old stranger outside a convenience store in Pontiac, Michigan. *Should youths such as Abraham be transferred to criminal courts for trials? Why or why not?*

Uncontested adjudications are generally brief. At the end, the youth or the youth's attorney admits the charges. *Why do you suppose most adjudications are uncontested?*

in juvenile justice is unknown, it is believed to be a common practice in many juvenile courts. Furthermore, in a nationwide study of plea bargaining in juvenile courts, it was found that "much of the country has either not addressed at all or has not fully developed standards regarding the guilty plea process in juvenile court." It was also discovered that there was considerable variability in the ways that plea bargaining was carried out in various courts. For example, urban courts were more likely to institute formal procedures to regulate plea bargaining than were suburban or rural courts.[58]

There are two types of adjudications: contested ones (in which juveniles dispute the charges) and uncontested ones. Contested adjudications are similar to trials in criminal courts, which were described in Chapter 8. They typically employ the same rules of evidence and procedure. Most contested adjudications are bench adjudications, in which the hearing officer—a judge, referee, court master, or commissioner—makes a finding of fact based on the evidence presented. A **hearing officer** is a lawyer empowered by the juvenile court to hear juvenile cases. In some jurisdictions, contested adjudications are jury trials. However, as noted earlier in this chapter, juveniles do not have a constitutional right to a jury trial, and even in states that give juveniles the right to a jury trial, jury trials are rare.

hearing officer A lawyer empowered by the juvenile court to hear juvenile cases.

Like their criminal court counterparts, the vast majority of juvenile court adjudications are uncontested. Uncontested adjudications are generally brief and consist of a reading of the charges, advice of rights, and possibly brief testimony by the youth or other parties, such as a probation officer. After this, the youth, or frequently the youth's attorney, admits the charges. In some states, an uncontested adjudication is called an arraignment.

The majority of cases that are not adjudicated are dismissed. Surprisingly, however, many juveniles whose cases are neither adjudicated nor dismissed are still placed on informal probation or treated in some other way. For example, of the estimated 318,500 delinquency cases filed but not adjudicated in 2005, 75% were dismissed. In 6%, the juvenile was placed on informal probation, and the remaining 19% were disposed of in other ways (see Figure 13.2). However, the majority of cases in which petitions are filed are adjudicated. In 2005, for example, 66% of the delinquency cases in juvenile courts were adjudicated (see Figure 13.2). Although 66% may not seem like a large percentage, keep in mind that many cases not adjudicated still receive some court supervision, such as informal probation.

Disposition **Disposition** is the juvenile court equivalent of sentencing in criminal court. At the disposition hearing, the court makes its final determination of what to do with the juvenile officially labeled delinquent. Some of the options available to juvenile courts are probation, placement in a diversion program, restitution, community service, detention, placement in foster care, placement in a long-term or short-term residential treatment program, placement with a relative, and placement with the state for commitment to a state facility. In addition, the court may order some combination of those dispositions, such as placement on probation, restitution, and a short stay in detention. However, disposition possibilities are limited by the available options in a particular jurisdiction. In a few jurisdictions, they are also limited by statutory sentencing guidelines. In practice, the disposition options available to most juvenile courts are quite narrow, consisting of probation or incarceration. When incarceration is used, an indeterminate period of commitment or incarceration is the norm.[59]

As part of the disposition, the court also enters various orders regarding the youth's behavior. Those orders consist of rules the youth must follow. Also, the court may enter orders regarding parents, relatives, or other people who live in the home. For example, the court may order parents to attend counseling or a substance abuse treatment program, a boyfriend to move out of the house, or parents to clean up their house and pay for court costs or services provided, such as counseling caseworker services. If parents fail to follow those orders, at least in some jurisdictions, they may be held in contempt of court and placed in jail.

In making the disposition, the hearing officer usually relies heavily on a presentence investigation report (sometimes called a predisposition report), which is completed by a probation officer or an investigator before the disposition. Presentence investigation reports for criminal courts were described in detail in Chapter 9. Although some research has failed to find evidence that extralegal factors, such as race or social class, influence disposition, the bulk of the research indicates that extralegal factors often play a role in disposition. For example, a number of studies have found that minority and lower-class youths are more likely to receive the most severe dispositions, even when seriousness of offense and prior record are taken into account.[60]

The most frequently used disposition in juvenile courts is probation, followed by placement. In 2005, for example, approximately 60% of the youths adjudicated delinquent were placed on probation; 22% received some type of commitment. Relatively few delinquency cases received other dispositions or were released after adjudication (see Figure 13.2).

Because of recent heightened concerns about violent juvenile offenders, many states have legislatively redefined the juvenile court's mission by de-emphasizing the goal of rehabilitation and stressing the need for public safety, punishment, and accountability in the juvenile justice system. Along with this change in purpose has been a fundamental philosophical change in the focus of juvenile justice, from offender-based dispositions to offense-based dispositions, which emphasize punishment or incapacitation instead of rehabilitation. These changes are reflected in new disposition or sentencing practices, including (1) the use of *blended sentences,* which combine both juvenile and adult sanctions (see Figure 13.3), (2) the use of mandatory minimum sentences for specific types of offenders or offense categories, and (3) the extension of juvenile court dispositions beyond the offender's age of majority, that is, lengthening the time an offender is held accountable in juvenile court.[61]

disposition The juvenile court equivalent of sentencing in criminal court. At the disposition hearing, the court makes its final determination of what to do with the juvenile officially labeled delinquent.

THINKING CRITICALLY

1. Which do you think is a better way to handle juvenile crime—the informal or formal process? Why?

2. Do you think juvenile offenders should be transferred to criminal courts for trial? Why or why not?

Figure 13.3

Blended Sentencing Options Create a "Middle Ground" Between Traditional Juvenile Sanctions and Adult Sanctions

Blended sentencing option:	State
Juvenile-exclusive blend: The juvenile court may impose a sanction involving either the juvenile or adult correctional systems. Juvenile court ⟨ or ⟩ Juvenile / Adult	None
Juvenile-inclusive blend: The juvenile court may impose both juvenile and adult correctional sanctions. The adult sanction is suspended pending a violation and revocation. Juvenile court ⟨ and ⟩ Juvenile / Adult	Alaska Connecticut Kansas Minnesota Montana Ohio Vermont
Juvenile-contiguous blend: The Juvenile court may impose a juvenile correctional sanction that may remain in force after the offender is beyond the age of the court's extended jurisdiction, at which point the offender may be transferred to the adult correctional system. Juvenile court _____ Juvenile _____ Adult	Colorado[1] Rhode Island Texas
Criminal-exclusive blend: The criminal court may impose a sanction involving either the juvenile or adult correctional systems. Criminal court ⟨ or ⟩ Juvenile / Adult	California Colorado[2] Illinois Kentucky Massachusetts Nebraska New Mexico Oklahoma Virginia West Virginia Wisconsin
Criminal-inclusive blend: The criminal court may impose both juvenile and adult correctional sanctions. The adult sanction is suspended, but is reinstated if the terms of the juvenile sanction are violated and revoked. Criminal court ⟨ and ⟩ Juvenile / Adult	Arkansas Florida Idaho Iowa Michigan Missouri Virginia[3]

Note: Blends apply to a subset of juveniles specified by state statute.

[1]Applies to those designated as "aggravated juvenile offenders."

[2]Applies to those designated as "youthful offenders."

[3]Applies to those designated as "violent juvenile felony offenders."

Source: Based on data from National Center for Juvenile Justice, "State Juvenile Justice Profiles" (2007) at www.ncjj.org/stateprofiles/overviews/faqbs.asp (accessed January 5, 2009).

Correctional Programs for Juveniles

As noted, when youths are adjudicated, a number of disposition options are available to juvenile courts, although the options typically used in any one jurisdiction are fairly narrow. Three general types of dispositions are these:

1. Dismissal of the case, which is used in a small percentage of cases.
2. The use of a community-based program.
3. The use of an institutional program.

Because both community-based and institutional correctional programs for adults were the subjects of previous chapters of this book, only the features of those programs that are unique to juveniles will be discussed in the following sections.

COMMUNITY-BASED CORRECTIONAL PROGRAMS FOR JUVENILES

Among the community-based correctional programs for juvenile offenders are diversion, pretrial release, probation, foster care, group home placement, and parole. Some of those programs are designed to provide services to youths in their own homes; others provide services to youths who have been removed from their homes, at least for short periods of time. Moreover, although all community-based programs are intended to control offenders and provide sanctions for their behavior, they are also designed to accomplish a variety of additional objectives. Those objectives include allowing youths to maintain existing ties with the community, helping them restore ties and develop new and positive ones with the community (reintegration), avoiding the negative consequences of institutional placement, providing a more cost-effective response to offenders, and reducing the likelihood of recidivism. Some of the community-based correctional programs for juveniles are examined in the following sections.

Probation Probation is the most frequently used correctional response for youths who are adjudicated delinquent in juvenile courts. Juvenile probation officers are referred to as "the workhorses of the juvenile justice system." In 2005 (the latest year for which data were available), juvenile probation officers processed about 1.7 million cases.[62] Although the actual practice of juvenile probation varies from one jurisdiction to the next, probation officers usually perform four important roles in the juvenile justice process:

1. They perform intake screening.
2. They conduct presentence investigations.
3. They supervise offenders.
4. They provide assistance to youths placed on probation.

In some jurisdictions, the same individual performs all of those roles. In other jurisdictions, each probation officer specializes in only one of the roles.

A recent trend in juvenile probation is the development of intensive-supervision (probation) programs, which in some jurisdictions involve home confinement. Intensive-supervision programs are intended to ensure regular contact between probationers and probation officers. They are also intended to serve as an intermediate response that is more restrictive than standard probation but less restrictive than incarceration. However, like standard probation programs, the frequency of contact between probation officers and probationers varies considerably.[63]

Although there is wide variation in the meaning of intensive supervision, there is some indication that programs that provide frequent supervision of offenders, as well as services, are as effective as incarceration at reducing recidivism.[64] The same research also suggests that intensive-supervision programs are more cost effective than incarceration, provided they actually divert a sizable number of youths from institutions.

A recent trend in intensive supervision of juveniles is the use of home confinement, which began to be used with juvenile offenders in the 1970s[65] and has grown in popularity since that time. Today, home confinement programs use two mechanisms to monitor youths: frequent probation officer contacts and electronic monitoring. Electronic monitoring requires an offender to wear a tamper-resistant electronic device that automatically notifies the probation department if the juvenile leaves home or another designated location.

The use of home confinement employing electronic monitoring of juvenile offenders began in the 1980s and has grown substantially.[66] However, because

CJ Online

OJJDP

Visit the Office of Juvenile Justice and Delinquency Prevention website at www.ojjdp.ncjrs.org to review the various programs offered by the organization. *Which programs do you think would help deter juvenile crime?*

My name is Kelly Webster. I am a deputy probation officer (P.O.) with Los Angeles County Probation Department. I work at Camp Scott, a boot camp housing females ages 12 through 19. Camp Scott is the only female boot camp in L.A. County. Minors sentenced to camp are wards of the court and spend from 4 months to a year incarcerated. They are sentenced to camp for any crime leading up to attempted murder, so their sentences vary.

To become a P.O., a 4-year degree is required, in any subject. I have a B.A. in social welfare from the University of California, Berkeley. However, I never intended on becoming a social worker. My interest has always been in the criminal justice system. I became a P.O. by looking into county job openings upon completing my undergraduate degree. The Probation Department had an opening as a detention services officer in juvenile hall. I worked there for a year before my promotion to a P.O. The only difference in the two jobs is the degree required, because of the court report writing.

I work a 56-hour shift, meaning that I work two days and then I have four and a half days off; I sleep at work for two nights. My routine consists of supervising approximately 115 minors at all times. Because camp is structured like the military, I wear fatigues, as do the minors. Minors must ask permission to speak, salute me when walking by, and march around the facility calling cadences.

During the week, the minors are in school. On the weekends, they are cleaning, receiving visits on Sunday, or writing letters in the dormitory. They do physical training every day and twice on the weekend.

When I am not with the whole group, I have time assigned to counsel my own caseload. I am responsible for about five minors at a time. I write court reports when the minor is scheduled for release, informing the judge of the minor's behavior in camp. I recommend release or more time, depending on how they have progressed. Camp's philosophy is family reunification, so I have as much contact with the minor's family as possible.

What I like most about being a juvenile P.O. is the ability to affect some minors. What I like least about the job is that some of these "hardened" children cannot be helped. It is difficult to hear about what some of these children have endured.

Which aspects of this job would you find most difficult? Why?

---

electronic monitoring technology is diverse, rapidly developing, and relatively new, little evidence of its effectiveness exists. Still, there are good reasons that some jurisdictions find electronic monitoring attractive:

1. It eases the problem of detention overcrowding.
2. It allows youths to participate in counseling, education, and vocational programs without endangering public safety.
3. It allows youth to live with supervision in an environment more natural than an institution.
4. It allows court workers to better assess the ability of youth to live in the community under standard probation after they leave the program.[67]

Besides probation, juvenile courts in some jurisdictions employ several other types of community-based interventions with juvenile offenders, such as restitution or community service programs, wilderness probation programs, and day treatment programs. In practice, probation is often combined with one of those other community-based interventions.

Restitution Restitution programs, as you may recall, require offenders to compensate victims for damages to property or for physical injuries. The primary goal of restitution programs is to hold youth accountable for their actions. In practice, there are three types of restitution:

1. *Monetary restitution*, a cash payment to the victim for harm done.
2. *Victim-service restitution*, in which the youth provides some service to the victim.
3. *Community-service restitution*, in which the youth provides assistance to a community organization.

Despite the growing popularity of juvenile restitution programs, as well as some programs' effective reduction of recidivism, there are potential problems with some of those programs. Problems include poorly managed, informal programs with low compliance rates; high recidivism rates in some programs; and hearing officers' ordering restitution that is unrealistic to expect juveniles to complete. There is also a potential for net widening, and restitution requirements can be subject to discretionary abuse; some jurisdictions, however, have established restitution guidelines to remedy this problem. Thus, rather than achieving the goals of accountability, offender treatment, and victim compensation, restitution programs may fail to protect community safety. Moreover, they are likely to produce negative perceptions of juvenile justice by both offenders and victims.

Wilderness Probation (Outdoor Adventure) Programs Wilderness probation or outdoor adventure programs for juvenile offenders are based, in part, on ideas derived from programs such as Outward Bound. (Outward Bound is a company that sells outdoor experiences, such as mountain climbing, backpacking, and mountain biking.) A basic assumption of those programs is that learning is best accomplished by acting in an environment where there are consequences for one's actions. Consequently, the programs involve youths in a physically and sometimes emotionally challenging outdoor experience intended to help them develop confidence in themselves, learn to accept responsibility for themselves and others, and develop a relationship of trust with program staff. This is done by engaging youths in a variety of activities, such as camping, backpacking, rock climbing, canoeing, sailing, negotiating rope courses, and a solo experience (spending one or more nights alone in the wilderness).[68]

Evaluations of several wilderness probation programs have shown that they can produce positive effects, such as increases in self-esteem and a decrease in criminal activity both during and after the program.[69] However, research also indicates that the positive effects of the programs may diminish over time or may be no greater than the effects produced by probation programs that provide regular and meaningful contacts between probation officers and probationers.[70]

Day Treatment Programs Day treatment programs for juvenile offenders operate in a number of jurisdictions around the United States. The programs often target serious offenders who would otherwise be candidates for institutionalization.

Some juvenile treatment programs strive to provide physically and emotionally challenging experiences to help youthful offenders gain confidence and learn responsibility for their actions. *What are the benefits and drawbacks of these kinds of programs?*

They provide treatment or services to youths during the day and allow them to return home at night. Because they are viewed as alternatives to incarceration, they are believed to be cost effective. Because they provide highly structured programs for youths during the day, it is assumed that they protect community safety as well. The range of services or treatments can be quite varied and may include academic remediation, individual and group counseling, job skills training, job placement, and social skills training. Although some evidence suggests that day treatment programs are as effective as, or more effective than, institutional placement, some programs may be no more effective at reducing recidivism than standard probation.[71]

Foster Homes Foster homes are out-of-home placements intended to resemble, as much as possible, a family setting. Foster parents are licensed to provide care for one or more youths (usually one to three) and are paid a daily rate for the costs of care. A court often uses foster placement when a youth's home life has been particularly chaotic or harmful. In such a case, foster care is used to temporarily separate the youth from the parents or guardian in an effort to resolve the problems that resulted in the youth's removal. Foster homes are also used to remove youths from particular neighborhoods and for some non-violent offenders instead of more restrictive placements, such as institutionalization. When used in those ways, they are considered "halfway-in programs." In other instances, foster homes are used as transitions to home and are considered "halfway-out programs."

Although foster homes are widely used by juvenile courts in some jurisdictions, there are few sound evaluations of their effectiveness. The limited research that exists indicates that foster care is generally not effective and may even be counterproductive.

Group Homes Similar to foster homes, group homes are open, nonsecure community-based facilities used in both halfway-in programs and halfway-out programs. However, they are somewhat larger and frequently less family like than foster homes. The purpose of many group homes is to avoid requiring

Group homes for delinquent youths are generally less impersonal than institutions and are less expensive than institutional placements. *What are some other advantages of group homes? What are some disadvantages?*

youths to accept "substitute parents," because many youths are in the process of developing emotional independence from parental figures. Nevertheless, group homes are generally less impersonal than institutions and are less expensive than institutional placements. In addition, their location allows residents to take advantage of community services. Youths who live in group homes usually go to school in the home or in the community or work in the community. Treatment typically consists of group or individual counseling provided by group-home staff or outside counselors.

Although group homes are used extensively in juvenile justice, relatively little sound, recent research has examined their effectiveness. One well-known, but older, study of a group home program, the Silverlake Experiment, found that youths placed in the program for approximately 6 months were no more likely to commit more crimes than similar youths who were randomly assigned to an institutional placement. In other words, placement in the program was neither more nor less effective than institutionalization at reducing recidivism.

INSTITUTIONAL PROGRAMS FOR JUVENILES

A variety of correctional institutions house juveniles within the United States, including detention centers, adult jails, shelter facilities (some of them are more community based), reception and diagnostic centers, ranches, forestry camps, farms, and training schools. These institutions hold a variety of youths, including those who are status offenders as well as those who have committed violent offenses against others. They are administered by either state or local governments or by private agencies.

Juvenile Correctional Institutions What distinguishes institutional programs from their community-based counterparts is that institutional programs typically restrict youths' access to the community more than community-based programs do. Indeed, institutional programs are the most restrictive placements available to juvenile courts. However, juvenile institutions vary in the extent to which they focus on custody and control.

For example, some juvenile institutions employ a variety of security hardware: perimeter fencing or walls, barbed or razor wire, and surveillance and detection devices, such as motion detectors, sound monitors, and security cameras. Those juvenile institutions, classified as secure facilities, closely monitor residents' movement within the facility and restrict residents' access to the community. Most public and private detention centers, reception and diagnostic centers, and state training schools are secure facilities. In contrast, other juvenile institutions rely much less on security devices. Those facilities have no perimeter fencing, and some do not lock entrances or exits at night. Classified as open institutions, they rely more heavily on staff than on physical security. Most private facilities, as well as most public shelters, ranches, forestry camps, and farms, are open institutions.[72]

In addition to differences in the use of security hardware, juvenile correctional institutions also differ in a number of other ways. Some of the institutions are privately operated institutions, although the majority are public institutions. The majority of both private and public institutions are small, housing 40 or fewer residents, although some large, state-operated institutions have a legal capacity of 800 or more. Some institutions are coed; others are single-gender institutions.

Institutions also differ in the average length of time that residents stay in the facility. Typically, youths stay longer in private facilities than in public facilities. However, some private and public facilities are for short-term placements, whereas others are for long-term placements. Institutions such as detention centers and diagnostic and reception centers are typically for short-term placements. Detention centers usually house youths awaiting adjudication or

MYTH

Most of the youths housed in juvenile correctional institutions pose an immediate threat to public safety.

FACT

As Jerome Miller notes in his book, *Last One Over the Wall: The Massachusetts Experiment in Closing Reform Schools* (1991), in Massachusetts only about 25% of youths committed to state correctional facilities had committed offenses against persons. Many of those offenses against persons did not actually involve physical violence or the threat of physical violence. Consequently, many youths placed in correctional facilities, including many of those placed for violent offenses, do not pose a grave threat to public safety.

those who have been adjudicated and are awaiting disposition. In some cases, youths are placed in those institutions for a period of time as a disposition. Other institutions, such as ranches, forestry camps, farms, and training schools, are generally for long-term placements. Youths are placed in them as a result of disposition or possibly assessment at a reception and diagnostic center.

Juvenile institutions also differ in types of programming and quality of care. Almost all juvenile correctional institutions offer basic educational and counseling programs for their residents. Moreover, more than half of all institutions offer family counseling, employment counseling, peer group meetings, a point system, or behavioral contracts. However, there is considerable variability in the extent to which institutions offer more specialized educational or counseling programs for clients and the extent to which residents participate in the programs. For example, research shows that many institutions do not offer vocational training, GED courses, tutoring, suicide prevention, or programs for special offender types, such as violent offenders, sex offenders, or drug offenders.[73]

In response to the significant increase in juvenile arrests and repeat offenses from the mid-1980s to the mid-1990s, a few states and many localities have established juvenile boot camps, modeled after adult boot camps. Evaluations of juvenile boot camps show they do not reduce the recidivism of graduates any better than incarceration or probation. Some research has found that boot camp graduates are more likely to be rearrested or rearrested more quickly than other offenders. Most boot camp programs have high dropout rates. In 2007, only four boot camps for juveniles (males) were in operation in the entire United States.[74] This number is misleading, however, because juvenile boot camps are called other names, such as residential treatment facilities, behavior-modification programs, and therapeutic boarding schools. It is estimated that at least 20,000 U.S. teenagers are confined in such facilities. A recent federal Government Accountability Office (GAO) report found thousands of allegations of abuse, some of which involved death, since the early 1990s. Lawmakers and witnesses during a recent government hearing compared the abuses to the kind of torture faced by prisoners at Iraq's Abu Ghraib prison. The GAO investigators attributed the abuses to ineffective management and operating practices and untrained staff, particularly in private residential programs, which are the least regulated. The private residential programs and their referral agencies were also accused of using deceptive marketing practices.[75]

An examination of the history of juvenile institutions reveals that children have often been subjected to abuse and inhumane treatment in juvenile correctional institutions. Certainly, the overall quality of institutional life in correctional facilities today is vastly improved over that experienced by most youths placed in houses of refuge and early reform and training schools. Competent, caring, and professional administrators, who oversee skilled and caring staff in delivering a variety of high-quality services to their residents, administer many juvenile institutions. Yet, many of the problems that have historically plagued juvenile correctional institutions are still evident. In a recent study of juvenile correctional institutions, for example, researchers learned that approximately 40% of the institutions were overcrowded (that is, they did not have enough beds for all of their residents and exceeded standards based on square footage, utility use, and/or fire codes).[76] Facilities with fewer standard beds were more likely to have transported residents to emergency rooms

Juvenile boot camps are popular in some jurisdictions. *What are some of the advantages and disadvantages of juvenile boot camps?*

Figure 13.4

Violent Crime Index Arrest Rates of Juveniles, 1980–2006

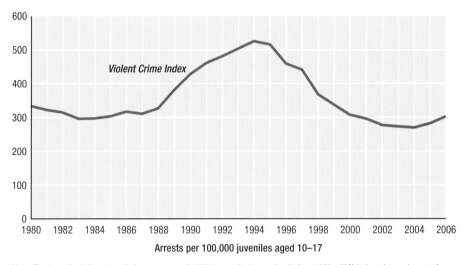

Arrests per 100,000 juveniles aged 10–17

Note: The juvenile violent crime index arrest rate in 2004 was at its lowest level since 1987—50% below the peak year of 1994. All the growth in the juvenile violent crime arrest rate that began in the latter part of the 1980s was erased by 2000. The rate increased 12% between 2004 and 2007. To place the extent of this increase in perspective, if the rate continued to increase annually by the same amount, it would be almost 14 years before it once again reached the peak level of 1994.

Source: Howard N. Snyder, "Juvenile Arrests 2006," U.S. Department of Justice, Office of Juvenile Justice and Delinquency Prevention, *Juvenile Justice Bulletin* (Washington, D.C.: GPO, November 2008), p. 5 at www.ncjrs.gov/pdffiles1/ojjdp/221338.pdf.

for treatment of injuries sustained at the institution. A recent survey by the Associated Press (AP) found more than 13,000 claims of abuse in juvenile correctional institutions nationwide from 2004 through 2007. The AP reported that the number was remarkable considering the total population of detainees at the time of the survey was about 46,000. However, authorities confirmed only 1,343 of the abuse claims, and investigators confirmed only 143 of the 1,140 sexual abuse claims. A study conducted by the U.S. Department of Justice in 2004 revealed 2,821 allegations of sexual abuse by juvenile-correction staffers. The higher number found in the Department of Justice study can be attributed to the inclusion of 194 private facilities. Experts noted that only a fraction of the claims are ever confirmed. In some cases the alleged abuses may not have actually occurred, but in many other cases abuses probably were not reported, because victims assumed no one would believe them. In the case of sexual abuse, some cases may not have been reported, because victims considered sexual relations with staff members as consensual. The Justice Department has filed suits against facilities in 11 states for supervision that is either "abusive" or "harmfully lax" and "shoddy."[77]

Despite the long history of juvenile correctional institutions, there is surprisingly little information on the effectiveness of this response to juvenile offenders. Moreover, what is known is not encouraging. Although there is some indication that effective institutional programs for juveniles exist,[78] the bulk of the evidence indicates that many juvenile institutions have little effect on recidivism. For example, a review of the rearrest rates of youths released in states that rely heavily on institutions found that the percentage of youths rearrested ranged from 51% to more than 70%.[79] The results may not be surprising, considering the quality of life in many juvenile institutions.

Recent Trends in Juvenile Incarceration Among recent trends in juvenile incarceration are (1) its increased use (at least until recently), (2) the use of both public and private facilities, (3) the disproportionately large percentage of males and racial or ethnic minorities that are incarcerated, and (4) the increasing number

Historically, large juvenile institutions have proven ineffective at preventing youths from offending again. *What do you think could be done to make these institutions more effective?*

MYTH

A new type of violent juvenile offender, one for whom violence is a way of life—a "superpredator"—emerged in the late 1980s and early 1990s.

FACT

Although evidence shows that in the early 1990s, juvenile arrest rates for violent crimes broke out of their historic range and increased to a level greater than in previous generations (see Figure 13.4), the evidence also shows that by 1995 arrest rates for juvenile violence had returned to a level comparable to that of a generation ago. Ironically, because of the myth of the "superpredator," nearly every state legislature made it easier to handle juveniles as adult offenders.

Source: "Challenging the Myths," U.S. Department of Justice, Office of Juvenile Justice and Delinquency Prevention, *1999 National Report Series: Juvenile Justice Bulletin* (Washington, D.C.: GPO, February 2000).

of juveniles being incarcerated in local adult jails and state prisons. Incarceration has become an increasingly popular response to delinquency, though that trend may be moderating somewhat. For example, in 2006, 92,854 juvenile offenders were held in residential placement facilities, about 4% fewer than in 2003 and about 12% fewer than in 1997.[80] South Dakota had the highest juvenile incarceration rate in 2006 (672 per every 100,000 juveniles in the population), while Vermont had the lowest (81). The juvenile incarceration rate for the United States in 2006 was 295 juveniles per every 100,000 juveniles in the population.

Ninety-five percent of juveniles placed in residential facilities in 2006 committed delinquency offenses; only 5% committed status offenses. The delinquency offenses included violent person offenses (34% of all offenses for which juveniles were incarcerated), property offenses (25%), drug offenses (9%), and public order offenses (11%). Another 16% of juveniles were confined for technical violations. Furthermore, whether a juvenile was placed in a public or private facility depended primarily on whether a delinquency or status offense was committed. Of the juveniles who were placed for delinquency offenses, 71% were placed in public facilities and 29% were placed in private facilities. Conversely, of the juveniles placed for status offenses, 28% were placed in public facilities and 72% were placed in private facilities. However, states varied greatly in the extent to which they used public or private residential facilities. At one extreme, Missouri placed 99% of its juvenile offenders in public facilities; at the other extreme, Pennsylvania placed 72% of its juvenile offenders in private facilities.

A disproportionately large percentage of males and racial or ethnic minorities are incarcerated in juvenile facilities. Although juvenile males constituted half of the U.S. juvenile population age 10 through 17 in 2006, 86% of all juveniles incarcerated in 2006 were males. However, a larger proportion of females was incarcerated for status offenses (41% of females compared to 59% of males). About 72% of all juveniles incarcerated for status offenses were placed in private as opposed to public facilities.

As for racial and ethnic minorities, in 2006, minorities (that is, nonwhites) made up about 35% of the American population age 10 through 17. Yet, minorities accounted for 65% of all juveniles in custody in 2006. About 68% of all juveniles in public facilities and about 59% of all juveniles in private facilities in 2006 were members of minority groups. Figure 13.5 illustrates the racial and

Figure 13.5

Racial and Ethnic Composition of Inmate Population of Public and Private
Juvenile Incarceration Facilities, 2006

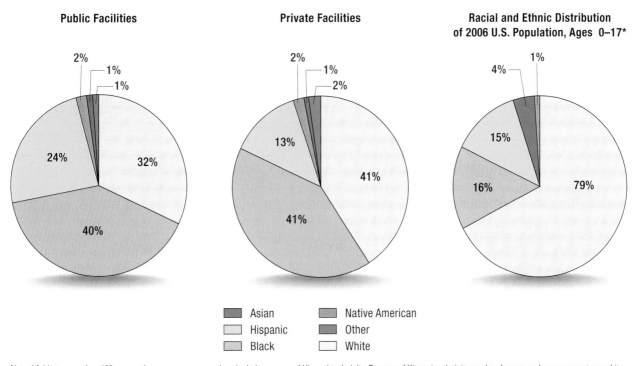

Public Facilities

2%
1%
1%
24%
32%
40%

Private Facilities

2%
1%
2%
13%
41%
41%

**Racial and Ethnic Distribution
of 2006 U.S. Population, Ages 0–17***

1%
4%
15%
16%
79%

Asian   Native American
Hispanic Other
Black   White

Note: *Adds to more than 100 percent because race proportions include persons of Hispanic ethnicity. Persons of Hispanic ethnicity can be of any race; however, most are white.

Source: Based on data in M. Sickmund, T. J. Sladky, W. Kang, and C. Puzzanchera (2008). "Easy Access to the Census of Juveniles in Residential Placement," http://ojjdp
.ncjrs.gov/ojstatbb/ezacjrp/ (accessed January 6, 2009).

ethnic composition of public and private juvenile incarceration facilities in
2006. Whites are underrepresented in both public and private facilities, blacks
are overrepresented in both, and Hispanics are overrepresented in public facilities and are underrepresented in private facilities, Asians are underrepresented
in both, and Native Americans are overrepresented in both. The Juvenile Justice and Delinquency Prevention Act of 1974, as amended, requires states to
determine whether minorities are disproportionately represented in confinement. If overrepresentation is found, the state must reduce it.

Juveniles have also been increasingly held in local adult jails and state
prisons. Those juveniles are not included in the aforementioned total of 92,854
juveniles who were incarcerated. At midyear 2007, local adult jails held 6,837
juveniles, an increase of about 1% from 2005 and a decrease of about 12%
from 1995. Eighty-three percent of the juveniles were being held as adults, and
17% were being held as juveniles. Another 2,639 juveniles were being held in
adult prisons at midyear 2007.[81]

Aftercare Programs Aftercare involves the provision of services to assist
youths in successfully making the transition from juvenile institutions to life
back in the community. The services are the same as those provided by other
types of community-based programs and may include foster care, shelter or
group-home placement, home placement, or efforts to help youths live on their
own. Parole, too, is one form of aftercare.

Unfortunately, the quality of many aftercare programs is questionable, and
in some cases, youths fail to receive any services after institutional release. As
in probation, parole supervision, in practice, may involve very little contact
between parole officers and parolees. Moreover, large caseloads carried by
aftercare workers may prevent the provision of meaningful services.

For those reasons and others (at the time, increasing juvenile crime rates, increasing numbers of juveniles requiring secure care, increasing costs, and the general failure to control or reduce the delinquent behavior of many juveniles in aftercare), the Office of Juvenile Justice and Delinquency Prevention in the late 1980s initiated an intensive community-based aftercare pilot project called the Intensive Aftercare Program (IAP).[82] The goal of IAP is to reduce recidivism among high-risk juvenile parolees. The creators of IAP describe it in this way:

> [IAP is a] correctional continuum consisting of three distinct, yet overlapping, segments: pre-release and preparatory planning during incarceration; structured transition that requires the participation of institutional and aftercare staff prior to and following community re-entry; and long-term, reintegrative activities that ensure adequate service delivery and the necessary level of social control.[83]

Table 13.3 shows the specific components of IAP as they were being implemented at three of the pilot project sites. An evaluation of the project

Table 13.3 Transition Components of IAP Programming

	IAP SITE		
Transition Component	**Colorado**	**Nevada**	**Virginia**
Early Parole Planning	Initial plan complete at 30 days after institutional placement; final plan complete at 60 days prior to release.	Initial plan complete at 30 days after institutional placement; final plan complete 30 days prior to furlough.	Initial plan complete 30 days after institutional placement; final plan complete 30 days prior to release.
Multiple perspectives incorporated in plan	Case manager, institutional staff, youth, parents, and community providers all routinely involved.	Parole officer, institutional community liaison, institutional staff, and youth; parent participation limited.	Parole officer, institutional case manager, youth, interagency "community assessment team," and parent.
Parole officer visits to institution	One to two times per week; routine.	Once per month; routine since spring 1997.	One to two times per month; routine.
Treatment begun in institution and continued in community	Via community providers. Includes multifamily counseling, life skills training, individual counseling, and vocational skills training, done routinely.	Via an institutional-community liaison and parole officers. Includes life skills and drug/alcohol curriculums; done routinely until liaison vacancy.	Via one provider at Hanover only. Drug/alcohol treatment; sporadic use. State policy discourages contract services by community providers for institutionalized youth.
Youth prerelease visits to community	Supervised day trips to community programs, beginning 60 days prior to release.	Not allowed.	Not allowed.
Preparole furlough	Overnight/weekend home passes, beginning 30 days prior to release.	Thirty-day conditional release to community, prior to official parole.	Not allowed.
Transitional residence	Not part of the design, but occurs for some youth.	Not part of the design.	Two group homes in Norfolk; 30- to 60-day length of stay; used for most youth.
Transitional day programming	Two-day treatment programs in Denver used for almost all youth during the first few months after release.	One-day-supervison/treatment program used for most youth.	Day treatment used for youth who do not go to group homes.
Phased supervision levels on parole	Informal system: contact once per week during the first few months, down to once per month later.	Four-phase system: contact four times per week during furlough; three times per week next 90 days; two times per week next 60–90 days; once per week next 30–60 days.	Four-phase system: group home; contact five to seven times per week next 60 days; three to five times per week next 60 days; three times per week last 30 days.

Source: Richard G. Wiebush, Betsy McNulty, and Thao Le, "Implementation of the Intensive Community-Based Aftercare Program," U.S. Department of Justice, Office of Juvenile Justice and Delinquency Prevention, *Juvenile Justice Bulletin* (Washington, D.C.: GPO, July 2000), p. 9, Table 3.

was published in 2005.[84] The IAP ran for almost 5 years at each of the three pilot project sites (fall 1995 through summer 2000) and, although all of the sites had some implementation problems, they operated programs that successfully incorporated most of the core features of the national IAP model. Several different measures were used to compare officially reported recidivism of the IAP and control groups during a 12-month follow-up period. At each site, IAP and control groups did not differ in the number of days at risk during the follow-up or in subsequent recidivism rates. Approximately 50% to 60% of both IAP and control group members at all three sites were rearrested for felony offenses, 60% to 70% for criminal offenses (felony and/or misdemeanor), and 80% to 85% for some type of offense. Also, at all three sites, IAP and control groups did not differ significantly in the prevalence, incidence, or seriousness of reoffending. Thus, like many other correctional programs for youths and adults, the Intensive Aftercare Program failed to achieve its primary goals.

In conclusion, twenty-first-century juvenile justice in the United States has several important problems to resolve. Many of the problems are the same ones that have plagued juvenile justice since the first specialized institutions for children were established in the early 1800s. The problems include:

1. Providing adequate due process protections to youths at all stages of the juvenile justice process.
2. Continuing to build on knowledge of effective correctional interventions and developing a range of effective and humane correctional responses, from diversion to institutional aftercare programs.
3. Eliminating the abusive treatment of youths placed in correctional programs.
4. Working out the appropriate balance between community-based and institutional correctional programs.
5. Conducting rigorous evaluations of juvenile justice agencies and programs.
6. Recognizing the limits of correctional responses in solving the juvenile crime problem.
7. Working out an appropriate balance between preventing and correcting delinquency.

THINKING CRITICALLY

1. Which of the community-based correctional programs described in the chapter (for example, restitution, wilderness probation, and day treatment) do you think would be most effective at rehabilitating youths? Why?

2. What do you think are the pros and cons of institutional programs for juveniles?

✳ Summary

1. Describe some of the early institutions used to respond to wayward and criminal youths.

   Among the early institutions used to respond to wayward and criminal youths were houses of refuge, placing out, reform schools, industrial schools, and training schools.

2. Explain the effects of some landmark U.S. Supreme Court cases on the juvenile justice system.

   Landmark Supreme Court cases on juvenile justice include *Ex parte Crouse*, *People* v. *Turner*, *Commonwealth* v. *Fisher*, *Kent* v. *United States*, *In re Gault*, *In re Winship*, and *McKeiver* v. *Pennsylvania*. Some of the effects of those cases on juvenile justice are the right to adequate notice of charges, protection against compelled self-incrimination, the right to confront and to cross-examine accusers, and the right to the assistance of counsel.

3. Identify and describe factors that influence the ways that police process juvenile cases.

   Among the factors that influence the ways that police process juvenile cases are (1) the seriousness of the offense, (2) the community, (3) the wishes of the complainant, (4) the demeanor of the youth, (5) the gender of the offender, (6) the race and social class of the offender, and (7) the police organization.

4. Summarize the rationale for the use of diversion in juvenile justice.

   Diversion programs in juvenile justice are based on the under-standing that formal responses to youths who violate the law, such as arrest and adjudication, do not always protect the best interests of children or the community. Indeed, some formal responses may be harmful to many youths and may increase the likelihood of future delinquent behavior. This is because formal processing may cause youths to develop negative or delinquent self-images, may stigmatize youths in the eyes of significant others, or may subject youths to inhumane treatment.

5. Describe the adjudication hearing in juvenile justice.

   There are two types of adjudication: contested ones (in which juveniles dispute the charges) and uncontested ones. Contested adjudications are similar to trials in criminal courts. Most contested adjudications are bench adjudications, in which the hearing officer makes a finding of fact based on the evidence presented. In some jurisdictions, contested adjudications are jury trials. At an uncon-tested adjudication hearing, the youth, or frequently the youth's attorney, admits to the charges. The vast majority of juvenile court adjudications are uncontested.

6. Describe the disposition hearing and the types of dispositions available to the juvenile court.

   The disposition is the juvenile court equivalent of sentencing in criminal court. At the disposition hearing, the court makes its final determination of what to do with the youth who is officially labeled delinquent. At the disposition, the court also enters various orders regarding the youth's behavior. Those orders consist of various rules the youth must follow. Also, the court may enter orders regarding parents, relatives, or other people who live in the home. Dispositions available to the juvenile court include probation, placement in a diversion program, restitution, community service, detention, placement in foster care, placement in a long-term or short-term residential treatment program, placement with a relative, and placement with the state for commitment to a state facility. Not all disposition alternatives are available in all jurisdictions.

7. Identify the types and describe the effectiveness of community-based correctional programs for juveniles.

   Community-based correctional programs include diversion, pretrial release, probation, foster care, group home placements, and parole. Evaluations of some programs indicate that they are effective at reducing recidivism or that they are as effective as institutional placement. In contrast, evaluations of other community-based programs indicate that they have little effect on subsequent offenses.

8. Summarize recent trends in juvenile incarceration.

   Among recent trends in juvenile incarceration are (1) its increased use (at least until recently), (2) the use of both public and private facilities, (3) the disproportionately large percentage of males and racial or ethnic minorities that are incarcerated, and (4) the increasing number of juveniles being incarcerated in local adult jails and state prisons.

9. Identify the types and describe the effectiveness of institutional programs for juveniles.

   In the United States, a variety of correctional institutions house juveniles, including detention centers, adult jails, shelter facilities, reception and diagnostic centers, ranches, forestry camps, farms, and training schools. There is some evidence that small, secure treatment facilities for violent or chronic offenders are effective at reducing recidivism. However, many institutions, particularly large state institutions, have often been found to have little positive effect on youths' subsequent delinquent behaviors. In fact, they may increase the likelihood that youths will commit further offenses.

✳ Key Terms

juvenile delinquency 506
apprenticeship system 507
binding-out system 507
houses of refuge 508
placing out 509

reform, industrial, or
   training schools 510
cottage reformatories 510
parens patriae 511
adjudication 514

informal juvenile justice 516
status offenses 516
radical nonintervention 521
intake screening 524
petition 525

transfer, waiver, or
   certification 526
hearing officer 528
disposition 529

✳ Review Questions

1. What changes occurred in the sixteenth and seventeenth centuries in the ways the young were viewed?
2. What were the purposes of houses of refuge?
3. What is *parens patriae,* and what was the legal context in which it arose?
4. What was the social and historical context in which the juvenile court was created?
5. Historically, what has been the fundamental difference between the procedures used in juvenile courts and those employed in criminal courts?
6. What is the informal juvenile justice process, and why is it important?
7. What are four typical responses that police officers employ when handling juvenile cases?
8. What are three recent trends in police processing of juveniles?
9. What are two relatively new juvenile diversion alternatives?
10. What are five possible intake decisions that might be made in the juvenile justice process?
11. What are five recent trends in the practice of transferring juvenile cases to criminal court, and what do they suggest about the current orientation of juvenile justice?
12. In practice, what two dispositions are typically available to juvenile court judges in most jurisdictions, and which one is most frequently used?
13. What are three new dispositional or sentencing practices employed by juvenile court judges?
14. What are six objectives of community-based correctional programs for juveniles?
15. What are four problems commonly found in juvenile correctional facilities?
16. What are some important problems that remain unresolved as juvenile justice in the United States enters the twenty-first century?

✳ In the Field

1. **Debate Juvenile Justice** With fellow students, family members, or friends, debate whether the juvenile justice system ought to be abolished and juvenile offenders treated as adults.
2. **Compare Correctional Facilities** Visit different juvenile correctional facilities in your community, both community-based facilities and institutional facilities.

Compare what you observe at these facilities based on the following criteria:
a. How do terms for similar offenses compare at each facility?
b. How are juveniles treated?
c. Are there educational or rehabilitation opportunities?
d. How does the way of life compare?

✳ On the Net

1. **Juvenile Information Center** Go to the Juvenile Information Center website at www.ncjrs.org. Click on Juvenile Justice and then choose one of the documents listed. Read the document and then write a brief summary of it.
2. **Research Parenting Issues** Go to the *Parenting Resources for the 21st Century* online guide at www.familyfirst

.com/parenting_resources_for_the_21.html. Select one or more of the major subject headings and then choose one or more of the specific topics to read. Write a report on the delinquency implications of the various parenting issues. (It may be helpful to review theories of delinquency in Chapter 3.)

✳ Critical Thinking Exercises

THE CASE OF PAUL

1. Paul, a 15-year-old, sexually assaulted, robbed, and killed Billy, an 11-year-old. Billy was missing for 2 days. Paul hid Billy's body for those 2 days in his family's garage before dumping it in a wooded area near the house. Neighbors describe Paul as quiet and introverted. His parents state that he grew increasingly violent after they kept him from a 43-year-old man named Smith who Paul had met in a chat room. Smith was subsequently charged with sexually assaulting Paul. The two apparently had sex in motels five times during the previous 4 months.

a. Should Paul be handled by the justice system (either juvenile or adult) or be diverted, perhaps to a mental health facility? Why?
b. Should he be charged with first-degree murder (as well as the other crimes)? Why or why not?
c. Should he be transferred to criminal court and tried as an adult?
d. If tried as an adult, should he enter a plea of not guilty by reason of insanity? A plea of guilty but insane? Why or why not?
e. If Paul is convicted of any of the charges, what sentence should be imposed? Why?

THE CASE OF JAMES

2. Seventeen-year-old James lives in a nice lower-middle-class neighborhood in central Florida. A few years ago, James began running with a bad crowd. His parents tried a variety of punishments, to no avail. James was eventually arrested for burglary, theft, and other crimes. A juvenile court judge placed him on probation and ordered him to receive counseling. James violated probation, stopped going to counseling sessions, and began committing crimes again. After a subsequent arrest, James was ordered into a residential rehabilitation program for several months. After finishing the program, he was placed in a special school, from which he soon ran away. He was next placed in another residential program, one designed for youths "needing more structure." He ran away. After he was caught, a juvenile court judge returned him to the residential program for about 6 months.

James's father states that the rehabilitation programs are a waste of time and money, because they are disorganized and ineffectual. He fears James will kill or be killed, and he wants James to be locked up until the age of 19. However, space is limited in the most secure juvenile institutions. In Florida, youths must commit an average of 12 crimes before they are placed in such institutions.

a. Should James be handled by the justice system (either juvenile or adult) or be diverted? Why?

b. If he is diverted, what type of program would benefit him most? Why?

c. If James is retained in the juvenile justice system, what disposition would be most appropriate and beneficial for him?

To access more information and resources, including study questions, chapter summaries, and links, go to: www.mhhe .com/bohm6e.

The Future of Criminal Justice in the United States

Chapter Objectives

After completing this chapter, you should be able to:

1. Describe the possible future of law enforcement if the crime control model dominates, and the possible future if the due process model dominates.

2. Describe the possible future of the administration of justice if the crime control model dominates, and the possible future if the due process model dominates.

3. Identify perhaps the most divisive issue that will confront correctional policy makers in the future.

4. Describe the possible future of corrections.

5. List some of the cost-reduction strategies likely to be advocated in corrections in the future.

6. Explain what identity theft is, and describe the extent of the problem in the United States.

7. Summarize the reasons why transnational organized crime poses special problems for law enforcement.

8. Describe some of the challenges faced by criminal justice in the Age of Terrorism.

CRIME STORY

On May 12, 2008, Walter Corea was sentenced to 15 years in a federal prison for his role in one of the nation's largest sex trafficking rings. Corea was the head smuggler, who brought Central American women and girls into the United States and forced them to work in bars and cantinas in the Houston area. Corea, jointly with his seven other co-defendants, also was ordered to pay more than $1.7 million in restitution to the victims. Corea had pleaded guilty to conspiracy to hold persons in a condition of peonage and to illegally and knowingly recruiting, harboring, and transporting persons for labor and services. Peonage is a condition of involuntary servitude imposed to extract repayment of indebtedness. He also pleaded guilty to conspiracy to bring, harbor and transport known illegal aliens for purposes of commercial advantage and private financial gain.

The smuggling ring was busted on November 13, 2005, following an investigation by the Human Trafficking

continued

Rescue Alliance of the Southern District of Texas. More than 100 officers from Immigration and Customs Enforcement, the FBI, the Harris County Sheriff's Office, the Harris County Constable Precinct Five Office, and the Texas Alcoholic Beverage Commission, raided five related bars and restaurants. They had expected to find 50 or 60 women. They rescued about 120 victims. The scantily-clad women, called "Bar Belles" by the FBI, told agents they had been forced to work six or seven nights a week and to allow men to buy them overpriced drinks in exchange for their company or sexual favors. They also were beaten, coerced into prostitution, and forced to have abortions. The ring's abortionist, Lorenza Nenez-Reyes, known as "La Comadre," pleaded guilty to an obstruction of justice charge, was sentenced to 19 months in a federal prison, and was deported to Honduras.

For years, the ring preyed on women and girls from Honduras, El Salvador, Nicaragua, and Guatemala, illegally luring them to Houston with false promises of legiti-mate work and then forcing them to labor in bars and cantinas to pay off smuggling fees of $8,000 to $15,000, as well as all living expenses. To control the women, the head of the ring, Maximino "El Chimino" Mondragon, kept records on each one that included the names of their mothers, brothers and children and locations of their homes and schools. He threatened to kill relatives or burn down family homes if they did not cooperate. In addition to Maximino Mondragon and Corea, other members of the ring included Mondragon's brother Oscar and their half brother, Victor Omar Lopez, Olga Mondragon, Oscar Mondragon's wife, Maria Fuentes, Maximino Mondragon's ex-wife and bookkeeper, and Kerin Silva, Corea's son. Oscar Mondragon was sentenced to a federal term of 15 years; Lopez to a term of about 9 years; Olga Mondragon to 7 years; and Maria Fuentes to 30 months. Fuentes is an illegal alien and will be deported. Kerin Silva was sentenced to 12 months home detention followed by three years probation. The ring's leader, Maximino Mondragon, has not been sentenced as of this writing.

Among the topics examined in Chapter 14 is transnational organized crime, of which the smuggling of human beings for illicit purposes is a major activity. The Mondragon operation is believed to be the first time an anti-human trafficking task force has taken down a powerful multinational smuggling ring. Buoyed by this success, other such task forces have been created in the United States. Are such task forces a good idea? What problems might arise from trying to coordinate the activities of different law enforcement agencies at the local, state, and federal levels? Should law enforcement agencies of other countries participate in these task forces? What problems might that cause? Should more resources be expended on this type of criminal activity? From where should the resources come? What should be done to help the victims of human smuggling and sex trafficking? As crime becomes more international, these types of questions will become increasingly important.

The Future of Criminal Justice

In the preceding chapters of this book, you have learned about the nature of crime and its consequences in the United States, theories of crime and delinquency causation, criminal law and its application, and the historical development of criminal and juvenile justice. You have also examined in detail the current operation of criminal and juvenile justice and have analyzed problems associated with each. In this last chapter, you will explore the directions that American criminal and juvenile justice might take in the future and consider some predictions. Excluded from this chapter are predictions about future trends in the most common types of crime and delinquency, because that subject is too far afield. However, we do examine two crimes that are likely to pose special problems for law enforcement and criminal justice in the twenty-first century: identity theft and transnational organized crime. We conclude the chapter with a summary of the criminal justice response to terrorism, the defining crime of the early twenty-first century.

The principal guide that informs predictions of the future directions of criminal and juvenile justice is Herbert Packer's model of the U.S. criminal justice process, which was introduced in Chapter 1.[1] For us, Packer's model has had considerable explanatory power for about 40 years, and it seems that its explanatory power will remain strong in the future. However, in making predictions, this text will not limit itself to Packer's vision of possible futures for criminal and juvenile justice, but will instead peer into its own crystal ball—and those of others—to venture some predictions in areas where Packer's model is silent.

THE FUTURE OF LAW ENFORCEMENT

The manner in which law is enforced in the future will vary substantially depending on whether it is driven by crime control model principles or due process model principles (see the discussion of these models in Chapter 1). Either way, advances in technology will play a huge role in law enforcement's future. This section addresses those issues.

Law Enforcement Under Crime Control If the future of law enforcement increasingly reflects the principles and policies of the crime control model, then you might expect fewer limitations on how the police attempt to combat crime. For example, the practice of detaining and arresting suspects for investigation without probable cause is likely to increase, as is the length of time a suspect may be held before being charged. The Supreme Court may augment those practices by granting good-faith exceptions to the Fifth Amendment protection against compelled self-incrimination. If the crime control model is fully embraced, it is possible that the Court's decision in *Miranda* v. *Arizona* could be overturned and that coerced confessions would be admissible at trial.

The investigative abilities of the police should be improved and made easier by the expansion of community policing. Although the current meaning of community policing remains vague (see Chapter 6), it will ultimately be defined by the way it is actually employed. If it is employed according to crime control principles, American citizens can expect greater intrusion into their lives. Privacy will be sacrificed for efficiency in crime control. The same is probably true if CompStat is widely adopted.

Greater intrusion into people's lives will be facilitated by advances in electronic surveillance. For example, advances in **bionics** (the replacing of human body parts with mechanical parts) may someday produce bionic eyes powerful enough for law enforcement officers to see for miles or through walls, and bionic ears sensitive enough to enable law enforcement officers, from a considerable distance, to clearly hear conversations held behind closed doors.[2] Already, computer-controlled supersensitive listening and video devices are able to accomplish the same things.[3] Miniaturization and remote-control technology will allow the creation of tiny eavesdropping aerial drones equipped with a camera and microphone that can fly into open spaces to record what is happening.[4] To the extent that the crime control model is followed, there may be fewer or, perhaps, no limitations on the future uses of electronic surveillance. According to this scenario, George Orwell's vision of a society monitored totally by Big Brother (the state and its agents) may become a reality in the United States, as it did to varying degrees in the totalitarian nations of Eastern Europe, Communist China, and the former Soviet Union. In other words, to facilitate efficient crime control, according to the logic of the crime control model, it is conceivable that every move you make, every word you say, and, possibly, every thought you think will be recorded for future incrimination, if the need arises.

New software is being developed that allows law enforcement agencies nationwide to share data in a timely manner.[5] The new software combines several public, private, and criminal databases and allows them to be searched simultaneously. An advanced feature of the software is the ability to take vague bits of information, such as a partial license tag number, and get lists of possible suspects or vehicles in seconds. The software is intended primarily for terrorism investigations, but it may also be used to help solve child abductions or other time-sensitive crimes. Another feature of the software is the ability to use digital driver's license photos to quickly generate a photo lineup that can be shown to witnesses. Critics of the new software contend that it infringes on civil liberties and privacy rights and could lead to racial profiling. It may even be possible, as depicted in Steven Spielberg's movie, *The Minority Report,* that

bionics The replacing of human body parts with mechanical parts.

 **CJ Online**

Bionics

Visit *Scientific American's* website at www.sciam.com to learn more about scientific research in bionics. *Do you think the use of bionics could have a significant impact on law enforcement in the future? Why?*

certain people or devices will be able to see into the future to identify criminals before they could do any harm. In any event, advanced electronic surveillance devices and other new technologies in law enforcement (to be discussed in more detail later in this chapter) should be available sooner than might normally be expected because of the war on terrorism.

Law Enforcement under Due Process However, if Americans see a shift to the principles and policies of the due process model, they should expect existing limitations on how the police combat crime to remain intact or even be expanded. Certainly, the practice of detaining and arresting suspects for investigation without probable cause will end or, at least, be decreased substantially. The present 48-hour limitation—with certain exceptions—on the length of time a suspect may be held before being charged will be standard operating procedure. Good-faith exceptions to protections against compelled self-incrimination will not be allowed, and current good-faith exceptions to the exclusionary rule may be eliminated. Adherence to the *Miranda* requirements will become even more routine among police officers than it is currently. Perhaps suspects will no longer be allowed to waive their rights.

To the extent that the due process model shapes future law enforcement practice, electronic surveillance will not be allowed under any circumstances or will at least be strictly limited to a few types of crimes (for example, crimes that threaten national security, such as treason and espionage).

As described more fully in Chapter 6, a recent development in criminal investigation is DNA profiling. Although this new technology is still controversial, it will probably become a routine law enforcement tool in the near future. Perhaps the most thorny issue with this new technology is how the DNA database will be collected and used. If the principles of the due process model prevail in the future, then the DNA database will probably comprise DNA samples taken only from booked suspects (and criminal justice personnel upon hiring), as is the current practice with fingerprints. Such a policy is unlikely to be very controversial or to attract much public resistance. However, if policy reflects the principles of the crime control model, then the DNA database may comprise DNA samples taken shortly after birth from all infants born in the United States. This latter strategy would clearly make the DNA database more

CJ Online

DNA

You can learn more about DNA profiling by visiting the National Institute of Justice's National Commission on the Future of DNA Evidence website at www.ojp.usdoj .gov/nij/topics/forensics/dna/ commission/welcome.html. *Do you think that DNA profiling will play an important role in the future of law enforcement? Why?*

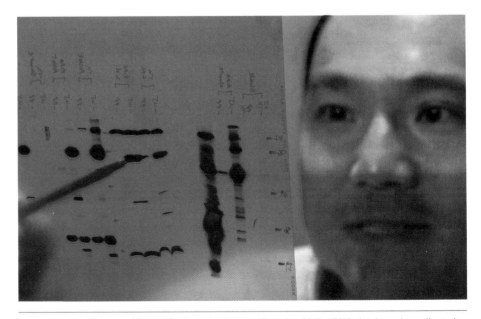

DNA profiling will be used increasingly in the future. *How should the DNA database be collected and used?*

complete and, therefore, a more efficient tool in the effort to solve crimes. It would also be much more controversial and would probably be resisted by a large segment of the population as a violation of privacy rights.

Advances in law enforcement technology are inevitable, but technology employed according to due process principles will be used to protect citizens and law enforcement personnel. For example, robots will be employed with greater frequency to perform a variety of law enforcement duties. Law enforcement personnel have used robots since the mid-1970s for handling bombs, and they are currently being used in other law enforcement situations, usually in SWAT or other dangerous circumstances.[6] In the future, they may be used routinely in hostage situations and in the arrest of dangerous suspects.

Some police departments are beginning to install digital video systems in their patrol cars to record and store pictures of every encounter their officers have.[7] Although many police departments already have camera systems in their cars to provide evidence in arrests and to protect themselves from lawsuits, the new systems record and store the data in computers. Also, unlike analog video systems, which usually are not activated until after a violation has occurred, the new digital systems allow the police to record the events preceding the infraction and the infraction, itself, while it is taking place. The new systems also come with small microphones that officers wear on their belts so they can record what is said outside their cars.

Some law enforcement agencies use robots to handle bombs and other dangerous assignments. *Should all law enforcement agencies have access to robots? If so, how should they be financed and distributed?*

When officers begin their shifts, they plug a portable hard drive into a computer mounted between the front seats of their patrol cars. They then activate a microphone and bi-directional camera that is mounted on the car's visor. The microphone and camera record continuously but only save 3 to 4 minutes at a time. When officers turn on their pursuit lights, the system automatically saves and stores the last few minutes and whatever comes next, until the system is turned off. Once their shifts are completed, officers take the portable hard drive to police headquarters and upload all the stored data to a central server.[8]

Some police departments have plans to put small wireless video cameras on police officers' lapels and to install equipment in patrol cars that will allow officers to remotely monitor video feeds from banks.[9]

Digital video surveillance cameras, many equipped with microphones, also are increasingly being used to provide around-the-clock surveillance in the public areas of cities and towns throughout the United States.[10] Many of these systems have been financed with Department of Homeland Security grants for the purpose of combating terrorism. They are being installed at possible attack targets, high-crime areas, and heavily trafficked areas. Most cameras have a 360-degree range of motion, can be remotely rotated, and zoom in and out. Few police departments, however, have written policies governing their use, formal training for users, or methods of evaluating whether they achieve results. Nevertheless, despite the privacy concerns of civil libertarians, studies showing that cameras are not effective in deterring terrorism or crime, and questions about whether live monitoring is the best use of limited police resources, most Americans support the use of surveillance cameras. According to a 2007 *ABC News/Washington Post* poll, 71% of Americans favored increased use of surveillance cameras, and only 25% opposed it. As for the concern with limited police resources and using "live" personnel to monitor the cameras, intelligent "video analytics" software has been developed to monitor live feeds. The software commands the cameras to be focused on specific things such as a crowd collecting in a particular neighborhood or the sound of a gunshot. It also allows

Digital video surveillance cameras are increasingly used to provide around-the-clock surveillance in the public areas of cities and towns throughout the United States. *Is this a good idea? Why or why not?*

one operator to monitor numerous cameras. The sale of the surveillance systems is big business. In the United States, alone, the market for the surveillance systems doubled between 2002 and 2008 to $9.2 billion, and is estimated to more than double again by 2010 to more than $21 billion. London, England began installing cameras in the early 1990s and has the most extensive network with about 500,000 cameras in its "Ring of Steel." Recently, the British Home Office approved funding to add thousands of "head-cams" mounted on the hats of police officers. With a countless number of private-surveillance cameras, it is estimated that the average Londoner is observed 300 times a day.

A related development gaining popularity in the United States and elsewhere is automatic license number plate recognition systems (ALPR or, more commonly, ANPR systems), which are replacing ordinary traffic-surveillance cameras in many locations. ANPR systems use infrared (IR) cameras and sophisticated software to recognize the letters and numbers on a plate and compare them with a database to detect vehicles of interest. Most systems now consist of multiple cameras, including both the IR cameras and color cameras to snap photos of vehicles. Systems can be mounted almost anywhere, and there are aerial units capable of reading a plate from an elevation of more than 1,600 feet. Most of the systems can detect, capture, and compare 1,500 to 3,000 plates per minute and do so at night, in rain, and through a chain-link fence or mild mud splatters. Patrol cars are typically equipped with at least three cameras to cover oncoming traffic, multilane traffic, and parked cars. An officer can record oncoming plates at a combined speed of 120 mph, or scan parked cars in a parking lot or on a neighborhood street without slowing down or taking his or her eyes off the road. The system can record the identification, photo, GPS location, and timestamp for any vehicle. The units currently cost $20,000 to $30,000 each and have been used for tracking stolen cars, felony warrants, Amber Alerts, and parking violations.[11]

New Law Enforcement Technology Some other ideas currently on drawing boards are these:

- A pocket-sized, voice-activated voice-stress analyzer that police officers could use to determine whether suspects or witnesses experienced stress during questioning, indicating possible dishonest answers (used like current polygraph machines).
- An ultrasmall, two-way cellular phone (like a Dick Tracy wrist communicator), possibly implanted in officers' larynxes, that would allow police officers to be in constant contact with headquarters, fellow officers, or anyone around the world.
- A wireless interoperability system, which connects the radio frequencies of various emergency first responders (federal, state, and local) and provides smooth, fast, and accurate real-time communications for emergency personnel who may need to coordinate activities at a large incident.[12]
- A universal translator (that is, an ultrasmall computer) that could instantly translate speech from one language to another, allowing police officers to

question suspects, witnesses, or crime victims without the language barrier they frequently confront today.[13]

- An ultra-wideband device that will allow police officers to detect motions through surfaces such as walls (for example, to determine whether there are people inside a room before they knock down a door).[14]
- Video-equipped, nearly unnoticeable pilotless drones for aerial surveillance that are guided by a remote operator or by GPS (Global Positioning System) that can hover above a target or just outside a window while transmitting real-time video.[15]
- A video stabilization system that electronically converts useless, unstable surveillance video into clear, court-presentable evidence.[16]
- A "smart" gun that would electronically disable itself if taken away from a police officer during a struggle.
- A microwave device to shut off a car's ignition, stopping fleeing suspects without the risk of a high-speed chase.
- A supersticky foam that could be sprayed on armed suspects, neutralizing them by temporarily gluing their arms to their bodies.
- Spikes embedded in retractable panels beneath roads that could be raised by remote control to blow out a getaway car's tires.[17]
- An exoskeleton suit using nanotechnology and artificial muscles to allow officers to run with minimal effort over prolonged periods at a speed of up to 20 mph with a top speed of 35 mph for shorter distances and to lift items up to four times their own weight.[18]
- A comprehensive, integrated modular tactical uniform that offers ballistic, chemical, and biological protection for special operations police officers such as SWAT officers and hazardous materials specialists.[19]
- Augmented reality technology that overlays computer-generated images onto a person's real-world vision that could be used by officers to have patrol car operator data and regional traffic management information on heads-up display to make driving safer and more efficient, especially during pursuit and rapid response situations; to identify friend-or-foe to reduce or eliminate friendly fire casualties by visually highlighting fellow officers both on and off duty; to project a display of officer location, activity, and status information on a three-dimensional map of the community; to manage the coordinated use of robots, aerial drones, and police officers to enhance surveillance activities; and to employ realistic training scenarios to simulate dangerous police environments while blending real-world equipment and fellow trainees into the scenario.[20]
- Jet packs that officers could wear on their backs so that they could patrol by air.[21]
- A handheld scanner that will allow remote body-cavity searches.[22]
- A mini buster secret compartment detector, a handheld device that senses density in solid objects, will allow police officers to scan over the body of a motor vehicle to locate hidden compartments used to smuggle contraband, terrorist devices, or other illegal items.[23]
- A handheld nonintrusive cargo inspection device that could be used at seaports, truck inspection facilities, airports, and ports of entry to reveal the presence of contraband in a sealed container and identify the contents (drugs, weapons, biological agents, or explosives) without expending costly time and resources searching by hand.[24]
- Nanosized computer chips that can be placed in the neural networks (such as the human brain) of police officers to give them access to billions of gigabytes of instantly accessible data (such as criminal records of suspects).[25]

New technology also promises to improve the police response to specific crimes, such as domestic violence and drunk driving. For example, in the case of domestic violence, one of the best ways of preventing reoccurrences is by having a court issue a protective order to keep the abuser separated from potential victims. Unfortunately, a police officer called to the scene of a domestic disturbance can verify the existence of a protective order only by calling the county clerk's office, assuming the disturbance occurred during business hours. Even then, the officer may not be able to verify the existence of a protective order if the county clerk has not received the order from the court. If the disturbance occurs after hours and the officer is unaware of the protective order, the officer's response to the situation, for example, not arresting the abuser, could result in tragedy. In the future, through comprehensive databases, all police officers will have access to every protective order at all times and virtually from the moment it has been issued.[26]

Similarly, in the case of drunk driving, courts routinely suspend a person's driver's license pending trial. The court then sends notification of the suspension by mail to the Bureau of Motor Vehicles (BMV), oftentimes taking weeks for the suspension to show up in the BMV's computers. It is conceivable that the drunk driver could leave the courtroom, get in his or her car, and drive to the nearest bar. An officer who stopped the drunk driver for a taillight violation, for example, would check the computer and not see that the driver's license was suspended and send the driver on his or her way. In the future, courts will routinely send suspension orders by computer directly to BMVs and law enforcement agencies and, in the process, save lives.[27]

The future of law enforcement in the United States is likely to be very different from law enforcement today. New styles of policing, such as community policing, will be embraced and new technologies employed. The form that the change ultimately takes, however, will depend substantially on whether there is a dramatic shift toward the principles and policies of the crime control model or toward the principles and policies of its due process counterpart. In the next section, possible future developments in the administration of justice are considered.

THE FUTURE OF THE ADMINISTRATION OF JUSTICE

Depending on whether the crime control model or the due process model dominates the future of criminal justice, there are likely to be many changes in the ways that justice is administered. Some of those changes may involve the right to counsel at various stages of the criminal justice process, the preliminary hearing, the grand jury, pretrial detention, plea bargaining, sentencing, appeals, and juvenile justice. The criminal courts will also have to adapt to the changing demographics of the population. Most of the conflicts currently processed by the criminal courts are likely to be handled by alternative dispute resolution programs that utilize mediation and arbitration. Restorative justice may play a greater role in the future. As recent events have so vividly illustrated, the criminal courts will have to be better prepared to deal with all sorts of disasters in the future. Finally, advances in technology will undoubtedly change the administration of justice.

Right to Counsel If, in the future, the administration of justice in the United States is more in line with the crime control model, then the right to legal counsel (both court-appointed and privately retained) at critical pre- and post-trial stages may be scaled back significantly. Advocates of the crime control model consider legal representation at any stage, other than perhaps at trial, a luxury and an unnecessary impediment to the efficient operation of the process. Advocates of the crime control model argue that prior to trial (for example, during interrogation), providing counsel to a suspect only hampers the ability of police to investigate a case. After trial, during the appellate process, the availability of legal counsel further reduces the speed with which a case can be brought to closure. Crime control model supporters maintain that in both situations, a crafty lawyer may be able to win the freedom of a factually guilty client by means of a legal technicality.

If the principles and policies of the due process model dominate the future of the administration of justice, however, then it is likely that the current right to counsel at a variety of critical stages in the process will be retained and, perhaps, even extended somewhat (for example, to appeals beyond the first one). Advocates of the due process model believe that legal counsel is crucial throughout the process and must be made available immediately after arrest. Otherwise, the likelihood that innocent people will be subject to harassment, or worse, by agents of the state (police officers and prosecutors) is increased to an intolerable level.

Preliminary Hearing Along with a greatly reduced role for legal counsel in the administration of justice, crime control model enthusiasts advocate the abolition of the preliminary hearing. They argue that it is a waste of time and money to conduct a preliminary testing of the evidence and the charges imposed, because prosecutors have no reason to pursue cases that are unlikely to lead to conviction. Recall from the discussion in Chapter 8 that prosecutors' reputations and chances of achieving higher political office depend at least partially on the proportion of convictions they are able to obtain. Besides, for several reasons, including the sheer volume of cases that must be handled in the lower courts, the evidence against a suspect is rarely tested at the preliminary hearing anyway. Today, the preliminary hearing is used mostly for making decisions about bail.

Due process model advocates, however, believe that the preliminary hearing is a critical stage in the administration of justice. Although they concede that this hearing is not currently being used as it is supposed to be, they argue that it needs reform instead of abandonment. As described previously, due process model advocates are skeptical about the motivations of prosecutors in criminal cases. History has certainly recorded numerous incidences of prosecutorial misbehavior. Because most criminal cases are resolved through plea bargaining rather than criminal trial, the preliminary hearing may be the only opportunity for a judicial officer to scrutinize the prosecutor's work. Elimination of the preliminary hearing (as it is supposed to operate in theory) would substantially reduce the effectiveness of the entire adversary process of justice.

Grand Jury Instead of elimination of the preliminary hearing, due process model enthusiasts are more inclined to argue for elimination of the grand jury. As described in Chapter 8, the grand jury is another vehicle by which the evidence and charges brought by a prosecutor against a suspect are examined by an impartial body. However, in practice, the grand jury is even more of a sham than the preliminary hearing, having become nothing more than a tool or a rubber stamp for the prosecutor. Invariably, a grand jury will indict or not indict a suspect if that is what the prosecutor wants. Moreover, abuses of the process are more likely to occur in grand jury proceedings, which are conducted in private—away from the watchful eyes of defense attorneys and the public—than in preliminary hearings, which allow the presence of defense attorneys and are open to the public.

Los Angeles Lakers' star Kobe Bryant arrives for his preliminary hearing. *Should the preliminary hearing be abolished, as crime control model proponents advocate? Why or why not?*

Pretrial Detention If the crime control model dominates the administration of justice in the future, it is likely that the use of pretrial detention will be expanded. Advocates of the crime control model maintain that expanded use of pretrial detention will encourage more factually guilty offenders to plead guilty—they would have nothing to gain by not doing so—and will better protect society from the crimes those people are likely to commit if not confined. As for the protection of society, perhaps in the future the pretrial detention of potentially dangerous suspects will be unnecessary because of technical advances in electronic monitoring. For example, the use of electronically monitored house arrest, in which suspects are connected to monitors by electrodes (perhaps surgically implanted in their bodies) that shock them intermittently when they are outside designated areas, may be sufficient to ensure that suspects do not pose a threat to society while awaiting trial.[28] If this type of monitoring is employed, it is likely that suspects would be given a choice between it and jail. Most suspects would probably choose electronic monitoring.

Due process model supporters argue that pretrial detention should be used sparingly if at all. They believe that people accused of crimes should be entitled to remain free until they are found guilty, unless they are unlikely to appear when required or they pose a significant threat to society. Regarding those two exceptions to pretrial release, due process model advocates believe that nonappearance problems can be handled adequately through the existing bail system. They do admit, however, that the present bail system discriminates against the poor. That discrimination is another problem that must be rectified. As for the pretrial detention of defendants who presumably pose a significant threat to society, due process model advocates doubt that prosecutors and judges can predict accurately which defendants actually pose a significant threat and which do not. The result is that many defendants who do not need to be jailed prior to trial will be jailed—or electronically monitored—because of inevitable false predictions. Due process model enthusiasts also suggest that both exceptions to pretrial release—nonappearance and potential threat to society—could be handled by methods other than pretrial detention—for example, by a prompt trial, as required by the Sixth Amendment.

Plea Bargaining As mentioned in Chapter 1, a key to the crime control model's efficiency in the administration of justice is heavy reliance on plea bargaining. Thus, if the crime control model dominates the administration of justice in the future, Americans should expect even fewer criminal trials than today. If there is instead a dramatic shift to the principles and policies of the due process model, plea bargaining will probably be discouraged, and the number of criminal cases that go to trial will increase substantially. For due process model supporters, a principal problem with plea bargaining is that after a guilty plea has been accepted, the possibility of any further judicial examination of earlier stages of the process is eliminated. In other words, with the acceptance of a guilty plea, there is no longer any chance that police or prosecutorial errors before trial will be detected. Plea bargaining will probably not be eliminated entirely, however, even in a legal atmosphere dominated by due process model principles and policies, because eliminating it would be impractical. The time and expense involved in subjecting every criminal case to a trial would be prohibitive.

Sentencing As discussed in Chapter 9 ("Sentencing, Appeals, and the Death Penalty"), more jurisdictions are eliminating or significantly reducing judicial discretion in sentencing by enacting mandatory sentencing statutes and using sentencing guidelines. This policy seems to reflect crime control model principles, although a due process model argument could be made that the restriction of judicial discretion in sentencing will reduce unwarranted judicial disparity in sentencing. In any event, if the trend continues, it is likely that in the area of sentencing, judges in the future will function simply as automatons, empowered only to apply the specific sentence dictated by law.

Appeals If the crime control model dominates the future of the administration of justice, it is likely that appeals—following the few trials that occur—will be strongly discouraged and limited. Crime control model advocates consider appeals a remote and marginal part of the process. They do recognize that the appellate process can correct errors in procedure or in the determination of factual guilt, and they endorse that role. They believe, however, that such errors occur only occasionally. For crime control model supporters, the appellate process can impede the efficient operation of the administration of justice.

If the due process model dominates the administration of justice in the future, there will probably be no limitations on the right to appeal. Due process model advocates, in contrast to their crime control model counterparts, believe that the right to appeal is a significant and indispensable part of the process, one where earlier errors and infringements of rights can be corrected. Perhaps even more important, due process model enthusiasts maintain that the prospect, if not the actual act, of appellate review can deter the commission of similar errors and other forms of misbehavior in subsequent cases. Due process model proponents argue that without the real prospect of appellate review, there would be no effective deterrent of police, prosecutorial, or judicial misbehavior or error.

Changing Demographics of the Population Because the population of the United States in the future will have greater cultural and racial diversity, criminal courts may be forced to adapt their routines and personnel to those changing demographics. Among the changes that may be required in the future:

1. A greater sensitivity of court personnel to cultural diversity issues.
2. An increased ability of court personnel to communicate effectively with non-English-speaking people (this will require the employment of interpreters and multilingual staff, as well as the provision of other language services, to ensure that due process rights are protected).
3. A more culturally and racially diverse workforce that better reflects the demographic characteristics of the population it serves.[29]

State and federal courts have a continuing need for qualified interpreters, especially in languages other than Spanish, and this need will only grow in the future. For example, on January 19, 2000, the New Mexico Supreme Court ruled that people cannot be disqualified from serving as jurors simply because they do not speak English. The decision will require the use of translators in New Mexico courtrooms.[30] Some states are so desperate for court interpreters that they have created training programs to increase the skills of borderline candidates. To identify people who have the minimally required knowledge, skills, and abilities to be a court interpreter, three major programs offer oral performance examinations. The first is the Federal Court Interpreter Certification Examination program, which was established in 1980 and tests and certifies Spanish interpreters for the federal courts. The second is the Consortium for State Court Interpreter Certification, which was founded in 1995 and currently consists of 36 member states. It develops and shares test instruments in twelve languages to certify state court interpreters. The third is the National Association of Judiciary Interpreters and Translators (NAJIT), which created a Spanish performance examination in 2001. To meet the growing demand for interpreters, judges and court administrators are likely to hire staff with bilingual skills for non-courtroom services and then arrange their calendars so they can use their bilingual staff inside the courtroom. Another

Table 14.1 Compensation for Salaried Court Interpreters, Select States, 2006

	Starting Salary	Maximum Salary
Arkansas	$26,000	$51,000
California	30,000	66,000
Colorado	34,980	60,036
Connecticut	38,036	49,565
Minnesota	30,326	54,808
New Jersey	50,000	71,000
New Mexico	38,168	59,634
Oregon	38,160	51,096
Pennsylvania	36,326	44,985

Note: Salaries are approximate. Some salaries are based on hourly or monthly rates.

Source: Flango et al., 2006. (For the full citation, see endnote 29.)

strategy is for different agencies within a jurisdiction to share interpreters.[31] Table 14.1 shows starting and maximum compensation for salaried court interpreters in select states in 2006.

As the number of people age 65 and over increases, the operation of criminal courts will probably have to change in other ways as well. (It is predicted that by 2030, 71 million people in the United States will be age 65 and over—double the number in the year 2000.[32]) In the first place, the types of cases routinely heard in criminal courts are likely to change somewhat and to reflect more and more the problems confronted by the elderly. For example, crimes committed by and against the elderly, such as elder abuse, domestic violence, and family violence, will probably increase, as will consideration of such issues as the right to die and the appropriate use of new medical technologies.[33] An older population will also put new demands on the way criminal courts conduct business. At the very least, courts will have to better accommodate people with physical disabilities such as hearing and visual impairments. For example, to serve hearing-impaired clients, a text telephone (telecommunications device for the deaf, or TDD) or an interpreter will probably become a standard fixture in courtrooms of the future. Likewise, court personnel might be trained to establish eye contact when addressing people with hearing impairments, to provide verbal prompts to people with visual impairments, and to sit down when talking to people who are confined to wheelchairs.[34] Interstate court collaboration will be needed to ensure that court orders are recognized and oversight is provided when older persons move from one state to another. For those unable to come to the courthouse, remote-access technology, such as videoconferencing, will need to be enhanced.[35]

Courts are already adapting to the future by employing signers for hearing-impaired persons. *In what other ways will courts of the future have to change?*

Juvenile Justice If the crime control model dominates the future, criminal courts will probably have to handle an increasing number of juvenile offenders, too, as the practice of transferring juvenile offenders to criminal court for trial increases (see the discussion in Chapter 13). Moreover, to the extent that crime control model principles guide the practice, Americans should expect younger and younger juvenile offenders to be transferred. If this trend becomes the norm, it is conceivable that sometime in the future the juvenile court, and possibly the entire juvenile justice system, could be eliminated entirely, in which case juvenile offenders would be treated similarly to adult criminal offenders.

Ironically, even if due process model principles guide the future, juvenile justice might be eliminated anyway. Juvenile courts are currently providing juvenile offenders with a greater number of procedural rights and are adopting more adversarial procedures (reflecting due process model principles). They are also increasingly replacing paternalistic, treatment-oriented correctional strategies with more punitive ones. As a result of those changes, there may be no practical need for a separate juvenile justice process in the future. In other words, if juvenile offenders are going to be treated exactly the same as adult criminal offenders, why have a separate juvenile justice process?

Alternative Dispute Resolution Programs and Restorative Justice Regardless of which model of criminal justice dominates the future, it is likely that most conflicts—with the possible exception of the more serious ones—dealt with today through the adversary process of justice will be handled differently through alternative dispute resolution programs. In other words, criminal courts will become the arenas of last resort for most conflicts, used only when all other methods of resolving disputes have been exhausted. The two alternative methods of dispute resolution that will probably be used most widely in the future are mediation and arbitration.

Gene Stephens, a criminologist who specializes in the future of crime and criminal justice, proposes a model, based on current neighborhood justice centers, that integrates mediation and arbitration into a process he calls "participatory justice."[36] **Mediation** brings disputants together with a third party (a mediator) who is trained in the art of helping people resolve disputes. The job of the mediator is to help the disputants talk out their problems, to offer suggestions about possible resolutions, and, if possible, to achieve consensus about how the dispute can be resolved to everyone's satisfaction. The agreed-on resolution is then formalized into a binding consent agreement. **Arbitration,** in contrast, brings disputants together with a third party (an arbitrator) who has the skills to listen dispassionately to evidence presented by both sides of a conflict. The arbitrator asks probing and relevant questions of each side and arrives at an equitable solution to the dispute. The process is concluded when the arbitrator imposes a resolution of the dispute, which is binding on all parties.

For Stephens, the goal of both methods is to resolve any conflicts through a consent agreement completed by all parties involved in the dispute. Mediation is the primary method of resolution. Arbitration is a backup procedure used only when mediation fails or is inappropriate (for example, in contract murder cases). In Stephens's model, appeals from mediation would be unnecessary because of the consent agreement, while appeals from arbitration would be limited to a single appeal to a three-member board of arbitrators. A variety of resolutions, whether by consent agreement or imposed arbitration, would be available. They include monetary restitution, community service, therapy, and even incarceration. Violations of consent agreements would be handled through arbitration, and violations of imposed arbitration resolutions would be dealt with through increasingly coercive measures—probably ending with incarceration. Stephens maintains that participatory justice would be cheaper, faster, and more equitable than the current adversary process of justice.[37] As of June

mediation A dispute resolution process that brings disputants together with a third party (a mediator) who is trained in the art of helping people resolve disputes to everyone's satisfaction. The agreed-on resolution is then formalized into a binding consent agreement.

arbitration A dispute resolution process that brings disputants together with a third party (an arbitrator) who has the skills to listen objectively to evidence presented by both sides of a conflict, to ask probing and relevant questions of each side, and to arrive at an equitable solution to the dispute.

Montana state Representative Karl Ohs helps mediate the end to the 81-day standoff between the Montana Freemen and the FBI. *Should mediation be used more often in criminal justice? Why or why not?*

restorative justice A process whereby an offender is required to contribute to restoring the health of the community, repairing the harm done, and meeting victims' needs.

reintegrative shaming A strategy in which disappointment is expressed for the offender's actions, the offender is shamed and punished, and, more importantly, following the expression of disappointment and shame is a concerted effort on the part of the community to forgive the offender and reintegrate him or her back into society.

2008, 43 states and the District of Columbia had victim-offender mediation (VOM) or VOM-type statutory authority in criminal cases. The only states without VOM programs or authority were Arkansas, Louisiana, Mississippi, North Dakota, Rhode Island, West Virginia, and Wyoming.[38]

Participatory justice is a form of restorative justice, an alternative to the punitive justice currently used in the United States and many other countries. The primary goals of **restorative justice** are to restore the health of the community, meet victims' needs, repair the harm done, and require the offender to contribute to those repairs. Another form of restorative justice that may be adopted in the United States in the future is Australian criminologist John Braithwaite's "reintegrative shaming."[39] **Reintegrative shaming** is a strategy in which disappointment is expressed for the offender's actions, the offender is shamed and punished, but, what is more important, following the expression of disappointment and shame is a concerted effort on the part of the community to forgive the offender and reintegrate him or her back into society. Braithwaite contends that the practice of reintegrative shaming is one of the primary reasons for Japan's relatively low crime rate.

Clearly, the future of the administration of justice in the United States should be quite different from what it is today. The exact differences will depend on which model's principles and policies dominate. Areas in which differences and changes are likely to be most pronounced include the availability of legal counsel at various stages in the process; retention or abolition of the preliminary hearing, the grand jury, and juvenile justice; and the extent of pretrial detention, plea bargaining, alternative dispute resolution procedures, judicial sentencing flexibility, and the appellate process. Courts of the future will also have to adapt to the needs of an increasingly older and more racially and culturally diverse population.

Better Preparation for Disasters One of the lessons learned from the tragedies of the 1995 bombing of the Alfred P. Murrah Federal Building in Oklahoma

Careers in Criminal Justice

BARJ Coordinator

My name is Donald J. Haldemann. I am the balanced and restorative justice (BARJ) coordinator for the Delaware County Juvenile Court in Southeastern Pennsylvania. I also supervise our Victim Services Unit with a staff of six. I have a Bachelor's in history, a Master's in administration of justice, and a Juris Doctor from Widener Law School in Delaware.

I worked with 1,300 juveniles as a juvenile probation officer for 21 years before embarking on the quest for restorative justice. In 1995, Pennsylvania's Juvenile Act was amended to include the concept of restorative justice. Slowly, with grant money from the Pennsylvania Commission on Crime and Delinquency, individual counties hired restorative justice specialists, and I jumped at the opportunity to join this elite fraternity. So, what is restorative justice and how can you join the movement?

A crime is considered to be an offense against the "State" under the traditional model, but restorative justice views crime as a harm against individual victims and the community. Offenders need to accept responsibility for the harm they have caused and participate in victim and community restoration.

On a daily basis my job consists largely of educating my staff, criminal justice professionals, social agencies, schools, and communities on restorative justice and how it can be a win/win proposition for all stakeholders in the process.

I can't possibly list all the positives about my job. I get to promote a philosophy of justice which is based on practices used in cultures all over the world for hundreds of years. What I find most difficult about my job is the reluctance of many criminal justice "players" to welcome a new way of looking at crime, opting instead to hang on to a process which has served no one's best interest. Offenders have not been helped to accept responsibility, victims have been ignored, and communities have been trained to believe that crime is a government problem and not their concern.

If you are thinking about becoming a restorative justice coordinator, I recommend you take a restorative justice training course like the one sponsored by Florida Atlantic University in partnership with the National Institute of Corrections. The more exposure you have to restorative justice philosophy and practitioners, the better.

Do you share this BARJ coordinator's enthusiasm for this philosophy of justice? Why or why not?

City, September 11, 2001, and the 2005 hurricanes is that criminal courts must be better prepared to protect court assets—people, facilities, and records—from future disasters. Currently, few courts have continuity of operations plans (COOPs).[40] However, experiences from the aforementioned disasters, especially the hurricanes, have provided some ideas of how courts can respond or how others can help the courts respond when the next disaster strikes. For example, after Hurricane Katrina, a special assessment team was sent to the Gulf states by the Administrative Office of the U.S. Courts to determine local court needs. To institutionalize the response, the College of William & Mary's Courtroom 21 Project is developing a conceptual plan for a national state court corps of first responders. Lawyers who needed court information, such as where to contact court officials, what special orders were in place, and how to seek extensions or continuances, were helped by representatives from the local, federal, and Louisiana Bar associations. Additionally, The Communications Center for Displaced Attorneys was established to help direct e-communications for relocated lawyers with Internet access.[41]

The aftermath of the hurricanes also revealed the importance of electronic filing of court documents. By filing court documents electronically, back-up files can more easily and efficiently be sent to alternate sites for protection, thereby minimizing the disruption of court business. The need for intranet data communication networks also became apparent. During emergencies, the networks allow the courts to maintain essential functions by providing remote access via private broadband Internet and dial-up services. The critical need for laptop computers during emergencies was realized as well. Other technologies that can aid the communication of judges, court executives, and essential staff during emergencies (or normal business operations) include an enterprise Blackberry network, cellular phones, and wireless personal-digital-assistant devices.[42]

Technology and the Administration of Justice Before considering the future of corrections in the United States, we emphasize that advances in technology are likely to influence the administration of justice in the future, just as they

The use of interactive television in the administration of justice is likely to be expanded in the future. *Besides those mentioned, what are some of the other benefits of having interactive television in the courtroom?*

will affect the future of law enforcement. The possible substitution of electronically monitored house arrest for pretrial detention and the use of technology during disasters has already been examined. Additionally, in many jurisdictions in the United States today it is no longer necessary for defendants to physically appear in court for the initial appearance, preliminary hearing, arraignment, or even trial. Interactive television can be used to administer justice to defendants without incurring the risks involved in physically transporting them to a courtroom. This development has allowed jails to be built in more remote areas of municipalities, affording greater protection to the citizens of a community and reducing the costs of constructing jails, because they need not be built in expensive urban locations. Courts are also allowing witnesses to provide videotaped depositions when they are physically unable to be present in court and allowing children to testify via interactive television in some child sex abuse cases.[43] Those practices are likely to continue and be expanded.

Developments in neuroscience also promise to transform the administration of justice.[44] For example, during the penalty phase of capital trials, lawyers frequently use the results of brain scans to argue mitigation, that a neurological impairment prevented a defendant from controlling his or her behavior. In fact, a Florida court recently held that the failure to admit neuroscience evidence during capital sentencing is grounds for a reversal. As a result of neuroscientific evidence, jurors have been persuaded to sentence defendants to life imprisonment rather than to death. Despite studies that question the reliability of neuroimaging evidence, courts have also admitted brain-imaging evidence during criminal trials to support claims that defendants are insane.

There are many other applications of neuroscience. For example, preliminary research suggests that brain activity in the prefrontal cortex is critical for selecting among punishments. Defense attorneys and prosecutors could use this information in the selection of jurors, or legislatures or sentencing commissions could use the information for devising sentencing guidelines acceptable to the public. Eyewitness identifications could be aided by using neuroscience. Brain scans can show activity in the parahippocampus, the area of the brain that

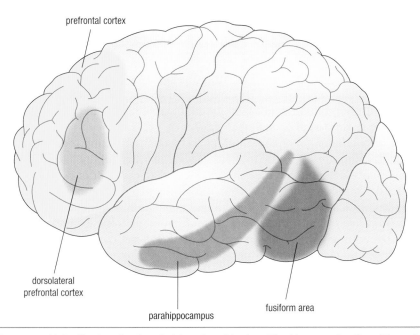

Brain areas with implications for the administration of justice. *Should neuroscientific evidence be used in the administration of justice? Why or why not?*

responds strongly to places and the recognition of scenes, and in the fusiform area of the brain, which is responsible for facial recognition. Findings from neuroscience were used in the 2005 decision in *Roper* v. *Simmons*, the case in which the Supreme Court struck down the death penalty for juveniles, that is, those under age 18 at the time of their crimes. The leading brief in the case, filed by the American Medical Association and other groups, argued that "adolescent brains are not fully developed" in the prefrontal regions; therefore, adolescents cannot control their impulses as adults do and should not be held fully culpable "for the immaturity of their neural anatomy." The brain region associated with deliberate problem solving and self-control is the dorsolateral prefrontal cortex. Currently, two lie-detection technologies rely on neuroimaging. The first, developed in the 1980s, is known as "brain fingerprinting" and measures changes in the frequency of brain waves. The second technology uses functional magnetic resonance imaging (f.M.R.I.) to distinguish between the brain activity of liars and truth tellers. So far, neither technology is more reliable than polygraphs, which are not considered reliable enough to use in most legal cases.

If the brain causes all behavior, including criminal behavior, then the concepts of retribution and criminal responsibility, which assume that criminal behavior is freely chosen, must seriously be reconsidered. Neuroscience may also change the focus of rehabilitation to repairing defective brains. For example, a new technique called transcranial magnetic stimulation (T.M.S.) has been employed to stimulate or inhibit specific areas of the brain. T.M.S. can temporarily alter how people feel and what they think.

Perhaps, someday, determination of guilt or innocence, as well as the truthfulness of testimony, will become a routine matter of simply employing mind-reading technology. For example, the transfer to the public domain, via computer or some other device, of ribonucleic acid (RNA) structures that form memories will make deception and privacy of thoughts nearly impossible.[45] Sometime in the future, it may even be possible to retrieve memories of the events of a crime from the stored RNA memory chains (or "memory banks") of deceased victims and witnesses.[46] Imagine the constitutional questions raised by such technological abilities.

Among other technological advances that people should expect in the administration of justice in the future (some are available today) are these:

1. More efficient processing and recording of information by computer, that is, electronic filing (thus eliminating the need for paper files).
2. Instantaneous long-distance communication among integrated court systems.
3. Use of artificial intelligence to assist in legal research and various decision-making duties, such as sentencing.
4. Use of computer-generated graphics to reconstruct crime incidents.
5. Use of computers to create a virtual reality in which court participants can experience an interactive three-dimensional re-creation of a crime scene.
6. Use of a computer that can extract the events of a crime from the conscious and unconscious memory of a witness.
7. Kiosk jurisprudence, that is, court information stations located throughout the community, where 24 hours a day, citizens can conduct court business such as filing complaints or paying fines, or receive court information such as the court's daily calendar, the estimated time of an arraignment, and the outcomes of cases that have already been heard.
8. A virtual courthouse, where all court business—including conferences, hearings, and trials—are conducted via the Internet.[47]

Perhaps as important as the new technologies is the development of national court technology standards. Draft versions of standards are already circulating for integrated computerized case management systems (CMS), electronic filing of court documents, and the electronic exchange of common forms and documents among courts, law enforcement, and other justice organizations. The nationwide exchange of information is the goal of the Global Justice XML Data Model (GJXDM). By way of uniform data semantics and structure, the GJXDM will allow organizations using different computer systems and databases to share information (XML is a software- and hardware-independent tool for transmitting information). The National Information Exchange Model (NIEM), a by-product of the GJXDM, is being developed through the sponsorship of the Departments of Justice and Homeland Security. The NIEM will include nonjustice agencies and will aid courts with exchanging information with all relevant partners.[48] Figure 14.1 shows the advances in court technology over the past three decades.

These developments, of course, will raise significant issues about privacy vs. public access, as well as data security concerns. For example, as more court records can be accessed over the Internet, they become more susceptible to identity thieves. (Identity theft is discussed later in this chapter.) Courts must therefore

Figure 14.1

Three Decades of Court Technology Advances

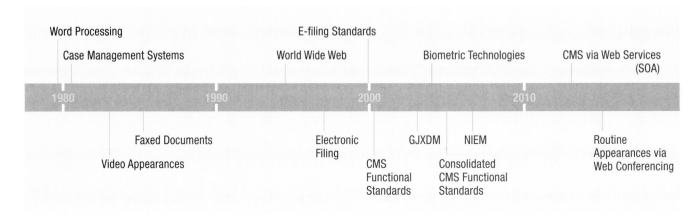

Source: Flango et al., 2006. (For full citation, see endnote 29.)

give greater consideration to what is included in a court record, and new policies and procedures must be created regarding access to court records. Of most concern are personal identifiers (such as social security numbers, cities and dates of birth, mothers' maiden name, children's names, street addresses); third-party identifications (victims, witnesses, informants, jurors); and unique identifying numbers (operators' licenses, financial accounts, state identifications). States are responding to this problem in different ways. Some states are obscuring information by using only the last four digits of a social security number, asking only for the year of birth, identifying children by initials, and asking only for city, state, and ZIP code. Other states are creating two records: a public record and a private record for sensitive information. Still other states are editing out sensitive information. Critics contend these methods have not been entirely effective. The hope is that new technology will provide a tamper-proof solution to the problem, perhaps in the form of more reliable editing software or better authentication processes.[49]

THE FUTURE OF CORRECTIONS

The crime control and due process models used in the previous sections do not lend themselves as well to a consideration of the future of corrections. The primary reason is that in the area of corrections, crime control is, and probably will remain, the paramount goal. This does not mean that due process concerns are unimportant, however. Whatever new strategies are employed in corrections in the future will have to conform to constitutional restrictions. Specifically, the Eighth Amendment protection against cruel and unusual punishment—however that phrase is interpreted in the future—will have to be respected and will no doubt set the outer limits of what corrections in the future might be.

The "New Penology" Perhaps the most divisive issue that will confront correctional policy makers in the future is whether increasingly scarce resources should be devoted more to punishment (to achieve the goals of retribution and incapacitation) or to rehabilitation (to achieve the goals of specific deterrence and successful reintegration). If the current trend continues, the answer is easy: scarce correctional dollars will be devoted primarily to punishment. In fact, it has recently been argued that a "new penology" has already emerged—a penology that has abandoned rehabilitation in favor of efficiently managing large numbers of prisoners.[50] Success for this new penology is not measured by reductions in recidivism (a standard measure of correctional success used in the past) but rather by how efficiently correctional systems manage prisoners within budgetary constraints.[51]

Alternatives to Incarceration Most people knowledgeable about corrections in the United States paint a rather bleak picture of its future. They believe that the number of citizens under correctional custody—in jail, in prison, on probation, or on parole—will continue to increase. Increasing numbers of offenders under correctional supervision, in turn, are likely to consume increasingly larger proportions of city, county, state, and federal budgets.

To make matters worse, scholars knowledgeable about corrections predict that alternatives to incarceration will not

The federal supermaximum-security prison in Florence, Colorado, was one of the first of the "new penology" institutions that has abandoned rehabilitation in favor of efficiently managing a large population of violent offenders. *What are some of the problems of abandoning rehabilitation as a goal of punishment?*

prevent the need to fund hundreds of costly new jails and prisons in the immediate future. In the first place, they contend, recent history demonstrates that increases in the use of alternatives to incarceration do not necessarily lead to decreases in the use of incarceration. Instead, increases in the use of alternatives coincide with increases in the use of incarceration, through net-widening, for example. This phenomenon occurred in the 1980s, when the use of community-based supervision nearly tripled and the use of incarceration almost doubled.[52]

A second reason that alternatives to incarceration will probably not reduce the need for more jails and prisons is that only a small percentage of future prisoners are likely to be good candidates for alternative programs. According to one authority, more than 95% of current prisoners are either violent offenders or repeat offenders with two or more felony convictions. Only 5% of prisoners can be considered low-risk offenders and thus good candidates for alternatives to incarceration.[53] This ratio of high-risk prisoners to low-risk prisoners is not likely to change dramatically in the future.

Cost-Reduction Strategies Future expenditures of tax dollars on corrections by governments at all levels will be made grudgingly, after much wrangling and debate. Every attempt will be made to carry out corrections functions as inexpensively as possible. Because the vast majority of correctional clientele will be members of the underclass, as is the case today, there will be little public resistance to low-cost management strategies. Indeed, corrections in the future is likely to take on "a kind of waste management function."[54]

Among the cost-reduction strategies likely to be advocated in the future are various alternatives to incarceration. For example, most persons convicted of minor offenses may be required to perform community service such as litter control and maintenance and construction of government buildings and grounds.[55] However, as described earlier, the cost savings of alternatives to incarceration tend to be illusory. In any case, most offenders who otherwise would be sent to prison will be considered poor candidates for the available alternatives.

Another cost-reduction strategy likely to receive increasing support in the future is the privatization of corrections. As described in Chapter 10 ("Institutional Corrections"), the private sector has been involved in corrections in various ways for a long time. Recently, private companies have entered the business of operating entire jails and prisons, and this practice, no doubt, will increase dramatically in the future.

However, a problem with the operation of jails and prisons by private companies—and a reason that cost savings from this strategy may prove minimal at best—is that private companies are in business to make a profit. If the companies are publicly owned, there is tremendous pressure on management to maximize shareholder value. As a result, it can be expected that private or public correctional companies will do all in their power to protect and enhance their interests by lobbying government officials for more favorable terms of operation and by using marketing to produce a greater demand for their products (that is, more offenders jailed or imprisoned).[56]

A third cost-reduction strategy—potentially the most effective one—is the use of new technology. For example, the use of cameras to watch prisoners and robots to service them, as well as the use of sensing devices on an institution's perimeter, would reduce the need for most correctional officers. The use of ultrasound may be the solution to costly prison riots. "Piping high-pitched sound over improved intercom systems would momentarily render everyone in the affected area unconscious and allow staff to enter, disarm, and regain custody."[57] If the death penalty continues to be employed in the United States, ultrasound may provide a more humane and cost-effective method of execution. In the near future, ultrasound could be provided at levels that would literally dematerialize the offender (eliminating the costs of disposing of the body).[58] Another possibility is instant death by laser ray.[59] The costs of building or enlarging more jails and prisons because of overcrowding would be reduced significantly in the future through the use of **cryonics** (freezing) and other forms of human hibernation.[60] Many prisoners could be "stored" in a small amount of space with the use of such technologies. In fact, they could literally be stacked on top of each other in coffin-like containers. Prisoners in the future also may be incarcerated in self-supporting undersea or space prisons, as the old practice of transporting prisoners is revived.[61]

You have already learned about the use of electronically monitored house arrest for pretrial detainees (using electrodes connected to a monitor, perhaps surgically implanted, that would intermittently shock clients while they were outside a designated area). The same technology could be used for probationers and parolees, reducing the number of probation and parole officers needed. In addition, a subliminal-message player might be implanted in probationers, parolees, and prisoners that would provide 24-hour anticrime messages, such as "Obey the law" or "Do what is required of you," or synthesized body chemicals could be implanted that would keep offenders under constant control.[62] The costs related to future violations could be reduced dramatically through such methods.

However, one must keep in mind that several possible factors might significantly reduce or negate the tremendous cost savings anticipated from new correctional technologies. For example, the success of the strategy may create incentives for net-widening, which will reduce or eliminate any anticipated cost savings.[63] In addition, technology has its own costs: Experts must be employed, staff must be trained, equipment must be serviced, and systems must be upgraded as new technologies are introduced.[64]

You may have noticed that this discussion did not cover an important subject: crime and delinquency prevention—the effort to prevent criminal and delinquent acts from being committed in the first place. Although crime and delinquency prevention will probably be a priority in the future, it will be mostly the responsibility of government agencies and philanthropic organizations outside the criminal justice process (for example, social, health, and welfare agencies). Because the focus of this book is criminal justice in the United States, we do not speculate here about future crime and delinquency prevention strategies.

Prison overcrowding could someday lead to the use of cryonics and other forms of human hibernation. *What problems might arise if cryonics were used to deal with prison overcrowding?*

cryonics A process of human hibernation that involves freezing the body.

THINKING CRITICALLY

1. What impact do you think DNA profiling will have on the future of law enforcement?

2. Do you think that people who don't speak English should be allowed to serve as jurors? Why or why not?

3. When it comes to corrections, to what do you think more money should be devoted: punishment or rehabilitation? Why?

Special Crime Problems of the Twenty-First Century

At the dawn of the twenty-first century, five interrelated crimes are likely to pose special problems for law enforcement agencies and criminal justice. The first three are drug crime, cybercrime, and terrorism—all of which have been examined in previous chapters. Terrorism is considered again in the final section of this chapter. The two other crimes are identity theft and transnational organized crime, which are considered next.

IDENTITY THEFT:
WHEN BAD THINGS HAPPEN TO YOUR GOOD NAME

Tania Collins of Apopka, Florida, had her purse snatched.[65] Among the items lost were her driver's license, Social Security card, and about $25 in cash. Although the incident scared her, and the loss of her personal belongings was an inconvenience, the theft of her purse and its contents was only the beginning of what would become a much bigger problem. Not long after the purse snatching, Tania discovered that someone else had been using her identity to accumulate more than $20,000 in credit card charges, bogus checks, grocery bills, phone bills, and other unpaid debt. Tania Collins had become a victim of identity theft.

Extent, Definition, and Types of Identity Theft Tania Collins is not alone. Identity theft is a much larger problem than even the experts suspected. A recent survey by the Federal Trade Commission (FTC) estimated that about 8.3 million adult Americans were victims of some form of identity theft in 2005. That 8.3 million estimate is not statistically different from the approximately 10 million victims estimate in 2002.[66] Figure 14.2 and Table 14.2 display identity theft victimization rates (per 100,000 population) by state in 2006.

Figure 14.2

Identity Theft Victims by State (per 100,000 Population),* January 1 Through December 31, 2006

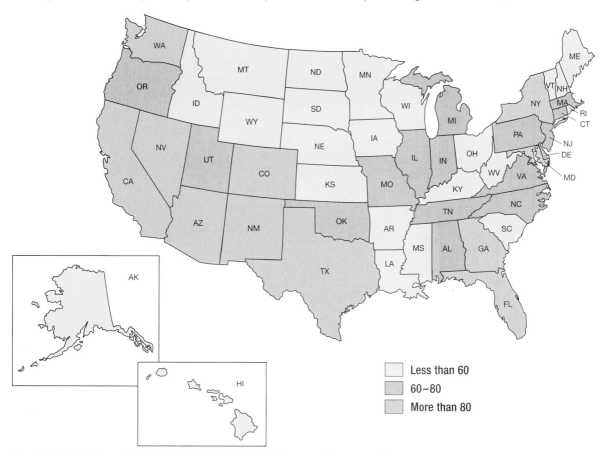

Less than 60

60–80

More than 80

Note: *Per 100,000 unit of population estimates are based on the 2006 U.S. Census population estimates (Table NST-EST2006-01–Annual Estimates of the Population for the United States and for Puerto Rico: April 1, 2000 to July 1, 2006). Numbers for the District of Columbia are 765 victims and 131.5 victims per 100,000 population.

Source: Federal Trade Commission, "Fighting Back Against Identity Theft," at www.ftc.gov/bcp/edu/microsites/idtheft/media-reference/writing.html (clearinghouse _2006.pdf).

Table 14.2 Identity Theft Victims by State (per 100,000 Population),*
          January 1 Through December 31, 2006

Rank	Victim State	Victims per 100,000 Population	Number of Victims
1	Arizona	147.8	9,113
2	Nevada	120.0	2,994
3	California	113.5	41,396
4	Texas	110.6	26,006
5	Florida	98.3	17,780
6	Colorado	92.5	4,395
7	Georgia	86.3	8,084
8	New York	85.2	16,452
9	Washington	83.4	5,336
10	New Mexico	82.9	1,621
11	Maryland	82.9	4,656
12	Illinois	78.6	10,080
13	Oregon	76.1	2,815
14	New Jersey	73.3	6,394
15	Virginia	67.2	5,137
16	Michigan	67.2	6,784
17	Delaware	66.7	569
18	Connecticut	65.8	2,305
19	Pennsylvania	64.9	8,080
20	North Carolina	64.9	5,748
21	Missouri	64.2	3,753
22	Massachusetts	63.7	4,102
23	Oklahoma	63.0	2,254
24	Indiana	62.2	3,928
25	Utah	61.8	1,577
26	Tennessee	61.3	3,700
27	Alabama	60.3	2,774
28	Ohio	59.9	6,878
29	Kansas	58.8	1,626
30	Rhode Island	57.6	615
31	Alaska	57.3	384
32	South Carolina	55.7	2,408
33	Minnesota	55.6	2,872
34	Arkansas	54.7	1,537
35	Louisiana	52.6	2,256
36	Mississippi	51.3	1,494
37	Nebraska	49.1	868
38	Idaho	49.0	718
39	Hawaii	47.8	615
40	New Hampshire	46.1	606
41	Montana	45.9	434
42	Wisconsin	45.6	2,536
43	Wyoming	42.3	218
44	Kentucky	42.0	1,766
45	Maine	39.7	525
46	West Virginia	39.3	715
47	Iowa	34.9	1,041
48	South Dakota	30.2	236
49	North Dakota	29.7	189
50	Vermont	28.5	178

Note: *Per 100,000 unit of population estimates are based on the 2006 U.S. Census population estimates (Table NST-EST2006-01—Annual Estimates of the Population for the United States and for Puerto Rico: April 1, 2000 to July 1, 2006). Numbers for the District of Columbia are 765 victims and 131.5 victims per 100,000 population.

Source: Federal Trade Commission, "Fighting Back Against Identity Theft," at www.ftc.gov/bcp/edu/microsites/idtheft/media-reference/writing.html (clearinghouse_2006.pdf).

Figure 14.3

How Victims' Information Is Misused,[*] January 1 Through December 31, 2006

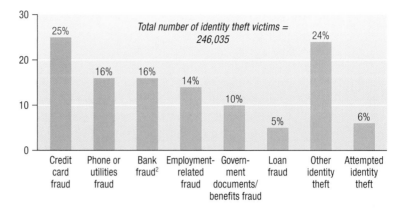

Note: *Per 100,000 unit of population estimates are based on the 2006 U.S. Census population estimates (Table NST-EST2006-01—Annual estimates of the Population for the United States and for Puerto Rico: April 1, 2000 to July 1, 2006). Numbers for the District of Columbia are 765 victims and 131.5 victims per 100,000 population.

Source: Federal Trade Commission, "Fighting Back Against Identity Theft," at www.ftc.gov/bcp/edu/microsites/idtheft/media-reference/writing.html (clearinghouse_2006.pdf).

identity theft The transfer or use without legal authority of the identity documentation of another person with the intent to commit, aid, or abet any activity that constitutes a felony.

Identity theft became a federal crime in 1998, when Congress passed the Identity Theft and Assumption Deterrence Act. The law stipulates that **identity theft** is committed "when anyone knowingly transfers or uses without legal authority the identification documentation of another person with the intent to commit, aid, or abet any unlawful activity that constitutes a felony."[67]

There are three general types of identity theft that vary in seriousness of victimization. From the most serious to least serious, identity theft may involve (1) *the misuse of personal information* to open new credit accounts, take out new loans, or engage in other types of fraud, such as misuse of the victim's name and identifying information when the thief is charged with a crime by law enforcement officers, when renting an apartment or home, when obtaining medical care, or when applying for a job; (2) *the misuse of existing accounts other than credit cards,* such as checking or savings accounts or telephone accounts; and (3) *the misuse of one or more existing credit cards or credit card account numbers.* Figure 14.3 shows how victims' information was misused in 2006.

Identity Theft Victimization Identity theft cost its victims about $15.6 billion in 2005 (the latest year for which reliable data were available, except for some 2006 data, as indicated). The bulk of that loss was from the misuse of a victim's personal information. The median annual loss per victim for all types of identity theft was approximately $500, but the per capita loss from the misuse of personal information was $1,350. Ten percent of all victims reported losing $6,000 or more, and 5% of all victims reported losing at least $13,000. Ten percent of misuse of personal information victims lost $15,000 or more, and 5% of such victims lost at least $30,000.

Businesses and financial institutions and not individuals incur most of the losses from identity theft, because a variety of laws protect individuals from the fraudulent actions of identity thieves. Thus, of the approximately $15.6 billion lost to identity theft in 2005, only a small fraction of the loss was borne by individuals. Victims incurred no out-of-pocket expenses in more than 50% of all ID thefts. Out-of-pocket expenses include any lost wages, legal fees, any payment of fraudulent debts, and other expenses such as notarization, copying, and postage. In the misuse of personal information category, victims had out-of-pocket expenses averaging $40; however, a quarter of those victims had out-of-pocket expenses averaging at least $1,000. The top 10% of misuse of personal information victims reported out-of-pocket expenses of at least $3,000, and the top 5% incurred out-of-pocket expenses of at least $5,000.

In 2005, victims of all three types of identity theft spent 4 hours, on average, attempting to resolve their problems. However, the top 10% of all victims spent at least 55 hours resolving their problems, while the top 5% of all victims spent at least 130 hours. Victims of personal information misuse spent the greatest amount of time resolving problems. The top 10% in this category spent 100 hours or more resolving problems; the top 5% spent at least 1,200 hours dealing with their problems. Besides out-of-pocket expenses and the expenditure of time resolving problems, more than a third of all victims experienced other types of problems, including being harassed by collections agents, being denied new credit, being unable to use existing credit cards, having difficulties obtaining or accessing bank accounts, being unable to obtain loans, having their utilities cut off, being subject of criminal investigation or civil suit, and being arrested.

When a victim's identity was stolen, it was sometimes misused for a relatively long period of time before the theft was discovered. As shown in Figure 14.4, 39% of identity-theft victims reported that they did not discover misused information for 7 months or more, and 9% reported not discovering the loss for 60 months or more. However, 40% of identity-theft victims discovered the misuse of their information within one week. The survey also found that the more quickly an identity theft was discovered, the smaller the loss incurred and the lower the out-of-pocket expenses.

Nearly 85% of identity-theft victims did not know the thief's identity, and 56% of them did not know how their identities were stolen. Among common techniques used in identity theft are "dumpster diving," "shoulder surfing," "spamming," and "phishing."[68] Thieves who "dumpster dive" go through dumpsters or trash cans to get copies of checks, credit card and bank statements, credit card applications, or other records with identifying information. "Shoulder surfers" look over victims' shoulders as they enter personal information into phones, computers, and ATMs. "Spammers" send unsolicited e-mail messages to victims, usually advertising a product, service, or get-rich-quick scheme, and ask the victim to provide identifying information in order to receive whatever is being advertised. "Phishers" send consumers e-mail messages claiming that there was a problem with their AOL account, for example. The messages warn consumers to update their billing information or risk losing their accounts and Internet access. The message directs consumers to click on a hyperlink to connect to the "AOL Billing Center." When consumers click on the link, they are sent to a look-alike AOL Web page, where they are asked to enter the numbers from the credit card they used to open the account and the numbers from a new credit card to correct the problem. They are also asked for additional identifying information. Identifying information can also be found on the Internet by accessing public record sites and fee-based information broker sites. Figure 14.5 shows the types of personal information obtainable on the Internet for a fee of $39.95. Other ways of obtaining personal information are by getting credit reports fraudulently by posing as an employer, loan officer, or landlord or by obtaining names and social security numbers from personnel or customer files in the workplace.[69]

The FTC survey revealed that the most common way victims discovered the misuse of their personal information was by monitoring the activity in their

Figure 14.4

Number of Months between Date Identity Theft First Occurred and Date First Discovered by Victim,* January 1–December 31, 2006

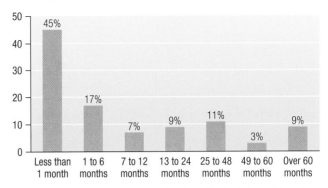

Notes: *Percentages are based on the total number of identity theft complaints where victims provided the dates on which the identity theft first occurred and on which they first discovered it (123,064). This information was reported by 52% of the victims who contacted the FTC directly. Because some victims experienced multiple instances where their information had been misused, these figures do not track the amount of time it took a victim to discover a particular instance of identity theft, but, rather, the amount of time between the initial misuse of the victim's information and when the victim first discovered that their information had been misused.

Source: Federal Trade Commission, "Fighting Back against Identity Theft," at www.ftc .gov/bcp/edu/microsites/idtheft/media-reference/writing.html (clearinghouse_2006.pdf).

Figure 14.5

Ease of Finding Personal Information Online

Current and previous addresses
Possible aliases
Phone numbers
Liens/Tax liens against them
Small claims/Civil judgments for or against them
Property ownership
Bankruptcies
List of neighbors
Possible names of relatives
National death index data revealing whether they are alive
Drug enforcement agency actions against them
Marriage status
Divorce status

Note: For $39.95 (an additional $20 for 1-hour e-mail delivery) you can obtain the following information about a person, knowing just his or her first and last names, by using an Internet people-search site.

Source: Flango et al., 2006 (for full citation, endnote 29).

accounts. Twelve percent of victims discovered their loss by monitoring their accounts through electronic means, 6% by monitoring their accounts with paper statements, and 11% of victims learned of their loss by being notified by a credit monitoring service that unusual activity was detected in their accounts. In 2006, 42% of victims contacted a credit reporting agency and were able to place a fraud alert, but 57% of victims had not contacted any credit reporting agency.[70]

Seventy-four percent of victims in 2006 did not notify a police department of the ID theft; 21% notified a police department and a report was taken; and

In an effort to thwart identity theft, the Mississippi Department of Public Safety is using special software that allows its driver's-license examiners to program computers to compare a driver's previous photograph with a newly taken one. *How effective do you think this system will be?*

5% notified a police department and a report was not taken.[71] Many victims of identity theft are too embarrassed to report the crime to the police. The FTC survey found that the higher the amount lost, the more likely that the theft was reported. In 81% of the identity thefts reported to the police, victims reported the local agency filed a formal report. The more quickly a theft was reported, the more likely the police filed a report. More than half of the victims who reported thefts to the police were "somewhat satisfied" (24%) or "very satisfied" (31%) with the law enforcement response, but more than 40% of them were "somewhat dissatisfied" (11%) or "very dissatisfied" (30%).

For many victims, identity theft can be a traumatic experience. It can provoke a host of emotions such as feelings of loss, helplessness, hopelessness, vulnerability, fear, denial, anger, isolation, betrayal, rage, and embarrassment.[72] A particularly common emotion felt by identity-theft victims is frustration with the very people to whom the victims turn for help, especially law enforcement and criminal justice personnel. Identity theft can be life altering. Many victims never see the world in the same way again. They lose their innocence. For other victims, the experience is life altering in another way: they are empowered; they develop an assertiveness and a boldness that they did not have before, and they discover who their true friends are.

Dealing with Identity Theft When asked to describe the most difficult part of their experience, nearly 40% of identity-theft victims who had spent at least 10 hours trying to resolve their problems (31% of all ID-theft victims) responded going through the dispute-resolution process. The dispute-resolution process involves communicating with consumer reporting agencies and companies to have debts absolved and credit reports corrected and replacing credit cards and other important documents. Respondents also mentioned the amount of time the dispute-resolution process took. About a third of the victims stated that dealing with the practical consequences of theft was the most difficult part of the experience, for example, dealing with losing money, inability to use credit cards and bank accounts, having utilities shut off, and being unable to open new accounts. Another quarter of the victims replied they were most affected by the emotional impact of the ID theft, for example, the effects of stress on their lives and health, the realization they were vulnerable, and/or the realization they had been betrayed.[73]

When asked what could be done to improve their victimization experience, identity-theft victims responded that law enforcement officers could improve the way they investigate the crime. Law enforcement officials counter that identity-theft cases are hard to investigate, because they often involve multiple jurisdictions, evidence problems, and complex financial matters. Law enforcement officials also complain of having too few investigators.[74] Still, victims wanted the police to (1) make a greater commitment to catch the thief or thieves, (2) follow up and communicate better with the victim, and (3) increase the assistance they provide victims. Victims also wanted offenders to receive stiffer penalties.

Many victims noted that people needed to be more aware of identity theft and better prepared to prevent and respond to it when it occurred. They recommended that people (1) use greater security precautions when handling personal information (for example, destroy materials containing personal information instead of putting them in the trash); (2) not place personal information on the Internet, (3) secure personal information in homes and at work, (4) more carefully monitor their mail, billing cycles, and credit reports, and (5) know whom to contact and notify the affected companies and credit reporting agencies more quickly when something wrong is detected.

Some victims wanted financial institutions to do a better job of preventing and detecting the crime. They listed (1) improving authentication measures (for

Fraud Alerts

The Fair Credit Reporting Act, which became law in December 2004, allows consumers who have a good faith suspicion they have been or are about to become ID-theft victims to place an initial 90-day "fraud alert" on their credit file that will appear on credit reports issued to potential users of the report. A potential creditor who receives a credit report containing a fraud alert is required to take reasonable steps to verify the identity of the person applying for credit. The Act also allows ID-theft victims to place an extended, 7-year fraud alert in their credit files. The alert contains a telephone number at which the consumer may be reached, and any potential creditor is required to contact the consumer either at the number or in person before extending any additional credit in the consumer's name.

Source: Federal Trade Commission-2006 Identity Theft Report (McLean, VA: Synovate, November 2007), pp. 46 and 48 at www.ftc.gov/os/2007/11/ SynovateFinalReportIDTheft2006.pdf (accessed January 10, 2009).

CJ Online

Survey of Identity-Theft Victims

To learn more about identity theft, read the results of the November 2007 FTC survey of victims. It can be accessed at www.ftc.gov/os/2007/11/ SynovateFinalReportIDTheft2006.pdf. *What did you learn from the report that surprised you?*

example, photos on credit cards), (2) more thorough identification procedures by employees during credit transactions, (3) better monitoring of account activity and notification of irregularities, and (4) better follow-up and assistance while repairing financial records (for example, having fewer documents for victims to sign, just listening to victims, and treating victims with understanding instead of suspicion).

Few things in life are worse than losing your good name. One would think that with the inevitable increase of financial transactions over the Internet and new, yet unknown ways of obtaining personal identifying information by thieves, identity theft is likely to become an even greater problem and headache for victims and law enforcement agencies. However, a comparison of the 2003 and 2006 FTC surveys suggests that the prevalence and costs of identity theft may be declining.

TRANSNATIONAL ORGANIZED CRIME: CRIME IN A GLOBAL CONTEXT

Transnational organized crime is a growing concern among law enforcement officials worldwide. As one leading authority on the subject puts it:

> Transnational organized crime will be one of the major problems facing policy makers in the 21st century. It will be a defining issue of the 21st century as the Cold War was for the 20th century and Colonialism was for the 19th. No area of international affairs will remain untouched as political and economic systems and the social fabric of many countries will deteriorate under the increasing financial power of international organized crime groups.[75]

Former FBI Director Louis Freeh and former CIA Director R. James Woolsey have both maintained that "transnational organized crime threatens the national security interests of the United States and other nations" and jeopardizes "the very fabric of democratic society" everywhere.[76]

A Definition of Transnational Organized Crime Unfortunately, there is no universally agreed-on definition of "transnational organized crime." So, following the lead of the framers of the United Nations Convention Against Transnational Organized Crime, we will define the key concept by combining the definitions of "organized crime group" and "transnational crime." An "organized crime group" is a "structured group of three or more persons existing for a period of time and acting in concert with the aim of committing one or more serious crimes or offenses in order to obtain, directly or indirectly, a financial or other material benefit."[77] A "serious crime" is defined as "an offense punishable by a maximum deprivation of liberty of at least four years or a more serious penalty."[78] A "transnational crime" is a crime that (a) "is committed in more than one State" [nation]; (b) "is committed in one State but a substantial part of its preparation, planning, direction or control takes place in another State"; (c) "is committed in one State but involves an organized criminal group that engages in criminal activities in more than one State"; or (d) "is committed in one State but has substantial effects in another State."[79]

Characteristics of Transnational Organized Crime Groups Until the last quarter of the twentieth century, organized crime, except for some cross-border smuggling, was primarily a local—or at worst, a national—problem. Organized crime became transnational with the expansion of multinational corporations, the opening of national borders to trade, and growing economic interdependence. However, unlike multinational corporations, transnational organized crime groups are not constrained by domestic and host country laws and regulations. They are able to exploit economic opportunities by using corruption, blackmail, and intimidation.[80]

Transnational organized crime groups vary widely in their structure, size, use of violence, scope of activities, level of transborder operations, corruption, level of political influence, extent of activity in the legitimate economy, and degree of cooperation with other organized crime groups.[81] Nevertheless, a survey of 40 selected transnational organized crime groups in 16 countries and 1 region by the United Nation's Centre for International Crime Prevention reveals some common characteristics:

- Two-thirds of the groups have a classical hierarchical type of structure [with a single leader, relatively clearly defined hierarchy, and strict systems of internal discipline], whereas one-third are more loosely organized.
- The majority of the groups are of moderate size, with between 20 and 50 participants.
- Violence is essential to the undertaking of their activities for the majority of the groups.
- Less than half the groups do not have a strong social or ethnic identity, while ethnic-based organizations represent less than a third of the organized crime groups.
- The largest number of groups are engaged in only one primary criminal activity.
- In the majority of cases, groups are engaged in criminal activities in multiple countries.
- The vast majority of the groups make use of corruption, either extensively or occasionally.
- Just under half of the groups are said to have no political influence, while one-third of the groups have an influence at the local/regional level.
- Less than half the groups have extensively penetrated the legitimate economy.
- The largest number of groups cooperates with other organized criminal groups, largely as a source of illicit commodities.[82]

Table 14.3 lists some of the "named" transnational organized crime groups, their base countries, and their criminal activities.

Criminal Activities of Transnational Organized Crime Groups Like most organized crime groups, transnational organized crime groups provide illegal goods and services for which there is public demand. The following is a list of some of the more significant criminal activities of transnational organized crime groups:

- Smuggling
    —Commodities (such as weapons and human beings)
    —Drugs
    —Protected species
- Contraband (goods subject to tariffs or quotas)
    —Stolen cars
    —Tobacco products
- Services
    —Immigrants
    —Prostitution
    —Indentured servitude
    —Money laundering
    —Fraud (such as bank or insurance fraud)[83]

The United Nations estimates that transnational organized crime groups bring in about $1.5 trillion a year, more than the GNP of many small countries. The criminal proceeds from money laundering worldwide are estimated to be between $600 billion and $1 trillion a year. An estimated $2 billion to $4 billion is earned annually from illegally dumping trash and hazardous waste.[84]

Table 14.3 Named Transnational Organized Crime Groups, Base Country, and Criminal Activities*

Transnational Organized Crime Group (Base Country)	Criminal Activities (Primary Activity Listed First)
Italian Group (Germany; controlled by La Cosa Nostra)	Large-scale tax evasion primarily through employment in construction industry; large-scale fraud; money laundering; illegal immigration; smuggling; loan sharking
Verhagen Group (The Netherlands)	Hashish trafficking; large-scale fraud/embezzlement; theft of electronic goods; fraud involving precious materials; trafficking in expensive jewelry; fraudulent real estate transactions
Outlaw Motorcycle Gangs (Australia)	Drug production and distribution (mainly amphetamines and cannabis); prostitution; trafficking of stolen vehicles; many other crimes
The McLean Syndicate (Australia)	Drug trafficking (mainly cannabis, but also cocaine); money laundering; illegal immigration/smuggling; armed robbery; theft of antiques; trafficking in women; prostitution; extortion; gambling; debt collection; murder; tax evasion
Japanese Yakuza (Australia)	Investment of the proceeds of crime from elsewhere; money laundering
The Orange Case (Caribbean)	Drug smuggling (mainly cannabis and cocaine)
Dream House Case (Caribbean)	Smuggling cocaine
The Meij Case (Caribbean)	Political corruption resulting in extensive penetration into the legal economy
The Fuk Ching (United States)	Extortion; smuggling of illegal immigrants; human trafficking; kidnapping; drug trafficking; armed robberies; money laundering; organized prostitution; environmental crimes
La Cosa Nostra (United States)	Gambling; loan sharking; extortion; drug trafficking (heroin, cocaine, and synthetic drugs); prostitution; murder; fraud; insurance scams; air cargo theft; environmental crimes; racketeering in labor unions and the construction, music, and garbage industries
Clan Paviglianiti (Italy)	Drug trafficking (mainly cocaine); forgery; large-scale fraud and embezzlement; armed robbery; vehicle theft and trafficking; manufacturing of firearms and ammunition; illegal trafficking in explosives
Syzranskaya Groopirovka (Russia)	Drug trafficking (heroin, cannabis, and opium)
Ziberman Group (Russia)	Smuggling of cigarettes and alcohol; theft of vehicles; illegal gambling; large-scale fraud and embezzlement; money laundering; armed robbery; extortion; murder
Vasi Iliev Security-2 (Bulgaria)	Insurance scams; illegal gambling; illegal import and export of food, equipment, alcohol, and cigarettes; many other crimes
The Cock Group (Lithuania)	Extortion; trafficking in heroin; vehicle theft; organized prostitution; many other crimes
Savlokhov Group (Ukraine)	Extortion; gambling; money laundering; forgery; fraud; loan sharking; usury; trafficking in illicit goods; prostitution; kidnapping; armed robbery
Juvenal Group (Colombia)	Drug trafficking; smuggling of migrants; money laundering
Hells Angels (Canada)	Drug manufacturing and trafficking (synthetic drugs, heroin, cannabis, and cocaine); prostitution; money laundering; insurance scams; vehicle theft and trafficking; extortion; gun running
The 28s Prison Gang (South Africa)	Drug trafficking (heroin, cannabis, cocaine, and synthetic drugs); illegal trading in firearms; organized prostitution; burglary; money laundering; gambling; vehicle theft and trafficking; armed robbery; extortion; trafficking in women and children for the sex industry
The Trapani Cosa Nostra (Italy)	Extortion; money laundering; trafficking in firearms; drug manufacturing and trafficking
The Licciardi Clan (Italy)	International drug trafficking; extortion; cigarette smuggling; loan sharking; counterfeiting; forgery; insurance scams; money laundering; armed robbery; organized prostitution; smuggling of firearms; trafficking of explosives; illegal gambling
Yamaguchi-Gumi (Japan)	Drug trafficking; extortion; gambling; organized prostitution; insurance scams; money laundering; armed robbery; trafficking in stolen goods; kidnapping; trafficking in firearms
The Liu Yong Syndicate (China)	Trafficking in illicit goods and services; racketeering; smuggling of human beings; organized prostitution; armed robbery; gambling; extortion
The Zhang Wei Syndicate (China)	Trafficking in illicit goods and services; racketeering; smuggling of human beings; prostitution; gambling; extortion; armed robbery
The Liang Xiao Min Syndicate (China)	Gambling; kidnapping; extortion; organized prostitution; armed robbery; racketeering; trafficking in illicit goods and services
Amezcua Contreras Organization (Mexico)	Producing and trafficking methamphetamine; supplying various chemicals to other trafficking organizations
Mocha Orejas Organization (Mexico)	Kidnapping; blackmail
Carillo Fuentes Organization (Mexico)	Transporting cocaine; trafficking in heroin and marijuana
Arellano-Felix Organization (Mexico)	Drug trafficking (cocaine, heroin, cannabis, and methamphetamine)

* Many transnational organized crime groups are not named, and not all named groups are included in this list. Also, some of the listed groups are no longer in operation, having been successfully dismantled by law enforcement efforts.

Source: *Results of a Pilot Survey of Forty Selected Organized Criminal Groups in Sixteen Countries,* Global Programme against Transnational Organized Crime, United Nations Office on Drugs and Crime (September 2002), Appendix B, at www.unodc.org/unodc/organized_crime.html.

Transnational organized crime groups have also been involved in hijackings, terrorism, and civil wars. In approximately 30 countries, insurgent or terrorist groups, in league with transnational organized crime groups, have financed all or part of their activities with income generated from taxes imposed on illegal drug production or from trafficking in illegal drugs themselves. Illegal trade in diamonds and oil has also financed civil wars and terrorist activities.[85]

Civil wars create refugees eager to escape to safer countries. This, too, provides a financial opportunity for transnational organized crime groups that smuggle people, especially women and children, across national borders. Poor women are also lured from their native countries by promises of good jobs in another country. Estimates of the number of women and children involved in these activities vary widely from 27 million to 200 million a year worldwide. Many of the women and children are enslaved in the countries to which they are smuggled or brought, often forced into prostitution to pay off the trafficker.[86]

Trying to Control Transnational Organized Crime Transnational organized crime poses special problems for law enforcement. Many transnational organized crime groups use legitimate import-export companies, service industries,

Drug Crime Revenue

The United Nations estimates that the international illicit drug trade generates $322 billion a year in revenue, making drug crime by far the world's most lucrative illegal activity.

Source: Matthew Levitt and Michael Jacobson, "The Money Trail: Finding, Following, and Freezing Terrorist Finances," The Washington Institute for Near East Policy, Policy Focus #89 (November 2008), p. 10 at www.washingtoninstitute.org/templateC04 .php?CID=302 (accessed December 7, 2008).

Transnational organized crime groups smuggle human beings into the United States. *How can this be prevented? Should it be prevented? Why?*

or multinational financial institutions as fronts for their illegal activities. Sometimes organized crime groups nest themselves inside legitimate businesses; other times they control them. Many groups employ experts in the use of global technology, such as the Internet and advanced wireless communications, and conduct market research to determine where to operate. They look for jurisdictions with weak law enforcement and criminal justice institutions. Transnational organized crime groups can also hide behind national borders and take advantage of the jurisdictional limitations or confusion of law enforcement.[87]

In addition, many transnational organized crime groups can claim among their members present and former state officials and military and state intelligence agency personnel. This is especially true of former communist nations, but it is not confined to them. The professional intelligence, police, and military skills provided by these members often give the crime groups an advantage over local law enforcement officials.[88]

Another problem is that some countries have no statutory or popular basis for preventing transnational organized crime. For example, in Russia as late as the 1990s no laws against organized crime existed; there were no criminal penalties for phony businesses or fictitious bankruptcies; and there was little financial or social support for law enforcement itself.[89]

Law enforcement agencies around the world are increasingly cooperating with each other to fight transnational organized crime. The legal bases for this cooperation are high-level bilateral and multilateral assistance treaties. The treaties provide rules for intelligence and evidence sharing and for determining jurisdiction in individual cases. The treaties also set standards for investigation techniques, the extradition of offenders, and the imposition of sanctions. Frequently, the treaties allow the exchanging of subject-matter experts and investigative expertise, the stationing of another nation's law enforcement officers in embassies, or the opening of a law enforcement headquarters or training facility in a foreign capital. The U.S. Departments of State, Justice, and Treasury, for example, have established international law enforcement academies in Budapest, Bangkok, and Gaborone (the capital of Botswana in Africa).[90]

A particularly promising development in this cooperative effort was the signing of the United Nations Convention Against Transnational Organized Crime by the United States and 123 other countries at a conference in Palermo, Italy, in December 2000. The convention was the first international instrument against this type of crime. It requires member countries to criminalize some of the major offenses committed by transnational organized crime groups, such as obstruction of justice, money laundering, corruption of public officials, and conspiracy.[91] The convention also encourages cooperation among member countries in the investigation, apprehension, and prosecution of transnational organized crime group members involved in serious crimes. This applies to countries with which the United States currently does not have a mutual legal assistance treaty. Cooperation can include exchanging information on organized crime groups, conducting joint investigations, employing special investigative methods (such as electronic or other forms of surveillance and undercover operations), the seizure and confiscation of the proceeds of illegal activities, the extradition of fugitives, and the protection of witnesses. However, at no time do member countries relinquish their sovereignty or jurisdictional integrity to another country. The convention also has three protocols that require member states to criminalize the trafficking in human beings, the smuggling of migrants, and the illicit manufacturing and trafficking in firearms. Additionally, the United States and other donor countries are to contribute funds to a special UN account to support developing countries that need technical assistance to implement the convention and its

FYI Interpol

Interpol is the world's largest international police organization with 182 member countries. It was created to enhance and facilitate international police cooperation and will undoubtedly play a major role in the fight against transnational organized crime. Every member country has an Interpol office called a National Central Bureau, which is staffed by the country's own police. The bureau is the point of contact for foreign governments needing assistance with overseas investigations. Contrary to popular belief, Interpol officers do not travel around the world to investigate cases in different countries. Rather, each member country employs its own officers to operate on its own territory and in accordance with its own national laws. The organization's General Secretariat is located in Lyon, France.

Source: "Interpol—An Overview," Interpol at www.interpol.int/Public/Icpo/FactSheets/Default .asp ("Interpol-an overview").

protocols. The convention and protocols have received the requisite number of signatures and are in force.

Currently, transnational organized crime is mainly addressed at the national level, when it is dealt with at all. Local law enforcement is ill-equipped to handle or even recognize it. Local law enforcement officers have neither the training nor the expertise to investigate sophisticated computer crimes or securities frauds, for example. When they work street-level drug sales, smuggling cases, and homicides, they rarely recognize that those crimes may be transnational organized crimes. Experts are divided on what the most promising strategy might be. Some of them believe that local law enforcement officers must be taught to recognize and respond to transnational organized crimes, especially since such crimes first surface at the local level. Others believe that transnational organized crime should be left to federal law enforcement agencies that are better able to deal with the technological, cultural, political, legal, and language complexities often involved in such crimes. Still others advocate greater cooperation among different levels of law enforcement through multiagency task forces, but they have problems as well. Some experts are dubious about the ability of any level of law enforcement to significantly reduce the illegal markets that sustain transnational organized crime groups. Those experts believe that significant reductions in illegal markets depend not on law enforcement, but primarily on social and economic changes, changes in public attitudes, advances in science, or shifts in profitability.[92] One thing is clear: while experts debate and law enforcement agencies fight over jurisdiction, transnational organized crime groups operate with relative impunity.

THINKING CRITICALLY

1. What do you think is the most effective way to deal with identity theft?

2. What do you think is the most effective way to deal with transnational organized crime?

Criminal Justice in the Age of Terrorism

The tragic events of September 11, 2001, have transformed the United States in many ways. A new kind of fear has gripped the American people, who no longer feel as safe as they did before that infamous day. The most notable change to occur is the war on terrorism—a financially costly war conceivably with no end. The war on terrorism, in turn, has altered criminal justice in the United States, as the fear of terrorism has joined the fear of crime in the nation's collective nightmares.

However, terrorism and crime are not separate phenomena. Although they may think of themselves as "freedom fighters," according to the FBI's counterterrorism policy, terrorists are criminals. Furthermore, as the U.S. government and its allies have increasingly succeeded in freezing their financial assets, al-Qaeda and other terrorist groups have turned to different types of crime to support their operations. Many of those crimes are the same ones committed by transnational organized crime groups: bootlegging cigarettes; counterfeiting compact discs, movies, and other products; drug trafficking; and smuggling human beings for profit to name a few.[93]

LEGISLATIVE RESPONSES TO TERRORISM

As for the response to terrorism, one of the more controversial developments in this new Age of Terror was the passage of the USA PATRIOT Act less than 2 months after the planes slammed into the World Trade Center and the Pentagon. As described in Chapter 4, the law gave the government broad new powers to address the menacing threat. For example, in terrorism-related matters, it expanded the government's search and surveillance powers and eliminated safeguards such as judicial oversight, the need for a warrant and probable cause, the ability to challenge certain searches in court, and public accountability. The law also created the new crime of "domestic terrorism," which is defined so broadly that it could include members of controversial activist groups such as Operation Rescue, the Earth Liberation Front, Greenpeace, or the World Trade Organization protesters, as long as they committed acts "dangerous to human life" to "influence the policy of a government by intimidation or coercion." Another provision of the law allows the Attorney General to detain noncitizens in the United States indefinitely without trial if there is reason to believe that the noncitizens endanger national security and a foreign country will not accept them for deportation. Critics contend that in removing traditional checks on law enforcement the PATRIOT Act and other similar legislation threaten the very rights and freedoms that the war on terrorism is trying to preserve.

Another legislative response to 9/11 was passage of the Homeland Security Act of 2002. As described in Chapter 5, the Act established the new Department of Homeland Security, the institutional apparatus whose mission in large part is to prevent terrorist attacks in the United States and to minimize the damage, and assist in the recovery, from terrorist acts that do occur. The creation of the Department of Homeland Security, which is ongoing, involves a massive reorganization of the federal law enforcement bureaucracy. Federal law enforcement agencies have been moved from their traditional departments, such as Justice or Treasury, to the new Department of Homeland Security. Other agencies have been combined or reconfigured. For example, the border and agency functions of the U.S. Customs Service, the Federal Protective Service, and the former Immigration and Naturalization Service have been reorganized into the Bureau of Immigration and Customs Enforcement under the Department of Homeland Security. New agencies have also been created, such as the Bureau of Citizenship and Immigration Services, the Office of State and Local Government Coordination, and the Office of Private Sector Liaison. Each of these new agencies is part of the Department of Homeland Security.

TERRORISM AND LAW ENFORCEMENT

As also discussed in Chapter 5, the FBI was *not* moved to the Department of Homeland Security (it remains in the Justice Department), but it has undergone some fundamental changes in response to 9/11. For example, its top priority has shifted from being a federal police agency to being an intelligence and counterterrorism agency. The management hierarchy at the FBI's headquarters in Washington has been restructured to support counterterrorism efforts. A quarter of the FBI's 11,000 agents have been reassigned to work on counterterrorism. A National Joint Terrorism Task Force has been established at FBI headquarters to coordinate the flow of information with task forces in each of the bureau's 56 field offices, and new FBI offices are being opened in foreign countries where al-Qaeda and other terrorist groups have a presence.

Local law enforcement officers have also become soldiers in the war on terrorism, as explained in Chapter 6. As "first responders" and the "front line of defense," local police officers and sheriffs' deputies not only must be able to respond to terrorist acts, but they also must be proactive in preventing them as well. Their job is especially difficult because they must be ever vigilant without engaging in racial or ethnic profiling. Local law enforcement agencies are increasingly trying to train their personnel for their new roles but, according to recent reports, are drastically underfunded and dangerously unprepared.

TERRORISM AND THE ADMINISTRATION OF JUSTICE

The war on terrorism has revealed the existence of a secretive federal court, previously unknown to most Americans. The Foreign Intelligence Surveillance Court, or FISA court, which is described in Chapter 8, has been in operation since the late 1970s. The court has approved thousands of Justice Department requests to conduct secret searches and surveillance of people in the United States who are suspected of having links to foreign agents or powers, often involving terrorism and espionage. Until recently, American citizens who were suspected of being terrorists or having ties to terrorist groups in the wake of 9/11 were arrested and detained without being charged with any crimes and were denied legal representation and access to the criminal courts to challenge their detention. Non-U.S. citizens accused of terrorism by the U.S. government were tried by military tribunals instead of federal courts, if they were charged and tried at all. In 2008, in *Boumediene* v. *Bush*, the U.S. Supreme Court ruled that the remaining approximately 260 Guantánamo detainees now have the constitutional privilege of *habeas corpus*, although this may not matter much, because President Obama has promised to close down the Guantánamo Bay prison.

TERRORISM AND CORRECTIONS

As noted above and described in Chapter 10, the U.S. government established a supermaximum-security prison at the Guantánamo Bay Naval Base in Cuba. Named Camp Delta, the purpose of the prison is to hold what Pentagon officials call the "worst of the worst enemies in the war on terror." The prisoners, originally from 42 different countries, are being held until they no longer have useful intelligence to provide, are cleared of criminal wrongdoing, and no longer pose a threat to the United States. Some of them may be held until the war on terrorism is over, whenever that might be. The U.S. government has not filed criminal charges against most of them or assigned them prisoner-of-war status, leaving them in legal limbo. If and when President Obama closes Camp Delta, the remaining prisoners will be moved to other prisons, either in the United States or perhaps abroad.

The United States is hated by people all over the world. *Why?*

Final Remarks

Few people question the threat to U.S. citizens' lives and well-being posed by twenty-first-century terrorism. The tragic events of September 11, 2001, provided a frightening wake-up call for most Americans. Unfortunately, there is no established roadmap to follow in fighting the war on terrorism. There are few precedents to guide decision makers in the difficult task of preserving domestic security. Critics contend that some government officials have been overzealous in their efforts. Some critics question the motives of particular government officials. Perhaps the most frequent criticism of the war on terrorism is that some of the legislation enacted and tactics allowed threaten the very rights and freedoms that the war on terrorism is trying to preserve. Some people worry that provisions of the PATRIOT Act and other similar legislation designed for the war on terrorism—provisions that override or set aside traditional procedural safeguards—will become a permanent part of the way criminal justice is administered in the United States. Some people are concerned that law enforcement strategies implemented to fight the war on terrorism—strategies that remove traditional constraints on law enforcement activity—will become commonplace in the ways law enforcement officers carry out their duties. There is no doubt that the collapse of the World Trade Center's twin towers changed the United States in unanticipated ways. The challenge faced by the United States in this Age of Terrorism is to defend domestic security without sacrificing the rights and freedoms of American citizens.

THINKING CRITICALLY

1. Do you think there should be legal limits on the ways the United States fights the war on terrorism? If so, what should they be? If not, why not?

2. Do you think it is acceptable to suspend traditional legal rights and freedoms in the war on terrorism? Why or why not? If your answer is in the affirmative, which legal rights and freedoms should be suspended, and which ones should not? Defend your choices.

✳ Summary

1. Describe the possible future of law enforcement if the crime control model dominates, and the possible future if the due process model dominates.

   If law enforcement in the future increasingly reflects the principles and policies of the crime control model, then Americans might expect fewer limitations on how the police attempt to combat crime. However, if there is a shift to the principles and policies of the due process model, Americans should expect existing limitations on how the police combat crime to remain intact or even to be expanded.

2. Describe the possible future of the administration of justice if the crime control model dominates, and the possible future if the due process model dominates.

   If the crime control model dominates the administration of justice in the future, then the right to legal counsel at critical pre- and post-trial stages may be scaled back significantly, the preliminary hearing may be abolished, and the use of pretrial detention may be expanded; there may be fewer criminal trials and more plea bargaining, and appeals may be strongly discouraged and limited. If the due process model dominates, then the current right to counsel at a variety of critical stages in the process is likely to be maintained or, perhaps, extended somewhat (for example, to appeals beyond the first one); the grand jury may be eliminated; plea bargaining probably will be discouraged, and the number of criminal cases that go to trial is therefore likely to increase substantially; and there will probably be no limitations on the right to appeal.

3. Identify the most likely divisive issue that will confront correctional policy makers in the future.

   Perhaps the most divisive issue that will confront correctional policy makers in the future is whether increasingly scarce resources will be devoted more to punishment (to achieve the goals of retribution and incapacitation) or to rehabilitation (to achieve the goals of specific deterrence and successful reintegration).

4. Describe the possible future of corrections.

   Most people knowledgeable about corrections in the United States paint a rather bleak picture of its future: an increasing number of offenders under correctional supervision, consuming larger and larger proportions of state and federal budgets. Future expenditures of tax dollars on corrections by governments at all levels will be made grudgingly, after much wrangling and debate. Every attempt will be made to carry out corrections functions as inexpensively as possible.

5. List some of the cost-reduction strategies likely to be advocated in corrections in the future.

   Among the cost-reduction strategies likely to be advocated in corrections in the future are various alternatives to incarceration.

   However, cost savings from those alternatives may be illusory. Another cost reduction strategy likely to receive increasing support in the future is the privatization of corrections. A third cost reduction strategy, and potentially the most effective one, is the use of new technology.

6. Explain what identity theft is, and describe the extent of the problem in the United States.

   Identity theft is the transfer or use without legal authority of the identification documentation of another person with the intent to commit, aid, or abet any unlawful activity that constitutes a felony. Identity theft is widespread. According to a recent survey commissioned by the Federal Trade Commission, more than 8 million Americans may have been victims of some type of identity theft in 2005.

7. Summarize the reasons why transnational organized crime poses special problems for law enforcement.

   One reason transnational organized crime poses special problems for law enforcement is that many transnational organized crime groups use legitimate import-export companies, service industries, and/or multinational financial institutions as fronts for their illegal activities. Sometimes organized crime groups nest themselves inside legitimate businesses; other times they control them. Many groups employ experts in the use of global technology and conduct market research to determine where to operate. They can also hide behind national borders and take advantage of the jurisdictional limitations or confusion of law enforcement. In addition, many transnational organized crime groups can claim among their members present and former state officials and military and state intelligence agency personnel whose expertise often gives the crime groups an advantage over local law enforcement officials. Another problem is that some countries have no statutory or popular basis for preventing transnational organized crime.

8. Describe some of the challenges faced by criminal justice in the Age of Terrorism.

   A major challenge for criminal justice is to fight the war on terrorism without threatening the very rights and freedoms that the war on terrorism is trying to preserve. Another challenge is to create the institutions, such as the Department of Homeland Security, to fight the war on terrorism. The FBI has the challenge of shifting its priorities from being a federal police agency to being an intelligence and counterterrorism agency. Local law enforcement agencies have the challenge of preventing terrorist acts and responding to them when they occur, without engaging in racial or ethnic profiling.

✳ Key Terms

✳ Review Questions

1. How might community policing based on the crime control model of criminal justice differ from community policing based on the due process model?

2. How might bionics affect law enforcement in the future?

3. What is perhaps the thorniest issue regarding the use of DNA technology as a law enforcement tool?

4. What is a principal problem with plea bargaining for due process model supporters?

5. How might the changing demographics of the U.S. population affect the operation of criminal courts?

6. What is the principal difference between mediation and arbitration?

7. What are restorative justice and reintegrative shaming, and how do they differ from punitive justice?

8. What is the *new penology,* and how is its measurement of success different from the measurement of correctional success in the past?

9. What is cryonics, and how might it be used in corrections in the future?

10. What are three general types of identity theft, and which one is considered the most serious for victims?

11. What are some of the ways that identity thieves obtain personal information?

12. What are some of the common characteristics of transnational organized crime groups?

13. What are some of the criminal activities of transnational organized crime groups?

✳ In the Field

1. **Criminal Justice in the Movies** There are numerous science fiction movies or videos that depict criminal justice in the future. Examples are *Blue Thunder, Escape from New York, Demolition Man, Blade Runner, Minority Report,* and the *RoboCop* series. Watch one or more of those movies or videos, and consider how plausible they seem in light of what you have read in this chapter. Have any of the innovations of these futuristic justice systems become a part of the current American justice system? Are any of these innovations discussed in this chapter?

2. **Identity Theft Vulnerability** Test how vulnerable family members or friends are to identity theft. If you live at home, go "dumpster diving" through trash cans looking for your family members' personal information, such as copies of checks, credit card and bank statements, credit card applications, or other records with identifying information. If you live in a dormitory or apartment, do the same with your roommate or roommates. Present what you find to the "victims." Discuss with them the problems that befall identity theft victims and how identity theft can be prevented.

✳ On the Net

1. **Explore New Technologies** Go to the Justice Technology Information Network at www.nlectc.org/. Click on "Technology Assistance" or "Equipment Needs." Survey the new technologies available, and write a three-page scenario of how criminal justice will change when the new technology is implemented.

2. **Evaluate Programs** Access "Creating a New Criminal Justice System for the 21st Century: Findings and Results from State and Local Program Evaluations" from the alphabetical index at www.ncjrs.org/AlphaTitles .html#C. Read some of the program evaluations. Write a short essay on why the programs may or may not be important in the twenty-first century.

✳ Critical Thinking Exercises

CORRECTIONS IN THE FUTURE

1. It is the year 2028, and you have been asked to serve on a citizens' committee charged with providing input about the creation of a new supermaximum-security federal prison. The prison will be built either several hundred feet beneath the ocean's surface off the east coast of the United States or on the moon. The rationale for these locations is to better isolate prisoners from the law-abiding population and to take advantage of prison labor for the high-risk jobs of either marine farming or

the mining of new and useful materials in space. The technology and the resources to build the prison, although expensive, are available.
a. Which location would be preferable? Why?
b. Should public tax dollars be used to fund the project, or should a private corporation be allowed to build and operate the facility at its own expense and keep any profits from the farming or mining business?
c. What special problems might arise because of the location of the prison?

LAW ENFORCEMENT IN THE FUTURE

2. It is the year 2028 in Washington, D.C., and public service officers, formerly called police officers, are flying routine patrol with the aid of their new jet packs. While flying over a condo near the city's center, two of the officers, using their bionic eyes and ears, detect what appear to be a half-dozen men plotting to bomb the White House. Surveying the condo from their sky perch, the officers see, stored in a bedroom closet, enough of a new, illegal, and largely undetectable hydrogen-based explosive to do the job. The officers, using the ultrasmall two-way communication devices implanted in their larynxes, communicate to headquarters what they have seen. They await further orders.

   a. Do the officers have probable cause to obtain a search warrant from a magistrate or to make an arrest? If you were a proponent of Packer's crime control model, what would your answer be? If you were a proponent of Packer's due process model, what would your answer be?

   b. How might the legal issues of the right to privacy, the admissibility of evidence, the exclusionary rule, and the plain-view doctrine affect the use of this new technology by law enforcement officers?

   c. What restraints, if any, should be imposed on the use of this new technology by law enforcement officers? If you were a proponent of Packer's crime control model, what would your answer be? If you were a proponent of Packer's due process model, what would your answer be?

To access more information and resources, including study questions, chapter summaries, and links, go to: www.mhhe .com/bohm6e.

1. The top crime news stories for 2008 are taken from *Time* magazine's "Top 10 Crime Stories" at www.time.com/time/specials/2008/top10/article/0,30583,1855948_1862222_1862233,00.html (accessed January 14, 2009); Joel Rubin and Ari B. Bloomekatz, Tami Abdollah, "Ninth Body Found at Scene of Christmas Eve Attack," *The Los Angeles Times* at http://articles.latimes.com/2008/dec/27/local/me-santa-shooting27 (accessed January 21, 2009); "UPDATE: Henderson Police Identify Atlantis Plastics Shooting Victims, Gunman," *Evansville Courier & Press* at www.courierpress.com/news/2008/jun/25/five-killed-atlantis-plastics-shooting-early-today/ (accessed January 21, 2009); "Eve Carson, UNC Chapel Hill Student Body President, Shot to Death," *The Huffington Post* at www.huffingtonpost.com/2008/03/06/eve-carson-unc-chapel-hi_n_90286.html (accessed January 21, 2009); Erin Gartner and Mike Baker, "Arrest Made in Eve Carson Murder, *The Huffington Post* at www.huffingtonpost.com/2008/03/12/arrest-made-in-eve-carson_n_91180.html (accessed January 21, 2009); "6 Shot Dead, Including Gunman, at Northern Illinois University," CNN.com/us at www.cnn.com/2008/US/02/14/university.shooting/ (accessed January 22, 2009); Robert Lenzner, "Bernie Madoff's $50 Billion Ponzi Scheme," Forbes.com at www.forbes.com/2008/12/12/madoff-ponzi-hedge-pf-ii-in_rl_1212croesus_inl.html (accessed January 23, 2009).

2. Our thanks to Professors Frank P. Williams III and Marilyn D. McShane for their help in securing these data.

3. Howard N. Snyder and Melissa Sickmund, *Juvenile Offenders and Victims: 2006 National Report.* Washington D.C.: U.S. Department of Justice, Office of Justice Programs, Office of Juvenile Justice and Delinquency Prevention (March 2006), p. 109 at www.ojjdp.ncjrs.gov/ojstatbb/nr2006/downloads/NR2006.pdf (accessed January 5, 2009). A rationale for concealing juvenile court records is to prevent, as much as possible, the labeling of juvenile offenders as delinquents, which could make them delinquents. (Labeling theory is discussed in Chapter 3.)

4. Herbert Packer, *The Limits of the Criminal Sanction* (Stanford, CA: Stanford University Press, 1968).

5. See, for example, Walter B. Miller, "Ideology and Criminal Justice Policy: Some Current Issues," *Journal of Criminal Law and Criminology* 64 (1973), pp. 141–162.

6. Robert M. Bohm, "'McJustice': On the McDonaldization of Criminal Justice," *Justice Quarterly* 23 (2006), pp. 127–146.

7. Unless otherwise indicated, the data in this section are from Steven W. Perry, "Justice Expenditure and Employment Extracts, 2006," *Bureau of Justice Statistics,* U.S. Department of Justice, at www.ojp.usdoj.gov/bjs/eande.htm#selected, filename: cjee0601.csv (date of version: 8/29/2008); Kristen Hughes, "Justice Expenditure and Employment Extracts, 2004," *Bureau of Justice Statistics,* U.S. Department of Justice, at www.ojp.usdoj.gov/bjs/eande.htm#selected, filename: cjee0401.csv (date of version: 11/15/2006); Sourcebook of Criminal Justice Statistics Online, Table 1.1.2005 at www.albany.edu/sourcebook/pdf/t112005.pdf (accessed January 21, 2009).

8. Kristen A. Hughes, "Justice Expenditure and Employment in the United States, 2003," *Bureau of Justice Statistics Bulletin,* U.S. Department of Justice (Washington, D.C.: GPO, April 2006).

9. Sourcebook of Criminal Justice Statistics 2002, p. 135, Table 2.40 at www.albany.edu/sourcebook/tost_2.html#2_u(t240.pdf).

10. Robert M. Bohm, *Deathquest III: An Introduction to the Theory and Practice of Capital Punishment in the United States,* 3rd ed. (Cincinnati, OH: Anderson, 2007).

11. Laurie A. Gould, "A Case Study of the Monetary Costs of Criminal Justice in a Local Jurisdiction" (unpublished manuscript, 2000).

12. D. Nimmo and J. E. Combs, *Subliminal Politics: Myths and Mythmakers in America* (Englewood Cliffs, NJ: Prentice Hall, 1980), p. 6.

13. Ibid., p. 16.

14. Many of the myths presented in this book were taken from the following sources: Robert M. Bohm and Jeffery T. Walker, *Demystifying Crime and Criminal Justice* (Los Angeles, CA: Roxbury, 2006); Jeffrey H. Reiman, *The Rich Get Richer and the Poor Get Prison: Ideology, Class, and Criminal Justice,* 7th ed. (Boston: Allyn & Bacon, 2004); Harold E. Pepinsky and Paul Jesilow, *Myths That Cause Crime,* 2nd ed. (Cabin John, MD: Seven Locks, 1985); Kevin N. Wright, *The Great American Crime Myth* (Westport, CT: Greenwood, 1987); also see Robert M. Bohm, "Myths about Criminology and Criminal Justice: A Review Essay," *Justice Quarterly* 4 (1987), pp. 631–642; William Wilbanks, *The Myth of a Racist Criminal Justice System* (Belmont, CA: Wadsworth, 1987); Victor E. Kappeler, Mark Blumberg, and Gary W. Potter, *The Mythology of Crime and Criminal Justice,* 3rd ed. (Prospect Heights, IL: Waveland, 2000); Samuel Walker, *Sense and Nonsense about Crime, and Drugs: A Policy Guide,* 5th ed. (Belmont, CA: Wadsworth, 2000). For a discussion of why these myths exist, see Robert M. Bohm, "Crime, Criminal and Crime Control Policy Myths," *Justice Quarterly* 3 (1986), pp. 193–214.

Chapter 2

1. Loony Laws at www.loonylaws.com/ (accessed January 31, 2009).

2. For additional examples and further discussion of this issue, see Robert M. Bohm, "Some Relationships That Arguably Should Be Criminal Although They Are Not: On the Political Economy of Crime," pp. 3–29 in K. D. Tunnell (ed.), *Political Crime in Contemporary America: A Critical Approach* (New York: Garland, 1993); Gregg Barak (ed.), *Crimes by the Capitalist State: An Introduction to State Criminality* (New York: State University of New York Press, 1991); Gregg Barak and Robert M. Bohm, "The Crimes of the Homeless or the Crime of Homelessness? On the Dialectics of Criminalization, Decriminalization, and Victimization," *Contemporary Crises* 13 (1989), pp. 275–288; James W. Coleman, *The Criminal Elite: Understanding White Collar Crime,* 4th ed. (New York: St. Martin's, 1998); David O. Friedrichs, *Trusted Criminals: White Collar Crime in Contemporary Society* (Belmont, CA: Wadsworth, 1995); Gary S. Green, *Occupational Crime,* 2nd ed. (Chicago: Nelson-Hall, 1996); David R. Simon, *Elite Deviance,* 8th ed. (Boston: Allyn & Bacon, 2006).

3. These elements and the discussion that follows are based on material from Edwin H. Sutherland and Donald R. Cressey, *Criminology,* 9th ed. (Philadelphia: J. B. Lippincott, 1974), pp. 13–15.

4. *M'Naghten's Case,* 8 Eng. Rep. 718 (1843).

5. American Psychiatric Association at www.psych .org/_public_info/insanity.cfm (accessed 7/17/2005).

6. Joe Lambe, "How Far Will 'Castle Doctrine' Defense Go?" *The Kansas City Star* (December 28, 2007), p. A1; Christopher Reinhart, "Castle Doctrine and Self-Defense" at www.cga.ct.gov/2007/rpt/2007-R-0052.htm.

7. The Gallup Poll at www.gallup.com/poll/1603/Crime .aspx (poll conducted October 3–5, 2008; accessed November 29, 2008).

8. Sutherland and Cressey, op. cit., p. 25.

9. Ibid. The remainder of the discussion in this section is based on material from the aforementioned source, pp. 25–30.

10. Ibid.

11. Calculated from data in Michael R. Rand, "Criminal Victimization, 2007," U.S. Department of Justice, Bureau of Justice Statistics, National Crime Victimization Survey (Washington, D.C.: GPO, December 2008), p. 6 at www.ojp.usdoj.gov/bjs/pub/pdf/cv07.pdf (accessed December 29, 2008).

12. Sutherland and Cressey, op. cit., pp. 27–28.

13. D. Seidman and M. Couzens, "Getting the Crime Rate Down: Political Pressure and Crime Reporting," *Law and Human Behavior* 8 (1974), pp. 327–342. See also L. DeFleur, "Biasing Influences on Drug Arrest Records: Implications for Deviance Research," *American Sociological Review* 40 (1975), pp. 88–103; W. L. Selke and H. E. Pepinsky, "The Politics of Police Reporting in Indianapolis, 1948–1978," *Law and Human Behavior* 6 (1982), pp. 327–342.

14. Wes Smith, "Report: Atlanta Hushed Crimes," *The Orlando Sentinel* (February 21, 2004), p. Al.

15. "Philly Underreports Crime," *The Orlando Sentinel* (September 15, 2000), p. A11.

16. "Crime Drop: More Fiction than Fact?" *The Orlando Sentinel* (May 11, 1997), p. B-1.

17. Darrell Steffensmeir, "Is the Crime Rate Really Falling? An 'Aging' U.S. Population and Its Effect on the Nation's Crime Rate, 1980–1984," *Journal of Research in Crime and Delinquency* 24 (1987), pp. 23–48.

18. Federal Bureau of Investigation, *Crime in the United States 2007* at www.fbi.gov/ucr/cius2007/data/ table_01.html.

19. Ibid.

20. "Serious Crimes Decline for 8th Consecutive Year," *The Orlando Sentinel* (May 8, 2000), p. A-7; "Violent Crimes Plummet 7%—Drop Biggest in 35 Years," *The Orlando Sentinel* (June 2, 1997), p. A-4; "FBI Report: Crime Rate Still Falling," *The Orlando Sentinel* (October 5, 1997), p. A-3.

21. Federal Bureau of Investigation, *Crime in the United States 2007* at www.fbi.gov/ucr/cius2007/about/ about_ucr.html.

22. Ibid.

23. Federal Bureau of Investigation, *Crime in the United States 2007* at www.fbi.gov/ucr/cius2007/offenses/ property_crime/larceny-theft.html.

24. Federal Bureau of Investigation, *Hate Crime Statistics 2007* at www.fbi.gov/ucr/hc2007/incidents.htm.

25. Ibid.

26. Federal Bureau of Investigation, *Crime in the United States 2007* at www.fbi.gov/ucr/cius2007/arrests/ index.html.

27. Ibid. at www.fbi.gov/ucr/cius2007/data/table_29.html.

28. Ibid.

29. Ibid. at www.fbi.gov/ucr/cius2007/arrests/index.html.

30. Ibid. at www.fbi.gov/ucr/cius2007/data/table_33.html.

31. *Crime in the United States 2007,* op. cit., at www.fbi .gov/ucr/cius2007/offenses/clearances/index.html.

32. Ibid.

33. Ibid.

34. Ibid.

35. *Crime in the United States 2003,* ibid. at 03sec5.pdf; *Crime in the United States 2004,* ibid. at www.fbi .gov/ucr/cius_04/special_reports/index.html.

36. Unless indicated otherwise, all information in this section is from Brian A. Reaves, "Using NIBRS Data to Analyze Violent Crime," U.S. Department of Justice, Bureau of Justice Statistics Technical Report (Washington, D.C.: GPO, October 1993). Federal Bureau of Investigation, "National Incident-Based Reporting System (NIBRS)" at www.fbi.gov/ucr/ faqs.htm.

37. *Crime in the United States 2007,* op. cit. at www.fbi .gov/ucr/cius2007/about/about_ucr.html.

38. Federal Bureau of Investigation, "National Incident-Based Reporting System (NIBRS)," op. cit.

39. U.S. Department of Justice, "Implementing the National Incident-Based Reporting System: A Project Status Report," (Washington, D.C.: GPO, July 1997).

40. "Crime Drop: More Fiction than Fact?" *The Orlando Sentinel* (May 11, 1997), p. B-1.

41. U.S. Department of Justice, Office of Justice Programs, Bureau of Justice Statistics, *Criminal Victimization in the United States, 1994* (Annapolis, MD: Bureau of Justice Statistics Clearinghouse, 1997).

42. See, for example, J. S. Wallerstein and C. J. Wylie, "Our Law-Abiding Lawbreakers," *Probation* 25 (1947), pp. 107–112; I. Silver, Introduction to *The Challenge of Crime in a Free Society* (New York: Avon, 1968). See also C. Tittle, W. Villemez, and D. Smith, "The Myth of Social Class and Criminality," *American Sociological Review* 43 (1978), pp. 643–656. Juvenile delinquency is also widespread. See, for example, Jerald Bachman, Lloyd Johnston, and Patrick O'Malley, *Monitoring the Future* (Ann Arbor: University of Michigan, Institute for Social Research, 1992); Martin Gold, "Undetected Delinquent Behavior," *Journal of Research in Crime and Delinquency* 3 (1966), pp. 27–46; Martin Gold, *Delinquent Behavior in an American City* (Belmont, CA: Brooks/Cole, 1970); Maynard Erickson and LaMar Empey, "Court Records, Undetected Delinquency, and Decision Making," *Journal of Criminal Law, Criminology, and Police Science* 54 (1963), pp. 446–469; James Short and F. Ivan Nye, "Extent of Unrecorded Delinquency," *Journal of Criminal Law, Criminology, and Police Science* 49 (1958), pp. 296–302.

43. Thomas Gabor, *Everybody Does It! Crimes by the Public* (Toronto: University of Toronto Press, 1994).

44. *Criminal Victimization in the United States 2006,* Statistical Tables, Table 82, www.ojp.usdoj.gov/bjs/pub/pdf/cvus/current/cv0682.pdf.

45. U.S. Department of Justice, Office of Justice Programs, Bureau of Justice Statistics, *Criminal Victimization in the United States, 1992* (Annapolis, MD: Bureau of Justice Statistics Clearinghouse, 1994), p. 148.

46. David R. Simon, *Elite Deviance,* 8th ed. (Boston: Allyn & Bacon, 2006) pp. 97, 107.

47. Ted R. Miller, Mark A. Cohen, and Brian Wiersema, "Victim Costs and Consequences: A New Look," U.S. Department of Justice, National Institute of Justice Report (Washington, D.C.: GPO, February 1996).

48. Wesley Skogan, "Fear of Crime and Neighborhood Change," in Albert J. Reiss, Jr., and Michael Tonry (eds.), *Communities and Crime,* Vol. 8 of *Crime and Justice: A Review of Research* (Chicago: University of Chicago Press, 1986).

49. The Gallup Poll at www.gallup.com/poll/1603/Crime.aspx (poll conducted October 3–5, 2008; accessed November 29, 2008).

50. Sourcebook of Criminal Justice Statistics Online at www.albany.edu/sourcebook/tost_2.html#2_k, Table 2.38 (accessed February 10, 2007).

51. Skogan, "Fear of Crime and Neighborhood Change," op. cit., p. 215.

52. Sourcebook of Criminal Justice Statistics Online at www.albany.edu/sourcebook/pdf/t2402007.pdf (accessed November 19, 2008).

53. Michael R. Rand, "Criminal Victimization, 2007," op. cit., p. 1.

54. Ibid., p. 3, Table 3.

55. Ibid.

56. Ibid.

57. Ibid.

58. Ibid., p. 4, Table 4. For 2005 data, see Shannon M. Catalano, "Criminal Victimization, 2005," U.S. Department of Justice, Bureau of Justice Statistics, National Crime Victimization Survey (Washington, D.C.: GPO, December 2006). More demographic categories were provided in the 2005 survey results. Data from the 2006 survey are unreliable.

59. Ibid., p. 5, Table 5. For 2004 data, see Shannon M. Catalano, "Criminal Victimization, 2005," ibid., p. 7, Table 5.

60. Ibid., p. 6, Table 6.

61. Ibid., p. 7, Table 7.

Chapter 3

1. Cesare Beccaria, *An Essay on Crimes and Punishments,* trans., with introduction, by Harry Paolucci (Indianapolis: Bobbs-Merrill, 1975), p. ix.

2. Ibid., p. 8.

3. Ibid., p. 42.

4. Ibid., p. 99.

5. Beccaria, op. cit.

6. See Irving M. Zeitlin, *Ideology and the Development of Sociological Theory,* 3rd ed. (Englewood Cliffs, NJ: Prentice Hall, 1987).

7. See Ian Taylor, Paul Walton, and Jock Young, *The New Criminology: For a Social Theory of Deviance* (New York: Harper and Row, 1974), pp. 24–32.

8. George B. Vold and Thomas J. Bernard, *Theoretical Criminology,* 3rd ed. (New York: Oxford, 1986), p. 48.

9. See William H. Sheldon, *Varieties of Delinquent Youth* (New York: Harper, 1949).

10. Diana H. Fishbein, *The Science, Treatment, and Prevention of Antisocial Behaviors: Application to the Criminal Justice System* (Kingston, NJ: Civic Research Institute, 2000).

11. See Diana H. Fishbein, "Biological Perspectives in Criminology," *Criminology* 28 (1990), pp. 27–72; Vold and Bernard, op. cit., pp. 87–92; Daniel J. Curran and Claire M. Renzetti, *Theories of Crime* (Boston: Allyn & Bacon, 1994), pp. 54–63; James Q. Wilson and Richard J. Herrnstein, *Crime and Human Nature* (New York: Simon & Schuster, 1985), pp. 75–81, 90–100.

12. See Curran and Renzetti, op. cit., p. 78; Fishbein, op. cit., pp. 38, 47.

13. See National Institute for Juvenile Justice and Delinquency Prevention, *Preventing Delinquency,* Vol. 1 (Washington, D.C.: GPO, 1977), pp. 120–122; Vold and Bernard, op. cit., pp. 101–103.

14. See Fishbein, op. cit., pp. 48, 53; National Institute, op. cit.; Curran and Renzetti, op. cit., pp. 73–77, 80–81.

15. Edwin H. Sutherland and Donald R. Cressey, *Criminology,* 9th ed. (Philadelphia: J. B. Lippincott, 1974), p. 152.

16. Robert Gordon, "Prevalence: The Rare Datum in Delinquency Measurement and Its Implications for

the Theory of Delinquency," in Malcolm W. Klein (ed.), *The Juvenile Justice System* (Beverly Hills, CA: Sage, 1976), pp. 201–84; Travis Hirschi and Michael J. Hindelang, "Intelligence and Delinquency: A Revisionist Review," *American Sociological Review* 42 (1977), pp. 572–587.

17. See Robert S. Woodworth and Mary R. Sheehan, *Contemporary Schools of Psychology,* 3rd ed. (New York: The Ronald Press Co., 1964).

18. Walter Bromberg and Charles B. Thompson, "The Relation of Psychosis, Mental Defect, and Personality Types to Crime," *Journal of Criminal Law and Criminology* 28 (1937), pp. 70–89; Karl F. Schuessler and Donald R. Cressey, "Personality Characteristics of Criminals," *American Journal of Sociology* 55 (1950), pp. 476–484; Gordon P. Waldo and Simon Dinitz, "Personality Attributes of the Criminal: An Analysis of Research Studies, 1950–1965," *Journal of Research in Crime and Delinquency* (1967), pp. 185–202; John Monahan and Henry J. Steadman, "Crime and Mental Disorder: An Epidemiological Approach," in Michael Tonry and Norval Morris (eds.), *Crime and Justice,* Vol. 4 (Chicago: University of Chicago Press, 1983).

19. Abraham H. Maslow, *Motivation and Personality,* 2nd ed. (New York: Harper and Row, 1970).

20. Seymour L. Halleck, *Psychiatry and the Dilemmas of Crime* (New York: Harper and Row, 1967).

21. Émile Durkheim, *Rules of Sociological Method* (New York: Free Press, 1964).

22. Vold and Bernard, op. cit., p. 160.

23. Robert E. Park, Ernest Burgess, and Roderick D. McKenzie, *The City* (Chicago: University of Chicago Press, 1928).

24. Clifford R. Shaw, *Delinquency Areas* (Chicago: University of Chicago Press, 1929); Clifford R. Shaw and Henry D. McKay, *Social Factors in Juvenile Delinquency* (Chicago: University of Chicago Press, 1931); Clifford R. Shaw and Henry D. McKay, *Juvenile Delinquency and Urban Areas* (Chicago: University of Chicago Press, 1942).

25. Clifford R. Shaw, *The Jackroller* (Chicago: University of Chicago Press, 1930); Clifford R. Shaw, *The National History of Delinquent Career* (Chicago: University of Chicago Press, 1931); Clifford R. Shaw, *Brothers in Crime* (Chicago: University of Chicago Press, 1938).

26. Robert K. Merton, "Social Structure and Anomie," *American Sociological Review* 3 (1938), pp. 672–682.

27. Albert K. Cohen, *Delinquent Boys: The Culture of the Gang* (New York: Free Press, 1955).

28. Richard A. Cloward and Lloyd E. Ohlin, *Delinquency and Opportunity: A Theory of Delinquent Gangs* (New York: Free Press, 1960).

29. See, for example, Albert Bandura, *Social Learning Theory* (Englewood Cliffs, NJ: Prentice Hall, 1977).

30. See, for example, Edwin H. Sutherland and Donald R. Cressey, *Criminology,* 9th ed. (Philadelphia: J. B. Lippincott, 1974).

31. Daniel Glaser, "Criminality Theories and Behavioral Images," *American Journal of Sociology* 61 (1956), pp. 433–444.

32. Definitions of learning theory concepts are from Howard Rachlin, *Introduction to Modern Behaviorism,* 2nd ed. (San Francisco: W. H. Freeman, 1976).

33. Michael R. Gottfredson and Travis Hirschi, *A General Theory of Crime* (Stanford, CA: Stanford University Press, 1990).

34. Edwin Lemert, *Social Pathology: A Systematic Approach to the Theory of Sociopathic Behavior* (New York: McGraw-Hill, 1951).

35. See Edwin M. Schur, *Radical Nonintervention* (Englewood Cliffs, NJ: Prentice Hall, 1973).

36. Robert J. Lilly, Francis T. Cullen, and Richard A. Ball, *Criminological Theory: Context and Consequences* (Newbury Park, CA: Sage, 1989), pp. 131–135.

37. John Braithwaite, *Crime, Shame and Reintegration* (Cambridge: Cambridge University Press, 1989).

38. Vold and Bernard, op. cit., p. 256.

39. George B. Vold, *Theoretical Criminology* (New York: Oxford, 1958).

40. William J. Chambliss, "Functional and Conflict Theories of Crime: The Heritage of Emile Durkheim and Karl Marx," in W. J. Chambliss and M. Mankoff (eds.), *Whose Law, What Order?* (New York: Wiley, 1976), p. 9.

41. Tony Platt, "Prospects for a Radical Criminology in the USA," in I. Taylor et al. (eds.), *Critical Criminology* (Boston: Routledge & Kegan Paul, 1975), p. 103.

42. Ibid.; for a similar definition, see also Herman Schwendinger and Julia Schwendinger, "Defenders of Order or Guardians of Human Rights?" in I. Taylor et al. (eds.), *Critical Criminology,* pp. 113–146.

43. See, for example, Richard Kinsey, John Lea, and Jock Young, *Losing the Fight Against Crime* (London: Basil Blackwell, 1976); Roger Matthews and Jock Young (eds.), *Confronting Crime* (London: Sage, 1986).

44. Jock Young, "Left Realism: The Basics," in B. D. MacLean and D. Milovanovic (eds.), *Thinking Critically about Crime* (Vancouver, BC: Collective Press, 1997), pp. 28–36.

45. Werner Einstadter and Stuart Henry, *Criminological Theory: An Analysis of Its Underlying Assumptions* (Fort Worth, TX: Harcourt Brace, 1995), p. 256.

46. Ibid., p. 257.

47. See Harold E. Pepinsky and Richard Quinney (eds.), *Criminology as Peacemaking* (Bloomington: Indiana University Press, 1991).

48. For two excellent reviews, see Kathleen Daly and Meda Chesney–Lind, "Feminism and Criminology," *Justice Quarterly* 5 (1988), pp. 497–538; Sally S. Simpson, "Feminist Theory, Crime, and Justice," *Criminology* 27 (1989), pp. 605–631.

49. See Einstadter and Henry, op. cit., p. 275.

50. Ibid.

51. Ibid., p. 278.

52. Ibid., p. 287.

53. Bruce Arrigo and T. R. Young, "Chaos, Complexity, and Crime: Working Tools for a Postmodern Criminology," in MacLean and Milovanovic, op. cit., p. 77. For an interesting postmodern analysis of the William Kennedy Smith rape trial, see Gregory M. Matoesian, *Law and the Language of Identity: Discourse*

in the William Kennedy Smith Rape Trial (New York: Oxford University Press, 2001).

54. Einstadter and Henry, op. cit., p. 291.

55. Arrigo and Young, op. cit., pp. 81–82; Stuart Henry and Dragan Milovanovic, *Constitutive Criminology: Beyond Postmodernism* (London: Sage, 1996).

56. Einstadter and Henry, op. cit., p. 294.

57. Ibid., p. 280.

Chapter 4

1. Jay A. Sigler, *Understanding Criminal Law* (Boston: Little, Brown, 1981), p. 3.

2. The discussion in the remainder of this section is based on material from Edwin H. Sutherland and Donald R. Cressey, *Criminology,* 9th ed. (Philadelphia: J. B. Lippincott, 1974), p. 8.

3. Most of the material in this section comes from Will Durant, *Our Oriental Heritage,* Part 1 of *The Story of Civilization* (New York: Simon & Schuster, 1954).

4. Most of the material in this section comes from Raymond J. Michalowski, *Order, Law, and Crime: An Introduction to Criminology* (New York: Random House, 1985).

5. See Archibald Cox, *The Court and the Constitution* (Boston: Houghton Mifflin, 1987), pp. 239–249.

6. For an examination of the influence of the Burger and Rehnquist Courts on criminal procedure, see Mary Margaret Weddington and W. Richard Janikowski, "The Rehnquist Court: The Counter-Revolution That Wasn't: Part II, The Counter-Revolution That Is," *Criminal Justice Review* 21 (1997), pp. 231–250.

7. In addition to the Supreme Court cases themselves, much of the information in the remainder of this chapter is from the following sources: John Ferdico, *Criminal Procedure for the Law Enforcement Officer* (St. Paul, MN: West, 1975); Yale Kamisar, Wayne R. LaFave, and Jerold H. Israel, *Modern Criminal Procedure,* 7th ed. (St. Paul, MN: West, 1990); Sanford H. Kadish and Monrad G. Paulsen, *Criminal Law and Its Processes,* 3rd ed. (Boston: Little, Brown, 1975); Wayne R. LaFave and Jerold H. Israel, *Criminal Procedure* (St. Paul, MN: West, 1984, Supp. 1991); Jerold H. Israel and Wayne R. LaFave, *Criminal Procedure in a Nutshell* (St. Paul, MN: West, 1975); John M. Scheb and John M. Scheb II, *Criminal Law and Procedure,* 2nd ed. (St. Paul, MN: West, 1994).

8. *Katz* v. *United States,* 389 U.S. 347 (1967).

9. *United States* v. *Jacobsen,* 466 U.S. 109 (1984).

10. Ibid.

11. "Boston Police Will Search Kids' Rooms—With Parents' Consent," *The Orlando Sentinel* (November 18, 2007), p. A2.

12. *Florida* v. *J. L.,* 529 U.S. 266 (2000).

13. *Illinois* v. *Wardlow,* 528 U.S. 119 (2000).

14. R. Erik Lillquist, "Absolute Certainty and the Death Penalty" (August 23, 2004). Seton Hall Public Law Research Paper No. 10. Available at SSRN: http://ssm .com/abstract=581281.

15. Ibid.

16. Unless indicated otherwise, information in this section is from www.epic.org/privacy/terrorism/hr3162.html,

which provides the full text of the USA PATRIOT Act; American Civil Liberties Union, "Surveillance under the USA PATRIOT Act," www.aclu.org/ SafeandFree/SafeandFree.cfm?ID512263&c5206, April 3, 2003; Electronic Frontier Foundation, "EFF Analysis of the Provisions of the USA PATRIOT Act," www.eff.org/Privacy/Surveillance/Terrorism_militias/ 20011031_eff_usa_patriot_analysis.htm, October 31, 2001; Lara Jakes Jordan, "FBI Admits Further Privacy Violations," *The Orlando Sentinel* (March 6, 2008), p. A3.

17. Department of Justice, "Fact Sheet: USA PATRIOT Act Improvement and Reauthorization Act of 2005" at www.usdoj.gov/opa/pr/2006/March/06_opa_113 .html; The American Civil Liberties Union, "The Patriot Act: Where It Stands" at http://action.aclu.org/ reformthepatriotact/whereitstands.html.

18. Information about the "Protect America Act of 2007" and the "FISA Amendments Act of 1978" is from the following sources: www.lifeandliberty.gov/docs/ text-of-paa.pdf, www.whitehouse.gov/news/releases/ 2007/08/20070806-5.html, www.aclu.org/safefree/ nsaspying/31203res20070807.html, www.govtrack.us/ congress/bill.xpd?bill=h110-3773; http://74.125.113.132/ search?q=cache:oTvSepr7yV8J:www.eff.org/files/filenode/ att/FISAINTRO_001_xml.pdf+FISA+Amendments+Act+ of+1978&hl=en&ct=clnk&cd=4&gl=us.

19. *Dickerson* v. *United States,* 530 U.S. 428 (2000).

20. Susan Clary, "Stunning: Remote-Control Belts Keep Peace in Courts," *The Orlando Sentinel* (December 1, 2001), p. H6.

21. See Raymond Paternoster, *Capital Punishment in America* (New York: Lexington, 1991), p. 51.

22. Barry Scheck, Peter Neufeld, and Jim Dwyer, *Actual Innocence: When Justice Goes Wrong and How to Make It Right* (New York: Signet, 2001), p. xx.

23. C. Ronald Huff, Arye Rattner, and Edward Sagarin, "Guilty until Proven Innocent: Wrongful Conviction and Public Policy," *Crime and Delinquency* 32 (1986), pp. 518–544.

24. Federal Bureau of Investigation, *Crime in the United States, 2007* at www.fbi.gov/ucr/cius2007/arrests/ index.html.

25. See Huff et al., op. cit., p. 523.

26. Scheck et al., op. cit., p. 95.

27. Ibid., p. 226.

28. Marcia Coyle, Fred Strasser, and Marianne Lavelle, "Fatal Defense," *The National Law Journal* 12 (1990), pp. 30–44.

29. Scheck et al., op. cit., p. 242.

30. Huff et al., op. cit., pp. 530–533; Scheck et al. op. cit.

31. Scheck et al., op. cit., pp. 351–357.

32. The National Institute of Justice, "The Effects of the Exclusionary Rule: A Study in California" (Washington, D.C.: U.S. Department of Justice, 1983).

33. Marvin Zalman, *Criminal Procedure: Constitution and Society,* 4th ed. (Upper Saddle River, NJ: Prentice Hall, 2005); American Bar Association Special Committee on Criminal Justice in a Free Society, "Criminal Justice in Crisis" (1988), at www.druglibrary.org/special/king/cjic.htm; F. Feeney,

F. Dill, and A. Weir, *Arrests Without Conviction: How Often They Occur and Why* (Washington, D.C.: U.S. Department of Justice, National Institute of Justice, 1983); P. Nardulli, "The Societal Cost of the Exclusionary Rule: An Empirical Assessment," *American Bar Foundation Research Journal* (1983), pp. 585–609; *Report of the Comptroller General of the United States, Impact of the Exclusionary Rule on Federal Criminal Prosecutions* (Washington, D.C.: U.S. General Accounting Office, 1979); K. Brosi, *A Cross City Comparison of Felony Case Processing* (Washington, D.C.: U.S. Department of Justice, Law Enforcement Assistance Administration, 1979); B. Forst, J. Lucianovic, and S. Cox, *What Happens after Arrest: A Court Perspective of Police Operations in the District of Columbia* (Washington, D.C.: U.S. Department of Justice, Law Enforcement Assistance Administration, 1978).

34. *Report of the Comptroller General of the United States,* op. cit.

35. Cited in Tamar Jacoby, "Fighting Crime by the Rules: Why Cops Like Miranda," *Newsweek* (July 18, 1988), p. 53.

36. Karen L. Guy and Robert G. Huckabee, "Going Free on a Technicality: Another Look at the Effect of the *Miranda* Decision on the Criminal Justice Process," *Criminal Justice Research Bulletin* 4 (1988), pp. 1–3.

37. Jacoby, op. cit.; Scheck et al., op. cit., p. 117.

38. Guy and Huckabee, op. cit.

39. See, for example, George C. Thomas, III, and Richard Leo, "The Effects of *Miranda* v. *Arizona*: 'Embedded' in Our National Culture?" in Michael Tonry (ed.), *Crime and Justice: A Review of Research* (2002), pp. 203–271.

40. For a different view, see Paul G. Cassell and Bret S. Hayman, "Police Interrogation in the 1990s: An Empirical Study of the Effects of *Miranda*," *UCLA Law Review* 43 (1996), pp. 839–931; and George C. Thomas, III, "Is *Miranda* a Real-World Failure? A Plea for More and Better Empirical Evidence," *UCLA Law Review* 43 (1996), pp. 821–837.

Chapter 5

1. Material in this section was taken from T. A. Critchley, *A History of Police in England and Wales,* 2nd ed. rev. (Montclair, NJ: Patterson Smith, 1972).

2. Ibid.

3. Maricopa County Sheriff's office at www.mcso.org/include/modules/Patrol_Duties/District_Facilities/enforcement_support.php (accessed November 23, 2008).

4. Patrick Pringle, *Hue and Cry: The Story of Henry and John Fielding and Their Bow Street Runners* (New York: William Morrow, 1965).

5. Material in this section was taken from A. C. Germann, F. Day, and R. Gallati, *Introduction to Law Enforcement and Criminal Justice* (Springfield, IL: Charles C. Thomas, 1962), pp. 54–55.

6. Edward Savage, *Police Records and Recollections, or Boston by Daylight and Gaslights for Two Hundred and Forty Years* (Boston: John P. Dale, 1873).

7. This material came from Carl Sifakis, *The Encyclopedia of American Crime* (New York: Smithmark, 1992), pp. 579–580.

8. Information in this section is from W. Marvin Dulaney, *Black Police in America* (Bloomington: Indiana University Press, 1996).

9. Center for Research on Criminal Justice, *The Iron Fist and the Velvet Glove: An Analysis of the U.S. Police* (Berkeley, CA: Center for Research on Criminal Justice, 1975); Hubert Williams and Patrick V. Murphy, "The Evolving Strategy of Police: A Minority View," *Perspectives on Policing,* No. 13 (Washington, D.C.: U.S. Department of Justice, January 1990).

10. Dulaney, op. cit., p. 2.

11. John Duff and Peter Mitchell, *The Nat Turner Rebellion: The Historical Event and the Modern Controversy* (New York: Harper & Row, 1971).

12. Thad Sitton, *Texas High Sheriffs* (Austin: Texas Monthly Press, 1988).

13. Adrian N. Anderson, Ralph A. Wooster, David G. Armstrong, and Jeanie R. Stanley, *Texas and Texans* (New York: Glencoe/McGraw-Hill, 1993).

14. Bruce Smith, *Police Systems in the United States* (New York: Harper & Row, 1960), pp. 178–205.

15. Samuel Walker, *A Critical History of Police Reform: The Emergence of Professionalism* (1977), Lexington, MA: Lexington, p. 76.

16. *Our Police* (Cincinnati Police Division, 1984).

17. Gene Carte and Elaine Carte, *Police Reform in the United States: The Era of August Vollmer* (Berkeley and Los Angeles: University of California Press, 1975).

18. Roy Robert, John Crank, and Jack Kuykendall, *Police and Society* (Los Angeles, CA: Roxbury Publishing Company, 1999), pp. 432–433.

19. Malcolm K. Sparrow, Mark H. Moore, and David M. Kennedy, *Beyond 911* (New York: Basic Books, 1990).

20. U.S. Department of Justice, *Response Time Analysis: Executive Summary* (Washington, D.C.: GPO, 1978).

21. Samuel Walker, *The Police in America: An Introduction,* 2nd ed. (New York: McGraw-Hill, 1992).

22. Robert C. Trojanowicz and Bonnie Bucqueroux, *Community Policing: A Contemporary Perspective* (Cincinnati: Anderson, 1989); Robert C. Trojanowicz and Bonnie Bucqueroux, *Community Policing: How to Get Started* (Cincinnati: Anderson, 1994).

23. Material about CompStat is from James J. Willis, Stephen D. Mastrofski, and David Weisburd, "The Myth That COMPSTAT Reduces Crime and Transforms Police Organization," in R. M. Bohm and J. T. Walker (eds.) *Demystifying Crime and Criminal Justice* (Los Angeles: Roxbury, 2006), pp. 111–119.

24. Information on the U.S. Marshals Service is from www.usmarshals.gov/history/index.html and www.usmarshals.gov/history/broad_range.htm.

25. Information on the U.S. Secret Service is from www.ustreas.gov/usss/history.shtml, www.ustreas.gov/usss/faq.shtml#faq1, and www.ustreas.gov/usss/mission.shtml (accessed October 29, 2008); www.treas.gov/usss/counterfeit.shtml (accessed January 4, 2009).

26. Information on the FBI is from www.fbi.gov/libref/historic/history/text.htm, www.fbi.gov/quickfacts.htm (both accessed October 29, 2008), Samuel Walker (1977) *A Critical History of Police Reform,* Lexington, MA: Lexington, and Frank J. Donner (1980) *The Age of Surveillance,* New York: Alfred A. Knopf.

27. Information on the DEA is from www.usdoj.gov/dea/history.htm and www.usdoj.gov/dea/agency/mission.htm. Other sources of information on America's War on Drugs are www.druglibrary.org/schaffer/history/e1910/harrisonact.htm, www.druglibrary.org/schaffer/Library/studies/cu/cu8.html; James A. Inciardi (1986) *The War on Drugs: Heroin, Cocaine, Crime, and Public Policy,* Palo Alto, CA: Mayfield; www.druglibrary.org/SCHAFFER/library/studies/wick/wick1b.html; www.nationmaster.com/encyclopedia/Bureau-of-Narcotics; www.nationmaster.com/encyclopedia/Harry-J.-Anslinger; www.druglibrary.org/SCHAFFER/hemp/taxact/mjtaxact.htm; www.deamuseum.org/dea_history_book/pre1970.htm; www.usdoj.gov/dea/pubs/history/1970-1975.html; Edward Jay Epstein (1977) *Agency of Fear: Opiates and Political Power in America,* New York: G.P. Putnam's Sons.

28. Federal Bureau of Investigation, *Crime in the United States,* 2007, www.fbi.gov/ucr/cius2007/.

29. Brian A. Reaves, *Federal Law Enforcement Officers, 2004,* U.S. Department of Justice, Bureau of Justice Statistics (Washington, D.C.: GPO, July 2006).

30. Matthew J. Hickman and Brian A. Reaves, *Local Police Departments, 2003* (Washington, D.C.: Bureau of Justice Statistics, May 2006).

31. V. A. Leonard, *Police Organization and Management* (New York: Foundation Press, 1964).

32. Matthew J. Hickman and Brian A. Reaves, *Sheriffs' Offices 2003,* Bureau of Justice Statistics (Washington, D.C.: GPO, May 2006).

33. Ibid.

34. Ibid.

35. Brian A. Reaves, *Census of State and Local Law Enforcement Agencies, 2004,* U.S. Department of Justice, Bureau of Justice Statistics *Bulletin* (Washington, D.C.: GPO, June 2007).

36. Reaves, *Federal Law Enforcement Officers, 2004,* op. cit.

37. Ibid.

38. Steven W. Perry, "Justice Expenditure and Employment Extracts, 2006," *Bureau of Justice Statistics,* U.S. Department of Justice at www.ojp.usdoj.gov/bjs/eande.htm#selected.filename:cjee0601.cvs (date of version: 8/29/08).

39. Reaves, *Federal Law Enforcement Officers, 2004,* op. cit.

40. Ibid.

41. Material on FLETC is from Reaves and Bauer, *Federal Law Enforcement Officers, 2002,* ibid., p. 11; the Federal Law Enforcement Training Center at www.fletc.gov.

42. Material on the Department of Homeland Security is from the U.S. Department of Homeland Security website at www.dhs.gov/ and www.dhs.gov/xabout/structure/.

43. *Terrorism in the United States, 1999,* op. cit., p. 10.

44. Material on Homeland Security and the FBI is from the following sources: Rebecca Carr, "FBI Chief: My Agency Can Handle Spying Job," *The Orlando Sentinel* (December 20, 2002), p. A11; Eric Lichtblau, "Pressure on FBI Grows from Within," *The Orlando Sentinel* (December 2, 2002), p. A9; Curt Anderson, "FBI Seeks to Expand Presence Overseas," *The Orlando Sentinel* (March 29, 2003), p. A3; "Senate Confirms Ridge as Head of Homeland Dept," *USA Today* (January 23, 2003), p. 12A; "FBI Tackles Fewer Cases, Focuses on Fighting Terrorists," The Orlando Sentinel (March 7, 2008), p. A4.

45. Richard B. Schmitt, "FBI Forecast Mortgage Crisis, Failed to Block It," *The Orlando Sentinel* (August 26, 2008), p. A6.

46. Eric Lichtblau, David Johnston, and Ron Nixon, "Uptick in Financial Crime Catches FBI Flat-footed," *The Orlando Sentinel* (October 19, 2008), p. A6.

47. Jeff Bliss, "FBI Told to Do Better Job of Tracking Terror Threats," *The Orlando Sentinel* (November 8, 2008), p. A5.

48. U.S. Department of State, Patterns of Global Terrorism 2003 at www.state.gov/s/ct/rls/pgtrpt/2003/c12153.htm (Introduction, p. v).

49. Ibid.

50. Ibid., pp. vi–vii.

51. Ibid.; Matthew Levitt and Michael Jacobson, "The Money Trail: Finding, Following, and Freezing Terrorist Finances," The Washington Institute for Near East Policy, Policy Focus #89 (November 2008), p. 16 at www.washingtoninstitute.org/templateC04.php?CID=302 (accessed December 7, 2008).

52. Federal Bureau of Investigation at www.fbi.gov/mostwant/topten/fugitives/laden.htm.

53. Matthew Levitt and Michael Jacobson, "The Money Trail: Finding, Following, and Freezing Terrorist Finances," The Washington Institute for Near East Policy, Policy Focus #89 (November 2008), p. 25 at www.washingtoninstitute.org/templateC04.php?CID=302 (accessed December 7, 2008).

54. *Occupational Outlook Handbook* at http://bls.gov/oco/ocos/159.htm (accessed May 2006).

55. Larry Margasak, "Low-Wage Security Has High Cost—Insecurity," *The Orlando Sentinel* (May 30, 2007), p. A3.

56. Unless indicated otherwise, most of the information in this section is from the *Occupational Outlook Handbook* at www.bls.gov/oco/ocos159.htm (accessed November 24, 2008); Bureau of Labor Statistics, Occupational Employment Statistics at www.bls.gov/oco/ocos159.htm#earnings accessed November 24, 2008).

57. Margasak op. cit.

58. Ibid.

Chapter 6

1. Keith Haley, "Training," in Gary Cordner and Donna Hale (eds.), *What Works in Policing? Operations and Administration Examined* (Cincinnati: Anderson, 1992).

2. Lee Rainwater, "The Revolt of the Dirty Workers," *Transaction* (November 1967), p. 2.

3. Jerome Skolnick, *Justice without Trial* (New York: Wiley, 1966).

4. U.S. Department of Justice, Federal Bureau of Investigation, "Law Enforcement Officers Killed & Assaulted" at www.fbi.gov/ucr/killed/2007/feloniouslykilled.html; Federal Bureau of Investigation, "Preliminary Statistics for Law Enforcement Officers Killed in 2005" (Press Release, May 15, 2006) at www.fbi.gov/pressrel/pressrel06/leoka.htm; U.S. Department of Justice, Federal Bureau of Investigation, *Uniform Crimes Reports, 2001, 2000, 1999,* www.fbi.gov/ucr/ucr.htm.

5. "Law Enforcement Officers Killed & Assaulted," ibid. at www.fbi.gov/ucr/killed/2007/data/table_19.html.

6. "Law Enforcement Officers Killed & Assaulted," ibid. at www.fbi.gov/ucr/killed/2007/accidentallykilled .html; "Preliminary Statistics for Law Enforcement Officers Killed in 2005," ibid.

7. Ibid.; *Sourcebook of Criminal Justice Statistics Online* at www.albany.edu/sourcebook/pdf/t31542006.pdf, Table 3.154.

8. James Q. Wilson, *Varieties of Police Behavior* (Cambridge, MA: Harvard University Press, 1968), pp. 140–227.

9. John Broderick, *Police in a Time of Change* (Morristown, NJ: General Learning Press, 1977), pp. 9–88.

10. William Muir, Jr., *Police: Streetcorner Politicians* (Chicago: University of Chicago Press, 1977).

11. Ellen Hochstedler, "Testing Types: A Review and Test of Police Types," *Journal of Criminal Justice* 9 (1981), pp. 451–466; also see Eugene A. Paoline, "The Myth of a Monolithic Police Culture," in Robert M. Bohm and Jeffery T. Walker (eds.), Demystifying Crime and Criminal Justice (Los Angeles: Roxbury, 2006).

12. G. Kelling, T. Pate, D. Dieckman, and C. Brown, *The Kansas City Preventive Patrol Experiment: A Summary Report* (Washington, D.C.: Police Foundation, 1974).

13. Gary Cordner, "Patrol," in Gary Cordner and Donna Hale (eds.), op. cit.

14. Daniel Mabrey, "Crime Mapping: Tracking the Hotspots," *Crime & Justice International* 18, no. 67 (2002), pp. 31–32.

15. Ibid.

16. James Q. Wilson and Barbara Boland, "The Effect of Police on Crime," *Law and Society Review* 12 (1978), pp. 367–384.

17. George Kelling, *The Newark Foot Patrol Experiment* (Washington, D.C.: Police Foundation, 1981).

18. Robert C. Trojanowicz, *The Neighborhood Foot Patrol Program in Flint, Michigan* (East Lansing, MI: National Neighborhood Foot Patrol Center, n.d.).

19. Bruce L. Berg and John J. Horgan, *Criminal Investigation,* 3rd ed. (Westerville: Glencoe/McGraw-Hill, 1998).

20. Alfred Blumstein and Joan Petersilia, "NIJ and Its Research Program," *25 Years of Criminal Justice Research* (Washington, D.C.: The National Institute of Justice, 1994), p. 13.

21. Christine Wicker, "Death Beat," in Keith N. Haley and Mark A. Stallo, *Texas Crime, Texas Justice* (New York: McGraw-Hill, 1996).

22. U.S. Department of Justice, Federal Bureau of Investigations, *Crime in the United States, 2007* at www.fbi .gov/ucr/cius2007/offenses/clearances/index.html.

23. Mark Willman and John Snortum, "Detective Work: The Criminal Investigation Process in a Medium-Size Police Department," *Criminal Justice Review* 9 (1984), pp. 33–39; V. Williams and R. Sumrall, "Productivity Measures in the Criminal Investigation Function," *Journal of Criminal Justice* 10 (1982), pp. 111–122; I. Greenberg and R. Wasserman, *Managing Criminal Investigations* (Washington, D.C.: U.S. Department of Justice, 1979); P. Greenwood and J. Petersilia, *The Criminal Investigation Process,* Vol. I, *Summary and Policy Implications* (Washington, D.C.: U.S. Department of Justice, 1975); B. Greenberg, C. Elliot, L. Kraft, and H. Procter, *Felony Investigation Decision Model: An Analysis of Investigative Elements of Information* (Washington, D.C.: GPO, 1975).

24. John Conklin, *Robbery and the Criminal Justice System* (New York: J. B. Lippincott, 1972), p. 149.

25. "Cops Clear JonBenet's Family," *The Orlando Sentinel* (July 10, 2008), p. A2; Catherine Tsai, "DNA Offers Hope JonBenet's Killer May Be Found," *The Orlando Sentinel* (July 11, 2008), p. A12.

26. Paisley Dodds, "After Ruling, Much of Britain's DNA Database May Be DOA," *The Orlando Sentinel* (December 5, 2008), p. A14.

27. Federal Bureau of Investigation, "CODIS—NDIS Statistics" at www.fbi.gov/hq/lab/codis/clickmap.htm.

28. Integrated Automated Fingerprint System at www.fbi .gov/hq/cjisd/iafis.htm (accessed November 26, 2008); Florida Department of Law Enforcement (personal communication, December 3, 2008). The FDLE was in the process of upgrading its system and adding 1.1 million prints that were on microfilm. The project was to be completed in January 2009.

29. Hollis Stambaugh, David Beaupre, David Icove, Richard Baker, Waynes Cassady, and Wayne P. Williams, *State and Local Law Enforcement Needs to Combat Local Crime,* National Institute of Justice, August 2000.

30. Ronald T. Holmes, Richard Tewksberry, and Stephen T. Holmes, "Pornography on the Internet," *Law and Order* 45, no. 9 (September 1997).

31. Stambaugh et al., op. cit.

32. Substance Abuse and Mental Health Services Administration, *2007 National Survey on Drug Use and Health* at www.oas.samhsa.gov/nsduh/2k7nsduh/2k7Results.cfm#1.1 (accessed November 27, 2008).

33. Unless indicated otherwise, information in this section on drug enforcement is from the following sources: Matthew J. Hickman and Brian A. Reaves, "Local Police Departments 2003," U.S. Department of Justice, Bureau of Justice Statistics (Washington, D.C.: GPO, May 2006), p. 15, Table 29, p. 16, Table 31; Peter Joseph Loughlin, "Does the Civil Asset Forfeiture Reform Act of 2000 Bring a Modicum of Sanity to the Federal Civil Asset Forfeiture System?" at www.malet .com/does_the_civil_asset_forfeiture_.htm; H. Williams, "Drug Control Strategies of United States Law Enforcement," United Nations, Office on Drugs and Crime at www.unoD.C..org/unoD.C./en/bulletin/bulletin_1990-01-01_1_page004.html#s005; Scott Ehlers, *Policy Briefing: Asset Forfeiture,* The Drug

Policy Foundation (Washington, D.C.: GPO, 1999); Samuel Walker, *Sense and Nonsense about Crime and Drugs: A Policy Guide,* 5th ed. (Belmont, CA: Wadsworth, 2001), chap. 13; Victor E. Kappeler, Mark Blumberg, and Gary W. Potter, *The Mythology of Crime and Criminal Justice,* 3rd ed. (Prospect Heights, IL: Waveland Press, 2000), chap. 8; "Long-Term Trends in Illicit Drug Use," U.S. Department of Health and Human Services, Office of Applied Studies at www.samhsa.gov/oas/nhsda/_2k1nhsda/vol1/_chapter9.htm#9.2.

34. Federal Bureau of Investigation, *Crime in the United States 2007,* www.fbi.gov/ucr/cius2007/data/table_29.html.

35. U.S. Drug Enforcement Administration, "Domestic Cannnabis Eradication/Suppression Program" at www.usdoj.gov/dea/programs/marijuana.htm.

36. Drug Abuse Resistance Education at www.dare.com; The Drug Reform Coordination Network, "A Different Look at D.A.R.E." at www.drcnet.org/DARE/section1.html and www.drcnet.org/DARE/section6.html.

37. Material on research studies based on information in Alfred Blumstein and Joan Petersilia, "NIJ and Its Research Program," *25 Years of Criminal Justice Research* (Washington, D.C.: The National Institute of Justice, 1994), pp. 10–14.

38. James Q. Wilson and George L. Kelling, "Broken Windows: The Police and Neighborhood Safety," *Atlantic Monthly,* 256 (1982), pp. 29–38.

39. Material in this subsection is based on information in the following sources: Community Policing Consortium, *Understanding Community Policing: A Framework for Action,* monograph, www.communitypolicing.org/conpubs.html, January 1998; U.S. Department of Justice, National Institute of Corrections, *Community Justice: Striving for Safe, Secure, and Just Communities* (Louisville, KY: LIS, 1996).

40. See William Oliver, "The Homeland Security Juggernaut: The End of the Community Policing Era?" *Crime & Justice International* 20 (2004), pp. 4–10.

41. Hickman and Reaves, *Local Police Departments, 2003,* op. cit., p. iii.

42. Federal Bureau of Investigation, *Terrorism in the United States, 1999,* p. 15, at www.fbi.gov/publications/terror/terroris.htm.

43. Ibid.

44. Ibid., p. 16.

45. U.S. State Department, *Patterns of Global Terrorism, 2001,* May 2002, p. v, at www.state.gov/s/ct/rls/pgtrpt/2000/pdf.

46. Ibid., p. 1.

47. *Terrorism in the United States, 1999,* op. cit., p. 15.

48. Ibid., p. i.

49. U.S. Department of Justice, Federal Bureau of Investigation, "Terrorism 2002–2005" at www.fbi.gov/publications/terror/terrorism2002_2005.htm.

50. U.S. State Department, *Patterns of Global Terrorism,* 2002, April 2003, p. xiii, at www.state.gov/s/ct/rls/pgtrpt/2002.

51. "Terrorism 2002–2005," op. cit.

52. Ibid.

53. Ibid., p. 18.

54. Ibid., p. 19.

55. Ibid., p. 20.

56. Ibid., pp. 25–26.

57. Ibid., p. 16.

58. Ibid., p. 23.

59. Ibid. p. xi; U.S. Department of State, Country Reports on Terrorism (April 28, 2006), www.state.gov/s/ct/rls/crt/2005/64337.htm.

60. *Terrorism in the United States, 1999,* op. cit., p. 23.

61. Ibid.

62. Ibid., pp. 38–40.

63. Ibid., p. i.

64. See Howard Zinn, *A People's History of the United States* (New York: Harper Colophon, 1980), chap. 4.

65. *Patterns of Global Terrorism, 2002,* op. cit., p. xi.

66. Eric Lichtblau, "Bush Issues Federal Ban on Racial Profiling," *The New York Times,* June 18, 2003.

67. Deborah Orin and David Kadison, "Government Still Knapping as New 9/11 Looms," *New York Post Online Edition,* June 30, 2003.

68. David Johnston, "Report Calls U.S. Agencies Understaffed for Bioterror," *The New York Times* (July 6, 2003).

69. "U.S. Not 'Well-Prepared' for Terrorism" at www.cnn.com/2005/US/12/04/911.commission/index.html (accessed November 28, 2008).

70. "The War on Terror: What Is It? Who Are Our Enemies and How Likely Are Different Types of Terrorist Attacks in the U.S.?" The Harris Poll #60, June 22, 2007 at www.harrisinteractive.com/harris_poll/index.asp?PID=776, Table 4.

Chapter 7

1. W. S. Wilson Huang and Michael S. Vaughn, "Support and Confidence: Public Attitudes toward the Police," in Timothy J. Flanagan and Dennis R. Longmire (eds.), *Americans View Crime and Justice: A National Public Opinion Survey* (Thousand Oaks, CA: Sage, 1996), pp. 31–45.

2. Humphrey Taylor, "Love Affair with NYPD Has Not Changed Nationwide Attitudes toward Police," *The Harris Poll* #13, March 20, 2002, at www.harrisinteractive.com/harris_poll/printerfriend/index.asp?PID=290; also see Bureau of Justice Statistics, *Sourcebook of Criminal Justice Statistics Online,* at www.albany.edu/sourcebook, Tables 2.14, 2.17, 2.24, 2.25, 2.28.

3. *Sourcebook,* op. cit. Table 2.18.

4. Larry Gaines and Victor Kappeler, "Police Selection," in Gary Cordner and Donna Hale (eds.), *What Works in Policing: Operations and Administration Examined* (Cincinnati: Anderson, 1992).

5. Robert B. Mills, "Psychological, Psychiatric, Polygraph, and Stress Evaluation," in Calvin Swank and James Conser (eds.), *The Police Personnel System* (New York: Wiley, 1981).

6. O. W. Wilson and Roy McLaren, *Police Administration* (New York: McGraw-Hill, 1972), p. 261.

7. Albert Reiss, *The Police and the Public* (New Haven, CT: Yale University Press, 1971).

8. Matthew J. Hickman and Brian A. Reaves, *Local Police Departments, 2003,* U.S. Department of Justice, Bureau of Justice Statistics (Washington, D.C.: GPO, 2006), and U.S. Census Bureau.

9. David Carter, Allen Sapp, and Darrel Stephens, *The State of Police Education: Policy Direction for the 21st Century* (Washington, D.C.: Police Executive Research Forum, 1989).

10. Information on the Police Corps is from The Police Corps Act, 42 U.S.C., sections 14091 et seq. as amended through November 2, 2002 (Title XX, Subtitle A, of the Violent Crime Control and Law Enforcement Act of 1994); U.S. Department of Justice, Office of the Police Corps at www.ojp.usdoj.gov/opclee/about.html.

11. *Hild* v. *Bruner,* 1980; *Bonsignore* v. *City of New York,* 1981.

12. Jack Gregory, "The Background Investigation and Oral Interview," in Calvin Swank and James Conser (eds.), op. cit.

13. Matthew J. Hickman and Brian A. Reaves, *Sheriffs' Offices, 2003,* U.S. Department of Justice, Bureau of Justice Statistics (Washington, D.C.: GPO, May 2006), p. 11, Table 20.

14. Jerome Skolnick, *Justice without Trial* (New York: Wiley, 1996).

15. Lawrence W. Sherman and Richard A. Berk, *The Minneapolis Domestic Violence Experiment* (Washington, D.C.: The Police Foundation, 1984).

16. Darren K. Carlson, "Racial Profiling Seen as Pervasive, Unjust," *The Gallup Organization* (July 20, 2004).

17. Matthew R. Durose, Erica L. Smith, and Patrick A. Langan, "Contacts between the Police and the Public, 2005," U.S. Department of Justice, Bureau of Justice Statistics Special Report (Washington, D.C.: GPO, April 2007) at www.ojp.usdoj.gov/bjs/pub/pdf/cpp05.pdf.

18. Jeff Kunerth and Pedro Ruz Gutierrez, "Is It Racial Profiling? A Matter of Perception," *The Orlando Sentinel* (October 10, 2006), p. A7.

19. Steve Lackmeyer and Ken Raymond, "City Leaders Balk at Ban on Police Profiling," *The Oklahoman* (June 3, 2000).

20. Alex Johnson, "Fear and Loathing on the Job," MSNBC (September 4, 2000).

21. NIOSH, "Stress at Work," www.cdc.gov/niosh/stresswk.html.

22. The Word Spy at www.LOGOPHILIA.com/WordSpy/c.html.

23. "10% of Police Shootings Found to Be 'Suicide by Cop,'" *Criminal Justice Newsletter* 29, no. 17 (September 1, 1998), pp. 1–2.

24. Alan Feuer, "Drawing a Bead on a Baffling Endgame: Suicide by Cop," *The New York Times* (June 25, 1998).

25. NIOSH, op. cit.

26. Matthew J. Hickman, "Citizen Complaints about Police Use of Force," U.S. Department of Justice, *Bureau of Justice Statistics Special Report,* June 2006.

27. Matthew J. Hickman and Brian A. Reaves, *Local Police Departments, 2003,* op. cit., p. 23.

28. Durose et al., "Contacts between the Police and the Public, 2005," op. cit.

29. Michael Doyle, "Ruling Backs Cops on Chase Tactics," *The Orlando Sentinel* (May 1, 2007), p. A3.

30. Ibid., p. 25, Table 55.

31. Sue Lindsey, "Sheriff, 19 Other Indicted in Long-Running Corruption," *The Orlando Sentinel* (November 3, 2006), p. A9.

32. *Facts on File World News Digest,* Vol. 66, no. 3409, April 13, 2006.

33. Jeff Leen, Gail Epstein, and Lisa Getter, "Dade Cops Like to Plan Collars for Dollars," *The Orlando Sentinel* (July 20, 1997), p. B-1.

34. Malcolm Gladwell, "Ex-Officer: We Beat, Stole, Pillaged," *The Charlotte Observer* (September 30, 1993), p. 2A.

35. Knapp Commission, *Report on Police Corruption* (New York: George Braziller, 1972).

36. Ellwyn R. Stoddard, "The Informal 'Code' of Police Deviancy: A Group Approach to Blue-Coat Crime," *Journal of Criminal Law, Criminology, and Police Science* 59 (1968), p. 204.

37. Candace McCloy, "Lawsuits against Police: What Impact Do They Have?" *Criminal Law Bulletin* 20 (1984), pp. 49–56.

Chapter 8

1. Administrative Office of the U.S. Courts, Federal Judiciary website, "Federal Judicial Vacancies" at www.uscourts.gov/judicialvac.html.

2. Administrative Office of the U.S. Courts, Federal Judiciary website, "Judicial Compensation" at www.uscourts.gov/salarychart.pdf (accessed November 30, 2008).

3. Supreme Court of the United States, "Chief Justice's Year-End Reports on the Federal Judiciary: 2008 Year-End Report," www.supremecourtus.gov/publicinfo/year-end/2008year-endreport.pdf (accessed January 11, 2009).

4. Ibid.

5. Administrative Office of the U.S. Courts, Federal Judiciary website, "About the U.S. Courts," at www.uscourts.gov.

6. Supreme Court of the United States, "Chief Justice's Year-End Reports on the Federal Judiciary: 2008 Year-End Report," op. cit.

7. Administrative Office of the U.S. Courts, Federal Judiciary website, "United States Courts of Appeals" at www.uscourts.gov/courtsofappeals.html.

8. Ibid.

9. "Federal Judicial Vacancies," op. cit.; "Judicial Compensation," op. cit.

10. "Federal Judicial Vacancies," op. cit.

11. "Judicial Compensation," op. cit.

12. Supreme Court of the United States, "Chief Justice's Year-End Reports on the Federal Judiciary: 2008 Year-End Report," op. cit.

13. Material on the state courts is based on information from the following sources: Richard Y. Schauffler, Robert C. LaFountain, Neal B. Kauder, and Shauna M. Strickland, *Examining the Work of State Courts, 2004. A National Perspective from the Court Statistics*

Project (Williamsburg, VA: National Center for State Courts, 2005); David B. Rottman, Carol R. Flango, Melissa T. Cantrell, Randall Hansen, Neil LaFountain, *State Court Organization 1998,* U.S. Department of Justice, Bureau of Justice Statistics (Washington, D.C.: GPO, June 2000); David W. Neubauer, *America's Courts and the Criminal Justice System,* 4th ed. (Pacific Grove, CA: Brooks/Cole, 1992); Christopher Smith, *Courts, Politics, and the Judicial Process* (Chicago: Nelson-Hall, 1993); N. Gary Holten and Lawson L. Lamar, *The Criminal Courts: Structures, Personnel, and Processes* (New York: McGraw-Hill, 1991); Lawrence Baum, *American Courts,* 3rd ed. (Boston: Houghton Mifflin, 1994). U.S. Department of Justice, Bureau of Justice Statistics, *Report to the Nation on Crime and Justice,* 2nd ed. (Washington, D.C.: GPO, 1988); H. Ted Rubin, *The Courts: Fulcrum of the Justice System* (Santa Monica, CA: Goodyear, 1976); James Eisenstein, Roy Flemming, and Peter Nadulli, *The Contours of Justice: Communities and Their Courts* (Boston: Little, Brown, 1988); Malcolm Feeley, *The Process Is the Punishment: Handling Cases in Lower Criminal Court* (New York: Russell Sage, 1979); Harry P. Stumpf and John H. Culver, *The Politics of State Courts* (New York: Longman, 1992); Paul Wice, *Chaos in the Courthouse: The Inner Workings of the Urban Criminal Courts* (New York: Praeger, 1985).

14. Unless indicated otherwise, material about specialty courts is from C. West Huddleston, III, Douglas B. Marlowe, and Rachel Casebolt, *Painting the Current Picture: A National Report Card on Drug Courts and Other Problem Solving Court Programs in the United States,* Vol. 2, No. 1 (Rockville, MD: National Drug Court Institute, May 2008); C. West Huddleston, III, Karen Freeman-Wilson, Douglas B. Marlowe, and Aaron Roussell, *Painting the Current Picture: A National Report Card on Drug Courts and Other Problem Solving Court Programs in the United States,* Vol. 1, No. 2 (Rockville, MD: National Drug Court Institute, May 2005); "Drug Courts: Overview of Growth, Characteristics, and Results," GAO/GGD-97-106, www.ncjrs.org/txtfiles/D.C.ourts.txt, July 31, 1997; Rottman et al., op. cit., p. 207.

15. John Wolfson and Sherri M. Owens, "Few Pay Back What They Took from Crime Victims," *The Orlando Sentinel* (February 23, 2003), p. B1.

16. Judith S. Kaye, "Making the Case for Hands-On Courts," *Newsweek* (October 11, 1999), p. 13.

17. Maya Bell, "Mentally Ill Get Court of Their Own—and Help," *The Orlando Sentinel* (July 13, 1997), p. A-1.

18. National Center for State Courts, "Appellate Court: Structure, Jurisdiction and Process," at www.ncsconline.org/WC/CourTopics/FAQs.asp?topic=AppCts (accessed November 30, 2008).

19. Ibid. at www.ncsconline.org/WC/CourTopics/FAQs.asp?topic=AppCts#FAQ159 (accessed November 30, 2008).

20. Ibid.

21. Rubin, op. cit.

22. In addition to the other sources cited, material on the key actors in the court process is from Neubauer, op.

cit.; David W. Neubauer, *Judicial Process: Law, Courts and Politics in the United States* (Pacific Grove, CA: Brooks/Cole, 1991); Smith, op. cit.; Holten and Lamar, op. cit.; Baum, op. cit.

23. Material about prosecutors is also taken from David Heilbroner, *Rough Justice: Days and Nights of a Young D.A.* (New York: Pantheon, 1990).

24. See, for example, Matthew R. Durose, "State Court Sentencing of Convicted Felons 2004—Statistical Tables," U.S. Department of Justice, Bureau of Justice Statistics at www.ojp.usdoj.gov/bjs/pub/html/scscf04/tables/scs04401tab.htm (accessed November 30, 2008).

25. Steven W. Perry, "Prosecutors in State Courts, 2005," U.S. Department of Justice, *Bureau of Justice Statistics Bulletin* (Washington, D.C.: GPO, July 2006).

26. Data in this section are from ibid.

27. In addition to the other sources cited, material on defense attorneys is from Elizabeth Loftus and E. Ketcham, *For the Defense* (New York: St. Martin's, 1991); Paul Wice, *Judges and Lawyers: The Human Side of Justice* (New York: Harper-Collins, 1991); Paul Wice, *Criminal Lawyers: An Endangered Species* (Newbury Park, CA: Sage, 1978); Seymour Wishman, *Confessions of a Criminal Lawyer* (New York: Penguin, 1982); Lisa J. McIntyre, *The Public Defender: The Practice of Law in the Shadows of Repute* (Chicago: University of Chicago Press, 1987).

28. Based on figures provided in C. Ronald Huff, Arye Rattner, and Edward Sagarin, "Guilty until Proven Innocent: Wrongful Conviction and Public Policy," *Crime and Delinquency* 32 (1986), pp. 518–544; U.S. Department of Justice, Federal Bureau of Investigation, *Crime in the United States,* 2004 at www.fbi.gov/ucr/cius_04/persons_arrested/index.html.

29. Information about indigent defense systems in 2005 is from The Spangenberg Group, "State and County Expenditures for Indigent Defense Services in Fiscal Year 2005," prepared for The American Bar Association, Bar Information Program (December 2006); The Spangenberg Group, "State Indigent Defense Commissions," prepared for the Bar Information Program upon Request of the Indigent Defense Advisory Group of the American Bar Association Standing Committee on Legal Aid and Indigent Defendants (October 2006). Both documents generously provided by Robert Spangenberg.

30. Bureau of Justice Statistics, "Indigent Defense Statistics," at www.ojp.usdoj.gov/bjs/id.htm.

31. Exodus 18:1–27.

32. In addition to the other sources cited, material on judges is from Paul Ryan, Allan Ashman, Bruce D. Sales, and Sandra Shane-DuBow, *American Trial Judges* (New York: Free Press, 1980); Robert Satter, *Doing Justice: A Trial Judge at Work* (New York: Simon & Schuster, 1990); Wice (1991), op. cit.; Wice (1985), op. cit.

33. Debbie Salamone and Gerald Shields, "Justice to ABA: Races Not Popularity Contests," *The Orlando Sentinel* (August 4, 1996), p. A-23.

34. Based on data from American Judicature Society, "Methods of Judicial Selection" at www.judicialselection.us/

judicial_selection/methods/selection_of_judges
.cfm?state= (accessed December 1, 2008).

35. In addition to the other sources cited, material on pretrial stages is from Neubauer (1992), op. cit.; Holten and Lamar, op. cit.

36. David C. Steelman, James E. McMillan, and John A. Goerdt, *Caseflow Management: The Heart of Court Management in the New Millennium* (Williamsburg, VA: National Center for State Courts, 2000).

37. G. Thomas Munsterman, Paula L. Hannaford, and G. Marc Whitehead (eds.), *Jury Trial Innovations* (Williamsburg, VA: National Center for State Courts, 1997).

38. Timothy R. Murphy, Paula L. Hannaford, Geneva Kay Loveland, and G. Thomas Munsterman, *Managing Notorious Cases* (Williamsburg, VA: National Center for State Courts, 1998).

39. Debbie Salamone Wickhan, "On the Run," *The Orlando Sentinel* (January 7, 2001), p. A-1.

40. Ibid.; Richard Willing, "Skipped Bail Is Taking Huge Bite," *USA Today* (10/13/2004) at www.usatoday .com/_news/nation/2004-10-13-bail-bonds_x.htm.

41. "Federal Grand Jury" at www.udayton.edu/~grandjur/index.htm.

42. In addition to the other sources cited, material on plea bargaining is from Neubauer (1992), op. cit.; Neubauer (1991), op. cit.; Holten and Lamar, op. cit.; Baum, op. cit.

43. In addition to the other sources cited, material on criminal trials is from Neubauer (1992), op. cit.; Neubauer (1991), op. cit.; Smith, op. cit.; Holten and Lamar, op. cit.

44. In addition to the other sources cited, material on juries is from Rottman et al., op. cit.; Holten and Lamar, op. cit.; Valerie P. Hans and Neil Vidmar, *Judging the Jury* (New York: Plenum, 1986); Harry Kalvan, Jr., and Hans Zeisel, *The American Jury* (Boston: Little, Brown, 1996); James P. Levine, *Juries and Politics* (Pacific Grove, CA: Brooks/Cole, 1992).

45. Paula Hannaford-Agor, "The Laborer Is Worthy of His Hire and Jurors Are Worthy of Their Jury Fees," *The Court Manager,* Vol. 2, No. 21, pp. 38–40 (2006) at www.ncsconline.org/Juries/JuryNews/JuryNewsCM21-2.pdf (accessed December 1, 2008).

46. "Just Under Three in Five Americans Believe Juries Can Be Fair and Impartial All or Most of the Time," The Harris Poll #9. January 21, 2008 at www.harrisinteractive.com/harris_poll/printerfriend/Index.asp?PID=861; C. Flango, A. McDowell, C. Campbell, and N. Kauder, *Future Trends in State Courts 2008* (Williamsburg, VA: National Center for State Courts, 2008), p. 3.

47. In addition to the other sources cited, material on the trial process is from Satter (1990), op. cit.

48. Cited in Scott E. Sundby, *A Life and Death Decision: A Jury Weighs the Death Penalty* (New York: Palgrave Macmillan, 2005), p. 154.

49. Ibid.

50. Ibid.

51. Ibid., pp. 205–206, n. 17.

52. *Examining the Work of State Courts, 2004,* op. cit.; Jeffrey Rosen, "One Angry Woman: Why Are Hung Juries on the Rise?" *The New Yorker* (February 24 & March 3, 1997), p. 55.

Chapter 9

1. In addition to the other sources cited, material on sentencing and appeals is from David W. Neubauer, *America's Courts and the Criminal Justice System,* 7th ed. (Belmont, CA: Wadsworth, 2002); Christopher Smith, *Courts, Politics, and the Judicial Process* (Chicago: Nelson-Hall, 1993); N. Gary Holten and Lawson L. Lamar, *The Criminal Courts: Structures, Personnel, and Processes* (New York: McGraw-Hill, 1991); Lawrence Baum, *American Courts,* 3rd ed. (Boston: Houghton Mifflin, 1994); David Garland, *Punishment and Modern Society: A Study in Social Theory* (Chicago: Univ. of Chicago Press, 1990); Paul Wice, *Chaos in the Courthouse: The Inner Workings of the Urban Criminal Courts* (New York: Praeger, 1985); John Paul Ryan, Allan Ashman, Bruce D. Sales, and Sandra Shane-DuBow, *American Trial Judges* (New York: Free Press, 1980); Robert Satter, *Doing Justice: A Trial Judge at Work* (New York: Simon & Schuster, 1990); Herbert Packer, *The Limits of the Criminal Sanction* (Stanford, CA: Stanford University Press, 1968).

2. Lauren E. Glaze and Thomas P. Bonczar, Probation and Parole in the United States, 2006, U.S. Department of Justice, *Bureau of Justice Statistics Bulletin* (Washington, D.C.: GPO, December 2007, revised July 2008), p. 6 at www.ojp.usdoj.gov/bjs/pub/pdf/ppus06 .pdf (accessed December 3, 2008).

3. Robert Carter, "Determinate Sentences," pp. 147–149, in M. D. McShane and F. P. Williams III (eds.), *Encyclopedia of American Prisons* (New York: Garland, 1996), p. 148.

4. Calculated from Matthew R. Durose and Patrick A. Langan, "Felony Sentences in State Courts, 2002," U.S. Department of Justice, *Bureau of Justice Statistics Bulletin* (Washington, D.C.: GPO, 2004), p. 5, Table 4.

5. *American Correctional Association 2008 Directory: Adult and Juvenile Correctional Departments, Institutions, Agencies and Probation and Parole Authorities* (Lanham, MD: American Correctional Association, 2008), p. 13; *American Correctional Association 2006 Directory: Adult and Juvenile Correctional Departments, Institutions, Agencies and Probation and Parole Authorities* (Lanham, MD: American Correctional Association, 2006), p. 15.

6. "Sentence Disparity in New York: The Response of Forty-One Judges," *The New York Times* (March 30, 1979), p. B3.

7. See Robert M. Bohm, "Retribution and Capital Punishment: Toward a Better Understanding of Death Penalty Opinion," *Journal of Criminal Justice* 20 (1992), pp. 227–235.

8. Michael Tonry, "Crime and Human Rights—How Political Paranoia, Protestant Fundamentalism, and Constitutional Obsolescence Combined to Devastate Black America: The American Society of Criminology 2007 Presidential Address," *Criminology* 46 (2008), p. 7.

9. Ibid.

10. "New Directions from the Field: Victims' Rights and Services for the 21st Century," U.S. Department of Justice, Office for Victims of Crime, *OVC Bulletin* (Washington, D.C.: GPO, December 2004).

11. *Report to the Nation 2003: Fiscal Years 2001 and 2002,* U.S. Department of Justice, Office for Victims of Crime; *Report to the Nation 2005: Fiscal Years 2003 and 2004,* U.S. Department of Justice, Office for Victims of Crime, www.ojp.usdoj.gov/ovc/welcovc/reporttonation2005/welcome.html, www.ojp.usdoj.gov/ovc/welcovc/reporttonation2003/_welcome.html.

12. *1996 Victims' Rights Sourcebook: A Compilation and Comparison of Victims' Rights Laws,* The National Center for Victims of Crime at www.ncvc.org/resources/reports/sourcebook; VictimLaw, "About Victim Rights" at www.victimlaw.info/victimlaw/pages/victimsRight.jsp (accessed December 3, 2008).

13. "New Directions from the Field: Victims' Rights and Services for the 21st Century," op. cit.

14. "Restorative Justice: An Interview with Visiting Fellow Thomas Quinn," *National Institute of Justice Journal,* No. 235 (March 1998), p. 10.

15. "Ordering Restitution to the Crime Victim," U.S. Department of Justice, Office for Victims of Crime, *Legal Series Bulletin #6* (Washington, D.C.: GPO, November 2002).

16. Unless indicated otherwise, material about the death penalty is from Robert M. Bohm, *Deathquest III: An Introduction to the Theory and Practice of Capital Punishment in the United States,* 3rd ed. (Cincinnati, OH: Anderson, 2007); James R. Acker, Robert M. Bohm, and Charles S. Lanier (eds.), *America's Experiment with Capital Punishment: Reflections on the Past, Present, and Future of the Ultimate Penal Sanction,* 2nd ed. (Durham, NC: Carolina Academic Press, 2003); Hugo Alan Bedau, *The Death Penalty in America; Current Controversies* (New York: Oxford University Press, 1997); Hugo Adam Bedau (ed.), *The Death Penalty in America,* 3rd ed. (London: Oxford University Press, 1982); William J. Bowers, with Glenn L. Pierce and John McDevitt, *Legal Homicide: Death as Punishment in America, 1864–1982* (Boston: Northeastern University Press, 1984); Raymond Paternoster, *Capital Punishment in America* (New York: Lexington, 1991); Robert M. Bohm, "Humanism and the Death Penalty, with Special Emphasis on the Post-*Furman* Experience," *Justice Quarterly* 6 (1989), pp. 173–195; Victoria Schneider and John Ortiz Smykla, "A Summary Analysis of Executions in the United States, 1608–1987: The Espy File," in R. M. Bohm (ed.), *The Death Penalty in America: Current Research* (Cincinnati: Anderson, 1991), pp. 1–19.

17. Death Penalty Information Center at www.deathpenaltyinfo.org.

18. Death Penalty Information Center, op. cit.; Amnesty International at web.amnesty.org/library/Index/ENGACT500072002? open&of=ENG-392.

19. Death Penalty Information Center, op. cit.

20. Tracy L. Snell, *Capital Punishment, 2005,* U.S. Department of Justice, *Bureau of Justice Statistics Bulletin* (Washington, D.C.: GPO, December 2006), p. 3, www.ojp.usdoj.gov/bjs/_abstract/cp05.htm.

21. Ibid., p. 16, Appendix table 4.

22. Paternoster, op. cit., pp. 208–209; Barry Scheck, Peter Neufeld, and Jim Dwyer, *Actual Innocence: When Justice Goes Wrong and How to Make It Right* (New York: Penguin Putnam, 2001); James S. Liebman, Jeffrey Fagan, and Valerie West, "A Broken System: Error Rates in Capital Cases, 1973–1995," The Justice Project at www.justice.policy.net/jpreport.html.

23. Snell, op. cit., p. 14, Appendix table 2.

24. Death Penalty Information Center, op. cit.

25. Ibid.; inmates who died in 2006 and 2007 from U.S. Department of Justice, Bureau of Justice Statistics, "Capital Punishment, 2007—Statistical Tables," Table 4 (last revised December 4, 2008) at www.ojp.usdoj.gov/bjs/pub/html/cp/2007/tables/cp07st04.htm and "Capital Punishment, 2006—Statistical Tables," Table 4 (last revised December 17, 2007) at www.ojp.usdoj.gov/bjs/pub/html/cp/2006/tables/cp06st04.htm (both accessed January 16, 2009).

26. Ibid.

27. Calculated from data in ibid.

28. Ibid.

29. Gallup Poll, May 19, 2005 (accessed through http://web.lexis-nexis.com).

30. Death Penalty Information Center, op. cit.

31. The survey was conducted in August and September of 2006. Originally, 193 religious organizations in the United States were identified from a listing provided by the Hartford Institute for Religion Research at http://hirr.hartsem.edu/org/faith_denominations_home pages.html. For various reasons, 67 of the organizations did not respond (22 of the organizations had invalid contact information), leaving 126 organizations that did respond (a 65% response rate, or a 74% response rate if the organizations with invalid contact information are excluded). My thanks to Gavin Lee for conducting the survey.

32. "The Shadow over America," *Newsweek* (May 29, 2000), p. 27.

33. Death Penalty Information Center, op. cit.

34. Bohm, *Deathquest III,* op. cit.

35. *Callins* v. *Collins,* 510 U.S. 1141 (1994).

36. Robert M. Bohm, Louise J. Clark, and Adrian F. Aveni, "Knowledge and Death Penalty Opinion: A Test of the Marshall Hypotheses," *Journal of Research in Crime and Delinquency* 28 (1991), pp. 360–387; Robert M. Bohm and Ronald E. Vogel, "A Comparison of Factors Associated with Uninformed and Informed Death Penalty Opinions," *Journal of Criminal Justice* 23 (1994), pp. 125–143; Robert M. Bohm, Ronald E. Vogel, and Albert A. Maisto, "Knowledge and Death Penalty Opinion: A Panel Study," *Journal of Criminal Justice* 21 (1993), pp. 29–45; Robert M. Bohm and Brenda L. Vogel, "More Than Ten Years After: The Long-Term Stability of Informed Death Penalty Opinions," *Journal of Criminal Justice* 32 (2004), pp. 307–327.

37. Jeffrey M. Jones, "Understanding Americans' Support for the Death Penalty," The Gallup Organization, Gallup Poll Tuesday *Briefing,* June 3, 2003.

38. Bohm, "Retribution and Capital Punishment," op. cit.; see also Bohm and Vogel, "A Comparison of Factors Associated with Uninformed and Informed Death Penalty Opinions," op. cit.

Chapter 10

1. See Robert Johnson, *Hard Time: Understanding and Reforming the Prison* (Monterey, CA: Brooks/Cole, 1987).
2. Michel Foucault, *Discipline and Punish: The Birth of the Prison* (New York: Pantheon, 1978).
3. See Graeme Newman, *The Punishment Response* (Albany, NY: Harrow and Heston, 1985).
4. Todd R. Clear and George F. Cole, *American Corrections,* 3rd ed. (Belmont, CA: Wadsworth, 1994).
5. Graeme Newman and Pietro Marongiu, "Penological Reform and the Myth of Beccaria," *Criminology* 28 (1990), pp. 325–346.
6. Ibid.
7. Clear and Cole, op. cit.
8. David J. Rothman, *The Discovery of the Asylum: Social Order and Disorder in the New Republic* (Boston: Little, Brown, 1971).
9. See Paul Takagi, "The Walnut Street Jail: A Penal Reform to Centralize the Powers of the State," *Federal Probation* (December 1975), pp. 18–26.
10. Rothman, op. cit.
11. Clear and Cole, op. cit.
12. Nicole Hahn Rafter, "Gender and Justice: The Equal Protection Issue," in L. Goodstein and D. L. MacKenzie (eds.), *The American Prison: Issues in Research and Policy* (New York: Plenum, 1989), pp. 89–109; see Nicole Hahn Rafter, *Partial Justice: Women in State Prisons, 1800–1935* (Boston: Northeastern University Press, 1985).
13. John Irwin, *Prisons in Turmoil* (Boston: Little, Brown, 1980).
14. Ibid., p. 3.
15. See Robert Martinson, "What Works? Questions and Answers about Prison Reform," *The Public Interest* 42 (1974), pp. 22–54; see also The American Friends Service Committee, *Struggle for Justice: A Report on Crime and Justice in America* (New York: Hill & Wang, 1971).
16. Heather C. West and William J. Sabol. "Prisoners in 2007," U.S. Department of Justice, Bureau of Justice Statistics Bulletin (Washington, D.C.: GPO, December 2008), p. 23, Appendix table 13 at www.ojp.usdoj.gov/bjs/pub/pdf/p07.pdf (accessed December 13, 2008).
17. *American Correctional Association 2008 Directory: Adult and Juvenile Correctional Departments, Institutions, Agencies and Probation and Parole Authorities* (Lanham, MD: American Correctional Association, 2008), pp. 26–27 (Data missing from Arizona, Connecticut, Delaware, Florida, Idaho, Louisiana, Nevada, South Dakota, Utah, and Washington); Federal Bureau of Prisons at www.bop.gov/; Reason Foundation, "Public Safety," Annual Privatization Report 2008 at www.reason.org/apr2008/public_safety.pdf (accessed January 14, 2007); James J.

Stephan and Jennifer C. Karberg, "Census of State and Federal Correctional Facilities, 2000," U.S. Department of Justice, Bureau of Justice Statistics (Washington, D.C.: GPO, August 2003).
18. Corrections Corporation of America website at www.correctionscorp.com/about/ (accessed December 9, 2008); The GEO Group, Inc. website at www.thegeogroupinc.com/facts.asp (accessed December 9, 2008); The Cornell Companies website at www.cornellcompanies.com/facilities.cfm (accessed December 9, 2008).
19. Meredith Kolodner, "Private Prisons Expect a Boom: Immigration Enforcement to Benefit Detention Companies" (July 26, 2006) at http:newsinitiative.org/story/2006/07/26/private_prisons_expect_a_boom.
20. W. Thomas, "Private Adult Correctional Facility Census: A 'Real-Time' Statistical Profile," www.crim.ufl.edu/pcp, September 4, 2001; James Austin and Gary Coventry, *Emerging Issues on Privatized Prisons,* U.S. Department of Justice, Bureau of Justice Statistics (Washington, D.C.: GPO, February 2001).
21. Doris Layton MacKenzie and James W. Shaw, "The Impact of Shock Incarceration on Technical Violations and New Criminal Activities," *Justice Quarterly* 10 (1993), pp. 463–487; also see Doris Layton MacKenzie and Claire Souryal, *Multisite Evaluation of Shock Incarceration,* U.S. Department of Justice, National Institute of Justice, November 1994; Dale Parent, "Correctional Boot Camps: Lessons from a Decade of Research," U.S. Department of Justice, National Institute of Justice, June 2003; David B. Wilson, Doris Layton MacKenzie, and Fawn Ngo Mitchell, "Effects of Correctional Boot Camps on Offending" (2005), A Campbell Collaboration systematic review at www.aic.gov.au/campbellcj/reviews/titles.html (accessed December 10, 2008).
22. Human Rights Watch World Report 1998: United States, www.hrw.org/worldreport/Back.htm; personal communication.
23. *American Correctional Association 2008 Directory,* op. cit., calculated from data on pp. 24–25 and the websites of all state departments of corrections for which information was not available in the 2008 Directory (accessed December 10, 2008); The Federal Bureau of Prisons, "About the Bureau of Prisons," at www.bop.gov/about/index.jsp (accessed December 10, 2008).
24. "Prisoners in 1992," United States Department of Justice, *Bureau of Justice Statistics Bulletin* (Washington, D.C.: GPO, May 1993).
25. West and Sabol, "Prisoners in 2007," op. cit.
26. Ibid.
27. Ibid.
28. Ibid., p. 7, Table 10 and p. 23, Appendix table 13.
29. Todd D. Minton and William J. Sabol, "Jail Inmates at Midyear 2008—Statistical Tables," U.S. Department of Justice, *Bureau of Justice Statistics Bulletin,* March 2009, p. 2, Table 1 at www.ojp.usdoj.gov/bjs/pub/pdf/jim08st.pdf.
30. Ibid., p. 8, Table 11.
31. West and Sabol, "Prisoners in 2007," op. cit., calculated from data on p. 18, Appendix table 6.

32. Minton and Sabol, "Jail Inmates at Midyear 2008—Statistical Tables," op. cit., calculated from data on p. 2, Table 1.

33. Adam Liptak, "Inmate Count in U.S. Dwarfs other Nations'," *The New York Times* (April 23, 2008), p. A1.

34. James P. Lynch, "A Cross National Comparison of the Length of Custodial Sentences for Serious Crimes," *Justice Quarterly* 10 (1993), pp. 639–660.

35. Liptak, op. cit.

36. *American Correctional Association 2008 Directory,* op. cit., calculated from data on pp. 15, 16, and 17. (States with missing or questionable data were augmented by examining their correctional budgets on their Department of Corrections websites; for some states, relevant data could not be found).

37. Ibid., p. 45.

38. Ibid., pp. 15, 16, and 17.

39. West and Sabol, "Prisoners in 2007," op. cit., p. 25, Appendix table 15.

40. Nils Christie, *Crime Control as Industry: Toward Gulags Western Style?* (New York: Routledge, 1993).

41. Michael Tonry, "Crime and Human Rights—How Political Paranoia, Protestant Fundamentalism, and Constitutional Obsolescence Combined to Devastate Black America: The American Society of Criminology 2007 Presidential Address," *Criminology* 46 (2008), p. 10.

42. Franklin E. Zimring, "The Great American Lockup," *Washington Post,* National Weekly Edition (March 1991), pp. 4–10.

43. West and Sabol, "Prisoners in 2007," op. cit., calculated from data on p. 1, Table 1.

44. Ibid., p. 4, Table 6.

45. See, for example, John Kramer and Darrell Steffensmeir, "Race and Imprisonment Decisions," *Sociological Quarterly* 34 (1993), pp. 357–376; Ronald L. Akers, *Criminological Theories: Introduction and Evaluation,* 2nd ed. (Los Angeles: Roxbury, 1997). For different views, see Edmund F. McGarrell, "Institutional Theory and the Stability of a Conflict Model of the Incarceration Rate," *Justice Quarterly* 10 (1993), pp. 7–28; Cassia Spohn and Jerry Cederblom, "Race and Disparities in Sentencing: A Test of the Liberation Hypothesis," *Justice Quarterly* 8 (1991), pp. 305–327.

46. West and Sabol, "Prisoners in 2007," op. cit., calculated from data on p. 22, Appendix table 12.

47. Center for Children of Incarcerated Parents: CCIP Data Sheet 3a, www.eccip.org/_publication.html; Christopher J. Mumola, "Incarcerated Parents and Their Children," U.S. Department of Justice, *Bureau of Justice Special Report* (Washington, D.C.: GPO, August 2000).

48. The Federal Bureau of Prisons, "Mission Statement," at www.bop.gov.

49. The Federal Bureau of Prisons, "The Bureau in Brief," op. cit.

50. Paige M. Harrison and Jennifer C. Karberg, "Prison and Jail Inmates at Midyear 2002," U.S. Department of Justice, *Bureau of Justice Statistics Bulletin* (Washington, D.C.: GPO, April 2003); West and Sabol, "Prisoners in 2007," op. cit., p. 2, Table 2; The Federal Bureau of Prisons, "Quick Facts about the Bureau of Prisons" at www.bop.gov/about/facts.jsp (accessed December 12, 2008).

51. American Correctional Association 2008 Directory, op. cit. (calculated from data on pp. 52–53; data were not available for Arizona, Connecticut, Delaware, Georgia, Hawaii, Illinois, Kentucky, Michigan, Mississippi, Nevada, South Dakota, Utah, and West Virginia).

52. "Prisons Favoring Electronic Security," *The Orlando Sentinel* (February 4, 2002), p. C3.

53. Francis X. Clines, "A Futuristic Prison Awaits the Hard Core 400" *The New York Times,* National Ed. (October 17, 1994), p. 1A.

54. Daniel P. Mears and Jamie Watson, "Towards a Fair and Balanced Assessment of Supermax Prisons," *Justice Quarterly* 23 (2006), pp. 232–270; Chase Riveland, "Supermax Prisons: Overview and General Considerations," U.S. Department of Justice, *National Institute of Corrections,* January 1999.

55. Material on Camp Delta is from Andrew Selsky and Jennifer Loven, "3 Gitmo Detainees Commit Suicide, Officials Report," *The Orlando Sentinel* (June 11, 2006), p. A12; "Profile: Guantánamo Bay," BBC News at http://news.bbc.co.uk/1/hi/world/americas/4720962.stm (June 29, 2006); Matthew Hay Brown, "Detainees Await an Unknown Fate," *The Orlando Sentinel* (July 20, 2003), p. A1; CBS News.com, "Camp Delta: Guantánamo Bay (June 23, 2004), www._cbsnews.com/stories/2003/09/16/60II/main573616.shtml; Ben Fox, "Assaults on Guards at Gitmo Drop 60%," *The Orlando Sentinel* (September 1, 2007), p. A5; Andrew O. Selsky, "U.S. Reveals Top-Secret al-Qaeda Jail at Gitmo," *The Orlando Sentinel* (February 7, 2008), p. A11.

56. Calculated from *Sourcebook of Criminal Justice Statistics 2003,* p. 503, Table 6.31 at www.albany.edu/sourcebook/pdf/t631.pdf (accessed December 14, 2008); West and Sabol, "Prisoners in 2007," op. cit., p. 3, Table 5.

57. West and Sabol, "Prisoners in 2007," ibid., p. 22, Appendix table 11.

58. *American Correctional Association 2008 Directory,* op. cit., calculated from data on p. 24–25.

59. Ibid.

60. John Ortiz Smykla and Jimmy J. Williams, "Co-Corrections in the United States, 1970–1990: Two Decades of Disadvantages for Women Prisoners," *Women and Criminal Justice* 8 (1996), pp. 61–76.

61. Harrison and Beck, "Prison and Jail Inmates at Midyear 2004," op. cit., p. 7; Harrison and Beck, "Prison and Jail Inmates at Midyear 2005," op. cit., p. 7.

62. Minton and Sabol, "Jail Inmates at Midyear 2008—Statistical Tables," op. cit.

63. Ibid.

64. John Irwin, *The Jail: Managing the Underclass in American Society* (Berkeley and Los Angeles: University of California Press, 1985).

65. John A. Backstrand, Don C. Gibbons, and Joseph F. Jones, "Who Is in Jail: An Examination of the Rabble

Hypothesis," *Crime and Delinquency* 38 (1992), pp. 219–229.

66. See Dale K. Sechrest and William C. Collins, *Jail Management and Liability Issues* (Miami: Coral Gables Publishing, 1989).

67. Unless indicated otherwise, information in this section on jail design is from Frank Schmalleger and John Ortiz Smykla, *Corrections in the 21st Century,* 3rd ed. (Columbus, OH: Glencoe/McGraw-Hill, 2007), pp. 220–223; *Podular, Direct Supervision Jails: Information Packet,* U.S. Department of Justice, National Institute of Corrections, Jails Division (January 1993) at www.nicic.org/resources/topics/ DirectSupervisionJails.aspx; Steve Fishback, "The Design of the New Anchorage Jail," *Alaska Justice Forum* 18, no. 3 (Fall 2001) at www.uaa.alaska.edu/ just/forum/f183fa01/c_anchjail.html.

68. Doris Bloodsworth, "Jail Ready to Debut Visitation by Video," *The Orlando Sentinel* (January 5, 2003), p. B1.

69. Mary Stohr-Gillman, Linda Zupan, Craig Curtis, Ben Menke, and Nicholas Lourich, "The Development of a Behavioral-Based Performance Appraisal System," *American Jails* 5 (1992), pp. 10–16.

70. Jeffrey D. Senese, "Evaluating Jail Reform: A Comparative Analysis of Popular/Direct and Linear Jail Inmate Infractions," *Journal of Criminal Justice* 25 (1997), pp. 61–73; Linda L. Zupan, *Jails: Reform and the New Generation Philosophy* (Cincinnati: Anderson, 1991); Schmalleger and Smykla, op. cit., p. 98; Fishback, op. cit.

71. *Direct Supervision Jails: 2006 Sourcebook,* U.S. Department of Justice, National Institute of Corrections (September 2006) at http://nicic.org/Library/021968.

72. James W. Marquart and Ben M. Crouch, "Coopting the Kept: Using Inmates for Social Control in a Southern Prison," in M. K. Carlie and K. I. Minor (eds.), *Prisons around the World: Studies in International Penology* (Dubuque, IA: Wm. C. Brown, 1992), pp. 124–138.

73. "Prison Rule Violators," United States Department of Justice, *Bureau of Justice Statistics Special Report* (Washington, D.C.: GPO, December 1989).

74. Amy L. Edwards, "Crackers and Water: Sheriff Cooks Up $161,000 in Meal Cuts," *The Orlando Sentinel* (July 10, 2008), p. A1.

75. Jay Reeves, "1.75 a Day Still Feeds Inmates in Alabama," *The Orlando Sentinel* (May 17, 2008), p. A9.

76. "Virginia Opens Special Prison for Aging Inmates," *The Dallas Morning News* (July 3, 1999), www .dallasnews.com/national/0703nat4prison.html, December 21, 2000.

77. Harrison and Beck, "Prisoners in 2005," op. cit., p. 8, Table 10; Kathleen Maguire, Ann L. Pastore, and Timothy J. Flanagan, *Sourcebook of Criminal Justice Statistics—1992,* U.S. Department of Justice, Bureau of Justice Statistics (Washington, D.C.: GPO, 1993), pp. 622 and 634, Tables 6.69 and 6.82; "Longer Sentences Mean Older Prisoners and New Set of Problems," *The Orlando Sentinel* (September 1, 1996), p. A-15.

78. Most of the information on the mentally ill is from Doris J. James and Lauren E. Glaze, "Mental Health Problems of Prison and Jail Inmates," U.S. Department of Justice, *Bureau of Justice Statistics Special Report* (Washington, D.C.: GPO, September 2006); "Fact Sheet: Criminalization of Americans with Severe Mental Illnesses," Treatment Advocacy Center at www.psychlaws.org/GeneralResources/Fact3.htm; Human Rights Watch, "Ill-Equipped: U.S. Prisons and Offenders with Mental Illness," www.hrw.org/ _reports/2003/usa1003/.

79. Doris J. James and Lauren E. Glaze, "Mental Health Problems of Prison and Jail Inmates," ibid., p. 9, Table 14.

80. Information in this section about HIV and AIDS is from Laura Maruschak, "HIV in Prisons, 2006," "U.S. Department of Justice, Bureau of Justice Statistics at www.ojp.usdoj.gov/bjs/pub/html/hivp/2006/hivp06 .htm (accessed December 13, 2008).

81. Phuong Le, "Prisons Go Green as Inmates Pitch In," *The Orlando Sentinel* (November 2, 2008), A10.

82. National Institute for Literacy, "FACT SHEET: Corrections Education," January 2001, at www.nifl.gov.

83. For reference, see Anthony Walsh, *Understanding, Assessing, and Counseling the Criminal Justice Client* (Pacific Grove, CA: Brooks/Cole, 1988); also see Patricia van Voorhis, Michael Braswell, and David Lester, *Correctional Counseling and Rehabilitation,* 4th ed. (Cincinnati: Anderson, 2000).

84. Ted Palmer, *A Profile of Correctional Effectiveness and New Directions for Research* (Albany, NY: State University of New York Press, 1994).

85. Johnson, op. cit.

Chapter 11

1. Erving Goffman, *Asylums* (New York: Doubleday, 1961), p. xiii.

2. James B. Jacobs, *Stateville: The Penitentiary in Mass Society* (Chicago: University of Chicago Press, 1977).

3. See Donald Clemmer, *The Prison Community* (New York: Holt, Rinehart & Winston, 1940); Gresham M. Sykes, *The Society of Captives: A Study of a Maximum Security Prison* (Princeton, NJ: Princeton University Press, 1958).

4. Clemmer, op. cit.

5. John Irwin and Donald R. Cressey, "Thieves, Convicts, and the Inmate Culture," *Social Problems* 10 (1962), pp. 142–155. Also see Clarence Schrag, "Some Foundations for a Theory of Corrections," in D. R. Cressey (ed.), *The Prison: Studies in Institutional Organization and Change* (New York: Holt, Rinehart & Winston, 1961), pp. 30–35.

6. See Richard Hawkins and Geoffrey P. Alpert, *American Prison Systems: Punishment and Justice* (Englewood Cliffs, NJ: Prentice Hall, 1989); John Irwin, *Prisons in Turmoil* (Boston: Little, Brown, 1980). Also see Leo Carroll, *Hacks, Blacks, and Cons: Race Relations in a Maximum Security Prison* (Lexington, MA: Heath, 1974); Geoffrey Hunt, Stephanie Riegel, Tomas Morales, and Dan Waldorf, "Changes in Prison Culture: Prison Gangs and the Case of the 'Pepsi Generation,'" *Social Problems* 40 (1993), pp. 398–409; James B.

Jacobs, *New Perspectives on Prisons and Imprisonment* (Ithaca, NY: Cornell University Press, 1983).

7. U.S. Department of Justice, Bureau of Justice Statistics, Deaths in Custody Statistical Tables," State Prison Deaths, 2001–2006" at www.ojp.usdoj.gov/bjs/D.C.rp/tables/D.C.st06spt1.htm (accessed December 14, 2008); Correctional Peace Officers Foundation, "Fallen Officers 2000–2007" at www.cpof.org/page/page/3363284.htm (accessed December 14, 2008).

8. Allen J. Beck and Paige M. Harrison, "Sexual Victimization in State and Federal Prisons Reported by Inmates, 2007," U.S. Department of Justice, *Bureau of Justice Statistics Special Report* (Washington, D.C.: GPO, December 2007).

9. Lee Bowker, *Prison Victimization* (New York: Elsevier, 1980).

10. Tony Rizzo, "Prisons Seek to Jam Cell Phone Signals," *The Kansas City Star* (December 21, 2008), p. A1.

11. Ann Cordilia, *The Making of an Inmate: Prison as a Way of Life* (Cambridge, MA: Schenkman, 1983).

12. Goffman, op. cit., p. 14.

13. Hans Toch, *Living in Prison: The Ecology of Survival* (New York: Free Press, 1977).

14. Robert Johnson, *Hard Time: Understanding and Reforming the Prison* (Monterey, CA: Brooks/Cole, 1987).

15. Irwin, op. cit.

16. David Ward and Gene Kassebaum, "Homosexuality: A Model of Adaptation in a Prison for Women," *Social Problems* 12 (1964), pp. 159–177.

17. Joycelyn Pollock-Byrne, *Women, Prison, and Crime* (Pacific Grove, CA: Brooks/Cole, 1990).

18. Christopher J. Mumola, "Incarcerated Parents and Their Children," U.S. Department of Justice, *Bureau of Justice Statistics Special Report* (Washington, D.C.: GPO, August 2000), p. 2, Table 1 and p. 3, Table 4.

19. Phyllis Jo Baunach, *Mothers in Prison* (New Brunswick, NJ: Transaction Books, 1985).

20. Rose Giallombardo, *Society of Women: A Study of a Women's Prison* (New York: Wiley, 1966); Esther Heffernan, *Making It in Prison: The Square, the Cool, and the Life* (New York: Wiley, 1972); Alice M. Propper, *Prison Homosexuality* (Lexington, MA: Heath, 1981).

21. Propper, op. cit.

22. Giallombardo, op. cit.

23. David Ward and Gene Kassebaum, *Women's Prison: Sex and Social Structure* (Chicago: Aldine, 1965).

24. Heffernan, op. cit.; Schrag, op. cit.

25. Gordon Hawkins, *The Prison: Policy and Practice* (Chicago: University of Chicago Press, 1976), p. 85.

26. *American Correctional Association 2008 Directory: Adult and Juvenile Correctional Departments, Institutions, Agencies and Probation and Parole Authorities* (Lanham, MD: American Correctional Association, 2008), calculated from data on pp. 32–33 and 42–43. Data for Arizona, Connecticut, Idaho, Illinois, Kansas, Nevada, and Vermont were not provided by this source. They were obtained from each department's website or through personal communication. Data for Illinois and Kansas were for 2005.

27. Calculated from data in ibid., p. 42–44 (missing and suspect data were obtained and verified from each department's website. Also, information about the percentage of custody staff, the ratio of correctional officers to inmates, and the turnover rate for the Federal Bureau of Prisons was obtained through a Freedom of Information request (received March 13, 2007).

28. American Correctional Association, *Corrections Compendium,* May/June 2007, pp. 19–20, Table 2; Federal Bureau of Prisons, www.bop.gov/jobs/job_descriptions/correctional_officer.jsp. Starting salaries for the Federal Bureau of Prisons is from U.S. Office of Personnel Management, Salaries and Wages, 2008 Salary Tables and Related Information at www.opm.gov/oca/08tables/TXT/leotbl.txt (accessed December 16, 2008).

29. *American Correctional Association 2008 Directory,* op. cit., p. 44. Turnover rate data were not provided for Arkansas, California, Connecticut, Idaho, Illinois, Kansas, Maryland, Nevada, Ohio, Utah, and Vermont.

30. Hawkins and Alpert, op. cit.

31. Ibid.

32. Sykes, op. cit.

33. John D. Hewitt, Eric D. Poole, and Robert M. Regoli, "Self-Reported and Observed Rule-Breaking in Prison: A Look at Disciplinary Response," *Justice Quarterly* 3 (1984), pp. 437–447.

34. Hawkins and Alpert, op. cit.

35. Lucien X. Lombardo, *Guards Imprisoned: Correctional Officers at Work,* 2nd ed. (Cincinnati: Anderson, 1989); and see Johnson, op. cit.

36. Catherine Tsai, "Supermax Understaffed, Guards Say," *The Orlando Sentinel* (November 8, 2006), p. A12.

37. Barbara A. Owen, "Race and Gender Relations among Prison Workers," *Crime and Delinquency* 31 (1985), pp. 147–159.

38. American Correctional Association, *Corrections Compendium* (July/August 2008), p. 12–14.

39. *American Correctional Association 2008 Directory: Adult and Juvenile Correctional Departments, Institutions, Agencies and Probation and Parole Authorities* (Lanham, MD: American Correctional Association, 2008), pp. 989–994; personal communication with Idaho, Indiana, Oklahoma, and South Carolina Departments of Corrections (December 5, 2008).

40. Jacobs, op. cit., pp. 36–37.

41. "Appendix B: Text of the Prison Litigation Reform Act of 1995" at http://ojjdp.ncjrs.org/PUBS/walls/appen-b.html; The American Civil Liberties Union, "The Prison Litigation Reform Act (PLRA)," at www.aclu.org/prison/gen/14769res20031113.html.

42. Calculated from *Sourcebook of Criminal Justice Statistics* Online, Table 5.65, 2007 at www.albany.edu/sourcebook/pdf/t5652007.pdf; *Sourcebook of Criminal Justice Statistics* Online, Table 6.13, 2007 at www.albany.edu/sourcebook/pdf/t6132007.pdf.

43. *Wilson* v. *Seiter,* 111 S.Ct. 2321 (1991).

44. Hawkins and Alpert, op. cit.

45. "5 States Let Dogs Attack Inmates, Rights Group Says." *The Orlando Sentinel* (October 12, 2006), p. A9.

46. ACLU National Prison Project, "Your Rights Regarding Environmental Hazards and Toxic Materials" at www.aclu.org/prison/conditions/14661res20031114.html.

47. Lauren E. Glaze and Thomas P. Bonczar, "Probation and Parole in the United States, 2006," U.S. Department of Justice, *Bureau of Justice Statistics Bulletin* (Washington, D.C.: GPO, December 2007, revised July 2, 2008), p. 6.

48. Unless indicated otherwise, information about recidivism is from Patrick A. Langan and David J. Levin, "Recidivism of Prisoners Released in 1994," U.S. Department of Justice, *Bureau of Justice Statistics Special Report* (Washington, D.C.: GPO, June 2002). Also see Miles D. Harer, *Recidivism among Federal Prison Releasees in 1987: A Preliminary Report,* Federal Bureau of Prisons, Office of Research and Evaluation, December 9, 1993; "Recidivism of Prisoners Released in 1983," United States Department of Justice, *Bureau of Justice Statistics Special Report* (Washington, D.C.: GPO, April 1989); "Recidivism of Young Parolees," United States Department of Justice, *Bureau of Justice Statistics Special Report* (Washington, D.C.: GPO, May 1987).

49. "Recidivism of Prisoners Released in 1983," op. cit.

50. *American Correctional Association 2008 Directory,* op. cit., p. 64.

51. Ben M. Crouch, "Is Incarceration Really Worse? Analysis of Offenders' Preferences for Prison over Probation," *Justice Quarterly* 10 (1993), pp. 67–88.

52. Kenneth D. Tunnell, "Choosing Crime: Close Your Eyes and Take Your Chances," *Justice Quarterly* 7 (1990), pp. 673–690.

53. Robert Martinson, "What Works? Questions and Answers about Prison Reform," *The Public Interest* 42 (1974), pp. 22–54.

54. Lynne Goodstein, "Inmate Adjustment to Prison and the Transition to Community Life," in R. M. Carter, D. Glaser, and L. T. Wilkins (eds.), *Correctional Institutions,* 3rd ed. (New York: Harper & Row, 1985), pp. 285–302.

55. Francis T. Cullen and Paul Gendreau, "Assessing Correctional Rehabilitation: Policy, Practice, and Prospects," in U.S. Department of Justice, Office of Justice Programs, *Criminal Justice 2000,* vol. 3, at www.ojp.usdoj.gov/nij/criminal_justice2000/vol3_2000.html.

56. "Civil Disabilities of Convicted Felons: A State-by-State Survey," U.S. Department of Justice, Office of the Pardon Attorney, October 1996, at www.usdoj.gov/pardon/readingroom.htm; Kevin G. Buckler and Lawrence F. Travis III, "Reanalyzing the Prevalence and Social Context of Collateral Consequence Statutes," *Journal of Criminal Justice* 31 (2003), pp. 435–453.

Chapter 12

1. David E. Duffee, "Community Corrections: Its Presumed Characteristics and an Argument for a New Approach," in D. E. Duffee and E. F. McGarrell (eds.), *Community Corrections: A Community Field Approach* (Cincinnati: Anderson, 1990), pp. 1–41.

2. Patricia M. Harris, Todd R. Clear, and S. Christopher Baird, "Have Community Supervision Officers Changed Their Attitudes Toward Their Work?" *Justice Quarterly* 6 (1989), pp. 233–246; and see Robert T. Sigler, "Role Conflict for Adult Probation and Parole Officers: Fact or Myth," *Journal of Criminal Justice* 16 (1988), pp. 121–129.

3. Lauren E. Glaze and Thomas P. Bonczar, "Probation and Parole in the United States, 2007 Statistical Tables," U.S. Department of Justice, *Bureau of Justice Statistics* (Washington, D.C.: GPO, December 2008), Table 4, www.ojp.usdoj.gov/bjs/pub/pdf/ppus07st.pdf.

4. John Augustus, *A Report of the Labors of John Augustus, For the Last Ten Years, In Aid of the Unfortunate* (Boston: Wright and Hasty, 1852); reprinted as John Augustus, *First Probation Officer* (New York: National Probation Association, 1939).

5. David J. Rothman, *Conscience and Convenience: The Asylum and Its Alternatives in Progressive America* (Boston: Little, Brown, 1980), p. 44; www.ohnd.uscourts.gov/U_S_Probation/U_S_Probation_Employment/u_s_probation_employment.html.

6. Tom Condon, "Prison Experiment: Sentenced to Read" at www.ctnow.com/templates/misc/printstory.jsp?slug5hc%2D.C.ondon1010%2Eartoct10.

7. Rolando V. del Carmen, "Legal Issues and Liabilities in Community Corrections," in T. Ellsworth (ed.), *Contemporary Community Corrections* (Prospect Heights, IL: Waveland Press, 1992), pp. 383–407.

8. www.defgen.state.vt.us/lawbook/ch38.html.

9. Jay S. Albanese, Bernadette A. Fiore, Jerie H. Powell, and Janet R. Storti, *Is Probation Working? A Guide for Managers and Methodologists* (New York: University Press of America, 1981), p. 65.

10. Ibid.

11. Joan Petersilia, Susan Turner, James Kahan, and Joyce Peterson, *Granting Felons Probation: Public Risks and Alternatives* (Santa Monica, CA: Rand, 1985).

12. "Recidivism of Felons on Probation, 1986–8," United States Department of Justice, *Bureau of Justice Statistics Special Report* (Washington, D.C.: GPO, February 1992).

13. Data generously provided by Thomas P. Bonczar, U.S. Department of Justice, Bureau of Justice Statistics (December 18, 2008).

14. Rothman, op. cit.

15. United States Parole Commission at www.usdoj.gov/uspc/mission.html.

16. Association of Paroling Authorities International, "Parole Board Surveys," www.apaintl.org/content/en/pdf/2005_ParolingAuthorities_Survey.pdf; John C. Runda, Edward E. Rhine, and Robert E. Wetter, *The Practice of Parole Boards* (Lexington, KY: Host Communications Printing, 1994).

17. Ibid.

18. Ibid.

19. Ibid.

20. Ibid.

21. "Charles Manson Denied 10th Parole Bid," CBSNEWS.com at www.cbsnews.com/stories/2002/04/25/national/main507237.shtml.

22. Association of Paroling Authorities International, op. cit.; Runda et al., op. cit.

23. "Georgia Parole Decision Guidelines" at www.pap .state.ga.us/opencms/export/sites/default/resources/ Proposed_Parole_Decision_Guidelines.pdf (accessed December 18, 2008).

24. Ibid.

25. Ibid.

26. Ibid.

27. Ibid.

28. Ibid.

29. Richard McCleary, *Dangerous Men: The Sociology of Parole* (Beverly Hills, CA: Sage, 1978).

30. Peggy B. Burke, *Abolishing Parole: Why the Emperor Has No Clothes* (Lexington, KY: American Probation and Parole Association, 1995); Peggy B. Burke, "Issues in Parole Release Decision Making," in C. A. Hartjen and E. E. Rhine (eds.), *Correctional Theory and Practice* (Chicago: Nelson-Hall, 1992), pp. 213–232.

31. Association of Paroling Authorities International, "Parole Board Survey 2005," op. cit.; Timothy A. Hughes, Doris James Wilson, and Allen J. Beck, "Trends in State Parole, 1990–2000," U.S. Department of Justice, *Bureau of Justice Statistics Special Report* (Washington, D.C.: GPO, October 2001), p. 2.

32. Paula M. Ditton and Doris James Wilson, "Truth in Sentencing in State Prisons," U.S. Department of Justice, *Bureau of Justice Special Report* (Washington, D.C.: GPO, January 1999), p. 3.

33. Burke, *Abolishing Parole,* op. cit.

34. John C. Watkins, Jr., "Probation and Parole Malpractice in a Noninstitutional Setting: A Contemporary Analysis," *Federal Probation* 53 (1989), pp. 29–34 (quotations from p. 30); also see Rolando V. del Carmen, op. cit.

35. Calculated from Lauren E. Glaze and Thomas P. Bonczar, "Probation and Parole in the United States, 2007 Statistical Tables," op. cit., p. 1, Table 3. Lauren E. Glaze, "Probation and Parole in the United States, 2001," U.S. Department of Justice, *Bureau of Justice Statistics Bulletin* (Washington, D.C.: GPO, August 2002), p. 1.

36. Jeffrey K. Liker, "Wage and Status Effects of Employment on Affective Well-Being among Ex-Felons," *American Sociological Review* 47 (1982), pp. 264–283 (quotation from p. 282).

37. Richard A. Berk and David Rauma, "Capitalizing on Nonrandom Assignment to Treatments: A Regression-Discontinuity Evaluation of a Crime-Control Program," *Journal of the American Statistical Association* 78 (1983), pp. 21–27. And see Peter H. Rossi, Richard A. Berk, and K. J. Lenihan, *Money, Work, and Crime: Experimental Evidence* (New York: Academic Press, 1980).

38. Information evaluating parole is from Timothy A. Hughes, Doris James Wilson, and Allen J. Beck, "Trends in State Parole, 1990–2000," U.S. Department of Justice, *Bureau of Justice Statistics Special Report* (Washington, D.C.: GPO, October 2001), pp. 10–14; Lauren E. Glaze, "Probation and Parole in the United States, 2002," op. cit., p. 6, Table 7; "U.S. Correctional Population Reaches 6.3 Million Men and Women Represents 3.1 Percent of the Adult U.S. Population," U.S. Department of Justice, Bureau of Justice Statistics Press Release, July 23, 2000, at www.ojp.usdoj.gov/ bjs/pub/pdf/pp99pr.pdf; "Recidivism of Young Parolees," U.S. Department of Justice, *Bureau of Justice Statistics Special Report* (Washington, D.C.: GPO, May 1987).

39. Calculated from Lauren E. Glaze and Thomas P. Bonczar, "Probation and Parole in the United States, 2007 Statistical Tables," op. cit., p. 8, Table 7.

40. Runda et al., op. cit. Also see United States G.A.O., *Intermediate Sanctions: Their Impacts on Prison Crowding, Costs, and Recidivism Are Still Unclear* (Washington, D.C.: General Accounting Office, 1990).

41. Billie S. Erwin and Lawrence A. Bennett, *New Dimensions in Probation: Georgia's Experience with Intensive Probation Supervision,* United States Department of Justice, National Institute of Justice, Research in Brief (Washington, D.C.: GPO, 1987), p. 4.

42. Joan Petersilia and Susan Turner, "Comparing Intensive and Regular Supervision for High-Risk Probationers: Early Results from an Experiment in California," *Crime and Delinquency* 36 (1990), pp. 87–111.

43. Joan Petersilia and Susan Turner, *Evaluating Intensive Supervision Probation/Parole: Results of a Nationwide Experiment,* U.S. Department of Justice, National Institute of Justice, Research in Brief (Washington, D.C.: GPO, 1993). For further detail see Joan Petersilia and Susan Turner, "Intensive Probation and Parole," in M. Tonry and A. J. Reiss (eds.), *Crime and Justice: A Review of Research,* Vol. 17 (Chicago: University of Chicago Press, 1993), pp. 281–335.

44. Dale G. Parent, *Day Reporting Centers for Criminal Offenders: A Descriptive Analysis of Existing Programs,* U.S. Department of Justice, National Institute of Justice, Issues and Practices (Washington, D.C.: GPO 1990).

45. William J. Sabol and Todd D. Minton, "Jail Inmates at Midyear 2007," U.S. Department of Justice, *Bureau of Justice Statistics Bulletin* (Washington, D.C.: GPO, June 2008), p. 10, Appendix table 5; Paige M. Harrison and Allen J. Beck, "Prison and Jail Inmates at Midyear 2005," U.S. Department of Justice, *Bureau of Justice Statistics Bulletin* (Washington, D.C.: GPO, May 2006), p. 7, Table 8; Paige M. Harrison and Allen J. Beck, "Prison and Jail Inmates at Midyear 2004," U.S. Department of Justice, *Bureau of Justice Statistics Bulletin* (Washington, D.C.: GPO, April 2005), p. 7, Table 8.

46. Material in this section is from *How to Use Structured Fines (Day Fines) as an Intermediate Sanction,* U.S. Department of Justice, Bureau of Justice Assistance, November 1996.

47. J. R. Lilly and R. A. Ball, "A Brief History of House Arrest and Electronic Monitoring." *Northern Kentucky Law Review* 13, no. 3 (1987), pp. 343–374.

48. Sabol and Minton, "Jail Inmates at Midyear 2007," op. cit.; Harrison and Beck, "Prison and Jail Inmates at Midyear 2005," op. cit.

49. Rolando V. del Carmen and Joseph B. Vaughn, "Legal Issues in the Use of Electronic Surveillance in Probation," in T. Ellsworth (ed.), *Contemporary*

Community Corrections (Prospect Heights, IL: Waveland Press, 1992), p. 426.

50. John P. Conrad, "Concluding Comments: VORP and the Correctional Future," in B. Galaway and J. Hudson (eds.), *Criminal Justice, Restitution, and Reconciliation* (Monsey, NY: Criminal Justice Press, 1990), p. 229.

51. 2008 data generously provided by Shari Britton, Chief, Bureau of Probation & Parole Field Services, Florida Department of Corrections; Rene Stutzman, "State Takes Eyes Off Inmates," *The Orlando Sentinel* (December 29, 2002), p. A1; Rene Stutzman, "Ankle Monitors Show a Higher Rate of Success," *The Orlando Sentinel* (December 29, 2002), p. A15; Florida Department of Corrections at www.d.c.state .fl.us; Camille Graham Camp and George M. Camp, *The 2001 Corrections Yearbook: Adult Systems* (Middletown, CT: Criminal Justice Institute, 2002), p. 206.

52. Unless indicated otherwise, material about halfway houses is from Belinda Rodgers McCarthy, Bernard J. McCarthy, Jr., and Matthew C. Leone, *Community-Based Corrections,* 4th ed. (Belmont, CA: Wadsworth, 2001).

53. David J. Hartmann, Paul C. Friday, and Kevin I. Minor, "Residential Probation: A Seven-Year Follow-Up Study of Halfway House Discharges," *Journal of Criminal Justice* 22 (1994), pp. 503–515.

54. Patrick G. Donnelly and Brian E. Forschner, "Client Success or Failure in a Halfway House," *Federal Probation* 48 (1984), pp. 38–44. Also see R. E. Seiter, H. Bowman Carlson, J. Grandfield, and N. Bernam, *Halfway Houses: National Evaluation Program: Phase I, Summary Report,* U.S. Department of Justice (Washington, D.C.: GPO, 1977).

55. Edward J. Latessa and Lawrence F. Travis, "Halfway House or Probation: A Comparison of Alternative Dispositions," *Journal of Crime and Justice* 14 (1991), pp. 53–75.

56. McCarthy et al., op. cit. Unless otherwise noted, the material in the remainder of this section draws on pp. 148–156 of this source.

57. Daniel P. LeClair and Susan Guarino-Ghezzi, "Does Incapacitation Guarantee Public Safety? Lessons from the Massachusetts Furlough and Prerelease Programs," *Justice Quarterly* 8 (1991), pp. 9–36 (quotation from p. 26).

Chapter 13

1. Philippe Aries, *Centuries of Childhood: A Social History of Family Life,* translated by Robert Baldick (New York: Random House, 1962).

2. Barry Krisberg and James F. Austin, *Reinventing Juvenile Justice* (Newbury Park, CA: Sage, 1993), p. 9.

3. Harry Elmer Barnes, *The Story of Punishment,* 2nd ed. (Montclair, NJ: Patterson Smith, 1972).

4. David J. Rothman, *The Discovery of the Asylum* (Boston: Little, Brown, 1971).

5. Thomas J. Bernard, *The Cycle of Juvenile Justice* (New York: Oxford University Press, 1992), p. 63; Rothman, op. cit., p. 207.

6. Robert M. Mennel, *Thorns and Thistles* (Hanover, NH: University Press of New England, 1973); Steven L. Schlossman, *Love and the American Delinquent* (Chicago: University of Chicago Press, 1977).

7. Alexander Pisciotta, "Treatment on Trial: The Rhetoric and Reality of the New York House of Refuge, 1857–1935," *The American Journal of Legal History* 29 (1985), pp. 151–181; Rothman, op. cit., p. 231.

8. Clemens Bartollas and Stuart J. Miller, *Juvenile Justice in America* (Englewood Cliffs, NJ: Regents/Prentice Hall, 1994), p. 136.

9. LaMar T. Empey and Mark C. Stafford, *American Delinquency: Its Meaning and Construction,* 3rd ed. (Belmont, CA: Wadsworth, 1991), p. 368.

10. Belinda R. McCarthy and Bernard J. McCarthy, *Community-Based Corrections,* 2nd ed. (Pacific Grove, CA: Brooks/Cole, 1991), p. 98.

11. Krisberg and Austin, op. cit., pp. 23–24; Hastings Hart, *Preventive Treatment of Neglected Children* (New York: Russell Sage, 1910), p. 70.

12. Bartollas and Miller, op. cit., p. 209; John T. Whitehead and Steven P. Lab, *Juvenile Justice: An Introduction* (Cincinnati: Anderson, 1990), p. 47.

13. Cited in Meda Chesney-Lind and Randall G. Shelden, *Girls, Delinquency, and Juvenile Justice* (Pacific Grove, CA: Brooks/Cole, 1992), p. 111.

14. Harold Finestone, *Victims of Change* (Westport, CT: Greenwood Press, 1976).

15. Anthony M. Platt, *The Child Savers: The Invention of Delinquency* (Chicago: University of Chicago Press, 1969), p. 99.

16. Ibid., pp. 101–102.

17. Bernard, op. cit., pp. 68–69.

18. Ibid., pp. 70–71.

19. Platt, op. cit., pp. 134–36; Bernard, op. cit., p. 73.

20. Empey and Stafford, op. cit. pp. 58–59.

21. Bartollas and Miller, op. cit., p. 92; Empey and Stafford, op. cit., p. 59.

22. Krisberg and Austin, op. cit., p. 30.

23. Bernard, op. cit., p. 96.

24. Ibid., pp. 96–97.

25. Walter Wadlington, Charles H. Whitebread, and Samuel M. Davis, *Cases and Materials on Children in the Legal System* (Mineola, NY: Foundation Press, 1983), p. 202; Bernard, op. cit., p. 110.

26. M. A. Bortner, *Delinquency and Justice: An Age of Crisis* (New York: McGraw-Hill, 1988), p. 60.

27. Bernard, op. cit., p. 141.

28. Charles Puzzanchera and Melissa Sickmund, *Juvenile Court Statistics 2005* (Pittsburgh, PA: National Center for Juvenile Justice, 2008), p. 58 at http://ncjj.servehttp .com/NCJJWebsite/pdf/jcsreports/jcs2005.pdf.

29. Ibid., p. 31.

30. Ibid., p. 82.

31. Douglas A. Smith, "The Organizational Context of Legal Control," *Criminology* 22 (1984), pp. 19–38.

32. Robert J. Sampson, "Effects of Socioeconomic Context on Official Reaction to Juvenile Delinquency," *American Sociological Review* 51 (1986), pp. 876–885; also see A. Cicourel, *The Social Organization of Juvenile Justice* (New York: Wiley, 1968).

33. Donald Black and Albert J. Reiss, "Police Control of Juveniles," *American Sociological Review* 35 (1970), pp. 63–77; Richard J. Lundman, Richard E. Sykes, and John P. Clark, "Police Control of Juveniles: A Replication," in Ralph Weisheit and Robert G. Culbertson (eds.), *Juvenile Delinquency: A Justice Perspective* (Prospect Heights, IL: Waveland Press, 1978), pp. 107–115; Irving Piliavan and Scott Briar, "Police Encounters with Juveniles," *American Journal of Sociology* 70 (1964), pp. 206–214.

34. Marvin D. Krohn, James P. Curry, and Shirley Nelson-Kilger, "Is Chivalry Dead? An Analysis of Changes in Police Dispositions of Males and Females," *Criminology* 21 (1983), pp. 417–437; Katherine Teilmann and Pierre H. Landry, "Gender Bias in Juvenile Justice," *Journal of Research in Crime and Delinquency* 18 (1981), pp. 47–80; see also William G. Staples, "Law and Social Control in Juvenile Justice Dispositions," *Journal of Research in Crime and Delinquency* 24 (1987), pp. 7–22; Meda Chesney-Lind, "Judicial Paternalism and the Female Status Offender: Training Women to Know Their Place," *Crime and Delinquency* 23 (1977), pp. 121–130.

35. Robert J. Sampson, "Sex Differences in Self-Reported Delinquency and Official Records: A Multiple-Group Structural Modeling Approach," *Journal of Quantitative Criminology* 1 (1985), pp. 345–367; Dale Dannefer and Russell K. Schutt, "Race and Juvenile Justice Processing in Court and Police Agencies," *American Journal of Sociology* 87 (1982), pp. 1113–1132.

36. Merry Morash, "Establishment of a Juvenile Police Record: The Influence of Individual and Peer Group Characteristics," *Criminology* 22 (1984), pp. 97–111; Krohn et al., op. cit.; D. Elliott and H. L. Voss, *Delinquency and Dropout* (Lexington, MA: Lexington Books, 1974).

37. Howard N. Snyder, "Juvenile Arrests 2006," U.S. Department of Justice, Office of Juvenile Justice and Delinquency Prevention, *Juvenile Justice Bulletin* (Washington, D.C.: GPO, November 2008), p. 3 at www.ncjrs.gov/pdffiles1/ojjdp/221338.pdf.

38. Federal Bureau of Investigation, *Crime in the United States 2007,* Table 43, www.fbi.gov/ucr/cius2007/data/table_43.html.

39. U.S. Census Bureau, *The 2009 Statistical Abstract*, Table No. 8 at www.census.gov/compendia/statab/tables/09s0008.pdf.

40. Delbert S. Elliott and David Huizinga, "Social Class and Delinquent Behavior in a National Youth Panel," *Criminology* 21 (1983), pp. 149–177.

41. *Sourcebook of Criminal Justice Statistics Online,* Table 4.26 at www.albany.edu/sourcebook/1995/pdf/t426.pdf; Federal Bureau of Investigation, *Crime in the United States 2007,* op. cit., Table 68.

42. Information about teen courts or youth courts is from Jeffrey Butts, Dean Hoffman, and Janeen Buck, "Teen Courts in the United States: A Profile of Current Programs," U.S. Department of Justice, Office of Juvenile Justice and Delinquency Prevention, Office of Juvenile Justice and Delinquency Prevention Fact Sheet #118 (Washington, D.C.: GPO, October 1999); Jeffrey A. Butts and Janeen Buck, "Teen Courts: A Focus on Research," *Juvenile Justice Bulletin* (Washington, D.C.: GPO, U.S. Department of Justice, Office of Juvenile Justice and Delinquency Prevention, October 2000); Jeffrey A. Butts, Janeen Buck, and Mark B. Coggeshall, *The Impact of Teen Court on Young Offenders* (Washington, D.C.: The Urban Institute, U.S. Department of Justice, Office of Juvenile Justice and Delinquency Prevention, April 2002); National Youth Court Center at www.youthcourt.net; National Association of Youth Courts at www.youthcourt.net/content/view/7/14/ (accessed December 29, 2008).

43. Information on restorative justice conferences or family group conferences is from Edmund F. McGarrell, "Restorative Justice Conferences as an Early Response to Young Offenders," *Juvenile Justice Bulletin* (Washington, D.C.: GPO, U.S. Department of Justice, Office of Juvenile Justice and Delinquency Prevention, August 2001); U.S. Department of Justice, Office of Juvenile Justice and Delinquency Prevention, *OJJDP Research 2000* (Washington, D.C.: GPO, May 2001).

44. Puzzanchera and Sickmund, op. cit., p. 32.

45. Calculated from data in William J. Sabol and Todd D. Minton, "Jail Inmates at Midyear, 2007," U.S. Department of Justice, *Bureau of Justice Statistics Bulletin* (Washington, D.C.: GPO, June 2008), p. 10, Appendix table 4.

46. Howard N. Snyder and Melissa Sickmund, *Juvenile Offenders and Victims: 1999 National Report* (Washington, D.C.: GPO, U.S. Department of Justice, National Center for Juvenile Justice, Office of Juvenile Justice and Delinquency Prevention, September 1999), p. 97.

47. U.S. Centers for Disease Control and Prevention (CD.C.), "Disturbing Facts about Juveniles in the Adult Court System," (Report released November 29, 2007), p. 2 at www.campaign4youthjustice.org/Downloads/PressReleases/CFYJ_CD.C._Report_11-29-07.pdf (accessed December 29, 2008).

48. Ted Rubin, "The Emerging Prosecutor Dominance of the Juvenile Court Intake Process," *Crime and Delinquency* 26 (1980), pp. 299–318.

49. For a review of this literature, see Chesney-Lind and Shelden, op. cit., pp. 137–139.

50. Michael Tonry, "Crime and Human Rights—How Political Paranoia, Protestant Fundamentalism, and Constitutional Obsolescence Combined to Devastate Black America: The American Society of Criminology 2007 Presidential Address," *Criminology* 46 (2008), p. 8.

51. Puzzanchera and Sickmund, op. cit., pp. 40–44.

52. Jeff Kunerth, "Adult Charges Harmful to Kids?" *The Orlando Sentinel* (March 22, 2007), p. B1.

53. National Center for Juvenile Justice, State Juvenile Justice Profiles at www.ncjj.org/stateprofiles/overviews/transfer3.asp (accessed January 5, 2009).

54. Howard N. Snyder and Melissa Sickmund, *Juvenile Offenders and Victims: 2006 National Report.* Washington D.C.: U.S. Department of Justice, Office

of Justice Programs, Office of Juvenile Justice and Delinquency Prevention (March 2006), p. 113 at www.ojjdp.ncjrs.gov/ojstatbb/nr2006/downloads/NR2006.pdf (accessed January 5, 2009).

55. Greg Krikorian, "Study: Many Kids Tried as Adults Don't Grasp System," *The Orlando Sentinel* (March 3, 2003), p. A3.

56. Snyder and Sickmund, op. cit., p. 113.

57. Unless indicated otherwise, material in this section is from the following sources: Ibid., pp. 111 and 116; Barry C. Feld, "Criminalizing the American Juvenile Court," in Michael Tonry (ed.), *Crime and Justice: A Review of Research,* Vol. 17 (Chicago: University of Chicago Press, 1993), pp. 197–280; Joseph B. Sanborn, Jr., "Policies Regarding the Prosecution of Juvenile Murderers: Which System and Who Should Decide," *Law & Policy* 18 (1996), pp. 151–178; Joseph B. Sanborn, Jr., "Certification to Criminal Court: The Important Policy Questions of How, When, and Why," *Crime and Delinquency* 40 (1994), pp. 262–281; Howard N. Snyder, *Juvenile Arrests 1995,* U.S. Department of Justice, Office of Juvenile Justice and Delinquency Prevention, *Juvenile Justice Bulletin* (Washington, D.C.: GPO, February 1997), p. 12; Barry C. Feld, "The Juvenile Court Meets the Principle of the Offense: Legislative Changes in Juvenile Waiver Statutes," *Journal of Criminal Law and Criminology* 78 (1987), pp. 471–533; Barry Krisberg, Ira M. Schwartz, Paul Litsky, and James Austin, "The Watershed of Juvenile Justice Reform," *Crime and Delinquency* 32 (1986), pp. 5–38; Donna Hamparian, Linda Estep, Susan M. Muntean, Ramon R. Prestino, Robert G. Swisher, Paul L. Wallace, and Joseph L. White, *Youth in Adult Court: Between Two Worlds* (Washington, D.C.: OJJDP, 1982); Sickmund, "Juveniles in Court," op. cit., p. 5; and personal communications from Donna M. Bishop and Joseph B. Sanborn, Jr.

58. Joseph B. Sanborn, Jr., "Pleading Guilty in Juvenile Court," *Justice Quarterly* 9 (1992), pp. 127–150.

59. Martin L. Forst, Bruce A. Fisher, and Robert B. Coates, "Indeterminate and Determinate Sentencing of Juvenile Delinquents: A National Survey of Approaches to Commitment and Release Decision-Making," *Juvenile and Family Court Journal* (Summer 1985), pp. 1–12.

60. Jeffrey Fagan, Ellen Slaughter, and Richard Hartstone, "Blind Justice: The Impact of Race on the Juvenile Justice Process," *Crime and Delinquency* 33 (1987), pp. 244–258; Belinda R. McCarthy and Brent L. Smith, "The Conceptualization of Discrimination in the Juvenile Justice Process," *Criminology* 24 (1986), pp. 41–64.

61. Snyder and Sickmund, op. cit.; Patricia Torbert, Richard Gable, Hunter Hurst IV, Imogene Montgomery, Linda Szymanski, and Douglas Thomas, *State Responses to Serious and Violent Juvenile Crime,* U.S. Department of Justice, Office of Juvenile Justice and Delinquency Prevention (Washington, D.C.: GPO, July 1996), chap. 3.

62. Patricia McFall Torbet, "Juvenile Probation: The Workhorse of the Juvenile Justice System," U.S. Department of Justice, Office of Juvenile Justice and Delinquency Prevention, *Juvenile Justice Bulletin* (Washington, D.C.: GPO, March 1996); Puzzanchera and Sickmund, op. cit., p. 58.

63. Troy L. Armstrong, "National Survey of Juvenile Intensive Supervision" (Parts I and II), *Criminal Justice Abstracts* 20 (1988), pp. 342–348 (Part I) and 497–523 (Part II).

64. Richard G. Wiebush, "Juvenile Intensive Supervision: The Impact on Felony Offenders Diverted from Institutional Placement," *Crime and Delinquency* 39 (1993), pp. 68–89; William H. Barton and Jeffrey A. Butts, "Viable Options: Intensive Supervision Programs for Juvenile Delinquents," *Crime and Delinquency* 36 (1990), pp. 238–256.

65. Richard A. Ball, Ronald Huff, and Robert Lilly, *House Arrest and Correctional Policy: Doing Time at Home* (Newbury Park, CA: Sage, 1988).

66. See Marc Renzema and David T. Skelton, "Use of Electronic Monitoring in the United States: 1989 Update," National Institute of Justice, Research in Brief (Washington, D.C.: National Institute of Justice, 1990); Daniel Ford and Annesley K. Schmidt, "Electronically Monitored Home Confinement," National Institute of Justice, Research in Action (Washington, D.C.: National Institute of Justice, 1985).

67. Joseph B. Vaughn, "A Survey of Juvenile Electronic Monitoring and Home Confinement Programs," *Juvenile and Family Court Journal* 40 (1989), pp. 1–36.

68. Kevin I. Minor and Preston Elrod, "The Effects of a Probation Intervention on Juvenile Offenders' Self-Concepts, Loci of Control, and Perceptions of Juvenile Justice," *Youth and Society* 25 (1994), pp. 490–511; Gerald L. Golins, *Utilizing Adventure Education to Rehabilitate Juvenile Delinquents* (Las Cruces, NM: Educational Resources Information Center, Clearinghouse on Rural Education and Small Schools, 1980).

69. See, for example, R. Callahan, "Wilderness Probation: A Decade Later," *Juvenile and Family Court Journal* 36 (1985), pp. 31–51; John Winterdyk and Ronald Roesch, "A Wilderness Experiential Program as an Alternative for Probationers: An Evaluation," *Canadian Journal of Criminology* 24 (1982), pp. 39–49.

70. H. Preston Elrod and Kevin I. Minor, "Second Wave Evaluation of a Multi-Faceted Intervention for Juvenile Court Probationers," *International Journal of Offender Therapy and Comparative Criminology* 36 (1992), pp. 247–262; John Winterdyk and Curt Griffiths, "Wilderness Experience Programs: Reforming Delinquents or Beating Around the Bush?" *Juvenile and Family Court Journal* 35 (1984), pp. 35–44; Winterdyk and Roesch, op. cit.

71. Ted Palmer, *The Re-Emergence of Correctional Intervention* (Newbury Park, CA: Sage, 1992); Office of Juvenile Justice and Delinquency Prevention, *Project New Pride: Replication* (Washington: OJJDP, 1979); LaMar T. Empey and Maynard L. Erickson, *The Provo Experiment: Evaluating Community Control of Delinquency* (Lexington, MA: Lexington Books, 1972).

72. Terrence P. Thornberry, Stewart E. Tolnay, Timothy J. Flanagan, and Patty Glynn, *Office of Juvenile Justice*

and Delinquency Prevention Report on Children in Custody 1987: A Comparison of Public and Private Juvenile Custody Facilities (Washington, D.C.: OJJDP, 1991).

73. Thornberry et al. (1991), op. cit.; Dale G. Parent, "Conditions of Confinement," *Juvenile Justice,* Vol. 1, no. 1 (Spring/Summer 1993), pp. 2–7, www.ncjrs.org/_pdffiles/jjjs93.pdf.

74. National Mental Health Association, "Juvenile Boot Camps" (2005), www.nmha.org/children/justjuv/bootcamp.cfm; *American Correctional Association 2008 Directory: Adult and Juvenile Correctional Departments, Institutions, Agencies and Probation and Parole Authorities* (Lanham, MD: American Correctional Association, 2008), pp. 28–31. Note that in the *ACA 2008 Directory,* many states did not provide information on boot camps.

75. Nancy Zuckerbrod "Youth Boot Camps Like Abu Ghraib, Witnesses Tell House," *The Orlando Sentinel* (April 25, 2008), p. A6; Nancy Zuckerbrod "Youth Boot Camps Panned," *The Orlando Sentinel* (April 24, 2008), p. A2.

76. Melissa Sickmund, "Juvenile Residential Facility Census, 2000: Selected Findings," U.S. Department of Justice, Office of Juvenile Justice and Delinquency Prevention, *Juvenile Offenders and Victims National Report Series Bulletin* (Washington, D.C.: GPO, December 2002), p. 3.

77. Holbrook Mohr, "Facilities for Juveniles Face Claims of Abuse," *The Orlando Sentinel* (March 3, 2008), p. A8.

78. See, for example, Barry Krisberg, "Juvenile Justice: Improving the Quality of Care," *National Council on Crime and Delinquency* (San Francisco: NCCD, 1992); Carol J. Garrett, "Effects of Residential Treatment on Adjudicated Delinquents," *Journal of Research in Crime and Delinquency* 22 (1985), pp. 287–308.

79. Barry Krisberg, Robert DeComo, and Norma C. Herrera, *National Juvenile Custody Trends 1978–1989* (Washington: OJJDP, 1992), p. 2; also see Steven Lab and John T. Whitehead, "A Meta-Analysis of Juvenile Correctional Treatment," *Journal of Research in Crime and Delinquency* 26 (1989), pp. 276–295; Norman G. Hoffmann, Ana M. Abrantes, and Ronald Anton, "Criminals, Troubled Youth, or a Bit of Both," *Addiction Professional* 1, no. 4 (July 2003); Snyder and Sickmund, op. cit., p. 234.

80. Unless indicated otherwise, data in this section are from Melissa Sickmund, T. J. Sladky, and Wel Kang, "Census of Juveniles in Residential Placement Databook" (2006), National Center for Juvenile Justice at www.ojjdp.ncjrs.gov/ojstatbb/cjrp/ (accessed January 6, 2009).

81. Paige M. Harrison and Allen J. Beck, "Prison and Jail Inmates at Midyear 2005," U.S. Department of Justice, *Bureau of Justice Statistics Bulletin* (Washington, D.C.: GPO, June 2006), p. 8, Table 9, and p. 5, Table 5; Sabol and Minton, "Jail Inmates at Midyear 2007," op. cit., p. 10, Appendix table 4; William J. Sabol and Heather Couture, "Prison Inmates at Midyear 2007," U.S. Department of Justice, *Bureau of Justice*

Statistics Bulletin (Washington, D.C.: GPO, June 2008), p. 9, Table 13 at www.ojp.usdoj.gov/bjs/pub/pdf/pim07.pdf (accessed January 6, 2009).

82. Richard G. Wiebush, Betsy McNulty, and Thao Le, "Implementation of the Intensive Community-Based Aftercare Program," U.S. Department of Justice, Office of Juvenile Justice and Delinquency Prevention, *Juvenile Justice Bulletin* (Washington, D.C.: GPO, July 2000).

83. Ibid., p. 2.

84. Richard G. Wiebush, Dennis Wagner, Betsie McNulty, Yanqing Wang, and Thao N. Lee, *Implemention and Outcome Evaluation of the Intensive Aftercare Program: Final Report.* U.S. Department of Justice, Office of Juvenile Justice and Delinquency Prevention (Washington, D.C.: GPO, March 2005).

Chapter 14

1. Herbert Packer, *The Limits of the Criminal Sanction* (Stanford, CA: Stanford University Press, 1968).

2. Gene Stephens, "High-Tech Crime: The Threat to Civil Liberties," *The Futurist* (July–August 1990), pp. 20–25.

3. Gene Stephens, "Law Enforcement," in G. T. Kurian and G. T. T. Molitor (eds.), *Encyclopedia of the Future* (New York: Simon & Schuster, Macmillan, 1996), p. 538; Jeff Kunerth, "You Have No Right to Privacy You Seek," *The Orlando Sentinel* (August 8, 1999), p. A1.

4. Scott Parks, "High-Tech's Time Is on Horizon in Security Business," *The Orlando Sentinel* (October 7, 2001), p. A10; Jeremiah Marquez, "A New Weapon against Crime?" *The Orlando Sentinel* (June 21, 2006), p. A17.

5. Etan Horowitz, "Speedy Database Helps Cops Put Pieces Together," *The Orlando Sentinel* (August 24, 2003), p. B1.

6. Gene Stephens, "Drugs and Crime in the Twenty-First Century," *The Futurist* (May–June 1992), pp. 19–22.

7. "Police to Use IBM's Digital Video System," *The Orlando Sentinel* (May 18, 2003), p. H3.

8. Ibid.

9. Ibid.

10. Material on surveillance cameras is from Charlie Savage, "U.S. Doles Out Millions for Street Cameras," *The Boston Globe* (August 12, 2007) at www.boston.com/news/nation/washington/articles/2007/08/12/us_doles_out_millions_for_street_cameras/; Demian Bulwa, "Future Fuzzy for Use of Public Surveillance Cameras," *The San Francisco Chronicle* (July 23, 2006) at www.sfgate.com/cgi-bin/article.cgi?f=/c/a/2006/07/23/CAMERAS.TMP; Allison Klein, "Police Go Live Monitoring D.C. Crime Cameras," washingtonpost.com at www.washingtonpost.com/wp-dyn/content/article/2008/02/10/AR2008021002726_pf.html; Alex Johnson, "Smile: More and More, You're on Camera," msnbc at www.msnbc.msn.com/id/25355673/; J. Douglas Walker, "Information Technology Advances Push the Privacy Boundaries Again," pp. 40–43 in C. Flango, A.

McDowell, C. Campbell, and N. Kauder, *Future Trends in State Courts 2008* (Williamsburg, VA: National Center for State Courts, 2008), p. 40.

11. J. Douglas Walker, "Information Technology Advances Push the Privacy Boundaries Again," op. cit., p. 41.

12. Ben Reed, "Future Technology in Law Enforcement," *Law Enforcement Bulletin,* Vol. 77, No. 5 (May 2008) at www.fbi.gov/publications/leb/2008/may2008/may2008leb.htm (accessed January 26, 2009).

13. Stephens (1996), op. cit., p. 539; "Police Test Voice Translator Box," *The Orlando Sentinel* (December 5, 1999), p. A17.

14. "New Ultra-Wideband Could Make Walls See-through," *The Orlando Sentinel* (June 15, 2000), p. A3.

15. J. Douglas Walker, "Information Technology Advances Push the Privacy Boundaries Again," op. cit., p. 40.

16. Ben Reed, "Future Technology in Law Enforcement," op. cit.

17. Cheevers, op. cit.

18. Ben Reed, "Future Technology in Law Enforcement," op. cit.

19. Ibid.

20. Ibid.

21. Stephens (1996), op. cit., p. 539.

22. Terry D. Anderson, Kenneth D. Gisborne, Marilyn Hamilton, Pat Holiday, John C. LeDoux, Gene Stephens, and John Welter, *Every Officer Is a Leader: Transforming Leadership in Police, Justice, and Public Safety* (Boca Raton, FL: St. Lucie Press, 2000), p. 368.

23. Ben Reed, "Future Technology in Law Enforcement," op. cit.

24. Ibid.

25. Ibid.

26. Randall T. Shepard, "Indiana Court Technology Is about Service, Not Bytes and Bandwith," pp. 26–28 in C. Flango, A. McDowell, C. Campbell, and N. Kauder, *Future Trends in State Courts 2008* (Williamsburg, VA: National Center for State Courts, 2008), p. 26.

27. Ibid., p. 27.

28. Stephens (1990), op. cit.

29. Anita Neuberger Blowers, "The Future of American Courts," in B. Maguire and P. Radosh (eds.), *The Past, Present, and Future of American Criminal Justice* (New York: General Hall, 1995); Carol R. Flango, Chuck Campbell, and Neal Kauder (eds.), *Future Trends in State Courts 2006* (Williamsburg, VA: National Center for State Courts, 2006).

30. "Court: Jurors Don't Have to Speak English to Serve," *The Orlando Sentinel* (January 20, 2000), p. A10.

31. Flango et al., op. cit.

32. Ibid.

33. Blowers, op. cit.

34. Ibid.

35. Richard Van Duizend, "The Implications of an Aging Population for the State Courts," pp. 76–80 in C. Flango, A. McDowell, C. Campbell, and N. Kauder, *Future Trends in State Courts 2008* (Williamsburg, VA: National Center for State Courts, 2008), pp. 77–78.

36. Gene Stephens, "Crime and Punishment: Forces Shaping the Future," *The Futurist* (January–February 1987), pp. 18–26.

37. Ibid.

38. Mark S. Umbreit, Jean Greenwood, Robert Schug, Jenni Umbreit, and Claudia Fercello, *Directory of Offender-Victim Mediation Programs in the United States,* U.S. Department of Justice, Office of Justice Programs, Office for Victims of Crime (Washington, D.C.: GPO, April 2000, updated June 26, 2008) at www.ojp.usdoj.gov/ovc/publications/infores/restorative_justice/96521-dir_victim-offender/welcome.html (accessed January 7, 2009).

39. John Braithwaite, *Crime, Shame and Reintegration* (Cambridge: Cambridge University Press, 1989).

40. Flango et al., op. cit.

41. Ibid.

42. Ibid.

43. Blowers, op. cit.; Flango et al., op. cit.

44. Material on neuroscience is from Jeffrey Rosen, "The Brain on the Stand," *The New York Times Magazine* (March 11, 2007), pp. 49–53, 70, 77, 82, and 84.

45. Stephens (1990), op. cit.

46. Ibid.

47. Blowers, op. cit.; Flango et al., op. cit.

48. Flango et al., ibid.

49. Ibid.

50. Malcolm M. Feeley and Jonathan Simon, "The New Penology: Notes on the Emerging Strategy of Corrections and Its Implications," *Criminology* 30 (1992), pp. 449–474.

51. Ibid.

52. John J. Dilulio, Jr., *No Escape: The Future of American Corrections* (New York: Basic Books, 1991), p. 4.

53. Ibid.

54. Feeley and Simon, op. cit., p. 470.

55. Stephens, "Prisons," op. cit.

56. See Francis T. Cullen and John P. Wright, "The Future of Corrections," in B. Maguire and P. Radosh (eds.), *The Past, Present, and Future of American Criminal Justice* (New York: General Hall, 1995).

57. Stephens (1990), op. cit.

58. Ibid.

59. Stephens, "Prisons," op. cit., p. 751.

60. Stephens (1990), op. cit.

61. Stephens, "Prisons," op. cit.

62. Stephens (1990), op. cit.

63. Cullen and Wright, op. cit.

64. Ibid.

65. Richard Burnett, "Putting Pieces Back Together," *The Orlando Sentinel* (August 20, 2003), p. C1.

66. *Federal Trade Commission–2006 Identity Theft Report* (McLean, VA: Synovate, November 2007) at www.ftc.gov/os/2007/11/SynovateFinalReportIDTheft2006.pdf (accessed January 7, 2009). (Unless indicated otherwise, survey material is from this source.) *Federal Trade Commission—Identity Theft Survey Report* (McLean, VA: Synovate, September 2003), at www.ftc.gov/reports/index.htm.

67. Pub. L. No. 105–318, 112 Stat. 3007 (Oct. 30, 1998).

68. "Identity Theft," The National White Collar Crime Center at www.nw3c.org/research_topics.html; "Identity Thief Goes 'Phishing' for Consumers' Credit Information," Federal Trade Commission,

July 21, 2003, at www.ftc.gov/opa/2003/07/
phishing.htm.

69. "Coping with Identity Theft: Reducing the Risk of
Fraud," Privacy Rights Clearinghouse, Fact Sheet
No. 17 (May 1995, revised February 2003), at
www.privacyrights.org/fs/fs17-it.htm.

70. Federal Trade Commission, "Fighting Back
against Identity Theft" at www.ftc.gov/bcp/edu/
microsites/idtheft/media-reference/writing.html
(clearinghouse_2006.pdf).

71. *Federal Trade Commission–2006 Identity Theft
Report,* op. cit., p. 50.

72. Linda Goldman-Foley, "Identity Theft—Overcoming
the Emotional Impact," The Identity Theft Resource
Center, Fact Sheet 17e (2000, revised November 26,
2001), at www.idtheftcenter.org/html/fs109.htm.
Material about the identity theft victimization
experience is from this source.

73. *Federal Trade Commission–2006 Identity Theft
Report,* op. cit., pp. 52–53.

74. Burnett, "Identity Theft Hits 'Epidemic' Levels," op. cit.

75. Louise Shelley, Director, Transnational Crime and
Corruption Center at www.american.edu/traccc.

76. *Transnational Organized Crime: Summary of a
Workshop,* The National Academy of Sciences, 2000,
p. 28, at www.nap.edu/books/0309065755/html.

77. United Nations Convention against Transnational
Organized Crime, 2000, Article 2(a) at www.unoD.C
.org/palermo/convmain.html.

78. Ibid., Article 2(b).

79. Ibid., Article 3(2).

80. Pino Ariacchi, "Nations Build Alliances to Stop
Organized Crime," *Global Issues: Arresting Transnational Crime,* U.S. Department of State, p. 1, at
http://usinfo.state.gov/journals/itgic/0801/gj08.htm.

81. *Results of a Pilot Survey of Forty Selected
Organized Criminal Groups in Sixteen Countries,*

Global Programme against Transnational Organized
Crime, United Nations Office on Drugs and Crime,
September 2002, p. 20, at www.unoD.C.org/unoD.C./
organized_crime.html.

82. Ibid., p. 28.

83. *Transnational Organized Crime: Summary of a
Workshop,* op. cit., pp. 11–12.

84. Wendy Chamberlin, "Intensifying the Fight against
Transnational Organized Crime," U.S. Department of
State, 2001, p. 1, at www.state.gov/g/inl/rls/rm/2001/
jan_apr/1078pf.htm.

85. Ariacchi, op. cit., p. 20.

86. Ibid.

87. Ariacchi, op. cit., pp. 1–2; Chamberlin, op. cit., p. 1.

88. Ariacchi, op. cit., p. 2.

89. *Transnational Organized Crime: Summary of a
Workshop,* op. cit., p. 32.

90. Ibid., p. 29; Chamberlin, op. cit., p. 2.

91. *Convention against Transnational Organized Crime,*
United Nations Crime and Justice Network, Centre for
International Crime Prevention, Office for Drug
Control and Crime Prevention at www.uncjin.org/
Documents/Conventions/conventions.html; Elizabeth
Verville, "U.S. Joins Global Convention Against Trans-
national Organized Crime," *Global Issues: Arresting
Transnational Crime,* U.S. Department of State, pp.
1–2, at http://usinfo.state.gov/journals/itgic/0801/ijge/
gj02.htm; Ariacchi, op. cit., pp. 3–5. Information
about the convention is from these sources.

92. *Transnational Organized Crime: Summary of a
Workshop,* op. cit., pp. 34–39.

93. Josh Meyer, "Diminished al-Qaeda Remains a Threat
to U.S.," *The Orlando Sentinel* (September 11, 2003),
p. A8.

Glossary

actus reus Criminal conduct—specifically, intentional or criminally negligent (reckless) action or inaction that causes harm. (2)

adjudication The juvenile court equivalent of a trial in criminal court, or the process of rendering a judicial decision regarding the truth of the facts alleged in a petition. (13)

administrative segregation The keeping of inmates in secure isolation so that they cannot harm others. (10)

aggravating factors or **circumstances** In death sentencing, facts or situations that increase the blameworthiness for a criminal act. (9)

aggressive patrol The practice of having an entire patrol section make numerous traffic stops and field interrogations. (6)

allocution The procedure at a sentencing hearing in which the convicted defendant has the right to address the court before the sentence is imposed. During allocution, a defendant is identified as the person found guilty and has a right to deny or explain information contained in the PSI if his or her sentence is based on it. (9)

anomie For Durkheim, the dissociation of the individual from the collective conscience. (3)

anomie For Merton, the contradiction between the cultural goal of achieving wealth and the social structure's inability to provide legitimate institutional means for achieving the goal. For Cohen, it is caused by the inability of juveniles to achieve status among peers by socially acceptable means. (3)

appellate jurisdiction The power of a court to review a case for errors of law. (8)

apprenticeship system The method by which middle- and upper-class children were taught skilled trades by a master. (13)

arbitration A dispute resolution process that brings disputants together with a third party (an arbitrator) who has the skills to listen objectively to evidence presented by both sides of a conflict, to ask probing and relevant questions of each side, and to arrive at an equitable solution to the dispute. (14)

arraignment A pretrial stage to hear the information or indictment and to allow a plea. (1)

arraignment A pretrial stage; its primary purpose is to hear the formal information or indictment and to allow the defendant to enter a plea. (8)

arrest The seizing and detaining of a person by lawful authority. (1)

arrest The seizure of a person or the taking of a person into custody, either actual physical custody, as when a suspect is handcuffed by a police officer, or constructive custody, as when a person peacefully submits to a police officer's control. (4)

arrest warrant A written order directing law enforcement officers to arrest a person. The charge or charges against a suspect are specified on the warrant. (8)

atavist A person who reverts to a savage type. (3)

Auburn system An early system of penology, originating at Auburn Penitentiary in New York, in which inmates worked and ate together in silence during the day and were placed in solitary cells for the evening. (10)

bail bond or **bail** Usually a monetary guarantee deposited with the court that is supposed to ensure that the suspect or defendant will appear at a later stage in the criminal justice process. (8)

bail Usually a monetary guarantee deposited with the court to ensure that suspects or defendants will appear at a later stage in the criminal justice process. (1)

banishment A punishment, originating in ancient times, that required offenders to leave the community and live elsewhere, commonly in the wilderness. (10)

bench trial A trial before a judge without a jury. (1 and 8)

bench warrant or *capias* A document that authorizes a suspect's or defendant's arrest for not appearing in court as required. (8)

beyond a reasonable doubt The standard of proof necessary to find a defendant guilty in a criminal trial. (4)

bifurcated trial A two-stage trial (unlike the one-stage trial in other felony cases) consisting of a guilt phase and a separate penalty phase. (9)

binding-out system Practice in which children were "bound over" to masters for care. However, under the binding-out system, masters were not required to teach youths a trade. (13)

biological inferiority According to biological theories, a criminal's innate physiological makeup produces certain physical or genetic characteristics that distinguish criminals from noncriminals. (3)

bionics The replacing of human body parts with mechanical parts. (14)

booking The administrative recording of an arrest. Typically, the suspect's name, the charge, and perhaps the suspect's fingerprints or photograph are entered in the police blotter. (1)

booking The process in which suspects' names, the charges for which they were arrested, and perhaps their fingerprints or photographs are entered on the police blotter. (8)

Chicago School A group of sociologists at the University of Chicago who assumed in their research that delinquent behavior was a product of social disorganization. (3)

civil law One of two general types of law practiced in the United States (the other is criminal law); a means of resolving conflicts between individuals. It includes personal injury claims (torts), the law of contracts and property, and subjects such as administrative law and the regulation of public utilities. (4)

class struggle For radical criminologists, the competition among wealthy people and among poor people and between rich people and poor people, which causes crime. (3)

classical theory A product of the Enlightenment, based on the assumption that people exercise free will and are thus completely responsible for their actions. In classical theory, human behavior, including criminal behavior, is motivated by a hedonistic rationality, in which actors weigh the potential pleasure of an action against the possible pain associated with it. (3)

classification facility A facility to which newly sentenced offenders are taken so that their security risks and needs can be assessed and they can be assigned to a permanent institution. (10)

clear and convincing evidence The standard of proof required in some civil cases and, in federal courts, the standard of proof necessary for a defendant to make a successful claim of insanity. (4)

cocorrectional facilities Usually small, minimum-security institutions that house both men and women with the goal of normalizing the prison environment by integrating the daytime activities of the sexes. (10)

collective conscience The general sense of morality of the times. (3)

college academies Schools where students pursue a program that integrates an associate's degree curriculum in law enforcement or criminal justice with the state's required peace officer training. (7)

community corrections The subfield of corrections in which offenders are supervised and provided services outside jail or prison. (12)

community policing A contemporary approach to policing that actively involves the community in a working partnership to control and reduce crime. (5)

commutation Reduction of the original sentence given by executive authority, usually a state's governor. (9 and 11)

complaint A charging document specifying that an offense has been committed by a person or persons named or described; usually used for misdemeanors and ordinance violations. (8)

CompStat A technological and management system that aims to make the police better organized and more effective crime fighters. It combines innovative crime analysis and geographic information systems, that is, crime

mapping (described in Chapter 6) with the latest management principles. (5)

conditional release A form of release that requires that a suspect/defendant maintain contact with a pretrial release program or undergo regular drug monitoring or treatment. (8)

confession An admission by a person accused of a crime that he or she committed the offense charged. (4)

conflict theory A theory that assumes that society is based primarily on conflict between competing interest groups and that criminal law and the criminal justice system are used to control subordinate groups. Crime is caused by relative powerlessness. (3)

conjugal visits An arrangement whereby inmates are permitted to visit in private with their spouses or significant others to maintain their personal relationship. (10)

constable The peacekeeper in charge of protection in early English towns. (5)

constable-watch system A system of protection in early England in which citizens, under the direction of a constable, or chief peacekeeper, were required to guard the city and to pursue criminals. (5)

contraband An illegal substance or object. (4)

contract security Protective services that a private security firm provides to people, agencies, and companies that do not employ their own security personnel or that need extra protection. (5)

convict code A constellation of values, norms, and roles that regulate the way inmates interact with one another and with prison staff. (11)

copicide A form of suicide in which a person gets fatally shot after intentionally provoking police officers. (7)

cottage reformatories Correctional facilities for youths, first developed in the late 1800s, that were intended to closely parallel family life and remove children from the negative influences of the urban environment. Children in those facilities lived with surrogate parents, who were responsible for the youths' training and education. (13)

crime control model One of Packer's two models of the criminal justice process. Politically, it reflects traditional conservative values. In this model, the control of criminal behavior is the most important function of criminal justice. (1)

crime index An estimate of crimes committed. (2)

crime index offenses cleared The number of offenses for which at least one person has been arrested, charged with the commission of the offense, and turned over to the court for prosecution. (2)

crime rate A measure of the incidence of crime expressed as the number of crimes per unit of population or some other base. (2)

criminal anthropology The study of "criminal" human beings. (3)

criminal law One of two general types of law practiced in the United States (the other is civil law); "a formal means of social control [that uses] rules. . . interpreted [and enforced] by the courts . . . to set limits to the conduct of the citizens, to guide the officials, and to define . . . unacceptable behavior." (4)

criminal sanctions or **criminal punishment** Penalties that are imposed for violating the criminal law. (9)

criminalization process The way people and actions are defined as criminal. (3)

criminological theory The explanation of criminal behavior, as well as the behavior of police, attorneys, prosecutors, judges, correctional personnel, victims, and other actors in the criminal justice process. (3)

crisis intervention A counselor's efforts to address some crisis in an inmate's life and to calm the inmate. (10)

cryonics A process of human hibernation that involves freezing the body. (14)

custody level The classification assigned to an inmate to indicate the degree of precaution that needs to be taken when working with that inmate. (10)

cybercrime The use of computer technology to commit crime. (6)

dark figure of crime The number of crimes not officially recorded by the police. (2)

day reporting centers Facilities that are designed for offenders who would otherwise be in prison or jail and that require offenders to report regularly to confer with staff about supervision and treatment matters. (12)

defendant A person against whom a legal action is brought, a warrant is issued, or an indictment is found. (1)

deprivation model A theory that the inmate society arises as a response to the prison environment and the painful conditions of confinement. (11)

determinate sentence A sentence with a fixed period of incarceration, which eliminates the decision-making responsibility of parole boards. (9)

differential association Sutherland's theory that persons who become criminal do so because of contacts with criminal patterns and isolation from anticriminal patterns. (3)

directed patrol Patrolling under guidance or orders on how to use patrol time. (6)

discretion The exercise of individual judgment, instead of formal rules, in making decisions. (7)

disposition The juvenile court equivalent of sentencing in criminal court. At the disposition hearing, the court makes its final determination of what to do with the juvenile officially labeled delinquent. (13)

diversion Organized, systematic efforts to remove individuals from further processing in criminal justice by placing them in alternative programs; diversion may be pretrial or posttrial. (12)

doctrine of fundamental fairness The rule that makes confessions inadmissible in criminal trials if they were obtained by means of either psychological manipulation or "third-degree" methods. (4)

doctrine of legal guilt The principle that people are not to be held guilty of crimes merely on a showing, based on reliable evidence, that in all probability they did in fact do what they are accused of doing. Legal guilt results only when factual guilt is determined in a procedurally regular fashion, as in a criminal trial, and when the procedural rules designed to protect suspects and defendants and to safeguard the integrity of the process are employed. (1)

domestic terrorism The unlawful use, or threatened use, of force or violence by a group or individual based and operating entirely within the United States or its territories without foreign direction committed against persons or property to intimidate or coerce a government, the civilian population, or any segment thereof, in furtherance of political or social objectives. (6)

double jeopardy The trying of a defendant a second time for the same offense when jeopardy attaches in the first trial and a mistrial was not declared. (4)

dual court system The court system in the United States, consisting of one system of state and local courts and another system of federal courts. (8)

due process model One of Packer's two models of the criminal justice process. Politically, it embodies traditional liberal values. In this model, the principal goal of criminal justice is at least as much to protect the innocent as it is to convict the guilty. (1)

due process of law The procedures followed by courts to ensure that a defendant's constitutional rights are not violated. (8)

due process of law The rights of people suspected of or charged with crimes. (4)

duress Force or coercion as an excuse for committing a crime. (2)

eight index crimes The Part I offenses in the FBI's uniform crime reports. They were (1) murder and nonnegligent manslaughter, (2) forcible rape, (3) robbery, (4) aggravated assault, (5) burglary, (6) larceny-theft, (7) motor vehicle theft, and (8) arson, which was added in 1979. (2)

electronic monitoring An arrangement that allows an offender's whereabouts to be gauged through the use of computer technology. (12)

entrapment A legal defense against criminal responsibility when a person, who was not already predisposed to it, is induced into committing a crime by a law enforcement officer or by his or her agent. (2)

ex post facto **law** A law that (1) declares criminal an act that was not illegal when it was committed, (2) increases the punishment for a crime after it is committed, or (3) alters the rules of evidence in a particular case after the crime is committed. (2)

excessive force A measure of coercion beyond that necessary to control participants in a conflict. (7)

exclusionary rule The rule that illegally seized evidence must be excluded from trials in federal courts. (4)

extinction A process in which behavior that previously was positively reinforced is no longer reinforced. (3)

feminist theory A perspective on criminality that focuses on women's experiences and seeks to abolish men's control over women's labor and sexuality. (3)

field interrogation A temporary detention in which officers stop and question pedestrians and motorists they find in suspicious circumstances. (6)

flat-time sentencing Sentencing in which judges may choose between probation and imprisonment but have little discretion in setting the length of a prison sentence. Once an offender is imprisoned, there is no possibility of reduction in the length of the sentence. (9)

frisking Conducting a search for weapons by patting the outside of a suspect's clothing, feeling for hard objects that might be weapons. (4)

full enforcement A practice in which the police make an arrest for every violation of law that comes to their attention. (7)

general deterrence The prevention of people in general or society at large from engaging in crime by punishing specific individuals and making examples of them. (3, 8, and 9)

general jurisdiction The power of a court to hear any type of case. (8)

GIS crime mapping A technique that involves the charting of crime patterns within a geographic area. (6)

good time The number of days deducted from a sentence by prison authorities for good behavior or for other reasons. (9 and 11)

grand jury A group of citizens who meet to investigate charges coming from preliminary hearings. (1)

grand jury Generally a group of 12 to 23 citizens who meet in closed sessions to investigate charges coming from preliminary hearings or to engage in other responsibilities. A primary purpose of the grand jury is to determine whether there is probable cause to believe that the accused committed the crime or crimes. (8)

grand jury indictment A written accusation by a grand jury charging that one or more persons have committed a crime. (8)

"grass eaters" Officers who occasionally engage in illegal and unethical activities, such as accepting small favors, gifts, or money for ignoring violations of the law during the course of their duties. (7)

habeas corpus A court order requiring that a confined person be brought to court so that his or her claims can be heard. (11)

halfway houses Community-based residential facilities that are less secure and restrictive than prison or jail but provide a more controlled environment than other community correctional programs. (12)

hands-off philosophy A philosophy under which courts are reluctant to hear prisoners' claims regarding their rights while incarcerated. (11)

harm The external consequence required to make an action a crime. (2)

hearing officer A lawyer empowered by the juvenile court to hear juvenile cases. (13)

highway patrol model A model of state law enforcement services in which officers focus on highway traffic safety, enforcement of the state's traffic laws, and the investigation of accidents on the state's roads, highways, and property. (5)

home confinement A program that requires offenders to remain in their homes except for approved periods of absence; commonly used in combination with electronic monitoring. (12)

houses of refuge The first specialized correctional institutions for youths in the United States. (13)

hung jury The result when jurors cannot agree on a verdict. The judge declares a mistrial. The prosecutor must decide whether to retry the case. (8)

identity theft The transfer or use without legal authority of the identity documentation of another person with the intent to commit, aid, or abet any activity that constitutes a felony (14)

imitation, or modeling A means by which a person can learn new responses by observing others without performing any overt act or receiving direct reinforcement or reward. (3)

importation model A theory that the inmate society is shaped by the attributes inmates bring with them when they enter prison. (11)

incapacitation The removal or restriction of the freedom of those found to have violated criminal laws. (8 and 9)

incarceration rate A figure derived by dividing the number of people incarcerated by the population of the area and multiplying the result by 100,000; used to compare incarceration levels of units with different population sizes. (10)

indeterminate sentence A sentence with a fixed minimum and maximum term of incarceration, rather than a set period. (9)

indictment A document that outlines the charge or charges against a defendant. (8)

informal juvenile justice The actions taken by citizens to respond to juvenile offenders without involving the official agencies of juvenile justice. (13)

information A document that outlines the formal charge(s) against a suspect, the law(s) that have been violated and the evidence to support the charge(s). (1 and 8)

initial appearance A pretrial stage in which a defendant is brought before a lower court to be given notice of the charge(s) and advised of her or his constitutional rights. (1)

insanity Mental or psychological impairment or retardation as a defense against a criminal charge. (2)

institution of social control An organization that persuades people, through subtle and not-so-subtle means, to abide by the dominant values of society. (1)

intake screening The process by which decisions are made about the continued processing of juvenile cases. Decisions might include dismissing the case, referring the youth to a diversion program, or filing a petition. (13)

intensive-supervision probation and parole (ISP) An alternative to incarceration that provides stricter conditions, closer supervision, and more treatment services than do traditional probation and parole. (12)

intermediate sanctions Sanctions that, in restrictiveness and punitiveness, lie between traditional probation and traditional imprisonment or, alternatively, between imprisonment and traditional parole. (12)

internal affairs investigations unit The police unit that ferrets out illegal and unethical activity engaged in by the police. (7)

international terrorism Violent acts dangerous to human life that are a violation of the criminal laws of the United States or any state, or that would be a criminal violation if committed within the jurisdiction of the United States or any state. These acts appear to be intended to intimidate or coerce a civilian population, influence the policy of a government by intimidation or coercion, or affect the conduct of a government by assassination or kidnapping. International terrorist acts occur outside the United States or transcend national boundaries in terms of the means by which they are accomplished, the persons they appear intended to coerce or intimidate, or the locale in which the perpetrators operate or seek asylum. (6)

jail A facility, usually operated at the local level, that holds convicted offenders and unconvicted persons for relatively short periods. (10)

jailhouse lawyer An inmate skilled in legal matters. (11)

job stress The harmful physical and emotional outcomes that occur when the requirements of a job do not match the capabilities, resources, or needs of the worker. (7)

jurisdiction The right or authority of a justice agency to act in regard to a particular subject matter, territory, or person. (1, 5, and 8)

just deserts The punishment rationale based on the idea that offenders should be punished automatically, simply because they have committed a crime—they "deserve" it—and the idea that the punishment should fit the crime. (9)

juvenile delinquency A special category of offense created for youths who, in most U.S. jurisdictions, are persons between the ages of 7 and 18. (2 and 13)

labeling theory A theory that emphasizes the criminalization process as the cause of some crime. (3)

learning theory A theory that explains criminal behavior and its prevention with the concepts of positive reinforcement, negative reinforcement, extinction, punishment, and modeling, or imitation. (3)

left realists A group of social scientists who argue that critical criminologists need to redirect their attention to the fear and the very real victimization experienced by working-class people. (3)

legal definition of crime An intentional violation of the criminal law or penal code, committed without defense or excuse and penalized by the state. (2)

legality The requirement (1) that a harm must be legally forbidden for the behavior to be a crime and (2) that the law must not be retroactive. (2)

less-eligibility principle The position that prisoners should receive no service or program superior to the services and programs available to free citizens without charge. (10)

limbic system A structure surrounding the brain stem that, in part, controls the life functions of heartbeat, breathing, and sleep. It also is believed to moderate expressions of violence; such emotions as anger, rage, and fear; and sexual response. (3)

lockup A very short-term holding facility that is frequently located in or very near an urban police agency so that suspects can be held pending further inquiry. (10)

mala in se Wrong in themselves. A description applied to crimes that are characterized by universality and timelessness. (2)

mala prohibita Offenses that are illegal because laws define them as such. They lack universality and timelessness. (2)

mandatory release A method of prison release under which an inmate is released after serving a legally required portion of his or her sentence, minus good-time credits. (11)

mandatory sentencing Sentencing in which a specified number of years of imprisonment (usually within a range) is provided for particular crimes. (9)

"meat eaters" Officers who actively seek ways to make money illegally while on duty. (7)

mediation A dispute resolution process that brings disputants together with a third party (a mediator) who is trained in the art of helping people resolve disputes to everyone's satisfaction. The agreed-upon resolution is then formalized into a binding consent agreement. (14)

medical model A theory of institutional corrections, popular during the 1940s and 1950s, in which crime was seen as symptomatic of personal illness in need of treatment. (10)

mens rea Criminal intent; a guilty state of mind. (2)

mere suspicion The standard of proof with the least certainty; a "gut feeling." With mere suspicion, a law enforcement officer cannot legally even stop a suspect. (4)

merit system A system of employment whereby an independent civil service commission, in cooperation with the city personnel section and the police department, sets employment qualifications, performance standards, and discipline procedures. (7)

milieu therapy A variant of group therapy that encompasses the total living environment so that the environment continually encourages positive behavioral change. (10)

mitigating factors or **circumstances** In death sentencing, facts or situations that do not justify or excuse a criminal act but reduce the degree of blameworthiness and thus may reduce the punishment. (9)

myths Beliefs based on emotion rather than analysis. (1)

national crime victimization surveys A source of crime statistics based on interviews in which respondents are asked whether they have been victims of any of the FBI's index offenses (except murder, nonnegligent manslaughter, and arson) or other crimes during the past 6 months. If they have, they are asked to provide information about the experience. (2)

necessity defense A legal defense against criminal responsibility used when a crime has been committed to prevent a more serious crime. (2)

negative reinforcement The removal or reduction of a stimulus whose removal or reduction increases or maintains a response. (3)

negligence The failure to take reasonable precautions to prevent harm. (2)

neoclassical theory A modification of classical theory in which it was conceded that certain factors, such as insanity, might inhibit the exercise of free will. (3)

net widening A phenomenon that occurs when the offenders placed in a novel program are not the offenders for whom the program was designed. The consequence is that those in the program receive more severe sanctions than they would have received had the new program remained unavailable. (12)

nolle prosequi (nol. pros.) The notation placed on the official record of a case when prosecutors elect not to prosecute. (8)

nolo contendere Latin for "no contest." When defendants plead *nolo*, they do not admit guilt but are willing to accept punishment. (8)

nonenforcement The failure to routinely enforce prohibitions against certain behaviors. (2)

norm Any standard or rule regarding what human beings should or should not think, say, or do under given circumstances. (2)

offenses known to the police A crime index, reported in the FBI's uniform crime reports, composed of crimes that are both reported to and recorded by the police. (2)

operational styles The different overall approaches to the police job. (6)

original jurisdiction The authority of a court to hear a case when it is first brought to court. (8)

overcriminalization The prohibition by the criminal law of some behaviors that arguably should not be prohibited. (2)

panopticon A prison design consisting of a round building with tiers of cells lining the inner circumference and facing a central inspection tower. (10)

pardon A "forgiveness" for the crime committed that stops further criminal processing. (9)

parens patriae The legal philosophy justifying state intervention in the lives of children when their parents are unable or unwilling to protect them. (13)

parole A method of prison release whereby inmates are released at the discretion of a board or other authority before having completed their entire sentences; can also refer to the community supervision received upon release. (1, 11, and 12)

parole guidelines Structured instruments used to estimate the probability of parole recidivism and to direct the release decisions of parole boards. (12)

patriarchy Men's control over women's labor and sexuality. (3)

peacemaking criminology An approach that suggests that the solutions to all social problems, including crime, are the transformation of human beings, mutual dependence, reduction of class structures, creation of communities of caring people, and universal social justice. (3)

Peel's Principles of Policing A dozen standards proposed by Robert Peel, the author of the legislation resulting in the formation of the London Metropolitan Police Department. The standards are still applicable to today's law enforcement. (5)

penal code The criminal law of a political jurisdiction. (4)

penal sanction An ideal characteristic of criminal law: the principle that violators will be punished or at least threatened with punishment by the state. (4)

Pennsylvania system An early system of U.S. penology in which inmates were kept in solitary cells so that they could study religious writings, reflect on their misdeeds, and perform handicraft work. (10)

penology The study of prison management and the treatment of offenders. (10)

personal jurisdiction A court's authority over the parties to a lawsuit. (8)

petition A legal form of the police complaint that specifies the charges to be heard at the adjudication. (13)

placing out The practice of placing children on farms in the Midwest and West to remove them from the supposedly corrupting influences of their parents and the cities. (13)

plea bargaining or **plea negotiating** The practice whereby the prosecutor, the defense attorney, the defendant, and—in many jurisdictions—the judge agree on a specific sentence to be imposed if the accused pleads guilty to an agreed-upon charge or charges instead of going to trial. (1 and 8)

police cadet program A program that combines a college education with agency work experience and academy training. Upon graduation, a cadet is promoted to police officer. (7)

politicality An ideal characteristic of criminal law, referring to its legitimate source. Only violations of rules made by the state, the political jurisdiction that enacted the laws, are crimes. (4)

positive reinforcement The presentation of a stimulus that increases or maintains a response. (3)

posses Groups of able-bodied citizens of a community, called into service by a sheriff or constable to chase and apprehend offenders. (5)

postmodernism An area of critical thought that, among other things, attempts to understand the creation of knowledge and how knowledge and language create hierarchy and domination. (3)

power differentials The ability of some groups to dominate other groups in a society. (3)

precedent A decision that forms a potential basis for deciding the outcomes of similar cases in the future; a by-product of decisions made by trial and appellate court judges, who produce case law whenever they render a decision in a particular case. (4)

preliminary hearing A pretrial stage used in about one-half of all states and only in felony cases. Its purpose is for a judge to determine whether there is probable cause to support the charge or charges imposed by the prosecutor. (1 and 8)

preponderance of evidence Evidence that more likely than not outweighs the opposing evidence, or sufficient evidence to overcome doubt or speculation. (4)

presentence investigation (PSI) An investigation conducted by a probation agency or other designated authority at the request of a court into the past behavior, family circumstances, and personality of an adult who has been convicted of a crime, to assist the court in determining the most appropriate sentence. (12)

presentence investigation reports Reports, often called PSIs or PSIRs, that are used in the federal system and the majority of states to help judges determine the appropriate sentence. They are also used in classifying probationers, parolees, and prisoners according to their treatment needs and security risk. (9)

presumptive sentencing Sentencing that allows a judge to retain some sentencing discretion, subject to appellate review. The legislature determines a sentence range for each crime. (9)

preventive detention Holding suspects or defendants in jail without giving them an opportunity to post bail, because of the threat they pose to society. (8)

preventive patrol Patrolling the streets with little direction; between responses to radio calls, officers are "systematically unsystematic" and observant in an attempt to both prevent and ferret out crime. Also known as random patrol. (6)

prisonization The process by which an inmate becomes socialized into the customs and principles of the inmate society. (11)

privatization The involvement of the private sector in the construction and the operation of confinement facilities. (10)

probable cause The amount of proof necessary for a reasonably intelligent person to believe that a crime has been committed or that items connected with criminal activity can be found in a particular place. It is the standard of proof needed to conduct a search or to make an arrest. (1 and 4)

probation A sentence in which the offender, rather than being incarcerated, is retained in the community under the supervision of a probation agency and required to abide by certain rules and conditions to avoid incarceration. (12)

probation conditions Rules that specify what an offender is and is not to do during the course of a probation sentence. (12)

procedural law The body of law that governs the ways substantive laws are administered; sometimes called *adjective* or *remedial* law. (4)

proportionality review A review in which the appellate court compares the sentence in the case it is reviewing with penalties imposed in similar cases in the state. The object is to reduce, as much as possible, disparity in death penalty sentencing. (9)

proprietary security In-house protective services that a security staff provides for the entity that employs it. (5)

protective custody The segregation of inmates for their own safety. (10)

psychopaths, sociopaths, or antisocial personalities Persons characterized by no sense of guilt, no subjective conscience, and no sense of right and wrong. They have difficulty in forming relationships with other people; they cannot empathize with other people. (3)

public safety officers Police department employees who perform many police services but do not have arrest powers. (7)

punishment The presentation of an aversive stimulus to reduce a response. (3) The imposition of a penalty for criminal wrongdoing. (8)

racial profiling The stopping and/or detaining of individuals by law enforcement officers based solely on race. (7)

radical nonintervention A practice based on the idea that youths should be left alone if at all possible, instead of being formally processed. (13)

radical theories Theories of crime causation that are generally based on a Marxist theory of class struggle. (3)

reasonable suspicion A standard of proof that is more than a gut feeling. It includes the ability to articulate reasons for the suspicion. With reasonable suspicion, a law enforcement officer is legally permitted to stop and frisk a suspect. (4)

recidivism The return of probationers to crime during or after probation. (11 and 12)

reform, industrial, or training schools Correctional facilities for youths, first developed in the late 1800s, that focused on custody. Today, those institutions are often called training schools, and although they may place more emphasis on treatment, they still rely on custody and control. (13)

regularity An ideal characteristic of criminal law: the applicability of the law to all persons, regardless of social status. (4)

rehabilitation The attempt to "correct" the personality and behavior of convicted offenders through educational, vocational, or therapeutic treatment and to return them to society as law-abiding citizens. (8 and 9)

reintegration The process of rebuilding former ties to the community and establishing new ties after release from prison. (12)

reintegrative shaming A strategy in which disappointment is expressed for the offender's actions, the offender is shamed and punished, and, more importantly, following the expression of disappointment and shame is a concerted effort on the part of the community to forgive the offender and reintegrate him or her back into society. (14)

relative deprivation Refers to inequalities (in resources, opportunities, material goods, etc.) that are defined by a person as unfair or unjust. (3)

relative powerlessness In conflict theory, the inability to dominate other groups in society. (3)

release on own recognizance (ROR) A release secured by a suspect's written promise to appear in court. (8)

restitution Money paid or services provided by a convicted offender to victims, their survivors, or the community to make up for the injury inflicted. (9 and 12)

restorative justice A process whereby an offender is required to contribute to restoring the health of the community, repairing the harm done, and meeting victims' needs. (14)

retribution A justification for punishment that implies repayment for an offense committed. (9)

revenge The punishment rationale expressed by the biblical phrase, "An eye for an eye, and a tooth for a tooth." People who seek revenge want to pay back offenders by making them suffer for what they have done. (9)

revocation The repeal of a probation sentence or parole, and substitution of a more restrictive sentence, because of violation of probation or parole conditions. (12)

role The rights and responsibilities associated with a particular position in society. (6)

role conflict The psychological stress and frustration that results from trying to perform two or more incompatible responsibilities. (6)

role expectation The behavior and actions that people expect from a person in a particular role. (6)

rules of discovery Rules that mandate that a prosecutor provide defense counsel with any exculpatory evidence (evidence favorable to the accused that has an effect on guilt or punishment) in the prosecutor's possession. (8)

searches Explorations or inspections, by law enforcement officers, of homes, premises, vehicles, or persons, for the purpose of discovering evidence of crimes or persons who are accused of crimes. (4)

seizures The taking of persons or property into custody in response to violations of the criminal law. (4)

selective enforcement The practice of relying on the judgment of the police leadership and rank-and-file officers to decide which laws to enforce. (7)

self-incrimination Being a witness against oneself. If forced, it is a violation of the Fifth Amendment. (4)

self-report crime surveys Surveys in which subjects are asked whether they have committed crimes. (2)

shire reeve In medieval England, the chief law enforcement officer in a territorial area called a *shire;* later called the *sheriff.* (5)

shock incarceration The placement of offenders in facilities patterned after military boot camps. (10)

slave patrols The earliest form of policing in the South. They were a product of the slave codes. (5)

snitch system A system in which staff learn from inmate informants about the presence of contraband, the potential for disruptions, and other threats to security. (10)

social contract An imaginary agreement to sacrifice the minimum amount of liberty necessary to prevent anarchy and chaos. (3)

social control theory A view in which people are expected to commit crime and delinquency unless they are prevented from doing so. (3)

social disorganization The condition in which the usual controls over delinquents are largely absent, delinquent behavior is often approved of by parents and neighbors, there are many opportunities for delinquent behavior, and there is little encouragement, training, or opportunity for legitimate employment. (3)

special jurisdiction The power of a court to hear only certain kinds of cases. (8)

special or **specific deterrence** The prevention of individuals from committing crimes again by punishing them. (3 and 9)

specificity An ideal characteristic of criminal law, referring to its scope. Although civil law may be general in scope, criminal law should provide strict definitions of specific acts. (4)

stare decisis The principle of using precedents to guide future decisions in court cases; Latin for "to stand by decided cases." (4)

state police model A model of state law enforcement services in which the agency and its officers have the same law enforcement powers as local police but can exercise them anywhere within the state. (5)

status offenses Acts that are not crimes when committed by adults but are illegal for minors (for example, truancy or running away from home). (2 and 13)

structured fines, or **day fines** Fines that are based on defendants' ability to pay. (12)

subject matter jurisdiction The power of a court to hear a particular type of case. (8)

subpoena A written order issued by a court that requires a person to appear at a certain time and place to give testimony. It can also require that documents and objects be made available for examination by the court. (4 and 8)

sub-rosa economy The secret exchange of goods and services among inmates; the black market of the prison. (11)

substantive law The body of law that defines criminal offenses and their penalties. (4)

summary or **bench trials** Trials without a jury. (1 and 8)

system A smoothly operating set of arrangements and institutions directed toward the achievement of common goals. (1)

tech prep (technical preparation) A program in which area community colleges and high schools team up to offer 6 to 9 hours of college law enforcement courses in the eleventh and twelfth grades, as well as one or two training certifications, such as police dispatcher or local corrections officer. Students who graduate are eligible for police employment at age 18. (7)

technical violations Failure to abide by the technical rules or conditions of probation or parole (for example, not reporting regularly to the probation officer), as distinct from commission of a new criminal act. (12)

temporary-release programs Programs that allow jail or prison inmates to leave the facility for short periods to participate in approved community activities. (12)

terrorism The systematic use of terror or unpredictable violence against governments, publics, or individuals to attain a political objective; the unlawful use of force and violence against persons or property to intimidate or coerce a government, the civilian population, or any segment thereof, in furtherance of political or social objectives; or premeditated, politically motivated violence perpetrated against noncombatant targets by subnational groups or clandestine agents, usually intended to influence an audience. (6)

theory An assumption (or set of assumptions) that attempts to explain why or how things are related to each other. (3)

three I's of police selection Three qualities of the American police officer that seem to be of paramount importance: intelligence, integrity, and interaction skills. (7)

tithing system A private self-help protection system in early medieval England, in which a group of 10 families, or a *tithing,* agreed to follow the law, keep the peace in their areas, and bring law violators to justice. (5)

tort A violation of the civil law. (4)

total institution An institutional setting in which persons sharing some characteristics are cut off from the wider society and expected to live according to institutional rules and procedures. (11)

traffic accident investigation crews In some agencies, the special units assigned to all traffic accident investigations. (6)

transfer, waiver, or **certification** The act or process by which juveniles who meet specific age, offense, and (in some jurisdictions) prior-record criteria are transferred to criminal court for trial. (13)

transportation A punishment in which offenders were transported from their home nation to one of that nation's colonies to work. (10)

trial *de novo* A trial in which an entire case is reheard by a trial court of general jurisdiction because there is an appeal and there is no written transcript of the earlier proceeding. (8)

undercriminalization The failure to prohibit some behaviors that arguably should be prohibited. (2)

uniform crime reports A collection of crime statistics and other law enforcement information gathered under a voluntary national program administered by the FBI. (2)

uniformity An ideal characteristic of criminal law: the enforcement of the laws against anyone who violates them, regardless of social status. (4)

unsecured bond An arrangement in which bail is set but no money is paid to the court. (8)

utility The principle that a policy should provide "the greatest happiness shared by the greatest number." (3)

venire The pool from which jurors are selected. (8)

venue The place of the trial. It must be geographically appropriate. (4)

victim-impact statements Descriptions of the harm and suffering that a crime has caused victims and their survivors. (9)

voir dire The process in which potential jurors who might be biased or unable to render a fair verdict are screened out. (8)

warrant A written order from a court directing law enforcement officers to conduct a search or to arrest a person. (4)

workhouses European forerunners of the modern U.S. prison, where offenders were sent to learn discipline and regular work habits. (10)

writ of *certiorari* A written order, from the U.S. Supreme Court to a lower court whose decision is being appealed, to send the records of the case forward for review. (8)

writ of *habeas corpus* An order from a court to an officer of the law to produce a prisoner in court to determine if the prisoner is being legally detained or imprisoned. (8)

Photo Credits

Chapter 1

p. 2: John Raoux/AP Images; p. 3: Orange County Sheriff's Office/AP Images; p. 7L: The Daily Tar Heel, Beth Ely/AP Images; p. 7M: HO/Reuters/Corbis; p. 7R: REUTERS/Brendan McDermid/Corbis; p. 8: Richard Lord/The Image Works; p. 12: Joel Gordon; p. 13: A. Ramey/PhotoEdit; p. 18: Elaine Thompson/AP Images; p. 21L: Bettmann/Corbis; p. 21R: REUTERS/Jim Bourg-Files/Corbis; p. 23: Giraudon/Bridgeman Art Library.

Chapter 2

p. 26: Akron Beacon Journal/Mike Cardew/AP Images; p. 27: Used with permission of the Orlando Sentinel, copyright 2009. Photographer: Roberto Gonzalez; p. 30: John Chiasson/Getty Images; p. 31: Kim Kulish/Corbis; p. 34L: Jeffrey Markowitz/Sygma/Corbis; p. 34R: Jeffrey Markowitz/Sygma/Corbis; p. 38: Larry W. Smith/Getty Images; p. 40: Mike Meadows/AP Images; p. 45: Tim Larsen/AP Images; p. 47: Courtesy of Tracy Snell; p. 50: Jose Luis Pelaez, Inc./Corbis; p. 53: ©Syracuse Newspapers/The Image Works; p. 55: Greg Smith/Corbis.

Chapter 3

p. 60: Department of Motor Vehicles/AP Images; p. 61: Gatehouse News Service/AP Images; p. 66: Bettmann/Corbis; p. 7T: U.S. Attorney's Office/AP Images; p. 067B: Hulton Archive/Getty Images; p. 69: Courtesy of Alida Merlo; p. 70L: Al Cohen/Getty Images; p. 70M: PhotoDisc/Getty Images; p. 70R: Image Source Limited/Index Stock Imagery; p. 74: Bettmann/Corbis; p. 76: Reuters NewMedia Inc./Corbis; p. 78: Bettmann/Corbis; p. 79: Marc Asnin; p. 81: A. Ramey/PhotoEdit; p. 84: Jonathan Drake/Reuters NewMedia Inc/Corbis; p. 88L: Marilyn Humphries/The Image Works; p. 8R: A. Ramey/PhotoEdit; p. 90: Vince Mannino/Corbis; p. 92: AFP Photo/Bert Maprangala.

Chapter 4

p. 98: Kenneth Garrett/Getty Images; p. 99: Courtesy of Wikipedia; p. 104: Charles Walker/Topfoto/The Image Works; p. 105: Bettmann/Corbis; p. 106: CSPAN via APTN/AP Images; p. 107: Syracuse Newspapers/Kevin Jacobus/The Image Works; p. 110ML: Wally McNamee/Corbis; p. 110MR: Shepard Sherbell/Corbis; p. 110R: AP Images; p. 110L: Brooks Kraft/Corbis; p. 113: Charles Bennett/AP Images; p. 120L: Mark Richards/PhotoEdit; p. 120M: Bettmann/Corbis; p. 120R: Daniel Sheehan/Liaison Agency/Newsmakers/Getty Images; p. 122: The Gazette, Lisa Powell/AP Images; p. 125: Davis Turner/CNP/Corbis; p. 128: Dave Weaver/AP Images; p. 131: Courtesy of Junior A. Barrett; p. 132: Bettmann/Corbis; p. 133: David Leeson/Dallas Morning News/The Image Works; p. 136: Courtesy of Renee Daniel.

Chapter 5

p. 142: Granger Collection; p. 144: Scott Olson/Getty Images; p. 145: Jeff Greenberg/The Image Works; p. 147: Topham/Fotomas/The Image Works; p. 149: Corbis; p. 150: Corbis; p. 151: Bettmann/Corbis; p. 152: ANA/The Image Works; p. 153: Courtesy of Texas Rangers Hall of Fame; p. 154: Bettmann/Corbis; p. 156: Bill Hudson/AP Images; p. 160: Granger Collection; p. 162: Ron Edmonds/AP Images; p. 163: Hulton Archive/Getty Images; p. 165TL: Hulton Archive/Getty Images; p. 165 TML: Katherine Young/Getty Images; p. 165TMR: Bettmann/Corbis; p. 165TR: Michael Ochs Archives/Getty Images; p. 165BL: Silver Screen Collection/Getty Images; p. 165BML: Corbis; p. 165BMR: Popperfoto/Getty Images; p. 165BR: Michael Ochs Archives/Getty Images; p. 168: Alex Wong/Getty Images; p. 169: Granger Collection; p. 170: Everett Collection; p. 171: Corbis; p. 172: Erik S. Lesser/Getty Images; p. 175: Hussein Akhtar/Sygma/Corbis;

p. 178: David Young-Wolff/PhotoEdit; p. 184: Chet Gordon/The Image Works; p. 185: Evy Mages/Reuters NewMedia Inc./Corbis; p. 189: Mike Segar/Reuters NewMedia/Corbis; p. 191: Courtesy of Jose Pagan; p. 196: Evy Mages/Reuters NewMedia Inc./Corbis; p. 197: Joe Marquette/AP Images; p. 198: David McNew/Getty Images.

Chapter 6

p. 204: Nancy Richmond/The Image Works; p. 205: Courtesy of the Dallas Police Department; p. 207: Spencer Ainsley/The Image Works; p. 212: Michael Newman/PhotoEdit; p. 215: Justin Sullivan/Getty Images; p. 217: Ed Bailey/AP Images; p. 222: Corbis; p. 223: Courtesy of Brenda Sue Collins; p. 225: Steve Liss/Sygma/Corbis; p. 227: Syracuse Newspapers/The Image Works; p. 230: Tony Savino/The Image Works; p. 233: Tom Carter/PhotoEdit; p. 234: Bernd Obermann/Corbis; p. 235: Bob Daemmrich; p. 237: PAUL K. BUCK/AFP/Getty Images; p. 239T: Animal Liberation Victoria, HO/AP Images; p. 239B: Jim Ruymen/Reuters/Corbis.

Chapter 7

p. 248: Mitch Wojnarowicz/Amsterdam Recorder/The Image Works; p. 249: Daily News LP; p. 253L: David McNew/Getty Images; p. 253R: Bob Daemmrich; p. 255: Greg Smith/Corbis; p. 256: Bob Daemmrich/The Image Works; p. 259: Sandy Felsenthal/Corbis; p. 261: Reuters/Brendan McDermid/Corbis; p. 263: Michael Newman/PhotoEdit; p. 265: Doug Martin; p. 266: Courtesy of Robert Bour; p. 268: Spencer Grant/PhotoEdit; p. 270: Joel Gordon; p. 273: Mark M. Lawrence/Corbis; p. 274: Ralf-Finn Hestoft/Corbis; p. 275: Mitchell Crooks/Getty Images; p. 279: Melanie Einzig/Getty Images.

Chapter 8

p. 286: Guy Cali/Corbis; p. 287: Department of Justice via Getty Images; p. 291: Paul Sakuma/Pool/Reuters NewMedia/Corbis; p. 294: MATTHEW CAVANAUGH/epa/Corbis; p. 296: Reuters NewMedia Inc./Corbis; p. 300: Bettmann/Corbis; p. 301: Gerry Broome/AP Images; p. 303: REUTERS/Jim Ruymen/Corbis; p. 304: Courtesy of Wilson Green; p. 307L: Carlo Allegri, Pool/AP Images; p. 307M: W. Garth Dowling; p. 307R: Dan Groshong/ReutersNewMedia/Corbis; p. 308: Shelley Gazin/Corbis; p. 313: Syracuse Newspapers/The Image Works; p. 318: Courtesy of Todd Nuccio; p. 320: Mary Kate Denny/PhotoEdit; p. 333: Lawrence Jackson/AP Images; p. 335: Courtesy of Debora Randolph.

Chapter 9

p. 340: Matt York/AP Images; p. 341: Nati Harnik/AP Images; p. 346: Damian Dovarganes/AP Images; p. 348: David Woo/Stock Boston; p. 352: Bettmann/Corbis; p. 354: Courtesy of Dori de Jong; p. 355: Reuters NewMedia Inc./Corbis; p. 356: Bob Daemmrich/

Case Index

Subject Index

psychological theories, 64t, 74
  humanistic psychological theory, 64t, 75–78
  intelligence theories, 64t, 74
  psychoanalytic theories, 64t, 74–75
psychopaths, **75**, 75t, **76**
public executions, *352*
public order crimes, 36, 37t
public safety officers, **261**
Pullman railroad strike, 159, *160*
punishment, **83–84**, **299**. *See also* criminal punishment
  caning, *84*
  corporal, 84
  as crime element, 30, 36
  cruel/unusual, 130–32
  in Enlightenment, 63, 65
  facts, 380
  myths, 380
  threat of, 36
  types of, 14
Puzzanchera, Charles, 525f

al-Qaeda, 192, 196–97, 236, 238, 378, 402
Quinney, Richard, 65t, 89

racial profiling, **271–72**
racism, 90
radical nonintervention, 87, **521**
radical theories, 65t, **89–91**. *See also* Marxist theory
Ramirez, Arthur J., 485
Rand, Michael R., 54f
Randolph, Debora, 335
random patrols, 157
rape, 51, 102
rational choice theory, 67
Reagan, Ronald, 34, 107
reasonable doubt, 118. *See also* beyond a reasonable doubt
reasonable suspicion, **117**, 117f
Reaves, Brian A., 175f, 182f, 183f, 186, 187t, 190, 210t, 216t, 235, 258t, 259t, 263t, 264t, 266t, 279t, 317f, 466
recidivism, **450**, 452f, **474**
  Blacks and, 450
  declining rates, 452, 452t
  defined, 450
  halfway houses, 496–97
  Hispanics and, 451
  parole, 484
  prison life and, 448–54
  probation, 474–75
  research, 453
Reckless, Walter C., 65t, 85
redlining, 80
reform schools, 509–**10**
reformatory movement, 382
regularity, 101f, **102**
rehabilitation, **299**, **352–53**
Rehnquist, William, 109, *110*
reintegration, **484**
reintegrative shaming, 87, 354, **560**
Reiss, Albert J., 65t, 85

relative deprivation, **92**
relative powerlessness, **88**
release on own recognizance (ROR), **324**
remedial law, 101
Reno, Janet, 305
Republican National Convention (1984), 107
residential parole, 477
"respect for the privacy of the home," 115
restitution, **343**, **471**, 532–33
restoration, 353–55
restorative justice, 523–24, 559–**60**
retribution, **351**
revenge, **351**, 372
revocation, **471**, 473
Rewards for Justice program, 197
Rey, Octave, 151
Ridge, Tom, 189
Ridgway, Gary, *18*
right-and-wrong test, 33
rights, 220, 258. *See also* Bill of Rights; due process rights; human rights; *Miranda* rights/warnings
  civil rights movement, 155
  to compulsory process for favorable witnesses, 128
  to confront opposing witnesses, 128
  to counsel, 128–30, 554–55
  due process, 19
  Eighth Amendment, 445–47
  First Amendment, 444–45
  Fourteenth Amendment, 447–48
  of inmates, 442–48, *444*
  to jury trial, 127
  to notice of accusation, 127–28
  Sixth Amendment, 126–30
  to speedy trial, 126–27
right-wing terrorism, 237–38
riots, 149
Ritz, Christina E., 81
RNA memory chains, 563
Roberts, John, Jr., 109, *110, 294*
robotics, 551, *551*
Rockefeller, John D., Jr., 170
role conflict, **206–8**
role expectation, **206–8**
role theory, 82
roles, **206–8**
Romans, Timothy, 505–6
Romero, Vincent, 505–6
Roosevelt, Theodore, 153, 162
ROR. *See* release on own recognizance
Rosecrance, John, 467
Rubin, Jerry, 35
Ruckleshaus, William, 166
Rudolph, Eric Robert, 238
rules of discovery, **303**
Rush, George E., 344

Sabol, William J., 389t, 390t, 395t, 405f
"Safe Homes," 115
SARA. *See* Scanning, Analysis, Response, Assessment

Scalia, Antonin, *294*
Scanning, Analysis, Response, Assessment (SARA), 234
Scheck, Barry, 133–34
Schrag, Clarence, 438
Schwarz, Charles, 275
SCLC. *See* Southern Christian Leadership Conference
Scott, John, 151
Scott, Timothy, 278
SDS. *See* Students for a Democratic Society
searches, **110**
  consent, 115
  defined, 110
  in Fourth Amendment, 111–15
  incident to arrest, 114
  search warrant, *112*
  with warrant, 111–13
  without warrant, 113–14
Seattle Police Department (SPD), 178–79, 179t, 256, 258t
secondary deviance, 86
second-generation jails, *408*, 408–9, 408f
Secret Service, 161, 174, 190
security. *See also* Department of Homeland Security; private security
  contract, 198
  national security letters, 119
  NSA, 122
  NSB, 195
  proprietary, 198
  TSA, 190
security level, **399**, 403f
Sedition Act of 1798, 159
seizures, **111–15**
selective enforcement, **269**
Selective Service Act, 162
self-incrimination, **124–26**
self-report crime surveys, **48–50**, *50*
sentencing, 342, 343t, 344t, 349f. *See also* appeals; death penalty
  blended sentences, 529, 530f
  commissions, 346
  in criminal justice future, 556–57
  determinate sentence, 345, 348–50
  facts, 346
  flat-time, 345
  good time, 345
  guidelines, 346, 347f
  intermediate sentence, 345
  by judge/jury, 342, 356–57
  longest, 344
  mandatory, 345
  myths, 346
  organizational considerations, 355–56
  personal characteristics of judges and, 356–57
  philosophical rationales, 350–55
  presumptive, 346, 348
  PSI and, 356
  Sentencing Commission, U.S., 346
  statutory provisions, 342–50

10 STEPS TO SUCCESS (CONTINUED)
AN INTRODUCTION TO CRIMINAL JUSTICE

AFTER REREADING THE CHAPTER, REREAD THE SUMMARY

Be sure you understand each of the main points and have completely mastered all the concepts listed under each chapter objective. These represent the minimum you need to know after your careful reading of the chapter. If you feel weak in any area, stop, reread, and review. Make sure your notes are complete and that you have not overlooked anything important.

STUDY THE KEY TERMS AGAIN

Try writing the definitions on a separate sheet of paper without looking them up first. You can refresh your memory of the key terms by looking at the page number where each first appears (see the list following the summary) or by skimming the chapter again and looking for the definitions in the margins. Make sure you are very familiar with the vocabulary of criminal justice before you go on.

ANSWER THE REVIEW QUESTIONS

If you miss any of these, go back through the chapter until you locate the text discussion, read the section over, and try the question again. Then go back and check the rest of your answers against the textbook. Don't proceed until you have answered each question correctly.